MODERN STATUTORY INTERPRETATION

FRAMEWORK, PRINCIPLES AND PRACTICE

Statutory interpretation is both a distinct body of law governing the determination of the meaning of legislation and a task that requires a set of skills. It is thus an essential area of legal practice, education and research. *Modern Statutory Interpretation: Framework, Principles and Practice* is an original, clear, coherent and research-based account of contemporary Australian statutory interpretation.

Written by experts in the field, the book provides a comprehensive coverage of statutory interpretation law as well as examining related areas such as legislative drafting, the parliamentary process, the modern history of interpretation, sources of doubt, and interpretation techniques. The content is structured in eight parts. Parts I–III introduce foundational matters, Parts IV–VII deal with the general principles of interpretation, and Part VIII examines special interpretative issues. A fully cross-referenced glossary is included.

With each chapter built around clear statements of principle and with numerous illustrations of the operation of the law, the work presents statutory interpretation in an accessible way. *Modern Statutory Interpretation* is an essential resource for legal professionals, legal researchers, and students undertaking advanced courses in statutory interpretation in Australia.

Jeffrey Barnes is an Associate Professor in La Trobe Law School at La Trobe University.

Jacinta Dharmananda is a Senior Lecturer at the Law School of the University of Western Australia.

Eamonn Moran is the Inspector at the Victorian Inspectorate, a former Chief Parliamentary Counsel in Victoria and former Law Draftsman, Department of Justice, Hong Kong.

Cambridge University Press acknowledges the Australian Aboriginal and Torres Strait Islander peoples of this nation. We acknowledge the traditional custodians of the lands on which our company is located and where we conduct our business. We pay our respects to ancestors and Elders, past and present. Cambridge University Press is committed to honouring Australian Aboriginal and Torres Strait Islander peoples' unique cultural and spiritual relationships to the land, waters and seas and their rich contribution to society.

MODERN STATUTORY INTERPRETATION

FRAMEWORK, PRINCIPLES AND PRACTICE

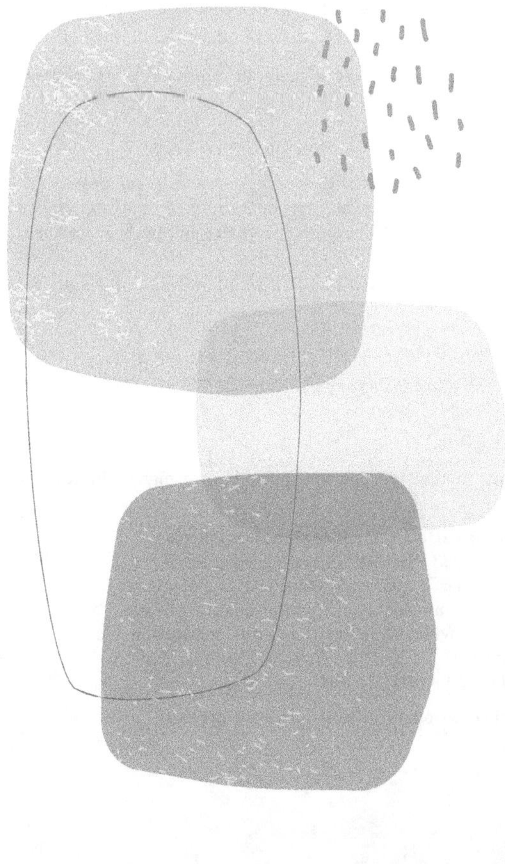

JEFFREY BARNES, JACINTA DHARMANANDA
AND EAMONN MORAN

CAMBRIDGE
UNIVERSITY PRESS

CAMBRIDGE
UNIVERSITY PRESS

Shaftesbury Road, Cambridge CB2 8EA, United Kingdom

One Liberty Plaza, 20th Floor, New York, NY 10006, USA

477 Williamstown Road, Port Melbourne, VIC 3207, Australia

314–321, 3rd Floor, Plot 3, Splendor Forum, Jasola District Centre, New Delhi – 110025, India

103 Penang Road, #05–06/07, Visioncrest Commercial, Singapore 238467

Cambridge University Press is part of Cambridge University Press & Assessment, a department of the University of Cambridge.

We share the University's mission to contribute to society through the pursuit of education, learning and research at the highest international levels of excellence.

www.cambridge.org
Information on this title: www.cambridge.org/highereducation/isbn/9781108816021

DOI: 10.1017/9781108895637

First published 2023
Cover and text designed by Sardine Design
Typeset by Straive

A catalogue record for this publication is available from the British Library

A catalogue record for this book is available from the National Library of Australia

ISBN 978-1-108-81602-1 Paperback

Additional resources for this publication at www.cambridge.org/highereducation/isbn/9781108816021/resources

Please be aware that this publication may contain several variations of Aboriginal and Torres Strait Islander terms and spellings; no disrespect is intended. Please note that the terms 'First Nations', 'Indigenous Australians' and 'Aboriginal and Torres Strait Islander peoples' may be used interchangeably in this publication.

FOREWORD

It has for some time been accepted that we live in an age of statutes. Given the volume and complexity of legislation it is unsurprising that a large part of the practice of the law in Australia involves statutory interpretation. The publication in recent years of texts on the subject confirms its importance and the difficulties associated with understanding why and how it is undertaken. This text by Jeffrey Barnes, Jacinta Dharmananda and Eamonn Moran is a welcome addition.

This text is a comprehensive account of the principles and practice of statutory interpretation in Australia today. It provides a detailed discussion of every aspect of the subject necessary for a proper understanding of it. It explains its constitutional setting and historical background, the development of its broader concepts and the approach of the courts to it, including the principles, presumptions and techniques that are employed. It discusses the use of extrinsic materials, interpretation and other statutes, and the place of international treaties and materials. It encourages the gaining of the skills necessary to undertake the process of statutory interpretation and deals with topics often overlooked such as methods of drafting and the process of enactment. Considerable reference is made in the text to case law and it will be a valuable resource for both student and practitioner.

The work seeks to ensure that the next generation of lawyers will be skilled in the 'art' and 'science' of statutory interpretation. That can only be achieved by providing a strong foundation for it in a lawyer's education. Whilst adopting an educative approach, the authors also provide a guide to practical techniques. The work benefits from the combined experiences of its authors and makes a valuable contribution to this most important topic.

The Hon Susan Kiefel AC
Chief Justice of Australia

CONTENTS

Foreword by Chief Justice Susan Kiefel *v*
Preface *xv*
List of examples *xvii*
Table of cases *xx*
Table of statutes *lvii*
About the authors *lxxxviii*
Acknowledgements *xc*

PART I BACKGROUND 1

1 The nature of statutory interpretation 3
Overview 3
Basic composition 3
Comparisons 6
Functions 14

2 A modern history of key concepts 17
Overview 17
Approach to statutory interpretation: 1900s to 1970s 17
Pivotal Interpretation Act amendments: 1980s 25
Common law developments – the 'modern' approach: 1990s 31
Changes to some Interpretation Acts: 2000s 33

3 Constitutional context 36
Overview 36
Sources of law and the separation of powers 36
The rule of law and parliamentary sovereignty 42

PART II THE FRAMEWORK OF STATUTORY INTERPRETATION 47

4 Legislative intent 49
Overview 49
The object of statutory interpretation 49
An objective concept 50
Distinct from 'purpose' 56
Statements of intent in legislation 57
Statement of intent in extrinsic materials 58

5 The judicial duty to be independent 62
Overview 62
Sole authoritative arbiters 62
Independence in reaching a decision 64

6 Text-based interpretation 72
Overview 72
The text-based principle 72
The meaning of the text-based principle 73
Consequences of transgressing the text 79

7 Context 83
Overview 83
Meaning of context 84
Duty to have regard to 86
Consequences of contextualism 90
Utility of regard to 93

8 Purpose 98
Overview 98
Statutory and common law requirement 98
Meaning of purpose 101
Assistance given by purpose 102
Finding the purpose 104
Limitations of the assistance given by purpose 110
Balancing purpose with the text 115

9 Practical techniques 117
Overview 117
Utilising models of interpretative skills 117
Making use of an overall method 118
Conducting legal research 121
Analysing the Act 123
Identifying interpretative factors 130
Formulating alternative constructions 135
Evaluating interpretative arguments 140
Determining the preferable construction 143
Presenting a legal opinion or reasons for judgment 144

PART III WORKING WITH LEGISLATION: BROADER SKILLS AND KNOWLEDGE 147

10 Legislative drafting 149
Overview 149
The drafting process 149
Role of parliamentary counsel 153
Drafting practices and techniques 156
Relationship between drafting and interpretation 161

11 Enactment procedure 163
Overview 163
The making of an Act 163
Classification of Bills and Acts 172
Powers and privileges of Parliament 175
Access to Acts 178

12 Commencement 181
Overview 181
What commencement means and how it is effected 181
Status of Act pre-commencement 190

13 Structure and components of an Act 194
Overview 194
Structure of an Act 194
Components of an Act 196

14 Problem analysis: sources of doubt 207
Overview 207
Nature of sources of doubt 207
Catalogues of potential sources of doubt 208
Utility of ascertaining sources of doubt 210

PART IV THE PROVISION, AND THE ACT AS A WHOLE 219

15 The language of the provision 221
Overview 221
The presumptive meaning 222
The nature of literal, grammatical, natural and ordinary meanings 223
Determining the presumptive meaning 226
Overcoming the presumptive meaning 229
When a text has a 'plain meaning' 229

16 The effect of drafting styles 231
Overview 231
Main drafting styles 231
Influence of drafting styles on interpretation 237
Drafting conventions of Australian parliamentary counsel 243

17 Special categories of legislation: the interpretation of remedial, penal and revenue provisions 245
Overview 245
Special categories of legislation 246
Remedial legislation 246
Penal provisions 250
Revenue Acts 256

18 Linguistic canons 260
Overview 260
Nature of linguistic canons 261
Canons that focus on the word in question 262
Canons that relate to other aspects of the provision 270
Canons that relate to the use of other relevant provisions 274

19 The 'always speaking' approach 283
Overview 283
Legislation can apply to circumstances unknown at enactment 283

Distinguish connotation from denotation 286
Changes in law since enactment 289
Limitations of approach 292

20 The scheme and components of an Act 295
Overview 295
Scheme of Act 295
Interpretative value of individual components 296
Impact on interpretation of where provisions are located 308

PART V LEGISLATIVE HISTORY 313

21 Legislative antecedents (evolution), including subsequent amending Acts 315
Overview 315
As part of wider context 315
Consolidation Acts 318
Use as interpretative aids 319
Presumptions about re-enacted words 323
Subsequent amending Acts 327

22 Pre-existing common law 330
Overview 330
As part of wider context 330
Interpretation of codes 333
Ways statute can impact pre-existing common law 335
Common law that triggers legislative enactment 338

23 Background facts and circumstances 340
Overview 340
As part of wider context 340
Range of matters 342
Rationality and parliamentary awareness 345
Use of judicial notice 348

24 Extrinsic materials: pre-parliamentary and parliamentary materials 350
Overview 350
Statutory and common law authority 350
Range of material 353
Statutory requirements 355
Common law requirements 358
Parliamentary awareness of material 359
Guidance on probative value 360
Text still paramount 366
Inference from parliamentary inaction 371

PART VI INTERPRETATION ACTS AND OTHER ACTS OF GENERAL APPLICATION 375

25 Interpretation Acts 377
Overview 377
Purpose of Interpretation Acts 377
Interpretation Acts are subject to contrary intention 378
Acts shortening provisions 381
General interpretative rules 394

26 Other Acts of general application 403
Overview 403
Human Rights Acts 403
Statutory review mechanisms 406
Criminal and sentencing Acts 410
Evidence Acts 412
Other facilitative Acts 413

PART VII THE WIDER CONTEXT 419

27 Consequences 421
Overview 421
Defining consequences 421
Taking into account consequences 422
Kinds of consequences that may be taken into account 429

28 The principle of legality 432
Overview 432
What is the principle of legality and how may it be rebutted? 433
Fundamental rights 440
Rationale for presumption 443
Applicability of presumption to delegated legislation and statutory rights 444

29 Use of the statute book and legislation of other jurisdictions 450
Overview 450
Relevance of other statutes 451
Statutes *in pari materia* 453
Statutes forming part of a single scheme 456
Comparable statutes 459

30 Use of precedent 464
Overview 464
Binding and persuasive precedent 464
Decisions on uniform and federal legislation 470
Decisions on statutes *in pari materia* 474
Doctrine of analogy 476

31 International treaties and materials 478
Overview 478
International obligations incorporated in domestic law 478

International obligations correspond to domestic law 481
Primacy of the text of domestic law 482
Presumption of consistency 483
International materials as extrinsic aids 487

32 Other common law presumptions and aids 489
Overview 489
Dictionaries and other works of reference 489
Surrounding law 497
Common sense 506

33 Inadmissible considerations 510
Overview 510
What makes a consideration inadmissible 510
Judicial policy 512
Certain executive government sources 514
Speculative matters 522

PART VIII SPECIAL INTERPRETATIVE ISSUES 525

34 Remedial constructions for drafting errors 527
Overview 527
Concepts central to remedial construction 527
Simple and obvious drafting errors 528
Guidance for remedial construction beyond simple errors 530
Gaps in legislation distinguished 535
Strained construction 537

35 Provisions in apparent conflict 539
Overview 539
Apparent conflict is an interpretative problem 539
Basic presumptions applied in resolving apparent conflict 541
Techniques for resolving apparent conflict 546

36 Statutory powers and their characterisation: discretion or duty? 553
Overview 553
Functions of statutory powers 553
Developments in drafting of statutory powers 556
Interpreting statutory powers – discretion or duty? 560

37 The effect of non-compliance with a statutory requirement 572
Overview 572
How the issue of the effect of non-compliance may arise 572
Is the requirement an essential condition? 573
Is breach of the requirement legally enforceable? 585

38 Statutory reasonableness 590
Overview 590
Concept 590
Importance in statute law 591

Definition and general characteristics 592
Interpretation 596

39 Presumption against retrospective operation 601
Overview 601
Concept of retrospectivity 601
Sources of the presumption 603
Justification for the presumption 605
When will the presumption be attracted? 607
Ousting the presumption 618

40 Presumption against application to government and other Crown entities 622
Overview 622
The presumption and its displacement 622
What is meant by the term 'the Crown' in this context? 627
Act may be binding on the Crown only partially or only in certain respects 630
Presumption may be modified or reversed by legislation 632
Immunity does not extend to a party dealing with the Crown 634

41 Presumption against extraterritorial operation 636
Overview 636
What is extraterritorial operation? 636
The presumption and when, how and why it arises 638
Rebutting the presumption 646

42 Mental ingredient of statutory offences 648
Overview 648
How state of mind for an offence is addressed in criminal law 648
The common law principle of mens rea 650
Applicability of the common law principle 654
Content of the common law principle 661
Position under the Criminal Codes 662

43 Delegated legislation 666
Overview 666
What is delegated legislation? 666
Ordinary interpretation principles generally apply 668
Terms have same meaning as in enabling Act 670
Retrospective operation 671
Grounds for invalidity 672
Severance of invalid portion 681
Effect of not making delegated legislation contemplated by the enabling Act 682

Glossary *685*
Bibliography *697*
Index *716*

PREFACE

In essence, statutory interpretation law governs the determination of the meaning of legislation. Statutory interpretation is of enormous importance to the work of the courts, the administration of the law by the executive branch of government, and the day-to-day practice of legal practitioners. Given its importance in practice, it is also an essential area of legal education and legal research.

The main aim of our work is to give those who engage in statutory interpretation an original, clear, coherent and research-based account of contemporary Australian statutory interpretation law. Given the nature of our work, we expect the primary audience to be the legal profession, legal researchers, and other professional users. Students taking advanced subjects on statutory interpretation that equip them for practice should also find it useful.

Three ideas have been fundamental in our preparation of this work.

The first is that it is important for the interpreter to have an understanding of the legislative process – that is, legislative drafting and parliamentary enactment procedure. This sets the context for the principles of interpretation and enhances an interpreter's understanding of many of those principles. These matters are covered in Part III.

Second, we have strived to arrange the book in a way that correlates, as best it can, with the overall method of interpretation and its practical application. Foundational matters are the subject of Parts I, II and III. Part I introduces statutory interpretation, taking in the essential nature and modern history of statutory interpretation and its constitutional context. Part II deals with the foundational principles of interpretation, including legislative intent and the well-known trilogy of text, context and legislative purpose. It also examines practical techniques of interpretation including overall method. Part III, as noted above, outlines the legislative process as well as basic aspects of legislation and sources of doubt and interpretative difficulty. After these foundational matters, Parts IV–VII deal with general principles of interpretation, starting with the intrinsic context and then moving through various components of external context. Part IV examines the guidance to be had from the words to be interpreted and the Act in question. Part V deals with legislative history. Part VI concerns Interpretation Acts and other Acts of general application. Part VII studies the remainder of the external context. Part VIII completes the body of the work with an examination of principles that deal with the resolution of special interpretative issues.

Third, we wished to present the law in an accessible way. Each chapter is built around a set of principles and uses detailed examples to provide concrete guidance on the operation of those principles. We believe this principle/example approach is well suited to stating and illuminating the law. At appropriate points, the principles are linked to research in the wider literature about controversial or unresolved questions. For convenience, the glossary at the end of the book collects together the basic terms that are explained in the work.

In the preparation of this work, Jeffrey Barnes assumed primary responsibility for the structure of the book. While each author has read and contributed to all of the chapters, primary responsibility for researching, drafting and finalising the various chapters was allocated as follows:

- Jeffrey Barnes: chapters 1, 5–7, 9, 14–15, 17–18, 27, 29, 32–33, 35–39, 41–42
- Jacinta Dharmananda: chapters 2–4, 8, 16, 19, 21–24, 30–31, 34
- Eamonn Moran: chapters 10–13, 20, 25–26, 28, 40, 43.

We are greatly honoured by the Hon Susan Kiefel AC, Chief Justice of the High Court of Australia, agreeing to write the Foreword and are most grateful to her for doing so.

As with any work of this nature and size, there are many people who assisted us and helped us bring the work to fruition. We thank Dr David Arnold for his skilled editorial work in the technicalities of referencing and for assistance in collating content for the glossary and bibliography. Dr Arnold's work was supported by the Social Research Assistance Platform of La Trobe University. We would also like to acknowledge the assistance of Dr Steven Churches in discussions around the original design of the work.

We thank the team at Cambridge University Press, especially Lucy Russell, Rose Albiston and Angela Damis, for their encouragement, patience and support. We are also most grateful for the feedback received from the anonymous reviewers engaged by the publisher.

We also have some individual thanks to make.

Jeffrey Barnes would like to thank Ken Millis for commenting on a draft of chapters 1 and 5 and Dr Steven Tudor for commenting on a draft of chapter 42. He would like to acknowledge the unstinting support of his wife Jane throughout the project.

Jacinta Dharmananda would like to thank her colleague Professor Sarah Murray for commenting on drafts of chapter 3. She also acknowledges that some of the research for this work (particularly for chapter 2 and Part V) is supported by an Australian Government Research Training Program ('RTP') Scholarship. Most importantly, special thanks and gratitude to her husband, Kanaga, for his unwavering encouragement and support, and to their daughters, Shivani and Nishka, for their quiet understanding.

Eamonn Moran would like to thank Victoria's former Special Minister of State, the Hon Gavin Jennings, for his support for him embarking on this project while holding office at the Victorian Inspectorate. Finally, and most importantly, his deep thanks go to his wife Anne for her encouragement for him to take on this work and accommodating it being done by him at inconvenient hours in the home environment.

To the best of our abilities, the law is stated as at 1 January 2022.

Jeffrey Barnes
Jacinta Dharmananda
Eamonn Moran
February 2022

EXAMPLES

1.1 *Dolheguy v Becker* 4
1.2 *ABC Developmental Learning Centres Pty Ltd v Secretary, Department of Human Services* 5
1.3 *Virgin Blue Airlines Pty Ltd v Federal Commissioner of Taxation* 8
1.4 *Minister for Immigration and Citizenship v Yucesan* 11
1.5 *WorldAudio Ltd v Australian Communications and Media Authority* 15
2.1 *Metropolitan Gas Company v Federated Gas Employees' Industrial Union* 21
3.1 *Treasurer of Victoria v Tabcorp Holdings Ltd* 39
4.1 *John Holland Pty Ltd v Victorian Workcover Authority* 57
4.2 *Nominal Defendant v GLG Australia Pty Ltd* 59
5.1 *Minister for Immigration and Citizenship v Yucesan* 64
5.2 *R v Hannan* 65
5.3 *Minister for Immigration and Citizenship v Yucesan* 67
5.4 *JAD v The Queen* 69
6.1 *Collett v Repatriation Commission* 76
6.2 *Smoker v Pharmacy Restructuring Authority* 78
6.3 *DPP v Moreno* 81
7.1 *SZTAL v Minister for Immigration and Border Protection* 85
7.2 *Beadle v La Bianca* 90
7.3 *LU Simon Builders Pty Ltd v Victorian Building Authority* 94
7.4 *LU Simon Builders Pty Ltd v Victorian Building Authority* 96
8.1 *AB v Western Australia* 107
8.2 *Medical Board of Australia v Kemp* 111
8.3 *Hunter Quarries Pty Ltd v Mexon* 113
9.1 *Chapman v South Eastern Sydney Local Health District* 121
9.2 *Talacko v Bennett* 123
9.3 *Tjungarrayi v Western Australia* 126
9.4 *Footscray City College v Ruzicka* 128
9.5 *LU Simon Builders Pty Ltd v Victorian Building Authority* 129
9.6 *LU Simon Builders Pty Ltd v Victorian Building Authority* 132
9.7 *Mansfield v The Queen* 135
9.8 *ZD v Secretary to the Department of Health and Human Services* 142
11.1 Passage of a Bill through the Commonwealth Parliament 169
12.1 *Guardianship and Administration Act 2019* (Vic) 188
13.1 Long title of the *Australia Act 1986* (Cth) 197
13.2 Preamble of the *Australia Act 1986* (Cth) 199
13.3 Short title clause of *Australia Act 1986* (Cth) 199
13.4 *Fair Work Act 2009* (Cth) s 10 201
13.5 Number and date of passing of the *Australia Act 1986* (Cth) 206
14.1 *R v PJ* 211

14.2 *Smoker v Pharmacy Restructuring Authority* 213
14.3 *Scott-Mackenzie v Bail* 214
15.1 *Healey v Royal Society for the Prevention of Cruelty to Animals Victoria* 224
15.2 *Merrick Tyler Pty Ltd v Commissioner of Main Roads* 227
15.3 *ZD v Secretary to the Department of Health and Human Services* 230
16.1 *Sea-Carriage of Goods Act 1909* (WA) 232
16.2 *Victims Compensation Fund Corporation v Brown* 238
16.3 *Quikfund (Australia) Pty Ltd v Airmark Consolidators Pty Ltd* 241
17.1 *AB v Western Australia* 247
17.2 *R v Rose* 252
17.3 *DPP (Cth) v Poniatowska* 255
17.4 *Federal Commissioner of Taxation v Multiflex Pty Ltd* 258
18.1 *Secretary, Department of Employment, Education, Training and Youth Affairs v Gray* 263
18.2 *CAG v Public Trustee of Queensland* 264
18.3 *R v Bentham* 264
18.4 *Herbert Adams Pty Ltd v Federal Commissioner of Taxation* 269
18.5 *Collett v Repatriation Commission* 271
18.6 *Collett v Repatriation Commission* 272
18.7 *CAG v Public Trustee of Queensland* 275
18.8 *United Firefighters' Union of Australia v Victorian Equal Opportunity and Human Rights Commission* 276
18.9 *CAG v Public Trustee of Queensland* 278
18.10 *ABC Developmental Learning Centres Pty Ltd v Secretary, Department of Human Services* 281
19.1 *Uber BV v Federal Commissioner of Taxation* 287
19.2 *Dionisatos (for the Estate of the Late George Dionysatos) v Acrow Formwork & Scaffolding Pty Ltd* 290
19.3 *A-G (Tas) v CL* 293
20.1 *R v Fyffe* 308
21.1 *Esso Australia Pty Ltd v Australian Workers' Union* 317
21.2 *Fremantle Lawyers Pty Ltd v Sarich* 320
21.3 *GBT v Western Australia* 322
22.1 *King v Philcox* 337
22.2 *Insurance Commission of Western Australia v Container Handlers Pty Ltd* 338
23.1 *Commissioner of State Revenue v EHL Burgess Properties Pty Ltd* 346
24.1 *Commissioner of Taxation v Murray* 359
24.2 *Re Bolton; Ex parte Beane* 367
24.3 *Mondelez Australia Pty Ltd v Automotive, Food, Metals, Engineering, Printing and Kindred Industries Union* 369
24.4 *Anderson v Commissioner of Highways* 371
26.1 *Victorian Civil and Administrative Tribunal Act 1998* (Vic) and *Freedom of Information Act 1982* (Vic) 408
27.1 *Berenguel v Minister for Immigration and Citizenship* 423
27.2 *Dietman v Brennan-Kuss* 425
27.3 *Alcan (NT) Alumina Pty Ltd v Commissioner of Territory Revenue (NT)* 427
28.1 *Coco v The Queen* 435
28.2 *X7 v Australian Crime Commission* 436
28.3 *R v Independent Broad-based Anti-corruption Commissioner* 437

28.4 *Vella v Minister for Immigration and Border Protection* 438
28.5 *Probuild Constructions (Aust) Pty Ltd v Shade Systems Pty Ltd* 440
28.6 *Evans v New South Wales* 445
29.1 *JAD v The Queen* 451
29.2 *Taylor v The Owners – Strata Plan 11564* 452
29.3 *Wilson v Transport Accident Commission* 455
29.4 *Liu v Stephen Grubits and Associates* 457
29.5 *Talacko v Bennett* 461
29.6 *Hughes v Janrule Pty Ltd* 463
30.1 *Weiss v The Queen* 466
30.2 *Metricon Qld Pty Ltd v Chief Commissioner of State Revenue (No 2)* 468
30.3 *Hill v Zuda Pty Ltd* 470
31.1 *Comptroller-General of Customs v Pharm-A-Care Laboratories Pty Ltd* 479
31.2 *FCS17 v Minister for Home Affairs* 482
31.3 *Cheedy v Western Australia* 485
32.1 *Doyle v Maypole Bakery Pty Ltd* 496
32.2 *Pinho v Andre* 500
32.3 *Zhang v Commissioner of Police* 501
32.4 *Coleman v Power* 502
32.5 *Minister for Immigration and Citizenship v Yucesan* 508
32.6 *ABC Developmental Learning Centres Pty Ltd v Secretary, Department of Human Services* 509
33.1 *Australian Education Union v Department of Education and Children's Services* 513
33.2 *Tom and Bill Waterhouse Pty Ltd v Racing New South Wales* 518
33.3 *Turner v Keegan* 520
33.4 *Barnes v Victoria* 521
34.1 *Commissioner for Corrective Services (WA) v Raj* 536
35.1 *Project Blue Sky Inc v Australian Broadcasting Authority* 543
35.2 *Commissioner of Police for New South Wales v Eaton* 546
35.3 *Saliba v Aziz* 550
36.1 *North Australian Aboriginal Justice Agency Ltd v Northern Territory* 556
36.2 *Leach v The Queen* 563
36.3 *Hall v Sheiban Pty Ltd* 564
36.4 *Re Griffiths* 566
37.1 *Ian Street Developer Pty Ltd v Arrow International Pty Ltd* 583
37.2 *Yarmirr v Australian Telecommunications Corporation* 589
38.1 *Taikato v The Queen* 599
39.1 *Dossett v TKJ Nominees Pty Ltd* 620
40.1 *Commonwealth v Anti-Discrimination Tribunal (Tas)* 631
40.2 *Australian Competition and Consumer Commission v Baxter Healthcare Pty Ltd* 635
41.1 *R v Nationwide News Pty Ltd* 640
41.2 *DPP v Sutcliffe* 647
42.1 *R v Lagan* (full mens rea) 657
42.2 *DPP v Hazelwood Pacific Pty Ltd (Ruling No 2)* (middle position) 658
42.3 *Stanojlovic v DPP* (absolute liability) 659
43.1 *Plaintiff M47/2012 v Director-General of Security* 675
43.2 *R v Toohey; Ex Parte Northern Land Council* 677
43.3 *King Gee Clothing Co Pty Ltd v Commonwealth* 680

TABLE OF CASES

Entries in bold indicate discussion in an Example

4Nature Inc v Centennial Springvale Pty Ltd (2017) 95 NSWLR 361, 669

A v Maughan (2016) 50 WAR 263, 290
AB v Conduct Division of the Judicial Commission (NSW) (2018) 365 ALR 163, 568
AB v Western Australia (2011) 244 CLR 390, **107–9**, 246, **247–9**, 250, 330, 513
Abbott v Minister for Lands [1895] AC 425, 609–10
ABC Developmental Learning Centres Pty Ltd v Secretary, Department of Human Services (2007) 15 VR 489, **5–6**, 138, **281–2**, 301, 508, **509**
Accident Compensation Commission v Murphy [1988] VR 444, 571
Adams v Director Fair Works Inspectorate (2017) 258 FCR 257, 474
Adams v Lambert (2006) 228 CLR 409, 401
ADCO Constructions Pty Ltd v Goudappel (2014) 254 CLR 1, 380, 395, 521, 601–2, 605, 618, 668–9, 671, 676
Addy v Federal Commissioner of Taxation (2021) 95 ALJR 911, 479
A-G v Fardon [2019] 2 Qd R 487, 595
A-G v Lamplough (1878) 3 Ex D 214, 201
A-G v Prince Ernest Augustus of Hanover [1957] AC 436, 32, 198, 296, 297
A-G v Smith (1985) 39 SASR 311, 397
A-G (Cth) v Foster (1999) 84 FCR 582, 387
A-G (Cth) v Oates (1999) 198 CLR 162, 33, 352
A-G (NSW) v Brewery Employes Union of New South Wales (1908) 6 CLR 469, 268
A-G (NSW) v Butterworth & Co (Australia) Ltd (1938) 38 SR (NSW) 195, 149–50, 178
A-G (NSW) v Markisic [2012] NSWSC 433, 400
A-G (NSW) v Melco Resorts & Entertainment Ltd (2020) 102 NSWLR 47, 447
A-G (NSW) v Quin (1990) 170 CLR 1, 38, 62–3, 409, 504
A-G (NSW) v World Best Holdings Ltd (2005) 63 NSWLR 557, 4
A-G (Qld) v Australian Industrial Relations Commission (2002) 213 CLR 485, 223, 380, 381, 602, 612, 613, 618–19
A-G (Qld) (ex rel Goldsbrough, Mort & Co Ltd) v A-G (Cth) (1915) 20 CLR 148, 284
A-G (SA) v Corporation of the City of Adelaide (2013) 249 CLR 1, 443, 445, 492, 673, 678
A-G (Tas) v CL [2018] TASFC 6, **293–4**, 366
A-G (Vic) v Commonwealth (1945) 71 CLR 237, 193
A-G (Vic) v Commonwealth (1962) 107 CLR 529, 18
A-G (WA) v Marquet (2003) 217 CLR 545, 176, 226
Agius v The Queen (2013) 248 CLR 601, 492
AGU v Commonwealth (No 2) (2013) 86 NSWLR 348, 626
Ahmed v HM Treasury (Justice Intervening) (Nos 1 and 2) [2010] 2 AC 534, 405
AIB Group (UK) Ltd v Martin [2002] 1 WLR 94, 273
Aid/Watch Inc v Commissioner of Taxation (Cth) (2010) 241 CLR 539, 289–90, 336–7

Ainsworth v Albrecht (2016) 261 CLR 167, 594–6
Ainsworth v Criminal Justice Commission (1992) 175 CLR 564, 262
Air-India v Wiggins [1980] 1 WLR 815, 645
AIT18 v Australian Information Commissioner (2018) 267 FCR 93, 247, 250
AJS v The Queen (2007) 235 CLR 505, 140
Alcan (NT) Alumina Pty Ltd v Commissioner of Territory Revenue (NT) (2009) 239 CLR 27, 6, 51, 74–5, 89, 100, 104, 109, 113, 124, 224, 256–8, 358, 363, 367–8, **427–8**
Alfonso v Northern Territory (1999) 131 NTR 8, 454
Al-Kateb v Godwin (2004) 219 CLR 562, 51, 101, 443, 483
Allan v Transurban City Link Ltd (2001) 208 CLR 167, 407
Allen v United Carpet Mills Pty Ltd [1989] VR 323, 659
Alley v Gillespie (2018) 264 CLR 328, 354, 362
Allina Pty Ltd v Commissioner of Taxation (1991) 28 FCR 203, 328
Alphapharm Pty Ltd v H Lundbeck A/S (2014) 254 CLR 247, 266, 367–8
Alqudsi v The Queen (2016) 258 CLR 203, 593
Amaca Pty Ltd v Novek (2009) 9 DDCR 199, 364
Amalgamated Society of Engineers v Adelaide Steamship Co Ltd (1920) 28 CLR 129, 18, 20, 91, 625
Amalgamated Television Services Pty Ltd v Australian Broadcasting Tribunal (1989) 91 ALR 363, 310
Amalgamated Wireless (A/asia) Ltd v Philpott (1961) 110 CLR 617, 324
Amatek Ltd v Googoorewon Pty Ltd (1993) 176 CLR 471, 107, 296
Ambrose v Edmonds-Wilson (1998) 48 SASR 514, 656
Amery v New South Wales (Director-General, NSW Department of Education and Training [2004] NSWCA 404, 262
AMT Planning Consultants Pty Ltd v Central Coast Council (2018) 238 LGERA 116, 472
Anderson v Commissioner of Highways (2019) 134 SASR 543, **371–2**
Anderson v Commissioner of Taxes (Vic) (1937) 57 CLR 233, 127, 256–7
Andrews v Thompson (2018) 340 FLR 439, 406
Andrews and Morrissy Developments Pty Ltd v Port Phillip City Council (2019) 241 LGERA 280, 361
Anglican Care v NSW Nurses and Midwives' Association (2015) 231 FCR 316, 447
Annetts v McCann (1990) 170 CLR 596, 504
Ansett Transport Industries (Operations) Pty Ltd v Wardley (1980) 142 CLR 237, 49
Anthony Horden and Sons Ltd v Amalgamated Clothing and Allied Trades Union of Australia (1932) 47 CLR 1, 276
Antico v Heath Fielding Australia Pty Ltd (1997) 188 CLR 652, 246, 249
Applicant A v Minister for Immigration and Ethnic Affairs (1997) 190 CLR 225, 479–80
Applicant S270/2019 v Minister for Immigration and Border Protection (2020) 94 ALJR 897, 486
AQO v Minister for Finance and Services (2016) 93 NSWLR 46, 129, 328, 362, 373, 429
Arnold v Hunt (1943) 67 CLR 429, 679
Arthur Yates & Co Pty Ltd v Vegetable Seeds Committee (1945) 72 CLR 37, 677
Assistant Registrar of Companies v Moses [2004] 3 NZLR 577, 226, 460
Associated Beauty Aids Pty Ltd v Commissioner of Taxation (Cth) (1965) 113 CLR 662, 183
Associated Minerals Consolidated Ltd v Wyong Shire Council [1975] AC 538, 3, 88, 133, 547
AstraZeneca AB v Apotex Pty Ltd (2015) 257 CLR 356, 355
Atkinson v Bardon (2018) 41 NTLR 35, 555, 558
Aubrey v The Queen (2017) 260 CLR 305, 251, 284, 287–8, 292, 294, 327, 465, 495

Australand Corporation (Qld) Pty Ltd v Johnson [2008] 1 Qd R 203, 465, 613–15
Australasian Meat Industry Employees Union v Hamberger (2000) 102 FCR 74, 85
Australasian Temperance and General Mutual Life Assurance Society Ltd v Howe (1922) 31 CLR 290, 268
Australia and New Zealand Banking Group Ltd v Federal Commissioner of Taxation (1994) 48 FCR 268, 373
Australian Boot Trade Employees' Federation v Whybrow & Co (1910) 11 CLR 311, 22, 674
Australian Broadcasting Corporation v Redmore Pty Ltd (1987) 11 NSWLR 621, 309
Australian Broadcasting Corporation v Redmore Pty Ltd (1989) 166 CLR 454, 309, 576, 579–81
Australian Broadcasting Tribunal v Bond (1990) 170 CLR 321, 15–16, 138–9
Australian Building and Construction Commissioner v Construction, Forestry, Mining and Energy Union (2017) 254 FCR 68, 129
Australian Building and Construction Commissioner v Construction, Forestry, Mining and Energy Union (2018) 262 CLR 157, 316, 371
Australian Building and Construction Commissioner v Molina (2020) 277 FCR 223, 37
Australian Capital Television Pty Ltd v Commonwealth (1992) 177 CLR 106, 44, 76, 275
Australian Coal & Shale Employees Federation v Aberfield Coal Mining Co Ltd (1942) 66 CLR 161, 672
Australian Communist Party v Commonwealth (1951) 83 CLR 1, 42, 106, 297, 490
Australian Competition and Consumer Commission v Australian Egg Corporation Ltd (2016) 337 ALR 573, 627
Australian Competition and Consumer Commission v Australian Egg Corporation Ltd (2017) 254 FCR 311, 627
Australian Competition and Consumer Commission v Australian Safeway Stores Pty Ltd (2003) 129 FCR 339, 254
Australian Competition and Consumer Commission v Australian Safeway Stores Pty Ltd (No 3) (2001) 119 FCR 1, 253
Australian Competition and Consumer Commission v Baxter Healthcare Pty Ltd (2007) 232 CLR 1, 630, **635**
Australian Competition and Consumer Commission v Yazaki Corporation (2018) 262 FCR 243, 303
Australian Crime Commission v Stoddart (2011) 244 CLR 554, 440
Australian Education Union v Department of Education and Children's Services (2012) 248 CLR 1, 3, 66, 74, 85, 109, 222, 362, 429, 512, **513–14**, 515
Australian Education Union v General Manager of Fair Work Australia (2012) 246 CLR 117, 422, 428–9, 440, 602, 606
Australian Finance Direct Ltd v Director of Consumer Affairs Victoria (2007) 234 CLR 96, 31
Australian Fisheries Management Authority v Su (2009) 176 FCR 95, 663–4
Australian Gas Light Co v Valuer-General (1940) 40 SR (NSW) 126, 268
Australian Investment and Development Pty Ltd v Commissioner of State Revenue [2019] VSCA 69, 258, 347–8, 473
Australian Mines and Metals Association Inc v Construction, Forestry, Maritime, Mining and Energy Union (2018) 268 FCR 128, 133, 145, 361
Australian Municipal, Administrative, Clerical and Services Union v Commonwealth [2018] FWCFB 1170, 274
Australian Postal Corporation v Sinnaiah (2013) 213 FCR 449, 113, 308, 446–7

Australian Prudential Regulation Authority v Holloway (2000) 104 FCR 521, 301
Australian Retirement Homes Ltd v Ash [2013] QCA 355, 299
Australian Securities and Investments Commission v Albarran (2008) 169 FCR 448, 597
Australian Securities and Investments Commission v DB Management Pty Ltd (2000) 199 CLR 321, 338, 439
Australian Securities and Investments Commission v King (2020) 270 CLR 1, 103, 355, 365
Australian Securities and Investments Commission v Westpac Securities Administration Ltd (2019) 272 FCR 170, 225, 270
Australian Securities Commission v Bank Leumi Le-Israel (1995) 134 ALR 101, 646
Australian Securities Commission v Bank Leumi Le-Israel (1996) 139 ALR 527, 646
Australian Securities Commission v Gallagher (1993) 11 WAR 105, 599
Australian Securities Commission v Marlborough Gold Mines Ltd (1993) 177 CLR 485, 470
Australian Tea Tree Oil Research Institute v Industry Research and Development Board (2002) 124 FCR 316, 670
Australian Unity Property Ltd v City of Busselton (2018) 237 LGERA 333, 39, 50, 528, 533
Automobile Fire and General Insurance Co of Australia Ltd v Davey (1936) 54 CLR 534, 387
Avel Pty Ltd v A-G (NSW) (1987) 11 NSWLR 126, 33, 361
Awada v Linknarf (in liq) (2002) 55 NSWLR 745, 301
Axon v Axon (1937) 59 CLR 395, 506

B v Medical Superintendent of Macquarie Hospital (1987) 10 NSWLR 440, 188–9
Babaniaris v Lutony Fashions Pty Ltd (1987) 163 CLR 1, 49, 285, 465
Baiada Poultry Pty Ltd v The Queen (2012) 246 CLR 92, 554, 562
Bail v Scott-Mackenzie [2016] VSC 563, 214
Bailey v Palombo [2020] NSWSC 1209, 265
Baini v The Queen (2012) 246 CLR 469, 324, 367–8, 466–7
Baker v The Queen (2012) 245 CLR 632, 477
Ballantyne v Workcover Authority of New South Wales [2007] NSWCA 239, 555, 561
Bampton v Viterra Ltd (2015) 123 SASR 80, 225
Bank of Australasia v Hall (1907) 4 CLR 1514, 302
Bank of New South Wales v Commonwealth (1948) 76 CLR 1, 629, 681
Barangaroo Delivery Authority v Lend Lease (Millers Point) Pty Ltd [2014] NSWCA 279, 304
Barbosa v Di Meglio [1999] NSWCA 307, 496
Barcelo v Electrolytic Zinc Co of Australasia Ltd (1932) 48 CLR 391, 639, 642, 645
Bare v Independent Broad-based Anti-corruption Commission (2015) 48 VR 129, 404
Barker v Campbell (1983) 153 CLR 52, 512
Barker v The Queen (1983) 153 CLR 338, 268
Barminco Investments Pty Ltd v O'Brien [2006] WASCA 88, 607, 609–10
Barnes v Jarvis [1953] 1 WLR 649, 507
Barnes v Victoria [2015] VSCA 343, **521–2**
Barns v Barns (2003) 214 CLR 169, 247
Barrie and Minister for Immigration, Citizenship, Migrant Services and Multicultural Affairs (Citizenship) [2020] AATA 287, 516
Bass v Permanent Trustee Co Ltd (1999) 198 CLR 334, 629–30
Bayside City Council v Telstra Corporation Ltd (2004) 216 CLR 595, 305
Beadle v La Bianca [2012] WASC 415, 88, **90**, 134, 253, 474–5
Beaumont v Yeomans (1934) 34 SR (NSW) 562, 604

Beckwith v The Queen (1976) 135 CLR 569, 251, 253
Bell v Tasmania (2021) 395 ALR 589, 651, 664
Bell Lawyers Pty Ltd v Pentelow (2019) 269 CLR 333, 289, 476
Bellino v Australian Broadcasting Corporation (1996) 185 CLR 183, 335
Benggong v Bougainville Copper Pty Ltd (1971) 124 CLR 47, 270
Bennett v Minister for Public Works (NSW) (1908) 7 CLR 372, 296, 318
Benning v Sydney City Council (1958) 100 CLR 177, 274
Berenguel v Minister for Immigration and Citizenship (2010) 264 ALR 417; 84 ALJR 251, 7, 135–6, 365, **423–4**, 430, 511
Berenguel v Minister for Immigration and Citizenship [2010] HCATrans 41, 424
Berowa Holdings Pty Ltd v Gordon (2006) 225 CLR 364, 576–7
Besmaw Pty Ltd v Sutherland Shire Council (2003) 127 LGERA 413, 273
BGM16 v Minister for Immigration and Border Protection (2017) 252 FCR 97, 8, 134, 138, 145–6, 361, 364, 366, 424, 430
Biga Nominees Pty Ltd v Commissioner of Taxation (Cth) (1991) 104 FLR 74, 499
Binetti v Feasey (2015) 249 A Crim R 305, 663
Binsaris v Northern Territory (2020) 270 CLR 549, 435, 477, 674
Birch v Allen (1942) 65 CLR 621, 21, 197, 296, 670
Bird v Commonwealth (1988) 165 CLR 1, 247
Birmingham City Council v Walker [2007] 2 AC 262, 304
Bitumen and Oil Refineries (Australia) Ltd v Commissioner for Government Transport (1955) 92 CLR 200, 24, 26
Black-Clawson International Ltd v Papierwerke Waldhof-Aschaffenburg AG [1975] AC 591, 63, 156, 341, 347–8, 359
Blacktown Workers' Club Ltd v O'Shannessy (2011) 183 LGERA 184, 491
Blashill v Chambers (1884) 14 QBD 479, 671
Bligh Consulting Pty Ltd v Ausgrid [2017] NSWCA 95, 14, 469
Blue Metal Industries Ltd v Dilley (1969) 117 CLR 651, 378, 380, 385
Bluebottle UK Ltd v Deputy Commissioner of Taxation (2007) 232 CLR 598, 319, 469
Blunn v Cleaver (1993) 47 FCR 111, 157
BMG Resources Ltd v Municipality of Beaconsfield [1988] Tas R 142, 633
BMW Australia Ltd v Brewster (2019) 269 CLR 574, 261, 284, 286, 288–9, 316
Boland v Yates Property Corporation Pty Ltd (1999) 167 ALR 575, 13
Borough of Glebe v Lukey (Australian Gaslight Co) (1904) 1 CLR 158, 19
Boughey v The Queen (1986) 161 CLR 10, 333–4
Bowtell v Goldsbrough, Mort & Co Ltd (1905) 3 CLR 444, 21, 297
Boyce v Hughes (1970) 72 SR (NSW) 54, 608
Bradken Consolidated Ltd v Broken Hill Pty Co Ltd (1979) 145 CLR 107, 623, 625, 633–5
Bradley v Commonwealth (1973) 128 CLR 557, 301
Bray v F Hoffman-La Roche Ltd (2003) 130 FCR 317, 639, 643
Brayson Motors Pty Ltd (in liq) v Commissioner of Taxation (Cth) (1985) 156 CLR 651, 519
Brennan v Comcare (1994) 50 FCR 555, 13, 210, 358, 465–6
Brennan v The King (1936) 55 CLR 253, 333, 663
Brett v Director General, Department of Education [2015] WASCA 66, 447
Briers v Skilled Group Ltd (2014) 23 Tas R 305, 390
Brighton v Australia and New Zealand Banking Group Ltd [2011] NSWCA 152, 271
Brisbane City Council v Amos (2019) 266 CLR 593, 261, 279, 324

Brisbane City Council v Group Projects Pty Ltd (1979) 145 CLR 143, 623, 633
British Railways Board v Pickin [1974] AC 765, 173
Broadcasting Co of Australia Pty Ltd v Commonwealth (1935) 52 CLR 52, 671
Broken Hill South Ltd v Commissioner of Taxation (NSW) (1937) 56 CLR 337, 20, 22
Brooks v Commissioner of Taxation (2000) 100 FCR 117, 305–6
Bropho v Human Rights and Equal Opportunity Commission (2004) 135 FCR 105, 592–5
Bropho v Western Australia (1990) 171 CLR 1, 31, 51, 92, 100, 433–4, 571, 623–5, 630–4
Brown v Tasmania (2017) 261 CLR 328, 38, 101–2, 104, 251, 254, 345, 354
Brownlie v State Pollution Control Commission (1992) 27 NSWLR 78, 637–8, 641, 645–6
Brunswick Corporation v Stewart (1941) 65 CLR 88, 678
Brunton v Acting Commissioner of Stamp Duties (NSW) [1913] AC 747, 256
Buck v Comcare (1996) 66 FCR 359, 446
Buddhist Society of Western Australia Inc v Commissioner of Taxation (No 2) [2021] FCA 1363, 238
Building Construction Employees v Minister for Industrial Relations (1986) 7 NSWLR 372, 512
Bull v The Queen (2000) 201 CLR 443, 543
Burch v South Australia (1998) 71 SASR 12, 365
Burchell and National Disability Insurance Agency [2019] AATA 1256, 516
Burns v Corbett (2018) 265 CLR 304, 345
Burns v Minister for Health (2012) 45 WAR 276, 352
Burridge v Chief Magistrate of the Magistrates Court (ACT) (No 2) (2018) 338 FLR 339, 390
Butler v A-G (Vic) (1961) 106 CLR 268, 395, 448, 541, 545, 549–50
Buzzacott v Minister for Sustainability, Environment, Water, Population and Communities (2013) 215 FCR 301, 594
BVG17 v BVH17 (2019) 268 FCR 448, 361
Byrne v Garrisson [1965] VR 523, 396, 605
Byrnes v Kendle (2011) 243 CLR 253, 51–2
Byrnes v The Queen (1999) 199 CLR 1, 50
Bywater Investments Ltd v Commissioner of Taxation (Cth) (2016) 260 CLR 169, 480, 482

C v Director-General of the Department of Youth & Community Services [1982] 1 NSWLR 65, 192–3
Cabell v Markham, 148 F 2d 737 (1945), 101, 491–2, 597
CAG v Public Trustee of Queensland [2008] 2 Qd R 419, **264**, **275**, **278–9**
Cain v Doyle (1946) 72 CLR 409, 630
Calidad Pty Ltd v Seiko Epson Corporation (2020) 94 ALJR 1044, 102, 465
Callanan v B (2005) 1 Qd R 348, 395
Campbell v Renton (Supreme Court of Victoria, Marks J, 18 August 1988), 239
Canadian Foundation for Children, Youth and the Law v A-G (Canada) [2004] 1 SCR 76, 591, 595, 597
Canadian Pacific Air Lines Ltd v Canadian Air Line Pilots Association [1993] 3 SCR 724, 224, 226
Cann's Pty Ltd v Commonwealth (1946) 71 CLR 210, 680
Cantor Management Services Pty Ltd v Booth (2017) 106 ATR 615, 470–1
Canty v Deputy Commissioner of Taxation (2005) 63 NSWLR 152, 274
Cappello v Roads and Maritime Services (2019) 100 NSWLR 259, 105
Cappello v Roads and Maritime Services [2019] NSWSC 439, 299
Carbines v Powell (1925) 36 CLR 88, 673–4

Cardinal Project Services Pty Ltd v Hanave Pty Ltd (2011) 81 NSWLR 716, 27
Carltona Ltd v Commissioner of Works (1943) 2 All ER 560, 391
Carr v Corporation of the Royal Exchange Assurance Co (1862) 121 ER 970, 296
Carr v Western Australia (2007) 232 CLR 138, 76, 92, 109, 111, 113, 114, 247, 249, 532
Carter v Bradbeer [1975] 1 WLR 1204, 467–8
Carter v Minister for Aboriginal Affairs (2005) 143 FCR 383, 555
Catlow v Accident Compensation Commission (1989) 167 CLR 543, 89
CCR v PS (No 2) (1986) 6 NSWLR 622, 188
Certain Lloyd's Underwriters v Cross (2012) 248 CLR 378, 44, 49, 53, 66, 79, 101, 105, 108–10, 295, 304, 352, 366–7, 457, 511–13
CGX20 v Minister for Immigration, Citizenship, Migrant Services and Multicultural Affairs (2021) 284 FCR 416, 529
Chakera v Kuzamanovic [2003] VSC 92, 309
Chakravarti v Advertiser Newspapers Ltd (1998) 193 CLR 519, 593
Chandler v DPP [1964] AC 763, 202, 301
Chang v Laidley Shire Council (2007) 234 CLR 1, 495, 602, 609, 614, 616
Channel Pastoral Holdings Pty Ltd v Federal Commissioner of Taxation (2015) 232 FCR 162, 238
Channel Seven Brisbane Pty Ltd v Australian Communications and Media Authority (2014) 227 FCR 162, 669
Chapman v Commonwealth Bank of Australia [2012] VSCA 162, 498–9
Chapman v South Eastern Sydney Local Health District (2018) 98 NSWLR 208, **121–2**
Chappell and Co Ltd v Associated Radio Co of Australia Ltd [1925] VLR 350, 288
Charlesworth v MJ Sterling Pty Ltd [1943] VLR 67, 296
Cheedy v Western Australia (2011) 194 FCR 562, 229–30, **485**
Chesterman v Federal Commissioner of Taxation (1923) 32 CLR 362, 225
Chevron Australia Holdings Pty Ltd v Federal Commissioner of Taxation (2017) 251 FCR 40, 344–5
Chevron USA Inc v Natural Resources Defense Council Inc, 467 US 837 (1984), 63, 515
Chew v The Queen (1992) 173 CLR 626, 307
Chief Adjudication Officer v Maguire [1999] 1 WLR 1778, 602, 615
Chief Commissioner of State Revenue v Benidorm Pty Ltd (2020) 104 NSWLR 232, 465
Chief Commissioner of State Revenue v Metricon Qld Pty Ltd (2017) 105 ATR 11, 469
Chilton v Progress Printing & Publishing Co [1895] 2 Ch 29, 296
China Ocean Shipping Co v South Australia (1979) 145 CLR 172, 623
Chiropedic Bedding Pty Ltd v Radburg Pty Ltd (2008) 170 FCR 560, 75
Chorlton v Lings (1868) LR 4 CP 374, 177
Chu Kheng Lim v Minister for Immigration, Local Government and Ethnic Affairs (1992) 176 CLR 1, 483
Chubb Insurance Co of Australia Ltd v Moore (2013) 302 ALR 101, 286, 637, 639, 644
Chugg v Pacific Dunlop Ltd (1990) 170 CLR 249, 34–5, 100
CIC Insurance Ltd v Bankstown Football Club Ltd (1997) 187 CLR 384, 32, 84, 88–90, 104, 229, 297, 300, 316, 330, 340, 342, 351–3, 358, 487–8
City of Swan v West Australian Shalom Group Inc [2017] WASC 217, 529, 668–9
Claydon v Green (1868) LR 3 CP 511, 205, 301–2
Clayton v Heffron (1960) 105 CLR 214, 169
Cleary v Australian Co-operative Foods (No 2) (1999) 32 ACSR 701, 567
Clegg v Western Australia (No 2) (2017) 265 A Crim R 201, 267–9

Clement v Comcare (2011) 194 FCR 24, 306
Clubb v Edwards (2019) 267 CLR 171, 38, 102, 107, 110, 113, 261, 298, 343, 354
Clunnies-Ross v Commonwealth (1984) 155 CLR 193, 296
Clyde Engineering Co Ltd v Cowburn (1926) 37 CLR 466, 675
Clyne v Deputy Commissioner of Taxation (1981) 150 CLR 1, 278
Coco v The Queen (1994) 179 CLR 427, **435–6**, 437, 444, 447
Cody v JH Nelson Pty Ltd (1947) 74 CLR 629, 272
Coffs Harbour and District Local Aboriginal Land Council v Lynwood [2017] NSWCA 317, 558, 569
Cole v Director-General of Department of Youth and Community Services (1986) 7 NSWLR 541, 296
Cole v Minister for Immigration and Border Protection (2018) 261 FCR 537, 366
Coleman v Caesarstone Australia Pty Ltd [2021] QSC 125, 531
Coleman v Power (2004) 220 CLR 1, 13, 64–5, 486, 492, 494–6, 501, **502–3**
Coleman v Shell Co of Australia (1943) 45 SR (NSW) 27, 602
Coles Supermarkets Australia Pty Ltd v Harris [2013] ACTSC 255, 288
Collector of Customs v Agfa Gevaert Ltd (1996) 186 CLR 389, 14, 222, 226, 265–8, 421, 427, 429–30, 495, 506, 508, 668
Collett v Repatriation Commission (2009) 178 FCR 39, **76–7**, 138, **271**, **272–3**, 430
Colley v Futurebrand FHA Pty Ltd (2005) 63 NSWLR 291, 607, 612
Colquhoun v Brooks (1887) 19 QBD 400, 274
Combet v Commonwealth (2005) 224 CLR 494, 265
Combined Gunggandji People v Queensland (2009) 179 FCR 187, 612, 614
Comcare v Lilley (2013) 216 FCR 216, 670, 680
Comcare v Martin (2016) 258 CLR 467, 87
Comcare v Martinez (No 2) (2013) 212 FCR 272, 597–8
Comcare v PVYW (2013) 250 CLR 246, 466
Commissioner, Australian Federal Police v Oke (2007) 159 FCR 441, 573, 578–80
Commissioner for Corrective Services (WA) v Raj (2014) 244 A Crim R 558, 533, **536–7**
Commissioner for Prices and Consumer Affairs (SA) v Charles Moore (Aust) Ltd (1977) 139 CLR 449, 24
Commissioner of Australian Federal Police v Hart (2018) 262 CLR 76, 562
Commissioner of Police v Kennedy [2007] NSWCA 328, 303
Commissioner of Police v Reid (2000) 9 Tas R 418, 567
Commissioner of Police v Thayli Pty Ltd [2020] WASC 43, 682
Commissioner of Police for New South Wales v Eaton (2013) 252 CLR 1, 3, 88, 126, 130, 133, 228, 280, 284, 456, 458, 523, 540–2, **546–8**
Commissioner of Stamp Duties v Permanent Trustee Co Ltd (1987) 9 NSWLR 719, 457
Commissioner of State Revenue v Bogong Ski Club Inc (2000) 2 VR 487, 279
Commissioner of State Revenue v EHL Burgess Properties Pty Ltd (2015) 209 LGERA 314, 320, 341, **346–8**, 473
Commissioner of State Revenue (Vic) v ACN 005 057 349 Pty Ltd (2017) 261 CLR 509, 317
Commissioner of State Revenue (Vic) v Royal Insurance Australia Ltd (1994) 182 CLR 51, 560–2
Commissioner of Taxation v Murray (1990) 21 FCR 436, 348, **359–60**
Commissioner of Taxation (Cth) v Anstis (2010) 241 CLR 443, 493
Commissioner of Taxation (Cth) v Australian Building Systems Pty Ltd (in liq) (2015) 257 CLR 544, 143, 278, 469, 474
Commissioner of Taxation (Cth) v BHP Billiton Ltd (2011) 244 CLR 325, 491

Commissioner of Taxation (Cth) v Jayasinghe (2017) 260 CLR 400, 84
Commissioner of Taxation (Cth) v Westraders Pty Ltd (1980) 144 CLR 55, 223
Commissioner of Taxation (Cth) v Whitfords Beach Pty Ltd (1982) 150 CLR 355, 29
Commissioner of Territory Revenue v Alcan (NT) Alumina Pty Ltd (2008) 156 NTR 1, 428
Commonwealth v Anti-Discrimination Tribunal (Tas) (2008) 169 FCR 85, 624, **631–3**
Commonwealth v Baume (1905) 2 CLR 405, 262
Commonwealth v Grunseit (1943) 67 CLR 58, 666–7
Commonwealth v Helicopter Resources Pty Ltd (2020) 94 ALJR 466, 326
Commonwealth v Human Rights and Equal Opportunity Commission (1998) 76 FCR 513, 250
Commonwealth v Huon Transport Pty Ltd (1945) 70 CLR 293, 682–3
Commonwealth v Progress Advertising and Press Agency Co Pty Ltd (1910) 10 CLR 457, 674
Commonwealth v SCI Operations Pty Ltd (1998) 192 CLR 285, 279
Commonwealth v Sterling Nicholas Duty Free Pty Ltd (1972) 126 CLR 297, 273
Commonwealth v Western Australia (Mining Act Case) (1999) 196 CLR 392, 625–6, 629
Commonwealth v Wright (1956) 96 CLR 536, 455
Commonwealth Custodial Services Ltd v Valuer-General (NSW) (2007) 156 LGERA 186, 101
Communications, Electrical, Electronic, Energy, Information, Postal, Plumbing & Allied Services Union of Australia v Australian Competition and Consumer Commission (2007) 162 FCR 466, 110
Communications, Electrical, Electronic, Energy, Information, Postal, Plumbing And Allied Services Union of Australia v Queensland Rail (2015) 256 CLR 171, 450
Comptroller-General of Customs v Pharm-A-Care Laboratories Pty Ltd (2020) 94 ALJR 182, **479–81**
Comptroller-General of Customs v Zappia (2018) 265 CLR 416, 253–4
Concrete Constructions (NSW) Pty Ltd v Nelson (1990) 169 CLR 594, 300
Connective Services Pty Ltd v Slea Pty Ltd (2019) 267 CLR 461, 254
Construction, Forestry, Maritime, Mining and Energy Union v Australian Building and Construction Commissioner (2020) 282 FCR 1, 358, 466
Construction, Forestry, Maritime, Mining and Energy Union v BHP Billiton Nickel West Pty Ltd (2018) 263 FCR 558, 358
Construction, Forestry, Mining and Energy Union v Hadgkiss (2007) 169 FCR 151, 253
Construction, Forestry, Mining and Energy Union v Mammoet Australia Pty Ltd (2013) 248 CLR 619, 113, 245–6, 254, 366, 425
Convex Ltd's Patent [1980] RPC 423, 608, 615
Conway v The Queen (2002) 209 CLR 203, 331
Cook v Cook (1986) 162 CLR 376, 476
Cooper Brookes (Wollongong) Pty Ltd v Commissioner of Taxation (Cth) (1981) 147 CLR 297, 31–2, 49, 75, 77, 91–2, 119, 280, 295, 421–2, 425, 430–1, 511, 529, 532, 534
Copyright Agency Ltd v New South Wales (2007) 159 FCR 213, 179
Corliss v The Queen (2020) 282 A Crim R 195, 54
Cormack v Cope (1974) 131 CLR 432, 166
Corocraft Ltd v Pan American Airways Inc [1969] 1 QB 616, 14
Corporate Affairs Commission (NSW) v Yuill (1991) 172 CLR 319, 22, 52–3, 262
Corporation of the City of Enfield v Development Assessment Commission (2000) 199 CLR 135, 63, 372, 515
Cottle v Commissioner of Police (NSW) (2020) 298 IR 202, 469
Country Carbon Pty Ltd v Clean Energy Regulator (2018) 267 FCR 126, 535
County Council of the County of Moray v Maclean [1962] SC 601, 609, 615

Coverdale v West Coast Council (2016) 259 CLR 164, 136, 371, 453–4
CPB Contractors Pty Ltd v Construction, Forestry, Maritime, Mining and Energy Union [2019] FCAFC 70, 99, 352
CPCF v Minister for Immigration and Border Protection (2015) 255 CLR 514, 57, 479, 483–6
CRI026 v Republic of Nauru (2018) 355 ALR 216, 507
Crick v Harnett (1907) 7 SR (NSW) 126, 168
CSR Ltd v Eddy (2005) 226 CLR 1, 12–13
CTM v The Queen (2008) 236 CLR 440, 422, 648–53, 655–6
Culve Engineering Pty Ltd v Apollo General Engineering (Aust) Pty Ltd (in liq) (2017) 53 VR 219, 562, 571
Cumerlong Holdings Pty Ltd v Dalcross Properties Pty Ltd (2010) 175 LGERA 433, 424
Cunliffe v Commonwealth (1994) 182 CLR 272, 101

D v Chief Executive Officer, Department for Child Protection and Family Support [2016] WASC 289, 558
D151 v New South Wales Crime Commission (2017) 94 NSWLR 738, 638, 641, 646
Dainford Ltd v Smith (1985) 155 CLR 342, 679
Dalton v NSW Crime Commission (2006) 227 CLR 490, 265
Daniels Corporation International Pty Ltd v Australian Competition and Consumer Commission (2002) 213 CLR 543, 285, 433, 436–7, 443–4
Dann v Gavranich (1989) 10 MVR 148, 499
D'Arcy v Myriad Genetics Inc (2015) 258 CLR 334, 354, 484
Davis (A Pseudonym) v The Queen (2016) 55 VR 1, 576, 578, 582
Dawson v Commonwealth (1946) 73 CLR 157, 297
Day v Harness Racing New South Wales (2014) 88 NSWLR 594, 528–9, 669
Day v Hunkin (1938) 61 CLR 65, 397
De Marco v Chief Commissioner of State Revenue (2013) 83 NSWLR 445, 264, 266, 498–9
De More Constructions Pty Ltd v Garpace Pty Ltd (2001) 53 NSWLR 132, 84
Deal v Kodakkathanath (2016) 258 CLR 281, 247
Department for Health and Ageing v Li (2018) 130 SASR 578, 533, 537
Deputy Commissioner of Taxation v Clark (2003) 57 NSWLR 113, 288, 290
Deputy Commissioner of Taxation v Dick (2007) 242 ALR 152, 270–1
Deputy Commissioner of Taxation (Cth) v Craddock (2006) 204 FLR 274, 254
Deputy Federal Commissioner of Taxation (NSW) v WR Moran Pty Ltd (1939) 61 CLR 735, 347
Deputy Federal Commissioner of Taxation (SA) v Ellis & Clark Ltd (1934) 52 CLR 85, 519
Deputy Federal Commissioner of Taxes (SA) v Elder's Trustee and Executor Co Ltd (1936) 57 CLR 610, 328–9
Dickinson v Motor Vehicle Insurance Trust (1987) 163 CLR 500, 339
Dietman v Brennan-Kuss (2015) 123 SASR 24, 63, **425–6**, 517, 519
Dionisatos (for the Estate of the Late George Dionysatos) v Acrow Formwork and Scaffolding Pty Ltd (2015) 91 NSWLR 34, **290–2**
Director-General of Education v Suttling (1987) 162 CLR 427, 393
Director of Public Works v Ho Po Sang [1961] AC 901, 607, 612–14
Dixie v Royal Columbian Hospital (1941) 2 DLR 138, 602
Dolheguy v Becker (2009) 52 MVR 462, **4–5**, 125, 280, 547
Dome Resources NL v Silver (2008) 72 NSWLR 693, 529
Dordevic v Moore (2017) 12 ACTLR 282, 598
Doro v Victorian Railways Commissioners [1960] VR 84, 606

Dossett v TKJ Nominees Pty Ltd (2003) 218 CLR 1, 380, 396, 515, 550, 604, 606–7, 615, 618–19, **620**
Doughty v Martino Developments Pty Ltd (2010) 27 VR 499, 328
Dowell Australia Ltd v Archdeacon (1975) 132 CLR 417, 498
Downer Engineering Power Pty Ltd v P & H Minepro Australasia Pty Ltd [2007] NSWCA 318, 262
Downey v Pryor (1960) 103 CLR 353, 683
Downs v Williams (1971) 126 CLR 61, 624
Doyle v Maypole Bakery Pty Ltd [1981] Tas R 376, 494, **496–7**, 508
DPP v Acme Storage Pty Ltd (2017) 264 IR 215, 267, 653
DPP v Bone (2005) 64 NSWLR 735, 656
DPP v Dale (2010) 30 VR 282, 65
DPP v Dickfoss (2011) 28 NTLR 71, 558, 567
DPP v George (2008) 102 SASR 246, 558
DPP v Gibson (2012) 61 MVR 261, 546
DPP v Hazelwood Pacific Pty Ltd (Ruling 2) [2019] VSC 871, 655–6, **658–9**
DPP v Kaba (2014) 44 VR 526, 440, 442, 444
DPP v Leys (2012) 44 VR 1, 27, 73, 85, 275, 531–4, 537
DPP v Moreno (2018) 57 VR 1, **81–2**, 140, 461, 533
DPP v Scheele (2016) 12 ACTLR 1, 80, 508, 533, 537, 541, 543
DPP v Spong (2018) 13 ACTLR 292, 472
DPP v Sutcliffe [2001] VSC 43, 637, 643, **647**
DPP v Walters (A Pseudonym) (2015) 49 VR 356, 40, 306
DPP v Williams (1998) 28 MVR 521, 272
DPP (Cth) v Easton (2018) 98 NSWLR 1077, 431
DPP (Cth) v Kamal (2011) 248 FLR 64, 279
DPP (Cth) v Keating (2013) 248 CLR 459, 254, 495
DPP (Cth) v Poniatowska (2011) 244 CLR 408, 254, **255–6**
DPP (Nauru) v Fowler (1984) 154 CLR 627, 529
DPP (NSW) v Starr (2012) 221 A Crim R 525, 253
DPP (SA) v Vella (1993) 61 SASR 379, 298
DPP (WA) v GTR [2007] WASC 318, 447
DPP (WA) v Hafner (2004) 28 WAR 486, 638
DPP (WA) v Williams (2007) 35 WAR 297, 562
DPP Reference No 1 of 2019 (2021) 95 ALJR 741, 324–5, 327
DQU16 v Minister for Home Affairs (2021) 95 ALJR 352, 482
DRJ v Commissioner of Victims Rights (No 2) (2020) 103 NSWLR 692, 636, 638, 641, 643–6
Dugan v Mirror Newspapers Ltd (1978) 142 CLR 583, 29
Duke of Devonshire v O'Connor (1890) 24 QBD 468, 205
Durham Holdings Pty Ltd v New South Wales (1999) 47 NSWLR 340, 608
Dyke v Elliott (1872) 4 LR PC 184, 250–1

Ealing London Borough Council v Race Relations Board [1972] AC 342, 151
Eastman v The Queen (2000) 203 CLR 1, 511
Eastman Photographic Materials Co Ltd v Comptroller-General of Patents, Designs and Trade Marks [1898] AC 571, 24
Echunga Football Club Inc v Hills Football League Inc (2014) 121 SASR 449, 669

Eckett v Eckett (2010) 237 FLR 324, 161
Eclipse Resources Pty Ltd v Minister for Environment (No 2) (2017) 223 LGERA 313, 362
Edwards v Kumarasamy [2016] AC 1334, 227
Edwards v The Queen (2021) 95 ALJR 808, 354
EFN v Lehmann [2018] 1 Qd R 126, 131
Egan v Willis (1998) 195 CLR 424, 177
Eichmann v Federal Commissioner of Taxation (2020) 280 FCR 10, 247
Electrolux Home Products Pty Ltd v Australian Workers' Union (2004) 221 CLR 309, 43, 93, 325, 434, 443–4, 512, 599
Elliott v Minister Administering Fisheries Management Act 1994 (2018) 97 NSWLR 1082, 447–8
Emanuele v Australian Securities Commission (1997) 188 CLR 114, 49, 422
Encyclopaedia Britannica (Australia) Inc v Director of Consumer Affairs [1988] VR 904, 571
Enernoc Australia Pty Ltd v Minister for Energy (WA) (No 2) [2017] WASC 113, 672
Environment East Gippsland Inc v VicForests (2010) 30 VR 1, 585
Esber v Commonwealth (1992) 174 CLR 430, 395–6, 602, 607, 612–15, 617
Escoigne Properties Ltd v Inland Revenue Commissioners [1958] AC 549, 305
Esmonds Motors Pty Ltd v Commonwealth (1970) 120 CLR 463, 674
Esso Australia Pty Ltd v Australian Workers' Union (2017) 263 CLR 551, 113, 115, 127, **317–18**, 320, 369, 535
Esso Australia Resources Ltd v Federal Commissioner of Taxation (1990) 201 CLR 49, 332, 476–7
Esso Australia Resources Ltd v Federal Commissioner of Taxation (2011) 199 FCR 226, 304, 355, 359
Evans v Job [2018] TASFC 3, 279
Evans v New South Wales (2008) 168 FCR 576, **445–6**, 672
Evans v Williams (1910) 11 CLR 550, 23
EWP Ltd v Moore [1992] 1 QB 460, 606
Exxon Corporation v Exxon Insurance Ltd [1982] Ch 119, 506

F, BV v Magistrates Court of South Australia (2013) 115 SASR 232, 27, 529, 532
Fagan v Dominitz (1957) 58 SR (NSW) 122, 186
FAI Insurances Ltd v Winneke (1982) 151 CLR 342, 504
Fair Trading Administration Corporation v Owners Corporation, SP 43551 [2002] NSWSC 624, 306
Farah Constructions Pty Ltd v Say-Dee Pty Ltd (2007) 230 CLR 89, 465, 470
Farnell v Chanbua (2016) 56 Fam LR 84, 274
Farnell Electronic Components Pty Ltd v Collector of Customs (1996) 72 FCR 125, 498–9
Fazzolari Pty Ltd v Parramatta City Council (2009) 237 CLR 603, 491
FCS17 v Minister for Home Affairs (2020) 276 FCR 644, 352, **482–3**, 486
Fearnley v Finlay [2014] 2 Qd R 392, 197, 296
Federal Commissioner of Taxation v Consolidated Media Holdings Ltd (2012) 250 CLR 503, 72, 89, 93, 133, 139, 319, 330, 345, 351, 353, 360, 366, 367
Federal Commissioner of Taxation v Henderson (1943) 68 CLR 29, 460
Federal Commissioner of Taxation v Indooroopilly Children Services (Qld) Pty Ltd (2007) 158 FCR 325, 63
Federal Commissioner of Taxation v Multiflex Pty Ltd (2011) 197 FCR 580, **258–9**, 554
Federal Commissioner of Taxation v Munro (1926) 38 CLR 153, 502
Federal Commissioner of Taxation v Ryan (2000) 201 CLR 109, 156

Federal Commissioner of Taxation v Tomaras (2018) 265 CLR 434, 11, 433, 440, 623–6, 630, 632
Federal Commissioner of Taxation v Traviati (2012) 205 FCR 136, 359
Federal Commissioner of Taxation v Wentworth District Capital Ltd (2011) 191 FCR 151, 89
Federal Council of the British Medical Association v Commonwealth (1949) 79 CLR 201, 307
Federated Engine-Drivers & Firemen's Association of Australasia v Broken Hill Pty Co Ltd (1911) 12 CLR 398, 278
Fei and Minister for Immigration and Border Protection (Citizenship) [2016] AATA 624, 516
Feldman v Nationwide News Pty Ltd (2020) 103 NSWLR 307, 353
Felman v Law Institute of Victoria [1998] 4 VR 324, 612
Fenton v Thorley & Co Ltd [1903] AC 443, 296
Ferdinands v Commissioner for Public Employment (2006) 225 CLR 130, 279, 539–42, 545, 549–50
Fernando v Minister for Immigration and Multicultural Affairs (2000) 97 FCR 407, 573, 580–1
Fielding v Morley Corporation [1899] 1 Ch 1, 197
Finance Facilities Pty Ltd v Commissioner of Taxation (Cth) (1971) 127 CLR 106, 554, 562
Financial Services Council Ltd v Industry Super Australia (2014) 222 FCR 455, 549
Firebird Global Master Fund II Ltd v Republic of Nauru (2015) 258 CLR 31, 99, 278, 292, 484
Fischer v Nemeske Pty Ltd (2016) 257 CLR 615, 491
Fisher v Bell [1961] 1 QB 394, 96, 267, 460, 497
Fisher v Fisher [1988] VR 1028, 298
Flaherty v Girgis (1987) 162 CLR 574, 93, 324
Flinn v James McEwen & Co Pty Ltd [1991] 2 VR 434, 184, 188
Foots v Southern Cross Mine Management Pty Ltd (2007) 234 CLR 52, 134
Footscray City College v Ruzicka (2007) 16 VR 498, **128**, 137–8, 430
Footscray Corporation v Maize Products Pty Ltd (1943) 67 CLR 301, 672
Forrest & Forrest Pty Ltd v Wilson (2017) 262 CLR 510, 246, 576, 580–1, 583
Forster v Jododex Australia Pty Ltd (1972) 127 CLR 421, 398–9
Forsyth v Deputy Commissioner of Taxation (2007) 231 CLR 531, 286, 289, 380
Fortress Credit Corporation (Australia) II Pty Ltd v Fletcher (2015) 254 CLR 489, 324, 327, 369
Foster's Case (1614) 77 ER 1222, 549
Frauenfelder v Reid (1963) 109 CLR 42, 301
Frederick v South Australia (2006) 94 SASR 545, 323, 325
Free Lanka Insurance Co Ltd v Ranasinghe [1964] AC 541, 602, 613–15
Fremantle Lawyers Pty Ltd v Sarich (2019) 54 WAR 113, 316, **320–1**
Frugtniet v Australian Securities and Investments Commission (2019) 266 CLR 250, 371

Gajjar v Minister for Immigration and Citizenship (2013) 87 ALJR 549, 265–6
Gala v Preston (1991) 172 CLR 243, 12–13
Gammon Ltd v A-G of Hong Kong [1985] 1 AC 1, 506
Garnett v Bradley (1878) LR 3 App Cas 944, 549
Gattellaro v Westpac Banking Corporation (2004) 204 ALR 258, 489
GBT v Western Australia [2019] WASCA 40, **322–3**, 683
Gentel v Rapps [1902] 1 KB 160, 675
George v Rockett (1990) 170 CLR 104, 594–5, 599

Gerlach v Clifton Bricks Pty Ltd (2002) 209 CLR 478, 555
Gerrard v Mayne Nickless Ltd (1996) 135 ALR 494, 612
Geschke v Del-Monte Home Furnishers Pty Ltd [1981] VR 856, 611
GF Heublein and Bro Inc v Continental Liqueurs Pty Ltd (1962) 109 CLR 153, 396, 619
Ghaidan v Godin-Mendoza [2004] 2 AC 557, 405
Giachin v Sandon (2013) 233 A Crim R 490, 656
Giannarelli v Wraith (1988) 165 CLR 543, 289
Gibb v Federal Commissioner of Taxation (1966) 118 CLR 628, 302
Gibbs v Mercantile Mutual Insurance (Australia) Ltd (2003) 214 CLR 604, 129
Gibson and Howes Ltd v Lennon (1917) 24 CLR 140, 278
Gifford v Strang Patrick Stevedoring Pty Ltd (2003) 214 CLR 269, 434, 440, 477
Gillies v Keogh [1989] 2 NZLR 327, 591
Giris Pty Ltd v Commissioner of Taxation (Cth) (1969) 119 CLR 365, 592
Glennan v Commissioner of Taxation (2003) 198 ALR 250, 585
Gnych v Polish Club Ltd (2015) 255 CLR 414, 573, 576, 578
Goodman (Official Assignee) v Mayor of Melbourne (1861) 1 W & W (L) 4, 310
Goodwin v Phillips (1908) 7 CLR 1, 280, 549–50
Graham v Minister for Immigration and Border Protection (2017) 263 CLR 1, 52, 292
Graham Barclay Oysters Pty Ltd v Ryan (2002) 211 CLR 540, 560
Grain Elevators Board (Vic) v Dunmunkle (1946) 73 CLR 70, 327–8
Grajewski v DPP (NSW) (2019) 264 CLR 470, 317, 319, 367
Grannall v C George Kellaway and Sons Pty Ltd (1955) 93 CLR 36, 645
Graovac v Minister for Immigration and Multicultural Affairs (1999) 56 ALD 709, 380
Greenway v Abishara [1964] VR 587, 301
Greiner v Independent Commission Against Corruption (1992) 28 NSWLR 125, 594
Grey v Pearson (1857) 10 ER 1216, 22
Grunwick Processing Laboratories Ltd v Advisory, Conciliation and Arbitration Service [1978] AC 655, 566
Gustavson Drilling (1964) Ltd v Minister of National Revenue [1977] 1 SCR 271, 602
Gypsy Jokers Motorcycle Club Inc v Commissioner of Police (No 2) [2008] WASC 166, 475

H v Minister for Immigration and Citizenship (2010) 188 FCR 393, 4, 144, 227, 305, 496
H Jones and Co Ltd v Warden, Councillors and Electors of the Municipality of Kingborough (1950) 82 CLR 282, 529
Hagan v Trustees of Toowoomba Sports Ground Trust [2000] FCA 1615, 300
Hall v Sheiban Pty Ltd (1989) 20 FCR 217, **564–5**
Hall v The Queen (2020) 136 SASR 535, 533
Halwood Corporation Ltd v Roads Corporation [1998] 2 VR 439, 558
Hamilton Gell v White [1922] 2 KB 422, 602, 609, 614–15
Hanau v Ehrlich [1912] AC 39, 465
Hancock v Edgell Birdseye (Ulverstone) Division of Petersville Industries Ltd [1998] TASSC 10, 617–18
Hanlon v The Law Society [1981] AC 124, 205
Harding v County Court of Victoria [2013] VSC 711, 131
Hardy Wine Co Ltd v Janevruss Pty Ltd [2006] VSCA 28, 303–4
Harrington v Lowe (1996) 190 CLR 311, 682
Harrison v Melhem (2008) 72 NSWLR 380, 62–3, 364–6, 511

Harrison v Moore (2018) 28 Tas R 99, 499
Hart v Commissioner of Taxation (2019) 272 FCR 612, 533
Harvey v Harvey (1951) 68 WN (NSW) 241, 222
Hatton v Beaumont [1977] 2 NSWLR 211, 575
Haureliuk v Furler (2012) 6 ACTLR 151, 364, 366
Hawthorne (Department of Health) v Morcam Pty Ltd (1992) 29 NSWLR 120, 654, 656
Hayman v Cartright (2018) 53 WAR 137, 334–5
He v Minister for Immigration and Citizenship (2009) 112 ALD 635, 598
He Kaw Teh v The Queen (1985) 157 CLR 523, 96, 162, 506, 648–57, 661–2
Healey v Royal Society for the Prevention of Cruelty to Animals Victoria (2018) 56 VR 414, **224–5**
Heatley v Tasmanian Racing and Gaming Commission (1977) 137 CLR 487, 295
Hepples v Commissioner of Taxation (Cth) (1992) 173 CLR 492, 256–7
Herald & Weekly Times Pty Ltd v Buckley (2009) 21 VR 661, 261
Herbert Adams Pty Ltd v Federal Commissioner of Taxation (1932) 47 CLR 222, 267, 268, **269–70**
Hersfield Developments Corporation Pty Ltd v Melbourne and Metropolitan Board of Works [1982] VR 608, 192
Heston and Isleworth UDC v Grout [1897] 2 Ch 306, 395
Hewitt v Benale Pty Ltd (2002) 27 WAR 91, 284
Heydon's Case (1584) 76 ER 637, 23
HFM043 v Republic of Nauru (2018) 92 ALJR 817, 534–5
Hickling v Laneyrie (1991) 21 NSWLR 730, 67
Hili v The Queen (2010) 242 CLR 520, 470
Hill v Council of Law Society of ACT [2019] ACTSC 79, 583
Hill v Council of Law Society of ACT (2020) 15 ACTLR 1, 583
Hill v Zuda Pty Ltd [2021] WASCA 59, **470–1**, 473
HKSAR v Tse Man Fei (Court of Final Appeal of the Hong Kong Special Administrative Region, FACC No 1 of 2016, 5 July 2016), 431
HML v The Queen (2008) 235 CLR 334, 226
Hoare v The Queen (1989) 167 CLR 348, 336
Hocking v Director-General, National Archives of Australia (2020) 94 ALJR 569, 354
Hofer v The Queen (2021) 95 ALJR 937, 466
Hoffmann v Chief of Army (2004) 137 FCR 520, 552
Holden v Nuttall [1945] VLR 171, 499
Holland v Jones (1917) 23 CLR 149, 348
Holloway v McFeeters (1956) 94 CLR 470, 522
Hopkins v Minister for Immigration, Citizenship, Migrant Services and Multicultural Affairs (2020) 275 FCR 42, 484
Hopper & Hopper [2016] FCCA 84, 117
Hore v Albury Radio Taxis Co-operative Society Ltd (2002) 56 NSWLR 210, 286
Hornsby Shire Council v Porter (1990) 19 NSWLR 716, 156
Horta v Commonwealth (1994) 181 CLR 183, 478
Hossain v Minister for Immigration and Border Protection (2018) 264 CLR 123, 505, 582
House of Peace Pty Ltd v Bankstown City Council (2000) 48 NSWLR 498, 227, 490–2
Houssein v Under Secretary, Department of Industrial Relations and Technology NSW (1982) 148 CLR 88, 274
HR Products Pty Ltd v Collector of Customs (1990) 20 ALD 340, 267

Huddart Parker & Co Pty Ltd v Moorehead (1909) 8 CLR 330, 20–1
Hughes v Janrule Pty Ltd (2011) 177 ACTR 1, 460, **463**
Hughes v The Queen (2017) 263 CLR 338, 240, 495
Hunt & Hunt Lawyers v Mitchell Morgan Nominees Pty Ltd (2013) 247 CLR 613, 355
Hunter Quarries Pty Ltd v Mexon (2018) 98 NSWLR 526, **113–15**, 134
Hunter Resources Ltd v Melville (1988) 164 CLR 234, 327, 515, 669
HZCP v Minister for Immigration and Border Protection (2019) 273 FCR 121, 513

I and L Securities Pty Ltd v HTW Valuers (Brisbane) Pty Ltd (2002) 210 CLR 109, 127
Ian Street Developer Pty Ltd v Arrow International Pty Ltd (2018) 54 VR 721, 358, 361
Ian Street Developer Pty Ltd v Arrow International Pty Ltd [2018] VSCA 294, 575, 578, **583–4**
Iannella v French (1968) 119 CLR 84, 653
ICI Australia Operations Pty Ltd v Workcover Authority of New South Wales (2004) 60 NSWLR 18, 570
In the Marriage of Harris (1987) 11 Fam LR 629, 557
Inco Europe Ltd v First Choice Distribution (A Firm) [2000] 1 WLR 586, 39, 527, 530–1, 533
Independent Commission Against Corruption v Cunneen (2015) 256 CLR 1, 102, 145, 229, 240, 302, 373, 422, 543
Inland Revenue Commissioners v Gittus [1920] 1 KB 563, 310–11
Inland Revenue Commissioners v Hinchy [1960] AC 748, 7, 136, 205
Inland Revenue Commissioners v Joiner [1975] 1 WLR 1701, 319
Insight Vacations Pty Ltd v Young (2011) 243 CLR 149, 638–9, 645
Institute of Patent Agents v Lockwood [1894] AC 347, 544, 548
Insurance Commission of Western Australia v Container Handlers Pty Ltd (2004) 218 CLR 89, **338–9**
Insurance Commissioner of the State Motor Car Insurance Office v Denning (1970) 120 CLR 437, 683
Interlego AG v Croner Trading Pty Ltd (1992) 39 FCR 348, 328
Interlego AG v Toltoys Pty Ltd (1974) 130 CLR 461, 491
International Finance Trust Co Ltd v New South Wales Crime Commission (2009) 240 CLR 319, 41, 42–3, 223, 502, 558
International Union v Massey-Ferguson Industries Ltd (1979) 94 DLR (3d) 743, 557
IOOF Holdings Ltd v Federal Commissioner of Taxation (2014) 224 FCR 535, 619
ISPT Nominees Pty Ltd v Chief Commissioner of State Revenue (2003) 53 ATR 527, 395
IW v City of Perth (1997) 191 CLR 1, 246–7, 250

JAD v The Queen [2012] NSWCCA 73, **69–71**, 253, **451–2**
Jagroop v Minister for Immigration and Border Protection (2016) 241 FCR 461, 613, 617–18
Joffe v The Queen (2012) 82 NSWLR 510, 238
John Beever (Aust) Pty Ltd v Paper Australia Pty Ltd (No 2) [2019] VSC 575, 541
John Fairfax Publications Pty Ltd v Gacic (2007) 230 CLR 291, 562
John Holland Pty Ltd v Victorian Workcover Authority (2009) 239 CLR 518, **57–8**
John v Commissioner of Taxation (Cth) (1989) 166 CLR 417, 275, 465, 469
Johns v Australian Securities Commission (1993) 178 CLR 408, 554
Jones v Australian Competition and Consumer Commission (2002) 76 ALD 424, 496
Jordan v Criminal Injuries Compensation Commissioner Neasey [2018] TASFC 10, 562

Julius v Lord Bishop of Oxford (1880) 5 App Cas 214, 554, 560
Jumbunna Coal Mine NL v Victorian Coal Miners' Association (1908) 6 CLR 309, 483–4, 639
Jurd v Public Trustee [2001] NSWSC 632, 603

K&S Lake City Freighters Pty Ltd v Gordon & Gotch Ltd (1985) 157 CLR 309, 32, 309–10
Kable v DPP (NSW) (1996) 189 CLR 51, 41, 44
Kabourakis v Medical Practitioners Board of Victoria [2006] VSCA 301, 555
Kahan v Strauss [2017] VSC 8, 240
Kaporonovski v The Queen (1973) 133 CLR 209, 333
Kartinyeri v Commonwealth (1998) 195 CLR 337, 176, 479, 483
Kay and Child Support Registrar [2015] AATA 429, 516–17
Kaye v A-G (Tas) (1956) 94 CLR 193, 633
Kearon v Grant [1991] 1 VR 321, 656
Kearsley v The Queen (2017) 265 A Crim R 233, 336
Keenan v The Queen [2020] VSCA 105, 578
Kelly v Saadat-Talab (2008) 72 NSWLR 305, 275
Kelly v The Queen (2004) 218 CLR 216, 113, 115, 303, 491
Kelly v Watson (1985) 10 FCR 305, 391
Kemppi v Adani Mining Pty Ltd (No 2) (2019) 271 FCR 423, 296
K-Generation Pty Ltd v Liquor Licensing Court (2009) 237 CLR 501, 351, 356, 502
Khoury v Government Insurance Office of New South Wales (1984) 165 CLR 622, 246–7, 249–50
Kim v Minister for Immigration and Multicultural and Indigenous Affairs (2004) 38 AAR 304, 570
King v Philcox (2015) 255 CLR 304, **337–8**, 424
King v The Queen (2012) 245 CLR 588, 493
King Gee Clothing Co Pty Ltd v Commonwealth (1945) 71 CLR 184, **680–1**
Kingsley's Chicken Pty Ltd v Queensland Investment Corporation [2006] ACTCA 9, 269
Kingston v Keprose Pty Ltd (1987) 11 NSWLR 404, 31, 78, 532
Kinning v Buchanan (1849) 137 ER 513, 62
Kioa v West (1985) 159 CLR 550, 96, 504
Kirin-Amgen Inc v Hoechst Marion Roussel Ltd [2005] 1 All ER 667, 84
Kiriwina Investment Co Pty Ltd v Green Lees Developments Pty Ltd [2018] NSWCA 210, 533
Kirk v Industrial Court of New South Wales (2010) 239 CLR 531, 409, 506
Kirkham v Industrial Relations Commission (2015) 121 SASR 471, 578–80, 582
Klein v Minister for Education (2007) 81 ALJR 582, 284
Klepp v Gibb (1988) 81 ALR 383, 401
Kline v Official Secretary to the Governor-General (2013) 249 CLR 645, 108, 367
Ko v Hall [2020] VSCA 224, 578, 580–2
Koowarta v Bjelke-Petersen (1982) 153 CLR 168, 479, 481
Kostrzewa v Southern Electric Authority of Queensland (1969) 120 CLR 653, 670
Kuczborski v Queensland (2014) 254 CLR 51, 354
Kurnell Passenger & Transport Service Pty Ltd v Randwick City Council (2009) 230 FLR 336, 535
Kutlu v Director of Professional Services Review (2011) 197 FCR 177, 573–5, 579–80

La Macchia v Minister for Primary Industry (1986) 72 ALR 23, 611
Lacey v A-G (Qld) (2011) 242 CLR 573, 37, 45, 50–1, 53, 76, 104, 109, 151, 367, 371, 440
Laird v Trustees of Clyde Navigation (1883) 8 App Cas 658, 285

Lake v Butler (1855) 119 ER 416, 398
Lake Macquarie Shire Council v Aberdare County Council (1970) 123 CLR 327, 286–7, 292
Lambe v Director-General of Social Services (1981) 38 ALD 362, 296
Lange v Australian Broadcasting Corporation (1997) 189 CLR 520, 37
Langton v Independent Commission Against Corruption (2000) 49 NSWLR 164, 670
Lansell House Pty Ltd v Federal Commissioner of Taxation (2010) 76 ATR 19, 268
Law Society of New South Wales v Glenorcy Pty Ltd (2006) 67 NSWLR 169, 638, 645
Lawson v Western Australia [No 3] [2018] WASCA 129, 528, 533
Leach v The Queen (2007) 230 CLR 1, 562, **563**
Leahy v Barnes [2013] QSC 226, 571
Leary v The Queen (1977) 74 DLR (3d) 103, 652
Leask v Commonwealth (1996) 187 CLR 579, 299, 649
Lednar v Magistrates' Court (2000) 117 A Crim R 396, 275
Lee v New South Wales Crime Commission (2013) 251 CLR 196, 56, 433, 439, 442–3
Legal Services Board v Gillespie-Jones [2012] VSCA 68, 305
Legal Services Board v Gillespie-Jones (2013) 249 CLR 493, 247, 421–2, 425, 430
Lennon v Gibson & Howes Ltd (1919) 26 CLR 285, 323
Leon Fink Holdings Pty Ltd v Australian Film Commission (1979) 141 CLR 672, 262
Lester v Garland (1808) 33 ER 748, 398
Lewis v Chief Executive Department of Justice and Community Safety (ACT) (2013) 280 FLR 118, 390
Liangsiriprasert v United States [1991] 1 AC 225, 643
LibertyWorks Inc v Commonwealth (2021) 95 ALJR 490, 104, 106, 108
Libman v The Queen [1985] 2 SCR 178, 643
Lim Chin Aik v The Queen [1963] AC 160, 652
Lindner v Wright (1976) 14 ALR 105, 529
Linfox Australia Pty Ltd v Federal Commissioner of Taxation (2019) 271 FCR 365, 348, 359
Lipohar v The Queen (1999) 200 CLR 485, 638, 642–5
Lithgow City Council v Jackson (2011) 244 CLR 352, 493
Littlewoods Mail Order Stores Ltd v Inland Revenue Commissioners [1963] AC 135, 278
Liu v Stephen Grubits and Associates (2019) 284 IR 475, **457–9**
Liversidge v Anderson [1942] AC 206, 594
Lloyd v Police (2004) 89 SASR 383, 499, 574
Lockrey v Historic Houses Trust of New South Wales (2012) 84 NSWLR 114, 498–9
Loges v Martin (1991) 13 MVR 405, 127
London and North Western Railway Co v Evans [1893] 1 Ch 16, 161–2
Lordianto v Commissioner of the Australian Federal Police (2019) 266 CLR 273, 319
Lottoland Australia Pty Ltd v Australian Communications and Media Authority (2019) 100 NSWLR 328, 129
Love v Commonwealth (2020) 270 CLR 152, 507
Lowe v The Queen (2015) 48 VR 351, 531, 533
Lowe Pty Ltd v Belgravia Nominees Pty Ltd [2020] WASCA 180, 364, 366
LU Simon Builders Pty Ltd v Victorian Building Authority [2017] VSC 805, 87, **94–5**, **96–7**, 127, **129–30**, **132**
Lucas-Smith v Coroners' Court (ACT) (2009) 166 ACTR 42, 644
Luna Park (NSW) Ltd v Tramways Advertising Pty Ltd (1938) 61 CLR 286, 88
Lygon Nominees Pty Ltd v Commissioner of State Revenue (2007) 23 VR 474, 279

Lynch v Rainbird [1968] Tas SR 30, 683
Lynn v New South Wales (2016) 91 NSWLR 636, 299

M v Scottish Ministers [2012] 1 WLR 3386, 450, 684
Ma v Police (SA) (2000) 137 SASR 159, 440
MacAlister v The Queen (1990) 169 CLR 324, 534
Macari v Celtic Football and Athletic Co Ltd [1999] SC 628, 276
Mack Fleet Pty Ltd v Transport for NSW (2020) 93 MVR 242, 570
Mackay v Davies (1904) 1 CLR 483, 325
Macleod v A-G (NSW) [1891] AC 455, 643
Macoun v Commissioner of Taxation (Cth) (2015) 257 CLR 519, 481, 484
Madras Electric Supply Corporation Ltd v Boarland [1955] AC 667, 632
Mainteck Services Pty Ltd v Stein Heurtey SA (2014) 89 NSWLR 633, 307
Makarov v Minister for Home Affairs [2021] FCAFC 129, 354
Makarov v Minister for Home Affairs (No 3) [2020] FCA 1655, 354
Malika Holdings Pty Ltd v Stretton (2001) 204 CLR 290, 434, 441, 443
Maloney v The Queen (2013) 252 CLR 168, 348
Mann v Paterson Constructions Pty Ltd (2019) 267 CLR 560, 440
Mansfield v The Queen (2012) 247 CLR 86, 134, **135**, 142, 253, 422, 430–1, 492, 513
Marbury v Madison, 5 US 137 (1803), 38, 63
Marchesano v Western Australia (2017) 52 WAR 176, 335
Marina Bay Developments Pty Ltd v Pittwater Council [2007] NSWLEC 41, 670
Marine Board of Strahan v Kirkpatrick [1967] Tas SR 179, 307
Marine Power Australia Pty Ltd v Comptroller-General of Customs (1989) 89 ALR 561, 267
Markell v Wollaston (1906) 4 CLR 141, 20, 24
Marks v GIO Australia Holdings Ltd (1998) 196 CLR 494, 127
Maroondah City Council v Fletcher (2009) 29 VR 160, 346
Mars Pension Trustees Ltd v County Properties and Developments Ltd [1999] SC 267, 276
Marshall v Director-General, Department of Transport (2001) 205 CLR 603, 75, 222–3, 261, 474
Marshall v Smith (1907) 4 CLR 1617, 395
Masson v Parsons (2019) 266 CLR 554, 75, 91, 222, 328–9
Master Education Services Pty Ltd v Ketchell (2008) 236 CLR 101, 517, 519, 576, 578, 669
Master Undertakers' Association of New South Wales v Crockett (1907) 5 CLR 389, 223
Mathieson v Burton (1971) 124 CLR 1, 602, 604, 608–9
Maughan Thiem Auto Sales Pty Ltd v Cooper (2013) 216 FCR 197, 323, 326
Maunsell v Olins [1975] AC 373, 4, 262, 267
Maurice Blackburn Cashman v Brown (2011) 242 CLR 647, 223
Maurici v Chief Commissioner of State Revenue (2001) 51 NSWLR 673, 274
Maxcon Constructions Pty Ltd v Vadasz (2018) 264 CLR 46, 475
Maxwell v Murphy (1957) 96 CLR 261, 317, 602–3, 607, 616–17, 619
Mayne Nickless Ltd v Mackintosh [1989] VR 878, 305
Mayor of Wellington v Compton [1916] NZLR 779, 301–2
McCarthy v Tasmania [1998] TASSC 124, 617
McDevitt v McArthur (1919) 15 Tas LR 6, 679
McGee v Gilchrist Humphrey (2005) 92 SASR 100, 485–6
McGlade v Native Title Registrar (2017) 251 FCR 172, 111
McGraw-Hinds (Aust) Pty Ltd v Smith (1979) 144 CLR 633, 278

McHugh v Minister for Immigration, Citizenship, Migrant Services and Multicultural Affairs (2020) 283 FCR 602, 285
McIvor v Allen (1943) 43 SR (NSW) 266, 679
McKechnie v Victorian Civil and Administrative Tribunal (2020) 62 VR 54, 408
McKenzie v Huybers [1929] SCR 38, 182
McKernan v Fraser (1931) 46 CLR 343, 24
McKinnon v Secretary, Department of Treasury (2006) 228 CLR 423, 593–5
McLaughlin v Dungowan Manly Pty Ltd (No 3) [2011] NSWSC 717, 306
McLeod-Dryden v Supreme Court (Vic) (2017) 270 A Crim R 352, 266
McNamara v Consumer Trader and Tenancy Tribunal (2005) 221 CLR 646, 465, 473–4, 628
McNeill v The Queen (2008) 168 FCR 198, 541, 549
Medical Board of Australia v Kemp (2018) 56 VR 51, **111–12**, 115, 425, 430
Mees v Roads Corporation (2003) 128 FCR 418, 178
Mei Ying Su v Australian Fisheries Management Authority (No 2) (2008) 251 ALR 135, 663–4
Melbourne Corporation v Barry (1922) 31 CLR 174, 325–7, 433
Mellifont v A-G (Qld) (1991) 173 CLR 289, 334
Melville v Chief Executive Officer, Department of Health and Families (2011) 30 NTLR 98, 639, 646
Merck Sharp & Dohme Corporation v Sandoz Pty Ltd [2021] FCA 947, 533
Mercorella v Secretary to the Departemtn of Justice (2015) 46 VR 646, 641
Merkur Island Shipping Corporation v Laughton [1983] 2 AC 570, 162
Merrick Tyler Pty Ltd v Commissioner of Main Roads [2015] WASCA 82, 11, **227–9**, 490–2
Meskovski v DPP (Vic) [2018] VSCA 293, 357
Messages On Hold Australia Pty Ltd v City of Perth [2007] WASC 226, 682
Metricon Qld Pty Ltd v Chief Commissioner of State Revenue (No 2) (2016) 102 ATR 781, **468–9**
Metropolitan Gas Co v Federated Gas Employees' Industrial Union (1925) 35 CLR 449, 20, **21–2**
Meyer Heine Pty Ltd v China Navigation Co Ltd (1966) 115 CLR 10, 639
Milanes v Minister for Immigration and Border Protection (2015) 234 FCR 508, 507–8
Milenkovski v Western Australia (2011) 42 WAR 99, 333
Military Rehabilitation and Compensation Commission v May (2016) 257 CLR 468, 52, 466
Millar v Taylor (1769) 98 ER 210, 24
Miller v Commonwealth (1904) 1 CLR 668, 23
Miller v Miller (2011) 242 CLR 446, 573
Mills v Commissioner of Taxation (2012) 250 CLR 171, 365
Mills v Meeking (1990) 169 CLR 214, 27, 51, 53, 99, 115, 361, 531–3
Mills v Wilkins (1703) 87 ER 822, 198
Milne v The Queen (2014) 252 CLR 149, 72, 79, 226, 492
Minister Administering the Crown Lands Act v NSW Aboriginal Land Council (2008) 237 CLR 285, 246–7, 343, 468
Minister for Aboriginal Affairs v Peko-Wallsend Ltd (1986) 162 CLR 24, 555
Minister for Foreign Affairs and Trade v Magno (1992) 37 FCR 298, 482
Minister for Home Affairs v Benbrika (2021) 95 ALJR 166, 41
Minister for Immigration and Border Protection v CED16 (2020) 94 ALJR 706, 240
Minister for Immigration and Border Protection v Han (2015) 231 FCR 113, 356
Minister for Immigration and Border Protection v Kumar (2017) 260 CLR 367, 247, 326, 495
Minister for Immigration and Border Protection v SZMTA (2019) 264 CLR 421, 582
Minister for Immigration and Border Protection v SZSSJ (2016) 259 CLR 180, 506
Minister for Immigration and Border Protection v WZAPN (2015) 254 CLR 610, 484

Minister for Immigration and Border Protection v WZARH (2015) 256 CLR 326, 486
Minister for Immigration and Citizenship v Anochie (2012) 209 FCR 497, 670
Minister for Immigration and Citizenship v Haneef (2007) 163 FCR 414, 285, 447
Minister for Immigration and Citizenship v Li (2013) 249 CLR 332, 505–7
Minister for Immigration and Citizenship v SZGUR (2011) 241 CLR 594, 555
Minister for Immigration and Citizenship v SZIZO (2009) 238 CLR 627, 582
Minister for Immigration and Citizenship v SZIZO [2009] HCATrans 71, 575
Minister for Immigration and Citizenship v SZJGV (2009) 238 CLR 642, 39, 80, 421–2, 430, 529, 532
Minister for Immigration and Citizenship v Yucesan (2008) 169 FCR 202, **11–12**, **64**, **67**, 227, **508–9**, 513
Minister for Immigration and Citizenship v Yucesan (2008) 216 FLR 252, 12, 64, 67
Minister for Immigration, Citizenship, Migrant Services and Multicultural Affairs v FAK19 [2021] FCAFC 153, 473
Minister for Immigration, Citizenship, Migrant Services and Multicultural Affairs v Moorcroft (2021) 391 ALR 270, 425, 431
Minister for Immigration and Ethnic Affairs v Teoh (1995) 183 CLR 273, 484–5, 487
Minister for Immigration and Multicultural Affairs v Bhardwaj (2002) 209 CLR 597, 555, 559, 573, 586
Minister for Immigration and Multicultural Affairs v Eshetu (1999) 197 CLR 611, 585, 587–8
Minister for Immigration and Multicultural Affairs v Savvin (2000) 98 FCR 168, 307
Minister for Immigration and Multicultural Affairs v WABQ (2002) 121 FCR 251, 341, 346
Minister for Immigration and Multicultural and Indigenous Affairs v Al Masri (2003) 126 FCR 54, 594
Minister for Immigration and Multicultural and Indigenous Affairs v B (2004) 219 CLR 365, 484
Minister for Immigration and Multicultural and Indigenous Affairs v Nystrom (2006) 228 CLR 566, 277
Minister for Immigration and Multicultural and Indigenous Affairs v QAAH of 2004 (2006) 231 CLR 1, 482, 484, 487
Minister for Immigration and Multicultural and Indigenous Affairs v SZAYW (2005) 145 FCR 523, 430, 489
Minister for Indigenous Affairs v MJD Foundation Ltd (2017) 250 FCR 31, 397
Minister for Urban Affairs and Planning v Rosemount Estates Pty Ltd (1996) 91 LGERA 31, 299
Minister for Works (WA) v Gulson (1944) 69 CLR 338, 632
Minister of Resources v Dover Fisheries Pty Ltd (1993) 43 FCR 565, 673
Minogue v Victoria (2018) 264 CLR 252, 254, 608, 613
Mitchell v Bailey (2008) 168 FCR 370, 115
Mitchell v Latrobe Regional Hospital (2016) 51 VR 581, 396, 604
Mitchell v Marshall (2014) 27 Tas R 1, 570
Mobil Oil Australia Pty Ltd v Victoria (2002) 211 CLR 1, 646
Mohammadi v Bethune [2018] WASCA 98, 456
Mokbel v A-G (Cth) (2007) 162 FCR 296, 387
Momcilovic v The Queen (2011) 245 CLR 1, 7, 49–51, 53, 222, 356–7, 404–6, 439–42, 476, 497, 531
Mondelez Australia Pty Ltd v Automotive, Food, Metals, Engineering, Printing and Kindred Industries Union (2020) 94 ALJR 818, 52, 116, 239–40, 356, 359, 361, 365–6, **369–70**, 440
Monis v The Queen (2013) 249 CLR 92, 115, 316

Moore v Smith (1859) 120 ER 1034, 622
Morgan v Rylands Brothers (Australia) Ltd (1927) 39 CLR 517, 274
Morgan v White (1912) 15 CLR 1, 639
Morton v Union Steamship Co of New Zealand Ltd (1951) 83 CLR 402, 673–4
Mount Beauty Gliding Club Inc v Jacob (2004) 10 VR 312, 65
Muin v Refugee Review Tribunal (2002) 190 ALR 601, 288, 491–2
Mulholland v Tasmania (2017) 25 Tas R 313, 570
Municipal Council of Sydney v Commonwealth (1904) 1 CLR 208, 19, 23–4
Municipal Officers' Association of Australia v Lancaster (1981) 54 FLR 129, 108, 299
Murphy v Farmer (1988) 165 CLR 19, 245–6, 253, 430
Murwangi Community Aboriginal Corporation v Caroll (2001) 166 FLR 247, 272
Muslimin v The Queen (2010) 240 CLR 470, 126
My Environment Inc v Vic Forests (2013) 42 VR 456, 111, 113
MYT Engineering Pty Ltd v Mulcon Pty Ltd (1999) 195 CLR 636, 266
MZAPC v Minister for Immigration and Border Protection (2021) 390 ALR 590, 504–5, 575–6, 582

NAGV and NAGW of 2002 v Minister for Immigration and Multicultural and Indigenous Affairs (2005) 222 CLR 161, 320, 328
Namoa v The Queen (2021) 95 ALJR 396, 333–4
National Disability Insurance Agency v McGarrigle (2017) 157 ALD 458, 595
National Disability Insurance Agency v WRMF (2020) 276 FCR 415, 595
National Mutual Life Association v Commissioner of State Taxation (2011) 110 SASR 536, 284–5
National Mutual Life Association of Australasia Ltd v Godrich (1909) 10 CLR 1, 23
National Rugby League Investments Pty Ltd v Singtel Optus Pty Ltd (2012) 201 FCR 147, 361
NBGM v Minister for Immigration and Multicultural Affairs (2006) 231 CLR 52, 482–3
Neindorf v Junkovic (2005) 80 ALJR 341, 332
Network Ten Pty Ltd v TCN Channel Nine Pty Ltd (2004) 218 CLR 273, 316
New South Wales Aboriginal Land Council v Minister Administering the Crown Lands (Consolidation) Act and the Western Lands Act (1988) 14 NSWLR 685, 608–9, 613–15, 617
New South Wales Aboriginal Land Council v Minister Administering the Crown Lands Act (2016) 260 CLR 232, 107, 249–50, 355, 469
New South Wales Aboriginal Land Council v Minister Administering the Crown Lands Act [2016] NSWLEC 157, 568
New South Wales Crime Commission v Kelaita (2008) 75 NSWLR 564, 459, 461
New South Wales Crime Commission v Kelly (2003) 58 NSWLR 71, 528–9
New South Wales v Betfair Pty Ltd (2009) 180 FCR 543, 153–4
New South Wales v Bujdoso (2007) 69 NSWLR 302, 311
New South Wales v Commonwealth (1975) 135 CLR 337, 637
New South Wales v Commonwealth (1990) 169 CLR 482, 193
New South Wales v Corbett [2007] HCATrans 119, 575
New South Wales v Williamson [2011] NSWCA 183, 79
New South Wales v Williamson (2012) 248 CLR 417, 304
New York Trust Co v Eisner, 256 US 345 (1921), 345
Newcastle City Council v A-G (NSW) (1983) 52 LGRA 75, 557
Newcastle City Council v GIO General Ltd (1997) 191 CLR 85, 33, 316, 352, 356, 369, 531, 537

Nguyen v Nguyen (1990) 169 CLR 245, 465
Niboyet v Niboyet (1878) 4 PD 1, 639, 642
Nicholls v Michael Wilson & Partners Ltd (2010) 243 FLR 177, 498
Nitro Circus Touring Australia Pty Ltd v Lenzoni [2016] NSWSC 178, 401
Nixon v A-G [1930] 1 Ch 566, 301
No 20 Cannon St Ltd v Singer & Friedlander Ltd [1974] 1 Ch 229, 385
Nominal Defendant v GLG Australia Ltd (2006) 228 CLR 529, **59–60**
Noone v Operation Smile (2012) 38 VR 569, 404
North Australian Aboriginal Justice Agency Ltd v Northern Territory (2015) 256 CLR 569, 41, 367, 371, 422, 430, 440, 443–4, 501–3, 541, 555, **556**, 676
Northbuild Construction Pty Ltd v Lockton [2000] 2 Qd R 600, 633
Northern Land Council v Olney (1992) 34 FCR 470, 268
Northern Territory v Arnhem Land Aboriginal Land Trust (2008) 236 CLR 24, 343
Northern Territory v Collins (2008) 235 CLR 619, 319
Northern Territory v Griffiths (2019) 269 CLR 1, 354
NSW Associated Blue-Metal Quarries Ltd v Federal Commissioner of Taxation (1956) 94 CLR 509, 228
NSW Commissioner of Police v Cottle (2022) 96 ALJR 304, 469
NT Power Generation Pty Ltd v Power & Water Authority (2002) 122 FCR 399, 627
NT Power Generation Pty Ltd v Power and Water Authority (2004) 219 CLR 90, 491

Oates v A-G (Cth) (2003) 214 CLR 496, 676
Obeid v Australian Competition and Consumer Commission (2014) 226 FCR 471, 302
O'Connell v Nixon (2007) 16 VR 440, 676
O'Connell v Palmer (1994) 53 FCR 429, 672
O'Connor v Healey (1967) 69 SR (NSW) 111, 638, 645
O'Donnell v Environment Protection Authority (2012) 192 LGERA 1, 379
O'Donoghue v Ireland (2008) 234 CLR 599, 560
Ogden Industries Pty Ltd v Lucas (1967) 116 CLR 537, 395, 605
Ogden Industries Pty Ltd v Lucas [1970] AC 113, 465, 469
Ogilvie v Lowe [1963] VR 225, 386
OKS v Western Australia (2019) 265 CLR 268, 240
Old UGC Inc v Industrial Relations Commission (NSW) (2006) 225 CLR 274, 645
Olin Corporation v Super Cartridge Co Pty Ltd (1977) 180 CLR 236, 491
Olsen v City of Camberwell [1926] VLR 58, 681
Ombudsman v Laughton (2005) 64 NSWLR 114, 261, 280
Ombudsman v Moroney (1983) 1 NSWLR 317, 301
O'Neill v The Queen (2020) 137 SASR 1, 337
One.Tel Ltd v Australian Communications Authority (2001) 110 FCR 125, 669
One.Tel Ltd (in liq) v Rich (2005) 190 FLR 443, 306
Onebev Pty Ltd v Encore Beverages Pty Ltd (2016) 50 VR 106, 399
O'Reilly v Rooney (1989) 10 MVR 19, 127
O'Reilly v State Bank of Victoria Commissioners (1983) 153 CLR 1, 391
Origin Energy LPG Ltd v Bestcare Foods Ltd [2007] NSWCA 321, 201
Ormond Investment Co v Betts [1928] AC 143, 256–7
O'Shaughnessy v Mirror Newspapers Ltd (1970) 125 CLR 166, 261
Ostrowski v Palmer (2004) 218 CLR 493, 649
Ousley v The Queen (1997) 192 CLR 69, 62

Owen v South Australia (1996) 66 SASR 251, 351, 366
Owens v Owens [2017] EWCA Civ 182, 284
Owens v Owens [2018] AC 899, 292
Owners of the Ship Shin Kobe Maru v Empire Shipping Co Inc (1994) 181 CLR 404, 303–4

P v Child Support Registrar (2014) 225 FCR 378, 516–17
Pac-Rim Printing Pty Ltd v Australian Postal Corporation (2000) 97 FCR 445, 270
Padfield v Minister for Agriculture, Fisheries and Food [1968] AC 997, 555
Palace Gallery Pty Ltd v Liquor and Gambling Commissioner (2014) 118 SASR 567, 365
Palace Gallery Pty Ltd v WorkCover Premium Review Panel (2014) 119 SASR 408, 321, 329
Palais Parking Station Pty Ltd v Shea (1977) 16 SASR 360, 184–5
Palgo Holdings Pty Ltd v Gowans (2005) 221 CLR 249, 109, 268, 317
Palmer v Western Australia (2021) 95 ALJR 868, 42
Palumpa Station Pty Ltd v Fox (1999) 132 NTR 1, 272
Pape v Commissioner of Taxation (Cth) (2009) 238 CLR 1, 292
Park v The Queen (2021) 395 ALR 193, 140, 144
Parkes Shire Council v South West Helicopters Pty Ltd (2019) 266 CLR 212, 75, 222–3
Partington v A-G (1869) LR 4 HL 100, 256
Pavic v Magistrates Court (Vic) (2003) 140 A Crim R 113, 274
Pearce v Florenca (1976) 135 CLR 507, 644
Pelka v Sundquist [2005] WASC 52, 96
Peniamina v The Queen (2020) 95 ALJR 85, 334
People v Harris, 885 NW 2d 832 (2016), 493–4
Pepper (Inspector of Taxes) v Hart [1993] AC 593, 178
Peppers Self Service Stores Pty Ltd v Scott (1958) 98 CLR 606, 189
Pepsi Seven-Up Bottlers Perth Pty Ltd v Commissioner of Taxation (1995) 62 FCR 289, 268
Perera-Cathcart v The Queen (2017) 260 CLR 595, 513
Perilya Broken Hill Ltd v Valuer-General (2015) 10 ARLR 235, 476
Perpetual Custodians Ltd v IOOF Investment Management Ltd (2013) 304 ALR 436, 261
Petch v The Queen (2020) 103 NSWLR 1, 656
Pfeiffer v Stevens (2001) 209 CLR 57, 223, 380, 397, 422, 554
PGA v The Queen (2012) 245 CLR 355, 331
Phillips v Lynch (1907) 5 CLR 12, 19, 23–4
Phillips v Police (2016) 125 SASR 427, 496
Phoenix Commercial Enterprises Pty Ltd v City of Canada Bay Council [2010] NSWCA 64, 268–9
Pickett v Western Australia (2020) 270 CLR 323, 333, 334, 335
Pidoto v Victoria (1943) 68 CLR 87, 502
Pilbara Infrastructure Pty Ltd v Australian Competition Tribunal (2012) 246 CLR 379, 355, 360, 562
Pilbara Infrastructure Pty Ltd v Brockman Iron Pty Ltd [2016] WASCA 36, 533, 668
Pilbara Infrastructure Pty Ltd v Brockman Iron Pty Ltd (No 2) [2014] WASC 345, 533
Pinho v Andre (Supreme Court of Victoria, Smith J, 20 December 1994), 498, 499, **500**
Pinkstone v The Queen (2004) 219 CLR 444, 493, 507–8
Pirrie v McFarlane (1925) 36 CLR 170, 625
PJ v The Queen (2012) 36 VR 402, 664–5
Plaintiff M47/2012 v Director-General of Security (2012) 251 CLR 1, 223, 280, 295, 669, **675–6**

Plaintiff M70/2011 v Minister for Immigration and Citizenship (2011) 244 CLR 144, 131, 276, 511
Plaintiff M79/2012 v Minister for Immigration and Citizenship (2013) 252 CLR 336, 667
Plaintiff M174/2016 v Minister for Immigration and Border Protection (2018) 264 CLR 217, 240
Plaintiff S4/2014 v Minister for Immigration and Border Protection (2014) 253 CLR 219, 497
Plaintiff S10/2011 v Minister for Immigration and Citizenship (2012) 246 CLR 636, 37, 50, 96, 344, 505–6
Plaintiff S157/2002 v Commonwealth (2003) 211 CLR 476, 38, 42, 223, 371, 409, 483, 485, 505, 585, 667
Plaintiff S195/2016 v Minister for Immigration and Border Protection (2017) 261 CLR 622, 478
Plaintiff S297/2013 v Minister for Immigration and Border Protection (2014) 255 CLR 179, 549
Plewa v Chief Adjudication Officer [1995] 1 AC 249, 614
PM v Childrens Court of the ACT (2018) 336 FLR 379, 398
PM v The Queen (2007) 232 CLR 370, 576–7
Police v Davis [1981] 1 DCRNZ 249, 475
Polites v Commonwealth (1945) 70 CLR 60, 478
Polo/Lauren Co LP v Ziliani Holdings Pty Ltd (2008) 173 FCR 266, 490–2
Polyukhovich v Commonwealth (1991) 172 CLR 501, 607, 643
Poniatowska v Channel Seven Sydney Pty Ltd (No 2) (2020) 136 SASR 455, 329
Popple v Rowe [1998] 1 VR 651, 215
Port of Brisbane Corporation v Commissioner of Taxation (2004) 140 FCR 375, 516–17
Port of Newcastle Operations Pty Ltd v Glencore Coal Assets Australia Pty Ltd (2021) 395 ALR 209, 99, 289, 351, 360
Porter v Bryan [1963] Tas SR 41, 385
Potter v Minahan (1908) 7 CLR 277, 23, 225, 433–4, 444
Povey v Qantas Airways Ltd (2005) 223 CLR 189, 13, 479–80
Powell v Kempton Park Racecourse Co [1897] 2 QB 242, 198, 296–7
Powell v Kempton Park Racecourse Co [1899] AC 143, 296
Power Rental Op Co Australia v Forge Group Power Pty Ltd (2017) 93 NSWLR 765, 365
Prabowo v Republic of Indonesia (1995) 61 FCR 258, 272
Pregelj v Manison (1987) 31 A Crim R 383, 663
President of the Shire of Arapiles v Board of Works (1904) 1 CLR 679, 23
President of the Shire of Charlton v Ruse (1912) 14 CLR 220, 205, 307
Prior v Mole (2017) 261 CLR 265, 593–4, 597
Prior v Sherwood (1906) 3 CLR 1054, 272
Probuild Constructions (Aust) Pty Ltd v Shade Systems Pty Ltd (2018) 264 CLR 1, 6, 134, 430, **440–1**, 475
Project Blue Sky Inc v Australian Broadcasting Authority (1998) 194 CLR 355, 7, 31, 45, 52, 56, 75–7, 100, 116, 125, 222–4, 262, 280, 297, 300, 422, 495, 505, 511, 515, 537, 540, 541, 542, **543–5**, 548, 560, 574–6, 578–9, 581–2, 665
Proudman v Dayman (1941) 67 CLR 536, 651, 653, 656
Province of Bombay v Municipal Corporation of Bombay [1947] AC 58, 623
Provincial Insurance Australia Pty Ltd v Consolidated Wood Products Pty Ltd (1991) 25 NSWLR 541, 11, 225, 228, 492
Prowse v McIntyre (1961) 111 CLR 264, 183, 397–8

Public Service Association v Industrial Relations Secretary [2015] NSWCA 386, 430
Public Service Association and Professional Officers' Association Amalgamated (NSW) v Director of Public Employment (2012) 250 CLR 343, 41, 491, 676
Public Service Association of New South Wales v Industrial Commission of New South Wales (1985) 1 NSWLR 627, 92
Public Service Association of South Australia Inc v Industrial Relations Commission (SA) (2012) 249 CLR 398, 50
Purcell v Electricity Commission of New South Wales (1985) 60 ALR 652, 280
Purvis v New South Wales (Department of Education and Training) (2002) 117 FCR 237, 428
Purvis v New South Wales (Department of Education and Training) (2003) 217 CLR 92, 246, 428
Pyneboard Pty Ltd v Trade Practices Commission (1983) 152 CLR 328, 433

Quarmby v Keating (2008) 18 Tas R 284, 290
Queensland v Central Queensland Land Council Aboriginal Corporation (2002) 125 FCR 89, 193
Queensland v Commonwealth (1977) 139 CLR 585, 474
Queensland v Congoo (2015) 256 CLR 239, 50, 53
Question of Law Reserved (No 1 of 2018) [2018] SASCFC 128, 570
Question of Law Reserved (No 2 of 1998) (1998) 70 SASR 502, 649, 656
Quikfund (Australia) Pty Ltd v Airmark Consolidators Pty Ltd (2014) 222 FCR 13, **241–2**
QUYD Pty Ltd v Marvass Pty Ltd [2009] 1 Qd R 41, 401

R v A2 (2019) 269 CLR 507, 6, 73–4, 80, 88, 91, 101, 116, 119, 229, 251, 253, 257, 284, 286, 288, 292, 294, 296, 301, 355, 358, 359, 366, 369, 430–1, 522
R v AL (A Pseudonym) (2016) 310 FLR 320, 328
R v Baines (1840) 113 ER 792, 310
R v Barlow (1997) 188 CLR 1, 663
R v Bentham [2005] 1 WLR 1057, 229–30, **264–5**, 494
R v Berchet (1688) 1 Show KB 106; 89 ER 480, 262
R v Birlut (1995) 39 NSWLR 1, 577
R v Bo (No 3) [2016] ACTSC 175, 649
R v Boland [1974] VR 849, 606
R v Bolton; Ex parte Beane (1987) 162 CLR 514, 49
R v Boucher [1995] 1 VR 110, 358
R v C [2002] QCA 156, 197
R v Casement [1917] 1 KB 98, 205
R v Chute (No 11) [2019] ACTSC 91, 140
R v Clarke (2008) 100 SASR 363, 657
R v Commissioner for Transport; Ex parte Cobb & Co Ltd [1963] Qd R 547, 164–5
R v Corporation of City of Ste Marie [1978] 2 SCR 1299, 651, 654
R v Deng (1996) 91 A Crim R 80, 577
R v Falconer (1990) 171 CLR 30, 506
R v Falzon (2018) 264 CLR 361, 472
R v Franke [1929] VLR 285, 646
R v Fyffe [1991] 2 VR 72, **308**
R v Gee (2003) 212 CLR 230, 290

R v Goreng-Goreng (2008) 220 FLR 21, 673
R v Griffiths [1991] 2 Qd R 29, 566–7
R v Hannan (2016) 259 A Crim R 558, **65–6**, 253, 430
R v Hellwig [2007] 1 Qd R 17, 577
R v Holley; Ex parte Attorney-General [1997] 2 Qd R 407, 571
R v Holliday (2017) 260 CLR 650, 355
R v Holmes; Ex parte Altona Petrochemical Co Ltd (1972) 126 CLR 529, 38
R v Hughes (2000) 202 CLR 535, 53
R v Hughes [2000] ACTSC 112, 662
R v Independent Broad-based Anti-corruption Commissioner (2016) 256 CLR 459, 422, 430, **437**
R v Ireland [1998] AC 147, 283
R v Janceski (2005) 64 NSWLR 10, 573–4, 577–8, 582
R v Justices of Leicestershire (1850) 117 ER 391, 499
R v Kirby; Ex parte Boilermakers' Society of Australia (1956) 94 CLR 254, 38
R v Lagan (2001) 127 A Crim R 262, 656, **657–8**, 662
R v Lavender (2005) 222 CLR 67, 245, 251, 317, 330, 336
R v LK (2010) 241 CLR 177, 334–5, 495
R v London County Council [1893] 2 QB 454, 175
R v Marks; Ex parte Australian Building Construction Employees and Builders Labourers' Federation (1981) 147 CLR 471, 266
R v Martin [1963] Tas SR 103, 650, 663
R v McLennan; Ex parte Carr (1952) 86 CLR 46, 679
R v McNeill (Ruling No 1) [2007] NFSC 2, 85
R v M'Cormick; Ex parte McMonigle (1884) 10 VLR (L) 268, 205
R v Miller (2001) 127 A Crim R 344, 70
R v Minister of Town and Country Planning; Ex parte Montague Burton Ltd [1951] 1 KB 1, 186
R v Mitchell [2008] 2 Qd R 142, 275
R v Momcilovic (2010) 25 VR 436, 404
R v Morton [1986] VR 863, 264, 619
R v Moylan; Ex parte Jenkins [1974] WAR 176, 557
R v Nationwide News Pty Ltd (2008) 22 VR 116, **640–1**, 645
R v Ng (2002) 5 VR 257, 682
R v Nguyen (2010) 204 A Crim R 246, 364
R v O'Connor (1980) 146 CLR 64, 652
R v Perry (No 3) (1981) 28 SASR 112, 272
R v Peters (1886) 16 QBD 636, 225, 490
R v PJ (2017) 270 A Crim R 439, **211–13**, 254
R v PLV (2001) 51 NSWLR 736, 534
R v Public Vehicles Licensing Appeals Tribunal (Tas); Ex parte Australian National Airways Pty Ltd (1964) 113 CLR 207, 176
R v Regos (1947) 74 CLR 613, 272
R v Reynhoudt (1962) 107 CLR 381, 93
R v Roach [1988] VR 665, 157
R v Rolfe (2021) 395 ALR 201, 308
R v Rose [2010] 1 Qd R 87, **252–3**
R v Scarlett; Ex parte McMillan (1972) 20 FLR 349, 605

R v Scarth [1945] St R Qd 38, 663
R v Schildkamp [1971] AC 1, 301–2
R v Secretary of State for the Environment; Ex parte Camden London Borough Council [1998] 1 WLR 615, 67
R v Secretary of State for the Environment, Transport and the Regions; Ex parte Spath Holme Ltd [2001] 2 AC 349, 76, 677
R v Secretary of State for the Home Department; Ex parte Fire Brigades Union [1995] 2 AC 513, 189, 193
R v Secretary of State for the Home Department; Ex parte Naughton [1997] 1 WLR 118, 507
R v Secretary of State for the Home Department; Ex parte Simms [2000] 2 AC 115, 443, 449
R v Sharma (2002) 54 NSWLR 300, 357
R v Sieders (2008) 72 NSWLR 417, 328
R v Skinner (2016) 126 SASR 120, 562
R v Slator (1881) 8 QBD 267, 268
R v Speyer [1916] 1 KB 595, 205
R v Sutton (1908) 5 CLR 789, 632
R v Tamawiwy (No 3) (2015) 302 FLR 79, 192
R v Taylor (1863) 2 W & W (L) 23, 310
R v Thompson (No 3) [2017] ACTSC 53, 569
R v Tolson (1889) 23 QBD 168, 648
R v Toohey; Ex parte Northern Land Council (1981) 151 CLR 170, **677**
R v Turnbull (1943) 44 SR (NSW) 108, 649, 661
R v Walsall Justices; Ex parte W [1990] 1 QB 253, 192
R v Wampfler (1987) 11 NSWLR 541, 650, 654
R v Wilson; Ex parte Kisch (1934) 52 CLR 234, 21, 23, 265–6
R v XY (2013) 84 NSWLR 363, 472
R v Young (1999) 46 NSWLR 681, 13, 72, 534
R v Yusoff (2013) 33 NTLR 113, 253
R (Black) v Secretary of State for Justice [2018] AC 215, 460
R (Quintavalle) v Secretary of State for Health [2003] 2 AC 687, 319
Radojevic v JDA Design Group Pty Ltd (No 2) [2017] VSC 796, 558
Ramaciotti v Federal Commissioner of Taxation (1920) 29 CLR 49, 24, 454
Ramos v Minister for Immigration and Multicultural Affairs (1999) 91 FCR 329, 311
Randren House Pty Ltd v Water Administration Ministerial Corporation [2020] NSWCA 14, 575
Randwick Municipal Council v Rutledge (1959) 102 CLR 54, 499
Rann v Olsen (2000) 76 SASR 450, 178
Re A Solicitor's Clerk [1957] 1 WLR 1219, 610
Re Alcan Australia Ltd; Ex parte Federation of Industrial, Manufacturing and Engineering Employees (1994) 181 CLR 96, 324
Re Application of the Fourth South Melbourne Building Society (1883) 9 VLR (Eq) 54, 302
Re Athlumney; Ex parte Wilson [1898] 2 QB 547, 602, 617
Re Australian Federation Construction Contractors; Ex parte Billing (1986) 61 ALJR 37, 356
Re Bidie [1948] 2 All ER 995, 32
Re Boaler [1915] 1 KB 21, 199, 298
Re Bolton; Ex parte Beane (1987) 162 CLR 514, 296, **367–8**, 371, 465
Re Bonner and Director-General of Health [1983] AATA 239, 398
Re Cathcart; Ex parte Campbell (1870) LR 5 Ch 703, 325
Re Citizen Limbo (1989) 92 ALR 81, 588

Re Collins; Ex parte Hocking (1989) 167 CLR 522, 307
Re Commercial Bank of Australia Ltd (1893) 19 VLR 333, 309
Re Commissioner of Water Resources and Leighton Contractors Pty Ltd [1991] 1 Qd R 549, 633
Re Credit Tribunal; Ex parte General Motors Acceptance Corporation (Australia) (1977) 137 CLR 545, 299
Re Davis (1947) 75 CLR 409, 555, 557, 566
Re DPP (Cth) Reference No 1 of 2008 (2008) 21 VR 111, 649, 663
Re Drake and Minister for Immigration and Ethnic Affairs (No 2) (1979) 2 ALD 634, 516
Re Dunsborough Districts Country Club Inc [1982] WAR 321, 570
Re East; Ex parte Nguyen (1998) 196 CLR 354, 295
Re Fogg (Dec'd) [1972] 1 NSWLR 416, 191
Re Foley (1952) 53 SR (NSW) 31, 201, 310
Re Griffiths [1991] 2 Qd R 29, 557, **566–7**
Re Health Act 1890 [1911] VLR 429, 205
Re Joybay Pty Ltd [2019] VSC 620, 533
Re Kierath, Minister for Heritage; Ex parte City of Fremantle (2000) 22 WAR 342, 555
Re Kumar and Minister for Immigration and Citizenship (2009) 107 ALD 178, 516
Re Lord Thurlow; Ex parte Official Receiver [1895] 1 QB 724, 557
Re Macks; Ex parte Saint (2000) 204 CLR 158, 298
Re MacTiernan; Ex Parte McKay (2007) 208 FLR 191, 305
Re Maurice's Application; Ex parte A-G (NT) (1987) 18 FCR 163, 341
Re McInnes (2014) 241 IR 158, 611
Re McIntyre v Transport Workers' Union of Australia; Ex parte A-G (Qld) (2000) 105 FCR 584, 612
Re Minister for Immigration and Multicultural and Indigenous Affairs; Ex parte Lam (2003) 214 CLR 1, 486
Re Minister for Immigration and Multicultural and Indigenous Affairs; Ex parte Palme (2003) 216 CLR 212, 573, 578, 580–1, 585
Re Minister of Primary Industries and Energy v Austral Fisheries Pty Ltd (1993) 40 FCR 381, 678
Re Pacific Coal; Ex parte Construction, Forestry, Mining and Energy Union (2000) 203 CLR 346, 381
Re Petroulias and Commissioner of Taxation (2010) 122 ALD 153, 516
Re Rebmik Contractors Pty Ltd and Commissioner of Taxation (2008) 101 ALD 445, 516–17
Re Rocha Pty Ltd (No 2) (2016) 312 FLR 309, 608, 612
Re Royce; Ex parte MacKaness and Avery Pty Ltd (1943) 43 SR (NSW) 239, 269
Re Samuel [1913] AC 514, 328
Re Sapronov and Minister for Immigration and Citizenship (2011) 120 ALD 362, 516
Re Seoud and Secretary, Department of Families, Housing, Community Services and Indigenous Affairs (2012) 126 ALD 593, 161
Re Settree Estates (2018) 98 NSWLR 910, 555
Re Sonnadere (1903) 5 WALR 11, 674
Re Woking Urban Council (Basingstoke Canal) Act, 1911 [1914] 1 Ch 300, 202
Re Woolley; Ex parte Applicants M276/2003 (2004) 225 CLR 1, 484
Reardon v Deputy Commissioner of Taxation (2013) 92 ATR 494, 328
Redman v Return to Work Corp (SA) (2021) 305 IR 326, 351, 365, 533–4
Reed v Motors Ltd [1926] SASR 128, 273

Regional Express Holdings Ltd v Australian Federation of Air Pilots (2017) 262 CLR 456, 278, 316, 320
Registrar of Births, Deaths and Marriages (NSW) v Norrie (2014) 250 CLR 490, 429
Registrar of Motor Vehicles v Vu (2013) 115 SASR 385, 578–80
Registrar of the Accident Compensation Tribunal v Commissioner of Taxation (Cth) (1993) 178 CLR 145, 624
Registrar of Titles (WA) v Franzon (1975) 132 CLR 611, 278
Renwick v Parole Board Queensland [2019] 2 QR 645, 279
Repatriation Commission v Keeley (2000) 98 FCR 108, 618
Residual Assco Group Ltd v Spalvins (2000) 202 CLR 629, 491, 503
Resort Management Services Ltd v Noosa Shire Council [1997] 2 Qd R 291, 602, 609–10, 615–16
Reynolds v Stacey (1957) 96 CLR 454, 318
Ribbon v The Queen (2019) 134 SASR 328, 43, 356, 361, 363
Richard G Bejah Insurance & Financial Services Pty Ltd v Maning [2002] TASSC 36, 704
Richards v McBride (1881) 8 QBD 119, 22
Richardson v Forestry Commission (1988) 164 CLR 261, 102
Riddle v The Queen (1911) 12 CLR 622, 327
Risk v Northern Territory (2002) 210 CLR 392, 454
River Wear Commissioners v Adamson (1877) 2 App Cas 743, 19, 22–3
Rizeq v Western Australia (2017) 262 CLR 1, 37, 131
RJE v Secretary to the Department of Justice (2008) 21 VR 526, 472
Roberts v Ahern (1904) 1 CLR 406, 623, 627
Robertson v City of Nunawading [1973] VR 819, 605, 606, 609, 612
Rodriguez v United States, 480 US 522 (1987), 113
Rodway v The Queen (1990) 169 CLR 515, 396, 601, 603, 616–18, 672
Rose v Hvric (1963) 108 CLR 353, 177, 540
Ross v Consumer, Trading and Teneacy Tribunal of NSW [2003] NSWSC 21, 274
Royal Women's Hospital v Medical Practitioners Board of Victoria (2006) 15 VR 22, 484
Ruhani v Director of Police (2005) 222 CLR 489, 274
Russo v Aiello (2003) 215 CLR 643, 106, 299
Ryde Municipal Council v Macquarie University (1978) 139 CLR 633, 307
Rylands Brothers (Australia) Ltd v Morgan (1927) 27 SR (NSW) 161, 274

SAAP v Minister for Immigration and Multicultural and Indigenous Affairs (2005) 228 CLR 294, 155
Saeed v Minister for Immigration and Citizenship (2010) 241 CLR 252, 89, 358, 371, 440, 512, 522, 562
Saif Ali v Sydney Mitchell & Co [1980] AC 198, 65
Saliba v Aziz (2013) 281 FLR 278, 540–1, 549, **550–2**
Salkeld v Johnson (1842) 1 Hare 196; 66 ER 1004, 296
Salkeld v Johnson (1848) 2 Ex 256, 198
Salomon v Salomon [1897] AC 22, 50
Samad v District Court of New South Wales (2002) 209 CLR 140, 554–5, 559, 561–2, 564–6
Samuels v Songaila (1977) 16 SASR 397, 617, 619
Saraswati v The Queen (1991) 172 CLR 1, 262, 506, 542, 550
Sargood Brothers v Commonwealth (1910) 11 CLR 258, 20, 433
SAS Trustee Corporation v Miles (2018) 265 CLR 137, 77, 84–5, 86–7, 91–2, 109, 359, 430
Scaffidi v Chief Executive Officer, Department of Local Government and Communities (2017) 52 WAR 368, 113

Schenker & Co (Aust) Pty Ltd v Maplas Equipment and Services Pty Ltd [1990] VR 834, 273
Scott-Mackenzie v Bail (2017) 16 ASTLR 449, 134, 145, 211, **214–15**, 229, 281, 508
Screen Australia v EME Productions No 1 Pty Ltd (2012) 200 FCR 282, 358
Seaford Court Estates Ltd v Asher [1949] 2 KB 481, 156
Secretary, Department of Employment, Education, Training and Youth Affairs v Gray (1999) 91 FCR 254, **263**
Secretary, Department of Family and Community Services v Hayward (A Pseudonym) (2018) 98 NSWLR 599, 341
Secretary, Department of Social Security v Kozhaya Dagher [1997] AATA 419, 387
Secretary, Department of Social Security v SRA (1993) 43 FCR 299, 246
Secure Funding Pty Ltd v Doneley [2010] QSC 91, 327
Selectrix Pty Ltd v Humphrys (2001) 159 FLR 348, 654
Shahi v Minister for Immigration and Citizenship (2011) 246 CLR 163, 421–2
Shanahan v Scott (1957) 96 CLR 245, 189, 295, 674
Shapowloff v Dunn (1981) 148 CLR 72, 594
Sharples v Arnison (2001) 160 FLR 194, 500
Sheahan v Carrier Air Conditioning Pty Ltd (1997) 189 CLR 407, 506
Sheldrake v DPP [2005] 1 AC 264, 405
Sherras v De Rutzen [1895] 1 QB 918, 649–50, 655
Sherzad v Minister for Immigration and Citizenship (2008) 170 FCR 105, 384–5
Shi v Migration Agents Registration Authority (2008) 235 CLR 286, 84
Shiel v Secretary, Department of Social Security (1999) 56 ALD 465, 570, 588
Shire of York v Rosmill Pty Ltd [2010] WASC 189, 288
Shore v A-G on the Relation of Wilson (1842) 8 ER 450, 225
Shorten v David Hurst Constructions Pty Ltd (2008) 72 NSWLR 211, 363, 365
Shuster v Minister for Immigration and Citizenship (2008) 167 FCR 186, 306
Silk Brothers Pty Ltd v State Electricity Commission of Victoria (1943) 67 CLR 1, 300
Simeon Wines Ltd v Bobos [2004] NSWCA 342, 272
Simonis v Perpetual Trustee Co Ltd (1987) 21 NSWLR 677, 266
Singh v Commonwealth (2004) 222 CLR 322, 4, 49–52, 55, 93, 102, 144, 286, 340, 346, 353
Singh v Minister for Immigration, Local Government and Ethnic Affairs (1989) 18 ALD 638, 389
Singh v Secretary of State for the Home Department [1992] 1 WLR 1052, 684
Slaveski v Smith (2012) 34 VR 206, 405
Slivak v Lurgi (Australia) Pty Ltd (2001) 205 CLR 304, 85
SM v The Queen (2013) 46 VR 464, 358
Smith v Motor Discounts Ltd (1935) 54 CLR 107, 395
Smith v The Queen (1994) 181 CLR 338, 279
Smith v Watson (1906) 4 CLR 802, 161
Smoker v Pharmacy Restructuring Authority (1994) 53 FCR 287, **78–9**, 93, **213–14**, 225, 496
Snedden v Minister for Justice (2014) 230 FCR 82, 237–8
Solomons v District Court of New South Wales (2002) 211 CLR 119, 593–4
Sonnet v The Queen (2010) 30 VR 519, 285, 288
South Australia v Collings (1996) 65 SASR 432, 602
South Australia v Commonwealth (1942) 65 CLR 373, 24
South Australia v Lampard Trevorrow (2010) 106 SASR 331, 516
South Australia v Tanner (1989) 166 CLR 161, 672, 678

South Australia v Totani (2010) 242 CLR 1, 41, 440, 442
South Australia Housing Trust v Development Assessment Commission (1994) 63 SASR 35, 568
South Australian Banking Co v Horner (1868) 2 SALR 263, 310
South-Eastern Drainage Board (South Australia) v Savings Bank of South Australia (1939) 62 CLR 603, 176–7, 540, 545, 549
South Western Sydney Local Health District v Gould (2018) 97 NSWLR 513, 491
Southern Cross Group Services Pty Ltd v Chief Commissioner of State Revenue (NSW) (2019) 110 ATR 16, 364, 366
Sovar v Henry Lane Pty Ltd (1967) 116 CLR 397, 4, 20, 23, 52, 143–4, 340, 512
Spear v Hallenstein [2018] VSC 169, 395, 607, 610, 612, 618
Spence v Queensland (2019) 268 CLR 355, 261–2, 274
Sports Centres Australia Pty Ltd v Commissioner for Australian Capital Territory Revenue (2019) 240 LGERA 311, 390
Srikantha v Commonwealth (No 2) (2020) 299 IR 302, 573
Stamford Property Services Pty Ltd v Mulpha Australia Ltd (2019) 99 NSWLR 730, 100
Stanford v Stanford (2012) 247 CLR 108, 597
Stanojlovic v DPP (2018) 273 A Crim R 215, 656, **659–61**
Starey v Graham [1899] 1 QB 406, 609
State Authorities Superannuation Board v Commissioner of State Taxation (WA) (1996) 189 CLR 253, 630
State of Utah v Rasabout, 356 P 3d 1258 (2015), 493
Stephenson v Taylor (1861) 12 ER 650, 205
Stevens v Kabushiki Kaisha Sony Computer Entertainment (2005) 224 CLR 193, 245–6, 340, 342, 353, 363
Stingel v Clark (2006) 226 CLR 442, 284
Stoke-on-Trent City Council v B & Q plc [1991] Ch 48, 490
Stowel v Lord Zouch (1569) 75 ER 536, 296
Strathfield Municipal Council v Elvy (1992) 25 NSWLR 745, 656
Stuart v Kirkland-Veenstra (2009) 237 CLR 215, 144
Stuart v O'Connor [2016] NSWSC 1179, 679
Stuart v The Queen (1974) 134 CLR 426, 334
Sue v Hill (1999) 199 CLR 462, 280, 295, 629
Suich v Northern Territory (2010) 27 NTLR 188, 424
Sullivan v Gordon (1999) 47 NSWLR 319, 291
Sun Zhan Qui v Minister for Immigration and Ethnic Affairs [1997] FCA 324, 585, 588
Sungravure Pty Ltd v Middle East Airlines Airliban SAL (1975) 134 CLR 1, 333–4
Sunland Group Ltd v Gold Coast City Council (2021) 95 ALJR 922, 680
Superannuation Fund Investment Trust v Commissioner of Stamps (SA) (1979) 145 CLR 330, 626
Surtees v Ellison (1829) 109 ER 278, 395
Sussex Peerage Case (1844) 8 ER 1034, 20–1, 296
Svikart v Stewart (1994) 181 CLR 548, 278
Sweet v Parsley [1970] AC 132, 650, 652–3
Switzerland Insurance Australia Ltd v Mowie Fisheries Pty Ltd (1997) 74 FCR 205, 475
Sydall v Castings Ltd [1967] 1 QB 302, 268
Sydney Local Health Network v QY (2011) 83 NSWLR 321, 298
Sydney Seaplanes Pty Ltd v Page (2021) 106 NSWLR 1, 104, 352

SZEEU v Minister for Immigration and Multicultural and Indigenous Affairs (2006) 150 FCR 214, 12–13
SZTAL v Minister for Immigration and Border Protection (2017) 262 CLR 362, 11, 80, **85–6**, 88, 99–100, 116, 225, 229, 323, 332, 340, 351, 355, 358, 360, 366, 451, 453–4, 481–2, 495
SZVBN v Minister for Immigration and Border Protection (2017) 254 FCR 393, 127

Tabcorp Holdings Ltd v Victoria (2016) 90 ALJR 376; 328 ALR 375, 278, 288, 317, 343–4
Taiapa v The Queen (2009) 240 CLR 95, 593
Taikato v The Queen (1996) 186 CLR 454, 591–2, 594–5, 597–8, **599–600**
Tajjour v New South Wales (2014) 254 CLR 508, 478–9, 484
Tal Life Ltd v Shuetrim (2016) 91 NSWLR 439, 491
Talacko v Bennett (2017) 260 CLR 124, 87, **123**, 125, 355, 460, **461–2**
Tame v New South Wales (2002) 211 CLR 317, 477
Tasker v Fullwood [1978] 1 NSWLR 20, 578, 580
Tasmania v Commonwealth and Victoria (1904) 1 CLR 329, 20–1, 23, 315, 340
Tasmania v Joseph (2017) 25 Tas R 327, 570
Tasmania v Thorpe [2011] TASSC 18, 618
Tasmanian Heritage Council v Cita Property Group Pty Ltd (2010) 181 LGERA 429, 567
Tattle v Grimwood (1826) 130 ER 603, 395
Taylor v A-G (Cth) (2019) 268 CLR 224, 344, 356, 361, 367, 533
Taylor v Centennial Newstan Pty Ltd (2009) 76 NSWLR 379, 535
Taylor v The Owners – Strata Plan No 11564 (2013) 83 NSWLR 1, 532–3
Taylor v The Owners – Strata Plan No 11564 (2014) 253 CLR 531, 13, 40, 73, 77, 79–80, 82, 115, 139, 295, 319, 451, **452–3**, 527–8, 532–5, 538
Taylor v Western Australia [2020] FCA 42, 296
TCN Channel Nine Pty Ltd v Australian Mutual Provident Society (1982) 62 FLR 366, 29
Telford v Severin (2007) 98 SASR 70, 607
Telstra Corporation Ltd v Australasian Performing Right Association Ltd (1997) 191 CLR 140, 288, 474
Telstra Corporation Ltd v Australian Competition and Consumer Commission (2008) 176 FCR 153, 670
Telstra Corporation Ltd v Hurstville City Council (2002) 118 FCR 198, 571
Telstra Corporation Ltd v Worthing (1999) 197 CLR 61, 630
Terasof Pty Ltd v Roads Corporation [2011] VSC 199, 605
Tervonen v Minister for Justice and Customs (No 2) (2007) 98 ALD 589, 387
Thai v DPP (No 2) (2009) 229 FLR 294, 646
The Great Fingall Consolidated Ltd v Sheehan (1905) 3 CLR 176, 517
The Owners – Strata Plan No 66375 v King [2018] NSWCA 170, 112, 115
Theo v Secretary, Department of Families, Community Services and Indigenous Affairs (2007) 45 AAR 403, 305
Theophanous v Herald & Weekly Times Ltd (1994) 182 CLR 104, 331, 341, 512
Thiess v Collector of Customs (2014) 250 CLR 664, 89, 99–101, 345, 360, 491
Thomas v Mowbray (2007) 233 CLR 307, 490, 591
Thomas v The King (1937) 59 CLR 279, 652, 663
Thompson v Byrne (1999) 196 CLR 141, 27, 53
Thompson v Groote Eylandt Mining Co Ltd (2003) 173 FLR 72, 498–9

Thompson v The Queen (1989) 169 CLR 1, 644–5
Thomson v Master and Fellows of St Catharine's College, Cambridge [1919] AC 468, 296
Tickle Industries Pty Ltd v Hann (1974) 130 CLR 321, 430
Tickner v Bropho (1993) 40 FCR 183, 299
Tillman v A-G (NSW) (2007) 70 NSWLR 448, 472
Tjungarrayi v Western Australia (2019) 269 CLR 150, 75, 113, **126**, 222, 355
Tohi v Minister for Immigration, Citizenship, Migrant Services and Multicultural Affairs (2021) 285 FCR 187, 533
Tokyo Mart Pty Ltd v Campbell (1988) 15 NSWLR 275, 535
Tom and Bill Waterhouse Pty Ltd v Racing New South Wales (2008) 72 NSWLR 577, **518–19**
Tonkin v Brand [1962] WAR 2, 189
Toolan v Metropolitan (Perth) Passenger Transport Trust (2001) 25 WAR 1, 379
Torrac Nominees Pty Ltd v Karabay (2007) 69 NSWLR 669, 603, 614
Total (Australia) Ltd v Registrar of Companies [1969] VR 821, 395
Tovir Investments Pty Ltd v Waverley Council [2014] NSWCA 379, 302–4, 669
Towne v Eisner, 245 US 418 (1918), 88
Townsville Hospitals Board v Townsville City Council (1982) 149 CLR 282, 628
Trade Practices Commission v TNT Management Pty Ltd (1985) 6 FCR 1, 254
Trajkoski v DPP (WA) (2010) 41 WAR 105, 456–7
Tran v Commonwealth (2010) 187 FCR 54, 300–1
Treacy v DPP [1971] AC 537, 645
Treasurer of Victoria v Tabcorp Holdings Ltd [2014] VSCA 143, **39–40**, 42, 73–4
Trinh v The Queen [2016] NSWCCA 110, 561
Tsolacis v McKinnon (2012) 38 VR 260, 401, 655–6
Tullamore Bowling & Citizens Club Ltd v Lander [1984] 2 NSWLR 32, 56
Turner v Keegan [2001] WASCA 9, **520**
Turner v Owen (1990) 26 FCR 366, 679

Uber BV v Federal Commissioner of Taxation (2017) 247 FCR 462, 268, **287**
Uebergang v Australian Wheat Board (1980) 145 CLR 266, 13
Uelese v Minister for Immigration and Border Protection (2015) 256 CLR 203, 421–2, 430
Ukley v Ukley [1977] VR 121, 296
Union Steamship Co of Australia Pty Ltd v King (1988) 166 CLR 1, 644
Unions NSW v New South Wales (2019) 264 CLR 595, 56, 101–4, 106, 109, 111, 115, 343
United Firefighters' Union of Australia v Victorian Equal Opportunity and Human Rights Commission [2018] VSCA 252, **276–7**
United States v Fisher, 6 US 358 (1805), 433

Vacher & Sons Ltd v London Society of Compositors [1913] AC 107, 199, 296, 298
Vallance v The Queen (1961) 108 CLR 56, 333–5, 654, 662–3
Van Dongen v Northern Territory (2005) 16 NTLR 169, 498–9
Van Heerden v Hawkins [2016] WASCA 42, 108, 272
Vanstone v Clark (2005) 147 FCR 299, 677–8
Varverakis v Police (2003) 38 MVR 247, 557
Vella v Commissioner of Police (NSW) (2019) 269 CLR 219, 324–5, 476
Vella v Minister for Immigration and Border Protection (2015) 90 ALJR 89, **438–9**

Vickers v Queensland Building and Construction Commission [2019] QCA 66, 638, 646
Victims Compensation Fund Corporation v Brown (2003) 201 ALR 260; 77 ALJR 1797, 113, 124–5, 134, 144, 229, **238**, 246, 249, 265–6, 425
Victoria v Commonwealth (1971) 122 CLR 353, 13
Victoria v Commonwealth (1975) 134 CLR 81, 24, 166
Victoria v Commonwealth (1996) 187 CLR 416, 101, 502
Victorian Building Authority v Andriotis (2019) 268 CLR 168, 236, 414, 558, 561–2, 570
Victorian Railway Commissioners v Herbert [1949] VLR 211, 630
Victorian Stevedoring and General Contracting Co Pty Ltd v Dignan (1931) 46 CLR 73, 42, 605, 676
Victorian Taxi Families Inc v Taxi Services Commission (2018) 61 VR 91, 178
Victrawl Pty Ltd v Telstra Corporation Ltd (1995) 183 CLR 595, 617
Vikpro Pty Ltd v Wyuna Court Pty Ltd (2016) 103 ATR 787, 326
Vincentia MC Pharmacy Pty Ltd v Australian Community Pharmacy Authority (2020) 280 FCR 397, 27, 116
Virgin Blue Airlines Pty Ltd v Federal Commissioner of Taxation (2010) 190 FCR 150, **8–9**, 496
Vumbaca v Baulkham Hills Shire Council (1979) 141 CLR 614, 225

WABZ v Minister for Immigration and Multicultural and Indigenous Affairs (2004) 134 FCR 271, 559
Wacal Developments Pty Ltd v Realty Developments Pty Ltd (1978) 140 CLR 503, 303, 493
Wacando v Commonwealth (1981) 148 CLR 1, 29, 107, 297
Wainohu v New South Wales (2011) 243 CLR 181, 41, 79, 107
Walker Corporation Pty Ltd v Sydney Harbour Foreshore Authority (2008) 233 CLR 259, 474
Wallaby Grip Ltd v QBE Insurance (Australia) Ltd (2010) 240 CLR 444, 517
Wallace v Kam (2013) 250 CLR 375, 507
Waller v Freehills (2009) 177 FCR 507, 639, 642–3
Wallersteiner v Moir [1974] 1 WLR 991, 557
Walton v Gardiner (1993) 177 CLR 378, 504
Wanganui-Rangitikei Electric Power Board (1934) 50 CLR 581, 638, 646
Ward v The Queen (1980) 142 CLR 308, 23, 637
Ward v Williams (1955) 92 CLR 496, 561
Warnink v J Townend & Sons (Hull) Ltd [1979] AC 731, 477
Waterfront Place Pty Ltd v Minister for Planning (2019) 59 VR 556, 378, 380, 399–400
Waters v Public Transport Corporation (1991) 173 CLR 349, 265, 595–6
Watson v Issell (1890) 16 VLR 607, 398
Waugh v Kippen (1986) 160 CLR 156, 245–6, 249, 251
Waverley Municipal Council v Swain [2003] Aust Torts Reports 81-694, 266
WBM v Chief Commissioner of Police (2010) 27 VR 469, 3, 66
Wei v Minister for Immigration and Border Protection (2015) 257 CLR 22, 421, 576, 579, 581
Weigall Constructions Pty Ltd v Melbourne & Metropolitan Board of Works [1972] VR 781, 192
Weiss v The Queen (2005) 224 CLR 300, 72, 79, 102, **466–7**
Wellington Diocesan Board of Trustees v Wairarapa Market Buildings Ltd [1974] 2 NZLR 562, 608
Welsbach Light Co of Australasia Ltd v Commonwealth (1916) 22 CLR 268, 21, 679

Wentworth District Capital Ltd v Federal Commissioner of Taxation (2010) 80 ATR 50, 89
Wentworth Securities Ltd v Jones [1980] AC 74, 530
West Australian Field and Game Association Inc v Pearce (1992) 8 WAR 64, 555
West Lakes Ltd v South Australia (1980) 25 SASR 389, 165
Western Australia v BLM (2009) 40 WAR 414, 342
Western Australia v Manado (2020) 270 CLR 81, 103, 354
Western Australia v Richards (2008) 37 WAR 229, 605, 617
Western Australia v Strickland (2000) 99 FCR 33, 85
Western Australia v Ward (2002) 213 CLR 1, 266, 422
Western Australian Planning Commission v Dungey [2010] WASC 52, 430
Western Australian Planning Commission v Southregal Pty Ltd (2017) 259 CLR 106, 110, 223, 262, 319–20, 354, 542, 548–9
Western Australian Trustee Executor & Agency Co Ltd v Commissioner of State Taxation (WA) (1980) 147 CLR 119, 256
Western Bank Ltd v Schindler [1977] Ch 1, 80, 82, 533
Westpac Securities Administration Ltd v Australian Securities and Investments Commission (2021) 270 CLR 118, 354
White v DPP (WA) (2011) 243 CLR 478, 226, 492
Whitton v Falkiner (1915) 20 CLR 118, 269
Wicks v State Rail Authority of New South Wales (2010) 241 CLR 60, 225, 422
Widgee Shire Council v Bonney (1907) 4 CLR 977, 663
Wik Peoples v Queensland (1996) 187 CLR 1, 51, 522
Wilderness Society Inc v Turnbull (2007) 166 FCR 154, 371
Wilkie v Commonwealth (2017) 263 CLR 487, 6, 326, 343, 343, 354, 355
Will v Brighton (2020) 104 NSWLR 170, 457, 491, 653
Williams v Commonwealth (No 2) (2014) 252 CLR 416, 372
Williams v Dunn's Assignee (1908) 6 CLR 245, 325
Williams v Melbourne Corporation (1933) 49 CLR 142, 673, 677–8
Williams v Oataway (2005) 11 VR 529, 308
Williams v Official Assignee of the Estate of William Dunn (1908) 6 CLR 425, 267, 327
Williams v Permanent Trustee Co of New South Wales Ltd [1906] AC 249, 318
Williams v The Queen (1978) 140 CLR 591, 499
Williams v Wreck Bay Aboriginal Community Council (2019) 266 CLR 499, 512
Wilson v Anderson (2002) 213 CLR 401, 37, 49, 51–2, 341
Wilson v Commissioner of Stamp Duties (1988) 13 NSWLR 77, 288–9
Wilson v Dagnall [1972] 1 QB 509, 191
Wilson v Gahan [1999] VSC 72, 657
Wilson v Safelite Group Inc, 930 F 3d 429 (2019), 493–4
Wilson v State Rail Authority of New South Wales (2010) 78 NSWLR 704, 58
Wilson v Transport Accident Commission (2017) 80 MVR 157, 453, 454, **455–6**
Wing v Earle (1653) 78 ER 468, 398
Wong v Commonwealth (2009) 236 CLR 573, 507
Woodcock v South Western Electricity Board [1975] 2 All ER 545, 499
Woodcrest Homes Pty Ltd v Fair Trading Tribunal [2002] NSWSC 552, 65
Woods v Multi-Sport Holdings Pty Ltd (2002) 208 CLR 460, 489
Woolcock Street Investments Pty Ltd v CDG Pty Ltd (2004) 216 CLR 515, 12–13
Woolworths Ltd v Crotty (1942) 66 CLR 603, 23

Work Health Authority v Outback Ballooning Pty Ltd (2019) 266 CLR 428, 50–1, 54–6, 101, 450
WorldAudio Ltd v Australian Communications and Media Authority (2006) 149 FCR 462, **15–16**
Wotton v State of Queensland (2002) 246 CLR 1, 229
Wright v TIL Services Pty Ltd (1956) 56 SR (NSW) 413, 679
Wynyard Investments Pty Ltd v Commissioner for Railways (NSW) (1955) 93 CLR 376, 628

X v Australian Prudential Regulation Authority (2007) 226 CLR 630, 223
X7 v Australian Crime Commission (2013) 248 CLR 92, **436–7**
XYZ v Commonwealth (2006) 227 CLR 532, 265–6, 636–7, 638, 639

Yarmirr v Australian Telecommunications Corporation (1990) 96 ALR 739, 554, 585, 588, **589**
Yarra City Council v Metropolitan Fire and Emergency Services Board (2017) 223 LGERA 135, 611
Yasmin v A-G (Cth) (2015) 236 FCR 169, 421
Yemshaw v Hounslow London Borough Council [2011] 1 WLR 433, 292
Yeo v A-G (Qld) [2012] 1 Qd R 276, 484
Young v Toacassie (1905) 2 CLR 470, 673
Yrttiaho v Public Curator of Queensland (1971) 125 CLR 228, 396, 603, 605, 612–13, 616–17
Yuill v Corporate Affairs Commission (NSW) (1990) 20 NSWLR 386, 444

ZD v Secretary to the Department of Health and Human Services [2017] VSC 806, 80, 137, **142–3**, **230**, 427, 507–8
Zerella Holdings Pty Ltd v Williams (2012) 113 SASR 573, 284
Zhang v Commissioner of Police (2021) 389 ALR 363, **501**, 503
Zhang v Zemin (2010) 79 NSWLR 513, 224, 356, 484, 488
Zheng v Cai (2009) 239 CLR 446, 37, 41, 45, 50–1, 53, 76
ZL v The Queen (2010) 208 A Crim R 325, 323

TABLE OF STATUTES

Entries in bold indicate discussion in an Example

Constitution

Constitution, 19, 36, 40, 42, 44, 164, 278, 344–5, 403, 489, 501–2, 507
ch I, 38
ch II, 38
ch III, 38
s 1, 36, 164
s 2, 164
s 49, 178
s 50(ii), 168
s 51, 643
ss 51-60, 36
s 51(xx), 415
s 51(xxxvii), 415
s 52(xxxvii), 414
s 53, 168–9, 172
s 54, 169
s 55, 169
s 56, 169
s 57, 166
s 58, 164–5, 172
s 64, 38
s 74, 164
s 75(iii), 409
s 75(v), 409
ss 106-107, 36
s 109, 57, 395, 550
s 122, 36

Commonwealth

A New Tax System (Goods and Services Tax) Act 1999, 258
pt 4-5 div 4, 287
s 35-5, 258–9
s 35-10, 258
s 144-5, 287
s 144-5(1), 287
s 195-1, 287
Aboriginal and Torres Strait Islander Commission Act 1989, 678
Aboriginal and Torres Strait Islander Peoples Recognition Act 2013, 198
Aboriginal Land Rights (Northern Territory) Act 1976, 343, 677
Acts Interpretation Act 1901, 24–5, 34, 131, 184, 377, 395, 605, 614, 618
s 2, 45, 50
s 2(1), 378
s 2(2), 379, 570
s 2B, 382–4
s 2C, 383
s 2D, 383
s 2F, 383
s 2K, 416
s 3, 182
s 3A, 182
s 4(4), 190
s 4(5), 190
s 6, 165, 206
s 7, 395, 603–4, 618, 671
s 7(2), 611–12
s 7(2)(c), 603–4
s 7(2)(e), 612
s 10, 290, 389
s 10(a), 388
s 10(b), 388
s 10(c), 388
s 10A(a), 388
s 10A(b), 388
s 10A(c), 388
s 12, 200
s 13, 25, 300, 459
s 13(1), 200–1, 203–5, 301, 308
s 13(2), 203
s 13(2)(a), 197
s 13(2)(b), 198

Acts Interpretation Act 1901 (cont.)
s 13(2)(d), 202
s 15A, 38, 401, 502–3
s 15AA, 25, 27, 28, 29, 31, 34–5, 92, 98–100, 108, 116, 513
s 15AA(1), 27
s 15AA(2), 28
s 15AB, 29–30, 32, 34–5, 88, 178, 316, 332, 351, 352, 355–7, 361, 364, 368
s 15AB(1), 92, 352, 357, 360
s 15AB(1)(a), 356, 459
s 15AB(1)(b)(i), 357
s 15AB(1)(b)(ii), 356
s 15AB(2), 352–3, 360
s 15AB(2)(a), 301
s 15AB(2)(a)–(h), 353
s 15AB(2)(d), 487
s 15AB(3), 30, 363
s 15AB(3)(a), 363
s 15AC, 326
s 15AD, 306
s 15AD(a), 306
s 15AD(b), 306
s 18A, 302, 382
s 19, 387
s 19(4), 387
s 21, 640
s 23, 385
s 23(a), 386
s 23(b), 384
s 25C, 400
s 28A(1)(a)(i), 392
s 28A(1)(a)(ii), 392
s 28A(1)(b), 392
s 29, 392
s 33(1), 397
s 33(2A), 402, 569–70
s 33(3), 185
s 33(4), 393
s 33A, 393
s 33AA, 393
s 33AB, 393, 582–3
s 34A, 389
s 34AA, 389
ss 34AA–34A, 389
s 34AAB, 391
s 34AB(1)(a), 389
s 34AB(1)(b), 389
s 34AB(1)(c), 390
s 34AB(1)(d), 390
s 34AB(2), 390
s 34AB(3), 390
s 35, 398
s 36(1), 398–9
s 36(2), 399
s 36(3), 399
s 37, 416
s 37A, 397
s 39, 206
s 40, 199
s 40(1A)(a)(ii), 206
s 46, 670
s 46(2), 401
Acts Interpretation Amendment Act 1984, 30
Acts Interpretation Amendment Act 2011, 34
s 23, 35
sch 1 cl 23, 99
Acts Interpretation Amendment Bill 1984, 29–30, 353
Administrative Appeals Tribunal Act 1975, 403, 407
s 25, 407
Administrative Decisions (Judicial Review) Act 1977, 15, 138, 403, 409
s 3(1), 15
s 5, 15–16
Admiralty Act 1988
s 4(2), 303
Airports (Business Concessions) Act 1959
s 7(1), 273
Appropriation Act (No 1) 2017–2018
s 10, 6, 343
s 10(1), 6
s 10(2), 6
Auditor-General Act 1997, 407
Australia Act 1986, 18, 44, 163, 183, **197**, **199**, **206**, 476
s 2(1), 665
s 3(1), 176
s 6, 176
s 7, 164
s 17(2), 183
Australian Broadcasting Act 1942
s 123, 310
s 123(1), 310
s 123(1A), 310
s 123(1AA), 310

s 123(2), 310
s 123(3), 310
s 123(4), 310
Australian Broadcasting Corporation Act 1983
pt IV, 309
pt VI, 309
s 6(2), 587
s 6(4), 587
s 8, 586
s 8(1), 587
s 8(2), 587
s 8(3), 587
s 70, 309
Australian Capital Territory (Self-Government) Act 1988, 36
s 21, 168
s 22, 164
s 24(2), 178
s 27, 625, 634
s 69A, 625
Australian Citizenship Act 2007
s 2A, 305
Australian Crime Commission Act 2002, 436, 437
s 19, 554
Australian Human Rights Commission Act 1986, 409
Australian Passports Act 2005, 414
Australian Securities and Investments Commission Act 2001
s 219(2A), 597
Australian Telecommunications Corporation Act 1989
s 27, 589
Austudy Regulations 1990, 263
reg 34, 263
reg 34(2), 263
reg 35(1), 263
reg 35(1)(a), 263
reg 35(1)(b), 263
Bankruptcy Act 1966
s 58, 462
s 58(3), 123, 462
s 60(2), 462
s 189AAA, 462
Biosecurity Act 2015
s 481, 417
s 484, 417
Broadcasting Act 1942
s 123, 310
Broadcasting Services Act 1992
s 3(e), 545
s 122, 543–4, 574
s 122(2)(b), 544
s 122(4), 545, 578
s 158, 543
s 160, 544, 567
s 160(b), 514
s 160(d), 125, 543–5, 574
Building and Construction Industry Improvement Act 2005
s 38, 131
Building and Construction Industry (Improving Productivity) Act 2016,
s 3, 42
Charter of Budget Honesty Act 1998
s 3(2), 587
sch 1, 587
Cheques Act 1986, 414
Child Care Act 1972
s 22A, 559
Child Support (Assessment) Act 1989
s 117(2)(a)(iv), 361
s 117(2)(b), 361
Commonwealth Conciliation and Arbitration Act 1904, 318
s 6, 22
s 6A, 21–2
Commonwealth Electoral Act 1918, 414
Commonwealth Employees' Compensation Act 1930
s 9A(1), 455
Commonwealth Employees' Rehabilitation and Compensation Act 1988, 612
Communist Party Dissolution Act 1950 (Cth), 297
Compensation (Commonwealth Government Employees) Act 1971, 612
Competition and Consumer Act 2010
s 4D, 303
s 5(1), 638
sch 2 s 18(1), 235–6
Copyright Act 1968, 180
pt III div 3, 179
pt VII, 178

Copyright Act 1968 (cont.)
s 8A, 627
s 8A(1), 178
s 8A(2), 179
s 29(6), 179
s 176, 179
s 177, 179
s 182A, 627
s 182A(1), 178
s 182A(3), 179
Corporations Act 2001, 112, 414, 627
s 9(b)(ii), 103
s 601FD(1), 103
s 1002G, 135
Crimes Act 1914, 403
s 4AA, 412
s 4B(3), 412
s 4F(1), 604
s 4F(2), 604
ss 4G–4H, 412
s 13, 344
s 50BA(1), 636–7
Criminal Code Act 1995, 113, 403, 662
sch, 410–11
ch 2, 650
pt 2.7, 646
s 1.1, 410, 411, 454
s 2.1, 663
s 2.2, 663
s 4.1(2), 255
s 4.3, 255
s 5.1, 157
s 5.2–5.5, 157
s 5.2(3), 454
s 5.2.3, 86
s 5.6, 663, 664
s 6.1, 663, 664
s 9.2, 663
s 9.3, 665
s 9.4, 665
s 11.5, 334
s 14.1, 646
s 14.1(2)(a), 645
s 92.3(1), 501
s 92.3(2), 501
s 135.2(1), 255
s 268.121, 344
s 471.12, 316
Criminal Code Amendment (Offences Against Australians) Act 2002, 602
Cross-Border Insolvency Act 2008
s 16, 462
Customs Act 1901
s 35A(1), 253
s 229(1)(i), 253
s 233B(1)(b), 661
s 233B(1)(c), 653, 661
Customs Tariff Act 1987, 267
Customs Tariff Act 1995
sch 3, 480
sch 3 ch 30, 480
sch 3 ch 30 note 1(a), 480
Defence Act 1903, 454, 682
Defence (Visiting Forces) Act 1963, 367
pt II, 367
pt III, 367
s 5(1), 367
s 8, 367
s 19, 367–8
Defence Force Discipline Act 1982, 552
Defence Housing Australia Act 1987
s 62, 587
Disability Discrimination Act 1992, 428
s 3, 105
Domicile Act 1982
s 6, 335
Electronic Transactions Act 1999, 413–14
pt 2 div 3, 413
s 5(1), 413
s 7A, 414
s 8, 413
ss 9–12, 413
Electronic Transactions Regulations 2020, 414
Enhancing Online Safety for Children Act 2015
s 22, 586
Evidence Act 1995, 412, 489
s 5, 174
s 143(a), 174
s 144, 490
Export Control Act 2020
s 326, 417
s 329, 417
Extradition Act 1988, 387
Fair Work Act 2009, 162, 201, 317–20, 370, 415, 457–8

pt 4-2, 458
pt 4-2 div 4, 458
s 10, **201**
s 40A, 459
s 79(1), 458
s 96, 369
s 96(1), 369
s 413, 318
s 413(5), 317
s 540(6), 320
s 569, 459
s 570, 458–9
s 570(1), 459
Fair Work (Registered Organisations) Act 2009
s 26A, 429
Family Law Act 1975, 597
Federal Court of Australia Act 1976
s 58DD, 462
Federal Circuit Court of Australia Act 1999, 458
s 79, 458–9
s 79(1), 458–9
Food Standards Australia New Zealand Act 1991
s 111(1), 559
Foreign Judgments Act 1991
s 15, 461
s 15(2), 123, 125, 462
Freedom of Information Act 1982, 403, 410
s 10, 515
s 15(2), 590
s 58(5), 594
Fringe Benefits Tax Assessment Act 1986
s 39A(1)(f), 8–9
s 58G, 9
Gambling Measures Act 2012
s 19(2), 586
s 198, 586
Governor-General Amendment (Salary) Act 2019
s 3, 311
Health Insurance Act 1973
s 84(3), 574
High Court Rules 2004, 417
Higher Education Funding Act 1988
s 2(2), 189
House of Representatives Standing Orders 2019
ord 138, 196
ord 139, 169
ord 140(b), 196
ord 141(a), 169
ord 143(a), 170
ord 143(b), 170
ord 143(b)–(c), 170
ord 144, 170
ord 147, 169
ord 149, 196
ord 149(a), 171
ord 149(b), 171
ord 149(d), 171
ord 150, 171
ord 158, 172
ord 162, 172
ord 161, 172
ord 215, 170
ord 222, 170
Human Rights (Parliamentary Scrutiny) Act 2011, 170, 403, 448
s 5, 170
s 7(a), 170
s 8, 152, 169
s 8(5), 169
ss 8–9, 354
Income Tax Assessment Act 1915
s 13, 454
Income Tax Assessment Act 1936, 254
s 99A, 592
s 254(1)(d), 469
s 255(1)(b), 469
Income Tax Assessment Act 1997, 203, 306, 553
Industrial Relations Act 1988, 298, 318
Inspector-General of Taxation Act 2003
s 9, 559
Insurance Act 1973
s 91, 462
Interactive Gambling Act 2001
s 8A, 129
International Tax Agreements Act 1953
s 5(1), 479
Judiciary Act 1903, 403
s 39B(1), 409
s 44(2A), 409
s 68, 290
Law Enforcement Integrity Commissioner Act 2006, 409

Legislation Act 2003
ch 2 pt 1, 667
ch 3 pt 2, 667
div 3, 530
pt 2, 667
s 9, 667
s 12(1A), 672
s 12(2), 672
s 12(4), 672
s 13, 681
s 13(1), 671
s 13(1)(a), 389, 401, 669, 671
s 13(1)(b), 670
s 13(2), 401
s 14, 680
s 15G, 574
s 15K, 574
s 15K(1), 667
s 15ZB, 166
s 17, 574
s 19, 574
s 42, 404, 448
s 43, 404
s 44, 667
s 50, 667
Life Insurance Act 1995
s 161, 462
s 165A, 574
Marriage Act 1961, 252
s 11, 252
Migration Act 1958, 8, 86, 481, 670
s 5(1), 85, 454
s 31(3), 675
s 36, 328, 482, 675
s 36(2)(aa), 85
s 36(2A), 85
s 473DD, 240
s 501, 675
s 501(3), 438
s 501(5), 438
s 501(6)(b), 447
s 501C, 438
s 503A, 438
s 503A(2), 438
s 504, 675
Migration Regulations 1994, 508
cl 300.214, 11, 64, 67, 508
cl 866.225, 675
cl 885.213(a), 423
reg 1.15(1)(c), 385
reg 1.15(1)(c)(ii), 598
reg 1.15B, 423
reg 1.15B(5), 423
Mutual Recognition Act 1992, 414
pt 2, 414
pt 3, 414
s 17(2), 414
s 20(1), 414
National Consumer Credit Protection Act 2009
s 278(2), 559
National Health Act 1953
s 99K, 79
s 99K(2), 78–9, 213
s 99L, 78
s 99L(1), 78
National Health (Australian Community Pharmacy Authority Rules) Determination 2011, 116
National Measurement Act 1960
s 8AA, 415
National Radioactive Waste Management Act 2012
s 17, 559
National Security (Prices) Regulations
reg 23, 680–1
reg 23(6), 681
reg 23(7), 681
reg 23(11), 681
National Sports Tribunal Act 2019
s 7(1), 622
Native Title Act 1993, 111, 126, 193, 485
s 14, 602
s 28, 574
s 38, 485
s 39, 485
s 43(1), 193
s 47B(1)(b)(i), 126
s 242(2), 126
Northern Territory (Self-Government) Act 1978, 36
s 6, 164
s 12, 178
s 30, 168
s 32(1), 164
s 51(1), 625

Occupational Health and Safety Act 1991, 57
s 4, 57
s 4(1), 57
Ombudsman Act 1976, 403, 409
Parliamentary Privileges Act 1987, 178
s 16, 178
s 16(1), 178
s 16(5)(b), 352
Parliamentary Service Act 1999
s 64KA(3), 587
s 64KA(6), 587
s 64MB(4), 587
s 64MB(9), 587
Patents Act 1952
s 69, 234
Patents Act 1989
s 13(1), 234
Petroleum Act 1984
s 57D, 574
Privacy Act 1988, 250, 403, 410
Privy Council (Appeals from the High Court) Act 1975, 164
Public Governance, Performance and Accountability Act 2013, 407, 415
Public Service Act 1999, 415
Racial Discrimination Act 1975
s 18D, 593
Radiocommunications Act 1992
s 111, 15–16
Regulatory Powers (Standard Provisions) Act 2014, 375, 417
pt 2, 417
pt 3, 417
pt 4, 417
pt 5, 418
pt 6, 418
pt 7, 418
ss 8–10, 417
s 17, 417
s 38, 417
s 47, 417
s 79, 417
s 79(2), 417
s 82, 418
s 100, 417
s 104(1)(f), 418
s 107(1)(a), 418
s 111, 417
s 115, 418
s 118, 417
Road Vehicle Standards Act 2018
s 52, 417
s 57, 418
s 58, 418
Royal Commissions Act 1902, 410
Safety, Rehabilitation and Compensation Act 1988
s 5A(1), 598
s 37(7), 446–7
s 57(2), 446
Sales Tax Act (No 1) 1930, 269
Sales Tax (Exemptions and Classifications) Act 1935, 359
Sales Tax Assessment Act (No 1) 1930, 269
first sch, 269
s 20(h), 269
Senate Standing Orders 2020 (Cth)
ord 23, 449
ord 24, 170
ord 111(3), 196
ord 111(4), 196
ord 111(5), 171, 173
ord 112, 171, 173
ord 115, 171, 173
ord 117, 171, 196
ord 118(1), 171
ord 120, 172
ord 121, 172
ord 122, 172
ord 123, 172
ord 131, 172
ord 132, 172
ord 139(1), 206
Sex Discrimination Act 1984
s 18(1), 235
s 28, 565
s 81(1), 564
Social Security Act 1991, 112, 553, 590–1
s 500J, 590
s 543A(2A)(f), 590
s 1061ZAAK(5)(a), 590
Social Security and Veterans' Affairs Legislation Amendment (One-off Payments and Other 2007 Budget Measures) Act 2007, 76, 271
sch 5 item 1, 76, 271, 272
sch 5 item 2(1)(b), 76, 271, 272

Special Broadcasting Service Act 1991
s 6(2), 587
s 6(4), 587
s 10(1), 587
s 10(2), 587
Sport Integrity Australia Act 2020
s 72, 417
s 73B, 418
Statute Law Revision Act 1981
sch 1, 98
Statute Law Revision Bill 1981, 26
sch 1, 27
Student and Youth Assistance Act 1973, 263
Succession to the Crown Act 2015, 198–9, 627
Superannuation Industry (Supervision) Regulations 1994
reg 6.17A, 470
Taxation Administration Act 1953, 258
Trade Practices Act 1974, 241, 634
pt V, 300
s 2A, 634
s 2B, 635
s 46, 634–5
s 47, 634–5
s 52, 300
Trans-Tasman Mutual Recognition Act 1997
s 39(4), 587
s 39(5), 587
Workplace Relations Act 1996, 298, 318
sch 19, 298

New South Wales

Aboriginal Land Rights Act 1983, 343
s 36(1), 468
Acts Shortening Act 1852, 25
Administrative Decisions Review Act 1997, 407
s 9, 407
Adoption Act 2000, 452
Adoption of Children Act 1965
s 19(1A), 71, 452
Ageing and Disability Commissioner Act 2019, 409
Anti-Discrimination Act 1977, 409
Building and Construction Industry Security of Payment Act 1999, 440, 475
Children and Young Persons (Care and Protection) Act 1998, 452
Civil and Administrative Tribunal Act 2013, 407
s 30, 407
s 34, 408
Civil Liability Act 2002, 290–1, 597, 201
s 12(2), 452, 532
s 12(2), 532
s 15(3), 364
s 15(3)(a), 364
s 15(3)(b), 364
s 15B, 290, 292
s 54, 573
Clean Waters Act 1970, 659
Community Protection Act 1994, 172
Community Relations Commission and Principles of Multiculturalism Act 2000, 199
Companies Act 1961, 380, 385
Compensation to Relatives Act 1897, 452
Constitution Act 1902, 36
s 5, 164
s 5A, 166, 197
s 5B, 166, 197
s 5C, 197
s 7A, 176
s 7B, 176
s 15, 168
Contracts Review Act 1980
s 4, 242
s 6, 242
s 6(2), 242
s 7, 242
s 7(1), 242
Corporations Law, 439
s 701, 439
Crime Commission Act 2012
s 35A, 638
Crimes Act 1900, 316, 411
pt 8A, 411
pt 9, 411
pts 11–11A, 411
s 7, 411
s 8, 411
s 10(2)(b), 646
ss 10A–10F, 411
s 10B(3), 646

s 10C(2)(a), 645
s 10D(2), 646
s 18, 336
s 45(1)(a), 284
s 73, 70
s 73(1), 69, 451
s 73(2), 211
s 73(2)(a), 212
s 73(3), 69, 212–13, 451
s 73(3)(a), 69, 212–13, 451
s 73(3)(b), 212–13
s 73(3)(c), 212–13
s 73(3)(d), 212–13
s 73(3)(e), 212–13
s 545E, 599
s 545E(1), 599
s 545E(2), 599
Crimes (Domestic and Personal Violence) Act 2007, 71, 452
Crimes (Sentencing Procedure) Act 1999
s 3A, 336
s 3A(a), 336
s 17, 412
s 19(1), 604
s 19(2), 604
Criminal Assets Recovery Act 1990, 459
Criminal Procedure Act 1986
ss 5–6, 412
s 126, 578
s 132(5), 593
Crown Lands Act 1989
s 90(2), 568
Crown Lands Act Amendment Act 1903, 23
Crown Lands Alienation Act 1861
s 13, 610
Defamation Act 1958, 333
Dust Diseases Tribunal Act 1989
s 12D, 290–2
s 12D(3)(e), 291–2
Electronic Transactions Act 2000, 413
pt 2 div 3, 413
s 5(1), 413
s 6A, 414
s 7, 413
ss 8–11, 413
Evidence Act 1995, 412
s 144, 489
s 97, 240
Government Information (Public Access) Act 2009, 410
Government Sector Employment Act 2013, 415
Guardianship Act 1987, 121
pt 5, 122
s 32(b), 122
s 33(1), 122
Health Care Liability Act 2001
s 9, 452
Human Tissue Act 1983, 122
s 36(1), 122
s 36(4), 122
Imperial Acts Application Act 1969
s 6, 177
Independent Commission Against Corruption Act 1988, 409, 594
s 8, 240, 373
Industrial Relations Act 1996, 415
ch 2 pt 6, 547
pt 6, 126
s 81(4), 546
Industrial Relations (Commonwealth Powers) Act 2009, 415
Interpretation Act 1897, 28, 385
s 8, 395
s 35(1), 398
Interpretation Act 1987, 200, 377, 392–3, 511, 603, 605
s 5, 50, 669
s 5(1), 378
s 5(2), 379, 570, 671
s 6, 302
s 7, 302, 382
s 8(a), 386
s 8(b), 384
s 8(c), 384
s 9, 402, 569–70
s 9(1), 569
s 9(2), 569
s 11, 670
s 12, 640
s 13(b), 626
s 15, 387
s 15(1)(b), 387
s 21(1), 382–4, 667
s 21C(1), 383
s 21C(2), 383
s 22(1), 181

Interpretation Act 1987 (cont.)
s 22(2), 165, 206
s 23, 182
s 23(2), 185
s 23(3), 184
s 23(4), 184
s 23(5), 184
s 23(7), 186
s 24, 182
s 25, 190
s 26, 190
s 28, 395
s 30, 395, 603, 671
s 30(1)(c), 395, 607
s 31, 401
s 32, 401, 681
s 33, 28, 99–100
s 34, 30, 178, 316, 332, 351, 364
s 34(2)(d), 487
s 34(3), 363
s 35(1), 202
s 35(1)(b), 200
s 35(2), 202
s 35(2)(c), 204
s 35(4), 202
s 35(4A), 203
s 35(5), 301
s 36(1), 398
s 36(2), 399
s 36(3), 400
s 37, 397
s 38, 398
s 39, 667
s 39(1), 672
s 40, 667
s 41, 667
s 42, 680
s 43, 185
s 45E, 530
s 46, 393
s 47(1)(a), 393, 397
s 47(1)(b)(i), 393
s 47(1)(b)(ii)–(iv), 393
s 47(2), 393
s 47(3), 393
s 48(1), 397
s 49, 389
s 49(1), 389
s 49(2)(a), 389
s 49(2)(b), 390
s 49(2)(c), 390
s 49(3), 391
s 49(4), 391
s 49(5), 391
s 49(6), 390
s 49(7), 389
s 49(8), 389
s 49(9), 390
s 49(10), 389, 391
s 52, 583
s 64, 200
s 64A, 200, 311
s 66, 199
s 66(1)(b), 206
s 68, 290, 389
s 68(1), 388, 670
s 68(2)(a), 388
s 68(3)(a), 388
s 69, 680
s 73, 175
s 74, 174
s 76, 392
s 78(1), 416
s 78(2), 416
s 80(1), 400
s 80(2), 400
Interpretation Amendment Act 2006
s 13A, 628
Judicial Officers Act 1986
s 10, 568
s 10(1)(a), 568
s 10(2)(c), 568
Land Tax Management Act 1956
s 10AA, 468–9
Landlord and Tenant (Amendment) Act 1948, 628
s 5(a), 628
Legislation Review Act 1987
s 9(1)(b)(i), 449
Legislative Assembly Standing Orders 2007
ch 29, 173
ord 117, 188
ord 188(1), 196
ord 209, 196
ord 239(6), 206
ord 358, 173
ord 361, 173

Legislative Council Standing Rules and Orders 2004
ord 136(3), 196
ord 136(4), 196
ord 143, 196
ord 162, 206
ord 164, 173
ord 165, 173
ord 166(1), 173
ord 166(3), 173
ord 168, 173
ord 170, 173
Local Government Act 1919
s 215, 683
Local Land Services Act 2013
s 200(6), 311
Mental Health Act 1983, 188
s 139, 188–9
Motor Accidents Act 1988, 59, 60
pt 5, 106, 299
s 3, 59
s 3(1), 59
s 69, 59
Motor Accidents Amendment Act 1995, 59
Motor Accidents Compensation Act 1999, 453
s 125, 452
Mutual Recognition (New South Wales) Act 1992, 414
Ombudsman Act 1974, 409
Parliamentary Evidence Act 1901, 178
Poisons and Therapeutic Goods Regulation 1994
cl 149, 554, 565, 566
Police Act 1990
s 80(3), 126, 546–8
Postage Act 1825, 316
Privacy and Personal Information Protection Act 1998, 410
Public Finance and Audit Act 1983, 407
Racing Administration Act 1998, 518
s 33, 518
s 33(b), 518
s 33A, 518
Racing Administration Regulation 2005
reg 15, 518
reg 15(1)(b), 518
Royal Commissions Act 1923, 410
Standard Time Act 1987
s 3, 416
s 4, 416
s 5, 416
s 6, 416
s 7, 416
s 8, 416
s 9, 416
s 10, 416
Statute Law (Miscellaneous Provisions) Act (No 2) 1992
sch 1, 33
Subordinate Legislation Act 1989
s 10, 667
Supreme Court Act 1970
s 69, 409
Tamworth Information Centre Bill 1992, 173
Transport (Division of Functions) Act 1932
s 4(2), 628
Transport Administration Act 1988
s 46(2)(b), 628
Uniform Civil Procedure Rules 2005, 417
Victims Support and Rehabilitation Act 1996, 124–5
sch 1 cl 5, 238
sch 1, cl 5(a), 124–5
Workers Compensation Act 1987, 453
pt 19H cl 5, 676
s 25, 114
s 66, 114–15
s 151I, 452
Workers' Compensation (Dust Diseases) Act 1942, 290
Workers Compensation Legislation Amendment Act 2012
sch 12[1], 676
World Youth Day Act 2006, 445
s 58, 445
World Youth Day Regulation 2008, 445
cl 7, 445

Queensland

Acts Interpretation Act 1954, 99, 101, 377, 603, 669
s 2, 378
s 4, 50, 379, 570

Acts Interpretation Act 1954 (cont.)
s 9, 401
s 9(1), 503
s 10, 200
s 11, 174–5
s 12, 175
s 12A, 174
s 13, 571, 632
s 14(2), 200, 202, 301
s 14(3), 204
s 14(5), 200, 204
s 14(6), 205, 308
s 14(7), 204
s 14A, 28, 34, 99
s 14B, 30, 178, 316, 332, 351
s 14B(2), 363
s 14B(3)(d), 487
s 14C, 326
s 14D(a), 306
s 14D(b), 306
s 14D(c), 306
s 14F, 199
s 14F(1)(b), 206
s 14H, 290, 389
s 14H(1)(a), 388
s 14H(1)(b), 388
s 15, 181
s 15A, 182
s 15B, 182
s 15C(1), 185
s 15C(2), 190
s 15D, 183
s 15D(2), 184
s 15DA(2), 186
s 15DA(3), 186
s 15DA(4), 186
s 17, 190
s 17(4), 190
s 19, 395
s 20, 395, 603, 671
s 20A, 395
s 20C(2), 604
s 20C(3), 604
s 23(1), 397, 554
s 24A, 393
s 24AA, 185
s 24B, 393
s 25(1)(b), 393
s 25(1)(b)(ii), 393
s 25(1)(b)(iv), 393
s 25(1)(b)(v), 393
s 25(1)(c), 393
s 25(2), 393
s 25(3), 393
s 25(4), 393
s 26, 393, 583
s 27A, 389
s 27A(1), 389
s 27A(2)(a), 389
s 27A(2)(c), 390
s 27A(3), 390
s 27A(3A), 390
s 27A(3B), 391
s 27A(3D), 390
s 27A(4), 391
s 27A(5), 391
s 27A(6), 391
s 27A(7), 390
s 27A(8), 389
s 27A(8A), 391
s 27A(8B), 391
s 27A(9), 389
s 27A(10), 390
s 27A(10A), 391
s 27A(11), 391
s 27A(12), 391
s 32, 302, 382
s 32A, 302
s 32B, 386
s 32C, 384
s 32CA, 402, 569–70
s 32CA(1), 569, 571
s 32CA(2), 569, 571
s 32D, 383
s 32DA, 383
s 33, 387
s 33(1)(b), 387
s 33A, 382
s 35, 640
s 36, 101
s 37, 398
s 38(1), 398–9
s 38(1)(a), 399
s 38(2), 399
s 38(3), 399
s 38(4), 400

s 38(5), 399
s 38A, 397
s 39(1)(a)(i), 392
s 39(1)(a)(ii), 392
s 39(1)(b), 392
s 39A, 392
s 48A(1), 400
s 48A(2), 400
sch 1, 101, 197–8, 381–4, 393
Acts Interpretation Amendment Act 1991, 28, 30
Anti-Discrimination Act 1991, 409
Auditor-General Act 2009, 407
Body Corporate and Community Management Act 1997, 595
s 276, 596
sch 5, 596
sch 5 item 10, 596
Builders' Registration and Home-owners' Protection Act 1979
s 52A(1), 566
s 52A(2), 566
Civil Liability Act 2003
s 45, 573
Commissions of Inquiry Act 1950, 410
Constitution Act 1867
s 2A, 164
Constitution of Queensland 2001, 36, 198
s 78, 176
s 9(1)(a), 178
s 9(1)(b), 178
Corrective Services Act 2006
s 193A(8), 279
Crime and Corruption Act 2001, 409
Criminal Code Act 1899, 411, 662
s 5, 411
s 8, 411
sch 1
s 5, 663
s 12, 645
s 22, 665
s 23(1)(b)(i), 663
s 24, 663, 664
s 24(2), 664
s 222, 252
Electronic Transactions (Queensland) Act 2001, 413
ch 2 pt 2, 413
ch 2 pt 3, 413
s 7A(2), 414
s 8, 413
sch 1, 414
sch 2, 413
Evidence Act 1977, 412
s 21AW(2), 577
s 43(d), 165
s 46A(2), 165, 206
Fair Work (Commonwealth Powers) and Other Provisions Act 2009, 415
Financial Accountability Act 2009, 407
Fire Service Legislation Amendment 1994
s 14, 34
Health Practitioner Regulation National Law Act 2009
sch, 159
Human Rights Act 2019, 152, 403
preamble, 42
pt 2 div 2, 404
pt 2 div 3, 404
s 13, 404
s 38, 354, 448
s 43, 177, 406
s 48, 177, 404, 406, 669
s 48(2), 404
s 48(3), 487
s 48(5), 406
s 53, 405
s 54, 405
Industrial Relations Act 2016, 415
Information Privacy Act 2009, 410
Integrated Planning Act 1997
s 5.4.2, 616
Invasion of Privacy Act 1971
s 43, 435
s 43(2)(c), 435
Judicial Review Act 1991, 409
s 41, 409
Local Government Act 1936
s 33(10)(a), 615
Local Government Act 1993, 397
s 860(1), 397
s 860(2), 397, 554
Mutual Recognition (Queensland) Act 1992, 414
Ombudsman Act 2001, 409

Parliament of Queensland Act 2001, 178
s 11, 168
Parliamentary Service and Other Acts Amendment Act 2011
s 4, 33
Penalties and Sentences Act 1992
s 5, 412
s 181B, 412
Personal Injuries Proceedings Act 2002, 531
s 6(3)(b), 531
Property Law Act 1974
pt 19, 264
s 71(2)(b), 303
s 283, 264, 275, 278–9
s 315, 275
Public Sector Act 2008, 415
Public Sector Ethics Act 1994, 415
Queensland Civil and Administrative Tribunal Act 2009, 407
s 6, 407
s 9, 407
Reprints Act 1992
pt 4, 530
Right to Information Act 2009, 410
Standard Time Act 1894
s 3, 416
s 4, 416
Standing Rules and Orders of the Legislative Assembly 2004
ord 127, 198
ord 145, 196
ord 151, 196
ord 152, 196
ord 169, 206
Statute Law (Miscellaneous Provisions) Act 1991
s 34, 571
Statutory Instruments Act 1992
pt 4 div 1, 669
pt 4 div 2, 669
s 4, 671
s 8, 667
s 14, 401
s 14(1), 671
s 21, 401, 681
s 23, 680
s 32, 672
s 34, 672
s 37, 670
s 47, 667
s 49, 667
s 50, 667
s 54, 667
sch 1, 401, 671
Uniform Civil Procedure Rules 1999, 417
Vagrants, Gaming and Other Offences Act 1931
s 7(1)(d), 502
Vicious Lawless Association Disestablishment Act 2013, 65
s 3, 65
s 5(1)(b), 65
s 7, 65
s 7(1)(b), 65

South Australia

Acts Interpretation Act 1915, 35, 351
s 18, 324
s 21, 284
s 22, 28
s 39, 184
Acts Interpretation Act Amendment Act 1986, 28
An Ordinance for Avoiding Unnecessary Repetitions 1843, 25
Building and Construction Industry Security of Payment Act 2009
s 12, 475
Civil Liability Act 1936, 337
s 20(1), 336
s 33, 337
s 43, 573
s 53, 337
s 53(1), 337
s 53(1)(a), 338
Constitution Act 1934, 36
s 4, 164, 198
s 10A, 176
s 38, 178
s 55, 168
s 56, 165
s 62, 168
COVID-19 Emergency Response Act 2020
s 19, 682
Criminal Law Consolidation Act 1935, 411

pt 1A, 411
pt 3 div 2, 411
pt 7B, 411
pt 8, 411
pt 9 div 2, 411
s 5G(2)(a), 645
s 5G(2)(b), 646
s 5G(2)(c), 646
s 48, 331
Criminal Procedure Act 1921
s 5, 412
Daylight Saving Act 1971
s 3, 416
s 4, 416
Education (Part-time Remuneration) Amendment Act 1991, 515
Education Act 1972
pt III, 514
s 9(4), 513–15
s 15, 514–15
Electronic Communications Act 2000
pt 2 div 3, 413
s 5(1), 413
s 6A, 414
s 7, 413
ss 8–11, 413
Equal Opportunity Act 1984, 409
Evidence Act 1929, 412
s 35A, 165, 206
Fair Work Act 1994, 415
Fair Work (Commonwealth Powers) Act 2009, 415
Fisheries Act 1982, 425
Fisheries Management Act 2007, 425
s 72(2)(b), 426
Fisheries Management (General) Regulations 2007, 425
Freedom of Information Act 1991, 410
Gaming Machine Regulations 2020
sch 1, 400
Independent Commissioner Against Corruption Act 2012, 409
Joint Standing Orders 1953
ord 14, 206
Kapunda Hospital (Variation of Trust) Act 2009, 198
Land Acquisition Act 1969, 372
s 22B, 372
s 25, 372
s 25(1)(a), 372
Legislation Interpretation Act 2021, 35, 324, 351, 365, 377–8, 397
s 3, 50, 378, 669
s 3(3), 379, 570, 671
s 4, 381–4, 387, 397, 626, 668
s 6, 302
s 7, 302, 382
s 9(1), 386
s 9(2), 386
s 9(3), 386
s 10(1), 384
s 10(2), 384
s 11, 402, 569
s 11(1), 569
s 11(2), 402, 568
s 11(3), 569
s 12, 670–1
s 14, 35, 99
s 14(2), 35
s 15, 401
s 15(1), 401
s 15(2), 401, 681
s 15(3), 401, 681
s 16, 35, 178, 316, 332, 351
s 16(2)(d), 487
s 16(3), 363
s 17, 284
s 18, 324
s 19, 201–2, 204, 301, 308
s 19(2)(a), 204
s 20(a), 306
s 20(b), 306
s 22, 633
s 22(3), 634
s 25, 174
s 26, 200
s 27(1), 182
s 27(3), 183
s 27(5), 185
s 27(6), 186
s 27(7), 186
s 28, 182
s 32, 395, 603, 671
s 35(1), 199
s 36, 290, 388
s 37(1), 397

Legislation Interpretation Act 2021 (cont.)
s 38, 190
s 38(3), 191
s 41(2)(a), 393
s 41(2)(c), 393
s 41(2)(d), 393
s 41(2)(e), 393
s 41(3), 393
s 41(8), 393
s 42(3), 393
s 43, 389
s 43(2), 389–90
s 43(3), 389
s 43(4), 389
s 43(5), 390
s 43(6), 390
s 43(7), 389
s 43(8), 389
s 43(9), 390–1
s 43(10), 390
s 43(11), 391
s 43(12), 390
s 44(1), 398–9
s 44(2), 399
s 44(2a), 399
s 44(3), 400
s 48, 398
s 49, 397
s 51(2), 392
s 51(2)(a), 392
s 51(2)(b), 392
s 51(2)(c), 392
s 51(3)(a), 392
s 51(3)(b), 392
s 51(4), 392
s 51(5), 392
s 52, 400
s 53(2)(a), 604
s 53(2)(b), 604
s 54, 412
sch 1 cl 23, 35
Legislation Interpretation Bill 2021, 397
Legislation Revision and Publication Act 2002
ss 4-7, 530
Legislative Assembly Standing Orders 2018
ch 22, 168
ord 234, 196
ord 246, 196
Legislative Council Standing Orders 1999
ch 23, 168
ord 272, 196
ord 276, 196
ord 290, 196
Legislative Instruments Act 1978, 668
s 16D, 672
s 16E(3), 680
Local Government Act 1934, 445
Magistrates Act 1983, 557
Magistrates (Miscellaneous) Amendment Act 2013, 557
Motor Vehicles Act 1959, 309
Mutual Recognition (South Australia) Act 1993, 414
Ombudsman Act 1972, 409
Professional Standards Act 2004, 159
Public Finance and Audit Act 1987, 407
Public Sector Act 2009, 415
Public Sector (Honesty and Accountability) Act 1995, 415
Real Property Act 1886
s 6, 176–7
Royal Commissions Act 1917, 410, 485
Sale of Goods Act 1895
s 25(2), 273
South Australian Civil and Administrative Tribunal Act 2013, 407
s 31, 407
Standard Time Act 2009
s 3, 416
s 4, 416
Uniform Civil Rules 2020, 417

Tasmania

Acts Interpretation Act 1931, 377
s 3, 401
s 4, 50, 379, 669, 671
s 4(1), 379, 570
s 5(2), 401
s 6(1), 200
s 6(2), 203
s 6(3), 200, 203–4
s 6(4)(a), 202
s 6(4)(b), 205
s 6(6), 571, 631–2
s 6(7), 174
s 8A, 28, 99

s 8B, 30, 178, 316, 332, 351
s 8B(2), 363
s 8B(3)(d), 487
s 9(3), 182
s 9(3A), 184–5
s 9(5), 182
s 10, 165, 206
s 10A, 402, 569
s 10A(1)(a), 569
s 10A(1)(b), 402, 570
s 10A(1)(c), 569
s 11, 190
s 11(3), 190
s 11(4), 190
s 13, 290
s 13(1), 199
s 13(1)(a)(ii), 206
s 13(5), 388, 670
s 13(6), 388
s 14, 395
s 14(1), 396
s 16, 395, 603, 671
s 16(1), 396, 604
s 16(2), 396
s 17, 290, 388
s 19, 670
s 20(a), 397
s 21(1)(a), 393
s 21(1)(b), 393
s 21(1)(c)–(d), 393
s 21(1B), 393
s 21(3), 393
s 21A, 393
s 22, 185
s 23A, 389
s 23AA, 389
s 23AA(1), 389
s 23AA(2)(a), 389
s 23AA(2)(b), 390
s 23AA(2)(c), 390
s 23AA(3), 391
s 23AA(4), 390
s 23AA(5), 390
s 23AA(5A), 391
s 23AA(6), 390
s 23AA(7), 391
s 23AA(8), 390
s 23AAB, 391
s 24, 385
s 24(b), 384
s 24(bb), 382
s 24(d), 384
s 24A, 386
s 24A(2), 386
s 25, 387
s 27, 640
s 28, 398
s 29(1), 398
s 29(2), 399
s 29(3), 399
s 29(6), 399
s 29AB(1)(a)(i), 392
s 29AB(1)(a)(ii), 392
s 29AB(1)(b), 392
s 30, 392
s 30A, 392
s 41(1), 383, 631
s 45, 384
s 45(1), 387
s 46, 382–4
s 47, 668
s 47(2), 400
s 47(3), 672
s 48, 416
Acts Interpretation Amendment Act 1992, 28, 30
Age of Majority Act 1973
s 4, 397
An Act for Shortening and Explaining the Language Used in Acts of Council, Legal Proceedings, Deeds and Other Documents 1853, 25
Anti-Discrimination Act 1998, 409, 631
s 3, 631–2
s 4, 631
s 16, 631
Audit Act 2008, 407
Civil Liability Act 2002
s 6, 573
Commissions of Inquiry Act 1995, 410
Constitution Act 1934, 36
s 10, 164
s 17, 168
s 42, 168
Criminal Code Act 1924, 333, 411, 650, 662
s 4(1), 663

Criminal Code Act 1924 (cont.)
s 4(3), 663
s 6, 411
s 8, 662, 664
s 10, 411
sch 1, 333
s 12, 665
s 13(1), 663
s 14, 664
Criminal Law (Territorial Application) Act 1995
s 4, 645
Crown Lands Act 1976
s 2, 454
Daylight Saving Act 2007
s 4, 416
s 5, 416
Electronic Transactions Act 2000, 413
pt 2 div 3, 413
s 3, 413
s 4A, 414
s 5, 413
ss 6–9, 413
Evidence Act 2001, 412
s 144, 489
Family Violence Act 2004, 293
s 2, 293
s 2(1), 293
Financial Management Act 2016, 407
House of Assembly Standing and Sessional Orders and Rules 2017
ord 200, 196
ord 210, 196
Industrial Relations Act 1984, 415
Industrial Relations (Commonwealth Powers) Act 2009, 415
Integrity Commission Act 2009, 409
Judicial Review Act 2000, 409
s 43, 409
Magistrates Court (Civil Division) Rules 1998, 417
Marine Act 1976, 475
Mutual Recognition (Tasmania) Act 1993
s 4, 414
s 5, 414
Ombudsman Act 1978, 409
Parliamentary Privilege Act 1858, 178
Penalty Units and Other Penalties Act 1987
s 4, 412
Personal Information Protection Act 2004, 410
Public Health Act 1962
s 63, 496
s 91(1), 496
Reproductive Health (Access to Terminations) Act 2013, 298
Right to Information Act 2009, 410
Sentencing Act 1997
s 99(1), 604
s 99(2), 604
Standard Time Act 1895
s 3, 416
s 4, 416
Standing Orders Legislative Council 2010
ord 259(2), 196
ords 269–274, 196
ord 306, 206
State Service Act 2000, 415
Subordinate Legislation Act 1992, 668
Subordinate Legislation Committee Act 1969
s 8(1)(a)(iii), 449
Supreme Court Rules 2000, 417
Tasmanian Civil and Administrative Tribunal Act 2020, 407
s 58, 407
Tasmanian Development Act 1983
s 11(1), 514
Valuation of Land Act 2001
s 3, 454
s 11(1), 454
Victims of Crime Assistance Act 1976, 293
s 2(1), 293
s 4, 293
Workplaces (Protection from Protesters) Act 2014, 345

Victoria

Aborigines Regulations 1957, 386
Accident Compensation Act 1985
s 2(2), 183
s 4(1), 183
s 5(1), 183
s 50(1), 128
s 50(1)(a), 128
s 50(2A), 128, 137
s 98, 128

s 98A, 128
Acts Interpretation Act 1958, 27, 396
s 17, 386
Administration and Probate Act 1958
s 90, 214
s 90A(1), 553
Administrative Law Act 1978, 409
Advancing the Treaty Process with Aboriginal Victorians Act 2018, 199
Age of Majority Act 1977
s 2, 397
An Act to Interpret and Shorten the Language of Acts of Council 1851, 25
Audit Act 1994, 407
Building Act 1993, 94, 129
pt 4, 95
pt 4 div 2, 95, 130
s 3(1), 130
s 37, 94, 97, 129–30
s 37B, 94–7, 130, 132
s 37B(2), 130
s 37C, 94, 96–7
s 37C(a)(i), 130
s 37C(a)(ii), 130
s 37C(b), 130
s 106(a), 95
Building and Construction Industry Security of Payment Act 2002, 583
s 3, 583
s 18, 583
s 22(4), 583–4
s 22(4)(a), 584
s 22(4)(b), 584
s 28(2), 584
Charter of Human Rights and Responsibilities Act 2006, 152, 403
pt 2, 404
s 7(2), 404
s 17(1), 143
s 28, 354, 448
s 31, 177, 406
s 31(6), 406
s 32, 177, 404, 406, 669
s 32(1), 404–6
s 32(2), 404, 487
s 32(3), 404
s 36, 405
s 36(5), 405
Child Wellbeing and Safety Act 2005
pt 2, 587
s 4(1), 587
s 4(2)(b), 587
s 41U(2), 587
s 41U(3)(b), 587
Children, Youth and Families Act 2005
s 263(7), 142, 230
Children's Services Act 1996, 5, 281
pt 5 div 1, 282
s 36, 282
s 36(1)(a)–(e), 281
s 36(1)(f), 5, 281, 509
s 41, 281–2, 509
Children's Services Regulations 2020
reg 127, 400
Commercial Passenger Vehicle Industry Act 2017
s 21, 587
Community Protection Act 1990, 172
Constitution Act 1975, 36
pt 1, 627
s 14, 165
s 15, 164
s 18, 176
s 19(1), 178
s 19(2), 178
s 1A(3)(b), 587
s 38, 167
s 43, 168
s 62(2), 168
s 64(2), 168
s 65, 167
s 65(5), 198
s 65(6), 198
s 65(8), 167
s 65A, 167
s 65C, 167
s 65E, 167
s 65F(3), 167
s 65F(5), 167
s 65G, 167
s 65G(8), 167
s 65G(9), 167
s 69, 165, 206

Consumer Affairs Legislation Amendment Act 2010
s 42(1), 298
Coroners Act 1985
s 59, 610
Corrections Act 1986
s 77(6A), 641
Corrections Amendment (Parole) Act 2014, 172
Creative Victoria Act 2017
s 4, 587
s 5, 587
Credit Act 1984, 195
Crimes (Family Violence) Act 1987, 298
Crimes Act 1958, 298
pt I divs 10–12, 411
pt IC, 411
s 3(1), 411
s 17, 325
s 21A, 637, 647
s 21A(2), 647
s 317(1), 308
s 568(1), 466–7
Criminal Procedure Act 2009
s 276, 467
Dangerous Goods Act 1985, 194
Disability Act 2006
s 8(2)(d), 522
s 9, 522
s 49, 521–2
s 49(2)(a), 521–2
Education and Training Reform Act 2006
ss 1.2.1–1.2.3, 587
Electronic Transactions (Victoria) Act 2000, 413
pt 2 div 3, 413
s 3(1), 413
s 6A, 414
s 7, 413
ss 8–11, 413
Environment Protection (Enforcement and Penalties) Act 2000, 658
Environment Protection Act 1970
s 1K, 659
s 39(1), 659
s 41, 658–9
s 41(1)(a), 658
s 41(1)(b), 658
s 41(1)(e), 658
s 59E, 659
s 62A(2), 611
s 62C, 659
Equal Opportunity Act 1984
s 17(5), 595
Equal Opportunity Act 2010, 276
s 151, 276–7
s 151(1), 277
s 151(2), 277
s 154, 409
s 157, 277
Evidence (Miscellaneous Provisions) Act 1958
s 28(2), 111–12
Evidence Act 2008, 412
s 144, 489
Fair Work (Commonwealth Powers) Act 2009, 415
s 4, 415
s 5, 415
s 5A, 415
Family Violence Protection Act 2008
s 144J(2), 587
s 144J(3), 587
s 144J(4)(a), 587
s 144J(4)(b), 587
Filming Approval Act 2014
s 5, 587
s 8, 587
Financial Management Act 1994, 407
Freedom of Information Act 1982, 410
s 50, **408**
s 50(1), **408**
s 52, **408**
s 54, **408**
s 55, **408**
Fundraising Act 1998
s 1, 105
s 18, 553
Gambling Legislation Amendment (Transition) Act 2012, 39
s 3.3, 39
Gambling Regulation Act 2003
s 3.6.3(1), 39–40
s 3.6.3A, 39–40
s 4.3.12, 343–4
Gender Equality Act 2020
s 1, 299
s 4, 299

Great Ocean Road and Environs Protection Act 2020, 198
Guardianship and Administration Act 2019
s 2, **188**
Health Practitioner Regulation National Law (Victoria) Act 2009
s 4, 159
Heritage Act 2017
s 17, 311
Imperial Acts Application Act 1980
s 8, 177
Independent Broad-based Anti-corruption Commission Act 2011, 410
pt 6, 437
s 144, 437
Inquiries Act 2014, 410
sch 2, 33
Interpretation Bill 1982, 27, 386
Interpretation of Legislation Act 1984, 27, 30, 377, 392
s 4, 50, 570, 669
s 4(1)(a), 379
s 6, 401
s 7, 200
s 9(1), 206
s 9(2), 206
s 10, 199
s 10(3), 197, 299
s 10A(1), 184
s 10A(2), 184
s 10A(4), 182
s 11(1), 182
s 11(2), 184
s 11(2A), 184
s 11(3), 181
s 11(4), 189
s 13, 190
s 13(2), 190
s 13(3), 191
s 13(4), 191
s 14, 395–6, 603, 610
s 14(2), 396, 604
s 14(2)(ea), 604
s 16(1)(b), 388
s 17, 290, 386, 389
s 17(1)(a), 388
s 17(1)(b), 388
s 17(1)(c), 388
s 22, 401, 681
s 23, 670–1
s 27, 185
s 28, 395–6
s 28(2), 671
s 32, 680
s 35, 27
s 35(a), 27, 99
s 35(b), 5, 30, 178, 316, 332, 351, 353, 357
s 35(b)(i), 308
s 36(1), 203
s 36(1A), 202
s 36(2), 200
s 36(2A), 202, 301
s 36(3), 204
s 36(3A), 204
s 36(3B), 205, 308
s 36(3C), 203
s 36(3D), 204
s 36(3E), 204
s 36(4), 301
s 36A(1)(a), 306
s 36A(1)(b), 306
s 36A(2), 306
s 37(a), 386
s 37(c), 384
s 37(d), 384
s 38, 382–4, 626
s 39, 302, 382
s 40, 393
s 40(a), 397
s 41(1)(a), 393
s 41(1)(b)–(c), 393
s 41(1)(d), 393
s 41(2), 393
s 41(3), 393
s 41AA, 393
s 42, 389
ss 42–42A, 389
s 42A(1)(a), 390
s 42A(1)(b), 389
s 42A(1)(c), 390
s 42A(2), 389
s 42AA(1)(a), 389
s 43, 398
s 44(1), 398
s 44(2), 398
s 44(3), 399

Interpretation of Legislation Act 1984 (cont.)
s 44(4), 399
s 44(6), 384
s 45, 402, 569, 571
s 45(1), 569
s 45(2), 569
s 45(3), 571
s 46A, 628
s 48, 640
s 49, 392
s 50, 416
s 53, 400
s 54A, 530
sch 1, 530
Interpretation of Legislation Bill 1984, 27, 30
Jury Directions Act 2013
s 25, 531
Land Tax Act 2005
s 64, 473
s 64(1), 346
s 65(1), 346
Legislative Assembly Standing Orders 2004
ord 66, 196
ord 83, 173
ord 84, 174
ord 85, 174
ord 86, 174
ord 60, 196
ord 14.13, 196
Legislative Council of Victoria Standing Orders 2020
ord 14.02, 196
ord 14.12, 196
ords 14.36–14.41, 174
Lord Mayor's Charitable Foundation Bill 2016 (Vic), 174
Legal Profession Act 2004, 203
ch 3, 305
Legal Profession Practice Act 1958
s 10(2), 289
Local Government (Whittlesea City Council) Act 2020
s 7(d), 582
Magistrates' Court Act 1989
s 126(2), 640
s 126(4), 640
Magistrates' Court (Family Violence Protection) Rules 2018, 417
Major Crime (Investigative Powers) Act 2004
s 3AA(2), 266
Marine Safety Act 2010
s 22, 587
Market Court Act 1978, 611
Melbourne and Metropolitan Board of Works Act 1958
s 201, 346
sch 3, 346
Melbourne College of Divinity Amendment Bill 2016, 174
Melbourne Strategic Assessment (Environment Mitigation Levy) Act 2020
s 9, 622
Members of Parliament (Standards) Act 1978
s 5(1), 587
s 5A(a), 587
s 5A(b), 587
Multicultural Victoria Act 2011
s 4, 587
s 5, 587
Mutual Recognition (Victoria) Act 1998, 414
Occupational Health and Safety Act 2004, 57
Ombudsman Act 1973, 409
Parliamentary Administration Act 2005
s 5(1), 587
s 5(3), 587
Parliamentary Committees Act 2003
s 17(a)(vi), 187
Police Regulation Act 1958
s 8AA(1), 676
Prevention of Cruelty to Animals Act 1986
s 24G, 224–5
s 24K, 224–5
s 38(2), 224–5
Prevention of Family Violence Act 2018
s 4, 587
Privacy and Data Protection Act 2014, 410
Private Security Act 2004
s 25, 240
Professional Standards Act 2003
s 34(2), 200
Prostitution Control Act 1994, 298
Public Administration Act 2004, 415

s 7(1), 587
s 7(4), 587
Road Safety (Drivers) Regulations 2009
reg 55(1), 660
Road Safety Act 1986, 4, 660
s 28(6), 4–5, 125
s 60(1), 81, 127
s 66(6), 4–5, 125
Sentencing Act 1991
s 109(1)–(2), 411
s 110, 412
s 112, 412
s 113D, 412
s 114(1), 604
s 114(2), 604
Serious Offenders Act 2018
pt 21, 587
s 339, 587
s 339(b), 587
Sex Work Act 1994, 298
Subordinate Legislation Act 1994
s 3(1), 667
s 5, 667
s 13, 152
s 15, 667
s 16(1), 672
s 17, 667
s 21(1)(f), 449
s 23, 667
Summer Time Act 1972
s 3, 416
s 4, 416
Supreme Court (General Civil Procedure) Rules 2015
ord 56, 408
r 56.01, 409
Supreme Court Act 1958
s 68, 158
Supreme Court Act 1986
s 3(6), 409
s 43(1), 416
s 43(2), 416
s 48, 158
s 52(1), 500
s 52(3), 500
Town and Country Planning Act 1961, 192
Transport Accident Act 1986
s 3(1A)(c), 455
s 233, 456
Transport Integration Act 2010
s 6, 587
ss 7–13, 587
s 22, 514
s 23, 236
s 23(d), 514
s 28, 587
Treasury and Finance Legislation Amendment Act 2018
s 18, 456
Victims' Charter Act 2006
s 22(1)(b), 587
s 22(2), 587
Victorian Civil and Administrative Tribunal Act 1998, 407
pt 2, **408**
s 3, **408**
s 40, **408**
s 42, 407
s 42(1), **408**
s 48(a), **408**
s 57, 514
s 67, **408**
Victorian Fisheries Authority Act 2016
pt 2 divs 2-3, 587
s 5, 587
Victorian Independent Remuneration Tribunal and Improving Parliamentary Standards Act 2019
s 2(2), 181
s 61, 181
Workplace Injury Rehabilitation and Compensation Act 2013
s 13, 587
s 14, 587
Wrongs Act 1958
s 14G, 573

Western Australia

Aboriginal Heritage Act 1972, 624
s 6, 623
s 10, 623
s 17, 623
s 18(1), 623
Age of Majority Act 1972
s 4, 397
Auditor General Act 2006, 407

Bail Act 1982, 333, 403
Building and Construction Industry Training Fund and Levy Collection Act 1990
s 6(3), 628
Children and Community Services Act 2004
s 36(2), 558
s 38(2), 558
s 38(4), 558
Constitution Act 1889, 36, 403
s 2, 164
s 34, 168
s 36, 178
s 73, 176
Constitution Acts Amendment Act 1899, 36, 403
Corruption and Crime Commission Act 2003
s 72(2), 475
Corruption, Crime and Misconduct Act 2003, 410
Crimes Act 1958, 411
Criminal Appeals Act 2004
s 30(4), 240
Criminal Code Act Compilation Act 1913, 411, 662
app B
s 4, 411, 663
s 7, 411
sch
ss 2–5, 403
s 7, 403
ss 11–17, 403
s 12, 645
s 22, 665
ss 22–26, 403
s 24, 663, 664
s 222, 334
Criminal Investigation Act 2006, 403
Criminal Procedure Act 2004, 403
Dangerous Sexual Offenders Act 2006, 322, 683
s 3, 322
s 14(2)(a), 322
Dangerous Sexual Offenders Legislation Amendment Act 2016, 322
Disability Act 2006
s 49(2)(a), 521
District Court Rules 2005, 417
Electoral Districts Act 1947–1955, 189
Electronic Transactions Act 2003
s 4, 205
s 5, 204
Electronic Transactions Act 2011, 413
pt 2 div 3, 413
s 5(1), 413
s 7, 414
s 8, 413
ss 9–12, 413
Equal Opportunity Act 1984, 409
Evidence Act 1906, 403, 412
Financial Management Act 2006, 403, 407
Fines, Penalties and Infringement Notices Enforcement Act 1994, 403
Firearms Act 1973
s 23(9), 520
s 23(9)(d)(ii), 520
Firearms Regulations 1974, 520
reg 11A, 520
reg 11A(1), 520
reg 11A(8), 520
Freedom of Information Act 1992, 410
Gender Reassignment Act 2000, 107
s 3, 248
s 14, 107–8
s 14(1), 248
s 15, 108
s 15(1)(b), 248
s 15(1)(b)(ii), 107, 248
s 16(1)(b), 248
Industrial Relations Act 1979, 415
Interpretation Act 1918, 28
Interpretation Act 1984, 182, 377, 604
pt VI, 668
s 3, 50, 379
s 3(1), 379, 570, 671
s 3(2), 379
s 5, 382–4, 668
s 7, 401
s 8, 284
s 9, 302, 382
s 10(a), 386
s 10(c), 384
s 12, 387
s 12(c), 387
s 13A, 383
s 13A(4), 383
s 13A(5), 383
s 16, 290
s 16(1), 388–9, 670
s 16(2), 389
s 16(3), 388

s 18, 28, 31, 99
s 19, 30, 178, 316, 332, 351
s 19(2)(a), 301
s 19(2)(d), 487
s 19(3), 363
s 20, 182
s 21, 182
s 22, 185
s 23, 184
s 24, 165, 206
s 25, 190
s 25(3), 190
s 25(4), 191
s 26, 199
s 26(1), 206
s 27, 190
s 28, 174
s 29, 200
s 31(1), 198, 296
s 31(2), 200, 202, 204–5
s 32(1), 203
s 32(2), 202, 205
s 34, 395
s 37, 395, 603, 671
s 37(1), 396, 619–20
s 37(2), 396, 619–21
s 39, 395
s 41(1), 672
s 42, 668
s 43(1), 674
s 43(4), 185
s 44(1), 670
s 48, 397
s 52(1)(a), 393
s 52(1)(b), 393
s 52(2), 393
s 52(3), 393
s 53, 393
s 56, 402, 569
s 56(1), 569
s 56(2), 569
s 57, 583
s 57(b), 393
s 58, 389
ss 58–59, 389
s 59(1)(a), 390
s 59(1)(b), 389
s 59(1)(c), 389
s 59(1)(d), 389
s 59(1)(e), 390
s 59(1)(f), 389
s 59(2)(a), 391
s 59(3), 390
s 61(1)(a), 399
s 61(1)(b), 398–9
s 61(1)(c), 399
s 61(1)(d), 398
s 61(1)(e), 399
s 61(1)(f), 399
s 61(1)(g), 399
s 61(2), 399
s 63, 400
s 65, 398
s 66, 416
s 66(2), 416
s 74, 400
s 75, 392
s 76(a), 392
s 76(b), 392
s 76(c), 392
s 76(d), 392
Joint Standing Rules and Orders of the Legislative Council and Legislative Assembly 2011
ord 9, 206
Land Administration Act 1997
s 241(7)(b), 228
Legislation Act 2021
pts 2–5, 530
s 50, 33
Legislative Council Standing Orders 2019
ch 20, 168
ord 122(1), 196
ord 122(2), 196
ord 122(3), 196
ord 126, 174
ord 130, 196
sch 1 ord 126, 174
Liquor Control Act 1988
s 5, 90
s 119, 90
s 119(7), 90, 474–5
Local Government Act 2020
s 328(5), 619
Mining Act 1978, 580, 583, 626
s 116(2), 583
Misuse of Drugs Act 1981, 267

Motor Vehicle (Third Party Insurance) Act 1943
s 3(7), 339
sch, 338–9
Municipal Corporations Act 1906, 321
Mutual Recognition (Western Australia) Act 2020, 414
Noongar (Koorah, Nitja, Boordahwan) (Past, Present, Future) Recognition Act 2016, 198
Parliamentary Commissioner Act 1971, 409
Parliamentary Privileges Act 1891, 178
s 1, 178
Planning and Development Act 2005
s 135, 320–1
Public Sector Management Act 1994, 403, 415
Reprints Act 1984
s 7, 530
s 7A, 530
Road Districts Act 1919, 321
Royal Commissions Act 1968, 410
Sea-Carriage of Goods Act 1909, 233
s 5, 232
Sentence Administration Act 2003, 536
s 7, 536
Sentencing Act 1995, 403, 536
s 10, 604
s 40(5), 412
s 40(5a), 412
s 85, 536
s 88(3), 536
Sentencing Legislation (Transitional Provisions) Amendment Act 2008, 342
Sentencing Legislation Amendment and Repeal Act 2003
sch 1 cl 3A, 342
Shortening Ordinance 1844, 25
Stamp Act 1921, 630
Standard Time Act 2005
s 4, 416
s 5, 416
Standing Orders of the Legislative Assembly 2017
ch 23, 168
ord 163, 196
ord 164, 196
ord 175, 196
State Administrative Tribunal Act 2004, 407
s 13, 407
Tobacco Products Control Act 2006, 102
s 3, 106
s 3(c), 102
Town Planning and Development Act 1928, 321
Transfer of Land Act 1893, 321
Workers' Compensation and Rehabilitation Act 1981, 620
Workers' Compensation and Rehabilitation Amendment Act 1999, 620
s 32(7), 620
Young Offenders Act 1994, 536

Australian Capital Territory

ACT Civil and Administrative Tribunal Act 2008, 407
s 9, 407
Administrative Decisions (Judicial Review) Act 1989, 409
Auditor-General Act 1996, 407
Civil Law (Wrongs) Act 2002
sch 4, 159
Court Procedures Rules 2006, 417
rr 3553-3554, 409
Crimes (Serious and Organised Crime) Legislation Amendment Act 2016, 543
Crimes Act 1900
s 27(3)(b), 657, 662
s 28(2)(a), 657
s 300, 140
Criminal Code 2002, 411, 662
s 6, 663
s 7, 663
s 22, 664
s 23, 664
s 24, 664
s 36, 663
s 63(3), 646
s 64(2)(a), 645
s 64(2)(b), 646
s 65(2), 646
Electronic Transactions Act 2001, 413
dictionary, 413
pt 2 div 2.3, 413
s 6A, 414
s 7, 413
s 8–11, 413
Evidence Act 2011, 412
s 144, 489

Financial Management Act 1996, 407
Firearms Act 1996
sch 1, 541, 543
Freedom of Information Act 2016, 410
Human Rights Act 2004, 152, 403
pt 3, 404
pt 3A, 404
s 28, 404
s 30, 177, 404, 406, 669
s 31(1), 404, 487
s 32, 405
s 32(3), 405
s 37, 354, 448
Human Rights Commission Act 2005, 409
Information Privacy Act 2014, 410
Integrity Commission Act 2018, 410
Interpretation (Amendment) Ordinance 1982, 28
Interpretation (Amendment) Ordinance 1985, 30
Interpretation Act 1967, 34
Interpretation Ordinance 1967
s 11A, 28
s 11B, 30
Legislation (Statutory Interpretation) Amendment Act 2003, 34
Legislation Act 2001, 34, 182, 377–9, 381, 390
ch 14, 34
ch 7, 668
dictionary pt 1, 381–4, 393
div 19.3.2, 393
pt 19.4, 389
s 4, 379, 669
s 6, 50, 379
s 6(2), 396, 570
s 6(3), 671
s 6(6), 379, 671
s 6(7), 379
s 13, 668
s 18, 668
s 26, 166
s 26(1)(a), 165
s 27, 206
s 28, 165
s 28(2)(b), 206
s 29, 181
s 43, 401, 681
s 45, 416
s 46, 185
s 47, 680
s 73(1), 182
s 74(1), 183
s 75, 185
s 75B, 672
s 76, 672
s 77(1), 183
s 77(2)–(3), 184
s 77(4), 184
s 79, 186
s 81, 190
s 81(6), 190
s 81(7), 190
s 84, 395–6, 603, 671
s 84(6), 604
s 84A(1), 604
s 84A(2), 604
s 84A(3), 604
s 86, 395–6
s 88, 395–6
s 100(1), 199
s 100(1)(b), 206
s 102, 290, 389
s 102(1)(a), 388
s 102(1)(b), 388
ss 114–118, 530
s 120, 401
s 121(1), 634
s 121(4), 634
s 122, 640
s 126(1), 203
s 126(2), 202, 301
s 126(3), 198
s 126(4), 204
s 126(5), 204, 204
s 126(6), 205, 308
s 126(7), 203
s 127(1), 205
s 127(2), 205
s 127(3), 202, 301
s 130, 312, 382
s 132(1)(a), 306
s 132(1)(b), 306
s 132(2), 306
s 133, 412
s 137, 100
s 138(a)–(c), 357

Legislation Act 2001 (cont.)
s 138(d), 357
s 139, 28, 34, 99
s 141, 30, 34, 316, 332, 357, 359
ss 141–143, 178, 351
s 141(1), 357
s 141(2), 363
s 141(2)(c), 359, 363
s 141(4), 359
s 142, 353, 357
s 142(1) item 7, 487
s 145(a), 386
s 145(b), 384
s 146, 402, 569
s 146(1), 569
s 146(2), 569
s 147, 326
s 148, 670
s 149, 397
s 150, 398
s 151(2), 398–9
s 151(3), 399
s 151A, 399
s 157, 302, 382
s 160, 383
s 162, 387
s 162(3), 387
s 169, 383
s 190, 412
s 197, 397
s 207, 393
s 208, 393
s 209, 393
s 212, 393, 583
s 231(1), 391
s 231(2), 389
s 232, 390
s 233, 389
s 234, 389
s 235, 390
s 236, 389
s 237, 390
s 238, 391
s 239(1), 389
s 239(2), 390
s 239(3), 389
s 239(4), 390
s 240, 390
s 241, 391
s 242(1), 390
s 242(2), 390
s 247(1)(a), 392
s 247(1)(b), 392
s 247(1)(c), 392
s 247(1)(d), 392
s 247(1)(e), 392
s 248(1)(b), 392
s 248(1)(c), 392
s 248(1)(d), 392
s 248(1)(e), 392
s 249, 392
s 250(1), 392
s 250(3), 392
s 250(4), 392
s 250(5), 392
s 255(4), 400
s 255(5)(c), 400
s 255(5)(d), 400
Legislative Assembly for the Australian Capital Territory: Standing Orders 2019
ord 169, 196
ord 170, 196
ord 180, 196
Mutual Recognition (Australian Capital Territory) Act 1992, 414
Ombudsman Act 1989, 409
Public Sector Management Act 1994, 415
Road Transport (Driver Licensing) Act 1999, 551
s 32, 550–1
s 32(2), 551
s 32(2)(a), 550
Road Transport (General) Act 1999, 551
s 61B(4)(d), 551
s 61C, 551–2
s 64, 551
Royal Commissions Act 1991, 410
Standard Time and Summer Time Act 1972
s 4, 416
s 5, 416
s 7, 416
Supreme Court Act 1933
s 37J, 463
s 37J(1)(k), 463

Northern Territory

Anti-Discrimination Act 1992, 409
Audit Act 1995, 407
Crimes (Victims Assistance) Act 1989
s 4(1), 454
Criminal Code Act 1983, 662
s 5, 663
sch 1, 411
s 3, 412
s 43AA, 663
s 43AM, 663–4
s 43AN, 663–4
s 43AO, 664
s 43AX, 663
s 43AY, 665
s 43BZ(3), 646
s 43CA(2)(a), 645
s 43CA(2)(b), 646
s 43CB(2), 646
Criminal Law Consolidation Act 1978
s 5, 563
Darwin Waterfront Corporation Act 2006
s 7, 628
Education Act 2015
s 122, 42
Electronic Transactions (Northern Territory) Act 2000, 413
pt 2 div 3, 413
s 5, 413
s 6A, 414
s 7, 413
ss 8–11, 413
Evidence (National Uniform Legislation) Act 2011, 412
Financial Management Act 1995, 407
Fisheries Act, 343
Independent Commissioner Against Corruption Act 2017, 410
Information Act 2002, 410
Inquiries Act 1945, 410
Interpretation Act 1978, 377
s 3, 50
s 3(1), 378
s 3(3), 379
s 3(4), 378
s 4, 669
s 5(3), 183
s 5(4), 182
s 6, 182
s 6(3), 185
s 6A, 182
s 6B(b), 189
s 7(1), 165, 206
s 8, 190
s 8(2), 190
s 9(b), 191
s 11, 395
s 12, 395, 603, 671
s 15(1), 388
s 15(2), 388
s 15(3), 388
s 17, 381–4
s 19, 387
s 19(2)(b), 387
s 19A(3), 383
s 20(1), 670
s 23, 302, 382
s 23A, 670
s 24(1), 386
s 24(2), 384
s 24AA, 383
s 25(1)(a)(i), 392
s 25(1)(a)(iii), 392
s 25(1)(b), 392
s 25(1)(d), 392
s 25(2), 392
s 25(4), 392
s 26, 384
s 27, 398
s 28(1), 398
s 28(1A), 398
s 28(2), 399
s 30, 397
s 38(1), 640
s 38DC, 412
s 40, 393
s 41(1), 393, 397
s 43, 185
s 44, 393
s 44A, 393
s 46, 391
s 46A, 389
s 46A(1), 389
s 46A(2), 389

Interpretation Act 1978 (cont.)
s 46A(3), 390
s 46A(4), 390
s 48, 389
s 49(1), 199
s 49(1)(b), 206
s 50, 290
s 50(1), 388–9, 671
s 54, 200
s 55(1), 203
s 55(2), 202, 301
s 55(4), 204–5
s 55(5), 200
s 55(6), 205
s 56, 206
s 59, 401
s 61, 401, 681
s 62A, 28, 99
s 62B, 30, 178, 316, 332, 351
s 62B(2)(d), 487
s 62C, 326
s 62D, 307
s 62D(a), 306
s 62D(b), 306
s 62D(c), 306
s 62E, 307
s 63, 668
s 63A, 668
s 63B(3), 672
s 63B(4), 672
s 63C, 668
s 66, 680
s 68, 400
Interpretation Amendment Act 1998, 28, 30
Interpretation Amendment Act 2021, 185
s 4, 185
Lands Acquisition Act 1978 (NT), 574
Legislative Assembly (Powers and Privileges) Act 1992, 178
Local Court Act 2015
s 48(2)(a), 417
Local Court (Adoption of Children) Rules 1994, 417
Local Government Act 2019
s 3, 622
Mutual Recognition (Northern Territory) Act 1992, 414
Northern Territory Civil and Administrative Tribunal Act 2014, 407
s 30, 407
s 33, 407
Ombudsman Act 2009, 409
Penalty Units Act 2009
s 5, 412
Personal Injuries (Liabilities and Damages) Act 2003
s 10, 573
Personal Violence Restraining Orders Act 2016
s 13, 555
Planning Act 1979, 677
Police Administration Act 1978
s 133AB, 556
s 133AB(3), 556
Public Sector Employment and Management Act 1993, 415
Sentencing Act 1995
s 29, 412
s 121(1), 604
s 121(2), 604
Sentencing (Crime of Murder) and Parole Reform Act 2003
s 18, 563
s 19, 563
s 19(5), 563
Standard Time Act 2005
s 4, 416
s 5, 416
Standing Orders 2016
ord 142, 196
ord 152, 196
ord 153, 196
Supreme Court Act 1979
s 9(2)(b), 409
s 86(3), 417
Supreme Court Rules 1987, 417
Taxation (Administration) Act 2007
div 8A, 427
s 4(1), 427
s 56N(2)(b), 427

Canada

Criminal Code, RSC 1985, 597

New Zealand

Sale of Liquor Act 1962
s 264, 475

United Kingdom

Acts of Parliament (Commencement) Act 1793, 182
Agricultural Holdings Act 1908, 615
Australia Act 1986, 18, 44, 163, 476
s 3(1), 176
s 6, 176
s 7, 164
Bill of Rights 1688, 177
art 9, 177–8, 351
Colonial Laws Validity Act 1865, 176
s 5, 176
Commonwealth of Australia Constitution Act 1900, 18
s 9, 36
Criminal Justice Act 1988
s 171(1), 189
Defence (General) Regulations 1939
reg 42C(1), 594
Explosive Substances Act 1883
s 9, 308
Fatal Accidents Acts 1846–1959, 191
Firearms Act 1968
s 17(2), 264–5
Housing Act 1985, 304
Human Rights Act 1998
s 3, 405
s 3(1), 405
Immigration Act 1971
s 18(1), 684
Interpretation Act 1850, 200, 377–8, 397
s 2, 200
Interpretation Act 1889, 395
Malicious Damage Act 1861, 317
Mental Health (Care and Treatment) (Scotland) Act 2003, 684
Social Security Act 1975
s 165A, 615
s 60, 615
Terrorism Act 2000
s 11(2), 405

International instruments

Australia–New Zealand Closer Economic Relations Trade Agreement, 544
Convention Against Torture and Other Cruel, Inhuman or Degrading Treatment or Punishment, 86
Convention Relating to the Status of Refugees, 482, 675
European Convention for the Protection of Human Rights and Fundamental Freedoms, 405
International Convention on the Harmonized Commodity Description and Coding System, 480
International Covenant on Civil and Political Rights, 485
Protocol on Trade in Services to the Australia-New Zealand Closer Economic Relations-Trade Agreement, 544–5
art 4, 544
art 5, 544
Vienna Convention on the Law of Treaties, 479–80
art 31(3), 481
art 32, 481

ABOUT THE AUTHORS

Dr Jeffrey Barnes is an Associate Professor in La Trobe Law School at La Trobe University. He assisted the Law Admissions Consultative Committee in preparing the *Statement on Statutory Interpretation* (Law Admissions Consultative Committee, 2010). Following that involvement, he was appointed the lead author of the *Council of Australian Law Deans Good Practice Guide to Teaching Statutory Interpretation* (Council of Australian Law Deans, 2015). He is the editor of *The Coherence of Statutory Interpretation* (Federation Press, 2019). He has a number of other publications in the areas of statutory interpretation, legislative drafting, the legislative process and administrative law. His doctorate was on the Plain Language Movement and legislation. In addition to producing scholarly writing, he has practised law widely, including as a parliamentary counsel for the NSW Parliamentary Counsel's Office, as Associate to the Chairman of and Law Reform Officer at the Australian Law Reform Commission, as Project Officer with the Administrative Review Council, and as a Legal Member (part-time) of the Social Security Appeals Tribunal. He has also been engaged by various government agencies as a consultant on statutory interpretation. His past academic appointments include Foundation Director of Teaching and Learning at La Trobe Law School, and Co-editor of *Legal Education Review*. In 2009 he developed and taught an elective subject on statutory interpretation, and since 2013 has developed and taught compulsory subjects wholly devoted to statutory interpretation for LLB and Juris Doctor students.

Jacinta Dharmananda is a Senior Lecturer at the Law School of the University of Western Australia ('UWA'). She has written widely in scholarly publications on statutory interpretation, and is co-author of the *Council of Australian Law Deans Good Practice Guide to Teaching Statutory Interpretation* (Council of Australian Law Deans, 2015). Her work on statutory interpretation has been cited by the High Court of Australia and shortlisted for the CALD 2020 Australian Legal Research awards (Article/Chapter ECR category). In 2017 she was the recipient of a Parliamentary Library Summer Research Scholarship to undertake research on legislation at the Parliamentary Library in Canberra. She is currently completing her doctorate at the Australian National University on the relationship between the legislative process and statutory interpretation law. In 2012 she designed, developed and taught an elective subject on statutory interpretation, a subject she has since taught to LLB and Juris Doctor students at UWA. In 2022 she designed, developed and commenced teaching to all Juris Doctor students a compulsory subject devoted to the interpretation of legal instruments, with a focus on statutory interpretation. Prior to joining UWA Law School, she worked as a commercial lawyer for over a decade in private practice and in-house in Melbourne, New York, Perth, Singapore and Tokyo.

Eamonn Moran PSM QC SBS is the Inspector at the Victorian Inspectorate, the key integrity body in Victoria. He commenced in that role in 2018. Immediately prior to that appointment, he was practising at the Victorian Bar and working as a consultant legislative counsel. Between 2012 and 2016 he was also a member of the Victorian Law Reform Commission. From 2008 until 2012 he was Law Draftsman in the Department of Justice, Hong Kong, and assumed primary responsibility for the development and publication of *Drafting Legislation in Hong Kong: A Guide to Styles and Practices* (Hong Kong Department of Justice, 2012). In 2012 he was awarded by the Hong Kong Government a Silver Bauhinia Star ('SBS') for his contribution to the development of plain language drafting in Hong Kong. He held the office of Chief Parliamentary Counsel in Victoria from 1999 until 2008. Before then he had worked as a parliamentary counsel in Victoria for more than 20 years and was appointed as Queen's Counsel in Victoria in 1998. He was awarded an Australian Public Service Medal ('PSM') in 2005 for service to legislative drafting and public law. His most recent publication was an article he contributed to *The Coherence of Statutory Interpretation* (Federation Press, 2019), edited by his co-author in this work, Dr Jeffrey Barnes. Mr Moran is a Past President of the Commonwealth Association of Legislative Counsel and a Past President of Clarity International. He has spoken at numerous conferences, both in Australia and overseas, on topics related to legislation.

ACKNOWLEDGEMENTS

Jacinta Dharmananda: Some of the research for this work (notably chapter 2 and Part V) is supported by an Australian Government Research Training Program ('RTP') Scholarship.

Permissions

PART I

BACKGROUND

Part I reviews the underpinnings of statutory interpretation from three perspectives. The first is functional: the basic characteristics of statutory interpretation. The second perspective is historical: the modern development of the law of statutory interpretation. The third perspective is constitutional: the key constitutional concepts relevant to statutory interpretation. These perspectives contribute to understanding the fundamental interpretative principles in Part II and many other principles covered in this book (such as the use of legislative history in Part IV).

Chapter 1 (*The Nature of Statutory Interpretation*) explains how statutory interpretation is both a distinct body of law and a task that requires the exercise of a set of skills, such as assembling arguments about alternative meanings. Statutory interpretation can therefore be distinguished from other legal tasks. It is different to formulating the legal rule of a case and should be distinguished from the task of applying the statute to the facts.

Chapter 2 (*A Modern History of Key Concepts*) considers the modern history of key contemporary concepts in statutory interpretation. It starts at the beginning of the 20th century, and includes the pivotal statutory and common law developments in the last quarter of the 1900s. This history reveals how the seeds of key contemporary concepts were evident in earlier statutory interpretation law and how they evolved. This enhances understanding of the modern approach to statutory interpretation.

Chapter 3 (*Constitutional Context*) explains statutory interpretation in the context of the Australian legal system. It focuses on fundamental constitutional concepts – the federal system, the separation of powers, the rule of law and parliamentary supremacy. These concepts are helpful to understand the institutions and sources of law relevant to statutory interpretation, as well as the function and limits of statutory interpretation.

THE NATURE OF STATUTORY INTERPRETATION

1

Overview

Statutory interpretation is a many-faceted thing. It is a substantive body of law and a process involving a set of skills. It is distinct from (but overlapping with) the application of the law. It is not wholly different from the interpretation of ordinary speech. But it is dissimilar in major respects from formulating the ratio decidendi or the rule of a case. Functionally, statutory interpretation resolves a question of law between parties to a dispute. It also contributes to law-making in the sense that the text of the statute, read with the interpretation, constitutes a new understanding of the law. [1.1]

Basic composition

Statutory interpretation is a substantive body of law [1.2]

According to Chief Justice Spigelman, writing extracurially, 'Statutory interpretation is not merely a collection of maxims. It is a distinct body of law.'[1] Several reasons may be given in support. First, sources. The sources of interpretative rules and presumptions are common law and statute law:

> [T]he judiciary is strictly involved in interpreting and applying principles of law, the source of which is either legislation or the common law. It is axiomatic, but critical, that in performing that role, no judge acts according to his or her own values or individual views.[2]

A court has no authority to legislate by using a 'judicially-constructed policy' – 'its own idea of a desirable policy'[3] – or personal values.[4]

Second, the rules and presumptions that are relevant to the statutory context and the circumstances of the case are binding. A judge has a duty to consider 'all available indications',[5]

---

1 Chief Justice JJ Spigelman, 'Principle of Legality and the Clear Statement Principle' (2005) 79 *Australian Law Journal* 769, 769.

2 *WBM v Chief Commissioner of Police* (2010) 27 VR 469, 481 [46] (Kaye J).

3 *Australian Education Union v Department of Education and Children's Services* (2012) 248 CLR 1, 14 [28] (French CJ, Hayne, Kiefel and Bell JJ).

4 See further **[33.4]**.

5 *Commissioner of Police for New South Wales v Eaton* (2013) 252 CLR 1, 19 [46] (Crennan, Kiefel and Bell JJ), quoting *Associated Minerals Consolidated Ltd v Wyong Shire Council* [1975] AC 538, 553–4 (Lord Wilberforce).

'the full range of relevant factors'[6] and 'the whole range of circumstances relevant upon a question of statutory interpretation'.[7]

It is true that most considerations are presumptions or aids to construction. As Lord Reid said:

> [R]ules of construction are relied on. They are not rules in the ordinary sense of having some binding force. They are our servants, not our masters. They are aids to construction, presumptions or pointers. Not infrequently one 'rule' points in one direction, another in a different direction. In each case we must look at all relevant circumstances and decide as a matter of judgment what weight to attach to any particular 'rule'.[8]

But that fact does not deprive the considerations of a legal quality.[9] It is an outdated conception of law to equate it with hard-and-fast rules.[10] The fact that the canons of statutory interpretation (the bulk of the interpretative criteria) are not hard-and-fast rules does not mean they are not binding and does not mean they are not 'law'. The following observation is endorsed:

> Seen from the perspective of the ordinary judge, the rules and principles of statutory interpretation are legally binding statements of the approach he [sic] should adopt, even if their content is more general and vaguer than other rules and principles of the legal system. They are more than mere counsels of good practice.[11]

Example 1.1 *Dolheguy v Becker*[12]

The plaintiff challenged the failure of the Court below to suspend the defendant's driver licence. At issue were two apparently conflicting provisions of the *Road Safety Act 1986* (Vic).[13] Under the main heading 'Principles of statutory interpretation without reference to extrinsic material', his Honour considered certain principles under the following headings:

'Purposive approach to statutory interpretation'[14]
'Principle that all the words of a statutory provision must be given effect'[15]
'Principle that general provisions are subject to specific provisions'[16]
'Principle of implied repeal of legislation'[17]

6 *A-G (NSW) v World Best Holdings Ltd* (2005) 63 NSWLR 557, 571 [53] (Spigelman CJ).

7 *Sovar v Henry Lane Pty Ltd* (1967) 116 CLR 397, 405 (Kitto J, Owen J agreeing at 417), affd *Singh v Commonwealth* (2004) 222 CLR 322, 335–6 [19] (Gleeson CJ); *H v Minister for Immigration and Citizenship* (2010) 188 FCR 393, 407 [51] (the Court).

8 *Maunsell v Olins* [1975] AC 373, 382 (Lord Reid).

9 Ruth Sullivan, 'Statutory Interpretation in a New Nutshell' (2003) 82(1) *Canadian Bar Review* 51, 53–5.

10 Ibid, criticising the realist John Willis.

11 John Bell and Sir George Engle, *Cross on Statutory Interpretation* (Oxford University Press, 3rd ed, 2005) 42.

12 (2009) 52 MVR 462.

13 Sections 28(6) and 66(6).

14 *Dolheguy v Becker* (2009) 52 MVR 462, 469 [37] (Kyrou J).

15 Ibid 470 [42].

16 Ibid 470 [44].

17 Ibid 470 [45].

'Principle that most recent statutory provision prevails'[18]
'Principle that ambiguity in a penal statute should be resolved in favour of an accused'.[19]

The Court separately considered the principle, set out in s 35(b) of the *Interpretation of Legislation Act 1984* (Vic), that 'permits the Court to have regard to extrinsic material, such as explanatory memoranda and parliamentary debates, as an aid to statutory interpretation'.[20]

Statutory interpretation is a process involving a set of skills [1.3]

Statutory interpretation is more than a body of substantive law. Bennion once described statutory interpretation as a 'collection of legal skills'.[21] From an advisor's standpoint, those skills include, in outline: finding the relevant law; closely reading the relevant provision or provisions, examining the context, formulating constructions, assembling the arguments for each construction, exercising judgement as to which is the preferable construction, and applying the law as interpreted to the facts.[22]

Example 1.2 *ABC Developmental Learning Centres Pty Ltd v Secretary, Department of Human Services*[23]

The plaintiff company objected to two letters sent to its head office seeking answers to specific questions and the provision of certain documents. The requests arose from two alleged incidents at its child care centres. In outline, the Court found the relevant law was the *Children's Services Act 1996* (Vic). It determined the relevant provision in issue, purportedly supporting the request, was s 36(1)(f). Examining the provision closely, while it authorised an authorised officer to 'require a person ... to answer a question to the best of that person's knowledge, information and belief', the provision did not state that the power was to be exercised at the child care premises.[24] The rival constructions as formulated by the parties were set out. The plaintiff construed the provision as limited to a person who 'is actually on the licensed premises at the time of the request'. The respondent department construed the provision as encompassing any person.[25] After considering the submissions of the parties and examining the provision and its context, the Court assembled the arguments for each construction. For the respondent, they comprised the literal reading of the provision[26] and a general purpose of the Act.[27] For the plaintiff, the Court

18 Ibid 471 [49].

19 Ibid 471 [50].

20 Ibid 472 [52]. The Court resolved the apparent conflict by holding that s 28(6) was an exception to s 66(6): at 472 [55].

21 FAR Bennion, *Understanding Common Law Legislation: Drafting and Interpretation* (Oxford University Press, 2009) 1.

22 Chapter 9 provides more detail on the skills.

23 (2007) 15 VR 489.

24 Ibid 493 [20] (Hollingworth J).

25 Ibid 493 [18].

26 Ibid.

27 Ibid 493 [19].

considered the surrounding provisions of the section,[28] the heading to the section,[29] other provisions of the Act,[30] extrinsic (parliamentary) materials,[31] interpretation legislation[32] and an important common law principle.[33] Exercising judgement as to which construction corresponded with Parliament's intention,[34] the Court favoured the plaintiff's construction.[35] Applying the law as interpreted to the facts, the Court concluded that a basis for relief being granted to the plaintiff had been established.[36]

Comparisons

[1.4] Statutory interpretation is distinct from application of the law

It is common for courts to distinguish statutory interpretation (or construction[37]) from application of the law to the facts. For example, in *Wilkie v Commonwealth*[38] the High Court noted that the question of construction (the meaning of s 10 of the *Appropriation Act (No 1) 2017–2018* (Cth)) was anterior to the question of application (the validity of the Finance Determination):

> **The construction of s 10 of Appropriation Act No 1 2017–2018**
>
> The plaintiffs' arguments concerning the validity of the Finance Determination were primarily directed to establishing that the precondition set out in s 10(1) of Appropriation Act No 1 2017–2018 to the exercise of the power of the Finance Minister to make a determination under s 10(2) was not met. Before addressing factual aspects of those arguments, it is convenient to isolate and address as a discrete topic those aspects of the arguments which bore on the construction of s 10(1).[39]

How is interpretation of legislation different to its application? Differences are apparent in their outcomes, their processes, and in the way the legislation is treated.

---

28 Ibid 493–4 [20]–[24].

29 Ibid 494 [25].

30 Ibid 494 [29]–[30].

31 Ibid 494 [26]–[27].

32 Ibid 494 [25].

33 Ibid 494 [31].

34 Ibid 493 [19].

35 Ibid 495 [32].

36 Ibid.

37 In this work, 'construe' and 'interpret' (and their respective nouns, 'construction' and 'interpretation') are regarded as synonymous. The High Court of Australia uses the terms interchangeably: see, eg, *R v A2* (2019) 269 CLR 507, 526 [55] (Kiefel CJ and Keane J, Nettle and Gordon JJ agreeing generally at 554 [148], Edelman J agreeing at 572 [193]), 559 [163] (Edelman J); *Probuild Constructions (Aust) Pty Ltd v Shade Systems Pty Ltd* (2018) 264 CLR 1, 22 [58] (Gageler J); *Alcan (NT) Alumina Pty Ltd v Commissioner of Territory Revenue (NT)* (2009) 239 CLR 27, 31 [4] (French CJ). This also accords with views in learned works, including Ray Finkelstein and David Hamer (eds), *LexisNexis Concise Australian Legal Dictionary* (LexisNexis Butterworths, 5th ed, 2015) 601; *Encyclopaedic Australian Legal Dictionary* (online at 3 May 2022) 'statutory interpretation'; Oliver Jones, *Bennion on Statutory Interpretation: A Code* (LexisNexis, 6th ed, 2013) 3–4, quoting Murray Gleeson, 'The Meaning of Legislation: Context, Purpose, and Respect for Fundamental Rights' (2009) 20(1) *Public Law Review* 26, 27 n 2.

38 (2017) 263 CLR 487.

39 Ibid 532–3 [96] (the Court).

Interpretation determines the meaning of legislation or, more precisely, its 'legal meaning'.[40] Legal meaning is 'the meaning that the legislature is taken to have intended [the words in question] to have'.[41] Heydon J has helpfully indicated that questions of meaning are about the 'scope' of the words in question.[42] This commonly takes in the scope of a particular element of a provision (express or implied) or the provision's legal effect.[43] As Bennion says, '[p]roblems of interpretation usually ... turn on *when* the enactment operates and *how* it operates'.[44]

Application, on the other hand, assumes that any issue of interpretation has been settled or is not in dispute. In applying the law, a court determines whether the facts fall within or outside the law as it is taken to mean.[45] In other words, application determines the legal position of a person in relation to particular facts. As Bell and Engle opine:

> [O]ne may say that interpretation is the process by which the courts determine the meaning of a statutory provision for the purpose of applying it to the situation before them. ... Throughout the rest of this book it is assumed that the word 'interpretation' is only apt in its application to statutes when there is a dispute about the meaning of words. This excludes the discussion of two procedures which certainly have claims to be described as 'interpretation', the process of determining how words of undisputed meaning apply to an undisputed situation of fact and the process of applying words of undisputed meaning after a conclusion has been reached with regard to disputed facts. These processes are best referred to as 'application' of the statute.[46]

Different processes are involved in reaching these different outcomes. An essential element of interpretation is framing alternative constructions.[47] They are the 'rival contentions as to the meaning [of the disputed provision]'.[48] As Justice Frankfurter said:

> When we talk of statutory construction we have in mind cases in which there is a fair contest between two readings, neither of which comes without respectable title deeds. A problem in statutory construction can seriously bother courts only when there is a contest between probabilities of meaning.[49]

A further distinction lies in the way the different tasks treat the wording of the legislation. With interpretation, the interpreter's words of clarification '[declare] or make explicit certain of its implied or unexpressed provisions'.[50] Either way, the legislative text is thereafter to be read with

---

40 *Project Blue Sky Inc v Australian Broadcasting Authority* (1998) 194 CLR 355, 384 [78] (McHugh, Gummow, Kirby and Hayne JJ).

41 Ibid.

42 *Momcilovic v The Queen* (2011) 245 CLR 1, 182 [450] (dissenting as to outcome).

43 For instances of questions of legal effect, see **[32.9]** (determination of jurisdictional error in administrative law) and chapter 37 (effect of non-compliance with a statutory requirement).

44 Oliver Jones, *Bennion on Statutory Interpretation: A Code* (LexisNexis, 6th ed, 2013) 401 (emphasis in original).

45 The application of law is binary: SI Strong, *How to Write Law Essays and Exams* (Oxford University Press, 3rd ed, 2010) 125.

46 John Bell and Sir George Engle, *Cross: Statutory Interpretation* (Oxford University Press, 3rd ed, 2005) 34.

47 *Berenguel v Minister for Immigration and Citizenship* (2010) 264 ALR 417, 423 [26] (the Court).

48 *Inland Revenue Commissioners v Hinchy* [1960] AC 748, 766 (Lord Reid).

49 Felix Frankfurter, 'Some Reflections on the Reading of Statutes' (1947) 47(4) *Columbia Law Review* 527, 527–8.

50 Oliver Jones, *Bennion on Statutory Interpretation: A Code* (LexisNexis, 6th ed, 2013) 475.

the gloss provided in the ruling. As the Federal Court noted in relation to an interpretation of a provision of the *Migration Act 1958* (Cth), 'In determining the scope and operation of the entire provision, it will be necessary to express or describe how the provision operates by using language other than that which appears in the statute.'[51] But an application of the law to the facts accepts the terms of the legislation (or the terms of the legislation read with a prior interpretation) and matches the facts with that wording to arrive at a result on the particular facts.

Nevertheless, as Bell and Engle suggested, the distinction between interpretation and application should not be pressed too far. Application of a statute is never mechanical and often involves an 'evaluative judgment'.[52] That judgement involves consideration of the statutory context as well as all the circumstances. And interpretation is in the light of the facts and does not travel beyond the dispute.[53] Therefore, interpretation and application share some common ground at a general level.

Example 1.3 *Virgin Blue Airlines Pty Ltd v Federal Commissioner of Taxation*[54]

The appellant paid for car parking for its employees at Melrose Car Park, within the confines of Melbourne Airport. The primary place of employment was Terminal 3 at the airport. The employees were taken by a shuttle bus from the car park to the bus stop at Terminal 4, from where they walked to Terminal 3. The trip from the car park took 15–20 minutes, including the time it took to walk from the bus stop to the Terminal 3 entrance. The Commissioner determined that the appellant was liable to pay fringe benefits tax and issued an assessment. Under the *Fringe Benefits Tax Assessment Act 1986* (Cth) ('FBTAA'), for the provision of car parking facilities to be a fringe benefit, s 39A(1)(f) had to be satisfied, namely that: 'during the period or periods, the car is parked at, or in the vicinity of, that primary place of employment'.

At first instance the Federal Court determined that the Melrose Car Park was 'in the vicinity of' Terminal 3. On appeal, the Full Court observed that a distinction ought to be made between interpretation and application of the subject phrase:

> The phrase 'in the vicinity of' in s 39A(1)(f) of the FBTAA refers to a relationship between two places. It is an expression capable of wide application. However, its reach requires consideration in its statutory context before its application to the facts.[55]

Accordingly, the Full Court first determined the reach of the phrase before applying it to the facts. The Full Court agreed with the primary judge that the ordinary meaning of 'in the vicinity of' was 'near, proximate or close', with case law pointing to the relevance of spatial and geographic

51 *BGM16 v Minister for Immigration and Border Protection* (2017) 252 FCR 97, 106 [51] (Mortimer and Wigney JJ).

52 *Virgin Blue Airlines Pty Ltd v Federal Commissioner of Taxation* (2010) 190 FCR 150, 163 [59] (Edmonds and Gilmour JJ); *Phillips v Police* (2016) 125 SASR 427, 433 [21] (Kourakis CJ).

53 See **[9.8]**.

54 (2010) 190 FCR 150.

55 Ibid 157 [31] (Edmonds and Gilmour JJ, Jessup J agreeing generally at 164 [63]).

separation.[56] But their Honours found that the primary judge had erred in putting weight on the fact that 'the two locations are part of *the same functional space* – Melbourne Airport'.[57] The Full Court found that whether the primary place of employment and the car park provided by the employer were part of the same functional space was irrelevant.[58]

In reaching this determination their Honours had regard to the purpose of the provision and the consequences, which were likely to have been unintended, if the functional space were treated as relevant. The Court found that the purpose of s 39A(1)(f) was not simply to tax a benefit. This was because s 39A(1)(f) was a 'carve out' from s 58G, which provided a blanket *exemption*. Therefore, 'the benefit to be taxed may be seen not as a car parking benefit per se ... but the additional benefit of having it provided "at or in the vicinity of" the employee's principal place of employment'.[59] Next, their Honours compared the promotion of the purpose in two scenarios: first, the current scenario, where the parking was provided 2 km from the primary place of employment but within the same functional space; and second, where the parking was provided in the CBD, also 2 km from the primary place of employment, but not within the same functional space. Edmonds and Gilmour JJ held:

> This divergence in tax result [that would occur should functional space be a relevant consideration] is not supported by the legislative purpose of s 39A(1)(f). The airport or hospital employee in the above example derives no greater benefit from the parking than does the CBD worker.[60]

Having determined that the general scope of the provision did not allow for consideration of whether the car parking was within the same functional space as the primary place of employment, their Honours applied the ordinary meaning to the facts – that is, they matched the facts with the law as interpreted. They noted that application in this case was 'a matter of evaluative judgment', and something courts are 'often required to make ... in various contexts'.[61] The fact that the employer considered it appropriate or convenient was not to the point given that not all car parking benefits were caught.[62] But the period of time taken by the shuttle bus[63] strengthened their Honours' conclusion, which was that the car parking provided by the appellant was not in the vicinity of their primary place of employment and therefore fringe benefits tax was not exigible in respect of the benefits.[64]

The interpretation of legislation is not wholly different from the interpretation of ordinary speech [1.5]

We are all familiar with conversational speech. Although speech is different in many ways from legislation and its interpretation, speech and legislation do share some common features. Differences between interpreting legislation and interpreting speech stem in part from

56 Ibid 162 [54].
57 Ibid 161 [50] (emphasis added by Edmonds and Gilmour JJ).
58 Ibid 162 [52].
59 Ibid 157 [30].
60 Ibid 162 [53].
61 Ibid 163 [59].
62 Ibid 163 [58].
63 Ibid 163 [60].
64 Ibid.

differences between the spoken and written word, which we will look at now in turn.[65] First, there is instinctiveness. Speech and social interaction is 'instinctive'; writing is not.[66]

Second, there is the audience. 'Speech presupposes the presence of a listener'.[67] In conversations 'we speak to those with whom we are on speaking terms. When we engage our conversational partners, we have an inkling of what they know and what they might be interested in learning'.[68] The audience for writing is more abstract,[69] for 'writing does not presuppose the presence (at the time of writing) of the reader'.[70]

Third, there are clues as to meaning. Speech involves some distinctive clues. 'In order to remain intelligible . . . oral language requires a great deal more repetition and redundancy'.[71] Also, with speech we have non-verbal cues. We have tone of voice.[72] And 'as we chat with [our conversational partner], we monitor their eyes, their face, and their posture'.[73]

Fourth, there is correctability. On the one hand, unlike writing, conversational speech involves a give-and-take – in conversation a listener can break into the conversation or follow up if 'they need clarification, or cannot swallow an assertion, or have something to add'.[74] On the other hand, while most speech acts are 'vanishing verbalizations', writing is recorded. As such it 'admits of correction'[75] and this facility 'brings a greater capacity for precision'.[76] Writing's permanence makes it a 'consultable product'.[77] It therefore offers more opportunities to distinguish between what is said and what is meant.[78]

Statutes add other differences. A statute is not 'an expression of individual thought to which is imparted the definiteness a single authorship can give'.[79] The legal interpreter cannot 'go to the

65 See generally Bernard S Jackson, *Making Sense in Law: Linguistic, Psychological and Semiotic Perspectives* (Deborah Charles Publications, 1995) 77–88.

66 Steven Pinker, *The Sense of Style: The Thinking Person's Guide to Writing in the 21st Century* (Penguin Books, 2014) 27, quoting Charles Darwin.

67 Bernard S Jackson, *Making Sense in Law: Linguistic, Psychological and Semiotic Perspectives* (Deborah Charles Publications, 1995) 83.

68 Steven Pinker, *The Sense of Style: The Thinking Person's Guide to Writing in the 21st Century* (Penguin Books, 2014) 27.

69 Robert J Connors, 'The Differences Between Speech and Writing: Ethos, Pathos, and Logos' (1979) 30(3) *College Composition and Communication* 285, 287.

70 Bernard S Jackson, *Making Sense in Law: Linguistic, Psychological and Semiotic Perspectives* (Deborah Charles Publications, 1995) 83.

71 Ibid 79.

72 Ibid 84.

73 Steven Pinker, *The Sense of Style: The Thinking Person's Guide to Writing in the 21st Century* (Penguin Books, 2014) 27.

74 Ibid 27–8.

75 Bernard S Jackson, *Making Sense in Law: Linguistic, Psychological and Semiotic Perspectives* (Deborah Charles Publications, 1995) 84.

76 Ibid 86.

77 Robert J Connors, 'The Differences Between Speech and Writing: Ethos, Pathos, and Logos' (1979) 30(3) *College Composition and Communication* 285, 288.

78 Bernard S Jackson, *Making Sense in Law: Linguistic, Psychological and Semiotic Perspectives* (Deborah Charles Publications, 1995) 86.

79 Felix Frankfurter, 'Some Reflections on the Reading of Statutes' (1947) 47 *Columbia Law Review* 527, 528.

writer and ask him or her what was intended'.[80] And a statute is read according to the 'rules' of statutory interpretation: 'A statute is not to be read as one would another document. Rather, a statute is read according to its own rules.'[81]

Despite these differences between speech and writing, and between speech and legislation, interpreting speech and statutory interpretation share common ground. Interpreting conversational speech 'is of an object',[82] namely words. Speech can be analysed according to constructions put on it. The starting point in arriving at legal meaning is the natural and ordinary meaning of the words used;[83] this is drawn from 'the ordinary usage of society'[84] or how a word is 'ordinarily understood in discourse'.[85] Speech is interpreted in the environment it is given – in other words, its 'context'.[86] In interpreting conversational speech, the making of implications is also a recognised method.[87] And the interpretation of speech is assisted by presumptions, 'a technique common to all speech acts, where inferences about meaning are drawn from expectations based upon past experience'.[88]

Example 1.4 *Minister for Immigration and Citizenship v Yucesan*[89]

A Sydney woman ('the first respondent') wished to marry a man who was a citizen of Turkey ('the visa applicant'). They had never met in person. They were introduced through their families – the custom in Turkish culture. The first respondent stated that she was shown photographs of the visa applicant and they communicated by SMS, email and telephone for three months before deciding to become engaged. The visa applicant applied for a Prospective Marriage (Temporary) (Class TO) visa. The first respondent was the sponsor. A delegate of the Minister refused the application on the basis that the applicant did not satisfy cl 300.214 of the *Migration Regulations 1994* (Cth). It provided that the parties to the proposed marriage must 'have met and be known to each other personally'. The delegate was not satisfied because they had never been physically in each other's company. On

80 Justice John Middleton, 'Statutory Interpretation: Mostly Common Sense?' (2016) 40 *Melbourne University Law Review* 626, 630. A legal interpreter is permitted to seek clarification of the mischief or purpose of a Bill that became the Act in question – see chapter 24.

81 Justice Susan Kenny, 'Current Issues in the Interpretation of Federal Legislation' (Speech, National Commercial Law Seminar Series, 3 September 2013) 4.

82 Joseph Raz, *Between Authority and Interpretation: On the Theory of Law and Practical Reason* (Oxford University Press, 2009) 226.

83 See **[15.2]** and **[15.3]**.

84 *Provincial Insurance Australia Pty Ltd v Consolidated Wood Products Pty Ltd* (1991) 25 NSWLR 541, 560 (Mahoney JA), approved in *Merrick Tyler Pty Ltd v Commissioner of Main Roads* [2015] WASCA 82, [41] (the Court).

85 *SZTAL v Minister for Immigration and Border Protection* (2017) 262 CLR 362, 368 [14] (Kiefel CJ, Nettle and Gordon JJ).

86 Robert J Connors, 'The Differences Between Speech and Writing: Ethos, Pathos, and Logos' (1979) 30(3) *College Composition and Communication* 285, 286, quoting Janet Emig, 'Writing as a Mode of Learning' (1977) 28(2) *College Composition and Communication* 124.

87 Oliver Jones, *Bennion on Statutory Interpretation: A Code* (LexisNexis, 6th ed, 2013) 460. For more detail see chapter 34.

88 *Federal Commissioner of Taxation v Tomaras* (2018) 265 CLR 434, 467 [100] (Edelman J).

89 (2008) 169 FCR 202.

appeal, the Migration Review Tribunal held that the ordinary meaning of the words 'met and be known to each other personally' extended to 'non physical person-to-person interactions'.[90]

The Minister applied for judicial review in the Federal Magistrates Court but that Court dismissed the application. The Minister appealed to the Full Court of the Federal Court. The Full Court allowed the appeal.

The intersection between the interpretation of speech and legal interpretation is briefly evident in the case. In considering the ordinary meaning of 'have met', the Court first consulted the *Macquarie Dictionary*. It noted that the primary dictionary meaning had the sense of two or more persons coming into each other's physical presence.

The Court added: 'Nevertheless it is true that the meaning of words evolves with time and also with technological progress. With the growth of the internet, the comment, "We met over the internet" would not surprise.'[91] From this passage it is evident that the Court took judicial notice of its experience with ordinary usage in the community, framed in the form of conversational speech, to assist it in arriving at the range of ordinary meanings. But whereas the Tribunal had implied that it was sufficient, legally speaking, for non-physical person-to-person interactions to be within the ordinary meaning,[92] the Full Court took account of factors other than the ordinary meaning,[93] as well as putting weight on the primary dictionary meaning.[94] It determined that 'have met' required 'the parties to have come into each other's company or physical presence'.[95]

Hence, the error made by the Tribunal and the Federal Magistrates Court was *not* in taking account of contemporary usage derived from ordinary speech; it was in placing determinative weight on that indication. Statutory interpretation is more than the determination of the range of ordinary meanings derived from current usage. When all the relevant interpretative factors were considered, the Magistrate had erred in holding that the construction adopted by the Tribunal was correct.[96]

[1.6] Statutory interpretation is dissimilar in major respects from formulating the rule of a case

Working with common law involves formulating the ratio decidendi or the rule of a case[97] arising from a dispute over common law. Working with legislation comparably involves its interpretation. At a general level these methods overlap. Both are concerned with ascertaining what the

90 Its reasons are quoted in *Minister for Immigration and Citizenship v Yucesan* (2008) 216 FLR 252, 255 [14] (Scarlett FM). See also *Minister for Immigration and Citizenship v Yucesan* (2008) 169 FCR 202, 204–5 [4] (the Court).

91 (2008) 169 FCR 202, 207 [17] (the Court).

92 Quoted in ibid 204–5 [4].

93 Namely the previous version of the law: ibid 207 [16]; statutory analogies: at 207–9 [18]–[26]; the legislative purpose: at 209 [27]–[28]; and common knowledge about marriage: at 209 [28]. The obligation of interpreters to take full account of the 'context' is considered in chapter 7 and following chapters.

94 Ibid 209 [28].

95 Ibid.

96 Ibid 209 [29].

97 Some judges make a distinction between the two. See *Woolcock Street Investments Pty Ltd v CDG Pty Ltd* (2004) 216 CLR 515, 542–3 [59]–[61] (McHugh J); *CSR Ltd v Eddy* (2005) 226 CLR 1, 11 [13] (Gleeson CJ, Gummow and Heydon JJ). For descriptions of the common law methods see *Woolcock Street Investments Pty Ltd v CDG Pty Ltd* (2004) 216 CLR 515, 542–3 [59]–[61] (McHugh J); *Gala v Preston* (1991) 172 CLR 243, 284 (Toohey J); *SZEEU v Minister for Immigration and Multicultural and Indigenous Affairs* (2006) 150 FCR 214, 247–8 [125]–[134] (Weinberg J).

law is. Both may involve ascertaining the reach of a statement of principle or the formulation of principle. For this purpose any such principle is read in context in both instances and a judge will attempt to harmonise the various sources. Both processes involve the exercise of judgement.

But at a specific level the respective methods are dissimilar in major respects. Indeed, '[t]he frequently repeated caution is against construing the terms of [common law] judgments as if they were the words of a statute'.[98] The tasks, the challenges and the contexts of common law and statutory interpretation are different. The tasks concern the workings of different arms of government. Put simply, the task in statutory interpretation concerns what a particular verbal formulation *means*. This involves 'the construction of the words the legislature has enacted'.[99] The task in ascertaining the rule of a case is more nebulous: to determine what principle an earlier case *stands for*.[100]

Arising from these different tasks, distinct challenges confront the 'interpreters' of common law and legislation. A court examining a general statement by the 'precedent court' may be confronted with the problem of whether the statement was a necessary element of the decision or whether it was merely obiter dictum (a mere passing observation).[101] Even if the statement is found to have been a necessary element, a further issue in determining the rule of the case is whether the point was in dispute.[102] A later court will also examine any proclaimed rule and may revise it if it determines it was stated too broadly or narrowly in the light of the material facts and other matters.[103] If no general rule is propounded, the later court will determine the principle the case stands for in the light of the reasons.[104] And in cases with multiple reasons for judgment, a particular problem can arise: what is the common ground?[105] Compare statutory interpretation: it involves a different challenge, namely resolving the ambiguity of particular words in legislation.

The contexts to which regard is had in meeting these respective challenges are vastly different. In ascertaining the ratio of a case, the contexts are primarily the case and the case system – the material facts, the issues, the reasoning, any ruling, the court order, and prior and subsequent cases.[106] In statutory interpretation, the contexts are those pertaining to the relevant parliament and executive rule-maker.[107] They include the parliamentary and rule-making processes.[108]

---

98 *Brennan v Comcare* (1994) 50 FCR 555, 572 (Gummow J).

99 *Taylor v The Owners – Strata Plan No 11564* (2014) 253 CLR 531, 549 [39] (French CJ, Crennan and Bell JJ). See also *R v Young* (1999) 46 NSWLR 681, 686 [5]–[6] (Spigelman CJ).

100 *Woolcock Street Investments Pty Ltd v CDG Pty Ltd* (2004) 216 CLR 515, 542–3 [59]–[61] (McHugh J); see also *Povey v Qantas Airways Ltd* (2005) 223 CLR 189, 216 [76] (McHugh J dissenting as to outcome in part).

101 *Gala v Preston* (1991) 172 CLR 243, 284 (Toohey J, quoting Julius Stone, *Precedent and Law* (Butterworths, 1985) 123); *SZEEU v Minister for Immigration and Multicultural and Indigenous Affairs* (2006) 150 FCR 214, 248 [135] (Weinberg J).

102 *Coleman v Power* (2004) 220 CLR 1, 44–5 [79] (McHugh J). See also *CSR Ltd v Eddy* (2005) 226 CLR 1, 11 [13] (Gleeson CJ, Gummow and Heydon JJ).

103 *Woolcock Street Investments Pty Ltd v CDG Pty Ltd* (2004) 216 CLR 515, 542–3 [59]–[61] (McHugh J).

104 Ibid 543–6 [63]–[71] (McHugh J).

105 *Victoria v Commonwealth* (1971) 122 CLR 353, 382 (Barwick CJ); *Uebergang v Australian Wheat Board* (1980) 145 CLR 266, 314 (Aickin J); *Boland v Yates Property Corporation Pty Ltd* (1999) 167 ALR 575, 616 [144] (Kirby J).

106 *SZEEU v Minister for Immigration and Multicultural and Indigenous Affairs* (2006) 150 FCR 214, 247 [129] (Weinberg J).

107 See chapter 7 and following chapters.

108 See chapter 24.

Functions

[1.7] Statutory interpretation contributes to law-making in the sense that the text of the statute, read with the interpretation, constitutes a new understanding of the law

Bennion pointed out that statutory interpretation 'keys into the whole system of law'.[109] It assists the resolution of disputes by providing for resolution of a question of law.[110]

Statutory interpretation also provides a precedent. The way in which it provides a precedent was recently described by Sackville AJA:

> The *ratio decidendi* of a case is:
>
> > Any rule of law expressly or implicitly treated by the [court] as a necessary step in reaching [its] conclusion having regard to the line of reasoning adopted by [it].
>
> Thus, if the meaning of a statute is disputed and the Court rules, as part of its justification for its conclusion, that it has one meaning rather than another, the ruling is the *ratio decidendi*.[111]

A court's ruling on an interpretative issue has been called a species of law-making:

> The dominance of statute law in our society might suggest that this interstitial or incremental law-making role of the judges has been much diminished. That is not the case because statutes require interpretation and contested interpretations require choices to be made between competing meanings. The making of such choices can be seen as a species of law-making.[112]

Nevertheless, the 'law-making' ability of the court is subject to several qualifications and constraints. First, the court's interpretation is not an independent source of law. It is the text passed by Parliament read with the court's interpretation that constitutes the new understanding of the law. As a result, courts contribute to, or bring about, law-making, but they are not legislators. In the memorable words of Donaldson J, '[judges] are not legislators, but finishers, refiners and polishers of legislation which comes to them in a state requiring varying degrees of further processing'.[113]

Second, as French CJ noted, in statutory interpretation the law-making contribution of a court is constrained by the language of the statute.[114] Third, it is also constrained by the requirement for there to be an issue between the parties.[115] Fourth, courts do not formulate legislative policy.[116] The effect of statutory interpretation is succinctly summed up by Gageler J, writing extracurially:

---

109 FAR Bennion, *Statutory Interpretation: A Code* (LexisNexis, 5th ed, 2008) 8.

110 A question of the sense of an expression, other than what it has in ordinary speech, is always a question of law: *Collector of Customs v Agfa-Gevaert Ltd* (1996) 186 CLR 389, 397 (the Court).

111 *Bligh Consulting Pty Ltd v Ausgrid* [2017] NSWCA 95, [121] (Sackville AJA, McColl JA agreeing at [1], Basten JA agreeing at [2]), quoting R Cross and JW Harris, *Precedent in English Law* (Clarendon Press, 4th ed, 1991) 72 (emphases in original judgment). Emphasis inserted by Sackville AJA. Sackville AJA added the interesting qualification that the ruling would be binding on a later case if the facts were not 'materially different': at [123].

112 Chief Justice Robert French, 'The Judicial Function in an Age of Statutes' (Speech, 2011 Goldring Memorial Lecture, 18 November 2011) 8.

113 *Corocraft Ltd v Pan American Airways Inc* [1969] 1 QB 616, 638.

114 Chief Justice Robert French, 'The Judicial Function in an Age of Statutes' (Speech, 2011 Goldring Memorial Lecture, 18 November 2011) 8. See also chapter 6.

115 See above discussion of ratio decidendi.

116 Stephen Gageler, 'Common Law Statutes and Judicial Legislation: Statutory Interpretation as a Common Law Process' (2011) 37(2) *Monash University Law Review* 1, 8.

> A court does not initiate legislation, nor does it formulate legislative policy. It is confined to the application of the statutory text, as enacted, to the case at hand and its declaration or exposition of the meaning of the statutory text occurs as an incident of that task. The legislative effect of such exposition of the statutory text as may be involved in the application of that text by a court to the case at hand is derivative and incidental.[117]

Example 1.5 *WorldAudio Ltd v Australian Communications and Media Authority*[118]

The applicants sought review of an alleged decision of the Australian Communications and Media Authority ('the Authority') under s 111 of the *Radiocommunications Act 1992* (Cth). That section expressly provided that the Authority may impose, vary or revoke a condition of an apparatus licence. The solicitors for the first applicant requested that the 'condition site' of the licence be changed. (Despite the condition, transmission had always occurred from another site.) The Authority replied that 'the [Authority] will not exercise its discretionary power under section 111 of the [Act] and vary the licence conditions in the terms proposed by [the first applicant]'.[119] The applicants challenged the alleged decision of the Authority not to exercise its power to change the condition of its licence.

In the Federal Court of Australia the Authority objected to the competency of the application, asserting the Court lacked jurisdiction under the *Administrative Decisions (Judicial Review) Act 1977* (Cth) ('ADJR Act') to try the application for review. To be reviewable under s 5 of that Act, the alleged decision was required to be a 'decision to which this Act applies'. That phrase is defined in s 3(1) and relevantly refers to 'a decision ... made ... under an enactment'. In *Australian Broadcasting Tribunal v Bond*[120] the High Court had interpreted the word 'decision', and the leading judgment of Mason CJ had established a precedent in this regard.[121] The *Bond* case had dealt with a challenge to certain interim findings of the Australian Broadcasting Tribunal in relation to broadcasting licences held by companies controlled by Alan Bond. In *WorldAudio* the Court cited the meaning that the High Court had given to 'decision' in the *Bond* case:

> In the further course of his reasons for judgment in *Bond* at 337, Mason CJ pointed out that 'a reviewable "decision" is one for which provision is made by or under a statute', which 'will generally, but not always, entail a decision which is final or operative and determinative, at least in a practical sense, of the issue of fact falling for consideration', so long of course 'that it be a substantive determination', as opposed to 'procedural determinations'.[122]

117 Ibid. The author explicitly elaborated on a point made by Lord Diplock: Sir Kenneth Diplock, 'The Courts as Legislators' in Brian W Harvey (ed), *The Lawyer and Justice* (Sweet & Maxwell, 1978) 263, 266–7.

118 (2006) 149 FCR 462.

119 Ibid 468 [14] (Conti J).

120 (1990) 170 CLR 321.

121 Brennan J agreed at ibid 365 and Deane J relevantly agreed at 369. The reasons of Toohey and Gaudron JJ differed.

122 (2006) 149 FCR 462, 472 [28] (Conti J).

The Authority argued that its decision-making merely constituted a withholding from consideration of a request of the applicants to change the site condition. Therefore, they continued, it had not exercised a power under s 111 and the application did not fall within s 5, read with the *Bond* interpretation that was binding on the Court.

The Court disagreed.[123] Applying the jurisdictional test in the ADJR Act read with the *Bond* precedent, the Court found against the respondent's objection to competency:

> Thus by way of reflection of the dictum I have cited from *Bond*, . . . the Authority indicated to the applicants the position which it had adopted or taken as inherently and essentially indicative of decision-making on its part, the same having for instance the 'character or quality of finality', and constituting and involving 'an outcome reflecting something in the nature of a determination of an application' within the scope of that dictum of Mason CJ in *Bond* I have earlier cited. That communication of the Authority constituted or involved a decision 'at least in a practical sense, of the issue of fact falling for consideration'. It was 'a substantive determination' as opposed to a 'procedural determination', to adopt the Chief Justice's further dictum in *Bond*.[124]

123 Ibid 483 [56].

124 Ibid 483 [59].

A MODERN HISTORY OF KEY CONCEPTS

2

Overview

Contemporary statutory interpretation law involves, broadly, consideration of the statutory text, taking account of its full context and having regard to its purpose. These three concepts have loosely existed in statutory interpretation law for centuries, providing the basis for determining the legislative intent of a statute to varying degrees. This chapter considers the relatively recent history of these key concepts, starting at the beginning of the 20th century. Having some basic knowledge and understanding of this recent history enhances understanding of contemporary concepts and provides historical context to the current law and older cases. Following federation in 1901, Australia continued to be bound, and influenced, by English law. The English approach to interpretation placed considerable emphasis on the grammatical meaning of text, with limited regard to context and purpose. Despite that, the seeds of contemporary concepts are discernible in that approach. In the second half of the 1900s, dissatisfaction with what was seen as the rigid and inconsistent approach of English law grew in both Australia and the United Kingdom. Ultimately, this led to pivotal statutory reforms in the Interpretation Acts of all Australian jurisdictions, commencing in the 1980s, which established new fundamental principles for interpretation. This was followed by similar developments in the common law in the 1980s and 1990s. These legislative and common law changes expanded on the concepts already existing in a limited form and provided the foundation for contemporary law. Since then, there have been further legislative changes in some jurisdictions, but these have consolidated fundamental principles rather than marking any significant shift. [2.1]

Approach to statutory interpretation: 1900s to 1970s

Understanding the recent evolution of statutory interpretation enhances understanding of contemporary concepts and prior case law [2.2]

Statutes in some form can be traced back at least to the 13th century.[1] But the courts 'had no ordered ideas on the subject'[2] of interpretation. Legislation and a body of law that modern lawyers might recognise arguably did not begin to develop until the 15th and 16th

1 JS Emmett, 'Early Statutes Shaping the Common Law' in JT Gleeson, JA Watson and RCA Higgins (eds), *Historical Foundations of Australian Law: Volume 1 Institutions, Concepts and Personalities* (Federation Press, 2013) 115, 116–24; Theodore FT Plucknett, *Concise History of the Common Law* (Little, Brown, 1956) 320–3.

2 Sir John Dyson, 'The Shifting Sands of Statutory Interpretation' (Conference Paper, Legislation and the Supreme Court, 9 October 2010) 3.

centuries.[3] The evolution of that law over the centuries has been long, complex and fascinating, inextricably linked to the development of the separation of powers doctrine, the emergence of parliamentary democracy, judicial attitudes to the common law, the development of statutes themselves, the growth of parliamentary law-making, drafting approaches, and the gradual dissolution of Australian ties to English law.

It is beyond the scope of this book to trace such an extensive history.[4] This chapter provides a snapshot of more recent developments, starting with the beginning of the 20th century. It is important to understand this relatively recent historical background for at least two reasons.

As a High Court judge has observed, we need to look at the history of a law and see how it 'took shape' to help us 'see more clearly the shape of the law of to-day'.[5] Understanding recent historical context enhances our understanding of the terminology and concepts of contemporary law because that history informs us how they 'took shape'. This knowledge also has pragmatic value. Understanding historical context helps the contemporary reader to read and appreciate judicial decisions from the 1900s when examining them for contemporary use.

[2.3] For a large part of the 20th century, the Australian approach to statutory interpretation was based on English law: legislative intent was inferred by an approach focusing on the plain, grammatical meaning of the text, with a limited regard to context and purpose

In 1901 the Commonwealth of Australia was established.[6] This marked a new era of evolving self-governance for Australia. With respect to the law, Australia would not cut all ties to the English legislature and court hierarchy until the final connections were extinguished in 1986.[7] Consequently, for a large part of the 20th century, Australian statutory interpretation law was heavily influenced, if not bound, by the 'settled rules of construction' enunciated by English superior courts.[8]

---

3 Ashley Black, 'Development of Principles of Statutory Interpretation' (Speech, Francis Forbes Society for Australian Legal History, 1 October 2013) 5, citing, among others, Theodore FT Plucknett, *Concise History of the Common Law* (Little, Brown, 1956); JS Emmett, 'Early Statutes Shaping the Common Law' in JT Gleeson, JA Watson and RCA Higgins (eds), *Historical Foundations of Australian Law – Volume 1 Institutions, Concepts and Personalities* (Federation Press, 2013); JH Baker, *An Introduction to English Legal History* (Oxford University Press, 4th ed, 2002).

4 For more extensive treatments, see Theodore FT Plucknett, *Statutes and Their Interpretation in the First Half of the Fourteenth Century* (Cambridge at the University Press, 1922); Samuel E Thorne, *A Discourse upon the Exposicion & Understandinge of Statutes, with Sir Thomas Egerton's Additions* (Huntington Library, 1942); Ashley Black, 'Development of Principles of Statutory Interpretation' (Speech, Francis Forbes Society for Australian Legal History, 1 October 2013); John Dyson, 'The Shifting Sands of Statutory Interpretation' (Conference Paper, Legislation and the Supreme Court, 9 October 2010); William D Popkin, *Statutes in Court: The History and Theory of Statutory Interpretation* (Duke University Press, 1999) 9; George Williams, Sean Brennan and Andrew Lynch, *Blackshield and Williams Australian Constitutional Law and Theory – Commentary and Materials* (Federation Press, 7th ed, 2018) 29.

5 *A-G (Vic) v Commonwealth* (1962) 107 CLR 529, 595 (Windeyer J).

6 *Commonwealth of Australia Constitution Act 1900* (Imp) 63 & 64 Vict, c 12.

7 *Australia Act 1986* (Cth) and *Australia Act 1986* (UK). See George Williams, Sean Brennan and Andrew Lynch, *Blackshield and Williams Australian Constitutional Law and Theory: Commentary and Materials* (Federation Press, 7th ed, 2018) ch 3.

8 *Amalgamated Society of Engineers v Adelaide Steamship Co Ltd* (1920) 28 CLR 129, 148 (Knox CJ, Isaacs, Rich and Starke JJ).

The seeds of the modern iterations of text, context and purpose are evident in 20th-century law. But the scope of, and weight given to, those notions differed. Further, a cohesive approach to statutory interpretation during this time is difficult to articulate. The emphasis on grammatical meaning coexisted with the mischief and, to a lesser extent, golden so-called rules as well as other indicia that permitted a limited regard to context and purpose. There was inconsistency in recourse to extraneous materials. Ultimately, this state of affairs precipitated the legislative and common law developments of the 1980s and 1990s, which amplified the notions of context and purpose and led to the broadly settled contemporary framework.

(a) **Legislative intent**

At the beginning of the 1900s, Australian courts were following the English approach to statutory interpretation, which included, just like contemporary law, the guiding concept of legislative intent. This concept has existed at common law in statutory interpretation for (literally) centuries. It has been traced back to the 16th century, with 'scattered examples' even earlier.[9] It has been suggested that the concept was used in the works of Aristotle more than two thousand years ago.[10] Very early notions of legislative intent were concerned with the *actual* subjective intent of the lawmakers. Judges may have had personal knowledge of the legislature's 'intent' due to the judge's role in law-making.[11] If they did not have actual knowledge, they may have consulted with their 'legislator brethren'.[12]

Over the centuries, institutional, political and other forces meant that the judiciary gradually separated from the legislature and such 'personal knowledge' was no longer possible.[13] One consequence of this was that the actual, subjective intent of the lawmakers was no longer the exclusive object of interpretation.[14] It remained, said our first Chief Justice of the High Court of Australia, 'the first duty of the Court . . . to ascertain, if possible, the intention of the legislature' when construing statutes.[15] At the beginning of the 20th century, this intent was understood as being expressed by the statutory language:

> The only safe and legitimate guide to the legislative intention is the language of the legislature itself fairly interpreted.[16]

---

9 Samuel E Thorne, *A Discourse upon the Exposicion & Understandinge of Statutes, with Sir Thomas Egerton's Additions* (Huntington Library, 1942) 59 n 125.

10 Horst Lucke, 'Statutes and the Intention of the Lawmaker as the Ultimate Guide to Their Applicability: History and Prospects' (2010) 45 *Supreme Court History Program Yearbook* 1, 2 n 2.

11 Theodore FT Plucknett, *Statutes and Their Interpretation in the First Half of the Fourteenth Century* (Cambridge at the University Press, 1922) 49–50.

12 Sir John Dyson, 'The Shifting Sands of Statutory Interpretation' (Conference Paper, Legislation and the Supreme Court, 9 October 2010) 4.

13 Theodore FT Plucknett, *Statutes and Their Interpretation in the First Half of the Fourteenth Century* (Cambridge at the University Press, 1922) 53–6; Theodore FT Plucknett, *Concise History of the Common Law* (Little, Brown, 1956) 331–2.

14 Horst Lucke, 'Statutes and the Intention of the Lawmaker as the Ultimate Guide to Their Applicability: History and Prospects' (2010) 45 *Supreme Court History Program Yearbook* 1, 7.

15 *Borough of Glebe v Lukey (Australian Gaslight Co)* (1904) 1 CLR 158, 175 (Griffith CJ).

16 *Phillips v Lynch* (1907) 5 CLR 12, 27–8 (Isaacs J). See also *Municipal Council of Sydney v Commonwealth* (1904) 1 CLR 208, 239 (O'Connor J), citing *River Wear Commissioners v Adamson* (1877) 2 App Cas 743, 763 (Lord Blackburn).

As with current law, legislative intent was expressed as an inference.[17] Fundamentally, this is still the notion of legislative intent.[18] There is some contemporary discourse about what 'intent' precisely represents.[19] But the more significant change has been how the language should be 'fairly interpreted' to arrive at the legislative intent.

(b) Focus on text, but within its intrinsic context

In the mid-1800s, Lord Chief Justice Tindal in the House of Lords stated in the *Sussex Peerage Case*:

> If the words of the statute are in themselves precise and unambiguous, then no more can be necessary than to expound those words in their natural and ordinary sense. The words themselves alone do, in such case, best declare the intention of the lawgiver.[20]

This approach was known as the 'literal rule'. It was inherited by the newly formed High Court of Australia in the early 1900s. The classic early Australian statement of this so-called rule is that of High Court Justice Higgins in the 1920 decision of *Amalgamated Society of Engineers v Adelaide Steamship Co Ltd*:[21]

> The question is, what does the language mean; and when we find what the language means, in its ordinary and natural sense, it is our duty to obey that meaning, even if we think the result to be inconvenient or impolitic or improbable.[22]

While this approach clearly emphasised the grammatical meaning of the text, it was not quite as clinical or restrictive as the above quotes might first suggest. First, as indicated by both Lord Tindal and Justice Higgins, the courts did consider the 'ordinary' meaning of statutory words.[23] Second, many of the syntactical canons of construction that we still use today, such as *ejusdem generis*, were well-established tools for providing guidance on word meaning.[24] These canons assume the relevance of intrinsic textual context to meaning.[25]

Third, in determining whether the language was clear, it was 'firmly established' that the 'whole document must be looked at' to ascertain the meaning of the text.[26] Both Higgins J and the other majority judges in *Amalgamated Society of Engineers v Adelaide Steamship Co Ltd*[27] confirmed this, as did many other cases.[28] Consequently, if, *when read in the context of the whole*

---

17 *Sovar v Henry Lane Pty Ltd* (1967) 116 CLR 397, 405 (Kitto J).

18 See **[4.4]**.

19 See **[4.5]**.

20 (1844) 11 Cl & Fin 85, 143; 8 ER 1034, 1057 (Lord Tindal CJ).

21 (1920) 28 CLR 129.

22 Ibid 162 (Higgins J). See also *Sargood Brothers v Commonwealth* (1910) 11 CLR 258, 279 (O'Connor J), citing *Tasmania v Commonwealth and Victoria* (1904) 1 CLR 329, 339 (Griffith CJ), which adopted the *Sussex Peerage Case* statement (1844) 11 Cl & Fin 85, 143; 8 ER 1034, 1057 (Lord Tindal CJ).

23 See also *Markell v Wollaston* (1906) 4 CLR 141, 150 (O'Connor J).

24 See Roy Wilson and Brian Galpin, *Maxwell on the Interpretation of Statutes* (Sweet & Maxwell, 11th ed, 1962) 320–30, citing decisions reaching back hundreds of years.

25 See chapter 18.

26 *Huddart Parker & Co Pty Ltd v Moorehead* (1909) 8 CLR 330, 388 (Isaacs J).

27 (1920) 28 CLR 129, 149 (Knox CJ, Isaacs, Rich and Starke JJ), 161–2 (Higgins J).

28 See, eg, *Metropolitan Gas Company v Federated Gas Employees' Industrial Union* (1925) 35 CLR 449, 455 (Isaacs and Rich JJ); *Broken Hill South Ltd v Commissioner of Taxation (NSW)* (1937) 56 CLR 337, 371 (Dixon J).

instrument, the meaning of a provision was 'literally clear and unambiguous' then the unqualified words were to be given effect.[29] The language of the whole instrument was to be applied through consideration of the subject matter of the statute.[30]

Consideration of the whole instrument did have limitations. For example, reference to the long title, headings and preambles was usually subject to the existence of ambiguity.[31] Some other components, such as marginal notes and punctuation, were regarded with greater scepticism and not routinely considered.[32]

Following is an illustration of the relevance of intrinsic context to meaning from the early 1900s.

Example 2.1 *Metropolitan Gas Company v Federated Gas Employees' Industrial Union*[33]

In 1925 there was a strike by members of the Federated Gas Employees' Industrial Union ('the Union'). These members were employed by two contractors performing work for the Metropolitan Gas Company ('the Company'). The Union had requested the contractors adopt certain working conditions. The Union and the Company were parties to a federal award, but the contractors were not parties to the award, nor bound by it.

Section 6A of the *Commonwealth Conciliation and Arbitration Act 1904* (Cth) provided:

> No person or organization bound by an award of the Court, or entitled to the benefit of an award of the Court, shall do anything in the nature of a lock-out or strike, or continue any lock-out or strike.
>
> Penalty: one thousand pounds.

The Company argued that the strike was prohibited under s 6A as the Union was bound by the federal award, and its members and the Union were doing something 'in the nature of a ... strike'. The Company argued that the word 'strike' was unqualified and grammatically could relate to any strike anywhere in Australia. The Union argued that 'strike' meant a strike in relation to a dispute for which an award had been made. As the dispute involving the contractors was not the subject of an award, s 6A was not applicable to the strike.

Isaacs and Rich JJ stated:

> It is a received canon of interpretation that every passage in a document must be read, not as if it were entirely divorced from its context, but as part of the whole instrument ...

29 *Metropolitan Gas Company v Federated Gas Employees' Industrial Union* (1925) 35 CLR 449, 455 (Isaacs and Rich JJ).

30 *Huddart Parker & Co Pty Ltd v Moorehead* (1909) 8 CLR 330, 388 (Isaacs J). See, eg, *Tasmania v Commonwealth and Victoria* (1904) 1 CLR 329, 339 (Griffith CJ); *Welsbach Light Co of Australasia Ltd v Commonwealth* (1916) 22 CLR 268, 276 (Griffith CJ); *R v Wilson; Ex parte Kisch* (1934) 52 CLR 234, 244 (Dixon J)

31 See, eg, *Sussex Peerage Case* (1844) 11 Cl & Fin 85, 143; 8 ER 1034, 1057 (Lord Tindal CJ) (discussing the preamble); *Bowtell v Goldsbrough, Mort & Co Ltd* (1905) 3 CLR 444, 451 (Griffith CJ) (discussing the preamble); *Birch v Allen* (1942) 65 CLR 621, 625–6 (Latham CJ) (discussing the long title).

32 See The Law Commission and the Scottish Law Commission, *The Interpretation of Statutes* (Report, Law Com No 21, Scot Law Com No 11, 9 June 1969) 25–7.

33 (1925) 35 CLR 449.

> If, when so read, the meaning of the section is literally clear and unambiguous, nothing remains but to give effect to the unqualified words. But, unless that so appears, other considerations arise to assist the Court to the true construction.[34]

Their Honours considered s 6A in the context of the other provisions in the Act. In particular, they noted s 6, which prohibited industrial action before an award as a means of settling the dispute by an award. Section 6A, they said, was its counterpart, forbidding action after the award had been made in relation to the dispute settled by the award. They also relied on other parts of the Act, including the long title, headings and a defined term, and noted the desirability of a construction that permitted the 'smooth working' of the statutory scheme.[35] They concluded:

> Consequently, both the general scheme of the Act, and the express heading governing the whole fasciculus of sections contained in Part II, operate to limit the generality of the words 'lock-out' and 'strike' in sec 6A.[36]

Those words, they said, mean a lock-out or strike in relation to a matter the subject of an award. They confirmed this preferred construction by noting that the Company's proposed construction led to inconsistent and absurd consequences.[37] Higgins J came to the same result on a different basis, but noted he was 'inclined to agree' with Isaacs and Rich JJ's 'view on the law'.[38]

The above case also illustrates that consideration of the consequences of a construction was a valid interpretative factor. This factor can be distinguished from the so-called golden rule that had emerged in the 19th century, usually traced back to *Grey v Pearson*[39] in 1857. This 'rule' provided that the grammatical meaning be adopted, unless it led to 'some absurdity, or some repugnance or inconsistency *with the rest of the instrument* ... but no farther'.[40] The absurdity must be 'so great' as to convince the court 'that the intention [of Parliament] could not have been to use them in their ordinary signification'.[41] The onus of showing that the words 'do not mean what they say' lay 'heavily' on the party who alleged it.[42]

It has been observed that the 'golden rule' was 'in less favour' in the 20th century than it was in the 19th century.[43] Its precise relationship to the relevance of 'consequences' is not clear, but

34 Ibid 455.

35 Ibid.

36 Ibid 456.

37 Ibid 455–7.

38 Ibid 461.

39 (1857) 6 HLC 61, 106; 10 ER 1216, 1234 (Lord Wensleydale).

40 Ibid (emphasis added).

41 *River Wear Commissioners v Adamson* (1877) 2 App Cas 743, 764–5 (Lord Blackburn).

42 *Australian Boot Trade Employees' Federation v Whybrow & Co* (1910) 11 CLR 311, 341 (Higgins J), citing *Richards v McBride* (1881) 8 QBD 119, 122 (Lord Tenterton CJ) and *Grey v Pearson* (1857) 6 HLC 61, 106; 10 ER 1216, 1234 (Lord Wensleydale).

43 Peter Brett, 'The Theory of Interpreting Statutes' (1953) 2(2) *University of Queensland Law Journal* 99, 101. However, it was not absent. See, eg, *Australian Boot Trade Employees' Federation v Whybrow & Co* (1910) 11 CLR 311, 341–2 (Higgins J); *Broken Hill South Ltd v Commissioner of Taxation (NSW)* (1937) 56 CLR 337, 371 (Dixon J); *Corporate Affairs Commission (NSW) v Yuill* (1991) 172 CLR 319, 340 (Gaudron J).

one commentator has suggested that its use by Australian courts in the 1900s was largely confined to correcting drafting mistakes in the wording of the statute that led to absurdity.[44]

(c) Limited regard to mischief or purpose

Twentieth-century law also recognised a limited version of legislative 'purpose'. The 'mischief rule' had been established in the 1584 decision of *Heydon's Case.*[45] *Heydon's Case* provided that, where the language of a statute is ambiguous on its face, the courts may look for the 'mischief' and 'defect' that the common law did not provide for, and the remedy that Parliament had resolved by statute to 'cure' that mischief.[46] It remained part of the law in the 1900s.[47] It was a limited tool, as ambiguity on the face of the statute was required, and the notion of 'mischief' was focused on the pre-existing deficiency of the common law. Thorne has described the mischief rule as evidence of an effort by the judiciary to make the interpretation of statutes 'something more than merely a grammatical exercise'.[48] Although the concept of mischief (as opposed to the rule) still has relevance today, it has been eclipsed to a large extent by the contemporary notion of purpose (see **[2.5]**).

Apart from the mischief rule, courts made not infrequent references to the 'object' or 'purpose' of a provision or Act, as apparent from the statute. For example, in the 1907 case of *Phillips v Lynch*,[49] the object of the Act, as evidenced by the statute and in particular the long title, was an important factor for determining the meaning of enabling words in the *Crown Lands Act Amendment Act 1903* (NSW).[50]

(d) Inconsistencies with respect to extrinsic context

In the 1900s it was accepted that if the words of the statute were ambiguous, it might be necessary to consider the background of the statute to assist in ascertaining the legislative intent. In *Tasmania v Commonwealth and Victoria*,[51] O'Connor J explained:

> The intention of the enactment is to be gathered from its words. If the words are plain, effect must be given to them; if they are doubtful, the intention of the legislature is to be gathered from the other provisions of the Statute aided by a consideration of *surrounding circumstances*.[52]

Such 'surrounding circumstances', his Honour said, included 'contemporaneous circumstances' such as the history of the law and historical facts.[53] This was generally taken to include the

44 DC Pearce, *Statutory Interpretation in Australia* (Butterworths, 1st ed, 1974) 15, referring to *President of the Shire of Arapiles v Board of Land and Works* (1904) 1 CLR 679, 687 (Griffith CJ).

45 *Heydon's Case* (1584) 3 Co Rep 7a; 76 ER 637.

46 Ibid 7b; 76 ER 637, 638.

47 See, eg, *National Mutual Life Association of Australasia Ltd v Godrich* (1909) 10 CLR 1, 9 (Griffith CJ), 34 (Isaacs J); *Woolworths Ltd v Crotty* (1942) 66 CLR 603, 618 (Latham CJ); *Ward v The Queen* (1980) 142 CLR 308, 332 (Stephen J).

48 SE Thorne, 'Equity of a Statute and Heydon's Case' (1936) 31(2) *Illinois Law Review* 202, 215.

49 (1907) 5 CLR 12.

50 Ibid 22–3 (O'Connor J), 31(Higgins J). See also *Municipal Council of Sydney v Commonwealth* (1904) 1 CLR 208, 239 (O'Connor J), citing *River Wear Commissioners v Adamson* (1877) 2 App Cas 743, 763 (Lord Blackburn); *Potter v Minahan* (1908) 7 CLR 277, 304, 306 (O'Connor J), 323 (Higgins J); *R v Wilson; Ex parte Kisch* (1934) 52 CLR 234, 244 (Dixon J).

51 (1904) 1 CLR 329.

52 Ibid 359 (O'Connor J) (emphasis added). See also *Evans v Williams* (1910) 11 CLR 550, 571 (Isaacs J).

53 *Tasmania v Commonwealth and Victoria* (1904) 1 CLR 329, 359 (O'Connor J). See also *Miller v Commonwealth* (1904) 1 CLR 668, 673–4 (Griffith CJ); *Sovar v Henry Lane Pty Ltd* (1967) 116 CLR 397, 405 (Kitto J).

common law and legislation that existed at enactment, and any matter generally known of which the court was prepared to give judicial notice. Recourse to statutes *in pari materia* was also permitted.[54] Further, dictionaries were regularly consulted for assistance with ascertaining an 'ordinary' meaning, just as today.[55]

Less clear was the permissibility of reference to extraneous materials reflecting the legislative history of the statute, such as speeches in Parliament, parliamentary committee reports and changes to a Bill during the parliamentary process. The so-called exclusionary rule stated that the intention of Parliament 'as expressed in the statute' should not be 'modified or controlled in a court by reference to any such material'.[56] But the precise scope of this 'rule' was unclear and the judicial rhetoric did not always match judicial practice. For example, in 1977 in *Commissioner for Prices and Consumer Affairs (SA) v Charles Moore (Australia) Ltd*[57] all High Court justices, except Murphy J, considered the prohibition on recourse to parliamentary material as absolute, even where the material had direct bearing on the interpretative issue.[58] Several noted that exclusion of such materials was a rule of longstanding and highest authority.[59] Mason J observed that the rule was 'so firmly entrenched' that it was 'a matter for Parliament to decide' whether an alteration should be made.[60] Yet, in *Municipal Council of Sydney v Commonwealth*,[61] Griffith CJ suggested that parliamentary debates may be referred to in order to see 'the subject-matter of discussion' and 'the evil to be remedied', seemingly alluding to the mischief rule.[62] There also appeared to be an exception for recourse to law reform and other committee reports where there was ambiguity.[63]

[2.4] **Interpretation Acts have existed in Australia since the 19th century, but these earlier versions did not suggest any particular interpretative approach and primarily consisted of presumptive rules to simplify and shorten legislative language**

The Bill for what became the *Acts Interpretation Act 1901* (Cth) ('the AIA') was the first Bill to be introduced into the newly established federal Parliament in 1901.[64] But it was not the first Australian

54 See, eg, *Phillips v Lynch* (1907) 5 CLR 12, 20 (O'Connor J); *Ramaciotti v Federal Commissioner of Taxation* (1920) 29 CLR 49, 53 (Knox CJ).

55 See, eg, *Markell v Wollaston* (1906) 4 CLR 141, 150 (O'Connor J); *McKernan v Fraser* (1931) 46 CLR 343, 360 (Dixon J), 373 (Evatt J)

56 *South Australia v Commonwealth* (1942) 65 CLR 373, 409 (Latham CJ); *Victoria v Commonwealth* (1975) 134 CLR 81, 152–4 (Gibbs CJ). The decision in *Millar v Taylor* (1769) 4 Burr 2303; 98 ER 210 is usually cited as the decision establishing the exclusionary rule. Cf John J Magyar, 'Debunking *Millar v Taylor*: The History of the Prohibition of Legislative History' (2020) 41(1) *Statute Law Review* 32.

57 (1977) 139 CLR 449.

58 Ibid 457 (Barwick CJ), 461 (Gibbs J), 470 (Stephen J), 477–8 (Mason J). Murphy J permitted recourse to parliamentary statements on the basis that the statute was ambiguous and the statements relevant: at 480.

59 Ibid 457 (Barwick CJ), 461 (Gibbs J), 477–8 (Mason J).

60 Ibid 478. See also at 461 (Gibbs J).

61 (1904) 1 CLR 208.

62 Ibid 213–14.

63 See, eg, *Eastman Photographic Material Co Ltd v Comptroller-General of Patents, Designs and Trade Marks* [1898] AC 571, 575 (Lord Halsbury); *Bitumen and Oil Refineries (Australia) Ltd v Commissioner for Government Transport* (1955) 92 CLR 200, 211–12 (the Court). For other cases, see Jocelynne A Scutt, 'Statutory Interpretation and Recourse to Extrinsic Aids' (1984) 58(9) *Australian Law Journal* 483, 484–6; P Brazil, 'Legislative History and the Sure and True Interpretation of Statutes in General and the Constitution in Particular' (1961) 4(1) *University of Queensland Law Journal* 1.

64 Commonwealth, House of Representatives, *Votes and Proceedings No 2* (10th May 1901) 11. It was the second Act to be enacted.

Interpretation Act. Many of the colonies had passed 'shortening' and other interpretation legislation as early as the 1840s and 1850s.[65] These early versions of interpretation legislation, including the AIA, were primarily language and drafting tools to shorten the need for repetition across legislation. As explained by then Attorney-General Deakin in relation to the Bill for the AIA, it was

> a measure providing for the simplification of the language of Acts of Parliament, and the shortening of their terminology. It constitutes in a sense a legal dictionary . . . which must be used over and over again in almost every Act of Parliament.[66]

Some early Acts provided technical rules relating to, for example, commencement and repeals. Some contained provisions more relevant to a common law principle. For example, the AIA provided that headings and schedules were deemed to form part of the Act – a legislative nod to the concept of intrinsic context.[67] But the Acts did not contain provisions requiring any particular approach to interpretation (other than reinforcing the centrality of the intention of Parliament by the use of the language of 'intent').[68] Statutory interpretation law remained dominated by the common law.

Pivotal Interpretation Act amendments: 1980s

By the 1970s, dissatisfaction with the state of the law was evident; this led to the enactment of s 15AA of the *Acts Interpretation Act 1901* (Cth), which paved the way for the broader contemporary concepts of purpose and context [2.5]

(a) Commonwealth developments

By the second half of the 20th century in both Australia and the United Kingdom, there was growing dissatisfaction with the state of statutory interpretation law. In the United Kingdom, this was reflected in two influential reports: one by the UK Law Commission and the Scottish Law Commission in 1969 ('the 1969 Report')[69] and one by a government-appointed committee chaired by The Right Honourable Sir David Renton in 1975, responsible for 'the Renton Report'.[70]

The 1969 Report examined the state of the law, noting the limitations of the literal, mischief and golden 'rules'.[71] It recommended 'limited' statutory intervention in four areas, one of which was to 'emphasise the importance in the interpretation of a provision of (i) the general legislative purpose'.[72] It also recognised that legislation was not 'made in a vacuum' and

---

65 See, eg, *Acts Shortening Act 1852* (NSW) 16 Vict, c 1; *An Ordinance for Avoiding Unnecessary Repetitions 1843* (SA) 7 Vict, c 1; *An Act for Shortening and Explaining the Language Used in Acts of Council, Legal Proceedings, Deeds and Other Documents 1853* (Tas) 17 Vict, c 1; *An Act to Interpret and Shorten the Language of Acts of Council 1851* (Vic) 15 Vict, c 1; *Shortening Ordinance 1844* (WA) 8 Vict, c 11. For further historical Acts, see Dennis Pearce, *Interpretation Acts in Australia* (LexisNexis, 1st ed, 2018) 3–4.

66 Commonwealth, *Parliamentary Debates*, House of Representatives, 6 June 1901, 789.

67 *Acts Interpretation Act 1901* (Cth) s 13, as enacted.

68 See **[25.3]**.

69 The Law Commission and the Scottish Law Commission, *The Interpretation of Statutes* (Report, Law Com No 21, Scot Law Com No 11, 9 June 1969).

70 Committee Appointed by the Lord President of the Council, *Committee on The Preparation of Legislation* (Comnd 6053, May 1975) ('the Renton Report').

71 The Law Commission and the Scottish Law Commission, *The Interpretation of Statutes* (Report, Law Com No 21, Scot Law Com No 11, 9 June 1969) 17–20.

72 Ibid 49.

examined the merits of recourse to a broad range of extrinsic materials, including parliamentary debates.[73]

The Renton Report focused on the drafting and making of legislation.[74] But it acknowledged the relationship between legislative drafting and interpretation, and endorsed the 1969 Report's recommendation to enact a statutory provision that required the adoption of a construction that promotes the legislative purpose of a provision.[75]

The situation in Australia, either precipitated by or reinforced by these English developments, reflected the English commentary.[76] The dissatisfaction was compounded by a period in the 1970s of what was perceived as an unnecessary literalist approach by the High Court. Commentators, legal and political, expressed concern about the High Court's 'emphasis on literalism and its refusal to look to the spirit of legislation *as well as* to its letter'.[77] Much of this criticism focused on a series of decisions of the High Court on Commonwealth tax legislation that were regarded as 'over-literal interpretations of Commonwealth statutes that have tended to defeat the intentions of the legislature'.[78]

Against this background, a symposium on statutory interpretation, attended by representatives of all arms of government, was held by the Commonwealth Attorney-General's Department in Canberra in March 1981. The general consensus of the symposium was that 'it cannot be pretended that the principles of statutory interpretation form the most stable, consistent or logically satisfying part of our jurisprudence'.[79] There were varying views about the adequacy of the mischief rule.[80] It was noted that, unlike the United Kingdom where a purposive approach was enjoying growing judicial support, there were still 'strong strands of literalism' in the Australian judiciary.[81]

A few months later, in May 1981, the government introduced the Statute Law Revision Bill 1981 (Cth) into the Senate. Among other things, it proposed a new provision, s 15AA, for

73 Ibid 27–37.

74 See **[10.7]**.

75 Committee Appointed by the Lord President of the Council, *Committee on The Preparation of Legislation* (Comnd 6053, May 1975) 135, 143–4, 157. A provision to this affect was in the UK Interpretation of Legislation Bill 1979, but was not enacted. See Jeffrey Barnes, 'Statutory Interpretation, Law Reform and Sampford's Theory of the Disorder of Law – Part One' (1994) 22(1) *Federal Law Review* 116, 149–54.

76 See, eg, Peter Brett 'The Theory of Interpreting Statutes' (1953) 2(2) *University of Queensland Law Journal* 99, 103; Herbert Mayo 'The Interpretation of Statutes' (1955) 29(4) *Australian Law Journal* 204. The High Court itself referred to the 'rigid rules of English law governing interpretation' in *Bitumen and Oil Refineries (Australia) Ltd v Commissioner for Government Transport* (1955) 92 CLR 200, 212 (the Court).

77 David Solomon, 'The Legislative Record of the Australian Parliament' in JR Nethercote (ed), *Parliament and Bureaucracy: Parliamentary Scrutiny of Administration: Prospects and Problems in the 1980s* (Hale & Iremonger, 1982) 135, 140 (emphasis in original).

78 Anonymous, 'Statutory Guidelines for Interpreting Commonwealth Statutes (Current Topics)' (1981) 55(10) *Australian Law Journal* 711, 711.

79 Patrick Brazil, 'Opening of Seminar' in Attorney-General's Department, *Another Look at Statutory Interpretation: A Symposium* (Australian Government Publishing Service, 1982) 1, citing Carlton Allen, *Law in Making* (7th ed, 1964).

80 Attorney-General's Department, *Another Look at Statutory Interpretation: A Symposium* (Australian Government Publishing Service, 1982) 1–8, 16–21.

81 Patrick Brazil, 'Purposive Versus Literal Approach' in ibid 18.

introduction into the AIA.[82] The objective of the new provision was to 'confirm that in interpreting provisions regard is to be had to the object or purpose underlying the Act in question'.[83]

As enacted in 1981, s 15AA(1) provided:

> In the interpretation of a provision of an Act, a construction that would promote the purpose or object underlying the Act (whether that purpose or object is expressly stated in the Act or not) shall be preferred to a construction that would not promote that purpose or object.

Initially there was 'a noticeable lack of enthusiasm by way of reaction to the new s 15AA, particularly among many members of the judiciary'.[84] For some, it was not a marked departure from the mischief rule, or it was regarded as a provision that merely legislated an approach that had been developing at common law.

But the belief that s 15AA contributed nothing new 'would be mistaken'.[85] Foremost, it imposed a statutory *requirement* to consider the purpose.[86] Second, as Dawson J clearly explained a few years later in *Mills v Meeking*,[87] the 'statutory injunction' of the wording of the provision is 'more than an instruction to adopt the traditional mischief or purpose rule in preference to the literal rule of construction'.[88] Unlike the mischief rule, it needs no ambiguity before a court should consider the purposes of an Act. It requires the court to consider the Act in the light of purpose as part of the interpretative process, and consideration of that purpose may assist in determining if there is more than one possible construction.[89]

(b) Enactment in other jurisdictions

In February 1984 the Interpretation of Legislation Bill 1984 was introduced into the Victorian Parliament. It was intended to replace the existing Interpretation Act, and to implement many recommendations of the 1983 report of the Legal and Constitutional Committee of the Victorian Parliament that had examined the provisions of a previous Bill, the Interpretation Bill 1982 (which had not been enacted).[90] That report contains a valuable and extensive discussion of the then existing state of the law and arguments for change. The 1984 Bill, enacted later in 1984, contained proposed s 35(a), a purpose provision substantially similar to s 15AA.[91]

---

82 Statute Law Revision Bill 1981 (Cth) sch 1.

83 Commonwealth, *Parliamentary Debates*, Senate, 28 May 1981, 2166 (Attorney-General Durack).

84 Anonymous, 'Statutory Guidelines for Interpreting Commonwealth Statutes (Current Topics)' (1981) 55(10) *Australian Law Journal* 711, 712.

85 RS Geddes, 'Purpose and Context in Statutory Interpretation' (2005) 2(1) *University of New England Law Journal* 5, 10.

86 See **[8.2]**.

87 (1990) 169 CLR 214.

88 Ibid 235 (in dissent as to outcome); 243 (McHugh J agreeing). Dawson J was referring to s 35 of the *Interpretation of Legislation Act 1984* (Vic), almost identical to the original s 15AA.

89 Ibid. Dawson J's statements have subsequently been approved on numerous occasions. See, eg, *Thompson v Byrne* (1999) 196 CLR 141, 159 [48] (Gaudron J); *Vincentia MC Pharmacy Pty Ltd v Australian Community Pharmacy Authority* (2020) 280 FCR 397, 412 [48] (Perry and Stewart JJ); *F, BV v Magistrates Court of South Australia* (2013) 115 SASR 232, 240 [11] (Kourakis CJ); *DPP v Leys* (2012) 44 VR 1, 23 [67] (the Court); *Cardinal Project Services Pty Ltd v Hanave Pty Ltd* (2011) 81 NSWLR 716, 726 [34] (Basten JA). See **[8.2]–[8.4]**.

90 Victoria, *Parliamentary Debates*, Legislative Council, 28 February 1984, 1602 (Attorney-General Kennan).

91 *Interpretation of Legislation Act 1984* (Vic), which repealed and replaced the *Acts Interpretation Act 1958* (Vic). There were also law reform inquiries: Law Reform Committee of South Australia, *Law Relating to Construction*

Other states and territories eventually enacted a purpose provision in their respective Interpretation Acts. The WA Parliament enacted its equivalent in 1984,[92] New South Wales in 1987,[93] South Australia in 1986,[94] Queensland in 1991,[95] the Australian Capital Territory and Tasmania in 1992,[96] and the Northern Territory in 1998.[97] All but the Queensland purpose provision were substantially the same as, or identical to, s 15AA as enacted in 1981. The Queensland provision used the language of 'best achieve the purpose' (see chapter 8) rather than the language of preference between a 'construction that would promote the purpose' and one 'that would not'. The Commonwealth, South Australia and the Australian Capital Territory have since adopted the language of 'best achieve the purpose' in their purpose provisions (see **[2.9]**).

[2.6] The enactment of 15AB of the *Acts Interpretation Act 1901* (Cth) and equivalent state and territory provisions marked a second critical point in the development of the contemporary approach to statutory interpretation

(a) Commonwealth developments

The enactment of s 15AA in 1981 did not affect the law regarding the use of extrinsic materials. In fact, sub-s (2) of the new s 15AA expressly retained the status quo. It provided:

> (2) Nothing in sub-section (1) shall be construed as authorizing, in the interpretation of a provision of an Act, the consideration of any matter or document not forming part of the Act for any purpose for which that matter or document could not be considered apart from that sub-section.

Despite that, the enactment of s 15AA established the foundation for change. It is clear from parliamentary debates and other executive material relating to s 15AA that it was seen as a stepping stone to permitting access to a broader range of extrinsic materials, especially parliamentary materials.[98] In October 1982 the Attorney-General's Department produced the policy discussion paper *Extrinsic Aids to Statutory Interpretation*. This formed the basis for a second Canberra symposium in February 1983.

---

of Statutes (Ninth Report, 1970); Northern Territory Law Reform Commission, *Report on Statutory Interpretation* (Report No 12, December 1987).

92 *Interpretation Act 1984* (WA) s 18, as originally enacted (repealing and replacing the *Interpretation Act 1918* (WA)).

93 *Interpretation Act 1987* (NSW) s 33, as originally enacted, replacing the *Interpretation Act 1897* (NSW).

94 *Acts Interpretation Act 1915* (SA) s 22, as inserted by *Acts Interpretation Act Amendment Act 1986* (SA). It replaced s 22 as originally enacted, which interestingly already required consideration of the object when a remedial Act.

95 *Acts Interpretation Act 1954* (Qld) s 14A, as inserted by the *Acts Interpretation Amendment Act 1991* (Qld).

96 *Interpretation Ordinance 1967* (ACT) s 11A, as inserted by the *Interpretation (Amendment) Ordinance 1982* (ACT) (since replaced by *Legislation Act 2001* (ACT) s 139 – see **[2.9]**). *Acts Interpretation Act 1931* (Tas) s 8A, as inserted by *Acts Interpretation Amendment Act 1992* (Tas).

97 *Interpretation Act 1978* (NT) s 62A, as inserted by the *Interpretation Amendment Act 1998* (NT).

98 See, eg, Commonwealth, *Parliamentary Debates*, Senate, 27 May 1981, 2166–7 (Attorney-General Durack); Commonwealth, *Parliamentary Debates*, Senate, 28 May 1981, 2312 (Senator Evans); Attorney-General (Cth), *New Guidelines for the Interpretation of Commonwealth Laws* (Press Release, 35/81, 27 May 1981); Office of Shadow Attorney-General, *Interpreting Tax Laws* (Press Release, 28 May 1981).

By this time even High Court judges were noting that the 'limits to the permissible use of material extrinsic to the legislation itself in aid of its interpretation are not clear'.[99] Despite, or because of, this obscurity, the practice of referring to extraneous materials, particularly Hansard, was 'growing' by the early 1980s.[100] The former intransigence towards parliamentary materials appeared to have softened, with numerous examples of references by the 1970s and early 1980s.[101] However, the limit on that recourse was that the materials could only be used to identify the mischief or 'evil' being remedied in the statute.[102]

The general sentiment of the symposium was that the law needed reform. Summing up in the symposium, then High Court of Australia Justice Mason summarised the situation:

> The law as it presently stands [on resort to extrinsic materials] is neither clear nor convincing . . . That there are anomalies in the present law is beyond question . . . It is generally felt that this doubt and uncertainty should be set at rest . . . preferably by the Parliament.[103]

The issue was more controversial than the proposal about purpose, especially regarding recourse to Hansard. Both the 1983 symposium (and the 1983 Victorian parliamentary committee report – see **[2.5](b)**) identified various concerns of principle and practice.[104] Despite this, in March 1984 the Acts Interpretation Amendment Bill 1984 was introduced into the Senate containing the new s 15AB. At the commencement of his second reading speech for the Bill, Attorney-General Evans stated:

> The purpose of this Bill is to facilitate the giving of effect to the intentions of the Parliament when Acts of Parliament fall to be interpreted.[105]

Although the new provision generated considerably more debate than had s 15AA, the Bill was passed with bipartisan support in May 1984. The details of s 15AB, which has not been amended since 1984, are discussed in **[24.5]–[24.7]**.

(b) Enactment of equivalent legislative provisions in other states and territories

The significance of a legislative enactment providing a cohesive and relatively expansive approach to the use of extrinsic materials should not be underestimated. Although perhaps difficult to appreciate now when lawyers regularly refer to many extrinsic sources, the enactment of s 15AB was 'ground-breaking'.[106] As explained extrajudicially by Justice Gageler:

---

99 *Dugan v Mirror Newspapers Ltd* (1978) 142 CLR 583, 599 (Stephen J).

100 Attorney-General's Department, *Extrinsic Aids to Statutory Interpretation* (Policy Discussion Paper No 285/1982, Attorney-General's Department, 1982) 9.

101 See, eg, *Dugan v Mirror Newspapers Ltd* (1978) 142 CLR 583, 594–601 (Stephen J); *Wacando v Commonwealth* (1981) 148 CLR 1, 25–6 (Mason J); *Commissioner of Taxation (Cth) v Whitfords Beach Pty Ltd* (1982) 150 CLR 355, 373–4 (Mason J); *TCN Channel Nine Pty Ltd v Australian Mutual Provident Society* (1982) 62 FLR 366, 379–80 (the Court).

102 See, eg, *Dugan v Mirror Newspapers Ltd* (1978) 142 CLR 583, 600 (Stephen J); *Wacando v Commonwealth* (1981) 148 CLR 1, 25 (Mason J); *Commissioner of Taxation (Cth) v Whitfords Beach Pty Ltd* (1982) 150 CLR 355, 373–4 (Mason J).

103 Attorney-General's Department, *Symposium on Statutory Interpretation* (Australian Government Publishing Service, 1983) 81–2 (Sir Anthony Mason).

104 See generally ibid; Legal and Constitutional Committee, Victorian Parliament, *Report on Interpretation Bill 1982* (Report No 21/1982–83, October 1983) 74–5.

105 Commonwealth, *Parliamentary Debates*, Senate, 8 March 1984, 582.

106 Stephen Gageler, 'Legislative Intention' (2015) 41(1) *Monash University Law Review* 1, 6.

> Save for the introduction of a modest statutory provision in Ghana in 1960, no other country to emerge from the former British Empire had then taken such a step. The section's enlargement of the matrix of material to which a court was entitled to look to ascertain the intention of the legislature set a precedent for similar provisions . . .[107]

All of the states and territories, except South Australia and the Australian Capital Territory, subsequently enacted a provision relating to the use of extrinsic material at the same time as they enacted their purpose provisions (see **[2.5]**).[108] Of those enacting jurisdictions, all but Victoria adopted provisions almost identical, or substantially similar, to s 15AB. The Australian Capital Territory enacted a provision almost identical to s 15AB in 1985.[109]

South Australia did not enact a statutory provision about extrinsic materials until 2021, when it enacted a new Interpretation Act (see **[2.9]**). Until that time, it relied solely on the common law.[110]

Although the Commonwealth provision is typically credited as the pioneering provision, the comparable Victorian provision, s 35(b) of the *Interpretation of Legislation Act 1984* (Vic), was enacted almost 'neck and neck' with s 15AB.[111] The latter was (and remains) a more simple provision. As enacted, it provided that 'any matter or document that is relevant' could be referred to (with a short list of examples). Unlike the restrictive three limbs in s 15AB (see **[24.7]**), the Victorian section does not prescribe any restrictions on recourse. The 1983 Victorian parliamentary committee report that preceded it (see **[2.5]**) considered and rejected an ambiguity threshold.[112] Nor does s 35(b) have an equivalent provision to s 15AB(3) about weight. (An equivalent provision to s 15AB(3) had been included by all other jurisdictions that enacted an extrinsic material provision except the Northern Territory.) The Victorian parliamentary committee explained:

> It is the job of the judge or magistrate to determine the relevance of all material coming before a court, and once relevance has been determined, to decide what weight might be given to it. There is no reason for judges to be less able to assess the relevance and weight of statements made in Parliament than they are able to assess relevance and weight of other extrinsic materials.[113]

---

107 Ibid.

108 *Interpretation Act 1987* (NSW) s 34, original Act; *Acts Interpretation Act 1954* (Qld) s 14B, as inserted by the *Acts Interpretation Amendment Act 1991* (Qld); *Acts Interpretation Act 1931* (Tas) s 8B, as inserted by the *Acts Interpretation Amendment Act 1992* (Tas); *Interpretation of Legislation Act 1984* (Vic) s 35(b), original Act; *Interpretation Act 1984* (WA) s 19, original Act; *Interpretation Act 1978* (NT) s 62B, as inserted by the *Interpretation Amendment Act 1998* (NT).

109 *Interpretation Ordinance 1967* (ACT) s 11B, as inserted by the *Interpretation (Amendment) Ordinance 1985* (ACT) (since replaced by the *Legislation Act 2001* (ACT) s 141 – see **[2.9]**).

110 See **[24.2]**.

111 The Interpretation of Legislation Bill 1984 (Vic), which included s 35(b), was introduced into the Victorian Legislative Council on 28 February 1984. The Acts Interpretation Amendment Bill 1984 (Cth), inserting s 15AB, was introduced into the Senate on 8 March 1984. The *Acts Interpretation Amendment Act 1984* (Cth) received Royal Assent on 15 May 1984. The *Interpretation of Legislation Act 1984* (Vic) was assented to on 22 May 1984.

112 Legal and Constitutional Committee, Victorian Parliament, *Report on Interpretation Bill 1982* (Report No 21/1982–83, October 1983) 118–20.

113 Ibid 91.

Common law developments – the 'modern' approach: 1990s

Despite the enactment of statutory provisions about purpose and extrinsic materials, the common law continued to develop in both respects [2.7]

Prior to the enactment of s 15AA of the AIA, there were indications that the High Court had started to place greater emphasis on considering the purpose of a statute independently of anticipated legislative change. The 1981 High Court decision of *Cooper Brookes (Wollongong) Pty Ltd v Commissioner of Taxation (Cth)*[114] is often cited as evidence of a 'shift in mood and emphasis' of the High Court, away from a literal approach and towards an 'openness to discerning policy'.[115] In that case, Mason and Wilson JJ identified some of the deficiencies of the literal and golden rules.[116] They did not dismiss having regard to a literal meaning, but stated that departing from it should extend to

> any situation in which for good reason the operation of the statute on a literal reading does not conform to the legislative intent as ascertained from the provisions of the statute, *including the policy* which may be discerned from those provisions.[117]

The reasons for the common law development towards a greater focus on purpose (and wider context) are 'several and complex'.[118] Be that as it may, by 1990 consideration of purpose was regarded as integral to the interpretative process, independent of statute. This was evident from *Bropho*, a High Court decision construing Western Australian legislation. In a unanimous judgment, the Court observed that legislative intent

> must, of course, be found in the provisions of the statute – including its subject matter and disclosed purpose and policy – when construed in a context which includes permissible extrinsic aids.[119]

No reference was made to s 18, the purpose provision of the *Interpretation Act 1984* (WA). The obligation to consider purpose at common law was confirmed in *Project Blue Sky Inc v Australian Broadcasting Authority*[120] in 1998. In 2007, Kirby J observed that 'acceptance of the purposive approach to the interpretation of legislation ... represents one of the most important doctrinal shifts in the reasoning of this Court in recent times'.[121] This was clearly a reference to the position at common law, as his Honour identified the purpose provisions in Interpretation Acts as being just one of the impetuses for the change.[122]

---

114 (1981) 147 CLR 297.

115 Justice Bryson, 'Statutory Interpretation: An Australian Judicial Perspective' (1992) 13(3) *Statute Law Review* 187, 194. See also RS Geddes, 'Purpose and Context in Statutory Interpretation' (2005) 2(1) *University of New England Law Journal* 5, 15–16.

116 (1981) 147 CLR 297, 319–21.

117 Ibid 321 (emphasis added).

118 *Australian Finance Direct Ltd v Director of Consumer Affairs Victoria* (2007) 234 CLR 96, 112 [35] where Kirby J suggests at least five reasons.

119 *Bropho v Western Australia* (1990) 171 CLR 1, 21–2 (Mason CJ, Deane, Dawson, Toohey, Gaudron and McHugh JJ), citing in part *Kingston v Keprose Pty Ltd* (1987) 11 NSWLR 404, 423 (McHugh J).

120 (1998) 194 CLR 355, 384 [78] (McHugh, Gummow, Kirby and Hayne JJ).

121 *Australian Finance Direct Ltd v Director of Consumer Affairs Victoria* (2007) 234 CLR 96, 112 [36].

122 Ibid.

The resilience of the common law is also evident by its development with respect to extrinsic materials. Perhaps even more so than for s 15AA, there was an 'analogical judicial development of the common law' following enactment of s 15AB.[123]

The notion of context was the key to this development. As noted in **[2.3]**, reference to 'surrounding circumstances' in cases of ambiguity had been accepted at common law well before the 1980s. With the door opened by s 15AB and its equivalents, the courts began to view this background more broadly. This was foreshadowed in the dissenting judgment of Mason J in the 1985 High Court decision of *K&S Lake City Freighters Pty Ltd v Gordon & Gotch Ltd.*[124] Partly influenced by *Cooper Brookes*, and relying on English authority, Mason J stated that the 'modern' approach to construction insists that 'context' be considered at the start of the interpretative process, not only when ambiguity arose, and included intrinsic context (the four corners of the Act) and the wider context such as the existing state of the law, other statutes and the 'mischief'.[125]

The broader concept of 'context' married well with the increasing judicial emphasis on legislative purpose. This connection is not surprising, given that one of the key reasons for enacting s 15AB was to allow recourse to relevant extrinsic materials to assist in identifying the purpose of the statute. In 1997, purpose and context converged. What is now referred to as the 'modern' common law approach to interpretation was summarised in *CIC Insurance Ltd v Bankstown Football Club Ltd.*[126] In the course of interpreting Commonwealth legislation, Brennan CJ, Dawson, Toohey and Gummow JJ stated:

> It is well settled that at common law, *apart from any reliance upon s 15AB* of the *Acts Interpretation Act 1901* (Cth), the court may have regard to reports of law reform bodies to ascertain the mischief which a statute is intended to cure. Moreover, the modern approach to statutory interpretation (a) insists that the *context be considered in the first instance*, not merely at some later stage when ambiguity might be thought to arise, and (b) uses 'context' *in its widest sense* to include such things as the existing state of the law and the mischief which, by legitimate means such as those just mentioned, one may discern the statute was intended to remedy.[127]

The elements of this statement are fully addressed in chapters 7 and 24. Briefly, it marked three pivotal changes to the previous common law on extraneous materials. First, consideration of context was no longer dependent on any ambiguity or other threshold but is an integral step in the interpretative process. Second, context means context in its 'widest sense' and so encompasses a non-exhaustive range of matters and materials beyond the statute itself. Finally, the statement made clear that the common law on recourse to extrinsic materials coexisted with, and is independent of, s 15AB and its statutory equivalents. In *CIC Insurance* the Court used these principles to refer to a law reform commission report. Later in the same year, several High Court judges relied on the principles enunciated in *CIC Insurance* to refer to an explanatory

---

123 Stephen Gageler, 'Legislative Intention' (2015) 41(1) *Monash University Law Review* 1, 7.

124 (1985) 157 CLR 309.

125 Ibid 315, citing *A-G v Prince Ernest Augustus of Hanover* [1957] AC 436, 461 (Viscount Simonds) and *Re Bidie* [1948] 2 All ER 995, 998 (Lord Greene MR).

126 (1997) 187 CLR 384.

127 Ibid 408 (emphasis added; citations omitted).

memorandum, as well as law reform commission materials.[128] Two years later, a unanimous High Court judgment referred to parliamentary debates.[129]

One consequence of the legislative and common law developments in the 1980s and 1990s is that the literal rule, mischief rule, and golden rule have been superseded [2.8]

To the extent that they represented the law, the three 'rules' have been subsumed by the legislative and common law developments in the last quarter of the 20th century. Indeed, these approaches no longer have much – if any – work to do. The literal rule is not equivalent to the contemporary principle to start with the ordinary meaning of the text. The former tended to place 'excessive emphasis on the words of a provision' without sufficient weight to other considerations.[130] In contemporary law the 'ordinary' meaning is only the starting point of statutory construction.[131] At the most, a literal approach may assist when other indicia are limited.[132]

The mischief rule, which required ambiguity on the face of the statute and only focused on the deficiency in the previous law, has been overtaken by the requirement to consider the broader notion of purpose from the outset of the interpretative process. The notion of 'mischief' remains, but tends to be considered under the umbrella of purpose.[133]

The golden rule was dependent on the literal approach to be operative. It is too restrictive in operation to be considered as equivalent to the contemporary principle that a particular construction may be tested by reference to its consequences.[134] Beyond the idea that the absurd consequence of a particular meaning may be relevant, it is difficult to identify any continued relevance for the rule given the contemporary requirement to consider context and purpose.

Changes to some Interpretation Acts: 2000s

Since the original enactment of ss 15AA and 15AB and their state and territory equivalents, the Australian Capital Territory, South Australia and the Commonwealth have made significant amendments to their provisions [2.9]

Since their original enactment, the Interpretation Act provisions on purpose and extrinsic materials in New South Wales, Queensland, Tasmania, Victoria, Western Australia and the Northern Territory have remained substantially unchanged. Amendments have been minor (such as to the list of examples of extrinsic materials in the provisions).[135] One possible exception is

128 *Newcastle City Council v GIO General Ltd* (1997) 191 CLR 85, 99–102 (Toohey, Gaudron and Gummow JJ). See also 112 (McHugh J).

129 *A-G (Cth) v Oates* (1999) 198 CLR 162, 175–6 [28–[30], citing both s 15AB and the common law.

130 The Law Commission and the Scottish Law Commission, *The Interpretation of Statutes* (Report, Law Com No 21, Scot Law Com No 11, 9 June 1969) 5. See **[15.3]**.

131 See **[6.5]**–**[6.7]**. For differences between 'literal' and 'ordinary' meaning see chapter 15.

132 See, eg, *Avel Pty Ltd v A-G (NSW)* (1987) 11 NSWLR 126. Kirby J noted that the legislative scheme was such 'a jumble of ill-matched and poorly integrated enactments' that 'the only safe approach' was 'an attention to the literal words of the legislation' (though he did then assess some extrinsic materials): at 127.

133 See **[8.3]**.

134 See chapter 27.

135 See, eg, *Parliamentary Service and Other Acts Amendment Act 2011* (Qld) s 4; *Statute Law (Miscellaneous Provisions) Act (No 2) 1992* (NSW) sch 1; *Inquiries Act 2014* (Vic) sch 2; *Legislation Act 2021* (WA) s 50 (not yet in force).

Queensland, which enacted a qualification to its purpose provision in 1994 that provides that the purpose provision does not create or extend criminal liability.[136]

The Australian Capital Territory, the Commonwealth and South Australia have made more substantive changes. In 2001 the ACT Parliament enacted the *Legislation Act 2001* (ACT) and began the process of transferring provisions from the *Interpretation Act 1967* (ACT) (formerly Ordinance) to that Act and updating and clarifying those provisions. After some initial stages,[137] the *Legislation (Statutory Interpretation) Amendment Act 2003* (ACT) ('the 2003 Amendment Act') completed the process and revised the purpose and extrinsic material provisions.

The 2003 Amendment Act enacted a new ch 14 to 'reflect significant common law developments' in statutory interpretation.[138] The new purpose provision, s 139, adopted the language of 'best achieve the purpose of the Act', similar to s 14A of the Queensland Act (see **[2.5]**). This was partly to consolidate the importance of purpose.[139] It was also to address a perceived limitation in the wording of the then s 15AA wording that had been highlighted in the 1990 High Court decision *Chugg v Pacific Dunlop Ltd.*[140] When considering the Victorian equivalent of s 15AA, Dawson, Toohey and Gaudron JJ observed that the provision only offered 'a limited choice' between a construction that would promote the purpose or object of an Act and one that would not promote that purpose or object.[141]

The new ch 14 also revised the extrinsic materials provision. The new s 141 abandoned the three limbs modelled on s 15AB, and simply stated that 'material not forming part of the Act may be considered', with various criteria stipulated to assess its weight. It is now similar to the Victorian provision (see **[2.6]**).

Neither of these revisions were intended to mark any dramatic change in the interpretation of ACT legislation.[142] They were regarded as legislative statements of the fundamental rules of statutory interpretation that had developed since the mid-1980s.[143]

The *Acts Interpretation Act 1901* (Cth) was reviewed in 1993 and 1998.[144] Both reviews were primarily driven by a desire to improve legislative drafting. Much later, the *Acts Interpretation Amendment Act 2011* (Cth) made numerous changes. Many were for clarification or modernisation, but some were substantive.[145] Among the latter was the adoption of the 'best achieve'

---

136 *Fire Service Legislation Amendment 1994* (Qld) s 14 amended the *Acts Interpretation Act 1954* (Qld) s 14A.

137 See Explanatory Statement, Legislation (Statutory Interpretation) Amendment Bill 2003 (ACT) 2–3.

138 Australian Capital Territory, *Parliamentary Debates*, Legislative Assembly, 13 March 2003, 999 (Mr Stanhope).

139 Explanatory Statement, Legislation (Statutory Interpretation) Amendment Bill 2003 (ACT) 1.

140 (1990) 170 CLR 249. See Explanatory Statement, Legislation (Statutory Interpretation) Amendment Bill 2003 (ACT) 10.

141 *Chugg v Pacific Dunlop Ltd* (1990) 170 CLR 249, 262. This was also the reason given for the Queensland Parliament to adopt 'best achieve' language in 1991. See Queensland, *Parliamentary Debates*, Legislative Assembly, 21 May 1991, 7641–2 (Attorney-General Wells).

142 Explanatory Statement, Legislation (Statutory Interpretation) Amendment Bill 2003 (ACT) 1 [3].

143 Ibid 1.

144 House of Representatives Standing Committee on Legal and Constitutional Affairs, Parliament of Australia, *Clearer Commonwealth Law: Report of the inquiry into Legislative Drafting by the Commonwealth* (Report, September 1993); Attorney-General's Department and Office of Parliamentary Counsel, *Review of the Commonwealth Acts Interpretation Act 1901* (Commonwealth of Australia, 1998).

145 See Jacinta Dharmananda, 'The Commonwealth Strikes Back: Clarifying Amendments to the *Acts Interpretation Act 1901* (Cth) (2011) 35(2) *Australian Bar Review* 116.

language for s 15AA.[146] Like the ACT amendment, the change was based on the limitations of the original language identified by *Chugg*.[147] No changes were made to s 15AB.

In 2021, South Australia enacted the *Legislation Interpretation Act 2021* (SA) ('the 2021 Act') to repeal and replace the *Acts Interpretation Act 1915* (SA).[148] The purpose provision in the 2021 Act, s 14, uses the 'best achieves the purpose' language.[149] Perhaps more significantly, the 2021 Act includes s 16, which is, for the first time in South Australia, a statutory provision on recourse to extrinsic materials. Section 16 mirrors s 15AB of the AIA. Neither of these provisions was regarded by the government as having a substantial effect on the approach to interpretation in South Australia.[150]

The impact (or lack of impact) of the 'best achieve' language in some of the purpose provisions is discussed in chapter 8.[151] More recently, the enactment of human rights legislation in Queensland, Victoria and the Australian Capital Territory has impacted the interpretation of legislation in those jurisdictions. This is discussed in chapter 26.

---

146 *Acts Interpretation Amendment Act 2011* (Cth) s 23.

147 Explanatory Memorandum, Acts Interpretation Amendment Bill 2011 (Cth) 19.

148 *Legislation Interpretation Act 2021* (SA) sch 1 cl 23. The *Legislation Interpretation Act 2021* (SA) commenced on 1 January 2022 (South Australia, *The South Australian Government Gazette*, No 82, 23 December 2021, 4619).

149 Section 14(2) also has a qualification regarding criminal liability similar to the Queensland qualification.

150 See, eg, South Australia, *Parliamentary Debates*, Legislative Council, Explanation of Clauses, 6 May 2021, 3367 (RI Lucas, Treasurer); South Australia, *Parliamentary Debates*, Legislative Council, 24 June 2021, 3903 (RI Lucas, Treasurer).

151 See **[8.2]**.

3 CONSTITUTIONAL CONTEXT

Overview

[3.1] The constitutional framework of legislation, federal and state, is relevant to statutory interpretation in various ways. At its most general level, the framework identifies the source of interpretative law for legislation. Further, three fundamental constitutional concepts – the separation of powers, the rule of law and parliamentary supremacy – both influence and provide a foundation for statutory interpretation law. Although these concepts are complex, and the subject of considerable discourse in constitutional law, it is important to understand their basic characteristics as a backdrop to the more detailed examination of statutory interpretation law that follows in this book.

Sources of law and the separation of powers

[3.2] **An understanding of the structure of the Australian legal system is needed to understand institutions and sources of law relevant to statutory interpretation**

Australia is a federation and parliamentary democracy. The body of law that constitutes its legislation consists of the laws enacted by the nine legislatures of the Commonwealth – namely, those of the states and the two self-governing territories – and the delegated legislation made pursuant to those laws.[1] Those parliaments are empowered to make legislation by a variety of sources and as a result of myriad historical developments. At a basic level, the *Australian Constitution*, contained within covering s 9 of the *Commonwealth of Australia Constitution Act 1900* (Imp) 63 & 64 Vic. c. 12, vests legislative power in the federal Parliament in relation to specified heads of power.[2] The legislative power of the state parliaments is founded in their respective state constitutions – these are preserved by the *Australian Constitution*, subject to the limits that it itself imposes on the states.[3] The legislative powers of the territory parliaments are established by federal legislation pursuant to the *Constitution*.[4] Issues arise as to the boundaries

---

1 This includes laws enacted by former colonial legislatures that are still in force. See Mark Leeming, *Resolving Conflicts of Laws* (Federation Press, 2011) 21.

2 *Australian Constitution* ss 1, 51–60.

3 Ibid ss 106–107. The state constitutions as currently made are *Constitution Act 1902* (NSW); *Constitution of Queensland 2001* (Qld); *Constitution Act 1934* (SA); *Constitution Act 1934* (Tas); *Constitution Act 1975* (Vic); *Constitution Act 1889* (WA); and *Constitution Acts Amendment Act 1899* (WA).

4 Australia has 10 territories but only the Australian Capital Territory and the Northern Territory are self-governing. Under s 122 of the *Constitution*, the federal Parliament gave the Northern Territory and the Australian Capital Territory self-government by the *Northern Territory (Self-Government) Act 1978* (Cth) and the *Australian Capital Territory (Self-Government) Act 1988* (Cth) respectively.

of the respective legislative powers of each parliament, and therefore the validity of legislation, and as to inconsistencies between legislation made by different parliaments. Those issues are the subject of constitutional law.[5] Understanding this framework at a general level is important for statutory interpretation, for at least two reasons. First, the framework identifies the institutions that enact the legislation the subject of the law of statutory interpretation. Second, this framework identifies the sources of the law that comprise statutory interpretation law. That law, like most law in Australia, is a composite of common law and statutory rules.[6]

Each Australian parliament has enacted its own Interpretation Act.[7] These Acts contain provisions about the role of purpose and extrinsic materials, as well as myriad important, but often 'idiosyncratic' or technical, rules about interpretation.[8]

In contrast to the separate Interpretation Acts, it is generally accepted that there is 'one common law' that prevails in Australia (with the ultimate arbiter being the High Court).[9] The doctrine of legislative supremacy (see **[3.5]**) directs that the provisions of the Interpretation Acts prevail over the common law to the extent of inconsistency. However, the relationship between the Acts and the common law is not so simply characterised. As will be seen from subsequent chapters, the common law principles, while in some instances altered or supplemented by the Interpretation Acts, tend to dominate the interpretative task.[10]

Statutory interpretation is an expression of the constitutional relationship between the three arms of government; the separation of powers between the courts and the legislature has particular significance [3.3]

The relevance of the constitutional framework to statutory interpretation has been expressly recognised by the High Court. In the 2009 decision of *Zheng v Cai*,[11] the Court explained:

> [J]udicial findings as to legislative intention are an *expression of the constitutional relationship* between the arms of government with respect to the making, interpretation and application of laws.[12]

This characterisation has been cited with approval on numerous occasions since 2011.[13] At a broad level, this statement serves to remind the interpreter of the different functions of the

5 Though interpretation of the impugned statutory provision is a key first step in determining constitutional validity: see **[32.8]**.

6 *Lacey v A-G (Qld)* (2011) 242 CLR 573, 592 [43] (French CJ, Gummow, Hayne, Crennan, Kiefel and Bell JJ).

7 See **[25.1]**.

8 Dennis Pearce, *Interpretation Acts in Australia* (LexisNexis Butterworths, 1st ed, 2018) 3.

9 *Lange v Australian Broadcasting Corporation* (1997) 189 CLR 520, 563–4 (Brennan CJ, Dawson, Toohey, Gaudron, McHugh, Gummow and Kirby JJ); *Rizeq v Western Australia* (2017) 262 CLR 1, 31 [78] (Bell, Gageler, Keane, Nettle and Gordon JJ).

10 Anthony Mason, 'The Interaction of Statute Law and Common Law' (2016) 90(5) *Australian Law Journal* 324, 324.

11 (2009) 239 CLR 446.

12 Ibid 455–6 [28] (French CJ, Gummow, Crennan, Kiefel and Bell JJ) (emphasis added). See also *Wilson v Anderson* (2002) 213 CLR 401, 418 [8] (Gleeson CJ).

13 See, eg, *Lacey v A-G (Qld)* (2011) 242 CLR 573, 591–2 [43] (French CJ, Gummow, Hayne, Crennan, Kiefel and Bell JJ); *Plaintiff S10/2011 v Minister for Immigration and Citizenship* (2012) 246 CLR 636, 666 [97] (Gummow, Hayne, Crennan and Bell JJ); *Australian Building and Construction Commissioner v Molina* (2020) 277 FCR 223, 242 [83] (the Court).

legislature and the judiciary: the legislature makes the law and the judiciary interprets it. In highlighting those distinct functions, the statement 'identifies the function of statutory interpretation as an important, if not critical, point of reference in determining where that boundary lies'.[14] Statutory interpretation law establishes the boundaries of legitimate interpretation and therefore the parameters of the judicial task when construing legislation. This is explored further in the next sections.

(a) The separation of powers between the legislature and the judiciary is one rationale for some principles of statutory interpretation

The doctrine of separation of powers can be traced back to Aristotle but became influential in the 18th century through the commentary of Charles Louis de Secondat, Baron de Montesquieu.[15] The essence of the doctrine is that the arms of government – the executive, the legislature and the judiciary – are to operate separately and independently, essentially to ensure a series of checks and balances against the exercise of excessive power by any one institution. The framers of the *Constitution*, as is reflected in chs I, II and III of the *Constitution*, adopted this separation of institutions framework from the United States.[16] However, they also departed from that framework: they provided for 'responsible government' according to the United Kingdom's Westminster model.[17] That is, under s 64 of the *Constitution*, the federal executive is integrated into the federal Parliament by the requirement that government ministers be members of Parliament, accountable to Parliament. Despite this 'dilution', the divide between legislative power and judicial power is regarded as 'deeply embedded' in the *Australian Constitution*.[18]

In a direct way, this separation is recognised in statutory interpretation. Most Interpretation Acts provide in some form that where there is a constructional choice that would place a statute within the limits of constitutional power and another that would place it outside those limits, the former is to be preferred.[19]

But the doctrine and statutory interpretation are linked at a more fundamental level. The High Court has emphasised that the attribution of meaning to statutory text is 'emphatically' seen as the province and duty of the judiciary.[20] An example of this manifesting in interpretation is the strict approach taken by the courts to the construction of privative clauses, provisions that purport to limit or oust the jurisdiction of courts.[21]

---

14 John Basten, 'Separation of Powers – Dialogue and Deference' (2018) 25(2) *Australian Journal of Administrative Law* 91, 92.

15 George Williams, Sean Brennan and Andrew Lynch, *Blackshield and Williams Australian Constitutional Law and Theory: Commentary and Materials* (Federation Press, 7th ed, 2018) 25.

16 Peter A Gerangelos et al, *Winterton's Australian Federal Constitutional Law: Commentary and Materials* (Thomson Reuters, 4th ed, 2017) 35.

17 Ibid.

18 *Clubb v Edwards* (2019) 267 CLR 171, 311 [408] (Edelman J), citing the leading case *R v Kirby; Ex parte Boilermakers' Society of Australia* (1956) 94 CLR 254. See also Cheryl Saunders, *The Constitution of Australia: A Contextual Analysis* (Hart Publishing, 2011) 198.

19 See, eg, *Acts Interpretation Act 1901* (Cth) s 15A. See **[32.8]**.

20 *Brown v Tasmania* (2017) 261 CLR 328, 480 [486], 486 [506] (Edelman J in dissent, but not with regard to this principle, citing *Marbury v Madison*, 5 US 137, 177 (Marshall CJ) (1803), *A-G (NSW) v Quin* (1990) 170 CLR 1, 35 (Brennan J) and *R v Holmes; Ex parte Altona Petrochemical Co Ltd* (1972) 126 CLR 529, 562 (Windeyer J).

21 *Plaintiff S157/2002 v Commonwealth* (2003) 211 CLR 476, 492–3 [32] (Gleeson CJ), 505 [72] (Gaudron, McHugh, Gummow, Kirby and Hayne JJ).

Conversely, the judiciary is wary of intruding into the legislative space and engaging in 'judicial legislation'.[22] Precisely how the constitutional relationship provides the foundation for statutory interpretation principles is a proposition that warrants a closer consideration than is permitted by this chapter.[23] But three key principles of statutory interpretation serve as examples.[24]

The first is the principle concerning the primacy to be given to the statutory text (chapter 6). This principle directs the interpreter to focus on the words that the legislating body has chosen. An example of this principle rationalised in the context of the separation of the judiciary and the courts follows.

Example 3.1 *Treasurer of Victoria v Tabcorp Holdings Ltd*[25]

For numerous years the Victorian gaming industry had operated as a duopoly gaming operator system, comprised of Tattersall and Tabcorp. Under gaming machine legislation, both had paid a levy each year in respect of the gaming machines they operated. In 2012 the Victorian Government introduced transitional legislation to facilitate a change to a new industry structure. For the levy the *Gambling Legislation Amendment (Transition) Act 2012* (Vic) introduced s 3.6.3A into the *Gambling Regulation Act 2003* (Vic), which provided:

> **3.6.3A Health benefit levy – financial year 2012 to 2013**
>
> (1) In respect of the financial year beginning on 1 July 2012 and ending on 30 June 2013, a gaming operator must pay to the Commission a health benefit levy calculated in accordance with the formula set out in section 3.6.3(1).
>
> (2) The Treasurer, in consultation with the Commission, is to determine the amount of the levy on each gaming operator in respect of the financial year and must notify each gaming operator of his or her determination as soon as practicable after making the determination.

Due to the change in the industry structure, Tabcorp and Tattersall only operated gaming machines up to August 2012. They argued that s 3.6.3A of the *Gambling Regulation Act 2003* (Vic) should be construed as granting the Treasurer a discretion to determine the levy otherwise than by the application of the mathematical formulae in s 3.6.3(1), which would require them to pay the levy on the gaming machines for the whole financial year. The Treasurer argued that the plain words of the section imposed an obligation on the Treasurer to apply the formulae regardless of the period of operation.

The Court of Appeal agreed with the Treasurer. As well as considering the legislative antecedents of the section and the legislative history, the Court relied on the 'unambiguous clarity' of

22 *Minister for Immigration and Citizenship v SZJGV* (2009) 238 CLR 642, 652 [9] (French CJ and Bell J, citing *Inco Europe Ltd v First Choice Distribution (A Firm)* [2000] 1 WLR 586, 592 (Lord Nicholls)).

23 For more detailed exposition of the proposition, see John Basten, 'Constitutional Dimensions of Statutory Interpretation' (Speech, Centre for Comparative Constitutional Studies, Melbourne Law School, 24 July 2015); Patrick Emerton and Lisa Burton Crawford, 'Statutory Meaning Without Parliamentary Intention: Defending the High Court's "Alternative Approach" to Statutory Interpretation' in Lisa Burton Crawford, Patrick Emerton and Dale Smith (eds), *Law Under a Democratic Constitution* (Hart Publishing, 2019) 39, 52–62.

24 These three principles as a reflection of the constitutional relationship are discussed in the context of the interpretative issue in *Australian Unity Property Limited v City of Busselton* (2018) 237 LGERA 333, 352–6 [77]–[91] (Buss P, Murphy and Mitchell JJA).

25 [2014] VSCA 143.

the plain meaning of the key words used by the legislature in their statutory context.[26] They determined that those words provided no basis for a construction that granted the Treasurer a discretion to calculate a levy other than by the formulae.[27] The Court explained:

> [T]here are powerful reasons of principle for giving primacy to the statutory text . . . the separation of powers requires nothing less. Axiomatically, it is for the Parliament to legislate and for the courts to interpret.[28]

A second example of how the doctrine influences the law is the requirement to consider the purpose of a statute (chapter 8). This principle can be seen as reflecting an assumption that the legislature enacts a statute to achieve a particular goal. But it also demands caution when attributing weight to that purpose. Purpose cannot be used to adopt a construction 'that departs too far from the statutory text . . . because too great a departure may violate the separation of powers in the Constitution'.[29]

The third example is the common law approach to implying words into statutes to fix a perceived drafting error or to fill a gap in the legislation (chapter 34). Given the function of the judiciary, there are limits on the judiciary's capacity to remedy those omissions through interpretation. In the absence of relevant statutory language, a remedial construction that attempts to fill a 'gap' in legislation will 'legislate, not . . . interpret'.[30]

The boundary between the functions of the legislature and the courts is not always an easy one to draw. Former Chief Justice French attempted to explain the acceptable demarcation:

> While there is no doubt that the choices which the judiciary makes in construing and applying statutes have a law-making dimension, they remain consistent with the separation of legislative and judicial powers if they are confined to functions, that is constructional choices or case-by-case development of principle, which have been left open by the Parliament.[31]

The nature of statutory interpretation, with its weighing and balancing of interpretative factors based in text, context and purpose, means that reasonable minds can differ as to the extent that Parliament has left choices 'open'. So, the appropriate point of demarcation between interpretation and legislation can lead to different views about construction.

(b) There is a question about the relevance of the separation of powers doctrine to state and territories; in practice little turns on this for statutory interpretation

There is, in theory at least, a question about the relevance of the separation of powers principle to the interpretation of state and territory legislation. As noted above, the constitutional framework of the states and territories differs substantially from that established by the *Australian Constitution*. It is well settled that there is no entrenched doctrine of separation of powers to

26 Ibid [6].

27 Ibid [31].

28 Ibid [101].

29 *Taylor v The Owners – Strata Plan No 11564* (2014) 253 CLR 531, 549 [40] (French CJ, Crennan and Bell JJ).

30 *DPP v Walters (A Pseudonym)* (2015) 49 VR 356, 360 [8] (the Court).

31 Robert French, 'The Courts and the Parliament' (2013) 87(12) *Australian Law Journal* 820, 829.

be derived from state constitutions.[32] This means that 'non-judicial functions may be conferred on the Supreme Courts' and other state courts so long as the conferral does not 'substantially impair the institutional integrity' of such a body.[33] The position of the self-governing territories is similar.[34] Common law developments have led to a recognition of certain values (through the idea of institutional integrity) as imposing some limitations on the power of state parliaments or the executive to constrain state courts.[35] There are also suggestions that foundational separation of powers principles have roots in Australia that predate the *Australian Constitution*, going back to the common law courts and the rule of law:

> The absence of an entrenched doctrine of separation of powers under the constitutions of the States at Federation and thereafter does not detract from the acceptance at Federation and the continuation today of independence, impartiality, fairness and openness as essential characteristics of the courts of the States. Nor does the undoubted power of State Parliaments to determine the constitution and organisation of State courts detract from the continuation of those essential characteristics. It is possible to have organisational diversity across the Federation without compromising the fundamental requirements of a judicial system.[36]

Accordingly, it has been suggested that, for state laws, the need to put statutory interpretation into a constitutional context recognising the arms of government 'may not depend on a strict separation of powers doctrine'.[37] It is also an open issue for the territories.

These are large questions. However, as a matter of practice, the common law of interpretation, as ultimately decided by the High Court, does not appear to make any distinction between Commonwealth and state or territory legislation when applying *Zheng v Cai*, or in emphasising the relevance of the separation of the legislative and judicial function.

(c) The separation of judicial and legislative functions is also relevant to the interpretation of delegated legislation

Delegated legislation is legislation made by a person or body, usually a member of the executive, where the power to make that legislation has been delegated to that person or body under a statute. In a constitutional structure based on the separation of powers, it might be thought that the delegation of power to the executive would raise issues about the separation of powers that are relevant to statutory interpretation.

Although arguments have been made that delegated legislation violates a number of constitutional principles, including the separation of powers,[38] it is established in a constitutional

32 *Kable v DPP (NSW)* (1996) 189 CLR 51, 67 (Brennan CJ), 77–8 (Dawson J), 93–4 (Toohey J), 109, 118 (McHugh J), 132 (Gummow J); *Public Service Association and Professional Officers' Association Amalgamated (NSW) v Director of Public Employment* (2012) 250 CLR 343, 368 [57] (Hayne, Crennan, Kiefel and Bell JJ).

33 *Minister for Home Affairs v Benbrika* (2021) 95 ALJR 166, 178 [20] (Kiefel CJ, Bell, Keane and Steward JJ) in the context of federal jurisdiction, citing *Kable v DPP (NSW)* (1996) 189 CLR 51.

34 *North Australian Aboriginal Justice Agency Ltd v Northern Territory* (2015) 256 CLR 569, 625 [146] (Keane J).

35 See, eg, *Kable v DPP (NSW)* (1996) 189 CLR 51; *International Finance Trust Co Ltd v New South Wales Crime Commission* (2009) 240 CLR 319; *Wainohu v New South Wales* (2011) 243 CLR 181.

36 *South Australia v Totani* (2010) 242 CLR 1, 45 [66] (French CJ).

37 John Basten, 'Separation of Powers – Dialogue and Deference' (2018) 25 *Australian Journal of Administrative Law* 91, 92.

38 See, eg, Gabrielle Appleby and Joanna Howe, 'Scrutinising Parliament's Scrutiny of Delegated Legislative Power' (2015) 15(1) *Oxford University Commonwealth Law Journal* 3, 4; Denise Meyerson, 'Rethinking the Constitutionality of Delegated Legislation' (2003) 11(1) *Australian Journal of Administrative Law* 45.

context that the principle has little impact on Parliament's ability to delegate its legislation-making.[39] The extent that it may otherwise influence the interpretation of delegated legislation is discussed in the chapter on delegated legislation (chapter 43).

The rule of law and parliamentary sovereignty

[3.4] The rule of law influences several principles of statutory interpretation

The notion of the rule of law has a long heritage. It has been described by the High Court as 'a useful shorthand description of a complex concept central to an appreciation of the form of government that inheres in the text and structure of the *Constitution*'.[40] Since Federation it has been '[a]cknowledged repeatedly' as a concept on which the *Australian Constitution* itself is framed.[41] That it is an element of Australia's representative and responsible government is accepted as axiomatic. Its ubiquitousness is such that it has even occasionally been referred to in legislation.[42]

While the rule of law 'is a much celebrated, historic ideal',[43] the content of it 'remains difficult to pin down'.[44] It is tolerably clear that at its 'core' it refers to the idea that all people and authorities, public or private, 'should be bound by and entitled to the benefit of laws publicly made, taking effect (generally) in the future and publicly administered in the courts'.[45]

Many of the elements generally accepted as giving content to the rule of law are recognisable in statutory interpretation law.[46] Perhaps the most immediately recognisable element is that the law should be clear and accessible. This is reflected in the principle that the starting point for the interpretative process is the ordinary meaning of the statutory text. This approach 'maximises the comprehensibility and accessibility of statute law'.[47] As French CJ in *International Finance Trust Co Ltd v New South Wales Crime Commission*[48] explained:

---

39 The leading case is *Victorian Stevedoring and General Contracting Company Co Pty Ltd v Dignan* (1931) 46 CLR 73. For discussion see Gabrielle Appleby and Joanna Howe, 'Scrutinising Parliament's Scrutiny of Delegated Legislative Power' (2015) 15(1) *Oxford University Commonwealth Law Journal* 3, 6–9; James Stellios, *Zines's The High Court and the Constitution* (Federation Press, 6th ed, 2015) 199–211.

40 *Palmer v Western Australia* (2021) 95 ALJR 868, 872 [8] (Kiefel CJ, Gageler, Keane, Gordon, Steward and Gleeson JJ).

41 Ibid. See also *Australian Communist Party v Commonwealth* (1951) 83 CLR 1, 193 (Dixon J); *Plaintiff S157/2002 v Commonwealth* (2003) 211 CLR 476, 492 [31] (Gleeson CJ), 513 [103] (Gaudron, McHugh, Gummow, Kirby and Hayne JJ).

42 See, eg, *Building and Construction Industry (Improving Productivity) Act 2016* (Cth) s 3; *Human Rights Act 2019* (Qld) Preamble; *Education Act 2015* (NT) s 122.

43 Richard H Fallon, Jr, '"The Rule of Law" as a Concept in Constitutional Discourse' (1997) 97(1) *Columbia Law Review* 1, 1.

44 George Williams, Sean Brennan and Andrew Lynch, *Blackshield and Williams Australian Constitutional Law and Theory: Commentary and Materials* (Federation Press, 7th ed, 2018) 23.

45 Tom Bingham, *The Rule of Law* (Penguin Books, 2010) 37.

46 See ibid, where the core elements referred to here are identified. See also Lisa Burton Crawford, *The Rule of Law and the Australian Constitution* (Federation Press, 2017) 100–2.

47 *Treasurer of Victoria v Tabcorp Holdings Ltd* [2014] VSCA 143, [102] (the Court).

48 (2009) 240 CLR 319,

> [T]hose who are required to apply or administer the law, those who are to be bound by it and those who advise upon it are generally entitled to rely upon the ordinary sense of the words that Parliament has chosen.[49]

This element is also used in reasoning related to the use of extrinsic materials. For example, some Interpretation Acts contain provisions providing that the desirability of persons being able to rely on the ordinary meaning should be considered when determining the weight of extrinsic materials.[50]

Other examples of statutory principles being influenced by the rule of law are consistency in interpretation (predictability),[51] the presumption against retrospectivity (statutes to operate prospectively),[52] the presumption that broadly worded statutory delegations of executive power are subject to implied limitations (no arbitrariness)[53] and the presumption that legislation be construed so as to be consistent with international law (the state to comply with international law).[54] One purported element of the rule of law that has received particular attention in statutory interpretation is adequate protection of human rights.[55] This is relevant to the common law presumption known as the 'principle of legality'.[56] That presumption is that the courts will not impute to the legislature an intention to abrogate or curtail fundamental rights or freedoms unless such an intention is clearly manifested by unmistakable and unambiguous language. It is expressed as

> not merely a common sense guide to what a Parliament in a liberal democracy is likely to have intended; it is a working hypothesis, the existence of which is known both to Parliament and the courts, upon which statutory language will be interpreted. The hypothesis is *an aspect of the rule of law*.[57]

Principles of interpretation that reflect elements of the rule of law operate as an 'expectation that Parliament *ought* to legislate in a certain manner' – that is, consistency with the rule of law.[58] But Parliament can rebut these principles, whether they are common law or embodied in Interpretation Act provisions. This brings us to the principle of legislative supremacy.

The principle of legislative or parliamentary supremacy informs debate about statutory interpretation principles [3.5]

In its traditional form, the principle of parliamentary sovereignty as proposed by AV Dicey in the late 1800s in England means 'neither more nor less ... that Parliament ... has ... the right to make or unmake any law whatever; and, further, that no person or body is recognised ... as

49 Ibid 349 [42].

50 See **[24.10]**. See also *Ribbon v The Queen* (2019) 134 SASR 328, 377 [114] (Peek J).

51 See **[18.12]**.

52 See chapter 39.

53 See chapter 36.

54 See chapter 31.

55 Tom Bingham, *The Rule of Law* (Penguin Books, 2010) 66–8. See also Robert French, 'Rights and Freedoms and the Rule of Law' (2017) 28(2) *Public Law Review* 109.

56 See chapter 28.

57 *Electrolux Home Products Pty Ltd v Australian Workers' Union* (2004) 221 CLR 309, 329 [21] (Gleeson CJ) (emphasis added).

58 Lisa Burton Crawford, *The Rule of Law and the Australian Constitution* (Federation Press, 2017) 102.

having a right to override or set aside the legislation of Parliament'.[59] Although the principle as enunciated by Dicey has been the subject of considerable criticism and discussion, parliamentary sovereignty 'is accepted as a keystone' of the British constitutional system.[60]

For Australia the principle of parliamentary sovereignty, like the doctrine of separation of powers, cannot be regarded as having been transferred 'wholesale' from England to our legal system. None of the Commonwealth, state or territory parliaments are absolutely sovereign or supreme. Federal Parliament is constrained by the limits in the *Australian Constitution*. State parliaments, while arguably facing fewer limits from their own constitutions, are still subject to various constraints, including those imposed by the *Australian Constitution*.[61] It is therefore perhaps more accurate to refer to our parliaments as being 'supreme' rather than sovereign.[62] For Australia the principle has been helpfully described as meaning that, subject to constitutional limitations on legislative power, 'every statute that Parliament enacts is legally valid, and therefore that all citizens and officials, including the courts, are legally obligated to obey it'.[63]

Accepting these qualifications and limits, parliamentary supremacy is regarded as a 'basic principle' of our legal system.[64] As such, like its cousin the separation of powers, it has an influence on statutory interpretation.

At its broadest level, parliamentary supremacy means that legislation enacted by Parliament prevails over the common law to the extent of any inconsistency between the two. Determining the extent of any inconsistency, or harmony, involves determining the scope and effect of the statute to determine its relationship to the common law.[65]

Another consequence of the principle is that, generally speaking, legislation made by one parliament cannot bind or restrain a successive parliament.[66] In other words, the successive parliament can enact legislation inconsistent with, or that repeals or amends, the legislation enacted by the earlier parliament. This drives common law and statutory principles that determine how all the statutes produced by a Parliament are reconciled in the statute book.

At a more specific level, the principle directs attention to the 'fundamental object' of the interpretative process, being the ascertainment of 'legislative intent'.[67] The concept of this 'intent' is discussed in chapter 4. But it is generally accepted that it refers to 'the meaning that

59 AV Dicey, *Introduction to the Study of the Law of the Constitution* (Macmillan and Co, 8th ed, 1915) 37–8.

60 Diggory Bailey and Luke Norbury, *Bennion on Statutory Interpretation* (LexisNexis, 7th ed, 2017) 25.

61 Other examples are the *Australia Act 1986* (Cth) and *Australia Act 1986* (UK), which also impose constraints.

62 Cheryl Saunders, 'Constitutional Dimensions of Statutory Interpretation' in Anthony J Connolly and Daniel Stewart (eds), *Public Law in the Age of Statutes* (Federation Press, 2015) 27, 42. It has been said that 'sovereignty' in Australia ultimately resides with the Australian people as electors. See, eg, *Australian Capital Television Pty Ltd v Commonwealth* (1992) 177 CLR 106, 138 (Mason CJ).

63 Jeffrey Goldsworthy, *Parliamentary Sovereignty: Contemporary Debates* (Cambridge University Press, 2010) 225.

64 *Kable v DPP (NSW)* (1996) 189 CLR 51, 74, 76 (Dawson J).

65 On the relationship generally, see Anthony Mason, 'The Interaction of Statute Law and Common Law' (2016) 90(5) *Australian Law Journal* 324; Stephen Gageler, 'Common Law Statutes and Judicial Legislation: Statutory Interpretation as a Common Law Process' (2011) 37(2) *Monash University Law Review* 1.

66 This is subject to valid and binding 'manner and form' provisions that can prevent a later state Parliament from repealing or amending a prior law of that state parliament unless certain procedural or enacting obstacles (such as a special parliamentary majority) are overcome.

67 *Certain Lloyd's Underwriters v Cross* (2012) 248 CLR 378, 411 [88] (Kiefel J).

the legislature is taken to have intended' the statutory text to have.[68] That attribution is determined by objective criteria applied in accordance with the principles of statutory interpretation. This language of 'intent' is also employed in interpretation legislation.[69] Subject to the debate about the precise nature of this intent, at the least the notion requires the interpreter to focus on the objective of Parliament in enacting legislation.

In addition to this fundamental objective, particular principles of statutory interpretation law may be regarded as both reflecting and restraining legislative supremacy. The notion of 'purpose' is an example of a reflective principle. The requirement under statutory and common law to identify the purpose of a statute is reflective of a fidelity to the product of Parliament. More generally, as statutory and common law rules are assumed to be accepted 'by all arms of government,'[70] they can be regarded as self-made (if statutory) or attributed (if common law) 'standing commitments'[71] to Parliament as to how the statutory text is expected to be interpreted, subject to contrary linguistic, purposive or other 'signs' from Parliament. That is, they will be displaced if an analysis of text, context and purpose indicates that the meaning to be attributed to the text, the product of Parliament, should be otherwise.

In contrast, some principles arguably have the effect of restraining legislature supremacy by requiring the legislature to produce a high degree of clarity in the statutory text. For example, as seen above, the common law principle of legality expects a Parliament to be abundantly clear about its 'intent' to abrogate certain fundamental rights. It has been argued that such common law principles may even go so far as to elevate the common law above parliamentary law.[72]

---

68 *Project Blue Sky Inc v Australian Broadcasting Authority* (1998) 194 CLR 355, 384 [78] (McHugh, Gummow, Kirby and Hayne JJ).

69 See, eg, *Acts Interpretation Act 1901* (Cth) s 2.

70 *Zheng v Cai* (2009) 239 CLR 446, 455 [28] (French CJ, Gummow, Crennan, Kiefel and Bell JJ); *Lacey v A-G (Qld)* (2011) 242 CLR 573, 592 [43] (French CJ, Gummow, Hayne, Crennan, Kiefel and Bell JJ).

71 Expression and distinction used by Jeffrey Goldsworthy, 'Parliamentary Sovereignty and Statutory Interpretation' in Rick Bigwood (ed), *The Statute: Making and Meaning* (LexisNexis, 2004) 187, 206.

72 See, eg, Jeffrey Goldsworthy, 'Is Legislative Supremacy Under Threat? Statutory Interpretation, Legislative Intention and Common Law Principles' (2016) 60(11) *Quadrant* 56.

PART II

THE FRAMEWORK OF STATUTORY INTERPRETATION

Part II concerns those aspects of statutory interpretation that underlie all interpretative practices. Broadly, they divide into fundamental interpretative principles (chapters 4–8) and practical interpretative techniques (chapter 9).

Chapter 4 (*Legislative Intent*) deals with the fundamental object and central question of statutory interpretation: discerning the legislative intent (or the intention of Parliament) with respect to the statutory provision being construed. Intention here refers to the presumed intention of Parliament. Ascertaining legislative intent is an objective exercise, meaning that evidence of the presumed intention is gathered from specific indications of meaning in the provision and its context. The indications or factors are manifestations of the interpretative criteria (Parts IV–VIII).

Chapter 5 (*The Judicial Duty to Be Independent*) concerns the independence of the judiciary in statutory interpretation. Constitutionally, judges are independent in the sense of being the sole authoritative arbiters of the meaning of legislation. Judges are also required to be independent in reaching their interpretations. They must base their decisions on sources of law and not on a personal desire to attain a particular outcome.

In statutory interpretation, 'the text' refers to the words whose meaning is in doubt. Chapter 6 (*Text-Based Interpretation*) explores the role of the text. The chapter demonstrates how the text is central to, and a constraint upon, interpretation.

'Context' in statutory interpretation is a legal term. It does not refer to everything outside the text. It refers to those matters of relevance to be considered together with the text. Chapter 7 (*Context*) states, elaborates and illustrates in a general way the duty to have regard to the context of the text whose meaning is in issue. It is not the purpose of this chapter to examine each of the individual contextual aids. Later Parts (Parts IV–VIII) elaborate in detail the contextual aids that may be considered.

Chapter 8 (*Purpose*) discusses legislative purpose: the goal the law is designed to achieve. Taking account of and promoting, where possible, the legislative purpose is the subject of common law principle and various mandates in the Interpretation Acts of the Commonwealth, the states and the territories. Indications of legislative purpose may be provided in several ways, including inferentially by the provision in question, expressly by an objects provision, and indicatively by extrinsic (parliamentary) materials.

Statutory interpretation is more than a body of legal doctrine. It is also an area of practical skill and technique. Chapter 9 (*Practical Techniques*) examines several of the skills and techniques. They relate to legal analysis of the Act, finding interpretative clues or indications of meaning ('interpretative factors'), formulating rival contentions as to the meaning of the words in question ('alternative constructions'), evaluating interpretative arguments, determining the preferable construction, and presenting a legal opinion or reasons for judgment. The chapter also illustrates the role of legal research in statutory interpretation, and locates the various skills relating to interpretation within an overall interpretative method.

LEGISLATIVE INTENT

4

Overview

The fundamental object of statutory interpretation is to ascertain the 'intention' of Parliament, or the 'legislative intent', in relation to the statute being construed. Legislative intent is an objective notion, representative of the constitutional relationship between the arms of government. The phrase can be misleading as the word 'intent' suggests something subjective. But it is clear that legislative intent is not the collective, or individual, subjective mental states of individuals involved in the making of legislation. The so-called intent of Parliament is to be ascertained from applying the principles of statutory interpretation to a piece of legislation. The legislative intent is the inference made about Parliament's intent following that application. Beyond that, there are differing views, mostly expressed in academic commentary, about what legislative intent more precisely represents. What is clear is that legislative intent is a useful device to guide the interpretative process, is distinguishable from the purpose of an Act, and must not be equated with statements of intent found in the legislation itself or extrinsic materials. [4.1]

The object of statutory interpretation

The fundamental object of statutory interpretation is to determine the 'legislative intention' [4.2]

It is axiomatic that the 'fundamental object' or 'central question' of statutory interpretation is to ascertain the legislative or parliamentary intent.[1] Sometimes, particularly in earlier decisions, references are made to the 'will' of Parliament, an equivalent concept.[2] But more often, questions of statutory interpretation 'are commonly formulated, and answered, by reference to legislative intention'.[3]

---

1 *Certain Lloyd's Underwriters v Cross* (2012) 248 CLR 378, 411 [88] (Kiefel J); *Momcilovic v The Queen* (2011) 245 CLR 1, 116 [261] (Gummow J); *Singh v Commonwealth* (2004) 222 CLR 322, 348 [52] (McHugh J); *Cooper Brookes (Wollongong) Pty Ltd v Commissioner of Taxation (Cth)* (1981) 147 CLR 297, 304 (Gibbs CJ), 320 (Mason and Wilson JJ); *Babaniaris v Lutony Fashions Pty Ltd* (1987) 163 CLR 1, 13 (Mason J); *Ansett Transport Industries (Operations) Pty Ltd v Wardley* (1980) 142 CLR 237, 280 (Aickin J).

2 See, eg, *Wilson v Anderson* (2002) 213 CLR 401, 418 [8] (Gleeson CJ); *R v Bolton; Ex parte Beane* (1987) 162 CLR 514, 518 (Mason CJ, Wilson and Dawson JJ); *Emanuele v Australian Securities Commission* (1997) 188 CLR 114, 146 (Kirby J).

3 *Singh v Commonwealth* (2004) 222 CLR 322, 335 [19] (Gleeson CJ).

The concept is used in the interpretation of all legislation, including delegated legislation.[4] The interpretation legislation of the Commonwealth, states and territories reinforces the centrality of the notion by using the language of 'intent'. For example, all Interpretation Acts provide that their provisions are subject to the contrary intent of the statute being interpreted.[5]

[4.3] **The concept of legislative intent has constitutional significance**

The concept of legislative intent, as the object of interpretation, has been expressly acknowledged as an 'expression of the constitutional relationship between the arms of government with respect to the making, interpretation and application of laws'.[6] This statement recognises the role of 'intent' in expressing the responsibility of the court, in its constitutional context, to give effect to the intent of the legislature, which has the responsibility for making the legislation.[7] The notion therefore operates as a 'boundary marker'[8] between legislating and interpreting. See further **[4.6]**. The constitutional context of statutory interpretation generally is discussed in chapter 3.

An objective concept

[4.4] **It is well accepted that legislative intent is an objective concept and represents an inference; it does not refer to a collection of the subjective, individual mental states of individuals comprising Parliament**

The expression 'legislative intent' can be misleading as it suggests that the interpreter should be concerned with the subjective thought processes of the individuals involved in making the legislation.[9] This might have been the situation hundreds of years ago in the United Kingdom when there was little separation between the judiciary and Parliament and the 'intention' of Parliament was a matter of personal knowledge of the judges.[10]

But, as explored in chapter 3, the doctrine of separation of powers is now central to Australian statutory interpretation law. Parliament manifests its intention by the use of language

4 *Australian Unity Property Ltd v City of Busselton* (2018) 237 LGERA 333, 352 [77] (the Court).

5 *Acts Interpretation Act 1901* (Cth) s 2; *Interpretation Act 1987* (NSW) s 5; *Acts Interpretation Act 1954* (Qld) s 4; *Legislation Interpretation Act 2021* (SA) s 3; *Acts Interpretation Act 1931* (Tas) s 4; *Interpretation of Legislation Act 1984* (Vic) s 4; *Interpretation Act 1984* (WA) s 3; *Legislation Act 2001* (ACT) s 6; *Interpretation Act* 1978 (NT) s 3. For discussion, see chapter 25.

6 *Lacey v A-G (Qld)* (2011) 242 CLR 573, 592 [43] (French CJ, Gummow, Hayne, Crennan, Kiefel and Bell J), citing *Zheng v Cai* (2009) 239 CLR 446, 455 [28]. See also *Public Service Association of South Australia Inc v Industrial Relations Commission (SA)* (2012) 249 CLR 398, 423 [64] (Gummow, Hayne, Crennan, Kiefel and Bell JJ); *Plaintiff S10/2011 v Minister for Immigration and Citizenship* (2012) 246 CLR 636, 666 [97] (Gummow, Hayne, Crennan and Bell JJ).

7 *Work Health Authority v Outback Ballooning Pty Ltd* (2019) 266 CLR 428, 461 [77] (Gageler J); *Singh v Commonwealth* (2004) 222 CLR 322, 336 [19] (Gleeson CJ); Richard Ekins, 'Statutes, Intentions and the Legislature: A Reply to Justice Hayne' (2014) 14(1) *Oxford University Commonwealth Law Journal* 3, 7.

8 Robert French, 'The Principle of Legality and Legislative Intention' (2019) 40(1) *Statute Law Review* 40, 45.

9 The misleading nature of the phrase has been acknowledged for a long time. Lord Wilson famously referred to it as a 'very slippery phrase' in *Salomon v Salomon* [1897] AC 22, 38. See also *Queensland v Congoo* (2015) 256 CLR 239, 275 [67] (Hayne J); *Momcilovic v The Queen* (2011) 245 CLR 1, 135 [322] (Hayne J); *Byrnes v The Queen (*1999) 199 CLR 1, 34 [80] (Kirby J).

10 See chapter 2.

in a statute, and courts give effect to the legislative will through interpretation.[11] That is why the text is often referred to as the 'surest' guide to the legislative intent.[12]

Consequently, it is well accepted in modern statutory interpretation that 'legislative intent' does not refer to the subjective mental intent of any individual parliamentarian, drafter or other individual involved in the authorship of the statute, nor to some aggregation of the collective individual mental states of those individuals.[13] As part of the interpretative process, we do not attempt to 'take the top off the heads of [the] authors . . . . – like soft-boiled eggs – to look inside for the truest account of their brain states at the moment that the texts were created'.[14] Such 'brain states' are not equivalent to the legislative intent.

There is also a practical reason for not equating legislative intent with the subjective intent of individuals. Even if we wished to collate the subjective mental states of those involved in creating the statutory text, it would not be possible. How would we do so? Members of the legislature are 'a mass of individuals with conflicting desires, emotions, and purposes'.[15] Those members

> may have radically unclear intentions regarding a proposed statute: their intentions may waver ... some members might not have been present when assent to the statute was given; some will have voted for it because they were told to do so; different members are likely to have been involved in the various stages of the bill's passage; and amendments to the bill may mean that the eventual statute no longer reflects, or no longer reflects only, the intentions of the original promoters.[16]

As legislative intent does not mean such 'subjective' intents, legislative intent and the process of construction are described as 'objective'.[17] Legislative intent is an objective notion in the sense that it is the intention to be inferred and attributed to Parliament by analysis of the statutory words in the light of their purpose and the surrounding circumstances. As summarised by Chief Justice Gleeson in *Singh v Commonwealth*:[18]

> The danger to be avoided in references to legislative intention is that they might suggest an exercise in psychoanalysis of individuals involved in the legislative process; the value of

---

11 *Wilson v Anderson* (2002) 213 CLR 401, 418 [8] (Gleeson CJ); *Bropho v Western Australia* (1990) 171 CLR 1, 21–2 (Mason CJ, Deane, Dawson, Toohey, Gaudron and McHugh JJ).

12 *Alcan (NT) Alumina Pty Ltd v Commissioner of Territory Revenue (NT)* (2009) 239 CLR 27, 47 [47] (Hayne, Heydon, Crennan and Kiefel JJ).

13 *Wik Peoples v Queensland* (1996) 187 CLR 1, 168–9 (Gummow J); *Singh v Commonwealth* (2004) 222 CLR 322, 336 [19] (Gleeson CJ); *Zheng v Cai* (2009) 239 CLR 446, 455–6 [28] (French CJ, Gummow, Crennan, Kiefel and Bell JJ); *Lacey v A-G (Qld)* (2011) 242 CLR 573, 592 [43] (French CJ, Gummow, Hayne, Crennan, Kiefel and Bell JJ); *Work Health Authority v Outback Ballooning Pty Ltd* (2019) 266 CLR 428, 460 [75] (Gageler J).

14 *Byrnes v Kendle* (2011) 243 CLR 253, 282 [95] (Heydon and Crennan JJ), citing Charles Fried, 'Sonnet LXV and the "Black Ink" of the Framers' Intention' (1987) 100(4) *Harvard Law Review* 751, 758–9 in the context of constitutional interpretation, which they said was matched in statutory interpretation: at 283 [97].

15 Philip Sales, 'Legislative Intention, Interpretation, and the Principle of Legality' (2019) 40(1) *Statute Law Review* 53, 58.

16 Neil Duxbury, *Elements of Legislation* (Cambridge University Press, 2013) 95. See also *Mills v Meeking* (1990) 169 CLR 214, 234 (Dawson J).

17 *Momcilovic v The Queen* (2011) 245 CLR 1, 136 [327] (Hayne J); *Wilson v Anderson* (2002) 213 CLR 401, 418 [8] (Gleeson CJ); *Al-Kateb v Godwin* (2004) 219 CLR 562, 622 [167] (Kirby J); *Work Health Authority v Outback Ballooning Pty Ltd* (2019) 266 CLR 428, 461 [77] (Gageler J), citing *Singh v Commonwealth* (2004) 222 CLR 322, 336 [19].

18 (2004) 222 CLR 322.

> references to legislative intention is that they express the constitutional relationship between courts and the legislature. ... it is through the meaning of the text, understood in the light of background, purpose and object, and surrounding circumstances, that the legislature expresses its intention, and it is from the text, read in that light, that intention is inferred.[19]

In other words, legislative intent is an imputed intent ascertained by the process of applying the laws of statutory construction to the text being construed. This notion of inference or attribution is well accepted. As has been routinely cited from *Project Blue Sky Inc v Australian Broadcasting Authority*,[20] the 'duty of a court is to give the words of a statutory provision *the meaning that the legislature is taken to have intended them to have*'.[21] The 'indicia' of that legislative intent[22] are found in the text, context and purpose of the statute.[23] The meaning of the statutory words that is determined using statutory interpretation law defines the boundaries of Parliament's 'intent,' which, as was seen in chapter 3, in turn marks the demarcation of functions between the legislature and the judiciary.

Justice Edelman has explained this attribution of intent in the context of conventional understandings about language. His Honour has stated:

> In common with how all speech acts are understood, the meaning is that which a reasonable person would understand to have been intended by the words used in their context ...[24]
>
> ... the prolific references by courts to parliamentary intention are not to a subjective intention of any or all of the members of Parliament. Rather, they are shorthand to describe the same general approach that people take to the understanding of language.[25]

[4.5] Though it seems well accepted that the concept of 'legislative intent' is an objective inference, it is unclear whether that inference represents anything more

Even though long accepted as the ultimate goal of the interpretative process, the role and meaning of legislative intent in statutory interpretation 'has always been contested terrain'.[26] Legal philosophers and scholars have engaged in debate for decades about what 'legislative intent'

19 Ibid 336 [19]. See also *Sovar v Henry Lane Pty Ltd* (1967) 116 CLR 397, 405 (Kitto J); *Byrnes v Kendle* (2011) 243 CLR 253, 283 [97] (Heydon and Crennan JJ).

20 (1998) 194 CLR 355.

21 Ibid 384 [78] (McHugh, Gummow, Kirby and Hayne JJ) (emphasis added).

22 *Corporate Affairs Commission (NSW) v Yuill* (1991) 172 CLR 319, 324 (Brennan J)

23 *Military Rehabilitation and Compensation Commission v May* (2016) 257 CLR 468, 473 [10] (French CJ, Kiefel, Nettle and Gordon JJ). See chapters 6–8.

24 *Mondelez Australia Pty Ltd v Automotive, Food, Metals, Engineering, Printing and Kindred Industries Union* (2020) 94 ALJR 818, 838 [95]. Gleeson CJ expressed intent in similar terms in *Wilson v Anderson* (2002) 213 CLR 401, 418 [8].

25 *Mondelez Australia Pty Ltd v Automotive, Food, Metals, Engineering, Printing and Kindred Industries Union* (2020) 94 ALJR 818, 839 [98]. See also *Graham v Minister for Immigration and Border Protection* (2017) 263 CLR 1, 37 [76] (Edelman J); James Edelman '2018 Winterton Lecture Constitutional Interpretation' (2019) 45(1) *University of Western Australia Law Review* 1, 11–16.

26 Cheryl Saunders, 'Constitutional Dimensions of Statutory Interpretation' in Anthony J Connolly and Daniel Stewart (eds), *Public Law in the Age of Statutes: Essays in Honour of Dennis Pearce* (Federation Press, 2015) 27, 38.

does or should represent. Much of this discourse has been in the international commentary.[27] But in Australia in recent decades, there has been increased discourse about what legislative intent represents in an Australian context, represented in considerable literature.[28] The core of this contemporary discussion is whether, even accepting that 'legislative intent' is an objective imputation about what Parliament intended, that inference or imputation may or may not represent something meaningful. More particularly, much of the discussion has focused on whether legislative intent is a label or metaphor that merely represents the outcome of the process of statutory interpretation and nothing more, or whether it represents an actual or so-called group intent of Parliament.[29]

A detailed examination and assessment of the conflicting views on this subject is beyond the scope of this work. For the purposes of this chapter, following is a brief summary of two views that have prominently featured in the Australian commentary.

First, statements made by the High Court in a number of cases have been taken, primarily by commentators, to suggest that the High Court views legislative intent as a fiction or label that serves little purpose, except as a representation of the outcome of the interpretative process.[30] These statements have been a catalyst for significant academic debate in Australia (and the United Kingdom) about the nature of the concept and whether it is appropriate to regard it as merely a 'fiction' or a meaningless label.[31]

---

27 A tiny sample: John F Manning, 'Without the Pretense of Legislative Intent' (2017) 130(9) *Harvard Law Review* 2397; Victoria Nourse, 'Elementary Statutory Interpretation: Rethinking Legislative Intent and History' (2014) 55(5) *Boston College Law Review* 1613; Richard Ekins, *The Nature of Legislative Intent* (Oxford University Press, 2012); Ronald Dworkin, *Law's Empire* (Hart, 1998); Kenneth A Shepsle, 'Congress Is a "They," Not an "It": Legislative Intent as Oxymoron' (1992) 12(2) *International Review of Law and Economics* 239; James Willard Hurst, *Dealing with Statutes* (Columbia University Press, 1982) 32–40; Gerald C MacCallum Jr, 'Legislative Intent' (1966) 75(5) *Yale Law Journal* 754; Max Radin, 'Statutory Interpretation' (1930) 43(6) *Harvard Law Review* 863.

28 Stephen Gageler, 'Legislative Intention' (2015) 41(1) *Monash University Law Review* 1, 7 has suggested that the emergence of this discourse is in part linked to the Australian statutory reforms in the 1980s that enlarged the range of extrinsic materials to which the courts are permitted to refer to as interpretative aids. See **[2.5]**, **[2.6]**.

29 For a helpful summary of the three dominant characterisations of legislative intent (label, imputation, or actual group intent), see Andrew Burrows, *Thinking About Statutes: Interpretation, Interaction, Improvement* (Cambridge University Press, 2018) 15–18.

30 Cases cited in support for this view include *Mills v Meeking* (1990) 169 CLR 214, 234 (McHugh J); *Thompson v Byrne* (1999) 196 CLR 141, 147 [13] (Gleeson CJ, Gummow, Kirby and Callinan JJ); *Zheng v Cai* (2009) 239 CLR 446, 455–6 [28] (French CJ, Gummow, Crennan, Kiefel and Bell JJ); *Lacey v A-G (Qld)* (2011) 242 CLR 573, 592 [43] (French CJ, Gummow, Hayne, Crennan, Kiefel and Bell JJ); *Corporate Affairs Commission (NSW) v Yuill* (1991) 172 CLR 319, 339–40 (Gaudron J), 345–6 (McHugh J); *R v Hughes* (2000) 202 CLR 535, 563 [60] (Kirby J). *Certain Lloyd's Underwriters v Cross* (2012) 248 CLR 378, 389 [25] (French CJ and Hayne J); *Momcilovic v The Queen* (2011) 245 CLR 1, 85 [146] (Gummow J), [315], [319] (Hayne J); *Queensland v Congoo* (2015) 256 CLR 239, 265–6 [36] (French CJ and Keane J). However, the notion of legislative intent as a fiction is hardly new. This perspective has been supported by many great legal minds including Ronald Dworkin, John F Manning, Andrew Burrows, and Max Radin.

31 See, eg, Richard Ekins 'Intentions and Reflections: The Nature of Legislative Intent Revisited' (2019) 64(1) *The American Journal of Jurisprudence* 139; Richard Ekins and Jeffrey Goldsworthy, 'The Reality and Indispensability of Legislative Intentions' (2014) 36 *Sydney Law Review* 39; Jim South, 'Are Legislative Intentions Real?' (2014) 40(3) *Monash University Law Review* 853; Kenneth Hayne, 'Statutes, Intentions and the Courts: What Place Does the Notion of Intention (Legislative or Parliamentary) Have in Statutory Construction?' (2013) 13(2) *Oxford University Commonwealth Law Journal* 27; Richard Ekins, 'Statutes, Intentions and the Legislature: A Reply to Justice Hayne' (2014) 14(1) *Oxford University Commonwealth Law Journal* 3; Philip Sales 'Legislative Intention, Interpretation, and the Principle of Legality' (2019) 40(1)

In the context of that discourse a second view has been expressed. That view is that the objective attribution to Parliament reached through interpretation is not just a label, but represents a 'real' intent of Parliament, with the statute being a deliberate group act. Advocates of this view appear to have been influenced by interdisciplinary social sciences research supporting the idea that groups can be viewed as autonomous entities.[32] For example, just as we refer to the 'intent' of a corporation, so too can we refer to the intent of Parliament as a meaningful concept that refers to a deliberate act by the group (Parliament) to further a particular objective.[33] This is a type of constructive intent. It is what 'a reasonable audience would conclude was the author's 'subjective' intention, given all the publicly available evidence of it'.[34]

The 'reality' of legislative intent as group intent appears to have received some support in the High Court from Justice Gageler. His Honour has questioned the scepticism about the characterisation of legislative intent as just a label and stated:

> Groups acting deliberatively according to established procedures can meaningfully be seen to have intentions, distinct from the subjective intentions of their constituent individuals, both as to what collectively they seek to achieve and as to how collectively they seek to achieve it. Legislative assemblies in representative democracies are the paradigm of groups acting deliberatively, as courts in representative democracies have for the most part done well to recognise when construing legislative output . . .[35]
>
> To reduce legislative intention to a label for the outcome of a constructional choice made by the court itself, is to miss the point of the traditional terminology. It is to ignore that the responsibility of the court, in making a constructional choice, is to adopt an authoritative construction of legislated text which accords with the imputed intention of the enacting legislature.[36]

The discussion awaits further clarification by the High Court.

Statute Law Review 53; Philip Sales, 'In Defence of Legislative Intention' (2019) 48(1) *Australian Bar Review* 6; Robert French, 'The Principle of Legality and Legislative Intention' (2019) 40(1) *Statute Law Review* 40; Andrew Burrows, *Thinking About Statutes: Interpretation, Interaction, Improvement* (Cambridge University Press, 2018) 18; Jeffrey Goldsworthy, 'Lord Burrows on Legislative Intention, Statutory Purpose, and the "Always Speaking' Principle" (2022) 43(1) *Statute Law Review* 79. For a direct comparison of views see Patrick Emerton and Lisa Burton Crawford, 'Statutory Meaning Without Parliamentary Intention: Defending the High Court's "Alternative Approach" to Statutory Interpretation' and Jeffrey Goldsworthy, 'Response to Contributors', both in Lisa Burton Crawford, Patrick Emerton and Dale Smith (eds), *Law Under a Democratic Constitution: Essays in Honour of Jeffrey Goldsworthy* (Hart Publishing, 2019) 39 and 270–6 respectively.

32 See the brief explanation in Stephen Gageler, 'Legislative Intention' (2015) 41(1) *Monash University Law Review* 1, 11–13, referring to Christian List and Philip Pettit, *Group Agency: The Possibility, Design and Status of Corporate Agents* (Oxford University Press, 2011) and Christian List, 'Collective Wisdom: Lessons From the Theory of Judgment Aggregation' in Hélène Landemore and Jon Elster (eds), *Collective Wisdom: Principles and Mechanics* (Cambridge University Press, 2012) 203. See also Richard Ekins and Jeffrey Goldsworthy, 'The Reality and Indispensability of Legislative Intentions' (2014) 36(1) *Sydney Law Review* 39, 64–5 who refer to, among others, the works of John Searle and Michael Bratman.

33 See also the useful explanation given in Philip Sales, 'Legislative Intention, Interpretation, and the Principle of Legality' (2019) 40(1) *Statute Law Review* 53, 59.

34 Richard Ekins and Jeffrey Goldsworthy, 'The Reality and Indispensability of Legislative Intentions' (2014) 36(1) *Sydney Law Review* 39, 46. See further at 48, 64, 67. See also Richard Ekins, 'Statutes, Intentions and the Legislature: A Reply to Justice Hayne' (2014) 14(1) *Oxford University Commonwealth Law Journal* 3, 5.

35 *Work Health Authority v Outback Ballooning Pty Ltd* (2019) 266 CLR 428, 460 [75] (Gageler J) (citations omitted).

36 Ibid 461 [77]. See also *Corliss v The Queen* (2020) 282 A Crim R 195, 214–5 [84]–[85] (Johnson J).

The differing views about what legislative intent represents do matter at a theoretical level; but at a practical level it is sufficient to recognise that the notion of legislative intent is useful as a device to provide focus for the interpretative task [4.6]

As Justice Basten has said extrajudicially, the issue about what legislative intent means is not just about semantics.[37] At the level of theory, the precise meaning of legislative intent does matter. Meta-theories of statutory interpretation, such as textualism, purposivism and intentionalism, depend on concepts of legislative intent. For example, the 'fiction' view is sometimes seen as a reflection of a textualist approach, whereas the use of 'group intent' arguments is sometimes more closely linked to purposivism or intentionalism.[38]

Our understanding of the concept of legislative intent is relevant at other theoretical levels. How we characterise this concept has implications for the reasoning behind many common law interpretative principles.[39] For example, scholars in Australia argue that how we rationalise the principle of legality, which is concerned with statutory provisions affecting fundamental rights or the general system of law (see chapter 28), depends on our presumptions about legislative intention. If the rationale for the principle is that it forces Parliament to squarely confront its abrogation of fundamental rights when passing legislation, then that depends on a presumption of actual group intent.[40]

At a practical level, in the day-to-day interpretation of statutes, it is probably sufficient to recognise that legislative intent represents the outcome of the application of statutory interpretation law, regardless of whether that intent is seen as a metaphor or label or as actual imputed group intent, or another characterisation. This is because, at the least, it is a legitimate term of legal analysis that guides the interpretative process.[41] It 'provides a specific and focused object of inquiry'.[42] The objective of finding a Parliament's intent directs the interpreter to a conclusion. It is 'a useful judicial construct because the judge is required to make the choices that best express the statutory text's meaning'.[43] That is why the concept has variously been referred to as a lodestar,[44]

37 John Basten, 'Legislative Intention' (2019) 93(5) *Australian Law Journal* 367, 368.

38 For a discussion on the relationship between legislative intent and 'intentionalism' in an Australian context, see Jamie Blaker, 'Is Intentionalist Theory Indispensable to Statutory Interpretation?' (2017) 43(1) *Monash University Law Review* 238.

39 See generally Richard Ekins and Jeffrey Goldsworthy, 'The Reality and Indispensability of Legislative Intentions' (2014) 36(1) *Sydney Law Review* 39, 42–5.

40 Bruce Chen, 'The Principle of Legality: Protecting Statutory Rights from Statutory Infringement?' (2019) 41(1) *Sydney Law Review* 73, 76. See also Philip Sales, 'Legislative Intention, Interpretation, and the Principle of Legality (2019) 40(1) *Statute Law Review* 53, 61–3. Cf Robert French, 'The Principle of Legality and Legislative Intention' (2019) 40(1) *Statute Law Review* 40.

41 *Work Health Authority v Outback Ballooning Pty Ltd* (2019) 266 CLR 428, 461 [77] (Gageler J); *Singh v Commonwealth* (2004) 222 CLR 322, 336 [19] (Gleeson CJ).

42 Philip Sales, 'Legislative Intention, Interpretation, and the Principle of Legality' (2019) 40(1) *Statute Law Review* 53, 60.

43 *Singh v Commonwealth* (2004) 222 CLR 322, 348 [52] (McHugh J), citing William Popkin, *Statutes in Court: The History and Theory of Statutory Interpretation* (Duke University Press, 1999) 211.

44 Cheryl Saunders, 'Constitutional Dimensions of Statutory Interpretation' in Anthony J Connolly and Daniel Stewart (eds), *Public Law in the Age of Statutes: Essays in Honour of Dennis Pearce* (Federation Press, 2015) 27, 36.

a constitutional compass[45] and 'a message for judges about judging'.[46] It is a device that reminds the interpreter that they operate under institutional and legal constraints.

Distinct from 'purpose'

[4.7] **Legislative intent is distinguishable from the concept of purpose**

Legislative intent is distinguishable from another key concept in statutory interpretation – purpose. Briefly, purpose is the object of the statute, or what it is designed to achieve (see chapter 8).

Determining legislative intent involves the application of the principles of statutory construction. A central principle is that we must endeavour to identify the purpose of the Act and adopt a construction that best achieves or is consistent with that purpose. The purpose or purposes of a statute, therefore, is just one of the factors (albeit a mandated consideration) that contribute to the task of determining the legislative intent (whatever view is taken of intent) and therefore the meaning.[47] Identification of statutory purpose is 'not logically congruent' with that of legislative intention, although sometimes the two may coincide.[48] To paraphrase Bennion, purpose relates to the object or policy to which the enactment is directed, while legislative intent is the imputed intent of Parliament represented by the legal meaning of the enactment.[49] The purpose is not what the law *means* – that is, the imputed intent – but what the law is *designed to achieve*.[50] Purpose can encompass a multitude of different objects or policies within a single statute; that in itself is inconsistent with the ultimate aim of interpretation being the determination of the (single) legislative intent.

It has been suggested in the academic literature that the distinction between purpose and legislative intent may be difficult to maintain.[51] If purpose is articulated as being, for example, the 'intended aim' or 'goal' of the legislature'[52] it is easy to see how the two concepts may overlap

45 Susan Kenny, 'Constitutional Role of the Judge: Statutory Interpretation' (2014) 1 *Judicial College of Victoria Online Journal* 4, 13.

46 Stephen Gageler, 'Legislative Intention' (2015) 41(1) *Monash University Law Review* 1, 14, citing Victoria F Nourse, 'A Decision Theory of Statutory Interpretation: Legislative History by the Rules' (2012) 122(1) *Yale Law Journal* 70, 85.

47 *Project Blue Sky Inc v Australian Broadcasting Authority* (1998) 194 CLR 355, 384 [78] (McHugh, Gummow, Kirby and Hayne JJ).

48 *Lee v New South Wales Crime Commission* (2013) 251 CLR 196, 226 [45] (French CJ). See also *Tullamore Bowling & Citizens Club Ltd v Lander* [1984] 2 NSWLR 32, 52–3 (Mahoney JA).

49 Oliver Jones, *Bennion on Statutory Interpretation* (LexisNexis, 6th ed, 2013) 455.

50 See Jeffrey Barnes, 'Contextualism: "The Modern Approach to Statutory Interpretation"' (2018) 41(4) *University of New South Wales Law Journal* 1083, 1109.

51 See, eg, Stephen Gageler, 'Legislative Intention' (2015) 41(1) *Monash University Law Review* 1, 10–11; Dale Smith, 'What is Statutory Purpose' in Lisa Burton Crawford, Patrick Emerton, Dale Smith (eds), *Law Under a Democratic Constitution: Essays in Honour of Jeffrey Goldsworthy* (Hart Publishing, 2019) 13, 16–19; Andrew Burrows, *Thinking About Statutes: Interpretation, Interaction, Improvement* (Cambridge University Press, 2018) 19–20.

52 *Unions NSW v New South Wales* (2019) 264 CLR 595, 656 [168], 657 [171] (Edelman J). See also *Work Health Authority v Outback Ballooning Pty Ltd* (2019) 266 CLR 428, 459 [72] (Gageler J). See chapter 8.

or be confused. Sometimes the two phrases are loosely used interchangeably, particularly in the context of describing the general purpose of a statute. But this is more a matter of indiscriminate expression rather than an intended equation of the two concepts.

Statements of intent in legislation

Statements of legislative intent in legislation inform but do not define construction [4.8]

The question sometimes arises as to the relevance of a statement in the statute itself about the legislative intent of that statute. For example, it is not uncommon to find statements in statutes about how an Act is intended to operate with the law of other Australian jurisdictions. Although there has been little attention given to such statements as a component of statutory interpretation, it is likely that they would be treated like provisions that state the purpose or object of an Act.[53] That is, such statements will be one of the intrinsic textual factors to be weighed and balanced in the interpretative process and so will inform, but not decide, the legislative intent. They are merely one of the provisions of a statute that must be considered in the context of the whole statute and other legitimate aids.

Example 4.1 *John Holland Pty Ltd v Victorian Workcover Authority*[54]

The plaintiff was charged with various offences relating to health and safety risks under the *Occupational Health and Safety Act 2004* (Vic) ('the Victorian Act'). After the alleged offences were committed, but before charges were laid, new licensing provisions came into force under the *Occupational Health and Safety Act 1991* (Cth) ('the Commonwealth Act'). The plaintiff became subject to the Commonwealth Act.

Section 4(1) of the Commonwealth Act relevantly provided:

> [T]his Act is intended to apply to the exclusion of any law of a State or Territory . . . to the extent that the law of the State or Territory relates to occupational health or safety and would otherwise apply in relation to employers, employees or the employment of employees.

An issue before the High Court was the proper construction of s 4 and the extent to which the Commonwealth Act, by virtue of s 109 of the *Constitution*, excluded the operation of the Victorian Act.

A unanimous judgment of the Court referred to s 4 as an 'express statement of legislative intent' in terms of the field that the law was intended to cover. The Court then said:

> But such a statement is only a statement of intention which informs the construction of the Act as a whole. It must be an intention which the substantive provisions of the Act are capable of supporting.[55]

53 Robert French, 'The Principle of Legality and Legislative Intention' (2019) 40(1) *Statute Law Review* 40, 50.

54 (2009) 239 CLR 518.

55 Ibid [20] 527. Cited with approval in *CPCF v Minister for Immigration and Border Protection* (2015) 255 CLR 514, 601 [282] (Kiefel J, dissenting).

The intention of a statute must be revealed by the application of the principles of statutory construction of which an express statement of intent in the legislation is just one indicator. In *John Holland* the Court concluded that the substantive provisions of the Act did support the statement of intention.[56]

Statement of intent in extrinsic materials

[4.9] **The intent expressed in parliamentary or other extrinsic materials does not equate to legislative intent**

As discussed above, 'legislative intent' does not refer to the aggregated subjective intentions of the individuals involved in the drafting and enactment of a statute, such as members of Parliament (including Ministers), legislative drafters, or departmental public servants. As a corollary to that proposition, the mental state or subjective intent of any one individual participant as revealed in extrinsic materials should not be conflated with the intent of Parliament. Extrinsic materials are materials that are extraneous to the Act in question.[57]

This is particularly important to bear in mind when referring to parliamentary and executive materials such as the Minister's second reading speech or explanatory memoranda.[58] The interpreter must avoid the danger of conflating the intention expressed by an individual involved in the making of the statute with the intent of the legislature.[59] The intent of the statute as expressed by any participant in extrinsic materials does not, of itself, equate to the intent of Parliament. So, to the extent that an individual, even the Minister introducing a Bill for an Act, expresses the intent of a Bill, that intent must not be considered as the final determination of meaning of the language of the statute, or the 'parliamentary intent'. As Allsop P has cautioned:

> I am mindful that any initial engagement with enactment history and context might be misunderstood as part of any enquiry as to the subjective intent of legislators or policy advisers so that such divined intent can be transferred to the words used by Parliament. Such an enquiry would be misdirected. It is the language of Parliament that must be interpreted and construed . . .[60]

This does not mean that those statements are irrelevant. As discussed in chapter 24, the second reading speech and other extrinsic materials can be of considerable probative value in the interpretative process. (Indeed, some advocates of the 'group theory' of intent consider the 'subjective' expressions about the statute by individuals involved in the making of the statute as important evidence for constructing the group intent.[61]) But evidence from such materials is only a factor in

56 *John Holland Pty Ltd v Victorian Workcover Authority* (2009) 239 CLR 518, 528 [22].

57 See Part V.

58 See chapter 24.

59 For practical difficulties with this conflation, see Neil Duxbury, *Elements of Legislation* (Cambridge University Press, 2013) 95–6, 108. For an anecdote highlighting the danger of the conflation, see Keith Mason, 'The Intent of Legislators' in Tom Gotsis (ed), *Statutory Interpretation: Principles and Pragmatism for a New Age* (Education Monograph 4, Judicial Commission of New South Wales, 2007) 33, 37.

60 *Wilson v State Rail Authority of New South Wales* (2010) 78 NSWLR 704, 707 [12] (Allsop P, Giles, Hodgson, Tobias and Macfarlan JJA agreeing).

61 Richard Ekins and Jeffrey Goldsworthy, 'The Reality and Indispensability of Legislative Intentions' (2014) 36(1) *Sydney Law Review* 39, 48.

the weighing and assessing of what are typically numerous factors when it comes to interpreting a statute. Further, to start from a presumption that any intent expressed by an individual is synonymous with the intent of Parliament is to work backwards. The interpretative task must start with the language and, as Allsop P states above, the ultimate meaning must be determined as a result of the weighing and balancing of interpretative factors, whether extrinsic materials, purpose, or intrinsic components, and ultimately must be reconciled with the text of the statute.

Example 4.2 *Nominal Defendant v GLG Australia Pty Ltd*[62]

The plaintiff, Mr Tleyji, was an employee of a labour hire company. That company supplied Mr Tleyji's services to another company, GLG Australia Pty Ltd ('GLG'). GLG occupied and operated a warehouse where the unloading of containers of goods took place. The usual method of operation for the unloading was for containers to be unloaded in the yard of the warehouse. A pallet was placed on a landing in front of the open container. The labourers would then place the boxes from the container onto the pallet. A forklift truck would go up the ramp to the landing. It would pick up the pallet and then reverse down the ramp. When the forklift truck went up the ramp it caused vibrations. These vibrations could be felt through the ramp, the landing and the container.

One day, Mr Tleyji was standing about a metre inside the container. The vibration caused by a forklift truck led to the boxes stacked in the container to fall and strike him. Mr Tleyji successfully sued the labour hire company and GLG, with the judge apportioning liability between them. GLG's insurer had gone into liquidation so its liabilities were taken over by the Nominal Defendant. The Nominal Defendant argued that it had no obligation under the third-party policy arrangements established by the *Motor Accidents Act 1988* (NSW) ('the Act') to indemnify GLG as Mr Tleyji's claim was outside the Act. GLG contended that Mr Tleyji's claim was a motor accident claim within the scope of the Act.

Section 69 of the Act provided for the award of damages in relation to injury to a person caused by the fault of the owner or driver of the vehicle. Injury was relevantly defined in s 3 of the Act as follows:

> [I]njury:
>
> (a) means personal or bodily injury caused by the fault of the owner or driver of a motor vehicle in the use or operation of the vehicle if, and only if, the injury is a result of and is caused during:
> (i) the driving of the vehicle, or
> (ii) a collision, or action taken to avoid a collision, with the vehicle, or
> (iii) the vehicle's running out of control, or
> (iv) such use or operation by a defect in the vehicle, . . .

The interpretative issue was whether Mr Tleyji's injury fell within the definition of 'injury' in s 3(1) of the Act.

The definition of 'injury' had been inserted by amendment in 1995.[63] One of the interpretative aids relied on by the Nominal Defendant to argue a narrow construction of 'injury' was the second reading speech of the Minister introducing the amendment Bill. In his speech the Minister

62 (2006) 228 CLR 529.

63 *Motor Accidents Amendment Act 1995* (NSW).

lamented the broad judicial interpretation that had been given to the Act provisions in the past, explaining that it had become 'critical to unambiguously impart the underlying aims and objectives of the *Motor Accidents Act* to the judiciary, lawyers and insurers'. He went on to say (referring to the Act scheme as the CTP policy):

> The CTP policy and the motor accidents scheme simply are not, and were never intended to be, a comprehensive accident compensation scheme providing substantial damages in all cases of injuries connected in some way to the use of a motor vehicle. Common sense and community expectations generally demand that the CTP policy provide coverage in respect of injuries which arise from crashes and *collisions on the roads or from vehicles running out of control*. Over the years the courts have interpreted the CTP policy as providing for a wide range of injuries often unrelated to motor accidents. For example, the CTP policy has been held to cover injuries sustained during the loading and unloading of vehicles, and injuries sustained while standing on the back of a stationary trailer, and injuries involved in the use of a firearm in a vehicle.[64]

The Nominal Defendant argued that this speech manifested the intent of Parliament to narrow the meaning of injury to certain types of injury, being those arising from clashes and collisions.

The majority, Gleeson CJ, Gummow, Hayne and Heydon JJ, held that the injury to Mr Tleyji had been caused by GLG's failure to design and implement a safe system of work in relation to the unloading of containers by the forklift, rather than being the result of the 'driving' of the forklift. Consequently, the injury was not within the meaning of para (a)(i) of the definition of 'injury' in the Act. In dissent, Kirby J held that Mr Tleyji's injury was within the section.

Despite these differing views, both judgments cautioned against the manner in which the Nominal Defendant had attempted to use the Ministerial speech. The majority stated that referring to the speech to identify the purpose of the amendment inserting the new definition of 'injury' was permissible. However, they also stated:

> It is not a permissible use of the speech, for example, to say that, because it referred to crashes and collisions on the roads, and vehicles running out of control, the post-1995 definition of 'injury' was limited to injuries caused in these ways, without paying regard to its precise terms. The speech criticised cases holding that the Act applied to injuries sustained during the loading and unloading of vehicles ... [but] ... The words of the statute, not non-statutory words seeking to explain them, have paramount significance.[65]

Kirby J also considered the speech with caution, referring to it as mainly providing 'an illustration of the political context in which the 1995 amendments to the Act were enacted'.[66] Like the majority, he said that 'the Second Reading and other speeches in Parliament may only be used to throw light on the meaning of legislative words, to the extent that such speeches are sustained by the legislative text as subsequently adopted'.[67] This caution, his Honour said, was 'not to discourage the proper use of such materials' but was to emphasise the primacy of the enacted law.[68]

64 *Nominal Defendant v GLG Australia Pty Ltd* (2006) 228 CLR 529, 554–5 [80] (Kirby J), citing New South Wales, *Parliamentary Debates*, Legislative Council, 16 November 1995, 3322 (emphasis in original).

65 Ibid 538 [22] (Gleeson CJ, Gummow, Hayne and Heydon JJ).

66 Ibid 555 [81].

67 Ibid 555 [82].

68 Ibid 556 [82].

In other words, content of parliamentary materials, even those making statements of intent, are not to be substituted for the process of ascertaining legislative intent. They may be a probative aid in that task, but they are just one indicator in the matrix of other relevant factors (such as intrinsic indicators and purpose) to weigh and balance before coming to a final determination of what Parliament intended. Statements of aspirations in parliamentary materials, including second reading speeches, about a statute must not be equated to the meaning of the statute. That conclusion is a result of the interpretative process.

5 THE JUDICIAL DUTY TO BE INDEPENDENT

Overview

[5.1] Judges are required to be independent in statutory interpretation in two main senses. First, they are independent in the sense of sovereign. In Australian law, judges are the sole authoritative arbiters of the meaning of legislation.

Second, judges are required to be independent in reaching their decisions. Courts are not dependent in a legal sense on parties for constructions. A judge is more than a mere selector between rival views. Courts are also independent of other interpretation agencies, whose statements of meaning are not relevant. And judges must not base their decisions on a personal desire to attain a particular outcome. Nevertheless, the duty to be independent permits individual judgement within the limits of legal method. Consequently, judges may disagree.

Sole authoritative arbiters

[5.2] **Courts are independent in the sense of sovereign; they are the sole authoritative arbiters of the meaning of legislation**

Courts are not the only interpretation agencies, in the sense of agencies that interpret the law in practice. The executive (principally, Ministers, government departments and statutory authorities) regularly interprets the law in the course of administering the law. For example, the Australian Taxation Office interprets taxation law. Executive decisions have presumptive validity.[1] Ministers sometimes express views of the meaning of a proposed law in the course of the passage of a Bill.[2] Laypersons frequently access the statute book[3] and presumably may form a view of what the law means.

Courts in the common law tradition have, however, the 'province and duty' to interpret the law. As Brennan J recalled in *Attorney-General for the State of New South Wales v Quin*:[4]

1 The 'presumption of regularity' is sometimes expressed in the Latin maxim *omnia praesumuntur rite et solemniter esse acta*; see, eg, *Ousley v The Queen* (1997) 192 CLR 69, 89 (Gaudron J), 107 (McHugh J), 129 (Gummow J, quoting *Kinning v Buchanan* (1849) 8 CB 271, 286; 137 ER 513, 519).

2 As occurred in *Harrison v Melhem* (2008) 72 NSWLR 380. See further chapters 24 and 33.

3 For a study of access by laypersons to statutory databases, see Alison Bertlin, 'What Works Best for the Reader? A Study on Drafting and Presenting Legislation' [2014] (2) *The Loophole: Journal of the Commonwealth Association of Legislative Counsel* 25.

4 (1990) 170 CLR 1.

> The duty and the jurisdiction of the courts are expressed in the memorable words of Marshall CJ in *Marbury v Madison:* 'It is, emphatically, the province and duty of the judicial department to say what the law is.'[5]

As a consequence, Australian courts are 'the sole authoritative arbiter of the meaning of the statutory expression of Parliament's will'.[6] This reflects the separation of powers in the Australian system, whereby '[t]he authoritative determination of the meaning of a statutory provision is an exercise of the judicial power, not of the legislative power, let alone of the executive power'.[7] Thus, it has been held that '[t]he courts have no reason to defer to the Executive Government's view of the meaning of a statutory provision'.[8]

The origin of the court's role in Anglo-Australian law lies in the history of the English courts:

> [It] is the function of the courts to say what the application of the words used to particular cases or individuals is to be. This power which has been devolved upon the judges from the earliest times is an essential part of the constitutional process by which subjects are brought under the rule of law – as distinct from the rule of the King or the rule of Parliament; and it would be a degradation of that process if the courts were to be merely a reflecting mirror of what some other interpretation agency might say . . .[9]

Australian law may be contrasted with the American position, where a doctrine of deference prevails in respect of certain administrative interpretations. The doctrine ('the *Chevron* doctrine' after the leading case[10]) applies 'where the statute [is] administered by a federal agency or regulatory authority [and it] is susceptible of several constructions, each of which may be seen to be (as it is put) a reasonable representation of Congressional intent'.[11] In other words, put simply, the regulatory agency need only arrive at a reasonable interpretation. In seriously considered dicta, the High Court of Australia has criticised the doctrine.[12] Following that case,

---

5 Ibid 35. His Honour was citing *Marbury v Madison*, 5 US (1 Cranch) 137, 177 (1803). Courts have often approved Brennan J's statement; see, eg, *Corporation of the City of Enfield v Development Assessment Commission* (2000) 199 CLR 135, 152–3 (Gleeson CJ, Gummow, Kirby and Hayne JJ, Gaudron J generally agreeing at 156 [53]). See also *Federal Commissioner of Taxation v Indooroopilly Children Services (Qld) Pty Ltd* (2007) 158 FCR 325, 327 [5] (Allsop J, Stone J agreeing at 326 [1]).

6 *Dietman v Brennan-Kuss* (2015) 123 SASR 24, 38 [45] (Kourakis CJ, Bampton J agreeing at 40 [55], Muecke DCJ agreeing at 40 [56]).

7 *Harrison v Melhem* (2008) 72 NSWLR 380, 384 [15] (Spigelman CJ). See chapter 3 for a general discussion of the doctrine of the separation of powers in the context of legislation and its interpretation.

8 *Dietman v Brennan-Kuss* (2015) 123 SASR 24, 38 [45] (Kourakis CJ, Bampton J agreeing at 40 [55], Muecke DCJ agreeing at 40 [56]). For statements made during parliamentary proceedings, see further chapter 24. For post-enactment statements see further **[33.5]**.

9 *Black-Clawson International Ltd v Papierwerke Waldhof-Aschaffenburg AG* [1975] AC 591, 629 (Lord Wilberforce). But since that statement, English courts have allowed ministerial statements made in Parliament to be given weight in determining the meaning of the law. See Jeffrey Barnes, 'Statements of Meaning in Parliamentary Debates: Revisiting *Harrison v Melhem*' [2018] 5 *University of New South Wales Law Journal Forum* 1, 3–4.

10 *Chevron USA Inc v Natural Resources Defense Council Inc*, 467 US 837 (1984).

11 *Corporation of the City of Enfield v Development Assessment Commission* (2000) 199 CLR 135, 151 [41] (Gleeson CJ, Gummow, Kirby and Hayne JJ; Gaudron J generally agreeing at 156 [53]).

12 Ibid 152 [41]–[42]. It is true that the High Court did not reject the *Chevron* doctrine in that case: Stephen Gageler, 'Deference' (2015) 22(3) *Australian Journal of Administrative Law* 151, 155. But, with respect, since the doctrine is not part of Australian law, the High Court had no need to do so. For a commentary on *Chevron* from an Australian perspective, see Gageler at 156.

the Full Federal Court held that '[i]t is clear that the *Chevron* doctrine is not a principle that applies in Australia'.[13]

The following case illustrates how an appeal court will correct a lower court if the appeal court perceives that the interpretative question was not determined independently.

Example 5.1 ***Minister for Immigration and Citizenship v Yucesan***[14]

As mentioned in chapter 1,[15] this case dealt with the meaning of 'have met' in cl 300.214 of the *Migration Regulations* (Cth). The Migration Review Tribunal had held that the words in question 'extended to non physical person-to-person interactions'.[16] As a result, the visa applicant (who was in Turkey) was eligible for a Prospective Marriage (Temporary) (Class TO) visa even though he had never met his fiancée (a Sydney woman) in person.

The Minister applied for judicial review in the Federal Magistrates Court, but the Court dismissed the application. Under the heading 'Conclusions', the Magistrate stated, among other things: 'In my view, it can be argued that meeting by internet or video telephony is at least as effective [sic] way for parties to meet and form an opinion about each other's compatibility as a future marriage partner as the current phenomenon of "speed dating".'[17]

Before the Full Court of the Federal Court, counsel for the Minister argued that the Federal Magistrate had erred. The Court recounted the argument:

> [T]he federal magistrate seemed to defer to the Tribunal in a manner reminiscent of the United States '*Chevron* doctrine' in considering whether the Tribunal's construction was 'arguable'. That doctrine, it was submitted, has no place in Australian law and the Tribunal should have asked itself whether the Tribunal's analysis was 'correct' and not whether it was arguable.[18]

The Court held that, to the extent that the Magistrate had deferred to the Tribunal, his Honour had erred.[19]

Independence in reaching a decision

[5.3] Courts are independent of the parties and are more than mere selectors between rival views

In *Coleman v Power*[20] Kirby J stated:

> Subject to considerations of procedural fairness, this Court may adopt a construction of legislation that has not been argued by the parties, and a fortiori it is

13 *Minister for Immigration and Citizenship v Yucesan* (2008) 169 FCR 202, 207 [15].

14 Ibid.

15 At **Example 1.4**.

16 Quoted in (2008) 169 FCR 202, 205 [4] (the Court).

17 *Minister for Immigration and Citizenship v Yucesan* (2008) 216 FLR 252 [49], quoted in ibid 205 [7] (the Court).

18 (2008) 169 FCR 202, 205–6 [9] (the Court).

19 Ibid 207 [15].

20 (2004) 220 CLR 1.

> not restricted to the interpretive principles argued by their representatives. As Lord Wilberforce said in *Saif Ali v Sydney Mitchell & Co*: 'Judges are more than mere selectors between rival views – they are entitled to and do think for themselves.'[21]

Courts have departed from the constructions of counsel for both parties in a number of cases.[22]

Example 5.2 *R v Hannan*[23]

The *Vicious Lawless Association Disestablishment Act 2013* (Qld) provided that when a court was sentencing a 'vicious lawless associate' for a declared offence, it must impose a further sentence of 15 years imprisonment: s 7(1)(b). The question arose as to the meaning of 'vicious lawless associate'. That term was defined as requiring, among other things, the person to be 'a participant in the affairs of an association': s 5(1)(b). In turn, 'association' was defined as including 'any other group of 3 or more persons by whatever name called, whether associated formally or informally and whether the group is legal or illegal': s 3. Each of the applicants had been charged with a number of offences, including trafficking in cannabis. It was alleged that each was a vicious lawless associate. Each applicant applied for a ruling that it was not established that he or she was such an associate at the time of offending. The evidence revealed that one of the applicants conducted an operation that involved the growing of cannabis plants and the sale of cannabis. The other applicants assisted him in achieving his purpose of conducting a profitable business of producing and selling cannabis.

The applicants contended that a group that breaks a limited class of law and does not have the attribute of general lawlessness was not an association.[24] The Crown contended that 'group' extended to 'an organised group of people who are united by a common object or purpose'.[25]

Neither of these constructions prevailed. The Court held for a construction that differed from that submitted by both parties:

> I conclude, therefore, that a person who acts with two or more others is not a vicious lawless associate, unless it is also shown that these persons when considered together have what I have referred to as a recognisable group existence, and a recognisable group identity.[26]

21 Ibid 94 [243], quoting *Saif Ali v Sydney Mitchell & Co* [1980] AC 198, 212.

22 See, eg, *Mount Beauty Gliding Club Inc v Jacob* (2004) 10 VR 312. Specific reference is made in that case to the Court effectively according the parties procedural fairness: the Court invited submissions from counsel on a construction originating from the bench: at 320 [21] (Callaway JA, Buchanan JA agreeing at 324 [34]). Other examples of cases in which a court departed from the constructions of counsel for both parties are *DPP v Dale* (2010) 30 VR 282 (Beach J) (dicta); *Woodcrest Homes Pty Ltd v Fair Trading Tribunal* [2002] NSWSC 552, [33] (Bell J); *R v Hannan* (2016) 259 A Crim R 558 (Peter Lyons J). The last-mentioned case is discussed below.

23 (2016) 259 A Crim R 558.

24 Ibid 563 [17] (Peter Lyons J).

25 Ibid 564 [21].

26 Ibid 569 [48]. Applying the law to the facts, the Court concluded that 'the evidence reveals that the applicants did not constitute an association for the purposes of the VLAD Act, and accordingly none of them was a "vicious lawless associate" for the purposes of s 7 of that Act': at 572 [62].

The Court's preferred construction was not as wide as the Crown's nor as narrow as each applicant's. But when applied to the facts, it resulted in a verdict for each applicant. The Court held that the evidence did not reveal the existence of a group, and nor therefore an association, under the Act.[27]

[5.4] **In interpreting legislation, judges must reason independently – that is, they must base their decisions on sources of law and not on a personal desire to attain a particular outcome**[28]

As in other areas of law, interpretation requires decisions to be based on legal sources:

> [T]he judiciary is strictly involved in interpreting and applying principles of law, the source of which is either legislation or the common law. It is axiomatic, but critical, that in performing that role, no judge acts according to his or her own values or individual views. Some of the functions of the judiciary – such as sentencing – do involve discretionary judgments, but those judgments are made according to established legal principles. They are not decided according to the judge's own set of values or individual idiosyncratic views of life.[29]

Thus, it is not acceptable for the court to presume a purpose for the legislation if there is no legislative basis for doing so:

> This approach, with respect, emphasised a judicially constructed policy at the expense of the requisite consideration of the statutory text and its relatively clear purpose. In construing a statute it is not for a court to construct its own idea of a desirable policy, impute it to the legislature, and then characterise it as a statutory purpose.[30]

And it is not acceptable for a judge to base their interpretation on a personal desire to attain a particular outcome:

> [Statutory interpretation] is, however, a species of law-making necessarily constrained by the requirement that the judges confine themselves to interpretation within the range of meanings which the words can bear *and not engage in rewriting laws to attain desired outcomes*.[31]

27 Ibid 571 [56], 572 [62].

28 See further **[33.4]**.

29 *WBM v Chief Commissioner of Police* (2010) 27 VR 469, 481 [46] (Kaye J).

30 *Australian Education Union v Department of Education and Children's Services* (2012) 248 CLR 1, 14 [28] (French CJ, Hayne, Kiefel and Bell JJ). See also, to similar effect, *Certain Lloyd's Underwriters v Cross* (2012) 248 CLR 378, 395 [41] (French CJ and Hayne J).

31 Chief Justice Robert French, 'The Judicial Function in an Age of Statutes' (Speech, 2011 Goldring Memorial Lecture, 18 November 2011) 8 (emphasis added).

Example 5.3 *Minister for Immigration and Citizenship v Yucesan*[32]

The facts and legislation the subject of *Yucesan* were introduced above (**Example 5.1**). The Federal Magistrate's reasons included the following:

> In my view, it can be argued that meeting by internet or video telephony is at least as effective [a] way for parties to meet and form an opinion about each other's compatibility as a future marriage partner as the current phenomenon of 'speed dating'. The face-to-face meeting for five or so minutes in speed dating would meet the definition of 'met' argued by counsel for the Minister, but a lengthy series of conversations over 'Skype' would not.[33]

On appeal, the Full Court rejected the relevance of this argument: 'Whether or not the federal magistrate is correct that "meeting by internet or video telephony is at least as effective a way for parties to meet and form an opinion about each other's compatibility as a future marriage partner" is not to the point.'[34] In other words, the Magistrate had to this extent unwittingly based his decision on his opinion of what the law ought to be rather than on cl 300.214 of the *Migration Regulations*, properly interpreted.

The judicial duty to be independent nevertheless permits individual judgement within the limits of legal method [5.5]

If the adjudication of the law was mechanical, the role of individual judgement would not arise. But the judicial process is not a 'slot machine';[35] 'the law is not a complete and coherent system, with fixed boundaries'.[36]

Judges, curially and extracurially, acknowledge the effect of individual judgement and impression. Kirby P has written that the task of 'classifying a provision on one side of the line or the other' is 'in part one of impression'.[37] A former Chief Justice of the High Court of Australia, Sir Anthony Mason, said that '[e]very judge brings to his or her office or, as I think is more often the case, develops while in office, a judicial philosophy'. He elaborated on the philosophy in this way: 'That philosophy may extend over a very wide range of matters related to the law, its place in society, the role of the courts and their relationship with other arms of government'.[38]

---

32 (2008) 169 FCR 202.

33 *Minister for Immigration v Yucesan* (2008) 216 FLR 252 [49], quoted in ibid 205 [7] (the Court).

34 (2008) 169 FCR 202, 209 [28] (the Court).

35 Julius Stone, *Legal System and Lawyers' Reasonings* (Maitland Publications, 1968) 235 n 5. But cf the rise of artificial intelligence: Tania Sourdin, 'Judge v Robot? Artificial Intelligence and Judicial Decision-Making' (2018) 41(5) *University of New South Wales Law Journal* 1114.

36 Justice John Basten, 'Constitutional Dimensions of Statutory Interpretation' (Speech, Constitutional Law Conference, Centre for Comparative Constitutional Studies, Melbourne Law School, 24 July 2015) 1.

37 *Hickling v Laneyrie* (1991) 21 NSWLR 730, 738. See also the similar statement by Lord Nolan in *R v Secretary of State for the Environment; Ex parte Camden London Borough Council* [1998] 1 WLR 615, 622.

38 Sir Anthony Mason, 'Rights, Values and Legal Institutions: Reshaping Australian Institutions' in Geoffrey Lindell (ed), *The Mason Papers: Selected Articles and Speeches by Sir Anthony Mason AC, KBE* (Federation Press, 2007) 80, 82. For a case study of a judge's judicial philosophy, see Jeffrey Barnes, 'Statutory Interpretation' in Ian Freckelton and Hugh Selby (eds), *Appealing to the Future: Michael Kirby and His Legacy* (Lawbook Co, 2009) 721.

The philosophy or set of values is one to which a judge may consciously or unconsciously subscribe.[39]

Inevitably, as another former Chief Justice of the High Court has acknowledged, the scope *in contested cases* for individual judgement and impression '[w]ithin the limits of legal method' gives rise, on occasion, to judicial disagreement.[40] Judges and lawyers may disagree about 'the values inherent in the law' or 'as to what the law requires'.[41] Bennion gives a name to the range of assessments of legal meaning that may result from different minds approaching the same problem of interpretation: 'differential readings'.[42] Therefore, it is well accepted that the practice of interpretation is more than a mechanical application of legal doctrine.

While some commentators take a different view,[43] the orthodox view is that a judge's individual judicial philosophy does not dominate legal reasoning.[44] The law provides several 'powerful constraints that serve to constrain a judge in giving effect to the philosophy or set of values to which he or she consciously or unconsciously subscribes'.[45] Accordingly, judges have 'sources of protection' against an accusation that 'under the guise of construing a statute, [they] are in truth amending it'.[46] They include:

- the presentation of argument, in which values play a relatively minor part;[47]
- the view that the principles by which disputes are resolved are 'reasonably well established, and generally accepted';[48]

---

39 Sir Anthony Mason, 'Rights, Values and Legal Institutions: Reshaping Australian Institutions' in Geoffrey Lindell (ed), *The Mason Papers: Selected Articles and Speeches by Sir Anthony Mason AC, KBE* (Federation Press, 2007) 80, 82.

40 Murray Gleeson, *The Rule of Law and the Constitution: Boyer Lectures 2000* (ABC Books, 2000) 134.

41 Ibid 137.

42 Oliver Jones, *Bennion on Statutory Interpretation: A Code* (LexisNexis, 6th ed, 2013) 99.

43 For instance, 'judicial decisions [are] largely unconstrained individualistic policy preferences' (David Robertson, *Judicial Discretion in the House of Lords* (Clarendon Press, 1998) 70) and '[judges] are not really constrained by legal language, precedents, rules, doctrines or principles': Robert W Benson, *The Interpretation Game: How Judges and Lawyers Make the Law* (Carolina Academic Press, 2008) xv. For references to other similar views, see Jeffrey Barnes, 'Statutory Interpretation' in Ian Freckelton and Hugh Selby (eds), *Appealing to the Future: Michael Kirby and his Legacy* (Lawbook Co, 2009) 721, 745–6. For a critical response, see Barnes at 747–9. See also another selection in Jeffrey Barnes, 'Statutory Interpretation and Administrative Law' in Matthew Groves (ed), *Modern Administrative Law in Australia: Concepts and Context* (Cambridge University Press, 2014) 119, 137.

44 The orthodox view is not just held by senior judges. See Oliver Jones, *Bennion on Statutory Interpretation: A Code* (LexisNexis, 6th ed, 2013) 101–2; Ruth Sullivan, 'Statutory Interpretation in a New Nutshell' (2003) 82 *Canadian Bar Review* 51, 82. John Braithwaite, in 'Rules and Principles: A Theory of Legal Certainty' (2002) 27 *Australian Journal of Legal Philosophy* 47, 64, argues that if judges do work 'bottom-up', the intuitions are 'grounded in professional training more than personal values', and with judges 'those professional intuitions are legal ones'. For a somewhat similar view, see the literary theorist Stanley Fish, *Doing What Comes Naturally: Change, Rhetoric, and the Practice of Theory in Literary and Legal Studies* (Clarendon Press, 1989) chs 6, 17.

45 Sir Anthony Mason, 'Rights, Values and Legal Institutions: Reshaping Australian Institutions' in Geoffrey Lindell (ed), *The Mason Papers: Selected Articles and Speeches by Sir Anthony Mason AC, KBE* (Federation Press, 2007) 80, 82.

46 Murray Gleeson, *The Rule of Law and the Constitution: Boyer Lectures 2000* (ABC Books, 2000) 130.

47 Sir Anthony Mason, 'Rights, Values and Legal Institutions: Reshaping Australian Institutions' in Geoffrey Lindell (ed), *The Mason Papers: Selected Articles and Speeches by Sir Anthony Mason AC, KBE* (Federation Press, 2007) 80, 82.

48 Murray Gleeson, *The Rule of Law and the Constitution: Boyer Lectures 2000* (ABC Books, 2000) 130.

- the requirement to give 'reasons which relate to the vast body of legal doctrine consisting of statute law and general law principles';[49]
- 'the perceptible influence of precedent and the overburden of doctrinal authority accumulated over centuries';[50]
- the appeal process, which 'results in a fairly large measure of conformity amongst judges in their approach to statutory interpretation';[51]
- the fact that Parliament has within it the power to amend a statute if it does not like the way the statute has been construed by a court.[52]

As evidence of the orthodox view, judges additionally point to the fact that it is 'a rare judge who strays so far from the ordinary canons of construction as to produce a result that leads to a charge not merely of error but of usurpation of legislative authority'.[53]

Example 5.4 *JAD v The Queen*[54]

The appellant was charged with a sexual offence that was perpetrated on the daughter of the appellant's de facto partner. At the time the complainant was 16 years old. Section 73(1) of the *Crimes Act 1900* (NSW) provided as follows:

> (1) Any person who has sexual intercourse with another person who:
> (a) is under his or her special care, and
> (b) is of or above the age of 16 years and under the age of 17 years,
> is liable to imprisonment for 8 years.

Subsection (3) then provided a definition of 'under his or her special care':

> (3) For the purposes of this section, a person (the victim) is under the special care of another person (the offender) if, and only if:
> (a) the offender is the step-parent, guardian or foster parent of the victim,
> ...

The defence argued that 'foster parent' in sub-s (3)(a) required an out-of-home care arrangement and did not extend 'to the situation where a couple were living in a de facto relationship together with the child of one of the people in that relationship'.[55]

49 Sir Anthony Mason, 'Rights, Values and Legal Institutions: Reshaping Australian Institutions' in Geoffrey Lindell (ed), *The Mason Papers: Selected Articles and Speeches by Sir Anthony Mason AC, KBE* (Federation Press, 2007) 80, 82.

50 Ibid 83.

51 Murray Gleeson, *The Rule of Law and the Constitution: Boyer Lectures 2000* (ABC Books, 2000) 130.

52 Ibid 130–1.

53 Ibid 130. For other similar judicial views, see Hilary Penfold, 'Legislation in the Courts' [2019] (1) *The Loophole: Journal of the Commonwealth Association of Legislative Counsel* 2, 12. For an instance of a judge criticised for a reason that was not to the point, see **Example 5.3** above.

54 [2012] NSWCCA 73.

55 Ibid [7] (Whealy JA).

Oddly, the Crown did not take an opposing view.[56] The opposing view was eventually taken by the majority of the NSW Court of Criminal Appeal. They held that 'the reference to "foster parent" in s 73 includes a reference to a de facto living in a familial relationship with a natural parent of a child of the ages specified in s 73'.[57]

The minority (Whealy JA) agreed with the defence counsel submission. He held that 'the intention in the 2003 amendment was to cover situations where children were fostered out to homes at which neither of their natural parents resided'.[58]

Whealy JA expressly differed from the majority in four respects. The first point of difference involved what was said in the parliamentary debates. In moving an amendment to the Bill that became s 73 as it was ultimately enacted, the member of Parliament said: 'The amendment does a number of things. First, it corrects the anomaly with respect to stepparents.'[59] The member did not elaborate on what that anomaly was. Nevertheless, the majority inferred that it was to overcome the 'anomaly' exposed by *R v Miller*,[60] which, according to Simpson J, had held that 'a de facto relationship between the parent of a child and another person does not, for the purposes of s 73 as it then stood, give rise to the relationship of step-parent and step-child between the de facto partner and the child'.[61] Whealy JA took a different impression of the evidence of the parliamentary debates:

> I think it is simply impossible to know what Mr Burke had in mind when he spoke of an 'anomaly with respect to step-parents'. . . . The history of the interpretation by Courts of Parliament's intention is littered with examples where speculation (however well-intentioned) must give way to the actual language used.[62]

The second point of difference between the majority and the minority concerned the consequences of the defence construction, should it be accepted. The majority were of the view that including a de factor partner did not give a 'strained interpretation' to the term 'foster parent'.[63] In contrast, the minority held:

> [T]he expression 'foster-parent' to my mind does not easily equate to a reference to a de facto partner living in a relationship with a natural parent of a child. Regretfully, I take the view that to equate the expression 'foster-parent' to a de facto is to give a 'strained interpretation' to the term 'foster-parent'.[64]

The third point of difference concerned use of the statute book and whether alternative words would have been used if Parliament had intended to include a de facto within the scope of 'foster parent'. The majority did not find references to 'foster parent' and definitions of 'de facto' in

56 Having initially conceded the correctness of defence counsel's position, the Crown later withdrew the concession and offered no argument beyond its written submissions: ibid [8]–[12].

57 Ibid [160] (Simpson J, Hoeben J agreeing at [170]).

58 Ibid [30].

59 New South Wales, *Parliamentary Debates*, Legislative Council, 27 May 2003, 1145 (Mr Burke), quoted in ibid [130] (Simpson J, Hoeben J agreeing at [170]).

60 (2001) 127 A Crim R 344.

61 [2012] NSWCCA 73, [59].

62 Ibid [23], [24].

63 Ibid [160] (Simpson J, Hoeben J agreeing at [170]).

64 Ibid [25].

other statutes[65] helpful, reasoning: 'a word in common parlance is given a specific statutory meaning but for the limited purpose of the statute in which it is used'.[66] In contrast, the minority was adamant that

> both the Parliamentary draftsperson and Parliament itself were well versed in expressions in legislation which defined a de facto relationship. . . .
>
> Equally, as [defence counsel's] examples show, the expression 'foster-parent' has been historically recognised in the Parliament of this State.
>
> It is clear that, had Parliament wished to amend s 73 to include persons in a de facto relationship, it could have done so by the use of language perfectly suited to that situation.[67]

Fourth, the majority and minority took a different view of the consequences of the construction that the majority favoured. The majority conceded that the following scenario might occur:

> It may be that it is not every de facto who will qualify for inclusion in the term 'foster parent'; whether he or she does come within that term will be a question of fact. It may be necessary to adduce evidence as to the nature of the actual relationship by including matters such as financial and/or emotional support, discipline, participation in family activities, and participation in educational or sporting or recreational activities. These are the sorts of things involved in bringing up a child or in 'tak[ing] the place of a father or mother in raising a child'.[68]

The minority thought that the consequence of a 'trial within a trial' weighed against the construction of Simpson J.[69]

In summary, the case illustrates different judgements within the limits of legal method: in inferring facts concerning the parliamentary history, in linguistic judgements as to what was a 'strained interpretation', and in the weight to be accorded provisions of other Acts and particular consequences.

---

65 *Adoption of Children Act 1965* (NSW) s 19(1A) and *Crimes (Domestic and Personal Violence) Act 2007* (NSW).

66 [2012] NSWCCA 73, [140] (Simpson J, Hoeben J agreeing at [170]).

67 Ibid [26], [28]–[29].

68 Ibid [31].

69 Ibid.

6 TEXT-BASED INTERPRETATION

Overview

[6.1] Statutory interpretation is to be 'text-based'. 'The text' here refers to the words whose meaning or effect is in issue. Rooted in constitutional principles, consideration of the text is the starting point of the interpretative process. The text supplies the basis for ascertaining the ordinary or grammatical meaning and similar meanings. In turn, that supplies a presumptive and weighty meaning. After having been read in context, the text is also the ending point of the interpretative process. It is where meaning is ultimately held to 'reside'. But, for an interpreter, the text is not limiting in the sense that he or she must choose between its grammatical or semantic possibilities, read in isolation. The paramount object remains to give effect to the intention of Parliament.

Although, read in isolation, the text is not a limit to its potential meaning, it is a constraint. Ultimately, the text, read in context, is a vehicle through which a court gauges whether an interpretation is constitutionally acceptable. A construction will not be preferred if its acceptance would give the appearance of 'judicial legislation'.

The text-based principle

[6.2] **Statutory interpretation is to be text-based**

The extent to which the text of legislation limits interpretation has been the subject of scholarly debate.[1] But as this chapter shows, the text is central to, and a constraint upon, interpretation.

Consideration of the text is pivotal:

> This Court has stated on many occasions that the task of statutory construction must begin with a consideration of the [statutory] text. So must the task of statutory construction end.[2]

To similar effect are other statements of the High Court, such as the following: '[p]urposive construction does not justify expanding the scope of a criminal offence beyond its textual limits'[3] and '[i]t is the words of the statute that ultimately govern'.[4] In short, '[c]onstruction must be text based'.[5]

But what is the meaning of the text-based principle and statements such as the above?

---

1 Compare Aharon Barak, *Purposive Interpretation in Law* (Trans Sari Bashi, Princeton University Press, 2005) ch 1 and Stanley Fish, 'Intention Is All There Is: A Critical Analysis of Aharon Barak's Purposive Interpretation in Law' (2008) 29(3) *Cardozo Law Review* 1109.

2 *Federal Commissioner of Taxation v Consolidated Media Holdings Ltd* (2012) 250 CLR 503, 519 [39] (the Court) (footnote omitted).

3 *Milne v The Queen* (2014) 252 CLR 149, 164 [38] (the Court).

4 *Weiss v The Queen* (2005) 224 CLR 300, 305 [9] (the Court).

5 *R v Young* (1999) 46 NSWLR 681, 687 [12] (Spigelman CJ).

The meaning of the text-based principle

The 'text' refers to the words whose meaning or effect is in issue [6.3]

A preliminary issue, for the purposes of the text-based principle, is what do courts mean by 'the text'? The answer is that the text is shorthand for 'the words being construed'.[6]

Learned commentators sometimes employ other terms to describe the words whose meaning or effect is in issue. Sullivan uses the term 'source of doubt' to describe the 'words or expressions whose meaning is doubtful in relation to the facts of the case'.[7] Bennion employs the term 'unit of inquiry' for the same purpose:

> For the purposes of statutory interpretation, the unit of inquiry is an enactment whose legal meaning in relation to a particular factual situation falls to be determined ... an 'enactment' is a legal *proposition* laid down in an Act or other legislative text ... Usually an enactment consists either of the whole or a part of a single sentence ...[8]

Some judicial discussion has occurred as to whether an exception to text-based interpretation in the above sense arises in relation to 'purposive construction'. In *Taylor v The Owners – Strata Plan No 11564*,[9] French CJ, Crennan and Bell JJ cited criticism by the Victorian Court of Appeal of a statement of Spigelman CJ characterising purposive construction as a process of construing 'the words actually used'.[10] According to French CJ, Crennan and Bell JJ, '[t]heir Honours said that the process [of construction] requires the court to determine whether the modified construction is reasonably open in light of the statutory scheme and against a background of the satisfaction of [certain conditions propounded by Lord Diplock]'.[11] French CJ, Crennan and Bell JJ did not agree with this characterisation, effectively affirming Spigelman CJ's characterisation of the focus of interpretation and what 'the text' comprised. Their Honours concluded: 'the task remains the construction of the words the legislature has enacted'.[12]

The text-based principle is rooted in constitutional principles [6.4]

Like other legal principles,[13] principles of interpretation are founded on 'certain values that are deserving of legal protection'.[14] In *Treasurer of Victoria v Tabcorp Holdings Ltd*[15] the Victorian Court of Appeal stated there were 'powerful reasons of principle for giving primacy to the statutory text'.[16] They first mentioned the separation of powers:

---

6 *R v A2* (2019) 269 CLR 507, 522 [36] (Kiefel CJ and Keane J, Nettle and Gordon JJ agreeing generally at 249 [148], Edelman J agreeing at 263 [193]).

7 Ruth Sullivan, 'Statutory Interpretation in a New Nutshell' (2003) 82(1) *Canadian Bar Review* 51, 66.

8 Oliver Jones, *Bennion on Statutory Interpretation* (LexisNexis, 6th ed, 2013) 374, 376, 378 (emphasis in original).

9 (2014) 253 CLR 531.

10 Ibid 547 [36] (French CJ, Crennan and Bell JJ), quoting *DPP v Leys* (2012) 296 ALR 96, 124 [92].

11 (2014) 253 CLR 531, 547–8 [36].

12 Ibid 549 [39] (footnote omitted).

13 Neil MacCormick, *Legal Reasoning and Legal Theory* (Oxford University Press, 1994) 105–6, referring to 'value preferences' being 'the bedrock' of legal reasoning.

14 Ruth Sullivan, *Sullivan on the Construction of Statutes* (LexisNexis, 5th ed, 2008) 2. See also, to similar effect, Neil D MacCormick and Robert S Summers, 'Interpretation and Justification' in Neil D MacCormick and Robert S Summers (eds), *Interpreting Statutes: A Comparative Study* (Dartmouth, 1991) 511, 532.

15 [2014] VSCA 143.

16 Ibid [101] (the Court).

> [T]he separation of powers requires nothing less. Axiomatically, it is for the Parliament to legislate and for the courts to interpret. Close adherence to the text, and to the natural and ordinary meaning of the words used, avoids the twin dangers of a court 'construct[ing] its own idea of a desirable policy', or making 'some a priori assumption about its purpose'.[17]

Next, they cited rule of law values and the values of a representative democracy: 'giving the text its natural and ordinary meaning maximises the comprehensibility and accessibility of statute law, and the accountability of the legislature'.[18] Lord Steyn has similarly invoked the 'democratic ideal' as anchoring the principle that 'the text of an enacted law must always be the touchstone'.[19]

Now, what does text-based interpretation involve or require?

[6.5] The text supplies the starting point of interpretation

In several decisions the High Court has propounded that it is proper technique to start with consideration of the text: 'This Court has stated on many occasions that the task of statutory construction must begin with a consideration of the text itself.'[20] A court analyses the '[t]he language which has actually been employed in the text of legislation'.[21]

There are several reasons why courts and other interpreters ought to start by considering the text. Two may be mentioned. First, it is 'a discipline guarding against the natural tendency to start at the destination and work back'.[22] Second, it also avoids the 'siren call' of parliamentary extrinsic material,[23] such as a statement by a Minister or a statement in an explanatory memorandum purportedly directly addressing the meaning of the provision in question.

[6.6] The text supplies the basis for ascertaining the ordinary or grammatical meaning and similar variations of the first-blush reading

Taken at 'first blush', the text supplies a starting point for ascertaining its meaning. The meaning that is taken varies a little. Sometimes it is referred to as the ordinary or grammatical meaning, as in the following: 'The process of construction begins with a consideration of the ordinary and grammatical meaning of the words of the provision having regard to their context and legislative purpose.'[24]

---

17 Ibid.

18 Ibid [102].

19 Lord Steyn, 'Interpretation: Legal Texts and Their Landscape' in BS Markesinis (ed), *The Clifford Chance Millennium Lectures: The Coming Together of the Common Law and the Civil Law* (Hart Publishing, 2000), quoted in Kenneth Keith, 'Sources of Law, Especially in Statutory Interpretation, with Suggestions about Distinctiveness' in John Prebble (ed), *Sir Kenneth Keith: Collected Papers* (Keith Paper 26, Victoria University of Wellington) 77, 87.

20 *Alcan (NT) Alumina Pty Ltd v Commissioner of Territory Revenue (NT)* (2009) 239 CLR 27, 46 [47] (Hayne, Heydon, Crennan and Kiefel JJ).

21 Ibid 47 [47] (footnote omitted).

22 Justice Susan Glazebrook, 'Filling the Gaps' in Rick Bigwood (ed), *The Statute: Making and Meaning* (LexisNexis, 2004) 153, 169.

23 Justice John Logan, 'Statutory Construction – Panel Discussion Presentation' [2016] *Federal Judicial Scholarship* 6.

24 *Australian Education Union v Department of Education and Children's Services* (2012) 248 CLR 1, 13 [26] (French CJ, Hayne, Kiefel and Bell JJ). See also *R v A2* (2019) 269 CLR 507, 520 [32] (Kiefel CJ and Keane J, Nettle and Gordon JJ agreeing generally at 554 [148], Edelman J agreeing at 572 [193]).

A similar expression is the natural or ordinary meaning. In *Masson v Parsons*[25] six members of the High Court stated that 'a court will not construe a provision in a way that departs from its natural and ordinary meaning unless it is plain that Parliament intended it to have some different meaning'.[26]

A further variation, though less used these days, is 'the literal and grammatical meaning'.[27]

These meanings clearly overlap but are not identical. They carry different nuances. Their differences are explored later in this work (chapter 15).

The first-blush reading may generate more than one possible meaning of the text. For instance, a word or phrase may have more than one ordinary meaning. If so, a court will put weight on the primary ordinary meaning or ordinary usage of the word.[28]

The text supplies a presumptive and weighty meaning [6.7]

The ordinary meaning of the words in question is presumptive: '[T]he rule that legislative provisions are to be construed according to their natural and ordinary meaning is a rule of general application'.[29]

For constitutional reasons described above at **[6.4]**, a court regards the ordinary meaning based on the text as weighty: 'The language which has actually been employed in the text of legislation is the surest guide to legislative intention.'[30]

Having ascertained the ordinary meaning, the question then becomes: is it appropriate to depart from that prima facie meaning? This approach was propounded in the influential reasons of Mason and Wilson JJ in *Cooper Brookes (Wollongong) Pty Ltd v Commissioner of Taxation (Cth)*:[31]

> [T]he propriety of departing from the literal interpretation is not confined to situations described by these labels ['absurd', 'extraordinary', 'capricious', 'irrational' or 'obscure']. It extends to any situation in which for good reason the operation of the statute on a literal reading does not conform to the legislative intent as ascertained from the provisions of the statute, including the policy which may be discerned from those provisions.[32]

The text is where meaning is ultimately held to 'reside' [6.8]

An interpreter must not read the text in isolation. Regard to context is necessary,[33] however plain or clear the text may first appear to be.[34] After having read the text in context and considered

---

25 (2019) 266 CLR 554 (Kiefel CJ, Bell, Gageler, Keane, Nettle and Gordon JJ).

26 Ibid 572 [26]. See also *Marshall v Director-General, Department of Transport* (2001) 205 CLR 603, 623 [37] (Gaudron J, Hayne J agreeing at 634 [67]); *Tjungarrayi v Western Australia* (2019) 269 CLR 150, 163–4 [31]–[32] (Kiefel CJ, Bell, Keane and Edelman JJ); *Parkes Shire Council v South West Helicopters Pty Ltd* (2019) 266 CLR 212, 225 [32] (Kiefel CJ, Bell, Keane and Edelman JJ).

27 *Project Blue Sky Inc v Australian Broadcasting Authority* (1998) 194 CLR 355, 382 [72], 384 [78] (McHugh, Gummow, Kirby and Hayne JJ).

28 See **[15.7]**.

29 *Marshall v Director-General, Department of Transport* (2001) 205 CLR 603, 623 [38] (Gaudron J, Hayne J agreeing at 634 [67]).

30 *Alcan (NT) Alumina Pty Ltd v Commissioner of Territory Revenue (NT)* (2009) 239 CLR 27, 47 [47] (Hayne, Heydon, Crennan and Kiefel JJ).

31 (1981) 147 CLR 297.

32 Ibid 321. See also to similar effect *Masson v Parsons* (2019) 266 CLR 554, 572 [26] (Kiefel CJ, Bell, Gageler, Keane, Nettle and Gordon JJ); *Chiropedic Bedding Pty Ltd v Radburg Pty Ltd* (2008) 170 FCR 560, 569 [39] (the Court).

33 See generally chapter 7.

34 See **[7.6]**.

which rival contention as to meaning ('construction') is preferable,[35] a court attributes the text's meaning to the legislature.[36] As was propounded in *Project Blue Sky Inc v Australian Broadcasting Authority*,[37] 'the duty of a court is to give *the words of a statutory provision* the meaning that the legislature is taken to have intended them to have'.[38]

Hence, meaning ultimately 'resides' in the text. The metaphor of 'residing' is taken from a judgment of the High Court in relation to legislative purpose:

> The purpose of a statute is not something which exists outside the statute. It resides in its text and structure, albeit it may be identified by reference to common law and statutory rules of construction.[39]

If the legislative purpose resides in the text, then, all the more so, the meaning must too. This consequence is obvious in the case where the text carries its ordinary or literal meaning. But it also applies in the case of non-literal meanings, such as where an implication is made. As Mason CJ pointed out in a constitutional context:

> It is essential to keep steadily in mind the critical difference between an implication and an unexpressed assumption upon which the framers proceeded in drafting the Constitution. *The former is a term or concept which inheres in the instrument and as such operates as part of the instrument*, whereas an assumption stands outside the instrument.[40]

Example 6.1 *Collett v Repatriation Commission*[41]

The appellant spent approximately two hours near a beach in Greece after his unit surrendered to the German forces during World War II. The advance elements of the enemy forces bypassed the appellant's unit during this time. After that period, the appellant, with two others, bravely escaped the surrender area, eventually finding safety. After the passing of the *Social Security and Veterans' Affairs Legislation Amendment (One-off Payments and Other 2007 Budget Measures) Act 2007* (Cth) the appellant (now nearing 100 years of age) applied for compensation under the Act. To be entitled, a person had to be relevantly 'interned by the military forces of an enemy State at any time during the designated war period': sch 5 item 2(1)(b).

The meaning of 'interned' was the issue. That word was defined in item 1 of sch 5 as meaning 'confined in a camp, building, prison, cave or *other place* (including a vehicle)' (emphasis added). The appeal to the Federal Court from a decision of the Administrative Appeals Tribunal turned on the meaning of 'other place'. The respondent Commission argued that 'other place' must fit the

35 This process is examined in chapter 9.

36 *Zheng v Cai* (2009) 239 CLR 446, 445 [28] (the Court).

37 (1998) 194 CLR 355.

38 Ibid 384 [78] (McHugh, Gummow, Kirby and Hayne JJ) (emphasis added). See, to similar effect, *R v Secretary of State for the Environment, Transport and the Regions; Ex parte Spath Holme Ltd* [2001] 2 AC 349, 396 (Lord Nicholls).

39 *Lacey v A-G (Qld)* (2011) 242 CLR 573, 592 [44] (French CJ, Gummow, Hayne, Crennan, Kiefel and Bell JJ).

40 *Australian Capital Television Pty Ltd v Commonwealth* (1992) 177 CLR 106, 135 (emphasis added) (citation omitted). The distinction made by Mason CJ was applied to interpretation of ordinary Acts (statutory interpretation) in *Carr v Western Australia* (2007) 232 CLR 138, 145–6 [11]–[16] (Gleeson CJ).

41 (2009) 178 FCR 39.

genus of the specific places mentioned.[42] The veteran argued that it was not necessary for a person to have been physically confined.[43] After a thorough examination of the provision at issue and its context, the Court found that 'other place' connoted 'a place of confinement of definite, restrictive physical limits'.[44] Of interest is the way the Court commented on where the meaning lay. The Court concluded: 'There is no need for the qualifying adjective "physically". The latter sense is *already present* reading the definition of "interned" as a whole and in context.'[45]

An interpreter is not limited by the grammatical or semantic possibilities of a text (read in isolation); the paramount object is to give effect to the intention of Parliament [6.9]

Although the text is considered at the start and end of the interpretative process, it is clear law that a court is not limited to its grammatical or semantic possibilities, read in isolation. In the oft-cited case of *Project Blue Sky*, it was held: 'Ordinarily, that meaning (the legal meaning) will correspond with the grammatical meaning . . . But not always.'[46] In *Taylor v The Owners – Strata Plan No 11564*,[47] Gageler and Keane JJ explained how consideration of the context could result in the legal meaning being 'ungrammatical':

> Context sometimes favours an ungrammatical legal meaning. Ungrammatical legal meaning sometimes involves reading statutory text as containing implicit words. Implicit words are sometimes words of limitation. They are sometimes words of extension. But they are always words of explanation.[48]

And, even more plainly, Edelman J has similarly held:

> Context can give words an interpretation that is the opposite of their ordinary meaning and grammatical sense. Context can also permit a construction of words that excludes their application to matters that would have fallen within the application of their literal meaning.[49]

If there is a tension between the text and the context, then the tension is resolved through the umbrella concept of the intention of Parliament:

> [T]here are cases in which inconvenience of result or improbability of result assists the court in concluding that an alternative construction which is reasonably open is to be preferred to the literal meaning because the alternative interpretation more closely conforms to *the legislative intent* discernible from other provisions in the statute.[50]

42 Ibid 49 [36] (Logan J).

43 Ibid 43 [12].

44 Ibid 47 [29].

45 Ibid 48 [33] (emphasis added).

46 *Project Blue Sky Inc v Australian Broadcasting Authority* (1998) 194 CLR 355, 384 [78] (McHugh, Gummow, Kirby and Hayne JJ).

47 (2014) 253 CLR 531.

48 Ibid 556 [65] (dissenting as to outcome).

49 *SAS Trustee Corporation v Miles* (2018) 265 CLR 137, 162–3 [64].

50 *Cooper Brookes (Wollongong) Pty Ltd v Commissioner of Taxation (Cth)* (1981) 147 CLR 297, 320 (Mason and Wilson JJ) (emphasis added). See also *Project Blue Sky Inc v Australian Broadcasting Authority* (1998) 194 CLR 355, 384 [78] (McHugh, Gummow, Kirby and Hayne JJ).

The way in which the intention of Parliament ultimately prevails over the grammatical possibilities of a text read in isolation was captured in a striking way by Wilcox J:

> [L]ike Humpty Dumpty in 'Alice through the Looking Glass', Parliament can give a word any meaning it wishes: 'When I use a word, it means just what I choose it to mean – neither more than [sic] less . . . The question is, which is to be the master [sic] – that's all.' Parliament is not bound by ordinary usage. Provided it makes its intention clear, Parliament can use any word it wishes, however much this may offend linguistic purists.[51]

In a number of cases, courts have given a strained (that is, non-grammatical) construction to statutory provisions.[52]

Example 6.2 *Smoker v Pharmacy Restructuring Authority*[53]

The applicant challenged the validity of guidelines purportedly issued by the Minister for Health pursuant to s 99L of the *National Health Act 1953* (Cth). Subsection (1) provided:

> The Minister must determine in writing the guidelines subject to which the Authority is to make recommendations under subsection 99K(1).

Section 99K(2) further provided:

> In making a recommendation under subsection (1), the Authority must comply with the relevant guidelines determined by the Minister under section 99L.

The Pharmacy Restructuring Authority and the Administrative Appeals Tribunal accepted that the guidelines were legally binding.

The issue before the Full Federal Court was whether, as counsel for the applicant argued, the guidelines 'do no more than provide guidance to the Authority; that the Authority retains a residual discretion regarding its ultimate decision'.[54]

All three members of the Court accepted that the ordinary meaning of 'guidelines' supported the argument of counsel for the applicant. Wilcox J said that the word is ordinarily used this way:

> Generally speaking, the function of 'guidelines' is to provide information and to point the way to a particular conclusion, without dictating that conclusion. Generally speaking, a residual discretion remains.[55]

Similarly, Burchett J argued that, according to its plain meaning and its 'ordinary understanding',

> language of that kind is not apt to withdraw the discretion from the person or body addressed. A guideline does not do that, just as guidance does not imply dictation, nor is a guide normally thought of as a commander.[56]

---

51 *Smoker v Pharmacy Restructuring Authority* (1994) 53 FCR 287, 289.

52 A helpful analysis and catalogue of precedents is provided by McHugh JA in *Kingston v Keprose Pty Ltd* (1987) 11 NSWLR 404, 421–3 (dissenting as to outcome).

53 (1994) 53 FCR 287.

54 Ibid 289 (Wilcox J).

55 Ibid.

56 Ibid 290.

Hill J (with whom Wilcox J and Burchett J agreed) argued that the normal meaning and 'ordinary usage' of the expression 'guideline' could be discerned from its dictionary meaning:

> 1. a line drawn as a guide for further writing, drawing, etc 2. (usu pl) a statement which defines policy or the area in which the policy is operative.[57]

But the Court unanimously found that 'guidelines' in s 99K did not bear its normal meaning. It meant rules.[58] The Court did so by reason that the intention of Parliament required such a reading:

> It follows, in my mind, in these circumstances that the legislative history as well as the context in the present case points to *an intention on the part of the legislature* to authorise what are referred to as 'guidelines' but what more properly should be described as *rules* which in fact circumscribe the discretion which the Authority has.[59]

The indications for a strained construction of 'guidelines' were: the mandatory language of s 99K(2) in the immediate context of 'guideline';[60] the nature of s 99K, which was expressed in terms of function rather than power;[61] and the legislative history. The word 'guidelines' had been employed originally in an agreement reached between the Minister and the Pharmacy Guild of Australia. The agreement contemplated the issue of mandatory rules, which it called 'guidelines'. The Court found that various provisions of the agreement, including in part its terminology, had been incorporated into the Act.[62]

Consequences of transgressing the text

A point may be reached when, as a matter of judgement, a court determines that a construction of the text would go too far by reason that, if the construction were accepted, it would give the appearance of 'judicial legislation'. [6.10]

It will be recalled that the High Court has said that '[p]urposive construction does not justify expanding the scope of a criminal offence beyond its textual limits'[63] and that '[i]t is the words of the statute that ultimately govern'.[64] Other statements are to similar effect. Justice Heydon in *Wainohu* has said that the construction must be 'open on the language [of legislation] and not inconsistent with it'.[65] In *Taylor*, French CJ, Crennan and Bell JJ held that the construction must be capable of being 'reconciled with the language that the Parliament has enacted'.[66] It is common for judges to canvass whether the text is 'sufficiently tractable to accommodate the meaning'.[67]

57 Ibid 298–9, quoting the *Macquarie Dictionary*.

58 Ibid 301 (Hill J, Wilcox J agreeing at 288, Burchett J agreeing at 291).

59 Ibid (emphasis, where first employed, added).

60 Ibid 299 (Hill J, Wilcox J agreeing at 288). Burchett J at 290 disagreed on this point.

61 Ibid 300 (Burchett J agreeing at 291).

62 Ibid.

63 *Milne v The Queen* (2014) 252 CLR 149, 164 [38] (the Court).

64 *Weiss v The Queen* (2005) 224 CLR 300, 305 [9] (the Court).

65 *Wainohu v New South Wales* (2011) 243 CLR 181, 238 [146] (dissenting as to outcome).

66 *Taylor v The Owners – Strata Plan 11564* (2014) 253 CLR 531, 550 [41].

67 *New South Wales v Williamson* [2011] NSWCA 183, [119] (Macfarlan JA), quoted in *Certain Lloyd's Underwriters v Cross* (2012) 248 CLR 378, 404 [66] (Crennan and Bell JJ).

And extracurially, Lord Justice Sales has said that '[t]he final outcome has to be compatible with the language used'.[68]

Although the grammatical possibilities of the text read in isolation are not a limit (see **[6.9]**), it is suggested that the references immediately above to the effect of the language of the text are not inapt provided that the role of the text is properly seen. At the point of judgement the text has been read in light of context.[69] References to 'textual limits' should therefore be taken to be shorthand for the limit posed by the text as read in context.[70] The limit is constitutional. In *Minister for Immigration and Citizenship v SZJGV*,[71] French CJ and Bell J helpfully recalled the judicial role in the separation of powers: 'The limits of the judicial role, as pointed out by Lord Nicholls, require that the courts "abstain from any course which might have the appearance of judicial legislation".'[72] Put another way, a judge has a duty of 'fidelity to the words of the relevant provision'.[73]

While the limits of the judicial role are conceptually clear (judges cannot legislate), there is no bright line separating interpreting from legislating: 'The line between judicial legislation, which our law does not permit, and judicial interpretation in a way best designed to give effect to the intention of Parliament is not an easy one to draw.'[74]

Ultimately, though, a line may have to be drawn. This calls for a judgement of matters of degree:

> The question whether the court is justified in reading a statutory provision as if it contained additional words or omitted words involves a judgment of matters of degree. That judgment is readily answered in favour of addition or omission in the case of simple, grammatical, drafting errors which if uncorrected would defeat the object of the provision. It is answered against a construction that fills 'gaps disclosed in legislation' or makes an insertion which is 'too big, or too much at variance with the language in fact used by the legislature'.[75]

---

68 Lord Justice Sales, 'Modern Statutory Interpretation' (2017) 38(2) *Statute Law Review* 125, 125. His Lordship qualified this statement by saying that '[the language] controls the exercise of interpretation, even if often only in a relatively loose sense'.

69 *SZTAL v Minister for Immigration and Border Protection* (2017) 262 CLR 362, 368 [14] (Kiefel CJ, Nettle and Gordon JJ). See also Justice Susan Kenny, 'Current Issues in the Interpretation of Federal Legislation' (Speech, National Commercial Law Seminar Series, Melbourne, 3 September 2013) 8.

70 See, to similar effect, *R v A2* (2019) 269 CLR 507, 560 [164] (Edelman J).

71 (2009) 238 CLR 642.

72 Ibid 652 [9] (citation omitted).

73 *ZD v Secretary to the Department of Health and Human Services* [2017] VSC 806, [103] (Osborn JA).

74 *Western Bank Ltd v Schindler* [1977] Ch 1, 18 (Lord Scarman), quoted in John Bell and George Engle, *Cross: Statutory Interpretation* (Oxford University Press, 3rd ed, 2005) 95. See also William Twining and David Miers, *How to Do Things with Rules: A Primer of Interpretation* (Cambridge University Press, 5th ed, 2010) 251.

75 *Taylor v The Owners – Strata Plan No 11564* (2014) 253 CLR 531, 548 [38] (French CJ, Crennan and Bell JJ) (citations omitted). For applications of the *Taylor* case, see **Example 6.3** and also *DPP v Scheele* (2016) 12 ACTLR 1, 14 [61], [64] (the Court). See also discussion of separation of powers at **[3.2]–[3.3]**.

Example 6.3 *DPP v Moreno*[76]

It was alleged in the Magistrates Court of Victoria that the defendant attended a department store in the company of the coaccused and an unknown female. They were observed leaving the store without attempting to pay for certain items of women's clothing. Outside the store, the three persons entered the suspect vehicle, but before they were able to exit the car park, store officers approached the vehicle and requested the defendant and coaccused to return to the security office. A short time after attending the security area, the coaccused decamped from the security staff and re-entered the suspect vehicle and exited the shopping centre.

During an interview at the nearby police station, the informant asked the defendant (who was the owner of the vehicle) about the driver of the vehicle. The defendant refused to answer the informant's questions. The defendant was later charged with theft and with a breach of s 60(1) of the *Road Safety Act 1986* (Vic). That provision read:

> **60 Duty of owner of motor vehicle to give information about driver**
>
> (1) An owner of a motor vehicle, or a relevant nominated person in relation to a motor vehicle, is guilty of an offence if, when required to do so by a police officer who is acting in the execution of duty, the person fails to give any information which it is within the power of the person to give and which may lead to the identification of any person who was the driver of the motor vehicle on any occasion or had possession or control of the motor vehicle on any occasion or fails to make all reasonable enquiries in order to obtain that information.

A Magistrate convicted the defendant of all charges.

On appeal to the County Court, the Court dismissed the charge under s 60(1) on the ground that the words 'under this Act' ought to be read into the provision after the words 'execution of duty'. The Court held that the request for information under cover of s 60(1) had nothing to do with any investigation of an alleged breach of the *Road Safety Act*.

The plaintiff sought judicial review by the Supreme Court of the decision of the County Court. Before the Supreme Court the defendant put forward an alternative construction of s 60(1). It was said that, after the words 'execution of duty' the provision should be read as if it contained the following words: 'where investigating an occasion in which an offence related to road safety or other driving related offence has occurred'.[77]

The Supreme Court observed that the alternative construction provided scope for police officers to utilise the investigative powers under s 60(1) to investigate driving-related offences under the *Crimes Act*, such as culpable driving. After a thorough review of the provision and its context, the Court rejected both the construction held by the County Court and the alternative formulation. It held that the implied power conferred upon police officers under s 60(1) was not confined to circumstances where the relevant offence is an offence under the *Road Safety Act* or a driving-related offence not contained within the Act.[78] Of particular interest is the assessment of the alternative construction. The Supreme Court observed that 'there is a lack of precision in the

76 (2018) 57 VR 1. The defendant's reported name is a pseudonym.

77 Ibid 26 [86] (Daly AsJ).

78 Ibid 2–3 [2].

phrase "related to road safety, or other driving related offence"'. The Court also thought that the alternative construction was not text-based within the principle advanced by Lord Scarman in *Western Bank Ltd v Schindler*[79] and approved in the majority judgment in *Taylor v The Owners – Strata Plan No 11564*.[80] The Supreme Court held that '[f]inally, the formulation could be said to be "too big, or too much at variance with the language in fact used by the legislature".'[81]

79 [1977] Ch 1, 18.

80 (2014) 253 CLR 531, 548 [38] (French CJ, Crennan and Bell).

81 (2018) 57 VR 1, 26 [87] (Daly AsJ).

CONTEXT 7

Overview

The aims of this chapter are to state, elaborate on and illustrate the context principle: the duty to have regard to the context of the text whose meaning is in issue. It is not the purpose of this chapter to examine each of the individual contextual aids. Later Parts (Parts IV–VIII) elaborate on the contextual aids that may be considered. [7.1]

We begin with the meaning of context. We note that 'text' and 'context' are notionally separate concepts, but in practice they tend to merge. 'Context' in statutory interpretation is a legal term. It does not refer to everything outside the text. It refers to those matters of relevance to be considered together with the text.

The duty to have regard to the context is briefly set out and explained. It is often grouped with the duty to give primacy to the text and the duty to promote the legislative purpose, for they are all foundational matters. The duty to have regard to the context is explained on the basis that it is essential before determining the meaning of legislation.

The context principle is explored. However plain a provision appears when read in isolation, an interpreter cannot determine the meaning of the provision without due regard to its context. 'Due regard' entails having regard to all relevant indications of meaning supplied by the text and context. Former restrictions on having regard to the context have been lifted by judicial decisions.

The consequences of the duty to have regard to the context, and of the lifting of restrictions relating to the context, are discussed. Inevitably, together they have brought about a sea change for statutory interpretation. Considering the text in its context ('contextualism') is the overall approach to interpretation; its rise has caused a number of former rules and other interpretative criteria to be adjusted in its wake.

The utility of regard to context is examined. Having regard to the context always has utility, even if it is to confirm the presumptive meaning apparent from the text. Specifically, the context typically supplies indications of varying weight as to the meaning that is taken to have been intended. But it may also supply a presumptive rule that is implied in the provision in question. In such a case the context is also important in determining whether there is a contrary intention to the application of the presumptive rule. Finally, although regard to the context is always useful, such regard is not necessarily free of dispute. The weight of a potential contextual aid may be contested or the 'aid' could itself be ambiguous.

Meaning of context

[7.2] **'Context' and 'text' are notionally separate concepts, but in practice they tend to merge**

Notionally, text and context are separate. Context is often distinguished from the text, as in the following passages:

> The word 'office', although a general word, must not be read in isolation; it must be read in context.[1]
>
> ... it is necessary to derive the meaning of s 303(1) from the context of the entirety of Div 3 of Pt 3 of the *Migration Act*, not just the sub-section read in isolation.[2]
>
> ... when s 4 of the Act is read in isolation from its context, the exemption which it provides from the prohibition it imposes is technically ambiguous.[3]

But, as explained below (**[7.5]**), words do not have meaning without regard to the context. Just as '[n]o one has ever made an acontextual statement',[4] 'the meaning produced by reading can never be a-contextual.'[5] Therefore, whenever we read the text of legislation in question, even 'in isolation', and form an impression of its meaning, it is in the light of *some* context, even if we are not conscious of the background assumptions. That context might include knowledge of the short title of the Act and the subject matter of the Act, and knowledge of the world and of language including ordinary meaning.[6] In other words, in practice, text and context merge. This idea is reflected in a statement of Edelman J: 'In ascertaining the reasonably intended meaning of Parliament *con*text is, literally, those matters to be considered (*simultaneously*) together with the text.'[7] The idea is also reflected in the legal boundaries of the term 'context', which is elaborated on below.

[7.3] **In statutory interpretation 'context' is a legal term and refers to those matters of relevance to be considered together with the text**

In statutory interpretation, 'context' is a legal term – that is, a term with legal boundaries around what is considered to be context in a particular case. It does not refer to everything outside a text whose meaning is in issue. It refers to the context of the text whose meaning is in doubt, *so far as relevant*.

Relevance is legally determined. The Victorian Court of Appeal has stated that '"[c]ontext", as discussed in ... *CIC Insurance*, imports all legitimate means by which the legislative intent may be

1 *Commissioner of Taxation (Cth) v Jayasinghe* (2017) 260 CLR 400, 412 [31] (Kiefel CJ, Keane, Gordon, Edelman JJ).

2 *Shi v Migration Agents Registration Authority* (2008) 235 CLR 286, 303 [53] (Kirby J) (footnote omitted).

3 *De More Constructions Pty Ltd v Garpace Pty Ltd* (2001) 53 NSWLR 132, 135 [13] (Fitzgerald AJA, Stein JA agreeing at 133 [1], Rolfe AJA agreeing at 133 [2]).

4 *Kirin-Amgen Inc v Hoechst Marion Roussel Ltd* [2005] 1 All ER 667, 689 [64] (Lord Hoffmann, Lord Hope agreeing at 703 [134], Lord Rodger agreeing at 703 [136], Lord Walker agreeing at 703 [137], Lord Brown agreeing at 704 [140]). See also Leonard Hoffmann, 'Language and Lawyers' (2018) 134(4) *Law Quarterly Review* 553, 554.

5 Ruth Sullivan, *Sullivan on the Construction of Statutes* (LexisNexis, 5th ed, 2008) 29.

6 Ruth Sullivan, *Statutory Interpretation* (Irwin Law, 3rd ed, 2016) 61; Ruth Sullivan, *Sullivan on the Construction of Statutes* (LexisNexis, 5th ed, 2008) 25–7.

7 *SAS Trustee Corporation v Miles* (2018) 265 CLR 137, 162 [64] (first emphasis in original; second emphasis added).

ascertained'.[8] To be a relevant aid in a particular case an interpretative factor must satisfy two broad requirements.

First, it must have a legal pedigree. It must be derived from (that is, be an application of) an interpretative criterion recognised by statute and common law.[9] As discussed above,[10] the law defines the general interpretative criteria for statutory interpretation. Thus, 'legal rules can sometimes exclude or restrict the use of some context'.[11] It is clearly impermissible, for instance, for a judge to base their decision on a 'judicially constructed policy'.[12] Instances of other impermissible considerations are the subject of later discussion in this work.[13]

The context can be structured in various ways.[14] In this work it is analysed in Parts IV–VIII as follows. The intrinsic context (the provision and the Act) is the subject of Part IV. This is followed in Parts V–VII with examination of the extrinsic context (the context beyond the Act). The extrinsic context comprises the historical context or the legislative history (Part V), Interpretation Acts and other Acts of general application (Part VI), and other contextual aids of a general nature (Part VII). Part VIII is concerned with special interpretative issues. These are issues thrown up in particular contexts that often demand the application of particular considerations.

To be relevant in a particular case, an interpretative factor must also satisfy a second requirement. Even if an argument is derived from a legitimate interpretative criterion, such as the provision of another statute, it must be relevant in the circumstances of the case – that is, relevant to the dispute concerning the provision in question.

Example 7.1 *SZTAL v Minister for Immigration and Border Protection*[15]

The appellants had sought protection visas. They argued that if removed from Australia they would suffer 'significant harm' under the 'complementary protection' regime in s 36(2)(aa) of the *Migration Act 1958* (Cth). 'Significant harm' was defined in s 36(2A) and included 'torture', 'cruel or inhuman treatment or punishment' and 'degrading treatment or punishment'. These terms were in turn defined in s 5(1). The first two terms referred to an act or omission 'intentionally

8 *DPP v Leys* (2012) 44 VR 1, 32 [94] (the Court) (citation omitted).

9 The concepts of interpretative factors and interpretative criteria draw upon the analysis by Bennion: Oliver Jones, *Bennion on Statutory Interpretation: A Code* (LexisNexis, 6th ed, 2013) 484. The term 'interpretative criteria', which was introduced in chapter 1 (**[1.2]**), describes all the general guides to legislative intention found in common law and statute law. For adoption of the term in case law, see *Slivak v Lurgi (Australia) Pty Ltd* (2001) 205 CLR 304, 316 [28] (Gleeson CJ, Gummow and Hayne JJ); *Western Australia v Strickland* (2000) 99 FCR 33, 45 [40] (the Court); *Australasian Meat Industry Employees Union v Hamberger* (2000) 102 FCR 74, 94 [42] (the Court); *R v McNeill (Ruling No 1)* [2007] NFSC 2, [42] (Weinberg CJ). See also chapter 9 for a practical application of these concepts.

10 At **[1.2]**.

11 *SAS Trustee Corporation v Miles* (2018) 265 CLR 137, 162 [64] (Edelman J).

12 At **[1.2]**. The phrase comes from *Australian Education Union v Department of Education and Children's Services* (2012) 248 CLR 1, 14 [28] (French CJ, Hayne, Kiefel and Bell JJ). The case is discussed at **Example 33.1**.

13 See chapter 33.

14 There is not as yet a complete consensus on the structure for analysis: Ruth Sullivan, 'Foreword to the Fourth Edition' in *Sullivan on the Construction of Statutes* (LexisNexis, 5th ed, 2008) ix, x.

15 (2017) 262 CLR 362.

inflicted' on a person. The last term referred to an act or omission 'intended to cause' extreme humiliation.

The Refugee Review Tribunal found that, because the appellants had left their country of origin, Sri Lanka, illegally, they would likely be held in remand in a prison for a short period in conditions that were poor and that may not meet international standards by reason of matters such as overcrowding, poor sanitary facilities, and limited access to food. The Tribunal concluded that the element of intention in the terms defining 'significant harm' was *not* satisfied.

After further unsuccessful appeals to the Federal Circuit Court and the Full Court of the Federal Court, the matter reached the High Court. The question was whether 'intentionally' took the ordinary meaning of 'to mean, to have in mind', or whether it was sufficient if 'a person does an act knowing that the act will, in the ordinary course of events, inflict pain or suffering, or cause extreme humiliation'.[16] By majority the Court found that the context did not tell against the ordinary meaning.[17]

Of present relevance is the Court's finding in relation to s 5.2(3) of the *Criminal Code* (Cth) (in sch to *Criminal Code Act 1995* (Cth)). It provided that '[a] person has intention with respect to a result if he or she means to bring it about *or is aware that it will occur in the ordinary course of events*'.[18] The lead judgment of Kiefel CJ, Nettle and Gordon JJ dismissed its relevance, holding: 'Turning to the *Criminal Code*, the alternative definition of 'intention' in s 5.2(3) does *not* form part of the context in which the complementary protection regime of the Act and the definitions contained in it are to be considered.'[19] Their Honours reasoned that 'it would have been a simple enough matter to have adopted the Criminal Code definition of intention ... but there is no reference to that definition and nothing to suggest that it was considered to be appropriate'.[20] In addition, the *Criminal Code*, and the *Migration Act* in its complementary protection provisions, gave effect to Australia's obligations under the *Convention Against Torture and Other Cruel, Inhuman or Degrading Treatment or Punishment* 'in different ways and for different purposes'.[21]

Duty to have regard to

[7.4] An interpreter must have regard to context

The High Court of Australia has stated on numerous occasions that regard to the context is essential in determining the meaning of legislative provisions. For example, in *SAS Trustee Corporation v Miles*[22] three members of the Court ruled: 'T]he starting point for ascertainment of the meaning of a statutory provision is, of course, the text of the provision considered in light of its

16 Ibid 367 [10] (Kiefel CJ, Nettle and Gordon JJ).

17 Ibid 369 [17].

18 Emphasis added by their Honours.

19 (2017) 262 CLR 362, 370 [20] (emphasis added).

20 Ibid 371 [23].

21 Ibid 371 [25].

22 (2018) 265 CLR 137.

context and purpose.'[23] And in *Talacko v Bennett*[24] the Court stated: 'The meaning of [the provision in doubt] is to be determined by reference to considerations of text, context and purpose.'[25]

Statements such as these raise a number of questions, such as why is regard to context necessary?

Regard to context is essential before determining the meaning of legislation [7.5]

Regard to context is essential because words in themselves carry merely a *capacity* to communicate meaning[26] or an indication of only general usage.[27] Thus, it is 'seriously misleading' to suggest words have a 'core' meaning, regardless of context.[28]

Extracurially, judges have helpfully commented on the nature of words in explaining the problems confronting statutory interpretation. Justice McHugh has observed that '[l]anguage, even plain English language, is necessarily imprecise'.[29] Justice Frankfurter has elaborated on this theme:

> [J]udicial construction ought not to be torn from its wider, non-legal context. Anything that is written may present a problem of meaning, and that is the essence of the business of judges in construing legislation. The problem derives from the very nature of words. They are symbols of meaning. But unlike mathematical symbols, the phrasing of a document, especially a complicated enactment, seldom attains more than approximate precision. If individual words are inexact symbols, with shifting variables, their configuration can hardly achieve invariant meaning or assured definiteness.[30]

If words are 'inexact symbols', how is meaning arrived at? It is *the use* to which language is put that enables it to be given meaning. In his treatise on language (published posthumously in 1953) Wittgenstein propounded that '[f]or a *large* class of cases ... in which we employ the word "meaning" it can be defined thus: the meaning of a word is its use in the language'.[31]

Justice Oliver Wendell Holmes had put a similar thesis: 'A word is not a crystal, transparent and unchanged; it is the skin of a living thought and may vary greatly in colour and content according to

---

23 Ibid 149 [20] (Kiefel CJ, Bell and Nettle JJ).

24 (2017) 260 CLR 124.

25 Ibid 145 [65] (Kiefel CJ, Bell, Keane, Gordon and Edelman JJ) (citation omitted). For another similar statement, see *Comcare v Martin* (2016) 258 CLR 467, 479 [42] (the Court).

26 Joseph Campbell and Richard Campbell, 'Why Statutory Interpretation Is Done as It Is Done' (2014) 39(1) *Australian Bar Review* 1, 13.

27 *LU Simon Builders Pty Ltd v Victorian Building Authority* [2017] VSC 805 [46] (Cavanough J).

28 Joseph Campbell and Richard Campbell, 'Why Statutory Interpretation Is Done as It Is Done' (2014) 39(1) *Australian Bar Review* 1, 12. See also Lon L Fuller, 'Positivism and Fidelity to Law – A Reply to Professor Hart' (1957) 71(4) *Harvard Law Review* 630, 661–9. Both these writers drew heavily on the work of Wittgenstein, discussed below.

29 Justice MH McHugh, 'The Growth of Legislation and Litigation' (1995) 69(1) *Australian Law Journal* 37, 46.

30 Justice Felix Frankfurter, 'Some Reflections on the Reading of Statutes' (1947) 47(4) *Columbia Law Review* 527, 528.

31 Ludwig Wittgenstein, *Philosophical Investigations*, tr GEM Anscombe (Basil Blackwell, 1953) 20 [43] (emphasis in original). As already noted, his work has been widely relied on in the statutory interpretation literature. See also Philip Sales, 'Legislative Intention, Interpretation, and the Principle of Legality' (2019) 40(1) *Statute Law Review* 53, 59.

the circumstances and the time in which it is used.'[32] The reference to the circumstances in which a word or phrase is used points to the 'particular context' in which it is used.[33]

Therefore, meaning depends on context. Jackson, an expert in language and in law, put it this way:

> For words are never used without any context whatsoever. We always presuppose some context, and it is in the light of our knowledge of that context that the words bear a meaning.[34]

[7.6] **An interpreter cannot decline to consider the context of a rule on the basis that the rule, read in isolation, is not ambiguous**

It is firmly accepted that an interpreter cannot decline to consider the context of a rule merely because, read in isolation, the rule is not ambiguous. The leading authority is the *CIC Insurance* case:

> It is well settled that at common law, apart from any reliance upon s 15AB of the *Acts Interpretation Act 1901* (Cth), the court may have regard to reports of law reform bodies to ascertain the mischief which a statute is intended to cure. Moreover, the modern approach to statutory interpretation (a) insists that *the context be considered in the first instance*, not merely at some later stage when ambiguity might be thought to arise, and (b) uses 'context' in its widest sense to include such things as the existing state of the law and the mischief which, by legitimate means such as those just mentioned, one may discern the statute was intended to remedy.[35]

Consequently, a court will err if, holding the provision in question is unambiguous, the court refuses to consider part of the context that casts doubt on that assumption.[36]

[7.7] **Regard to context imposes a duty to take account of all relevant indications of meaning, not just the intrinsic context**

The duty to have regard to the context requires a court to consider 'all available indications':

> [T]he question as to the operation of the statutes remains a matter to be gleaned by reference to legislative intention. That intention is to be extracted 'from all available indications'.[37]

This goes beyond the Act concerned ('the intrinsic context').

---

32 *Towne v Eisner*, 245 US 418, 425 (1918), cited with approval in *Luna Park (NSW) Ltd v Tramways Advertising Pty Ltd* (1938) 61 CLR 286, 309–10 (Dixon J).

33 Philip Sales, 'Legislative Intention, Interpretation, and the Principle of Legality' (2019) 40(1) *Statute Law Review* 53, 54.

34 Bernard S Jackson, *Making Sense in Law: Linguistic, Psychological and Semiotic Perspectives* (Deborah Charles Publications, 1995) 43. See also Robyn Carston, 'Legal Texts and Canons of Construction: A View from Current Pragmatic Theory' in Michael Freeman and Fiona Smith (eds), *Law and Language: Current Legal Issues* (Oxford University Press, 2013) vol 15, ch 2; Brian G Slocum, 'Ordinary Meaning and Empiricism' (2019) 40 (1) *Statute Law Review* 13, 14; James Boyd White, *Justice as Translation: An Essay in Cultural and Legal Criticism* (University of Chicago Press, 1990) 137.

35 *CIC Insurance Ltd v Bankstown Football Club Ltd* (1997) 187 CLR 384, 408 (Brennan CJ, Dawson, Toohey and Gummow JJ; Gaudron J generally agreeing at 412) (emphasis added) (citations omitted). This passage was endorsed in *SZTAL v Minister for Immigration and Border Protection* (2017) 262 CLR 362, 368 [14] (Kiefel CJ, Nettle and Gordon JJ), 374 [36]–[37] (Gageler J); and in *R v A2* (2019) 269 CLR 507, 521 [33] (Kiefel CJ and Keane J, Nettle and Gordon JJ agreeing generally at 249 [148], Edelman J agreeing at 263 [193]).

36 *Beadle v La Bianca* [2012] WASC 415, [23] (Pritchard J). The case is discussed below at **Example 7.2**.

37 *Commissioner of Police for New South Wales v Eaton* (2013) 252 CLR 1, 19 [46] (Crennan, Kiefel and Bell JJ, quoting *Associated Minerals Consolidated Ltd v Wyong Shire Council* [1975] AC 538, 553–4).

It is true that in *Alcan (NT) Alumina Pty Ltd v Commissioner of Territory Revenue (NT)*[38] the High Court emphasised the text over the context:

> This Court has stated on many occasions that the task of statutory construction must begin with a consideration of the text itself. Historical considerations and extrinsic materials cannot be relied on to displace the clear meaning of the text. The language which has actually been employed in the text of legislation is the surest guide to legislative intention. The meaning of the text may require consideration of the context, which includes the general purpose and policy of a provision, in particular the mischief it is seeking to remedy.[39]

And a little later, in *Saeed v Minister for Immigration and Citizenship*,[40] extrinsic materials were contrasted with 'the ordinary rules of statutory construction': 'As was pointed out in *Catlow v Accident Compensation Commission* it is erroneous to look at extrinsic materials before exhausting the application of the ordinary rules of statutory construction.'[41]

On their face, the statements in *Alcan* and *Saeed* were not wholly consistent with the earlier authority of *CIC Insurance Ltd v Bankstown Football Club Ltd* in which, in unqualified terms, the High Court had required reference to the context in its 'widest sense' before meaning is determined.[42] Questions were raised in case law[43] and the literature[44] about the consistency of these rulings.

Whatever these statements meant, the High Court soon clarified (and confirmed[45]) the position:

> This Court has stated on many occasions that the task of statutory construction must begin with a consideration of the [statutory] text. So must the task of statutory construction end. The statutory text must be considered in its context. That context includes legislative history and extrinsic materials. Understanding context has utility if, and in so far as, it assists in fixing the meaning of the statutory text.[46]

---

38 (2009) 239 CLR 27.

39 Ibid 46–7 [47] (Hayne, Heydon, Crennan and Kiefel JJ) (citations omitted).

40 (2010) 241 CLR 252.

41 Ibid 265 [33] (French CJ, Gummow, Hayne, Crennan and Kiefel JJ) (citation omitted). The reference to the *Catlow case* made in *Saeed* is to *Catlow v Accident Compensation Commission* (1989) 167 CLR 543, 550 (Brennan and Gaudron JJ).

42 See **[7.6]** above.

43 *Wentworth District Capital Ltd v Federal Commissioner of Taxation* (2010) 80 ATR 50, 59–60 [34–[35] (Perram J), affirmed in *Federal Commissioner of Taxation v Wentworth District Capital Ltd* (2011) 191 FCR 151.

44 Justice Susan Kenny, 'Constitutional Role of the Judge: Statutory Interpretation' (2014) 1 *Judicial College of Victoria Online Journal* 4, 10, 11. See also Jeffrey Barnes, 'Contextualism: "The Modern Approach to Statutory Interpretation"' (2018) 41(4) *University of New South Wales Law Journal* 1083, 1102–5.

45 *Thiess v Collector of Customs* (2014) 250 CLR 664, 671 [22] (the Court).

46 *Federal Commissioner of Taxation v Consolidated Media Holdings Ltd* (2012) 250 CLR 503, 519 [39] (the Court) (citations omitted), citing *Alcan (NT) Alumina Pty Ltd v Commissioner of Territory Revenue (NT)* (2009) 239 CLR 27, 46–7 [47].

Example 7.2 *Beadle v La Bianca*[47]

Section 119(7) of the *Liquor Control Act 1988* (WA) ('the Act') provided:

> Where a person is the occupier or has or takes part in the care, management, or control of any unlicensed premises (other than a place or premises to which subsection (2) or (3) applies) and allows those premises to be kept or used as a place of resort for the consumption of liquor, the person commits an offence.

The respondent was prosecuted in the Magistrates Court for an offence against the provision. The Magistrate acquitted the accused on the basis of an interpretation of 'place of resort'. He held that the prosecution must prove that there was frequency of the use of the premises at times when they were unlicensed. As the prosecution had relied on only one occasion when the premises were unlicensed and kept or used as a place of resort for the consumption of alcohol, it was held that the prosecution had not proved their case beyond reasonable doubt. The Magistrate regarded the phrase 'place of resort' as having an unambiguous meaning.[48] The Magistrate referred to dictionaries, other subsections in s 119, and to the utility of the rule if it were to be satisfied by an isolated instance.[49] But the Magistrate refused to consider the objects of the Act in question, stating: 'It follows that I find there is no need to refer to the objects of the Liquor Control Act to resolve any issue of statutory interpretation.'[50]

According to the Supreme Court, the objects of the Act were set out in the long title and s 5 of the Act.[51] The latter provided that an object was 'to minimise harm or ill-health caused to people, or any group of people, due to the use of liquor'. The Court noted that that purpose would be promoted more by a construction that did not require frequency or repetition of use.[52] After referring to the 'modern approach to statutory construction' and the principle in the *CIC Insurance* case set out above at **[7.6]**, the Court held that the Magistrate had erred in law[53] for the following reason: 'The legislative purpose (together with all aspects of the legislative context) should be considered at the outset, in conjunction with the ordinary meaning of the words, to construe a provision in a statute.'[54]

Consequences of contextualism

[7.8] **Considering the text in its context ('contextualism') is the overall approach to interpretation; its rise has caused a number of former rules and other interpretative criteria to be adjusted in its wake**

The *CIC Insurance Case* (**[7.6]**) and later authorities (**[7.7]**) strongly indicate that the overall approach to statutory interpretation may fairly be described as contextual. Previously, regard to

47 [2012] WASC 415.

48 Quoted in ibid [15].

49 As quoted in ibid.

50 Quoted in ibid.

51 Ibid [42]–[44].

52 Ibid [45].

53 Ibid [23].

54 Ibid [22].

the context had been seriously truncated by particular 'rules'. Now, under the umbrella of 'contextualism' (the approach to interpretation that considers the text in its context), all relevant indications are considered even if the text, read in isolation, is not ambiguous (see the principle discussed at **[7.6]**). And their weight is not preordained but depends largely on the context.

Unlike a rule-oriented approach, contextualism in practice is not a top-down method; it is more the reverse. As Justice Crennan insightfully pointed out, the overall contemporary approach accentuates the circumstances of the case and the particular context:

> The current approach to establishing the meaning of a provision in a statute, by reference not only to the plain meaning of words but also by reference to context, purpose, legality or fairness, or some combination of such considerations, exemplifies the proposition that no single theory of, or approach to, statutory interpretation or construction is invariably more useful than, or to the exclusion of, others. It is the problems which are thrown up by the cases, and the particular statutes under consideration in individual cases, which determine which approach is useful, rather than it being the other way round.[55]

As a consequence of greater regard to context, widespread changes have occurred to the law.[56] A few illustrations are now briefly given.

The former literal rule[57] was expressly disapproved.[58] It was reduced in status to a literal *reading*.[59] Though the ordinary or grammatical meaning is the presumptive meaning,[60] it may be departed from 'for good reason' to give effect to the legislative intention[61] or where 'it is plain that Parliament intended [the words in question] to have some different meaning'.[62] Context supplies the justification for doing so:

> It is now accepted that even words having an apparently clear ordinary or grammatical meaning may be ascribed a different legal meaning after the process of construction is complete. This is because consideration of the context for the provision may point to factors that tend against the ordinary usage of the words of the provision.[63]

The weight of the ordinary or grammatical meaning now depends on the context, including how clear that meaning is:

> Context can give words an interpretation that is the opposite of their ordinary meaning and grammatical sense. Context can also permit a construction of words that excludes their application to matters that would have fallen within the application of their literal

55 Justice Susan Crennan, 'Blackstone's "Signs" and Statutory Interpretation' (CLE Lecture, Victorian Bar, Melbourne, 28 November 2007) 11–12.

56 For a wider discussion of historical developments, see chapter 2.

57 For Australia, the most well-known statement of the literal rule was in *Amalgamated Society of Engineers v Adelaide Steamship Co Ltd* (1920) 28 CLR 129, 161–2 (Higgins J). See *Cooper Brookes (Wollongong) Pty Ltd v Commissioner of Taxation (Cth)* (1981) 147 CLR 297, 319–20 (Mason and Wilson JJ).

58 *Cooper Brookes (Wollongong) Pty Ltd v Commissioner of Taxation (Cth)* (1981) 147 CLR 297, 319–21 (Mason and Wilson JJ).

59 Ibid 321.

60 See **[6.7]** and chapter 15.

61 *Cooper Brookes (Wollongong) Pty Ltd v Commissioner of Taxation (Cth)* (1981) 147 CLR 297, 321 (Mason and Wilson JJ).

62 *Masson v Parsons* (2019) 266 CLR 554, 572 [26] (Kiefel CJ, Bell, Gageler, Keane, Nettle and Gordon JJ).

63 *R v A2* (2019) 269 CLR 507, 521 [32] (Kiefel CJ and Keane J; Nettle and Gordon JJ agreeing generally at 554 [148], Edelman J agreeing at 572 [193]).

> meaning. However, as with contractual interpretation, where 'the clearer the natural meaning the more difficult it is to justify departing from it', so too in statutory interpretation 'questions of degree arise' and it will be more difficult to displace an interpretation that 'has a powerful advantage in ordinary meaning and grammatical sense'.[64]

The former 'golden rule', which had permitted departures from the literal rule, was eclipsed by the rise of contextualism.[65] It was held that departure from the ordinary or grammatical sense is not restricted to cases of absurdity and inconsistency.[66]

Added emphasis is now given to the legislative purpose.[67] Notwithstanding s 15AA of the *Acts Interpretation Act 1901* (Cth) and its equivalents,[68] the presumption that Parliament intends the legislative purpose to be promoted has not been elevated into a rule that would 'swamp' consideration of other contextual factors.[69] Rather, the weight of an argument from legislative purpose (if the purpose is ascertainable) depends on the context, including the level of specificity of the purpose.[70] If a court can discern 'a more specific purpose' in the text, this is more likely to be of assistance.[71]

Recourse to parliamentary materials (such as Hansard) was for a long time prohibited by a self-imposed 'exclusionary rule'.[72] Now, under the common law, and some statutory regimes, indications of the mischief and the purpose may be ascertained without having to satisfy the controls in the federal statutory regime.[73] Their utility depends on their relevance in the particular context.[74]

An enhanced regard to context has also caused a reassessment of the 're-enactment presumption':[75]

> There is a presumption, useful in statutory interpretation, that where a provision of legislation has been passed upon by authoritative decisions of the courts and is later re-enacted, Parliament can be taken, in the absence of a clear intention to the contrary, to know and accept the interpretations given to the legislation.[76]

---

64 *SAS Trustee Corporation v Miles* (2018) 265 CLR 137, 162–3 [64] (Edelman J) (citations omitted).

65 For former authorities on the golden rule, and its demise, see *Cooper Brookes (Wollongong) Pty Ltd v Commissioner of Taxation (Cth)* (1981) 147 CLR 297, 320 (Mason and Wilson JJ).

66 *Cooper Brookes (Wollongong) Pty Ltd v Commissioner of Taxation (Cth)* (1981) 147 CLR 297, 320 (Mason and Wilson JJ).

67 *Bropho v Western Australia* (1990) 171 CLR 1, 20 (the Court).

68 See **[8.2]**.

69 See **[8.2]**. On the prevalence of context as a determinant of legal meaning, see Michael Kirby, 'The Never-Ending Challenge of Drafting and Interpreting Statutes – A Meditation on the Career of John Finemore QC' (2012) 36(1) *Melbourne University Law Review* 140, 170–2. See also Chief Justice JJ Spigelman, 'The Intolerable Wrestle: Developments in Statutory Interpretation' (2010) 84(12) *Australian Law Journal* 822, 827.

70 See **[8.7]**.

71 *Carr v Western Australia* (2007) 232 CLR 138, 143 [6] (Gleeson CJ).

72 An exception existed for reports of expert bodies where the report had been tabled in the Parliament and had led to the legislation in question: see chapter 24.

73 *Acts Interpretation Act 1901* (Cth) s 15AB(1). This regime is less illustrative of the rise of contextualism as, if invoked, it imposes restrictions on use of the extrinsic material to which it relates.

74 See chapter 24.

75 This presumption is considered in chapter 21.

76 *Public Service Association of New South Wales v Industrial Commission of New South Wales* (1985) 1 NSWLR 627, 640 (Kirby P).

At one time the presumption was criticised as 'artificial', with the High Court stating that '[a]t most the principle affords a presumption of no great weight concerning the meaning of the words used'.[77] But now its weight is seen to turn on the context. In a case involving the 'specialised and politically sensitive field' of industrial relations,[78] the High Court had no doubt the presumption was applicable to the provision concerned.[79] Gleeson CJ remarked:

> No doubt there are circumstances in which it is artificial, and unpersuasive, to attribute to Parliament a consciousness of a judicial interpretation which might have been placed upon an expression, perhaps years before, and in some different context. But it is hard to think of a clearer case of parliamentary adoption of an expression, with a judicially settled meaning, to be applied in a particular context, than the present.[80]

Utility of regard to

Regard to context assists in fixing meaning [7.9]

Regard to the context assists in fixing meaning:

> The statutory text must be considered in its context. That context includes legislative history and extrinsic materials. Understanding context has utility if, and in so far as, it assists in fixing the meaning of the statutory text.[81]

The role of context varies according to the circumstances. To quote Gleeson CJ in *Singh v Commonwealth*,[82] '[m]eaning is always influenced, and sometimes controlled, by context'.[83] Context *influences* meaning by, for example, clarifying or confirming the ordinary or grammatical meaning of the text.[84] It may be seen to *control* meaning in a more determinative sense where the context supplies indications that compel the court to arrive at a meaning other than the ordinary or grammatical meaning.[85] And where the indications of meaning supplied by the text are competing, consideration of the context may compel a court to give the words in question the meaning that the context so indicates.[86]

---

77 *Flaherty v Girgis* (1987) 162 CLR 574, 594 (Mason ACJ, Wilson and Dawson JJ). The 'artificial' comment was made by Dixon CJ in *R v Reynhoudt* (1962) 107 CLR 381, 388. In *Flaherty*, Mason ACJ, Wilson and Dawson JJ endorsed it: 594.

78 *Electrolux Home Products Pty Ltd v Australian Workers' Union* (2004) 221 CLR 309, 346–7 [81] (McHugh J).

79 Ibid 324–5 [8] (Gleeson CJ), 346–7 [81] (McHugh J), 371 [162] (Gummow, Hayne and Heydon JJ).

80 Ibid 324–5 [8].

81 *Federal Commissioner of Taxation v Consolidated Media Holdings Ltd* (2012) 250 CLR 503, 519 [39] (French CJ, Hayne, Crennan, Bell and Gageler JJ). With respect, the word 'if' in this quotation is troublesome. It ought not be read as implying that the context might not have utility in some cases. It always has utility, at least in confirming the ordinary meaning of the words in question. It may be taken to imply that the context may or may not be determinative.

82 (2004) 222 CLR 322.

83 Ibid 332 [12] (Gleeson CJ).

84 The ordinary or grammatical meaning, and other meanings found by a first-blush reading, are more fully discussed in chapter 15.

85 *Smoker v Pharmacy Restructuring Authority* (1994) 53 FCR 287, 290 (Burchett J).

86 This includes giving the provision a meaning that is not within its grammatical or semantic possibilities: see chapter 6 (**[6.9]**).

Example 7.3 *LU Simon Builders Pty Ltd v Victorian Building Authority*[87]

The first plaintiff was specified as the 'builder' in the building permits for six apartment buildings in Melbourne. The second and third plaintiffs were directors of the first plaintiff. One of them was named as the responsible building practitioner in the relevant building permits. The Victorian Building Authority gave a direction to fix in respect of the six buildings. In each case the direction was given after a certificate of final inspection or an occupancy permit had been issued for the building, and up to nine years after the permits were issued. The reason for each direction appeared to relate to allegations that the cladding on the building may not be compliant with the requirements of the *Building Act 1993* (Vic) ('the Act'), the building regulations or the relevant building permits. The plaintiffs challenged the validity of the directions.

The directions were purportedly given under s 37B of the Act:

> **37B Direction by authorised person to fix building work**
>
> (1) This section applies if, after the inspection of building work, an authorised person believes on reasonable grounds that the building work fails to comply with this Act, the building regulations or the building permit issued in relation to the building work.
>
> (2) The authorised person may give a direction to fix the building work to a relevant person in accordance with this Division.

The Act defined 'authorised person' as including the Victorian Building Authority (s 37). The plaintiff's construction of s 37B was that the power was unavailable after a certificate of final inspection or an occupancy permit had been issued. The defendant's construction was that there was power to give a builder a direction to fix under s 37B at any time at all or, alternatively, within a reasonable period.

The defendant's principal argument was that s 37B 'does not contain any express time limit or cut-off point'.[88] This argument was given weight by the Court. But the Court found the text also gave rise to indications for the plaintiff's construction. As a matter of ordinary English, the Court found the words 'direction to fix' 'connotes intervention in an ongoing process, more so than intervention after the fact'.[89]

The Court ultimately agreed with the plaintiff's construction[90] and issued a declaration to that effect. The main reason for so holding appeared to be that examination of the context of the provision revealed numerous indications pointing to the construction put by the plaintiff. Together with the text, these indications were 'overwhelming'.[91] The Court's analysis is meticulous and detailed. The relevant indications it found included the following.

The immediately succeeding provision, s 37C, was helpful. It provided that a direction to fix building work may be given as an oral direction. This went against the defendant's construction, for '[s]uch a direction would be wildly out of place in relation to an alleged defect emerging long after the builder had departed the former building site'.[92]

87 [2017] VSC 805.

88 Ibid [32] (Cavanough J).

89 Ibid [46].

90 Ibid [6].

91 Ibid.

92 Ibid [47].

Grammatical analysis of relevant provisions was helpful. Neighbouring sections in the same division as s 37B, which bore upon the construction issue, were all expressed in the present tense. This contrasted with the past tense used in a comparable provision in s 106(a) of the Act.[93]

The Court examined the immediately surrounding provisions. It found that they were arranged in a sequence that broadly matched the stages of a building project. Part 4, which included s 37B, came between a Part dealing with building permits and a Part dealing with occupancy permits.

Having regard to the provision and the context provided by the Act, the Court considered that the case for the plaintiff was so strong that it was not necessary to take account of the plaintiff's submissions regarding the wider context: the likely operation of the Act if the defendant's construction were accepted, and extrinsic materials. The plaintiff had pointed to 'inconvenient, improbable and irrational consequences that would follow from the defendant's construction of Division 2 of Part 4'.[94] The plaintiff had also based arguments on the principle of legality, including the impact of a direction to fix on a person who might no longer hold a relevant building permit that is currently in force, and on the owner's common law property rights.[95] Although not determinative, these contextual arguments fortified the plaintiffs' case.[96] The Court also considered certain extrinsic materials, namely the prior statute law and the Minister's second reading speech to the Bill that put forward the proposed s 37B. The purposes identified in the second reading speech – early intervention, the prevention of defective, non-compliant work, and retaining the same power as previously held by the relevant building surveyor[97] – did not assist the defendant.[98]

Therefore, while the text in question (s 37B) was the basis for arguments for each of the opposing constructions, the context of the provision – comprising other provisions of the Act, the likely operation of the Act if the defendant's construction was accepted, and extrinsic materials (the prior law and the Minister's second reading speech) – overwhelmingly pointed to the plaintiff's construction. The case illustrates how, in respect of a provision that is ambiguous when read in isolation, examination of the context may provide compelling evidence of the legal meaning.

Context typically assists by supplying indications of meaning; it can also assist by supplying a presumptive rule from the general law [7.10]

In the typical case of statutory interpretation the context supplies various indications of meaning. These assist by 'pointing' to one of the constructions contended for in respect of the provision in doubt. **Example 7.3** is illustrative.

The context of a provision in doubt also potentially includes surrounding law. Prior to his appointment to the High Court, Justice Stephen Gageler wrote: 'The meaning of a statutory text is also informed, and reinformed, by the need for the courts to apply the text each time, not in isolation, but as part of the totality of the common law and statute law as it then exists.'[99] Knowledge of the general law is thus presumed:

93 Ibid [52].

94 Ibid [56].

95 Ibid [57].

96 Ibid [58].

97 Ibid [69]–[70].

98 Ibid [68].

99 Stephen Gageler, 'Common Law Statutes and Judicial Legislation: Statutory Interpretation as a Common Law Process' (2011) 37(1) *Monash University Law Review* 1, 1–2.

> [A]ny statute must of course be looked at in the light of the general law of the country. Parliament in its wisdom in passing an Act must be taken to know the general law.[100]

The general law may supply a relevant presumptive rule, which is taken to be implied in a statutory provision unless the statute in question manifests a contrary intention. Examples from the general (common) law include: the presumption that mens rea is an essential element of every statutory offence;[101] and '[t]he presumption that the principles of natural justice condition the exercise of a statutory power'.[102] Both principles come under the umbrella of the principle of legality.[103]

[7.11] Regard to context is not necessarily free of dispute; the weight of a potential contextual aid may be contested or the 'aid' could itself be ambiguous

Although regard to the context is usually productive, context is not necessarily an area free of dispute. Potential aids may themselves be contested in a number of ways. The weight of a potential interpretative aid may be contested[104] or the 'aid' may be ambiguous itself.

Example 7.4 *LU Simon Builders Pty Ltd v Victorian Building Authority*[105]

The facts and legislation for this case were given in **Example 7.3**. It will be recalled that the central provision whose meaning was in doubt was s 37B of the *Building Act 1993* (Vic). The central issue was whether a direction to fix building work given under that provision was subject to implied temporal limitations.

In the context of s 37B was s 37C:

> **37C Method of giving directions**
>
> A direction to fix building work may be given as –
>
> (a) an oral direction to either or both of the following persons –
> (i) the builder;
> (ii) the person who is apparently in charge of the site on which the building work is being carried out; or
>
> (b) a written direction to the builder.

Although a potential aid to interpreting s 37B, s 37C itself became briefly embroiled in an interpretative dispute in this case. First, the defendant argued that the capacity for a direction to

100 *Fisher v Bell* [1961] 1 QB 394, 399 (Lord Parker CJ; Ashworth J agreeing at 401 and Elwes J agreeing at 401), followed in *Pelka v Sundquist* [2005] WASC 52, [47]–[48].

101 *He Kaw Teh v The Queen* (1985) 157 CLR 523, 528, discussed at **[42.4]**.

102 *Plaintiff S10/2011 v Minister for Immigration and Citizenship* (2012) 246 CLR 636, 658 [66] (Gummow, Hayne, Crennan and Bell JJ), quoting with approval *Kioa v West* (1985) 159 CLR 550, 619 (Brennan J). For discussion of the principle of natural justice generally in relation to statutory interpretation, see Jeffrey Barnes, 'How Statutory Interpretation Sustains Administrative Law' (2015) 22(3) *Australian Journal of Administrative Law* 163, 165–9; Jeffrey Barnes, 'Statutory Interpretation and Administrative Law' in Matthew Groves (ed), *Modern Administrative Law in Australia: Concepts and Context* (Cambridge University Press, 2014) 119, 124–7. See also Mark Aronson, Matthew Groves and Greg Weeks, *Judicial Review of Administrative Action and Government Liability* (Thomson Reuters, 6th ed, 2017) ch 7.

103 See chapter 28.

104 Chapter 9 deals with critical analysis of interpretative arguments at **[9.9]**.

105 [2017] VSC 805.

fix to be given as an oral direction did not favour the plaintiff's time-bound construction. This was because the section provided for both oral and written directions. The defendant implied that, in cases such as the present, a written direction was appropriate. The Court found this argument lacked cogency because it was still the case that the provision provided for oral directions and, further, other Parts of the Act (in a different time sequence) did not.[106]

Next, the defendant argued that the term 'the builder' in s 37C could be read in a way that was consistent with its construction of s 37B that there is power to give a builder a direction to fix under that provision at any time. The term was defined in s 37 in relation to building work as 'the person who *is* specified as the builder in the building permit issued in relation to that building work'.[107] The defendant submitted that 'the definition [of builder] would cover a person whose name appears in an existing document that *in the past* was a building permit that was in force'. The Court was unpersuaded by this construction of the definition:

> Once again, I note the use of the present tense. . . . I regard this as a strained reading of the definition. There is little or nothing in the Act to suggest that such a strained reading of the definition should be adopted.[108]

---

106 Ibid [47] (Cavanough J).

107 Emphasis added.

108 *LU Simon Builders Pty Ltd v Victorian Building Authority* [2017] VSC 805, [53] (Cavanough J).

8 PURPOSE

Overview

[8.1] The law of statutory interpretation directs us to ascertain the 'purpose' of an Act when construing a provision of that Act. This is one of the few *general* principles of statutory interpretation law that is the subject of a legislative mandate, though the common law has developed an equivalent principle. The mandate is that we must have regard to the purpose of an Act and choose the construction that promotes or best achieves that purpose. This does not warrant neglect of the statutory text or context, but instead requires the interpreter to have regard to the purpose in the context of the broader analysis of text and context required by the rules of statutory interpretation. Sometimes the purpose will be critical to the task of attributing meaning and sometimes it will be of little value. The value that purpose can provide to the task may depend on the degree of specificity with which it can be expressed. Many Acts embody multiple purposes or the purpose of the Act may be general. For these reasons, the purpose of the provision being construed can be more helpful for the interpretative task than the purpose of the Act as a whole. Evidence or indications of the purpose of an Act or a provision may be found in extrinsic materials. But ultimately the purpose must be evident from the statutory text itself and that text must be able to bear the meaning that the identified purpose promotes. The notion of purpose is not a licence to rewrite the text.

Statutory and common law requirement

[8.2] **Both the statutory and common law require an interpreter to ascertain the purpose of the statute**

The interpretation legislation of each Australian jurisdiction and the Australian common law both require the interpreter to consider the purpose of the statute being construed as part of the interpretative task.

(a) There is a statutory provision requiring consideration of purpose in the interpretation legislation of each jurisdiction

The interpretation legislation of each Australian jurisdiction contains a provision effectively directing an interpreter to ascertain the 'purpose' of an Act when construing it.

The first of these provisions was enacted in Australia in 1981. It was s 15AA of the Commonwealth *Acts Interpretation Act 1901* ('the AIA').[1]

1 Section 15AA was introduced by the *Statute Law Revision Act 1981* (Cth) sch 1. For background see chapter 2.

The version of s 15AA passed in 1981 was as follows:

> 15AA (1) In the interpretation of a provision of an Act, a construction that would promote the purpose or object underlying the Act (whether that purpose or object is expressly stated in the Act or not) shall be preferred to a construction that would not promote that purpose or object.

The states and territories each subsequently enacted a purpose provision in their respective Acts. New South Wales, Tasmania, Victoria, Western Australia and the Northern Territory each enacted a provision reflecting the 1981 version of s 15AA and their provisions remain substantially the same as, or identical to, that version.[2]

In 2011 the originally enacted s 15AA was repealed and substituted.[3] The new, and still current, provision contains different 'best achieve the purpose' language:

> In interpreting a provision of an Act, the interpretation that would best achieve the purpose or object of the Act (whether or not that purpose or object is expressly stated in the Act) is to be preferred to each other interpretation.

The Queensland *Acts Interpretation Act 1954* has contained the language of 'best achieve the purpose' since its original enactment of a purpose provision in 1991.[4] The purpose provisions of the Acts of the Australian Capital Territory and South Australia originally reflected the 1981 version of s 15AA, but in 2003 and 2021 respectively the 'best achieve' language was adopted.[5]

These purpose provisions impose a statutory 'instruction' or requirement.[6] Consideration of purpose is not a factor to be engaged with at the discretion of the judiciary. Nor is there any need for the existence of any ambiguity or any other condition before purpose can be taken into account.[7] Purpose must be considered not only where the provisions 'on their face offer more than one construction, but also in determining whether more than one construction is open'.[8]

(b) The difference in the language of the two versions of the purpose provision is of little practical consequence

The difference in the language of the two versions of the purpose provision gives rise to the question of whether they have different requirements or scope. The broader wording of the 'best achieve' language might suggest that greater weight or emphasis be given to purpose in the interpretative task than is required by the other version. But this does not seem to have come to pass.[9] The better view of

---

2 *Interpretation Act 1987* (NSW) s 33; *Interpretation Act 1978* (NT) s 62A; *Acts Interpretation Act 1931* (Tas) s 8A; *Interpretation of Legislation Act 1984* (Vic) s 35(a); *Interpretation Act 1984* (WA) s 18.

3 *Acts Interpretation Amendment Act 2011* (Cth) sch 1 cl 23.

4 *Acts Interpretation Act 1954* (Qld) s 14A.

5 *Legislation Act 2001* (ACT) s 139; *Legislation Interpretation Act 2021* (SA) s 14. For background to the current provisions see chapter 2.

6 *Port of Newcastle Operations Pty Ltd v Glencore Coal Assets Australia Pty Ltd* (2021) 395 ALR 209, 227–8 [89] (the Court); *Firebird Global Master Fund II Ltd v Republic of Nauru* (2015) 258 CLR 31, 56–7 [69] (French CJ and Kiefel J); *SZTAL v Minister for Immigration and Border Protection* (2017) 262 CLR 362, 375 [39] (Gageler J); *Thiess v Collector of Customs* (2014) 250 CLR 664, 672 [23] (French CJ, Hayne, Kiefel, Gageler and Keane JJ).

7 *SZTAL v Minister for Immigration and Border Protection* (2017) 262 CLR 362, 375 [39] (Gageler J in dissent but not as to principle); *Mills v Meeking* (1990) 169 CLR 214, 235 (Dawson J).

8 *Mills v Meeking* (1990) 169 CLR 214, 235 (Dawson J).

9 See, eg, *CPB Contractors Pty Ltd v Construction, Forestry, Maritime, Mining and Energy Union* [2019] FCAFC 70, [46]–[47], citing *Thiess v Collector of Customs* (2014) 250 CLR 664, 672.

the 'best achieve' language of the Commonwealth, Queensland, ACT and South Australian purpose provisions is that they are an explicit statutory recognition of the varying degrees of choice that were already recognised judicially.[10] This is supported by the fact that the difference in wording of the statutory provisions does not appear to have impacted the consistent approach to purpose taken by the High Court when construing statutes from different Australian jurisdictions. This is likely attributable to the analogical development of the common law (see (c) below).

As discussed in **[2.9]**, the enactment of the 'best achieve' language in the Commonwealth, Queensland and the Australian Capital Territory was prompted, at least in part, by observations in the 1990 High Court decision of *Chugg v Pacific Dunlop Ltd* about the 'limited choice' offered by the original s 15AA wording between 'a construction that would promote the purpose or object [of the Act]' and one 'that would not promote that purpose or object'.[11] These observations may reflect an unnecessarily strict reading of the original s 15AA provision. But even if that reading is accepted, practically it may be of little consequence. The common law principle about purpose, discussed below, means that even if the 'limited choice' wording means that the purpose section is inapplicable, the common law will step in so that purpose must still be considered.[12]

(c) **The common law requires consideration of purpose as part of the interpretative task**

Since the 1990s, consideration of purpose has been an integral part of the interpretative process at common law, independent of statute.[13] The relevance of purpose to the interpretative task was made clear, without reference to a statutory provision, in the oft-cited *Project Blue Sky Inc v Australian Broadcasting Authority*:[14]

> The primary object of statutory construction is to construe the relevant provision so that it is consistent with the language *and purpose* of all the provisions of the statute.[15]

It is now difficult to discern any meaningful distinction between the statutory mandate and the common law principle. Indeed, the legislative provisions on purpose have been described as a 'statutory reflection of a general systemic principle'.[16] The principles that follow apply equally regardless of the legal authority used for referring to purpose.

---

10 See Michael Kirby 'The Never-Ending Challenge of Drafting and Interpreting Statutes – A Meditation on the Career of John Finemore QC' (2012) 36(1) *Melbourne University Law Review* 140, 168–72.

11 (1990) 170 CLR 249, 262. Cf South Australia, *Parliamentary Debates*, Legislative Council, Explanation of Clauses, 6 May 2021, 3367 (RI Lucas, Treasurer).

12 See, eg, *Stamford Property Services Pty Ltd v Mulpha Australia Ltd* (2019) 99 NSWLR 730 where McCallum JA, in dissent, observed on appeal that the primary judge's determination that s 33 of the *Interpretation Act 1987* (NSW) (a purpose provision containing the so-called limited choice wording) was not applicable did not mean that purpose should not be considered, given the common law: at 753 [99]. Leeming JA, with whom Emmett AJA substantially agreed, did not directly address the point but considered the purpose of the Act, though concluded it did not materially assist: at 751 [90].

13 See chapter 2.

14 (1998) 194 CLR 355.

15 Ibid 381 [69] (McHugh, Gummow, Kirby and Hayne JJ) (emphasis added). See also *SZTAL v Minister for Immigration and Border Protection* (2017) 262 CLR 362, 368 [14] (Kiefel CJ, Nettle and Gordon JJ); *Alcan (NT) Alumina Pty Ltd v Commissioner of Territory Revenue (NT)* (2009) 239 CLR 27, 47 [47] (Hayne, Heydon, Crennan and Kiefel JJ); *Bropho v Western Australia* (1990) 171 CLR 1, 21–2 (Mason CJ, Deane, Dawson, Toohey, Gaudron and McHugh JJ).

16 *SZTAL v Minister for Immigration and Border Protection* (2017) 262 CLR 362, 375 [39] (Gageler J), citing *Thiess v Collector of Customs* (2014) 250 CLR 664, 672 [23] (French CJ, Hayne, Kiefel, Gageler and Keane JJ). See also *Legislation Act 2001* (ACT) s 137.

Meaning of purpose

It is difficult to articulate a precise meaning of 'purpose', but a working meaning is the goal that the law is designed to achieve [8.3]

Despite the centrality of the concept under statute and at common law, what constitutes the 'purpose' or 'object' (often used interchangeably) of an Act in Australian statutory interpretation law remains imprecise.

There have been various efforts at describing purpose: the 'intended aim' or 'goal' of the legislature,[17] 'the public interest sought to be protected and enhanced,'[18] the 'intended practical operation of the law or to what the law is designed to achieve in fact'[19] or 'the object for the advancement or attainment of which [the] law was enacted'.[20] It is sometimes equated with 'policy'.[21] The *Acts Interpretation Act 1954* (Qld) provides that the word 'purpose' in a Queensland Act includes 'policy objective'.[22]

All of these descriptions are essentially synonyms for describing the goal that the statute was enacted to achieve. They reflect the idea that purpose be understood as concerned with 'the functional role that the statute plays within the legal system'.[23] Legislation is not enacted in a vacuum – statutes 'always have some purpose or object to accomplish'.[24]

The old term 'mischief' is sometimes used when purpose is considered. This is understandable given the historical background.[25] The concept of 'mischief' refers to some defect or gap in the existing law that needs to be addressed.[26] In that respect it might be considered an aspect or subset of purpose. The 'mischief' might be the, or a, trigger for why the statute was enacted.[27] So it will usually be useful for ascertaining the statutory purpose. But purpose is a broader concept than mischief. The 'trigger' for a statute will not necessarily comprise the totality of the statutory purpose and so the two should not necessarily be equated. In modern times, when volumes of legislation are not necessarily directed towards rectifying a 'defect' or 'evil,' the concept of mischief does not always have utility.[28]

---

17 *Unions NSW v New South Wales* (2019) 264 CLR 595, 656 [168], 657 [171] (Edelman J).

18 *Brown v Tasmania* (2017) 261 CLR 328, 392 [209] (Edelman J), citing *Cunliffe v Commonwealth* (1994) 182 CLR 272, 300.

19 *Work Health Authority v Outback Ballooning Pty Ltd* (2019) 266 CLR 428, 459 [72] (Gageler J) (citations omitted).

20 *Al-Kateb v Godwin* (2004) 219 CLR 562, 608 [121] (Gummow J), citing *Victoria v Commonwealth* (1996) 187 CLR 416.

21 See, eg, *Certain Lloyd's Underwriters v Cross* (2012) 248 CLR 378, 389 [24] (French CJ and Hayne J), 405 [70] (Crennan and Bell JJ).

22 Section 36; sch 1.

23 Dale Smith, 'What Is Statutory Purpose?' in Lisa Burton Crawford, Patrick Emerton and Dale Smith (eds), *Law Under a Democratic Constitution: Essays in Honour of Jeffrey Goldsworthy* (Hart Publishing, 2019) 13, 15.

24 *Thiess v Collector of Customs* (2014) 250 CLR 664, 672 [23] (the Court), citing *Cabell v Markham*, 148 F 2d 737, 739 (1945).

25 See chapter 2.

26 *R v A2* (2019) 269 CLR 507, 521 [33] 524 [44] (Kiefel CJ and Keane J).

27 See *Commonwealth Custodial Services Ltd v Valuer-General (NSW)* (2007) 156 LGERA 186, 191 [16] (Spigelman CJ).

28 For further discussion, see Samuel L Bray, 'The Mischief Rule' (2021) 109 *Georgetown Law Journal* 967. Cf Timothy J Bradley, 'Getting into Mischief: Reflections on Statutory Interpretation and the Mischief Rule' (2021) 109(5) *Georgetown Law Journal Online* 199.

The concept of purpose is distinguishable from other concepts. First, the purpose of a statute is not to be equated with 'the subjective motives or purposes of the various members of the Parliament which enacted the law'.[29] We are concerned with 'the purpose or object of the law itself – that which it can be seen to be designed to serve or achieve'.[30] Consequently, it has been characterised as a 'construct' and one that is to be objectively discerned.[31]

Second, the purpose of a statute is to be distinguished from the means in the statute of attaining that purpose. So, for example, the object of the *Tobacco Products Control Act 2006* (WA) may be to reduce the incidence of illness and death related to the use of tobacco products, but one of the means by which it does so is to have provisions that restrict the promotion of smoking.[32]

Third, the purpose of a statute or provision is distinct from its effect or its foreseeable consequences.[33] Justice Edelman provides a useful example in a High Court decision concerning a statute that places caps on political donations. His Honour explained:

> [T]he distinction can be seen in a law that places caps on political donations for the *purpose* of reducing corruption but with the foreseeable *effect* or *consequence* of restricting the funds available to political parties and candidates to meet the costs of political communication.[34]

Fourth, as was discussed in chapter 4, purpose is distinct from 'legislative intent'.[35] Purpose is one factor that must be weighed in the interpretative task, whereas 'legislative intent' encompasses the final conclusion about meaning that is attributable to the legislature.

Assistance given by purpose

[8.4] **Identification of purpose may assist in making constructional choices, but it must always be balanced with text and context, and other relevant indicia and given appropriate weight**

Statutory construction requires us to 'choose from among the range of possible meanings the meaning which Parliament should be taken to have intended'.[36] Having regard to purpose assists this task in at least two ways. First, it recognises that the 'task of construing ... is not accomplished by simply taking the text of the statute in one hand and a dictionary in the other'.[37] Like all legal instruments, the statute is created to communicate an object or design.

---

29 *Richardson v Forestry Commission* (1988) 164 CLR 261, 311 (Deane J); *Unions NSW v New South Wales* (2019) 264 CLR 595, 656 [169] (Edelman J).

30 *Richardson v Forestry Commission* (1988) 164 CLR 261, 311 (Deane J).

31 *Calidad Pty Ltd v Seiko Epson Corporation* (2020) 94 ALJR 1044 [91] (Kiefel CJ, Bell and Keane JJ); *Unions NSW v New South Wales* (2019) 264 CLR 595, 656 [169] (Edelman J); *Singh v Commonwealth* (2004) 222 CLR 322, 336 [19] (Gleeson CJ).

32 *Tobacco Products Control Act 2006* (WA) s 3(c). Gordon J notes this distinction in *Brown v Tasmania* (2017) 261 CLR 328, 432–3 [322].

33 *Clubb v Edwards* (2019) 267 CLR 171, 360 [257] 281 [309] (Nettle J); *Brown v Tasmania* (2017) 261 CLR 328, 362–3 [100] (Kiefel CJ, Bell and Keane JJ), 392 [209] (Gageler J).

34 *Unions NSW v New South Wales* (2019) 264 CLR 595, 656–7 [170] (Edelman J) (emphasis in original).

35 See **[4.7]**.

36 *Independent Commission Against Corruption v Cunneen* (2015) 256 CLR 1, 28 [57] (French CJ, Hayne, Kiefel and Nettle JJ).

37 *Weiss v The Queen* (2005) 224 CLR 300, 305 [10] (Gleeson CJ, Gummow, Kirby, Hayne, Callinan and Heydon JJ).

Part of understanding written text is to have regard to that object. Regard to purpose, like the notion of context, therefore accords with ordinary conventions about understanding language.[38] It helps guide the preferred meaning to be given to the words being construed.

The notion of purpose serves to remind the interpreter about the separation of powers imperative that underpins statutory interpretation. Only one institution, the legislature, has the power to set the parameters of the policy of a statute. The role of the judiciary is to explain (interpret) those parameters, not to create them.

These points help us to understand why, if and when a relevant purpose is identified (which, as discussed further below, is sometimes difficult), purpose is important and so why a construction that would best achieve or promote that purpose is to be preferred. But the purpose of legislation must always be balanced against other factors, and the extent to which purpose guides the choice of preferred meaning may be dependent on that balancing. If there are two plausible constructions of the text available and one is consistent with the statutory purpose and one is not, then the purpose will provide a strong reason for the former to be chosen. It has been observed that 'it is the duty of the Court to avoid, so far as the text of the Act permits, a construction inconsistent with the purpose of a provision and instead "look to see whether any other meaning produces a more reasonable result"'.[39]

An example is *Australian Securities and Investments Commission v King*.[40] Mr King had been an executive director and chief executive officer of the parent of a group of companies. That group included MFSIM, the corporate entity responsible for a managed investment scheme. The Australian Securities and Investments Commission brought proceedings against Mr King as an officer of MFSIM pursuant to s 601FD(1) of the *Corporations Act 2001* (Cth) ('the Act') in relation to MFSIM's conduct regarding the managed investment scheme. Mr King was not a director of MFSIM at the relevant time. Section 9(b)(ii) of the Act provided that an 'officer of a corporation' included someone who had 'the capacity to affect significantly the corporation's financial standing'. The High Court was required to determine whether Mr King was an 'officer of a corporation'.

The Court of Appeal of the Supreme Court of Queensland concluded that for Mr King to be an 'officer' of a corporation within s 9(b)(ii) Mr King had to act in an 'office' of the entity. In the High Court, Kiefel CJ, Gageler and Keane JJ (Nettle and Gordon JJ agreeing) rejected this construction. Part of the reasoning of Kiefel CJ, Gageler and Keane JJ was that a primary purpose of the relevant provisions of the Act was to protect shareholders and creditors, and the Court of Appeal's construction was 'not apt to achieve' that purpose.[41] Their Honours observed that '[i]t would be an extraordinary state of affairs if those who actually determine the course of a company's financial affairs could avoid responsibility for their conduct by the simple expedient of deliberately eschewing any formal designation of their responsibilities'.[42]

In contrast to the *King* scenario, if there are two plausible constructions available and both are consistent with the statutory purpose, then the textual and other interpretative factors may carry more weight to determine the boundary of how far Parliament intended to go to achieve the purpose.[43]

38 *Unions NSW v New South Wales* (2019) 264 CLR 595, 656 [169] (Edelman J). On the subject of context, see chapter 7.

39 *Western Australia v Manado* (2020) 270 CLR 81 [58] (Nettle J), citing numerous authorities.

40 (2020) 270 CLR 1.

41 Ibid 22 [46].

42 Ibid.

43 See **[8.8]** on balancing text and purpose.

It is not unusual for the approach to statutory interpretation in Australia to be described as 'purposive'. This is an understandable and convenient shorthand label for referring to the centrality of purpose in statutory interpretation. But it is apt to mislead. In theoretical discourse a purposive theory of interpretation typically refers to an interpretative methodology where purpose is the primary concern, so that a construction that best promotes purpose is the key determinant of meaning.[44] Effecting the policy of the statute is paramount, even if it is difficult to explain how that accords with the text of the statute.[45]

In Australia it has been said that 'the importance of regard to the legislative purpose does not mean it amounts to a general approach'.[46] Sullivan makes a useful distinction. She distinguishes between a purposive approach and a purposive analysis. As opposed to a purposive approach, a purposive analysis requires the interpreter to 'always carry out an analysis to determine the relevant purpose ... but the results of this analysis are not necessarily controlling'.[47] A 'purposive analysis' more accurately reflects the state of current Australian law. The statutory provisions direct us to prefer a construction that best achieves or promotes the purpose, but the common law provides that, despite that directive, it is to be balanced with text and context. This means that sometimes the purpose will compel a particular choice between alternative constructions and sometimes it will be less determinative. This spectrum of utility becomes clearer in the next sections.

Finding the purpose

[8.5] The purpose of a statute must be found in the text and structure of the statute

Although notionally context and purpose are separate, purpose will be revealed by an examination of the Act's context.[48] This means that the intrinsic context (the text within the four corners of the Act) and the extrinsic context (matters and materials outside the Act) may provide evidence of what the Act is trying to achieve (or what mischief it addresses). Consequently, identifying purpose is 'necessarily interconnected' with contextual analysis.[49] They are 'concurrent' considerations – purpose 'must be identified by the same context, and hence the same extrinsic materials, that elucidate the meaning of the words'.[50]

In other words, purpose is to be found by 'ordinary processes of construction'.[51] What this means in a practical sense is explained in a short summary from *Lacey v Attorney-General (Queensland)*[52] where the High Court stated that the statutory purpose

---

44 See, eg, John F Manning, 'What Divides Textualists from Purposivists' (2006) 106(1) *Columbia Law Review* 70.

45 Ruth Sullivan, *Sullivan on the Construction of Statutes* (LexisNexis, Canada, 6th ed, 2014) 262–3 where she likens a 'purposive' approach to the (historical) "equity of the statute"'.

46 Jeffrey Barnes, 'Contextualism: "The Modern Approach to Statutory Interpretation"' (2018) 41(4) *University of New South Wales Law Journal* 1083, 1108.

47 Ruth Sullivan, *Sullivan on the Construction of Statutes* (LexisNexis, Canada, 6th ed, 2014) 262.

48 *Alcan (NT) Alumina Pty Ltd v Commissioner of Territory Revenue (NT)* (2009) 239 CLR 27, 47 [47] (Hayne, Heydon, Crennan and Kiefel JJ); *CIC Insurance Ltd v Bankstown Football Club Ltd* (1997) 187 CLR 384, 408 (Brennan CJ, Dawson, Toohey and Gummow JJ); *Sydney Seaplanes Pty Ltd v Page* (2021) 106 NSWLR 1, 11 [31] (Bell P).

49 RS Geddes, 'Purpose and Context in Statutory Interpretation' (2005) 2(1) *University of New England Law Journal* 5, 45.

50 *Unions NSW v New South Wales* (2019) 264 CLR 595, 656 [169] (Edelman J) and generally 656–7 [168]–[172].

51 *LibertyWorks Inc v Commonwealth* (2021) 95 ALJR 490, 532 [183] (Gordon J), citing *Brown v Tasmania* (2017) 261 CLR 328, 362 [96] (Kiefel CJ, Bell and Keane JJ).

52 (2011) 242 CLR 573.

> may appear from an express statement in the relevant statute, by inference from its terms and by appropriate reference to extrinsic materials. The purpose of a statute is not something which exists outside the statute. It resides in its text and structure, albeit it may be identified by reference to common law and statutory rules of construction.[53]

This section (**[8.5]**) addresses the intrinsic context referred to in the *Lacey* quotation (express statements and the statute's terms). The next section **[8.6]** addresses the reference to extrinsic materials.

(a) A purpose provision of an Act or some other express statement of purpose is a useful starting point for ascertaining the purpose of the Act, but such statements are not conclusive

Purpose or objects provisions are increasingly common in statutes. These are, as their headings suggest, often provisions that purport to state what the legislation is trying to achieve. A particular part of an Act may have its own purpose or objects provision.[54]

The headings of 'purpose' and 'objects' for these provisions are sometimes used interchangeably. But care should be taken to examine what the provision *does*, rather than assuming they contain relevant statements about purpose based merely on their heading. For example, in Victoria a purpose clause may be descriptive of what an Act does, like a long title, as opposed to providing for its intended aim.[55] This is illustrated in the *Fundraising Act 1998* (Vic):

> **1 Purpose**
> The purpose of this Act is to regulate the raising and application of money and other benefits for non-commercial purposes from the public.

By way of contrast, 'objects' and 'purpose' clauses in Commonwealth legislation appear to be very similar. Drafting materials provide that they are the appropriate place for 'aspirational material', such as goals, so as to distinguish them from the simplified outline.[56] An example is s 3 of the *Disability Discrimination Act 1992* (Cth), which provides as follows:

> **3. Objects**
> The objects of this Act are:
> (a) to eliminate, as far as possible, discrimination against persons on the ground of disability in the areas of:
>   (i) work ...
> (b) to ensure, as far as practicable, that persons with disabilities have the same rights to equality before the law as the rest of the community; and
> (c) to promote recognition and acceptance within the community of the principle that persons with disabilities have the same fundamental rights as the rest of the community.

53 Ibid 592 [44] (French CJ, Gummow, Hayne, Crennan, Kiefel and Bell JJ). See also *Certain Lloyd's Underwriters v Cross* (2012) 248 CLR 378, 389 [25] (French CJ and Hayne J).

54 See **[8.5](c)**.

55 Cf *Cappello v Roads and Maritime Services* (2019) 100 NSWLR 259, 269 [40] n 1 (Payne JA) equating an objects provision with preambles.

56 Office of Parliamentary Counsel, *Drafting Direction No 1.3A: Simplified Outlines* (Australian Government, November 2016) 9 [57]–[59]. For Act components, see chapter 13.

Other purpose provisions may contain a mixture of the Act's purpose and the means to achieve that purpose. In the following example from the *Tobacco Products Control Act 2006* (WA), the first sentence states the intended aim of the statute, but paras (a) and (b) refer to some of the *means* by which to achieve it.

> **3. Purposes of the Act**
>
> The purposes of this Act are to reduce the incidence of illness and death related to the use of tobacco products –
>
> (a) by prohibiting the supply of tobacco products and smoking implements to young persons; and
>
> (b) by discouraging the use of tobacco products; ...

To the extent that a provision does contain express statements about the Act's goals, these provisions are a useful starting point in the purposive analysis.[57] They may also assist in giving 'practical content' to protean expressions such as 'reasonable', 'justification' and 'satisfactory'.[58]

But objects or purpose provisions should not be regarded as conclusive of the purpose.[59] They are not a short-cut analysis. This is because they, like any other provision in an Act, must be read and understood in the context of the statute as a whole.[60] This is a reflection of contextual principle. It recognises the way a statute works, with each provision having a particular role in implementing the overall object of the Act and so providing evidence of the scope of that object. As Justice Edelman explained:

> In circumstances where a statute expressly sets out its own objects or purposes, that express statement will almost always be relevant to identifying the objects and purposes of a particular provision. But a court should not blindly accept that the high-level, abstract purposes of the whole Act must be the exhaustive statement of the purposes of a single provision.[61]

In other words, an express purpose provision may not express the purpose or purposes to the 'appropriate level' of generality or specificity required for the interpretation of a particular provision or part.[62] Consequently, though it is 'tempting', as Geddes has warned, 'to seize upon a statement of purpose in an Act and to strive for an interpretation that furthers the purpose as defined, the task of relevantly defining purpose may be more complex'.[63] Express statements of purpose in a statute or in a part in a statute should not be *automatically* ascribed to that Act or part. A holistic analysis of the statute is always required.

57 *Unions NSW v New South Wales* (2019) 264 CLR 595, 627 [79] (Gageler J).

58 *Russo v Aiello* (2003) 215 CLR 643 [5] (Gleeson CJ), referring to the objects of pt 5 of the *Motor Accidents Act 1988* (NSW).

59 *LibertyWorks Inc v Commonwealth* (2021) 95 ALJR 490, 537 [204] (Edelman J), citing *Australian Communist Party v Commonwealth* (1951) 83 CLR 1.

60 For this principle see **[18.15]**.

61 *Unions NSW v New South Wales* (2019) 264 CLR 595, 657 [172]. Cf Gageler J, 627 [79].

62 *LibertyWorks Inc v Commonwealth* (2021) 95 ALJR 490, 537 [204] (Edelman J), citing *Unions NSW v New South Wales* (2019) 264 CLR 595.

63 RS Geddes, 'Purpose and Context in Statutory Interpretation' (2005) 2(1) *University of New England Law Journal* 5, 45.

(b) If there is no objects or purpose provision, then determining the purpose falls entirely to the subject matter, terms and other components of the statute

If there is no objects or purpose provision then the purposive analysis falls to be determined in its entirety 'inferentially by reference to its subject matter, text and context' of the Act.[64] This requires an evaluation of the provisions of the Act as well as its other components. For example, the long title or the preamble of an Act may contain statements about the scope of the Act or what it is trying to achieve. The common law permits the long title to be used to assist in the identification of the statute's purpose.[65] Preambles, too, though less common in much modern legislation, may be considered at common law.[66] In some jurisdictions these common law principles are no longer necessary as the long titles or preambles are now considered part of an Act pursuant to interpretation legislation.[67] Therefore, they become part of the analysis of the Act as a whole. Following is an example of the purpose of an Act being discerned inferentially by reference to its entirety.

Example 8.1 *AB v Western Australia*[68]

Both AB and AH had been born with the gender characteristics of a female but had identified themselves as male from an early age. Each had been diagnosed as suffering from gender dysphoria. Both had altered their external appearance by various means, including by mastectomy and testosterone therapy. Neither wished to have a hysterectomy. The appearance of each of AB and AH was that of a male person.

AB and AH wished to be recognised legally as male. As they lived in Western Australia, they sought registration of a change to the official records of their gender under the *Gender Reassignment Act 2000* (WA) ('the GRA'). The GRA provided for the issue of a 'recognition certificate', which is conclusive evidence of the sex stated in the certificate.

The issuing of certificates is done by the Gender Reassignment Board ('the Board'). Section 14 required that a person applying for a certificate had undergone a 'reassignment procedure'. Section 15(1)(b) of the GRA provided that a further three conditions must be satisfied, one of which was that the person:

> (ii) had adopted the lifestyle and had the gender characteristics of a person of the gender to which the person has been reassigned; . . .

The sole issue before the High Court was whether AB and AH had the 'gender characteristics' of a male as required by s 15(1)(b)(ii) given that each retained a female reproductive system. The expression 'gender characteristics' was defined in the GRA to mean 'the physical characteristics by virtue of which a person is identified as male or female'. The statutory interpretation issue was whether 'physical characteristics' referred only to external characteristics, in which case AB and AH would be entitled to a certificate, or whether it meant all physical characteristics including internal characteristics.

---

64 *Clubb v Edwards* (2019) 267 CLR 171, 233 [186] (Gageler J).

65 *Amatek Ltd v Googoorewon Pty Ltd* (1993) 176 CLR 471, 477 (the Court); *Wainohu v New South Wales* (2011) 243 CLR 181, 192 [8] (French CJ and Kiefel J).

66 *Wacando v Commonwealth* (1981) 148 CLR 1, 23 (Mason J); *New South Wales Aboriginal Land Council v Minister Administering the Crown Lands Act* (2016) 260 CLR 232, 301 [187] (Nettle and Gordon JJ).

67 See **[13.4]** and **[13.6]**.

68 (2011) 244 CLR 390.

There was no express objects or purpose provision in the GRA. The Court inferred its purpose from a number of contextual indicators. For example, the Court referred to the long title of the GRA, which stated that the GRA was to 'promote equality of opportunity and to provide remedies in respect of discrimination'.[69] Second, the definition of 'gender characteristics' referred to the physical characteristics by which a person is 'identified', suggesting an emphasis on outward appearance.[70] Third, the other conditional provision, s 14, required a medical *or* surgical procedure. As s 14 was the only provision in the GRA expressly requiring a physical procedure, this suggested that it was the minimum procedure required under the Act.[71] The Court compared s 14, about physical bodily state, to s 15, which contained provisions about perception, lifestyle and self-belief.[72]

This analysis led the Court to conclude that the GRA was about 'social recognition'.[73] Its primary object was not for the applicant to achieve a certain abstract notion of physicality, although some physical change was relevant, but its object was to 'remove impediments to the way in which a person lives within society'.[74] Having regard to that purpose, supported by the text of the Act, the Court concluded that 'physical characteristics' should be attributed the more liberal construction of observable physical characteristics.[75]

(c) **The purpose of the part or provision being construed may also assist interpretation**

Section 15AA and its equivalents, as well as the common law principle about purpose, are framed by reference to the purpose of an Act. But 'legislators pursue narrow objectives to accomplish broader purposes'.[76] The purpose or purposes of an Act are effectuated by its individual provisions. Those individual provisions are the method by which Parliament accomplishes the broader Act purpose.[77] So, having regard to the purpose of a particular provision is consistent with the requirement to consider the purpose of the Act, and is a regular part of the interpretative exercise.[78] For instance, in *AB v State of Western Australia* (**Example 8.1**), the Court's conclusion about the object of s 15, to address social perception, was a relevant part of its overall purposive analysis. Ascertaining the purpose of other provisions may be a helpful interpretative aid. The purposes of the statute may be 'cast at a higher level of generality than the particular purposes of its disparate parts'.[79] The more specific purpose of a provision may provide a stronger indication of the preferred meaning.[80] Again, in *AB v State of Western Australia* the Court's analysis of the function of s 14, about medical procedures, was a point of comparison to the function of s 15 and

69 Ibid 397 [5].

70 Ibid 403–4 [29]–[32].

71 Ibid 404 [32].

72 Ibid 404–5 [33]–[34].

73 Ibid 405 [34]–[35].

74 Ibid 405 [34].

75 The GRA was a beneficial Act: ibid 406 [38]. For the principle that beneficial or remedial legislation is to be given a liberal construction, see **[17.3]**.

76 Kent Greenawalt, *Statutory and Common Law Interpretation* (Oxford University Press, 2013) 97.

77 *Van Heerden v Hawkins* [2016] WASCA 42, [176] (Murphy JA), citing *Municipal Officers' Association of Australia v Lancaster* (1981) 54 FLR 129, 153 (Evatt and Northrop JJ).

78 *Kline v Official Secretary to the Governor-General* (2013) 249 CLR 645, 659–60 [32] (French CJ, Crennan, Kiefel and Bell JJ); *Certain Lloyd's Underwriters v Cross* (2012) 248 CLR 378, 405 [70] (Crennan and Bell JJ).

79 *LibertyWorks Inc v Commonwealth* (2021) 95 ALJR 490, 537 [204] (Edelman J).

80 For further discussion see **[8.7]**.

contributed to its conclusions about the purpose of the GRA. This is part of the interpreter striving for a construction that provides a coherent working of the Act as a whole.[81]

Reference to extrinsic materials may assist in identifying the purpose, but the converse of the proposition that the purpose must be found in the text and structure of the Act is that the purpose must not be constructed by an idea of desirable policy derived from extrinsic materials or otherwise [8.6]

In the case of *AB v Western Australia* the Court found the purpose of the Act in its text and context. The converse of this proposition is that the interpreter must not impute a policy to the legislature without having done the analysis of the Act that justifies that conclusion. On numerous occasions, the High Court has declared that

> it is not for a court to construct its own idea of a desirable policy, impute it to the legislature, and then characterise it as a statutory purpose.[82]

Ideas about desirable policy may arise from an interpreter having preconceptions about the policy that the Act is intended to implement. These preconceptions might arise from extrinsic materials.

As stated in *Lacey v Attorney-General (Queensland)*, it is well accepted that the purpose of an Act can be identified by 'appropriate reference to extrinsic materials'.[83] It might also be discerned from other extrinsic context, including the statutory evolution of the relevant provision and the historical background.[84] Recourse is regularly made to parliamentary materials, such as a second reading speech or a law reform report, or to the evolution of the Act, or both, to assist in determining the object of a particular provision or of the Act itself.[85]

On its face, the common law principle that the purpose must be found in the text and structure of the Act may appear to be difficult to reconcile with the ability to have recourse to external context to assist with ascertaining the purpose. Reconciling these two interpretative principles is a matter of weight. Materials outside the Act can provide ideas about purpose, or indicate a 'more specific purpose which helps to answer the [interpretative] question'.[86] But these indications are not sufficient *by themselves* to justify a conclusion about purpose.

The use of legislative history as an interpretative aid, including for identification of purpose, is discussed more fully in Part V. For the purposes of this chapter, it is sufficient to note that evidence gained from legislative history about the purpose may assist in the identification of purpose but, as a general proposition, does not prevail over what may be plausibly revealed from the statutory text. Ideas about purpose found in the extrinsic context, including parliamentary materials, are not a warrant for 'attributing a wider operation to a statute than its language and

81 *SAS Trustee Corporation v Miles* (2018) 265 CLR 137, 149 [20] (Kiefel CJ, Bell and Nettle JJ), 157 [41], [43] (Gageler J).

82 *Australian Education Union v Department of Education and Children's Services* (2012) 248 CLR 1, 14 [28] (French CJ, Hayne, Kiefel and Bell JJ). See also *Certain Lloyd's Underwriters v Cross* (2012) 248 CLR 378, 390 [26] (French CJ and Hayne J); *Alcan (NT) Alumina Pty Ltd v Commissioner of Territory Revenue (NT)* (2009) 239 CLR 27, 48 [52] (Hayne, Heydon, Crennan and Kiefel JJ); *Palgo Holdings Pty Ltd v Gowans* (2005) 221 CLR 249, 262 [28] (McHugh, Gummow, Hayne and Heydon JJ).

83 *Lacey v Attorney-General (Queensland)* (2011) 242 CLR 573, 592 [44] (French CJ, Gummow, Hayne, Crennan, Kiefel and Bell JJ).

84 *Clubb v Edwards* (2019) 267 CLR 171, 328 [457], citing *Unions NSW v New South Wales* (2019) 264 CLR 595, 657 (Edelman J).

85 See Part V.

86 *Carr v Western Australia* (2007) 232 CLR 138, 143 [6] (Gleeson CJ).

evident operation permit'.[87] This is a reflection of the principle that the language of the statute must reveal the purpose.

> It is not legitimate to identify a legislative purpose not apparent from the text of the relevant provisions (or in this case even expressed in some extrinsic material), to examine extrinsic material and notice that there is nothing positively inconsistent with the identified purpose, and then to answer the question of construction by reference to the purpose that was initially assumed. That reasoning is not sound.[88]

This does not mean that legislative history and other extrinsic materials cannot play a role in determining the purpose. For example, in *Western Australian Planning Commission v Southregal Pty Ltd*[89] the purpose of a provision as determined by extrinsic materials and the statutory evolution played an important part in the judgment of Gageler and Nettle JJ in determining what the relevant provision was intended to achieve.[90] The text of the statute alone was equivocal. The key is for the purpose identified by such means to be able to be reconciled with the statutory text.

The use of extrinsic materials is a clear example of the utility of the distinction between a purposive analysis and a purposive approach. In a purposive analysis, the identification of a purpose in extrinsic materials that is broader than what the statutory language can bear does not warrant such a broader construction. A purpose revealed by extrinsic materials will sometimes be 'confounded by the construction which the court places on the words actually used'.[91]

Limitations of the assistance given by purpose

[8.7] **Consideration of purpose is integral but there are limitations as to how far purpose can assist in the interpretative task; those limitations may depend on the level of specificity with which purpose can be expressed**

As at least one Australian judge has noted extrajudicially there are many challenges in identifying and applying the concept of purpose.[92] Although an essential component of interpretation, its probative value will vary and sometimes be limited or even negligible. To reflect on why this is, it is helpful to remember that a statute is the product of a legislative process. Legislating is a complex process and 'nearly always an inescapably political activity'.[93] A Bill presented to Parliament for enactment is subject to negotiations and tactics among the political parties, as well as being governed by extensive parliamentary procedural rules and conventions. It might be subject to amendment, political compromise, or truncated scrutiny opportunities. As well, statutes are executive tools. They may embody complex, interrelated or broad policy objectives, which

87 *Certain Lloyd's Underwriters v Cross* (2012) 248 CLR 378, 412 [89] (Kiefel J).

88 Ibid 395 [41] (French CJ and Hayne J).

89 (2017) 259 CLR 106.

90 Ibid 127–38 [69]–[87].

91 *Communications, Electrical, Electronic, Energy, Information, Postal, Plumbing & Allied Services Union of Australia v Australian Competition and Consumer Commission* (2007) 162 FCR 466, 518 [197] (the Court).

92 John Middleton, 'Statutory Interpretation – Mostly Common Sense?' (2016) 40(2) *Melbourne University Law Review* 626, 635.

93 David Feldman, 'Beginning at the Beginning: The Relationships between Politics and Law' in David Feldman (ed), *Law in Politics, Politics in Law* (Hart Publishing, 2015) 3, 12.

nevertheless must be reduced to textual expression as clear as possible by the parliamentary drafter. It is not surprising therefore that there are nuances and challenges of using 'purpose'.[94]

(a) An Act or provision may have multiple or competing purposes and so the interpretative task involves assessing how the Act or provision balances those purposes or which purposes are relevant to the interpretative task

A statute may address a broad or complex policy or a wide range of matters, sometimes disparate. Underlying statutes or provisions may have multiple purposes, or purposes that are competing or divisive.[95] For example, the *Native Title Act 1993* (Cth) has been described as reflecting a 'series of political compromises, worked out sometimes in a highly reactive way, to judicial and political developments' that have 'resulted in a textually dense and prescriptive legislative scheme' not susceptible to the easy discovery of a purpose.[96] In these situations, purpose may be of 'little assistance' as the interpreter seeks to determine the balance sought by Parliament.[97] These instances are likely to mark a shift in the weight to be given to purpose in the interpretative exercise. The structure, language, extrinsic materials and historical context become more critical to determine the meaning of the words. **Example 8.2** illustrates a provision with competing interests.

Example 8.2 *Medical Board of Australia v Kemp*[98]

Three patients of Dr Kemp complained about his conduct to the Medical Board of Australia in relation to his prescription of medication and other management practices. The Board referred the complaints to the responsible body, the Victorian Civil and Administrative Tribunal ('VCAT'), on the basis that it was possible professional misconduct. In order to conduct the hearing, the Board applied to VCAT for a summons to Dr Kemp to produce all medical records of the relevant patients.

Section 28(2) of the *Evidence (Miscellaneous Provisions) Act 1958* (Vic) provided:

> No physician or surgeon shall without the consent of his patient divulge in any civil suit action or proceeding any information which he has acquired in attending the patient and which was necessary to enable him to prescribe or act for the patient.

Two of the patients refused to provide their consent. Dr Kemp therefore argued that pursuant to s 28(2) he was not obliged to produce their medical records. VCAT argued that disciplinary proceedings were not caught by the words 'any civil suit action or proceeding'.

One of Dr Kemp's arguments was that the primary purpose of s 28(2) was to protect medical confidences. Consequently, 'proceeding' should be construed broadly, with the qualification of 'civil' only meant to exclude criminal matters.[99] The Board argued that the purpose of s 28(2) was to protect medical confidence in the context of civil suits, actions and proceedings, which are

94 For a useful summary of the authorities and propositions about the limitations of purpose see *My Environment Inc v Vic Forests* (2013) 42 VR 456, 459–62 [4]–[16] (Warren CJ).

95 *Unions NSW v New South Wales* (2019) 264 CLR 595, 656 [168] (Edelman J); *Carr v Western Australia* (2007) 232 CLR 138, 143 [5] (Gleeson CJ).

96 *McGlade v Native Title Registrar* (2017) 251 FCR 172, 241 [351] (Mortimer J).

97 *Carr v Western Australia* (2007) 232 CLR 138, 143 [5], [7] (Gleeson CJ).

98 (2018) 56 VR 51.

99 Ibid 64 [62].

brought to vindicate private interests or claims.[100] Consequently, they argued, disciplinary proceedings were not within the ambit of the section.

Niall JA, with whom Maxwell P and Tate JA agreed, acknowledged that the phrase 'suit action or proceeding' were words of 'considerable breadth' only qualified by the word 'civil'.[101] While acknowledging that one of the purposes of the provision was to protect medical confidences, his Honour said it was not possible to state that this was its paramount purpose. He said s 28(2) operated 'at the intersection of various interests' and in a specific context.[102]

> First, there is the interest of the patient in protecting medical confidence. Second, there are the interests of the parties to the suit, action or proceeding who will be denied access to the material that, it must be assumed, would otherwise be obtainable and probative of some issue in dispute. Third, there is the public interest that the administration of justice shall not be frustrated by the withholding of documents or evidence which must be produced if justice is to be done.[103]

In other words, s 28(2) purported to balance these private and public interests. The difficulty was determining the precise nature of that balancing act and therefore the provision's scope.

In his analysis, Niall JA relied on interpretative factors to determine that scope, such as the limiting word 'civil' in the provision, the fact that s 28(2) did not confer substantive rights of medical confidence on a patient, the legislative history, earlier court decisions, and the consequences of denying access to medical records in a regulatory setting.[104]

On this basis, Niall JA determined that

> the words of s 28(2) best describe a function of determining the rights of the parties in a curial setting and are not apt to describe administrative or regulatory functions.[105]

The disciplinary proceedings, being regulatory, were not within s 28(2).

(b) Even if a single purpose of an Act can be determined, it may be too general to be helpful; the greater the specificity of the purpose the more likely it will influence the attribution of meaning

Purpose can only be used rationally and meaningfully in the interpretative task if it is identified 'at the appropriate level of generality'.[106] The more specific the purpose can be articulated, the more useful it may be at suggesting a particular construction.[107] Consequently, difficulties arise if purpose can only be expressed at a high level of generality. The size of much modern legislation contributes to this – the Act may be too large, the scope too wide or the provisions too disparate for the purpose of the statute to be identified except in a general way. Consider, for example, the *Corporations Act 2001* (Cth) (over 1,600 sections and over 4,000 pages), *Social Security Act 1991*

100 Ibid 63–4 [59].

101 Ibid 65 [66].

102 Ibid 73 [108].

103 Ibid 73–4 [108].

104 Ibid; see summary at 54–5 [10].

105 Ibid 67 [75].

106 *Clubb v Edwards* (2019) 267 CLR 171, 328 [457] (Edelman J). See Murray Gleeson, 'Statutory Interpretation' (Speech, Justice Hill Memorial Lecture, Taxation Institute of Australia, 24th National Convention, 11 March 2009) 12–14.

107 *The Owners – Strata Plan No 66375 v King* [2018] NSWCA 170, [290] (Ward JA).

(Cth) (over 1,200 sections and over 2,000 pages excluding schedules) and *Criminal Code Act 1995* (Cth) (nearly 500 sections and over 1,000 pages).

A purpose expressed at a high level of generality may not be helpful as it may not compel any particular construction of the words in doubt.[108] The example often cited is the one given by Chief Justice Gleeson in *Carr v Western Australia*:[109]

> [I]t may be said that the underlying purpose of an *Income Tax Assessment Act* is to raise revenue for government. No one would seriously suggest that s 15AA of the *Acts Interpretation Act* has the result that all federal income tax legislation is to be construed so as to advance that purpose.[110]

The statement from a United States decision, that 'no legislation pursues its purposes at all costs',[111] succinctly expresses this idea.

Consequently, the interpreter must not assume that 'whatever furthers the statute's primary objective must be the law'.[112] This is a type of imputation to the text being construed which risks overwhelming or ignoring the statutory text and context.[113]

It can assist to break down the statute into its Parts or Divisions to see if a purpose may be identifiable in relation to that Part or Division that is at a level of specificity that may assist.[114] Further, as noted previously, the Act pursues its purpose through its individual provisions. So, the purpose of the particular provision being construed may provide a further level of specificity. If that purpose can be identified, and it is consistent with the general purpose, then it has a more persuasive connection with the particular interpretative task. There are numerous instances of the court considering the purpose of a particular provision as an aid to construction where the purpose of the Act is too general to be helpful. **Example 8.3** illustrates a number of the points discussed in this section.

Example 8.3 *Hunter Quarries Pty Ltd v Mexon*[115]

Mr Messenger was an employee of Hunter Quarries Pty Ltd. In 2014 he was in the cabin of an excavator when the excavator tipped on its side and Mr Messenger suffered a severe injury to his

108 *Kelly v The Queen* (2004) 218 CLR 216, 233 [43] (Gleeson CJ, Hayne and Heydon JJ).

109 (2007) 232 CLR 138.

110 Ibid 143 [6]. Other examples where the purpose was too general to be of rational assistance include *Victims Compensation Fund Corporation v Brown* (2003) 77 ALJR 1797, 1804 [33] (Heydon J, other judges agreeing); *Esso Australia Pty Ltd v Australian Workers' Union* (2017) 263 CLR 551, 588 [69] (Gageler J, in dissent); *Australian Postal Corporation v Sinnaiah* (2013) 213 FCR 449, 456 [27] (the Court).

111 *Rodriguez v United States*, 480 US 522, 525–6 (1987). This statement has been cited numerous times by Australian judges. See, eg, *Tjungarrayi v Western Australia* (2019) 269 CLR 150, 166 [46] (Gageler J); *Construction, Forestry, Mining and Energy Union v Mammoet Australia Pty Ltd* (2013) 248 CLR 619, 633 [41] (Crennan, Kiefel, Bell, Gageler and Keane JJ); *My Environment Inc v Vic Forests* (2013) 42 VR 456, 459 [6] (Warren CJ).

112 *Rodriguez v United States*, 480 US 522, 525–6 (1987).

113 *Alcan (NT) Alumina Pty Ltd v Commissioner of Territory Revenue (NT)* (2009) 239 CLR 27, 47–8 [51] (Hayne, Heydon, Crennan and Kiefel JJ), citing *Carr v Western Australia* (2007) 232 CLR 138, 143.

114 See, eg, *Scaffidi v Chief Executive Officer, Department of Local Government and Communities* (2017) 52 WAR 368, 400 [155] (the Court).

115 (2018) 98 NSWLR 526.

upper body. He was unconscious for a few minutes, and then he died. It was accepted that Mr Messenger's death resulted from an injury during employment and so his dependents sought (and received) a lump sum death benefit from Hunter Quarries pursuant to s 25 the *Workers Compensation Act 1987* (NSW) ('the WCA').

In 2015 the administrator of Mr Messenger's estate sought compensation under s 66 of the WCA. Section 66 provided:

> **66 Entitlement to compensation for permanent impairment**
>
> (1) A worker who receives an injury that results in a degree of permanent impairment greater than 10% is entitled to receive from the worker's employer compensation for that permanent impairment as provided by this section. Permanent impairment compensation is in addition to any other compensation under this Act.

Hunter Quarries resisted the claim. On appeal to the NSW Court of Appeal, one of the company's arguments was that 'permanent impairment' in s 66 did not encompass impairment so serious that death would inevitably follow within a short time. Rather, it referred to impairment where there is some continued and enduring experience of living. The administrator argued that 'permanent' was the opposite of temporary, and so an impairment that persisted until death, even if that period was only a few minutes or a few seconds, constituted 'permanent impairment'.[116]

There was no objects clause in the WCA, but s 3 of another Act was found to be relevant to the WCA.[117] Section 3 provided that the purpose of the Act was to establish a workplace injury management and workers compensation system with various objectives, including securing the health, safety and welfare of workers, providing injured workers and their dependants with income support for work-related injuries, and being fair, affordable and financially viable.

Payne JA, with whom Gleeson JA and Sackville JA agreed,[118] stated:

> It is true that one purpose of the *Workers Compensation Act* is to benefit workers but it is going too far to say that every grant of an entitlement should be construed broadly because it is part of a beneficial scheme... Where, as here, the problem is one of doubt about the extent to which the legislation pursues a purpose, stating the purpose is unlikely to solve the problem.[119]

To determine the meaning of 'permanent impairment' in s 66, Payne JA was required to weigh and balance other indicators. These included the language employed by s 66 (such as the examples in the section that referred to 'degree' of impairment),[120] the surrounding provisions (such as the heading of the Division containing s 66),[121] the evidence from the second reading speech during the enactment of s 66,[122] and the legislative evolution of s 66.[123] From this analysis Payne JA held that the words 'permanent impairment' in s 66 meant impairment where there is 'some continued

116 Ibid 536–7 [47].

117 The WCA was required to be construed in accordance with this other Act.

118 Basten JA and Simpson AJA agreed with the outcome and with Payne JA in many respects.

119 *Hunter Quarries Pty Ltd v Mexon* (2018) 98 NSWLR 526, 541–2 [65]–[66], citing, in part, *Carr v Western Australia* (2007) 232 CLR 138, 142–3 [5] (Gleeson CJ).

120 Ibid 540–1 [59]–[63].

121 Ibid 543 [72].

122 Ibid.

123 Ibid 544 [78], 545–6 [87] [88]. Payne JA also rejected the relevance of previous authority.

and enduring experience of living'.[124] As Simpson JA expressly explained (agreeing with Payne JA), the more specific purpose of s 66 was to compensate an employee for loss of quality of life caused by the workplace injury that will continue for the duration of the worker's life.[125]

(c) There may be instances where both the purpose of the Act and the purpose of the provision are elusive or unhelpful

The purpose of the Act or the provision or both may be elusive or unhelpful.[126] This could be for various reasons. Acts that have been subject to multiple amendments over time or that operate to address an assortment of matters may suffer from this phenomenon. For example, in *Medical Board of Australia v Kemp* (**Example 8.2**) the purpose of the Act itself (rather than the provision) was regarded as elusive: it was a 'miscellany of provisions ... that do not coalesce into a single coherent whole'.[127] It may be difficult to ascertain due to the complexity of the statute,[128] unclear drafting[129] or because the text and context offer no meaningful information about purpose.[130] In this case the interpretative task falls entirely on other statutory interpretation principles to determine meaning.

Balancing purpose with the text

Purpose is not a licence to rewrite the statute but may indicate that the ordinary and grammatical meaning is not preferred [8.8]

Purpose cannot be relied on to adopt a construction 'that departs too far from the statutory text'.[131] It is the legislature's function to enact the words that communicate the policy of the statute. It is the court's function to construe it, 'not to rewrite it, in the light of its purposes'.[132] A construction that departs too far from the text risks violating the separation of powers or engaging in 'judicial legislation'.[133]

But determining the line between construction and 'legislation' in interpretation gives rise to an important question: to what extent is it permissible for the text to accommodate an identified legislative purpose? Reasonable minds can differ on the evaluation about where it is appropriate to draw that line.

It is accepted that consideration of purpose, like context, recognises that various meanings of words may be possible, including a meaning that does not correspond with the ordinary

124 Ibid 547 [95].

125 Ibid 550 [114].

126 *Unions NSW v New South Wales* (2019) 264 CLR 595, 656 [168] (Edelman J).

127 (2018) 56 VR 51, 77 [129].

128 *The Owners – Strata Plan No 66375 v King* [2018] NSWCA 170, [290].

129 *Esso Australia Pty Ltd v Australian Workers' Union* (2017) 263 CLR 551, 570–1 [29] (Kiefel CJ, Keane, Nettle and Edelman JJ).

130 *Mitchell v Bailey* (2008) 168 FCR 370, 378 [31] (Tracey J); *Monis v The Queen* (2013) 249 CLR 92, 112 [20] (French CJ); *Kelly v The Queen* (2004) 218 CLR 216, 233 [43].

131 *Taylor v The Owners – Strata Plan No 11564* (2014) 253 CLR 531, 549 [40] (French CJ, Crennan and Bell JJ).

132 *Mills v Meeking* (1990) 169 CLR 214, 235 (Dawson J).

133 *Taylor v The Owners – Strata Plan No 11564* (2014) 253 CLR 531, 549 [40] (French CJ, Crennan and Bell JJ).

grammatical meaning. This is beyond doubt since *Project Blue Sky*.[134] It was reaffirmed in *SZTAL v Minister for Immigration and Border Protection*:[135]

> Considerations of context and purpose simply recognise that . . . some other meaning of a word may be suggested, and so too, if its ordinary meaning is not consistent with the statutory purpose, that meaning must be rejected.[136]

An example is *Vincentia MC Pharmacy Pty Ltd v Australian Community Pharmacy Authority*.[137] In this case the Full Federal Court was required to consider the definition of 'large medical centre' in the *National Health (Australian Community Pharmacy Authority Rules) Determination 2011* (Cth).[138] Being in a 'large medical centre' was one of the criteria for a pharmacist to be able to provide pharmaceutical benefits. The definition relevantly provided that it was a medical centre that operates, and has one or more medical practitioners, for 'at least 70 hours each week'.

One of the issues was whether the word 'week' in the definition should be given its ordinary and grammatical meaning, being a period of seven successive days in each calendar year (narrow construction), or whether it meant an 'ordinary week', meaning a calendar week of seven successive days except where a public holiday occurred (broad construction). The majority, Perry and Stewart JJ, accepted that both constructions were open and that the ordinary meaning of 'week' favoured the narrow construction. But, they said, although the legislation had competing purposes, its primary purpose was to ensure access by the public to pharmaceutical benefits.[139] The broad construction, in line with s 15AA, best achieved that purpose. Accordingly, the 'apparent ordinary meaning of . . . "each week" . . . must . . . give way to the legislative purpose'.[140] Jackson J, dissenting, concluded that neither the context nor any purpose of the legislation threw any real doubt on the ordinary meaning.[141]

Purpose, therefore, like context, may indicate that the preferred interpretation is a narrow meaning, or a broad meaning. Achieving consistency with statutory purpose may lead to a 'strained construction'.[142]

This balancing between legislative text and legislative purpose gives rise to a number of specific interpretative issues that are explored in separate chapters in this book. These include the 'always speaking' principle (chapter 19), the use of parliamentary and other extrinsic materials (Part V), the principle of legality (chapter 28), and the rectification of drafting errors (chapter 34). As we saw at the beginning of this chapter, one of the functions of purpose is to remind the interpreter that attributing meaning to statutory text is about deferring to the 'intent' of the legislature. At the heart of many of the issues arising in these topics is the challenge of balancing interpretative indicators regarding legislative purpose and those in relation to the statutory text.

134 (1998) 194 CLR 355, 384 [78] (McHugh, Gummow, Kirby and Hayne JJ).

135 (2017) 262 CLR 362.

136 Ibid 368 [14] (Kiefel CJ, Nettle and Gordon JJ). See also *R v A2* (2019) 269 CLR 507, 522 [37] (Kiefel CJ and Keane JJ).

137 (2020) 280 FCR 397.

138 For delegated legislation see chapter 43.

139 (2020) 280 FCR 397, 415 [60].

140 Ibid 416 [65], citing *Mondelez Australia Pty Ltd v Automotive, Food, Metals, Engineering, Printing and Kindred Industries Union* (2020) 94 ALJR 818 [3] (Kiefel CJ, Nettle and Gordon JJ), 841 [109] (Edelman J), discussed in **[24.13]**.

141 (2020) 280 FCR 397, 423 [96].

142 See **[6.9]** and **[34.9]**.

PRACTICAL TECHNIQUES 9

Overview

As well as a body of legal doctrine, statutory interpretation is an area of skill and technique. To a degree these techniques can be described and modelled. With reference to actual cases, this chapter models techniques for undertaking legal analysis of an Act, identifying interpretative clues or indications of meaning ('interpretative factors'), formulating alternative constructions (rival contentions as to the meaning of the words in question), evaluating interpretative arguments, determining the preferable construction, and presenting a legal opinion and reasons for judgment.[1] It also illustrates how legal research is conducted, and locates the various skills relating to interpretation within an overall interpretative method. [9.1]

Utilising models of interpretative skills

Many of the skills necessary to practise interpretation can be modelled [9.2]

As noted in Chapter 1 (**[1.3]**), statutory interpretation is more than a body of law; it is an area of practice comprising a set of skills. This chapter explores that point and takes it further. Its object is to show that many of the skills can be described and modelled.[2] In other words, interpretation is an activity where *techniques* are applied.[3] Theorising about skills provides benefits for the experienced practitioner as well as the novice. For the novice, a model provides a useful starting point for analysis and thinking. For the practitioner, it provides a framework for reflection and a test of their (often well-developed) intuitive approach.

The skills that an interpreter of statute law needs are sometimes generic and sometimes unique to the statute field. Analysing facts is an example of a generic skill that applies to the handling of statute law as well as common law. For instance, developing a chronology of events is equally useful in handling statute law.[4] Another example of a generic skill often used in handling

---

1 For convenience, a technique allied to interpretation (the identification of sources of doubt) is the subject of chapter 14.

2 And if the skills can be modelled they can be taught. Cf Lord Wilberforce, 'A Judicial Viewpoint' in Attorney-General's Department, *Symposium on Statutory Interpretation* (AGPS, 1983) 5, 6.

3 The *Oxford English Dictionary* defines 'technique' as follows: '1. The formal or practical aspect of any art, occupation, or field; manner of execution or performance with regard to this. Also more generally: way of doing something.': *Oxford English Dictionary* (3rd ed, 2009, online at 8 May 2022) 'technique' (def 1).

4 For discussion of a chronology of events, see Inns of Court School of Law, *Case Preparation* (Blackstone Press, 1996) 134 and see example in *Hopper & Hopper* [2016] FCCA 84, [82] (Judge Harman). For a useful work on factual analysis for law students, see Howard Gensler, 'Law School Examinations and Factual Analysis' (1997) 31(2) *The Law Teacher* 198. For a useful work on factual analysis for practitioners, see Inns of Court School of Law, *Case Preparation* (Blackstone Press, 1996) ch 14.

statute law is analysing cases.[5] Even in statute law, ascertaining the ratio of a case is an important skill.[6] The present work focuses on skills that are more or less unique to statute law. They include:

- conducting legal research pertaining to legislation – for example, finding extrinsic materials relevant to a piece of legislation;
- undertaking analysis of legislative text;
- identifying relevant interpretative factors;
- formulating constructions;
- undertaking critical assessment and weighing of interpretative factors;
- determining which construction ought to be preferred; and
- presenting a legal opinion and a judgment about interpretation as far as possible in plain English.

Each of these skills is discussed in detail below, with greater attention paid to those skills that can be modelled.

In a work such as the present – which caters for practitioners as well as students – it is worth reflecting on the fact that the skills that an interpreter needs to develop will vary according to where they are on the novice/expert continuum. An experienced practitioner will be able to relate a model to their own experience. They will be able to interpret the model. They will not treat the model as a panacea. By comparison, the novice needs to develop an awareness that a model gives them a basis to develop skills but it is not sufficient in itself.

This last point leads to the role of the present chapter. It cannot be a substitute for practising interpretation. Like other professional skills, interpretation will develop with regular practice and reflection. The role of this chapter is to provide guidance by elaborating on and where possible modelling the practice. Worked examples accompany this work.[7] These examples provide feedback and the opportunity for reflection. Like driving a car or playing the piano, the technique must be attempted and practised and reflected upon before it is truly learned. For the law student, this entails practice *throughout the degree program*, otherwise the learning risks withering on the educational vine.[8]

Making use of an overall method

[9.3] **The process of interpretation cannot be reduced to a formula, but an overall method for interpretation can be described**

Like its sister activity, legislative drafting,[9] interpretation is both an art and a science.[10] Its 'artistic' side is evident in the fact that interpretation does not lend itself to being reduced to a comprehensive formula. There is no precise set of rules or even presumptions that apply in an exhaustive way to every problem. As famously put by Justice Frankfurter:

5 Michael Zander, *The Law-Making Process* (Hart Publishing, 7th ed, 2015) ch 5.

6 FAR Bennion, *Understanding Common Law Legislation: Drafting and Interpretation* (Oxford University Press, 2009) 181.

7 See the publisher's website for worked examples.

8 Jeffrey Barnes et al, *Council of Australian Law Deans Good Practice Guide to Teaching Statutory Interpretation* (Council of Australian Law Deans, 2015) 18–9.

9 See chapter 10.

10 Cf Johan Steyn, 'The Intractable Problem of the Interpretation of Legal Texts' (2003) 25(1) *Sydney Law Review* 5, who says: 'Interpretation is not a science. It is an art.' But despite his protestations, his Lordship did allude to what appear to be 'scientific' aspects: at 8.

> Unhappily, there is no table of logarithms for statutory construction. No item of evidence has a fixed or even average weight. One or another may be decisive in one set of circumstances, while of little value elsewhere.[11]

One reason is that the factors that 'present themselves'[12] for consideration vary from problem to problem. As Mason and Wilson JJ said in *Cooper Brookes (Wollongong) Pty Ltd v Commissioner of Taxation of the Commonwealth*,[13] the factors depend on 'the particular case'.[14] In that vein, and more recently, Justice Crennan has elaborated extracurially on the significance of the particular problem that a court is faced with:

> The current approach to establishing the meaning of a provision in a statute, by reference not only to the plain meaning of words but also by reference to context, purpose, legality or fairness, or some combination of such considerations, exemplifies the proposition that no single theory of, or approach to, statutory interpretation or construction is invariably more useful than, or to the exclusion of, others. *It is the problems which are thrown up by the cases, and the particular statutes under consideration in individual cases, which determine which approach is useful, rather than it being the other way round.*[15]

But just because no formula is available does not mean that interpretation lacks an objective approach that is able to give some general guidance. In *R v A2*[16] Kiefel CJ and Keane J[17] reviewed some of the regular features of interpretative method.[18] They began by noting that '[t]he method to be applied in construing a statute to ascertain the intended meaning of the words used is well settled'.[19] Several aspects of interpretative method may be distilled from the judgment:

1. The object of interpretation is 'to ascertain the intended meaning of the words used'.[20]
2. The process of construction 'commences with a consideration of the words of the provision itself';[21] namely, 'the text'.[22]
3. Even if the words in doubt have an 'apparently clear ordinary or grammatical meaning' the process of construction 'does not end there'.[23] Consideration of the context is always necessary.[24]

---

11 Justice Felix Frankfurter, 'Some Reflections on the Reading of Statutes' (1947) 47(4) *Columbia Law Review* 527, 543.

12 FAR Bennion, *Bennion on Statutory Interpretation: A Code* (LexisNexis, 5th ed, 2008) 9.

13 (1981) 147 CLR 297.

14 Ibid 320–1.

15 Justice Susan Crennan, 'Blackstone's "Signs" and Statutory Interpretation' (CLE Lecture, Victorian Bar, Melbourne, 28 November 2007) 11–12 (emphasis added).

16 (2019) 269 CLR 507.

17 Nettle and Gordon JJ generally agreed at ibid 554 [148] and Edelman J agreed at ibid 572 [193].

18 Their description is not held out by their Honours to be exhaustive. As would be expected their Honours had an eye to what features were particularly relevant to the case in hand.

19 (2019) 269 CLR 507, 520 [32] (Kiefel CJ and Keane J, Nettle and Gordon JJ agreeing generally at 554 [148], Edelman J agreeing at 572 [193]).

20 See further chapter 4.

21 *R v A2* (2019) 269 CLR 507, 520–1 [32]. See further chapters 6, 15.

22 Ibid 522 [36]. See further chapter 6.

23 Ibid 520 [32]. See further **[7.6]**.

24 Ibid 521 [33], 522 [37]. See further chapter 7.

4. Interpretation involves a multifactorial assessment, for the context may supply 'factors' that support or go against the ordinary usage.[25]
5. What factors are relevant 'depends [much] upon the terms of the particular statute and what may be drawn from the context for and purpose of the provision'.[26]
6. A court will consider how much 'context' a factor provides.[27] The 'evident purpose or policy of the particular provision' is likely to provide more assistance than a 'very general purpose of a statute'.[28]
7. '[T]he words of the provision [being construed] should not be lost sight of in the process of construction'.[29]
8. The process of construction ends with the court ascribing the words used their 'legal meaning'.[30]

While recognising that all interpretations are different in some way, several writers have attempted to describe the overall method.[31] The Council of Australian Law Deans model[32] is representative of the models that offer a simpler statement.[33] Without purporting to being definitive, it provides that key aspects of a 'general method' include:

- locating the provision in question;
- reading it in context;
- identifying the relevant and multiple interpretative criteria for the problem at hand;
- critically analysing how and to what extent those factors assist in determining the legal meaning of the provision;
- formulating opposing and available constructions of the provision in the light of the indications of meaning gathered so far; and,
- after comparing the support each rival construction accrues from the interpretative factors, making a judgment as to which of the constructions, on balance, carries more weight and is to be regarded as expressing the legal meaning.[34]

25 Ibid 521 [32]. See further **[9.6]** (interpretative factors) and **[9.7]** (identification). On ordinary usage see chapter 15.

26 Ibid 522 [36].

27 Ibid 521 [34]. See further **[9.9]** for evaluation of interpretative arguments.

28 Ibid 521–2 [34]–[37]. See further chapter 8.

29 Ibid 521–2 [34]–[36]. See further chapter 6.

30 Ibid 521 [32]. See further **[1.4]** (legal meaning) and **[9.10]** (determining the preferable construction).

31 See Jeffrey Barnes, 'Is There an Overall Method to Interpreting Legislation?' in Jeffrey Barnes (ed), *The Coherence of Statutory Interpretation* (Federation Press, 2019) 78, 79–89. Barnes states that the models differ to some extent. This is partly due to different audiences addressed. It is also due to the difficulty of modelling a practice which is fact-dependent, potentially complex, and non-linear: at 87. See also Johan Steyn, 'The Intractable Problem of the Interpretation of Legal Texts' (2003) 25(1) *Sydney Law Review* 5, 8.

32 Jeffrey Barnes et al, *Council of Australian Law Deans Good Practice Guide to Teaching Statutory Interpretation* (Council of Australian Law Deans, 2015) 15–17. Two of the authors of that report, including the lead author, are co-authors of the present work.

33 See further Jeffrey Barnes, 'Is There an Overall Method to Interpreting Legislation?' in Jeffrey Barnes (ed), *The Coherence of Statutory Interpretation* (Federation Press, 2019) 78, 87.

34 Jeffrey Barnes et al, *Council of Australian Law Deans Good Practice Guide to Teaching Statutory Interpretation* (Council of Australian Law Deans, 2015) 16. The reference to 'carries more weight' should be understood as referring to the weight of the interpretative factors that support the preferred construction. See **[9.10]**.

For those who wish to test their understanding against a more detailed model, the literature affords further guidance.[35]

Conducting legal research

An interpreter is often required to engage in legal research, especially to probe the context of the relevant Act [9.4]

The word 'research' is derived from Middle French *recercher*, meaning to look for with care.[36] In law, research varies according to the purpose.[37] In interpretation, research can be necessary at the preliminary stage of finding the relevant Act. And if a large Act is found to be relevant, an interpreter may be required to search the Act for the key provisions or for clues as to their meaning. Another form of research is probing the context, especially to discover relevant extrinsic materials.

It is impossible in a work of the present nature to map fully steps which are helpful in these tasks. More specialist works are able to deal with this topic in detail.[38] But it is possible to illustrate legal research associated with statutory interpretation in such a way as to give some idea of the steps involved. **Example 9.1** illustrates the process of finding the law.

Example 9.1 *Chapman v South Eastern Sydney Local Health District*[39]

The plaintiff was the widow of the late Joel Chapman. Following complications arising from a medical procedure in a Sydney hospital, Mr Chapman was unconscious on 27 March 2018 when the plaintiff received advice that Mr Chapman was unlikely to survive. The plaintiff commenced enquiries about the possibility of recovering and preserving her husband's sperm. She was informed by the hospital that this required authorisation by a court order. A judge of the Supreme Court of New South Wales (Garling J) made orders ex parte at 6.30 pm on 28 March, including declaring that under the *Guardianship Act 1987* (NSW) the plaintiff was lawfully entitled to consent to the open testicular sperm extraction procedure being performed upon her husband. Mr Chapman was pronounced dead the next morning (29 March). The sperm retrieval procedure was carried out later that day.

Most of the orders of Garling J were now spent. The plaintiff sought further orders from the Supreme Court, including a declaration that she was entitled to the possession of the sperm recovered from the body of her late husband. The Court (Fagan J) began with the basic consideration that '[t]he procedure is invasive and would have constituted an assault or trespass to the person, unlawful both criminally and civilly in the absence of consent or other justification'.[40]

35 The study by Barnes (Jeffrey Barnes, 'Is There an Overall Method to Interpreting Legislation?' in Jeffrey Barnes (ed), *The Coherence of Statutory Interpretation* (Federation Press, 2019) 78) found that Bennion's model was the most comprehensive of those surveyed: at 87. But even that model was found to have shortcomings: at 85–6. The study accordingly restated the Bennion model: at 87–9.

36 *Oxford English Dictionary* (3rd ed, 2010, online at 8 May 2022) 'research' (def 1).

37 *Australian Law Dictionary* (3rd ed, 2017) 'research'.

38 See, eg, Robin Creyke et al, *Laying Down the Law* (LexisNexis Butterworths, 10th ed, 2018) pt 4, especially ch 18; Bruce Bott and Ruth Talbot-Stokes, *Nemes and Coss' Effective Legal Research* (LexisNexis Butterworths, 6th ed, 2015), especially ch 6.

39 (2018) 98 NSWLR 208.

40 Ibid 214 [12].

The Court then examined whether there was authority for sperm extraction from a living, unconscious patient. The Court first examined the *Human Tissue Act 1983* (NSW). The Court held that this Act specifically prohibited a person removing 'tissue' from the body of any other person, whether living or deceased (s 36(1)), and this prohibition applied to the removal of sperm.[41]

Under s 36(4) of the *Human Tissue Act*, however, the prohibition in s 36(1) did not apply to or in respect of

> anything authorised by or under . . .
>
> . . .
>
> (c) any other law.

The Court proceeded to investigate whether any other law authorised the removal of sperm. The Court first considered that no recourse could be had to the Court's inherent jurisdiction.[42]

The Court next considered its parens patriae jurisdiction. This jurisdiction was not available for extraction of sperm from an unconscious and moribund patient because '[s]uch an operation could not be for his benefit, welfare or protection'.[43]

Finally, the Court considered pt 5 of the *Guardianship Act 1987* (NSW). This Act empowered a 'person responsible' to give consent to 'medical treatment' (s 33(1)) carried out on a person, but only 'for the purpose of promoting their health and well-being': s 32(b). After interpreting 'medical treatment', this Act was found not to be available for medical personnel to extract sperm from an unconscious patient who had not given his own prior consent.[44]

The Court also considered authority for sperm extraction from a deceased male, and concluded that '[t]here does not appear to me any legal foundation for the court to make an order authorising removal of sperm from a deceased male body in New South Wales'.[45]

The upshot was that the prohibition upon removing tissue from the body of another person (whether living or deceased) under s 36(1) of the *Human Tissue Act* was the relevant law that applied to the removal of sperm without the written consent of the donor.[46]

Nevertheless, the Court declared that the plaintiff was entitled to the possession of the sperm (on conditions). This was because: (1) although the orders of Garling J ought not have been made, the recovered sperm samples had been lawfully obtained[47] and (2) pursuant to court orders, work and skill had been applied in crypopreserving the sample and as a result the sample was the property of the widow at whose behest the work and skill had been applied.[48]

The case illustrates how finding the relevant law can be a complicated process. Essentially, though, after identifying potential law, the interpreter matches the facts to the law (resolving constructional choices where necessary) until satisfied that the relevant law has been found or that there is no relevant law. As Sullivan writes, '[t]o identify [provisions in doubt] the interpreter tests how clearly each word in the relevant provision applies (or does not apply) to the facts of the case'.[49]

---

41 Ibid 215 [13]–[15].

42 Ibid 216 [21].

43 Ibid 220 [37].

44 Ibid 223 [47].

45 Ibid 225 [58].

46 Ibid 216 [20], 223 [47] (unconscious patient), 225–6 [58] (deceased male body).

47 Ibid 229–30 [75]. The sample had been obtained under orders of a judge of the Supreme Court, a superior court of general jurisdiction. Its orders are valid unless set aside: at 224–5 [53].

48 Ibid 230 [76]–[77].

49 Ruth Sullivan, 'Statutory Interpretation in a New Nutshell' (2003) 82(1) *Canadian Bar Review* 51, 66.

Example 9.2 illustrates the use of research to probe extrinsic materials for indications of the legislative purpose.

Example 9.2 *Talacko v Bennett*[50]

The case raised the question of 'whether a "stay of enforcement" of a judgment within the meaning of s 15(2) of the *Foreign Judgments Act* [1991 (Cth)] is brought about by s 58(3) of the *Bankruptcy Act 1966* (Cth)'.[51] The respondents argued for a restrictive meaning: that 'stay of enforcement of a judgment' had a technical, legal meaning and referred to 'a stay ordered by a court that operates directly on an order or judgment and not, in contrast, on the party who might otherwise seek enforcement of that judgment'.[52] In contrast, the appellant contended that 'nothing in the text of s 15(2) qualifies the words [in question] so as to limit the provision exclusively to judicially ordered stays'.[53]

The Court allowed the appeal. The elaborate course by which the Court found the indication of the legislative purpose from extrinsic materials is described in summary form below:

> The evident purpose of s 15(2) is to prevent an application for a certificate which, if granted, would facilitate the enforcement by execution by a foreign legal system of a judgment which is not enforceable by execution under the law in Australia. In this regard, the explanatory memorandum for the *Foreign Judgments Bill 1991* (Cth) explained in cl 2 that the Bill was largely modelled on the *Foreign Judgments (Reciprocal Enforcement) Ordinance 1954* (ACT), which was in turn substantially modelled on the *Foreign Judgments (Reciprocal Enforcement) Act 1933* (UK). The UK Act was the product of the work of the Foreign Judgments (Reciprocal Enforcement) Committee (the Greer Committee). In the Report of the Greer Committee in relation to a measure that was the precursor to s 15(2) of the *Foreign Judgments Act*, it was said that the certified copy of the British judgment was 'not to be issued if *execution* has been stayed' (emphasis added).[54]

Analysing the Act

Interpretation cannot occur without prior analysis of the Act [9.5]

(a) To determine the object of interpretation, analysis of the statute and sometimes of a provision is required

In statutory interpretation, particular words are in dispute: 'The starting point … is the ordinary and grammatical sense of *the statutory words to be interpreted* having regard to

50 (2017) 260 CLR 124. See also **Example 29.5**.

51 Ibid 130 [1] (Kiefel CJ, Bell, Keane, Gordon and Edelman JJ, Gageler J agreeing at 148 [78] and Nettle J agreeing at 148 [79]).

52 Ibid 143 [60].

53 Ibid 142 [57].

54 Ibid 145–6 [68] (footnote omitted).

their context and the legislative purpose.'[55] The term used to describe these words is the 'object of interpretation'.[56]

It has been pointed out that '[w]ith philosophy of language and linguistics, the typical focus is on the sentence as the relevant unit of meaning'.[57] The author of that statement appears to maintain that the same focus must apply in law:

> the meaning of a sentence, which is the proper object of interpretation ... what is relevant is the ordinary meaning of the sentences in which the words appear. ... the object of the ordinary meaning determination is the sentence and not individual words ...[58]

But in statutory interpretation the sentence as a whole is far from the universal focus of our attention. In legislation, sentences can be very long and are often divided into paragraphs (and sometimes paragraphs are divided further into subparagraphs). Each paragraph, though linked by a common purpose to other paragraphs in the same sentence and to the stem (called 'the chapeau'), has a legal effect all of its own. And even if a sentence is not given a parallel structure, it is composed of a number of grammatical clauses. As for a paragraph or subparagraph, a grammatical clause (which may be a single word) has a distinct legal effect also. This is the crucial reason for why particular words are in dispute: it is not just that parties dispute their scope or effect; it is that the words in question are divisible from other parts of the provision or statute that are *not* in dispute. The object of interpretation in statutory interpretation reflects this capacity for division. To clarify, the object of interpretation is not always a part of a sentence. It has been emphasised that part of a sentence may be an object of interpretation to make the contrast with linguistic theory. A whole sentence or more may be in doubt. It all depends on the circumstances of the case and what is in dispute. As Sullivan says:

> The interpreter's first step is to identify which words in the relevant provision are possible candidates for dispute. These are words or expressions whose meaning is doubtful in relation to the facts of the case.[59]

In short, the object of interpretation is as wide or as narrow as the words in dispute. Bennion's term for the words in question is helpful. It is 'unit of inquiry'.[60] The word 'unit' does not have a predetermined boundary. The word 'inquiry' does not mean that a 'unit of inquiry' is an issue; rather, that a particular part ('unit') of the statute is the *subject* of an inquiry.

Some examples will now further explain the concept of the text or the object of interpretation.

A case in which a single word was at issue is *Victims Compensation Fund Corporation v Brown.*[61] The Act in question was the *Victims Support and Rehabilitation Act 1996* (NSW). Clause 5(a) of sch 1 to the Act read as follows:

---

55 *Alcan (NT) Alumina Pty Ltd v Commissioner of Territory Revenue (NT)* (2009) 239 CLR 27, 31 [4] (French CJ) (emphasis added).

56 Joseph Raz, *Between Authority and Interpretation: On the Theory of Law and Practical Reason* (Oxford University Press, 2009) 226; Brian G Slocum, 'Ordinary Meaning and Empiricism' (2019) 40(1) *Statute Law Review* 13, 20.

57 Brian G Slocum, 'Ordinary Meaning and Empiricism' (2019) 40(1) *Statute Law Review* 13, 20.

58 Ibid 20, 21.

59 Ruth Sullivan, 'Statutory Interpretation in a New Nutshell' (2003) 82(1) *Canadian Bar Review* 51, 66.

60 Oliver Jones, *Bennion on Statutory Interpretation* (LexisNexis, 6th ed, 2013) 374–6.

61 (2003) 201 ALR 260.

> The following applies to the compensable injury of shock:
>
> (a) Compensation is payable only if the symptoms *and* disability persist for more than 6 weeks.[62]

The critical element – the element in doubt – was a single word: 'and'.

> The first and second respondents each had 'symptoms' of shock which persisted for 6 weeks, but neither had a 'disability'. Their entitlement to claim for shock thus rested on the answer to a single question. In cl 5(a), did 'and' mean 'and' or 'or'?
>
> ...
>
> The question is a narrow one ... In the expression 'symptoms and disability' the word 'and' should be construed conjunctively ...[63]

An example where a phrase was at issue is *Talacko v Bennett*.[64] Section 15(2) of the *Foreign Judgments Act 1991* (Cth) read:

> An application may not be made until the expiration of any stay of enforcement of the judgment in question.

The High Court isolated a phrase within that provision as the element in doubt:

> It is against that legislative background that the question of statutory construction in this case is to be considered: the proper construction of the phrase 'any stay of enforcement of the judgment' in s 15(2) of the *Foreign Judgments Act* and, in particular, whether that phrase extends to include the operation of s 58(3) of the *Bankruptcy Act*.[65]

A case in which an entire provision (falling short of a sentence) was the subject of doubt is *Project Blue Sky Inc v Australian Broadcasting Authority*.[66] That case dealt with the meaning of s 160(d) of the *Broadcasting Services Act 1992* (Cth). That provision read as follows:

> The ABA is to perform its functions in a manner consistent with:
>
> ...
>
> (d) Australia's obligations under any convention to which Australia is a party or any agreement between Australia and a foreign country.

A question in that case was whether a broadcasting standard made in breach of s 160(d) was invalid. This entailed examining whether, by implication, breach of the provision was intended to have that consequence.

A case in which an entire sentence was at issue is *Dolheguy v Becker*.[67] It involved a clash between two subsections of the *Road Safety Act 1986* (Vic): ss 28(6) and 66(6).

---

62 Emphasis added.

63 (2003) 201 ALR 260, 262 [8], 263 [12] (Heydon J, McHugh AJA agreeing at 261 [1], Gummow J agreeing at 261 [2], Kirby J agreeing at 261 [3], Hayne J agreeing at 261 [4]).

64 (2017) 260 CLR 124. The case is considered above at **Example 9.2**.

65 Ibid 136 [34] (Kiefel CJ, Bell, Keane, Gordon and Edelman JJ).

66 (1998) 194 CLR 355.

67 (2009) 52 MVR 462.

A case in which the scope of more than a sentence (an entire Part) was at issue was *Commissioner of Police for New South Wales v Eaton*.[68] There, pt 6 of the *Industrial Relations Act 1996* (NSW) was held not applicable to a decision made under s 80(3) of the *Police Act 1990* (NSW).[69]

(b) Close attention to the text is required

The High Court has spoken of the need to 'give close attention' to statutory provisions.[70] If close attention is not given, significant distinctions may be overlooked. It is necessary to read legislation this way because of one of its key functions – to change the law[71] – and because of the way legislation is written. A legislative drafter explains:

> [T]he legislative drafter . . . operates in an environment where all the words count and have equal weight. . . . the drafter's literary environment is a stark one. Statutory language is by its nature compressed and spare. The drafter is generally denied some of the techniques available to other writers – such as repetition, explanation and emphasis.[72]

Example 9.3 *Tjungarrayi v Western Australia*[73]

The *Native Title Act 1993* (Cth) ('the Act' or 'NTA') provided for claims to be made even though title to the land had previously been extinguished. But this exemption from the normal rule was *not* applicable if the area was covered by a 'lease': s 47B(1)(b)(i). In the case the areas in question were covered by a petroleum exploration permit and a mineral exploration licence. These fell outside the definition of 'lease' in the Act. The Act, however, included a definition of 'mining lease' in s 242(2): 'In the case only of *references* to a mining lease, the expression *lease* also includes a licence issued, or an authority given, by or under a law of the Commonwealth, a State or a Territory.'[74]

The court below, the Full Federal Court, held that, as mining leases were leases, the permit and licence were a 'lease' and hence the claim was not permitted. The High Court disagreed, paying close attention to the words of s 242(2):

> Section 242(2) is expressly conditioned in its operation by the prefatory words, '[i]n the case only of references to a mining lease'. This condition requires a 'reference' to a mining lease in the operative provision of the NTA in any particular case. The condition is not satisfied by an operative provision that does not make reference to a mining lease.
>
> In each matter, the Full Court's reasoning fails to recognise that, according to the ordinary and natural meaning of s 242(2), it is engaged *only* where the operative provision of the NTA contains an express textual reference to a 'mining lease'. In each case, the Full Court applied s 242(2) as if the opening words of s 242(2), '[i]n the case only of references to a mining lease', were '[i]n the case of a mining lease'.[75]

---

68 (2013) 252 CLR 1.

69 Ibid 7 [9], 14 [31] (Heydon J), 32 [92] (Crennan, Kiefel and Bell JJ).

70 *Muslimin v The Queen* (2010) 240 CLR 470, 475 [4] (The Court).

71 Geoffrey Bowman, 'The Art of Legislative Drafting' (2005) 7 *European Journal of Law Reform* 3, 7.

72 Ibid 8, 9.

73 (2019) 269 CLR 150. For another example of close attention by the High Court, see Jeffrey Barnes, 'Contextualism: "The Modern Approach to Statutory Interpretation"' (2018) 41(4) *University of New South Wales Law Journal* 1083, 1091–4.

74 Emphasis added.

75 (2019) 269 CLR 150, 163 [30]–[31] (Kiefel CJ, Bell, Keane and Edelman JJ, Gageler J agreeing at 165 [42]).

(c) **Elemental analysis is almost always necessary**

To understand fully a provision, a court may find it necessary to find the 'discrete elements' of a provision.[76] Elemental analysis is the breaking up of a provision into its constituent elements and sub-elements. An interpreter does this to facilitate close attention to the text and to ascertain which, if any, elements have been clearly satisfied and which, if any, are not clearly satisfied and are in doubt.

Bennion refers to the elements as expressed by the Parliament as the 'statutory factual outline' and the elements as interpreted as the 'judicial factual outline'. The word 'outline' indicates that statutory provisions are expressed in general terms. If the actual facts fall within the factual outline then this triggers the legal thrust or legal effect intended.[77] Enright puts forward a similar model. He describes law as 'a generalisation of the facts to which it applies'. His technique of analysis of a statutory provision is called 'micro analysis':

> This breaks each law into two parts. (i) One part is the consequences which the law brings when it applies to facts. ... (ii) The other part consists of the elements which define the types of facts to which the law applies.[78]

As Enright suggests, it is helpful to set these elements out in a checklist.[79] That way an interpreter can ensure close and comprehensive attention is given to the statute.

In a simple case of elemental analysis a court will divide up a provision into grammatical clauses.[80] *O'Reilly v Rooney*[81] illustrates a more complex case. The Supreme Court of Victoria divided an 85-word sentence[82] into six clauses. It found only two were at issue in the case.[83]

(d) **Grammatical analysis is frequently employed**

Many cases involve grammatical analysis.[84] In case law, grammatical analysis ranges from simple observations on present tense[85] and active voice[86] to more sophisticated analysis, such as differences between the present tense and the present perfect tense.[87] **Example 9.4** illustrates attention to the humble comma.

---

76 *I and L Securities Pty Ltd v HTW Valuers (Brisbane) Pty Ltd* (2002) 210 CLR 109, 126 [50] (Gaudron, Gummow and Hayne JJ), quoting and approving *Marks v GIO Australia Holdings Ltd* (1998) 196 CLR 494, 526–7 [95] (Gummow J).

77 Oliver Jones, *Bennion on Statutory Interpretation* (LexisNexis, 6th ed, 2013) 396–401.

78 Christopher Enright, *Legal Technique* (Federation Press, 5th ed, 2002) 344 [29.10].

79 Ibid 344 [29.10], ch 32.

80 For example, *I and L Securities Pty Ltd v HTW Valuers (Brisbane) Pty Ltd* (2002) 210 CLR 109, 126 [50] (Gaudron, Gummow and Hayne JJ), quoting and approving *Marks v GIO Australia Holdings Ltd* (1998) 196 CLR 494, 526–7 [95] (Gummow J); *Anderson v Commissioner of Taxes (Vic)* (1937) 57 CLR 233, 237–8 (Latham CJ).

81 (1989) 10 MVR 19.

82 *Road Safety Act 1986* (Vic) s 60(1).

83 (1989) 10 MVR 19, 23 (Gobbo J). The analysis was followed in *Loges v Martin* (1991) 13 MVR 405, 410 (Nathan J).

84 See Michael Meehan and Graham Tulloch, *Grammar for Lawyers* (LexisNexis Butterworths, 3rd ed, 2013). Another useful work is Nichola Corbett-Jarvis and Brendan Grigg, *Effective Legal Writing: A Practical Guide* (LexisNexis Butterworths, 2nd ed, 2017) ch 2.

85 *LU Simon Builders Pty Ltd v Victorian Building Authority* [2017] VSC 805, [52], [53] (Cavanough J)

86 *SZVBN v Minister for Immigration and Border Protection* (2017) 254 FCR 393, 413 [88] (Griffiths J).

87 *Esso Australia Pty Ltd v Australian Workers' Union* (2017) 263 CLR 551, 570–1 [29], 574–5 [36]–[38], 581–2 [51] (Kiefel CJ, Keane, Nettle and Edelman JJ), 588 [67] (Gageler J).

Example 9.4 *Footscray City College v Ruzicka*[88]

In a workers compensation matter, a worker had succeeded in her claim for weekly payments but not for lump sum compensation under ss 98 and 98A of the *Accident Compensation Act 1985* (Vic) ('the Act'). The employer appealed a decision of a County Court judge that there should be no order as to costs of the unsuccessful claim for lump sum compensation.

The Act imposed a duty on the Court to award costs against the party against whom a judgment or decision is made: s 50(1)(a). The duty was expressed to be '[s]ubject to this Act'. Subsection (2A), however, stated as follows:

> (2A) In proceedings before the County Court under this Act which relate to a claim under section 98 or 98A, if a judgment or order is made by the County Court for the payment of an amount of compensation to the claimant –
>
> (a) which is not less than 90 per cent of the claimant's counter statutory offer but is greater than the statutory offer made by the Authority, employer or self-insurer – the Authority, employer or self-insurer must pay the claimant's party and party costs and must bear their own costs; or
>
> (b) which is equal to or less than the statutory offer made by the Authority, employer or self-insurer – the claimant must pay the party and party costs of the Authority, employer or self-insurer and bear his or her own costs; or
>
> (c) which is greater than the statutory offer made by the Authority, employer or self-insurer but less than 90 per cent of the counter statutory offer made by the claimant – each party must bear their own costs –
>
> and the County Court must not otherwise make an award of costs.

Counsel for the respondent worker argued that 's 50(2A) constitutes a code in respect of all s 98/98A claims, such that the court is required to make costs orders as prescribed by paras (a)–(c), but otherwise it has no power to make any costs order on such an application'.[89] The opposing construction was that s 50(2A) was not a code; rather, in the words of Chernov JA who gave the leading judgment, 'the opening words of [the subsection] do no more than provide a description of the proceeding in respect of which the court is compelled to award costs in accordance with one of the succeeding paragraphs'.[90]

In preferring the latter construction, Chernov JA placed weight on the comma in sub-s (2A) after '98A':

> It seems to me that the comma . . ., rather than supporting the respondent's argument that it compels the subsection to read that the prohibition applies in respect of all s 98/98A proceedings, supports the opposite view. The comma, I think, is not a mere reflection of grammatical correctness but demonstrates that the legislature intended to place a demarcation between the words preceding the comma and those following it such that the mandatory provisions in paras (a)–(c), and thus the concluding words of the subsection, apply only to the situation where an order for compensation has been made.[91]

Hence, if a party was unsuccessful in a s 98/98A application for lump sum compensation, s 50(1) operated to compel the losing party to pay the party and party costs in respect of the application.[92]

---

88 (2007) 16 VR 498.

89 Ibid 500 [6] (Chernov JA, Warren CJ agreeing at 499 [1], Maxwell P agreeing at 499 [2]).

90 Ibid 504 [14].

91 Ibid 503–4 [14] (footnote omitted).

92 Ibid 503 [13], 506 [21].

(e) Tracing (following the legislative chain) is often required in complex legislation

Much legislation is complex. In *AQO v Minister for Finance and Services*[93] Basten JA describes how the Court was taken by counsel through what his Honour describes as an 'extraordinarily complex chain' by which a member of the community may discover that they have a right of appeal to the Appeal Panel of the New South Wales Civil and Administrative Tribunal.[94] The chain of linked provisions wound its way through three Acts.[95]

Sometimes the legislative chain is a series of definition provisions, called 'cascading definitions'.[96] Here a term is defined, then an element of that definition is defined, and sometimes the definitional process continues even further. In *Australian Building and Construction Commissioner v Construction, Forestry, Mining and Energy Union*[97] the Full Court of the Federal Court observed that 'it is necessary to proceed through a labyrinthine series of complex definitional provisions'.[98] A much shortened summary follows. Section 38 of the *Building and Construction Industry Improvement Act 2005* (Cth) provided that '[a] person must not engage in unlawful industrial action'. The term 'unlawful industrial action' was then defined in terms of four elements (the first-level definitions). Each of those elements were then defined separately (the second-level definitions). Finally, some of the elements of the second-level definitions were in turn defined (third-level definitions).

Another instance of a chain is when a rule is subject to exceptions, and the exceptions are themselves subject to exceptions. In *Lottoland Australia Pty Ltd v Australian Communications and Media Authority*[99] the Court encountered such a regime.[100] After expressing difficulty, the Court recast the scheme into a list of elements.[101]

Example 9.5 *LU Simon Builders Pty Ltd v Victorian Building Authority*[102]

The *Building Act 1993* (Vic) relevantly included the following provisions:

Division 2 – Directions to fix building work

37 Definitions

In this Division –

...

builder in relation to building work, means the person who is specified as the builder in the building permit issued in relation to that building work;

...

93 (2016) 93 NSWLR 46.

94 Ibid 74 [123] (Ward JA agreeing at 87 [177]).

95 Ibid 73–4 [120–[123].

96 *Gibbs v Mercantile Mutual Insurance (Australia) Ltd* (2003) 214 CLR 604, 649 [134] (Kirby J) (dissenting as to outcome).

97 (2017) 254 FCR 68.

98 Ibid 77 [39] (the Court).

99 (2019) 100 NSWLR 328.

100 *Interactive Gambling Act 2001* (Cth) s 8A, discussed at (2019) 100 NSWLR 328, 363 [156] (Sackar J).

101 (2019) 100 NSWLR 328, 363 [157].

102 [2017] VSC 805.

relevant person means a person referred to in section 37C who can be, or has been, given a direction to fix building work.

...

37B Direction by authorised person to fix building work

...

(2) The authorised person may give a direction to fix the building work to a relevant person in accordance with this Division.

37C Method of giving directions

A direction to fix building work may be given as –

(a) an oral direction to either or both of the following persons –
   (i) the builder;
   (ii) the person who is apparently in charge of the site on which the building work is being carried out; or
(b) a written direction to the builder.

The central issue in the case was the scope of s 37B(2) – was the power available after a certificate of final inspection or an occupancy permit had been issued? The plaintiff argued that it was not.[103] It became relevant to ascertain to whom and how the direction could be given, for this would indicate the scope of the power in s 37B. In this regard the Court paid close attention to s 37C and its connection with s 37B.[104] The legislative chain linking the provisions is relatively straightforward. Beginning with s 37B(2), the person to whom the direction may be issued is specified as 'a relevant person'. The reader is expected first to read in context and notice definitions for div 2 of pt 4 in s 37. That section defines a 'relevant person' as 'a person referred to in section 37C'. Reading that provision, one sees that it refers to 'the builder' (s 37C(a)(i), (b)) and 'the person who is apparently in charge of the site on which the building work is being carried out': s 37C(a)(ii). For elaboration of 'the builder', one is again expected to access definitions. 'Builder' is defined in s 37 and 'building work' is defined in s 3(1).

This example shows that following the legislative chain may require a combination of reading in context and following specific references to other provisions.

Identifying interpretative factors

[9.6] **To know what aids to look for, an interpreter must first grasp the relationship between, on the one hand, general interpretative criteria, and, on the other hand, interpretative indications or interpretative factors that are derived from those criteria**[105]

Interpretation is a practical business. As Lord Sales pointed out extracurially, a court requires '*evidence* regarding the meaning of the statute' to be adduced.[106] The High Court of Australia refers to such evidence as 'indications [that] point towards a legislative intention'[107] and as

103 Ibid [6] (Cavanough J).

104 Ibid [47]–[50].

105 This section develops the distinction between interpretative criteria and interpretative factors that is made in Oliver Jones, *Bennion on Statutory Interpretation* (LexisNexis, 6th ed, 2013) 477–81, 484–5. See also **[7.3]**.

106 Philip Sales, 'Legislative Intention, Interpretation, and the Principle of Legality' (2019) 40(1) *Statute Law Review* 53, 60 (emphasis added).

107 *Commissioner of Police for New South Wales v Eaton* (2013) 252 CLR 1, 27 [72] (Crennan, Kiefel and Bell JJ).

'matters [that] point' to or against a construction.[108] Another term that is used to refer to the indications of legislative intention is 'interpretative factors'.[109] These indications are specific – indeed unique – to the context. As French CJ said, what a court looks for is 'the text, context and purpose *of the relevant statutory provision*'.[110]

For example, if the meaning of a provision is in doubt, the interpreter will normally weigh the ordinary and grammatical meaning *of the words in question*. If the interpreter is able to ascertain the purpose of the provision, the interpreter will also give that factor weight. But if there is no prior version of the provision in doubt that has received a judicial interpretation, there is no relevant factor to weigh derived from the norm that when Parliament re-enacts a provision that had previously been judicially interpreted, Parliament intends the words to have that meaning. Similarly, if the explanatory memorandum to the Bill that became the Act in question is not helpful, there is no relevant factor based on the Interpretation Act or the common law that the court may weigh.

These examples show that a court does not weigh the general norms of statutory interpretation, either in toto or selectively. It cannot weigh the norms in toto, since some norms may not be relevant. And even if a general norm is relevant, the court weighs the manifestation of the norm, not the norm itself.

To elaborate briefly on the distinction between interpretative criteria and interpretative factors, they are distinct in terms of where they are established, their function and relationship to legislative intention, and whether they present in a case. Interpretative criteria are established in statute or common law. By comparison, an interpretative factor is established in a particular context. The function of an interpretative criterion is to supply a general guide to legislative intention (across all legislation of the jurisdiction), whereas the function of an interpretative factor is to act as a guide to legislative intention in a particular case. An interpretative criterion is not necessarily relevant to a particular case. By comparison an interpretative factor, where it manifests in the context of the words in question, is relevant as a matter of course. Though conceptually distinct, interpretative criteria and interpretative factors are closely related in practice. An interpretative factor is the offspring of an interpretative criterion: the manifestation in a particular context of a relevant interpretative criterion. Another way of expressing the relation is to say that an interpretative factor is the result of applying an interpretative criterion to a provision or its context in circumstances in which the criterion is relevant.

To sum up: an interpreter of particular words in question needs to have a general knowledge of the interpretative criteria, for some of the general norms will be relevant to the determination of the meaning of the words. And an interpreter of particular words needs to be able to identify and weigh the interpretative factors, for these are the considerations that directly impact upon the determination of the preferable construction of the words.

---

108 *Rizeq v Western Australia* (2017) 262 CLR 1, 66 [183] (Edelman J).

109 Cases that have used this concept include *Harding v County Court of Victoria* [2013] VSC 711, [14] (Macaulay J); *EFN v Lehmann* [2018] 1 Qd R 126, 130 [9] (North J).

110 *Plaintiff M70/2011 v Minister for Immigration and Citizenship* (2011) 244 CLR 144, 162 [13].

Example 9.6 *LU Simon Builders Pty Ltd v Victorian Building Authority*[111]

It will be recalled (see **Example 9.5**) that the question in this case was whether the power to give a direction to fix building work in s 37B of the *Building Act 1993* (Vic) was available after a certificate of final inspection or an occupancy permit had been issued. In the case the directions were issued up to nine years after the issue of an occupancy permit.

The Court referred to an interpretative criterion that the plaintiffs invoked:

> Appropriately, in my view, the plaintiffs also invoke the principle that a construction that would produce inconvenient, improbable or irrational consequences should be avoided if there is a competing construction that is reasonably open and would not produce such consequences.[112]

Stated in that form (including with reference to authorities that have been presently omitted), the principle is abstract and general. It is not itself something that can be weighed. It will be recalled that a court requires '*evidence* regarding the meaning of the statute' to be adduced.[113] The evidence comprises the indications of meaning from the text and the context. In due course the Court considered indications from the particular statutory context that were authorised by, and applications of, the interpretative criterion referred to.

> The plaintiffs say that it is inconceivable that Parliament intended that a direction to fix might be given to a person who does not hold a relevant building permit that is currently in force. Generally speaking, it is a serious criminal offence to carry out 'building work' without a building permit or relevant exemption, and all the more so to do it knowingly. ... As indicated above, the plaintiffs also submit that other inconvenient, improbable and irrational consequences would follow from the defendant's construction of Division 2 of Part 4. Among other things, the plaintiffs submit, correctly in my view, that, on the defendant's construction, a direction to fix could be issued long after the event to a person who was no longer a builder or who bore absolutely no responsibility or blame for the alleged defect(s) or who answered both of those descriptions; or who, because of the passage of time, could no longer enforce any rights of contribution the person may have otherwise have had. Examples could be multiplied.[114]

These particular consequences are relevant indications of meaning because they are consequences that arise in the context. The likelihood of them arising marks them out as not speculative. Further, they are not abstract and general as is the criterion from which they are derived. They arise for consideration from the facts of the case and are specific to the statutory provision in question.

[9.7] A number of methods are available to assist in identifying interpretative factors

The number of interpretative criteria recognised by statute and common law is quite large. The Full Federal Court has referred to the 'wide range of more specific principles of statutory

111 [2017] VSC 805.

112 Ibid [29] (Cavanough J); footnotes omitted.

113 Philip Sales, 'Legislative Intention, Interpretation, and the Principle of Legality' (2019) 40(1) *Statute Law Review* 53, 60 (emphasis added).

114 [2017] VSC 805, [54], [56] (Cavanough J).

construction'.[115] Bennion's checklist of 'possible guides to legal meaning of the enactment' contains 50 interpretative criteria.[116] Sanson's index of 'rules of statutory interpretation' numbers 186.[117] Each statute is unique in some way.[118] A statute may provide some obvious indications of how it is to be read (such as definition provisions and objects provisions) but it does not present a code of interpretative indications. '[A]ll available indications' need to be identified.[119] Therefore, the problem arises: how does an interpreter identify all of the contextual indications of meaning? A number of methods to assist exist. Some are more applicable to novices; others more to experts. The following are considered briefly: intuition; a 'spiral approach'; 'text, context and purpose'; a series of analyses; and the use of checklists.

The least useful method to novices was cited by Barwick CJ: 'Perhaps it may be said that [the 'rules'] denote elements of approach to construction which a well-furnished Judge will almost intuitively carry in mind as possible factors in his endeavour to discover meaning.'[120] Here a former Chief Justice suggests that an expert can identify indications of meaning intuitively – that is, by relying on experience. Justice Callaway echoes this statement, observing that he had not 'so recently' opened a particular Australian textbook.[121] But, for obvious reasons, intuition cannot take a novice very far.

More relevant for novices and practitioners is when judges reflect on the precise method they have taken.[122] Justice Susan Glazebrook's 'spiral' approach to statutory interpretation is a well-structured statutory interpretation methodology.[123] She suggests that the interpreter first consider what the provision in question has to offer, then spiral out progressively to the remainder of the Act, the legislative (enacting) history of the Bill, and finally to the wider legal context. The model is not intended to be used rigidly. Justice Glazebrook advances several advantages of the approach. It is 'a discipline guarding against the natural tendency to start at the destination and work back'.[124] It offers 'some predictability'. It assures 'a logical progression will be followed'. And it still gives interpreters 'flexibility to meet the requirements of the individual case'.[125] Other strengths are apparent. It is consistent with High Court authority[126]

115 *Australian Mines and Metals Association Inc v Construction, Forestry, Maritime, Mining and Energy Union* (2018) 268 FCR 128, 147 [78] (the Court).

116 FAR Bennion, *Bennion on Statutory Interpretation: A Code* (LexisNexis, 5th ed, 2008) app B.

117 Michelle Sanson, *Statutory Interpretation* (Oxford University Press, 2nd ed, 2016) 332–44.

118 Geoffrey Bowman, 'The Art of Legislative Drafting' (2005) 7(1/2) *European Journal of Law Reform* 3, 4–5.

119 *Commissioner of Police for New South Wales v Eaton* (2013) 252 CLR 1, 19 [46] (Crennan, Kiefel and Bell JJ), quoting *Associated Minerals Consolidated Ltd v Wyong Shire Council* [1975] AC 538, 553–4 (PC).

120 Sir Garfield Barwick, 'Foreword to the First Edition' in DC Pearce and RS Geddes, *Statutory Interpretation in Australia* (Butterworths, 3rd ed, 1988) vii, vii.

121 Justice Frank Callaway, 'Judges and Statutes' [2005] Winter *Bar News* 25, 27.

122 The following commentary draws on Jeffrey Barnes, 'Is There an Overall Method to Interpreting Legislation?' in Jeffrey Barnes (ed), *The Coherence of Statutory Interpretation* (Federation Press, 2019) 78.

123 Justice Susan Glazebrook, 'Filling the Gaps' in Rick Bigwood (ed), *The Statute: Making and Meaning* (LexisNexis, 2004) 153, 169–76.

124 Ibid 169. Cf John Braithwaite, 'Rules and Principles: A Theory of Legal Certainty' (2002) 27 *Australian Journal of Legal Philosophy* 47, arguing that if judges do work 'bottom-up', the intuitions are 'grounded in professional training more than personal values', and with judges 'those professional intuitions are legal ones': at 64.

125 Justice Susan Glazebrook, 'Filling the Gaps' in Rick Bigwood (ed), *The Statute: Making and Meaning* (LexisNexis, 2004) 153, 170.

126 *Federal Commissioner of Taxation v Consolidated Media Holdings Ltd* (2012) 250 CLR 503, 519 [39] (French CJ, Hayne, Crennan, Bell and Gageler JJ).

to begin with the provision in question. It does not dictate inappropriately the consideration of any particular interpretative criterion, regardless of whether there is evidence of it in the particular context and circumstances. It steps the reader through the three stages of the context. And its brevity (four steps) makes it simple to remember and apply. A similar analysis of the context has been advocated by Lord Sales.[127] The spiral approach is reflected in a number of cases.[128] A limitation of the model is that the interpreter has to work out for themselves what indications appear. It is not a formula. It affords general guidance only.

A method that has a catchy title is 'text, context and purpose'.[129] The trilogy of general sources has been influential in the structure of some judgments.[130] The method usefully highlights the legislative purpose and reminds the user to attend to the context. But it is not as logical and easy to use as the Glazebrook spiral approach because it does not step the user through the context.

Ruth Sullivan proposes a series of analyses for the interpreter, in order to ascertain 'the relevant indicators of legislative meaning and intent'.[131] The analyses include 'textual analysis', 'purposive analysis', 'scheme analysis', 'extrinsic aids', 'policy analysis' and 'consequential analysis'.[132] Her article examines each of the categories. She adds the rider that

> [o]thers might prefer fewer, or more, or different categories. The important thing is not how this preliminary work is categorized, but how it is carried out. The goal is to be as comprehensive and as explicit as possible.[133]

Finally, some writers advocate checklists for interpreters to use.[134] These lists are valuable as they conveniently bring together in a concise way a large body of knowledge. But they are not exhaustive. Furthermore, they are not intended as a substitute for learning the law.[135] If a student generates their own list (using the checklists as a check on the accuracy and comprehensiveness of their own list), they can learn through that experience.[136]

---

127 Philip Sales, 'Legislative Intention, Interpretation, and the Principle of Legality' (2019) 40(1) *Statute Law Review* 53, 56.

128 See the analysis of *Victims Compensation Fund Corporation v Brown* (2003) 201 ALR 260 in Jeffrey Barnes, 'Contextualism: "The Modern Approach to Statutory Interpretation"' (2018) 41(4) *University of New South Wales Law Journal* 1083, 1088–90. Other cases that evidence it include *Scott-Mackenzie v Bail* (2017) 16 ASTLR 449, 458–61, [36]–[49] (the Court); *Beadle v La Bianca* [2012] WASC 415, [25]–[55] (Pritchard J); *Mansfield v The Queen* (2012) 247 CLR 86. The last-mentioned case is illustrated in **Example 9.7** below.

129 An early use was by Kirby J in *Foots v Southern Cross Mine Management Pty Ltd* (2007) 234 CLR 52, 93 [130] (dissenting as to outcome). It is now commonly cited by the High Court – see, eg, *Probuild Constructions (Aust) Pty Ltd v Shade Systems Pty Ltd* (2018) 264 CLR 1, 14 [34] (Kiefel CJ, Bell, Keane, Nettle and Gordon JJ).

130 *Hunter Quarries Pty Ltd v Mexon* (2018) 98 NSWLR 526, 539–45 [56] –[80] (Payne JA, Gleeson JA agreeing at 531 [16], Sackville AJA agreeing at 549 [105], Simpson AJA generally agreeing at 550 [113]). See also *BGM16 v Minister for Immigration and Border Protection* (2017) 252 FCR 97, 108–12 [58]–[81] (Mortimer and Wigney JJ).

131 Ruth Sullivan, 'Statutory Interpretation in a New Nutshell' (2003) 82(1) *The Canadian Bar Review* 51, 58.

132 Ibid 59–64.

133 Ibid 58 (citation omitted).

134 Oliver Jones, *Bennion on Statutory Interpretation: A Code* (LexisNexis, 6th ed, 2013) app B; Michelle Sanson, *Statutory Interpretation* (Oxford University Press, 2nd ed, 2016) 332–44.

135 Bennion advocates that users read his treatise from beginning to end: Oliver Jones, *Bennion on Statutory Interpretation: A Code* (LexisNexis, 6th ed, 2013) xxxv. In the checklist in her work Sanson supplies references to the body of her work 'so that readers can locate statutory provisions and/or cases relating to each rule': Michelle Sanson, *Statutory Interpretation* (Oxford University Press, 2nd ed, 2016) 332.

136 David Boud, Ruth Cohen and David Walker, 'Introduction: Understanding Learning from Experience' in David Boud, Ruth Cohen and David Walker (eds), *Using Experience for Learning* (Society for Research into Higher Education & Open University Press, 1993) 1, 9.

Example 9.7 ***Mansfield v The Queen***[137]

Section 1002G of the *Corporations Act 2001* (Cth) prohibited persons who were in possession of information of a certain character from trading in shares. The offence is commonly known as insider trading.

The appellants were charged with conspiracy to commit a contravention of s 1002G. The information they possessed was false. The central question in these appeals was as follows: did the appellants possess 'information' that was not generally available? The prior interpretative question was whether 'information' had to be true. Finding against the appellants, the Court held that 'information' included false information.[138]

The reasoning of the joint judgment of Hayne, Crennan, Kiefel and Bell JJ proceeded generally as follows. At [29]–[30] under the heading 'Ordinary usage of "information"' they examined the word 'information', considering its ordinary usage and dictionary definitions. At [31]–[35] under the heading 'Other statutory provisions', the joint judgment considered other aspects of the section in question, touching on the reasons of a judge of the court below, the Court of Appeal of the Supreme Court of Western Australia. This is broadly consistent with the first stage of the Glazebrook approach – examining the provision in question.

At [36] the joint judgment considered a report on insider trading in Australia by the Standing Committee on Legal and Constitutional Affairs of the House of Representatives.

At [37]–[43] the joint judgment further considered other provisions of the Act. This is consistent with the second stage of the Glazebrook approach – examining the remainder of the Act in question.

At [44]–[47], under the heading 'Purpose of prohibiting insider trading', the joint judgment considered indications of the legislative purpose informed by the legislative history. This is consistent with the third Glazebrook stage of examining the legislative history.

At [48]–[50], under the heading 'International practice', the joint judgment considered an argument based on laws of other jurisdictions. Potentially, the consideration of such laws would be consistent with the Glazebrook fourth stage of 'the wider context'.[139]

In summary, the reasons of the joint judgment broadly match the spiral approach advocated by Glazebrook J.

Formulating alternative constructions

Formulating alternative constructions is an essential skill [9.8]

(a) Constructions are rival contentions as to the meaning of the words in question

The word 'construction' has several meanings in statutory interpretation. It is often used synonymously with the process of interpretation, as in, for example: '[The heading] may therefore inform their construction.'[140] It can also refer to the specific final interpretation or conclusion reached by a court or interpreter. The present section uses it in a third sense – the

137 (2012) 247 CLR 86.

138 Ibid 96 [28] (Hayne, Crennan, Kiefel and Bell JJ), 106 [73] (Heydon J).

139 But the Court rejected the use made of such material: ibid 100 [48]–[50] (Hayne, Crennan, Kiefel and Bell JJ), 106 [74]–[76] (Heydon J).

140 *Berenguel v Minister for Immigration and Citizenship* (2010) 264 ALR 417, 423 [26] (the Court).

sense used by the High Court in the following passage from *Berenguel v Minister for Immigration and Citizenship*:

> [I]n this case, the construction for which the minister contends leads to such plain unfairness and absurdity that it is not to be preferred. The *alternative* construction for which the plaintiff contends does not compromise the purpose of the Migration Regulations.[141]

The key word here is 'alternative'. In this passage 'construction' refers to what Lord Reid has described as 'the rival contentions as to the meaning of [the provision in question]'.[142] Or, put another way, in relation to a dispute about the meaning of a statutory provision, it refers to the interpretation of the provision that is proposed by a party to the dispute.[143] The High Court refers to the task of choosing between the rival contentions as to meaning as 'constructional choice'.[144]

The significance of this distinction is that a construction in the sense of a rival contention is formulated by a party or an adviser. Normally a court will choose between the constructions so formulated.[145] Formulating a construction is an important, indeed a central, practical skill.

(b) Formulating constructions, and choosing between them, are central to the practice of interpretation

Many judges and other commentators rightly place constructions at the centre of their theory of the interpretative process.[146] Lord Steyn places constructions at the core of his definition of interpretation: 'Interpretation . . . is an exercise involving the making of choices between feasible interpretations.'[147] Justice Frankfurter introduced his classic discussion of interpretation through a focus on constructions:

> When we talk of statutory construction we have in mind cases in which there is a fair contest between two readings, neither of which comes without respectable title deeds. A problem in statutory construction can seriously bother courts only when there is a contest between probabilities of meaning.[148]

According to Bennion, '[t]he art of determining precisely which is the most helpful yet plausible construction to advance to the court is an important forensic accomplishment'.[149] And Sullivan's assessment of the importance of constructions is one that is strongly endorsed:

---

141 Ibid (emphasis added).

142 *Inland Revenue Commissioners v Hinchy* [1960] AC 748, 766.

143 Exceptionally, a court may propose a construction that is not sourced in a submission of counsel. See **[5.3]**.

144 *Coverdale v West Coast Council* (2016) 259 CLR 164, 172 [23] (the Court).

145 A court will not do so if it comes to the view that a construction of its own devising represents the law.

146 Unfortunately, some models of the interpretative process do not give a place to the formulation of constructions. See, eg, Robin Creyke et al, *Laying Down the Law* (LexisNexis Butterworths, 10th ed, 2018) 447–8 ('practical guide to interpretation of legislation'); Catherine Brown, Judith McNamara and Cheryl Treloar, *Good Practice Guide (Bachelor of Laws): Statutory Interpretation* (Australian Learning and Teaching Council, 2011) 6–8 and app C ('eight step guide'); Elizabeth Ellis, *Principles and Practice of Australian Law* (Thomson Reuters, 3rd ed, 2013) 255 [7.71] ('main steps in the interpretation process').

147 Johan Steyn, 'The Intractable Problem of the Interpretation of Legal Texts' (2003) 25(1) *Sydney Law Review* 5, 8.

148 Felix Frankfurter, 'Some Reflections on the Reading of Statutes' (1947) 47(4) *Columbia Law Review* 527, 527–8.

149 Oliver Jones, *Bennion on Statutory Interpretation: A Code* (LexisNexis, 6th ed, 2013) 413.

> The second step is to develop an interpretation of the doubtful language that effectively clarifies whether the legislation applies and leads to the preferred result. Such an interpretation usually takes the form of a paraphrase or definition, or in some cases a set of criteria that operates as a legal test. ... Coming up with an effective definition, paraphrase or set of criteria is perhaps the most challenging and important task in interpretation. It is here that the skill and imagination of counsel can make a real difference.[150]

(c) Constructions are not applications

A construction is a party's attempt to clarify the law in a way that suits their interests. Like statute law for the most part, a construction is general and (if accepted by a court) applies to all persons affected by the statute. In contrast, an application of the law (as interpreted) to the facts matches the actual facts to the preferred construction and arrives at the legal position of the parties in dispute.

Footscray City College v Ruzicka,[151] presented in **Example 9.4**, is illustrative. The case concerned the meaning of s 50(2A) of the *Accident Compensation Act 1985* (Vic). Counsel for the respondent worker argued that 's 50(2A) constitutes a code in respect of all s 98/98A claims, such that the court is required to make costs orders as prescribed by paras (a)–(c), but otherwise it has no power to make any costs order on such an application'.[152] The opposing construction was that s 50(2A) was not a code; rather, in the words of Chernov JA who gave the leading judgment, 'the opening words of [the subsection] do no more than provide a description of the proceeding in respect of which the court is compelled to award costs in accordance with one of the succeeding paragraphs'.[153] Though each construction is general, they present a constructional choice; the facts of the case are not matched to arrive at the outcome for the parties until the preferred construction is chosen.

(d) Constructions are formulated to resolve a dispute

Constructions are formulated to resolve a dispute over the meaning of a provision, and to go no further. As Gageler J has stated extracurially:

> [A] court is justified and obliged authoritatively to determine the meaning of a statutory text only so far as the attribution of meaning to the text is necessary to enable that court to discern the content of the law that must be applied to determine the rights of the parties who are in dispute in the individual case.[154]

Therefore, if a party's construction would make an implication in a statute, the other side's construction may simply be to reject the implication.[155] If the court takes the latter view,[156] the court will not have determined the meaning of the legislation except to the extent of rejecting a proposed implication.

150 Ruth Sullivan, 'Statutory Interpretation in a New Nutshell' (2003) 82(1) *Canadian Bar Review* 51, 67.

151 (2007) 16 VR 498.

152 Ibid 500 [6].

153 Ibid 504 [14].

154 Stephen Gageler, 'Common Law Statutes and Judicial Legislation: Statutory Interpretation as a Common Law Process' (2011) 37(1) *Monash University Law Review* 1, 3.

155 As occurred in *ZD v Secretary to the Department of Health and Human Services* [2017] VSC 806, [56] (Osborn JA).

156 As occurred in ibid [82].

Of course, a court may offer obiter views on the persuasiveness of arguments addressing an interpretative issue that is not necessary for the court to resolve.[157]

(e) Constructions always involve the interpreter employing words that are not in the text in question

In formulating a construction an interpreter must employ words that are not in the provision in question. Otherwise, no clarification of the words in question could be effected. This point was made by the Full Federal Court:

> The construction issue in this appeal is not about the meaning of an individual word in a statute, nor even about the meaning of a phrase. It is about the scope and operation of an entire provision. In determining the scope and operation of the entire provision, *it will be necessary to express or describe how the provision operates by using language other than that which appears in the statute.*[158]

For example, in *Footscray City College v Ruzicka*[159] (**Example 9.4**) the respondent introduced the notion of a 'code', while the opposing construction ultimately accepted by the Court used the language of 'description of the proceeding'.

(f) To formulate a construction a number of methods can assist

Three methods have been suggested.[160] The first method is based on a practitioner's duty to act in the client's interests to the best of their ability (subject to the overriding duty to the Court).[161] The method leverages the outcome that the client wants or would want. Working backwards from that outcome, the interpreter intuits a construction that would likely deliver that outcome. A law student given a hypothetical can also use this method, albeit with a hypothetical client. A weakness of this method is that it has a superficial attractiveness. A construction proffered by counsel that promotes the client's interests, but that is without interpretative support, will not be helpful.

Second, an interpreter may draw on dicta in earlier cases on the exact same legislation, or on holdings on similar legislation. But while earlier holdings would be likely to be considered, a court may have to start afresh if it identifies problems in the earlier view.[162]

Third, the interpreter may, based on the indications, formulate the constructions inductively. A court may also use this method if dissatisfied with the constructions of counsel for both parties.[163] Here the interpreter begins by asking 'where' the indications of meaning point to. The interpreter is then called upon to formulate a construction that would support such indications. This occurred in *Australian Broadcasting Tribunal v Bond*.[164] In that case the word in doubt was 'decision' in the *Administrative Decisions (Judicial Review) Act 1977* (Cth). Mason CJ began by

157 See, eg, *ABC Developmental Learning Centres Pty Ltd v Secretary, Department of Human Services* (2007) 15 VR 489, 495–6 [33]–[41] (Hollingworth J).

158 *BGM16 v Minister for Immigration and Border Protection* (2017) 252 FCR 97, 106 [51] (Mortimer and Wigney JJ) (emphasis added).

159 (2007) 16 VR 496.

160 The following draws upon Jeffrey Barnes, 'Is There an Overall Method to Interpreting Legislation?' in Jeffrey Barnes (ed), *The Coherence of Statutory Interpretation* (Federation Press, 2019) 78, 85.

161 Alex Chernov, 'The Lawyer and Morality' (1991) 18(1) *Brief* 6, 6, 7.

162 As occurred in *Collett v Repatriation Commission* (2009) 178 FCR 39, 45–6 [23] (Logan J).

163 On a court's independence from the parties (more than mere selectors from rival views), see **[5.3]**.

164 (1990) 170 CLR 321.

noting wider constructions: '[I]n the context of judicial or administrative proceedings it ordinarily refers to an announced or published ruling or adjudication . . . or, more narrowly, a determination effectively resolving an actual substantive issue.'[165] His Honour then showed how 'other considerations point to the word having a relatively limited field of operation'.[166] These included various textual indications: the immediate context, examples of 'decision', a provision apparently extending the concept of 'decision', and separate provision for the review of 'conduct'. After considering contextual indications (including adverse consequences of the wider constructions) he formulated the construction to which the latter set of indications pointed:

> [The] answer is that a reviewable 'decision' is one for which provision is made by or under a statute. That will generally, but not always, entail a decision which is final or operative and determinative, at least in a practical sense, of the issue of fact falling for consideration.[167]

(g) **Constructions are related to the text**

Interpretation by a court must be text-based.[168] The scope of this requirement was discussed in an earlier chapter.[169] Of course, the same requirement applies to a party's construction. If a party's construction 'cannot be reconciled with the language that the Parliament has enacted', the construction cannot be preferred.[170]

(h) **Formulating a construction is an exercise in legal drafting, and the form of a construction affects its weight as an interpretative consideration**

Speaking generally, formulating a construction should be seen as an exercise in legal drafting.[171] Legal drafting is different to other forms of legal writing, such as arguments in a written submission to a court by a barrister and essay writing in academic journals. A drafter needs to be aware of the function of legal drafting:

> Legal drafting is legal thinking made visible. This visible legal thinking is to precipitate legal rights, duties, privileges and functions in definitive form.[172]

A construction as formulated by a party to a dispute should be seen as a form of drafting because, if accepted by a court, it will precipitate legal rights in that form. It will be held to be implied in, or a justifiable gloss on, the statute. Formulating a construction should be seen as an extension of legislative drafting engaged in by parliamentary counsel.[173]

---

165 Ibid 335.

166 Ibid 336.

167 Ibid 337.

168 *Federal Commissioner of Taxation v Consolidated Media Holdings Ltd* (2012) 250 CLR 503, 519 [39] (the Court) (footnote omitted).

169 Chapter 6. See also chapter 3.

170 *Taylor v The Owners – Strata Plan 11564* (2014) 253 CLR 531, 550 [41] (French CJ, Crennan and Bell JJ). See generally **[3.3]**.

171 Several articles on teaching statutory interpretation recognise the importance of drafting. See, eg, Jacinta Dharmananda and Patricia Lane, 'Teaching Statutory Interpretation in Australia: What's Next?' (2018) 39(1) *Statute Law Review* 27, 38; Patricia Lane, 'Colloquium on Teaching Legal Interpretation: A Report' (2013) 87(9) *Australian Law Journal* 575, 577; Oliver Jones, 'Statutory Interpretation: The Case for a Core Subject' (2007) 5(2) *Journal of Commonwealth Law and Legal Education* 85, 95.

172 Robert C Dick, *Legal Drafting in Plain Language* (Carswell, 3rd ed, 1995) 5.

173 See chapter 10.

Drafting of constructions is therefore a critical skill for interpreters to foster and develop. Sullivan's advice on how to formulate and present a construction is sound: 'the formulation should be as precise and concise as possible and should be set out as the initial claim in the argument: "In this provision, properly understood, the words in dispute mean . . ."'.[174]

The way a construction is formulated is also of interpretative interest. A court will consider the effect the formulation would have in practice as part of the bundle of interpretative factors that are weighed in order to determine which is the preferable construction. To give an example, s 300 of the *Crimes Act 1900* (ACT) states, in part:

> ***serious offence*** means –
>
> (a) an offence *involving* actual or threatened violence and punishable by imprisonment for longer than 12 months; . . .[175]

The interpretative question in *R v Chute (No 11)*[176] related to 'involving' and was whether it was enough that the violence be closely connected with the offence, or whether the violence must form part of the conduct which constituted the offence. In preferring the latter construction the Court considered the form and operation of the alternative constructions:

> Ultimately, the issue turns on what is meant by 'involving'. . . . In my view, the latter interpretation is preferable because:
>
> . . .
>
> (b) it provides a clearer criterion for the application of the definition . . .[177]

In another case a 'lack of precision' attending a construction was one of the grounds for not preferring it.[178]

Evaluating interpretative arguments

[9.9] Interpretative arguments are evaluated using tools of critical thinking[179]

An interpreter determines the preferable construction by having regard to which construction, on balance, the interpretative factors favour or point to.[180] But in order to do this the interpreter needs to have evaluated each interpretative argument – that is, they need to have determined the level of 'support' such argument affords a particular construction.[181] The level of support is also known as 'weight'.[182]

---

174 Ruth Sullivan, 'Statutory Interpretation in a New Nutshell' (2003) 82(1) *Canadian Bar Review* 51, 67.

175 Emphasis added.

176 [2019] ACTSC 91.

177 Ibid [18] (Mossop J).

178 *DPP v Moreno* (2018) 57 VR 1, 26 [87] (Daly AsJ).

179 Some material in this section is drawn from Jeffrey Barnes, 'Is There an Overall Method to Interpreting Legislation?' in Jeffrey Barnes (ed), *The Coherence of Statutory Interpretation* (Federation Press, 2019) 78, 85–6.

180 See **[9.10]** below.

181 *Park v The Queen* (2021) 395 ALR 193, 199 [26] (the Court).

182 *AJS v The Queen* (2007) 235 CLR 505, 512 [14] (Gleeson CJ, Hayne, Heydon and Crennan JJ).

The general criteria by which legal arguments are evaluated are 'validity ... cogency and ... appropriateness'.[183] Validity in this context means 'permissible, but not necessarily conclusive'.[184] Cogency goes to weight or persuasiveness.[185] And appropriateness has regard to conventions of style in a particular context.[186]

An interpretative argument is *valid* if it is derived from an interpretative criterion recognised by law.[187]

The *cogency* of an argument is not determined in the abstract.[188] Rather, as Lord Sales has written:

> It is impossible to specify in abstract terms what weight each of these ingredients should be given, both in relation to the text and as between themselves. They each reflect different values which have varying and different force depending on the particular context.[189]

When presented with an interpretative argument a judge objectively evaluates it. This process is referred to as 'critical thinking'.[190] In legal and non-legal fields critical thinking is an essential tool of intellectual inquiry,[191] without which a person does not possess full understanding of a discipline.[192] '[C]ritical thinking has both general and topic-specific components',[193] meaning that, while to some extent specific to law, critical thinking supplies 'a common core of basic principles that apply in most fields (though not every principle applies in every field)'.[194] Critical thinking has been defined as 'disciplined, self-directed thinking which exemplifies ... clarity, precision, accuracy, relevance, consistency, and logicalness'.[195] Critical thinking is used in

183 William Twining and David Miers, *How to Do Things with Rules: A Primer of Interpretation* (Cambridge University Press, 5th ed, 2010) 363.

184 Ibid 359.

185 Ibid 360.

186 Ibid.

187 See **[1.2]** and chapter 33.

188 See **[9.3]**.

189 Lord Justice Sales, 'Modern Statutory Interpretation' (2017) 38(2) *Statute Law Review* 125, 129–30.

190 William Twining and David Miers, *How to Do Things with Rules: A Primer of Interpretation* (Cambridge University Press, 5th ed, 2010) 344.

191 Peter A Facione, *Critical Thinking: A Statement of Expert Consensus for Purposes of Educational Assessment and Instruction: Executive Summary: The Delphi Report* (California Academic Press, 1990) 2.

192 Robert H Ennis, 'The Degree to Which Critical Thinking Is Subject Specific: Clarification and Needed Research' in Stephen P Norris (ed), *The Generalizability of Critical Thinking: Multiple Perspectives on an Educational Ideal* (Teachers College Press, 1992) 21, 30.

193 Robert H Ennis, 'A Taxonomy of Critical Thinking Dispositions and Abilities' in Joan Boykoff Baron and Robert J Sternberg (eds), *Teaching Thinking Skills: Theory and Practice* (W H Freeman & Co, 1987) 9, 21.

194 Robert H Ennis, 'The Degree to Which Critical Thinking is Subject Specific: Clarification and Needed Research' in Stephen P Norris (ed), *The Generalizability of Critical Thinking: Multiple Perspectives on an Educational Ideal* (Teachers College Press, 1992) 21, 31.

195 Robert Cogan, 'Preface' in *Critical Thinking: Step by Step* (University Press of America, 1998), quoting Richard Paul, *Critical Thinking: What Every Person Needs to Survive in a Rapidly Changing* World (Center for Critical Thinking and Moral Critique, Sonoma State University, 1990) 51. Other definitions exist: see, eg, Mark Mason, 'Critical Thinking and Learning' (2007) 39(4) *Educational Philosophy and Theory* 339, 344.

interpretation to analyse arguments, identify and handle irrelevance, seek evidence and counter-evidence, make value judgements, and to weigh, balance, and ultimately decide.[196]

Critical thinking is evident in the reasoning of the High Court[197] and other courts.

Example 9.8 *ZD v Secretary to the Department of Health and Human Services*[198]

The Children's Court made an interim accommodation order ('IAO') providing for out-of-home care by foster parents in respect of three young children. The mother of the children appealed a condition of the order. The order was purportedly made under s 263(7) of the *Children, Youth and Families Act 2005* (Vic) ('the Act'), which read:

> An interim accommodation order may include any conditions that the Court or bail justice considers should be included in the best interests of the child.

The condition provided that each child may be immunised in accordance with an approved immunisation program.

The mother's construction of the provision in question was that the power did not extend to making decisions that have significant long-term consequences for the child. The Secretary's opposing construction was that no such implication should be made. The Court agreed with the Secretary's contention[199] and dismissed the appeal.

Counsel for the mother put four main arguments to the Court, following which the Court evaluated their agency. The first argument was that the word 'interim' in the provision indicated that the purpose of an IAO was to make interim provision only for the welfare of a child – that is, the order had short-term consequences only.[200] The Court found this argument lacked cogency. The Act did not provide a time limit for an IAO.[201] Also, the fact that the order was preliminary in nature 'does not logically of itself mean that a requirement to resolve issues with long-term consequence may not arise during its currency'.[202] The Court also used common sense and consequentialist reasoning in evaluating the argument. The Court instanced children suffering from severe chronic illnesses, saying: 'It cannot sensibly be the intention of the legislation that the magistrate's power to impose conditions with respect to the safe accommodation of a child suffering from such conditions is limited by the application of the suggested criterion.'[203]

The second argument put by the mother was that, read as a whole, the Act recognises that decisions that have significant long-term consequences for the child require the consent of the

196 Robert H Ennis, 'A Taxonomy of Critical Thinking Dispositions and Abilities' in Joan Boykoff Baron and Robert J Sternberg (eds), *Teaching Thinking Skills: Theory and Practice* (W H Freeman & Co, 1987) 9, 12–15.

197 See Jeffrey Barnes, 'Contextualism: "The Modern Approach to Statutory Interpretation"' (2018) 41(4) *University of New South Wales Law Journal* 1083, 1094–7. The case that is analysed is *Mansfield v The Queen* (2012) 247 CLR 86.

198 [2017] VSC 806.

199 Ibid [82] (Osborn JA).

200 Ibid [55], [86].

201 Ibid [85].

202 Ibid [84].

203 Ibid [81].

children's parents.[204] This argument was also found to lack cogency. While a number of provisions in the Act fettered the Secretary's powers in relation to a 'major long-term issue', no such fetters were placed on the Children's Court.[205] The Act prioritised the best interests of the child,[206] and consideration of the parents' position was specifically provided for.[207] In short, the mother's argument lacked evidence from the Act.

The third argument of the mother was that 'the Legislature cannot have intended that the making of an IAO would impact on parental responsibility with respect to major long-term issues'. But this argument went against the evidence of the background law as well as the Act. At common law the overriding consideration of the child's best interests limited parental power to control decisions with respect to the appropriateness of medical procedures.[208] And the Court was the repository of the parens patriae power to make orders with respect to medical treatment in the best interests of a child and contrary to the wishes of a parent.[209]

Finally, counsel for the mother attempted to invoke the *Charter of Human Rights and Responsibilities Act 2006* (Vic). Section 17(1) of the Charter stated: 'Families are the fundamental group unit of society and are entitled to be protected by society and the State.' The Court found that this argument lacked relevance because the provision of the Act in question was 'not capable of more than one interpretation'.[210]

In summary, in evaluating the cogency of the arguments put by the mother, the Court used a variety of critical thinking tools: the evidence or support from the Act, logic and common sense, the evidence of a long history in the background law, and relevance in the circumstances.

Determining the preferable construction

An interpreter determines the preferable construction by having regard to which construction, on balance, the interpretative factors favour or point to [9.10]

After each argument has been evaluated as indicated (**[9.9]**), the interpreter weighs the arguments that favour one construction or the other. The preferable construction is the construction that, on balance, the interpretative factors favour or that command the greater 'weight' overall.[211] A leading authority is *Sovar v Henry Lane Pty Ltd*:[212]

> [T]he question ... here is ... one of statutory interpretation. ... The legitimate endeavour of the courts is to determine what inference really arises, *on a balance of considerations*, from the nature, scope and terms of the statute, including the nature of the evil against

204 Ibid [55], [68].

205 Ibid [72]–[73].

206 Ibid [74]–[75].

207 Ibid [77].

208 Ibid [78].

209 Ibid [79].

210 Ibid [106].

211 Oliver Jones, *Bennion on Statutory Interpretation: A Code* (LexisNexis, 6th ed, 2013) 486. See, eg, *Commissioner of Taxation (Cth) v Australian Building Systems Pty Ltd (in Liq)* (2015) 257 CLR 544, 564–5 [42] (French CJ and Kiefel J).

212 (1967) 116 CLR 397.

> which it is directed, the nature of the conduct prescribed, the pre-existing state of the law, and, generally, the whole range of circumstances relevant upon a question of statutory interpretation ...[213]

Another metaphor used in determining the preferable construction is to examine which construction the indications of meaning 'point' more to. An example is *Victims Compensation Fund Corporation v Brown*,[214] where Heydon J stated: '[I]t can be said that the Act as a whole, and its background, point more to a conjunctive construction than a disjunctive construction.'[215]

Presenting a legal opinion or reasons for judgment

[9.11] Presenting a legal opinion or reasons for judgment benefits from a well-structured, plain English approach

A well-thought-out legal opinion or reasons for judgment will suffer greatly if it is not presented well. This section gives some guidance in presenting it effectively. Worked examples that accompany this work illustrate the approach.

As Martin Cutts explains in *The Oxford Guide to Plain English*, a writer ought to aim for 'a reader-centred structure'. The author defines it as a structure organised 'so that readers can grasp the important information early and navigate through the document easily'.[216]

Three principles stand out as helping to achieve a reader-centred structure in the present context. These principles are for general guidance and may not apply in certain circumstances. In employment you may be required to follow a particular format. The same applies to a law student.

First, state the question you have to answer at the outset.[217] If you have been given a task in the form of an instruction, such as 'Advise Joan as to what are her rights, if any, in relation to her Centrelink claim', convert it into a question, such as 'What are Joan's rights in relation to her Centrelink claim?'.[218] Opening with the question the client wants answered brings a number of benefits. 'Questions tend to provoke interest in readers by bringing them into the action.'[219] Questions spice up the communication. They 'convert dull, plodding label-headings into verb-rich information'.[220] The question also 'helps your reader know what to expect'.[221] This is

213 Ibid 405 (Kitto J, Owen J agreeing at 417) (emphasis added). This passage was approved in *Singh v Commonwealth* (2004) 222 CLR 322, 336 [19] (Gleeson CJ) and *Stuart v Kirkland-Veenstra* (2009) 237 CLR 215, 253 [110] (Gummow, Hayne and Heydon JJ), and followed in *H v Minister for Immigration and Citizenship* (2010) 188 FCR 393, 407 [51] (the Court).

214 (2003) 201 ALR 260.

215 Ibid 267 [28] (Heydon J, McHugh ACJ agreeing at 261 [1], Gummow J agreeing at 261 [2], Kirby J agreeing at 261 [3], Hayne J agreeing at 261 [4]). See also *Park v The Queen* (2021) 395 ALR 193: 'contextual considerations point decisively away from [the appellant's] interpretation' (at 197 [15] (the Court)).

216 Martin Cutts, *Oxford Guide to Plain English* (Oxford University Press, 4th ed, 2013) 165.

217 As advocated by Alan L Dworsky, *The Little Book on Legal Writing* (FB Rothman, 2nd ed, 1992) 102.

218 However, a law student completing an examination paper need not open with the question if the question is stated on the examination paper and there is no instruction to start by addressing the question.

219 Martin Cutts, *Oxford Guide to Plain English* (Oxford University Press, 4th ed, 2013) 170.

220 Ibid.

221 SI Strong, *How to Write Law Essays and Exams* (Oxford University Press, 3rd ed, 2010) 180.

because the question describes 'the aim of your written work' and it 'defines the scope of the following discussion'.[222] And by giving the question you are more likely to stay focused on the task at hand. In advice to law students, Strong says, like a professional, 'answer only the question asked'.[223]

Second, the answer (to the question presented) should be given at or near *the beginning* of your written work, rather than at the end.[224] This brings a number of benefits relating to ease of use, recall and comprehension.[225] It ensures that the task you have been set is answered. By placing the answer *next* to the question presented, it ensures a degree of rigour, because you are more likely to respond directly to the question that is asked. Also, the answer is the main information the client wants; and it is desired 'at once'.[226] Only then can the client relax and turn their attention to what seems to them secondary matters of detail.[227] In addition, the reader is better placed to follow your reasoning. Knowing the answer at the outset makes it easier for the reader to follow the advice 'because it provide[s] a context in which to make sense of the facts and information the lawyer-writer [is] presenting in the earlier sections'.[228] As Cutts succinctly says: 'Then readers can see, right from the start, exactly what you're getting at.'[229]

Third, the discussion phase should be tailored to the nature of statutory interpretation. Not all legal problems are the same. An opinion writer should not follow a model premised on rule *application* such as IRAC ('Issue, Rule, Application, Conclusion').[230]

It is helpful, after ascertaining the unit of inquiry or words in doubt, to juxtapose the opposing constructions of the unit of inquiry at the outset of the discussion. Judges often helpfully do this in their reasons for judgment.[231] Then set out the arguments for the construction that will *not* be preferred. As they are followed by the arguments for the preferred construction, this structure will allow you to explain why the former set of arguments are not preferred. Alternatively, a separate evaluation phase could be employed. In setting out the

---

222 Ibid.

223 Ibid 43.

224 As advocated for practitioners in Inns of Court School of Law, *Opinion Writing* (Blackstone Press, 1996) 80, 82.

225 For empirical support, see Jeffrey Barnes, 'Statutory Objects Provisions: How Cogent is the Research and Commentary?' (2013) 34(1) *Statute Law Review* 12, 15–17 (summaries), 23–4 (topic specifiers); Robert Eagleson, 'Drafting Matters – Letters of Advice' (2007) 58 *Clarity* 23.

226 Robert Eagleson, 'Drafting Matters – Letters of Advice' (2007) 58 *Clarity* 23, 24, 25.

227 Ibid 25.

228 Ibid 27.

229 Martin Cutts, *Oxford Guide to Plain English* (Oxford University Press, 4th ed, 2013) 165.

230 It also places the conclusion at the end instead of at the start.

231 See, eg, *Independent Commission Against Corruption v Cunneen* (2015) 256 CLR 1, 10 [2] (French CJ, Hayne, Kiefel and Nettle JJ); *BGM16 v Minister for Immigration and Border Protection* (2017) 252 FCR 97, 99–100 [13] (Mortimer and Wigney JJ); *Australian Mines and Metals Association Inc v Construction, Forestry, Maritime, Mining and Energy Union* (2018) 268 FCR 128, 132 [4]–[5] (the Court); *Scott-Mackenzie v Bail* (2017) 16 ASTLR 449 [35] (the Court).

arguments for each construction, it is sensible to start with arguments from the provision (as the High Court suggests[232]) and spiral out to the wider context, one stage at a time.[233] The authority of each argument will be clearer if the interpretative criterion from which the interpretative argument is derived is set out.[234] And the interpretative discussion should conclude with the preferred construction and the relationship it has with the text.[235]

232 See **[6.5]** and chapter 15.

233 This is the approach advocated by Glazebrook J and discussed above at **[9.7]**. See also Jeffrey Barnes, 'Is There an Overall Method to Interpreting Legislation?' in Jeffrey Barnes (ed), *The Coherence of Statutory Interpretation* (Federation Press, 2019) 78, 91–2.

234 Ibid 90–1.

235 Ibid 92–4. The relationship is either an implication or a justifiable gloss: see above **[9.8]**, citing *BGM16 v Minister for Immigration and Border Protection* (2017) 252 FCR 97, 106 [51] (Mortimer and Wigney JJ).

PART III

WORKING WITH LEGISLATION: BROADER SKILLS AND KNOWLEDGE

A competent interpreter needs to have more than a knowledge of basic principles (Parts I and II) and interpretative approaches (Parts IV–VIII). An interpreter needs a broader knowledge about legislation. Part III is concerned with equipping the reader in this regard. Specifically, the focus of Part III is on the development, drafting, enactment and commencement of legislation and on how, through that process, sources of doubt can emerge.

The Part begins with chapter 10 (*Legislative Drafting*). This chapter explains the mechanics of legislative drafting, who does it, the styles of drafting adopted, and the value that users of legislation can derive from knowledge of the drafting process.

Chapter 11 (*Enactment Procedure*) examines who makes Acts of Parliament in Australia and the relevant procedures. The procedures followed in the Commonwealth Parliament are described in detail. There is discussion of how Bills and Acts may be classified and of the rights and privileges enjoyed by Parliaments in going about their law-making business. The chapter ends with an explanation of who has the right to print and publish Acts across Australia.

While an Act may come into operation on the day it is passed by Parliament, usually it does not. Chapter 12 (*Commencement*) explains how Acts are brought into operation, their status before then and the circumstances in which powers contained within them may be exercised pre-commencement.

Chapter 13 (*Structure and Components of an Act*) examines the structure of Acts, the various components that make up an Act (some mandatory and others optional) and the status of those components – that is, whether or not they are treated as part of the Act.

Chapter 14 (*Problem Analysis: Sources of Doubt*) ends the Part with an analysis of the potential root sources or causes of doubt as to the meaning or effect of a law. The origin of a doubt may be traced to something in the way in which a law was developed, drafted or made, or it may arise out of a subsequent event or development. Whatever the cause, being able to identify sources of doubt provides a launching pad for interpretative arguments. It also promotes greater awareness, for those involved in the process of developing laws, of potential sources of doubt.

LEGISLATIVE DRAFTING 10

Overview

Australia has nine legislatures[1] that between them produce a vast mass of written law each year.[2] [10.1]
This chapter focuses on legislative drafting, on how legislative drafting work is carried out within government and on the specialist lawyers who perform that work for government. In presenting a draft to their instructors in response to a set of drafting instructions, these lawyers provide legal advice that the draft is consistent with those instructions and gives legal effect to them. The style of drafting used by these lawyers in their work has evolved over time, with a plain language style now preferred. While there is a common commitment to plain language drafting, particular drafting practices and techniques vary from jurisdiction to jurisdiction within Australia, presenting a challenge to the enactment of uniform legislation. Finally, it is noted that clear drafting limits the need for canons of construction on or presumptions about legislative intent to be applied in interpreting legislative text.

The drafting process

Drafting of legislation is a function of executive government [10.2]

An Act begins life as a Bill. A Bill is a proposed law that is to be considered by Parliament.[3] While very occasionally a Bill proposed by an individual parliamentarian may pass into law, the vast majority of Acts result from Bills put before Parliament by a Minister on behalf of the government. These Bills are usually drafted by government lawyers known as parliamentary counsel or (in jurisdictions with a legislature that is not a Parliament) legislative counsel.[4] These lawyers specialise in the drafting of legislation. Although not the source of the policy ideas embedded in legislation, and occasionally required to reproduce a form of wording for a particular concept that has been agreed during policy making, these lawyers can properly be regarded as being effectively the authors of legislation.[5] The role of parliamentary counsel as authors of legislation is not always understood. In *Attorney-General (NSW) v Butterworth & Co (Australia) Ltd*[6] Long Innes CJ

1 The Parliament of the Commonwealth of Australia, the Parliaments of each of the six states and the legislatures of the Australian Capital Territory and the Northern Territory.

2 In 2020 there were 502 Acts passed in Australia and close to 5,000 items of delegated legislation of different kinds made.

3 For convenience, the term 'Parliament' is used in this chapter to refer to all Australian legislatures.

4 For convenience, the term 'parliamentary counsel' is used in this chapter to refer to all such lawyers.

5 Their work may, of course, be edited by others during a Bill's passage through Parliament.

6 (1938) 38 SR (NSW) 195, 259.

in Eq observed that, like any piece of writing, a Bill must have an author but that identifying its author may be as difficult as ascertaining the paternity of a child.

In Australia, Bills proposed by the executive government of any of the nine jurisdictions emerge from a highly regulated process conducted within government.[7] Legislative proposals are initially developed within government departments. Sources of these proposals include:

- the governing party's platform put forward at an election;
- work done by a specialist body such as a law reform commission or other advisory body;
- experience gained in administering an area of public policy; and
- an event that led to a public campaign for a change to the law on a particular matter.

Whatever the source, detailed policy development work on the proposal is done by officials within one or more government departments who then set about preparing instructions for the drafting of a Bill to give effect to the proposal. Broad consultation across government will occur and the policy development work may also involve confidential consultations with affected entities outside government.

Drafting instructions should cover all aspects of the legislative proposal. This includes:

- a statement about its background and what is intended to be achieved by it;
- details of any proposed administrative arrangements, including whether a new entity is to be created, or the functions of an existing entity expanded, for the purpose of administering the proposed new law;
- information on whether new staff are required to be employed and, if so, how;
- particulars of any new offences to be created;
- an explanation of the implementation path proposed for the new law, including any proposed staged commencement arrangements and tailored transitional arrangements; and
- details of what is to be left to be covered by delegated legislation to be made under the proposed new law.[8]

Well-thought-through policy is the foundation of good legislation. Sound policy development at the initial stage means policymakers can avoid having to make policy shifts during drafting that cannot then comfortably be fitted by parliamentary counsel into the scheme of the Bill within the time available.

Parliamentary counsel is usually consulted about the form and content of the drafting instructions. It is they who will have the task of drafting a Bill based on those instructions so their feedback on their adequacy for the purpose is invaluable. It will be for parliamentary counsel to take the legislative policy detailed in those instructions and shape it into a Bill that is fit to be enacted by Parliament.

---

7 For information on this process within particular jurisdictions see Office of Parliamentary Counsel, *OPC's Drafting Services: A Guide for Clients* (Australian Government, 2016); General Counsel for the New South Wales Department of Premier and Cabinet, *Ministerial Handbook* (New South Wales Department of Premier and Cabinet, 2011); Office of the Chief Parliamentary Counsel, *The Legislative Process* (Victorian Government, June 2020); Queensland Department of the Premier and Cabinet, *The Queensland Legislation Handbook* (Queensland Government, 6th ed, 2019); Office of Parliamentary Counsel, *Manual for the Preparation of Bills* (Tasmanian Government, 2011); ACT Parliamentary Counsel's Office, *Developing Legislation and Working with PCO* (ACT Government, 2020). See also chapter 11.

8 A useful checklist for drafting instructions is set out at Office of Parliamentary Counsel, *OPC's Drafting Services: A Guide for Clients* (Australian Government, 2016) para 117.

Ultimately the responsible Minister will take a submission[9] to Cabinet (or to a legislation committee of Cabinet, as applicable) seeking approval to proceed with the proposal. If approval is given, the formal drafting work begins.

During its preparation a Bill may go through multiple drafts and parliamentary counsel may schedule many rounds of detailed discussion with departmental instructing officers. Parliamentary counsel relies on the instructing officers to answer their detailed questions arising out of their analysis of the policy, explain technical issues and generally help them understand the background to the proposed new law and the context in which it is to operate. Parliamentary counsel also expects that each draft will be carefully reviewed by the instructing officers and further instructions issued to address any perceived deficiencies in it.

The role of parliamentary counsel extends beyond coming up with words that translate policy ideas into legislation and placing them within a coherent structure. They are adept at policy analysis, such a critical part of constructing a workable legislative scheme. Through experience gained over many years, they are aware of what a legislative scheme needs to cover and will seek further instructions from policy officers to cover identified gaps in the policy outlined in the drafting instructions. They are skilled advisers with deep knowledge of legislative policy and practice as well as parliamentary procedure. They are familiar with the approaches to statutory interpretation taken by the courts.[10] They are also experts on the local statute book (the body of enacted laws in force in the jurisdiction) and know how best to work the new piece of drafting into that book so that it can operate effectively and in harmony with essential elements of the administrative and legal framework of the jurisdiction. Parliamentary counsel are concerned about the integrity of the statute book. They are sometimes referred to as its guardians or keepers.[11] As such they seek to ensure that its overall coherence is not in any way impaired by new additions to it. But fundamentally they are 'counsel' in the true sense of the word, advising their instructors on a broad range of legal and other issues relating to Bills.

Following back-and-forth communications between parliamentary counsel and instructing officers, ultimately a point is reached when they both are satisfied that the Bill as drafted gives effect to the drafting instructions. Clearly, not all Bills are of the same complexity or length and therefore the time required for their drafting varies. At the same time governments have a legislative agenda that they wish to pursue in accordance with an agreed timeline. It is a common experience of parliamentary counsel that they would like to have more time to perfect the drafting of their Bills. However, they have no option but to endeavour to produce the best draft possible within the time available.[12]

---

9 Other than for the purpose of obtaining Commonwealth government policy approval, the drafting instructions will usually be attached to the submission. For the Commonwealth government process, see Department of Prime Minister and Cabinet, *Legislation Handbook* (Australian Government, 2017).

10 In *Lacey v A-G (Qld)* (2011) 242 CLR 573, French CJ, Gummow, Hayne, Crennan, Kiefel and Bell JJ referred in their joint judgment to 'the rules of construction, common law and statutory . . . which are known to parliamentary drafters and the courts': at 592 [43]. In *Ealing London Borough Council v Race Relations Board* [1972] AC 342, Lord Simon referred to the rules of construction as being 'part of that common code of juristic communication by which the draftsman signals legislative intention': at 361.

11 See Ronan Cormacain, 'Legislation, Legislative Drafting and the Rule of Law' (2017) 5(2) *The Theory and Practice of Legislation* 115, 115, 132–3.

12 See Christopher Jenkins, 'The Language of Legislation' [1997] (December) *The Loophole: Journal of the Commonwealth Association of Legislative Counsel* 9–11. Jenkins writes: 'Almost all legislation is produced under pressure of time . . . In these circumstances the first priority has to be to produce in time a draft which achieve [sic] the desired policy. The resulting provisions will not necessarily be in the form which would be most helpful to the reader' (at 10).

With the drafting of the Bill finalised, approval for its introduction into Parliament may be sought from Cabinet, or a Cabinet committee, as applicable. As part of this approval process, a statement about the Bill's compatibility with human rights may need to be prepared.[13] It may also be necessary for a statement to be prepared examining the likely financial, environmental or other impact of the Bill. Responsibility for the preparation of such statements lies with departmental officials.

If approval is given for the Bill to proceed, it is then printed for Parliament and introduced on a date determined by the government. The date of introduction may depend on the priority given to the Bill. The government may have a large legislative agenda requiring that priorities for introduction into Parliament be allocated to the available Bills to better manage the parliamentary process.

As governments want, or need, to legislate on a wide range of matters, the work demand on parliamentary counsel offices is at times such that some legislative drafting work must be outsourced to consultants. Almost invariably, these consultants will be persons who have many years of legislative drafting experience gained from working within a parliamentary counsel office. However, ultimate control of the form and substance of a Bill being drafted by a consultant generally remains with the parliamentary counsel office. That office, in effect, settles the Bill and ensures that it accords with its drafting style.

The practice with respect to the drafting of delegated legislation varies across Australia.[14] In some jurisdictions such legislation is drafted by parliamentary counsel while in others it is drafted by departmental officials and settled by parliamentary counsel. For certain kinds of delegated legislation parliamentary counsel may be required to issue a certificate specifying whether the instrument as drafted is within the power conferred by the enabling Act and is in a proper form.[15] However, irrespective of who holds the pen, the actual drafting process is similar to that applying to Bills. Drafting instructions will have been prepared and one or more instructing officers appointed to work collaboratively with the drafter. Usually there is no need, however, for the draft instrument to be submitted to Cabinet for approval. This is unsurprising given that the instrument is being made in the exercise of a power of delegation contained in a previously approved Bill.

[10.3] Legislative drafting is an integral part of the law-making process

Without a Bill there is no Act. Acts emerge out of the deliberations of Parliament on a written legislative proposal put before it. The Bill may emerge in the same form in which it was introduced, or it may be amended during the parliamentary process, even extensively.[16] Policy compromises may have had to be reached to secure the Bill's passage through Parliament. Usually, parliamentary counsel are charged with the task of preparing amendments on the instructions of the government or, in some jurisdictions, by working directly on a confidential basis with individual members of Parliament or a non-government party. However, individual parliamentarians and non-government parties are at liberty to make whatever arrangements they choose

---

13 See *Human Rights Act 2019* (Qld); *Charter of Human Rights and Responsibilities Act 2006* (Vic); *Human Rights Act 2004* (ACT). The *Human Rights (Parliamentary Scrutiny) Act 2011* (Cth) s 8 requires that a statement of compatibility be prepared for each Bill and presented to each House of the Commonwealth Parliament.

14 Delegated legislation is legislation made by an entity under a power delegated to it by an Act. See chapter 43. For a description of the process in Victoria for the drafting of delegated legislation, including parliamentary counsel's requirements, see Office of the Chief Parliamentary Counsel of Victoria, *Notes for Guidance on the Preparation of Statutory Rules* (Victorian Government, 2017).

15 See, eg, *Subordinate Legislation Act 1994* (Vic) s 13.

16 See chapter 11.

for the drafting of their own proposed amendments. This may even include a member doing their own drafting or seeking the assistance of a parliamentary officer for this purpose.

Amendments need to be confined to what is strictly necessary to give effect to the policy change. It is not possible to rewrite the entire Bill, no matter how many or how major the amendments are, even if that is what parliamentary counsel would have done had such extensive policy shifts occurred during drafting and there was time to do it.

Delegated legislation also forms part of the legal framework of the jurisdiction. These instruments, like Bills, are products of a legislative drafting process. They are also usually subject to a form of scrutiny by Parliament or a specialist parliamentary committee and may be disallowed by a House of Parliament in whole or in part.[17]

Role of parliamentary counsel

Parliamentary counsel are non-political [10.4]

Just like other public servants, staff of parliamentary counsel offices are non-political. They are not driven by policy considerations. It is the relevant Minister who has responsibility for the policy reflected in a Bill. The aim of parliamentary counsel is to produce a legally sound and effective law. Importantly, however, they have regard to the other laws in force in the jurisdiction. They seek to ensure that the proposed new law will fit seamlessly with those laws and will be in a form that is compatible with, and is supported by, the jurisdiction's legal, financial and administrative framework, thus rendering it capable of being administered and enforced as a law.

The policy underlying the Bill, so long as it is coherent and well thought through, is not the particular concern of parliamentary counsel. They are technical experts focused solely on producing as good a product as is possible in the circumstances.

However, it may happen during drafting, or while reviewing draft drafting instructions at the pre-drafting stage, that parliamentary counsel may suggest to the departmental instructors a variation to the policy framework intended to enhance the workability of the scheme. It is up to the instructors whether to act on that suggestion and vary the drafting instructions accordingly.

A parliamentary counsel provides legal advice [10.5]

In *New South Wales v Betfair Pty Ltd*[18] a Full Court of the Federal Court of Australia observed that instructions to parliamentary counsel seeking the preparation of draft legislation were instructions to provide legal advice. The provision of draft legislation by parliamentary counsel in response to those instructions constitutes the provision of that legal advice. The Full Court stated:

> Parliamentary Counsel do not merely type or format the legislation. Parliamentary Counsel apply legal skill and knowledge to give written expression to the policy underlying the proposed legislation. Parliamentary Counsel would be expected, and perhaps under a duty, to advise upon the legality or effectiveness of the legislation being sought by the instructors. In the case of subordinate legislation, if regarded as beyond power, Parliamentary Counsel would presumably advise of this view. Similarly, if an Act of Parliament was considered unconstitutional, or inconsistent with another Act of Parliament, this is a matter Parliamentary Counsel would be expected to advise upon, even if the only express instruction was to draft the legislation.

---

17 See chapter 43.

18 (2009) 180 FCR 543.

> Where no problem of this kind arises, Parliamentary Counsel, in drafting the legislation and presenting the draft to the government agency, is in effect advising that the draft legislation is in accordance with the instructions given and gives legal effect to those instructions. The draft itself is not legal advice, but the communication in providing the draft legislation contains implicitly the advice of Parliamentary Counsel endorsing the draft legislation as being effective and valid.[19]

[10.6] Legislative drafting is both an art and a science

Over the years there has been much debate as to whether legislative drafting is an art or a science.[20] In reality, legislative drafting is both.

While a parliamentary counsel is a writer, they are not operating in the same free-form uninhibited world that, for example, a novelist or poet inhabits.[21] There are many fixed rules applying to their product. These include the numbering system to be used, the description to be applied to individual components, how provisions are to be formatted, and the need to include a long title and a short title as well as standard words of enactment. On top of that, the jurisdiction may have a drafting manual with which the parliamentary counsel is expected to comply. There are also common law and statutory rules of construction that parliamentary counsel must bear in mind.[22] Further, there is a dictionary of defined terms in the local Interpretation Act that must be considered.[23] The need for consistency with other laws in force in the jurisdiction is also a limiting factor on literary choices.

These are all objective matters of which a parliamentary counsel must have knowledge and consider in drafting. The parliamentary counsel acquires that knowledge through a mixture of study, training (both formal and on the job) and experience. Complying during drafting with the format rules and instructions in the local drafting manual promotes the predictability and accessibility of the law as it gives that written law a common look and feel.

There are many other skills that a parliamentary counsel must possess. These include subject-matter expertise, knowledge of constitutional and administrative law, familiarity with the overall statute book, awareness of government processes, particularly Cabinet processes affecting legislation, and a sound knowledge of parliamentary procedure.

It is the need to be on top of all these knowledge requirements and to draft compatibly with them that constitutes the science element of legislative drafting.

There is, however, a definite literary element to legislative drafting. Subject to the restraints referred to above, a parliamentary counsel has freedom over word choice (including the appropriate level of generality to adopt) and document structure. While the plain language approach

19 Ibid 549.

20 See, eg, Geoffrey Bowman, 'The Art of Legislative Drafting' (2005) 7(1–2) *European Journal of Law Reform* 3; Sandra C Markman, 'Legislative Drafting: Art, Science or Discipline?' [2011] (4) *The Loophole: Journal of the Commonwealth Association of Legislative Counsel* 5.

21 In her book *Bring Up The Bodies* (Fourth Estate, 2012) Hilary Mantel writes: 'A statute is written to entrap meaning, a poem to escape it' (at 414).

22 The Hon Michael Kirby AC CMG, a former High Court judge, observed: '[A] highly accomplished legislative drafter will necessarily perform the drafting function keeping in mind the approach that the courts are likely to adopt to elucidate the meaning of words used. Any other approach would be potentially self-defeating': see Michael Kirby, 'The Never-Ending Challenges of Drafting and Interpreting Statutes – A Meditation on the Career of John Finemore QC' (2012) 36(1) *Melbourne University Law Review* 140, 150.

23 See **[25.4]**.

now generally adopted by Australian drafting offices affects word choice to some degree,[24] there is still much scope for individual creativity.

An important part of the drafting process is conceptualising the overall structure of the Bill. Subject to any fixed rules applying within the jurisdiction as to the location of particular components,[25] parliamentary counsel will adopt a structure that appeals to them and that they believe will best assist the reader to understand the Bill.[26] Views on structure, and on the words to be chosen, will differ among parliamentary counsel. Given the same set of instructions, no two parliamentary counsel will come up with a Bill that is in exactly the same terms and adopts exactly the same structure.[27]

In *SAAP v Minister for Immigration and Multicultural and Indigenous Affairs*[28] Kirby J recognised the important role of parliamentary counsel in providing structure to a Bill:

> It is conventional for parliamentary counsel to arrange provisions of an Act of Parliament in an order which will appear logical to the mind of the administrator or other person called upon to apply the law and to the lawyer called upon to interpret it. However, in the nature of legislation, required, as it commonly is, to address multiple and unforeseeable circumstances, it is almost impossible to envisage, and provide for, every case to which the statute will apply. If a general logic in the presentation of statutory provisions is attained, that is as much as can usually be hoped for.[29]

The personal flair that a parliamentary counsel brings to implementing the policy underlying a legislative proposal arises out of their practice of the art of drafting. It represents the counsel's sense of how best to communicate the message. Like artists, the parliamentary counsel starts with a blank canvas.[30] The final product reflects their individual choice and sense of literary style.

There are, however, other limitations on a parliamentary counsel's literary choices. They cannot, for example, state the same thing within a Bill more than once to give it greater impact. They cannot use different words within the same Bill to describe the same thing.[31] Such practices would unduly complicate the interpretative process as well as the wording of the Bill. Parliamentary counsel aim for consistency in their use of language and avoid stating something that does not need to be stated. Word choice itself is always challenging. It is not in the nature of

---

24 The Parliamentary Counsel Office in the Australian Capital Territory has published a document to assist with word choice: ACT Parliamentary Counsel's Office, *Words and Phrases Guide: A Guide to Plain Legal Language* (ACT Government, 2016).

25 See chapter 13.

26 A consistent structure of legislation in a jurisdiction is, however, desirable and parliamentary counsel should work with that objective in mind. See Eamonn Moran, 'The Coherence of Statutory Interpretation: Drafting Perspectives' in Jeffrey Barnes (ed), *The Coherence of Statutory Interpretation* (Federation Press, 2019) 50, 50–1.

27 Parliamentary counsel should, however, be alive to the weight that a court may give, in interpreting an Act, to how provisions are aligned within the Act.

28 (2005) 228 CLR 294.

29 Ibid 341.

30 If drafting an amending Bill, there is, of course, an existing Act that the counsel must work on.

31 If drafting a Bill that amends an existing Act, the freedom of counsel over word choice is further limited as they need to maintain consistency with wording already used in that Act.

words to convey meaning with scientific precision.[32] In *Black-Clawson International Ltd v Papierwerke Waldhof-Aschaffenburg AG*[33] Lord Simon stated:

> [M]ost words in the English language have a number of shades of meaning. Even the bright isolating rays of the draftsman's technical skills – his juxtapositions and differentiations – are rarely sufficient in themselves to pick out without any possibility of mistake by a court of construction the exact shade of meaning intended, to the exclusion of a penumbra of other possible meanings.[34]

In making their literary choices (the art aspect of legislative drafting) and assembling the various necessary elements that technically need to be in the Bill (the science aspect of legislative drafting), the parliamentary counsel is operating at two levels. They are operating as a visionary, seeing the big picture, keeping the overall purpose in mind and ensuring that all essential matters of substance are covered. At the same time, they are sweating over the small stuff, obsessively keeping an eye on the details and ensuring that all necessary administrative and procedural issues are dealt with appropriately.

An effective parliamentary counsel needs to be able to operate at those two levels. They also need to have the requisite writing and composition skills as well as the necessary technical know-how.

Drafting practices and techniques

[10.7] Different drafting styles have evolved over time

In May 1973 a committee was appointed in the United Kingdom with terms of reference that included reviewing the form in which public Bills are drafted '[w]ith a view to achieving greater simplicity and clarity in statute law'. The committee, chaired by Sir David Renton, and accordingly known as the Renton Committee, reported to Parliament in May 1975.[35]

Chapter VI and app B of the Committee's report details some of the then widespread criticism of statute law being made by judges and others. Complaints included that the language used was obscure and complex, that the desire for certainty had led to over-elaboration and that the structure of individual statutes was often illogical and unhelpful to readers. The Committee made several recommendations for changes to drafting techniques aimed at improving the comprehensibility of legislation. These included simplifying vocabulary and syntax where possible without sacrificing certainty, using statements of principle within statutes, indexing definitions and increasing the size of the type in which Schedules to Acts are printed.

In Australia in the 1970s the state of statute law was no better than it was in the United Kingdom. Traditional legal language was regarded as appropriately dignified for use in an Act of Parliament. The quest for precision (spurred on by the highly literal approach to interpretation then in vogue at the High Court of Australia[36]) had led to detailed drafting, with sentences being frequently long and complex and archaic words being not uncommon. On top of that, printed legislation had a cramped look to it when viewed on the page and was not even accompanied by a table of contents.

---

32 See *Seaford Court Estates Ltd v Asher* [1949] 2 KB 481, 499 (Denning LJ); *Hornsby Shire Council v Porter* (1990) 19 NSWLR 716, 718 (Kirby P).

33 [1975] AC 591.

34 Ibid 646.

35 Renton Committee, *The Preparation of Legislation* (Cmd 6053, 1975).

36 In *Federal Commissioner of Taxation v Ryan* (2000) 201 CLR 109, Kirby J referred to 'the dark days of literalism': at 146.

In the 1980s pressure for the adoption of a simpler drafting style was mounting. In Victoria the then Attorney-General, the Hon J H Kennan MLC, made a Ministerial Statement to the Legislative Council entitled 'Plain English Legislation' on 7 May 1985.[37] In that Statement Mr Kennan announced changes to be made to the format of Victorian legislation aimed at simplifying it. He followed up that Statement by giving, on 10 September 1985, the then Law Reform Commission of Victoria a reference to 'inquire into and review current techniques, principles and practices of drafting legislation . . . in order to recommend what steps should be taken to adopt a plain English drafting style'. The Commission published a landmark report in 1987.[38] Appended to the report was a Drafting Manual.

The Commission advocated the adoption of a plain English style of drafting in place of the then current style, which, in the Commission's opinion, suffered from linguistic defects, excessive sentence length, the creation and use of unnecessary concepts, poor organisation of material and unattractive layout.

From the mid-1980s to the early 1990s there was a move towards adopting a plain English style of drafting in each of the Australian jurisdictions.[39] There was also at this time discussion around a 'general principles' style of drafting under which only general principles would be stated in primary legislation, leaving it to courts to fill in any necessary details.[40] The Renton Committee stated that it would like to see such an approach adopted as it would lead to greater simplicity and clarity. They recognised, however, that such a style of drafting would sacrifice immediate certainty and would be likely to be unacceptable in fiscal and other public law legislation. As stated above, the Renton Committee, however, encouraged the use of statements of principle. It suggested that if the legislation itself required those statements to be supplemented by matters of detail, that detail should be relegated to Schedules, leaving the main body of the Act confined to statements of principles.[41]

Despite some judicial criticism in earlier days,[42] plain language drafting is now the style adopted in all Australian jurisdictions.[43] An early illustration of the difference it can make can be found by comparing how a provision drafted in the traditional style was rewritten to overcome its apparent deficiencies (long sentences, multiple words being used for the one concept, and the use of archaic language).

***Supreme Court Act 1958* (Vic) s 68**

68. No action suit or process whatever shall be had maintained or prosecuted against any person in whose house chamber stable barn or other building or on whose estate any fire

37 Victoria, *Parliamentary Debates*, Legislative Council, 7 May 1985, 432–7 (JH Kennan, Attorney-General).

38 Law Reform Commission of Victoria, *Plain English and the Law* (Report No 9, June 1987).

39 See IML Turnbull, 'Clear Legislative Drafting: New Approaches in Australia' (1990) 11(3) *Statute Law Review* 161.

40 See I Turnbull, 'Legislative Drafting in Plain Language and Statements of General Principle' (1997) 18(1) *Statute Law Review* 21. 'Fuzzy law' was another term used to refer to drafting in general principles. See Lisbeth Campbell, 'Legal Drafting Styles: Fuzzy or Fussy?' (1996) 3(2) *Murdoch University Electronic Journal of Law* 17.

41 Renton Committee, *The Preparation of Legislation* (Cmd 6053, 1975) para 10.13. An example where detail is relegated not to Schedules but to subsequent subsections is the *Criminal Code Act 1995* (Cth) sch s 5. Section 5.1 states in a bold font: '**A fault element for a particular physical element may be intention, knowledge, recklessness or negligence**.' Sections 5.2–5.5 then explain what is meant by each of those terms in ordinary font.

42 See, eg, *R v Roach* [1988] VR 665; *Blunn v Cleaver* (1993) 47 FCR 111.

43 See **[16.2]** for a discussion of traditional, plain language and general principles styles of drafting.

No action to lie against person on whose estate a fire accidentally begins. No 3783 s 68.

accidentally begins and no recompense shall be made by such person for any damage suffered thereby any law usage or custom to the contrary notwithstanding. And in such case if any action be brought the defendant may plead the general issue and give this Act and the special matter in evidence at any trial thereupon to be had: Provided that no contract or agreement made between landlord and tenant shall be hereby defeated or made void.

***Supreme Court Act 1986* (Vic) s 48**

48 Proceeding does not lie against person on whose land fire accidentally begins

(1) Despite anything to the contrary, a proceeding cannot be brought or maintained against any person in whose building or on whose land a fire accidentally begins and that person is not liable to make any recompense for any damage caused by that fire.

(2) Nothing in this section defeats or makes void a contract or agreement between a landlord and a tenant.

To facilitate plain language drafting, parliamentary counsel offices in Australia and elsewhere have adopted plain language policies. A well-developed example of a plain language policy is the *Plain English Manual* published by the Commonwealth Office of Parliamentary Counsel.[44] Another example of helpful information on the use of plain language published by a parliamentary counsel office is the *Drafting Guidance* document published by the United Kingdom Office of Parliamentary Counsel.[45] It covers, among other matters, document and sentence structure, vocabulary and the use of gender-neutral language.

[10.8] Drafting practices and techniques vary across jurisdictions

Despite sharing the same common law system and operating within the one federation, the drafting practices and techniques practised by parliamentary counsel vary from jurisdiction to jurisdiction within Australia. Some of those variations are as follows:

- Commonwealth legislation refers to units of text below the level of a section by referencing directly that unit by its name – for example, 'paragraph 9(1)(a)' – whereas state and territory legislation does so by referencing the section containing that unit – for example, 'section 9(1)(a)'.
- Commonwealth legislation sometimes provides simplified outlines of groups of provisions whereas state and territory legislation usually does not.
- Some jurisdictions, such as Queensland and the Australian Capital Territory, make extensive use of notes and examples whereas other jurisdictions, such as Victoria and Tasmania, make only a limited use of them.
- The form in which amendments are made varies greatly. For example, Victorian legislation uses a whole sentence structure approach such as 'In section 9, for "dog" substitute "cat".'. Now compare Queensland legislation. To effect the same amendment, its legislation would provide as follows:

44 See Office of Parliamentary Counsel, *Plain English Manual* (Australian Government, 2016). Apart from describing good writing habits and setting out writing practices to avoid, it has a chapter on the planning necessary for an effective drafting project. It also has hints on structuring a Bill and suggestions on readability aids that might be employed. An Appendix gives simple alternatives to a number of expressions in traditional language.

45 Office of the Parliamentary Counsel of the United Kingdom, *Drafting Guidance* (The National Archives, 2020).

Section 9, 'dog'–

- *omit, insert* –

cat

- Some jurisdictions – for example, the Commonwealth – have a practice of including all amendments and repeals in a Schedule to the Act while others – for example, Victoria – generally include amendments and repeals in the body of the Act.
- Some jurisdictions, such as South Australia, include the definitions applicable to the Act in a section near the beginning of the Act. Others – for example, Queensland – place definitions in a Schedule at the back of the Act.

Another factor giving rise to variations in drafting is the fact that interpretation legislation is not the same across all the jurisdictions.[46] The Interpretation Acts in force in Australia vary both in terms of the technical rules of construction and the collections of defined terms that they contain.

The differences in drafting practices and techniques across Australia create a special challenge when governments wish to enact national uniform legislation on a particular subject matter. This issue has been addressed by a committee comprised of the heads of the parliamentary counsel offices for the Commonwealth, the states and the territories. The committee is known as the Parliamentary Counsel's Committee. It has adopted a Protocol on Drafting National Uniform Legislation designed to promote consistency in its drafting.[47]

Legislation that operates uniformly across Australia can be achieved in several different ways including:

- by one jurisdiction enacting legislation and other jurisdictions applying it, as in force from time to time, as a law of their jurisdiction;[48] and
- all or multiple jurisdictions enacting the same item of legislation, drafted as model legislation by the Parliamentary Counsel's Committee, and it being agreed by the jurisdictions that only such local variations as are absolutely necessary to achieve the agreed policy will be permitted.[49]

The Protocol sets out techniques to be adopted to promote consistency in national uniform legislation. They include:

- jurisdictions adopting uniform numbering of sections, Parts and other components and agreeing on how to number additional sections that are subsequently inserted;
- jurisdictions agreeing not to use decimal numbering, other than for the numbering of Parts in large Bills that are divided into Chapters;

46 See chapter 25.

47 Parliamentary Counsel's Committee, *Protocol on Drafting National Uniform Legislation* (Australasian Parliamentary Counsel's Committee, 2018). The agreed official versions of national uniform legislation are available at <http://www.pcc.gov.au>.

48 An example of an applied law scheme is the Health Practitioner Regulation National Law. This Law is set out in the Schedule to the *Health Practitioner Regulation National Law Act 2009* (Qld) and then applied as a law of their jurisdiction by Acts of the other states and the two territories. See, eg, *Health Practitioner Regulation National Law (Victoria) Act 2009* (Vic) s 4.

49 An example of mirror uniform legislation is the Professional Standards Acts of all the states and the Northern Territory. See, eg, *Professional Standards Act 2004* (SA). For the Australian Capital Territory the relevant provisions are in the *Civil Law (Wrongs) Act 2002* (ACT) sch 4.

- the Commonwealth version adopting the state/territory system of referring to units of text below the level of a section by referencing the section containing that unit – for example, 'section 9(1)(a)';
- placing definitions in a section at the beginning of the legislation and not in a dictionary at the end of the legislation; and
- not using 'their' as a singular pronoun in legislation and avoiding the use of 'he or she'.

[10.9] There is value in publishing drafting practices and techniques

Parliamentary counsel offices have developed, and use consistently in their work, particular drafting practices and techniques. Knowledge of those practices and techniques would undoubtedly be of great value to the users of legislation, particularly courts and lawyers whose job it is to interpret legislation. Some parliamentary counsel offices do publish extensive material relevant to the drafting process while others are more limited in the information they provide.[50]

The Commonwealth Office of Parliamentary Counsel has made available on its website a drafting manual, an amending forms manual, a plain English manual (already mentioned) and numerous drafting directions.[51] The Parliamentary Counsel's Office in the Australian Capital Territory makes similar documents available on its website, including a useful resource called *Words and Phrases Guide: A Guide to Plain Legal Language*.[52]

The NSW Parliamentary Counsel's Office has published a broad range of drafting practice documents on the NSW legislation website.[53] There are documents on plain language policy and gender-neutral language policy and, supported with references to relevant cases, documents on the drafting of savings and transitional provisions and legislative definitions. These documents contain information of value to anyone interpreting legislation.[54] They explain the basis on which parliamentary counsel in the Office tackle various aspects of the drafting process and what the approaches that they take indicate.

Published by the Office of the Chief Parliamentary Counsel, Victoria, the document *The Legislative Process* (June 2020) contains many details relating to the Victorian legislative process.[55] It has a chapter on the basic features of Acts. It lists those aspects of Acts that are fixed and explains at a high level how Acts are structured and numbered. It provides some basic material on examples and notes, preambles, long and short titles, commencement options, definitions and transitional provisions.

---

50 See **[16.5]** for a discussion on publicly available Australian drafting manuals and directions and their value. A useful overseas example of a comprehensive guide to legislative styles and practices is Law Drafting Division, *Drafting Legislation in Hong Kong: A Guide to Styles and Practices* (Hong Kong Department of Justice, 2012).

51 See <https://www.opc.gov.au>.

52 See ACT Parliamentary Counsel's Office, *Words and Phrases Guide: A Guide to Plain Legal Language* (ACT Government, 2016).

53 See <https://www.legislation.nsw.gov.au/information>.

54 One of those drafting practice documents is NSW Parliamentary Counsel's Office, *DP1: Using PCO Drafting Practice Documents* (NSW Government, May 2017). It states that 'the published drafting practices of the PCO may be relevant material that can help in interpreting legislation (including ascertaining the purpose or object of particular kinds of legislative provisions)': at [17].

55 See Office of the Chief Parliamentary Counsel of Victoria, *The Legislative Process* (Victorian Government, June 2020).

It is surprising that more use is not made of such materials by courts and other interpreters of legislation.[56] Given that they are public and official documents, there seems no reason why a court could not have regard to them.[57] A likely explanation is that counsel and judges are unaware of their existence. Occasional references in case law to legislative information material published by parliamentary counsel offices may be found. Thus in *Eckett v Eckett*[58] the Family Court referred to the published drafting manuals of the Commonwealth Office of Parliamentary Counsel when describing application and transitional provisions and commented that 'the policies prescribed in those manuals are reflected in all legislation of the Commonwealth Parliament'.[59] The Commonwealth *Drafting Direction No 4.4* regarding the correction of errors in legislation is referenced in *Re Seoud and Secretary, Department of Families, Housing, Community Services and Indigenous Affairs*.[60]

Courts expect parliamentary counsel to be familiar with the approaches they take to statutory interpretation. In return, parliamentary counsel could reasonably expect the legal profession and other users of legislation, including courts, to seek to be familiar with the legislative drafting styles and techniques adopted by them. A necessary first step is for parliamentary counsel offices to publish guides to those styles and techniques and to promote those publications to users, including courts.

The production of comprehensive guides to the working practices of parliamentary counsel would help all who need to understand legislation gain a deeper appreciation of the considerations that influence its shape and form. This would undoubtedly assist users in understanding how Bills are constructed, the assumptions that are made by parliamentary counsel and the considerations that they take account of in going about their work.

Relationship between drafting and interpretation

Clear drafting limits the need for the application of canons of interpretation on or presumptions about legislative intent [10.10]

There is an obvious relationship between drafting and interpretation. If the meaning of a provision is clear, a reader does not need to apply canons of interpretation on or presumptions (common law or statutory) about legislative intent to resolve an ambiguity or uncertainty.[61] This point has been made a number of times in case law. In *Smith v Watson*[62] Barton J found that 'the plain English of the Act now in question' rendered the statutory canons of interpretation superfluous. In doing so, he adopted what Bowen LJ had said in *London and North Western Railway Co v Evans*[63] about the use of various rules or canons of construction in interpreting statutes:

56 There is also a wealth of material on legislative drafting available at the website of the Commonwealth Association of Legislative Counsel, <http://www.calc.ngo/>.

57 See Jacinta Dharmananda, 'Drafting Statutes and Statutory Interpretation: Express or Assumed Rules?' (2019) 45 *Monash University Law Review* 401.

58 (2010) 237 FLR 324.

59 Ibid 336 [73].

60 (2012) 126 ALD 593, 597 [13] (Deputy President Forgie).

61 See chapters 32 and 39–41. See also Eamonn Moran, 'The Coherence of Statutory Interpretation: Drafting Perspectives' in Jeffrey Barnes (ed), *The Coherence of Statutory Interpretation*, (Federation Press, 2019) 50, 53–5.

62 (1906) 4 CLR 802, 820.

63 [1893] 1 Ch 16.

> These canons do not override the language of a Statute where the language is clear; they are only guides to enable us to understand what is inferential. In each case the Act of Parliament is all-powerful, and, when its meaning is unequivocally expressed, the necessity for rules of construction disappears and reaches its vanishing point.[64]

A similar point was also made in *He Kaw Teh v The Queen*[65] by Dawson J. He observed that '[r]ules of construction must give way to actual expressions of legislative intent'.[66]

It follows that initiatives by parliamentary counsel to make the law clear should have an impact on the need for the application of canons of interpretation on or presumptions about legislative intent. Any complexity in legislation should not be caused by the language used or the overall design adopted. It may, however, be the case that the legislation is dealing with a complex subject matter and the intended meaning of the legislation may not be readily apparent. While some conceptual complexity in policy may be unavoidable, every effort should be made to keep it to a minimum.[67] This requires both the critical examination of the policy proposals being put forward for adoption by legislation, to see whether they can be simplified in any way, and the careful application of drafting techniques designed to make complex policy as intelligible as possible.[68]

---

64 Ibid 27.

65 (1985) 157 CLR 523.

66 Ibid 594.

67 See *Merkur Island Shipping Corporation v Laughton* [1983] 2 AC 570, 595 (Sir John Donaldson MR).

68 See Office of Parliamentary Counsel, *Reducing Complexity in Legislation* (Australian Government, June 2016). It has a section containing examples of kinds of policy decisions that can cause complexity and cites the *Fair Work Act 2009* (Cth) as an example of a complex policy Act rendered as readable as possible by using specified drafting techniques.

ENACTMENT PROCEDURE 11

Overview

This chapter examines how Acts are made. The procedure for that (enactment procedure) is traced from the introduction of a legislative proposal (a Bill) into Parliament through to the conversion of that Bill into an Act. [11.1]

Australia has nine jurisdictions (the Commonwealth, the states and the two territories within mainland Australia) for which a Parliament or (in the case of the territories) an Assembly is constitutionally vested with the power to make Acts.[1] Each of these bodies comprises at least one elected legislative chamber or House and, except for South Australia and the Australian Capital Territory, the Queen or a vice-regal representative of the Queen. With the exception of the Australian Capital Territory, the Queen or her representative must consent to a Bill passed by the elected House or Houses for it to become an Act. With some exceptions, where there are two Houses each must agree to a Bill that is in exactly the same terms.

A Bill needs to pass through various stages in a House of Parliament. In New South Wales and Victoria different procedures apply to Bills that are classified as private Bills. Once enacted, an Act only has the force of law from the date or dates it is commenced. That date is usually a date after the date of enactment but may be before that date if the Act, or any of its provisions, has a retrospective commencement.[2]

The doctrine of parliamentary sovereignty has the effect that, except as permitted by the Australia Acts,[3] a Parliament cannot prevent itself or a subsequent Parliament from exercising the power to repeal or amend an Act passed by it or limit how that power may be exercised.

Australian parliaments enjoy a broad range of privileges, including the right not to have their proceedings questioned in court.

The Crown has a prerogative right to print and publish Acts and may also own copyright in them. Despite this, the trend by Australian governments is not to impede access to legislative material.

The making of an Act

Acts are made by bodies constitutionally vested with legislative power [11.2]

An Act is a written law directly made by a body (a Parliament) that is constitutionally vested with plenary legislative power. An Act may empower a Minister or other entity to make an instrument

1 For convenience, the term 'Parliament' is used in this chapter to refer to all Australian legislatures and 'House' to refer to each elected legislative chamber.

2 See chapter 12.

3 *Australia Act 1986* (Cth); *Australia Act 1986* (UK).

of a legislative nature on a defined matter. Such an instrument is not an Act but an item of delegated legislation.[4]

For the Commonwealth[5] and Victoria,[6] Parliament is comprised of the Queen and two elected Houses of Parliament. For Tasmania,[7] Parliament is comprised of the Governor, as the Queen's representative, and two elected Houses of Parliament. For Queensland,[8] Parliament is comprised of the Queen and one elected House of Parliament. For New South Wales[9] and Western Australia,[10] it is the Queen acting with the advice and consent of two elected Houses of Parliament that has the power to make Acts.

The position in South Australia is different.[11] There the Queen or the Governor does not form part of the Parliament as such. That Parliament consists of two elected Houses. However, Bills passed by the Parliament of South Australia must be assented to by the Governor in the name and on behalf of the Queen.

For the Australian Capital Territory,[12] an elected Assembly alone has the power to make Acts. For the Northern Territory,[13] an elected Assembly with the assent of the Administrator of the Territory,[14] or of the Governor-General (if the Administrator reserves it for the Governor-General's pleasure), has the Act-making power.

While the *Australian Constitution* formally vests the legislative power of the Commonwealth in a federal Parliament consisting of the Queen, a Senate and a House of Representatives,[15] in practice the powers and functions of the Queen as part of the federal Parliament are exercisable by the Governor-General.[16]

All the powers and functions of the Queen in relation to the making of an Act by a state Parliament are exercisable only by the Governor of the state. However, if the Queen is personally present in a State, she is not precluded from exercising any of those powers and functions.[17]

The consent of the Queen (or, in practical terms, her representative) is an essential part of the process for the making of Commonwealth and State Acts. Without that consent, a Bill does not become an Act. In *R v Commissioner for Transport; Ex parte Cobb & Co Ltd*[18] Stanley J, sitting as a member of the Full Court of the Queensland Supreme Court, stated:

4 See chapter 43.

5 *Australian Constitution* s 1.

6 *Constitution Act 1975* (Vic) s 15.

7 *Constitution Act 1934* (Tas) s 10.

8 *Constitution Act 1867* (Qld) s 2A.

9 *Constitution Act 1902* (NSW) s 5.

10 *Constitution Act 1889* (WA) s 2.

11 *Constitution Act 1934* (SA) s 4.

12 *Australian Capital Territory (Self-Government) Act 1988* (Cth) s 22.

13 *Northern Territory (Self-Government) Act 1978* (Cth) s 6.

14 The Administrator is appointed by the Governor-General. See *Northern Territory (Self-Government) Act 1978* (Cth) s 32(1).

15 *Australian Constitution* s 1.

16 Ibid ss 2, 58. The requirement under s 74 for certain proposed laws relating to appeals to the Privy Council to be reserved by the Governor-General for Her Majesty's pleasure has not had any practical effect since the passing of the *Privy Council (Appeals from the High Court) Act 1975* (Cth).

17 *Australia Act 1986* (Cth) s 7; *Australia Act 1986* (UK) s 7.

18 [1963] Qd R 547.

> But the fundamental conception of parliamentary legislation in Queensland is that the combined powers of the Queen and the Legislative Assembly are manifested by the conversion of Bills into Acts which have the force of law ...
>
> Thus the Legislative Assembly sends forward the Bill containing the provisions which if assented to by the Sovereign, become an Act. The Queen does not legislate by her own power, nor does the Legislative Assembly by its own power. The combined powers of both are required to convert a Bill into an Act.[19]

Having regard to the critical function of the Queen's representative in assenting to a Bill, a relevant issue is whether the exercise of that function is subject to the advice of Ministers and whether such advice may be to refuse to do so.

In *West Lakes Ltd v South Australia*[20] Zelling J expressed the view that it would not accord with constitutional precedent for Ministers to advise the Governor to refuse assent to a Bill that had been passed by both Houses of Parliament.

Academics hold differing views. Professor Twomey has argued that there is much to be said for the view that the Queen or her vice-regal representative acts on the advice of the House(s) of Parliament when giving royal assent but recognises that Ministers have a discretion to advise the refusal of assent (albeit a discretion that is heavily circumscribed by constitutional convention).[21] Professor Lindell holds the view that the function of assent is only exercisable in accordance with the wishes of the government.[22]

There is provision at the Commonwealth level, and also in South Australia and Victoria, for the Governor-General or the Governor, as the case requires, to suggest amendments to a Bill presented for assent that, if accepted by both Houses of the relevant Parliament, are then incorporated in the Bill as assented to.[23]

The date appearing on authorised versions of Acts passed in all jurisdictions, except Victoria and the Australian Capital Territory, and purporting to be the date on which the Act was assented to is evidence of the date of assent.[24] In Victoria the date of assent endorsed on an Act is part of the Act and, accordingly, has effect as a legislative declaration as to the date of assent.[25] In the Australian Capital Territory proposed laws passed by the Assembly are notified by the parliamentary counsel.[26] Proof is not required of that notification.[27]

---

19 Ibid 568.

20 (1980) 25 SASR 389, 415.

21 See Anne Twomey, 'The Refusal or Deferral of Royal Assent' [2006] *Public Law* 580, 601.

22 See Geoffrey Lindell, 'Assent or Refusal to Assent to Legislation – On Whose Advice? (2009) 11(3) *Constitutional Law and Policy Review* 126, 127.

23 *Australian Constitution* s 58; *Constitution Act 1934* (SA) s 56; *Constitution Act 1975* (Vic) s 14.

24 *Acts Interpretation Act 1901* (Cth) s 6; *Interpretation Act 1987* (NSW) s 22(2); *Evidence Act 1977* (Qld) s 46A(2) (s 43(d) of that Act provides that judicial notice must be taken of when every Act was assented to); *Evidence Act 1929* (SA) s 35A; *Acts Interpretation Act 1931* (Tas) s 10; *Interpretation Act 1984* (WA) s 24; *Interpretation Act 1978* (NT) s 7(1).

25 *Constitution Act 1975* (Vic) s 69.

26 Under the *Legislation Act 2001* (ACT) s 28, on the passing of a proposed law by the Legislative Assembly the Speaker must ask the parliamentary counsel to notify its making and, on being asked, the parliamentary counsel must do so by publishing its text in the ACT Legislation register or in another place allowed under that section.

27 *Legislation Act 2001* (ACT) s 26(1)(a).

Section 15ZB of the *Legislation Act 2003* (Cth) provides that in proceedings in a court or tribunal, proof is not required about the assent, or the day of assent, of a Commonwealth Act. A court or tribunal may inform itself of those matters from an authorised version of the Act or any other reliable source of information. Similar provision is made by s 26 of the *Legislation Act 2001* (ACT).

[11.3] Each House of Parliament must agree to the Bill in exactly the same terms

In Australia where there are two elected Houses of Parliament in a jurisdiction, as is the case for the federal Parliament and each state Parliament other than that of Queensland, the general rule is that both Houses must agree to a Bill that is in exactly the same terms as that to which each other House has agreed in order for that Bill to progress to being an Act.

However, if the two Houses cannot come to an agreement on the passage of a Bill, some jurisdictions have provisions that result in the consent of one of those Houses being dispensed with.

For the Commonwealth, if the Senate on two occasions, at least three months apart, rejects or fails to pass a particular Bill that has been passed by the House of Representatives, or passes it with amendments to which the House of Representatives does not agree, both Houses may be dissolved simultaneously. Following the general election consequential on that dissolution, if the House of Representatives again passes the same Bill and the Senate again rejects or fails to pass it, or passes it with amendments to which the House of Representatives does not agree, the Governor-General may convene a joint sitting of the members of both Houses. If at the joint sitting an absolute majority of those members agree to the Bill as passed by the House of Representatives with amendments, if any, made by one House and not agreed to by the other, the Bill is taken to have been passed by both Houses.[28]

In New South Wales the consent of the Legislative Council may be dispensed with in the case of a Bill appropriating revenue or money for the ordinary annual services of the government. This can occur if the Bill is passed by the Legislative Assembly but the Legislative Council rejects or fails to pass it within one month after its transmission to the Legislative Council, or returns it to the Legislative Assembly with a message suggesting any amendment to which the Legislative Assembly does not agree.[29] The consent of the Legislative Council may also be dispensed with in the case of any other Bill deadlocked in the same way if the Bill is approved at a referendum.[30]

---

28 *Australian Constitution* s 57. In *Victoria v Commonwealth* (1975) 134 CLR 81, 118–9 (Barwick CJ), 163–5 (Gibbs J), 180 (Stephen J agreeing with Barwick CJ and Gibbs J) and 181–2 (Mason J) it was held that the procedures established by s 57 are justiciable and that a failure to follow them results in invalidity. In *Cormack v Cope* (1974) 131 CLR 432, Barwick CJ (at 454–5 and 460–1) and Gibbs J (at 466–7) expressed the view that the Court had jurisdiction to intervene pre-enactment in the legislative process to ensure compliance with the s 57 procedures but ordinarily would not as a sufficient remedy was available post-enactment. McTiernan J (at 461), Menzies J (at 464–6) and Stephen J (at 472) were of the view that the Court did not have jurisdiction to intervene pre-enactment while Mason J (at 473) said that it was not necessary to finally decide the question.

29 *Constitution Act 1902* (NSW) s 5A.

30 Ibid s 5B. Before a referendum may be held there must be a 'free conference' between managers of both Houses followed by a joint sitting of the members of both Houses at which the Bill is deliberated on but not voted on. In *Clayton v Heffron* (1960) 105 CLR 214 Dixon CJ, McTiernan, Taylor and Windeyer JJ concluded that invalidity did not ensue from a failure to hold a meeting of managers in a free conference: at 248. They stated that, according to the traditional view, courts do not inquire into the lawfulness and regularity of the parliamentary process before it is completed: at 234–5. They added: 'The process of law-making is one thing: the power to make the law as it has emerged from the process is another. It is the latter which the court must always have jurisdiction to examine and pronounce upon' (at 235).

In Victoria the consent of the Legislative Council may be dispensed with for a Bill that appropriates money for the ordinary annual services of the government. The circumstances allowing the consent of the Legislative Council to be dispensed with are that the Bill is passed by the Legislative Assembly but, within one month after that passing, it is not passed by the Legislative Council or is passed with a message suggesting any amendment to which the Legislative Assembly does not agree.[31]

Victoria has fixed four-year terms for the Legislative Assembly[32] but the Assembly may be dissolved sooner where there is a disputed Bill. A 'disputed Bill' is a Bill that has been passed by the Assembly but, within two months after it is sent to the Legislative Council for passing, it is either not passed by the Legislative Council or is passed with amendments with which the Legislative Assembly does not agree.[33] The Legislative Assembly may refer the disputed Bill to a special committee of both Houses known as the Dispute Resolution Committee.[34] If the Committee cannot reach a dispute resolution within 30 days, or either House fails to give effect to a dispute resolution reached by the Committee, the Premier may advise the Governor that the Assembly be dissolved.[35]

If, after the general election held following that dissolution, the Bill (in the same form as introduced into or passed by the previous Legislative Assembly or in a form that is consistent with a resolution of the Dispute Resolution Committee) is passed by the next elected Legislative Assembly but, within two months after it is sent to the Legislative Council for passing, is either not passed by the Legislative Council or is passed with amendments with which the Legislative Assembly does not agree, a joint sitting of both Houses may be convened by the Governor.[36] At that joint sitting the disputed Bill is considered and, if agreed to by an absolute majority of the total number of the members of both Houses, with or without any amendments, the Bill is taken to have been passed by both Houses.[37] A certificate of the Speaker of the Legislative Assembly to the effect that the Bill is a Bill to which the special procedure applies is endorsed on the Bill when presented to the Governor for assent and that certificate is conclusive evidence for all purposes and cannot be questioned in any court.[38]

South Australia, Tasmania and Western Australia each have two elected Houses of Parliament but they do not have any legislative provisions in place that could result in the consent of one of those Houses being dispensed with. The result is that unless both Houses are in agreement on a

---

31 *Constitution Act 1975* (Vic) s 65. Section 65(8) provides that the certificate of the Speaker that the Bill has been passed in accordance with the special procedure 'is conclusive evidence for all purposes and cannot be questioned in any court'. This is clearly intended to prevent a court inquiring into whether the prescribed procedure has been properly followed.

32 Ibid s 38.

33 Ibid s 65A.

34 Ibid s 65C.

35 Ibid s 65E. The Speaker of the Legislative Assembly certifies to the Governor that the Bill is a Bill to which s 65E applies. That certificate is 'conclusive evidence for all purposes and cannot be questioned in any court'.

36 Ibid s 65F(3). The Speaker of the Legislative Assembly certifies to the Governor that the Bill is a Bill to which s 65F(3) applies. That certificate is 'conclusive evidence for all purposes and cannot be questioned in any court'. See s 65F(5).

37 Ibid s 65G.

38 Ibid s 65G(8), (9).

Bill, the Bill will not progress. However, both South Australia[39] and Western Australia[40] have provision for a conference of managers representing each House to meet with a view to reaching agreement on a disputed Bill.

[11.4] Bills are read three times in each House of Parliament

Each House of Parliament may adopt rules to regulate its procedure in dealing with legislation (referred to as standing orders).[41] While there are minor variations in the detailed procedural rules applied to the handling of Bills in legislatures across Australia, there is broad consistency as to the stages that a Bill must pass through in the course of its Parliamentary journey.

A Bill is formally presented to a House of Parliament by a member of that House[42] (first reading stage), then its broad principles are debated (second reading stage) followed by (if required) a consideration of the Bill in detail during which amendments are capable of being made to the text of the Bill (consideration in detail stage) and finally a vote is taken on the Bill, as amended if applicable (third reading stage). Despite the use of the word 'reading' in the title of these various stages, the text of the body of the Bill is not actually read aloud at any of these stages.[43]

After its introduction a Bill may be referred for consideration and report to a committee comprised of members of the House or of both Houses. A House may establish a standing committee under its standing orders or by a specific resolution. Joint committees of both Houses may be established by legislation or by resolution of both Houses.

Where there are two Houses of Parliament in the jurisdiction, the same process is repeated in the other House with any amendments[44] made in that House being returned to the first House for consideration. The first House may accept, reject or amend those amendments. Amendments may move back and forth between the Houses as often as is necessary until agreement is reached. When agreement is reached a print of the Bill is prepared incorporating the amendments agreed to by both Houses. The Bill may then proceed to royal assent. If both Houses are not in agreement, the Bill cannot proceed unless a special procedure of a kind outlined in **[11.3]** is available.

The process followed in the Commonwealth Parliament in respect of a Bill first introduced in the House of Representatives is set out in **Example 11.1** as an illustration of the process followed in all Australian jurisdictions.

---

39 *Legislative Council Standing Orders 1999* (SA) ch 23; *Legislative Assembly Standing Orders 2018* (SA) ch 22.

40 *Legislative Council Standing Orders 2019* (WA) ch 20; *Standing Orders of the Legislative Assembly 2017* (WA) ch 23.

41 *Australian Constitution* s 50(ii); *Australian Capital Territory (Self-Government) Act 1988* (Cth) s 21; *Constitution Act 1902* (NSW) s 15; *Northern Territory (Self-Government) Act 1978* (Cth) s 30; *Parliament of Queensland Act 2001* (Qld) s 11; *Constitution Act 1934* (SA) s 55; *Constitution Act 1934* (Tas) s 17; *Constitution Act 1975* (Vic) s 43; *Constitution Act 1889* (WA) s 34. In *Crick v Harnett* (1907) 7 SR (NSW) 126 the NSW Supreme Court held that a standing order allowing the suspension of a member charged with an offence was outside the power of the Legislative Assembly as it did not regulate the orderly conduct of the Assembly. The relevant power to make a standing order under the *Constitution Act 1902* (NSW) s 15 was limited to that purpose.

42 While very occasionally a Bill presented by an individual member may pass into law, the vast majority of Acts result from Bills presented by a Minister on behalf of the government. See **[10.2]**.

43 Standing orders may provide for two or more Bills that are complementary to each other to be debated together (cognate debate).

44 For certain kinds of financial legislation, the upper House of Parliament may be constitutionally prohibited from making amendments to the legislation but may instead suggest amendments. See *Australian Constitution* s 53; *Constitution Act 1934* (SA) s 62; *Constitution Act 1934* (Tas) s 42; *Constitution Act 1975* (Vic) ss 62(2), 64(2).

Example 11.1 Passage of a Bill through the Commonwealth Parliament

The Houses of the Commonwealth Parliament are the Senate and the House of Representatives. With some exceptions a Bill may be introduced in either House. Proposed laws appropriating revenue or money[45] or imposing taxation[46] must start in the House of Representatives.[47]

House of Representatives

A member of the House of Representatives who intends to introduce a Bill must give written notice of that intention to the Clerk of the House. The notice must be signed by at least that member and one other and specify the Bill's title and the date on which it is to be introduced.[48] The member must then give the Clerk a signed legible copy of the Bill.[49] The member may also present a signed explanatory memorandum explaining the reasons for the Bill and must do so if the member is a Minister and the Bill is not an Appropriation or Supply Bill.[50]

Section 8 of the *Human Rights (Parliamentary Scrutiny) Act 2011* (Cth) requires a Member of Parliament who introduces a Bill into a House of the Parliament to cause a statement to be presented to the House as to the compatibility of the Bill with the rights and freedoms recognised or declared by certain specified international instruments.[51] The statement may be incorporated in the explanatory memorandum.

On the Bill being presented to the House, it is read a first time without a question being put.[52] This is a formal stage. This first reading only involves the long title of the Bill being read aloud by the Clerk.

The member who introduced the Bill, either immediately after the first reading or at a later time, may move a motion that the Bill be read a second time and, on moving that motion, give a speech about the Bill.[53] If the Bill provides for the appropriation of revenue or money, it is necessary for the Governor-General to send a message to the House recommending the purpose of the appropriation.[54] The message is announced immediately after the second reading of the Bill.[55] Only a Minister can introduce a Bill that requires an appropriation message from the Governor-General. The requirement for a message from the Governor-General preserves the exclusive right of the executive government to initiate appropriations.[56]

---

45 Such a proposed law must only deal with appropriating revenue or money. The purpose of the appropriation must be recommended by message of the Governor-General to the House of Representatives. See *Australian Constitution* ss 54, 56.

46 Such a proposed law must only deal with imposing taxation. See ibid s 55.

47 Ibid s 53.

48 *House of Representatives Standing Orders 2019* (Cth) ord 139.

49 Ibid ord 140(a).

50 Ibid ord 141(b).

51 A failure to do so for a Bill that becomes an Act does not affect the validity, operation or enforcement of the Act. See *Human Rights (Parliamentary Scrutiny) Act 2011* (Cth) s 8(5). See also **[26.2]**.

52 *House of Representatives Standing Orders 2019* (Cth) ord 141(a).

53 Ibid ord 142(a).

54 *Australian Constitution* s 56.

55 *House of Representatives Standing Orders 2019* (Cth) ord 147. For an Appropriation or Supply Bill, the message is announced before the Bill is introduced. See ord 180(b).

56 Rosemary Laing (ed), *Odgers' Australian Senate Practice* (Department of the Senate Canberra, 14th ed, 2016) 364.

At this stage the Bill may be referred to a parliamentary committee for an advisory report.[57] The House of Representatives Standing Orders require the appointment of a Selection Committee with the function of selecting Bills that the Committee regards as controversial or as requiring further consultation or debate for referral to the relevant standing or joint committee.[58]

There are also several standing parliamentary committees that play a role in relation to each Bill introduced in the federal Parliament.

The *Human Rights (Parliamentary Scrutiny) Act 2011* (Cth) has established a Parliamentary Joint Committee on Human Rights. It consists of 10 members, five from each House of the federal Parliament.[59] Among its functions is to examine Bills that come before either House for compatibility with human rights, and to report to both Houses of Parliament on that issue.[60]

The Senate Standing Orders require the appointment, at the commencement of each Parliament, of a Standing Committee for the Scrutiny of Bills to report, in respect of the clauses of Bills introduced into the Senate, or the provisions of Bills not yet before the Senate, whether such Bills, by express words or otherwise:

- trespass unduly on personal rights and liberties;
- make rights, liberties or obligations unduly dependent upon insufficiently defined administrative powers;
- make rights, liberties or obligations unduly dependent upon non-reviewable decisions;
- inappropriately delegate legislative powers; or
- insufficiently subject the exercise of legislative power to parliamentary scrutiny.[61]

After a standing or joint committee has reported on a Bill, a time is set for the consideration in detail of the Bill.[62] Alternatively, the Bill may be referred to a committee of the House, known as the Federation Chamber,[63] and there considered in detail.[64]

Consideration in detail in the House may be skipped if the House grants leave for the immediate moving of the question that the Bill be read a third time.[65] This will occur where the Speaker is of the view that members do not wish to debate the Bill in detail, but instead wish to proceed to the third reading immediately. Any one member objecting can prevent this occurring and cause the Bill to go through the consideration in detail stage.

Where a Bill is referred to the Federation Chamber, consideration in detail may be skipped if the Federation Chamber grants leave for the immediate moving of a motion that the Bill be reported to the House without amendment.[66]

57 *House of Representatives Standing Orders 2019* (Cth) ord 143(b)–(c).

58 Ibid ord 222. Standing Order 215 provides for the appointment of a range of general purpose standing committees.

59 *Human Rights (Parliamentary Scrutiny) Act 2011* (Cth) s 5.

60 Ibid s 7(a).

61 *Senate Standing Orders 2020* (Cth) ord 24.

62 *House of Representatives Standing Orders 2019* (Cth) ord 144. Under Standing Order 143(b), on receipt of the advisory report the Bill may be referred to the Federation Chamber.

63 Ibid ord 143(a).

64 Ibid ords 143(a), 183.

65 Ibid ord 148(a).

66 Ibid ord 148(b).

Consideration in detail is bypassed in approximately 75 per cent of Bills.[67]

If a Bill is considered in detail, unless a motion is passed for it to be considered as a whole, its clauses are considered in numerical order followed by its schedules, with its preamble (if any) and title being finally considered.[68] In practice, however, by leave of the House usually the Bill is taken as a whole or groups of clauses or schedules are taken together.[69] An amendment may be moved to any part of the Bill during the consideration in detail stage in the House or the Federation Chamber provided it is relevant to the subject matter of the Bill and otherwise conforms to the standing orders.[70] Amendments made by the Federation Chamber must be reported to the House and considered by it.[71] The House must pass a motion agreeing to the Bill, as amended (if applicable), before it may proceed to the third reading stage.[72]

At the third reading stage the question that the Bill 'be now read a third time' is put to the House. If that motion is carried the Bill has passed the House and a copy of it, certified by the Clerk of the House, is sent to the Senate with a message asking that it agree to the Bill.[73]

Senate

On receipt of the Bill from the House of Representatives the President of the Senate formally puts the question to the Senate that the Bill be read a first time.[74] When a motion is moved for the second reading of the Bill, debate on the motion is adjourned at the conclusion of the speech of the senator who moved it.[75] The next step is for the Bill to be considered in a committee of the whole Senate.[76] This is the Senate's equivalent to the House of Representative's consideration in detail stage. The Senate Standing Orders require that the clauses of the Bill are considered in numerical order followed by its schedules, with its preamble (if any) and title being finally considered.[77] However, in practice virtually all Bills are considered as a whole and amendments moved to any part of the Bill.[78]

In committee of the whole Senate an amendment may be made to any part of the Bill provided it is relevant to the subject matter of the Bill and is otherwise in conformity with the rules and orders of the Senate.[79] However, the Senate may not amend a Bill imposing taxation or

67 DR Elder (ed), *House of Representatives Practice* (Department of the House of Representatives Canberra, 7th ed, 2018) ch 10.

68 *House of Representatives Standing Orders 2019* (Cth) ord 149(a), (b). For certain types of Bill, schedules are considered before clauses. See Standing Order 149(d).

69 DR Elder (ed), *House of Representatives Practice* (Department of the House of Representatives Canberra, 7th ed, 2018) 374.

70 *House of Representatives Standing Orders 2019* (Cth) ord 150.

71 Ibid ord 153.

72 A member may move that the Bill be reconsidered in detail. See ibid ord 154.

73 Ibid ords 155, 157.

74 *Senate Standing Orders 2020* (Cth) ord 112. The question is not debated unless the Bill is one that the Senate may not amend.

75 Ibid ord 111(5).

76 Ibid ord 115. This step is delayed until any standing or select committee to which the Bill is referred has reported on the Bill.

77 Ibid ord 117.

78 Rosemary Laing (ed), *Odgers' Australian Senate Practice* (Department of the Senate Canberra, 14th ed, 2016) 330.

79 *Senate Standing Orders 2020* (Cth) ord 118(1).

appropriating revenue or money for the ordinary annual services of the Government.[80] Nor may the Senate amend a Bill so as to increase any proposed charge or burden on the people.[81] However, the Senate may, by message sent to the House of Representatives, request it to make an amendment to a Bill that the Senate is incapable of making.[82]

At the conclusion of the consideration of the Bill in committee of the whole Senate, the committee may agree to the Bill, as amended, being reported to the Senate.[83] The report is considered by the Senate and, if adopted, the Bill proceeds to the third reading and, after the third reading, the Bill is taken to have been passed by the Senate.[84]

If a Bill received from the House of Representatives is amended by the Senate in the course of its passage through the Senate, a schedule of the amendments is sent by the Clerk of the Senate to the House of Representatives and its concurrence to them sought.[85] The House of Representatives may agree to, or disagree with, any Senate amendment and may make an amendment to a Senate amendment.[86] The Senate is informed by message of the outcome, including written reasons for not agreeing to any amendment.[87] A committee of the whole Senate then considers that message and may insist, or not insist, on its amendments or make further amendments to the Bill consequent on the rejection of its amendments or as an alternative to the rejected amendments.[88] This back-and-forth process may continue.[89] If ultimately a stage is reached where both Houses are in agreement, the Speaker of the House of Representatives presents the Bill to the Governor-General for the Queen's assent in accordance with s 58 of the *Australian Constitution*.[90]

Classification of Bills and Acts

[11.5] Bills may be classified in particular ways

The parliaments of New South Wales and Victoria, unlike those in all the other Australian jurisdictions, may classify a Bill as a private Bill. All other Bills are public Bills.

Private Bills are for the benefit of particular individuals or organisations. They may be contrasted with public Bills (the sole classification applicable outside New South Wales and Victoria), which apply to the general community.[91] A public Bill that affects a particular private

80 *Australian Constitution* s 53.

81 Ibid.

82 Ibid.

83 *Senate Standing Orders 2020* (Cth) ord 120.

84 Ibid ord 122. The Bill may be recommitted in whole or in part. See *Senate Standing Orders 2020* (Cth) ords 121, 123.

85 Ibid ord 131.

86 *House of Representatives Standing Orders 2019* (Cth) ord 158.

87 Ibid ord 161.

88 *Senate Standing Orders 2020* (Cth) ord 132.

89 *House of Representatives Standing Orders 2019* (Cth) ord 162; *Senate Standing Orders 2020* (Cth) ord 132.

90 *House of Representatives Standing Orders 2019* (Cth) ord 162.

91 A public Act may, however, apply only to a specified person. See *Community Protection Act 1994* (NSW); *Community Protection Act 1990* (Vic); *Corrections Amendment (Parole) Act 2014* (Vic).

interest in a manner different from the private interests of other persons or bodies of the same category or class is treated as a hybrid Bill.[92]

Chapter 29 of the Standing Orders of the NSW Legislative Assembly makes provision for private Bills. The promoter of a private Bill must petition the Legislative Assembly to introduce the Bill. However, at least three months before presenting the petition, the promoter must cause a notice of intention to petition the Legislative Assembly to introduce the Bill, containing a statement of its general objects, to be published once a week for four consecutive weeks in the Government Gazette and in at least one major newspaper published in Sydney and in the district affected by the Bill. A petition, to which is attached a printed copy of the proposed Bill and that contains proof of the publication of the notice in the Government Gazette and the relevant newspapers, may then be presented to the Legislative Assembly and notice of motion for the introduction of the Bill given. After being introduced the Bill is referred to a select committee. The Clerk of the Assembly is entitled to claim from the Bill's promoter such expenses as the Clerk deems reasonable.[93]

Chapter 26 of the Standing Rules and Orders of the Legislative Council in New South Wales makes similar provision for the introduction of private Bills. Before a private Bill is read a first time in the Legislative Council, sufficient copies of it are printed, in the same form as public Bills, at the expense of its promoter[94] and the sum of $50 towards expenses is paid to the Parliament.[95] The promoter is liable for the payment of any additional sum required to fully cover any expenses incurred.[96] After its first reading the Bill is referred to a select committee that may take evidence as required, hear submissions and decide on matters in issue between persons supporting and opposing the Bill.[97]

However, a private Bill coming to one House from the other is proceeded with as a public Bill.[98]

Despite the special provision made for them, private Bills are rare in New South Wales. The last successful private Bill in New South Wales was the Tamworth Information Centre Bill 1992. The modern trend is for governments to assist private bodies, such as churches and community organisations, with securing the passage of legislation by allowing them to proceed as public Bills.

In Victoria the Standing Orders of the Legislative Assembly provide that after the second reading speech of a Bill is made, the Speaker may rule that the Bill is a private Bill. The Legislative Assembly may, however, agree to treat the Bill as a public Bill. If that is not done the Speaker is required to publish a statement about the general nature of the Bill in a newspaper circulating generally in Victoria and, if applicable, in a newspaper circulating in the relevant locality.[99]

Persons who consider that the Bill has a direct and adverse effect on them may send a written objection to the Speaker within 14 days after the publication of the statement. If objection is made, the Speaker must appoint a panel of examiners to consider the objection and report back to

---

92 See *British Railways Board v Pickin* [1974] AC 765, 797 (Lord Wilberforce), 800 (Lord Simon).

93 *Legislative Assembly Standing Orders 2007* (NSW) ord 358.

94 *Legislative Council Standing Rules and Orders 2004* (NSW) ords 164, 165.

95 Ibid ord 166(1).

96 Ibid ord 166(3).

97 Ibid ord 168.

98 *Legislative Assembly Standing Orders 2007* (NSW) ord 361; *Legislative Council Standing Rules and Orders 2004* (NSW) ord 170.

99 *Legislative Assembly Standing Orders 2004* (Vic) ord 83.

the Speaker on whether the objection raises sufficiently important matters for a select committee to be appointed to consider the Bill.[100]

The promoter of a private Bill must pay a deposit of $1,000 before the Bill is read a second time and remains liable for all expenses involved in its preparation and passage unless the Legislative Assembly dispenses with fees.[101]

Subject to the above, a private Bill is dealt with in the Legislative Assembly in the same way as a public Bill.[102]

Broadly similar provision is made by the Standing Orders of the Legislative Council. However, in the Legislative Council the period for lodging objections is 21 days, not 14, and the deposit amount is not prescribed.[103]

Private Bills are more common in Victoria than in New South Wales. Recent examples are the Lord Mayor's Charitable Foundation Bill 2016 (Vic) and the Melbourne College of Divinity Amendment Bill 2016 (Vic). Each of those Bills was, however, treated as a public Bill and fees were dispensed with.

A private Bill must not be confused with a private member's Bill. A private member's Bill is a public Bill introduced by a Member of Parliament who is not a Minister. Private member's Bills may be introduced in any of the Australian parliaments.

The Standing Orders of the Western Australian Legislative Council[104] provide for a Bill to be classified as a Uniform Legislation Bill if it ratifies or gives effect to a bilateral or multilateral intergovernmental agreement or introduces a uniform scheme or uniform laws throughout the Commonwealth. A Uniform Legislation Bill is required to be referred, for inquiry and report, to the Standing Committee on Uniform Legislation and Statutes Review[105] at the conclusion of the second reading speech. The Bill cannot proceed through the second reading stage until the Committee has reported.

[11.6] **Acts may be classified in a number of different ways**

In all Australian states, except New South Wales and Victoria, Acts passed after certain specified dates are taken to be public Acts unless the Act otherwise expressly provides.[106]

In New South Wales and Queensland it is expressly provided that a private Act does not become a public Act merely because it is amended by or under a public Act.[107] It is also provided in New South Wales and Queensland that a private Act must not be construed so as to prejudicially affect existing rights of, or to impose liabilities in relation to previous acts or omissions on, the Crown or any other person, other than a person at whose instance, or for whose special benefit, the Act is passed or some other person claiming by, through or

100 Ibid ord 84.

101 Ibid ord 85.

102 Ibid ord 86.

103 *Legislative Council of Victoria Standing Orders 2020* (Vic) ords 14.36–14.41.

104 *Legislative Council Standing Orders 2019* (WA) ord 126.

105 Established by ibid sch 1 ord 6.

106 *Acts Interpretation Act 1954* (Qld) s 11 (Acts passed after 26 July 1852); *Legislation Interpretation Act 2021* (SA) s 25 (Acts passed after 1 January 1873); *Acts Interpretation Act 1931* (Tas) s 6(7) (Acts passed after 5 August 1853); *Interpretation Act 1984* (WA) s 28 (Acts passed after 13 April 1853). The Tasmanian and Western Australian provisions further provide for all Acts to be judicially noticed as public Acts. The *Evidence Act 1995* (Cth) s 143(a) (as extended by s 5) now requires judicial notice to be taken by Australian courts of all Acts.

107 *Interpretation Act 1987* (NSW) s 74; *Acts Interpretation Act 1954* (Qld) s 12A.

under such a person.[108] Given that all Queensland Acts passed after 26 July 1852 are taken to be public Acts,[109] these provisions are only relevant to Queensland Acts passed before that date.

When passed, an Act may be classified in a number of different ways apart from the public Act/private Act distinction. One way is according to the extent of the Act's operation. In this case the classification is between general Acts and local or personal Acts. Frequently a hybrid classification is appropriate, such as 'public general Act'.

In *R v London County Council*[110] Bowen LJ stated:

> Now, a general Act, prima facie, is that which applies to the whole community. In the natural meaning of the term it means an Act of Parliament which is unlimited both in its area and, as regards the individual, in its effects; and as opposed to that you get statutes which may well be public because of the importance of the subjects with which they deal and their general interest to the community, but which are limited in respect of area – a limitation which makes them local – or limited in respect of individuals or persons – a limitation which makes them personal.[111]

Another way is between principal and amending Acts. A principal Act contains new substantive provisions that together form a new Act[112] whereas an amending Act changes the law by amending or repealing provisions of one or more other Acts. An amending Act may also be classified as an omnibus Act if its provisions range across diverse and unrelated topics.[113]

There are several classifications applied to Acts that do not make any substantive change to the law. These are consolidation Acts (Acts that gather together in the one place provisions scattered across a number of Acts), statute law revision Acts (Acts that formally repeal spent Acts, correct minor errors or otherwise tidy up the statute book without effecting any substantive changes), declaratory Acts (Acts that merely declare what the law is) and codifying Acts (these are similar to consolidation Acts but also incorporate a statutory re-statement of relevant common law).

Powers and privileges of Parliament

Parliament cannot bind a subsequent Parliament not to repeal or amend legislation or to use specified words to effect an amendment [11.7]

A Parliament of a jurisdiction can repeal or amend any Act passed by the then current Parliament, or any previous Parliament, of that jurisdiction. Further, a Parliament cannot purport to restrict

108 *Interpretation Act 1987* (NSW) s 73; *Acts Interpretation Act 1954* (Qld) s 12.

109 *Acts Interpretation Act 1954* (Qld) s 11.

110 [1893] 2 QB 454.

111 Ibid 462.

112 A principal Act may contain provisions that make amendments to other Acts that are consequential on the new substantive provisions.

113 See Standing Committee on Administration and Procedure, Parliament of the Australian Capital Territory, *Omnibus Bills* (Report 2, May 2017) made following a resolution passed by the ACT Legislative Assembly on 16 February 2017, noting that omnibus amendment Bills are a useful tool to make policy, technical and editorial amendments to various pieces of legislation and enable legislation to be kept up to date and respond to changing circumstances and/or fix errors.

or remove the power of a subsequent Parliament to repeal or amend any Act passed by it.[114] This is a necessary corollary of the doctrine of parliamentary sovereignty.[115]

In *R v Public Vehicles Licensing Appeal Tribunal (Tas); Ex parte Australian National Airways Pty Ltd*[116] the High Court stated:

> The will of a Parliament is expressed in a statute or Act of Parliament and it is the general conception of English law that what Parliament may enact it may repeal.[117]

In *Kartinyeri v Commonwealth*[118] Brennan CJ and McHugh J said:

> The power to repeal a law may be exercised from time to time as the Parliament chooses. One Parliament cannot deny or qualify the power of itself or of a later Parliament to exercise that power. The Parliament cannot bind itself or its successor Parliaments not to amend the laws it makes.[119]

Ordinarily a simple majority of the members of a House of Parliament voting on a motion for the passage of a Bill is all that is required for the Bill to be passed by that House. There may, however, be a special requirement to be complied with, such as obtaining a particular majority in a House of Parliament or approval at a referendum, before a Bill respecting the constitution, powers or procedure of a state Parliament may be effectively passed.[120] Such 'manner and form' requirements are provided for in each state Constitution Act except that of Tasmania.[121]

In *South-Eastern Drainage Board (South Australia) v Savings Bank of South Australia*[122] the High Court considered the effect of s 6 of the *Real Property Act 1886* (SA), which provided that no future law, inconsistent with that Act, applied to land subject to that Act unless that future law used a specified form of words to do so. The High Court held that not using the specified form of words in a law did not prevent that law applying to land subject to the 1886 Act provided that the intention to do so was clear. The Court rejected an argument that the requirement was made effective by the 'manner and form' provisions of s 5 of the *Colonial Laws Validity Act 1865* (Imp).[123] Latham CJ stated:

> But the proviso with respect to manner and form applies only to laws respecting the constitution of the legislature, the powers of the legislature, and the procedure of the legislature. Sec. 6 is plainly not a provision affecting in any way the constitution of the legislature. Nor does it affect the powers of the legislature. It only purports to prescribe the contents of an Act which the legislature has power to pass. Nor does the

---

114 There may, however, be a 'manner and form' requirement to be complied with. See below.

115 See AV Dicey, *Introduction to the Study of the Law of the Constitution* (Macmillan, 8th ed, 1915).

116 (1964) 113 CLR 207 (Dixon CJ, Kitto, Taylor, Menzies, Windeyer and Owen JJ).

117 Ibid 226.

118 (1998) 195 CLR 337.

119 Ibid 357 [16].

120 See *Australia Act 1986* (Cth) s 6; *Australia Act 1986* (UK) s 6; *A-G (WA) v Marquet* (2003) 217 CLR 545, 572–3 (Gleeson CJ, Gummow, Hayne and Heydon JJ).

121 See *Constitution Act 1902* (NSW) ss 7A and 7B; *Constitution of Queensland 2001* (Qld) s 78; *Constitution Act 1934* (SA) s 10A; *Constitution Act 1975* (Vic) s 18; *Constitution Act 1889* (WA) s 73.

122 (1939) 62 CLR 603.

123 The *Colonial Laws Validity Act 1865* (Imp) was disapplied from state laws by the *Australia Act 1986* (Cth) s 3(1) and *Australia Act 1986* (UK) s 3(1).

> section relate to any part of the procedure of the legislature in passing statutes. Accordingly, in my opinion, sec. 6 of the *Real Property Act* cannot operate to deprive of effect any subsequent legislation of the South-Australian Parliament which, upon the natural construction of its terms, enacts a provision which is inconsistent with the *Real Property Act 1886*.[124]

In the same case Evatt J stated:

> [I]t is worth while to note what [sec. 6 of the *Real Property Act*] purports to do. It purports to control future parliaments of South Australia in any legislation affecting land under the *Real Property Act* by requiring that unless such legislation is couched in a certain literary form ... it cannot affect land under the Act ...
>
> In my opinion the legislature of South Australia has plenary power to couch its enactments in such literary form as it may choose. It cannot be effectively commanded by a prior legislature to express its intention in a particular way ...
>
> [Section 6] purports to lay down a rigid rule binding upon all future parliaments. It declares that, however clearly the intention of such parliaments may be expressed in an enactment, that intention shall not be given effect to unless it contains the magic formula. I think the command in sec. 6 was quite ineffective and inoperative.[125]

Parliament may, however, enact interpretative provisions that purport to give meaning to words or expressions used in future Acts. This is what Interpretation Acts do. Such Acts are, however, subject to a contrary intention being expressed in a future Act.[126] Human Rights Acts are another example of legislation that purports to affect the interpretation of future Acts.[127] However, the Human Rights Acts in force in Australia do not purport to bind future parliaments.[128]

Parliaments in Australia enjoy a broad range of privileges [11.8]

In England the supremacy of Parliament was secured by the passing of the *Bill of Rights 1688*.[129] Among the rights declared by that Act was 'That the Freedome of Speech and Debates or Proceedings in Parlyament ought not to be impeached or questioned in any Court or Place out of Parlyament'. This declaration, contained in art 9 of the Bill of Rights, still has the force of law in Australia today.[130]

---

124 (1939) 62 CLR 603, 618. See also 623 (Starke J), 625 (Dixon J) and 636 (McTiernan J).

125 Ibid 633–4. See also *Rose v Hvric* (1963) 108 CLR 353. In this case the High Court held that the expression 'Except where otherwise expressly enacted' in an Act did not exclude that requirement being satisfied by implication where 'that is the necessary result of the operation of another enactment according to the intention it manifests' (Kitto, Taylor and Owen JJ at 358) as 'to do more would be exceeding the competency of parliament with respect to future legislation' (Kitto, Taylor and Owen JJ at 357, quoting Keating J in *Chorlton v Lings* (1868) LR 4 CP 374, 395).

126 See **[25.3]**.

127 See *Human Rights Act 2019* (Qld) s 48; *Charter of Human Rights and Responsibilities Act 2006* (Vic) s 32; *Human Rights Act 2004* s 30 (ACT). See **[26.2]**.

128 See *Human Rights Act 2019* (Qld) s 43; *Charter of Human Rights and Responsibilities Act 2006* (Vic) s 31.

129 The Act actually only received royal assent on 16 December 1689. See <http://www.legislation.gov.uk/aep/WillandMarSess2/1/2#reference-c2144673>.

130 See *Egan v Willis* (1998) 195 CLR 424, 444–5 [22]–[24] (Gaudron, Gummow and Hayne JJ), 462 [69] (McHugh J), 488–9 [128–9] (Kirby J), 509–10 [180] (Callinan J). See also *Imperial Acts Application Act 1969* (NSW) s 6; *Imperial Acts Application Act 1980* (Vic) s 8.

Parliaments in Australia have power to legislate about the privileges, immunities and powers that they hold[131] and, subject to such legislation, some of them are expressly stated as having all the privileges held by the British House of Commons as at specified dates.[132] Some have enacted either general legislation about privileges or specific legislation conferring particular privileges.[133]

Section 16(1) of the *Parliamentary Privileges Act 1987* (Cth) declares that the provisions of art 9 of the Bill of Rights apply to the Commonwealth Parliament but then further states that 'as so applying, are to be taken to have, in addition to any other operation, the effect of the subsequent provisions of this section'. Section 16 then proceeds to define the term 'proceedings in Parliament' and make provision as to what is admissible and inadmissible in proceedings in courts or tribunals.[134]

While all jurisdictions have provisions in interpretation legislation expressly permitting reference to parliamentary debates to determine the meaning of statutes,[135] it is clear that even without those provisions art 9 does not prevent a court referring to them for that purpose.[136]

Access to Acts

[11.9] The Crown has a prerogative proprietary right to print and publish Acts

It is in the public interest for Acts to be widely available in the community on which they are binding. The right to print and publish Acts is a prerogative right of the Crown.[137] While this prerogative right has given the Crown the exclusive right to print and publish Acts, there has for a long time been a recognition that the public interest requires that it should not generally be relied on to restrict publication.[138]

This prerogative right sits alongside Crown copyright subsisting in an Act under pt VII of the *Copyright Act 1968* (Cth) ('the *Copyright Act*').[139]

131 *Australian Constitution* s 49; *Constitution of Queensland 2001* (Qld) s 9(1)(a); *Constitution Act 1975* (Vic) s 19 (2); *Constitution Act 1889* (WA) s 36; *Australian Capital Territory (Self-Government) Act 1988* (Cth) s 24(2); *Northern Territory (Self-Government) Act 1978* (Cth) s 12.

132 *Australian Constitution* s 49 (1 January 1901); *Constitution of Queensland 2001* (Qld) s 9(1)(b) (1 January 1901); *Constitution Act 1934* (SA) s 38 (24 October 1856); *Constitution Act 1975* (Vic) s 19(1) (21 July 1855); *Parliamentary Privileges Act 1891* (WA) s 1 (1 January 1989).

133 See, eg, the *Parliamentary Privileges Act 1987* (Cth); *Parliamentary Evidence Act 1901* (NSW); *Parliament of Queensland Act 2001* (Qld); *Parliamentary Privilege Act 1858* (Tas); *Parliamentary Privileges Act 1891* (WA); *Legislative Assembly (Powers and Privileges) Act 1992* (NT).

134 As to whether s 16 merely codifies art 9 or extends its operation or effect see *Rann v Olsen* (2000) 76 SASR 450 and *Mees v Roads Corporation* (2003) 128 FCR 418.

135 *Acts Interpretation Act 1901* (Cth) s 15AB; *Interpretation Act 1987* (NSW) s 34; *Acts Interpretation Act 1954* (Qld) s 14B; *Legislation Interpretation Act 2021* (SA) s 16; *Acts Interpretation Act 1931* (Tas) s 8B; *Interpretation of Legislation Act 1984* (Vic) s 35(b); *Interpretation Act 1984* (WA) s 19; *Legislation Act 2001* (ACT) ss 141–143; *Interpretation Act 1978* (NT) s 62B.

136 See *Pepper (Inspector of Taxes) v Hart* [1993] AC 593; *Victorian Taxi Families Inc v Taxi Services Commission* (2018) 61 VR 91, 125 [93(j)] (Derham AJ).

137 *A-G (NSW) v Butterworth & Co (Australia) Ltd* (1938) 38 SR (NSW) 195 ('*Butterworth*'). Long Innes CJ stated that the basis for this prerogative right was 'the duty resting upon the King, as first executive magistrate, to superintend the publication of acts of the legislature ... carrying with it a corresponding prerogative': at 229.

138 Long Innes CJ in *Butterworth* referred to a United Kingdom Treasury Minute dated 31 August 1887 that stated that, with certain exceptions, the reproduction of Acts should not be restricted as it was desirable that they be made known to the public as widely as possible: at 236.

139 The *Copyright Act* s 8A(1) provides that the Act does not affect any prerogative right or privilege of the Crown. Section 182A(1) expressly refers to the 'copyright, including any prerogative right or privilege of the Crown

Crown copyright subsists under the *Copyright Act* (if it would not otherwise subsist) in Bills drafted by parliamentary counsel employed by the Commonwealth, a state or a territory and acting within the scope of their employment.[140]

Crown copyright also subsists under the *Copyright Act* in a non-government Bill drafted personally by a member of the Commonwealth or a state or territory Parliament or by someone under their direction or control (and thus not done under the direction or control of the Commonwealth, the state or the territory) if the Bill is first published[141] in Australia by, or under the direction or control of, the Commonwealth, the state or the territory and with the approval of the author.[142]

The *Copyright Act* places prerogative rights and privileges of the Crown that are in the nature of copyright in the same position with respect to infringement as copyright subsisting by virtue of that Act.[143] Accordingly, the fair dealing and other provisions in pt III div 3 of the *Copyright Act*, which provide that certain acts do not constitute an infringement of copyright in works, are equally applicable to works in which a prerogative right or privilege of the Crown subsists.

Despite owning copyright (including any prerogative right or privilege of the Crown in the nature of copyright) in legislation, the trend by Australian governments has been not to impede access to legislative material.

Thus the Commonwealth allows all content on the Federal Register of Legislation to be freely used under a Creative Commons licence.[144] New South Wales,[145] Queensland[146] and South Australia[147] similarly treat material on their legislation websites.

The Northern Territory authorises the publication and other dealing with its legislative material on specified conditions including that it must not indicate directly or indirectly that it is an official version of the material.[148]

Tasmania grants users of its legislation website a licence to download, print and otherwise reproduce the information on it for non-commercial purposes only.[149]

Western Australia expressly permits users of its legislation website to download, store in cache, display, print and otherwise reproduce, the whole or any part of any material on the website in an unaltered form only for non-commercial use.[150]

---

in the nature of copyright, in a prescribed work'. Section 182A(3) defines a 'prescribed work' as including 'an Act or State Act, an enactment of the legislature of a Territory or an instrument (including an Ordinance or a rule, regulation or by-law) made under an Act, a State Act or such an enactment'.

140 *Copyright Act* s 176. See also *Copyright Agency Ltd v New South Wales* (2007) 159 FCR 213.

141 The *Copyright Act* s 29(6) provides that any unauthorised publication is to be disregarded in determining whether a publication of a work is the first publication of the work.

142 *Copyright Act* s 177.

143 *Copyright Act* s 8A(2).

144 See <https://www.legislation.gov.au/Content/Disclaimer>.

145 See <https://legislation.nsw.gov.au/copyright>.

146 See <https://www.legislation.qld.gov.au/copyright>.

147 See<https://www.legislation.sa.gov.au/Web/Footer/Copyright/Copyright.aspx>.

148 See <https://legislation.nt.gov.au/en/Footer/Terms-of-Use>.

149 See <https://www.tas.gov.au/stds/codi.htm>.

150 See <https://www.legislation.wa.gov.au/legislation/statutes.nsf/copyright.html>.

The Australian Capital Territory permits users of its legislation website to download, display, distribute, print and reproduce any material on it, in unaltered form only, for personal, educational or non-commercial use.[151]

Western Australia and the Australian Capital Territory rely on their copyright in legislative material to prevent any other use, apart, of course, from uses permitted by the *Copyright Act*.

Victoria asserts its copyright in all Victorian legislation and publications printed with the authority of the Victorian Government Printer.[152]

151 See <https://www.act.gov.au/copyright>.

152 See <http://www.legislation.vic.gov.au/>.

COMMENCEMENT 12

Overview

An Act is passed when the final stage of the enactment process is completed. It may not come into operation for some time after it is passed. It may come into operation wholly at the one time or in stages over a period. [12.1]

The time of its commencement may be fixed by the Act itself or be left to an instrument to be made under the Act. Such an instrument may be made even if the provision authorising its making is not itself in operation. Whether, and when, a commencement instrument is to be made is at the discretion of the Executive. Some jurisdictions set a default date for the commencement of legislation.

Even if not in operation, an Act can still have effect for some purposes. Powers conferred by it may be exercised for limited purposes. It may be amended by another Act. However, as a general rule courts do not take account of an uncommenced Act.

What commencement means and how it is effected

Passing and commencement are different concepts [12.2]

Chapter 11 examined the process for making Acts in Australia. On the date on which the final stage in that process is completed, the Act is passed.[1] Some jurisdictions have a provision to the effect that a reference in legislation to the date of passing of an Act is a reference to the date on which that final stage is completed.[2]

While the date of the passing of an Act may also be the date of its commencement, usually it is not. An Act, or a provision of an Act, comes into force on its commencement date, which may be months or even years after the date of the Act's passing.[3] Indeed it may even be before the date of passing if the Act, or provision, has a retrospective commencement.[4]

---

1 This should not be confused with the passing of a Bill by a legislative chamber in the course of the legislative process.

2 *Interpretation Act 1987* (NSW) s 22(1); *Acts Interpretation Act 1954* (Qld) s 15; *Interpretation of Legislation Act 1984* (Vic) s 11(3); *Legislation Act 2001* (ACT) s 29.

3 See **[12.3]**.

4 An example is the *Victorian Independent Remuneration Tribunal and Improving Parliamentary Standards Act 2019* (Vic), passed on 19 March 2019. Section 2(2) provides that s 61 is to be taken to have come into operation on 1 July 2018.

[12.3] An Act commences on the day(s) fixed by or under it or, in default of that, as determined by interpretation legislation

An Act almost invariably makes provision for its own commencement. Commencement may be on a day or days specified in the Act or may be set by reference to an event specified in the Act such as the commencement of another Act. Frequently, an Act makes provision for the making of an instrument (a proclamation or commencement notice) under it to specify commencement.[5]

The detailed rules about commencement are spelt out in the interpretation legislation in force in the particular jurisdiction.[6] There is no uniformity across Australia in those rules.

If an Act contains no provision for its commencement, it commences as follows:

- Queensland and South Australia – on the day on which it receives royal assent;[7]
- Northern Territory – on the day after the day on which the assent to the Act is declared;[8]
- Australian Capital Territory – on the day after its notification day;[9]
- Tasmania – 14 days after royal assent;[10]
- Commonwealth[11], New South Wales[12] and Western Australia[13] – 28 days after royal assent; and
- Victoria – on a day or days to be proclaimed, or on the first anniversary of the Act's passing, whichever is the earlier.[14]

Where an Act or a provision is to commence on a particular day, for every Australian jurisdiction, except Tasmania, it commences at the beginning of that day.[15] In Tasmania[16] it commences at the end of the preceding day. Despite their differences in wording, there is no difference in effect

5 In *McKenzie v Huybers* [1929] SCR 38 Anglin CJC held that the fixing of a commencement date by a proclamation made under a statute 'had the same effect as if that date had been fixed by the statute itself': at 41.

6 At common law the rule was that an Act was deemed to have come into operation on the first day of the parliamentary session in which it was passed. The obvious inconvenience caused by this rule was overcome in England by the *Acts of Parliament (Commencement) Act 1793* (UK) (33 Geo 3, c 13), which made the date of the Act's passing the date of its commencement in the absence of a contrary intention.

7 *Acts Interpretation Act 1954* (Qld) s 15A; *Legislation Interpretation Act 2021* (SA) s 27(1).

8 *Interpretation Act 1978* (NT) s 5(4). Under s 6 of that Act, if the Act is reserved for the signification of the pleasure of the Governor-General, it does not have effect before the day on which notification of that assent is published in the *Gazette*.

9 *Legislation Act 2001* (ACT) s 73(1).

10 *Acts Interpretation Act 1931* (Tas) s 9(3).

11 *Acts Interpretation Act 1901* (Cth) s 3A: 'An Act to alter the Constitution commences on the day on which it receives royal assent.'

12 *Interpretation Act 1987* (NSW) s 23. However, the Governor may, by proclamation, appoint a day for the commencement of an Act that does not provide for its commencement, being a day that is not earlier than the date of assent and not later than 28 days after the date of assent.

13 *Interpretation Act 1984* (WA) s 20.

14 *Interpretation of Legislation Act 1984* (Vic) s 10A(4).

15 *Acts Interpretation Act 1901* (Cth) s 3; *Interpretation Act 1987* (NSW) s 24; *Acts Interpretation Act 1954* (Qld) s 15B; *Legislation Interpretation Act 2021* (SA) s 28; *Interpretation of Legislation Act 1984* (Vic) s 11(1); *Interpretation Act 1984* (WA) s 21; *Legislation Act 2001* (ACT) s 74(1); *Interpretation Act 1978* (NT) s 6A.

16 *Acts Interpretation Act 1931* (Tas) s 9(5).

between these provisions. In *Prowse v McIntyre*[17] Kitto J stated that '[t]he beginning of a day is nothing but the end of the day before, and the end of the day is nothing but the beginning of the next' while Windeyer J[18] referred to the instance of midnight as 'being both the end of one day and the beginning of the next, for there are no rests in time'.[19]

In Queensland,[20] South Australia,[21] the Australian Capital Territory[22] and the Northern Territory[23] a proclamation or commencement notice may also fix the time on a day for commencement as well as the day, thereby enabling the default rule in the jurisdiction to be displaced. An individual Act may, of course, also displace the default rule by making special provision for the Act, or a provision, to commence at a specified time on a day.

While there is no Commonwealth general provision allowing a proclamation to fix the time on a day of commencement, an example at the Commonwealth level of commencement at a time, other than the beginning of a day, is the *Australia Act 1986* (Cth) – it commenced at 0500 Greenwich Mean Time on 3 March 1986.[24] However, in that case the commencement provision, s 17(2), provided that the Act 'shall come into operation on a day and at a time to be fixed by Proclamation'.[25]

It may be desirable to have an Act come into operation in two or more stages. This could be simply directly provided for in its commencement provision by it specifying different days for the commencement of specified provisions. If left to a proclamation or commencement notice made under the Act, the rule varies across Australia as to whether the empowering provision in the Act needs to expressly provide for that instrument to fix multiple commencement days.

In Queensland,[26] South Australia,[27] the Australian Capital Territory[28] and the Northern Territory,[29] if an Act provides for commencement on a day to be fixed by proclamation or notice, the proclamation or notice may fix a single day or time for the Act to come into operation or different days or times for different provisions of the Act to come into operation.

17 (1961) 111 CLR 264, 274.

18 Ibid 278.

19 See also *Associated Beauty Aids Pty Ltd v Commissioner of Taxation (Cth)* (1965) 113 CLR 662, 669–70 (Windeyer J).

20 *Acts Interpretation Act 1954* (Qld) s 15D.

21 *Legislation Interpretation Act 2021* (SA) s 27(3).

22 *Legislation Act 2001* (ACT) ss 74(1), 77(1).

23 *Interpretation Act 1978* (NT) s 5(3).

24 See Commonwealth, *Gazette: Special*, No S 85, 2 March 1986.

25 A confusing scenario is presented by the *Accident Compensation Act 1985* (Vic). Section 2(2) provided for pt VII to come into operation on the day fixed by proclamation of the Governor in Council published in the Government Gazette. Section 5(1) defined that day as the 'proclaimed day'. That day was fixed as 1 September 1985 by a proclamation published in the Government Gazette on 30 August 1985 at p 3401. However, the application clause of the Act (s 4(1)) operated by reference to the 'appointed day', which term in turn is defined by s 5(1) as 'four o'clock in the afternoon of the day before the proclaimed day'. Providing for the proclamation to fix both a date and time would have been a much clearer approach to take.

26 *Acts Interpretation Act 1954* (Qld) s 15D.

27 *Legislation Interpretation Act 2021* (SA) s 27(3).

28 *Legislation Act 2001* (ACT) s 77(1).

29 *Interpretation Act 1978* (NT) s 5(3).

In New South Wales,[30] Tasmania,[31] Victoria[32] and Western Australia,[33] express provision needs to be made in the Act if power to appoint different days for different provisions of the Act is required.

The *Acts Interpretation Act 1901* (Cth) contains no general provision as to the content of proclamations, but the standard form of commencement provision used in Commonwealth Acts makes it clear whether the proclamation may fix a single day or multiple days.

Express provision is made in a number of jurisdictions as to whether a proclamation or commencement notice fixing a day or time for commencement has to be published before that day or time in order for it to be effective.

In New South Wales,[34] Queensland,[35] Victoria[36] and the Australian Capital Territory,[37] it is provided that the proclamation or notice cannot fix a day before the day of publication but, if it is not in fact published until after the day fixed, the instrument does not wholly fail but has effect from the day of publication or, in the case of the Australian Capital Territory, the day after that day. In those jurisdictions without any express provision, the ordinary presumption against retrospective operation of an instrument would apply.[38]

In *Flinn v James McEwen & Co Pty Ltd*[39] the Full Victorian Supreme Court had to consider what constituted publication of a proclamation of commencement. In that case the published 'proclamation' in the *Government Gazette* did not contain the representation of the seal,[40] the name of the Governor or the expression 'By His Excellency's Command'. The Full Court held that, as a result of those omissions, the Act had not come into operation. Murphy J stated:

> 'Publication' in the present context means, I believe, make generally known and available to the public so that it may be read, and this requires that the proclamation itself be printed, so that its authority and provenance may be seen in the *Gazette* itself. The fact, if it be the fact, that it has passed under the Great Seal – or in Victoria the Public Seal of Victoria, must be seen ... Next, it must be seen to have been signed by his Excellency, the Governor in Council. ...
>
> The publication must, in my opinion, show on its face that the necessary solemnity attendant upon a Royal proclamation has preceded the proclamation.[41]

Can a proclamation or notice fixing the commencement day or time of an Act be subsequently amended so as to delay that commencement? In a South Australian case, *Palais Parking Station Pty Ltd v Shea*,[42] Bray CJ held that it could not as proclamations were not included in s 39 of the *Acts Interpretation Act 1915* (SA), which provided power to vary regulations and other instruments. He

30 *Interpretation Act 1987* (NSW) s 23(4).

31 *Acts Interpretation Act 1931* (Tas) s 9(3A).

32 *Interpretation of Legislation Act 1984* (Vic) s 10A(1), (2).

33 *Interpretation Act 1984* (WA) s 23.

34 *Interpretation Act 1987* (NSW) s 23(3), (5).

35 *Acts Interpretation Act 1954* (Qld) s 15D(2).

36 *Interpretation of Legislation Act 1984* (Vic) s 11(2), (2A).

37 *Legislation Act 2001* (ACT) s 77(2)–(3). Section 77(4) excepts from this rule a commencement notice that is authorised to provide for an earlier date or time.

38 See chapter 39 and **[43.5]**.

39 [1991] 2 VR 434.

40 That is, the symbol '(L.S.)'.

41 [1991] 2 VR 434, 442–3 (Fullagar J agreeing at 447, Hampel J agreeing at 448).

42 (1977) 16 SASR 350.

stated that the power to make a proclamation of commencement 'is one of those powers which can only be exercised once and the exercise of which cannot be revoked or altered'.[43]

In South Australia s 27(5) of the *Legislation Interpretation Act 2021* (SA) now provides that the Governor may, by subsequent proclamation made before the date fixed for commencement, vary the proclamation so as to fix a different day or time for the Act or provision to come into operation.

In the Commonwealth,[44] Queensland,[45] Tasmania,[46] Victoria,[47] Western Australia,[48] the Australian Capital Territory[49] and the Northern Territory[50] there are general provisions applying to delegated legislation that have the effect of providing that the power to make a proclamation or commencement notice includes power to vary or revoke it. The equivalent provision in New South Wales, however, applies only to statutory rules (which a proclamation is not) and orders.[51]

Accordingly, the position in South Australia is clear but everywhere else in Australia, apart from New South Wales, there would still seem to be a statutory basis for amending a proclamation or commencement notice, given that such instruments are not expressly excluded from the general provisions in force in those places.

A commencement provision is operative even if not expressly commenced [12.4]

The power to make a proclamation or notice fixing a day or time for the commencement of an Act or provision of an Act is to be found in the commencement provision of the Act.[52] If the commencement provision of the Act is itself not commenced, how can an instrument be made under it?

A number of jurisdictions overcome this problem by providing that the commencement provision comes into operation on the day on which the Act receives the royal assent.[53] In the Australian Capital Territory the rule is that the commencement provision automatically commences on the notification day of the Act or on any earlier date on which any provision of the Act is taken to have commenced.[54] In the Northern Territory, up until the commencement of the *Interpretation Amendment Act 2021* on 1 January 2022, there was a provision to the effect that the commencement provision commenced on the day on which the Administrator's assent was declared or, if the Act was reserved for the Governor-General's assent, on the day on which notice of that assent was published in the Government Gazette.[55] That provision was repealed by s 4 of the 2021 Act.

43 Ibid 358.

44 *Acts Interpretation Act 1901* (Cth) s 33(3).

45 *Acts Interpretation Act 1954* (Qld) s 24AA.

46 *Acts Interpretation Act 1931* (Tas) s 22.

47 *Interpretation of Legislation Act 1984* (Vic) s 27.

48 *Interpretation Act 1984* (WA) s 43(4).

49 *Legislation Act 2001* (ACT) s 46.

50 *Interpretation Act 1978* (NT) s 43.

51 *Interpretation Act 1987* (NSW) s 43.

52 Ibid s 23(2) empowers the Governor to make a proclamation to appoint a day (between assent and 28 days after assent) for the commencement of an Act that does not provide for its commencement.

53 *Acts Interpretation Act 1954* (Qld) s 15C(1); *Acts Interpretation Act 1931* (Tas) s 9(3A); *Interpretation Act 1984* (WA) s 22.

54 *Legislation Act 2001* (ACT) s 75.

55 *Interpretation Act 1978* (NT) s 6(3).

New South Wales addresses the problem directly by providing that a proclamation may be made under the commencement provision even though that provision has not commenced.[56]

Of course there is no issue if the Act itself makes express provision for the commencement provision to come into operation at the earliest time at which reliance needs to be placed on it, without the need for any proclamation or commencement notice. In any event reliance can be placed on the common law.

In *Fagan v Dominitz*[57] Street CJ stated that a commencement provision must 'be regarded as an immediate grant of power independently of any proclamation, and a grant coming into existence upon the date when the Act received the Royal Assent'.

The Court of Appeal in England had earlier addressed this issue in *R v Minister of Town and Country Planning; Ex parte Montague Burton Ltd.*[58] Counsel had argued that the relevant Act could never come into operation because the Minister could not appoint a day under it for its commencement until the Act had commenced and the Act could not commence until the Minister had appointed a day. Tucker LJ dismissed the argument, stating:

> That ingenious argument does not appeal to me because I think that an ordinary and natural interpretation must be given to a section which itself brings the Act into operation, namely, that it must necessarily come into operation with the passing of the Act ... Any other interpretation would really make nonsense of the provisions of the Act.[59]

[12.5] The power of the Executive to delay commencement may be limited

If Parliament delegates to the Executive the power to fix a commencement date, does the Executive have total discretion as to when that date will be fixed or indeed as to whether a date will be fixed at all? In some jurisdictions interpretation legislation provides for automatic commencement of an Act after a specified period of time, if a date has not been fixed by then, while in others the provision empowering the fixing of the date itself puts limits on the exercise of the power.

In Queensland, for Acts enacted after 31 December 1994, automatic commencement of an Act happens on the first anniversary of it receiving the royal assent.[60] That period of one year may be extended to a period of up to two years by regulation.[61] In South Australia, for Acts passed after 1 January 2022 or within two years before that date, automatic commencement happens on the second anniversary of the Act receiving the royal assent unless this provision is disapplied.[62] In the Australian Capital Territory an Act that does not commence until a day or time fixed by a commencement notice automatically commences on the sixth month anniversary of the day on which the making of the Act is notified by the parliamentary counsel.[63]

---

56 *Interpretation Act 1987* (NSW) s 23(7).

57 (1957) 58 SR (NSW) 122, 126.

58 [1951] 1 KB 1.

59 Ibid 5.

60 *Acts Interpretation Act 1954* (Qld) s 15DA(2). This rule may be disapplied by the Act.

61 Ibid s 15DA(3), (4).

62 *Legislation Interpretation Act 2021* (SA) s 27(6), (7).

63 *Legislation Act 2001* (ACT) s 79. This automatic commencement may be displaced by a provision made by or under an Act.

In Commonwealth and Victorian legislation the practice is to include a specific limiting provision in Acts all or part of which do not commence until a day fixed by proclamation made under the Act.

Drafting Direction No 1.3 issued by the Commonwealth Parliamentary Counsel gives the background to the adoption of this practice.[64] In the late 1980s certain Senators criticised the government over the increasing number of Acts not proclaimed to commence for long periods after passage, sometimes years. Senate Standing Order 139(2) now provides:

> There shall be laid on the table, on or before 31 August each year, details of all provisions of Acts which come into effect on proclamation and which have not been proclaimed, together with a statement of reasons for their non-proclamation and a timetable for their operation.[65]

The Department of the Prime Minister and Cabinet has adopted a policy imposing restrictions on the period within which an Act, or a provision of an Act, may be proclaimed. Generally that period should not be longer than six months with the need for a longer period being explained in the explanatory memorandum that accompanies the Bill. The Senate Standing Committee for the Scrutiny of Bills in practice seeks an explanation for any commencement provision that departs from the standard required by the policy.

These Commonwealth developments were taken note of by the Scrutiny of Acts and Regulations Committee of the Victorian Parliament. On 19 April 1993 it published a report entitled *Report On Commencement By Proclamation*.[66] The report endorsed a practice for restricted proclamation clauses. It states:

> Commencement by proclamation can allow an unacceptable delay in the starting of an Act which the Parliament has thought fit to pass or even allow the Executive to decline to bring into operation an Act (or portions of an Act) which the Parliament has passed. It can also be a method of quieting a noisy lobby group (at least temporarily) by Parliament passing an Act to the benefit of the group with the Executive having no intention of bringing the Act into operation, for lack of money or resources. There is an added difficulty for users of the law, who not only must consult the Statute Book but also search separately for publication of proclamation dates. This leaves Acts which commence by proclamation in an unacceptable state of uncertainty.[67]

Example 12.1 illustrates the current Victorian practice for restricting the length of the period within which an Act, or provisions of an Act, must be proclaimed to come into operation.[68]

---

64 See Office of Parliamentary Counsel, *Drafting Direction No 1.3* (Australian Government, January 2017) [21]–[27].

65 Department of Prime Minister and Cabinet, Commonwealth Parliament, *Report on Unproclaimed Legislation* (Australian Government, August 2019) lists 12 Acts all or part of which have not been proclaimed, including provisions of an Act that received royal assent on 2 July 1998.

66 Scrutiny of Acts and Regulations Committee, Parliament of Victoria, *Report on Commencement by Proclamation* (Report No 37, April 1993).

67 Ibid 2.

68 The Scrutiny of Acts and Regulations Committee of the Victorian Parliament considers whether any delay to commencement of more than 12 months from the date on which a Bill is first introduced into Parliament is reasonable and justified relying on the *Parliamentary Committees Act 2003* (Vic) s 17(a)(vi). This provision gives the Committee a function of reporting to Parliament on whether a Bill directly or indirectly 'inappropriately delegates legislative power'. It has issued a Practice Note to government legal and legislation officers indicating its expectation that information should be provided to Parliament explaining and justifying a delay to commencement of longer than 12 months. Scrutiny of Acts and Regulations Committee, *Practice Note* (Parliament of Victoria, 26 May 2014).

Example 12.1 ***Guardianship and Administration Act 2019*** **(Vic)**

2 Commencement

(1) Subject to subsection (2), this Act comes into operation on a day or days to be proclaimed.[69]

(2) If a provision of this Act does not come into operation before 1 March 2020, it comes into operation on that day.

No similar practice is followed in New South Wales,[70] Tasmania, Western Australia or the Northern Territory. Accordingly, open-ended commencement clauses may be found in Acts passed in those jurisdictions.

If an Act contains an open-ended commencement clause, the Executive could seek to delay for a long period, or even indefinitely, the making of a proclamation or notice fixing the commencement date of the Act or of a provision of the Act. The difficulties to which this can give rise were highlighted in two cases in New South Wales concerning the *Mental Health Act 1983* (NSW).

The issue in *CCR v PS (No 2)*[71] was that while the operative provision of the 1983 Act providing for the discharge of a 'mentally ill person' (s 139) had been proclaimed, the provision in s 5 of that Act defining the term 'mentally ill person' had not. That definition differed from the definition of the same term in the predecessor Act under which the person had been detained. Powell J stated:

> It is but little short of scandalous that, in relation to matters directly affecting the liberty of the subject, there should exist such doubts ... which doubts are a product of the recent pernicious practices of delaying the proclamation of Acts of the Parliament and of proclaiming different dates of operation for different provisions within an Act of Parliament.[72]

In a case before the NSW Court of Appeal, *B v Medical Superintendent of Macquarie Hospital*,[73] involving the same Act, Kirby P stated:

> [T]here has been a lengthy, and almost unprecedented, delay on the part of the Executive Government in proclaiming relevant sections of the 1983 Act, including the definition provisions in s. 5 upon which depend many provisions of that Act ...
>
> It should not be assumed that Parliament intended provisions of a machinery character ... to operate, disconnected from a crucial definition provision ...
>
> The purpose of Parliament is thus frustrated, and not in a minor or incidental matter but in a provision vital to the whole operation of the new Act ...
>
> No argument was addressed to the Court as to whether the proclamation which brought s139 into operation without s5, was valid.[74]

69 In *Flinn v James McEwen & Co Pty Ltd* [1991] 2 VR 434 Fullagar and Hampel JJ held that a provision of this kind enables the Act to be proclaimed to come into operation in part on one day and by another proclamation to come into operation as to another part on another day: at 448.

70 *Legislative Assembly Standing Orders 2007* (NSW) ord 117 provides that on the second sitting day of each session and then every 15th sitting day thereafter, the Speaker must table a list of legislation remaining unproclaimed 90 days after assent.

71 (1986) 6 NSWLR 622.

72 Ibid 624.

73 (1987) 10 NSWLR 440.

74 Ibid 447–9.

In that case Priestley JA observed that the result was so bizarre that he was clinging 'to the hope that somewhere there is a gazetted proclamation which puts the apparent blunder to rights'.[75] McHugh JA touched on the validity point in stating that 'a serious question must also arise as to whether the proclamation seeking to bring s139 into effect without the aid of s5 is valid: cf *Shanahan v Scott* (1957) 96 CLR 245 and *Peppers Self Service Stores Pty Ltd v Scott* (1958) 98 CLR 606'.[76]

In *Tonkin v Brand*[77] the Full Supreme Court of Western Australia had to consider a provision of the *Electoral Districts Act 1947–1955* (WA) that provided that a proclamation on the division of areas into electoral districts 'shall be issued' in specified circumstances. The Court made a declaration that the Executive Council members were under a legal duty to advise the Governor to issue such a proclamation in the circumstances that then existed.

In *R v Secretary of State for the Home Department; Ex parte Fire Brigades Union*[78] the House of Lords considered s 171(1) of the *Criminal Justice Act 1988* (UK) – it provided that the Act (other than some provisions for which specific provision for their commencement was made) 'shall come into force on such day as the Secretary of State may . . . appoint'. By December 1993 a day had not been appointed for the commencement of provisions establishing a statutory scheme of compensation for victims of crime. At that time the government announced in a White Paper that those provisions would not be implemented.[79] The Court held that the Act did not impose an enforceable duty on the Secretary of State to bring the provisions into force at any particular time but that it did impose a continuing obligation on the Secretary of State to consider whether to bring the relevant provisions into force.

If Parliament does intend to give the executive government the discretion to leave an Act or a provision of an Act unproclaimed, it should state that intention clearly. An example of this is the *Higher Education Funding Act 1988* (Cth), s 2(2) of which provided that certain provisions 'commence on such date (if any) as is . . . fixed by Proclamation'. While the Minister would still be under an ongoing duty to consider whether to recommend the making of a proclamation or commencement notice, there would be no expectation of one being made reasonably promptly or at all.

Internal references to commencement of the Act are construed differently across Australia [12.6]

What is the meaning of a reference in an Act to the commencement of that Act or of another Act where that Act or the other Act did not come, or is not to come, into operation on the one day?

Victoria[80] and the Northern Territory[81] provide that such a reference is a reference to the first day on which the whole Act is in operation. Western Australia treats such a

75 Ibid 459.

76 Ibid 463.

77 [1962] WAR 2.

78 [1995] 2 AC 513.

79 Lord Lloyd in ibid stated: 'It might cause surprise to the man on the Clapham omnibus that legislative provisions in an Act of Parliament, which have passed both Houses of Parliament and received the Royal Assent, can be set aside in this way by a member of the executive' (at 568).

80 *Interpretation of Legislation Act 1984* (Vic) s 11(4).

81 *Interpretation Act 1978* (NT) s 6B(b).

reference as a reference to 'the day of coming into operation of the appropriate provisions of that written law'.[82]

Queensland treats a reference in a provision of an Act to the commencement of that Act, where the Act does not all (except for its citation and commencement) commence on a single day or at a single time, as a reference to the commencement of that provision.[83]

New South Wales treats a reference in an Act to the commencement of another Act, where that other Act provides that all of its provisions (with specified exceptions) commence at the same time, as a reference to the commencement of all of its provisions, with those specified exceptions.[84]

Status of Act pre-commencement

[12.7] Powers may be exercised between passing and commencement for limited purposes

A common reason for a period of delay between passing and commencement is to enable necessary things to be done before the Act may be put into operation. Those things may include the making of regulations, the appointment of members to a board being established by the Act, the setting up of arrangements for the administration of the Act, the engagement of new public officials, the training of staff, the designing of forms and the programming of computers to process applications.[85]

Each jurisdiction has a provision in its interpretation legislation to empower the doing of things under an Act or provision (including a provision being inserted in another Act) before it has come into operation.[86] The drafting of these provisions is not consistent.

Some provide that an appointment or instrument made before commencement does not take effect before commencement.[87] Some provide that the thing done can only have effect before commencement to the extent necessary for the effective operation of the Act.[88] Some make it expressly clear that the exercise of a power does not confer a right or impose an obligation on a person before commencement except to the extent necessary for bringing the Act or provision into operation or making it fully effective at or after commencement.[89] The NSW provision is limited to the making of instruments of a legislative or administrative character with the instruments not taking effect before commencement.[90] In Tasmania and Western Australia an instrument, notice or other document made or given before commencement does not take effect before commencement.[91]

---

82 *Interpretation Act 1984* (WA) s 27.

83 *Acts Interpretation Act 1954* (Qld) s 15C(2).

84 *Interpretation Act 1987* (NSW) s 25.

85 Lord Thring, the inaugural First Parliamentary Counsel in London (1869–86), wrote that 'great inconvenience arises from bringing a complicated Act into operation immediately on the date of its passing, and it is almost always advisable to postpone its operation for some little time, in order at all events that the public may become acquainted with its provisions'. See Madeleine MacKenzie and David Purdie (eds) *Thring's Practical Legislation: the Composition and Language of Acts of Parliament and Business Documents* (Luath Press, 3rd ed, 2015) 101.

86 *Acts Interpretation Act 1901* (Cth) s 4(4); *Interpretation Act 1987* (NSW) s 26; *Acts Interpretation Act 1954* (Qld) s 17; *Legislation Interpretation Act 2021* (SA) s 38; *Acts Interpretation Act 1931* (Tas) s 11; *Interpretation of Legislation Act 1984* (Vic) s 13; *Interpretation Act 1984* (WA) s 25; *Legislation Act 2001* (ACT) s 81; *Interpretation Act 1978* (NT) s 8.

87 *Acts Interpretation Act 1901* (Cth) s 4(5); *Legislation Act 2001* (ACT) s 81(7) (unless s 81(6) applies).

88 *Acts Interpretation Act 1954* (Qld) s 17(4); *Interpretation Act 1978* (NT) s 8(2).

89 *Acts Interpretation Act 1901* (Cth) s 4(4); *Interpretation of Legislation Act 1984* (Vic) s 13(2).

90 *Interpretation Act 1987* (NSW) s 26.

91 *Acts Interpretation Act 1931* (Tas) s 11(3); *Interpretation Act 1984* (WA) s 25(3).

Tasmania,[92] Victoria[93] and Western Australia[94] have provisions specifically applying to the appointment of persons to offices, or the establishment of bodies, under an uncommenced Act or provision. They expressly allow an appointee to act in the office, and a body to meet and operate, for the purpose of giving full effect to the uncommenced Act or provision at its commencement. The Victorian and Western Australian legislation provide that despite so acting or operating, the term of office of an appointee or member of a body does not officially begin until commencement. The Victorian provision also expressly gives appointees and members of bodies an entitlement to the same remuneration or allowances (if any) for work done before commencement as if the Act or provision had been in operation at the relevant time.

South Australia has a general provision allowing a power to be exercised before commencement, if expedient, but with any such exercise of power (other than the appointment of a person to a position) only having effect on commencement. However, anything done by an appointee has no effect until commencement.[95]

An Act may be amended before it commences [12.8]

Can an Act passed by Parliament be amended before it comes into operation? Northern Territory legislation expressly provides for this.[96] However, even in the absence of an express statutory provision, it is clear that an Act may be amended before it commences. In *Re Fogg (Dec'd)*[97] Helsham J stated:

> It is not, to my mind, impossible to amend an Act which has not yet commenced so that it will commence in its amended form, and to do that it is, of course, necessary that the amending Act should operate upon the amended Act immediately. It does not seem to me that because the amending Act must commence for these purposes it turns on, as it were, the prior Act as a result.[98]

As a general rule courts do not take account of uncommenced legislation [12.9]

An Act, or a provision of an Act, that has not yet commenced is not part of the 'in force' statute law of the jurisdiction. Can a court, however, have regard to it for any purpose?

In *Wilson v Dagnall*[99] the issue before the English Court of Appeal was whether a court in assessing damages in an action by a widow under the *Fatal Accidents Acts 1846–1959* (UK) was required to take her prospects of remarriage into account. While at the time the case was being heard a court was required to do so, an amending Act, due to come into operation five days later, would reverse that position. The trial judge did not take the widow's prospects of remarriage into account, considering that it would be unjust and wrong to do so in the circumstances of the amending Act due to become operational very shortly. On appeal the majority held that the trial judge was wrong. Megaw LJ stated:

---

92 *Acts Interpretation Act 1931* (Tas) s 11(4).

93 *Interpretation of Legislation Act 1984* (Vic) s 13(3), (4).

94 *Interpretation Act 1984* (WA) s 25(4).

95 *Legislation Interpretation Act 2021* (SA) s 38(3).

96 *Interpretation Act 1978* (NT) s 9(b).

97 [1972] 1 NSWLR 416.

98 Ibid 420.

99 [1972] 1 QB 509.

> Parliament has unambiguously said that the Act is to come into operation on 1st August 1971. To my mind there is no ambiguity about that nor any doubt as to its effect. It means that Parliament has ordained that up to that date, 1st August 1971, the law is to remain as before.[100]

However, Lord Denning MR, in a dissenting judgment, held that the trial judge was right to have regard to the new Act but should have directed the judgment to be post-dated so as to take effect on 2 August 1971. He was of the view that it was wrong that the amount of damages should be affected by the expedition of the Court in giving judgment.[101]

A similar situation arose in *R v Walsall Justices; Ex parte W*,[102] where the rule of law requiring that unsworn testimony had to be corroborated was to be abolished under legislation proclaimed to come into operation on the day after the trial. The presiding justices decided that in the interests of justice the trial should be adjourned. The Divisional Court held that that was not a legitimate basis for an adjournment. Their Honours stated:

> [I]t is the function of courts to apply the law ... If a particular law is thought to cause injustice, it is for Parliament to change it. Here Parliament has considered that in the interests of justice the law should be changed. It determined (through subordinate legislation) that 12 October 1988 should be the date on which that change should come into effect. Until that date, it was in our judgment the duty of the court to apply the existing law.[103]

Limited account for interpretative purposes was taken of an uncommenced amendment in *Hersfield Developments Corporation Pty Ltd v Melbourne and Metropolitan Board of Works*.[104] In that case there was a dispute over the meaning of the expression 'advertising signs' in a schedule to the *Town and Country Planning Act 1961* (Vic). It was argued that support for the view that the expression did not include a sign that was directory in nature was provided by an unproclaimed amendment to the Act that, in defining 'advertisement', expressly included the concept of directory signs. This was said to be recognition that such signs were not then currently covered. McGarvie J stated that the unproclaimed amendment

> provides some support for the appellant's submission, but it is not of great weight. By the new definition Parliament may have been intending to put beyond argument the meaning of 'advertising' or 'advertises', instead of recognizing any limited ambit of those words.[105]

However, in *C v Director-General of the Department of Youth & Community Services*[106] a similar question was approached in a different way. In that case Waddell J had to consider whether it was legitimate for the purpose of interpreting an existing subsection of a section to have regard to the

100 Ibid 519.

101 Ibid 513–4.

102 [1990] 1 QB 253.

103 Ibid 261 (Woolf LJ and Saville J).

104 [1982] VR 608.

105 Ibid 613. See also *Weigall Constructions Pty Ltd v Melbourne & Metropolitan Board of Works* [1972] VR 781. In this case the issue was whether a right of appeal against a condition of a subdivision permit existed not only in a person in whose favour a determination to grant a permit had been made but also in a person to whom a permit had already been issued. Pape J referred to an unproclaimed amendment to the relevant legislation and stated that it 'would seem to support the view that without it there was no right of appeal against a condition in a permit already issued': at 789.

106 [1982] 1 NSWLR 65.

terms of an additional subsection to be added by a later unproclaimed Act. He held that it was not legitimate to do so, stating:

> It seems to me that on the question of interpretation of earlier legislation regard should not be had to the terms of later legislation which will not commence until a date to be proclaimed and which is, accordingly, not yet law ... Although it happens very seldom, it is always possible that the necessary proclamation will not be made and that the legislation will not pass into law. It seems to me that while such a possibility exists it would be wrong for a court to take the terms of later legislation into account in interpreting earlier.[107]

Despite as a general rule not taking account of uncommenced Acts or provisions, courts do not treat them as if they did not exist. They may be regarded as having legal relevance for some purposes.

In *Queensland v Central Queensland Land Council Aboriginal Corporation*[108] the status of an Act that had been enacted, but which was not in force, was discussed. The *Native Title Act 1993* (Cth) allowed the relevant Commonwealth Minister to determine that alternative provisions provided for by 'a law of a State' have effect in place of particular provisions of that Act. The issue before the Full Federal Court was whether for this purpose an Act that was not in force was 'a law of a State'.

The primary judge had been of the view that an Act passed but not in operation was an 'Act in escrow' and legally non-existent for any purpose affecting the legal position of the parties. Beaumont J, as a member of the Full Federal Court, stated that there was an abundance of high authority 'to the effect that, upon enactment, a statute may have legal relevance for particular purposes, even if not yet in force'.[109] He referred[110] to cases in which the constitutional validity of enacted, but not in force, legislation was challenged[111] and he rejected[112] the characterisation of an enacted statute not yet in force as 'legally non-existent' or as an 'Act in escrow'.[113]

Kiefel J stated that in general terms 'it is doubtless correct that statutory provisions do not affect the legal position of persons until they become operative' but that that did not mean that they were 'ineffective for all purposes'.[114] Moreover, in Her Honour's view, in the context of s 43(1) of the *Native Title Act 1993* (Cth), the requirement for there to be a state law providing for alternative provisions 'merely requires the Act to contain the alternative provisions', without any necessity for those provisions to be in force.[115]

---

107 Ibid 71.

108 (2002) 125 FCR 89.

109 Ibid 102.

110 Ibid 103.

111 *A-G (Vic) v Commonwealth* (1945) 71 CLR 237 and *New South Wales v Commonwealth* (1990) 169 CLR 482, 495, 513.

112 *Queensland v Central Queensland Land Council Aboriginal Corporation* (2002) 125 FCR 89, 103.

113 In *R v Secretary of State for the Home Department; Ex parte Fire Brigades Union* [1995] 2 AC 513, Lord Lloyd of Berwick, referring to uncommenced sections of an Act, stated that it was a mistake 'to treat these sections as if they did not exist. True, they do not have statutory force. But that does not mean that they are writ in water. They contain a statement of Parliamentary intention, even though they create no enforceable rights': at 570.

114 (2002) 125 FCR 89, 119.

115 Ibid. Lee J was also of the view that 'alternative provisions' may be found in an Act that had not yet commenced: at 112.

13 STRUCTURE AND COMPONENTS OF AN ACT

Overview

[13.1] This chapter looks at the structure of Acts and their various components. An Act begins life as a Bill and its components flow through into the Act when passed. Certain components of a Bill are mandated by legislation[1] or parliamentary standing orders.[2] Others reflect the choices made by a jurisdiction about Act structure.

When a Bill is passed and becomes an Act, the rules vary across Australian jurisdictions as to whether certain components of the Bill are treated as part of the Act. Increasingly, however, the trend is for everything that forms part of the text of the Act, as enacted, to be treated as part of the Act.

The role played for interpretative purposes by any particular component, whether treated as a part of an Act or not, and by how an Act is structured, is dealt with in chapter 20. This chapter is confined to identifying the various components and indicating whether they are treated as part of an Act.

Structure of an Act

[13.2] Provisions should be organised in a logical way

Chapter 10 focused on legislative drafting, the process by which Bills are developed for introduction into Parliament. A Bill becomes an Act if it completes all stages on its journey through Parliament.[3] An important first step in the legislative drafting process, certainly in the case of long and complex Bills, is the drawing up by parliamentary counsel of a detailed plan for the drafting project. A key matter to be dealt with in the drafting plan is how provisions within the Bill are to be arranged – that is, how to structure the legislative scheme.[4]

Poor organisation of material in legislation, both within sections and within an Act as a whole, was criticised by the Law Reform Commission of Victoria in its report *Plain English and the Law*.[5] The Commission used the *Dangerous Goods Act 1985* (Vic) as an example of poor organisation of material. It pointed to how, before a general reader gets to the provisions likely to be important to them (those dealing with licensing and the duties of licensees and of other people handling

---

1 Principally Interpretation Acts but also, in some jurisdictions, provisions contained in Constitution Acts.

2 These are procedural orders applicable to proceedings in Parliament.

3 See chapter 11.

4 See Office of Parliamentary Counsel, *Plain English Manual* (Australian Government, 2016) ch 2 for a description of how to plan a drafting project for Commonwealth legislation.

5 Law Reform Commission of Victoria, *Plain English and the Law* (Report No 9, June 1987) [47]–[56].

dangerous goods), the reader must wade through a substantial amount of technical and administrative material. The Commission was also critical of the separation of closely related provisions and pointed to the *Credit Act 1984* (Vic) as an example.[6] The Commission returned to this theme in a later report, stating: 'If complex messages are to be understood, the ideas must not only be coherent; they must also be presented in an orderly flow.'[7]

At the Commonwealth level a 1993 report by the House of Representatives Standing Committee on Legal and Constitutional Affairs, while acknowledging the importance of the principle of putting the main message first as an aid to communication, supported the continued inclusion of preliminary provisions (such as commencement provisions and definitions) at the beginning of an Act.[8] That report also recommended a greater use of schedules 'to deal with discrete topics, such as procedural matters, constitution of authorities etc., that do not go to the essence of the scheme established by legislation'.[9] It further supported a recommendation of the Administrative Review Council in a report entitled *Rule Making by Commonwealth Agencies*[10] on the kinds of matters that should be dealt with by Acts and not left to delegated legislation.[11]

Guidance on the arrangement of Commonwealth Bills may be found in chapter 5 of the *Plain English Manual* published by the Commonwealth Office of Parliamentary Counsel.[12] It recommends arranging provisions so that the relationship between them is as clear as possible and advises putting 'general or important propositions first, then particular or less important propositions, then exceptions, then administrative provisions, then offences, etc.'.[13]

The way in which provisions of an Act are arranged, and how they are set out, can impact on how they are interpreted.[14]

Structural rules dictate the form of a Bill [13.3]

In drawing up a drafting plan for a Bill, a parliamentary counsel needs to work within certain fixed parameters. Some components of a Bill are made mandatory by the standing orders of the House or Houses of Parliament in which they are introduced. A Bill that does not comply with any

---

6 Ibid [56]. The Law Reform Commission set out a comment on the *Credit Act*'s organisation of material from Warren Pengilley, *Credit Act 1984* (Longman Professional, 1984) 12: 'The Act believes in "the treasure trove" principle of statutory interpretation. By this method, the draftsman drops clues in certain sections of the Act which enable the astute seeker of truth to see the possibility of the relevance of other sections, and thus by shuttling back and forth, hopefully to arrive at the correct conclusion'.

7 Law Reform Commission of Victoria, *Access to the Law: The Structure and Format of Legislation*, (Report No 33, May 1990) 8 [2.2].

8 House of Representatives Standing Committee on Legal and Constitutional Affairs, Parliament of Australia, *Clearer Commonwealth Law, Report of the Inquiry into Legislative Drafting by the Commonwealth* (Report, September 1993).

9 Ibid [7.26].

10 Administrative Review Council, *Report to the Attorney General: Rule Making by Commonwealth Agencies* (Report No 35, 1992).

11 Ibid [7.20]. Those matters were significant questions of policy, rules with significant impacts on individual rights and liberties, administrative and significant criminal penalties, taxes and significant fees and charges, procedural matters going to the essence of the legislative scheme and amendments of Acts. See also, for Commonwealth legislation, Department of Prime Minister and Cabinet, *Legislation Handbook* (Commonwealth of Australia, 2017) [1.10], [1.11].

12 Office of Parliamentary Counsel, *Plain English Manual* (Australian Government, 2016).

13 Ibid [103].

14 See chapter 20.

such standing order may be required to be withdrawn.[15] Other legislation within the jurisdiction may also mandate particular content – for example, the words of enactment to be used.[16]

Interpretation legislation in each jurisdiction also contemplates that an Act, and therefore a Bill, will contain certain components such as sections with headings and that it may contain schedules. Standing orders determine the order in which clauses (the description given to sections in a Bill) and schedules are considered in Parliament.[17]

Matters of layout such as font size, line spacing and heading style are pre-determined by the software program designed by the jurisdiction for the drafting and printing of its legislation. However, except for preliminary provisions such as commencement clauses and clauses containing definitions, the arrangement of clauses within a Bill is generally at the discretion of parliamentary counsel. This discretion may be limited, however, by the requirements of an in-house drafting manual with which the counsel must comply.

Components of an Act

[13.4] A Bill must have a long title

A long title is an essential component of a Bill. This is a title placed at the start of a Bill that describes its general objects.[18] It has significance for its passage through Parliament as each clause of a Bill must come within the scope of the Bill as defined by the long title.[19] The long title passes through the same parliamentary processes as the rest of a Bill.

---

15 For example, ord 138 of *House of Representatives Standing Orders 2019* (Cth) states that 'A bill not prepared according to the standing orders of the House shall be ordered to be withdrawn.' See also *Senate Standing Orders 2020* (Cth) ord 111(4); *Legislative Council Standing Rules and Orders 2004* (NSW) ord 136(4); *Legislative Council Standing Orders 1999* (SA) ord 276; *Legislative Assembly Standing Orders 2004* (Vic) ord 60; *Legislative Council of Victoria Standing Orders 2020* (Vic) ord 14.02; *Standing Orders of the Legislative Assembly 2017* (WA) ord 164; *Legislative Council Standing Orders 2019* (WA) ord 122(3); *Legislative Assembly for the Australian Capital Territory Standing Orders 2019* (ACT) ord 170.

16 See **[13.5]**.

17 *House of Representatives Standing Orders 2019* (Cth) ord 149; *Senate Standing Orders 2020* (Cth) ord 117; *Legislative Assembly Standing Orders 2007* (NSW) ord 209; *Legislative Council Standing Rules and Orders 2004* (NSW) ord 143; *Standing Rules and Orders of the Legislative Assembly 2004* (Qld) ord 145; *Legislative Assembly Standing Orders 2018* (SA) ord 246; *Legislative Council Standing Orders 1999* (SA) ord 290; *House of Assembly Standing and Sessional Orders and Rules 2017* (Tas) ord 200; *Standing Orders Legislative Council 2010* (Tas) ords 269–274; *Legislative Assembly Standing Orders 2004* (Vic) ord 66; *Legislative Council of Victoria Standing Orders 2020* (Vic) ord 14.12; *Standing Orders of the Legislative Assembly 2017* (WA) ord 175; *Legislative Council Standing Orders 2019* (WA) ord 130; *Legislative Assembly for the Australian Capital Territory: Standing Orders 2019* (ACT) ord 180; *Standing Orders 2016* (NT) ord 152.

18 *Legislative Assembly Standing Orders 2007* (NSW) ord 188(1) provides that it is not necessary to specify in the long title every Act that the Bill proposes to amend.

19 *House of Representatives Standing Orders 2019* (Cth) ord 140(b); *Senate Standing Orders 2020* (Cth) ord 111(3); *Legislative Assembly Standing Orders 2007* (NSW) ord 188(1); *Legislative Council Standing Rules and Orders 2004* (NSW) ord 136(3); *Standing Rules and Orders of the Legislative Assembly 2004* (Qld) ords 151, 152; *Legislative Assembly Standing Orders 2018* (SA) ord 234; *Legislative Council Standing Orders 1999* (SA) ord 272; *House of Assembly Standing and Sessional Orders and Rules 2017* (Tas) ord 210; *Standing Orders Legislative Council 2010* (Tas) ord 259(2); *Legislative Assembly Standing Orders 2004* (Vic) ord 14.13; *Standing Orders of the Legislative Assembly 2017* (WA) ord 163; *Legislative Council Standing Orders 2019* (WA) ord 122(1), (2); *Legislative Assembly for the Australian Capital Territory: Standing Orders 2019* (ACT) ord 169; *Standing Orders 2016* (NT) ords 142, 153.

On a Bill becoming an Act, in all Australian jurisdictions, except Victoria, the long title forms part of the Act. At common law, from the middle of the 19th century onwards, a long title was regarded as part of an Act. In *Fielding v Morley Corporation*[20] the English Court of Appeal stated:

> [N]ow, and for some years past, the title of an Act of Parliament has been part of the Act. In old days it used not to be so, and in the old law books we were told not so to regard it; but now the title is an important part of the Act, and is so treated in both Houses of Parliament.[21]

Its status as part of an Act is confirmed by Commonwealth and Queensland legislation.[22] However, in Victoria for Acts passed on or after 1 September 1985, the long title of the Bill for the Act does not form part of the Act.[23] In other Australian jurisdictions the common law treatment of a long title as part of an Act applies.

Example 13.1 Long title of the *Australia Act 1986* (Cth)

An Act to bring constitutional arrangements affecting the Commonwealth and the States into conformity with the status of the Commonwealth of Australia as a sovereign, independent and federal nation

A Bill must have words of enactment [13.5]

Words of enactment (sometimes referred to as enacting words) are words that appear at the start of a Bill[24] and are included for the purpose of evidencing, when the Bill is passed, that Parliament has approved the Bill and that any other consent necessary for the making of a valid Act[25] has been obtained.

In New South Wales s 5C of the *Constitution Act 1902* (NSW) prescribes the words of enactment to be used in Bills presented for royal assent in accordance with s 5A[26] or 5B[27] of that Act. The form of the enacting words to be included in Queensland Bills is set out in the

20 [1899] 1 Ch 1, 3–4 (Lindley MR, Chitty and Collins LJJ). Quoted with approval by Latham CJ in *Birch v Allen* (1942) 65 CLR 621, 626.

21 See also *Fearnley v Finlay* [2014] 2 Qd R 392 where Jackson J stated that 'highest authority supports the conclusion that, at common law, the long title is part of an Act' (at 401 [48]) and *R v C* [2002] QCA 156 where Williams JA stated that '[i]t is clear that the long title is part of a statute': at [20].

22 *Acts Interpretation Act 1901* (Cth) s 13(2)(a); *Acts Interpretation Act 1954* (Qld) sch 1 (definition of 'provision').

23 *Interpretation of Legislation Act 1984* (Vic) s 10(3). In practice the long title as included in the Bill for the Act is set out in an endnote to the printed Act.

24 They appear immediately after the long title (in Victoria, immediately after the title at the beginning of the Bill) or, if there is a preamble, immediately after the preamble.

25 See **[11.2]**.

26 Section 5A dispenses with the consent of the Legislative Council to an annual appropriation Bill in the event of disagreement between it and the Legislative Assembly.

27 Section 5B dispenses with the consent of the Legislative Council to a Bill (other than an annual appropriation Bill) where there is disagreement between it and the Legislative Assembly, and the Bill is approved at a referendum.

Standing Orders of the Legislative Assembly.[28] In Victoria the words of enactment for an Annual Appropriation Bill that is presented for royal assent in accordance with s 65(5) of the *Constitution Act 1975* (Vic)[29] are set out in s 65(6) of that Act.

For all other Australian Bills the form of the enacting words to be included in them is not mandated by legislation or parliamentary standing orders.

The following are the general enacting words used in Australian legislation:

- **Commonwealth**: The Parliament of Australia enacts:
- **New South Wales**: The Legislature of New South Wales enacts:
- **Queensland**: The Parliament of Queensland enacts –
- **South Australia**: The Parliament of South Australia enacts as follows:[30]
- **Tasmania**: Be it enacted by Her Excellency the Governor of Tasmania, by and with the advice and consent of the Legislative Council and House of Assembly, in Parliament assembled, as follows:
- **Victoria**: The Parliament of Victoria enacts:
- **Western Australia**: The Parliament of Western Australia enacts as follows:
- **Australian Capital Territory**: The Legislative Assembly for the Australian Capital Territory enacts as follows:
- **Northern Territory**: The Legislative Assembly of the Northern Territory enacts as follows:

[13.6] A Bill may have a preamble immediately before the enacting words

A Bill may have a preamble immediately before the enacting words.[31] The function of a preamble is to explain the background to the Bill and the reason why the legislation is desirable. Preambles are now generally only included in public Bills that are of constitutional significance.[32]

At common law, upon a Bill containing a preamble being passed, the preamble was regarded as part of the Act.[33] This position is confirmed by legislation in some Australian jurisdictions.[34]

---

28 *Standing Rules and Orders of the Legislative Assembly* 2004 (Qld) ord 127.

29 This provision enables a Bill to be presented for royal assent despite the rejection by the Legislative Assembly of amendments suggested by the Legislative Council.

30 As noted at **[11.2]**, while Bills passed by the Parliament of South Australia must be assented to by the Governor in the name and on behalf of the Queen, under the *Constitution Act 1934* (SA) s 4 the Queen or the Governor does not form part of the Parliament. Accordingly, the South Australian enacting words do not cover all necessary consents to a Bill.

31 If the Bill has a preamble, the word 'therefore' used to be generally inserted before 'enacts' or 'enacted' (as applicable) in the enacting words. As the preamble set out the background to the Bill, the word 'therefore' linked the fact of enactment to that background. However, the trend now, in some Australian jurisdictions, is for Acts with preambles not to include this word in the enacting words. See, eg, *Aboriginal and Torres Strait Islander Peoples Recognition Act 2013* (Cth); *Kapunda Hospital (Variation of Trust) Act 2009* (SA).

32 See, eg, *Succession to the Crown Act 2015* (Cth); *Constitution of Queensland 2001* (Qld); *Great Ocean Road and Environs Protection Act 2020* (Vic); *Noongar (Koorah, Nitja, Boordahwan) (Past, Present, Future) Recognition Act 2016* (WA).

33 *Mills v Wilkins* (1703) 6 Mod Rep 62; 87 ER 822; *Salkeld v Johnson* (1848) 2 Ex 256, 283 (Pollock CB); *Powell v Kempton Park Racecourse Co* [1897] 2 QB 242, 289 (Rigby LJ); *A-G v Prince Ernest Augustus of Hanover* [1957] AC 436, 467 (Lord Normand). See also Anne Winckel, The Contextual Role of a Preamble in Statutory Interpretation (1999) 23(1) *Melbourne University Law Review* 184, 205–6.

34 *Acts Interpretation Act 1901* (Cth) s 13(2)(b); *Acts Interpretation Act 1954* (Qld) sch 1 (definition of 'provision'); *Interpretation Act 1984* (WA) s 31(1); *Legislation Act 2001* (ACT) s 126(3).

Example 13.2 Preamble of the *Australia Act 1986* (Cth)

WHEREAS[35] the Prime Minister of the Commonwealth and the Premiers of the States at conferences held in Canberra on 24 and 25 June 1982 and 21 June 1984 agreed on the taking of certain measures to bring constitutional arrangements affecting the Commonwealth and the States into conformity with the status of the Commonwealth of Australia as a sovereign, independent and federal nation: AND WHEREAS in pursuance of paragraph 51 (xxxviii) of the Constitution the Parliaments of all the States have requested the Parliament of the Commonwealth to enact an Act in the terms of this Act:

An Act is given a short title for ease of reference [13.7]

Except for Victoria, a Bill for an Act has a clause setting out a name for the Act. The name of an Act is generally referred to as its short title. The word 'short' distinguishes it from the long title.[36] As it is contained within a section, the short title forms part of the Act. For Victorian Acts since 1985 the title appearing before the enacting words, or before the preamble if there is one, serves the same purpose as a short title and forms part of the Act.[37]

A short title is merely a label[38] given to an Act to facilitate reference to it.[39] Express authorisation is given by each jurisdiction for Acts to be referred to in legislation and other documents by their short title.[40]

Example 13.3 Short title clause of *Australia Act 1986* (Cth)

(1) This Act may be cited as the *Australia Act 1986*.

A Bill must be divided into clauses [13.8]

A Bill must be divided into clauses. Clauses deal with a single theme or topic.[41]

---

35 The word 'Whereas' was traditionally used at the start of preambles but is now generally omitted in Australian legislation with preambles. See, eg, the preambles to the *Succession to the Crown Act 2015* (Cth), *Community Relations Commission and Principles of Multiculturalism Act 2000* (NSW) and *Advancing the Treaty Process with Aboriginal Victorians Act 2018* (Vic).

36 See **[13.4]**.

37 *Interpretation of Legislation Act 1984* (Vic) s 10.

38 In *Re Boaler* [1915] 1 KB 21, 40 Scrutton J stated that 'the short title being a label, accuracy may be sacrificed to brevity'.

39 In *Vacher & Sons Ltd v London Society of Compositors* [1913] AC 107, 128 Lord Moulton referred to short titles as 'a statutory nickname to obviate the necessity of always referring to the Act under its full and descriptive title'. It is described in DR Elder, *House of Representatives Practice* (Department of the House of Representatives, 7th ed, 2018) ch 10, 346 as 'a convenient name for the Act, a label which assists in identification and indexing'.

40 *Acts Interpretation Act 1901* (Cth) s 40; *Interpretation Act 1987* (NSW) s 66; *Acts Interpretation Act 1954* (Qld) s 14F; *Legislation Interpretation Act 2021* (SA) s 35(1); *Acts Interpretation Act 1931* (Tas) s 13(1); *Interpretation Act 1984* (WA) s 26; *Legislation Act 2001* (ACT) s 100(1); *Interpretation Act 1978* (NT) s 49(1).

41 On the passing of a Bill, the clauses are referred to as sections.

In Great Britain before the enactment of Lord Brougham's Act of 1850[42] it was the practice to commence every clause with the words 'be it enacted' or 'be it further enacted'. Section 2 of that Act provided that each section of an Act has effect as a substantive enactment without introductory words, thus rendering the insertion of words of enactment at the beginning of a clause unnecessary.[43] A provision to this effect is now included in the interpretation legislation in force in the various Australian jurisdictions, other than the Australian Capital Territory.[44]

A clause may be divided into subclauses. A subclause must be connected with the theme or topic of the clause.[45]

Generally a clause that is not divided into subclauses, or a subclause itself, is comprised of a single sentence. Some jurisdictions, however, allow there to be more than one sentence in a clause or subclause if that is considered appropriate in the circumstances – for example, to avoid an overly long sentence.[46]

A sentence within a clause or subclause may be paragraphed. If so, the clause or subclause will begin with words that apply to each of the paragraphs. These words are referred to as 'the chapeau'. Paragraphs must flow on grammatically from the chapeau and have a thematic connection with each other.

Similarly a paragraph that contains subparagraphs will begin with a chapeau from which each subparagraph must flow on grammatically. The subparagraphs must have a thematic connection with each other. If any further level of paragraphing is employed, the same rules apply.

[13.9] An Act may contain schedules

Schedules are used for a variety of purposes. They may set out ancillary or technical matters or matters of detail. They may contain provisions that repeal or amend other legislation. They may contain provisions of a savings or transitional nature. Schedules in turn may be divided into clauses and subclauses and employ paragraphing techniques in the same way as a section or subsection within the body of the Act.

If the schedule comprises a list of items, the items may be numbered sequentially using Arabic numerals or consecutive alphabetical letters or any other numbering system used for schedules within the jurisdiction.

In each Australian jurisdiction, other than New South Wales and South Australia, legislation expressly states that schedules are part of the Act in which they appear.[47] In New South Wales the *Interpretation Act 1987* (NSW) provides that headings to schedules are part of the Act[48] and that a schedule has effect according to its tenor whether or not the Act declares that the schedule has effect.[49] This latter provision renders it unnecessary to have a provision in the body of an Act introducing the schedule. The NSW provisions effectively treat a schedule as part of the Act. In

---

42 *Interpretation Act 1850,* 13 & 14 Vict, c 21.

43 The enacting words at the beginning of the Act apply to the whole Act.

44 *Acts Interpretation Act 1901* (Cth) s 12; *Interpretation Act 1987* (NSW) s 64; *Acts Interpretation Act 1954* (Qld) s 10; *Legislation Interpretation Act 2021* (SA) s 26; *Acts Interpretation Act 1931* (Tas) s 6(1); *Interpretation of Legislation Act 1984* (Vic) s 7; *Interpretation Act 1984* (WA) s 29; *Interpretation Act 1978* (NT) s 54.

45 On the passing of a Bill, the subclauses are referred to as subsections.

46 An example of a subsection containing more than one sentence is the *Professional Standards Act 2003* (Vic) s 34(2).

47 *Acts Interpretation Act 1901* (Cth) s 13(1); *Acts Interpretation Act 1954* (Qld) s 14(5); *Acts Interpretation Act 1931* (Tas) s 6(3); *Interpretation of Legislation Act 1984* (Vic) s 36(2); *Interpretation Act 1984* (WA) s 31(2); *Legislation Act 2001* (ACT) s 126(5); *Interpretation Act 1978* (NT) s 55(5).

48 Section 35(1)(b).

49 Section 64A.

South Australia s 19 of the *Legislation Interpretation Act 2021* provides that everything (with a few exceptions not including a schedule) appearing in an Act is part of the Act.

In any event, at common law schedules are treated as part of an Act.[50] Thus in *Attorney-General v Lamplough*[51] Brett LJ stated that a schedule 'is as much a part of the statute, and is as much an enactment as any other part'.[52] In *Re Foley*[53] Roper CJ accepted the status of a schedule as a 'legislative enactment'.[54]

An Act may be divided into chapters, parts, divisions and subdivisions [13.10]

An Act, and accordingly a Bill, may be divided into chapters, although normally this is reserved for very large Bills.[55] A chapter is divided into parts. If not divided into chapters, then parts are the primary unit into which a Bill may be divided. Parts may be divided into divisions. Divisions may be divided into subdivisions.

The Commonwealth uses simplified outlines in legislation. These give a guide to what is in the Act or in a chapter, part, division or subdivision of an Act. They are placed within a text box to highlight them. They are part of the Act in which they appear.[56] An example of a simplified outline of a part may be found in s 10 of the *Fair Work Act 2009* (Cth).

Example 13.4 *Fair Work Act 2009* (Cth) s 10

10 Guide to this Part

This Part is about the terms that are defined in this Act.

Division 2 has the Dictionary (see section 12). The Dictionary is a list of every term that is defined in this Act. A term will either be defined in the Dictionary itself, or in another provision of this Act. If another provision defines the term, the Dictionary will have a signpost to that definition.

Division 3 has definitions relating to the meanings of employee and employer.

Division 4 has some other definitions that apply across this Act.

Each component into which a Bill is divided has a heading [13.11]

A Bill has headings to clauses, and in some jurisdictions subclauses.[57] Chapters, parts, divisions, subdivisions and schedules also have headings. A heading is a brief indication of the contents of the provision to which it is a heading.

50 In *Origin Energy LPG Ltd v Bestcare Foods Ltd* [2007] NSWCA 321, [13] Handley JA, relying on *A-G v Lamplough* (1878) 3 Ex D 214, 229 (Brett LJ) stated that a schedule to the *Civil Liability Act 2002* (NSW) was part of the Act.

51 (1878) 3 Ex D 214.

52 Ibid 229.

53 (1952) 53 SR (NSW) 31.

54 Ibid 36.

55 See, eg, the *Fair Work Act 2009* (Cth).

56 *Acts Interpretation Act 1901* (Cth) s 13(1).

57 Subsection headings are to be found in sections in Commonwealth legislation containing more than four subsections. They are printed in italics to distinguish them from section headings, which are bolded. They are treated as part of the Act by the *Acts Interpretation Act 1901* (Cth) s 13(1).

When the Bill is passed, clause headings in it become section headings in the Act. At common law section headings, or marginal notes (also referred to as side notes),[58] were not regarded as forming part of the statute in which they were printed. The reason commonly given by courts for adopting this position was that such section headings or marginal notes were not strictly enacted by Parliament. Thus, in *Chandler v Director of Public Prosecutions*[59] Lord Reid stated:

> I have never heard of it being supposed in recent times that an amendment to alter a side note could be proposed in either House of Parliament. Side notes in the original Bill are inserted by the draftsman. During the passage of the Bill through its various stages amendments to it or other reasons may make it desirable to alter a side note. In that event I have reason to believe that alteration is made by the appropriate officer of the House – no doubt in consultation with the draftsman. So side notes cannot be said to be enacted in the same sense as the long title or any part of the body of the Act.[60]

For Commonwealth legislation, and in Queensland, South Australia, Victoria, the Australian Capital Territory and the Northern Territory, section headings are now treated as part of the Act,[61] while in New South Wales, Tasmania and Western Australia they continue not to be so treated.[62]

The way in which clause headings were dealt with in Parliament in the past, and how editorial changes were frequently made to them in the course of preparing reprints of legislation, explains why those states and territories that moved away from the common law position only made the change operate prospectively to headings enacted, amended or inserted after specified dates. Victoria took the strictest approach and only made section headings enacted or inserted on or after 1 January 2001 part of the Act, treating a parliamentary amendment to a heading of dubious provenance as insufficient to legitimise it as part of the Act.[63]

Headings to schedules (excluding the Northern Territory and possibly Western Australia),[64] chapters (excluding Tasmania and Western Australia), parts, divisions and subdivisions are part of the Act.[65] Subsections 36(1A) and (2A) of the *Interpretation of Legislation Act 1984* (Vic) also

---

58 Instead of clause headings it was common in the past to have a note in the margin of the printed page of a Bill briefly indicating the contents of the clause opposite the note.

59 [1964] AC 763, 789–90.

60 In *Re Woking Urban Council (Basingstoke Canal) Act, 1911* [1914] 1 Ch 300, Phillimore LJ referred to marginal notes being 'inserted not by Parliament nor under the authority of Parliament, but by irresponsible persons': at 302.

61 *Acts Interpretation Act 1901* (Cth) s 13(1); *Acts Interpretation Act 1954* (Qld) s 14(2) (if enacted, amended or inserted after 30 June 1991); *Legislation Interpretation Act 2021* (SA) s 19 (except section headings to amending provisions in Bills introduced before 1 January 2022); *Interpretation of Legislation Act 1984* (Vic) s 36(2A) (if enacted or inserted on or after 1 January 2001); *Legislation Act 2001* (ACT) ss 126(2), 127(3) (if enacted, amended or inserted after 1 January 2000); *Interpretation Act 1978* (NT) s 55(2) (if enacted, amended or inserted after 1 July 2006).

62 *Interpretation Act 1987* (NSW) s 35(2), (4) (unless the heading is expressly referred to in some other part of the Act otherwise than being merely set out in parentheses); *Acts Interpretation Act 1931* (Tas) s 6(4)(a); *Interpretation Act 1984* (WA) s 32(2).

63 *Interpretation of Legislation Act 1984* (Vic) s 36(2A).

64 The *Interpretation Act 1984* (WA) s 31(2) makes a schedule to a written law part of the written law. It is silent as to whether this covers the heading to the schedule. Certain other headings are excluded from being part of a written law by s 32(2). It may be argued that the net result is that a heading to a schedule forms part of the written law.

65 *Acts Interpretation Act 1901* (Cth) s 13(1), (2)(d); *Interpretation Act 1987* (NSW) s 35(1); *Acts Interpretation Act 1954* (Qld) s 14(2) (if enacted, amended or inserted after 30 June 1991); *Legislation Interpretation Act 2021*

make the headings to parts, divisions, subdivisions, sections, clauses or items into which a schedule to an Act is divided part of the Act if the Act is passed on or after 1 January 2001 or the heading is inserted on or after that date. The breadth of s 13(1) and (2) of the *Acts Interpretation Act 1901* (Cth) would also make such headings part of the Act, irrespective of when the Act was passed or the heading was inserted.

Each component into which an Act is divided has a number [13.12]

Every provision of an Act, including subsections, paragraphs and subparagraphs, is assigned a number. This facilitates cross-referencing within the Act and external referencing to provisions of the Act.

Provisions within an Act are numbered in accordance with the jurisdiction's practices. Chapters, parts and divisions[66] are generally numbered using Arabic numerals – that is, 1, 2, 3 etc. Sections are generally similarly numbered but subsections are numbered using Arabic numerals within round brackets – that is, (1), (2), (3) etc. A series of paragraphs within a section or subsection is numbered using alphabetical letters within round brackets – that is, (a), (b), (c) etc. A series of subparagraphs is numbered by using small Roman numerals within round brackets – that is, (i), (ii), (iii) etc. While their use is generally discouraged, if sub-subparagraphs are used, they are generally numbered using alphabetical letters in capitals and within round brackets – that is (A), (B), (C) etc.

Variants to the numbering system described above may be found in Australian legislation. Occasionally a form of decimal numbering is used.[67] Other variants include, for Commonwealth legislation, a numbering system under which a section number is made up of two components separated by a dash, the first component being the division number (with division numbers being consecutive throughout the Act and not starting again at the start of a part) and the second being the section number within that division – for example, 14-9.[68]

The number of a provision is treated as part of Commonwealth Acts,[69] Victorian Acts[70] and ACT Acts.[71] Section and subsection numbers included in the heading to the section or subsection are treated as part of NSW Acts, even though the heading is not.[72] Other jurisdictions do not make express provision as to the status of the number.

Acts generally group definitions together [13.13]

Definitions of terms used within an Act tend to be gathered together in a single location within the Act, either in an early section of the Act or a schedule or a dictionary at the end of the Act.

(SA) s 19; *Acts Interpretation Act 1931* (Tas) s 6(2), (3); *Interpretation of Legislation Act 1984* (Vic) s 36(1); *Interpretation Act 1984* (WA) s 32(1); *Legislation Act 2001* (ACT) s 126(1); *Interpretation Act 1978* (NT) s 55(1).

66 A division may be divided into subdivisions. The numbering used for them differs across Australian jurisdictions. Commonwealth Acts letter them as A, B, C etc whereas, for example, Victorian Acts number subdivisions using Arabic numerals – that is 1, 2, 3 etc.

67 See, eg, the *Legal Profession Act 2004* (Vic). This style of numbering indicates clearly where a provision is located within the Act – for instance, s 2.2.1 is located within pt 2.2.

68 See the *Income Tax Assessment Act 1997* (Cth) for an example of this style of numbering.

69 *Acts Interpretation Act 1901* (Cth) s 13(1).

70 *Interpretation of Legislation Act 1984* (Vic) s 36(3C).

71 *Legislation Act 2001* (ACT) s 126(7).

72 *Interpretation Act 1987* (NSW) s 35(4A).

However, if the term being defined is only used in one section or in one division or part, the definition may be found in that section, division or part.

A dictionary at the end of a Commonwealth Act is part of the Act so long as it does not appear after the end of the last schedule to the Act.[73] A dictionary in an appendix of an Act is treated as part of a Queensland Act,[74] a Tasmanian Act[75] and a Western Australian Act.[76] Wherever it appears, a dictionary is treated as part of a South Australian Act[77] and an Australian Capital Territory Act.[78] Of course, if included in a schedule to any Australian Act, a dictionary would be part of the Act.

[13.14] An Act may contain an example, a note or other reader's aid

An Act may include one or more examples illustrating the application of a provision to particular facts. It may have notes cross-referring the reader to other relevant provisions of that or any other Act or giving other appropriate information. It may even contain mathematical formulas, diagrams, flow charts, tables or other devices that can convey meaning in a manner more helpfully and simply to readers than plain text. Before the 1980s such devices were rare in legislation. They are no longer uncommon.

An example is part of Commonwealth Acts,[79] Queensland Acts,[80] South Australian Acts,[81] Victorian Acts (in certain circumstances),[82] ACT Acts[83] and Northern Territory Acts.[84] In other jurisdictions, an example included within a provision of an Act would clearly form part of the Act.[85]

Notes and other reader's aids that appear in the printed text of a Commonwealth Act as enacted by Parliament are part of the Act.[86] Elsewhere in Australia some of them are excluded from being part of an Act. New South Wales and Victoria exclude marginal notes, footnotes and endnotes.[87] Queensland excludes footnotes, editor's notes and endnotes.[88] South Australia excludes editorial notes.[89] Tasmania excludes marginal notes, footnotes (unless appended to a

---

73 *Acts Interpretation Act 1901* (Cth) s 13(1).

74 *Acts Interpretation Act 1954* (Qld) s 14(5).

75 *Acts Interpretation Act 1931* (Tas) s 6(3).

76 *Interpretation Act 1984* (WA) s 31(2).

77 *Legislation Interpretation Act 2021* (SA) s 19.

78 *Legislation Act 2001* (ACT) s 126(5).

79 *Acts Interpretation Act 1901* (Cth) s 13(1).

80 *Acts Interpretation Act 1954* (Qld) s 14(3).

81 *Legislation Interpretation Act 2021* (SA) s 19.

82 *Interpretation of Legislation Act 1984* (Vic) s 36(3A). The circumstances are if the example is at the foot of a provision under the heading 'Example' or 'Examples' in an Act passed on or after 1 January 2001 or the example was inserted in an earlier Act by an Act passed on or after 1 January 2001.

83 *Legislation Act 2001* (ACT) s 126(4).

84 *Interpretation Act 1978* (NT) s 55(4).

85 See, eg, *Electronic Transactions Act 2003* (WA) s 5 (definition of 'data storage device').

86 *Acts Interpretation Act 1901* (Cth) s 13(1).

87 *Interpretation Act 1987* (NSW) s 35(2)(c); *Interpretation of Legislation Act 1984* (Vic) s 36(3). The *Interpretation of Legislation Act 1984* (Vic) in s 36(3D) and (3E) expressly excludes an explanatory memorandum or table of provisions printed with an Act before its title, and an index or other material printed with an Act after its endnotes, from being part of the Act.

88 *Acts Interpretation Act 1954* (Qld) s 14(7).

89 *Legislation Interpretation Act 2021* (SA) s 19(2)(a).

prescribed form) and endnotes from being part of an Act.[90] Western Australia excludes marginal notes and footnotes[91] and expressly makes tables, together with any notes to the table, part of an Act.[92] The Australian Capital Territory excludes from being part of an Act footnotes, endnotes and other notes, tables of contents, reader's guides and indexes[93] and expressly makes diagrams part of an Act.[94] The Northern Territory makes notes in the text part of an Act and excludes from being part of an Act notes (including marginal notes, footnotes and endnotes) that are not part of the text.[95] Specific provision may also be made in an Act about the status of notes of any kind in that Act.[96]

Acts are punctuated in accordance with the prevailing rules of grammar [13.15]

Acts, like any other item of formal writing, are punctuated in accordance with the prevailing rules of grammar. Punctuation helps make the relationship of the various components of a sentence more apparent to the reader, thus helping the reader understand the sentence more quickly.

It used to be the clearly established rule that punctuation marks were not regarded as forming part of the Act.[97] This view seems to have been based on the belief that in England punctuation marks were not entered on the Parliament Roll on which, until 1850, Acts were engrossed.[98] There is no basis for a similar belief in relation to Australian statutes. Thus, in *President of the Shire of Charlton v Ruse*[99] Isaacs J, referring to the apparent fact of the Rolls of the Imperial Parliament not being punctuated, stated:

> That is not so, however, in Victoria; the original Acts assented to and signed by the Governor on behalf of the Sovereign are punctuated.[100]

Punctuation is treated as part of Commonwealth Acts,[101] Queensland Acts,[102] Victorian Acts (in certain circumstances)[103] and Australian Capital Territory Acts.[104]

---

90 *Acts Interpretation Act 1931* (Tas) s 6(4)(b).

91 *Interpretation Act 1984* (WA) s 32(2).

92 Ibid s 31(2).

93 *Legislation Act 2001* (ACT) s 127(1), (2).

94 *Legislation Act 2001* (ACT) s 126(4).

95 *Interpretation Act 1978* (NT) s 55(4), (6).

96 See, eg, *Electronic Transactions Act 2003* (WA) s 4.

97 *Stephenson v Taylor* (1861) 1 B & S 95; 121 ER 650, 654 (Cockburn CJ); *Claydon v Green* (1868) LR 3 CP 511, 522 (Willes J); *R v M'Cormick; Ex parte McMonigle* (1884) 10 VLR (L) 268, 272 (Higinbotham J); *Duke of Devonshire v O'Connor* (1890) 24 QBD 468, 478 (Lord Esher MR); *Re Health Act 1890* [1911] VLR 429, 441 (Cussen J); *R v Speyer* [1916] 1 KB 595, 614 (Lord Reading CJ); *R v Casement* [1917] 1 KB 98, 123 (Lord Reading CJ).

98 *Stephenson v Taylor* (1861) 1 B & S 95; 121 ER 650, 654 (Cockburn CJ); *Claydon v Green* (1868) LR 3 CP 511, 519 (Bovill CJ), 521–2 (Willes J); *President of the Shire of Charlton v Ruse* (1912) 14 CLR 220, 229 (Isaacs J); *Inland Revenue Commissioners v Hinchy* [1960] AC 748, 765 (Lord Reid); *Hanlon v The Law Society* [1981] AC 124, 197 (Lord Lowry).

99 (1912) 14 CLR 220.

100 Ibid 229.

101 *Acts Interpretation Act 1901* (Cth) s 13(1).

102 *Acts Interpretation Act 1954* (Qld) s 14(6).

103 *Interpretation of Legislation Act 1984* (Vic) s 36(3B). The circumstances are if the Act was passed on or after 1 January 2001 or the punctuation was inserted in an earlier Act by an Act passed on or after 1 January 2001.

104 *Legislation Act 2001* (ACT) s 126(6).

[13.16] Acts are given a number when passed and show the date of their passing

Bills, when given royal assent, are assigned a number[105] and have the date of royal assent endorsed on them.[106] Except for South Australian Acts, an Act may be referred to by its number and the year in which it was passed.[107] The date of assent shown on an official copy of an Australian Act is evidence that that date is the date of assent.[108] For the Australian Capital Territory, there is no assent process as such but the making of the Act is notified in the register, the Gazette or otherwise under s 28(2)(b) of the *Legislation Act 2001* (ACT).

Example 13.5 Number and date of passing of the *Australia Act 1986* (Cth)

No. 142, 1985
[*Assented to 4 December 1985*]

---

105 *Acts Interpretation Act 1901* (Cth) s 39; *Interpretation of Legislation Act 1984* (Vic) s 9(1); *Legislation Act 2001* (ACT) s 27; *Interpretation Act 1978* (NT) s 56. In other states the provision for numbering is in standing orders. See *Legislative Assembly Standing Orders 2007* (NSW) ord 239(6); *Legislative Council Standing Rules and Orders 2004* (NSW) ord 162; *Standing Rules and Orders of the Legislative Assembly 2004* (Qld) ord 169; *Joint Standing Orders 1953* (SA) ord 14; *Standing Orders Legislative Council 2010* (Tas) ord 306; *Joint Standing Rules and Orders of the Legislative Council and Legislative Assembly 2011* (WA) ord 9.

106 *Legislative Council Standing Rules and Orders 2004* (NSW) ord 162; *Standing Rules and Orders of the Legislative Assembly 2004* (Qld) ord 169; *Joint Standing Orders 1953* (SA) ord 14; *Standing Orders Legislative Council 2010* (Tas) ord 306; *Joint Standing Rules and Orders of the Legislative Council and Legislative Assembly* 2011 (WA) ord 9. For Commonwealth and Northern Territory Acts there is no specific requirement for the date of assent to be included on them but *Senate Standing Orders 2020* (Cth) ord 139(1) recognises the practice of showing the date of assent for Bills that originated in the Senate. In Victoria, the *Constitution Act 1975* (Vic) s 69 directs the Clerk of the Parliaments to indorse the date of assent on every Act and provides that the indorsement is part of the Act.

107 *Acts Interpretation Act 1901* (Cth) s 40(1A)(a)(ii); *Interpretation Act 1987* (NSW) s 66(1)(b); *Acts Interpretation Act 1954* (Qld) s 14F(1)(b); *Acts Interpretation Act 1931* (Tas) s 13(1)(a)(ii); *Interpretation of Legislation Act 1984* (Vic) s 9(2); *Interpretation Act 1984* (WA) s 26(1); *Legislation Act 2001* (ACT) s 100(1)(b); *Interpretation Act 1978* (NT) s 49(1)(b).

108 *Acts Interpretation Act 1901* (Cth) s 6; *Interpretation Act 1987* (NSW) s 22(2); *Evidence Act 1977* (Qld) s 46A(2); *Evidence Act 1929* (SA) s 35A; *Acts Interpretation Act 1931* (Tas) s 10; *Interpretation Act 1984* (WA) s 24; *Interpretation Act 1978* (NT) s 7(1). In Victoria, under the *Constitution Act 1975* (Vic) s 69, the date of assent indorsed on an Act is part of the Act.

PROBLEM ANALYSIS: SOURCES OF DOUBT

14

Overview

Sources of doubt are socio-legal phenomena that are the root causes of interpretative doubt. [14.1]

Potential sources of doubt have been catalogued extensively in the literature. Some analyses are language-based. Other analyses are based on the legislative process, including events after the creation of the rule.

Ascertaining sources of doubt is part of the practice of interpretation. It is a skill for deepening knowledge of the problem or potential problem. Sources of doubt provide a launching pad for interpretative arguments. Knowledge of potential sources of doubt is also a valuable resource for participants in the legislative process – law reformers, instructors and parliamentary counsel – because it assists them to anticipate potential sources of doubt.

Sources of doubt have other uses for interpreters and participants in the law-making process. They can assist in locating responsibility for errors in legislation that need not have been there. And as drafting styles are closely connected with sources of doubt, knowledge of potential sources of doubt provides food for thought about the appropriate drafting style.

Nature of sources of doubt

Sources of doubt are the root causes of interpretative doubt[1] [14.2]

In this work 'sources of doubt' does not refer to the words whose meaning is in doubt ('the unit of inquiry'). Nor do they comprise legal doctrine in the strict sense. Rather, they are socio-legal phenomena: the root *causes* of doubt. Examples are lack of clear policy objectives, poor drafting, and an unforeseeable event. Comparable expressions in the literature are 'sources of ambiguity';[2] 'factors that cause objective doubt as to the meaning of legislative texts';[3] 'doubt-factors';[4] 'root cause of ambiguity';[5] 'condition of doubt';[6] 'difficulties for drafters and interpreters';[7] 'what

1 This section draws on Jeffrey Barnes, 'Sources of Doubt and the Quest for Legal Certainty' (2008) 2(2) *Legisprudence: International Journal for the Study of Legislation* 119, 120.

2 Sanford A Schane, *Language and the Law* (Continuum, 2006) 17.

3 FAR Bennion, *Bennion on Statute Law* (Longman, 3rd ed, 1990) 229.

4 Ibid 213.

5 Christopher Enright, *Legal Technique* (Federation Press, 2002) 137 [12.17].

6 William Twining and David Miers, *How to Do Things with Rules: A Primer of Interpretation* (Cambridge University Press, 5th ed, 2010) ch 6.

7 DC Pearce and RS Geddes, *Statutory Interpretation in Australia* (LexisNexis Butterworths, 8th ed, 2014) 4–6 [1.4].

makes legal language difficult to understand';[8] 'difficulties that give rise to the need for interpretation';[9] and 'how misunderstandings arise'.[10]

Sources of doubt arise in two main situations: doubts as to the general meaning or effect of a law (interpretation, strictly speaking) and doubts as to the application of a law to a particular set of circumstances.[11] Though sharing common ground at a general level, these processes are distinct in fundamental respects.[12] The differences are evident in sources of doubt. An example is the use of broad terms, or general principles drafting.[13] Issues with these terms are more commonly associated with difficulties of application rather than interpretation.[14] Further, the use of a broad term is a deliberate strategy in which the law-maker, foreseeing a penumbra of doubt in its application, is nevertheless comfortable in leaving it to a future court to determine the application of the term in a particular context. Now compare doubt about the scope or meaning of a rule – it is generally *unforeseen* since, for obvious reasons, a drafter 'is trying to ensure that there are no ambiguities or uncertainties in the language he or she chooses'.[15]

Catalogues of potential sources of doubt

[14.3] Potential sources of doubt have differing origins

A number of writers have attempted an overview of potential sources of doubt. The literature comprises two main schools of thought, each of which draws on disciplines outside the law.[16] One, drawing on linguistics, holds that sources of doubt are language-based.[17] Examples are lexical ambiguity ('whenever a word has more than one objective or dictionary meaning');[18] syntactic

8 Peter M Tiersma, *Legal Language* (University of Chicago Press, 1999) ch 12.

9 RI Carter, *Burrows and Carter: Statute Law in New Zealand* (LexisNexis NZ Ltd, 5th ed, 2015) 189.

10 Mark Adler and Daphne Perry, *Clarity for Lawyers: Effective Legal Language* (The Law Society, 3rd ed, 2017) 175.

11 William Twining and David Miers, *How to Do Things with Rules: A Primer of Interpretation* (Cambridge University Press, 5th ed, 2010) 176. See also FAR Bennion, *Bennion on Statute Law* (Longman, 3rd ed, 1990) 256.

12 For instance, a dispute over application to the facts is a dispute over the result on the facts, not a dispute over competing constructions. See **[1.4]**.

13 On its relationship to sources of doubt, see **[14.7]**. For an introduction to general principles drafting, see **[10.7]**. For its effect on interpretation, see chapter 16 and the case study on statutory reasonableness in chapter 38, especially **[38.11]**.

14 See, in relation to the application of statutory reasonableness, **[38.3]**, **[38.10]**.

15 Hilary Penfold, 'Legislative Drafting and Statutory Interpretation' (2006) 7 *The Judicial Review* 471, 487. This explains why 'Australian drafters don't generally draft in reliance on maxims' and 'most of the rules of statutory interpretation should only apply if the drafters haven't done a good job, and the meaning is later found to be ambiguous': Peter Quiggin, 'Statutory Construction: How to Construct, and Construe, a Statute' in Neil Williams (ed), *Key Issues in Judicial Review* (Federation Press, 2014) 78, 88. At the time of their writing, Penfold was a former First Parliamentary Counsel, Commonwealth Office of Parliamentary Counsel, and Quiggin was the current First Parliamentary Counsel.

16 This is another example of how law is continuously invaded by other disciplines, yet never conquered: Roger Cotterrell, 'Why Must Legal Ideas Be Interpreted Sociologically?' (1998) 25(2) *Journal of Law and Society* 171, 178, referring to JM Balkin, 'Interdisciplinarity as Colonization' (1996) 53 *Washington and Lee Law Review* 949.

17 Sanford A Schane, *Language and the Law* (Continuum, 2006) ch 1; Mark Adler and Daphne Perry, *Clarity for Lawyers: Effective Legal Language* (The Law Society, 3rd ed, 2017) pt D; Jeffrey Barnes, 'Sources of Doubt and the Quest for Legal Certainty' (2008) 2(2) *Legisprudence: International Journal for the Study of Legislation* 119, 145–7.

18 Sanford A Schane, *Language and the Law* (Continuum, 2006) 15.

ambiguity ('whenever a given word order may allow for more than one grammatical relationship');[19] referential ambiguity ('uncertainty of reference');[20] vagueness of categorisation[21] ('vagueness of [a term's] application to the classification of particular items');[22] and 'contextual ambiguity' ('where there is a conflict between the enactment and its internal or external context').[23]

A second school of thought approaches the field from the perspective of rule processes. The seminal work is by Twining and Miers.[24] The authors contend that 'any particular problem of interpretation needs to be set in the context of some conception of a wider process – a series of events and decisions which have led up to the moment when the interpreter is faced with a choice and which will continue after that moment'.[25] Their work sets out the relevant events and decisions in four stages. They are: prior to the creation of the rule; the rule-making stage; after the creation of the rule; and special features of the present case. The model is detailed and comprises 36 'conditions of doubt'.

Other writers have applied the Twining and Miers model in different ways to legislation. Bennion took the perspective of the drafter. His model comprises five 'doubt-factors', each of which in one way or another is 'linked to the drafter'.[26] They are: 'ellipsis', the technique of omitting to state what to the drafter seems to be obvious;[27] the 'broad term', a technique of brevity by which Parliament delegates to 'the processors' the task of working out the detailed effect of the law;[28] 'politic uncertainty',[29] where it is 'considered politic to shroud a legislative text in obscurity';[30] 'unforeseeable developments',[31] such as changes in language, technology, social practice and the surrounding law;[32] and 'error',[33] a reference to 'all defects in the text which need not have been there'.[34]

19 Ibid.

20 Ibid 22.

21 Ibid 22–6.

22 Ibid 23.

23 Oliver Jones, *Bennion on Statutory Interpretation: A Code* (LexisNexis Butterworths, 6th ed, 2013) 425.

24 William Twining and David Miers, *How to Do Things with Rules: A Primer of Interpretation* (Cambridge University Press, 5th ed, 2010).

25 Ibid 4.

26 FAR Bennion, *Bennion on Statute Law* (Longman, 3rd ed, 1990) 213.

27 Ibid ch 15. The equivalent condition of doubt in Twining and Miers is condition 13(e): see William Twining and David Miers, *How to Do Things with Rules: A Primer of Interpretation* (Cambridge University Press, 5th ed, 2010) 179.

28 FAR Bennion, *Bennion on Statute Law* (Longman, 3rd ed, 1990) ch 16. The equivalent condition of doubt in Twining and Miers is condition 14: *How to Do Things with Rules: A Primer of Interpretation* (Cambridge University Press, 5th ed, 2010) 180.

29 FAR Bennion, *Bennion on Statute Law* (Longman, 3rd ed, 1990) ch 17. The equivalent condition of doubt in Twining and Miers is condition 13(f): *How to Do Things with Rules: A Primer of Interpretation* (Cambridge University Press, 5th ed, 2010) 179.

30 FAR Bennion, *Bennion on Statute Law* (Longman, 3rd ed, 1990) 248.

31 Ibid ch 18.

32 Ibid 252. The equivalent conditions of doubt in Twining and Miers are conditions 17–20, 25: *How to Do Things with Rules: A Primer of Interpretation* (Cambridge University Press, 5th ed, 2010) 180–1.

33 FAR Bennion, *Bennion on Statute Law* (Longman, 3rd ed, 1990) ch 19, 214. The chapter heading, 'The Fallible Drafter', is misleading.

34 Ibid 255. The equivalent condition of doubt focusing on the drafter in Twining and Miers is condition 13: *How to Do Things with Rules: A Primer of Interpretation* (Cambridge University Press, 5th ed, 2010) 179–80.

The work by Barnes takes a wider legal perspective. Drawing widely on the legal literature pertaining to sources of doubt, the author showed how the Twining and Miers approach applied to legislation.[35]

Utility of ascertaining sources of doubt

[14.4] **Ascertaining sources of doubt is an aspect of the practice of interpretation, but does not replace the presumptions used to justify legal meaning**

Sources of doubt as to the meaning of a legislative provision typically become apparent in its implementation, the post-enactment phase in the life cycle of legislation in which legislation is tested by conflicts and pressures of various kinds.[36] As Samek says:

> Law, in fact, does not operate in a straightforward manner as a package of rules. There are practices, conventions, discretions, expenses and delays – a host of countervailing forces, lurking like an iceberg below the surface.[37]

Ascertaining sources of doubt as to the meaning of legislation is recognised as an aspect of the practice of interpretation (a key part of the implementation phase). For instance, Bennion includes '[d]iagnose the cause of the doubt' in his model of interpretative technique by advocates.[38] Ascertaining sources of doubt is a skill for deepening knowledge of the problem or potential problem. It thereby provides a launching pad for interpretative arguments.

Although sources of doubt as to the meaning of a legislative provision typically manifest in the implementation phase, their origins may lie in the pre-enactment phases: emergence, drafting, and parliamentary consideration. As scholarly writings on sources of doubt are concerned with expounding *potential* sources of doubt, these writings[39] are a valuable resource for law reformers, instructors and parliamentary counsel.[40] They assist participants in the legislative process to anticipate sources of doubt in the law they are developing.

As an analytical tool for courts and other interpreters, sources of doubt are, however, subject to two major limitations. First, a judicial interpreter may not be as aware of the development of the law as is a member of the executive.[41] Therefore, it may not be possible for a court to ascertain, from admissible materials, what all the sources of doubt are. For this reason, ascertaining sources of doubt is to a degree speculative and contestable.

Second, even if the interpreter can ascertain the sources of doubt with some confidence, this may not deliver the solution on a plate. For example, if the interpretative problem is diagnosed as the terms of the words in question not being coextensive with the purpose of the

35 Jeffrey Barnes, 'Sources of Doubt and the Quest for Legal Certainty' (2008) 2(2) *Legisprudence: International Journal for the Study of Legislation* 119, 126–45.

36 Stephen Bottomley and Simon Bronitt, *Law in Context* (Federation Press, 4th ed, 2012) 331.

37 RA Samek, 'A Case for Social Law Reform' (1977) 55(3) *Canadian Bar Review* 409, 411.

38 Oliver Jones, *Bennion on Statutory Interpretation* (LexisNexis Butterworths, 6th ed, 2013) 1177 (step 10).

39 The major sources are William Twining and David Miers, *How to Do Things with Rules: A Primer of Interpretation* (Cambridge University Press, 5th ed, 2010) ch 6; FAR Bennion, *Bennion on Statute Law* (Longman, 3rd ed, 1990) chs 15–19; and Jeffrey Barnes, 'Sources of Doubt and the Quest for Legal Certainty' (2008) 2(2) *Legisprudence: International Journal for the Study of Legislation* 119, 126–47.

40 For an example of its use to predict potential interpretative issues, see Jeffrey Barnes, 'Crimes Act 1914 (Cth) – Part VIIC – Division 3: Sections 85ZV, 85ZW and Associated Definitions: Potential Interpretative Issues and their Impact', *Zenodo* (Web Page, 8 July 2019) <https://doi.org/10.5281/zenodo.3271515>.

41 *Brennan v Comcare* (1994) 50 FCR 555, 573 (Gummow J, Burchett J agreeing generally at 556).

Act,[42] the interpretative answer is not immediately obvious. The court will need to analyse the weight of the indications from the text and the purpose, and seek out other relevant indications from the context. Thus, analysing the problem and diagnosing the sources of doubt is not an alternative to, nor does it replace, the interpretative criteria of the law such as the various presumptions of interpretation (which of course provide the legal justification for the legal meaning). Rather, analysing the sources of doubt supports the process of identifying the relevant indications of meaning.

Identifying sources of doubt enables a court to understand better the interpretative problem; it may also provide a launching pad for interpretative arguments [14.5]

Twining and Miers argue that if an interpreter is puzzled about the general scope or meaning of a rule, or about its application to a particular set of circumstances, reference to learning on sources of doubt may assist 'to tease out the factors which are giving rise to difficulty, in order to arrive at a better understanding of what problems of interpretation are involved and to identify the main starting points for arguments about possible competing interpretations'.[43]

Bennion agrees. Like Twining and Miers,[44] he saw sources of doubt as presenting an opportunity for a 'new approach'.[45] Bennion expanded on the inquiry:

> Precisely what, in the text we are examining, causes the doubt? What is its etiology, as a medical practitioner would say? Only when we understand that can we proceed further along the road to resolving it.[46]

Three case examples are now given.[47] In **Example 14.1** *R v PJ*, identifying the source of doubt enabled the court to arrive at a deeper understanding of the problem presented to it, thereby assisting its solution. In **Examples 14.2** and **14.3**, the *Smoker* case and *Scott-Mackenzie v Bail* respectively, identifying the source of doubt provided a launching pad for interpretative arguments, as well as furnishing an explanation for the doubt.

Example 14.1 *R v PJ*[48]

The defendant (respondent), who was employed at the relevant time as a personal health, development and physical education teacher, was charged with offending against s 73(2) of the *Crimes Act 1900* (NSW), read with s 73(3)(c). Section 73(2) provided as follows:

> (2) Any person who has sexual intercourse with another person who:
> (a) is under his or her special care, and
> (b) is of or above the age of 17 years and under the age of 18 years,
> is liable to imprisonment for four years.

42 William Twining and David Miers, *How to Do Things with Rules: A Primer of Interpretation* (Cambridge University Press, 5th ed, 2010) 179 (condition 11). See **[8.4]**, **[8.7]**.

43 Ibid 185–6.

44 Ibid 186.

45 FAR Bennion, *Bennion on Statute Law* (Longman, 3rd ed, 1990) 215.

46 Ibid.

47 For discussion of four case studies, each identifying multiple sources of doubt, see Jeffrey Barnes, 'When "Plain Language" Legislation is Ambiguous – Sources of Doubt and Lessons for the Plain Language Movement' (2010) 34(3) *Melbourne University Law Review* 671.

48 (2017) 270 A Crim R 439.

Subsection (2)(a) was expanded on in sub-s (3) (emphasis added):

> (3) For the purposes of this section, a person (the victim) is under the special care of another person (the offender) if, and only if:
> (a) the offender is the step-parent, guardian or foster parent of the victim, or the de facto partner of a parent, guardian or foster parent of the victim, or
> (b) the offender is a school teacher and the victim is a pupil of the offender, or
> (c) the offender has an established personal relationship with the victim *in connection with* the provision of religious, sporting, musical or other instruction to the victim, or
> (d) the offender is a custodial officer of an institution of which the victim is an inmate, or
> (e) the offender is a health professional and the victim is a patient of the health professional.

The interpretative question that arose was the meaning of 'in connection with' in s 73(3)(c).

The factual background to the dispute concerned the conduct of the respondent in relation to the alleged female victim. At the time of the alleged offence, the alleged victim was 17 years old and attending the school at which the defendant was employed. Though she had been a former pupil of the defendant teacher in 2011, 2012 and 2013, at the time of the alleged offences (2015) she was not a pupil of the defendant.

To catch the relationship of 'special care' in s 73(2)(a), the Crown invoked the definition in s 73(3)(c). The Crown argued that, in that paragraph, 'in connection with the provision of ... sporting ... instruction to the victim' did not require a temporal connection between the act of sexual intercourse and the provision of instruction, so long as a personal relationship of the kind specified in para (c) had been established in the past.[49] Counsel for the respondent put the opposing construction that such a temporal connection was required.[50]

The puzzle for the Court was created by the fact that, on the one hand, the definitions of 'special care' in s 73(3)(a), (b), (d) and (e) were 'all expressed in terms of the *present* existence of defined relationships',[51] whereas, in relation to para (c), there was a 'latent ambiguity or obscurity'[52] as to whether 'in connection with' required a temporal connection between the instruction and the act of sexual intercourse. Latham J, who gave the leading judgment,[53] posed the question – why did the legislature choose to cast the circumstances giving rise to liability under s 73(3)(c) in different terms?[54] Her Honour gave this response:

> The fact that the legislature chose to cast the circumstances giving rise to liability under s 73(3)(c) in different terms calls for an explanation. One explanation for that difference in expression lies in the contrast between the position of authority occupied by offenders in the categories (3)(a), (b), (d) and (e) and the position of authority occupied by a tutor or instructor of the kind envisaged by (3)(c).

---

49 Ibid 444 [23] (Latham J, Bellew J agreeing at 449 [41], Campbell J agreeing at 449 [42]).

50 Ibid 443 [11] (before trial judge).

51 Ibid 444 [24] (emphasis added).

52 Ibid 445 [29].

53 Bellew J agreeing at ibid 449 [41], Campbell J agreeing at 449 [42].

54 Ibid 445 [26].

> The type of instruction referred to in (3)(c) may be of a casual or permanent nature, and may be undertaken daily, weekly, fortnightly or monthly, for less or more than an hour's duration, over the course of months or years (depending on the purpose underlying the instruction). The circumstances of the instruction vary as greatly as the nature and purpose of the instruction dictates.
>
> For these reasons, it cannot be assumed in every case that a tutor who has provided or is providing instruction to a 17 year old necessarily exercises the type of authority and control over his/her pupil that gives rise to the capacity to exploit that influence. The question is one of fact and degree which depends upon the circumstances of each case.[55]

The case appears to be an illustration of a condition arising prior to the creation of the rule – namely, the '[s]heer complexity of the original situation'.[56] Instruction took many forms and occurred in a wide variety of circumstances. In this way it differed from the other 'special care' categories in s 73(3). This appreciation gave the Court a deeper understanding of the problem, though it did not itself resolve it. As Latham J reflected: 'Whilst this analysis might assist in understanding the formulation of s 73(3)(c), it does not resolve the latent ambiguity or obscurity in the sub-section.'[57]

Example 14.2 *Smoker v Pharmacy Restructuring Authority*[58]

In this case the problem for the Full Federal Court was the meaning of 'guidelines' in s 99K(2) of the *National Health Act 1953* (Cth), which read:

> In making a recommendation under subsection (1), the Authority must comply with the relevant guidelines determined by the Minister under section 99L.

The puzzle raised by the text was whether, as the Minister argued, 'guidelines' that had been determined by the Minister were legally binding on the Pharmacy Restructuring Authority, or whether, as the appellant argued, they provided no more than mere guidance, the Authority retaining a residual discretion regarding its ultimate decision. Hill J (who gave the leading judgment)[59] traced the source of doubt to a background agreement between the Minister and the Pharmacy Guild of Australia. He found: 'That agreement provided for amendments to be made to the Act, inter alia, to establish the Authority and empowering it to make recommendations.'[60] Upon inspection of the agreement, Hill J found that 'the agreement contemplated the issue of mandatory rules which it called "guidelines"'.[61] Further, he found: 'The provisions of the

55 Ibid 445 [26]–[28].

56 William Twining and David Miers, *How to Do Things with Rules: A Primer of Interpretation* (Cambridge University Press, 5th ed, 2010) 178.

57 (2017) 270 A Crim R 439, 445 [29]. The Court ultimately preferred the construction of the respondent: at 449 [39].

58 (1994) 53 FCR 287. This example draws on aspects of the analysis of the *Smoker* case in Jeffrey Barnes, 'When "Plain Language" Legislation is Ambiguous – Sources of Doubt and Lessons for the Plain Language Movement' (2010) 34(3) *Melbourne University Law Review* 671, 680–3. The article identifies other related sources of doubt.

59 Burchett J agreed with Hill J's conclusion at (1994) 53 FCR 287, 291. Wilcox J agreed with Hill J's views, though he would have been prepared to reach the same conclusion without the extrinsic material: at 288.

60 Ibid 300 (Hill J, Wilcox J agreeing at 288).

61 Ibid 301.

agreement including, in part, its terminology were incorporated into the Act and the "guidelines" ultimately promulgated reflect largely the matters agreed with the Pharmacy Guild.'[62] It can be supposed that, following the background agreement, a cause of doubt for the puzzling use of the term 'guidelines' lay in a political imperative to ensure the legislation implemented the agreement *in the terms used in the agreement*. Political imperatives are mentioned in the source of doubt literature as a potential source of doubt.[63]

Identifying the source of doubt in the background agreement provided a launching pad for interpretative argument, the Court identifying 'legislative history' as an interpretative factor favouring the Minister's construction.[64] The Court ultimately preferred that construction.[65]

Example 14.3 *Scott-Mackenzie v Bail*[66]

In this case the scope of certain provisions defining eligibility for a family provision order were in doubt. A family provision order is an order of a court that makes provision out of the estate of a deceased person for the proper maintenance and support of an eligible person.

The respondent (applicant) was a child of the deceased's former domestic partner, Ms H. The relationship between the deceased and Ms H, extending over 40 years, ended with the death of Ms H in 2001. The deceased later commenced a domestic relationship with Ms R, and left his estate to her.

Section 90 of the *Administration and Probate Act 1958* (Vic) defined 'eligible person' as including a 'stepchild of the deceased'. The primary judge construed 'stepchild of the deceased' as including a person who was a child of the deceased's domestic partner.[67] As a result, he found the applicant eligible for the order.[68]

The executor appealed to the Victorian Court of Appeal. The executor argued that the phrase 'stepchild of the deceased' is restricted to a person whose parent was *married* to the deceased. For the ordinary meaning of the phrase in question, the executor relied on, among other things, dictionary definitions of 'stepchild' and dicta in a 1998 decision of the Victorian Court of Appeal in which '[t]he Court regarded marriage as being integral to the existence of a stepchild relationship and determined that for a claimant to be a stepchild of another person, it is essential that the claimant's mother or father is or was married to that other person'.[69]

But doubt over the ordinary meaning of 'stepchild of the deceased' was raised by certain changes in the factual context. The Court of Appeal observed that domestic relationships were 'considerably more common than they were, say, 30 years ago', adding, '[t]he fact that the word 'stepchild' came into existence at a time before domestic partnerships became more common

62 Ibid.

63 Hilary Penfold, 'Legislative Drafting and Statutory Interpretation' (2006) 7 *The Judicial Review* 471, 483; Jeffrey Barnes, 'Sources of Doubt and the Quest for Legal Certainty' (2008) 2(2) *Legisprudence: International Journal for the Study of Legislation* 119, 132–3.

64 (1994) 53 FCR 287, 300–1 (Hill J, Wilcox J agreeing at 288, Burchett J agreeing at 291).

65 Ibid 301 (Hill J, Wilcox J agreeing at 288, Burchett J agreeing in the conclusion at 291).

66 (2017) 16 ASTLR 449, 451 [10].

67 *Bail v Scott-Mackenzie* [2016] VSC 563, [118] (Derham AsJ).

68 Ibid [120].

69 451 [10] (the Court), referring to *Popple v Rowe* [1998] 1 VR 651.

explains why definitions have previously referred to either an original marriage and a subsequent marriage, or merely a subsequent marriage'.[70]

In other words, changes in the factual context, and changes in mores or prevailing values since the 1998 *Popple* case and the publication of the dictionaries,[71] gave a deeper understanding of the problem presented and led to arguments favouring the respondent's construction. The contemporaneity of the changes pointed to the ordinary meaning of the phrase in question being different to that evidenced in dictionaries and the 1998 case.[72] The Court of Appeal ultimately preferred the respondent's construction.[73]

Ascertaining sources of doubt can assist in locating responsibility for errors in legislation [14.6]

Locating the responsibility for error can assist in preventing future errors occurring in like circumstances. Somewhat unfairly, legislative drafters are often, perhaps usually, blamed for errors in legislation. Lord Oliver writes: 'Whenever anyone finds a provision difficult to understand with certainty, his first and instantaneous reaction is to blame the draftsman.'[74] Mason P agrees that there is a 'tendency to blame the drafter' when a judge is 'faced with apparently contradictory statutory commands'.[75]

Yet the sources of doubt literature suggests that automatically blaming the drafter is apt to mislead. 'Poor drafting' is just one of 36 conditions of doubt in the Twining and Miers model.[76] More specifically, as Mason P is quick to recognise, 'many policies and legal principles are ambiguous and contradictory in their nature'.[77] And as Lord Oliver says: 'It is [the drafter's] job as well as his misfortune to seek to reduce to writing concepts and ideas fashioned and implanted by somebody else.'[78] In other words (the words of Quiggin, the First Parliamentary Counsel of the Office of Parliamentary Counsel (Cth)), 'OPC does not have any policy making role'.[79] According to Penfold, a predecessor of Quiggin, a litany of inherent difficulties in the legislative process (largely beyond the control of the drafter) are prone to cause doubt. They include: the need to write for different audiences, timelines caused by workloads or political demands that do not allow for much

70 Ibid [461].

71 This illustrates condition 17 ('[c]hange in factual content since creation of the rule') and condition 18 ('[c]hange in mores or prevailing values since creation of the rules) in William Twining and David Miers, *How to Do Things with Rules: A Primer of Interpretation* (Cambridge University Press, 5th ed, 2010) 178.

72 *Scott-Mackenzie v Bail* (2017) 16 ASTLR 449 [460–1].

73 Ibid [461].

74 Lord Oliver of Aylmerton, 'A Judicial View of Modern Legislation' (1993) 14(1) *Statute Law Review* 1, 4.

75 Justice Keith Mason, 'The Intent of Legislators: How Judges Discern It and What They Do if They Find It' (2006) 27(3) *Australian Bar Review* 253, 255.

76 Condition 13: William Twining and David Miers, *How to Do Things with Rules: A Primer of Interpretation* (Cambridge University Press, 5th ed, 2010) 179–80.

77 Justice Keith Mason, 'The Intent of Legislators: How Judges Discern It and What They Do if They Find It' (2006) 27(3) *Australian Bar Review* 253, 255.

78 Lord Oliver of Aylmerton, 'A Judicial View of Modern Legislation' (1993) 14(1) *Statute Law Review* 1, 4.

79 Peter Quiggin, 'Statutory Construction: How to Construct, and Construe, a Statute' in Neil Williams (ed), *Key Issues in Judicial Review* (Federation Press, 2014) 78, 81. The author acknowledges that parliamentary counsel have an influence on lower levels of policy-making: at 81–2.

reflection or research, inadequate consultation by instructors with outside experts, political imperatives to use certain expressions, the drafting of parliamentary amendments by persons outside the Office of Parliamentary Counsel, and demands for questionable pre-emptive amendments (where administrators are not confident that their preferred interpretation of the law will survive judicial scrutiny).[80] Quiggin endorses many of these difficulties, including how, in a number of drafting jobs, the instructing department has submitted inadequate or flawed instructions.[81]

[14.7] Knowledge of potential sources of doubt provides food for thought about the appropriate drafting style[82]

Drafting styles express the main ways in which legislation is written. As introduced earlier,[83] the main drafting styles are the traditional style,[84] the general principles style[85] and the plain language style.[86] The styles can be combined.[87] The traditional style is intended to be 'very precise' and to give 'exact effect to the wishes of the policy-makers'.[88] The general principles style is 'the style used when the drafter deliberately states the law in general principles and leaves the details to be filled in by the courts, by subordinate legislation or in some other way'.[89] The main precepts of the plain language style, as described by Turnbull, are 'use the rules of simple writing', 'identify and avoid traditional forms of expression if they could be expressed more simply' and 'use aids to understanding that are not merely concerned with language'.[90]

Each of these drafting styles has repercussions for the raising of sources of doubt. Braithwaite points out that '[i]n legal scholarship it is mostly assumed that tightly specified rules increase legal certainty'.[91] Put another way, the assumption is that the traditional style increases legal certainty whereas the general principles style does not. But judicial opinion and empirical

80 Hilary Penfold, 'Legislative Drafting and Statutory Interpretation' (2006) 7 *The Judicial Review* 471, 481–4.

81 Peter Quiggin, 'Statutory Construction: How to Construct, and Construe, a Statute' in Neil Williams (ed), *Key Issues in Judicial Review* (Federation Press, 2014) 78, 78, 80.

82 For effects of drafting styles on interpretation, see chapter 16.

83 At **[10.7]**.

84 Other names include 'the detailed form': Office of Parliamentary Counsel, *Plain English Manual* (Australian Government, 2016) [18], [20]; 'the prescriptive style': Justice Steven Rares, 'Legality, Rights and Statutory Interpretation' (Conference Paper, 2013 AGS Administrative Law Conference, Canberra, 20–21 June 2013) [58]; 'micro-management of decision-making': Justice John Logan, 'Statutory Construction – Panel Discussion Presentation' [2016] *Federal Judicial Scholarship* 6.

85 I Turnbull, 'Legislative Drafting in Plain Language and Statements of General Principle' (1997) 18(1) *Statute Law Review* 21. This style is also known by these names: 'principles based legislative drafting': Justice Steven Rares, 'Legality, Rights and Statutory Interpretation' (Speech, 2013 AGS Administrative Law Conference, Canberra, 20–21 June 2013) [59]; 'conceptual specification': Justice John Logan, 'Statutory Construction – Panel Discussion Presentation' [2016] *Federal Judicial Scholarship* 6; 'general prescriptions': Justice Nye Perram, 'The Perils of Complexity: Why More Law Is Bad Law' (2010) 39 *Australian Tax Review* 179, 185.

86 I Turnbull, 'Legislative Drafting in Plain Language and Statements of General Principle' (1997) 18(1) *Statute Law Review* 21.

87 Ibid 29–31.

88 Ibid 22.

89 Ibid 26.

90 IML Turnbull, 'Clear Legislative Drafting: New Approaches in Australia' (1990) 11(3) *Statute Law Review* 161, 166, 169.

91 John Braithwaite, 'Rules and Principles: A Theory of Legal Certainty' (2002) 27 *Australian Journal of Legal Philosophy* 47, 50.

evidence suggest that the traditional style can often be a source of doubt,[92] casting doubt on the assumption referred to. The then Chief Justice of the High Court, French CJ, commented extracurially: 'Combinations of words may narrow their individual indeterminacies, but may also have the reverse effect.'[93] In another address, he was more emphatic: 'The more words that are used in conditioning the exercise of an executive power, the more scope there can be for debate about what they mean and therefore about the circumstances in which the power can be exercised.'[94] And several state and federal judges have, in a forthright manner, drawn attention to interpretative difficulties caused by overly prescriptive legislation.[95] Some have called for greater use of the general principles style.[96]

Empirical support for the effects of the traditional and general principles styles is provided by Braithwaite.[97] On the back of this he advances a theory of legal certainty regarding 'rules' and 'principles'. (Similar to traditional and general principles styles, he conceives 'rules' as 'specific prescriptions', and 'principles' as 'unspecific or vague prescriptions'.[98]) His theory comprises three main propositions:

1. When the type of action to be regulated is simple, stable (not changing unpredictably across time) and does not involve huge economic interests, rules regulate with greater certainty than principles.[99]
2. With complex actions in changing environments where large economic interests are at stake principles are more likely to enable legal certainty than rules.[100]

---

92 It should not be assumed that the drafter is automatically responsible for the drafting style. See **[14.6]**. The role of the instructing agency in reducing complexity is suggested in Peter Quiggin, 'Statutory Construction: How to Construct, and Construe, a Statute' in Neil Williams (ed), *Key Issues in Judicial Review* (2014) 78, 85–6. For a trenchant critique of Commonwealth instructing agencies in the 1980s, see Geoffrey Hackett-Jones, 'The Scar of Odysseus and the Role of Parliamentary Counsel in the Legislative Process' in David St L Kelly (ed), *Essays on Legislative Drafting in Honour of J Q Ewens* (1988) 43, 51.

93 Chief Justice Robert French, 'The Courts and the Parliament' (Speech, Queensland Supreme Court Seminar, Brisbane, 4 August 2012) 9.

94 Chief Justice Robert French, 'The Judicial Function in an Age of Statutes' (2011 Goldring Memorial Lecture, Wollongong, 18 November 2011) 15.

95 Justice Mark Weinberg, 'Of Mozart, Modern Drafting and the Criminal Lawyers' Lament' (Speech, Victoria Law Foundation Oration, Supreme Court of Victoria, Melbourne, 21 July 2016) [51]–[96]; Justice Steven Rares, 'Legality, Rights and Statutory Interpretation' (Conference Paper, 2013 AGS Administrative Law Conference, Canberra, 20–21 June 2013) [60], [85]; Justice John Logan, 'Statutory Construction – Panel Discussion Presentation' [2016] *Federal Judicial Scholarship* 6; Justice Nye Perram, 'The Perils of Complexity: Why More Law Is Bad Law' (2010) 39(4) *Australian Tax Review* 179, 184–6. Perram J maintains the problem is 'Commonwealth legislation in general': at 184.

96 Justice Steven Rares, 'Legality, Rights and Statutory Interpretation' (Speech, 2013 AGS Administrative Law Conference, Canberra, 20–21 June 2013) [85]–[86]; Justice Nye Perram, 'The Perils of Complexity: Why More Law Is Bad Law' (2010) 39(3) *Australian Tax Review* 179, 185.

97 John Braithwaite, 'Rules and Principles: A Theory of Legal Certainty' (2002) 27 *Australian Journal of Legal Philosophy* 47.

98 Ibid 47.

99 Ibid 52. This theory correlates with findings in the plain language area. Empirical studies show that 'where the subjects are knowledgeable of the specialist subject matter and the rules are simple and concrete, considerable success [in comprehension levels] can be achieved': Jeffrey Barnes, 'The Plain Language Movement and Legislation: Does Plain Language Work?' (PhD Thesis, La Trobe University, 2013) 258–9. But the studies do not show success in the case of 'substantial and reasonably complex Acts': at 258.

100 John Braithwaite, 'Rules and Principles: A Theory of Legal Certainty' (2002) 27 *Australian Journal of Legal Philosophy* 47, 53.

3. When the type of action to be regulated is complex, changing and involves large economic interests, principles or rules alone are less certain than a prudent mix of rules and principles.[101]

The author explains the advantages of principles: 'Principles may be more important than rules for engendering legal certainty because they are simpler, shorter, fewer and therefore can be better discussed from board meetings down to factory floor in drawing out the lessons from valued stories.'[102] He concedes that empirical support for his theory is 'extremely limited',[103] but that 'the propositions are advanced as more consistent with the little we know than the competing formulations considered'.[104]

As regards the plain language style, there is evidence that it reduces uncertainty and increases comprehension by removing unnecessary obscurity, by raising fewer difficulties and by making legislation easier to read and understand.[105] Nevertheless, plain language has its limits:

> [I]t is naïve to claim or assume, as so many less compromising advocates of plain English do, that legislation has the capacity to 'communicate' the law, across the board, unhindered by sources of doubt. The cases and the general literature on legislation demonstrate that there are simply too many uncontrollable factors potentially at work.[106]

101 Ibid 65.

102 Ibid 75.

103 The author concedes there is a lack of data relating to judicial decision-making: ibid 60. In its absence, he draws on various sources, including fieldwork concerning styles of regulation of nursing homes in Australia and the United States, and private law.

104 Ibid 75.

105 Jeffrey Barnes, 'The Plain Language Movement and Legislation: Does Plain Language Work?' (PhD Thesis, La Trobe University, 2013) ch 6. For an earlier and brief overview, see Jeffrey Barnes, 'The Continuing Debate about "Plain Language" Legislation: A Law Reform Conundrum' (2006) 27(2) *Statute Law Review* 83, 128–9.

106 Jeffrey Barnes, 'When "Plain Language" Legislation is Ambiguous – Sources of Doubt and Lessons for the Plain Language Movement' (2010) 34(3) *Melbourne University Law Review* 671, 706 (footnotes omitted).

PART IV

THE PROVISION, AND THE ACT AS A WHOLE

Parts IV–VIII explore the so-called rules of interpretation, better known as the interpretative criteria of the law. When the criteria are manifested in a particular statutory context they provide indications of meaning and are known as interpretative factors. Part IV begins with the criteria that may be manifested in the text or provision, and in the remainder of the Act concerned.

Chapter 15 (*The Language of the Provision*) examines how particular presumptive meanings are derived from the language of the text in question. The courts use a variety of expressions to describe the meanings generated by reading the words in question – primarily the 'literal', 'grammatical', 'natural' and 'ordinary' meanings. While the meanings are much alike, each carries particular nuances and emphases. The meaning generated from the language of the text is to be applied unless good reason is shown to depart from it.

Drafting styles describe the manner in which legislation is written. The main drafting styles for legislation are traditional, plain language, and general principles, though provisions may comprise a hybrid of these styles. Chapter 16 (*The Effect of Drafting Styles*) examines how drafting styles influence statutory interpretation.

In interpreting legislation, courts can take into account whether the provision in question comes within a particular category of legislation. The categories most frequently mentioned are remedial, penal and taxing. Chapter 17 (*Special Categories of Legislation: The Interpretation of Remedial, Penal and Revenue Provisions*) examines their significance for statutory interpretation.

Linguistic canons recognise and put into effect general language conventions – that is, conventions relating to the use of language generally. Chapter 15 dealt with the 'ordinary and grammatical meaning' and the 'natural and ordinary meaning' of the words in question. Chapter 18 (*Linguistic Canons*) examines other linguistic canons, which often have Latin tags. Examples of linguistic canons dealt with in chapter 18 are the presumption against surplusage, *noscitur a sociis* (the importance of the immediate context), and *expressio unius est exclusio alterius* (the express mention of one thing indicates the exclusion of another).

Chapter 19 (*The 'Always Speaking' Approach*) deals with the principle that we approach, where possible, the interpretation of statutory text as if it is speaking continuously in the present. Application of the principle may enable the text to apply to a state of affairs, or to incorporate a state of the law, that did not exist at the time of enactment.

Chapter 20 (*The Scheme and Components of an Act*) considers the role that the various components of an Act play for interpretative purposes, whether or not treated as formally part of the Act. The components that are discussed include an objects clause, punctuation and an example. The chapter also discusses how the components of an Act give an Act structure and help explain its scheme.

THE LANGUAGE OF THE PROVISION 15

Overview

An earlier chapter (chapter 6) established the importance of the text in statutory interpretation. The present chapter examines how particular presumptive meanings may be derived from the particular words in doubt. The primary meanings are the 'literal', 'grammatical', 'natural' and 'ordinary' meanings. Often combined, the presumptive meaning that reading a provision generates may be described, for instance, as the 'ordinary and grammatical meaning' and the 'natural and ordinary meaning'. [15.1]

Although the presumptive meanings are much alike, they carry individual nuances and emphases. For instance, when a court refers to the literal meaning of particular words, it goes by the express provision alone. By comparison, the ordinary meaning is a meaning drawn from the meaning that the words ordinarily convey in society.

Various methods are deployed to find the presumptive meaning in practice. A judge's immediate or first-blush reading of the words in question is intuitive, but grounded in professional training. In determining the ordinary meaning, a judge often uses dictionaries and other works of scholarly reference for support. If a word has more than one ordinary meaning, a court will put greater weight on the primary ordinary meaning – in other words, its primary ordinary usage. Ordinary meanings can themselves change over time also. In the end a judge has the capacity to determine for themself the ordinary and grammatical meaning.

Despite its prima facie significance, the presumptive meaning will not necessarily prevail; the context may compel the judge to give the words in question another meaning. But if, after regard is had to the context, it is concluded that the meaning of the words in question is clear and not open to more than one interpretation, the text is assigned a legal meaning that is sometimes called the 'plain meaning'.

The chapter does not deal exhaustively with all the indications of meaning that may be gathered from the words in question. Those words may be the basis for a variety of interpretative arguments that, because they are not necessarily exclusively sourced in the words in question, are dealt with elsewhere in this work. They include arguments based on other linguistic canons,[1] the presumption that the legislative purpose be promoted,[2] the style of legislative drafting[3] and the presumption that a construction be tested by reference to its consequences.[4]

1 See chapter 18.

2 See chapter 8.

3 See chapter 16. Styles of drafting are introduced in **[10.7]** and **[14.7]**. See also chapter 16.

4 See chapter 27.

The presumptive meaning

[15.2] **Consideration of the text ordinarily generates a presumptive meaning: the ordinary, grammatical, literal or natural meaning**

As discussed in chapter 6, consideration of the words in question ('the text') constitutes the starting point in statutory interpretation.[5] The meaning it generates constitutes a presumptive and weighty meaning, which applies unless good reason is shown to depart from it.[6]

The courts use a variety of expressions to describe the meanings that are generated by reading the provision at issue – primarily the ordinary, grammatical, literal and natural meanings. The expressions are often combined. Although the meanings are much alike, they carry individual nuances and emphases.

One expression is the 'ordinary or grammatical meaning', as in this holding: 'It is now accepted that even words having an apparently clear ordinary or grammatical meaning may be ascribed a different legal meaning after the process of construction is complete.'[7] It has been similarly put: 'The process of construction begins with a consideration of the ordinary and grammatical meaning of the words of the provision having regard to their context and legislative purpose.'[8]

Sometimes, reference is made to the literal or grammatical meaning:

> Ordinarily, that meaning (the legal meaning) will correspond with the *grammatical meaning* of the provision. But not always. The context of the words, the consequences of a literal or grammatical construction, the purpose of the statute or the canons of construction may require the words of a legislative provision to be read in a way that does not correspond with the *literal or grammatical meaning*.[9]

Another similar expression is the 'natural and ordinary meaning'. In *Masson v Parsons*[10] six members of the High Court stated that 'a court will not construe a provision in a way that departs from its natural and ordinary meaning unless it is plain that Parliament intended it to have some different meaning'.[11]

Alternatively, a more general reference to the meaning that is generated may be made – for example: '[t]reating the section in its then form purely *as a piece of English*'.[12]

---

5 See **[6.5]**.

6 See **[6.7]**.

7 *R v A2* (2019) 269 CLR 507, 521 [32] (Kiefel CJ and Keane J, Nettle and Gordon JJ agreeing generally at 554 [148], Edelman J agreeing at 572 [193]).

8 *Australian Education Union v Department of Education and Children's Services* (2012) 248 CLR 1, 13 [26] (French CJ, Hayne, Kiefel and Bell JJ). See also *Collector of Customs v Agfa-Gevaert Ltd* (1996) 186 CLR 389, 401 (Brennan CJ, Dawson, Toohey, Gaudron and McHugh JJ), citing with approval EA Driedger, 'Statutes: The Mischievous Literal Golden Rule' (1981) 59(4) *Canadian Bar Review* 780, 785–6; *Momcilovic v The Queen* (2011) 245 CLR 1, 52 [56] (French CJ).

9 *Project Blue Sky Inc v Australian Broadcasting Authority* (1998) 194 CLR 355, 384 [78] (McHugh, Gummow, Kirby and Hayne JJ) (footnote omitted; emphasis added).

10 (2019) 266 CLR 554.

11 Ibid 572 [26] (Kiefel CJ, Bell, Gageler, Keane, Nettle and Gordon JJ). See also *Marshall v Director General, Department of Transport* (2001) 205 CLR 603, 623 [37] (Gaudron J, Hayne J agreeing at 634 [67]); *Tjungarrayi v Western Australia* (2019) 269 CLR 150, 163–4 [31]–[32] (Kiefel CJ, Bell, Keane and Edelman JJ); *Parkes Shire Council v South West Helicopters Pty Ltd* (2019) 266 CLR 212, 225 [32] (Kiefel CJ, Bell, Keane and Edelman JJ).

12 *Harvey v Harvey* (1951) 68 WN (NSW) 241, 243 (Street CJ, Owen and Herron JJ agreeing at 244) (emphasis added).

The above meanings serve an important purpose:

> It is a basic rule of statutory construction that legislative provisions are to be construed according to their natural and ordinary meaning unless that would lead to a result that the legislature must be taken not to have intended. The rule serves the important purpose of ensuring that those who are subject to the law understand the nature and extent of their rights and obligations.[13]

The meanings of the various expressions are explored below.

The nature of literal, grammatical, natural and ordinary meanings

When a court refers to the literal or grammatical or natural meaning of particular words, the words are read in isolation from the rest of the Act [15.3]

The literal meaning, grammatical meaning[14] and natural meaning[15] are found by reading the words in isolation from the rest of the Act.

The literal meaning emphasises the actual words whose meaning is in doubt.[16] A literal meaning is the meaning 'readily ascertained from the language used'.[17] A literal approach goes by the 'express provisions'[18] or 'literal words' of the provision concerned.[19] Thus, a 'literalist' approach 'insist[s] that only the words of an Act should be looked at'.[20] It is contrasted with a contextual approach,[21] which may identify the mischief or legislative purposes (assisted by extrinsic materials that are relevant) and take account of 'basic principles and presumptions that are attributed to the lawmaker'.[22]

---

13 *Marshall v Director General, Department of Transport* (2001) 205 CLR 603, 623 [37] (Gaudron J, Hayne J agreeing at 634 [67]) (citations omitted). See also *International Finance Trust Co Ltd v New South Wales Crime Commission* (2009) 240 CLR 319, 349 [42] (French CJ).

14 *Project Blue Sky Inc v Australian Broadcasting Authority* (1998) 194 CLR 355, 385 [80] (McHugh, Gummow, Kirby and Hayne JJ); *Plaintiff M47/2012 v Director-General of Security* (2012) 251 CLR 1, 77 [173] (Hayne J).

15 *Attorney-General (Qld) v Australian Industrial Relations Commission* (2002) 213 CLR 485, 505 [53] (Gaudron, McHugh, Gummow and Hayne JJ); *Master Undertakers' Association of New South Wales v Crockett* (1907) 5 CLR 389, 395 (Isaacs J).

16 The *Oxford English Dictionary* (3rd ed, 2011, online at 8 May 2022) eloquently defines 'literal' as '[o]f, relating to, or designating the primary, original, or etymological sense of a word, or the exact sense expressed by the actual wording of a phrase or passage, as distinguished from any extended sense, metaphorical meaning, or underlying significance'.

17 *Plaintiff S157/2002 v Commonwealth* (2003) 211 CLR 476, 523 [126] (Callinan J).

18 *Western Australian Planning Commission v Southregal Pty Ltd* (2017) 259 CLR 106, 146 [114], 152 [136] (Keane J) (dissenting as to outcome).

19 *Parkes Shire Council v South West Helicopters Pty Ltd* (2019) 266 CLR 212, 248 [123] (Gordon J).

20 *Commissioner of Taxation (Cth) v Westraders Pty Ltd* (1980) 144 CLR 55, 79 (Murphy J) (dissenting as to outcome).

21 *Maurice Blackburn Cashman v Brown* (2011) 242 CLR 647, 660 [34] (the Court); *X v Australian Prudential Regulation Authority* (2007) 226 CLR 630, 664 [116] (Kirby J). See chapter 7.

22 *Pfeiffer v Stevens* (2001) 209 CLR 57, 82 [92] (Kirby J) (dissenting as to outcome). See also *Project Blue Sky Inc v Australian Broadcasting Authority* (1998) 194 CLR 355, 384 [78] (McHugh, Gummow, Kirby and Hayne JJ), approving *Bennion on Statutory Interpretation* (3rd ed, 1997) 343–4 (evidencing the mischief being drawn from the context).

A similar legal term is 'grammatical meaning'.[23] As its name implies, it emphasises the rules and usages of grammar.[24]

The 'natural meaning' is another similar expression.[25] It emphasises the meaning of the words as a whole. The Supreme Court of Canada has referred to 'the natural meaning' of a provision as the meaning arrived at after the provision is 'simply read through as a whole'.[26] A natural meaning is contrasted with a 'strained meaning'.[27]

Example 15.1 *Healey v Royal Society for the Prevention of Cruelty to Animals Victoria*[28]

Under ss 24G and 24K of the *Prevention of Cruelty to Animals Act 1986* (Vic) ('the Act'), the Department Head has the power to approve an inspector applying to a magistrate for the issue of a search warrant in relation to premises where there are at-risk animals. Section 38(2) of the Act is a power of delegation:

> **38 Delegation**
>
> ...
>
> (2) The Department Head may by instrument of delegation delegate to any person any power, duty or function of the Department Head under this Act or [Regulations] other than this power of delegation.

Purportedly pursuant to this provision, the Department Head delegated to 'the person or class of persons appointed to a position or acting in or performing the duties of a position described in [the Delegation]'. Relevantly, except for two positions, the listed delegates were all public officials, such as 'Chief Veterinary Officer' and 'Senior Police Officers' (as defined). The exceptions were the Chief Executive Officer and the Chief Operating Officer of the Royal Society for the Prevention of Cruelty to Animals Victoria (the respondent).

---

23 See *Project Blue Sky Inc v Australian Broadcasting Authority* (1998) 194 CLR 355, 384 [78] (McHugh, Gummow, Kirby and Hayne JJ). The plurality approved a passage in FAR Bennion, *Statutory Interpretation* (3rd ed, 1997) 343–4, a work that treats the grammatical meaning (or the preferred grammatical meaning) as substantively equivalent to the 'literal meaning'; see now Oliver Jones, *Bennion on Statutory Interpretation* (LexisNexis, 6th ed, 2013) 429.

24 Oliver Jones, *Bennion on Statutory Interpretation* (LexisNexis, 6th ed, 2013) 429 (an earlier edition of which was approved in *Project Blue Sky Inc v Australian Broadcasting Authority* (1998) 194 CLR 355, 384 [78]) defines the grammatical meaning as 'the meaning it bears when, as a piece of English prose, it is construed according to the rules and usages of grammar, syntax and punctuation, and the accepted linguistic canons of construction': at 423.

25 The *Macquarie Dictionary* (online version) gives for one meaning of 'literal': 'in accordance with, involving, or being the natural or strict meaning of the words or word'.

26 *Canadian Pacific Air Lines Ltd v Canadian Air Line Pilots Association* [1993] 3 SCR 724, 735 (Gonthier J, Lamer CJ, La Forest and Iacobucci JJ agreeing at 730).

27 *Alcan (NT) Alumina Pty Ltd v Commissioner of Territory Revenue (NT)* (2009) 239 CLR 27, 47 [48] (Hayne, Heydon, Crennan and Kiefel JJ, French CJ agreeing at 30 [1]); *Zhang v Zemin* (2010) 79 NSWLR 513, 535 [126] (Spigelman CJ, Allsop P generally agreeing at 540 [157], McClellan CJ at CL agreeing at 543 [174]). For discussion of 'strained' meanings, see **[6.9]** and chapter 34.

28 (2018) 56 VR 414.

The applicant was a dog breeder. After complaints were made to the respondent about the conditions of the dogs and their living conditions, an employee of the respondent, Mr P, applied to the Magistrates' Court for search warrants. The employee had been purportedly authorised under the Act by the Chief Operating Officer of the respondent. The warrants were executed and 54 out of a total of 90 dogs on the applicant's property were seized. The applicant commenced a judicial review proceeding challenging the validity of the warrants and their execution. After the trial judge dismissed the proceeding, the applicant sought leave to appeal against the decision on several grounds. The appeal to the Court of Appeal of the Supreme Court of Victoria succeeded on one ground.

One of the unsuccessful grounds alleged that the trial judge had erred in holding that s 38(2) authorised the delegation to the Chief Operating Officer of the respondent of the powers of the Department Head under ss 24G and 24K of the Act. The applicant submitted that s 38(2) authorised the delegation of the Department Head's powers only to a named person or to the holder of a public office, being a statutory office or an office in the public service. For a number of reasons, the Court of Appeal found the ground lacked merit. Its reasons had regard to the natural meaning of the words 'to any person' in s 38(2):

> The natural meaning of the words 'to any person' in the phrase 'The Department Head may ... delegate to any person' in s 38(2) is any person to whom the Department Head choses [sic] to delegate the relevant powers. There is nothing in the section which confines the words to a named natural person or the holder of a public office.[29]

The ordinary meaning is the meaning that the words ordinarily convey [15.4]

The 'ordinary meaning' refers to 'the meaning which the words ordinarily convey'.[30] This in turn is to be understood as the meaning that the words ordinarily convey outside the Act – that is, in society. This understanding is confirmed by synonymous expressions for the ordinary meaning. They include 'how [a word] is ordinarily understood in discourse',[31] 'usual' meaning,[32] 'meaning in general usage',[33] 'common usage',[34] 'meaning given to [a word] in daily life',[35] 'their sense in common parlance',[36] 'the ordinary usage of society'[37] and 'the way in which the word is ordinarily used in Australia'.[38]

29 Ibid 432 [51] (the Court).

30 *Wicks v State Rail Authority of New South Wales* (2010) 241 CLR 60, 77 [50] (the Court).

31 *SZTAL v Minister for Immigration and Border Protection* (2017) 262 CLR 362, 368 [14] (Kiefel CJ, Nettle and Gordon JJ).

32 *Australian Securities and Investments Commission v Westpac Securities Administration Ltd* (2019) 272 FCR 170, 179–80 [25] (Allsop CJ).

33 *Bampton v Viterra Ltd* (2015) 123 SASR 80, 119 [187] (Blue J).

34 *Vumbaca v Baulkham Hills Shire Council* (1979) 141 CLR 614, 617 (Stephen J).

35 *Chesterman v Federal Commissioner of Taxation* (1923) 32 CLR 362, 381 (Isaacs J).

36 *Potter v Minahan* (1908) 7 CLR 277, 320 (Higgins J).

37 *Provincial Insurance Australia Pty Ltd v Consolidated Wood Products Pty Ltd* (1991) 25 NSWLR 541, 560 (Mahoney JA), citing *Shore v A-G on the Relation of Wilson* (1842) 9 Cl & Fin 355, 527; 8 ER 450, 518 (Coleridge J) and *R v Peters* (1886) 16 QBD 636, 641 (Lord Coleridge CJ).

38 *Smoker v Pharmacy Restructuring Authority* (1994) 53 FCR 287, 289 (Wilcox J).

If, as commonly occurs, a word has more than one ordinary meaning, a court may deduce what is the 'relevant ordinary meaning'.[39] In such a case more than the ordinary meaning is relied on. In the light of the statutory context the court determines which ordinary meaning is relevant.

Example 15.2 below is a case applying the ordinary meaning.

Determining the presumptive meaning

[15.5] **A judge's immediate or 'first blush' reading of the words in question is intuitive, but grounded in professional training**

A rule, even a clear rule, does not 'speak for itself'.[40] The way in which a grammatical or natural meaning is found has been the subject of judicial comment and also of psychological research. Judicially, the process has been described as 'the first blush' sense,[41] 'the interpreter's immediate ... response to the words'[42] and the result of the provision being 'simply read through'.[43]

Kirby J has further suggested that the grammatical reading is intuitive.[44] As Kirby J himself recognised,[45] a body of work in social psychology supports this claim. Reviewing the evidence, Crowe writes about the nature of intuition in 'easy cases' – characterised as 'cases where this intuitive process yields a clear and determinate outcome':[46]

> These intuitive judgments are not a result of a conscious process of applying rules and principles to the facts, but rather are formed without (consciously) thinking about it. As a result, they may sometimes seem so obvious as to go without saying. The intuitive judgments formed by judges will be holistic, in the sense that they incorporate the judges' assessment of both the facts of the case and the applicable law. ... This does not mean, however, that the process is genuinely effortless in the sense that it lacks the exercise of judgment or does not rely on extensive cognitive processing. Nor does it mean that the judgments in question fail to accurately apply the law. Judges are highly trained legal specialists and the heuristics they use to form holistic judgments will reflect their legal training and experience in the courtroom. Their judgments are therefore likely to track the law at both a rule-based and principled level. Indeed, one might expect the readiness with which judges form such intuitions to be reflective of their skill and experience.[47]

---

39 See, eg, *Milne v The Queen* (2014) 252 CLR 149, 163 [33] (French CJ, Hayne, Bell, Gageler and Keane JJ); *White v DPP (WA)* (2011) 243 CLR 478, 487–8 [21] (French CJ, Crennan and Bell JJ).

40 Aharon Barak, *Purposive Interpretation in Law* tr Sari Bashi (Princeton University Press, 2005) 13, quoting G Tedeschi, *Masot B'mishpat [Essays in Law]* 1 (1978).

41 *Collector of Customs v Agfa-Gevaert Ltd* (1996) 186 CLR 389, 401 (Brennan CJ, Dawson, Toohey, Gaudron and McHugh JJ), quoting with approval EA Driedger, 'Statutes: the Mischievous Literal Golden Rule' (1981) 59(4) *Canadian Bar Review* 780, 785–6; *Assistant Registrar of Companies v Moses* [2004] 3 NZLR 577, 580, [11] (Keith J, McGrath and Glazebrook JJ agreeing at 578) (CA).

42 *A-G (WA) v Marquet* (2003) 217 CLR 545, 590 [133] (Kirby J) (dissenting as to outcome).

43 *Canadian Pacific Air Lines Ltd v Canadian Air Line Pilots Association* [1993] 3 SCR 724, 735 (Gonthier J, Lamer CJ, La Forest, Iacobucci JJ agreeing at 730).

44 *A-G (WA) v Marquet* (2003) 217 CLR 545, 590 [133] (Kirby J) (dissenting as to outcome). For a similar view, see Johan Steyn, 'The Intractable Problem of the Interpretation of Legal Texts' (2003) 25(1) *Sydney Law Review* 5, 8.

45 *HML v The Queen* (2008) 235 CLR 334, 365 [52].

46 Jonathan Crowe, 'Not-So-Easy Cases' (2019) 40(1) *Statute Law Review* 75, 79.

47 Ibid 78–9. For a similar view see John Braithwaite, 'Rules and Principles: A Theory of Legal Certainty' (2002) 27 *Australian Journal of Legal Philosophy* 47, 64 (intuitions are 'grounded in professional training more than

The intuitive element in the first blush or immediate response by a reader should not disguise the challenges that readers of legislation face at this level. Legislation is usually complex and dense; every word nearly always counts. The high degree of precision usually achieved by parliamentary counsel calls for an equally careful response by the reader.[48] A too hasty reading may lead to error.[49] A close attention to the wording is always required.[50]

In determining the ordinary or grammatical meaning, a judge often uses dictionaries and other works of scholarly reference for support [15.6]

In many cases courts have used dictionaries in support of determinations about the ordinary meaning.[51] A court may be assisted in determining the ordinary meaning by other scholarly works, such as historical works.[52]

Dictionaries are an extrinsic aid. The use of dictionaries and other scholarly works is discussed in more detail elsewhere in this work (chapter 32).

A word in question may have more than one ordinary meaning; if so, a court will put greater weight on the primary ordinary meaning or ordinary usage of the word [15.7]

It is a commonplace for a word to possess more than one ordinary meaning. The fact that more than one ordinary meaning exists does not itself generate an interpretative issue. Where the parties disagree over the ordinary meaning, and opposing constructions are advanced, a court will resolve the dispute along normal lines,[53] having regard to the context.[54]

Where opposing constructions are advanced and an issue in the dispute is the ordinary meaning, a court will place greater weight on the 'primary ordinary meaning'[55] – in other words, the primary ordinary usage of the word in question.

Example 15.2 *Merrick Tyler Pty Ltd v Commissioner of Main Roads*[56]

The appellant owned two parcels of land that were within the one lot and listed on the one certificate of title. One parcel was on the western side of Old Coast Road (the western parcel) and the other was on the eastern side of that road (the eastern parcel). The two parcels did not share a

personal values'). For an early view of intuitive judgments in handling statute law, see Lon L Fuller, 'Positivism and Fidelity to Law – A Reply to Professor Hart' (1957) 71(4) *Harvard Law Review* 630, 663.

48 Oliver Jones, *Bennion on Statutory Interpretation* (LexisNexis, 6th ed, 2013) 390.

49 Elizabeth Ellis, *Principles and Practice of Australian Law* (Lawbook Co, 3rd ed, 2013) 248 [7.62].

50 See **[9.5]**.

51 *House of Peace Pty Ltd v Bankstown City Council* (2000) 48 NSWLR 498, 504–5 [27] (Mason P, Stein JA agreeing at 511 [56], Giles JA agreeing at 511 [57]). A search of 'dictionary' on the High Court of Australia database on AustLII alone (<http://classic.austlii.edu.au/>; as at 11 January 2021) results in 648 hits.

52 *H v Minister for Immigration and Citizenship* (2010) 188 FCR 393, 405 [47] (the Court) ('parent').

53 For practical techniques see chapter 9.

54 *Edwards v Kumarasamy* [2016] AC 1334, 1342 [17] (Lord Neuberger, Lord Wilson, Lord Sumption and Lord Reed JJSC agreeing at 1338, Lord Carnwath JSC agreeing at 1354 [62]). See also **[15.10]**.

55 *Merrick Tyler Pty Ltd v Commissioner of Main Roads* [2015] WASCA 82, [42], [44] (the Court). Another Full Court case in which this occurred is *Minister for Immigration and Citizenship v Yucesan* (2008) 169 FCR 202, 207 [17], 209 [28] (the Court) ('met').

56 [2015] WASCA 82.

common boundary or have any other point of connection between the two. The respondent compulsorily acquired part of the eastern parcel. Section 241(7)(b) of the *Land Administration Act 1997* (WA) provided for compensation for land compulsorily acquired. This included compensation for damage to the reduction of the value of 'adjoining land':

> If the fee simple in land is taken from a person who is also the holder in fee simple of adjoining land, regard is to be had to the amount of any damage suffered by the claimant –
>
> ...
>
> (b) due to a reduction of the value of that adjoining land ...

The trial judge found that the western parcel was not 'adjoining land'. On appeal to the Court of Appeal of the Supreme Court of Western Australia, the appellant submitted that 'adjoining land' meant neighbouring land, when not separated by other privately owned land. The appellant relied on the primary judge's observation that the *Oxford English Dictionary* (online) defined 'adjoining' as 'adjacent, contiguous, *neighbouring*' (emphasis added). The trial judge had also observed that the *Macquarie Dictionary* (online) had defined 'adjoining' to mean 'bordering or contiguous'.

For several reasons the Court of Appeal preferred the construction that supported the decision of the respondent. In its reasons it gave added weight to the more popular of the ordinary meanings: 'The word "adjoining" when used to describe two parcels of land in relation to each other *primarily denotes, in its ordinary signification*, that the two parcels are contiguous in the sense of sharing at least some point of contact with each other.'[57]

[15.8] The ordinary meaning of a word in doubt may change over time

Linguistically, the ordinary meanings of words are 'in a constant state of flux'.[58] If the meaning of a word changes after the enactment of the statute, the question may arise as to whether the ordinary meaning should be 'updated'. The presumption is that an Act is 'always speaking' or, as Gageler J put it, 'the text of a statute is ordinarily to be read as speaking continuously in the present'.[59] For a detailed discussion of the presumption, see chapter 19.

[15.9] In the end a judge has the capacity to determine for themself the ordinary and grammatical meaning

A judge has the capacity, through the doctrine of judicial notice,[60] to determine for themself the ordinary and grammatical meaning. On the ordinary meaning, Kitto J stated that 'in the end the conclusion must depend on one's own understanding of the sense in which the words are currently used'.[61] Hence, a court may find the ordinary meaning without relying upon a

57 Ibid [42] (emphasis added). It is not clear whether, for this finding, the Court was relying on the dictionaries or its own knowledge, or both.

58 Kate Burridge and Alexander Bergs, *Understanding Language Change* (Routledge, 2016) 52. Chapter 3 contains many vivid illustrations.

59 *Commissioner of Police for New South Wales v Eaton* (2013) 252 CLR 1, 32 [97] (citation omitted) (Gageler J, dissenting as to outcome).

60 See **[32.2]** for reference to the general law doctrine and the relevant provisions of Evidence Acts.

61 *NSW Associated Blue-Metal Quarries Ltd v Federal Commissioner of Taxation* (1956) 94 CLR 509, 514 (Kitto J). See also discussion of 'ordinary parlance' at 512. Kitto J's view was followed in *Provincial Insurance Australia Pty Ltd v Consolidated Wood Products Pty Ltd* (1991) 25 NSWLR 541, 560 (Mahoney JA) and the latter passage

dictionary.[62] And it may determine the ordinary meaning even though this goes against all or most dictionary meanings drawn to the court's attention.[63]

Overcoming the presumptive meaning

The presumptive meaning will not necessarily prevail; the context may suggest or indeed compel a judge to give the words in question another meaning [15.10]

Despite its prima facie significance, as stated above (**[15.2]**) the ordinary and grammatical meaning is merely presumptive. In *SZTAL v Minister for Immigration and Border Protection*[64] three members of the High Court of Australia pointed out that the context may suggest the provision be given another meaning:

> The starting point for the ascertainment of the meaning of a statutory provision is the text of the statute whilst, at the same time, regard is had to its context and purpose ... Considerations of context and purpose simply recognise that, understood in its statutory, historical or other context, some other meaning of a word may be suggested ...[65]

The role of context in determining legal meaning is discussed in chapter 7.

When a text has a 'plain meaning'

If, after regard is had to the context, it is concluded that the meaning of the words in question is clear and not open to more than one interpretation, the legal meaning that is assigned to those words is sometimes called the 'plain meaning' [15.11]

The 'plain meaning' of statutory words has been contrasted with such words having 'uncertain connotation'.[66] This suggests that plain meaning is synonymous with clear meaning.[67]

A court may hold that statutory words have a plain meaning ('meaning A') even following argument being put for an opposing construction ('meaning B'). This may occur if, after full

---

was in turn approved in *Merrick Tyler Pty Ltd v Commissioner of Main Roads* [2015] WASCA 82, [41] (the Court).

62 See, eg, *Victims Compensation Fund Corporation v Brown* (2003) 201 ALR 260, 263 [13] (Heydon J, McHugh ACJ agreeing at 261 [1], Gummow J agreeing at 261 [2], Kirby J agreeing at 261 [3], Hayne J agreeing at 261 [4] ('and'); *Wotton v State of Queensland* (2002) 246 CLR 1, 25 [62] (Heydon J) ('obtains').

63 *Scott-Mackenzie v Bail* (2017) 16 ASTLR 449, 460–1 [46]–[47] ('stepchild'). Several dictionaries were surveyed. One dictionary 'loosely defined' the word consistent with the ordinary meaning found by the Court: at [36]. The others were not consistent.

64 (2017) 262 CLR 362.

65 Ibid 368 [14] (Kiefel CJ, Nettle and Gordon JJ). See also to similar effect *CIC Insurance Ltd v Bankstown Football Club Ltd* (1997) 187 CLR 384, 408 (Brennan CJ, Dawson, Toohey and Gummow JJ).

66 *Independent Commission Against Corruption v Cunneen* (2015) 256 CLR 1, 29–30 [62] (French CJ, Hayne, Kiefel and Nettle JJ).

67 A synonymous term is 'routine reading': William Twining and David Miers, *How to Do Things with Rules: A Primer of Interpretation* (Cambridge University Press, 5th ed, 2010) 175–6. A number of commentators are of the view that plainness is the typical property of statute law: see Jeffrey Barnes, 'Sources of Doubt and the Quest for Legal Certainty' (2008 2(2) *Legisprudence: International Journal for the Study of Legislation* 119, 122–4. For a postmodern perspective of plain meaning, see Margaret Davies, 'Authority, Meaning, Legitimacy' in Jeffrey Goldsworthy and Tom Campbell (eds), *Legal Interpretation in Democratic States* (Ashgate, 2002) 115, 123–5.

regard to the words and their context, the court concludes that the words in question are not 'open to more than one interpretation'.[68] In other words, there is only 'one possible meaning'.[69] In such a situation, despite the court finding that there is no ambiguity in the sense mentioned,[70] the interpretative criteria of statutory interpretation still have a role to play.[71] They may be used to show that the legal meaning of the words in question has support (albeit, one-sided) from interpretative factors.[72]

Example 15.3 *ZD v Secretary to the Department of Health and Human Services*[73]

The mother of three young children challenged, in the Supreme Court of Victoria, a condition imposed by the Children's Court of Victoria in an interim accommodation order. That order provided for out-of-home care by foster parents. The condition was purportedly imposed under s 263(7) of the *Children, Youth and Families Act 2005* (Vic) ('the Act'), which read:

> An interim accommodation order may include any conditions that the Court or bail justice considers should be included in the best interests of the child.

The condition objected to provided that each child may be immunised in accordance with an approved immunisation program. The mother's construction of the provision in question was that the power did not extend to making decisions that have significant long-term consequences for the child. The Secretary's opposing construction was that no such implication should be made.

None of the mother's arguments (critically analysed elsewhere[74]) were found to carry any weight. Hence, the Supreme Court concluded, 's 263(7) of the [Act] is not capable of more than one interpretation'.[75] Accordingly, the Court held that the relevant provision had a 'plain meaning [by which] the [Children's] Court is given a wide discretion governed by the overriding principle of the best interests of the child'.[76] It followed that the Secretary's contention was correct,[77] and the Supreme Court dismissed the appeal.

---

68 *Cheedy v Western Australia* (2011) 194 FCR 562, 583 [107] (the Court). See also *ZD v Secretary to the Department of Health and Human Services* [2017] VSC 806, [11], [71], [74], [82]; *R v Bentham* [2005] 1 WLR 1057, 1061 [10] (Lord Bingham, Lord Steyn agreeing at 1062 [12], Lord Phillips agreeing at 1062 [13], Lord Carswell agreeing at 1062 [15]).

69 *Cheedy v Western Australia* (2011) 194 FCR 562, 583 [107] (the Court). See further Oliver Jones, *Bennion on Statutory Interpretation* (LexisNexis, 6th ed, 2013) 507–10; David Lowe and Charlie Potter, *Understanding Legislation: A Practical Guide to Statutory Interpretation* (Hart, 2018) 32 [3.13].

70 *Cheedy v Western Australia* (2011) 194 FCR 562, 583 [106]–[109] (the Court).

71 Cf *R v Bentham* [2005] 1 WLR 1057, 1061 [10] (Lord Bingham, Lord Steyn agreeing at 1062 [12], Lord Phillips agreeing at 1062 [13], Lord Carswell agreeing at 1062 [15]).

72 See, eg, *ZD v Secretary to the Department of Health and Human Services* [2017] VSC 806 (discussed **Example 15.3**); *R v Bentham* [2005] 1 WLR 1057, 1061–2 [8]–[11] (Lord Bingham, Lord Steyn agreeing at 1062 [12], Lord Phillips agreeing at 1062 [13], Lord Carswell agreeing at 1062 [15]).

73 [2017] VSC 806.

74 See **Example 9.8**.

75 [2017] VSC 806, [106] (Osborn JA).

76 Ibid [11].

77 Ibid [82].

THE EFFECT OF DRAFTING STYLES 16

Overview

This chapter builds on chapter 10 where the nature of legislative drafting is discussed. It addresses the main styles of legislative drafting and their impact on interpretation. In common law jurisdictions there are three main recognised styles of drafting: traditional, plain language and general principles. Since the 1980s, Australian parliamentary counsel have largely adopted the plain language style of drafting, though other styles, notably general principles, are also used whenever appropriate. Plain language drafting will vary in its detail and prescription. It is helpful when interpreting a statute to be able to identify the drafting style or combination of styles that are used in that statute. Recognising and understanding that style may guide the relative weight to be given to text, context and purpose. Apart from style, each Australian jurisdiction adopts its own drafting format and conventions that differ to some extent from each other. To the extent that drafting practices are accessible in authoritative, publicly available drafting manuals, there is merit in becoming familiar with those manuals for interpretation. All Australian drafters adopt a textual style of amendment. [16.1]

Main drafting styles

The main drafting styles for legislation are traditional, plain language, and general principles, though most drafting comprises a hybrid of these styles [16.2]

Legislative language is a 'distinct literary genre'.[1] Broadly the writing must be disciplined, deliberate, spare, consistent and logically structured, and avoid superfluous language and embellishments.[2] But that does not mean that there is one 'right' style of drafting legislation. Moreover, the style of drafting in Australia has evolved since the establishment of parliamentary counsel's offices in each of its jurisdictions.[3]

There are three main styles of drafting recognised in common law jurisdictions: traditional, plain language and general principles drafting. Plain language drafting can vary considerably in its detail.

These styles are not mutually exclusive. A statute may be drafted in a combination of styles. For the interpreter these style labels are useful as signposts, as they can have a significant effect on interpretation. A description of the main features of each follows. Their relevance to interpretation is discussed in **[16.3]**–**[16.4]**.

---

1 Ruth Sullivan, 'Statutory Interpretation in Canada' in Tom Gotsis (ed), *Statutory Interpretation: Principles and Pragmatism for a New Age* (Education Monograph 4, Judicial Commission of New South Wales, 2007) 105, 116.

2 See **[10.6]**.

3 See generally Carmel Meiklejohn, *Fitting the Bill: A History of Commonwealth Parliamentary Drafting* (Office of Parliamentary Counsel, 2012) and **[10.7]**.

(a) Traditional style is a formalised style

Australia inherited a 'traditional' style of drafting legislation from the United Kingdom in the 19th century, which continued to be used following Federation.[4] Other terms for this style are 'detailed' or 'fussy' drafting.[5] This is a formalised style, often incorporating traditional or Latin legal expressions, archaic words, tautologies and long sentences.[6] It focuses on precision, detail and certainty as its primary goals.[7] One of the perceived advantages of this style of drafting is that, if deployed with sufficient skill, it can provide certainty in relation to the detailed circumstances that it covers.[8] However, the emphasis on precision and certainty can lead to more words being used and longer provisions. For example, instead of using the plain words 'anything done', the traditional style might state 'any act or thing done, step taken, or decision made'.[9] A major criticism of this style is that the emphasis on certainty and detail leads to unnecessarily complex provisions that are unclear to the reader.[10] **Example 16.1** shows a provision drafted in the traditional style.

Example 16.1 *Sea-Carriage of Goods Act 1909* (WA)

5. Certain clauses prohibited in bills of lading

Where any bill of lading or document contains any clause, covenant, or agreement whereby –

(a) the owner, charterer, master, or agent of any ship, or the ship itself, is relieved from liability for loss or damage to goods arising from the harmful or improper condition of the ship's hold, or any other part of the ship in which goods are carried, or arising from negligence, fault, or failure in the proper loading, stowage, custody, care, or delivery of goods received by them or any of them to be carried in or by the ship; or

...

that clause, covenant or agreement shall be illegal, null and void, and of no effect.

---

4 Office of Parliamentary Counsel, *Plain English Manual* (Australian Government, 2016) 5 [7]; Ian Turnbull, 'Plain Language and Drafting in General Principles' [1995] *The Loophole: Journal of the Commonwealth Association of Legislative Counsel* 25, 25.

5 Lisbeth Campbell, 'Drafting Styles: Fuzzy or Fussy?' (1996) 3(2) *Murdoch University Electronic Journal of Law* [1].

6 Ian Turnbull, 'Legislative Drafting in Plain Language and Statements of General Principle' (1997) 18(1) *Statute Law Review* 21, 22; Law Reform Commission of Victoria, *Plain Language and the Law: The 1987 Report Republished* (Report, Law Reform Commission of Victoria, 2017) 9 [17].

7 Lisbeth Campbell, 'Legal Drafting Styles: Fuzzy or Fussy?' (1996) 3(2) *Murdoch University Electronic Journal of Law* [10]–[12].

8 Committee Appointed by the Lord President of the Council, *Committee on the Preparation of Legislation (the 'Renton Report')* (Cmnd 6053, May 1975) 55 [9.14].

9 Example from Office of Parliamentary Counsel, *Plain English Manual* (Australian Government, 2016) app 3, 39.

10 IML Turnbull, 'Clear Legislative Drafting: New Approaches in Australia' (1990) 11(3) *Statute Law Review* 161, 162; Office of Parliamentary Counsel, *Plain English Manual* (Australian Government, 2016) 5 [7]–[8]; Committee Appointed by the Lord President of the Council, *Committee on the Preparation of Legislation* (Cmnd 6053, May 1975) 55 [9.14].

Since the mid-1980s this style has largely been superseded by plain language drafting in Australia as the dominant style of preference of drafters (see (b) below). But this does not mean that Australian interpreters will not have to interpret legislation drafted in traditional style. Due to the longevity of statutes there is still legislation on the statute books drafted in this way. The *Sea-Carriage of Goods Act 1909* (WA) extracted in **Example 16.1** is one such instance. As well, although archaic and convoluted language has been mostly discarded from contemporary legislative drafting, it is still the case that contemporary statutory provisions may be drafted using plain language style with considerable detail. See (b) below and **[16.3](a)**.

(b) Plain language style focuses on clear language and structure

In the 1980s in Australia the limitations of the traditional style for legislation and other forms of legal writing led to a movement for the adoption of a 'plain English' drafting style for all legal documents, including legislation. A brief summary of this development is provided in **[10.7]**. This drafting style is now often referred to in Australia simply as 'plain language' drafting.[11] On the basis of publically available publications, Australian parliamentary counsel offices appear to have adopted a plain language drafting policy.[12]

Plain language drafting style focuses on direct language that is 'clear and effective for its intended audience'.[13] There is no one definitive way to draft in 'plain' language.[14] The main elements of the style are short, well-constructed sentences, simplicity of syntax and vocabulary, and the avoidance of archaic, legalistic, obscure or longwinded expressions.[15] The publicly available *Plain English Manual* ('the OPC *Plain English Manual*') is the foundation of the 'plain language' drafting style for federal legislation.[16] It provides a table of numerous examples of 'traditional' expressions that are no longer acceptable and their appropriate 'simple' replacements.[17]

---

11 See, eg, Office of Parliamentary Counsel, *OPC Drafting Manual* (Australian Government, July 2019) 13 [90].

12 See, eg, Parliamentary Counsel's Committee, *Protocol on Drafting National Uniform Legislation* (Australasian Parliamentary Counsel's Committee 4th ed, 2018) 11; Office of Parliamentary Counsel, *OPC Drafting Manual* (Australian Government, July 2019) 13 [89]–[92]; ACT Parliamentary Counsel's Office, *Words and Phrases Guide: A Guide to Plain Legal Language* (ACT Government, December 2016); NSW Parliamentary Counsel's Office, *DP2: PCO Plain Language Policy* (NSW Government, May 2017); Department of Premier and Cabinet, *The Legislation Handbook* (Queensland Government, November 2019) 18; Office of the Chief Parliamentary Counsel of Victoria, *The Legislative Process* (Victorian Government, June 2020) 2; Parliamentary Counsel's Office of Western Australia, *How to Read Legislation: A Beginner's Guide* (Western Australian Government, May 2011) 6. See also Eamonn Moran, 'The Coherence of Statutory Interpretation: Drafting Perspectives' in Jeffrey Barnes (ed), *The Coherence of Statutory Interpretation* (Federation Press, 2019) 50, 57; Duncan Berry, 'A Comparative Study of Legal Jargon in Australian Statutes' [2014] (3) *The Loophole: Journal of the Commonwealth Association of Legislative Counsel* 3 where Berry concludes from a survey of numerous Australian statutes over several decades that there has been a clear trend away from 'legalese' (the attributes associated with traditional drafting).

13 Peter Butt, *Modern Legal Drafting: A Guide to Using Clearer Language* (Cambridge University Press, 3rd ed, 2013) 103.

14 Robert D Eagleson, 'Efficiency in Legal Drafting' in David St L Kelly (ed), *Essays on Legislative Drafting* (Adelaide Law Review Association, 1988) 13, 14; I Turnbull, 'Legislative Drafting in Plain Language and Statements of General Principle' (1997) 18(1) *Statute Law Review* 21, 23; Office of Parliamentary Counsel, *Plain English Manual* (Australian Government, 2016) 6 [13].

15 Office of Parliamentary Counsel, *Plain English Manual* (Australian Government, 2016) chs 3–4; IML Turnbull, 'Clear Legislative Drafting: New Approaches in Australia' (1990) 11(3) *Statute Law Review* 161, 166–9. See also Helen Xanthaki, *Drafting Legislation: Art and Technology of Rules for Regulation* (Hart Publishing, 2014) ch 6.

16 Office of Parliamentary Counsel, *OPC Drafting Manual* (Australian Government, July 2019) 13 [91]. See n 12 for other relevant parliamentary counsel drafting guides.

17 Office of Parliamentary Counsel, *Plain English Manual* (Australian Government, 2016) app 3.

Set out below is an example of the difference between traditional drafting and plain language drafting.[18] The plain language version contains shorter sentences, refers to general terms rather than a list of specific terms, and avoids repetitious words.

Traditional *Patents Act 1952* (Cth)	**Plain Language *Patents Act 1989* (Cth)**
Effect of patent s 69 Subject to this Act, the effect of a patent is to grant to the patentee the exclusive right, by himself, his agents and licensees, during the term of the patent, to make, use, exercise and vend the invention in such manner as he thinks fit, so that he shall have and enjoy the whole profit and advantage accruing by reason of the invention during the term of the patent.	Exclusive rights given by patent s 13(1) Subject to this Act, a patent gives the patentee the exclusive rights, during the term of the patent, to exploit the invention and to authorise another person to exploit the invention.

An important feature of plain language drafting is that it adopts a holistic approach to legislative drafting that is not just about the language; this style encompasses the organisation, arrangement and design of legislation. As explained in the NSW Plain Language Policy for legislation:

> [T]he principles of plain language aim for clarity in the language of legislation, in the structure of the legal ideas contained in legislation, and in the physical layout and presentation of legislation.[19]

Drafters may employ plain language reader aids. These are tools used to improve the readability and understanding of the statutory language. They include items such as objects provisions, examples, graphics, tables, outlines and notes.[20]

It has been noted that the use of the word 'plain' as a description of this style of drafting is unfortunate as it suggests language that is unsophisticated or simplistic.[21] Instead, it is more helpful to think of 'plain' as a style that focuses on clarity and strives not to use unnecessarily complicated or convoluted language.[22] This doesn't mean that the resultant legislation will always be clear or not be detailed or complex.[23] Plain language drafting can be highly prescriptive. For example, attempts to amend the Corporations Law using plain language drafting have not prevented it from being lengthy, detailed and complex.[24]

18 Example from IML Turnbull 'Clear Legislative Drafting: New Approaches in Australia' (1990) 11(3) *Statute Law Review* 161, 175. Mr Turnbull was First Parliamentary Counsel of the Commonwealth Office of Parliamentary Counsel and spearheaded the adoption of 'plain language drafting' for Commonwealth legislation in the 1990s.

19 NSW Parliamentary Counsel's Office, *DP2: PCO Plain Language Policy* (NSW Government, May 2017) 1 [5].

20 See **[20.7]–[20.12]**. See also Office of Parliamentary Counsel, *Plain English Manual* (Australian Government, 2016) 32–4 [154]–[169].

21 Peter Butt, *Modern Legal Drafting* (Cambridge University Press, 3rd ed, 2013) 102.

22 Ibid, citing, in part, Law Reform Commission of Victoria, *Legislation, Legal Rights and Plain English* (Discussion Paper No 1, August, 1986) 3.

23 See generally Thomas E Webb and Robert Greyer, 'The Drafters' Dance: The Complexity of Drafting Legislation and the Limitations of "Plain Language" and "Good Law" Initiatives' (2020) 41(2) *Statute Law Review* 129.

24 See Andrew Godwin, Vivienne Brand and Rosemary Teele Langford, 'Legislative Design – Clarifying the Legislative Porridge' (2021) 38(5) *Company and Securities Law Journal* 280, 287–92.

To some extent this may be the result of the policy reflected in the statute. As explained in a Western Australian guide, 'how hard legislation is to read and understand will always be related to some extent to how complex are the things that it has to communicate'.[25] Further, as is evident from chapters 10 and 11, the process of statute making is a complex one, with numerous stakeholders, actors and factors influencing the final product.

(c) General principles-based drafting contemplates that detail be addressed elsewhere

General principles-based drafting is where the law is drafted deliberately in general or broad terms. A broad statement contains a norm-based principle that might be helpfully described as being about 'an intended outcome in a general field'.[26] The principle is expressed at a high level of generality 'rather than itemising a list of outcomes for every conceivable case'.[27]

General principles drafting involves a 'conscious intention to leave matters of detail to be determined elsewhere'.[28] That is, the details of the law are to be filled in by delegated legislation, the courts, or 'in some other way'.[29] Some 'other way' may include by administrative decision makers.[30] This style is sometimes referred to as 'fuzzy' law or 'European' or 'continental' style drafting.[31] For Commonwealth legislation the term 'coherent principles' drafting has also been used.[32] It is essentially the same as 'general principles' drafting.[33] The following is an example.

> *Competition and Consumer Act 2010* (Cth), Schedule 2, Australian Consumer Law
>
> **18 Misleading or deceptive conduct**
>
> (1) A person must not, in trade or commerce, engage in conduct that is misleading or deceptive or is likely to mislead or deceive.

General principles in statutory provisions that state an operative legislative rule are distinct from statutory provisions that state principles that operate as a guide to interpretation

---

25 Parliamentary Counsel's Office of Western Australia, *How to Read Legislation: A Beginner's Guide* (Department of the Attorney General (WA), May 2011) 6.

26 Greg Pinder, 'The Coherent Principles Approach to Tax Law Design' [2005] *Treasury Economic Roundup* (Autumn) 75, 77.

27 Ibid 78.

28 Ian Turnbull, 'Plain Language and Drafting in General Principles' [1995] *The Loophole: Journal of the Commonwealth Association of Legislative Counsel* 25, 29.

29 Office of Parliamentary Counsel, *Plain English Manual* (Australian Government, 2016) 7 [15].

30 See Peter Bayne, 'Fuzzy Drafting and the Interpretation of Statutes in the Administrative State' (1992) 66(8) *Australian Law Journal* 523.

31 The label 'fuzzy' can be attributed to solicitor John Green who argued for general principles drafting in corporations law: House of Representatives Standing Committee on Legal and Constitutional Affairs, Parliament of Australia, *Clearer Commonwealth Law: Report of the Inquiry into Legislative Drafting by the Commonwealth* (Final Report, September 1993) 128. The label 'European' or 'continental' style arises from the European legislative tradition of drafting in general principles.

32 Office of Parliamentary Counsel, *OPC's Drafting Services: Guide for Clients* (Australian Government, July 2016) 33 [142]–[144]. This term appears to have emerged when the Australian Government was considering a redesign of the tax laws in the mid-noughties. For background, see Greg Pinder, 'The Coherent Principles Approach to Tax Law Design' [2005] *Treasury Economic Roundup* (Autumn) 75; Michael Dirkis and Brett Bondfield, 'At the Extremes of a Good Tax Policy Process: A Case Study Contrasting the Role Accorded to Consultation in Tax Policy Development in Australia and New Zealand' (2005) 11(2) *New Zealand Journal of Taxation Law and Policy* 250.

33 Office of Parliamentary Counsel, *Reducing Complexity in Legislation* (Australian Government, June 2016) 3 [16].

or to administration of the statute.[34] Gageler J explained the distinction in *Victorian Building Authority v Andriotis*:[35]

> In some contexts, a principle can be a guide to statutory interpretation or a consideration to be taken into account in curial or administrative decision-making. In other contexts, a principle can be a statutory rule that forms a fundamental tenet of the statutory scheme of which it forms part.[36]

The former 'principles' provide guidance for interpretation, including being part of context, but are not operative in the sense of having direct application to the facts.[37] The following example illustrates the distinction.

> *Transport Integration Act 2010* (Vic)
>
> **23 Interpretation**
>
> It is the intention of Parliament that this Act is to be administered and interpreted having regard to the following –
>
> (a) the vision statement;
> (b) the transport system objectives;
> (c) the decision making principles;
> (d) any statement of policy principles.

In contrast, the example from the *Competition and Consumer Act 2010* (Cth) has direct application to a factual situation.

The OPC *Plain English Manual* acknowledges that general principles drafting is an important technique when used appropriately.[38] For instance, it might be useful for the drafter where it is not possible for the instructor to identify the wide range of circumstances in which the provision might apply,[39] or where the policy is so complex that it is not possible to keep the law simple.[40] A provision drafted in general principles is likely to generate a body of case law to define its parameters.[41]

---

34 'Principles-based' drafting appears to refer only to *operative* legislative rules: Greg Pinder, 'The Coherent Principles Approach to Tax Law Design' [2005] *Treasury Economic Roundup* (Autumn) 75, 78; Daniel Lovric, 'Principles-Based Drafting: Experiences from Tax Drafting' [2010] (3) *The Loophole: Journal of the Commonwealth Association of Legislative Counsel* 16, 17, 21.

35 (2019) 268 CLR 168.

36 Ibid 190 [68]. Cf 213–4 [155] (Edelman J).

37 Daniel Lovric, 'Principles-Based Drafting: Experiences from Tax Drafting' [2010] (3) *The Loophole: Journal of the Commonwealth Association of Legislative Counsel* 16, 17. Sometimes it may be difficult to identify whether a statutory principle is an operative rule or a mere guide.

38 Office of Parliamentary Counsel, *Plain English Manual* (Australian Government, 2016) 7 [16]. See also I Turnbull 'Legislative Drafting in Plain Language and Statements of General Principle' (1997) 18(1) *Statute Law Review* 21, 30–1.

39 Office of Parliamentary Counsel, *Plain English Manual* (Australian Government, 2016) 7 [17].

40 Ian Turnbull, 'Plain Language and Drafting in General Principles' [1995] *The Loophole: Journal of the Commonwealth Association of Legislative Counsel* 25, 35.

41 Daniel Lovric, 'Principles-Based Drafting: Experiences from Tax Drafting' [2010] (3) *The Loophole: Journal of the Commonwealth Association of Legislative Counsel* 16, 17 n 3 states that case law is not a 'necessary' feature of principles-based drafting, but is a 'likely' feature if the provision is important and been in existence for some time.

(d) **Contemporary legislative drafting often uses a hybrid of styles**

A single statute or even a provision will not always be drafted exclusively in one or other of these styles. As explained by a former Commonwealth First Parliamentary Counsel:

> They [the styles] have names because in their typical form each is easily recognisable, but in practice they can merge into each other. A law may fall anywhere within this spectrum, and indeed different provisions of the same law may have aspects of all three styles.[42]

For example, general principles drafting may be used in combination with more detailed plain language drafting.[43] A general principle may be stated in one provision, and then other provisions provide for 'clarifications, add-ons and carve-outs' from the general principle.[44] There may also be readability aids to assist in explaining the general principle provision.[45] Although the formalism, elaboration and legalese of the traditional style are rarely used in contemporary Australian drafting, plain language drafting can be used to express various degrees of detail. See **[16.3](a)**.

Influence of drafting styles on interpretation

The drafting style of a provision forms part of its intrinsic context and so identifying the style may assist in the interpretation of that provision [16.3]

Drafting style contributes to the way that statutory language is assembled and to how the statute communicates its message.[46] It is therefore a part of the intrinsic context of the words being construed. So, understanding the drafting style of the statute may assist in the interpretation of that statute. As explained in *Snedden v Minister for Justice*:[47]

> The relative importance of context and purpose may vary depending on the subject matter and *structure of the statute, as well as the general manner of expression used by the drafter.*[48]

Set out below are some of the ways in which understanding the drafting style may influence interpretation.

(a) **Drafting that is detailed and precisely worded, whether in traditional or plain language style, may support a construction that is specific and precise about the circumstances covered by the Act, and therefore is a factor against a broader construction**

Statutes that are drafted in a 'closely structured and finely worded' manner with detailed language, whether in the traditional or plain style, may emphasise the weight to be given to

---

42 Ian Turnbull, 'Plain Language and Drafting in General Principles' [1995] *The Loophole: Journal of the Commonwealth Association of Legislative Counsel* 25, 25.

43 Dennis Murphy, 'Plain English in Drafting Legislation and Regulations' (Speech, Plain Legal Language for Public Sector Administrators', Parliament House, Sydney, 29 July 1992) 11; I Turnbull 'Legislative Drafting in Plain Language and Statements of General Principle' (1997) 18(1) *Statute Law Review* 21, 31.

44 Daniel Lovric, 'Principles-Based Drafting: Experiences from Tax Drafting' [2010] (3) *The Loophole: Journal of the Commonwealth Association of Legislative Counsel* 16, 18–21; Greg Pinder, 'The Coherent Principles Approach to Tax Law Design' [2005] *Treasury Economic Roundup* (Autumn) 75, 83.

45 Greg Pinder, 'The Coherent Principles Approach to Tax Law Design' [2005] *Treasury Economic Roundup* (Autumn) 75, 84 refers to the process of explanation and clarification as 'unfolding' the principle.

46 Wim Voermans, 'Styles of Legislation and Their Effects' (2011) 32(1) *Statute Law Review* 38, 39.

47 (2014) 230 FCR 82.

48 Ibid 100 [99] (Middleton and Wigney JJ, Pagone J agreeing in part at 126 [242]) (emphasis added).

the text.[49] Such prescriptive drafting supports a construction that the provision is only intended to cover the specific circumstances of the precisely detailed wording. Where a statute is detailed, the text may not be as 'flexible' for interpretation as statutes expressed in more general terms.[50] (Certain revenue statutes have been identified as having this characteristic.[51]) **Example 16.2** illustrates this point.

Example 16.2 *Victims Compensation Fund Corporation v Brown*[52]

After answering a knock on the door one day, Mr Brown, the first respondent, was violently attacked. Ms Lewis, the second respondent, witnessed the attack. Both claimed compensation for shock under the *Victims Support and Rehabilitation Act 1996* (NSW). Compensation for shock was specified in detail in cl 5 of sch 1 to the Act. It relevantly provided:

> (a) Compensation is payable only if the symptoms and disability persist for more than 6 weeks.

Both respondents had 'symptoms' of shock that persisted for six weeks, but neither had a 'disability'. The interpretative issue was whether the 'and' in 'symptoms and disability' was to be construed disjunctively or conjunctively.

Heydon J, with all other members of the Court agreeing, determined that the 'and' should be read conjunctively so that, to be entitled to compensation for shock, both symptoms and disability must persist for more than six weeks. His Honour acknowledged the broad beneficial purpose of the Act, as one providing for compensation, and the presumption that a beneficial Act attracts a liberal construction (see **[17.2]**). However, Heydon J balanced that broad object against the detail provided in the text of the Act.

> Although the purpose of the Act is beneficial, it does not follow that recovery is contemplated for every act of violence or every consequence that could be described as an injury. The numerous injuries set out in the Table to Sch 1 (which extends over 12 pages) are identified with considerable precision. The clauses in Sch 1 which precede the Table, too, are drafted with some attempt at precision. . . . in dealing with specific limited words like those of cl 5, it is not open to apply much liberality of construction . . . The legislation has endeavoured to define these circumstances [of compensation] in precise language which does not permit universal recovery . . .[53]

In other words, the precise, detailed language of the Act supported a legislative intent that only the particular and precise circumstances indicated by the ordinary meaning of the text were covered.[54] Clearly, the degree to which an expansive meaning can be persuasively attributed to the text may be diminished if the text is written in a precise and detailed manner.

---

49 *Joffe v The Queen* (2012) 82 NSWLR 510, 518 [36] (Allsop P).

50 *Channel Pastoral Holdings Pty Ltd v Federal Commissioner of Taxation* (2015) 232 FCR 162, 165 [6] (Allsop CJ).

51 Ibid; followed in *Buddhist Society of Western Australia Inc v Commissioner of Taxation (No 2)* [2021] FCA 1363, [36] (McKerracher J).

52 (2003) 77 ALJR 1797.

53 Ibid 1804 [33].

54 See also *Snedden v Minister for Justice* (2014) 230 FCR 82, 100–1 [100]–[106] (Middleton and Wigney JJ, Pagone J agreeing in part) for similar reasoning.

(b) The immediate context of the words in doubt is more important in plain language drafting than traditional drafting style

The traditional style of drafting assumes that each sentence of a legislative provision must be self-contained and 'context free'.[55] For example, cross-references are used within a group of subsections in order to be precise about how the subsections relate to one another. In contrast, plain language drafting involves a more 'narrative style' that assumes that a provision, or group of provisions, will be read as a whole and as part of the statute as a whole.[56] The following example is extracted from a longer example in the OPC *Plain English Manual*.[57]

> *Traditional:*
>
> (1) A person may apply to the Minister under this section for a licence.
> (2) An application under subsection (1) must be accompanied by the prescribed fee.
>
> *Plain language drafting:*
>
> (1) A person may apply to the Minister for a licence.
> (2) The application must be accompanied by the prescribed fee.

In plain language drafting, sub-s (2) must be read in the context of sub-s (1) for the relevant application to be identified. This closely reflects the common law principle that a provision must be read in the context of the statute as a whole, discussed in **[18.15]**. But the relative weight of that intrinsic context is emphasised if the drafting is in plain language style.

(c) Plain language drafting may support a construction adopting an ordinary meaning of the text

Plain language drafting eschews archaic expressions and legalisms. One of its aims is readability and ease of understanding through the use of plain, familiar or 'ordinary' language. It might therefore be seen to mirror the common law rebuttable presumption that we start the interpretative process by assuming that words have their ordinary and grammatical meaning.[58] The link between that presumption and plain language drafting was identified in the following comment by Edelman J in the High Court:

> One presumption ... is that when Parliament uses words with a common or ordinary meaning then the words are intended to bear that ordinary meaning. That presumption also reflects the expressed goal of parliamentary drafting for clarity and familiarity in order to ensure the transparency and intelligibility of statute law.[59]

Text drafted in plain language arguably lends weight to an argument that the ordinary meaning of the text is intended.[60] This is subject to two cautionary notes. First, plain language drafting is not

---

55 Risto Hiltunen, 'The Grammar and Structure of Legal Texts' in Peter M Tiersma and Lawrence M Solan (eds), *The Oxford Handbook of Language and Law* (Oxford University Press, 2012) 39, 41.

56 Office of Parliamentary Counsel, *Plain English Manual* (Australian Government, 2016) 26 [110].

57 Ibid 21–22 [88].

58 See **[6.7]**.

59 *Mondelez Australia Pty Ltd v Automotive, Food, Metals, Engineering, Printing and Kindred Industries Union* (2020) 94 ALJR 818, 838 [95] (Edelman J), citing the Office of Parliamentary Counsel, *Plain English Manual* (Australian Government, 2016) (other citations omitted).

60 See, eg, *Campbell v Renton* (Supreme Court of Victoria, Marks J, 18 August 1988) 9–10, commenting on the Act before the Court being 'a product of the new "plain English" movement'.

always directed to the 'ordinary' reader. Drafters will consider the target audience for a statute, and recognise that a complex policy or particular subject reflected in a statute may have a particular audience or one that is experienced in reading legislation.[61] Second, plain language will not prevent the attribution of a non-ordinary meaning if that is considered to be the legislative intent.[62]

(d) Interpretation of provisions using general principles drafting generally requires greater weight to be given to purpose or context (intrinsic and extrinsic) than to the text of the particular provision

A provision drafted using general principles drafting is

> flexible and covers a wide range of circumstances at a high level of abstraction. Broad principles have a degree of uncertainty at their edges; they have a core of relatively clear application surrounded by a penumbra of uncertain application.[63]

Given this nature, general principles drafting will often use indefinite or imprecise terms.[64] These are words or phrases that, when read in isolation, are vague or indeterminate. Their meaning is protean, highly dependent on the context in, and subject for which, they are used. Extrajudicially, Justice Leeming, drawing on American commentary, has referred to statutes using broadly expressed concepts as '[o]pen-ended statutes' that 'naturally and indeed necessarily attract a more purposive and less minutely textual mode of construction'.[65] Examples of broad concepts are 'adversely impact',[66] 'public interest',[67] 'significant probative value',[68] 'reasonable excuse',[69] 'substantial miscarriage of justice'[70] and 'exceptional circumstances'.[71]

One of the results of broad or general statutory language is lack of certainty about its application in certain factual circumstances. This is one of the concerns usually raised for general principles drafting.[72] Leaving merits aside, a consequence of the generality and imprecision of

---

61 Office of Parliamentary Counsel, *Plain English Manual* (Australian Government, 2016) 13 [50]; Office of Parliamentary Counsel, *Reducing Complexity in Legislation* (Australian Government, June 2016) 1–2 [7].

62 *Mondelez Australia Pty Ltd v Automotive, Food, Metals, Engineering, Printing and Kindred Industries Union* (2020) 94 ALJR 818, 838 [96] (Edelman J): discussed in **[24.13]**. See also *Minister for Immigration and Border Protection v CED16* (2020) 94 ALJR 706, 711–12 [28] (Edelman J).

63 Daniel Lovric, 'Principles-Based Drafting: Experiences from Tax Drafting' [2010] (3) *The Loophole: Journal of the Commonwealth Association of Legislative Counsel* 16, 17.

64 This is not to say that plain language drafting does not contain indefinite terms. All styles of drafting may incorporate imprecise terms.

65 Justice Mark Leeming, 'Equity: Ageless in the 'Age of Statutes' (2015) 9(2) *Journal of Equity* 108, 116.

66 *Independent Commission Against Corruption v Cunneen* (2015) 256 CLR 1 (*Independent Commission Against Corruption Act 1988* (NSW) s 8).

67 *Kahan v Strauss* [2017] VSC 8 (*Private Security Act 2004* (Vic) s 25).

68 *Hughes v The Queen* (2017) 263 CLR 338 (*Evidence Act 1995* (NSW) s 97).

69 See chapter 38.

70 *OKS v Western Australia* (2019) 265 CLR 268, 280–1 [34] (Edelman J) (*Criminal Appeals Act 2004* (WA) s 30(4)).

71 *Plaintiff M174/2016 v Minister for Immigration and Border Protection* (2018) 264 CLR 217, 229 [30] (Gageler, Keane and Nettle JJ) (*Migration Act 1958* (Cth) s 473DD).

72 Committee Appointed by the Lord President of the Council, *Committee on the Preparation of Legislation (the 'Renton Report')* (Cmnd 6053, 1975) 60 [10.13]. For some advantages and disadvantage of general principles drafting see Standing Committee on Legal and Constitutional Affairs, *Clearer Commonwealth Law: Report of the Inquiry into Legislative Drafting by the Commonwealth* (Final Report, September 1993) 128–35.

general principles language is that the 'ordinary' meaning of the text may be less helpful than it would be for precise, particular plain language. This does not change fundamentally the interpretative process. But it means that, in the weighing and balancing of text, context and purpose, the concepts of context and purpose are likely to have more work to do. General language and broad terms must necessarily lean more heavily on context and purpose to give them content. As explained wryly by one commentator:

> It is fair to say that judges, when interpreting [such] provisions ... can expect to spend more quality time with their imaginary friends than with their more tangible friend, the plain meaning of the text. Rather, the difficulty faced ... is that often the judge's more reliable friend, the plain meaning of the text, has little to say about the meaning ...[73]

Extrinsic context, including legislative history, may therefore have a strong role to play. Case law on the meaning of a general principles provision is another category of extrinsic context that is central to setting the boundaries of the broad concept contained in the provision. This is illustrated in **Example 16.3**.

Example 16.3 *Quikfund (Australia) Pty Ltd v Airmark Consolidators Pty Ltd*[74]

Two companies, the respondents, entered into rental agreements with two finance companies, the appellants, in respect of office equipment on the basis of misleading and deceptive conduct by third parties. The respondents' obligations under the rental agreements had been guaranteed by their respective directors, being natural persons, who were also the shareholders of the respondents. The respondents defaulted under the rental agreement. The appellant financiers sued the corporate respondents under the rental agreements and also sought to enforce the guarantees given by the directors.

The Full Court of the Federal Court considered two issues. The first was whether certain financial services provisions of the (then) *Trade Practices Act 1974* (Cth) meant that the appellant financiers were liable for conduct of the third parties. In explaining statutory interpretation principles, the Court acknowledged:

> Often, the relationship between context (including pre-enactment history), purpose and text will be illuminated by the subject matter of the statute, as well as by the approach to expression by the drafter. Statutes drafted in broad simple language that set a principled framework for a well-known body of law may well be approached with an eye to context, and especially pre-existing law.[75]

Although the Court did not expressly engage with this statement in their analysis of the *Trade Practices Act* provisions, their statement about interpretation formed a relevant backdrop to their

73 Justice Timothy Ginnane, 'Indefinite Terms and Broad Discretions: Statutory Interpretation Against an "Infinite Variety of Facts"' in Jeffrey Barnes (ed), *The Coherence of Statutory Interpretation* (Federation Press, 2019) 95, 97. His Honour is referring to the interpretation of indefinite terms, but the sentiment is equally apt for general principles drafting. See also Committee Appointed by the Lord President of the Council, *Committee on the Preparation of Legislation (the 'Renton Report')* (Cmnd 6053, 1975) 60 [10.13].

74 (2014) 222 FCR 13.

75 Ibid 30 [75].

treatment of the second issue. This was the claim by the directors that the guarantees were 'unjust' under s 7(1) of the *Contracts Review Act 1980* (NSW) ('the CRA'). Section 7(1) provided:

> (1) Where the Court finds a contract or a provision of a contract to have been unjust in the circumstances relating to the contract at the time it was made, the Court may, if it considers it just to do so, and for the purpose of avoiding as far as practicable an unjust consequence or result, do any one or more of the following . . .

Section 4 of the CRA provided that 'unjust' 'includes unconscionable, harsh or oppressive'. Section 6(2) of the CRA was a 'carve-out' to the general principle in s 7. Section 6(2), drafted as a general proposition, relevantly provided:

> **6 Certain restrictions on grant of relief**
>
> . . .
>
> (2) A person may not be granted relief under this Act in relation to a contract so far as the contract was entered into in the course of or for the purpose of a trade, business or profession carried on by the person . . ., other than a farming undertaking . . .

The primary judge had determined that the persons who had executed the guarantees, the directors, were not the persons who had entered the contracts during the course of a business carried on by them, given that the persons carrying on the relevant businesses were the corporate respondents. On appeal the financiers argued that the directors were precluded by s 6(2) from relief. They argued that s 6(2) extended to an individual who carried on the business through a company.

The Full Court noted that the CRA was a 'short, clearly drafted and powerful statute',[76] the aim of which was to protect those who might be referred to as 'consumers' (and unincorporated farmers).[77] Section 6 therefore excluded relief for unjust contracts from corporations and other persons if the contract was entered into in the course of or for the purposes of a trade, business or profession carried on by that person. However, while the principle was clear, the boundary of its operation was the critical issue.[78]

In the absence of weighty probative textual factors or determinative legislative history, the Court turned to a line of NSW authorities that supported the primary judge's construction that s 6(2) only precluded relief if the person who sought relief and the person who entered the contract in the course of business were the same entity. Notably, the Court said, this line of precedent had not led to any action by Parliament.[79] As this 'stable interpretation' by the authorities was clearly available linguistically on the text and had provided a straightforward framework of some certainty to the commercial world, it was to be accepted.[80] Consequently, the financiers were not successful on this issue.

76 Ibid 38 [120].

77 Ibid 39 [122].

78 Ibid.

79 Ibid 40 [127].

80 Ibid 43 [134]–[136].

Understanding drafting style, including its evolution, may assist in interpretation in other ways [16.4]

There is a common law presumption that where a predecessor statute contains a word or phrase that is then changed in an amendment Act or a successive statute on the same subject matter, we start from the premise that a change in meaning was intended.[81] This presumption may be rebutted if the change can be attributed to a mere change in drafting style. Several jurisdictions have express provisions in their Interpretation Acts that state that a change in words due to a change in style should not be taken to be a change in meaning.[82] Knowledge of drafting styles may assist with determining whether a change in wording across successive statutes indicates a change in meaning, or simply the adoption of a new style.

Further, knowledge of the evolution of legislative drafting may assist in reading a statute. So, by way of simple example, understanding that plain language drafting only began to be adopted in the mid-1980s in Australia may lead the interpreter to read, say, a 1970s Act (likely drafted in the traditional style) from a different perspective.

Drafting conventions of Australian parliamentary counsel

As well as drafting style, there are drafting conventions and techniques adopted by parliamentary counsel, though these may differ between jurisdictions [16.5]

Although plain language is the dominant drafting style in Australia, each jurisdiction has its own template for the overall design for each new Bill.[83] This format, as well as specific techniques and drafting conventions, may vary across jurisdictions. Some of these variations are identified in **[10.8]**. Sometimes a convention is adopted consistently by many jurisdictions. For example, gender-neutral legislative drafting has become a preferred drafting convention in Australia.[84]

In some jurisdictions, drafting manuals, policies or drafting directions used by parliamentary counsel are publicly available on their office's website. The Commonwealth Office of Parliamentary Counsel's Office is most notable in this regard; it has a comprehensive and authoritative set of drafting directions and drafting manuals for statutes and legislative instruments available.[85] At the least, these publicly available documents, produced by those who draft the legislation, can provide insight into the overall structure and design of the legislation of that jurisdiction. Where the public materials about drafting practices are more detailed, such as with the Commonwealth, there is considerable scope for these materials to provide specific insight into drafting techniques, conventions and word usage for legislation of that jurisdiction.[86] A number

81 See **[21.7]**, **[18.13]**.

82 See **[21.9]**.

83 Eamonn Moran, 'The Coherence of Statutory Interpretation: Drafting Perspectives' in Jeffrey Barnes (ed) in *The Coherence of Statutory Interpretation* (Federation Press, 2019) 50, 51.

84 See, eg, Office of Parliamentary Counsel, *Drafting Direction No 2.1: English Usage, Gender-Specific and Gender-Neutral Language, Grammar, Punctuation and Spelling* (Australian Government, 2016) 3–4; NSW Parliamentary Counsel's Office, *DP3: PCO Gender Neutral Language Policy* (NSW Government, May 2017).

85 See **[10.9]** for more detail.

86 See Jacinta Dharmananda, 'Drafting Statutes and Statutory Interpretation: Express or Assumed Rules?' (2019) 45(2) *Monash University Law Review* 401 for a discussion of the value that can be derived from the Commonwealth publicly available drafting manuals. See also Diggory Bailey, 'Bridging the Gap: Legislative Drafting Practice and Statutory Interpretation' [2020] (April) *Public Law* 220, arguing for greater understanding in the UK context.

of parliamentary counsel (former and current) have raised the desirability and merit of interpreters being more familiar with drafting practices.[87]

[16.6] One consistent technique is that all drafters in Australia adopt a textual style of amendment

In relation to amending Acts, all Australian drafting offices adopt a 'textual amendment' style of amending Acts. This involves 'identifying particular bits of text and either inserting or adding other text after it, omitting that text or omitting the text and substituting other text for it'.[88]

This amendment technique is distinct from the 'referential' amending style (also known as 'legislation by reference'). A 'referential' approach is where a statute is enacted that modifies the operation of an existing provision, but the amending law does not become part of the statute it amends.[89] That is, the amending Act or instrument 'changes the effect of the Act or instrument being amended without altering the text of that Act or instrument'.[90] Both the referential style and textual style of amendment are used in the United Kingdom.[91]

---

87 Hilary Penfold, 'Legislation in the Courts' [2019] (1) *The Loophole: Journal of the Commonwealth Association of Legislative Counsel* 2, 6–7; Eamonn Moran, 'The Coherence of Statutory Interpretation: Drafting Perspectives' in Jeffrey Barnes (ed) *The Coherence of Statutory Interpretation* (Federation Press, 2019) 50, 57; Daniel Lovric, 'Legislative Counsel and the Judiciary: Divergences in Statutory Interpretation?' [2015] (2) *The Loophole: Journal of the Commonwealth Association of Legislative Counsel* 42.

88 Office of Parliamentary Counsel, *OPC Drafting Manual* (Australian Government, July 2019) 10 [60].

89 Committee Appointed by the Lord President of the Council, *Committee on The Preparation of Legislation (the 'Renton Report')* (Cmnd 6053, May 1975) 76 [13.2].

90 Office of Parliamentary Counsel, *Amending Forms Manual* (Australian Government, 15th ed, May 2019) 11 [2].

91 Office of the Parliamentary Counsel of the United Kingdom, *Drafting Guidance* (The National Archives, 2020) 38–53.

SPECIAL CATEGORIES OF LEGISLATION: THE INTERPRETATION OF REMEDIAL, PENAL AND REVENUE PROVISIONS

17

Overview

In interpreting legislation, courts can take into account whether the provision in question comes within a 'special category' of legislation[1] – in other words, its particular 'character'.[2] The categories most frequently mentioned are remedial, penal and taxing. [17.1]

Remedial legislation – legislation providing benefits and remedies – is to be given a 'fair, large and liberal' interpretation. But this is not a hard-and-fast rule.

Penal provisions include provisions imposing civil penalties. Penal provisions are construed by reference to the ordinary principles of statutory interpretation. But if those principles have 'run out' and failed to resolve an issue concerning the scope of a penal provision, then, as a last resort, a penal provision is read in favour of the subject. A penal law is also read with the expectation that it should be certain and its reach ascertainable by those who are subject to it.

It is highly likely that taxing Acts and other revenue Acts are no longer subject to special interpretative rules. Nevertheless, they are read in their taxation context.

In comparison with previous eras, the rules for special categories of legislation have a diminished importance.[3] This has been attributed to the demise of literalism[4] and to recognition by courts of the legitimacy of modern parliaments.[5]

---

1 *Stevens v Kabushiki Kaisha Sony Computer Entertainment* (2005) 224 CLR 193, 260 [227] (Kirby J).

2 *Waugh v Kippen* (1986) 160 CLR 156, 164 (Gibbs CJ, Mason, Wilson and Dawson JJ); *Murphy v Farmer* (1988) 165 CLR 19, 28–9 (Deane, Dawson and Gaudron JJ); *Construction, Forestry, Mining and Energy Union v Mammoet Australia Pty Ltd* (2013) 248 CLR 619, 634 [48] (the Court).

3 *Stevens v Kabushiki Kaisha Sony Computer Entertainment* (2005) 224 CLR 193, 260 [227] (Kirby J).

4 Ibid 260 [227].

5 *R v Lavender* (2005) 222 CLR 67, 97 [94] (Kirby J).

Special categories of legislation

[17.2] **Courts can take into account whether the provision in question comes within a special category of legislation**

There are at least three 'special categories' of legislation[6] that a provision might be analysed under, in order to determine its particular 'character': [7] remedial, penal and taxing. Others are also of significance.[8]

Remedial legislation

[17.3] **Remedial legislation is to be given a fair, large and liberal interpretation**

(a) Remedial legislation is widespread

Remedial legislation is 'legislation intended for beneficial and remedial purposes'.[9] It provides benefits and remedies.[10]

Many instances of remedial legislation have been identified in the case law. Examples[11] are Acts awarding victims compensation,[12] furthering industrial safety,[13] allowing the reassignment of gender so as to promote equality of opportunity,[14] providing social security,[15] regulating insurance contracts,[16] furthering anti-discrimination,[17] affording Aboriginal land rights,[18]

---

6 *Stevens v Kabushiki Kaisha Sony Computer Entertainment* (2005) 224 CLR 193, 260 [227] (Kirby J).

7 *Waugh v Kippen* (1986) 160 CLR 156, 164 (Gibbs CJ, Mason, Wilson and Dawson JJ); *Murphy v Farmer* (1988) 165 CLR 19, 28–9 (Deane, Dawson and Gaudron JJ); *Construction, Forestry, Mining and Energy Union v Mammoet Australia Pty Ltd* (2013) 248 CLR 619, 634 [48] (the Court).

8 See, eg, the effect of 'a statutory regime [that] confers power on the executive government of a State to grant exclusive rights to exploit the resources of the State': *Forrest & Forrest Pty Ltd v Wilson* (2017) 262 CLR 510, 529 [64] (Kiefel CJ, Bell, Gageler and Keane JJ) discussed briefly at **[37.3](c)**.

9 *Minister Administering the Crown Lands Act v NSW Aboriginal Land Council* (2008) 237 CLR 285, 300 [44] (Hayne, Heydon, Crennan and Kiefel JJ).

10 *IW v City of Perth* (1997) 191 CLR 1, 58 (Kirby J), followed in *Purvis v New South Wales (Department of Education and Training)* (2003) 217 CLR 92, 111 [45] (McHugh and Kirby JJ).

11 A more detailed list appears in DC Pearce and RS Geddes, *Statutory Interpretation in Australia* (LexisNexis Butterworths, 8th ed, 2014) 360–3 [9.3].

12 *Victims Compensation Fund Corporation v Brown* (2003) 201 ALR 260, 268 [31], 269 [33] (Heydon J, McHugh ACJ agreeing at 261 [1], Gummow J agreeing at 261 [2], Kirby J agreeing at 261 [3], Hayne J agreeing at 261 [4]).

13 *Waugh v Kippen* (1986) 160 CLR 156, 164 (Gibbs CJ, Mason, Wilson and Dawson JJ).

14 *AB v Western Australia* (2011) 244 CLR 390, 397 [5] (the Court).

15 *Secretary, Department of Social Security v SRA* (1993) 43 FCR 299, 303 (Black CJ, Heerey J agreeing at 328).

16 *Khoury v Government Insurance Office of New South Wales* (1984) 165 CLR 622, 638 (Mason, Brennan, Deane and Dawson JJ), 640 (Murphy J); *Antico v Heath Fielding Australia Pty Ltd* (1997) 188 CLR 652, 659 (Brennan CJ), 675 (Dawson, Toohey, Gaudron and Gummow JJ).

17 *IW v City of Perth* (1997) 191 CLR 1, 12 (Brennan CJ and McHugh J).

18 *Minister Administering the Crown Lands Act v NSW Aboriginal Land Council* (2008) 237 CLR 285, 292–3 [17]–[19] (Kirby J), 300 [44] (Hayne, Heydon, Crennan and Kiefel JJ).

granting employee's compensation,[19] regulating videotaped interviews of accused persons,[20] providing for testator's family maintenance,[21] compensating clients of defaulting legal practitioners,[22] promoting occupational health and safety,[23] affording privacy[24] and providing tax relief to small business.[25]

(b) A court determines whether legislation is remedial as a matter of interpretation

A court will have regard to the ordinary aids to interpretation to determine whether legislation is remedial. This includes the statutory objects, general principles laid down in the Act, and extrinsic materials.[26]

(c) Remedial legislation is to be liberally construed

As a general principle, 'beneficial and remedial legislation is to be given a "fair, large and liberal" interpretation'.[27] More specifically, the provisions of such legislation are to be 'beneficially construed so as to provide the most complete remedy of the situation with which they are intended to deal'.[28] Or, as put by Nettle J, 'remedial legislation ... should be construed in a manner that gives effect to the remedy and secures the result which it is the purpose of the legislation to achieve'.[29] The approach is contrasted with a 'literal or technical' construction.[30]

Example 17.1 *AB v Western Australia*[31]

This case concerned the meaning of a provision of the *Gender Reassignment Act 2000* (WA) ('the Act'). The Act's long title, as amended in 2003, was as follows:

> An Act to allow the reassignment of gender and establish a Gender Reassignment Board with power to issue recognition certificates; to make consequential amendments ... to promote equality of opportunity, and provide remedies in respect of discrimination, on gender history grounds in certain cases; and for connected purposes.

19 *Bird v Commonwealth* (1988) 165 CLR 1, 6 (Mason CJ, Brennan and Toohey JJ), 9 (Deane and Gaudron JJ).

20 *Carr v Western Australia* (2007) 232 CLR 138, 153 [40] (Gummow, Heydon and Crennan JJ).

21 *Barns v Barns* (2003) 214 CLR 169, 187–8 [44] (Gummow and Hayne JJ), 210 [124] (Kirby J).

22 *Legal Services Board v Gillespie-Jones* (2013) 249 CLR 493, 509 [50] (French CJ, Hayne, Crennan and Kiefel JJ).

23 *Deal v Kodakkathanath* (2016) 258 CLR 281, 295 [36] (French CJ, Kiefel, Bell and Nettle JJ).

24 *AIT18 v Australian Information Commissioner* (2018) 267 FCR 93, 115 [82] (the Court).

25 *Eichmann v Federal Commissioner of Taxation* (2020) 280 FCR 10, 22–3 [38]–[40] (the Court).

26 *Deal v Kodakkathanath* (2016) 258 CLR 281, 295 [36] (French CJ, Kiefel, Bell and Nettle JJ); *Minister Administering the Crown Lands Act v NSW Aboriginal Land Council* (2008) 237 CLR 285, 300 [44] (Hayne, Heydon, Crennan and Kiefel JJ).

27 *AB v Western Australia* (2011) 244 CLR 390, 402 [24] (the Court).

28 *Khoury v Government Insurance Office of New South Wales* (1984) 165 CLR 622, 638 (Mason, Brennan, Deane and Dawson JJ).

29 *Minister for Immigration and Border Protection v Kumar* (2017) 260 CLR 367, 395 [72] (Nettle J, dissenting as to outcome) (citation omitted).

30 *IW v City of Perth* (1997) 191 CLR 1, 12 (Brennan CJ and McHugh J).

31 (2011) 244 CLR 390.

A recognition certificate is conclusive evidence that the person 'is of the sex stated in the certificate': s 16(1)(b). On its production the certificate is required to be registered by the Registrar of Births, Deaths and Marriages. Before a person can apply to the Board for a certificate, it is necessary that the person has undergone a 'reassignment procedure' (s 14(1)), defined as a 'medical or surgical procedure ... to alter the genitals and other gender characteristics of a person': s 3. Section 15(1)(b) provided that the Board must be satisfied that the person applying for a recognition certificate

> ...
>
> (ii) has adopted the lifestyle and has the gender characteristics of a person of the gender to which the person has been reassigned ...

Section 3 defined 'gender characteristics' as 'the physical characteristics by virtue of which a person is identified as male or female'.

Each of the appellants identified as male although they retained some gender characteristics of a female. Each of them had undergone gender reassignment procedures, in the nature of a bilateral mastectomy and testosterone therapy. On applying to the Board for a recognition certificate stating that each was of the male sex,

> [t]he Board was satisfied in each case that the appearance of each of the appellants is that of a male person and that all the indications were that they had adopted the lifestyle of such a person. The sole reason why it determined not to issue a certificate to them was they retained a female reproductive system.[32]

On appeal the State Administrative Tribunal granted each application for a recognition certificate. On appeal to the Court of Appeal of the Supreme Court of Western Australia, the majority allowed appeals from the Tribunal's decisions.

On a further appeal to the High Court of Australia, the principal interpretative issue was the scope of the term 'gender characteristics' in s 15(1)(b)(ii) and, in particular, the meaning of 'identified' in the Act's definition of the term.

According to the High Court, the majority in the Court of Appeal (Martin CJ and Pullin JA) 'appear to have considered that it required the Board to determine the extent to which a person had assumed the characteristics of the opposing sex [and] it appears to have been assumed [by the majority] that there is some point which is reached, in the transition, when a person might be regarded as male not female or female not male'.[33] The minority (Buss JA) held that the physical characteristics by which a person is identified as male or female are confined to external physical characteristics.[34]

The High Court unanimously allowed each appeal. At the forefront of their Honours' reasoning was the remedial presumption. After quoting the Act's long title, they said:

> These statutory objects and their nature, which is remedial and beneficial, assume importance in these appeals. ... It is generally accepted that there is a rule of construction that beneficial and remedial legislation is to be given a 'fair, large and liberal' interpretation ... Those requirements, including those of s 15(1)(b)(ii), are to be given a fair and liberal interpretation in order that they achieve the Act's beneficial purposes.[35]

32 Ibid 398 [12] (the Court).

33 Ibid 403 [29].

34 As cited in ibid 401 [21].

35 Ibid 397 [5], 402 [24], 406 [38] (citation omitted).

For the remedial presumption to be fully engaged, the Court found it necessary to elaborate on the Act's objects before matching the objects to the provision in question.[36] The Court explained the Act's broad objects as 'to remove impediments to the way in which a person lives within society [and] to facilitate the acceptance of a person, as being of the gender to which they are reassigned, within society so that they may fully participate within it'.[37] The Court then matched those objects to the provision: '[The Act's] objects suggest that the question for the Board is to be approached from a social perspective, which is to say, by reference to what other members of society would perceive the person's gender to be.'[38]

Thus, rather than requiring the Board to determine the extent to which a person had assumed the characteristics of the opposite sex, the test laid down by the provision in question was one of 'social recognition':[39]

> The question [s 15(1)(b)(ii)] raises is what gender the person exhibits to other members of society, by reference to the gender characteristics they now have and to their lifestyle. That conclusion would be reached by reference to the person's appearance and behaviour, amongst other things. It does not require detailed knowledge of their bodily state.[40]

(d) **It ought not be assumed at the outset of the interpretative process that the remedial presumption will apply; the presumption is limited by the text and the purpose of the Act**

The remedial presumption is limited by the text and purpose of the Act. As regards the text, the High Court has said: '[T]he rule that remedial provisions are to be beneficially construed . . . must, as has been said, be restrained within the confines of "the actual language employed" and what is "fairly open" on the words used.'[41] Also, '[the presumption] should not be read as doing more work than that disclosed by its subject, scope and purpose'.[42]

In *Victims Compensation Fund Corporation v Brown*[43] the High Court warned against *beginning* with the assumption that, because the legislation was remedial, it should be construed by taking a 'liberal approach'. It reiterated its view that the text is the starting point: 'To begin consideration of issues of construction by positing that a "liberal", "broad" or "narrow" construction will be given tends to obscure the essential question, that of determining the meaning the relevant words used require.'[44] Thus, in this case, although the legislation should not be construed restrictively, the adoption by the drafter of 'precise language which does not permit universal recovery' did not permit 'much liberality of construction'.[45]

---

36 See **[8.5]** for a general discussion of the determination of the legislative purpose.

37 (2011) 244 CLR 390, 405 [34], [36].

38 Ibid 405 [34].

39 Ibid.

40 Ibid.

41 *Khoury v Government Insurance Office of New South Wales* (1984) 165 CLR 622, 638 (Mason, Brennan, Deane and Dawson JJ). See also *Waugh v Kippen* (1986) 160 CLR 156, 164 (Gibbs CJ, Mason, Wilson and Dawson JJ); *Antico v Heath Fielding Australia Pty Ltd* (1997) 188 CLR 652, 659 (Brennan CJ), 675 (Dawson, Toohey, Gaudron and Gummow JJ); *New South Wales Aboriginal Land Council v Minister Administering the Crown Lands Act* (2016) 260 CLR 232, 271 [92] (Gageler J).

42 *Carr v Western Australia* (2007) 232 CLR 138, 153 [40] (Gummow, Heydon and Crennan JJ).

43 (2003) 201 ALR 260.

44 *Victims Compensation Fund Corporation v Brown* (2003) 201 ALR 260, 269 [33] (Heydon J; McHugh ACJ agreeing at 261 [1], Gummow J agreeing at 261 [2], Kirby J agreeing at 261 [3], Hayne J agreeing at 261 [4]).

45 Ibid.

(e) **The presumption does not mean that in all cases it is appropriate that remedial legislation be given the most expansive construction**

The courts sometimes say that the requirement to construe remedial legislation beneficially is a 'rule',[46] as if it were applied to the facts on its own. But this nomenclature is just shorthand – a convenience. As indicated by Gageler J, the presumption is not a hard-and-fast rule:

> The principle that, as beneficial legislation, the Land Rights Act is to be construed beneficially does not mean that the most expansive view of claimable Crown lands must be taken whenever constructional choice arises in the application of that definition.[47]

His Honour explained why and how the remedial principle was limited in its effect:

> The principle that beneficial legislation is to be construed beneficially is a manifestation of the more general principle that all legislation is to be construed purposively. . . . Neither in its general application nor in its particular manifestation can that principle be applied other than on the understanding that legislation 'rarely pursues a single purpose at all costs' and that '[u]ltimately, it is the text, construed according to such principles of interpretation as provide rational assistance in the circumstances of the particular case, that is controlling'.[48]

(f) **Exceptions in remedial legislation are read neither restrictively nor expansively**

Where exemptions in remedial legislation contain provisions designed to 'strike a careful and practical balance between competing community interests', a court will be careful not to distort the balance struck.[49] Hence, the Administrative Appeals Tribunal did not err when it determined that exceptions in the *Privacy Act 1988* (Cth) should 'neither [be] read restrictively nor expansively'.[50]

Penal provisions

[17.4] **In general, penal provisions are construed by reference to the ordinary 'rules' of construction**

(a) **Formerly, penal statutes were required to be read strictly**

Formerly, there was a rule that

> all penal Statutes are to be construed strictly, that is to say, the Court must see that the thing charged as an offence is within the plain meaning of the words used, and must not strain the words on any notion that there has been a slip or a *casus omissus*, that the thing

46 *Khoury v Government Insurance Office of New South Wales* (1984) 165 CLR 622, 638 (Mason, Brennan, Deane and Dawson JJ); *AB v Western Australia* (2011) 244 CLR 390, 402 [24]; *IW v City of Perth* (1997) 191 CLR 1, 12 (Brennan CJ and McHugh J).

47 *New South Wales Aboriginal Land Council v Minister Administering the Crown Lands Act* (2016) 260 CLR 232, 271 [94].

48 Ibid 270–1 [92] (Gageler J) (citation omitted).

49 *AIT18 v Australian Information Commissioner* (2018) 267 FCR 93, 116 [86] (the Court), quoting with approval *Commonwealth v Human Rights and Equal Opportunity Commission* (1998) 76 FCR 513, 520 (Burchett J, Drummond J agreeing at 528).

50 Ibid 117 [89].

> is so clearly within the mischief that it must have been intended to be included and would have been included if thought of.[51]

(b) The ordinary 'rules' of construction are applied in the first instance

In *R v A2*[52] Kiefel CJ and Keane J remarked that '[t]he old rule, that statutes creating offences should be strictly construed, has lost much of its importance'.[53] They stated the general rule: 'A statutory offence provision is to be construed by reference to the ordinary rules of construction.'[54] In this regard there is no distinction between civil statutes and penal provisions.[55]

(c) As a last resort, penal provisions are construed in favour of the subject

A qualification to the general rule mentioned above is that, as a last resort, penal provisions are construed in favour of the subject. The leading statement is by Gibbs J in *Beckwith v The Queen*:[56]

> The rule formerly accepted, that statutes creating offences are to be strictly construed, has lost much of its importance in modern times. In determining the meaning of a penal statute the ordinary rules of construction must be applied, but if the language of the statute remains ambiguous or doubtful the ambiguity or doubt may be resolved in favour of the subject by refusing to extend the category of criminal offences ... The rule is perhaps one of last resort.[57]

This statement has been approved in a number of subsequent High Court of Australia cases, including *Waugh v Kippen*,[58] *Aubrey v the Queen*[59] and *R v A2*.[60] These cases have confirmed that the penal presumption rule is 'one of last resort'.[61] This means that the rule 'comes into operation when the normal principles of interpretation have "run out" [and] if "all other indicia [have] failed" to provide guidance'.[62] It has been observed that the rule regarding penal provisions is a 'second-order principle'.[63]

---

51 *Dyke v Elliott* (1872) 4 LR PC 184, 191, quoted with approval in *Scott v Cawsey* (1907) 5 CLR 132, 145 (Barton J).

52 (2019) 269 CLR 507.

53 Ibid 525 [52] (Kiefel CJ and Keane J, Nettle and Gordon JJ agreeing generally at 554 [148], Edelman J agreeing at 572 [193]).

54 Ibid.

55 Ibid 559–60 [163] (Edelman J).

56 (1976) 135 CLR 569.

57 Ibid 576 (Gibbs J).

58 (1986) 160 CLR 156, 164 (Gibbs CJ, Mason, Wilson and Dawson JJ). In this case the remedial presumption took priority over the penal presumption, the latter being a 'last resort': at 165.

59 (2017) 260 CLR 305, 325–6 [39] (Kiefel CJ, Keane, Nettle and Edelman JJ).

60 (2019) 269 CLR 507, 525–6 [52] (Kiefel CJ and Keane J, Nettle and Gordon JJ agreeing generally at 554 [148], Edelman J agreeing at 572 [193]).

61 *Aubrey v The Queen* (2017) 260 CLR 305, 325 [39] (Kiefel CJ, Keane, Nettle and Edelman JJ). See also *R v A2* (2019) 269 CLR 507, 525–6 [52] (Kiefel CJ and Keane J, Nettle and Gordon JJ agreeing generally at 554 [148], Edelman J agreeing at 572 [193]). In other words, the 'perhaps' qualification has not been included.

62 *R v Lavender* (2005) 222 CLR 67, 96–7 [93] (Kirby J) (citations omitted).

63 *Brown v Tasmania* (2017) 261 CLR 328, 497 [542] (Edelman J) (dissenting as to outcome).

Example 17.2 *R v Rose*[64]

The appellant was convicted by the District Court of Queensland of offences of incest with his de facto wife's daughter. At the time of some of the offences the victim was 17, and at the time of other offences she was 18. Section 222 of the *Criminal Code* (Qld) (in Schedule 1 to the *Criminal Code Act 1899* (Qld)) provided:

> **222 Incest**
>
> (1) Any person who –
>
> (a) has carnal knowledge with or of the person's offspring or other lineal descendant, or sibling, parent, grandparent, uncle, aunt, nephew or niece; and
>
> (b) knows that the other person bears that relationship to him or her, or some relationship of that type to him or her;
>
> commits a crime.
>
> Maximum penalty – imprisonment for life.
>
> ...
>
> (5) A reference in this section to an offspring or other lineal descendant, or a sibling or a parent includes a relationship of that type that is a half, adoptive or step relationship.
>
> (6) For subsection (5), a reference to a step relationship includes a relationship corresponding to a step relationship arising because of cohabitation in a de facto relationship or because of a foster relationship or a legal arrangement.
>
> ...
>
> (8) This section does not apply to carnal knowledge between persons who are lawfully married or entitled to be lawfully married.

On appeal to the Court of Appeal of the Supreme Court of Queensland, it was common ground that sub-ss (5) and (6) applied to the appellant. The issue was the scope of sub-s (8) and the words 'persons who are ... entitled to be lawfully married' in particular.[65] A narrower construction was that 'entitled to be lawfully married' meant given a right, or 'an absolute entitlement'.[66] A broader construction was that the words in question were satisfied if a person has 'grounds for laying a claim to be able to lawfully marry'.[67]

Section 11 of the *Marriage Act 1961* (Cth) provides that a person is of marriageable age at 18 years. The Crown conceded that the convictions, in relation to counts applying to conduct occurring when the complainant was 18 years old, must be quashed.

But, as mentioned above, other counts applied to conduct occurring when the complainant was 17 years old. Under the *Marriage Act*, in the case of a person who has attained the age of 16 years but has not attained the age of 18 years, a judge or magistrate may, in their discretion, make an order authorising the applicant to marry a particular person.

After reviewing the terms of s 222(8), its ordinary meanings as evidenced in a particular dictionary, parliamentary debate on the proposed provision in question, case law on other unrelated enactments, and the *Marriage Act*, McMurdo P opined that 'it is not easy to definitively determine whether the parliament, in enacting s 222(5)–(8), was intending to include conduct

64 [2010] 1 Qd R 87.

65 Ibid 92 [14] (McMurdo P, Muir JA agreeing at 97 [36], Atkinson J agreeing at 98 [43]).

66 Ibid 93 [20], 94 [21].

67 Ibid 94 [22].

like the appellant's [in the other counts].' Her Honour (while critical of the defendant's conduct)[68] then proceeded to apply the *Beckwith* last-resort rule so as to exonerate him:

> In such circumstances, the principle of construction adopted, effectively as a last resort, in construing a criminal statute creating a serious offence punishable by a lengthy period of imprisonment, is that an ambiguous term should be strictly construed in favour of the person charged: *Beckwith v R*. This case is within that unusual category of cases where it is prudent to adopt that principle of construction.[69]

(d) A construction of an offence provision that does not favour the subject may be warranted

If (as usually occurs) the ordinary principles of statutory interpretation are able to resolve an interpretative issue relating to the scope of a penal provision, it follows that '[a] broad construction of an offence provision may be warranted in a particular case'.[70] A number of cases instance a broader construction being taken in relation to a statutory offence,[71] particularly if the purpose of the provision is protective.[72]

(e) The scope of the last-resort principle extends beyond criminal offences

In *Beckwith v The Queen*[73] Gibbs J described the last-resort principle as applying to 'statutes creating offences'.[74] Later cases have extended the principle to analogous aspects of the civil realm. The leading case is *Murphy v Farmer*.[75] It concerned the interpretation of s 229(1)(i) of the *Customs Act 1901* (Cth). The provision provided for goods to be forfeited to the Crown in certain circumstances. Deane, Dawson and Gaudron JJ stated:

> The provision is, in our view, properly to be seen as penal or quasi-penal in character and as attracting the rule that '[t]hose who contend that [a] penalty may be inflicted, must shew that the words of the Act distinctly enact that it shall be incurred under the present circumstances. They must fail, if the words are merely equally capable of a construction that would, and one that would not, inflict the penalty'...[76]

The holding in *Murphy v Farmer* has been applied to civil penalties.[77]

---

68 The defendant's conduct is censured at ibid 89 [3]. McMurdo P made an interesting observation that '[i]mmoral behaviour does not, however, always equate to criminal behaviour': at 89 [4].

69 Ibid 94 [22] (citation omitted).

70 *R v A2* (2019) 269 CLR 507, 526 [55] (Kiefel CJ and Keane J, Nettle and Gordon JJ agreeing generally at 554 [148], Edelman J agreeing at 572 [193]).

71 *R v A2* (2019) 269 CLR 507; *Mansfield v The Queen* (2012) 247 CLR 86; *JAD v R* [2012] NSWCCA 73; *Construction, Forestry, Mining and Energy Union v Hadgkiss* (2007) 169 FCR 151; *R v Yusoff* (2013) 33 NTLR 113; *Beadle v La Bianca* [2012] WASC 415; *R v Hannan* (2016) 259 A Crim R 558; *Director of Public Prosecutions (NSW) v Starr* (2012) 221 A Crim R 525.

72 *R v A2* (2019) 269 CLR 507, 526–7 [55] (Kiefel CJ and Keane J, Nettle and Gordon JJ agreeing generally at 554 [148], Edelman J agreeing at 572 [193]).

73 (1976) 135 CLR 569.

74 Ibid 576.

75 (1988) 165 CLR 19.

76 Ibid 28–9 (footnote omitted). In *Comptroller-General of Customs v Zappia* (2018) 265 CLR 416, Kiefel CJ, Bell and Gageler JJ deprecated use of the appellation 'quasi-penal' to characterise the civil liability under s 35A(1) of the *Customs Act 1901* (Cth): at 431 [40].

77 *Australian Competition and Consumer Commission v Australian Safeway Stores Pty Ltd (No 3)* (2001) 119 FCR 1, 226 [983] (Goldberg J) (pecuniary penalties), varied on other grounds in *Australian Competition and Consumer*

(f) Penal consequences are part of the context of the legislation

Despite the last-resort rule, it has been observed that the 'potential penal consequences are part of the context within which [a provision] falls to be interpreted and applied'.[78] This suggests that the penal consequences may be considered as a first-order principle – that is, as part of the normal weighing operation where a provision is open to more than one construction. Having said this, the content of this contextual principle is not entirely clear. It probably recognises that, where penal consequences may deprive a person of their liberty, the consequences are a first-order consideration.[79] It may also include the expectation of clarity principle (see below).[80]

(g) A penal law is read with the expectation that it should be certain and its reach ascertainable by those who are subject to it

In *DPP (Cth) v Keating*[81] the High Court stated that there is 'an idea that is fundamental to criminal responsibility: that the criminal law should be certain and its reach ascertainable by those who are subject to it'.[82] In practice this means that 'penal provisions will be construed in a manner that gives rise to as much clarity as possible'.[83] Edelman J has helpfully referred to the principle as 'an expectation of clarity in penal provisions'[84] and has pointed out that the principle is longstanding.[85] He has also raised the question whether this principle is 'appropriately characterised as part of any second-order principle of construction that penal provisions are construed narrowly or is better seen merely as involving recognition of the context of the provision as penal'.[86]

The principle is illustrated in a number of cases, including **Example 17.3**.[87]

Commission v Australian Safeway Stores Pty Ltd (2003) 129 FCR 339; *Deputy Federal Commissioner of Taxation (Cth) v Craddock* (2006) 204 FLR 274, 286 [40] (Cavanough J) (penalty notices under the *Income Tax Assessment Act 1936* (Cth)). See also *Trade Practices Commission v TNT Management Pty Ltd* (1985) 6 FCR 1, 47–8 (Franki J).

78 *Connective Services Pty Ltd v Slea Pty Ltd* (2019) 267 CLR 461, 472 [19] (the Court).

79 In *Minogue v Victoria* (2018) 264 CLR 252, 271 [47] (Kiefel CJ, Bell, Keane, Nettle and Edelman JJ) members of the High Court stated that 'a penal statute, or one affecting a person's liberty, should be construed strictly'. This apparent equation of penal statutes with statutes affecting a person's liberty may explain why the potential consequences of imprisonment were considered as a first-order principle in *R v PJ* (2017) 270 A Crim R 439, 446 [31] (Latham J, Bellew J agreeing at [41], Campbell J agreeing at [42]).

80 *Brown v Tasmania* (2017) 261 CLR 328, 497 [542] (Edelman J) (dissenting as to outcome).

81 (2013) 248 CLR 459.

82 Ibid 479 [48] (the Court). The Court was drawing on *DPP (Cth) v Poniatowska* (2011) 244 CLR 408, 424 [44] (French CJ, Gummow, Kiefel and Bell JJ).

83 *Brown v Tasmania* (2017) 261 CLR 328, 497 [542] (Edelman J) (dissenting as to outcome).

84 Ibid 496–7 [542].

85 Ibid 497 [542].

86 Ibid (citations omitted).

87 See also *Comptroller-General of Customs v Zappia* (2018) 265 CLR 416, 431 [40] (Kiefel CJ, Bell and Gageler JJ). See also *Construction, Forestry, Mining and Energy Union v Mammoet Australia Pty Ltd* (2013) 248 CLR 619, 634–5 [48] (the Court).

Example 17.3 *DPP (Cth) v Poniatowska*[88]

The respondent was charged with 17 counts of obtaining a financial advantage, contrary to s 135.2(1) of the *Criminal Code* (Cth) (in sch to *Criminal Code Act 1995* (Cth)):

> (1) A person is guilty of an offence if:
> (a) the person engages in conduct; and
> (aa) as a result of that conduct, the person obtains a financial advantage for himself or herself from another person; and
> (ab) the person knows or believes that he or she is not eligible to receive that financial advantage; and
> (b) the other person is a Commonwealth entity.
> ...

Paragraph (a) of sub-s (1) had to be read with the definitions in the Code of 'conduct' and 'engage in conduct' in s 4.1(2):

> (2) In this Code:
> *conduct* means an act, an omission to perform an act or a state of affairs.
> *engage in conduct* means:
> (a) do an act; or
> (b) omit to perform an act.

Section 4.3 added requirements in relation to what was an 'omission to perform an act' for the purposes of the above definition:

> *Omissions*
> An omission to perform an act can only be a physical element if:
> (a) the law creating the offence makes it so; or
> (b) the law creating the offence impliedly provides that the offence is committed by an omission to perform an act that by law there is a duty to perform.

Thus, for an offence provision in the Code to catch an omission to perform an act, the provision has to satisfy either of the paragraphs of s 4.3.

Each charge related to the respondent's receipt of part-payments of the Parenting Payment Single ('PPS') from Centrelink. The allegation in each case was that, because she had failed to advise Centrelink of her receipt of payments of commission from her employer, she was not entitled to part-payment of the PPS. It was not alleged that the respondent was under a duty imposed by a law of the Commonwealth to advise Centrelink of the receipt of those payments.

The appellant Director did not rely on para (b) of s 4.3. The issue in the appeal to the High Court was the scope of para (a) of s 4.3 and whether 'the introduction of the expression "engages in conduct" [in s 135.2(1)] operates to bring the offence created by s 135.2(1) within s 4.3(a)'. If so, the Director's appeal would succeed. The Director's construction of para (a) was that s 4.3(a) did not require the offence provision to specify an omission to perform an act, and an intentional failure to do something that causes the person to receive a financial advantage satisfied the paragraph. The opposing construction of para (a) was that, for it to apply, it required the offence provision to 'identify a specific omission to [perform an] act'.[89] On this construction, as

88 (2011) 244 CLR 408.

89 Ibid 422 [35] (French CJ, Gummow, Kiefel and Bell JJ).

s 135.2(1) did not identify a specific omission to perform an act, then s 4.3(a) did not apply and in the absence of para (b) applying, the offence did not catch an omission to perform an act.

The majority of the Court preferred the latter construction of s 4.3(a).[90] In reaching that conclusion, they referred to a number of considerations. Notably, the Court drew on the expectation of clarity principle:

> The principles of criminal responsibility stated in the Code proceed from the view that the criminal law should be certain and that its reach should be able to be ascertained by those who are the subject of it. Section 4.3 is a reflection of those ideas. The exceptions to the general principle that it states do not extend to criminalising the omission of [sic] *any* act which is able to be causally related to a result of conduct.[91]

Revenue Acts

[17.5] Revenue Acts are read in the light of their taxation context

(a) Special rules formerly applied to the interpretation of taxing and other revenue statutes

Revenue statutes include taxation statutes and statutes imposing a duty.[92] Until relatively recently these Acts were subject to special rules of interpretation.[93] The formerly leading case was *Anderson v Commissioner of Taxes (Vic)*.[94] In that case three members of the High Court expressed approval for a strict construction. Latham CJ stated: 'The subject is not taxable by inference or by analogy, but only by the plain words of a statute applicable to the facts and circumstances of his case.'[95] His Honour also approved the following principle: '[I]f the Crown, seeking to recover the tax, cannot bring the subject within the letter of the law, the subject is free, however apparently within the spirit of the law the case might otherwise appear to be'.[96]

Similarly, Rich and Dixon JJ approved the following statement: 'The intention to impose a tax or duty, or to increase a tax or duty already imposed, must be shown by clear and unambiguous language and cannot be inferred from ambiguous words.'[97] They also approved the following:

> It is well established that one is bound, in construing Revenue Acts, to give a fair and reasonable construction to their language without leaning to one side or the other, that

---

90 Ibid 422 [35], 423 [37].

91 Ibid 424 [44].

92 *Brunton v Acting Commissioner of Stamp Duties (NSW)* [1913] AC 747, 760, quoted with approval in *Anderson v Commissioner of Taxes (Vic)* (1937) 57 CLR 233, 243 (Rich and Dixon JJ); *Hepples v Commissioner of Taxation (Cth)* (1992) 173 CLR 492, 511 (Deane J), quoting with approval *Western Australian Trustee Executor & Agency Co Ltd v Commissioner of State Taxation (WA)* (1980) 147 CLR 119, 126 (Gibbs J).

93 *Ormond Investment Co v Betts* [1928] AC 143, 162 (Lord Atkinson), approved in *Anderson v Commissioner of Taxes (Vic)* (1937) 57 CLR 233, 243 (Rich and Dixon JJ). In *Hepples v Commissioner of Taxation (Cth)* (1992) 173 CLR 492, 511 Deane J maintained that special rules of the kind set out in *Anderson* applied.

94 (1937) 57 CLR 233. The authority of this case was recognised by the High Court in *Alcan (NT) Alumina Pty Ltd v Commissioner of Territory Revenue (NT)* (2009) 239 CLR 27, 49 [57] (Hayne, Heydon, Crennan and Kiefel JJ, French CJ agreeing at 30 [1]).

95 (1937) 57 CLR 233, 239 (Latham CJ).

96 Ibid, quoting *Partington v A-G* (1869) LR 4 HL 100, 122 (Lord Cairns).

97 Ibid 243, quoting *Brunton v Acting Commissioner of Stamp Duties (NSW)* [1913] AC 747, 760 (Lord Parker).

> no tax can be imposed on a subject by an Act of Parliament without words in it clearly showing an intention to lay the burden upon him, that the words of the statute must be adhered to, and that so-called equitable constructions of them are not permissible.[98]

All interpretative rules are expressions of values that courts have identified are deserving of protection.[99] In *Hepples v Commissioner of Taxation (Cth)*[100] Deane J argued that the principles enunciated by Rich and Dixon JJ in *Anderson* were 'supported by strong reasons in both law and common sense'.[101] His Honour expanded on this:

> For one thing, statutes imposing taxation derogate from the ordinary rights of the citizen in that they represent a compulsory exaction of money. For another, the framing of the provisions of such legislation is essentially within the control of government.[102]

(b) There is little or no room, in contemporary law, for special general rules of interpretation applying to revenue Acts

Since *Anderson* was decided in 1937, many changes have occurred in statutory interpretation.[103] Principal among these have been the requirement to examine the context in its widest sense in all cases[104] and the requirement to have regard, and give appropriate weight, to the legislative purpose to the extent to which it may be identified.[105] The contemporary law of interpretation eschews literalism or a narrow form of textualism.[106] The text is the starting point[107] and grounds interpretation,[108] but non-grammatical readings are possible if, on balance, the permissible considerations favour that reading.[109]

The leading contemporary statement on the approach to the interpretation of taxing legislation (albeit dicta[110]) is *Alcan (NT) Alumina Pty Ltd v Commissioner of Territory Revenue (NT)*.[111] After setting out the general principles of statutory interpretation,[112] the Court stated: '[T]ax

98 Ibid, quoting *Ormond Investment Co v Betts* [1928] AC 143, 162 (Lord Atkinson).

99 Ruth Sullivan, *Sullivan on the Construction of Statutes* (LexisNexis Canada, 5th ed, 2008) 2.

100 (1992) 173 CLR 492.

101 Ibid 511.

102 Ibid.

103 See chapter 2.

104 See **[7.6]**, **[7.7]**.

105 See **[8.2]**.

106 *R v A2* (2019) 269 CLR 507, 522 [37] (Kiefel CJ and Keane J, Nettle and Gordon JJ generally agreeing at 554 [148], Edelman J agreeing at 572 [193]); Sir Anthony Mason, 'Changing the Law in a Changing Society' (1993) 67(8) *Australian Law Journal* 568, 569. See generally chapter 2. See also Jeffrey Barnes, 'Contextualism: "The Modern Approach to Statutory Interpretation"' (2018) 41(4) *University of New South Wales Law Journal* 1083, 1102–5.

107 See **[6.5]**.

108 See **[6.10]**.

109 See **[6.9]**.

110 See *Alcan (NT) Alumina Pty Ltd v Commissioner of Territory Revenue (NT)* (2009) 239 CLR 27, 49 [57] (Hayne, Heydon, Crennan and Kiefel JJ, French CJ agreeing at 30 [1]).

111 (2009) 239 CLR 27.

112 Ibid 46–7 [47] (Hayne, Heydon, Crennan and Kiefel JJ, French CJ agreeing at 30 [1]).

statutes do not form a class of their own to which different rules of construction apply; they are to be construed by application of the settled principles referred to above.'[113]

(c) The fact that an Act is a taxing Act is part of the Act's context and is therefore relevant to the task of construing such an Act

After stating that tax statutes are to be construed by application of the general settled principles of statutory interpretation, the High Court in *Alcan* added a rider:

> [T]he fact that a statute is a taxing Act, or contains penal provisions, is part of the context and is therefore relevant to the task of construing the Act in accordance with those settled principles. Whether or when 'rules' of the kind considered in *Anderson* and *Waugh v Kippen* may be relied upon need not be decided.[114]

When the Court says that 'a taxing Act . . . is part of the context' it means that, in the case of a taxing Act, relevant considerations in the context of such an Act will arise as a result of the Act being a taxing Act.

Example 17.4 *Federal Commissioner of Taxation v Multiflex Pty Ltd*[115]

The respondent taxpayer lodged business activity statements with the Commissioner, claiming to be entitled to refunds of goods and services tax ('GST') in the amount of $970,759. The Commissioner suspected the documentary foundation for input tax credits was wholly or substantially fraudulent and did not make the refund, but proceeded with an investigation 'with all due expedition'.[116]

The Act in question, *A New Tax System (Goods and Services Tax) Act 1999* (Cth) ('the GST Act'), provided:

> **35-5 Entitlement to refund**
>
> (1) If the *assessed net amount for a tax period is less than zero, the Commissioner must, on behalf of the Commonwealth, pay that amount (expressed as a positive amount) to you.

Section 35-10 of that Act further provided that this entitlement to a refund arises, 'when you give the Commissioner your GST return'.

The case turned on whether a particular implication was appropriate in s 35-5 of the GST Act. The Commissioner argued that there was to be implied in the provision such time as was reasonably necessary to determine by investigation whether the claimed net amount was truly payable by the company concerned.[117] The opposing construction for the company was that the relevant provisions of the GST Act and the *Taxation Administration Act 1953* (Cth) ('TAA') did not

113 Ibid 49 [57]. For a detailed survey of cases on the approach to interpreting taxation legislation, see *Australian Investment and Development Pty Ltd v Commissioner of State Revenue* [2019] VSCA 69.

114 *Alcan (NT) Alumina Pty Ltd v Commissioner of Territory Revenue (Northern Territory)* (2009) 239 CLR 27, 49 [57] (Hayne, Heydon, Crennan and Kiefel JJ, French CJ agreeing at 30 [1]) (citations omitted).

115 (2011) 197 FCR 580.

116 As found by the primary judge: see ibid 584 [12] (the Court).

117 Ibid 581–2 [1], 589–90 [28] (the Court).

contemplate the withholding of a payment under s 35-5 pending the ascertainment, by the Commissioner, of the true state of affairs with respect to GST and input tax credits.[118]

For various reasons the Full Federal Court dismissed the appeal by the Commissioner. It held that the language of s 35-5 *did* give rise to an implication, but only that a refund must be made within a time that is reasonable in the circumstances of the duty concerned – the duty to make the refund.[119]

Among the indications to which the Court gave weight, were contextual factors that arose by virtue of the Act in question being a taxing Act. First, the Court had regard to other elements of the statutory scheme. The GST Act was not administratively self-contained, but was connected to, and relied on, provisions in the TAA.[120] Second, the Court had regard to the wording of the comparable New Zealand Act, an Act that 'provided much inspiration in the drafting of the core concepts of Australia's GST system'.[121] The Court noted that the Australian Act lacked the wording of the New Zealand Act, which expressly allows the Commissioner to give notice of their intention to investigate the circumstances of a registered person's return within a specified period.[122] Third, guided by precedents from the New Zealand courts[123] as well as a previous decision of the Court,[124] the Court had regard to 'the business environment' in which the GST legislation must operate.[125] It also observed that confidence in the GST system might be eroded by delay on the part of the Commissioner in making refunds.[126] This background to s 35-5, 'with consequential ramifications for its construction',[127] suggested 'the importance of a prompt refund, as calculated by an entity, being made by the Commissioner to that entity'.[128] Fourth, and equally, the Court had regard to the consequences of the respondent's construction for the administration of the GST scheme. The Court noted that the Commissioner was not without remedy if they know the business activity statement to be wrong. The Court pointed out that the Commissioner is entitled at any time to make an assessment of the net amount.[129]

In summary, the *Multiflex* case illustrates several contextual factors that arose by virtue of the Act in question being a taxing Act: other elements of a taxation scheme; the consequences of the rival constructions (for taxpayers, for confidence in the taxation system, and for the workable administration of the Act); and comparable Acts and interpretations of those Acts.

---

118 Ibid 582 [3], 584–5 [13].

119 Ibid 592–3 [40].

120 Ibid 585 [15], 589 [26].

121 Ibid 582 [2].

122 Ibid 591 [35].

123 Ibid 591–2 [35]–[36].

124 Ibid 592 [37].

125 Ibid.

126 Ibid 592 [39].

127 Ibid 592 [37].

128 Ibid 592 [38].

129 Ibid 589 [26].

18 LINGUISTIC CANONS

Overview

[18.1] Linguistic canons recognise and put into effect general language conventions – that is, conventions relating to the use of language generally. Chapter 15 has dealt with the canon that the 'ordinary and grammatical meaning' and the 'natural and ordinary meaning' of the words in question are the presumptive legal meaning and are to be applied unless good reason is shown to depart from it.

The present chapter examines other linguistic canons. In statutory interpretation the canons often have Latin tags. The canons are regularly drawn upon by courts, some more so than others. They roughly divide into three categories: canons that focus on the words whose meaning is in question; canons that relate to other aspects of the provision containing the words in question; and canons that relate to the use of other relevant provisions of the Act in question. Each of these categories is now briefly examined.

Canons that focus on the words whose meaning is in question include the presumption against surplusage; the practice of taking careful note of the words used as compared with words that could have, but were not, chosen; a canon regarding the interpretation of a composite expression; and a canon regarding words that have previously acquired a technical meaning.

Canons that relate to other aspects of the provision containing the words in question include a canon that emphasises the importance of the immediate context of the words in question (*noscitur a sociis*); a subsidiary canon that prescribes how to interpret a general word that completes a list of two or more specific words (*ejusdem generis*); and a canon that deals with the approach to the assignment of plural objects to distinct matters (*reddendo singula singulis*).

Canons that normally relate to the use of other relevant provisions of the Act include a canon that treats the express mention of one thing (in another provision) as indicating the exclusion of another (in the provision in question) (*expressio unius est exclusio alterius*); a canon that no implication is to be made on a topic with respect to which provision has been made (*expressum facit cessare tacitum*); a canon dealing with the use of the same words in the Act in question, and a canon dealing with the opposite situation – namely, when different words are used in the statute; a canon dealing with apparent conflict between a general provision and a specific provision (*generalia specialibus non derogant*); and a general canon relating to use of all relevant provisions of the Act (an Act is to be read as a whole).

Nature of linguistic canons

Linguistic canons are general language conventions that are presumptively applied in statutory interpretation [18.2]

The presumptive meaning of a statutory provision is the meaning it bears read as a piece of English.[1] That rule 'serves the important purpose of ensuring that those who are subject to the law understand the nature and extent of their rights and obligations'.[2] It also enables members of Parliament to read draft legislation put before them in a cooperative way.[3]

Giving weight to linguistic canons is one of the primary means by which the courts seek to effectuate these purposes.[4] The canons are sometimes described in case law as 'general language conventions'.[5] As Bennion's definition of linguistic canons has been judicially approved,[6] it may usefully be cited:

> Linguistic canons of construction are not confined to statutes, even to the field of law. They are based on the rules of logic, grammar, syntax and punctuation; and the use of language as a medium of communication generally.[7]

Barak's extracurial description is similar. It has also been judicially approved.

> The canons reflect semantic rules, not legal rules. They are not unique to law but rather are rules of general applicability for understanding language . . . They are common to all legal systems and systems of interpretation. They belong to the field of language. They help determine the range of a legal text's semantic possibilities.[8]

As linguistic canons are general language conventions, they are applicable to a wide range of language use. For example, in legal discourse the hendiadys canon (a type of composite expression[9]) has been applied to a newspaper article,[10] a statement of claim,[11] a reasons for judgment,[12] and a

1 See **[6.7]**, **[15.2]**.

2 *Marshall v Director-General, Department of Transport* (2001) 205 CLR 603, 623 [37] (Gaudron J; Hayne J agreeing at 634 [67]) (citation omitted).

3 Philip Sales, 'Legislative Intention, Interpretation, and the Principle of Legality' (2019) 40(1) *Statute Law Review* 53, 59.

4 Related matters that are examined elsewhere are rules of grammar (**[9.5](d)**) and the ordinary, natural and grammatical meanings (chapter 15).

5 *Brisbane City Council v Amos* (2019) 266 CLR 593, 612 [36] (Kiefel CJ and Edelman J, Nettle J expressing support at 382 [54]) (discussing *generalia specialibus non derogant*); *BMW Australia Ltd v Brewster* (2019) 269 CLR 574, 652 [206] (Edelman J, dissenting as to outcome) (discussing *generalia specialibus non derogant*). See also *Spence v Queensland* (2019) 268 CLR 355, 490–1 [302] (Edelman J, dissenting as to outcome) (discussing *expressio unius est exclusio alterius*).

6 *Perpetual Custodians Ltd v IOOF Investment Management Ltd* (2013) 304 ALR 436.

7 Ibid 456 [82] (Leeming JA, McColl JA agreeing at 438 [1], Gleeson JA agreeing at 438 [2]).

8 Aharon Barak, *Purposive Interpretation in Law* (Princeton University Press, 2005) 107, quoted with approval in *Ombudsman v Laughton* (2005) 64 NSWLR 114, 119 [24] (Spigelman CJ, Handley JA agreeing at 119 [28], Basten JA agreeing generally at 120 [39]).

9 See **[18.5]** below.

10 *O'Shaughnessy v Mirror Newspapers Ltd* (1970) 125 CLR 166, 177 (Windeyer J).

11 *Herald & Weekly Times Pty Ltd v Buckley* (2009) 21 VR 661, 669 [27] (the Court).

12 *Clubb v Edwards* (2019) 267 CLR 171, 329–30 [461] (Edelman J).

contract.[13] In non-legal discourse, the canons are readily evident in literary works for the layperson.[14]

The linguistic canons are often loosely described as 'rules', but like other so-called rules of construction they are merely 'aids to construction, presumptions or pointers'.[15] With language conventions 'much depends on context'.[16] Thus, in a case where there are opposing constructions of the provision in doubt, each with interpretative support, a linguistic canon is not determinative; uppermost is what the legislature is likely to have intended.[17]

Canons that focus on the word in question

[18.3] **Endeavours should be made to avoid treating words chosen by the legislature as redundant: this is the presumption against surplusage**

The presumption against surplusage mandates that

> a court construing a statutory provision must strive to give meaning to every word of the provision. In *The Commonwealth v Baume* Griffith CJ cited *R v Berchet* to support the proposition that it was 'a known rule in the interpretation of Statutes that such a sense is to be made upon the whole as that no clause, sentence, or word shall prove superfluous, void, or insignificant, if by any other construction they may all be made useful and pertinent'.[18]

Nevertheless, courts recognise that 'Parliament is sometimes guilty of "surplusage" or even "tautology"'.[19] The reason why this occurs is that '[f]rom time to time provisions will be inserted for more abundant caution to guard against the possibility that the general might be read as not including the particular'.[20]

If material is mere surplusage, the Court may 'ignore' it.[21]

---

13 *Downer Engineering Power Pty Ltd v P & H Minepro Australasia Pty Ltd* [2007] NSWCA 318, [19] (Basten JA).

14 The work *This is Shakespeare* by Emma Smith (Pelican Books, 2019) contains several applications of linguistic canons that lawyers would find familiar. For example, the author compares the uses of the word 'complexion' in *The Merchant of Venice* (same word, same meaning): at 102; analyses a famous speech by Shylock in the same play that begins with 'If you prick us do we not bleed?', observing the drafting structure of consecutive parallel sentences each beginning with 'If you' (*noscitur a sociis*): at 106; considers the context of other passages of the work (Act as a whole): at 106; and, for Shakespeare's use of 'adore' in *Twelfth Night*, examines the playwright's oeuvre (statute book): at 182–3.

15 *Maunsell v Olins* [1975] AC 373, 382 (Lord Reid), approved in *Corporate Affairs Commission (NSW) v Yuill* (1991) 172 CLR 319, 347 (McHugh J) (dissenting as to outcome). Lord Reid was referring to 'rules of construction'. These include linguistic canons.

16 *Spence v Queensland* (2019) 268 CLR 355, 490 [302] (Edelman J, dissenting as to outcome).

17 *Ainsworth v Criminal Justice Commission* (1992) 175 CLR 564, 575 (Mason CJ, Dawson, Toohey and Gaudron JJ), speaking of *expressio unius est exclusio alterius* and *expressum facit cessare tacitum*. On legislative intention generally see chapter 4.

18 *Project Blue Sky Inc v Australian Broadcasting Authority* (1998) 194 CLR 355, 382 [71] (McHugh, Gummow, Kirby and Hayne JJ), quoting *Commonwealth v Baume* (1905) 2 CLR 405, 414 (Griffith CJ). The statement of Griffith CJ is in substance a quotation from *R v Berchet* (1688) 1 Show KB 106, 108 [89 ER 480, 481].

19 *Western Australian Planning Commission v Southregal Pty Ltd* (2017) 259 CLR 106, 122 [55] (Kiefel CJ and Bell J).

20 *Leon Fink Holdings Pty Ltd v Australian Film Commission* (1979) 141 CLR 672, 679 (Mason J).

21 *Amery v New South Wales (Director-General, NSW Department of Education and Training)* [2004] NSWCA 404, [49] (Beazley JA, Cripps AJA agreeing at 208), citing *Saraswati v The Queen* (1991) 172 CLR 1, 22 (McHugh J).

Example 18.1 ***Secretary, Department of Employment, Education, Training and Youth Affairs v Gray***[22]

Austudy is an income support payment scheme for full-time students. The respondent, who was enrolled as a student for the degree of Arts/Law, applied for Austudy benefits. He was denied benefits on the ground that he did not meet the full-time study requirements in the *Austudy Regulations 1990* (Cth), made under the *Student and Youth Assistance Act 1973* (Cth).

Regulation 34 stated:

> **34. Workload: tertiary students**
>
> (1) A tertiary student must study full-time.
>
> (2) To be a full-time student, a student must be enrolled in and undertake at least three-quarters of the normal amount of full-time work for a period as set out in regulation 35.

Regulation 35(1) effectively defined the normal amount of full-time work. It stated:

> (a) the normal amount of full-time work for a year of the course is the standard student load determined by the institution for the purposes of HECS; and
>
> (b) the normal amount of full-time work for a semester of the course is 0.5 of the standard student load.

In the relevant year the student undertook 0.8 (80 per cent) of the standard student load. He therefore satisfied reg 35(1)(a), read with reg 34(2). But in the second semester he had undertaken 0.3 (30 per cent) of the full-year standard student load. According to the Department, this was less than the workload required by reg 35(1)(b) read with reg 34(2).[23]

The issue was whether the student had to satisfy para (b). The Department argued that 'and' in reg 35(1) indicated a conjunction, so that paras (a) and (b) were cumulative requirements that had to be met. Otherwise, a student could complete the requirements for a full-year course in one semester, do nothing in the second, but continue to receive the Austudy benefit.

The respondent argued that paras (a) and (b) described alternative tests and alternative periods. On this construction a student was required to satisfy only one of them to qualify for an Austudy benefit.

The Court gave little or no weight to the consequentialist argument of the Department because it found that the scenario it envisaged would be 'extremely rare'.[24] Ultimately the Court agreed with the construction put by the respondent. It held that 'paras (a) and (b) are alternatives intended to deal respectively with courses that are full year courses and those which are not'.[25] Among the considerations that led to this conclusion was the presumption against surplusage. It found that when this consideration was applied, it strongly favoured the respondent. The Court reasoned that 'compliance with the requirements of para (b) . . . would invariably render the need to comply with para (a) otiose'.[26] Hence, the 'interpretation [put by the Department] leaves para (a) of reg 35(1) with no work to do and as mere surplusage'.[27]

---

22 (1999) 91 FCR 254.

23 Under reg 34(2) three-quarters of 0.5 = 0.375 or 37.5 per cent. His second semester workload of 30 per cent was less than this amount.

24 *Secretary, Department of Employment, Education, Training and Youth Affairs v Gray* (1999) 91 FCR 254, 260 [21] (Hill J).

25 Ibid 262 [30].

26 Ibid 260 [21].

27 Ibid 262 [30].

[18.4] 'Alternative words could have been used'

A court may bolster an interpretation it favours by saying that, if Parliament *had* intended an alternative meaning, it could have used words that made such an intention clear.[28] For example, it may say: 'If that had been the intention of Parliament the words "..." would have been inserted after the word "..."'.[29] The inference is stronger if the circumstances in which a missing qualification would arise could not be said to be unexpected.[30]

Example 18.2 illustrates the inference. **Example 18.3** illustrates how a court may bolster its reasoning by supplying the alternative wording.

Example 18.2 *CAG v Public Trustee of Queensland*[31]

Section 283 of the *Property Law Act 1974* (Qld) gave a certain right to a former de facto partner:

> After a de facto relationship has ended, a de facto partner may apply to a court for an order adjusting interests in the property of either or both of the de facto partners.

The appellant had applied to the Supreme Court under this provision after her former de facto partner died. The Public Trustee responded by applying to have the application struck out on the basis that the proceeding was commenced after the death of the former partner, and the Act did not have that reach. The appellant submitted that pt 19 of the Act, which included s 283, covered people in the applicant's position even where they had not commenced proceedings before the death of the de facto partner against whom a claim for a property adjustment order had been made. At first instance the Supreme Court agreed with the Public Trustee's construction and acceded to the Trustee's application.

On appeal the Court of Appeal agreed with the primary judge.[32] In doing so they found support in the present canon:

> If it were the intention of the legislature that the operation of s 283 of the Act is to extend to claims against deceased de facto spouses, one would expect ... that such an intention would be made clear by the text of the Act ...[33]

Example 18.3 *R v Bentham*[34]

In this case the provision in question was s 17(2) of the *Firearms Act 1968* (UK), which read:

> If a person, at the time of his committing or being arrested for an offence specified in Schedule I to this Act, has in his possession a firearm or imitation firearm, he shall be

28 Ruth Sullivan, *Statutory Interpretation* (Irwin Law, 3rd ed, 2016) 149.

29 *R v Morton* [1986] VR 863, 866 (the Court).

30 *De Marco v Chief Commissioner of State Revenue* (2013) 83 NSWLR 445, 460 [75] (Basten JA).

31 [2008] 2 Qd R 419.

32 Ibid [28] (Keane JA, de Jersey CJ agreeing at 420 [1], Fraser JA agreeing at 431 [32]).

33 Ibid 430 [25].

34 [2005] 1 WLR 1057.

> guilty of an offence under this subsection unless he shows that he had it in his possession for a lawful object.

The issue was whether possession of an imitation firearm extended to any thing, including (as here) a hand inside clothing, that gave the impression of a gun. In finding for the accused the Court indicated the wording that could have been adopted if Parliament *had* intended to catch such an act:

> Parliament might have created an offence of falsely pretending to have a firearm (although not an imitation firearm). But it has not done so.[35]

The Court then contrasted the different wording of the Act in question: 'the appellant was not accused of falsely pretending to have a firearm but of *possessing* an imitation firearm'.[36]

Composite expressions comprise grammatical components that are read together [18.5]

A composite expression, also called a 'composite phrase'[37] or a 'compound expression',[38] 'is a compound created out of at least two elements or integers which is different from each of them'.[39] For example, the composite expression 'above the table' consists of the preposition 'above' and the nominal expression 'the table'.[40] In case law, examples of expressions that have been held to be composite are 'external affairs',[41] 'civil and criminal process',[42] 'departmental expenditure',[43] 'more onerous terms',[44] 'was not given by the applicant for the purpose of the application'[45] and 'de facto relationship'.[46]

A particular kind of composite expression is an hendiadys.[47] It has been described as 'an expression in which a single idea is conveyed by two words connected by a conjunction, and in

35 Ibid 1061 [9] (Lord Bingham, Lord Steyn agreeing at 1062 [12], Lord Phillips agreeing at 1062 [13], Lord Carswell agreeing at 1062 [15]).

36 Ibid 1061 [9] (emphasis added).

37 *Collector of Customs v Agfa-Gevaert Ltd* (1996) 186 CLR 389, 401, 402 (the Court); *XYZ v Commonwealth* (2006) 227 CLR 532, 544 [19] (Gleeson CJ).

38 *R v Wilson; Ex parte Kisch* (1934) 52 CLR 234, 244 (Dixon J).

39 *Victims Compensation Fund Corporation v Brown* (2003) 201 ALR 260, 269–70 [34] (Heydon J, McHugh ACJ agreeing at 261 [1], Gummow J agreeing at 261 [2], Kirby J agreeing at 261 [3], Hayne J agreeing at 261 [4]). The term 'composite expression' is also deployed in *Collector of Customs v Agfa-Gevaert Ltd* (1996) 186 CLR 389, 402 (the Court). For a linguistic analysis see Ronald W Langacker, 'Possession and Possessive Constructions' in John R Taylor and Robert E MacLaury (eds), *Language and the Cognitive Construal of the World* (Mouton de Gruyter, 1995) 51, 54.

40 Ronald W Langacker, 'Possession and Possessive Constructions' in John R Taylor and Robert E MacLaury (eds), *Language and the Cognitive Construal of the World* (Mouton de Gruyter, 1995) 51, 54.

41 *XYZ v Commonwealth* (2006) 227 CLR 532, 568 [102] (Kirby J).

42 *Dalton v NSW Crime Commission* (2006) 227 CLR 490, 527 [115] (Kirby J).

43 *Combet v Commonwealth* (2005) 224 CLR 494, 527 [21] (Gleeson CJ).

44 *Waters v Public Transport Corporation* (1991) 173 CLR 349, 366 (Mason CJ and Gaudron J, Deane J generally agreeing at 382).

45 *Gajjar v Minister for Immigration and Citizenship* (2013) 87 ALJR 549, 552 [19] (Kiefel J).

46 *Bailey v Palombo* [2020] NSWSC 1209, [108] (Hallen J).

47 Oliver Jones, *Bennion on Statutory Interpretation: A Code* (LexisNexis, 6th ed, 2013) 1072.

which each word in the expression tends to colour the other with its qualities'.[48] An example[49] is 'systemic and continuing' in the following provision:

> An offence satisfies this subsection if the offence –
>
> ...
>
> (b) forms part of *systemic and continuing* criminal activity . . .[50]

Composite expressions need to be read having regard to their constitution as a single expression.[51] It is apt to mislead, and can lead to error, to 'dissect a composite legislative expression into separate parts, giving each part a meaning which the part has when used in isolation, then combine the meanings to give that composite expression a meaning at odds with the meaning it has when construed as a whole'.[52]

To properly construe a composite expression, it is appropriate to begin by taking each element into account. But each throws light on the meaning of the rest.[53] Ultimately, the compound expression must be read as a whole.[54] Thus, each element

> may only be analysed separately to an extent. To ascertain how the provision is intended to apply, the elements need to be read together and in light of the object of [the section].[55]

When the component parts are read together, a different meaning may be arrived at than would occur by taking the disintegrated parts alone. For example, a 'deed of company arrangement' did not require that it should be executed as a deed.[56] And 'building operations' did not require that what was being built was a 'building'. As the adjective 'building' was derived from the verb 'to build', the composite expression included the building of bridges, towers and other structures as well as buildings.[57]

The High Court has cautioned against adopting a rigid rule in this area, which would deny the utility of the meaning of a component part of a composite expression.[58] Thus, for example, if a

48 *McLeod-Dryden v Supreme Court (Vic)* (2017) 270 A Crim R 352, 359 [25] (the Court). See also *Waverley Municipal Council v Swain* [2003] Aust Torts Reports 81-694, 63765 [12] (Spigelman CJ, Handley JA and Ipp JA relevantly agreeing at 63782 [145]; *Victims Compensation Fund Corporation v Brown* (2003) 201 ALR 260, 269–70 [34] (Heydon J, McHugh ACJ agreeing at 261 [1], Gummow J agreeing at 261 [2], Kirby J agreeing at 261 [3], Hayne J agreeing at 261 [4]).

49 *McLeod-Dryden v Supreme Court of Victoria* (2017) 270 A Crim R 352, 359 [25] (the Court). For another example see *De Marco v Chief Commissioner of State Revenue* (2013) 83 NSWLR 445, 459 [71] (Basten JA).

50 *Major Crime (Investigative Powers) Act 2004* (Vic) s 3AA(2) (emphasis added).

51 *Simonis v Perpetual Trustee Co Ltd* (1987) 21 NSWLR 677, 685 (Kearney J).

52 *Alphapharm Pty Ltd v H Lundbeck A/S* (2014) 254 CLR 247, 271–2 [61] (Crennan, Bell and Gageler JJ) (citations omitted). See also *XYZ v Commonwealth* (2006) 227 CLR 532, 543–4 [19] (Gleeson CJ); *R v Wilson; Ex parte Kisch* (1934) 52 CLR 234, 244 (Dixon J); *Western Australia v Ward* (2002) 213 CLR 1, 93 [89] (Gleeson CJ, Gaudron, Gummow and Hayne JJ).

53 *XYZ v Commonwealth* (2006) 227 CLR 532, 568 [102] (Kirby J).

54 *R v Wilson; Ex parte Kisch* (1934) 52 CLR 234, 244 (Dixon J).

55 *Gajjar v Minister for Immigration and Citizenship* (2013) 87 ALJR 549, 552 [19] (Kiefel J).

56 *MYT Engineering Pty Ltd v Mulcon Pty Ltd* (1999) 195 CLR 636, 644–5 [14] (Gleeson CJ, Gaudron, Gummow and Hayne JJ).

57 *R v Marks; Ex parte Australian Building Construction Employees and Builders Labourers' Federation* (1981) 147 CLR 471, 490 (Murphy J, Mason J agreeing at 488).

58 *Collector of Customs v Agfa-Gevaert Ltd* (1996) 186 CLR 389, 398, 400–1 (the Court).

composite expression does not, taken as a whole, have a trade meaning,[59] but a distinct element or elements of the expression does have a trade meaning, 'it will ordinarily make sense for a court or tribunal to take notice of the trade meaning of a word or words within that expression'.[60]

It is presumed that where the word in question has previously acquired a technical meaning, the legislature used the word in that technical sense [18.6]

(a) Words in statutes may be used in a technical sense

The statute book deals with an enormous range of matters – from everyday road rules to matters of scientific expertise. Many words and expressions in statutes have been held to carry technical meanings: for example, 'derivative' in a chemistry setting under the *Misuse of Drugs Act 1981* (WA),[61] 'programmable controllers' in the *Customs Tariff Act 1987* (Cth),[62] 'pastry' in federal sales tax legislation[63] and 'offer for sale' in offensive weapons legislation.[64]

(b) A word that has acquired a technical meaning attracts a presumption that the legislature used the word in its technical sense

In the first place words are presumed to carry their ordinary and grammatical meaning. An exception arises:

> Words in statutes should be taken to have been used by the legislature in their ordinary sense unless there is something in their context, phrasing or the subject matter with which they deal to lead to the conclusion that they are intended to assume a technical meaning or to be used in a specialised or trade sense.[65]

It follows that '[w]here a word or phrase has a technical meaning in relation to an area of trade, business, technology or other non-legal expertise, in the absence of any indication to the contrary, it should be given its technical meaning'.[66]

The presumption in relation to words that have acquired a technical meaning is stronger if the setting deals with that expertise: 'Where a word or phrase has a technical meaning in relation to a particular expertise, and is used in a context dealing with that expertise, it is to be given that meaning unless the contrary intention appears.'[67]

The presumption in relation to words that have acquired a technical meaning recognises an Act's 'register'. This refers to 'the semantic level appropriate to the subject matter and to the audience addressed'.[68] Having regard to the meaning the audience would give to the words in

---

59 Trade and technical meanings are dealt with in **[18.6]** below.

60 *Collector of Customs v Agfa-Gevaert Ltd* (1996) 186 CLR 389, 401 (the Court).

61 *Clegg v Western Australia (No 2)* (2017) 265 A Crim R 201.

62 *HR Products Pty Ltd v Collector of Customs* (1990) 20 ALD 340.

63 *Herbert Adams Pty Ltd v Federal Commissioner of Taxation* (1932) 47 CLR 222.

64 *Fisher v Bell* [1961] 1 QB 394.

65 *Marine Power Australia Pty Ltd v Comptroller-General of Customs* (1989) 89 ALR 561, 572 (Lockhart J), approved in *DPP v Acme Storage Pty Ltd* (2017) 264 IR 215, 229 [66] (the Court). For an earlier authority see *Williams v Official Assignee of the Estate of William Dunn* (1908) 6 CLR 425, 447–8 (O'Connor J).

66 *Marine Power Australia Pty Ltd v Comptroller-General of Customs* (1989) 89 ALR 561, 572 (Lockhart J).

67 *Clegg v Western Australia (No 2)* (2017) 265 A Crim R 201, 211 [55] (the Court) (citations omitted).

68 *Maunsell v Olins* [1975] AC 373, 391 (Lord Simon), approved in *Collector of Customs v Agfa-Gevaert Ltd* (1996) 186 CLR 389, 398 (the Court).

question assists the court in finding 'the most natural and ordinary meaning which is appropriate in the circumstances'.[69]

(c) The presumption in favour of technical meanings applies to legal terms

According to Lord Diplock, the use by lawyers of terms of art in the drafting of legal documents has a 'social justification'. This includes achieving 'a more precise meaning'.[70] As terms of art used in statutes are technical words, a presumption thereby arises: 'Where words have been used which have acquired a legal meaning, it will be taken, prima facie, that the legislature has intended to use them with that meaning'.[71] In the case of a legal term the presumption is said to be a 'strong' one,[72] indicating that the presumption is difficult to rebut.

(d) Expert evidence is admissible to inform a court of the technical meaning, but this rule is not applicable to legal terms of art

Unlike an ordinary English word or phrase, for which expert evidence is not admissible,[73] 'evidence is admissible for the purpose of ascertaining the technical meaning of a non-legal term used in a statute'.[74] The evidence that is admissible includes expert evidence of witnesses. In addition, a court may have regard to trade manuals, industry journals, textbooks and other trade and industry evidence.[75]

The purpose of providing the evidence is to inform the court of the technical meaning the word has previously acquired and thereby engage the presumption that technical words carry technical meanings. As the Federal Court put it, 'evidence could be called both to assist the conclusion that the expression is used in a technical sense and to elucidate that technical meaning if differing from its ordinary meaning'.[76] The role of such evidence is limited. It remains the task of the court to interpret the Act[77] and to state whether particular articles are properly included

69 Ibid. The statement was applied in *Collector of Customs v Agfa-Gevaert Ltd* (1996) 186 CLR 389, 400, 401 (the Court).

70 *Sydall v Castings Ltd* [1967] 1 QB 302, 313–4 (Lord Diplock), quoted with approval in *Phoenix Commercial Enterprises Pty Ltd v City of Canada Bay Council* [2010] NSWCA 64, [168] (Campbell JA, Spigelman CJ generally agreeing at [1]).

71 *A-G (NSW) v Brewery Employes Union of New South Wales* (1908) 6 CLR 469, 531 (O'Connor J). For similar statements see *Australasian Temperance and General Mutual Life Assurance Society Ltd v Howe* (1922) 31 CLR 290, 302 (Isaacs J); *Barker v The Queen* (1983) 153 CLR 338, 341 (Mason J), 355–6 (Brennan and Deane JJ); *Palgo Holdings Pty Ltd v Gowans* (2005) 221 CLR 249, 280–1 [96] (Kirby J) (dissenting as to outcome).

72 *A-G (NSW) v Brewery Employes Union of NSW* (1908) 6 CLR 469, 531 (O'Connor J), quoting *R v Slator* (1881) 8 QBD 267, 272 (Denman J).

73 *Australian Gas Light Co v Valuer-General* (1940) 40 SR (NSW) 126, 137 (Jordan CJ); *Uber BV v Federal Commissioner of Taxation* (2017) 247 FCR 462, 487 [104] (Griffiths J); *Lansell House Pty Ltd v Federal Commissioner of Taxation* (2010) 76 ATR 19, 33 [60] (Sundberg J).

74 *Clegg v Western Australia (No 2)* (2017) 265 A Crim R 201 [56] (the Court).

75 *Herbert Adams Pty Ltd v Federal Commissioner of Taxation* (1932) 47 CLR 222, 226 (Starke J), 227 (Dixon J, Rich J agreeing at 225); *Clegg v Western Australia (No 2)* (2017) 265 A Crim R 201, 238 [77] (the Court).

76 *Northern Land Council v Olney* (1992) 34 FCR 470, 480 (the Court). For a more detailed analysis of the uses of expert evidence, see *Pepsi Seven-Up Bottlers Perth Pty Ltd v Commissioner of Taxation* (1995) 62 FCR 289, 298–9 (Hill J).

77 *Clegg v Western Australia (No 2)* (2017) 265 A Crim R 201, 211 [56] (the Court).

under the statutory designation.[78] The evidence cannot take the place of a statutory definition.[79] Furthermore, the evidence must demonstrate uniformity in the specialised use.[80]

The rule regarding the admissibility of expert evidence does not apply to legal terms. Here '[t]he Court is able to know the meaning of technical legal terms without the calling of extrinsic evidence'.[81]

Example 18.4 is illustrative of a term that had previously acquired a non-legal technical meaning.[82]

Example 18.4 *Herbert Adams Pty Ltd v Federal Commissioner of Taxation*[83]

Under the *Sales Tax Assessment Act (No 1) 1930* (Cth) and the *Sales Tax Act (No 1) 1930* (Cth), sales tax was imposed upon the sale value of goods manufactured in Australia. The tax was payable by the manufacturer. Section 20(h) of the *Sales Tax Assessment Act (No 1) 1930* provided that sales tax was *not* payable under that Act upon the sale value of the goods specified in the First Schedule. The schedule included the following: 'Pastry but not including cakes or biscuits.'

The appellant manufactured a class of goods described in a return to the Commissioner of Taxation as 'sponge'. It was described as a 'mixture of eggs, sugar, flour, and water, and is baked either in round tins or as oblong blocks'.[84] The appellant claimed that the sponge was 'pastry' within the exemption and was not cake or biscuits.

The first question was whether a sponge was generally not liable to sales tax by reason it was 'pastry'. Starke J held that there was no difference between the commercial understanding and common speech as regards the meaning of 'pastry'.[85] But three other members of the High Court (Rich, Dixon and McTiernan JJ) differed. They thought that there was an issue as to whether the legislature had used the word in its ordinary or technical sense. Dixon J (with whom Rich J agreed[86]) observed that in its popular meaning pastry would *not* include cakes or biscuits.[87] His Honour was assisted by evidence that showed that in the pastry cook trade pastry had a wider meaning than its popular meaning: 'It appears, however, both from the evidence of witnesses and from trade manuals and text-books that among pastry-cooks the word "pastry" is used as a general expression describing most of the products of their art.'[88]

---

78 *Whitton v Falkiner* (1915) 20 CLR 118, 127 (Isaacs J).

79 *Re Royce; Ex parte MacKaness and Avery Pty Ltd* (1943) 43 SR (NSW) 239, 244 (Jordan CJ).

80 *Herbert Adams Pty Ltd v Federal Commissioner of Taxation* (1932) 47 CLR 222, 229 (Dixon J, Rich J agreeing at 225). But the evidence of one, uncontradicted expert witness may be sufficient: *Clegg v Western Australia (No 2)* (2017) 265 A Crim R 201, 203 [3], 215 [77] (the Court).

81 *Phoenix Commercial Enterprises Pty Ltd v City of Canada Bay Council* [2010] NSWCA 64, [175] (Campbell JA, Spigelman CJ generally agreeing at [1].

82 For an illustration of the interpretation of terms ('offer' and 'accepts') that had previously acquired a legal meaning, see *Kingsley's Chicken Pty Ltd v Queensland Investment Corporation* [2006] ACTCA 9.

83 (1932) 47 CLR 222.

84 Ibid 225 (Starke J).

85 Ibid 226.

86 Ibid 225.

87 Ibid 227 (Dixon J, Rich J agreeing at 225).

88 Ibid.

This evidence raised the presumption that the word 'pastry' carried its technical meaning, but it did not determine the issue of whether the word carried its ordinary or technical meaning. Dixon J looked to the legislation and aids of interpretation to determine the legal meaning. He concluded that 'the Legislature has expressed itself in a manner which amounts to a recognition, if not an adoption, of the trade meaning'.[89] Two factors were influential. The first was *noscitur a sociis* (discussed below in **[18.7]**). The non-inclusion of 'cakes or biscuits' in the 'pastry' exception indicated that 'pastry' did not carry its popular meaning.[90] The second was the statutory context: 'A revenue law directed to commerce usually employs the descriptions and adopts the meanings in use among those who exercise the trade concerned.'[91]

On the second question, whether the sponge was a 'cake', trade usage was again relied on to press the issue.[92] But this time the evidence was insufficient to raise the presumption.[93] His Honour also observed that, in any case, the legislation was not expressed in such a form as to show, as it had done with 'pastry', that a specialised meaning was intended.[94]

In conclusion, while sponge was provisionally excluded from liability to sales tax by reason that, according to its technical meaning, it was 'pastry', it was in the end not excluded by reason that it fell within the provision for 'cakes'.

Canons that relate to other aspects of the provision

[18.7] The immediate context is an indication of meaning: *noscitur a sociis*

This canon stipulates that '[w]ords may be known by the company they keep'.[95] Put another way, it is 'a maxim pointing to immediate context as an indication of meaning'.[96] It holds that 'a statutory provision should be read and construed as a whole and not as a series of isolated words'.[97] The canon is illustrated in a number of cases, including the one presented in **Example 18.5**.[98]

89 Ibid. McTiernan J agreed with Dixon and Rich JJ that the word 'pastry' carried its wider, technical meaning: at 230.

90 Ibid 228 (Dixon J, Rich J agreeing at 225). McTiernan J took a similar approach at 230. The reason appears to be this: if the word 'pastry' carried its narrower, ordinary meaning, the exclusions of cakes and biscuits would not have been necessary. Therefore (applying the presumption against surplusage – see **[18.3]**), the exclusion was consistent with a broader meaning of 'pastry'.

91 Ibid 227.

92 Ibid 228.

93 Ibid 229.

94 Ibid 228.

95 *Benggong v Bougainville Copper Pty Ltd* (1971) 124 CLR 47, 58 (Windeyer J). See also *Deputy Commissioner of Taxation v Dick* (2007) 242 ALR 152, 154 [12] (Spigelman CJ).

96 *Pac-Rim Printing Pty Ltd v Australian Postal Corporation* (2000) 97 FCR 445, 450 [14] (the Court).

97 *Australian Securities and Investments Commission v Westpac Securities Administration Ltd* (2019) 272 FCR 170, 247 [332] (O'Bryan J).

98 For an additional illustration, see *Pac-Rim Printing Pty Ltd v Australian Postal Corporation* (2000) 97 FCR 445, 450 [14], 451 [17] (the Court).

Example 18.5 *Collett v Repatriation Commission*[99]

As recounted in a previous chapter (**Example 6.1**), the appellant former soldier spent approximately two hours near a beach in Greece after his unit surrendered to the German forces during World War II. The advance elements of the enemy forces bypassed the appellant's unit during this time. After that period, the appellant, with two others, bravely escaped the surrender area, eventually finding safety. Much later, after the passing of the *Social Security and Veterans' Affairs Legislation Amendment (One-off Payments and Other 2007 Budget Measures) Act 2007* (Cth), the appellant (now nearing 100 years of age) applied for compensation under the Act. To be entitled he had to be relevantly 'interned by the military forces of an enemy State at any time during the designated war period': sch 5 item 2(1)(b).

The meaning of 'interned' was the issue. That word was defined in item 1 of sch 5. The definition relevantly provided:

> **interned** means:
>
> (a) confined in a camp, building, prison, cave or *other place* (including a vehicle) . . .[100]

The appeal to the Federal Court from a decision of the Administrative Appeals Tribunal turned on the meaning of 'other place'. The Repatriation Commission argued that 'other place' must fit the genus of the specific places mentioned.[101] The veteran argued that it was not necessary for a person to have been physically confined.[102]

The Court found that '[t]he construction of the alternative "or other place" in para (a) of the definition offers a paradigm example of the utility of the statutory interpretation maxims *noscitur a sociis* and *ejusdem generis*'.[103] The first-mentioned canon was evident in a number of ways, including the way the Court drew on the words 'confined in' in the relevant paragraph. It held that each of the places in para (a) of the definition of 'interned', including the critical words 'other place', were 'governed by the verb "confined" and the preposition "in"'.[104] The word 'confined' itself suggested an actual physical restriction.[105] After a thorough examination of other aspects of the provision at issue and its context, the Court found that 'other place' connoted physical confinement.[106] The surrender area was not an 'other place'[107] and the veteran was not entitled to compensation.

General words at the end of a list of specific items may be restricted to the same genus as the specific items: *ejusdem generis* [18.8]

The *ejusdem generis* canon is a subcategory of *noscitur a sociis*.[108] The canon specifies that 'where there are general words following particular or specific words, the general words should be

99 (2009) 178 FCR 39.

100 Emphasis added.

101 *Collett v Repatriation Commission* (2009) 178 FCR 39, 49 [36] (Logan J).

102 Ibid 43 [12].

103 Ibid 47 [29]. *Ejusdem generis* is considered below at **[18.8]**.

104 Ibid 47 [30].

105 Ibid.

106 Ibid 48 [33].

107 Ibid 49 [36].

108 *Brighton v Australia and New Zealand Banking Group Ltd* [2011] NSWCA 152, [96] (Campbell JA, Giles JA agreeing at [1], Hodgson JA agreeing at [2]); *Deputy Commissioner of Taxation v Dick* (2007) 242 ALR 152, 154 [13] (Spigelman CJ).

confined to things of the same kind as those specified'.[109] But before the canon can be applied it is necessary to identify some class or genus that comprehends the specific cases for which provision is made.[110] In other words, 'it must appear that the specified things "possess some common and dominant feature" so that they can be described as constituting a genus distinguished by that feature'.[111] A further requirement is that there is 'a reference to two or more specifics before the general expression',[112] for 'it is trite law that one species cannot make a genus for the purpose of the ejusdem generis rule'.[113]

The greater the number of specific items that are enumerated, the easier it will be to find a genus.[114] While the canon has been applied in a number of cases, including the one presented in **Example 18.6**,[115] it may not be possible to find a genus. In that case the canon is not applied.[116]

Example 18.6 *Collett v Repatriation Commission*[117]

The *Collett* case described above (**Example 18.5**) also illustrates the *ejusdem generis* canon of construction. It will be recalled that the case for compensation turned on the scope of 'interned' in item 2(1)(b) of sch 5 of the *Social Security and Veterans' Affairs Legislation Amendment (One-off Payments and Other 2007 Budget Measures) Act 2007* (Cth). Item 1 of sch 5 relevantly defined the word as follows:

> **interned** means:
>
> (a) confined in a camp, building, prison, cave or other place (including a vehicle) ...

The words in question were 'other place'. The Court held that the case was a paradigm case also for the application of *ejusdem generis*.[118] It explained:

> 'Or other place' takes its meaning from its context and its meaning is limited by the more specific words which surround it. Each of the words 'camp', 'building', 'prison', 'cave' and 'vehicle' connotes a place of confinement of definite, restrictive physical limits.[119]

109 *Cody v JH Nelson Pty Ltd* (1947) 74 CLR 629, 639 (Starke J). For similar definitions see *Prior v Sherwood* (1906) 3 CLR 1054, 1072 (Barton J); *R v Regos* (1947) 74 CLR 613, 623 (Latham CJ, McTiernan J agreeing at 628); *Brighton v Australia and New Zealand Banking Group Ltd* [2011] NSWCA 152, [96] (Campbell JA, Giles JA agreeing at [1], Hodgson JA agreeing at [2]); *Simeon Wines Ltd v Bobos* [2004] NSWCA 342, [17] (Sheller JA, Santow JA agreeing at [31], Young CJ in Eq agreeing at [32]).

110 *R v Regos* (1947) 74 CLR 613, 623 (Latham CJ, McTiernan J agreeing at 628); *Brighton v Australia and New Zealand Banking Group Ltd* [2011] NSWCA 152, [96] (Campbell JA, Giles JA agreeing at [1], Hodgson JA agreeing at [2]).

111 *R v Regos* (1947) 74 CLR 613, 624 (Latham CJ, McTiernan J agreeing at 628). This holding was applied in *Palumpa Station Pty Ltd v Fox* (1999) 132 NTR 1, 6 [21] (Bailey J) and the latter case was followed in this respect in *Murwangi Community Aboriginal Corporation v Caroll* (2001) 166 FLR 247, 251–2 [22] (Thomas J).

112 *DPP v Williams* (1998) 28 MVR 521, 526 [16] (Smith J).

113 *R v Perry (No 3)* (1981) 28 SASR 112, 116 (Cox J).

114 *Prabowo v Republic of Indonesia* (1995) 61 FCR 258, 265 (Hill J).

115 See also *Prior v Sherwood* (1906) 3 CLR 1054, 1072–3, 1077, 1082 (Barton J), 1085 (O'Connor J).

116 *Van Heerden v Hawkins* [2016] WASCA 42, [114] (Buss JA).

117 (2009) 178 FCR 39.

118 Ibid 47 [29] (Logan J).

119 Ibid.

For this and other reasons 'other place' was read as a place of definite, restrictive physical limits.[120] As the surrender area did not qualify,[121] the veteran was not entitled to compensation.

Distinct matters with particular objects are assigned distributively: *reddendo singula singulis* [18.9]

This canon means, in short, 'render each to each'.[122] It provides for a 'distributive interpretation', whereby 'particular phrases are to be read so as to relate to their particular objects'.[123] A more full description is given by Lord Millett: 'This [principle] simply means that, when plurals are broken down, each singular component must be attributed to its respective singular and not to every other possible singular.'[124]

An example is in the following subsection:

> Where a person having bought or agreed to buy goods obtains, with the consent of the seller, possession of the goods or the documents of title to the goods, the *delivery* or *transfer* by that person, or by a mercantile agent acting for him, of the *goods* or *documents of title* . . .[125]

'[D]elivery or transfer . . . of the goods or documents of title' is read as if it stated 'delivery of the goods, or transfer of the documents of title'.[126]

Another example pertains to the paragraph below:

> [A] person shall not, within an airport, . . .
>
> (a) *sell*, for delivery within the airport, or *supply*, any *goods* or *services*; . . .[127]

Applying the canon, para (a) is read as if it stated that a person shall not 'sell any goods or supply any services'.[128]

Like other 'rules' of construction, it is not applied if to do so would not 'bring out the intended effect' of the legislation in question.[129]

---

120 Ibid 48 [33].

121 Ibid 49 [36].

122 *Besmaw Pty Ltd v Sutherland Shire Council* (2003) 127 LGERA 413, 433 [98] (Talbot J).

123 *Schenker & Co (Aust) Pty Ltd v Maplas Equipment and Services Pty Ltd* [1990] VR 834, 841 (McGarvie J, Kaye J agreeing at 835, Ormiston J substantially agreeing at 850) (footnote omitted).

124 *AIB Group (UK) Ltd v Martin* [2002] 1 WLR 94, 98–9 [16] (dissenting as to outcome). Though disagreeing on the construction, Lord Rodger agreed on the value of the canon at 104 [47], as did Lord Irvine LC at 95 [1].

125 *Sale of Goods Act 1895* (SA) s 25(2) (emphasis added).

126 *Reed v Motors Ltd* [1926] SASR 128, 137 (Napier J) (reversed on other grounds in [1926] SASR 128).

127 *Airports (Business Concessions) Act 1959* (Cth) s 7(1) (emphasis added).

128 *Commonwealth v Sterling Nicholas Duty Free Pty Ltd* (1972) 126 CLR 297, 313 (Windeyer J) (dissenting as to outcome).

129 *AIB Group (UK) Ltd v Martin* [2002] 1 WLR 94, 104 [47] (Lord Rodger, Lord Hutton agreeing at 95 [3]).

Canons that relate to the use of other relevant provisions

[18.10] An affirmative catalogue excludes every other case: *expressio unius est exclusio alterius*

The maxim *expressio unius est exclusio alterius* 'treats the express mention of one thing as indicating the exclusion of another'.[130] The canon needs a brief elaboration. First, the exclusion that the canon speaks of is implied.[131] Second, the implication relates to the catalogue or class that is expressly enumerated. As Kirby J explains, 'an affirmative catalogue necessarily excludes every other case'.[132] Bell and Engle are also helpful in this regard. They define the canon similarly: '[M]ention of one or more things of a particular class may be regarded as by implication excluding all other members of the class'.[133]

The courts often sound warnings about this presumption; for example:

> That maxim must always be applied with care, for it is not of universal application and applies only when the intention it expresses is discoverable upon the face of the instrument. It is 'a valuable servant, but a dangerous master'.[134]

The reason for the warning is that '[t]he failure to make the "expressio" complete very often arises from accident, very often from the fact that it never struck the draftsman that the thing supposed to be excluded needed specific mention of any kind'.[135]

In giving weight to the canon, factors a court will take into account include:

- the precision in the drafting;
- the similarity of the subject matter in the provisions being considered; and
- the extent to which the Act has been amended, since extensive alteration of the statute increases the risk of provisions being inconsistent unintentionally.[136]

---

130 *Spence v Queensland* (2019) 268 CLR 355, 490 [302] (Edelman J, dissenting as to outcome).

131 *Maurici v Chief Commissioner of State Revenue* (2001) 51 NSWLR 673, 679 [11] (Handley JA, Beazley JA agreeing at 688 [62], Giles JA agreeing at 688 [63]; *Canty v Deputy Commissioner of Taxation* (2005) 63 NSWLR 152, 163 [66] (Handley JA, Beazley JA agreeing at 165 [81], Santow JA agreeing at 165 [82]).

132 *Ruhani v Director of Police* (2005) 222 CLR 489, 547 [180].

133 John Bell and George Engle, *Cross: Statutory Interpretation* (Oxford University Press, 3rd ed, 2005) 140.

134 *Houssein v Under Secretary, Department of Industrial Relations and Technology NSW* (1982) 148 CLR 88, 94 (the Court) (citations omitted).

135 *Colquhoun v Brooks* (1887) 19 QBD 400, 406 (Wills J). This statement has been approved in a number of judgments, including *Rylands Brothers (Australia) Ltd v Morgan* (1927) 27 SR (NSW) 161, 169 (Long Innes J) (reversed on appeal on other grounds in *Morgan v Rylands Brothers (Australia) Ltd* (1927) 39 CLR 517); *Benning v Sydney City Council* (1958) 100 CLR 177, 196 (Fullagar J) (dissenting as to outcome); *Ross v Consumer, Trading and Tenancy Tribunal of NSW* [2003] NSWSC 218, [35] (Harrison M); *Australian Municipal, Administrative, Clerical and Services Union v Commonwealth* [2018] FWCFB 1170, [62] (the Commission).

136 *Farnell v Chanbua* (2016) 56 Fam LR 84, 140 [288] (Thackray CJ) (citations omitted). The last factor was particularly evident in *Pavic v Magistrates Court (Vic)* (2003) 140 A Crim R 113. The Court referred to how 'the random and disparate nature of the amendments which have been made to the subdivision over its history renders problematical any idea of unifying principle or drafting practice sufficient to generate an implication of *expressio unius personae vel rei, est exclusio alterius*': at 117 [14] (Nettle J).

Example 18.7 *CAG v Public Trustee of Queensland*[137]

The facts of this case were set out above at **[18.2]**. The case dealt with the interpretation of s 283 of the *Property Law Act 1974* (Qld) ('the Act'). In agreeing with the primary judge's conclusion in favour of the respondent, the first, and one of the primary, reasons given by the Court of Appeal was based on *expressio unius est exclusio alterius*. The Court drew inferences based on s 315 of the Act:

> **Effect on proceeding of death of party**
>
> If a party to a proceeding for a property adjustment order dies before a final order has been made, a court may make an order if it considers –
>
> (a) it would have adjusted interests in property if the deceased party had not died; and
> (b) it is still appropriate to adjust the interests despite the death of the deceased party.

The primary judge had applied the *expressio unius canon*, stating:

> An obvious conclusion to be drawn from the form of [s 315] is that the power in the court to make an order where a de facto partner dies exists only if that partner was already a party to a proceeding commenced while he or she was still alive.[138]

Of course, the express reference in s 315 to 'party to a proceeding . . . dies before a final order has been made' assumed the applicant for the order was a party to the proceeding before the death. Applying the *expressio unius* canon, the Court of Appeal agreed with the primary judge that s 315 had 'negative implications' for s 283:[139] the applicant could *not* apply after the death of the partner, *except* as provided in s 315. In other words, s 315 pointed to s 283 presupposing that each of the parties was alive at the time of the application.[140]

No implication is to be made on a topic with respect to which provision has been made: *expressum facit cessare tacitum* [18.11]

The canon *expressum facit cessare tacitum* is closely related to *expressio unius*.[141] The former has been described as an 'aspect' and a 'restatement'[142] of the latter.[143] The *expressum facit* maxim states that 'where there is specific statutory provision on a topic there is no room for implication of any further matter on that same topic'.[144] The canon 'only bites where what is expressed is co-

137 [2008] 2 Qd R 419.

138 As quoted in ibid 423 [13] (Keane JA, de Jersey CJ agreeing at 420 [1], Fraser JA agreeing at 431 [32]).

139 Ibid 428 [18].

140 Ibid 428 [19].

141 *Australian Capital Television Pty Ltd v Commonwealth* (1992) 177 CLR 106, 213 (Gaudron J, Deane and Toohey JJ agreeing at 169).

142 *DPP v Leys* (2012) 44 VR 1, 53 n 239 (the Court).

143 *Kelly v Saadat-Talab* (2008) 72 NSWLR 305, 310 [13] (Allsop P, Ipp J agreeing at 314 [31]).

144 *John v Commissioner of Taxation (Cth)* (1989) 166 CLR 417, 434 (Mason CJ, Wilson, Dawson, Toohey and Gaudron JJ). For similar statements, see *Australian Capital Television Pty Ltd v Commonwealth* (1992) 177 CLR 106, 213 (Gaudron J, Deane and Toohey JJ agreeing at 169); *R v Mitchell* [2008] 2 Qd R 142, 154 [47] (Keane JA, Williams JA agreeing at 152 [37], Mullins J agreeing at 157 [60]); *Lednar v Magistrates' Court* (2000) 117 A Crim R 396, 432 [321] (Gillard J).

extensive in ambit with what would otherwise be implied'.[145] Or, put another way, the canon applies when the implication would be 'directly contradictory of the terms that are expressed'.[146]

An application of the *expressum facit* maxim is the 'Anthony Hordern principle'.[147] In *Anthony Hordern and Sons Ltd v Amalgamated Clothing and Allied Trades Union of Australia*[148] Gavan Duffy CJ and Dixon J held:

> When the Legislature explicitly gives a power by a particular provision which prescribes the mode in which it shall be exercised and the conditions and restrictions which must be observed, it excludes the operation of general expressions in the same instrument which might otherwise have been relied upon for the same power.[149]

Example 18.8 *United Firefighters' Union of Australia v Victorian Equal Opportunity and Human Rights Commission*[150]

The Secretary to the Department of Justice and Regulation of Victoria wrote to the Victorian Equal Opportunity and Human Rights Commission 'regarding behavioural issues and increasing workforce diversity within the Country Fire Authority and the Metropolitan Fire and Emergency Services Board'. The letter contained a request, purportedly pursuant to certain provisions of the *Equal Opportunity Act 2010* (Vic) ('the Act'):

> The government requests the [Commission] to undertake a review under section 151 of the [Act] and section 41(c) of the [Charter]. This would include any relevant research in accordance with [the Commission's] function under s 157 of the [Act].

The United Firefighters' Union of Australia raised concerns about the proposed review. In the first place it contended the review was not authorised under s 151 of the Act. That provision stated:

> **151 Commission may conduct review of compliance**
>
> (1) On request of *a person*, the Commission may enter into an agreement with *the person* to review *that person's* programs and practices to determine their compliance with this Act.
>
> ...
>
> (2) If, after undertaking a review, the Commission gives *the person* advice about whether programs or practices are compliant with this Act, the giving of that advice does not give rise to –
>
> (a) any liability of, or other claim against, the Commission; or

145 *Macari v Celtic Football and Athletic Co Ltd* [1999] SC 628, 653 (Lord Marnoch).

146 *Mars Pension Trustees Ltd v County Properties and Developments Ltd* [1999] SC 267, 270 (Lord Prosser) (footnote omitted).

147 *Plaintiff M70/2011 v Minister for Immigration and Citizenship* (2011) 244 CLR 144, 177 [50] (French CJ); *United Firefighters' Union of Australia v Victorian Equal Opportunity and Human Rights Commission* [2018] VSCA 252, [152] (Tate JA) (dissenting as to outcome).

148 (1932) 47 CLR 1.

149 Ibid 7 (Gavan Duffy CJ and Dixon J).

150 [2018] VSCA 252.

(b) any right, expectation, duty or obligation that would not otherwise be conferred or imposed on *the person* who has been given the advice; or

(c) any defence that would not otherwise be available to *that person*.[151]

The Union argued that the programs and practice to be reviewed were those of the Country Fire Authority ('CFA') and the Metropolitan Fire and Emergency Services Board ('MFB'), and as they had not requested the review, the review was not authorised by s 151.

It was common ground that the phrases 'a person', 'the person' and 'that person' in s 151(1) and (2) all referred to the same person. Nevertheless, the Secretary argued that this requirement was satisfied as the programs and practices of the MFB and the CFA were programs and practices of the 'Executive Government' of Victoria (in other words, the state government). As the Secretary had requested the review, it followed, so the argument ran, that the review was a review of the programs and practice of the person who had made the request of the Commission.

The Court of Appeal of the Supreme Court of Victoria unanimously disagreed. It held that where the review was of the employment practices of independent legal entities (here the MFB and the CFA), the employment practices could not be characterised as the programs and practices of any other legal person. Therefore, the review was not authorised under s 151.[152]

The Secretary then put the alternative argument that the review was authorised by s 157 of the Act. That provision read:

(1) The Commission may undertake research into any matter arising from, or incidental to, the operation of this Act that it considers would advance the objectives of this Act.

(2) The Commission may collect and analyse data relevant to the operation and the objectives of this Act.

Invoking the Anthony Hordern doctrine,[153] the majority of the Court of Appeal held that s 157 did not authorise the review.[154] In the terms of that doctrine, s 151 was 'a power . . . which prescribes the mode in which it shall be exercised and the conditions and restrictions which must be observed'. The condition that s 151 prescribed was that the employer whose compliance with the Act is to be reviewed must have requested the review. Section 157, on the other hand, was a general expression in the same instrument. Therefore, it was held, '[o]n well-established principles, a general power like s 157 cannot be relied on to authorise a compliance review free of that condition'.[155] In other words, the statute 'confers only one power to take the relevant action', and that was s 151.[156]

151 Emphases added by Maxwell P and Priest JA.

152 [2018] VSCA 252, [56], [61] (Maxwell P and Priest JA), [90] (Tate JA).

153 Ibid [79] n 27 (Maxwell P and Priest JA).

154 Ibid [76], [79], [83] (Maxwell P and Priest JA). Tate JA dissented at [91].

155 Ibid [79].

156 Ibid, quoting *Minister for Immigration and Multicultural and Indigenous Affairs v Nystrom* (2006) 228 CLR 566, 589 [59] (Gummow and Hayne JJ).

[18.12] It is presumed that in a statute the same word is used with the same meaning

An 'essential ingredient' of legislative drafting is consistency,[157] including consistency in the use of language.[158] The use of the same words in a statute attracts a presumption: '[A]ccording to ordinary canons of statutory construction, an Act must be construed so far as possible to give the same meaning to the same words wherever those words appear in the statute.'[159]

The presumption is stronger where a provision in the same Act 'serves similar purposes and uses identical or substantially similar language'.[160] So, for example, if provisions 'overlap', that strengthens the presumption.[161] Also, if the words share a common legislative history, the presumption will be stronger.[162] But the presumption 'readily yields to the context';[163] 'it is "only a presumption"'.[164] For example, 'the presumption has little force in Income Tax Acts because they deal with a wide variety of topics'.[165] It is even possible and 'well recognized that a word may be used in two different senses in the same section of the one Act'.[166]

Example 18.9 *CAG v Public Trustee of Queensland*[167]

The facts of this case were set out above at **Example 18.2**. It will be recalled that the case concerned the meaning of s 283 of the *Property Law Act 1974* (Qld) ('the Act'):

> After a de facto relationship has ended, a de facto partner may apply to a court for an order adjusting interests in the property of either or both of the de facto partners.

The central question was whether the applicant could apply under this section for an order adjusting interests in the property of a de facto partner who had died prior to the application being made. This entailed ascertaining the meaning of the reference to 'de facto partners'. The

157 Eamonn Moran, 'The Coherence of Statutory Interpretation: Drafting Perspectives' in Jeffrey Barnes (ed), *The Coherence of Statutory Interpretation* (Federation Press, 2019) 50, 56.

158 Ibid 51.

159 *Firebird Global Master Fund II Ltd v Republic of Nauru* (2015) 258 CLR 31, 86 [190] (Nettle and Gordon JJ) (citations omitted). For similar statements see *Regional Express Holdings Ltd v Australian Federation of Air Pilots* (2017) 262 CLR 456, 467 [21], 468 [25] (the Court); *Tabcorp Holdings Ltd v Victoria* (2016) 328 ALR 375, 389 [65] (the Court); *Commissioner of Taxation (Cth) v Australian Building Systems Pty Ltd (in liq)* (2015) 257 CLR 544, 560 [27] (French CJ and Kiefel J); *Registrar of Titles (WA) v Franzon* (1975) 132 CLR 611, 618 (Mason J); *Gibson and Howes Ltd v Lennon* (1917) 24 CLR 140, 148 (Barton J); *Federated Engine-Drivers & Firemen's Association of Australasia v Broken Hill Pty Co Ltd* (1911) 12 CLR 398, 417 (Barton J).

160 *Commissioner of Taxation (Cth) v Australian Building Systems Pty Ltd (in liq)* (2015) 257 CLR 544, 560 [27] (French CJ and Kiefel J).

161 *Svikart v Stewart* (1994) 181 CLR 548, 580 (Gaudron J) (a case on the *Australian Constitution*).

162 *Commissioner of Taxation (Cth) v Australian Building Systems Pty Ltd (in liq)* (2015) 257 CLR 544, 560–1 [27] (French CJ and Kiefel J).

163 Ibid 560 [27] (French CJ and Kiefel J), quoting *Clyne v Deputy Commissioner of Taxation* (1981) 150 CLR 1, 15 (Mason J, with whom Aickin and Wilson JJ agreed).

164 *McGraw-Hinds (Aust) Pty Ltd v Smith* (1979) 144 CLR 633, 643 (Gibbs J), quoting *Littlewoods Mail Order Stores Ltd v Inland Revenue Commissioners* [1963] AC 135, 159.

165 *Commissioner of Taxation (Cth) v Australian Building Systems Pty Ltd (in liq)* (2015) 257 CLR 544, 560 [27] (French CJ and Kiefel J).

166 *McGraw-Hinds (Aust) Pty Ltd v Smith* (1979) 144 CLR 633, 643 (Gibbs J).

167 [2008] 2 Qd R 419.

Court considered the 'same word, same meaning' presumption. It first observed that 'de facto partner', when first mentioned in the section, had a clear meaning:

> It is impossible to suppose that the right to apply conferred on a de facto partner by s 283 of the Act could be exercisable by the estate of a deceased de facto partner; and CAG's counsel did not suggest otherwise. The reference to the right of a de facto partner to apply under s 283 of the Act must be to a living de facto partner.[168]

It then applied the presumption: 'There is no reason evident from the text of the Act to treat the later reference in s 283 to de facto partners as having a different and more expansive meaning encompassing deceased de facto partners.' [169]

Parliament is taken to have intended different meanings when it has used different words[170] [18.13]

Logically complementing the 'same word, same meaning' presumption[171] is a presumption that 'the legislature [intends] different words . . . to have different meanings'.[172] The presumption is also a logical extension of the presumption against surplusage.[173]

The present presumption is applicable even if the words appear similar.[174] Indeed, the presumption is all the more important in such a case, since it counters the tendency to conflate the meanings of similar, but different, words.

General provisions do not detract from the specific: *generalia specialibus non derogant* [18.14]

The canon *generalia specialibus non derogant* applies to intersecting laws and determines a rule of priority for them. It provides that 'a statute of general provision will not normally be taken to override one with special provisions governing the circumstances with greater particularity'.[175] The canon only applies if there is an apparent conflict – that is, '[t]he rule applies only when the

168 Ibid 429 [21] (Keane JA, de Jersey CJ agreeing at 420 [1], Fraser JA agreeing at 431 [32].

169 Ibid.

170 *Commissioner of State Revenue v Bogong Ski Club Inc* (2000) 2 VR 487, 492 [22] (Hansen J).

171 See **[18.12]** above.

172 *Renwick v Parole Board Queensland* [2019] 2 QR 645, 654 [22] (Holmes CJ, Gotterson JA agreeing at 657 [35], McMurdo JA agreeing at 657 [36]). For similar statements, see *Evans v Job* [2018] TASFC 3, [16] (Estcourt J) (dissenting as to outcome); *Lygon Nominees Pty Ltd v Commissioner of State Revenue* (2007) 23 VR 474, 482 [31] (Redlich JA, Ashley JA agreeing at 475 [1], Bell AJA agreeing at 499 [92]); *DPP (Cth) v Kamal* (2011) 248 FLR 64, 84 [67] (Martin CJ); *Commissioner of State Revenue v Bogong Ski Club Inc* (2000) 2 VR 487, 492 [22] (Hansen J).

173 *Commissioner of State Revenue v Bogong Ski Club Inc* (2000) 2 VR 487, 492 [22] (Hansen J). See **[18.3]**.

174 *Renwick v Parole Board Queensland* [2019] 2 QR 645, 654–5 [22]–[23] (Holmes CJ, Gotterson JA agreeing at 657 [35], McMurdo JA agreeing at 657 [36]) ('location' and 'place' in definition of 'victim's location' in s 193A (8) of the *Corrective Services Act 2006* (Qld)).

175 *Ferdinands v Commissioner for Public Employment* (2006) 225 CLR 130, 162 [106] (Kirby J) (dissenting as to outcome). For similar statements see *Brisbane City Council v Amos* (2019) 266 CLR 593, 612 [36] (Kiefel CJ and Edelman J, Nettle J expressing support at 382 [54]); *Smith v The Queen* (1994) 181 CLR 338, 348 (Mason CJ, Dawson, Gaudron and McHugh JJ); *Commonwealth v SCI Operations Pty Ltd* (1998) 192 CLR 285, 305 [39] (Gaudron J).

general provision would otherwise encompass the matter dealt with by the special or more limited provision'.[176] The operation of the canon has been described this way:

> Where there is a general provision which, if applied in its entirety, would neutralise a special provision dealing with the same subject matter, the special provision must be read as a proviso to the general provision, and the general provision, in so far as it is inconsistent with the special provision, must be deemed not to apply.[177]

The logic behind the principle was expressed thus: 'It is but common sense that Parliament having before it two apparently conflicting sections at the same time cannot have intended the general provision to have deprived the specific provision of effect.'[178]

It has been suggested that the rule is *only* a tie-breaker or a last resort: 'The maxim applies only where there are two inconsistent provisions which cannot be reconciled as a matter of ordinary interpretation.'[179] It has been held that it is still useful in the process of reconciliation: 'The proposition that the *generalia specialibus* maxim applies only where two provisions cannot be reconciled ... does not prevent the underlying principle being invoked when determining whether or not a conflict is in fact irreconcilable.'[180]

As mentioned, the canon is used to resolve apparent conflict between statutory provisions. For discussion of the application of the canon, see **[35.7]** and the illustrative case of *Commissioner of Police for New South Wales v Eaton*[181] (**Example 35.2**).

[18.15] An Act is to be read as a whole and consideration given to all relevant provisions

The meaning of any statutory provision must be determined 'by reference to the language of the instrument viewed as a whole'.[182] This canon therefore calls for consideration of all of the relevant provisions in the rest of the statute or legislative instrument concerned.[183] The object of ascertaining those references is to ensure, as far as possible, that the provision in question is read consistently with the rest of the document. This object in turn rests on the assumption that '[statutory] provisions are intended to give effect to harmonious goals'.[184] Reference to the Act as a whole has been described as a 'fundamental proposition'.[185]

As the principle is both far-reaching and overarching, several matters concerning the Act as a whole are dealt with elsewhere in this work. The language of the provision is the subject of

176 *Sue v Hill* (1999) 199 CLR 462, 514 [128] (Gaudron J).

177 *Goodwin v Phillips* (1908) 7 CLR 1, 14 (O'Connor J).

178 *Smith v The Queen* (1994) 181 CLR 338, 348 (Mason CJ, Dawson, Gaudron and McHugh JJ) (citation omitted).

179 *Purcell v Electricity Commission of New South Wales* (1985) 60 ALR 652, 657 (Mason ACJ, Wilson, Brennan and Dawson JJ).

180 *Ombudsman v Laughton* (2005) 64 NSWLR 114, 118 [23] (Spigelman CJ, Handley JA agreeing at 119 [28]).

181 (2013) 252 CLR 1. This case illustrates the canon in relation to apparent conflict between provisions of different statutes. For an illustration of the application of the canon in relation to apparent conflict between provisions in the one statute, see *Dolheguy v Becker* (2009) 52 MVR 462.

182 *Cooper Brookes (Wollongong) Pty Ltd v Federal Commissioner of Taxation (Cth)* (1981) 147 CLR 297, 320 (Mason and Wilson JJ), approved in *Project Blue Sky Inc v Australian Broadcasting Authority* (1998) 194 CLR 355, 381 [69] (McHugh, Gummow, Kirby and Hayne JJ).

183 *Project Blue Sky Inc v Australian Broadcasting Authority* (1998) 194 CLR 355, 381 [69] (McHugh, Gummow, Kirby and Hayne JJ).

184 Ibid 382 [70].

185 *Plaintiff M47/2012 v Director-General of Security* (2012) 251 CLR 1, 72 [162] (Hayne J).

chapter 15. The scheme and standard components of an Act, such as a definitions provision, are considered in chapter 20. Linguistic canons that draw on the Act in certain respects have been examined earlier in the present chapter. And the boundary line as to what is formally part of an Act (as distinct from other material on the face of the document) is considered in chapter 13.

Presently, the focus is on residual indications of meaning supplied by other provisions of the Act in question. Where the indications are found varies. Some indications may be found in neighbouring provisions that are part of the same legislative sentence.[186] Alternatively, an indication may be found in a different section of the Act[187] or from a synthesis of related provisions of the Act.[188]

Example 18.10 *ABC Developmental Learning Centres Pty Ltd v Secretary, Department of Human Services*[189]

As related earlier (**Example 1.2**), the plaintiff company objected to two letters sent to its head office by an authorised officer, purportedly acting under the *Children's Services Act 1996* (Vic) ('the Act'). The officer had sought answers to specific questions and the provision of certain documents. The requests arose from two alleged incidents at the plaintiff's childcare centres. The Supreme Court of Victoria determined that the provision in issue was s 36(1)(f) of the Act. It empowered an authorised officer to 'require a person . . . to answer a question to the best of that person's knowledge, information and belief'. The provision did not state that the power was to be exercised at the childcare premises. Nevertheless, the plaintiff read the provision as limited to a person who 'is actually on the licensed premises at the time of the request'.[190] The respondent department read the provision as encompassing any person at any place.[191]

The Court considered various arguments from the Act as a whole. The Department argued that it should be inferred that a general purpose of the Act was to protect young children from harm, and that Parliament would have wished departmental officers to have the widest possible powers to achieve that end.

In opposition the Court considered several provisions that favoured the plaintiff's construction. Two examples may be noticed.[192] First, the Court drew on previous paragraphs in the same subsection – that is, s 36(1)(a)–(e). As each of these paragraphs concerned a power of entry to the licensed premises, or powers upon entry of the premises, it drew the inference that '[t]hat structure tends to suggest that the power in sub-section [sic] (f) is simply another power to be exercised at premises entered pursuant to sub-section [sic] (a)'.[193] Second, the Court drew on s 41 of the Act. It

186 See **Example 18.10**.

187 See ibid.

188 For an illustration of ascertainment of legislative policy, see *Scott-Mackenzie v Bail* (2017) 16 ASTLR 449, 458–60 [37]–[45] (the Court).

189 (2007) 15 VR 489.

190 Ibid 493 [18] (Hollingworth J).

191 Ibid.

192 The Court also drew on the heading to the section in question, but this was extrinsic material: ibid 494 [25]. And it made an *expressio unius* argument based on other provisions of the Act: at 494 [29].

193 Ibid 494 [24].

provided that an authorised officer may not exercise any of the powers under div 1 of pt 5 (which included s 36) if they failed to produce, on request, their identity card 'for the inspection by the occupier of the premises'. The Court could not see how s 41 could be complied with if (as argued by the Department) the request could be made by mail, email or over the telephone. The Court inferred that the words of s 41 – 'inspection by the occupier of the premises' – provided further support for the plaintiff's construction that the power is one to be exercised at the licensed premises and is not at large. For these and other reasons the plaintiff's construction was ultimately preferred by the Court.[194]

194 Ibid 495 [32].

THE 'ALWAYS SPEAKING' APPROACH

19

Overview

Statutes often operate for many years. Yet the passage of time may mean that a statute is operating in circumstances quite different to the circumstances in which it was enacted. The question is how these changes affect the interpretation of the statute. The principle of interpretation that a statute is to be interpreted as 'always speaking' is typically invoked in this context. It provides that, where appropriate, a word or phrase in a statute is to be construed as speaking continuously in the present. This means that it may be possible for statutory text to apply to a state of affairs or a legal environment that was not known or understood at the time the statute was enacted. The potential to construe statutory text as 'always speaking' is a matter of construction. In this context courts have emphasised the distinction between the connotation, or 'essential' meaning, of text, which does not change, and its denotation, or application, which may. If the essential meaning can be expressed at a sufficiently broad level, consistent with statutory purpose, then it may apply to a class of things or a state of affairs that exists at the time of interpretation, but not at the time of enactment. The principle is not a licence to 'update' the meaning of a word or phrase in a statute, though this may be its effect. As part of the interpretative exercise, a penal provision may be approached with particular caution. [19.1]

Legislation can apply to circumstances unknown at enactment

The 'always speaking' principle is that we approach, where possible, the interpretation of statutory text as if it is speaking continuously in the present; this may enable the text to apply to a state of affairs that did not exist at the time of enactment [19.2]

The notion of the words of a statute as 'always speaking' is long established. It has been traced back to a drafting convention recommended by George Coode in 1845,[1] and then English drafter Lord Thring, in the late 19th century.[2] That drafting convention encouraged parliamentary counsel to draft statutes as speaking continuously in the present, as 'it would be most inconvenient if courts could never rely in difficult cases on the current meaning of statutes'.[3]

---

1 George Coode, *On Legislative Expression: Or, The Language of the Written Law* (William Benning and Co, 1845) 23, 66.

2 Henry Thring, *Practical Legislation: The Composition and Language of Acts of Parliament and Business Documents* (John Murray, 1902) 83. Lord Thring acknowledged the contribution of Coode: at 61. For more detail on its origins, see Chad Jacobi, *Interpretation Acts: Origins and Meaning* (Lawbook, 2019) 129–33.

3 *R v Ireland* [1998] AC 147, 158 (Lord Steyn), referring to the drafting convention.

This drafting convention appears to have morphed into a common law approach to *interpreting* statutes, so that they are 'ordinarily to be read as speaking continuously in the present'.[4] This means that 'if things not known or understood at the time an Act came into force fall, on a fair construction, within its words, those things should be held to be included'.[5] This approach has long been recognised in Australia;[6] the High Court referred to it as early as 1915.[7]

Those 'things not known or understood at the time' of enactment may include 'changes in our understanding of the natural world, technological changes, changes in social standards and ... changes in societal attitudes'.[8] It may also include legislative and common law developments (see **[19.6]**). The outcome is that the statute may be applied in a contemporary context, despite that context being different from the context in which the statute was enacted.

This common law approach is recognised in the Interpretation Acts of two Australian jurisdictions – South Australia and Western Australia.[9] The courts treat these legislative provisions as having the same effect as the common law.[10]

The principle recognises that when Parliament enacts legislation, it cannot always envisage the variety of facts that may arise; nor can it foresee how society, and laws, will evolve. Consequently, the 'metes and bounds'[11] of the application of the statute cannot always be determined. A particular issue may 'trigger' the legislation, but that does not mean that the application of the legislation is confined to that issue. For example, in *R v A2*[12] the Court was required to consider the phrase 'otherwise mutilates' in s 45(1)(a) of the *Crimes Act 1900* (NSW), which provided an offence in relation to female genital mutilation. The offence was enacted in 1994. One of the arguments of the respondents was that in 1994 there were only three practices of mutilation contemplated by Parliament, and so the application of the section should be confined to those practices. Edelman J, rejecting this argument, explained:

> [T]hose understandings of the forms of the practice should not conclusively define the scope of s 45(1)(a) ... Where legislation does not expressly delimit the scope of its application then its scope is usually to be determined by the contemporary application of its essential meaning that will best give effect to the legislative purpose. This is what is meant by statutes 'always speaking'.[13]

---

4 *Commissioner of Police for New South Wales v Eaton* (2013) 252 CLR 1, 32 [97] (Gageler J, in dissent but not on principle).

5 *Aubrey v The Queen* (2017) 260 CLR 305, 321 [29] (Kiefel CJ, Keane, Nettle and Edelman JJ); see also *BMW Australia Ltd v Brewster* (2019) 269 CLR 574, 598 [44] (Kiefel CJ, Bell and Keane JJ).

6 *Klein v Minister for Education* (2007) 81 ALJR 582, 593 [54] (Kirby J).

7 *A-G (Qld) (ex rel Goldsbrough, Mort & Co Ltd) v A-G (Cth)* (1915) 20 CLR 148, 174 (Isaacs J).

8 *BMW Australia Ltd v Brewster* (2019) 269 CLR 574, 638 [171] (Edelman J dissenting but not as to principle) citing *Owens v Owens* [2017] 4 WLR 74 [39] (Munby P).

9 *Legislation Interpretation Act 2021* (SA) s 17 (formerly *Acts Interpretation Act 1915* (SA) s 21), *Interpretation Act 1984* (WA) s 8.

10 For Western Australia see, eg, *Klein v Minister for Education* (2007) 81 ALJR 582, 593 [54] (Kirby J); *Hewitt v Benale Pty Ltd* (2002) 27 WAR 91, 98–9 [35]–[36] (Scott J). For South Australia see, eg, *Zerella Holdings Pty Ltd v Williams* (2012) 113 SASR 573, 595–6 [93]–[95] (Gray J in dissent); *National Mutual Life Association v Commissioner of State Taxation* (2011) 110 SASR 536, 565–6 [110]–[111] (Gray J, Sulan J agreeing at 576 [154], Vanstone J agreeing at 576 [155]).

11 *Stingel v Clark* (2006) 226 CLR 442, 459 [27] (Gleeson CJ, Callinan, Heydon and Crennan JJ).

12 (2019) 269 CLR 507.

13 Ibid 562 [168]–[169].

Sometimes the term 'ambulatory' (literally, 'moving about; not stationary')[14] is used interchangeably with 'always speaking'. This former term seems more appropriate as a description of the nature and character of the language that is 'always speaking,' rather than of the principle itself. This is because the term 'ambulatory' is used broadly in statutory interpretation. For example, connecting phrases such as 'in relation to' and 'in connection with' have been described as being of 'ambulatory significance' given that their range of application depends entirely on the statutory context in which they are used.[15]

The 'always speaking' approach is distinguishable from the maxim *contemporanea expositio est optima et fortissima in lege,* which now has little relevance given the contemporary approach to interpretation [19.3]

The 'always speaking' approach is distinguishable from the Latin interpretative maxim *contemporanea expositio est optima et fortissima in lege,* which provides that 'the best way of determining the meaning of an instrument is to read it in the sense in which it would have been understood when it was drawn up'.[16] This maxim is based on a search for the 'original' intent of Parliament, and is arguably more consistent with a search for the subjective intent of the legislators.[17] The maxim is difficult to reconcile with the modern approach to statutory interpretation, which eschews any consideration of the subjective intent of parliamentarians and adopts an objective approach to determining legislative intent.[18] That is probably why, in recent times, the maxim has been described as a 'dubious rule'[19] or 'largely ... abandoned'.[20] In Western Australia and South Australia, where there are legislative provisions directing an 'always speaking' approach, its relevance is highly doubtful.[21] To the extent that the maxim might still be relevant at common law, judicial commentary suggests that its use is confined to the construction 'of ambiguous language in statutes which are sufficiently old for the words to have had a previous different meaning'.[22] Speaking in 1883 about the maxim when construing an 1858 statute, Lord Watson described an 'old' statute as one of 'one or two centuries ago'![23]

The dwindling relevance of the *contemporanea expositio* maxim does not mean that statutory text is never confined to the application originally intended. As is discussed in **[19.5]**, there will be instances where the legislature has demonstrated an intent for the meaning and application of

14 *Macquarie Concise Dictionary* (7th ed, 2017) 'ambulatory.'

15 See, eg, *McHugh v Minister for Immigration, Citizenship, Migrant Services and Multicultural Affairs* (2020) 283 FCR 602, 655 [227]–[229] (Mortimer J), in part citing *Minister for Immigration and Citizenship v Haneef* (2007) 163 FCR 414, 442 [106] (Black CJ, French and Weinberg JJ).

16 *Encyclopaedic Australian Legal Dictionary* (LexisNexis, online at 15 December 2021) '*contemporanea expositio est optima et fortissima in lege*'.

17 For a discussion of the historical relationship between this maxim and the 'always speaking' approach, see Chad Jacobi, *Interpretation Acts: Origins and Meaning* (Lawbook Co, 2019) 133–9.

18 See chapter 4.

19 *Daniels Corporation International Pty Ltd v Australian Competition and Consumer Commission* (2002) 213 CLR 543, 571 [71] n 46 (Kirby J).

20 *National Mutual Life Association v Commissioner of State Taxation* (2011) 110 SASR 536, 566 [111] (Gray J, Sulan J agreeing at 576 [154], Vanstone J agreeing at 576 [155]).

21 Ibid.

22 *Babaniaris v Lutony Fashions Pty Ltd* (1987) 163 CLR 1, 23 (Wilson and Dawson JJ).

23 *Laird v Trustees of Clyde Navigation* (1883) 8 App Cas 658, 673 (Lord Watson). Cf *Sonnet v The Queen* (2010) 30 VR 519, 532 [48] (the Court) where the maxim was considered for a 1958 Act.

the words to be confined to that envisaged at enactment.[24] But this is an outcome of the interpretative process, rather than an application of the maxim. Accordingly, perhaps the better view is that the application of the maxim is confined to 'ancient' statutes, but contemporary interpretation law can have a similar outcome.

Distinguish connotation from denotation

[19.4] **The 'always speaking' approach does not automatically permit an application of the statute to contemporary circumstances; first the essential meaning (connotation) of the text must be determined and then its application to contemporary circumstances considered**

Characterisation of the 'always speaking' principle as a rebuttable presumption, is

> apt to mislead. What it bespeaks is an exercise in statutory interpretation which seeks to discern what is called the intention of the legislature in enacting the specific provision, having regard to its context, scope and purpose.[25]

Whether statutory text can be construed as applying to a new state of affairs must be determined by the principles of interpretation. To determine whether text is ambulatory, courts highlight the distinction between meaning and application. More specifically, they refer to the difference between the connotation, or 'essential meaning',[26] of the word and the denotation of the word.

Use of labels such as connotation and 'essential meaning' are not in themselves overly helpful. To borrow an explanation from constitutional law, the connotation is essentially the meaning of the word – the 'qualities and only those qualities that a thing must have in order to come within the term'.[27] It might be described as the 'essential attributes'[28] of the word.

In contrast, the denotation of a word

> is the class of things that, from time to time, may be seen to possess those essential attributes sufficiently to justify the application of the word or phrase to them.[29]

The decision of *Lake Macquarie Shire Council v Aberdare County Council*[30] is often cited as an example of the connotation/denotation distinction. The High Court considered the word 'gas' in

---

24 *National Mutual Life Association v Commissioner of State Taxation* (2011) 110 SASR 536, 566 [111] (Gray J, Sulan J agreeing at 576 [154], Vanstone J agreeing at 576 [155]).

25 *Forsyth v Deputy Commissioner of Taxation* (2007) 231 CLR 531, 548 [39] (Gleeson CJ, Gummow, Hayne, Callinan, Heydon and Crennan JJ). See also *Hore v Albury Radio Taxis Co-operative Society Ltd* (2002) 56 NSWLR 210, 223 [43] (Campbell J). The precise role of the principle in the context of the modern approach to interpretation has been queried: see Jacinta Dharmananda, 'The 'Always Speaking' Principle: Not Always Needed?' (2017) 28(3) *Public Law Review* 199. See also Neal Goldfarb, '"Always Speaking?" Interpreting the Present Tense in Statutes' (2013) 58(1) *Canadian Journal of Linguistics* 63.

26 *R v A2* (2019) 269 CLR 507, 563 [170]–[171] (Edelman J); *BMW Australia Ltd v Brewster* (2019) 269 CLR 574, 638 [171] (Edelman J); *Singh v Commonwealth* (2004) 222 CLR 322, 343 [38] (McHugh J dissenting) in a constitutional context.

27 James Stellios, *Zines's the High Court and the Constitution* (Federation Press, 6th ed, 2015) 19.

28 *Chubb Insurance Co of Australia Ltd v Moore* (2013) 302 ALR 101, 119 [82] (Emmett JA and Ball J; Bathurst CJ, Beazley P and Macfarlan JA agreeing 103–4).

29 Ibid.

30 (1970) 123 CLR 327.

NSW legislation. When the legislation was enacted the only 'gas' known to Parliament for lighting and heating was coal gas. The issue was whether the more recently available liquid petroleum gas could be 'gas'. Barwick CJ explained that while 'the connotation of the word "gas" will be fixed' its denotation can change with changing technologies and so could apply to a gas not known at the time of enactment.[31]

Determining the essential meaning, or connotation, of text is therefore critical to determining whether the text is always speaking and the extent to which it can apply to previously unknown circumstances.

Example 19.1 *Uber BV v Federal Commissioner of Taxation*[32]

The issue was whether an uberX driver had to be registered for GST purposes under s 144-5 of the *A New Tax System (Goods and Services Tax) Act 1999* (Cth) (the 'GST Act'). Section 144-5(1) of div 144 of pt 4-5 of the GST Act required people who supplied 'taxi travel' to be registered. Section 195-1 defined 'taxi travel' as meaning 'travel that involves transporting passengers, by taxi or limousine, for fares'.

Uber BV argued that the GST Act was intended to target a specific industry – namely, the taxi industry or 'taxi operators' – and not a new service, known as 'ridesharing', that did have the core characteristics of a 'taxi'.[33]

Griffiths J determined that the meaning of the word 'taxi' was 'a vehicle available for hire by the public and which transports a passenger at his or her direction for the payment of a fare'.[34] His Honour rejected various arguments about the 'essential characteristics' of the word 'taxi'.[35] In particular, while acknowledging that a fare will often be calculated by reference to a taximeter, he did not consider this 'an essential aspect' of the meaning of 'taxi' that a vehicle must have such a device.[36] Consequently, as the GST Act provisions are 'always speaking',

> merely because software technology of the type used in providing the uberX service may not have been known at the time that Div 144 was inserted into Pt 4-5 of the GST Act is not determinative.[37]

His Honour concluded that the uberX driver was suppling 'taxi travel' and so had to be registered for GST purposes.

---

31 Ibid 331. A more recent acknowledgement of the denotation/connotation distinction is *Aubrey v The Queen* (2017) 260 CLR 305 321–2 [29] (Kiefel CJ, Keane, Nettle and Edelman JJ). For further High Court examples, see James Edelman, '2018 Winterton Lecture Constitutional Interpretation' (2019) 45(1) *University of Western Australia Law Review* 1, 17–18 n 68.

32 (2017) 247 FCR 462.

33 Ibid 480 [70]–[71].

34 Ibid 497 [135].

35 Ibid 497–8 [138].

36 Ibid 497 [135] [138].

37 Ibid 494 [130].

[19.5] **The higher the level of generality of the text, the greater the possibility that the essential meaning can be expressed at a broad level and so may apply to changed circumstances; conversely, the more specific the language, the narrower the scope of application**

The extent to which the essential meaning can be expressed broadly is critical to its capacity to speak continuously in the present. There are various judicial formulations of the level of expression required: 'a high level of generality',[38] of 'indeterminate scope',[39] 'open textured'[40] 'sufficiently wide'[41] and having a 'generic sense'[42] are a few. General or indeterminate words may be, in themselves, 'indicia of an intention that the application of a section should vary over time'.[43] As well as the examples of the words 'gas,' 'taxi' and 'otherwise mutilates' referred to above, 'document',[44] 'construction' and 'installation',[45] 'diffusion service'[46] and 'inflicts grievous bodily harm'[47] are further examples of words that have been attributed a meaning at a sufficiently high level of generality to apply to circumstances not known at the time of their enactment.

But even where the meaning of a word or phrase is general enough to apply to a changed state of affairs, the question still remains as to whether it applies to the facts before the court. For example, in *Deputy Commissioner of Taxation v Clark,* [48] Spigelman CJ (Handley and Hodgson JA agreeing) determined that 'other good reason' in a defence provision for company directors was sufficiently general to be construed as 'always speaking' and so included the changed statutory and common law environment. The Court, however, held the text did not apply to the particular facts before the Court.[49]

In contrast, if a statutory word or phrase is attributed a specific or particular meaning, that text will be limited in its capacity to apply to new things or circumstances. For example, in *Tabcorp Holdings Ltd v Victoria*[50] the argument that a provision concerning 'licences' in a gambling licence Act was generic and ambulatory and so extended to new licences granted under a replacement licensing regime was rejected. The Court determined, on the basis of various interpretative factors, including the use of the word in other sections, that 'licences' referred only to the specific licences issued under the previous legislative scheme.[51]

There may be instances where the outcome of the interpretative process is that the essential meaning of statutory text is so narrow that it only applies to the circumstances that existed at the

38 *R v A2* (2019) 269 CLR 507, 563 [170] (Edelman J); *Deputy Commissioner of Taxation v Clark* (2003) 57 NSWLR 113, 145 [142] (Spigelman CJ).

39 *Coles Supermarkets Australia Pty Ltd v Harris* [2013] ACTSC 255, [26] (Burns J).

40 *BMW Australia Ltd v Brewster* (2019) 269 CLR 574, 638 [171] (Edelman J).

41 *Chappell and Co Ltd v Associated Radio Co of Australia Ltd* [1925] VLR 350, 361 (Cussen J).

42 *Deputy Commissioner of Taxation v Clark* (2003) 57 NSWLR 113, 145 [141] (Spigelman CJ).

43 *Sonnet v The Queen* (2010) 30 VR 519, 532 [48] (the Court).

44 *Muin v Refugee Review Tribunal* (2002) 76 AJLR 966, 985–6 [104] (McHugh J).

45 *Shire of York v Rosmill Pty Ltd* [2010] WASC 189, [44]–[45] (Hall J).

46 *Telstra Corporation Ltd v Australasian Performing Right Association Ltd* (1997) 191 CLR 140, 193-4 (Kirby J).

47 *Aubrey v The Queen* (2017) 260 CLR 305, 325-6 [38]–[40] (Kiefel CJ, Keane, Nettle and Edelman JJ).

48 (2003) 57 NSWLR 113.

49 Ibid 146 [148], 148 [158], 149 [164]–[168].

50 (2016) 90 ALJR 376.

51 Ibid 387 [65]. *Coles Supermarkets Australia Pty Ltd v Harris* [2013] ACTSC 255, [26] (Burns J) and *Wilson v Commissioner of Stamp Duties* (1988) 13 NSWLR 77, 79–80 (Kirby J) are other examples of specific meaning not applying to new situations.

time of its enactment, or another particular time. Provisions such as these are sometimes referred to as a 'fixed time' or 'fixed date' provision.[52]

For example, in *Giannarelli v Wraith*[53] the High Court considered s 10(2) of the *Legal Profession Practice Act 1958* (Vic). This section provided that a barrister's liability for negligence to a client was 'to the same extent as a solicitor was on the twenty-third day of November One thousand eight hundred and ninety-one liable' to his client. Wilson J (with whom Mason CJ agreed on the interpretative issue[54]) considered that the words 'to the same extent as a solicitor was on [23 November 1891] liable to his client' were words of limitation.[55] That, together with the legislative history of the provision, led his Honour to conclude that s 10(2) was 'plainly a "fixed-time" provision'.[56] Accordingly, to determine whether a barrister was liable for in-court negligence under s 10(2) it was necessary to determine the extent of a solicitor's liability for in-court negligence on 23 November 1891.[57]

Ultimately, the level of generality or specificity of the meaning of any word is a matter of construction given 'the precise words used, their context in the legislation, the legislative and Parliamentary history of the statute and the apparent purposes to which the words are directed in their context'.[58] It requires analysis using the ordinary principles of interpretation.

Changes in law since enactment

The 'always speaking' approach may operate so that a provision is construed in the context of contemporary law, even if that law has developed since enactment [19.6]

The 'always speaking' approach may apply so that text incorporating common law concepts or other legislation includes 'changes in the law since the legislation was enacted'.[59] This approach was adopted in a High Court case concerning the meaning of 'charitable institution' in various Commonwealth tax Acts.[60] The majority, accepting that the statutory phrase derived its meaning from the common law, explained:

> Where [sic] statute *picks up as a criterion for its operation a body of the general law*, such as the equitable principles respecting charitable trusts, then, in the absence of a contrary indication in the statute, the statute speaks continuously to the present, and *picks up the case law as it stands from time to time.*[61]

52 *Forsyth v Deputy Commissioner of Taxation* (2007) 231 CLR 531, 544 [22] (Gleeson CJ, Gummow, Hayne, Callinan, Heydon and Crennan JJ). Kirby J, dissenting, acknowledged the possibility of a 'fixed time' meaning (563 [96]) but found such a construction 'unconvincing' (554 [63]).

53 (1988) 165 CLR 543.

54 Ibid 561.

55 Ibid 566.

56 Ibid 567.

57 Ibid 567–8.

58 *Wilson v Commissioner of Stamp Duties* (1988) 13 NSWLR 77, 78 (Kirby P).

59 *BMW Australia Ltd v Brewster* (2019) 269 CLR 574, 638 [171] (Edelman J). See also *Bell Lawyers Pty Ltd v Pentelow* (2019) 269 CLR 333, 363–4 [83] (Edelman J); *Port of Newcastle Operations Pty Ltd v Glencore Coal Assets Australia Pty Ltd* (2021) 395 ALR 209, 227 [86] (the Court).

60 *Aid/Watch Incorporated v Commissioner of Taxation (Cth)* (2010) 241 CLR 539.

61 Ibid 549 [23] (French CJ, Gummow, Hayne, Crennan and Bell JJ) (emphasis added). See chapter 22 for statutes incorporating common law.

The term 'charitable institutions' was therefore construed to refer to the common law as it existed from time to time.

Ambulatory language may also take into account the 'current legislative environment'[62] as part of the context relevant to its interpretation. For example, s 68 of the *Judiciary Act 1903* (Cth), which operates by reference to the jurisdiction of state and territory jurisdictions in respect of particular offences, has been characterised as ambulatory, picking up state and territory law as it exists from time to time.[63] The Interpretation Acts have a similar ambulatory effect where Acts refer to specific legislation.[64] For example, each Interpretation Act provides that a reference in an Act to other legislation in the same jurisdiction is to be construed to refer to that legislation as amended from time to time.[65]

A statute construed to speak to both the current common law and legislative environment was the subject of the case in **Example 19.2**.

Example 19.2 *Dionisatos (for the Estate of the Late George Dionysatos) v Acrow Formwork & Scaffolding Pty Ltd*[66]

In the late 1960s, Mr Dionysatos was employed as a scaffolder by a company constructing the Sydney Opera House. In 2012 he was diagnosed with mesothelioma and died shortly afterwards. His personal representative continued his claim for damages against the company in the Dust Diseases Tribunal ('the Tribunal'), alleging his illness was caused by exposure to asbestos dust when working for the company. In 2013 the Tribunal found that Mr Dionysatos had been exposed to asbestos and upheld the estate's claim, making an award of damages. The damages included a component in respect of his loss of capacity to provide gratuitous domestic services to his wife, who had dementia and physical difficulties. This category of damages was permitted under s 15B of the *Civil Liability Act 2002* (NSW) ('the *Civil Liability Act*').

Prior to that finding, in late 2012, the Dust Diseases Board ('the Board') had awarded compensation to Mr Dionysatos' widow pursuant to the *Workers' Compensation (Dust Diseases) Act 1942* (NSW) ('the Workers' Compensation Act'). That Act allowed compensation to spouses partially dependent on the worker for support.

The Tribunal deducted the compensation awarded to Mr Dionysatos' widow under the Workers Compensation Act from the damages awarded to Mr Dionysatos' estate under the *Civil Liability Act*. The Tribunal had determined that s 12D of a third Act – the *Dust Diseases Tribunal Act 1989* (NSW) ('the Tribunal Act') – had no application. Section 12D relevantly provided:

62 *A v Maughan* (2016) 50 WAR 263, 296 [122] (Martin CJ). See also *Deputy Commissioner of Taxation v Clark* (2003) 57 NSWLR 113, 148 [158] (Spigelman CJ).

63 *R v Gee* (2003) 212 CLR 230, 240–1 [3]–[7] (Gleeson CJ), 244 [24] (McHugh and Gummow JJ), 269 [114] (Kirby J).

64 Noted in *Quarmby v Keating* (2008) 18 Tas R 284, 308–9 [56]–[57] (Evans J, Crawford CJ agreeing 287 [1]), referring to *Acts Interpretation Act 1931* (Tas) ss 13, 17.

65 *Acts Interpretation Act 1901* (Cth) s 10; *Interpretation Act 1987* (NSW) s 68; *Acts Interpretation Act 1954* (Qld) s 14H; *Legislation Interpretation Act 2021* (SA) s 36; *Acts Interpretation Act 1931* (Tas) s 13; *Interpretation of Legislation Act 1984* (Vic) s 17; *Interpretation Act 1984* (WA) s 16; *Legislation Act 2001* (ACT) s 102; *Interpretation Act 1978* (NT) s 50. See further **[25.4](e)**.

66 (2015) 91 NSWLR 34.

12D Damages for non-economic loss not to be reduced by certain compensation payments

(1) This section applies to proceedings before the Tribunal . . . for damages in relation to dust-related conditions.

(2) In determining damages for non-economic loss in any such proceedings, no deduction is to be made for any amount of compensation already paid or payable, or payable in the future, under the *Workers' Compensation (Dust Diseases) Act 1942*.

(3) In this section:

damages for non-economic loss means damages or compensation for the following:

. . .

(e) the need for services of a domestic nature . . .which have been or are to be provided to a person by another person, and for which the first person has not paid and is not liable to pay any fee or charge.

Section 12D had been inserted into the Tribunal Act in 1998. The estate appealed the Tribunal's decision to make the deduction.

One of the grounds of dispute was the language of s 12D(3)(e), which identified one of the categories of damages of 'non-economic loss' from which no deduction should be made. The company argued that, though they accepted that the ordinary meaning of 'services . . . provided to a person by another person' was wide enough to include the domestic services provided by a worker to their spouse, it could not have been the intent of the legislature for damages for such services to be excluded from deduction. One reason, they argued, was that at the time of the enactment of s 12D, the 2002 *Civil Liability Act* had not been enacted. As well, the 1999 New South Wales judicial decision of *Sullivan v Gordon*,[67] which recognised damages for domestic services, did not exist. So, they reasoned, those kind of awards could not have been contemplated by the legislature when it enacted the s 12D exception to deduction in 1998.

In separate judgments, Basten JA and Gleeson JA (Macfarlan JA agreeing with the judgments of both) rejected this argument. Both referred to the 'always speaking' principle. Basten JA noted that, in the absence of a contrary indication in the statute, the Tribunal Act was to be given an ambulatory effect and was 'intended to operate in the context of the general law'.[68] Gleeson JA (as an alternative basis to his finding on s 12D) described the interpretative arguments as 'finely balanced'[69] but explained:

> Whether or not *Sullivan v Gordon* type damages, which are now recognised in a modified form by s 15B of the *Civil Liability Act*, were in the contemplation of the drafter of s 12D is not the point. The question is whether the language used in the definition in s 12D(3)(e), when read into the operative provision, describes a claim for damages for non-economic loss that answers the description of s 15B damages.[70]

67 (1999) 47 NSWLR 319.

68 (2015) 91 NSWLR 34, 40–1 [14]–[15].

69 Ibid 83 [264].

70 Ibid [263].

Gleeson JA noted that the language of s 12D was 'sufficiently general to apply to things not then recognised or enacted'.[71] Accepting the 'always speaking' approach to the interpretation of s 12D, he concluded that s 12D operated to exclude the deduction of Mrs Dionysatos' statutory benefit from the s 15B damages.[72]

Limitations of approach

[19.7] **The 'always speaking' approach may have an updating effect, but it is not a licence to 'update' the meaning of statutory text; the latter would suggest that the essential meaning can change**

Although courts have sometimes loosely referred to the 'always speaking' approach as resulting in the meaning of a word changing over time, the High Court has consistently stated that the connotation or essential meaning of a statute does not change.[73] To consider otherwise would result in 'two contradictory meanings at different times, each of which is correct at one time but not another, without any intervention from the legislature which enacted it'.[74] This has, at least, constitutional and separation of powers concerns.

The proposition that meaning does not change is consistent with the 'always speaking' approach given the distinction made between the connotation (essential meaning) and denotation. Consequently, while an ambulatory construction may have an 'updated operation'[75] or *effect*, this should not be taken to mean that the *meaning* is updated.

The High Court has observed the distinction between the 'always speaking' principle and an approach that updates *meaning*, noting that the latter is different to accepted Australian common law.[76] The distinction is be demonstrated by considering reasoning in the UK decision of *Yemshaw v Hounslow London Borough Council.*[77] It has been argued that Lady Hale's reasoning suggests that it is legitimate to update the *meaning* of legislative text in light of contemporary conditions.[78] This is a 'far more controversial' interpretative approach as it permits a change in the state of affairs to drive a change in meaning.[79] Extracurially, Edelman J has explained:

> The effect of this reasoning [in *Yemshaw*] is that the core meaning of a statute can change. Matters which are not within the meaning of the statute one year will fall within the

71 Ibid 84 [264].

72 Ibid [268].

73 *R v A2* (2019) 269 CLR 507, 553 [144] (Bell and Gageler JJ, dissenting), 563 [170] (Edelman J); *Aubrey v The Queen* (2017) 260 CLR 305, 322 [29] (Kiefel CJ, Keane, Nettle and Edelman JJ), citing *Lake Macquarie Shire Council v Aberdare County Council* (1970) 123 CLR 327, 331 (Barwick CJ).

74 *Pape v Commissioner of Taxation (Cth)* (2009) 238 CLR 1, 145 [423] (Heydon J).

75 *Firebird Global Master Fund II Ltd v Republic of Nauru* (2015) 258 CLR 31, 92 [208]–[209] (Nettle and Gordon JJ).

76 *Aubrey v The Queen* (2017) 260 CLR 305, 322 [30] n 82 ((Kiefel CJ, Keane, Nettle and Edelman JJ), referred to in *R v A2* (2019) 269 CLR 507, 553 [143] (Bell and Gageler JJ), 563 [170] n 223 (Edelman J).

77 [2011] 1 WLR 433, 442–3 [26]–[27] (Baroness Hale of Richmond JSC). Cf *Owens v Owens* [2018] AC 899, 921 [46] (Baroness Hale of Richmond PSC).

78 See, eg, James Edelman, '2018 Winterton Lecture: Constitutional Interpretation' (2019) 45(1) *University of Western Australia Law Review* 1, 23–8; Richard Ekins, 'Case Comment – Updating the Meaning of Violence' (2013) 129 (January) *Law Quarterly Review* 17.

79 *Graham v Minister for Immigration and Border Protection* (2017) 263 CLR 1, 38 [83] (Edelman J, in dissent).

> statute in the next. This is very different from an approach which permits the scope of words of a genus to encompass circumstances which did not previously exist, such as now construing the word 'mail' in 1970's legislation to include 'e-mail'.[80]

His Honour elsewhere described such 'updating' as a 'wholly dynamic approach' to interpretation that gives rise to a number of difficulties.[81]

Example 19.3 illustrates the distinction between an ambulatory construction and an approach that 'updates' word meaning merely due to developments in contemporary circumstances.

Example 19.3 *A-G (Tas) v CL*[82]

The respondent had separated from their partner and had been involved in lengthy Family Court proceedings. The partner was described as a heavy drinker, controlling and obsessive. The respondent applied for compensation pursuant to the *Victims of Crime Assistance Act 1976* (Tas) (the 'VOCA Act').

Section 4 of the VOCA Act provided that compensation may be awarded where a person suffers injury 'as a result of the act of another person that constitutes an offence'. Further, s 2(1) of the VOCA provided:

> ***offence*** means an offence that involves violence by one person against another and includes a crime under section 127, 127A, 185, 186, 191A or 192 of the Criminal Code.

The respondent did not allege that they had suffered physical violence, or the threat of physical violence. Their claim was based on allegations of economic and emotional abuse and intimidation, behaviours that were offences under the *Family Violence Act 2004* (Tas). The issue on appeal was whether the word 'violence' in s 2(1) meant only physical violence or the threat of physical violence, or whether it extended to non-physical violence such as emotional or economic abuse.

The primary judge found in favour of the respondent. One of the grounds for His Honour's reasoning was to use the 'always speaking' approach to adopt a meaning of the word 'violence' that extended beyond physicality and force and included notions of coercion, intimidation, and economic abuse.

On appeal, Porter JA (Blow CJ and Wood J agreeing) determined that the primary judge had erred in applying the principle.[83] Porter JA recognised that the approach did not abrogate the need for proper construction of the statute.[84] His Honour considered numerous textual, contextual and purposive factors. For example, he noted the character of the criminal offences referred to in the definition and determined that the *Family Violence Act 2004* (Tas) was not a statute *in paria materia* to the VOCA Act. He also noted that it was 'quite clear' from parliamentary material relating to the enactment of s 2 that the purpose of the definition was to 'restrict the range of

---

80 James Edelman, 'Uncommon Statutory Interpretation' (2012) 11(1) *The Judicial Review* 71, 91.

81 James Edelman, '2018 Winterton Lecture: Constitutional Interpretation' (2019) 45(1) *University of Western Australia Law Review* 1, 27–8. See also Jeffrey Goldsworthy, 'Lord Burrows on Legislative Intention, Statutory Purpose, and the "Always Speaking" Principle' (2022) 43(1) *Statute Law Review* 79.

82 [2018] TASFC 6.

83 Ibid [83].

84 Ibid [46].

criminal conduct for which claims could be made' in light of concerns about the increasing demands on the existing compensation regime.[85]

This process of construction led Porter JA to conclude:

> Whatever the social and moral desirability of the construction contended for by the respondent may be, I am persuaded that a fair reading of the VOCA Act does not allow an interpretation of the definition to include extended notions of what might be understood as 'domestic violence' or 'family violence' . . .
>
> In my view, the words 'offence involving violence by one person against another' *in the context in which they appear*, have the more common meaning of physical force or the threat of it . . .[86]

[19.8] In the course of determining whether text is ambulatory, the penal nature of a provision may be of particular relevance

It has been suggested that the penal nature of a criminal offence provision will be of particular significance to determining whether the provision is ambulatory. In *R v A2*[87] Bell and Gageler JJ (dissenting) cautioned:

> It is one thing to recognise that the application of a statutory word or phrase may change over time, particularly in light in [sic] advances in science and technology. It is another thing to contemplate that the meaning of statutory language creating an offence can expand etymologically such that conduct that is not proscribed at the date of the enactment of the offence may come to fall within the proscription at some undefined time thereafter. That is because, accepting that the fixity or variability through time of the content of any statutory language is a question of interpretation, statutory language which creates a criminal offence is to be interpreted in light of the fundamental principle that a criminal norm should be certain and its reach ascertainable by those who are subject to it.[88]

It is unlikely that these comments are a 'gloss' on the 'always speaking' principle. It is arguably more appropriate to view them as reflecting the ordinary approach to interpretation that the penal character of a provision or Act may be taken into account.[89] That is, it is a contextual factor relevant to determining whether the criminal provision is ambulatory. Even so, as statements made in dissent, the application of the principle to criminal statutes 'would benefit from clarification at the highest level'.[90]

---

85 Ibid [81]. See also [14].

86 Ibid [83]–[84] (emphasis added).

87 (2019) 269 CLR 507.

88 Ibid 552 [141]. Cf Dan Meagher, 'The "Always Speaking" Approach to Statutes (and the Significance of Its Misapplication in *Aubrey v The Queen*)' (2020) 43(1) *University of New South Wales Law Journal* 191, 214–6 where he argues that the principle has been used to extend criminal liability.

89 See **[17.4]**.

90 John-Patrick Asimakis, '"Always Speaking" Statutes' (2021) 95(11) *Australian Law Journal* 869, 874.

THE SCHEME AND COMPONENTS OF AN ACT

20

Overview

Chapter 13 explained how Acts are structured, identified their various components (such as preambles, titles, headings and examples) and explained whether each component is treated as part of the Act. This chapter deals with the role that those components play for interpretative purposes, whether treated as part of the Act or not. Collectively the components help explain the scheme of the Act. [20.1]

Of least value for interpretative purposes are short titles, section headings and simplified outlines. Long titles, preambles, and headings to groups of sections form part of the context for interpretative purposes. Objects clauses may help identify the purposes of an Act. Reader's aids, such as examples and notes, may assist in the interpretative process as can punctuation. Definitions play a key role in conveying meaning.

This chapter also sets out inferences that can be drawn about the meaning of a provision from where it is located within the Act.

Scheme of Act

The components of an Act give an Act structure and help explain its scheme [20.2]

Judges often refer to the scheme of an Act that they are in the process of interpreting.[1] They deduce the scheme of the Act from looking at the overall arrangement of its components and their general content. Doing so gives them a high-level overview of the structure or framework of the Act, or of the relevant portion of the Act, and what the individual components are about. This in turn guides the judge in harmonising the meaning of doubtful individual components with the overall scheme of the Act.[2]

The focus in this section has been on the scheme created by an individual Act. Two or more Acts may also be said to form a legislative scheme where they have a common purpose and some connection with each other and are intended to operate together.[3] This latter kind of legislative scheme is discussed in **[29.4]**.

---

1 *Shanahan v Scott* (1957) 96 CLR 245, 256 (Kitto J); *Heatley v Tasmanian Racing and Gaming Commission* (1977) 137 CLR 487, 505, 507 (Aickin J); *Re East; Ex parte Nguyen* (1998) 196 CLR 354, 364–5 [25] (Gleeson CJ, Gaudron, McHugh, Gummow, Hayne and Callinan JJ); *Plaintiff M47/2012 v Director-General of Security* (2012) 251 CLR 1, 21 [3] (French CJ).

2 *Cooper Brookes (Wollongong) Pty Ltd v Federal Commissioner of Taxation (Cth)* (1981) 147 CLR 297, 322 (Mason and Wilson JJ); *Sue v Hill* (1999) 199 CLR 462, 564 [267] (Kirby J); *Taylor v The Owners – Strata Plan No 11564* (2014) 253 CLR 531, 549 [39] (French CJ, Crennan and Bell JJ).

3 *Certain Lloyd's Underwriters v Cross* (2012) 248 CLR 378, 414 [97] (Kiefel J).

Interpretative value of individual components

[20.3] A long title may be used to determine the object and scope of an Act and to resolve an ambiguity but not to contradict clear language

Courts use the long title of an Act to help them ascertain its object or purpose[4] and determine its scope.[5] While the long title may assist in resolving an ambiguity, courts will not use it to override clear and unambiguous language in the body of the Act.[6]

The long title constitutes part of the context in which any particular provision of an Act should be considered.[7]

[20.4] A preamble forms part of the context of an Act and as such plays a role in the interpretative process

The function of a preamble is to explain the background to the Act and the reasons why Parliament considers its enactment desirable. As part of an Act,[8] it plays a role in the interpretative process.

A preamble has been described as 'a key to open the minds of the makers of the Act, and the mischiefs which they intended to redress'[9] and as 'the key to the intention of the Legislature'.[10] It is seen as providing evidence of the intention of Parliament in enacting the legislation.[11] Its recitals are to set out the background to the Act – the facts that led Parliament to enact it.[12] A preamble gives an indication of the scope of the Act.[13]

In Western Australia s 31(1) of the *Interpretation Act 1984* (WA) provides that the preamble is to be construed as a part of the Act 'intended to assist in explaining its purport and object'. This is consistent with the common law treatment of a preamble.[14]

---

4 *Fenton v Thorley & Co Ltd* [1903] AC 443, 447 (Lord Macnaghten); *Lambe v Director-General of Social Services* (1981) 4 ALD 362, 366–8 (Full Court of the Federal Court of Australia); *Amatek Ltd v Googoorewon Pty Ltd* (1993) 176 CLR 471, 477 (the Court); *R v A2* (2019) 269 CLR 507, 556–7 [155] (Nettle and Gordon JJ).

5 *Fenton v Thorley & Co Ltd* [1903] AC 443, 447 (Lord Macnaghten); *Vacher & Sons Ltd v London Society of Compositors* [1913] AC 107, 128 (Lord Moulton); *Birch v Allen* (1942) 65 CLR 621, 625 (Latham CJ, Rich, Starke, McTiernan and Williams JJ agreeing at 627); *Ukley v Ukley* [1977] VR 121, 123 (the Court); *Cole v Director-General of Department of Youth and Community Services* (1986) 7 NSWLR 541, 549 (McHughJA).

6 *Birch v Allen* (1942) 65 CLR 621, 625–6 (Latham CJ, Rich, Starke, McTiernan and Williams JJ agreeing at 627); *Bennett v Minister for Public Works (NSW)* (1908) 7 CLR 372, 383 (Isaacs J); *Charlesworth v MJ Sterling Pty Ltd* [1943] VLR 67, 69 (O'Bryan J); *Clunnies-Ross v Commonwealth* (1984) 155 CLR 193, 199 (Gibbs CJ, Mason, Wilson, Brennan, Deane and Dawson JJ).

7 *Re Bolton; Ex parte Beane* (1987) 162 CLR 514, 530 (Deane J); *Fearnley v Finlay* [2014] 2 Qd R 392, 401 (Jackson J); *R v A2* (2019) 269 CLR 507, 559 [162] (Edelman J).

8 See **[13.6]**.

9 *Stowel v Lord Zouch* (1569) 1 Pl 353; 75 ER 536, 560–1 (Dyer CJ).

10 *Carr v Corporation of the Royal Exchange Assurance Co* (1862) 1 B&S 956, 960; 121 ER 970, 971 (Wightman J).

11 *Sussex Peerage Case* (1844) 11 CL&F 85; 8 ER 1034, 1056–7 (Tindal LCJ); *Powell v Kempton Park Racecourse Co* [1897] 2 QB 242, 266 (Lopes LJ); *Thomson v Master and Fellows of St Catharine's College, Cambridge* [1919] AC 468, 487 (Lord Atkinson); *Taylor v Western Australia* [2020] FCA 42, [63] (Mortimer J).

12 *Kemppi v Adani Mining Pty Ltd (No 2)* (2019) 271 FCR 423, 448 [61] (Rares ACJ and Robertson J).

13 *Salkeld v Johnson* (1842) 1 Hare 196; 66 ER 1004, 1008–9 (Wigram V-C); *Chilton v Progress Printing & Publishing Co* [1895] 2 Ch 29, 33 (Lord Halsbury); *Powell v Kempton Park Racecourse Co* [1899] AC 143, 157 (Earl of Halsbury LC); *A-G v Prince Ernest Augustus of Hanover* [1957] AC 436, 467 (Lord Normand).

14 See **[13.6]**.

In *Wacando v Commonwealth*[15] Gibbs CJ, affirming what had been earlier stated by Griffith CJ in *Bowtell v Goldsbrough, Mort & Co Ltd*,[16] observed that 'if the words of the section are plain and unambiguous their meaning cannot be cut down by reference to the preamble'.[17]

It is suggested that limiting the use of a preamble to where there is an ambiguity in the body of the Act is inconsistent with the modern approach to statutory interpretation with its emphasis on context.[18] This is reflected in the judgment of Mason J in *Wacando v Commonwealth*[19] where he stated:

> It has been said that where the enacting part of a statute is clear and unambiguous it cannot be cut down by the preamble. But this does not mean that a court cannot obtain assistance from the preamble in ascertaining the meaning of an operative provision. The particular section must be seen in its context; the statute must be read as a whole and recourse to the preamble may throw light on the statutory purpose and object.[20]

The extent to which the preamble may assist in interpreting the Act depends on the nature of the preamble itself. If it is written in very general terms or is very brief or is itself ambiguous,[21] it is not of much use in the interpretative process.[22]

Reciting a statement as a fact in a preamble is not conclusive proof of that fact [20.5]

Courts are not bound to accept without question the accuracy of facts set out in a preamble. They are 'prima-facie evidence'[23] only of those facts.

Parliament cannot use a statement of facts in a preamble to conclusively establish a constitutional basis for an Act. In *Australian Communist Party v Commonwealth*[24] the High Court held that the *Communist Party Dissolution Act 1950* (Cth) was invalid. That Act had an extensive preamble outlining the perceived threat to Australia from activities engaged in by the Australian Communist Party. Williams J stated:

> [W]here the constitutional validity of an Act is in issue, the recitals cannot, in my opinion, be more than a statement of the reasons why Parliament enacted the law. They indicate to the Court what Parliament believes to be the constitutional basis of the Act ...
>
> Where the constitutional validity of an Act is challenged, it is the actual facts and only the actual facts which count ...[25]

---

15 (1981) 148 CLR 1.

16 (1905) 3 CLR 444, 451.

17 (1981) 148 CLR 1, 15–6.

18 *CIC Insurance Ltd v Bankstown Football Club Ltd* (1997) 187 CLR 384, 408 (Brennan CJ, Dawson, Toohey and Gummow JJ, Gaudron J agreeing at 412); *Project Blue Sky Inc v Australian Broadcasting Authority* (1998) 194 CLR 355, 381–2 (McHugh, Gummow, Kirby and Hayne JJ).

19 (1981) 148 CLR 1.

20 Ibid 23.

21 *Powell v Kempton Park Racecourse Co* [1897] 2 QB 242, 289–90 (Rigby LJ); *A-G v Prince Ernest Augustus of Hanover* [1957] AC 436, 467 (Lord Normand).

22 *Powell v Kempton Park Racecourse Co* [1897] 2 QB 242, 290 (Rigby LJ), 299 (Chitty LJ); *A-G v Prince Ernest Augustus of Hanover* [1957] AC 436, 463 (Viscount Simonds), 471 (Lord Morton), 474–5 (Lord Somervell).

23 *Dawson v Commonwealth* (1946) 73 CLR 157, 175 (Latham CJ).

24 (1951) 83 CLR 1.

25 Ibid 224.

[20.6] A short title has little interpretative value

The short title of an Act is really only a label. It sacrifices accuracy to brevity.[26] In *Vacher & Sons Ltd v London Society of Compositors*[27] Lord Moulton said of short titles:

> That is a title given to the Act solely for the purpose of facility of reference. If I may use the phrase, it is a statutory nickname to obviate the necessity of always referring to the Act under its full and descriptive title. It is not legitimate, in my opinion, to use it for the purpose of ascertaining the scope of the Act. Its object is identification and not description.[28]

A short title may, however, be drafted in such a way that it can assist in the interpretative process.[29] In *Clubb v Edwards*[30] the High Court had to consider a Tasmanian Act with the short title of *Reproductive Health (Access to Terminations) Act 2013*. Edelman J described that short title as providing 'a clear indication of the general purposes of the Act'.[31]

Apart from its brevity, a difficulty with using a short title as an interpretative aid is that it may not even be particularly accurate. In *Fisher v Fisher*[32] Nathan J criticised the short title of the *Crimes (Family Violence) Act 1987* (Vic) in the following terms:

> This Act is referred to as the *Crimes (Family Violence) Act*. It purports to amend the *Crimes Act* . . . the Act does not amend the *Crimes Act* at all, but introduces new, necessary and defined procedures to deal with episodes of threatened family violence. To do so, it has established a civil remedy . . . and has set out the civil proceedings by which those injunctive remedies can be obtained. They are not criminal matters, and to call them so does not change the essential characterisation of the Act. A duck does not become an emu merely because it is called one. This Act, which is discreet in its operation from the *Crimes Act* 1958, does not become an amendment to that Act . . . merely because it is recited as being so. Nothing I have said destroys the efficacy of the Act or the remedies which it creates. It is plainly inappropriately entitled, and this should be remedied, but I must look to the substance of the legislation and not strike it down merely because of its inaccurate title.[33]

A short title may even be used to convey a political slogan.[34] Used as such, it does not even help inform the reader about whether the Act is a principal or an amending Act.

The short title of an Act may be amended by a subsequent Act.[35] This can create difficulties for users wanting to trace the legislative history of an Act.

---

26 *Re Boaler* [1915] 1 KB 21, 40 (Scrutton J).

27 [1913] AC 107.

28 Ibid 128–9.

29 *DPP (SA) v Vella* (1993) 61 SASR 379, 385 [12] (Olsson J); *Re Macks; Ex parte Saint* (2000) 204 CLR 158, 251 [261], 257 [277] (Kirby J); *Sydney Local Health Network v QY* (2011) 83 NSWLR 321, 332 [63] (Campbell JA).

30 (2019) 267 CLR 171.

31 Ibid 328 [458].

32 [1988] VR 1028.

33 Ibid 1039–40.

34 See Paul O'Brien, 'Legislative Titles – What's in a Name?' (2012) (3) *The Loophole: Journal of the Commonwealth Association of Legislative Counsel* 17.

35 In Victoria the *Prostitution Control Act 1994* (Vic) became the *Sex Work Act 1994* (Vic) as a result of the *Consumer Affairs Legislation Amendment Act 2010* (Vic) s 42(1). More remarkably, the *Industrial Relations Act 1988* (Cth) became the *Workplace Relations Act 1996* (Cth) as a result of the *Workplace Relations and Other Legislation Amendment Act 1996* (Cth) sch 19.

An objects clause, while not determinative of the purposes of the Act, assists in identifying those purposes [20.7]

An Act may contain a section that expressly states the purposes for which it is enacted or the object or objects it seeks to achieve.[36] Such a section is referred to in this chapter as an objects clause. An objects clause is treated by courts as relevant to the proper construction of the Act.[37] A broadly formulated objects clause may be of limited or no value, however, for the purpose of construction.[38]

While account may be taken of an objects clause to resolve uncertainty or ambiguity, it cannot 'control clear statutory language . . . or command a particular outcome of exercise of discretionary power'.[39]

An objects clause is not determinative of the purposes of an Act, let alone the purposes of a particular section. Accordingly, if an Act with an objects clause provided that a power may be exercised 'for any of the purposes of this Act', a court may look beyond the objects in the objects clause to all the provisions of the Act to determine its purposes.[40] It is recognised that the objects of an Act may be 'directed to disparate ends and are not necessarily harmonious'.[41]

A reference in an objects clause to an object that could be constitutionally achieved by the Act does not protect the Act from invalidity. In *Leask v Commonwealth*[42] Brennan CJ observed that '[t]he Parliament cannot legislate a measure into power merely by declaring its measure to be enacted for a valid object'.[43]

A Commonwealth Act may contain a provision indicating whether a matter dealt with by it is or is not intended to exclude state laws on that matter. Such a provision, while valid, does not itself affect the validity or operation of a state law.[44]

36 In *Russo v Aiello* (2003) 215 CLR 643, 645 [5] Gleeson CJ described the *Motor Accidents Act 1988* (NSW) pt 5 as being 'replete with legislative declarations of its objects'. Since 1 September 1985 when the long title of Bills for Victorian Acts ceased to be part of the Act by force of the *Interpretation of Legislation Act 1984* (Vic) s 10(3), the practice has been for all Victorian Acts to contain a purpose section as the first section of the Act. The nature of that section is more akin to that of a long title than an objects clause. An objects clause may also be included. See, eg, *Gender Equality Act 2020* (Vic) ss 1 and 4.

37 *Tickner v Bropho* (1993) 40 FCR 183, 191–2 (Black CJ), 207–9 (Lockhart J) 215–16 (French J). In *Russo v Aiello* (2003) 215 CLR 643 Gleeson CJ described statutory statements of objects as not being 'an exercise in apologetics' but as giving practical content to certain terms used in the Act such as 'reasonable', 'justification' and 'satisfactory': at 645 [5].

38 In *Australian Retirement Homes Ltd v Ash* [2013] QCA 355 Gotterson JA described a particular statutory objective as being 'so broadly formulated that debating points can be made for and against each of the competing constructions in terms of consistency with it': at [37]. See also **[8.5]**.

39 *Minister for Urban Affairs and Planning v Rosemount Estates Pty Ltd* (1996) 91 LGERA 31, 78 (Cole JA). See also *Lynn v New South Wales* (2016) 91 NSWLR 636, 648 (Beazley P).

40 *Cappello v Roads and Maritime Services* [2019] NSWSC 439. Similarly in *Municipal Officers' Association of Australia v Lancaster* (1981) 37 ALR 559 the Federal Court looked beyond an objects clause in interpreting a provision requiring a discretion to be exercised 'having regard to the objects of the Act'.

41 *Lynn v New South Wales* (2016) 91 NSWLR 636, 648 (Beazley P).

42 (1996) 187 CLR 579.

43 Ibid 591.

44 *Re Credit Tribunal; Ex parte General Motors Acceptance Corporation (Australia)* (1977) 137 CLR 545, 562–4 (Mason J), Barwick CJ, Gibbs and Stephen JJ agreeing at 552, Jacobs J agreeing at 565.

[20.8] Part, division and subdivision headings form part of the context of an Act and play a role in the interpretative process

The headings to any part, division or subdivision into which the body of an Act is divided form part of the Act.[45] They contribute to the context in which a provision that appears under that heading is to be construed.[46]

In *Concrete Constructions (NSW) Pty Ltd v Nelson*[47] the majority judges limited the situations in which a heading of a part may be taken into consideration to cases of ambiguity.[48] Despite the heading of pt V of the *Trade Practices Act 1974* (Cth) being 'Consumer Protection', they construed a section in that part, s 52, as prohibiting a corporation from engaging in misleading or deceptive conduct 'in trade or commerce' regardless of whether the conduct is misleading to, or deceptive of, a person in the capacity of a consumer. They stated:

> The general heading 'Consumer Protection' at the commencement of Pt V is part of the Act (*Acts Interpretation Act 1901* (Cth), s 13). It constitutes part of the context within which the substantive provisions of Pt V must be construed and should be taken into consideration in determining the meaning of those provisions in case of ambiguity. The heading does not, however, control the permissible scope of the substantive provisions of Pt V and cannot properly be used to impose an unnaturally constricted meaning upon the words of those substantive provisions ... As a matter of language, s 52 prohibits a corporation from engaging in misleading or deceptive conduct 'in trade or commerce' regardless of whether the conduct is misleading to, or deceptive of, a person in the capacity of a consumer. In these circumstances, it is not permissible to give to the heading of Pt V the effect of confining the general words of s 52 to cases involving the protection of consumers alone.[49]

Brennan J[50] and McHugh J[51] construed s 52 in the light of the heading to pt V and held that its scope is limited to conduct that misleads or deceives, or is likely to mislead or deceive, a person in their capacity as a consumer.

McHugh J in that case observed that to limit the situations in which a heading of a part may be taken into consideration to cases of ambiguity may represent 'too limited an approach to the construction of federal statutes and that their headings must always be taken into account in determining the meaning of provisions'.[52] In light of the modern approach of reading an Act as a whole and always considering context (which includes headings),[53] a limitation on the use of headings to cases of ambiguity is inconsistent with that approach.

---

45 See **[13.11]**.

46 *Hagan v Trustees of Toowoomba Sports Ground Trust* [2000] FCA 1615, [34] (Drummond J); *Tran v Commonwealth* (2010) 187 FCR 54, 70–1 [63]–[64] (Rares J), 98 [193] (Besanko J).

47 (1990) 169 CLR 594 (Mason CJ, Deane, Dawson and Gaudron JJ).

48 A similar view had been expressed by Latham CJ in *Silk Brothers Pty Ltd v State Electricity Commission of Victoria* (1943) 67 CLR 1, 16 (Rich J agreeing at 18 and McTiernan J at 23). See also *Tran v Commonwealth* (2010) 187 FCR 54, 70 [63] (Rares J).

49 (1990) 169 CLR 594, 601–2 (Mason CJ, Deane, Dawson and Gaudron JJ). Toohey J expressed the same view at 609.

50 Ibid 605.

51 Ibid 618–24.

52 Ibid 618.

53 *CIC Insurance Ltd v Bankstown Football Club Ltd* (1997) 187 CLR 384, 408 (Brennan CJ, Dawson, Toohey and Gummow JJ, Gaudron J agreeing at 412); *Project Blue Sky Inc v Australian Broadcasting Authority* (1998) 194 CLR 355, 381–2 (McHugh, Gummow, Kirby and Hayne JJ).

While account is taken of a part or division heading, its brevity may limit its usefulness.[54] In *Tran v Commonwealth*[55] Besanko J observed that while a division heading 'can be an important contextual matter ... it is only a heading and it is by no means uncommon for legislation to contain headings which do not reflect the full scope and effect of the sections which follow'.[56]

Section headings are rarely of value as an interpretative aid [20.9]

The purpose of a section heading, or its predecessor, the marginal note, is to give an indication of the contents of the section to which it relates.[57] At common law such headings were not regarded as forming part of the statute in which they were printed.[58] That common law position is now reversed in some Australian jurisdictions.[59]

Having regard to the common law view of the status of section headings, courts traditionally regarded them as having no value as an interpretative aid.[60] This has now changed with the move to a contextual, whole-of-instrument approach to statutory interpretation. In *R v A2*[61] Keifel CJ and Keane J stated:

> A modern approach to statutory construction may take account of headings. Whilst headings of a provision are not always reliable and do not form part of a statute, and so may not govern what follows in the provision, headings may be used in a similar way to extrinsic materials. They may point the way towards and be used to identify the mischief to which the provision is directed and its purpose.[62]

---

54 *Australian Prudential Regulation Authority v Holloway* (2000) 104 FCR 521, [50] (Mansfield J); *Awada v Linknarf (in liq)* (2002) 55 NSWLR 745, 749–50 (Barrett J).

55 (2010) 187 FCR 54.

56 Ibid 98 [193].

57 *R v Schildkamp* [1971] AC 1, 20 (Viscount Dilhorne).

58 See **[13.11]**.

59 *Acts Interpretation Act 1901* (Cth) s 13(1); *Acts Interpretation Act 1954* (Qld) s 14(2) (if enacted, amended or inserted after 30 June 1991); *Legislation Interpretation Act 2021* (SA) s 19 (except section headings to amending provisions if the Bill for the Act was introduced before 1 January 2022); *Interpretation of Legislation Act 1984* (Vic) s 36(2A) (if enacted or inserted on or after 1 January 2001); *Legislation Act 2001* (ACT) ss 126(2), 127(3) (if enacted, amended or inserted after 1 January 2000); *Interpretation Act 1978* (NT) s 55(2) (if enacted, amended or inserted after 1 July 2006).

60 See *Claydon v Green* (1868) LR 3 CP 511; *Mayor of Wellington v Compton* [1916] NZLR 779; *Nixon v A-G* [1930] 1 Ch 566; *Frauenfelder v Reid* (1963) 109 CLR 42; *Chandler v DPP* [1964] AC 763; *Greenway v Abishara* [1964] VR 587; *R v Schildkamp* [1971] AC 1, 20 (Viscount Dilhorne); *Bradley v Commonwealth* (1973) 128 CLR 557. However, in *Ombudsman v Moroney* (1983) 1 NSWLR 317, 324–5 Street CJ was prepared to give a role to 'authenticated' marginal notes in the interpretative process.

61 (2019) 269 CLR 507.

62 Ibid 523 [40] (citations omitted). For section headings that are not part of the Act being treated as extrinsic material see *ABC Developmental Learning Centres Pty Ltd v Secretary, Department of Human Services* (2007) 15 VR 489, 494 (Hollingworth J); *Tran v Commonwealth* (2010) 187 FCR 54, 59 [9] (Lander J), 71 [65] (Rares J), 99 [202] (Besanko J). In *R v Rolf* (2021) 395 ALR 201, in a joint judgment of all seven judges, it is stated that 'a modern approach to statutory construction often takes account of headings, much in the same way as use is made of extrinsic materials': [18]. Section headings are specifically treated as extrinsic material by the *Interpretation Act 1987* (NSW) s 35(5) and *Interpretation of Legislation Act 1984* (Vic) s 36(4). The same outcome may apply under the *Acts Interpretation Act 1901* (Cth) s 15AB(2)(a) and *Interpretation Act 1984* (WA) s 19(2)(a).

In those jurisdictions in which section headings are treated as part of the Act, their treatment would mirror that of other headings that are part of the Act.[63]

Given their brevity, section headings will seldom be of any value in the interpretative process. In *Mayor of Wellington v Compton*[64] it was said that there were marginal notes in New Zealand statutes 'which state the very opposite of what the statute.[65] In *R v Schildkamp*[66] Lord Upjohn referred to a marginal note as being 'a very brief precis of the section' and as therefore forming 'a most unsure guide to the construction of the enacting section'.[67] The marginal note has been described as 'a guide to a hasty inquirer'[68] and as 'a rude sign-post for the guidance of travellers through the Act'.[69]

[20.10] By specifying how a word or expression used in an Act is to be understood, definitions play an important role in the interpretative process

The purpose of a definition[70] in an Act is to specify how a word or expression used in the Act is to be understood.[71] As such, definitions play an important role in the interpretative process. A definition may be specified as applying to each provision in which the word or expression appears or its application may be limited to provisions in a particular portion of the Act or even to a specified provision of the Act.[72]

The context may show that a defined word or expression is not used in its defined sense.[73] The section in which the definition appears may expressly state this limitation by including a phrase such as 'unless the context otherwise requires'. Even if such a restriction is not included, it 'must always of necessity be understood'.[74] In New South Wales, Queensland and South Australia, interpretation legislation makes this restriction clear across all Acts.[75]

---

63 See **[20.8]**.

64 [1916] NZLR 779.

65 Ibid 785 (Stout CJ).

66 [1971] AC 1.

67 Ibid 28.

68 *Claydon v Green* (1868) LR 3 CP 511, 522 (Willes J).

69 *Bank of Australasia v Hall* (1907) 4 CLR 1514, 1555 (Higgins J).

70 The *Legislation Act 2001* (ACT) s 130 defines a 'definition' as a provision of an Act that gives meaning to a term or limits or extends the meaning of a term. In *Independent Commission Against Corruption v Cunneen* (2015) 256 CLR 1, 33 Gageler J described the definition of a term as 'the creation of the most basic building block of a statutory structure'.

71 See *Gibb v Federal Commissioner of Taxation* (1966) 118 CLR 628, 635 (Barwick CJ, McTiernan and Taylor JJ).

72 Other parts of speech of the defined word or expression have corresponding meanings. See *Acts Interpretation Act 1901* (Cth) s 18A; *Interpretation Act 1987* (NSW) s 7; *Acts Interpretation Act 1954* (Qld) s 32; *Legislation Interpretation Act 2021* (SA) s 7; *Interpretation of Legislation Act 1984* (Vic) s 39; *Interpretation Act 1984* (WA) s 9; *Legislation Act 2001* (ACT) s 157; *Interpretation Act 1978* (NT) s 23.

73 In *Tovir Investments Pty Ltd v Waverley Council* [2014] NSWCA 379 Basten JA stated that 'in most circumstances, to treat a definition clause as handmaiden rather than mistress is to acknowledge the possibility of its exclusion in a particular context, by implication': at [16].

74 *Re Application of the Fourth South Melbourne Building Society* (1883) 9 VLR (Eq) 54, 58 (Holroyd J); *Obeid v Australian Competition and Consumer Commission* (2014) 226 FCR 471, 487 [53] (the Court).

75 *Interpretation Act 1987* (NSW) s 6; *Acts Interpretation Act 1954* (Qld) s 32A; *Legislation Interpretation Act 2021* (SA) s 6.

A definition of a word or expression should not itself enact substantive law.[76] Its purpose is to allow the user of legislation to read and construe a substantive provision containing a word or expression to which a definition applies as if for that word or expression there were substituted the words of the definition. Using the device of defining a word or expression facilitates the shortening of the substantive provision. The interpretative task is to construe the substantive provision with the definition read into it, not to construe the definition itself as a stand-alone component.[77]

However, the words of a definition may not be capable of being comfortably read into the substantive enactment. In this situation 'the exercise of construction will need to address any logical or grammatical infelicities that arise'.[78] To do this requires 'some understanding of the meaning of the definition itself'.[79]

In construing a definition, can a court have regard to the ordinary meaning of a phrase or expression that forms part of the term that is being defined? Up until recent years the general view taken by courts was that this was impermissible.

In *Owners of the Ship Shin Kobe Maru v Empire Shipping Co Inc*[80] ('*Shin Kobe Maru*') the High Court had to consider the meaning of 'proprietary maritime claim' in the *Admiralty Act 1988* (Cth). That term was defined by s 4(2) of that Act as including a claim relating to ownership of a ship. The relevant issue was whether the use of the word 'proprietary' in the defined term so coloured the definition as to read it down to a claim with respect to the claimant's ownership, excluding a claim that a third party is entitled to ownership. While accepting that in their natural and ordinary meaning 'a claim relating to ownership' would be wide enough to encompass a claim with respect to a third party's ownership,[81] the High Court, in an unanimous judgment, held that the use of the word 'proprietary' in the defined term did not colour the meaning to be given to the definition. The Court added that '[i]t would be quite circular to construe the words of a definition by reference to the term defined'.[82] In so holding the Court referenced *Wacal Developments Pty Ltd v Realty Developments Pty Ltd*.[83] In that case the High Court considered the definition of 'instalment contract' in s 71(2)(b) of the *Property Law Act 1974* (Qld). At issue was whether the word 'instalment' in the defined term coloured the meaning to be given to the definition. Gibbs J, in rejecting that proposition, stated: '[I]t is impermissible to construe a definition by reference to the term defined. The expression is given by the statute a special meaning which must be applied whether or not it accords with the ordinary meaning.'[84]

In *Hardy Wine Co Ltd v Janevruss Pty Ltd*,[85] Callaway JA in the Victorian Court of Appeal, referring to a definition of 'fair market price' in an agreement between the parties to a contractual

76 In *Australian Competition and Consumer Commission v Yazaki Corporation* (2018) 262 FCR 243 the Federal Court held that the definition of 'exclusionary provision' in s 4D of the *Competition and Consumer Act 2010* (Cth) enacted substantive law: at 272 [114].

77 See *Kelly v The Queen* (2004) 218 CLR 216, 253 [103] (McHugh J).

78 *Commissioner of Police v Kennedy* [2007] NSWCA 328, [44] (Basten JA).

79 *Tovir Investments Pty Ltd v Waverley Council* [2014] NSWCA 379, [16] (Basten JA).

80 (1994) 181 CLR 404.

81 Ibid 418.

82 Ibid 419.

83 (1978) 140 CLR 503.

84 Ibid 507.

85 [2006] VSCA 28.

dispute, observed that it may be impermissible to take the words in the defined term into account in construing the definition but added in a footnote that he did not think the proposition from the *Shin Kobe Maru* case to that effect was 'universally true'.[86] A similar sentiment was expressed by Leeming JA in *Barangaroo Delivery Authority v Lend Lease (Millers Point) Pty Ltd*.[87] Leeming JA stated that, especially for a complex definition 'where reliance on the mere literal or grammatical meaning is unlikely to be determinative', the first step is to 'consider the structure and purpose, as well as the text' of the definition.[88] In *Tovir Investments Pty Ltd v Waverley Council*[89] Basten JA expressed the view that in a Local Environmental Plan lacking 'the degree of precision and formality one expects in a statute' reliance may be placed on the term being defined in giving meaning to a definition.[90]

In *Birmingham City Council v Walker*[91] Lord Hoffmann, giving a judgment in the House of Lords with which the other judges agreed,[92] expressed the view that, in construing a definition of 'successor' in the *Housing Act 1985* (UK), 'the ordinary meaning of the word is part of the material which can be used to construe the definition'.[93]

In *Esso Australia Resources Ltd v Federal Commissioner of Taxation*[94] the Federal Court, while applying the principle established in the *Shin Kobe Maru* case, stated: 'It may be that this approach is difficult to reconcile with the general approach to interpreting statutes which requires that the meaning of a provision be determined "by reference to the language of the instrument as a whole": *Project Blue Sky* at [69] and the authorities there cited. The phrase or expression is just as much a part of the statute as any other part.'[95]

The trend of authority in Australia now leans towards allowing the text of a term being defined to be considered in construing the definition. It would seem likely that in deciding what term to define, the parliamentary counsel would wish to use a term that captures the essence of the concept.

If Act A defines a term as having the same meaning as in Act B, the meaning of the term in Act A is not affected by the operation or application of Act B. For example, if Act B defines 'personal injury damages' but excludes from the coverage of Act B damages incurred in specified circumstances, the fact that Act A defines 'personal injury damages', as used in Act A, as having the same meaning as in Act B does not bring with it those coverage exclusions. Act A is referring to the meaning of 'personal injury damages' in Act B – that is, to how it is defined in Act B, not to how Act B operates in any particular situation.[96]

---

86 Ibid [4] (Eames JA agreeing at [15], Ashley JA agreeing at [16]).

87 [2014] NSWCA 279.

88 Ibid [11]–[12] (Beazley P agreeing at [1], Tobias AJA agreeing at [104]).

89 [2014] NSWCA 379.

90 Ibid [21] (Macfarlan JA agreeing at [46], Leeming JA agreeing at [47]).

91 [2007] 2 AC 262.

92 Ibid 268–9.

93 Ibid 268 [11].

94 (2011) 199 FCR 226.

95 Ibid 257 [104] (the Court).

96 See *Certain Lloyd's Underwriters v Cross* (2012) 248 CLR 378, 393 (French CJ and Hayne J), 412 (Kiefel J). See also *New South Wales v Williamson* (2012) 248 CLR 417, 425 (French CJ and Hayne J).

Simplified outlines are of limited value in the interpretative process [20.11]

While simplified outlines have been described as 'helpful'[97] and as providing 'a conveniently simplified outline'[98] of the operation of provisions and have also been relied on for descriptions of the provisions of which they are an outline,[99] their limited value in the construction process is recognised. In *H v Minister for Immigration and Citizenship*[100] the Full Court of the Federal Court, in referring to s 2A of the *Australian Citizenship Act 2007* (Cth), which provided a simplified outline of the Act, stated:

> Section 2A is part of the Citizenship Act and cannot be ignored in the process of construction. Perhaps such an outline may help resolve ambiguities in, or doubts about the scope of, other provisions of the Act. Since it is only a 'simplified outline', however, it is improbable that s 2A would alter the clear meaning of a provision or, indeed, resolve a constructional issue of any complexity.[101]

A simplified outline of ch 3 of the *Legal Profession Act 2004* (Vic) was criticised by the Victorian Court of Appeal in *Legal Services Board v Gillespie-Jones*[102] as being 'really a synopsis of only some of the more populist objectives of the legislation' and as being in 'disconformity' with the terms of certain substantive provisions. The Court observed that it was not clear to it how or why such simplified provisions 'are thought to aid in the accurate construction of the operative provisions of Chapter 3. If anything, they tend to obscure the task of construing operative provisions which do not mirror those broadly stated objectives'.[103]

Examples, notes and other reader's aids may assist in the interpretative process [20.12]

An Act may set out an example of how the provision to which the example relates operates in a specified factual situation. As part of the Act, account can be taken of the example in construing the Act.[104]

Prior to the 1990s examples were rarely included as stand-alone statements in Australian legislation.[105] This was the case even though judges had occasionally highlighted the value to be obtained from considering examples.[106]

---

97 *Theo v Secretary, Department of Families, Community Services and Indigenous Affairs* (2007) 45 AAR 403, [15] (the Court).

98 *Re MacTiernan; Ex Parte McKay* (2007) 208 FLR 191, 195 [22] (Martin CJ).

99 *Bayside City Council v Telstra Corporation Ltd* (2004) 216 CLR 595, 617 [8]–[9], 618 [12] (Gleeson CJ, Gummow, Kirby, Hayne and Heydon JJ).

100 (2010) 188 FCR 393.

101 Ibid 417 [88].

102 [2012] VSCA 68, [37] (Nettle, Redlich and Hansen JJA).

103 Ibid.

104 *Brooks v Commissioner of Taxation* (2000) 100 FCR 117, 134 [64] (the Court).

105 Examples were occasionally incorporated within a sentence preceded by words such as 'for example'.

106 In *Escoigne Properties Ltd v Inland Revenue Commissioners* [1958] AC 549 Lord Denning stated that 'one of the best ways, I find, of understanding a statute is to take some specific instances which, by common consent, are intended to be covered by it . . . Section 50 of the Finance Act, 1938 . . . is a section which I would not be able to understand unless I was first given an instance of what it was intended to cover': at 566–7. In *Mayne Nickless Ltd v Mackintosh* [1989] VR 878 Murphy J, with whose judgment Gobbo and Phillips JJ agreed at 896, observed that he found 'it easier to visualise the way in which the section is intended to work in practice by considering examples': at 885.

Nowadays examples are reasonably common as stand-alone statements in Australian Acts. Interpretation legislation in all but three[107] Australian jurisdictions defines the extent to which an example may be used as an interpretative aid by providing that an example is not exhaustive[108] (clearly, this would be the situation even in the absence of such a provision[109]) and makes it clear that an example does not limit the meaning of the provision.[110]

Except for New South Wales, Tasmania, Western Australia and the Northern Territory, interpretation legislation in all Australian jurisdictions provides that an example may extend the meaning of the provision.[111] Queensland and the Northern Territory expressly state that if there is an inconsistency between the example and the provision, the provision prevails.[112] Even in the absence of such a legislative statement, this would be the situation.[113]

The Victorian provision applies only to examples included at the foot of a provision under the heading 'Example' or 'Examples',[114] whereas the ACT provision[115] applies to examples at the end of a provision or forming part of the provision, whether or not the words 'for example' are used.[116]

If forming part of the Act,[117] notes, tables, diagrams, maps and other reader's aids that appear in the text of an Act as enacted by Parliament may be considered in the course of the interpretative process.[118] Even if not part of the Act in a formal sense, as extrinsic material they may assist as interpretative aids.[119]

---

107 New South Wales, Tasmania and Western Australia.

108 *Acts Interpretation Act 1901* (Cth) s 15AD(a); *Acts Interpretation Act 1954* (Qld) s 14D(a); *Legislation Interpretation Act 2021* (SA) s 20(a); *Interpretation of Legislation Act 1984* (Vic) s 36A(1)(a) (Acts passed on or after 1 January 2001); *Legislation Act 2001* (ACT) s 132(1)(a); *Interpretation Act 1978* (NT) s 62D(a).

109 In *Brooks v Commissioner of Taxation* (2000) 100 FCR 117 the Federal Court stated, in relation to examples contained in the *Income Tax Assessment Act 1997* (Cth): 'An example is just that, an example, it is not intended to be exhaustive of cases which might fall within the section' (at 135 [66]).

110 *Acts Interpretation Act 1901* (Cth) s 15AD (example is not exhaustive); *Acts Interpretation Act 1954* (Qld) s 14D(b); *Legislation Interpretation Act 2021* (SA) s 20(b); *Interpretation of Legislation Act 1984* (Vic) s 36A(1)(b) (Acts passed on or after 1 January 2001); *Legislation Act 2001* (ACT) s 132(1)(b); *Interpretation Act 1978* (NT) s 62D(b). While the wording of the Commonwealth provision differs, in *Fair Trading Administration Corporation v Owners Corporation, SP 43551* [2002] NSWSC 624 Burchett AJ stated that s 15AD 'appears merely to confirm the approach the ordinary principles of construction would generally require a court to take' as examples 'cannot have a narrowing effect, so as to exclude other things that fall fairly within the language of the provision': at [17].

111 *Acts Interpretation Act 1901* (Cth) s 15AD(b); *Acts Interpretation Act 1954* (Qld) s 14D(b); *Legislation Interpretation Act 2021* (SA) s 20(b); *Interpretation of Legislation Act 1984* (Vic) s 36A(1)(b) (Acts passed on or after 1 January 2001); *Legislation Act 2001* (ACT) s 132(1)(b).

112 *Acts Interpretation Act 1954* (Qld) s 14D(c); *Interpretation Act 1978* (NT) s 62D(c).

113 *McLaughlin v Dungowan Manly Pty Ltd (No 3)* [2011] NSWSC 717, [22] (Pembroke J).

114 *Interpretation of Legislation Act 1984* (Vic) s 36A(2).

115 *Legislation Act 2001* (ACT) s 132(2).

116 Without the benefit of such a provision, an example forming part of a provision would be construed in the same way as any other substantive provision included in the Act.

117 See **[13.14]**.

118 See *One.Tel Ltd (in liq) v Rich* (2005) 190 FLR 443, 459–60 [54] (Bergin J). In *DPP v Walters (A Pseudonym)* (2015) 49 VR 356 the majority judges stated that 'if two interpretations are open on the text of the substantive provision, a note might assist in determining which of the two interpretations was to be preferred . . . however, if there is conflict between the substantive provision and the note, the note must give way': at 370 [51] (Maxwell P, Redlich, Tate and Priest JJA).

119 See *Clement v Comcare* (2011) 194 FCR 24, 29 [34] (Cowdroy J); *Shuster v Minister for Immigration and Citizenship* (2008) 167 FCR 186, 188–9 [11] (Bennett J).

In the Northern Territory a note in the text of an Act is part of the Act.[120] Section 62E of the *Interpretation Act 1978* (NT) makes the same provision with respect to notes as it makes by s 62D with respect to examples (a note is not exhaustive and does not limit or extend the meaning of the provision; if inconsistent with the provision, the provision prevails to the extent of the inconsistency).

In 2010 the Commonwealth Office of Parliamentary Counsel conducted a survey[121] of user attitudes to various aids to understanding, such as examples, notes and diagrams, used in Commonwealth legislation. For those aids, just over 80 per cent of respondents (56 per cent of respondents who were judges or magistrates) were satisfied with the usefulness of examples, 87 per cent (78 per cent of respondents who were judges or magistrates) were satisfied with the usefulness of notes and 63 per cent (87 per cent of respondents who were judges or magistrates) were satisfied with the usefulness of diagrams. Clearly there is strong user support for the use of reader's aids in legislation.

Punctuation has a role to play in the interpretative process[122] [20.13]

In Australia the view was taken in the early 20th century that courts may take account of punctuation but must not allow it to control the meaning if the meaning is otherwise reasonably clear. Thus, in *President of the Shire of Charlton v Ruse*[123] Griffith CJ stated that punctuation marks 'which may be due to a printer's or proof reader's error, ought not to control the sense if the meaning is otherwise tolerably clear'.[124]

By late in the 20th century a more robust attitude to punctuation was being taken by courts in Australia.

In *Re Collins; Ex parte Hockings*[125] Toohey and McHugh JJ, in construing a definition containing a comma, stated that there was 'no reason why the use of a comma ... should be discarded or thought to serve no purpose'.[126] In *Minister for Immigration and Multicultural Affairs v Savvin*[127] Katz J said that the hesitant judicial attitude to punctuation displayed in cases like *Charlton* 'is on the wane, certainly so far as the construction of domestic legislation by national courts is concerned'. [128]

Just how valuable punctuation is as an aid depends on the court's perception of how carefully the Act has been punctuated.[129]

---

120 See **[13.14]**.

121 For a review of the survey see Peter Quiggin, 'A Survey of User Attitudes to the Use of Aids to Understanding in Legislation' (2011) (1) *The Loophole: Journal of the Commonwealth Association of Legislative Counsel* 96.

122 See also **[13.15]**.

123 (1912) 14 CLR 220.

124 Ibid 225. See also Isaacs J at 229–230. See *Federal Council of the British Medical Association v Commonwealth* (1949) 79 CLR 201, 254–5 (Rich J).

125 (1989) 167 CLR 522.

126 Ibid 525. See also *Ryde Municipal Council v Macquarie University* (1978) 139 CLR 633, 636 (Gibbs ACJ); *Chew v The Queen* (1992) 173 CLR 626, 631 (Mason CJ, Brennan, Gaudron and McHugh JJ).

127 (2000) 98 FCR 168.

128 Ibid [76]–[80].

129 See *Marine Board of Strahan v Kirkpatrick* [1967] Tas SR 179, 191 (Crawford J); *Mainteck Services Pty Ltd v Stein Heurtey SA* (2014) 89 NSWLR 633, 659–60 [105] (Leeming JA).

Even if not treated as part of a Victorian Act,[130] statutory recognition of the role of punctuation in interpretation is given in Victoria. Section 35(b)(i) of the *Interpretation of Legislation Act 1984* (Vic) provides that in the interpretation of a provision of an Act consideration may be given to any matter or document that is relevant including, but not limited to, all indications provided by the Act as printed by authority, including punctuation.[131]

Apart from Victoria, punctuation is recognised as being part of an Act in a formal sense in the Commonwealth, Queensland, South Australia and the Australian Capital Territory.[132] As such, a court may take account of it just as it does any other part of the Act.

Example 20.1 shows how the use of punctuation can assist in conveying meaning while its absence can create doubt and ambiguity.[133]

Example 20.1 *R v Fyffe*

An issue in this case was the meaning of para (b) of the definition of 'explosive substance' in s 317(1) of the *Crimes Act 1958* (Vic). That paragraph included as an explosive substance 'any apparatus machine implement or materials used or intended to be used or adapted for causing or aiding in causing any explosion in or with any explosive substance'. The question was whether the words 'intended to be' attach to the word 'adapted' as well as to the word 'used' in the definition.

Murphy J[134] contrasted the Victorian definition with s 9 of the *Explosive Substances Act 1883* (UK), which contained the expression 'any apparatus, machine, implement, or materials used, or intended to be used, or adapted for causing, or aiding in causing, any explosion in or with any explosive substance'. He pointed out that the 'use of commas in this definition in the English Act would seem to make reasonably clear that in that section the words "intended to be" attach only to the word "used" and not to the word "adapted"', which is how he interpreted the Victorian provision.[135]

Impact on interpretation of where provisions are located

[20.14] **The context provided by sections immediately surrounding a particular provision can affect the interpretation of that provision**

While the modern approach to statutory interpretation is to read the text of an Act in the context of the Act as a whole, for an Act divided into parts the particular context of a part can affect the interpretation of provisions in that part.[136]

130 Under the *Interpretation of Legislation Act 1984* (Vic) s 36(3B) punctuation is treated as part of Acts passed on or after 1 January 2001 and as part of an earlier Act if the punctuation is inserted by an Act passed on or after that date.

131 See *Williams v Oataway* (2005) 11 VR 529, 537–8 (Batt JA).

132 *Acts Interpretation Act 1901* (Cth) s 13(1); *Acts Interpretation Act 1954* (Qld) s 14(6); *Legislation Interpretation Act 2021* (SA) s 19 (no express reference to punctuation but the section covers 'everything' appearing in the Act except a few specified things); *Legislation Act 2001* (ACT) s 126(6).

133 See also discussion of grammatical analysis at **[9.5]**.

134 *R v Fyffe* [1991] 2 VR 72, 79.

135 McGarvie J at ibid 86 expressed the same view as did Brooking J at ibid 104–5.

136 *Australian Postal Corporation v Sinnaiah* (2013) 213 FCR 449, 456 [24] (the Court). In *R v Rolfe* (2021) 395 ALR 201 [20] the location of a section within a division was relied on to identify its purpose (the Court).

In *Australian Broadcasting Corporation v Redmore Pty Ltd*[137] both the majority and minority judges in the High Court relied on the general structure of the *Australian Broadcasting Corporation Act 1983* (Cth) in concluding that the contractual power granted to the ABC by a section in pt IV of that Act (headed 'Powers and Duties of the Corporation') was not limited by s 70 in pt VI of that Act (headed 'Finance'). Section 70 provided that the ABC must not, without the Minister's approval, enter into a contract under which it had to pay more than $500,000. It was held that s 70 was merely directory as to the manner of exercising contractual powers and did not confine those powers to agreements involving expenditure of not more than $500,000.

The majority judges in the High Court upheld the decision of the majority judges in the NSW Court of Appeal (Samuels and McHugh JJA).[138] Those judges had placed great weight on the inference to be drawn from the location of the two sections involved. McHugh JA stated:

> If s 70 was intended to limit rather than to regulate the contractual powers of the ABC, it is surprising that it was not placed in Pt IV which defines the ambit of the powers of the ABC. The deliberate removal of the provisions of s 70 from Pt IV to Pt VI which deals with 'Finance' seems explicable only on the basis that Parliament did not intend to affect the legal capacity of the ABC to enter into a contract even though it involves more than $500,000.[139]

In the much earlier Victorian case *Re Commercial Bank of Australia Ltd*,[140] the view was taken that a prima facie presumption that sections in a group relate to the same subject matter could be drawn. Holroyd J stated:

> When an Act is divided and cut up into parts or heads, *prima facie* it is, we think, to be presumed that those heads were intended to indicate a certain group of clauses as relating to a particular subject ... The object is *prima facie* to enable everybody who reads to discriminate as to what clauses relate to such and such a particular subject matter. It must be perfectly clear that a clause introduced into a part of an Act relating to one subject matter is meant to relate to other subject matters in another part of the Act before we can hold that it does so.[141]

In *K&S Lake City Freighters Pty Ltd v Gordon & Gotch Ltd*[142] the majority judges in the High Court were of the view that the context provided by the part of the *Motor Vehicles Act 1959* (SA) in which a section was included (a part headed 'Third Party Insurance') did not lead to the scope of that section being limited to contracting out of liability for death or bodily injury (the subject

---

137 (1989) 166 CLR 454.

138 *Australian Broadcasting Corporation v Redmore Pty Ltd* (1987) 11 NSWLR 621.

139 Ibid 635 (Samuels JA agreeing at 630). The dissenting judge, Kirby P, considered the arrangement of the Act merely to be an 'instance of the draftsman's sense of logic': at 629. The equivalent provision to s 70 in the repealed *Broadcasting and Television Act 1942* (Cth) was in a Division headed 'Powers and functions of the Commission'.

140 (1893) 19 VLR 333.

141 Ibid 375. Referring to this case and to the presumption that when an Act is divided into parts, each part relates to a particular subject and is not affected by clauses in another part, in *Chakera v Kuzamanovic* [2003] VSC 92 Nettle J observed that 'modern Acts of Parliament tend to contain many more sections than Acts used to do' and that '[i]t may be doubted that the same sort of precision as was contemplated in [*In*] *Re Commercial Bank of Australia Limited* is to be expected these days': at [19].

142 (1985) 157 CLR 309.

matter of third party insurance). It was noted that the part included another section that expressly extended to claims for damage to property.[143]

The presumption that sections in a group relate to the same subject matter is just that, a presumption. It may be displaced when regard is had to the context of the Act as a whole.

[20.15] An inference may be drawn from other subsections of a section about the scope of a particular subsection

How a subsection is interpreted may be affected by the content of other subsections of the same section.

In *Amalgamated Television Services Pty Ltd v Australian Broadcasting Tribunal*,[144] the Full Court of the Federal Court had to consider s 123 of the *Broadcasting Act 1942* (Cth). Subsections (1), (1A), (1AA), (2) and (3) of that section clearly only related to the provision of information about financial matters whereas sub-s (4), on a literal reading, extended to any information concerning the broadcasting or television activities of the licensee. The Court stated:

> [W]e think that it is hardly likely that the legislature would, in a section dealing with financial matters, append as the last sub-section of that section a general obligation to make available documents for inspection or to furnish information of a general kind. In our opinion, the books and documents and information to which s 123(4) refers are books and documents and information relevant to financial matters and the obligation is restricted to such matters.[145]

[20.16] An Act's schedule is not of lesser importance than a provision in the body of the Act

There is a long line of 19th-century authorities to the effect that if there was a conflict between an Act's schedule and a section that set out the purpose of the schedule, the schedule must yield to, and be controlled by, that section.[146] This reflected a view that a schedule was inferior in standing to a section. However, in *Re Foley*[147] the NSW Supreme Court approved the following statement of the relevant principles made by Lord Sterndale MR in *Inland Revenue Commissioners v Gittus*:[148]

> It seems to me there are two principles or rules of interpretation which ought to be applied to the combination of Act and schedule. If the Act says that the schedule is to be used for a certain purpose and the heading of the part of the schedule in question shows that it is prima facie at any rate devoted to that purpose, then you must read the Act and the schedule as though the schedule were operating for that purpose, and if you can satisfy the language of the section without extending it beyond that purpose you ought to do it. But if in spite of that you find in the language of the schedule words and terms that go clearly outside that purpose, then you must give effect to them and you must not consider them as limited by the heading of that part of the schedule or by the purpose

143 In a dissenting judgment Mason J stated that the context of the Part of the Act in which the section was located 'demands that the section be read more narrowly than if it had stood alone': ibid 318.

144 (1989) 91 ALR 363.

145 Ibid 371 (Morling, Burchett and Hill JJ).

146 See *R v Baines* (1840) 12 Ad & E 210; 113 ER 792, 799 (Lord Denman CJ); *Goodman (Official Assignee) v Mayor of Melbourne* (1861) 1 W & W (L) 4, 6 (Stawell CJ); *R v Taylor* (1863) 2 W & W (L) 23, 29 (Stawell CJ); *South Australian Banking Co v Horner* (1868) 2 SALR 263, 264 (Gwynne J).

147 (1952) 53 SR (NSW) 31, 36 (Roper CJ in Eq).

148 [1920] 1 KB 563.

> mentioned in the Act for which the schedule is prima facie to be used. You cannot refuse to give effect to clear words simply because prima facie they seem to be limited by the heading of the schedule and the definition of the purpose of the schedule contained in the Act.[149]

This view treats schedules and sections as components of an Act equal in status and to be construed having regard to the Act as a whole and the overall context. It also reflects the reality that legislative drafters place provisions in a schedule not out of any belief that those provisions are in any way subordinate to provisions in the body of the Act but out of the belief that to do so improves the presentation and readability of the Act.

In any event it is common currently for a schedule to be introduced by a section providing simply for it to have effect or to have effect according to its terms, without stating a purpose for the schedule.[150] Even such a provision is unnecessary in NSW legislation.[151]

---

149 Ibid 576. See also *Ramos v Minister for Immigration and Multicultural Affairs* (1999) 91 FCR 329, 334 [28] (the Court); *New South Wales v Bujdoso* (2007) 69 NSWLR 302, 323 [89] (Basten JA).

150 See, eg, *Governor-General Amendment (Salary) Act 2019* (Cth) s 3; *Local Land Services Act 2013* (NSW) s 200(6); *Heritage Act 2017* (Vic) s 17.

151 *Interpretation Act 1987* (NSW) s 64A.

PART V

LEGISLATIVE HISTORY

Context – a fundamental notion in statutory interpretation (chapter 7) – includes the wider context. Part V deals with a major component of this wider context – the legislative history of an Act. In this book the term legislative history is used to refer broadly to the materials, law and circumstances that reflect the genesis and historical development of an Act or a provision of an Act up to the version being interpreted. Examining legislative history can provide information about what Parliament intended. Part V divides legislative history into four categories: legislative antecedents; pre-existing common law; background facts and circumstances; and pre-parliamentary, executive and parliamentary materials. Each has its own chapter. A category of materials that might have some claim to be included in this Part is international treaties and materials. Although the current Part does refer to general international historical context (chapter 23), the use of international treaties and materials is more conveniently addressed separately in chapter 31.

Chapter 21 (*Legislative Antecedents (Evolution), Including Subsequent Amending Acts*) focuses on the historical legislative evolution of the statutory provision being interpreted. This may start with the original enactment, or a relevant statute made by another Parliament, and then includes the successive enactments, amendments and repeals that led to the version of the statutory provision being construed. For convenience, this chapter also discusses use of amending Acts made *after* the version of the provision being interpreted.

Chapter 22 (*Pre-existing Common Law*) deals with the common law that existed prior to the statute being enacted, where that common law has been replaced, codified, abolished, modified or supplemented by that statute or incorporated into it. Reference to the historical common law is distinct from using common law as a precedent, which is addressed in chapter 30.

Chapter 23 (*Background Facts and Circumstances*) addresses the matrix of facts and circumstances that formed the background to the enactment of the Act or provision being construed. These matters help place the enactment of the statutory language in its broader historical, social, political and economic setting.

Chapter 24 (*Extrinsic Materials: Pre-parliamentary and Parliamentary Materials*) examines the use and probative value of various materials that are rationally connected to a statute and created in the pre-legislative stage (such as a law reform commission report or white paper) or during the legislative process (such as a second reading speech or an explanatory memorandum).

LEGISLATIVE ANTECEDENTS (EVOLUTION), INCLUDING SUBSEQUENT AMENDING ACTS 21

Overview

Legislative antecedents are the enactments that constitute the historical legislative development of the statute or statutory provision being interpreted, such as repealed statutes and successive amendments to the statute made by the same Parliament. Antecedents may also include statutes made by other parliaments where it can be inferred that the statute being interpreted is derived from that other statute. [21.1]

The common law has permitted recourse to legislative antecedents for a long time. But the contemporary wider context principle makes it clear that this history is to be considered from the outset of the interpretative process, without any need for doubt or ambiguity on the face of the statutory text. Knowledge of historical legislative development, like other wider context, provides a better understanding of the pre-existing law, which in turn may assist in understanding the meaning or purpose of the statute being construed. Practically, legislative antecedents are often considered with other pieces of legislative history, such as parliamentary materials.

The common law has developed certain presumptions where words used in a previous enactment are carried over to a subsequent statute, such as the re-enactment presumption. Caution must be exercised in applying these presumptions, especially where there is a change in drafting practice or the statute is a consolidation statute.

Subsequent amending Acts are clearly not 'historical' and therefore arguably not part of 'context'. Despite that, there is a common law principle that permits recourse to subsequent enactments in certain circumstances.

As part of wider context

Courts have considered legislative antecedents for a long time, but the contemporary 'wider context' principle requires consideration from the start of the interpretative process [21.2]

Courts in Australia have been permitted to refer to legislative antecedents in statutory interpretation since at least the start of the 20th century.[1] As with many extrinsic sources in earlier times, this was sometimes dependent on the statutory text being ambiguous.[2] Under the 'modern' common law, legislative antecedents are a legitimate component of context 'in its widest sense' and must be considered 'in the first instance, not merely at some later stage when ambiguity

1 See **[2.3]**.

2 See, eg, *Tasmania v Commonwealth and Victoria* (1904) 1 CLR 329, 359 (O'Connor J).

might be thought to arise'.[3] It is well accepted that 'a court is permitted to have regard to the words used by the legislature in their legal and historical context'.[4] That context 'includes reference to the legislative history of the provision'.[5]

It is readily understandable why legislative antecedents are relevant contextual material. As then Justice Allsop noted: 'The law at any given point cannot be divorced from how it reached that point.'[6] Legislative antecedents potentially enhance our understanding of what Parliament was trying to achieve, including a statute's object or the 'mischief' it was trying to remedy. By examining how the text has changed, remained consistent, evolved, or been placed in a different statutory context, the interpreter may be able to identify relevant indicators about meaning.

The Interpretation Acts of the states, territories and the Commonwealth all contain provisions allowing recourse to extrinsic materials.[7] All these provisions potentially cover legislative antecedents. But they are not, in practice, used as legal authority for recourse to this material. The common law continues to be the legal authority engaged for this category of legislative history.

[21.3] Legislative antecedents refers to the pre-enactment statutory history of the Act or provision being interpreted

Legislative antecedents refers to the historical *legislative* development of an Act or a statutory provision.[8] Some international commentators refer to the 'legislative evolution' of a statute or statutory provision.[9] This is a useful term that helps distinguish these materials from the broader term 'legislative history', but to date it does not seem to be used with regularity in Australia.

The historical legislative development of an Act or provision may start with the first version of that Act or provision enacted by the same Parliament, a predecessor statute, or an earlier statute enacted by a Parliament of another jurisdiction if that earlier statute can logically be regarded as its genesis or otherwise relevant. Examples are the *Postage Act 1825* (NSW) as the source of s 471.12 of the *Criminal Code* (Cth) (in sch to *Criminal Code Act 1995* (Cth))[10] and the *Malicious*

---

3 *CIC Insurance Ltd v Bankstown Football Club Ltd* (1997) 187 CLR 384, 408 (Brennan CJ, Dawson, Toohey and Gummow JJ). See **[2.7]**, **[7.3]–[7.6]**.

4 *Network Ten Pty Ltd v TCN Channel Nine Pty Ltd* (2004) 218 CLR 273, 280 [11] (McHugh ACJ, Gummow and Hayne JJ), citing *Newcastle City Council v GIO General Ltd* (1997) 191 CLR 85, 112 (McHugh J).

5 *Fremantle Lawyers Pty Ltd v Sarich* (2019) 54 WAR 113, 146 [140] (Buss P), citing *CIC Insurance Ltd v Bankstown Football Club Ltd* (1997) 187 CLR 384, 408 (Brennan CJ, Dawson, Toohey and Gummow JJ) and *Newcastle City Council v GIO General Ltd* (1997) 191 CLR 85, 112–113 (McHugh J); *BMW Australia Ltd v Brewster* (2019) 269 CLR 574, 598 [43] (Kiefel CJ, Bell and Keane J).

6 James Allsop, 'Statutes: Context, Meaning and Pre-enactment History' [2005] (Winter) *Bar News* 19, 21.

7 *Acts Interpretation Act 1901* (Cth) s 15AB; *Interpretation Act 1987* (NSW) s 34; *Acts Interpretation Act 1954* (Qld) s 14B; *Legislation Interpretation Act 2021* (SA) s 16; *Acts Interpretation Act 1931* (Tas) s 8B; *Interpretation of Legislation Act 1984* (Vic) s 35(b); *Interpretation Act 1984* (WA) s 19; *Legislation Act 2001* (ACT) s 141; *Interpretation Act 1978* (NT) s 62B. Prior to 2022, South Australia relied solely on the common law: see **[2.9]**, **[24.2]**.

8 The term is not uncommon. See, eg, *Regional Express Holdings Ltd v Australian Federation of Air Pilots* (2017) 262 CLR 456, 475 [45] (the Court); *Australian Building and Construction Commissioner v Construction, Forestry, Mining and Energy Union* (2018) 262 CLR 157, 186 [91] 192 [107] (Keane, Nettle and Gordon JJ).

9 See, eg, James Steele, 'Statutory Forebears: Legislative Evolution as a Means of Statutory Interpretation' (2018) 39(3) *Statute Law Review* 303, 305–6; Ruth Sullivan, *Sullivan on the Construction of Statutes* (LexisNexis Canada, 6th ed, 2014) 660.

10 *Monis v The Queen* (2013) 249 CLR 92, 118 [32] (French CJ).

Damage Act 1861 (UK) as the origin of the *Crimes Act 1900* (NSW).[11] In one instance the concepts in an Act were found to have originated in the Book of Genesis.[12]

From there, an Act's evolution is traced through ensuing versions up to the version of the statute or provision being interpreted. This category of legislative history is about the lineage of the statute – the sequence of 'ancestors' from which it descended. Examples include:

- prior enacted versions of the statute or statutory provision, including amendments to those prior versions;
- amendments to the statute;
- relevant statutes enacted by another Parliament;
- repealed statutes and provisions;
- transitional and savings Acts that regulate amendments and repeals; and
- portions of earlier or repealed Acts where those portions have been combined or enacted in a successor Act.

There is old common law authority that suggests that repealed legislation should be regarded as never having been enacted, subject to certain exceptions.[13] But it is clear that it is permissible to look at repealed provisions to assist in determining the meaning of a statute.[14] This position is consistent with the 'wider context' principle. Recourse to repealed provisions or Acts is now routine when considering the enacting history of a statute.[15] **Example 21.1** is an illustration of the court attributing probative value to repealed provisions.

Example 21.1 *Esso Australia Pty Ltd v Australian Workers' Union*[16]

An employer, Esso Australia, and the union representing its employees, the Australian Workers Union ('AWU'), were negotiating a new enterprise agreement. In support of its claims the AWU organised industrial action. Esso obtained an order from the Fair Work Commission requiring the AWU to stop organising certain action, but the AWU continued, causing it to be in contravention of the order. The AWU subsequently claimed that industrial action was 'protected' industrial action within the meaning of the *Fair Work Act 2009* (Cth) ('the *Fair Work Act*'). Section 413(5) set out the requirements for industrial action to qualify as 'protected' industrial action, including:

> (5) The following persons must not have contravened any orders that apply to them and that relate to, or relate to industrial action relating to, the agreement or a matter that arose during bargaining for the agreement:
>
> (a) if the person organising or engaging in the industrial action is a bargaining representative for the agreement – the bargaining representative ...

---

11 *Grajewski v DPP (NSW)* (2019) 264 CLR 470, 476–7 [14] (Kiefel CJ, Bell, Keane and Gordon JJ).

12 *Palgo Holdings Pty Ltd v Gowans* (2005) 221 CLR 249, 257 [16] n 19 (McHugh, Gummow, Hayne and Heydon JJ). The Book of Genesis is the first book of the Old Testament.

13 See, eg, *Maxwell v Murphy* (1957) 96 CLR 261, 266–7 (Dixon CJ). The old common law position was not definitive: see Thomas MacLeod, *The High Court on the Interpretation of Statutes* (Law Book Co, 1924) 188–90.

14 *R v Lavender* (2005) 222 CLR 67, 79–80 [31], 83 [41] (Gleeson CJ, McHugh, Gummow and Hayne JJ).

15 See, eg, *Commissioner of State Revenue (Vic) v ACN 005 057 349 Pty Ltd* (2017) 261 CLR 509, 525–8 [39]–[45] (Bell and Gordon JJ); *Tabcorp Holdings Ltd v Victoria* (2016) 90 ALJR 376, 382 [30], 389–90 [78]–[84] (the Court).

16 (2017) 263 CLR 551.

The issue was whether the words 'must not have contravened any orders that apply to them' in the provision referred only to orders continuing at the time of the proposed protected industrial action, or whether they extended to past contraventions of orders, even if the order had ceased to operate by the time of the proposed industrial action.

The majority judgment of Kiefel CJ, Keane, Nettle and Edelman JJ considered the legislative antecedents of s 413. They commenced with the first statutory definition of 'industrial action' in the *Commonwealth Conciliation and Arbitration Act 1904* (Cth), then noted that the concept of 'protected' industrial action was introduced by a 1993 amendment to the *Industrial Relations Act 1988* (Cth). That Act was renamed and amended and became the *Workplace Relations Act 1996* (Cth). The equivalent section to s 413 was subject to further repeal and re-enactment. That prior section, said the majority, conveyed the sense of referring to the situation where an organisation had not complied with an order where it was still possible to do so before the proposed industrial action.[17]

The relevant provisions of the *Workplace Relations Act 1996* (Cth) were repealed and replaced by the *Fair Work Act* in 2009. The majority compared the language of the predecessor sections with the current section and noted a change. From this, they determined that the understanding of the meaning of the repealed provisions could not be carried over to s 413. The change, they said, 'bespeaks an explicit change in emphasis from a state of *compliance* with orders to a state of *absence of past contravention* of orders'.[18] The analysis, they said, 'resolves any doubt' arising from the textual difficulties of the Act.[19]

Consolidation Acts

[21.4] **There is old authority that suggests that consolidation Acts should be interpreted without reference to their legislative antecedents, but this approach is not consistent with the contemporary principle of context**

A consolidation Act is a statute that repeals a current statute, or a number of statutes or statutory provisions on a subject matter, including their amendments, and brings them together into a single Act to consolidate the law in the area.[20] That instrument is enacted to consolidate and replace all previous legislative enactments on a particular subject area. Its purpose, therefore, is to bring the law together in one place, not to change it. Whether an Act consolidates the law or changes it will itself be a matter of statutory construction.

A consolidation Act in this formal sense is different from the way the term is often used in online databases. In that instance 'consolidation' is used to describe a version online that incorporates all amendments and repeals currently in force so that the Act online is a complete and current version for the convenience of the user.

There is authority that suggests that consolidation Acts, in the formal sense, should be construed without reference to their legislative antecedents, unless there is textual ambiguity.[21] In the House of Lords it was explained:

---

17 Ibid 574 [35].

18 Ibid (emphasis in original).

19 Ibid 576 [41]. Cf Gageler J, in dissent, who considered the legislative antecedents 'ambiguous': at 588–9 [70].

20 *Australian Law Dictionary* (online at 25 November 2021) 'consolidating statute'.

21 *Bennett v Minister for Public Works (NSW)* (1908) 7 CLR 372, 379 (O'Connor J), citing *Williams v Permanent Trustee Co of New South Wales Ltd* [1906] AC 249, 252 (Lord Macnaghten); *Reynolds v Stacey* (1957) 96 CLR 454, 466 (Dixon CJ and McTiernan J).

> The process of consolidation would lose much of its point if, whenever a question as to its construction arose, reference had to be made to the individual Acts consolidated.[22]

Many of these authorities pre-date the development of the current principle about context. Now, any limitation on recourse to the antecedents of a consolidation Act seems inconsistent with the well-established principle that 'context', including statutory and historical context, is to be regarded from the start of the interpretation process and is not dependent on any ambiguity. It is also inconsistent with the High Court's rejection of 'rigid rules' of interpretation.[23] So, rather than applying any automatic prohibition, the better approach is for the nature of the statute as a consolidation Act to be considered as a relevant purposive and contextual factor when interpreting the statute.

Use as interpretative aids

Like all extrinsic aids the probative value to be given to legislative antecedents will vary, but there are some common strands about their use [21.5]

Legislative antecedents contribute to the story of the statute. They reveal its genesis and development. This is relevant because we presume that Parliament, when amending or replacing legislation, generally acts deliberately to make some change.[24] Like all extrinsic aids their value and weight will depend on the degree to which they provide information that contributes to an understanding of the provision being construed, and on how that is balanced against other interpretative factors. Sometimes they will be have significant weight,[25] sometimes they will be used to demonstrate consistency with a construction arrived at from other interpretative factors[26] and sometimes they will be of limited or no assistance.[27] But, as with legislative history generally, information derived from legislative antecedents cannot displace the statutory text.[28] Examination of it 'should not deflect the Court from its duty in resolving an issue of statutory construction which ultimately is always a text based activity'.[29]

There are few specific 'rules' about how to use legislative antecedents to illuminate meaning, but some common law strands provide guidance.

First, antecedents may assist in identifying what Parliament is trying to achieve – in other words, the statutory purpose. An examination of the wording of successive enactments can highlight the course, or changes in course, that Parliament has adopted and therefore provide information about the development of the policy behind the statute or the function of a

22 *Inland Revenue Commissioners v Joiner* [1975] 1 WLR 1701, 1709 (Viscount Dilhorne).

23 *Taylor v The Owners – Strata Plan No 11564* (2014) 253 CLR 531, 549 [37] (French CJ, Crennan and Bell JJ).

24 *R (Quintavalle) v Secretary of State for Health* [2003] 2 AC 687, 695 (Lord Bingham).

25 See, eg, *Western Australian Planning Commission v Southregal Pty Ltd* (2017) 259 CLR 106, 127–39 [69]–[90] (Gageler and Nettle JJ).

26 See, eg, *Lordianto v Commissioner of the Australian Federal Police* (2019) 266 CLR 273, 313 [106] (Kiefel CJ, Bell, Keane and Gordon JJ).

27 See, eg, *Bluebottle UK Ltd v Deputy Commissioner of Taxation* (2007) 232 CLR 598, 632 [91] (the Court).

28 *Grajewski v DPP (NSW)* (2019) 264 CLR 470, 478 [19] (Kiefel CJ, Bell, Keane and Gordon JJ); *Federal Commissioner of Taxation v Consolidated Media Holdings Ltd* (2012) 250 CLR 503, 519 [39] (French CJ, Hayne, Crennan, Bell and Gageler JJ).

29 *Northern Territory v Collins* (2008) 235 CLR 619, 623 [16] (Gummow ACJ and Kirby J), citing numerous authorities.

provision.[30] They may be particularly helpful 'in statutes with a clear pedigree'.[31] The *Fair Work Act 2009* (Cth) in the decision of *Esso Australia Pty Ltd v AWU* (**Example 21.1**) is an illustration. The clear lineage of the *Fair Work Act* permitted the majority to identify a change in wording in the current provision as indicative of a change in policy scope. Amending acts may be of particular significance as the introduction or removal of particular provisions or statutory text may be revelatory, depending on 'what has been retained and what has been removed'.[32]

Second, legislative evolution may assist in identifying the preferred meaning of a statutory provision, 'especially where its meaning appears equivocal'.[33] For example, in *Regional Express Holdings Ltd v Australian Federation of Air Pilots*[34] the Federation of Air Pilots purported to represent some cadets in a dispute with an aviation company. The cadets were not members of the Federation and so the company argued that the Federation was not 'entitled to represent the industrial interests' of the cadets as required by s 540(6) of the *Fair Work Act 2009* (Cth). The Federation argued that a person being *eligible* for membership of an industrial association was sufficient for the association to be 'entitled to represent the industrial interests of' that person.

The Court noted that the expression 'entitled to represent the industrial interests of the person' did not have a 'plain and ordinary meaning.'[35] As part of its analysis, the Court traced the expression from case law in 1957, through subsequent successive amendments, enactments and repeals until its final home in the *Fair Work Act*. Against this background, the Court concluded that 'the prior well-established meaning of the expression' was used in the new setting of s 540.[36]

Third, legislative antecedents may indicate whether or not the 'ordinary meaning' of text is or is not appropriate. This potential value is illustrated in **Example 21.2**.

Example 21.2 *Fremantle Lawyers Pty Ltd v Sarich*[37]

In his will the deceased had devised land he owned to his sons, daughter-in-law, and grandchildren. The land, in the shape of a battleaxe, comprised a single lot, but he devised the 'handle' to one son and the 'blade' to the other beneficiaries. Section 135 of the *Planning and Development Act 2005* (WA) ('the PDA') relevantly provided:

> (1) A person is not to –
> (a) subdivide any lot; . . .
> without the approval of the [Western Australian Planning] Commission.

30 See, eg, *Commissioner of State Revenue v EHL Burgess Properties Pty Ltd* (2015) 209 LGERA 314, 329 [51]–[52] (the Court); *NAGV and NAGW of 2002 v Minister for Immigration and Multicultural and Indigenous Affairs* (2005) 222 CLR 161, 187 [84] (Kirby J).

31 James Allsop, 'Statutes: Context, Meaning and Pre-enactment History' [2005] (Winter) *Bar News* 19, 21.

32 *Commissioner of State Revenue v EHL Burgess Properties Pty Ltd* (2015) 209 LGERA 314, 329 [51] (the Court).

33 *Western Australian Planning Commission v Southregal Pty Ltd* (2017) 259 CLR 106, 127 [69] (Gageler and Nettle JJ).

34 (2017) 262 CLR 456.

35 Ibid 465 [19].

36 Ibid 476 [48]. See also 475–6 [45]–[47].

37 (2019) 54 WAR 113.

In the course of proceedings about the construction of the will, the Supreme Court held that the devising of the land was void as contrary to s 135 of the PDA. The solicitors who prepared the will appealed to the Court of Appeal. The issue was the scope of the word 'subdivide'. One proposed construction was that 'subdivide' should be given its ordinary meaning in that it encompassed any act that created a physical division of a lot.[38] The alternative construction proposed was that 'subdivide' had a more specific meaning, confined to the situation where a person makes an application to create new lots.

Buss P, with whom Murphy and Beech JJA substantially agreed,[39] engaged in an examination of the extensive legislative antecedents to provisions of the PDA that had used the term 'subdivide' in relation to the regulation of land. This commenced with provisions of the *Road Districts Act 1919* (WA), *Municipal Corporations Act 1906* (WA) and *Transfer of Land Act 1893* (WA). The *Town Planning and Development Act 1928* (WA) ('the TPD Act') then repealed relevant sections of the *Road Districts Act 1919* (WA) and *Municipal Corporations Act 1906* (WA)), and the TPD Act and the *Transfer of Land Act 1893* (WA) became a precursor scheme in relation to the subdivision of lots.[40]

Although acknowledging that legislative history cannot displace the meaning of statutory text,[41] the meaning of 'subdivide', Buss P said, is 'shaped by' its context.[42] The statutory context of the legislative antecedents revealed that the term 'subdivide' was not broadly referring to the creation of a new proprietary interest, but was directed to the process of application and approval to remedy the 'mischief' of 'do-it-yourself' subdivisions.[43]

Having established that historical context, the task then turned to the current s 135 in the PDA (which had repealed and replaced the TPD Act). Though acknowledging some drafting restructure in the PDA, Buss P concluded that the prohibition against 'subdividing' was not materially different from its legislative predecessors.[44] At all times the word was not intended to have an 'ordinary' meaning, but was intended to capture the instance of lodgement of an application for the creation of new lots.[45] The meaning of 'subdivide' in the PDA did not, therefore, prohibit the deceased from devising part of a lot by will.

To obtain a clear understanding of the evolution of the statute, legislative antecedents are often considered with other legislative history, such as parliamentary materials or pre-existing common law [21.6]

The process of statutory construction would be 'subverted if a piecemeal, isolated, historical construction' of a statutory provision was conducted.[46] At the least it would undermine the concept of 'context'. It may be that legislative antecedents alone may be relevant, but in many

38 Ibid 145 [128], 150 [162] (Buss P), 171–2 [287]–[288] (Murphy and Beech JJA).

39 Murphy and Beech JJA agreed with Buss P's construction. One of their reasons was the conclusion drawn by Buss P about the legislative evolution: ibid 174 [297].

40 Ibid 150 [156].

41 Ibid 146 [142].

42 Ibid 150 [162].

43 Ibid 152–3 [172]. See also 156 [193].

44 Ibid 158 [200]–[201], using the explanatory memorandum to confirm this observation. See also 160 [231].

45 Ibid 158–9 [205]–[206].

46 *Palace Gallery Pty Ltd v WorkCover Premium Review Panel* (2014) 119 SASR 408, 418 [29] (Kourakis CJ).

instances the value to be derived from legislative antecedents will be enhanced by other legislative history. Extrinsic materials, particularly the parliamentary materials that relate to amendments or predecessor statutes, may assist understanding of successive changes.[47] (Similarly, if the history includes common law then an understanding of that common law is required.[48]) **Example 21.3** is a simple instance of how parliamentary material may assist understanding of a legislative antecedent.

Example 21.3 *GBT v Western Australia*[49]

The Supreme Court of Western Australia made a continuing detention order in respect of the appellant under the *Dangerous Sexual Offenders Act 2006* (WA) ('the DSO Act'). In making the order the primary judge relied on the reports of a psychiatrist and a psychologist, who had been named as 'qualified experts' under the DSO Act. Section 14(2)(a) of the DSO Act provided:

> (2) If the court is satisfied as described in subsection (1) –
> (a) the court must order that the offender undergo examinations by 2 qualified experts named by the court, at least one of whom is to be a psychiatrist, for the purposes of preparing reports in accordance with section 37 to be used on the hearing of the application ...

Section 3 of the DSO Act defined a 'qualified expert' to mean a psychiatrist or a qualified psychologist and 'qualified psychologist' was defined to mean 'a psychologist holding a qualification or accreditation prescribed for the purposes of this definition'. The appellant appealed the detention order, arguing that the psychologist was not a 'qualified psychologist' on the ground that no regulations prescribing qualifications or accreditation were in existence at the relevant time.

As originally enacted, s 14(2)(a) of the DSO Act required the Court to order that the offender undergo examinations by two psychiatrists. The *Dangerous Sexual Offenders Legislation Amendment Act 2016* (WA) ('the Amendment Act'), modified the provision to its current form. The explanatory memorandum to the Bill for the Amendment Act gave the following explanation of the purpose of amending s 14(2)(a) of the Act:

> to allow suitably qualified psychologists to conduct examinations and provide reports, in addition to requiring that at least one of the qualified experts that the court orders the offender to undergo examination by ... must be a psychiatrist ...[50]

The explanatory memorandum was used by the Court of Appeal to elucidate the Amendment Act. The Court, in a unanimous decision, accepted that the Amendment Act expanded the range of experts who could give a report, but noted that 'as stated in the explanatory memorandum, it was proposed only to allow "suitably qualified psychologists" to undertake the examination and make the report'.[51] The Amendment Act, as explained by this extrinsic material, was one of the three

47 See chapter 24.

48 See chapter 22.

49 [2019] WASCA 40.

50 Ibid [68] (Mazza JA, Mitchell JA and Beech JA), citing the Explanatory Memorandum, Dangerous Sexual Offenders Legislation Amendment Bill 2015 (WA).

51 Ibid [70].

factors that led the Court to determine that the better construction of 'qualified psychologist' and therefore 'qualified expert' was that the person must hold a prescribed qualification or accreditation.[52] As no such prescription had existed, the psychologist was not a 'qualified expert' under s 14(2).[53]

Presumptions about re-enacted words

The re-enactment in a statute of the same word that was in a prior statute may give rise to the presumption that Parliament intended to incorporate the same concept [21.7]

Where a predecessor statute contains a word that is then re-enacted in a successive statute 'in a similar connection' it may be presumed that Parliament 'intended to attach the same meaning to the same words'.[54] This is based on the presumption that the legislature may be taken to be 'aware' of the concepts in the predecessor legislation.

This presumption can be explained in the context of the new and predecessor statutes being *in pari materia*.[55] Statutes *in pari materia* are, broadly, statutes that deal with the same subject matter along the same lines.[56] They can be antecedent statutes, or current statutes from the same or different jurisdictions. Predecessor legislation can be regarded as a particular type of *in pari materia* statute. In the absence of other textual or contextual indicators to the contrary, predecessor legislation can be assumed to have a 'similar connection' to the subsequent or amending statute by virtue of being part of its evolution. As explained in a South Australian decision:

> There are some circumstances in which it is appropriate to have regard to the other statutes enacted by the one Parliament … Assistance is more likely to be gained if the comparable statutory provisions were predecessor provisions dealing with the same subject matter, or are a part of a group of enactments dealing with different aspects of the one subject matter, or where it is plain that the provision under consideration has been derived from another provision …[57]

The converse of the presumption also applies. Where a predecessor statute contains a word or phrase that is then changed in an amendment Act or a successive statute on the same subject matter, we start from the premise that the 'change in terminology was not accidental – that there must have been a purpose behind it'.[58]

---

52 Ibid [63]–[73].

53 The Court then held that the absence of a second report from a 'qualified expert' did not deprive the primary judge of the power to make the continuing detention order.

54 *Lennon v Gibson & Howes Ltd* (1919) 26 CLR 285, 287 (the Court).

55 *SZTAL v Minister for Immigration and Border Protection* (2017) 262 CLR 362, 371 [24] (Kiefel CJ, Nettle and Gordon JJ); *ZL v The Queen* (2010) 208 A Crim R 325, 329 [19] (Nettle JA, Bongiorno JA and Ross AJA agreeing).

56 See **[29.3]**.

57 *Frederick v South Australia* (2006) 94 SASR 545, 558 [49] (White J).

58 *Maughan Thiem Auto Sales Pty Ltd v Cooper* (2013) 216 FCR 197, 203 [32] (Katzmann J, Greenwood and Besanko JJ agreeing at 198 [1]).

[21.8] Except in South Australia, where Parliament re-enacts a word that has been given a meaning by a court, then Parliament can be taken to have intended the meaning given by the court; this is the 're-enactment presumption'

There is a common law presumption that '[w]here Parliament repeats words which have been judicially construed, it can be taken to have intended the words to bear the meaning already judicially attributed to them'.[59] This has been termed the 're-enactment presumption'.[60]

The presumption is based on a court being able to draw 'an inference as to parliamentary approval' of the judicial interpretation.[61] It is long established and has 'abundant authority'.[62] More recently it has been explained as a requirement of the 'modern contextual approach'[63] or, more broadly, for the 'stability of the law'.[64] The presumption has been abrogated in South Australia in the *Legislation Interpretation Act 2021* (SA).[65]

It has been suggested that the converse of the presumption may also be presumed:

> [The presumption] equally requires that, changes of drafting style aside, statutory language re-enacted in an altered form after it has acquired a settled judicial meaning be taken to have a different meaning.[66]

The application of the presumption is not limited to the re-enactment of judicially considered words from legislation in the same jurisdiction. The key is the inference that can be drawn about Parliament's awareness and approval. For example, in *Vella v Commissioner of Police (NSW)*[67] a provision of a 2016 NSW Act was the subject of interpretation. The NSW Act was modelled on 2007 UK legislation. In 2010, being in the period between the UK enactment and the NSW enactment, the Court of Appeal of England and Wales construed a provision of that UK legislation that was equivalent to the NSW provision now being construed. Kiefel CJ noted that the legislative history of the NSW Act, specifically the parliamentary debates, revealed that the Court of Appeal decision was 'known' to the NSW

59 *DPP Reference No 1 of 2019* (2021) 95 ALJR 741, 754 [51] (Gageler, Gordon and Steward JJ), citing *Re Alcan Australia Ltd; Ex parte Federation of Industrial, Manufacturing and Engineering Employees* (1994) 181 CLR 96, 106 (Mason CJ, Brennan, Deane, Dawson, Toohey, Gaudron and McHugh JJ) and numerous other High Court authorities.

60 *Fortress Credit Corporation (Australia) II Pty Ltd v Fletcher* (2015) 254 CLR 489, 502 [15] (the Court), citing DC Pearce and RS Geddes, *Statutory Interpretation in Australia* (LexisNexis Butterworths, 8th ed, 2014) 136–45.

61 *DPP Reference No 1 of 2019* (2021) 95 ALJR 741, 747 [15] (Kiefel CJ, Keane and Gleeson JJ, dissenting but not as to principle), citing *Flaherty v Girgis* (1987) 162 CLR 574, 594 (Mason ACJ, Wilson and Dawson JJ).

62 *Fortress Credit Corporation (Australia) II Pty Ltd v Fletcher* (2015) 254 CLR 489, 502 [15] (the Court), citing *Re Alcan Australia Ltd; Ex parte Federation of Industrial, Manufacturing and Engineering Employees* (1994) 181 CLR 96, 106 (Mason CJ, Brennan, Deane, Dawson, Toohey, Gaudron and McHugh JJ).

63 *Baini v The Queen* (2012) 246 CLR 469, 484 [43] (Gageler J) (dissenting, but not as to principle).

64 *Brisbane City Council v Amos* (2019) 266 CLR 593, 615 [45] (Gageler J).

65 *Legislation Interpretation Act 2021* (SA) s 18. The abrogation is not new. It was also contained in the predecessor Act: *Acts Interpretation Act 1915* (SA) s 18.

66 *Baini v The Queen* (2012) 246 CLR 469, 484–5 [43] (Gageler J) (dissenting, but not as to principle), citing *Amalgamated Wireless (A/asia) Ltd v Philpott* (1961) 110 CLR 617, 624 (Dixon CJ, Kitto, Taylor and Windeyer JJ).

67 (2019) 269 CLR 219.

Parliament.[68] Her Honour determined that in these circumstances it was possible to assume that the legislature has adopted the interpretation given to the earlier enactment by the Court of Appeal.[69]

The presumption may even apply where the exact words the subject of the judicial decision are not themselves the focus of the re-enactment. For example, in *Director of Public Prosecutions Reference No 1 of 2019*[70] the High Court considered the meaning of the word 'recklessly' in s 17 of the *Crimes Act 1958* (Vic). In 1995 the Court of Appeal of Victoria had attributed a meaning to the word that had remained the law in Victoria. Following that decision two enactments were passed that concerned s 17, though they did not expressly address the word 'recklessly'. Gageler, Gordon and Steward JJ, after considering the amendments and the extrinsic materials relating to them, attributed to Parliament awareness and approval of the Court of Appeal decision and applied the presumption.[71]

The courts have identified various factors that might rebut or shore up the presumption. These include the similarity of language (if too general an inference may not be reasonable),[72] the content of other legislative history such as Hansard, explanatory memoranda and expert reports,[73] whether the subsequent Act is a consolidating Act,[74] whether the legislation is in a specialised and politically sensitive field (where it might be expected that legislation is carefully scrutinised)[75] and the temporal proximity between the judicial interpretation and the subsequent enactment.[76] Older case law suggests that the judicial decision on the interpretation of the prior Act must be a 'considered'[77] decision and one made by a superior court.[78] Given the modern contextual approach, these points are better considered as factors relevant to whether an inference can reasonably be drawn about what Parliament 'knew'. Ultimately, the application of the presumption to a statute 'will turn on its own circumstances having regard to the history of the specific statute'.[79]

---

68 Ibid 233–4 [19].

69 Ibid 233–4 [19]–[20]. See also 244 [52] (Bell, Keane, Nettle and Edelman JJ).

70 (2021) 95 ALJR 741.

71 Ibid 754–6 [51]–[59] (Gageler, Gordon and Steward JJ). Cf Edelman J agreeing as to outcome but relying on other factors: at 758 [66] and n 137. Kiefel CJ, Keane and Gleeson J, dissenting, determined that the presumption was not applicable: at 750 [31]–[32].

72 See, eg, *Frederick v South Australia* (2006) 94 SASR 545, 558 [50] (White J).

73 See, eg, *DPP Reference No 1 of 2019* (2021) 95 ALJR 741, 752–4 [43]–[50] (Gageler, Gordon and Steward JJ).

74 See **[21.9](b)**.

75 *DPP Reference No 1 of 2019* (2021) 95 ALJR 741, 754 [51] (Gageler, Gordon and Steward JJ), 747–8 [16] (Kiefel CJ, Keane and Gleeson J, dissenting); *Electrolux Home Products Pty Ltd v Australian Workers' Union* (2004) 221 CLR 309, 346–7 [81] (McHugh J).

76 *DPP Reference No 1 of 2019* (2021) 95 ALJR 741, 755 [51] (Gageler, Gordon and Steward JJ), citing *Electrolux Home Products Pty Ltd v Australian Workers' Union* (2004) 221 CLR 309, 324–5 [8] (Gleeson CJ), 346–7 [81] (McHugh J), 370–1 [161–2] (Gummow, Hayne and Heydon JJ) and 398 [251] (Callinan J).

77 *Williams v Dunn's Assignee* (1908) 6 CLR 245, 452 (O'Connor J), citing *Mackay v Davies* (1904) 1 CLR 483, 491 (Griffith J); see also 445–6 (Barton J).

78 *Melbourne Corporation v Barry* (1922) 31 CLR 174, 181 (Knox CJ) citing *Re Cathcart; Ex parte Campbell* (1870) LR 5 Ch 703, 706 (James LJ).

79 *DPP Reference No 1 of 2019* (2021) 95 ALJR 741, 755 [52] (Gageler, Gordon and Steward JJ).

[21.9] Presumptions about the meaning of words being carried over to subsequent statutes should be used with particular caution where there is a change in drafting style or a consolidation Act

Neither of the presumptions described in **[21.7]** and **[21.8]** are 'rigid doctrine ... forcing the hands of the Court'.[80] As is the nature of common law presumptions, they should never be applied as rules of automatic application, but as presumptions to be considered in the context of the entire interpretative task.

In this regard, we highlight two instances for caution.

(a) Change in drafting style

As indicated in the quote in **[21.8]** about the converse of the re-enactment presumption, caution needs to be exercised in applying these presumptions where a change in wording can be explained by reference to a change in drafting style. Although 'plain language' style was adopted by the Commonwealth and states in the early 1990s, this was not always the case. Drafting styles have evolved, and continue to evolve.[81]

These presumptions can create challenges for the parliamentary drafter where the drafter wishes to adopt a new style or terminology in an Act 'dealing with a subject matter that is already referred to in the Act' or another Act but is 'virtually obliged to use like terminology to that which is already there'.[82] To accommodate this, several jurisdictions, including the Commonwealth, have provisions in their interpretation legislation that provide, in general terms, that where an Act has a particular form of words that expresses an idea and then a different form of words is used in a later Act or an amendment, the ideas in the later Act or amendment should not be taken to be substantively different if that change can be attributed to a change in drafting style.[83]

For example, in *Maughan Thiem Auto Sales Pty Ltd v Cooper*[84] the Court, referring to s 15AC of the *Acts Interpretation Act 1901* (Cth), concluded that the substitution of the word 'decision' for the word 'judgment' in a replacement Act was a change in style, rather than substance, with 'decision' being an 'apt compendious word'.[85] Other examples include changes to remove 'duplicated verbiage',[86] to 'rewrite into "plain English"',[87] to accommodate the drafting style of a particular jurisdiction[88] or to be 'in line with modern drafting conventions'.[89]

Whether a jurisdiction has a provision in its Interpretation Act about drafting style or not, the challenge in any interpretative task is to determine whether a change in language can be

80 *Melbourne Corporation v Barry* (1922) 31 CLR 174, 186, 187 (Isaacs J).

81 See **[10.7]**.

82 Dennis Pearce, *Interpretation Acts in Australia* (LexisNexis Butterworths, 2018) 90 [3.84].

83 *Acts Interpretation Act 1901* (Cth) s 15AC; *Acts Interpretation Act 1954* (Qld) s 14C; *Legislation Act 2001* (ACT) s 147; *Interpretation Act 1978* (NT) s 62C.

84 (2013) 216 FCR 197.

85 Ibid 205 [43] (Katzmann J, Greenwood and Besanko JJ agreeing at 198 [1]).

86 See, eg, *Wilkie v Commonwealth* (2017) 263 CLR 487, 536 [107] (Kiefel CJ, Bell, Gageler, Keane, Nettle, Gordon and Edelman JJ).

87 See, eg, *Vikpro Pty Ltd v Wyuna Court Pty Ltd* (2016) 103 ATR 787, 798 [35] (Philippides JA, in dissent).

88 See, eg, *Commonwealth v Helicopter Resources Pty Ltd* (2020) 94 ALJR 466, 479 [52] (Edelman J).

89 See, eg, *Minister for Immigration and Border Protection v Kumar* (2017) 260 CLR 367, 376 [20] (Bell, Keane, Gordon JJ).

attributed to a stylistic change, or signifies a substantive change in policy. Parliamentary and other extrinsic materials may assist this determination. The age of the earlier statute may also be a factor.[90]

(b) **Consolidation Acts**

As explained in **[21.4]** the function of a consolidating statute is to consolidate the law; when enacting it, Parliament is considering 'not *what* it should enact but *how* existing law should be arranged'.[91] We assume that it does not alter the pre-existing law.[92] Accordingly, it is assumed that when Parliament enacts a consolidation statute, it does not address the meaning of any statutory provision, nor therefore any judicial interpretation of that provision, and so does not endorse any particular judicial decision.

There are some inconsistencies in the case law about the relationship between the re-enactment presumption and consolidating Acts.[93] But recent authority suggests that, in the absence of other interpretative criteria indicating otherwise, the re-enactment presumption is inapplicable, or at best weak, in relation to consolidating Acts.[94]

Similar issues arise in relation to the interpretation of codes. See **[22.4]**.

Subsequent amending Acts

Although not 'history,' in some circumstances it is permissible to rely on a subsequent amending statute as an aid to the interpretation of a statute in its unamended form [21.10]

In certain circumstances an amending statute can be an interpretative aid for construing the statute it amends in its unamended form. This is the inverse of historical evolution. Rather than being antecedent the amendment Act is a 'successor'.

As extrinsic material created subsequent to the version of the Act being construed (assuming the amending Act does not operate retrospectively), it is debateable as to whether taking account of a subsequent amending Act can be rationalised by reference to the principle of context. Nevertheless, there is a line of authority that permits reference to subsequent amending Acts as an interpretative aid.

The authority often cited is *Grain Elevators Board (Vic) v Dunmunkle Shire*[95] where Dixon J opined that amending legislation may be taken into account in determining the scope of prior legislation to avoid a result that would render the amendment unnecessary or futile.[96] This was later extended to the situation where it would render the amendment deficient.[97] It has also been

---

90 See, eg, *Secure Funding Pty Ltd v Doneley* [2010] QSC 91 where Martin J noted that 'one would expect' that language in a 1994 Act would differ from language used in 1861 and 1877 Acts: at [50].

91 *Melbourne Corporation v Barry* (1922) 31 CLR 174, 188 (Isaacs J) (emphasis in original). See also 441 (Griffith CJ).

92 Ibid 186 (Isaacs J). See also *Riddle v The Queen* (1911) 12 CLR 622, 632 (Barton J).

93 See generally CJF Kidd, 'The Construction of Consolidating Statutes and the *Barras* Principle: The Significance of *Farrell v Alexander*' (1977) 51(5) *Australian Law Journal* 256.

94 *DPP Reference No 1 of 2019* (2021) 95 ALJR 741, 754 [51] (Gageler, Gordon and Steward JJ); *Aubrey v The Queen* (2017) 260 CLR 305, 333 [60] (Bell J dissenting), citing *Williams v Official Assignee of the Estate of William Dunn* (1908) 6 CLR 425, 441 (Griffith CJ) and *Melbourne Corporation v Barry* (1922) 31 CLR 174, 188 (Isaacs J); *Fortress Credit Corporation (Australia) II Pty Ltd v Fletcher* (2015) 254 CLR 489, 503 [15] n 77 (the Court).

95 (1946) 73 CLR 70.

96 Ibid 86.

97 *Hunter Resources Ltd v Melville* (1988) 164 CLR 234, 255 (Dawson J).

suggested that the approach may not be confined to an Act that amends an earlier Act, but may extend to other subsequent amending enactments where the two Acts comprise the same scheme.[98]

Subsequent amending Acts have also been used to indicate that the provision in question does not cover a particular circumstance. For example, in *NAGV and NAGW of 2002 v Minister for Immigration and Multicultural and Indigenous Affairs*,[99] Kirby J turned to subsequent amendments to s 36 of the *Migration Act 1958* (Cth) to reinforce his preferred construction of the section.[100] The amendments, due to their commencement date, were not applicable to the facts before the Court. Kirby J noted that one of the amendments was to add a subsection to s 36 confining the scope of the section.[101] Kirby J used this subsequent amendment to support his broad construction of s 36, stating that the amendment showed that legislative techniques were available to Parliament to limit the scope of the section and they had not been used.[102] His Honour argued that the Court 'should not strain itself to import' a limitation on the section 'when the Parliament, with the power to do so, has not enacted them expressly'.[103]

There are difficulties as a matter of principle in using a subsequent amending Act as an interpretative aid. As Gummow J has noted, such an approach is 'a curious way of revealing parliamentary intention at the time of passing the earlier provision'.[104] Further, caution about the inference to be drawn from subsequent amendments is required 'because there are a number of assumptions, usually implicit, underlying later legislation'.[105]

There are also identified limits to their use.[106]

First, the amending statute may only be referred to when the words of the earlier Act are ambiguous or obscure.[107] This restriction would not seem to be affected by the principle of 'wider' context, with its absence of any ambiguity threshold, which focuses on past, not post, circumstances.

Second, the reasoning in the *Grain Elevators* case 'has no application where the amending words have been included to remove possible doubts as to the meaning of the original provision'.[108] As was observed by Viscount Haldane LC in *Re Samuel*:[109]

> It is not a conclusive argument as to the construction of an earlier Act to say that unless it be construed in a particular way a later enactment would be surplusage. The later Act may have been designed, ex abundante cautela, to remove possible doubts.[110]

---

98 *Reardon v Deputy Commissioner of Taxation* (2013) 92 ATR 494, 504–5 [32] (Holmes JA).

99 (2005) 222 CLR 161.

100 Ibid 187 [85], citing *Hunter Resources Ltd v Melville* (1988) 164 CLR 234, 254 (Dawson J).

101 Ibid 188 [87].

102 Ibid 188 [88].

103 Ibid.

104 *Interlego AG v Croner Trading Pty Ltd* (1992) 39 FCR 348, 382.

105 *AQO v Minister for Finance and Services* (2016) 93 NSWLR 46, 79 [143] (Basten JA).

106 For a summary of numerous authorities see *R v Sieders* (2008) 72 NSWLR 417, 431–4 [118]–[128] (Campbell JA).

107 *Masson v Parsons* (2019) 266 CLR 554, 573–4 [28] (Kiefel CJ, Bell, Gageler, Keane, Nettle and Gordon JJ); *Allina Pty Ltd v Commissioner of Taxation* (1991) 28 FCR 203, 212 (the Court); *Deputy Federal Commissioner of Taxes (SA) v Elder's Trustee and Executor Co Ltd* (1936) 57 CLR 610, 625–6 (Dixon, Evatt and McTiernan JJ).

108 *R v AL (A Pseudonym)* (2016) 310 FLR 320, 327 [25] (Maxwell P, Weinberg and Kyrou JJA), citing *Doughty v Martino Developments Pty Ltd* (2010) 27 VR 499, 511 [33] (Nettle JA); *Allina Pty Ltd v Commissioner of Taxation* (1991) 28 FCR 203, 212 (the Court).

109 [1913] AC 514.

110 Ibid 526. The Latin phrase *ex abundante cautela* means 'from an abundance of caution'.

Third, care must be taken as to whether the legislature has adopted a view about the meaning of the earlier statute in the amending Act. Subsequent legislation proceeding on a mistaken construction of previous legislation 'does not alter the law by merely betraying an erroneous opinion of it'.[111] This principle

> reflects the accepted objective theory of statutory construction and the constitutional separation of powers between the Parliament and the courts. The courts are the sole interpreters of, and attributors of meaning to, the statutes enacted by the Parliament . . .[112]

Finally, the subsequent amendment must actually be enacted. The 'possibility of an amendment' is not material that can be used to construe an Act.[113]

111 *Masson v Parsons* (2019) 266 CLR 554, 573–4 [28] (Kiefel CJ, Bell, Gageler, Keane, Nettle and Gordon JJ), citing *Deputy Federal Commissioner of Taxes (SA) v Elder's Trustee and Executor Co Ltd* (1936) 57 CLR 610, 625–6 (Dixon, Evatt and McTiernan JJ).

112 *Palace Gallery Pty Ltd v WorkCover Premium Review Panel* (2014) 119 SASR 408, 417–18 [26] (Kourakis CJ).

113 *Poniatowska v Channel Seven Sydney Pty Ltd (No 2)* (2020) 136 SASR 455, 467 [86] (the Court).

22 PRE-EXISTING COMMON LAW

Overview

[22.1] This chapter addresses the common law where it is part of the history of an Act and so forms part of its wider context. This is distinct from using common law as a precedent, or as part of the wider contextual surrounding law.

The requirement to consider context includes the Act's legislative history. Common law becomes part of the legislative history of a statute where that statute addresses something that was previously governed by the common law. The doctrine of legislative supremacy means that Parliament's legislation takes precedence over the judiciary's decisions to the extent of the scope of that legislation. That scope is determined by principles of statutory interpretation. The pre-existing common law provides background to the statute. It places the statutory language in its historical and legal setting, which may assist in identifying the object of the statutory enactment or the meaning to be attributed to the text.

The common law may become part of legislative history in a number of ways. A statute may codify the common law, in whole or in part, abolish it or modify, supplement or incorporate it. A statute may be a response to a judicial decision. All of these scenarios are variations on how the common law can form part of the chain of history of a statute.

As part of wider context

[22.2] **The wider context of a statute includes its historical and legal context; this includes common law that existed prior to the enactment of a statute or statutory provision where the legislation addresses that common law area**

It is well accepted at common law that the words used by the legislature must be considered in their context, and that context includes the statute's legal and historical context, including prior legislative and common law on the subject.[1] Examination of that wider context is no longer dependent on an ambiguity threshold and should be undertaken from the start of the interpretative task.[2]

1 *CIC Insurance Ltd v Bankstown Football Club Ltd* (1997) 187 CLR 384, 408 (Brennan CJ, Dawson, Toohey, and Gummow JJ); *AB v Western Australia* (2011) 244 CLR 390, 398 [10] (the Court); *R v Lavender* (2005) 222 CLR 67, 81–2 [33]–[36] (Gleeson CJ, McHugh, Gummow and Hayne JJ); *Federal Commissioner of Taxation v Consolidated Media Holdings Ltd* (2012) 250 CLR 503, 519 [39] (French CJ, Hayne, Crennan, Bell and Gageler JJ). See **[7.3]–[7.6]**.

2 See **[7.6]**.

Recourse to the pre-existing common law as part of context may assist in analysing the meaning of the statutory provisions that now cover, in whole or part, that area of law:

> When a statute enters a field that has been governed by the common law, the pre-existing common law almost invariably gives guidance as to the statute's meaning and purpose. That is because the meaning of legislation usually depends on a background of concepts, principles, practices and circumstances that the drafters 'took for granted or understood, without conscious advertence, by reason of their common language or culture'.[3]

The antecedent common law provides a point of contextual comparison to the law stated in the statute. Knowing what came before may assist our understanding of what has replaced it.

Antecedent common law refers to the common law as it has existed and developed over time up to the point of enactment of the statutory provision being construed. It includes case law on legislative antecedents to the statute.[4] For example, in *PGA v The Queen*[5] the High Court considered s 48 of the *Criminal Law Consolidation Act 1935* (SA) ('the CLC Act'). Section 48 criminalised rape but did not identify the elements of the crime. The section was taken to have imported the common law on what comprised the offence of rape (for statutes incorporating common law see **[22.6]**). The issue was whether that common law included any presumption of consent by a wife to sexual intercourse with her husband in marriage. If it did, the appellant could not be found guilty of raping his wife. In considering the common law relevant to s 48, the Court considered the long history of the offence of rape, starting with the extrajudicial writings of Sir Matthew Hale, Chief Justice of the Court of King's Bench, in 1736 that had referred to such a presumption. From there the Court considered the development of the common law, legislative antecedents to s 48 that purported to incorporate that common law, and case law on those antecedents. It was primarily this historical analysis that led the majority to conclude: 'By the time of the enactment in 1935 of the CLC Act, if not earlier ... at common law a husband could be guilty of a rape committed by him upon his lawful wife.'[6]

Examining pre-existing common law as part of the historical background to the statute is distinct from using the common law as a precedent in relation to the meaning of particular statutory text.[7] It is also distinct from where the common law forms part of the wider context by being part of the 'surrounding law' of the statute.[8] This chapter addresses the common law prior to the enactment of a statutory provision to the extent that it can be identified as part of the chain of history of that provision. It is accepted that sometimes the line between these characterisations may be difficult to draw (such as where a statute incorporates common law concepts).

Similarly to legislative antecedents, prior common law, as matter extrinsic to the statute, could potentially be covered by the provisions of the Interpretation Acts of the states, territories

3 *Conway v The Queen* (2002) 209 CLR 203, 207 [5] (Gaudron ACJ, McHugh, Hayne and Callinan JJ), citing, in part, *Theophanous v Herald & Weekly Times Ltd* (1994) 182 CLR 104, 196 (McHugh J).

4 For legislative antecedents see chapter 21.

5 (2012) 245 CLR 355.

6 Ibid 384 [64] (French CJ, Gummow, Hayne, Crennan and Kiefel JJ).

7 See chapter 30.

8 See **[32.6]**.

and the Commonwealth that allow recourse to extrinsic materials or matters.[9] But, in practice, these legislative provisions are not typically used as legal authority for recourse to this material. The common law principles continue to be relied on.

[22.3] The existence of prior common law on the same subject does not displace the ordinary process of statutory interpretation: an interpreter must start the interpretative task with the statutory text

Due to the doctrine of legislative supremacy that underpins our legal system, '[l]egislation of a Parliament, acting within its constitutional powers, has an authority that displaces the common law to the extent of the statutory provisions'.[10] Bennion has a helpful analogy to explain the relationship between the common law and statute where the latter replaces the former as the statement of the law:

> [O]ne can use the image of a floor upon which rugs are spread. The floor consists of ... common law ... An Act is like a rug laid down on this floor. The Act conceals, for the area it covers, the texture underneath.[11]

Accepting this, even where there is longstanding and established common law that has governed an area of law, we must still start with the words of the statute that have been enacted to address that law. As Kirby J in *Neindorf v Junkovic*[12] cautioned:

> This Court has repeatedly said in recent times that ... it is the duty of Australian courts to start their analysis of the legal liability of parties affected not with the pre-existing common law but with the statutory prescription. The reason for this requirement is simple. ... Where Parliament has spoken, it is a mistake to start with common law authority.[13]

In other words, the 'starting point for the ascertainment of the meaning of a statutory provision is the text of the statute'.[14] This is a well-established and fundamental interpretative principle.[15]

Examining the 'interrelation and interaction between common law and statute may trigger varied and complex questions'.[16] In the context of legislative history, the pre-existing common law can form part of the wider context in a number of ways. All are essentially variations on how the prior common law has been affected by the statute (the determination of which requires the application of statutory interpretation law). This chapter has characterised those variations in

9 *Acts Interpretation Act 1901* (Cth) s 15AB; *Interpretation Act 1987* (NSW) s 34; *Acts Interpretation Act 1954* (Qld) s 14B; *Legislation Interpretation Act 2021* (SA) s 16; *Acts Interpretation Act 1931* (Tas) s 8B; *Interpretation of Legislation Act 1984* (Vic) s 35(b); *Interpretation Act 1984* (WA) s 19; *Legislation Act 2001* (ACT) s 141; *Interpretation Act 1978* (NT) s 62B. Prior to 2022, South Australia relied solely on the common law: see **[2.9]**, **[24.2]**.

10 *Neindorf v Junkovic* (2005) 80 ALJR 341, 350–1 [42] (Kirby J). See **[3.5]**.

11 Oliver Jones, *Bennion on Statutory Interpretation* (LexisNexis, 6th ed, 2013) 168.

12 (2005) 80 ALJR 341.

13 Ibid 350–1 [42] (dissenting, but not as to principle) (citations omitted).

14 *SZTAL v Minister for Immigration and Border Protection* (2017) 262 CLR 362, 368 [14] (Kiefel CJ, Nettle and Gordon JJ).

15 See **[6.2]**, **[6.5]**.

16 *Esso Australia Resources Ltd v Federal Commissioner of Taxation* (1999) 59–60 [18] (Gleeson CJ, Gaudron and Gummow JJ).

four groupings: codification; abolition; incorporation, modification and supplementation; and legislative response. Each is now addressed in turn.

Interpretation of codes

Where a statute has codified an area of law, there is authority that limits recourse to the antecedent common law [22.4]

Where a statute replaces the previous law on a subject and purports to be a comprehensive statement of the law on that subject, then that enactment is known as a code.[17] The code may be a legislative statement of an area previously covered by common law only, or it may be a comprehensive legislative statement that replaces a combination of common law principles, old statute law, statutory modifications to common law concepts or re-enacted statute law.[18] Whatever the combination, the prior common or legislative law is no longer relevant as a representation of the *current* law.

Codes can be a comprehensive statement on one aspect of the law in an area, or on the whole area. For example, in *Sungravure Pty Ltd v Middle East Airlines Airliban SAL*[19] Mason J found that the *Defamation Act 1958* (NSW) preserved certain protections and privileges in the law of defamation, but 'within the ambit which it seeks to cover' was a code.[20] By way of contrast, in *Milenkovski v Western Australia*[21] the Court found that the *Bail Act 1982* (WA) 'is intended to be a comprehensive code on the subject of bail'[22] that displaces the common law.[23]

There is long established authority on a particular interpretative approach to a code. As a purported exhaustive and comprehensive statement of the law, its language

> should be construed according to its natural meaning and without any presumption that it was intended to do no more than restate the existing law. It is not the proper course to begin by finding how the law stood before the Code, and then to see if the Code will bear an interpretation which will leave the law unaltered.[24]

In a modern context, there is nothing remarkable about these principles. Starting with the ordinary meaning of the statutory text, rather than legislative history, is a well-established current principle for all statutes.[25] Moreover, just as a court must not construct its own idea of

---

17 *Australian Law Dictionary* (online at 27 November 2021) 'code'. Cf a consolidated statute: see **[21.4]**.

18 See, eg, Windeyer's description of the Tasmanian *Criminal Code* in *Vallance v The Queen* (1961) 108 CLR 56, 74–5.

19 (1975) 134 CLR 1.

20 Ibid 22.

21 (2011) 42 WAR 99.

22 Ibid 108 [31] (McLure P, Pullin JA agreeing at 111 [50]; Hall J substantially agreeing at 111 [51]).

23 Ibid 108 [34].

24 *Brennan v The King* (1936) 55 CLR 253, 263 (Dixon and Evatt JJ). This statement has been approved many times by the High Court. See, eg, *Namoa v The Queen* (2021) 95 ALJR 396, 398 [11] (Gleeson J, Kiefel CJ, Gageler, Keane, Gordon, Edelman and Steward JJ agreeing at 397 [1]–[6] respectively); *Pickett v Western Australia* (2020) 270 CLR 323, 337–8 [22]–[24] (Kiefel CJ, Bell, Keane and Gordon JJ), 360–1 [92] (Nettle J); *R v LK* (2010) 241 CLR 177, 220 [97] (Gummow, Hayne, Crennan, Kiefel and Bell JJ); *Boughey v The Queen* (1986) 161 CLR 10, 30 (Brennan J); *Kaporonovski v The Queen* (1973) 133 CLR 209, 236 (Gibbs J, Stephen J agreeing).

25 See **[6.6]**.

a desirable policy from extrinsic materials and impute it to the text, so must a court come to a code without preconceptions about what it has or has not incorporated from the previous law.[26]

More important are the well-established extrapolations from those principles. The principles have been taken to mean that we must interpret a code 'without reference to the pre-existing law,'[27] save in certain circumstances where it would be justifiable to do so: 'where the Code contains provisions of doubtful import, *or* uses language which had previously acquired a technical meaning, *or* on some such special ground'.[28]

The threshold of 'doubtful import' refers to ambiguity on the face of the statute.[29] The pre-existing law (that is, the wider context) cannot be used to create an ambiguity in the text.[30]

The second ground addresses the situation where a code uses language 'conventionally used to express a general common law principle'[31] or that expressly or impliedly had acquired an established legal or other technical meaning under the prior common law. For example, in *R v LK*[32] one issue was the meaning of 'conspiracy' and 'conspire' in s 11.5 of the *Criminal Code* (Cth) (in sch to *Criminal Code Act 1995* (Cth)). French CJ stated:

> The Code provisions relating to the offence of conspiracy are written against the background of the common law, which, subject to their text, informs their content.[33]

That background of the common law was found, by French CJ, to stem back to a UK decision in 1868.[34] The Court concluded that the use of the term in the Code was to be understood by reference to the common law meaning.[35]

Where a code uses an expression that is not defined in the code, and that expression or term has an established common law meaning, that may be an indication that the legislature intended the common law meaning or principle to be referred to. This was the case in, for example, *R v LK*.[36] In contrast, if the term is defined in the code, that definition may indicate that the common law meaning was not intended.[37]

---

26 Regarding imputation of policy, see **[8.6]**.

27 *Boughey v The Queen* (1986) 161 CLR 10, 30 (Brennan J). See also *Mellifont v A-G (Qld)* (1991) 173 CLR 289, 309 (Mason CJ, Dean, Dawson, Gaudron and McHugh JJ).

28 *Stuart v The Queen* (1974) 134 CLR 426, 437 (Gibbs J, Mason J agreeing at 445) (emphasis added), cited in *Pickett v Western Australia* (2020) 270 CLR 323, 337–8 [23] (Kiefel CJ, Bell, Keane and Gordon JJ). See also 360–1 [92] (Nettle J). See also *R v LK* (2010) 241 CLR 177, 220 [97] (Gummow, Hayne, Crennan, Kiefel and Bell JJ); *Boughey v The Queen* (1986) 161 CLR 10, 30 (Brennan J); *Sungravure Pty Ltd v Middle East Airlines Airliban SAL* (1975) 134 CLR 1, 22 (Mason J); *Vallance v The Queen* (1961) 108 CLR 56, 75–6 (Windeyer J).

29 *Namoa v The Queen* (2021) 95 ALJR 396, 399 [11] (Gleeson J, Kiefel CJ, Gageler, Keane, Gordon, Edelman, and Steward JJ agreeing at 397 [1]–[6] respectively), citing *Mellifont v A-G (Qld)* (1991) 173 CLR 289, 309 (Mason CJ, Deane, Dawson, Gaudron and McHugh JJ).

30 Ibid.

31 *Boughey v The Queen* (1986) 161 CLR 10, 30 (Brennan J).

32 (2010) 241 CLR 177.

33 Ibid 206 [59].

34 Ibid 207 [62] (French CJ).

35 Ibid 210 [72] (French CJ) (Gummow, Hayne, Crennan, Kiefel and Bell JJ agreeing at 224 [107], subject to certain statutory modifications; Heydon J agreeing with the plurality at 235 [145]). See also, eg, *Peniamina v The Queen* (2020) 95 ALJR 85, 90 [13] (Bell, Gageler and Gordon JJ), 1010 [80] (Keane and Edelman JJ).

36 *R v LK* (2010) 241 CLR 177, 220 [97] (Gummow, Hayne, Crennan, Kiefel and Bell JJ).

37 See, eg, *Hayman v Cartright* (2018) 53 WAR 137 where the Court determined that the term 'assault', defined in s 222 of the *Criminal Code* (WA) (in sch to app B of *Criminal Code Act Compilation Act 1913* (WA)), was to be

These principles are usually expressed in the context of a code replacing the common law. However, given that it is the character of a code that underpins them, there seems no reason why they should not be equally applicable to a code and its relationship to legislative antecedents.[38]

It is difficult to see how the restrictions on recourse to historical context, in particular the ambiguity threshold, can be reconciled with the modern principle to consider context in its 'widest sense' even if there is no ambiguity. It has been suggested that the modern principles of interpretation, including the context principle, should be read '[s]ubject to' the particular interpretative principles for codes.[39]

Further, as a matter of practicality the restrictions are questionable. One of the circumstances that permits recourse to antecedent law is where the statute is considered to have imported a common law concept. Yet it may be difficult to determine if a code has imported a common law concept without first referring to that prior law.

It is timely, perhaps, for the relevance of these restrictions to be reconsidered. It is noteworthy that they have their origin in an era prior to the development of the wider context principle.[40] For consistency with modern interpretative law and method, it may be more appropriate to regard the object and nature of a code (a comprehensive statement of the law) as a relevant and important contextual indicator in the interpretative process, rather than as a trigger for different interpretative rules.

Ways statute can impact pre-existing common law

Where a statute abolishes common law, whether in whole or part, that antecedent common law is a part of its legislative history [22.5]

Legislation abolishing common law without enacting a replacement legal framework is not common. Where done, it is typically to abolish 'anachronistic common law actions' that no longer reflect current societal attitudes.[41] An example is s 6 of the *Domicile Act 1982* (Cth), which abolished the common law rule that a married woman has at all times the domicile of her husband.

Where the common law is abolished by statute, in whole or in part, that prior common law becomes a historical part of the context. As such it may assist in determining the meaning or scope of the abolishing statutory provision.

On a cautionary note it should not be assumed that a statute has abolished the common law merely because alternative language has been used. The common law *principles* may be imported

---

construed by reference to that definition and not the prior common law meaning of the term: at 149–50 [58]–[62]. See also *Vallance v The Queen* (1961) 108 CLR 56, 75 (Windeyer J).

38 *Pickett v Western Australia* (2020) 270 CLR 323, 360–1 [92] (Nettle J). His Honour included 'statutory antecedents' when referring to these principles. See also *R v LK* (2010) 241 CLR 177, 219 [96] (Gummow, Hayne, Crennan, Kiefel and Bell JJ referring to a passage in DC Pearce and RS Geddes, *Statutory Interpretation in Australia* (LexisNexis Butterworths, 6th ed, 2006), which included prior statutes); *Bellino v Australian Broadcasting Corporation* (1996) 185 CLR 183, 220–1 (Dawson, McHugh and Gummow JJ referring to a predecessor statute).

39 *Marchesano v Western Australia* (2017) 52 WAR 176, 201 [97] (Buss P). See also *Pickett v Western Australia* (2020) 270 CLR 323, 361 [92] where Nettle J appears to make a similar suggestion; *Hayman v Cartright* (2018) 53 WAR 137, 149–50 [60] (the Court).

40 For history see chapter 2.

41 Barbara McDonald, 'Legislative Intervention in the Law of Negligence: The Common Law, Statutory Interpretation and Tort Reform in Australia' (2005) 27(3) *Sydney Law Review* 443, 448.

into the statute even though the common law *term* is not. For example, s 3A(a) of the *Crimes (Sentencing Procedure) Act 1999* (NSW) provides:

> The purposes for which a court may impose a sentence on an offender are as follows –
>
> (a) to ensure that the offender is adequately punished for the offence, ...

Prior to the enactment of s 3A, the common law principles governing sentencing included, among others, the principle of proportionality. That principle requires that a sentence for an offence 'should never exceed that which can be justified as appropriate or proportionate to the gravity of the crime considered in the light of its objective circumstances'.[42] Despite no reference to the term 'proportionality' in s 3A(a), the provision has been taken to reflect this principle.[43]

[22.6] Where a statute incorporates, supplements or modifies common law, that antecedent common law will be a part of its legislative history

Where legislation incorporates, supplements or modifies the common law, that prior common law, to the extent that it has governed the subject area now covered by the statute, forms part of the statute's historical context. This is so even where a statute incorporates the common law concepts. This is because that 'imported' common law, while of significant probative value, is no longer the statement of the current law. The statutory text is now the current law, albeit it may be interpreted with the aid of common law concepts.[44]

Determining the extent to which a statute overrides, or imports, the common law can be complex.[45] Section **[22.6]** considers other ways statutes can impact antecedent common law.

(a) Statute incorporates the common law

A statute may incorporate concepts or phrases from the prior common law. This may be done, as seen in **[22.4]**, as part of a code's exhaustive statement of the law. This may also occur on a more piecemeal basis in any statute.[46]

Sometimes the incorporation of the common law will be expressly provided. For example, s 20(1) of the *Civil Liability Act 1936* (SA) provides: 'Subject to this Part, the liability of the occupier of premises for injury, damage or loss attributable to the dangerous state or condition of the premises *shall be determined in accordance with the principles of the law of negligence*.'

More commonly, an analysis of the statute using principles of statutory interpretation, including reference to legislative history, will be required. For example, in *Aid/Watch Inc v Commissioner of Taxation (Cth)* ('*Aid/Watch*')[47] the issue was whether Aid/Watch Incorporated, an organisation that promoted the more efficient use of Australian and multinational foreign aid for the relief of poverty, was a 'charitable institution' under various Commonwealth Tax Acts. If so, it would be entitled to exemption from tax liability under those Acts. The term was not defined in any

42 *Hoare v The Queen* (1989) 167 CLR 348, 354 (Mason CJ, Deane, Dawson, Toohey and McHugh JJ) (emphasis omitted).

43 *Kearsley v The Queen* (2017) 265 A Crim R 233, 237 [11] (Macfarlan JA) (footnotes omitted).

44 For statutory text incorporating a common law concept as it changes over time, see chapter 19.

45 See, eg, the issues raised by occupiers' liability legislation, as discussed in Peter Handford and Brenda McGivern, 'Two Problems of Occupiers' Liability: Part One – The Occupiers' Liability Acts and the Common Law' (2015) 39(2) *Melbourne University Law Review* 128.

46 See, eg, *R v Lavender* (2005) 222 CLR 67 where the Court considered whether s 18 of the *Crimes Act 1900* (NSW) had incorporated the common law of unlawful homicide by involuntary manslaughter.

47 (2010) 241 CLR 539.

of the relevant Acts. The majority judgment considered the long history of legislative and common law antecedents, as well as similar statutes. The majority concluded that the legislation employed 'as an integer for its operation a term with a content given by the common law as established from time to time'.[48] Therefore, 'charitable institution' was to 'be understood by reference to its source in the general law',[49] in which case Aid/Watch qualified as charitable.[50]

As can be seen from *Aid/Watch*, where the general law is incorporated into statute, its use is twofold. First, it forms part of the legislative history of the statute that may assist in determining whether the statute incorporates the general law. Second, if the statute is found to incorporate a common law concept, then the common law becomes an interpretative aid for the statutory text.

(b) Statute modifies or supplements the common law

A statute that modifies or supplements the common law of an area alters the law of that area, but does not displace it in its entirety. This may be expressly provided for in the statute or inferred from the process of interpretation. **Example 22.1** is an illustration of modification.[51]

Example 22.1 *King v Philcox*[52]

Mr Philcox's brother died in a car accident as a result of a driver's negligence. Mr Philcox had driven past the scene of the accident several times and seen that someone had been seriously hurt but had not been aware it was his brother. Later, he was told of the death and realised that it had been his brother in the accident that he had seen. Mr Philcox was devastated and later diagnosed with mental harm consisting of a recognised psychiatric illness. He sued the driver of the car for mental harm under the *Civil Liability Act 1936* (SA) ('CLA').

Section 33 of the CLA relevantly provided that a person did not owe a duty to another person not to cause them mental harm unless a certain test of foreseeability was met. Further, s 53 provided:

> (1) Damages may only be awarded for mental harm if the injured person –
> (a) was physically injured in the accident or was present at the scene of the accident when the accident occurred; . . .

The Court, in three separate judgments, determined that Mr Philcox was prevented from recovery for damages by s 53(1). All judgments considered the common law principles of negligence, and two judgments considered the legislative antecedents and parliamentary materials for the provisions at length.[53] It was noted that the CLA was not attempting to codify the law of negligence.[54] While the judgments varied in their views about the extent to which s 33 was consistent with the common law, it was accepted that s 53 modified the common law position. As

48 Ibid 548–9 [20] (French CJ, Gummow, Hayne, Crennan and Bell JJ).

49 Ibid 550 [24].

50 See also **[19.6]**.

51 For an example of a statute supplementing the common law, see *O'Neill v The Queen* (2020) 137 SASR 1, 12 [41] (Nicholson J, Stanley J agreeing at 2 [1], Hughes J agreeing at 16 [65]).

52 (2015) 255 CLR 304.

53 Ibid 313–19 [10]–[20] (French CJ, Kiefel and Gageler JJ), 347–51 [120]–[128] (Nettle J).

54 Ibid 318 [18] (French CJ, Kiefel and Gageler JJ).

Keane J explained, it was 'the unmistakable intention of s 53(1)(a) of the Act to cut back common law rights on a selective basis'.[55]

Further, his Honour said:

> [I]t would be out of place to insist upon an artificial construction in order to preserve common law rights ... 'It is of little assistance, in endeavouring to work out the meaning of parts of [a legislative] scheme, to invoke a general presumption against the very thing which the legislation sets out to achieve.'[56]

These latter comments serve as a reminder that the prior common law, even when incorporated into a statute, is always subject to the statutory text.

Common law that triggers legislative enactment

[22.7] **Where a judicial decision triggers a legislative enactment, the probative value of the antecedent common law may be more apparent**

The enactment of a legislative provision may be triggered by a particular judicial decision that, for political, financial or other reasons, is not acceptable to the government of the day and so prompts a legislative response. In this instance, the object of the statutory provision may be readily discernible, particularly where parliamentary materials refer to that decision. **Example 22.2** is an illustration.

Example 22.2 *Insurance Commission of Western Australia v Container Handlers Pty Ltd*[57]

Mr Sutton was a passenger with a driver transporting a truck in the north of Western Australia. The truck was being carried by a prime mover and low loader combination. The driver was an employee of Container Handlers Pty Ltd, which owned the prime mover and loader.

On the journey the low loader and prime mover combination suffered mechanical problems, and the driver decided that some wheels would have to be removed. In the course of assisting the driver to do this, Mr Sutton's hand was crushed.

Mr Sutton successfully sued Container Handlers (as the driver's employer) for damages for negligence. Container Handlers claimed indemnification under their third-party insurance policy with the WA Insurance Commission under the *Motor Vehicle (Third Party Insurance) Act 1943* (WA) ('the MV Act'). The Commission refused to pay.

The MV Act provided, in the schedule to the Act, that the Commission would insure the owner of a motor vehicle

> in respect of all liability for negligence which may be incurred by the owner ... in respect of the death of or bodily injury to any person directly caused by, or by the driving of, that motor vehicle in any part of the Commonwealth ...

55 Ibid 326 [42].

56 Ibid, citing in part *Australian Securities and Investments Commission v DB Management Pty Ltd* (2000) 199 CLR 321, 340 [43] (Gleeson CJ, Gaudron, Gummow, Hayne and Gaudron JJ). See also 322–23 [29]–[31] (French CJ, Kiefel and Gageler JJ).

57 (2004) 218 CLR 89.

Section 3, entitled 'Interpretation', provided:

> (7) For the purposes of this Act, the death of or bodily injury to any person shall not be taken to have been caused by a vehicle if it is not a consequence of the driving of that vehicle ...

The interpretative issue was whether the injury was 'directly' caused by the driving or by the vehicle. The textual indicators of the MV Act formed an important part of the reasoning of most of the members of the High Court. Each judge also referred to the legislative history of the schedule.

Prior to 1987 the schedule had used the language 'caused by *or arising out of* the use of such [a] motor vehicle' (emphasis added). In the 1987 decision of *Dickinson v Motor Vehicle Insurance Trust* ('*Dickinson*')[58] the High Court had considered that language in relation to a child who has sustained injuries while playing with a box of matches in a parked car. In *Dickinson* the Court had concluded that the injury was covered by the schedule for the following reason:

> The test posited by the words 'arising out of' is wider than that posited by the words 'caused by' and the former ... does not require the direct or proximate relationship which would be necessary to conclude that the injuries were caused by the use of the vehicle.[59]

After *Dickinson* Parliament amended the language of the schedule to the version before the Court. The parliamentary materials relating to the Amendment Act revealed that its object was to overcome the effect of *Dickinson*.[60] They showed that the executive saw the decision as adversely impacting the price of compulsory third-party insurance premiums.[61] This pre-existing case law, as highlighted by the parliamentary materials, made it clear that the object of the new wording was therefore to narrow the scope of the legislative policy. All the judgments relied at least in part on this history in coming to the view that the injury was not within the scope of the schedule.[62] Container Handlers was therefore not entitled to indemnification.

---

58 (1987) 163 CLR 500.

59 *Insurance Commission of Western Australia v Container Handlers Pty Ltd* (2004) 218 CLR 89, 117 [77] (Gummow J), citing *Dickinson v Motor Vehicle Insurance Trust* (1987) 163 CLR 500, 505 (Mason CJ, Wilson, Brennan, Dawson and Toohey JJ).

60 (2004) 218 CLR 89, 97 [14], 113 [63] (McHugh J).

61 Ibid 117 [79] (Gummow J).

62 Ibid 113 [63] (McHugh J), 117 [79] (Gummow J), 127 [115] (Kirby J), 130–1 [130]–[131] (Callinan J) 140–1 [152] (Heydon J). However, views differed as to whether this was dependent on the wording of the schedule or of s 3(7), which informed the schedule.

23 BACKGROUND FACTS AND CIRCUMSTANCES

Overview

[23.1] The legislative history of a statute includes its legislative antecedents (chapter 21), the pre-existing common law (chapter 22) and pre-parliamentary and parliamentary materials (chapter 24). These tend to be readily identifiable aspects of a statute's historical context. But the 'wider context' of a statute is more than just these matters and documents. It extends to the background of facts and circumstances that led up to and surrounded the enactment of a statute, such as the social, political, economic and commercial facts of that time. These facts and circumstances might be characterised as a residual category of a statute's legislative history. There is no exhaustive description of what matters might constitute a statute's 'background'. Despite that breadth, only contextual matters that have a rational connection to the interpretative issue being considered will have probative value. There is also authority that suggests that the background matters and facts that may be relevant for interpretation are limited to matters and facts that are well known to the public, or that Parliament can be taken to be 'aware' of at the time of enactment. Courts may use the doctrine of judicial notice to refer to background facts and circumstances without the need for proof.

As part of wider context

[23.2] **The 'wider context' of a statute includes the background to, and the circumstances in which, the statute was enacted**

For decades, courts have referred to, in certain circumstances, 'the historical facts surrounding the bringing of law into existence'.[1] Like the legislative history considered in chapters 21, 22 and 24, background facts and circumstances may be considered under the modern common law principle that context must be considered in its 'widest sense' and in the first instance.[2]

This aspect of wider context concerns the circumstances in which the statute was written.[3] This means the 'time, place, and any other circumstance that could rationally assist understanding of meaning' of the statutory text.[4] Another way of describing this aspect of context is as the

1 *Tasmania v Commonwealth and Victoria* (1904) 1 CLR 329, 359 (O'Connor J); *Sovar v Henry Lane Pty Ltd* (1967) 116 CLR 397, 405 (Kitto J, Owen J agreeing at 417). See chapter 2.

2 *CIC Insurance Ltd v Bankstown Football Club Ltd* (1997) 187 CLR 384, 408 (Brennan CJ, Dawson, Toohey and Gummow JJ); *SZTAL v Minister for Immigration and Border Protection* (2017) 262 CLR 362, 368 [14] (Kiefel CJ, Nettle and Gordon JJ), 374 [36]–[37] (Gageler J). See **[2.7]**, **[24.2]** and chapter 7.

3 Murray Gleeson, 'The Meaning of Legislation: Context, Purpose and Respect for Fundamental Rights' (2009) 20(1) *Public Law Review* 26, 29–30.

4 *Singh v Commonwealth* (2004) 222 CLR 322, 332 [12] (Gleeson CJ). See also *Stevens v Kabushiki Kaisha Sony Computer Entertainment* (2005) 224 CLR 193, 230 [124] (McHugh J).

'matrix of facts' in which the statute was created.[5] This historical information assists the court to understand the 'background of concepts, principles, practices, facts, rights and duties which the authors of the text', the Parliament, 'took for granted or understood' when enacting the statute.[6] Former Chief Justice Gleeson referred, extrajudicially, to considering such matters as engaging in 'informed' interpretation.[7]

Understanding the historical background to a statute beyond the pre-existing law recognises that statutes are not made in a vacuum. They are intended to achieve a purpose or to reflect a policy that, to some extent at least, is a product of the time when they were enacted. The relevance of the circumstances surrounding the making of a statute can also be rationalised by reference to notions of how language conveys meaning. As Leonard Hoffmann has explained:

> The meaning conveyed by any utterance, whether orally or in writing, always requires a consideration of both the rules ... of the language and the background against which those words were used. The background may be other parts of the same utterance ..., or facts which the speaker expected the audience to know, assumptions which they expected the audience to make, and so on ... There can be no speech act without some background.[8]

To put it another way, understanding the background to a statute is a reflection of the 'important function of context in the dynamics of communication'.[9] This context, together with the pre-existing law and extrinsic materials, helps to build a more complete picture of the statute's history. This may assist the interpreter to make reasonable inferences about what Parliament intended to be communicated by the text.[10]

Sometimes the background to a statute will be revealed by reference to extrinsic documents. For example, white papers, law reform commission reports, second reading speeches and committee reports all reveal aspects of the statute's background. These 'extrinsic materials' are discussed in chapter 24.

---

5 *Commissioner of State Revenue v EHL Burgess Properties Pty Ltd* (2015) 209 LGERA 314, 329 [52] (the Court), citing *Minister for Immigration and Multicultural Affairs v WABQ* (2002) 121 FCR 251, 281 [106] (Moore J), which in turn cites *Black-Clawson International Ltd v Papierwerke Waldhof-Aschaffenburg AG* [1975] AC 591, 646 (Lord Simon). See also *Minister for Immigration and Multicultural Affairs v WABQ* (2002) 121 FCR 251, 271 [71] (Hill J); *Re Maurice's Application; Ex parte A-G (NT)* (1987) 18 FCR 163, 171–2 (Beaumont J).

6 *Theophanous v Herald & Weekly Times Ltd* (1994) 182 CLR 104, 196 (McHugh J, dissenting). Although dealing with a constitutional issue, McHugh J was making a point for all legal instruments: see *Secretary, Department of Family and Community Services v Hayward (A Pseudonym)* (2018) 98 NSWLR 599, 608 [27] (the Court) ('the proposition holds true for statutes'). See also *Wilson v Anderson* (2002) 213 CLR 401, 418–19 [9] (Gleeson CJ).

7 Murray Gleeson, 'The Meaning of Legislation: Context, Purpose and Respect for Fundamental Rights' (2009) 20(1) *Public Law Review* 26, 29, citing Francis Bennion, *Bennion on Statutory Interpretation* (5th ed, LexisNexis, 2008) 589.

8 Leonard Hoffmann, 'Language and Lawyers' (2018) 134 (October) *Law Quarterly Review* 553, 554. See also Reed Dickerson, *The Interpretation and Application of Statutes* (Little, Brown, & Co 1975) 108.

9 Reed Dickerson, 'Statutory Interpretation: The Uses and Anatomy of Context' (1972) 23(2) *Case Western Reserve Law Review* 353, 356.

10 Leonard Hoffmann, 'Language and Lawyers' (2018) 134 (October) *Law Quarterly Review* 553, 558.

Range of matters

[23.3] **There is no exhaustive description of what matters may be included in 'surrounding circumstances'**

The concept of 'surrounding circumstances' can be regarded as a residual category of legislative history. Legislative antecedents, prior common law and extrinsic materials will likely capture the bulk of historical context. The notion of background circumstances captures other relevant historical matters that assist understanding the statute.

The nature of this legislative history means that there is some difficulty in describing or identifying its boundaries. As Chief Justice Spigelman has stated, when writing of the contextual principle of *CIC Insurance* extracurially, 'no judgment has attempted to identify a list of matters capable of being encompassed within the concept of "context" when understood "in its widest sense"'.[11]

The indeterminate character of this type of legislative history is unsurprising. Given the political context of legislation, the range of subject matters addressed by legislation and the diversity of factors that drive its enactment, it would not be useful or meaningful to attempt to provide an exhaustive description of what constitutes this history. The notion of 'surrounding circumstances' effectively allows a court to consider 'any material that may throw light on the meaning that the enacting legislature intended to give to the provision'.[12] Attempting to compile a definitive list of matters is made more problematic by the fact that, often, the court will not expressly identify these matters as matters of context.

Consequently, rather than attempt a categorical description of what may be encompassed in the concept of 'surrounding circumstances', the following examples serve to illustrate the wide range of the background matters that might be considered.

(a) ***Specialist field context***: Facts about a particular field in existence at the time of enactment of the statute may contribute towards an inference about what Parliament intended by a statute in that field. One example is *Western Australia v BLM*.[13] The Court was required to consider a new cl 3A in sch 1 of the *Sentencing Legislation Amendment and Repeal* Act *2003* (WA), as inserted by the *Sentencing Legislation (Transitional Provisions) Amendment Act 2008* (WA). One of the issues was whether the clause granted a discretion to the court when sentencing and, if so, what criteria should be used. As well as reviewing legislative antecedents and various extrinsic materials, Wheeler and Pullin JJA referred to the historical context of the Act, including times in custody, the high rate of imprisonment in Western Australia, the desire to avoid that rate increasing, and the difficulties the courts had in achieving consistency of sentencing.[14] Their Honours referred to tables of information about imprisonment and community correction rates, and historical sentencing statistics.[15] Against that factual background they considered it an 'obvious construction'[16] that cl 3A required the court to engage in a particular method of arriving at appropriate minimum custodial periods.

11 Chief Justice Spigelman, 'The Intolerable Wrestle: Developments in Statutory Interpretation' (2010) 84(11) *Australian Law Journal* 822, 827, referring to *CIC Insurance Ltd v Bankstown Football Club Ltd* (1997) 187 CLR 384.

12 *Stevens v Kabushiki Kaisha Sony Computer Entertainment* (2005) 224 CLR 193, 230 [124] (McHugh J).

13 (2009) 40 WAR 414.

14 Ibid 424–6 [19]–[23] (Owen JA agreeing; Buss JA and Miller JA disagreeing on construction: at 481 [267]).

15 Ibid 425 [20], [23].

16 Ibid 426 [25].

(b) ***Social context***: When attempting to identify the purpose of legislation at the appropriate level of generality, a court may refer to the 'social objective' of that legislation.[17] To identify that objective, the social context of the Act can be important. For example, in *Northern Territory v Arnhem Land Aboriginal Land Trust*,[18] a central issue was whether grants of land under the *Aboriginal Land Rights (Northern Territory) Act 1976* (Cth) conferred rights to exclude persons who wished to fish pursuant to a licence under the *Fisheries Act 1988* (NT) from tidal waters within the boundaries of the grant. Kirby J's analysis included consideration of the

> background of the particular place that such Aboriginal rights now enjoy, having regard to their unique character as legally *sui generis*, their history, their belated recognition, their present purposes and the 'moral foundation' (now recognised in legislation) for respecting them.[19]

Similarly, in a decision shortly after Northern Territory v Arnhem Land Aboriginal Land Trust, Kirby J stated that the *Aboriginal Land Rights Act 1983* (NSW) must be understood in its historical, legal, social and human rights context, which included a background of discrimination with respect to the rights to traditional lands of the Indigenous people of Australia.[20]

(c) ***Political context***: In *Wilkie v Commonwealth*,[21] an issue was whether s 10 of the *Appropriation Act (No 1) 2017–2018* (Cth) permitted a determination providing the Australian Bureau of Statistics with $122 million for a voluntary postal plebiscite on same sex marriage. One of the issues was the extent of the power of the Minister to allocate expenditure under s 10 and whether it permitted expenditure for a 'new policy'. The Court considered the parliamentary practice since 1965 with respect to the content of Appropriation Acts agreed by the House of Representatives and the Senate, and whether they had historically included money for 'new policy'. Recent history revealed that there had ceased to be any clear distinction between 'new' policies and modifications of existing policy.[22] It was open, the Court said, to draw an implication as to the scope of the appropriations contained in the Act from that historical parliamentary practice.[23]

(d) ***Commercial context***: The commercial or economic context in which a statute is enacted may have relevance. For example, in *Tabcorp Holdings Ltd v Victoria*[24] s 4.3.12 of the *Gambling Regulation Act 2003* (Vic) provided that 'on the grant of new licences', the person holding the former licences was entitled to a payment. Tabcorp had been the holder of wagering and gaming licences under a duopoly scheme. That regime was replaced and Tabcorp was allocated 'gaming machine entitlements' under the new licensing regime. The Court was required to determine whether 'grant of new licences' only referred to the

---

17 See, eg, *Clubb v Edwards* (2019) 267 CLR 171, 328 [457] (Edelman J) citing *Unions NSW v New South Wales* (2019) 264 CLR 595, 657 [171] (Edelman J). See also *Minister Administering the Crown Lands Act v NSW Aboriginal Land Council* (2008) 237 CLR 285, 293 [21] (Kirby J).

18 (2008) 236 CLR 24.

19 Ibid 69 [69] (footnotes omitted).

20 *Minister Administering the Crown Lands Act v NSW Aboriginal Land Council* (2008) 237 CLR 285, 291 [12], [13].

21 (2017) 263 CLR 487.

22 Ibid 541 [126]–[127] (the Court).

23 Ibid 541 [126]. See also 524 [64].

24 (2016) 90 ALJR 376.

duopoly of wagering and gaming licences previously granted to Tabcorp, or whether it extended to the newly created gaming machine entitlements. The Court referred to the history of the legislation, noting that the duopoly licensing scheme had produced the wagering and gaming licences as 'an instrument of commerce, not merely an abstract legal concept', and that such commerciality was an essential part of the machinery of the previous scheme.[25] Once that commercial context was appreciated, then, when the duopoly scheme was dissolved, a reference to 'new licences' in s 4.3.12 as being confined to new licences under the previous regime was 'unmistakable', according to the Court.[26]

(e) ***International context***: International extrinsic materials, such as conventions and treaties, and presumptions made about international law and domestic legislation are addressed in chapter 31. The ability of courts to consider background generally enables them to consider the international context more broadly, beyond the scope of those presumptions and materials. Developments or events in other countries may provide context if they can be rationally linked to the interpretative issue. For example, in *Taylor v Attorney-General (Cth)*[27] a private prosecution had been brought against Ms Aung San Suu Kyi, Minister of the Office of the President and Foreign Minister of the Republic of the Union of Myanmar, for alleged crimes against humanity in contravention of the *Criminal Code* (Cth) (in sch to *Criminal Code Act 1995* (Cth)) ('the Code'). One issue was how s 268.121 of the Code operated with s 13 of the *Crimes Act 1914* (Cth). Section 268.121 of the Code provided that such a prosecution had to have the consent of the Attorney-General and must be brought in their name. Section 13 of the *Crimes Act* permitted 'any person' to institute such proceedings. As part of the analysis of s 268.121, under the heading 'Contextual Indications', Nettle and Gordon JJ (in dissent) fortified their conclusion that the Code provisions did not exclude private prosecutions by noting:

> [A]t the time of drafting s 268.121, the drafters would almost certainly have had in front of them the forms of legislation earlier enacted in New Zealand, the United Kingdom and Canada [to give effect to certain international obligations] ... And since the drafters did not adopt the Canadian form of words, but rather combined the United Kingdom and New Zealand pattern with a provision, long familiar in this country, for the institution of proceedings in the name of the Attorney-General, the logical conclusion is that they eschewed the Canadian approach in favour of the more orthodox United Kingdom and New Zealand course of retaining the private right of prosecution and subjecting it to a requirement first to obtain the Attorney-General's consent.[28]

(f) ***Constitutional context***: The *Australian Constitution* of 1900 provides the central framework for the Australian system of government, and the roles of the respective arms of government. The principles of statutory interpretation are regarded as the 'product of ... the interaction between the three branches of government established by the *Constitution*'.[29] The *Constitution* is background to all Australian legislation. There are

25 Ibid 390 [90]–[91] (the Court).

26 Ibid 390 [91]. See generally 390–1 [89]–[95]. For the relevance of commercial context, see also *Chevron Australia Holdings Pty Ltd v Federal Commissioner of Taxation* (2017) 251 FCR 40, 43–6 [3]–[15] (Allsop CJ).

27 (2019) 268 CLR 224.

28 Ibid 254 [79]. See also 259 [97]–[98] (Edelman J, also dissenting).

29 *Plaintiff S10/2011 v Minister for Immigration and Citizenship* (2012) 246 CLR 636, 666 [97] (Gummow, Hayne, Crennan and Bell JJ). See **[3.3]**.

fundamental constitutional concepts that guide statutory interpretation law and so the meaning of statutes.[30] The *Constitution* provisions themselves may also provide relevant contextual material.[31] See **[32.8]** for presumptions of interpretation arising from the *Constitution*.

Rationality and parliamentary awareness

To be used in statutory interpretation, the background circumstances must have some rational connection to the interpretative task [23.4]

In his seminal article on statutory interpretation, former US Supreme Court Justice Felix Frankfurter, quoting former Justice Oliver Holmes, stated that 'a page of history is worth a volume of logic'.[32] Background to the enactment of a statute frames the statute – context 'gives the place, the wholeness and the relational reality to words'.[33] However, like any other extrinsic context, that context will only have utility 'if, and in so far as, it assists in fixing the meaning of the statutory text'.[34] That is, it must be relevant to the interpretative task.[35] Relevance, and weight, will depend on the statute, the interpretative issue, the background circumstances and other relevant interpretative factors. If we think of contextual matter as evidence, this is no different to assessing whether any evidence has a rational connection to an issue and, if it does, the weight to be given to it.

In statutory interpretation, background circumstances may indicate the object or mischief that the statute is intended to address. It is well established that evidence of the mischief or purpose is relevant to construction.[36] For example, in *Brown v Tasmania*[37] the Court considered certain provisions of the *Workplaces (Protection from Protesters) Act 2014* (Tas). In assessing the purpose of that Act, Kiefel CJ, Bell and Keane JJ considered the long history of protests, including onsite protests, in Tasmania. They noted:

> There is also a particular historical, social and legislative background to forest operations and public access to forests in Tasmania, and demonstrations in forests appear to have been the catalyst for the Protesters Act.[38]

Further, the factual background may provide evidence of which 'concepts, principles, practices, facts, rights and duties' (see **[23.2]**) Parliament might be taken to have been aware of at the time of enactment. This may enable reasonable inferences to be drawn about Parliament's object or intent that can be weighed and balanced as part of the basket of all relevant interpretative factors. **Example 23.1** illustrates this scenario.

---

30 See generally chapter 3.

31 See, eg, *Burns v Corbett* (2018) 265 CLR 304, 412 [256] (Edelman J).

32 Felix Frankfurter, 'Some Reflections on the Reading of Statutes' (1947) 47(4) *Columbia Law Review* 527, 543, citing *New York Trust Co v Eisner*, 256 US 345, 349 (1921).

33 *Chevron Australia Holdings Pty Ltd v Federal Commissioner of Taxation* (2017) 251 FCR 40, 43 [3] (Allsop CJ).

34 *Thiess v Collector of Customs* (2014) 250 CLR 664, 671 [22] (French CJ, Hayne, Kiefel, Gageler and Keane JJ), quoting *Federal Commissioner of Taxation v Consolidated Media Holdings Ltd* (2012) 250 CLR 503, 519 [39] (French CJ, Hayne, Crennan, Bell and Gageler JJ).

35 See **[7.3]**.

36 See chapter 8.

37 (2017) 261 CLR 328.

38 Ibid 341 [6]. See also 346 [33], 371 [134].

Example 23.1 *Commissioner of State Revenue v EHL Burgess Properties Pty Ltd*[39]

A rural property, named 'Lockerbie', was used primarily for primary production. Section 65(1) of the *Land Tax Act 2005* (Vic) ('the LTA') provided a land tax exemption as follows:

> Land outside greater Melbourne that is used primarily for primary production is exempt land.

The issue in contention was whether some of the land comprising Lockerbie was within 'greater Melbourne' and therefore *not* entitled to the tax exemption. The term 'greater Melbourne' was defined in s 64(1) of the LTA and then provided:

> *greater Melbourne* means –
>
> (a) *metropolitan area* within the meaning of section 201 of the *Melbourne and Metropolitan Board of Works Act 1958* . . .; or
>
> (b) any area declared by the Governor in Council under subsection (3) to be the metropolitan area.

The term 'metropolitan area' was defined in the 1958 Act by reference to a Third Schedule to that Act, which listed various cities and shires, and any other area declared by the Governor in Council to be a metropolitan area. However, the cities and shires – other than one – referred to in the Third Schedule had ceased to exist. Indeed, the vast majority of the cities and shires listed had not had the status of a municipality since 1994. The LTA had been enacted in 2005. As well, the Governor in Council had made no declarations concerning metropolitan area.

EHL Burgess' preferred construction was that the term 'greater Melbourne' should be interpreted by reference to the legal entities, the municipalities, listed in the Third Schedule. If the municipality had ceased to exist as a legal entity then the area within the boundaries of the entity was not a 'metropolitan area' and so was outside 'greater Melbourne'. An opposing construction, preferred by the Commissioner, was that 'greater Melbourne' was determined by reference to the physical areas covered by the municipalities, and so the legal existence or not of the entities did not affect the identification of that area.

The Court acknowledged that context could include time, place and any other circumstance that could rationally assist understanding of meaning.[40] Therefore, the Court stated, they may have regard to the 'matrix of facts in which the statute was enacted'.[41] There were two main important historical facts. The first was that it had been a 'matter of public record of considerable notoriety'[42] at the time of the enactment of the LTA that the cities and shires had ceased to exist as municipalities. The second was that the Governor in Council had not exercised their powers to alter the areas falling within the Third Schedule. The Court said:

> Despite knowing these facts, when Parliament enacted the LTA in 2005, it assigned a meaning to 'greater Melbourne' by reference to the Third Schedule. This could only have

39 (2015) 209 LGERA 314 ('*EHL Burgess*').

40 Ibid 329 [52] (the Court), citing *Singh v Commonwealth* (2004) 222 CLR 322 [12] (Gleeson CJ) and *Maroondah City Council v Fletcher* (2009) 29 VR 160, 166 [27] (Warren CJ and Osborne AJA).

41 Ibid 329 [52] (the Court), citing *Minister for Immigration and Multicultural Affairs v WABQ* (2002) 121 FCR 251, 281 [106] (Moore J).

42 Ibid 341 [104].

> been on the basis that the areas within the boundaries of the Cities and Shires . . . of that schedule had continuing relevance to the definition of 'metropolitan area', and, in turn, the definition of 'greater Melbourne', notwithstanding the cessation of the legal entities previously associated with those municipalities.[43]

These historical facts, together with the Court's analysis of the statutory language and legislative history, led the Court to conclude that the Commissioner's construction was the preferred one.

Whether surrounding circumstances can rationally assist may be linked to whether Parliament can be taken to be aware of those circumstances [23.5]

The example of *EHL Burgess* above demonstrates that if Parliament can be taken to have known or been aware of particular circumstances that existed at the time of enactment then that may establish a rational connection between the background facts and the enacted statutory text. This is consistent with the linguistic rationale for considering background circumstances (see **[23.2]**). If Parliament, as the author of the text, can be taken to be aware of particular circumstances, then those circumstances form part of the collection of assumptions that frame the enactment of the statute. This was implicitly acknowledged by the Court in *EHL Burgess*.[44]

This proposition is often traced back to the House of Lords decision *Black-Clawson International Ltd v Papierwerke Waldhof-Aschaffenburg AG*,[45] where Lord Reid stated:

> An Act is addressed to all the lieges and it would seem wrong to take into account anything that was not public knowledge at the time. That may be common knowledge at the time or it may be some published information which Parliament can be presumed to have had in mind.[46]

Parliament may be aware of particular circumstances because they are commonly or publicly known. As was noted even before the modern approach to interpretation, 'the court is not bound to shut its eyes to public general knowledge of the circumstances in which the legislation was passed'.[47] It may also be possible to infer that Parliament is aware of particular historical circumstances from material available to Parliament at the time of enactment.

The notion of Parliament's 'awareness' is not uncommon in statutory interpretation. It can be found in other interpretative principles such as the principle of legality,[48] the re-enactment presumption[49] and the presumption that Parliament makes laws consistent with international law.[50] It does not require empirical proof, but a reasoned inference. It is a construct by which knowledge is attributed to Parliament where it can be reasonably inferred.

---

43 Ibid 344 [117]. The process of construction by the Court in *EHL Burgess* was reconsidered in *Australian Investment and Development Pty Ltd v Commissioner of State Revenue* [2019] VSCA 69, where the applicant unsuccessfully argued that the construction of 'greater Melbourne' determined by the Court in *EHL Burgess* was wrong. See also **[30.7]**.

44 *EHL Burgess* (2015) 209 LGERA 314, 344 [117].

45 [1975] AC 591.

46 Ibid 614.

47 *Deputy Federal Commissioner of Taxation (NSW) v WR Moran Pty Ltd* (1939) 61 CLR 735, 793 (Evatt J).

48 See chapter 28.

49 See chapter 21.

50 See chapter 31.

There is limited Australian authority expressly endorsing the *Black-Clawson* principle on Parliament awareness.[51] It seems to be more of an unstated assumption when courts are referring to a statute's background. The proposition has received some attention in the context of the recent discourse on legislative intent.[52] Yet it remains open to question this limitation. Material or matters that are capable of assisting the particular interpretative task are not always confined to materials or matters that it can be inferred Parliament 'knew' at the time of enactment. Other interpretative aids involve consideration of contemporary context or post-enactment materials.[53]

Use of judicial notice

[23.6] **To refer to background facts, courts sometimes make use of the doctrine of 'judicial notice'**

The general rule for matters adjudicated before a court is that 'all the facts in issue or relevant to the issue in a given case must be proved by evidence'.[54] The doctrine of judicial notice provides an exception to this general rule that is relevant to consideration of historical facts and circumstances.[55] Judicial notice permits a court to take 'notice' of this history in certain circumstances without requiring a party to prove it by evidence.

The common law doctrine of judicial notice allows courts to take into account, without the burden of proving them, facts that are 'notorious', being a fact that is

> so generally known that every ordinary person may be reasonably presumed to be aware of it, the Court 'notices' it, either *simpliciter* if it is at once satisfied of the fact without more, or after such information or investigation as it considers reliable and necessary in order to eliminate any reasonable doubt.
>
> The basic essential is that the fact is to be of a class that is so generally known as to give rise to the presumption that all persons are aware of it.[56]

Background or surrounding circumstances to the enactment of legislation may be 'noticed' by the Court. This was the case in the example of *EHL Burgess* (**Example 23.1**). The Court noted that it was 'notorious' that, at the time of enactment of the LTA, the cities and shires in the Third Schedule, other than one, had ceased to exist.[57] Despite this device, judges do not always specify that they are referring to historical matters using the doctrine.

---

51 Though the idea has been endorsed. See, eg, *Linfox Australia Pty Ltd v Federal Commissioner of Taxation* (2019) 271 FCR 365, 388 [117] (the Court), citing *Commissioner of Taxation v Murray* (1990) 21 FCR 436, 449 (Hill J); *Australian Investment and Development Pty Ltd v Commissioner of State Revenue* [2019] VSCA 69, [60].

52 See, eg, Richard Ekins and Jeffrey Goldsworthy, 'The Reality and Indispensability of Legislative Intentions' (2014) 36(1) *Sydney Law Review* 39, 48–51, 66–7; Larry Alexander, 'Goldsworthy on Interpretation of Statutes and Constitutions: Public Meaning, Intended Meaning and the Bogey of Aggregation' in Lisa Burton Crawford, Patrick Emerton and Dale Smith (eds), *Law Under a Democratic Constitution: Essays in Honour of Jeffrey Goldsworthy* (Hart Publishing, 2019), 5, 10–11.

53 See, eg, chapter 19, **[21.10]** and **[24.16]**.

54 JD Heydon, LexisNexis, *Cross on Evidence* (online at 29 November 2021) [3001].

55 Judicial notice is also relevant to non-historical matters. See chapters 19, 32.

56 *Holland v Jones* (1917) 23 CLR 149, 153 (Isaacs J). For detailed treatment of judicial notice, see JD Heydon, LexisNexis, *Cross on Evidence* (online at 29 November 2021) ch 2, esp [3015]–[3025].

57 *EHL Burgess* (2015) 209 LGERA 314, 336 [82] (the Court). Another example is *Maloney v The Queen* (2013) 252 CLR 168, 240 [194] where Bell J noted that '[t]he link between the excessive consumption of alcohol and violence is notorious' and this was relevant to the legislative purpose of the Act being construed.

The doctrine of judicial notice may permit a court to 'notice' a historical fact or matter that is regarded as a 'legislative fact'. As explained in *Cross on Evidence*:

> A legislative fact ... is a fact which helps the court determine the content of law and policy and to exercise its discretion or judgment in determining what course of action to take. ... It is clear from the cases that judges have felt themselves relatively free to apply their own views of and to make their own enquiries about social ethics, psychology, politics and history where relevant without requiring evidence or other proof.[58]

As noted in **[32.2]**, the doctrine of judicial notice has been incorporated or modified, in whole or in part, by legislation in many Australian jurisdictions.

58 JD Heydon, LexisNexis, *Cross on Evidence* (online at 29 November 2021) [3005]. A 'legislative fact' is to be contrasted with an 'adjudicative fact'.

24 EXTRINSIC MATERIALS: PRE-PARLIAMENTARY AND PARLIAMENTARY MATERIALS

Overview

[24.1] The legislative history of a statute includes the extrinsic materials relating to that history. Pre-parliamentary materials and parliamentary materials are a significant category of those extrinsic materials. There is a common law principle that permits access to extrinsic materials. As well, each state and territory has provisions in their respective Interpretation Acts governing consideration of extrinsic materials. These statutory and common law gateways to extrinsic materials coexist, although their requirements vary. The doctrine of 'parliamentary privilege' is not a barrier to using parliamentary materials for interpretation. There is no exhaustive list of the pre-parliamentary and parliamentary materials that might be relevant for statutory interpretation, although it is assumed that they are materials that were publicly available, or at least known to Parliament, at the time of the enactment of the legislation being construed. Once it is established that there is legal authority to consider these extrinsic materials, the next step is to determine their probative value. There is no established hierarchy of the utility of different types of materials, but there are some guiding strands evident from the case law, including the extent to which the materials identify the purpose of an Act or provision. Silence in parliamentary material may be a relevant indicator. The existence of parliamentary or pre-parliamentary material that is directly relevant to an interpretative issue does not displace the fundamental principle that the interpretative task must start and end with the text; nor can the words in those materials displace the statutory text. Generally, materials that come into existence after the enactment of the statute being construed are not relevant to its interpretation.

Statutory and common law authority

[24.2] **There is statutory and common law authority for recourse to extrinsic materials and they are not the same**

When courts refer to 'extrinsic materials' they are often, though not always, referring to parliamentary and pre-parliamentary materials. These are a category of extrinsic materials relating to the legislative history of an Act. For the purposes of this chapter, parliamentary materials are non-legislative materials relating to a Bill that are generated, or presented to Parliament, during the enactment process for that Bill to become an Act. Pre-parliamentary materials are non-legislative materials related or connected to a Bill that were created prior to a Bill being introduced into Parliament. There is statutory and common law authority for recourse to these extrinsic materials. Their requirements vary.

(a) Statutory authority

All Australian jurisdictions have provisions in their respective Interpretation Acts permitting access to extrinsic materials. The Commonwealth provision is s 15AB of the *Acts Interpretation Act 1901* (Cth) ('the AIA'). New South Wales, the Northern Territory, Queensland, South Australia, Tasmania and Western Australia have identical or very similar wording to s 15AB.[1] The Victorian and ACT Interpretation Acts have provisions that are drafted more broadly.[2] Details of these provisions are discussed in **[24.7]**.

(b) Common law authority

As explained in chapter 7, the so-called modern approach to statutory interpretation is the common law principle expressed in *CIC Insurance Ltd v Bankstown Football Club Ltd*.[3] In that decision, the joint judgment of Brennan CJ, Dawson, Toohey and Gummow JJ stated:

> [T]he modern approach to statutory interpretation (a) insists that the context be considered *in the first instance*, not merely at some later stage when ambiguity might be thought to arise, and (b) uses 'context' *in its widest sense* to include such things as the existing state of the law and the mischief which, by legitimate means ... one may discern the statute was intended to remedy.[4]

It is well established that the 'widest' context includes legislative history and extrinsic materials that relate to that legislative history.[5] In South Australia, as explained in **[2.9]**, a statutory provision on extrinsic materials was only enacted in 2021 in the *Legislation Interpretation Act 2021* (SA) and came into operation on 1 January 2022. Prior to that enactment the previous Act, the *Acts Interpretation Act 1915* (SA), did not contain any provision on extrinsic materials, and so the question of whether extrinsic materials could be considered in South Australia was answered solely by reference to the common law.[6]

Parliamentary privilege does not prevent courts from referring to parliamentary materials for the interpretation of a statute [24.3]

Words spoken in Parliament or documents presented in Parliament for parliamentary use are subject to the doctrine of 'parliamentary privilege'. This means that members of Parliament are protected from being the subject of legal proceedings due to the words they have spoken, or the documents used, in Parliament. One consequence of this privilege is that those words and documents are not permitted to be referred to in proceedings of courts or tribunals. The privilege originates from art 9 of the *Bill of Rights 1688* (UK).

---

1 *Interpretation Act 1987* (NSW) s 34; *Acts Interpretation Act 1954* (Qld) s 14B; *Legislation Interpretation Act 2021* (SA) s 16; *Acts Interpretation Act 1931* (Tas) s 8B; *Interpretation Act 1984* (WA) s 19; *Interpretation Act 1978* (NT) s 62B.

2 *Interpretation of Legislation Act 1984* (Vic) s 35(b); *Legislation Act 2001* (ACT) ss 141–143.

3 (1997) 187 CLR 384.

4 Ibid 408 (emphasis added).

5 *Port of Newcastle Operations Pty Ltd v Glencore Coal Assets Australia Pty Ltd* (2021) 395 ALR 209, 227 [87] (the Court); *SZTAL v Minister for Immigration and Border Protection* (2017) 262 CLR 362, 368 [14] (Kiefel CJ, Nettle and Gordon JJ), 374 [36]–[37] (Gageler J); *Federal Commissioner of Taxation v Consolidated Media Holdings Ltd* (2012) 250 CLR 503, 519 [39] (French CJ, Hayne, Crennan, Bell and Gageler JJ).

6 *K-Generation Pty Ltd v Liquor Licensing Court* (2009) 237 CLR 501, 521–2 [51]–[52] (French CJ), referring to *CIC Insurance v Bankstown Football Club Ltd* (1997) 187 CLR 384; *Redman v Return to Work Corp (SA)* (2021) 305 IR 326, 354–5 [104]–[105] (Livesey JA, Bleby JA agreeing at 365 [149]); *Owen v South Australia* (1996) 66 SASR 251, 255–6 (Cox J, Prior J agreeing at 257).

Does reference to parliamentary materials in court proceedings to construe legislation breach parliamentary privilege? Some Australian jurisdictions have legislation expressly exempting interpretative use. For example, s 16(5)(b) of the *Parliamentary Privileges Act 1987* (Cth) provides that the record of proceedings and statements in Parliament are not subject to the privilege in court and tribunal proceedings so far as they relate to 'the interpretation of an Act'. However, even where there is no such legislative exemption, the doctrine does not appear to be a barrier to their use for statutory interpretation in Australia.

[24.4] **The statutory and common law authorities are coexisting, but independent, authorities for recourse to extrinsic materials**

Section 15AB and its equivalents and the common law operate as coexisting gateways for consideration of extrinsic materials. This is indicated by *CIC Insurance* itself, as the plurality prefaced the context principle with 'apart from any reliance upon s 15AB of the *Acts Interpretation Act 1901* (Cth)'.[7] It is therefore possible to use either authority for recourse to parliamentary and other materials. So if the limitations contained in, for example, s 15AB (discussed in **[24.7]**) prevent recourse to extrinsic materials, the common law may offer an alternative avenue. These coexisting gateways have been confirmed many times.[8] This state of affairs gives rise to an anomalous position in the law, discussed in **[24.7]**.

[24.5] **Under both the statutory and common law gateways, there is no exhaustive typology of materials that may be considered**

(a) **The statutory gateway**

None of the statutory provisions on extrinsic materials contained in any of the Australian Interpretation Acts impose any limitation on the *type* of material that may potentially be considered for interpretation.

Section 15AB(1) of the AIA, mirrored substantially in the equivalent provisions of New South Wales, Queensland, South Australia, Tasmania, Western Australia and the Northern Territory, reads as follows:

> (1) [I]n the interpretation of a provision of an Act, if any material not forming part of the Act is capable of assisting in the ascertainment of the meaning of the provision, consideration may be given to that material [in certain circumstances (discussed in **[24.7]**)].

The words 'any material not forming part of the Act' in s 15AB(1) indicate that the material that may be considered is open-ended. The breadth of that language is confirmed in s 15AB(2):

> (2) Without limiting the generality of subsection (1), the material that may be considered in accordance with that subsection in the interpretation of a provision of an Act includes ...

7 *CIC Insurance Ltd v Bankstown Football Club Ltd* (1997) 187 CLR 384, 408 (Brennan CJ, Dawson, Toohey and Gummow JJ).

8 See, eg, *Newcastle City Council v GIO General Ltd* (1997) 191 CLR 85, 99 (Toohey, Gaudron and Gummow JJ), 112 (McHugh J); *A-G (Cth) v Oates* (1999) 198 CLR 162, 175 [28] (Gleeson CJ, McHugh, Gummow, Kirby and Hayne JJ); *Certain Lloyd's Underwriters v Cross* (2012) 248 CLR 378, 406 n 100 [70] (Crennan and Bell JJ); *Sydney Seaplanes Pty Ltd v Page* (2021) 106 NSWLR 1, 13 [41] (Bell P); *CPB Contractors Pty Ltd v Construction, Forestry, Maritime, Mining and Energy Union* [2019] FCAFC 70, [61] (O'Callaghan and Wheelahan JJ); *FCS17 v Minister for Home Affairs* (2020) 276 FCR 644, 647 [8] (Allsop CJ); *Burns v Minister for Health* (2012) 45 WAR 276, 284 [27]–[28] (Martin CJ, Newnes JA agreeing at 296 [81]).

A list of items then follows in s 15AB(2)(a)–(h). The words 'without limiting the generality of subsection (1)' and 'includes' confirm that this list is by way of example and is not exhaustive. The equivalent provisions of the Interpretation Acts of New South Wales, Queensland, South Australia, Tasmania, Western Australian and the Northern Territory similarly contain a list preceded by the word 'includes'.

Section 142 of the *Legislation Act 2001* (ACT) also provides a list of examples of material in a table, and states that the list in the table 'does not limit the material that may be considered in working out the meaning of an Act'. Section 35(b) of the *Interpretation of Legislation Act 1984* (Vic) permits consideration of 'any matter or document that is relevant'. This language is broader than the word 'material' used in all the other Acts, and on its face extends to extrinsic matters, and not just materials. Section 35(b), which contains a short list of examples, similarly provides that a 'matter or document' is 'not limited' to that list.

In other words, the categories of potentially relevant extrinsic material available under the Interpretation Act statutory provisions are not closed.[9]

(b) The common law principle

The common law principle of 'wider context' reflected in *CIC Insurance* clearly extends to parliamentary and pre-parliamentary materials. Wider context includes:

> 'extrinsic materials' such as reports of statutory bodies or commissions and parliamentary speeches – indeed any material that may throw light on the meaning that the enacting legislature intended to give to the provision.[10]

Like the statutory authority, the categories of materials that might be encompassed in the common law 'wider context' principle are not closed.[11]

Range of material

The non-exhaustive nature of the statutory and common law gateways means that a wide range of parliamentary and pre-parliamentary materials may be available to be considered as interpretative aids [24.6]

The open-ended nature of both the statutory and the common law gateways to extrinsic materials means that a wide range of parliamentary and pre-parliamentary materials may be available to be examined as extrinsic interpretative aids. References in judicial decisions to explanatory memoranda,[12] second reading speeches[13] and law reform commission reports are familiar. And,

9 *Singh v Commonwealth* (2004) 222 CLR 322, 336 [20] (Gleeson CJ); *Feldman v Nationwide News Pty Ltd* (2020) 103 NSWLR 307, 323 [68] (Bell P, Macfarlan JA agreeing at 351 [209], Payne JA agreeing at 351 [210]). See also Explanatory Memorandum, Acts Interpretation Amendment Bill 1984 (Cth) 3 where it states that s 15AB(2) 'sets forth, in a non-exhaustive way, the main categories of extrinsic materials that can assist in the interpretation of Acts'.

10 *Stevens v Kabushiki Kaisha Sony Computer Entertainment* (2005) 224 CLR 193, 230 [124] (McHugh J). See also *Federal Commissioner of Taxation v Consolidated Media Holdings Ltd* (2012) 250 CLR 503, 519 [39] (French CJ, Hayne, Crennan, Bell and Gageler JJ). See **[7.3]**.

11 See also **[23.2]–[23.3]**.

12 Referred to as the 'Explanation of Clauses' in South Australia, 'Explanatory Statement' in the Australian Capital Territory and the Northern Territory, 'Explanatory Notes' in New South Wales and Queensland and the 'Fact Sheet' and 'Clause Notes' in Tasmania.

13 Referred to as the explanatory speech in Queensland and the 'presentation speech' in the Australian Capital Territory.

as noted above, all Interpretation Act provisions provide, in varying degrees, a list of examples. Set out below are examples of other parliamentary and pre-parliamentary materials that have been examined (though not necessarily given probative weight – see **[24.10]**) for a statutory interpretation task:

- parliamentary committee inquiry reports;[14]
- submissions made to a parliamentary committee inquiry;[15]
- parliamentary debates after the second reading speech (including statements by members who are not Ministers,[16] comments in the committee stage,[17] and the Minister's speech in reply[18]);
- ministerial statements in Parliament;[19]
- proposed amendments to Bills and debates about those amendments;[20]
- supplementary or revised explanatory memorandum (usually consequent upon an amendment being made to a Bill during enactment);[21]
- materials tabled in Parliament, such as a government response to a report;[22]
- a human rights statement of compatibility for a Bill[23] (required for legislation of the Commonwealth, Victoria, Queensland and the Australian Capital Territory);[24]
- a Commonwealth Bills Digest;[25] and
- a contemporaneous parliamentary briefing paper.[26]

Legislative history can also include parliamentary materials relating to Bills other than the Bill for the statute being construed. Examples include parliamentary materials relating to legislative antecedents,[27] the second reading speech for another Bill,[28] explanatory memoranda for other

---

14 *Northern Territory v Griffiths* (2019) 269 CLR 1, 137 [333] (Edelman J).

15 *Hocking v Director-General, National Archives of Australia* (2020) 94 ALJR 569, 585–6 [60]–[62] (Kiefel CJ, Bell, Gageler and Keane JJ), 613 [208] (Edelman J).

16 *Brown v Tasmania* (2017) 261 CLR 328, 499–500 [549] (Edelman J).

17 *Western Australia v Manado* (2020) 270 CLR 81, 88 [3] (Kiefel CJ, Bell, Gageler, Keane and Gordon JJ).

18 *Western Australian Planning Commission v Southregal Pty Ltd* (2017) 259 CLR 106, 120–1 [47]–[48] (Kiefel and Bell JJ).

19 *Kuczborski v Queensland* (2014) 254 CLR 51, 78–9 [62] (Hayne), 98–9 [141] (Crennan, Kiefel, Gageler and Keane JJ), 136 [293] (Bell J).

20 *D'Arcy v Myriad Genetics Inc* (2015) 258 CLR 334, 355–6 [36] (French CJ, Kiefel, Bell and Keane JJ).

21 *Westpac Securities Administration Ltd v Australian Securities and Investments Commission* (2021) 270 CLR 118, 133 [21] (Kiefel CJ, Bell, Gageler, and Keane JJ), 135–7 [28]–[34] (Gordon J).

22 *Wilkie v Commonwealth* (2017) 263 CLR 487, 533–4 [99] (the Court).

23 *Clubb v Edwards* (2019) 267 CLR 171, 206 [90] (Kiefel CJ, Bell and Keane JJ), 270–5 [279] [283] [286] [289] (Nettle J).

24 *Human Rights (Parliamentary Scrutiny) Act 2011* (Cth) ss 8–9; *Human Rights Act 2019* (Qld) s 38; *Charter of Human Rights and Responsibilities Act 2006* (Vic) s 28; *Human Rights Act 2004* (ACT) s 37. See **[28.10]**.

25 *Makarov v Minister for Home Affairs (No 3)* [2020] FCA 1655, [94] (Katzmann J), affd *Makarov v Minister for Home Affairs* [2021] FCAFC 129. A Bills Digest is a publicly available written analysis of a Commonwealth Bill produced by the Parliamentary Library of the Australian Parliament. See <https://www.aph.gov.au/Parliamentary_Business/Bills_Legislation/Bills_Digests>.

26 *Edwards v The Queen* (2021) 95 ALJR 808, 817 [52] (Edelman and Steward JJ).

27 See **[21.6]**.

28 *Alley v Gillespie* (2018) 264 CLR 328, 338–9 [21] (Kiefel CJ, Bell, Keane and Edelman JJ).

Bills[29] and parliamentary committee reports of other jurisdictions.[30] Pre-parliamentary materials can vary even more widely. Examples include:

- government position or discussion papers;[31]
- a media release;[32]
- a public departmental information paper;[33]
- ministerial communiques;[34]
- a government response to an independent report;[35]
- drafting instructions;[36]
- model Bill provisions, exposure drafts of Bills or commentary on those Bills;[37]
- reports of independent bodies such as the Australian Bureau of Statistics,[38] the Productivity Commission[39] and the Family Law Council;[40] and
- reports by international bodies.[41]

While this is a broad range of material, the critical question is whether any particular document has relevance for the particular interpretative task (see **[24.10]**).

Statutory requirements

Although the categories of extrinsic materials are not closed, some Interpretation Acts set conditions for recourse to that material [24.7]

(a) Commonwealth, New South Wales, Queensland, South Australia, Tasmania, Western Australia and the Northern Territory

While the categories of extrinsic materials are not closed (**[24.5]**), the statutory provisions on extrinsic materials in the Interpretation Acts of the Commonwealth, New South Wales, Queensland, South Australia, Tasmania, Western Australia and the Northern Territory do limit the circumstances in which recourse can be made to those materials. Section 15AB of the AIA

29 *SZTAL v Minister for Immigration and Border Protection* (2017) 262 CLR 362, 370 [22] (Kiefel CJ, Nettle and Gordon JJ).

30 *Talacko v Bennett* (2017) 260 CLR 124, 146 [68] (Kiefel CJ, Bell, Keane, Gordon and Edelman JJ).

31 *New South Wales Aboriginal Land Council v Minister Administering the Crown Lands Act* (2016) 260 CLR 232, 297 [176] (Nettle and Gordon JJ).

32 *Tjungarrayi v Western Australia* (2019) 269 CLR 150, 183 [97] (Nettle J).

33 Ibid 180–2 [93]–[96] (Nettle J).

34 *Hunt & Hunt Lawyers v Mitchell Morgan Nominees Pty Ltd* (2013) 247 CLR 613, 643–4 [78] (Bell and Gageler JJ).

35 *AstraZeneca AB v Apotex Pty Ltd* (2015) 257 CLR 356, 369 [16] (French CJ).

36 *Esso Australia Resources Ltd v Federal Commissioner of Taxation* (2011) 199 FCR 226, 275–6 [156]–[157] (the Court).

37 *Australian Securities and Investments Commission v King* (2020) 270 CLR 1, 42 [117] fn 177, 44 [122] (Nettle and Gordon JJ); *R v Holliday* (2017) 260 CLR 650, 664 [49]–[51] (Kiefel CJ, Bell and Gordon JJ).

38 *Wilkie v Commonwealth* (2017) 263 CLR 487, 545 [145] (the Court).

39 *Pilbara Infrastructure Pty Ltd v Australian Competition Tribunal* (2012) 246 CLR 379, 409–10 [72], [75] (French CJ, Gummow, Hayne, Crennan, Kiefel and Bell JJ).

40 *R v A2* (2019) 269 CLR 507, 517–8 [21]–[24] (Kiefel CJ and Keane J).

41 Ibid 515 [16], 516 [19] (Kiefel CJ and Keane J), 549–60 [135]–[137] (Bell and Gageler JJ). For international materials see also chapter 31.

again serves as an example. It provides that consideration may be given to material not forming part of an Act in only three specific instances:

> (a) to confirm that the meaning of the provision is the ordinary meaning conveyed by the text of the provision taking into account its context in the Act and the purpose or object underlying the Act; or
> (b) to determine the meaning of the provision when:
> (i) the provision is ambiguous or obscure; or
> (ii) the ordinary meaning conveyed by the text of the provision taking into account its context in the Act and the purpose or object underlying the Act leads to a result that is manifestly absurd or is unreasonable.

The Interpretation Acts of New South Wales, Queensland, South Australia, Tasmania, Western Australia and the Northern Territory have substantially similar conditions in their provisions. These limitations give rise to some curious results.

The limitations mean that if the meaning of statutory text is clear on its face and does not lead to an absurd or manifestly unreasonable outcome, recourse to extrinsic material is only permitted to 'confirm' that meaning (s 15AB(1)(a)).[42] Section 15AB(1)(b)(i) permits recourse to 'determine' meaning if the provision is 'ambiguous' or 'obscure'. The ambiguity 'must arise from the words themselves before recourse to the extrinsic material is permitted'.[43] Section 15AB(1)(b)(ii) also permits recourse to 'determine' meaning if the ordinary meaning gives rise to an 'absurd' or 'unreasonable' result. Further, the provisions of s 15AB(1)(a) and (b)(ii) appear to assume that the ordinary meaning of a provision has been identified, taking into account intrinsic context and purpose, before recourse can be made to the extrinsic material.

These limitations have been recognised by the courts.[44] They do give rise to some perplexing situations. For example, extrinsic materials of probative value might be identified, but then cannot be used to support a non-ordinary meaning unless sub-s (1)(b)(i) or (1)(b)(ii) are available. This requires the interpreter to have some sort of 'amnesia' about what the extrinsic materials have revealed to them should it not be a 'confirmation'.[45] As well, the requirement of ambiguity on the face of the statute under sub-s (1)(b)(i) means that if it is the extrinsic source itself that reveals an ambiguity, that source cannot be used unless either of the other two gateways are available.

In practice, the technicalities of these provisions are less significant than they might otherwise be, for two reasons. First, the alternative gateway of the common law does not require any condition to be met for recourse to extrinsic context (see **[24.8]**). So, if the statutory provision cannot be satisfied the common law will still permit recourse.

---

42 *Re Australian Federation Construction Contractors; Ex parte Billing* (1986) 61 ALJR 37, 39 (the Court); *Ribbon v The Queen* (2019) 134 SASR 328, 376–7 [112]–[114] (Peek J, Parker J agreeing at 418 [255], Doyle J agreeing at 418 [256]).

43 *Newcastle City Council v GIO General Ltd* (1997) 191 CLR 85, 112 (McHugh J).

44 *Mondelez Australia Pty Ltd v Automotive, Food, Metals, Engineering, Printing and Kindred Industries Union* (2020) 94 ALJR 818, 834 [69] (Gageler J); *Taylor v A-G (Cth)* (2019) 268 CLR 224, 256 [87] (Nettle and Gordon JJ); *Momcilovic v The Queen* (2011) 245 CLR 1, 154 [389] n 692 (Heydon J); *K-Generation Pty Ltd v Liquor Licensing Court* (2009) 237 CLR 501, 521–2 [50]–[52] (French CJ); *Newcastle City Council v GIO General Ltd* (1997) 191 CLR 85, 112 (McHugh J). *Minister for Immigration and Border Protection v Han* (2015) 231 FCR 113, 126 [61] (the Court); *Zhang v Zemin* (2010) 79 NSWLR 513, 537 [138] (Spigelman CJ).

45 Matthew T Stubbs, 'From Foreign Circumstances to First Instance Considerations: Extrinsic Material and the Law of Statutory Interpretation' (2006) 34(1) *Federal Law Review* 103, 113.

Secondly, the limb of 'ambiguity' in s 15AB(1)(b)(i) is broadly construed. As explained by Spigelman CJ in the context of the NSW provision:

> 'Ambiguity' is not limited to lexical or verbal ambiguity and syntactic or grammatical ambiguity. It often extends to circumstances in which the meaning is, for whatever reason, doubtful.[46]

Consequently, the limb of 'ambiguity' will be wide enough to permit recourse to extrinsic materials for most interpretative tasks.

The differences between the statutory pathway of s 15AB and its equivalents, and the common law pathway, do give rise to an anomalous position in the law. The common law appears to undermine the restrictions of those statutory provisions.[47] Moreover, it is difficult to reconcile how the statutory and common law gateways operate together coherently.[48] This may be why it is not always clear in the cases which legal gateway is relied on when referring to extrinsic materials, or why one gateway has been cited over another.

(b) Australian Capital Territory and Victoria

Section 141(1) of the *Legislation Act 2001* (ACT) provides:

> In working out the meaning of an Act, material not forming part of the Act may be considered.

The phrase 'working out the meaning of an Act' is defined in s 138 to mean:

> (a) resolving an ambiguous or obscure provision of the Act; or
> (b) confirming or displacing the apparent meaning of the Act; or
> (c) finding the meaning of the Act when its apparent meaning leads to a result that is manifestly absurd or is unreasonable; or
> (d) finding the meaning of the Act in any other case.

The limbs in sub-ss 138(a)–(c), while similar to s 15AB(1), permit 'displacing' the 'apparent' meaning as well as confirming it. Second, the additional sub-s 138(d), which has no s 15AB equivalent, is a broad 'catch all'. This subsection, in combination with ss 141 and 142, appears effectively to remove any statutory restrictions on consideration of extrinsic materials.

The Victorian legislation is the most broadly drawn of all the Interpretation Acts. It does not contain the ambiguity or other thresholds for recourse of s 15AB.[49] Section 35(b) of the *Interpretation of Legislation Act 1984* (Vic) provides that 'consideration may be given to any matter or document that is relevant'. This provision is the statutory provision most consistent with the common law.

---

46 *R v Sharma* (2002) 54 NSWLR 300, 312–13 [55] (Spigelman CJ, Mason P agreeing at 318 [86], Barr J agreeing at 318 [87], Bell J agreeing at 318 [88], McClellan J agreeing at 318 [89]).

47 RS Geddes, 'Purpose and Context in Statutory Interpretation' (2005) 2(1) *University of New England Law Journal* 5, 23. See also Jacinta Dharmananda, 'Outside the Text: Inside the Use of Extrinsic Materials in Statutory Interpretation' (2014) 32 *Federal Law Review* 333, 342.

48 See Matthew T Stubbs, 'From Foreign Circumstances to First Instance Considerations: Extrinsic Material and the Law of Statutory Interpretation' (2006) 34(1) *Federal Law Review* 103, 123–4.

49 *Meskovski v DPP (Vic)* [2018] VSCA 293, [85] n 62 (the Court); *Momcilovic v The Queen* (2011) 245 CLR 1, 154 [389] n 692 (Heydon J).

(c) **All statutory provisions are discretionary**

All of the Interpretation Act provisions that allow recourse to extrinsic materials provide that the recourse is discretionary and not mandatory. This is indicated by the use of the word 'may' in all the provisions.[50] This discretion is in contrast to the common law, discussed in the next section.

Common law requirements

[24.8] **Unlike some of the statutory provisions, the common law does not require the satisfaction of any conditions for consideration of extrinsic materials; conversely, consideration of the wider context is required**

Unlike the statutory provisions of the Interpretation Acts of the Commonwealth, New South Wales, Queensland, South Australia, Tasmania, Western Australia and the Northern Territory, the common law 'wider context' principle does not require that the text be ambiguous or the satisfaction of any other condition before extrinsic sources can be considered. The common law 'insists' that context, including wider context, 'be considered in the first instance' and not at some later stage in the interpretative process, whether or not there is ambiguity on the face of the text.[51]

Further, unlike all the statutory provisions, a consideration of the wider context is not discretionary: the common law *requires* context be considered before meaning is determined.[52]

There was a period when statements about the importance of the text by the High Court in cases such as *Alcan (NT) Alumina Pty Ltd v Commissioner of Territory Revenue (NT)*[53] and *Saeed v Minister for Immigration and Citizenship*[54] were taken to suggest a retreat from the 'wider context' principle. Some authorities suggested that the common law had reverted to a more textualist approach, where extrinsic materials should only be referred to if other means of statutory construction were exhausted or a threshold of ambiguity met.[55]

The notion that the common law principle requires satisfaction of any ambiguity or other threshold is not consistent with High Court authority.[56] The High Court has made it clear that consideration of the context, including the wider context, of a provision is to be undertaken at the first stage of the process of construction.[57] The earlier judicial statements about the importance of the text have been explained by the High Court as serving to remind the interpreter

50 *Screen Australia v EME Productions No 1 Pty Ltd* (2012) 200 FCR 282, 293 [48] (the Court), citing *Brennan v Comcare* (1994) 50 FCR 555, 573 (Gummow J). See also *R v Boucher* [1995] 1 VR 110, 124 (the Court).

51 *CIC Insurance Ltd v Bankstown Football Club Ltd* (1997) 187 CLR 384, 408.

52 See **[7.7]**.

53 (2009) 239 CLR 27, 46–7 [47] (Hayne, Heydon, Crennan and Kiefel JJ).

54 (2010) 241 CLR 252, 265 [33] (French CJ, Gummow, Hayne, Crennan and Kiefel JJ).

55 See, eg, *Ian Street Developer Pty Ltd v Arrow International Pty Ltd* (2018) 54 VR 721, 733 [55] (Riordan J); *Construction, Forestry, Maritime, Mining and Energy Union v BHP Billiton Nickel West Pty Ltd* (2018) 263 FCR 558, 563 [25]–[26] (Rangiah J); *SM v The Queen* (2013) 46 VR 464, 477 [49] (Weinberg JA).

56 *Construction, Forestry, Maritime, Mining and Energy Union v Australian Building and Construction Commissioner (The Bay Street Appeal)* (2020) 282 FCR 1, 6 [5] (Allsop CJ).

57 *R v A2* (2019) 269 CLR 507, 521 [33] (Kiefel and Keane JJ); *SZTAL v Minister for Immigration and Border Protection* (2017) 262 CLR 362, 368 [14] (Kiefel CJ, Nettle and Gordon JJ), 374 [36]–[37] (Gageler J). See **[7.4]**–**[7.7]**.

> that the text of a statute is important . . . [but] [n]one of these cases suggest a return to a literal approach to construction. They do not suggest that the text should not be read in context and by reference to the mischief to which the provision is directed.[58]

The lack of any threshold to consider extrinsic materials at common law, and the coexisting statutory and common law gateways to those materials, mean that, in effect, there is little in the way of a barrier to recourse to parliamentary materials for interpretative purposes.[59] This state of affairs has meant that most of the issues surrounding the use of extrinsic materials concern the interpretative value of that material, rather than access (see **[24.10]**).

Parliamentary awareness of material

There is an underlying assumption that extrinsic materials, to be legitimately used as interpretative aids, must have been publicly available, or otherwise 'known' to Parliament, at the time of the enactment of the provision being construed [24.9]

Despite the scope of the statutory and common law principles to extend to a wide range of materials, there appears to be an implicit assumption in the case law that only extrinsic materials that were publicly available, or otherwise known to Parliament, at the time of the enactment can be legitimately used as interpretative aids for construing that enactment. This assumption is often traced back to Lord Reid in the House of Lords decision *Black-Clawson International Ltd v Papierwerke Waldhof-Aschaffenburg AG,*[60] referred to in **[23.5]**.

Section 141 of the *Legislation Act 2001* (ACT) is the only Interpretation Act that expressly addresses this notion. It provides that 'the accessibility of the material to the public' is a matter that must be 'taken into account' when deciding whether to consider extrinsic material or not.[61] The other Interpretation Act provisions do not contain a similar direction. To the extent there are authorities expressly addressing this matter, the rejection of materials not publicly available or known at the time of enactment has been based on them not being 'capable of assisting'[62] as required by most of the Interpretation Acts.

Example 24.1 *Commissioner of Taxation v Murray*[63]

The Court was required to construe the words 'works of art' in the *Sales Tax (Exemptions and Classifications) Act 1935* (Cth) ('the Act'). It was asked to consider material from the files of the

58 *R v A2* (2019) 269 CLR 507, 522 [36]–[37] (Kiefel CJ and Keane JJ). See similar explanations in *Mondelez Australia Pty Ltd v Automotive, Food, Metals, Engineering, Printing and Kindred Industries Union* (2020) 94 ALJR 818, 833 [66] (Gageler J); *SAS Trustee Corporation v Miles* (2018) 265 CLR 137, 162 [64] (Edelman J).

59 See Jacinta Dharmananda, 'Outside the Text: Inside the Use of Extrinsic Materials in Statutory Interpretation' (2014) 42(2) *Federal Law Review* 333, 342–4.

60 [1975] AC 591.

61 Section s 141(2)(c). Material on the ACT legislation register is 'taken to be accessible to the public': s 141(4).

62 *Linfox Australia Pty Ltd v Federal Commissioner of Taxation* (2019) 271 FCR 365, 388 [117] (the Court); *Federal Commissioner of Taxation v Traviati* (2012) 205 FCR 136, 145–6 [45]–[46] (Middleton J). Cf *Esso Australia Resources Ltd v Federal Commissioner of Taxation* (2011) 199 FCR 226, 268 [111], 275 [156] where the Full Court endorsed the primary judge's use of internal correspondence between a government department and the Australian Tax Office.

63 (1990) 21 FCR 436.

Commissioner of Taxation relating to the Bill for the Act, including correspondence between the Minister and the Treasurer, an internal minute to the Commissioner, and a copy of notes that went to Parliament with the Bill. Hill J noted that sub-s 15AB(2) of the AIA did not limit the classes of material that could be considered under s 15AB(1).[64] However, Hill J determined that these materials were not 'capable of assisting' within s 15AB(1) given that they were not materials to which the legislature could be taken to have contemplated. His Honour explained:

> At best such material may suggest the mischief which some person had in mind when framing a Bill before it is put before Parliament. But if the Parliament is not appraised of that mischief by the proponent of the Bill in a second reading speech, by an explanatory memorandum or in debate, it will be hard to be sure that the mischief was in truth that which Parliament sought to overcome.[65]

The source of this implicit assumption at common law is less obviously apparent. One possibility is that materials cannot be considered 'contextual' in the formation of the statute if they were not contemplated or known by the enacting Parliament.[66]

Guidance on probative value

[24.10] **Once it is established that there is legal authority to consider extrinsic materials, the next step is to determine their probative value, if any**

Once it is established that the statutory or common law permits consideration of extrinsic materials, the next step is to determine the probative value, if any, to be attributed to those materials. The existence of material, even large volumes of material, does not of itself mean that there will be something of interpretative value.[67]

In broad terms, consideration of extrinsic materials, including parliamentary and pre-parliamentary materials, 'has utility if, and in so far as, it assists in fixing the meaning of the statutory text'.[68] Essentially this means that 'to be taken into account the contextual materials must be relevant to the matter in issue'.[69] Just like any other contextual aid, extrinsic materials must be evaluated to determine if they have utility and to identify any factors that can assist, or that suggest a construction not otherwise readily apparent.[70] The statutory provisions reflect this

64 Ibid 449 (Sheppard J agreeing at 436 with Hill J's statements on s 15AB).

65 Ibid.

66 See Justice James Edelman, '2018 Winterton Lecture Constitutional Interpretation' (2019) 45(1) *University of Western Australia Law Review* 1, 13–14. See also **[23.5]**.

67 See, eg, *Pilbara Infrastructure Pty Ltd v Australian Competition Tribunal* (2012) 246 CLR 379, 408–10 [71]–[75] (French CJ, Gummow, Hayne, Crennan, Kiefel and Bell JJ) (where extensive reference was made to a 'very large body of extrinsic material' with most of it being unhelpful).

68 *Port of Newcastle Operations Pty Ltd v Glencore Coal Assets Australia Pty Ltd* (2021) 35 ALR 209, 227 [87] (the Court), citing *Thiess v Collector of Customs* (2014) 250 CLR 664, 671 [22] (the Court) and *Federal Commissioner of Taxation v Consolidated Media Holdings Ltd* (2012) 250 CLR 503, 519 [39] (the Court).

69 Justice Susan Kenny, 'Current Issues in the Interpretation of Federal Legislation' (Speech, National Commercial Law Seminar Series, Melbourne, 3 September 2013) 6.

70 *SZTAL v Minister for Immigration and Border Protection* (2017) 262 CLR 362, 368 [14] (Kiefel CJ, Nettle and Gordon JJ). See chapter 7.

notion of relevance with the language of 'capable of assisting' or, for Victoria, simply using the word 'relevant'.[71]

A simple example of the need for relevance is *BVG17 v BVH17*.[72] In that decision, Collier and Rangiah JJ rejected an argument by one of the parties that an explanatory memorandum supported a particular construction of s 117(2)(b) of the *Child Support (Assessment) Act 1989* (Cth). They said that the passage relied on by the party related to a different provision, s 117(2)(a)(iv), and it was not 'capable of assisting' construction under s 15AB of the AIA;[73] that is, it was not relevant.

If the material is relevant, then the next step is to decide what weight is to be given to the material. The case law does not reveal any detailed criteria for this task. Evaluating the weight, if any, to be given to parliamentary, and pre-parliamentary materials, is task specific. It will vary depending on the particular interpretative task and other relevant interpretative aids and principles. The interpreter must, on each occasion, determine what aspect of context, including the extrinsic context, is pertinent to the particular interpretative issue.[74]

Some judicial observations about parliamentary materials include:

- materials containing contradictory or ambiguous statements are unlikely to be of use;[75]
- unequivocal statements are more helpful;[76]
- political rhetoric in second reading speeches is unlikely to be helpful;[77]
- importance of the timing of statements – for example, statements about a version of a provision that is subsequently amended in Parliament before enactment are unlikely to assist;[78]
- the quality and provenance of parliamentary materials is relevant to their assessment;[79] and
- parliamentary materials themselves should not be subject to interpretation.[80]

There have been judicial statements that have suggested that certain materials have less weight or even lack relevance. For example, it has been suggested that statements made by members of Parliament not being the Minister introducing the Bill may often be unhelpful,[81] or that the

71 See **[24.7]**.

72 (2019) 268 FCR 448.

73 Ibid 475 [104].

74 Justice John Basten, 'Statutory Interpretation: Choosing Principles of Interpretation' (2017) 91(11) *Australian Law Journal* 881, 881, 884.

75 *Ian Street Developer Pty Ltd v Arrow International Pty Ltd* (2018) 54 VR 721, [75] (Riordan J); *Taylor v A-G (Cth)* (2019) 268 CLR 224, 277 [148] (Edelman J).

76 *Australian Mines and Metals Association Inc v Construction, Forestry, Maritime, Mining and Energy Union* (2018) 268 FCR 128, 162 [137] (the Court).

77 *BGM16 v Minister for Immigration and Border Protection* (2017) 252 FCR 97, 119 [102] (Mortimer and Wigney JJ); *Andrews and Morrissy Developments Pty Ltd v Port Phillip City Council* (2019) 241 LGERA 280, 287 [32] (Osborn JA).

78 *National Rugby League Investments Pty Ltd v Singtel Optus Pty Ltd* (2012) 201 FCR 147, 168 [81] (the Court); *Avel Pty Ltd v Attorney-General (NSW)* (1987) 11 NSWLR 126, 128–9 (Kirby J).

79 *Mondelez Australia Pty Ltd v Automotive, Food, Metals, Engineering, Printing and Kindred Industries Union* (2020) 94 ALJR 818, 834 [67] (Gageler J), referring to Jacinta Dharmananda, 'Using Parliamentary Materials in Interpretation: Insights from Parliamentary Process' (2018) 41(1) *University of New South Wales Law Journal* 4. The case is presented at **Example 24.3**.

80 *Ribbon v The Queen* (2019) 134 SASR 328, 381 [126] (Peek J, Parker J agreeing at 418 [255], Doyle J agreeing at 418 [256]).

81 *Mills v Meeking* (1990) 169 CLR 214, 236 (Dawson J).

speech in reply of a Minister at the end of a debate is not legitimate material.[82] Yet there are numerous examples of authorities where such statements in the parliamentary debates have been considered.[83]

Ultimately, the relevance and weight of parliamentary and pre-parliamentary materials depends on the nature, content and timing of the material itself, the existence of other relevant interpretative indicators, and the particular interpretative task. Bright-line assertions about the value of any particular category of material run the risk of creating an arbitrary assessment of the material.

Subject to the above qualifications, there are some strands of guidance evident from the authorities.

(a) Use of parliamentary and other extrinsic materials is not to be understood as being part of an inquiry into the subjective intent of the legislators

The fundamental object of statutory interpretation is to ascertain the legislative intention of Parliament. As discussed in chapter 4, legislative intent is an objective concept. So, when considering parliamentary and other extrinsic materials, we are not seeking to determine the subjective thought processes of the individuals involved in enacting the legislation.[84]

(b) Statements in extrinsic materials about the meaning or effect of legislation already enacted when the statements were made carry no weight

There may be statements made in Parliament by a member of the executive, including a Minister, about the effect of a law *already in force* at the time of the statement. Of themselves, these statements carry no probative weight when construing that already enacted statute. This is a logical position based on the notion that opinions by a parliamentary member about the meaning, purpose or effect of a provision *already enacted* do not have any greater weight than the opinion of any other individual merely by virtue of them holding executive office. See **[33.5]**. The same reasoning is relevant to statements in law reform commission reports that postdate the statutory enactment being construed,[85] and ministerial documents made after the legislation has come into effect.[86]

(c) Statements about purpose in parliamentary materials are relevant to interpretation, but the purpose of an Act or provision must ultimately be found to reside in the statute itself

As discussed in chapter 8, consideration of the purpose of a statute is integral to the interpretative process. Extrinsic materials may assist to identify that purpose (see **(e)** below). A purpose identified from parliamentary or other extrinsic materials must not be imputed to the statute without more. The purpose must be found to reside in the text and structure of the statute itself. See **[8.5]–[8.6]**.

---

82 *Alley v Gillespie* (2018) 264 CLR 328, 343 [36] (Kiefel CJ, Bell, Keane and Edelman JJ) though the basis for the rejection was not clear.

83 See **[24.6]**.

84 See **[4.4]** and **[4.9]**.

85 *AQO v Minister for Finance and Services* (2016) 93 NSWLR 46, 79–80 [151] (Basten JA, Ward JA agreeing at 87 [177]). See also **[24.16]**.

86 *Eclipse Resources Pty Ltd v Minister for Environment (No 2)* (2017) 223 LGERA 313, 371 [231] (the Court), citing *Australian Education Union v Department of Education and Children's Services* (2012) 248 CLR 1, 16 [33] (French CJ, Hayne, Kiefel and Bell JJ).

(d) The Interpretation Acts of the Commonwealth, New South Wales, Queensland, South Australia, Tasmania, Western Australia and the Australian Capital Territory provide that when determining the weight of extrinsic material (or whether to consider it at all), certain factors must be considered, including the desirability of persons being able to rely on the ordinary meaning of the statute

The extrinsic material provisions of each of the Interpretation Acts of the Commonwealth, New South Wales, Queensland, South Australia, Tasmania, Western Australia and the Australian Capital Territory include a provision mandating certain factors to be taken into account when considering whether, and, if so, what weight, should be given to extrinsic material.[87] Section 15AB(3) of the AIA serves as an example:

> (3) In determining whether consideration should be given to any material in accordance with subsection (1), or in considering the weight to be given to any such material, regard shall be had, in addition to any other relevant matters, to:
> (a) the desirability of persons being able to rely on the ordinary meaning conveyed by the text of the provision taking into account its context in the Act and the purpose or object underlying the Act; and
> (b) the need to avoid prolonging legal or other proceedings without compensating advantage.

Though specifying the above matters, the language of the provisions leaves open the possibility of considering other relevant matters. As noted in **[24.9]**, s 141(2)(c) of the *Legislation Act 2001* (ACT) also requires that 'accessibility of the material to the public' be taken into account. These provisions permit the court to 'decline to consider extrinsic material or give it limited weight'.[88] Neither the Victorian nor the Northern Territory Interpretation Acts have equivalent provisions.

The common law approach of starting with the ordinary meaning, and having regard to context and purpose, has been stated to apply 'to like effect' to s 15AB(3)(a).[89] The 'desirability' of persons being able to rely on the ordinary meaning has been characterised as a reflection of an aspect of the rule of law.[90] The direction to consider the avoidance of prolonging legal proceedings may not be reflected in the common law.[91]

Despite provisions such as s 15AB(3) being mandatory, they have not assumed a significant role in modern statutory interpretation. This may be due to the reliance on the common law principle that the process of construction begins with a consideration of the ordinary and grammatical meaning of the text.[92]

---

87 *Acts Interpretation Act 1901* (Cth) s 15AB(3); *Interpretation Act 1987* (NSW) s 34(3); *Acts Interpretation Act 1954* (Qld) s 14B(2); *Legislation Interpretation Act 2021* (SA) s 16(3); *Acts Interpretation Act 1931* (Tas) s 8B(2); *Interpretation Act 1984* (WA) s 19(3); *Legislation Act 2001* (ACT) s 141(2).

88 *Shorten v David Hurst Constructions Pty Ltd* (2008) 72 NSWLR 211, 217 [26] (Basten JA) referring to the *Interpretation Act 1987* (NSW) s 34(3).

89 *Alcan (NT) Alumina Pty Ltd v Commissioner of Territory Revenue (NT)* (2009) 239 CLR 27, 31–2 [5] (French CJ).

90 See **[3.4]**. See also *Ribbon v The Queen* (2019) 134 SASR 328, 377 [114] (Peek J, Parker J agreeing at 418 [255], Doyle J agreeing at 418 [256]).

91 See *Stevens v Kabushiki Kaisha Sony Computer Entertainment* (2005) 224 CLR 193, 230 [124] (McHugh J) who suggested the entirety of s 15AB(3) probably modified the common law.

92 See **[6.6]–[6.7]**.

(e) There is authority that suggests that parliamentary statements about the purpose of an Act or provision are admissible, but that parliamentary statements about an Act or a provision's meaning or effect are not; this proposition is open to question

Parliamentary materials, like other extrinsic materials, may contain information pertaining to the general context of an Act, the mischief to be addressed by the Act, the Act's legislative purpose, or the intended meaning or effect of the Act.[93] In Australia there is a line of authority for the proposition that, when considering statements made in Parliament by Ministers or other members about a Bill that becomes the Act being construed, a distinction should be made between statements about the purpose of, or mischief underlying, that Bill, which is admissible, and statements about its intended meaning or effect, which are not. This proposition is often traced back to statements made in the NSW decision of *Harrison v Melhem.*[94]

In *Harrison* the Court was construing s 15(3) of the *Civil Liability Act 2002* (NSW). The interpretative issue was whether the word 'and' between sub-ss 15(3)(a) and (b) should be construed conjunctively or disjunctively. The legislative history was extensive and included numerous parliamentary statements.[95] One such statement was by a Minister in relation to an amendment to another Act that formed part of the legislative history of the *Civil Liability Act*. The Minister's statement was taken to reveal the Minister's understanding of the meaning of 'and' as conjunctive, requiring both (a) and (b) to be satisfied.[96]

Mason P (Beazley JA and Giles JA agreeing) said:

> Statements in Parliament, even by ministers during the Second Reading debate, will however seldom be available to elucidate the meaning of the later-enacted text. Identification of mischief and purpose is one thing, statement of meaning is another.[97]

Spigelman CJ made similar comments.[98] Mason P considered the distinction between mischief or purpose, on the one hand, and statement of meaning on the other, as relevant under both s 34 of the *Interpretation Act* 1987 (NSW) (the s 15AB equivalent) and the common law.[99] Spigelman CJ determined that the material was not 'capable of assisting' within the words of s 34.[100]

Although they appear to be obiter dicta, the statements in *Harrison* on this distinction have been followed or referred to in superior courts.[101] South Australian decisions have identified a

---

93 Ruth Sullivan, *Sullivan on the Construction of Statutes* (LexisNexis Canada, 6th ed, 2014) 680. For the distinction between mischief and purpose see **[8.3]**.

94 (2008) 72 NSWLR 380.

95 For a summary, see Jeffrey Barnes, 'Statements of Meaning in Parliamentary Debates: Revisiting *Harrison v Melhem*' (2018) (5) *UNSW Law Journal Forum* 1, 4–6.

96 *Harrison v Melhem* (2008) 72 NSWLR 380, 390–1 [118].

97 Ibid 399 [162]. See also 401 [172]. Beazley JA's agreement was subject to qualifications expressed by Spigelman CJ on another principle of interpretation. Basten JA dissented.

98 Ibid 384 [12]–[14].

99 Ibid 401 [172].

100 Ibid 384 [12].

101 See, eg, *Lowe Pty Ltd v Belgravia Nominees Pty Ltd* [2020] WASCA 180, [207] (the Court); *Southern Cross Group Services Pty Ltd v Chief Commissioner of State Revenue (NSW)* (2019) 110 ATR 16, 28 [53] (Ward CJ); *BGM16 v Minister for Immigration and Border Protection* (2017) 252 FCR 97, 119 [103] (Mortimer and Wigney JJ); *Haureliuk v Furler* (2012) 6 ACTLR 151, 162 [30] (the Court); *R v Nguyen* (2010) 204 A Crim R 246, 250 [18]–[19] (Barr AJ, Beazley JA and Buddin J agreeing); *Amaca Pty Ltd v Novek* (2009) 9 DDCR 199, 214–5 [72]–[78] (Campbell JA).

similar distinction, but appear to have adopted their own line of common law authority separate from *Harrison*.[102]

There is no doubt that, in Australia, one of the primary reasons to refer to contextual material, including parliamentary statements, is to obtain indications about the mischief or the statutory purpose. The relevance of purpose is clear under common law, and the Interpretation Acts provide statutory mandates to consider purpose.[103] However, for a number of reasons, caution should be exercised in taking *Harrison* as authority for a definitive rule that statements of meaning or effect in parliamentary materials can never have interpretative relevance or weight.

First, it is possible to identify High Court cases where the Court has relied on statements in parliamentary materials that may be regarded as statements of effect or meaning. For example, in the High Court decision of *Mondelez* (**Example 24.3**) the Court readily referred to examples about the operation of a provision in explanatory memoranda. Another example is *Berenguel v Minister for Immigration and Citizenship*,[104] where a statement in an explanatory statement about the effect of an amendment was relied on.[105] It is possible to identify other High Court decisions where statements of meaning or effect have been considered.[106]

Second, there are practical objections to the distinction. It is open to argument that there is a level of artificiality in attempting to distinguish which statements constitute statements about linguistic meaning or intent and what qualifies as statements about purpose. Conceptually, it is also questionable. As has been noted judicially, as a matter of communication, 'linguistic meaning and purpose are inexorably interwoven'.[107] The line between statements of meaning or effect, and statements about purpose or mischief is not always easy to draw.

Third, it is open to question why parliamentary materials in particular, as compared to other extrinsic materials, should attract this sort of analysis. One possible answer is that statements of intent or effect in parliamentary materials by members of Parliament tend to be lightning bolts for attention in the interpretative process, given that they may ostensibly offer a clear statement on the issue at hand. The distinction in this case serves to remind us that the role of attributing meaning to legislation is the court's function, and not the executive's.

It may be possible in most, if not all, cases to characterise statements in parliamentary materials about the operation of a statute or its effect as enabling inferences to be made about the purpose of the statute, rather than as a reliance on the actual example or statement of effect.[108] For example, in *Mondelez* (**Example 24.3**) Justice Gageler stated that examples in

---

102 See, eg, *Redman v Return to Work Corp (SA)* (2021) 305 IR 326, 354–5 [104] (Livesey JA, Bleby JA agreeing at 365 [149]), citing *Burch v South Australia* (1998) 71 SASR 12, 38–9 (Bleby J); *Palace Gallery Pty Ltd v Liquor and Gambling Commissioner* (2014) 118 SASR 567, 581–2 [49] (the Court). Note that these are decisions relying solely on common law principles as they were delivered prior to the enactment of the *Legislation Interpretation Act 2021* (SA), which contains a provision on extrinsic materials. See **[24.2]**.

103 See chapter 8.

104 (2010) 84 ALJR 251.

105 Ibid 254–5 [21] (the Court).

106 See, eg, *Australian Securities and Investments Commission v King* (2020) 270 CLR 1, 41 [115], 44 [123] (Nettle and Gordon JJ); *Mills v Commissioner of Taxation* (2012) 250 CLR 171, 187–8 [27]–[28] (Gageler J). See also Jeffrey Barnes, 'Statements of Meaning in Parliamentary Debates: Revisiting *Harrison v Melhem*' [2018] 5 *UNSW Law Journal Forum* 1, 11–16.

107 *Shorten v David Hurst Constructions Pty Ltd* (2008) 72 NSWLR 211, 217 [27] (Basten JA). See also *Power Rental Op Co Australia v Forge Group Power Pty Ltd* (2017) 93 NSWLR 765, 785 [87] (Ward JA).

108 Jeffrey Barnes, 'Statements of Meaning in Parliamentary Debates: Revisiting *Harrison v Melhem*' [2018] 5 *UNSW Law Journal Forum* 1, 13 n 97.

explanatory memoranda can help explain the overall legislative design.[109] However characterised, a statement in materials should not automatically be deemed irrelevant 'simply because it is couched in terms of intention'.[110] This may be why their Honours in *Harrison* used the language of 'rarely'[111] and 'seldom'[112] in relation to the proposition. Many subsequent authorities have used similarly open language when referring to *Harrison* and its statements on use of parliamentary materials.[113]

It is clear that parliamentary statements of intent or meaning should not be *equated with* or *determinative of* meaning by themselves (see **[24.10](a)**). They are not an answer to the meaning of statutory text. Like any other extrinsic material, the content of parliamentary materials must be evaluated for reliance and weight. In the absence of an express statement by the High Court on this issue,[114] and in the light of the cautionary points raised above, it may be that the proposition highlighted by *Harrison* is better characterised as a cautionary one about parliamentary materials, rather than as a decision establishing a determinative distinction.

Text still paramount

[24.11] **The existence of relevant parliamentary and other materials does not displace the interpretative principle that the interpretative task must start and end with the text**

As discussed in chapter 6, the interpretative task must start, and end, with the statutory text. This is the correct approach even where there are extraneous materials of considerable probative value.[115] Extrinsic materials are an aid to interpretation. They inform; their examination is not 'an end in itself'.[116] Consideration of these materials may point to factors that assist in determining a constructional choice. They may indicate for or against an ordinary meaning, a strained meaning or a particular meaning where the text is imprecise or open textured.[117] But the text remains paramount. This is why words such as 'elucidate',[118] 'support',[119] 'confirm',[120]

109 *Mondelez Australia Pty Ltd v Automotive, Food, Metals, Engineering, Printing and Kindred Industries Union* (2020) 94 ALJR 818, 834 [71] (Gageler J). His Honour also noted that examples can yield insight into 'grammatical sense': at 834 [71].

110 *Owen v South Australia* (1996) 66 SASR 251, 256 (Cox J).

111 *Harrison v Melhem* (2008) 72 NSWLR 380, 384 [12] (Spigelman CJ).

112 Ibid 399 [162] (Mason P).

113 See, eg, *Lowe Pty Ltd v Belgravia Nominees Pty Ltd* [2020] WASCA 180, [207] (the Court); *Southern Cross Group Services Pty Ltd v Chief Commissioner of State Revenue (NSW)* (2019) 110 ATR 16, 28 [54] (Ward CJ); *A-G (Tas) v CL* (2018) 28 Tas R 70, 97 [81] (Porter AJ); *BGM16 v Minister for Immigration and Border Protection* (2017) 252 FCR 97, 119 [103] (Mortimer and Wigney JJ); *Haureliuk v Furler* (2012) 6 ACTLR 151, 162 [30] (the Court).

114 *Harrison* has been cited by the High Court for other reasons.

115 *SZTAL v Minister for Immigration and Border Protection* (2017) 262 CLR 362 [14] (Kiefel CJ, Nettle and Gordon JJ).

116 *Federal Commissioner of Taxation v Consolidated Media Holdings Ltd* (2012) 250 CLR 503, 519 [39] (French CJ, Hayne, Crennan, Bell and Gageler JJ)

117 *R v A2* (2019) 269 CLR 507, 520–2 [32]–[37] (Kiefel CJ and Keane J); *SZTAL v Minister for Immigration and Border Protection* (2017) 262 CLR 362 [14] (Kiefel CJ, Nettle and Gordon JJ), 374–5 [37]–[40] (Gageler J). See **[24.13]**.

118 *Certain Lloyd's Underwriters v Cross* (2012) 248 CLR 378, 405 [70] (Crennan and Bell JJ).

119 *Cole v Minister for Immigration and Border Protection* (2018) 261 FCR 537, 553 [53] (the Court).

120 *Construction, Forestry, Mining and Energy Union v Mammoet Australia Pty Ltd* (2013) 248 CLR 619, 633 [45] (Crennan, Kiefel, Bell, Gageler and Keane JJ).

'indicative',[121] 'fortify',[122] 'reinforce',[123] 'illuminate'[124] and 'infer'[125] are often used to describe the role of extrinsic materials.

Even where extrinsic materials are highly probative, extrinsic materials cannot be used to displace the clear meaning of text [24.12]

As a corollary to the principle of the paramountcy of the text, it is uncontroversial that legislative history, including parliamentary materials, 'cannot displace the meaning of the statutory text'.[126] For parliamentary and non-parliamentary materials, this means that the words of a Minister, the executive or other party involved in the legislative process in extrinsic materials cannot be substituted for the statutory words, even when the materials provide compelling evidence about legislative intent. This does not mean that the words in extrinsic materials cannot be probative; it means that they are not determinative or alone sufficient to provide the answer to the interpretative issue. **Example 24.2** serves as an illustration for this principle.

Example 24.2 *Re Bolton; Ex parte Beane*[127]

Mr Beane was a US citizen who was a member of the US Marine Corp and was serving in Vietnam. In 1970 he allegedly deserted and left Vietnam, going to Australia where he became an Australian resident.

In 1986, after living in Australia for 16 years, he was arrested by the NSW police pursuant to a warrant, issued by the Commonwealth, for his transfer to the custody of US authorities. The issue before the Court was whether the request for his apprehension had been validly made by the United States under the *Defence (Visiting Forces) Act 1963* (Cth) ('the Visiting Forces Act').

Section 19 in pt III of the Visiting Forces Act permitted, upon the request of the US authority, an Australian authorised officer to apprehend a deserter by issuing a warrant for the police force to do so. However, s 8 in pt II contained the only express power for the authority of a foreign country to deal with a person handed over under s 19. The power that authorities of a foreign country had over persons in Australia was in relation to 'members of any visiting force of that country'. The term 'visiting force' was defined in s 5(1) to mean:

> any body, contingent or detachment of the forces of a country that is for the time being *present in Australia* by arrangement of the Minister. (emphasis added)

The question was whether s 19 authorised the arrest of Mr Beane, given that he had not been from a 'visiting force' as defined.

121 *Alphapharm Pty Ltd v H Lundbeck A/S* (2014) 254 CLR 247, 264 [39].

122 *Kline v Official Secretary to the Governor-General* (2013) 249 CLR 645, 664 [48].

123 *Baini v The Queen* (2012) 246 CLR 469, 482 [34] (French CJ, Hayne, Crennan, Kiefel and Bell JJ).

124 *North Australian Aboriginal Justice Agency Ltd v Northern Territory* (2015) 256 CLR 569, 608 [86] (Gageler J).

125 *Lacey v A-G (Qld)* (2011) 242 CLR 573, 592 [44] (French CJ, Gummow, Hayne, Crennan, Kiefel and Bell JJ).

126 *Federal Commissioner of Taxation v Consolidated Media Holdings Ltd* (2012) 250 CLR 503, 519 [39] (French CJ, Hayne, Crennan, Bell and Gageler JJ). See also *Taylor v A-G (Cth)* (2019) 268 CLR 224, 256 [87] (Nettle and Gordon JJ); *Grajewski v DPP (NSW)* (2019) 264 CLR 470, 478–9 [19] (Kiefel CJ, Bell, Keane and Gordon JJ); *Certain Lloyd's Underwriters v Cross* (2012) 248 CLR 378, 405 [70] (Crennan and Bell JJ); *Alcan (NT) Alumina Pty Ltd v Commissioner of Territory Revenue (NT)* (2009) 239 CLR 27, 47 [47] (Hayne, Heydon, Crennan and Kiefel JJ); *Northern Territory v Collins* (2008) 235 CLR 619, 642 [99] (Crennan J).

127 (1987) 162 CLR 514.

Using s 15AB of the AIA, the Court considered the second reading speech of the Minister introducing the Bill for the Visiting Forces Act. That speech relevantly stated:

> Part III of the bill relates to deserters and absentees without leave from the forces of countries within the Commonwealth of Nations, and other countries to which the part may be applied by regulation. *They need not be deserters or absentees from a visiting force.*[128]

Mason CJ, Wilson and Dawson JJ, in a joint judgment, stated that the speech 'unambiguously' asserted that pt III was to apply whether or not deserters and absentees were from a visiting force.[129] But, while they recognised that this meant that the speech deserved 'serious consideration,' they said:

> The words of a Minister must not be substituted for the text of the law ... It is always possible that through oversight or inadvertence the clear intention of the Parliament fails to be translated into the text of the law. However unfortunate it may be when that happens, the task of the Court remains clear. The function of the Court is to give effect to the will of Parliament as expressed in the law.[130]

That is, the speech was not determinative as the words of the statute itself did not reflect its executive intent. Deane J made similar comments.[131] It was held that s 19 only provided power in relation to a 'visiting force'.[132]

This principle does not deny the importance of legislative history. It reminds us that

> [t]he pre-existing law and the legislative history should not deflect the Court from its duty to resolve an issue of statutory construction, which is a text-based activity.[133]

A variation of the principle is that paraphrases of statutory language in parliamentary materials should not be substituted for the text.[134] Essentially, this principle guides the balance that must be struck between probative extrinsic materials and the statutory text: it supports the principle that the text is the surest guide.[135]

---

128 Ibid 541 (Toohey J), citing Commonwealth, *Parliamentary Debates*, House of Representatives, 24 October 1963, 2263 (Sir Garfield Barwick) (emphasis added).

129 (1987) 162 CLR 514, 518.

130 Ibid 518.

131 Ibid 532.

132 Brennan and Gaudron JJ agreed with the outcome but did not refer to the speech. In contrast, Toohey J, in dissent, did not rely on the speech determinatively but said the speech 'resolved' any doubt: ibid 540–1.

133 *Alphapharm Pty Ltd v H Lundbeck A/S* (2014) 254 CLR 247, 265 [42] (Crennan, Bell and Gageler JJ).

134 *Baini v The Queen* (2012) 246 CLR 469, 476 [14] (French CJ, Hayne, Crennan, Kiefel and Bell JJ).

135 *Alcan (NT) Alumina Pty Ltd v Commissioner of Territory Revenue (NT)* (2009) 239 CLR 27, 47 [47] (Hayne, Heydon, Crennan and Kiefel JJ). One possible qualification to this principle is where there are drafting errors or implied words are permissible. See chapter 34.

Although words in extrinsic materials cannot displace statutory text, they can be used to support a non-ordinary or strained meaning of the text [24.13]

Consideration of the context, including extrinsic materials, may point to factors that indicate a non-ordinary or strained meaning of the words of the provision.[136] But that construction must be reasonably open on the text.[137]

Example 24.3 *Mondelez Australia Pty Ltd v Automotive, Food, Metals, Engineering, Printing and Kindred Industries Union*[138]

Mondelez Australia Pty Ltd ('Mondelez') employed workers at a Cadbury chocolate plant under an enterprise agreement. This matter was in relation to two of those employees. The enterprise agreement specified that those employees work 36 hours per week averaged over a four-week cycle. They worked an average of three 12-hour shifts per week.

Section 96 of the *Fair Work Act 2009* (Cth) provided:

> (1) For each year of service with his or her employer, an employee is entitled to 10 days of paid personal/carer's leave.
>
> (2) An employee's entitlement to paid personal/carer's leave accrues progressively during a year of service according to the employee's ordinary hours of work, and accumulates from year to year.

Mondelez' method of calculation under s 96 meant that the employees were entitled to paid leave for eight 12-hour shifts over a year of service. Mondelez sought a declaration in the Full Court of the Federal Court that their method of calculation of personal/carer's leave under the enterprise agreement complied with s 96(1). The respondent union argued that the employees were entitled to 10 paid absences per year. The Federal Court upheld the union's construction and Mondelez appealed to the High Court.

The issue turned on the meaning of the word 'day' in s 96(1) (where it appears as plural 'days'). The union argued that 'day' meant 'working day', being the portion of a 24-hour day that would otherwise be allocated to work. This construction would provide an entitlement of 10 absences to each employee. Mondelez argued that 'day' should be construed as a 'notional day', being a day consisting of one-tenth of the equivalent of an employee's ordinary hours of work in a two-week period. This construction would mean the calculation would be based on an individual employee's ordinary hours of work and so would reduce the two employees' entitlement to eight absences.

The plurality of Kiefel CJ, Nettle and Gordon JJ, and Edelman J in a separate judgment, agreed with Mondelez that 'day' meant a 'notional day'.

The plurality affirmed the accepted approach to 'start with the statute' and to construe it 'as a whole' and 'in light of the relevant extrinsic materials and the legislative history'.[139] They considered that numerous intrinsic indicators and the scheme purpose were consistent with a 'notional day' construction, and that that construction was 'reinforced' by the explanatory

136 *R v A2* (2019) 269 CLR 507, 520–1 [32] ((Kiefel CJ and Keane J).

137 *Esso Australia Pty Ltd v Australian Workers' Union* (2017) 263 CLR 551, 582 [52] (Kiefel CJ, Keane, Nettle and Edelman JJ); *Fortress Credit Corporation (Australia) II Pty Ltd v Fletcher* (2015) 254 CLR 489, 503 [16] (French CJ, Hayne, Kiefel, Gageler and Keane JJ); *Newcastle City Council v GIO General Ltd* (1997) 191 CLR 85, 113 (McHugh J).

138 (2020) 94 ALJR 818.

139 Ibid 823 [13].

memorandum to the Fair Work Bill 2008.[140] As well as referring to statements in the Memorandum, their Honours relied on three examples in the Memorandum that were intended to 'illustrate the intended operation' of the provisions.[141] Each of these, they said, were 'consistent with the "notional day" construction'.[142]

Edelman J expressly acknowledged the interpretative presumption that words are intended to bear an ordinary meaning and that this might lead a 'reasonable reader' of the Act to be surprised about a 'notional day' construction, as opposed to a 'working day' meaning.[143] However, unusual meanings, he said, can be countenanced from a range and combination of circumstances, one of which was

> where the ordinary meaning of the words is inconsistent with the expressed understanding of the legislative operation in extrinsic materials.[144]

After considering the 'full context'[145] of the provision, his Honour concluded that, counter-intuitively to the ordinary meaning that a reasonable reader might reach from first reading the legislation, a 'reasonable, informed reader' would understand that 'day' meant 'notional day'.[146]

Gageler J, in dissent, did not dispute the relevant statutory principles.[147] Like the other judges he gave considerable attention to the explanatory memorandum. His Honour acknowledged the potential interpretative value of explanatory memoranda.[148] But in this instance, Gageler J opined, the Memorandum should not be used 'to attribute a complicated and contestable and ungrammatical meaning to the uncomplicated and grammatically meaningful text'.[149]

[24.14] If a statutory provision abrogates a fundamental right, the courts will be particularly cautious about attributing weight to extrinsic materials even when they offer compelling evidence of legislative intent

There is a common law presumption known as the 'principle of legality', discussed in chapter 28. One aspect of the principle is that, where common law 'fundamental rights' are impacted by a statutory provision, the principle favours a construction, if available, that avoids or minimises the provision's abrogation of that right by requiring any such encroachment to be stated in clear and unambiguous language in the statute.

There is authority that suggests that courts will be reluctant to attribute significant value to parliamentary materials where those materials support a broad construction of text that diminishes a fundamental right, and the principle of legality can operate to support a narrower construction that minimises that abrogation. In these instances, the principle that extrinsic

140 Ibid 826 [29].

141 Ibid 827 [31]

142 Ibid 827 [32]. The plurality also referred to the explanatory memorandum to the legislative antecedent to the *Fair Work Act 2009* (Cth) to show continuity. See **[21.6]**.

143 Ibid 821, 837–8 [93]–[95].

144 838 [96].

145 Ibid 841 [107]

146 Ibid 841 [109].

147 Ibid 833–4 [66]–[67].

148 Ibid 834 [71]. Though he also expressed caution about the probative weight to be given to the material, given its nature and provenance: at 834 [67], 835 [72].

149 Ibid 835 [73].

materials do not displace the clear meaning of text (addressed in **[24.12]**) is used with considerable force. **Example 24.2**, *Re Bolton,* illustrates this point. One well-established fundamental right is personal liberty.[150] In *Re Bolton* Mason CJ, Wilson and Dawson JJ stated that the proposition that the words of a Minister must not be substituted for the text of the law was particularly apt 'when the intention stated by the Minister but unexpressed in the law is restrictive of the liberty of the individual'.[151] Deane J made a similar point.[152] Other examples that suggest a correlation between the principle of legality and the diminished weight of extrinsic materials are *Lacey v Attorney-General of Queensland,*[153] *Saeed v Minister for Immigration and Citizenship,*[154] *Plaintiff S157/2002 v Commonwealth*[155] and *North Australian Aboriginal Justice Agency Ltd v Northern Territory.*[156]

Inference from parliamentary inaction

When construing an amendment or replacement Act, the absence of any mention of a fundamental change in the parliamentary materials relating to the effect of the amendment or replacement Act may support a construction that no fundamental change in meaning is intended [24.15]

If a provision in a statute is amended or replaced by another statute so that it contains different wording, that textual change may suggest a change in meaning for the new provision.[157] Conversely, silence in the parliamentary materials relating to the amending Act may be used to support an argument that the new words are *not* intended to make a fundamental change, particularly if the earlier wording had an established meaning. The logic is that if Parliament had intended to make a significant change to the previously well-known position, then it is to be expected that such a change would have been noted in the parliamentary materials.[158]

Example 24.4 *Anderson v Commissioner of Highways*[159]

The Commissioner of Highways ('the Commissioner') acquired land in which Mr Anderson had an interest. Mr Anderson, the appellant, claimed that he suffered from an adjustment disorder with

150 See **[28.6]** fn 58.

151 *Re Bolton; Ex parte Beane* (1987) 162 CLR 514, 518. See also 520.

152 Ibid 532.

153 (2011) 242 CLR 573, 583 [20] 598 [61] (French CJ, Gummow, Hayne, Crennan, Kiefel and Bell JJ).

154 (2010) 241 CLR 252, 259 [15] 264–5 [31] (French CJ, Gummow, Hayne, Crennan and Kiefel JJ).

155 (2003) 211 CLR 476, 499 [55], 505 [72] (Gaudron, McHugh, Gummow, Kirby and Hayne JJ).

156 (2015) 256 CLR 569, 647–8 [222], 649–50 [229] (Nettle and Gordon JJ). See Dan Meagher, 'The "Modern Approach" to Statutory Interpretation and the Principle of Legality: An Issue of Coherence?' (2018) 46(3) *Federal Law Review* 397, which discusses the relationship between the principle of legality and the contextual principle.

157 See **[21.7]**.

158 See, eg, *Frugtniet v Australian Securities and Investments Commission* (2019) 266 CLR 250, 259 [21] (Kiefel CJ, Keane and Nettle JJ); *Australian Building and Construction Commissioner v Construction, Forestry, Mining and Energy Union* (2018) 262 CLR 157, 192 [107] (Keane, Nettle and Gordon JJ); *Coverdale v West Coast Council* (2016) 259 CLR 164, 177 [40] (the Court); *Wilderness Society Inc v Turnbull* (2007) 166 FCR 154, 158–9 [17]–[18] (Branson and Finn JJ).

159 (2019) 134 SASR 543.

post-traumatic stress disorder type symptoms following notice of the acquisition. He sought compensation under the *Land Acquisition Act 1969* (SA) ('the Land Act') for this personal injury arising from the acquisition of the land. Section 22B of the Land Act provided for compensation for an acquisition and s 25(1)(a) of the Land Act provided that the compensation must be

> such as adequately to compensate him for any loss that he has suffered by reason of the acquisition of the land . . .

The Land Act had replaced its 1925 predecessor Act. Mr Anderson accepted that personal injury had not been compensable under that predecessor Act. One of his arguments was that the textual and contextual differences between the Land Act and the predecessor Act supported a construction of 'any loss' that extended to compensation for loss by way of personal injury.

Stanley J, with whom Kelly and Blue JJ agreed,[160] rejected this argument. Stanley J held that the textual and contextual differences between the predecessor and new provisions did not support a construction of an extended scope. His Honour considered the second reading speech given by the Minister to the Land Act Bill and said:

> [H]ad such a fundamental change been intended by the legislature it would be expected that would have been unequivocally identified in the Second Reading Speech. The absence of such an expression of intention provides strong support for the rejection of the appellant's construction.[161]

Blue J made a similar point in relation to the second reading speech.[162] The Court held that ss 22B and 25 only permitted compensation for a loss of, or diminution of interest in, the acquired land.

It is improbable that the absence of express statements about a fundamental change in parliamentary materials would, by itself, be sufficient to warrant a particular construction. As with *Anderson* the better view is that plausible inferences can only be drawn about absence when considered together with other compelling interpretative factors.

[24.16] Generally, materials that come into existence after the enactment of the statute being construed are not relevant to its interpretation, but may assist if inferences can be drawn from parliamentary inaction

Parliamentary and executive materials that come into existence after the enactment of the statute being construed are 'post-enactment' materials. Generally, post-enactment extrinsic materials, such as executive guides or policy documents, about an enacted statute are not regarded as legitimate extrinsic aids.[163] In contrast to the United States, the High Court of Australia has not endorsed any general principle of 'deference' to post-enactment executive interpretations of legislation.[164]

---

160 Though Blue J framed the interpretative question in a slightly different way and provided some additional reasoning.

161 *Anderson v Commissioner of Highways* (2019) 134 SASR 543, 563 [75].

162 Ibid 548 [14].

163 See **[33.5]**. Though note subsequent Amendment Acts may be used as interpretative aids: see **[21.10]**.

164 *Corporation of the City of Enfield v Development Assessment Commission* (2000) 199 CLR 135, 153 [39]–[44] (Gleeson CJ, Gummow, Kirby and Hayne JJ), 158 [59] (Gaudron J); *Williams v Commonwealth (No 2)* (2014) 252 CLR 416, 458 [39]–[41] (French CJ, Hayne, Kiefel, Bell and Keane JJ).

It is possible to identify instances of courts referring to post-enactment materials for interpretation.[165] It is not easy to identify the basis on which those materials are considered. More readily understandable is a slightly different situation where it might be argued that post-enactment material to a particular provision has been given interpretative weight. This is in the particular situation where a provision is enacted, extrinsic material is subsequently created about that provision, and then the Act containing the provision is amended but not the provision itself. In this instance the extrinsic material postdates the enactment of the provision in question. There is precedent for an inference to be drawn from the extrinsic material where Parliament has had the opportunity to address the issue raised in the post-enactment material about the provision, but did not do so. This is a variation on the principle discussed in **[24.15]**.

An example is the dissenting judgment of Gageler J in *Independent Commission Against Corruption v Cunneen.*[166] The Court was construing s 8 of the *Independent Commission Against Corruption Act 1988* (NSW) ('the Act'). A report of an independent review of the Act, including s 8, was published in 2005. The report contained statements about the meaning of s 8. Later in the same year, Parliament amended the Act, adopting some recommendations of the report but not amending s 8. The report was therefore post-enactment material for the purposes of s 8. In those circumstances Gageler J stated:

> That a legislature has refrained from amending a statutory provision following receipt of a report explaining the provision to have a particular textually available meaning is a factor which tells in favour of not departing from that meaning in construing the provision in the context of the statute as otherwise amended.[167]

Similar reasoning was adopted by McColl JA, in dissent, in *AQO v Minister for Finance and Services*.[168] Parliamentary inaction with respect to the provision being construed in the face of material that postdates that provision may be used to infer something about that provision.

The weight to be afforded to these materials must 'vary with the circumstances'.[169] For practical and conceptual reasons, caution should be exercised in attaching significance to parliamentary inaction.[170]

165 See, eg, *Australia and New Zealand Banking Group Ltd v Federal Commissioner of Taxation* (1994) 48 FCR 268, 291–2 (Hill J) (used to indicate mischief).

166 (2015) 256 CLR 1.

167 Ibid 44 [113]. Cf the majority who dismissed the value of the statement in the report: at 16 [16] (French CJ, Hayne, Kiefel and Nettle JJ).

168 (2016) 93 NSWLR 46, 67 [89]. Cf Basten JA's judgment in the same case: at 80 [146]–[147].

169 (2015) 256 CLR 1, 44 [113] (Gageler J).

170 See generally Diggory Bailey, 'Interpreting Parliamentary Inaction' (2020) 79(2) *Cambridge Law Journal* 245.

PART VI

INTERPRETATION ACTS AND OTHER ACTS OF GENERAL APPLICATION

Part V examined the role played by legislative history as part of the extrinsic context of legislation. Part VI deals with the extrinsic context provided by Acts of general application, and how they impact the interpretation and operation of an individual Act.

An Act passed by Parliament does not stand alone. It forms part of the body of written law within the relevant jurisdiction. Within that body of written law are general Acts, such as Interpretation Acts (chapter 25), that apply to all Acts, irrespective of their subject matter. Other general Acts apply if relevant to the subject matter of the Act in question or if called up by an individual Act (chapter 26). It is with these general Acts that Part VI deals.

Chapter 25 (*Interpretation Acts*) examines Acts, enacted by each Australian jurisdiction, which apply to the interpretation of all other Acts passed by that jurisdiction, in the absence of a contrary intention. They contain definitions of terms commonly used in legislation, facilitate the use of brief operative provisions (such as commencement and delegation provisions) and provide general rules of construction. They vary somewhat across Australia in the range of matters they cover and in their terms. Knowledge of these Acts is critical to interpreting legislation. Other chapters of this work also highlight provisions of these Acts. Chapter 25 deals with the remaining notable features of Interpretation Acts as well as giving a general description of their main purposes.

Chapter 26 (*Other Acts of General Application*) focuses on a range of other general Acts that support the operation of individual Acts. They include human rights Acts, Acts dealing with the review of administrative decisions, crime and sentencing Acts, evidence Acts, electronic transaction Acts, mutual recognition Acts and public sector employment Acts. Mention is also made of the *Regulatory Powers (Standard Provisions) Act 2014* (Cth), which enables monitoring and investigation powers to be readily called up by other Commonwealth Acts.

INTERPRETATION ACTS 25

Overview

Each Australian jurisdiction has an Act dealing with the interpretation of the Acts of that jurisdiction.[1] Such Acts are referred to in this book, including in this chapter, as 'Interpretation Acts', irrespective of their actual title. [25.1]

Familiarity with the relevant Interpretation Act is critical to understanding the legislation of a jurisdiction as legislation is drafted on the assumption that the reader has that familiarity.

The main purposes of an Interpretation Act are to shorten other legislation, by enacting provisions that apply across the statute book without any need for them to be specifically set out, and to put in place general interpretative principles applicable to legislation.

This chapter does not set out to give an exhaustive description of all the provisions contained in these Acts. It highlights the more important ones that are not otherwise dealt with in this work.[2]

An Act may displace the relevant Interpretation Act, wholly or partly, by evincing a contrary intention. This chapter discusses what is required to establish such a contrary intention.

Purpose of Interpretation Acts

The main purposes of an Interpretation Act are to shorten legislation and provide general interpretative rules [25.2]

The heritage of Australia's Interpretation Acts can be traced back to Lord Brougham's Act of 1850 in the United Kingdom.[3] The aim of that Act was to bring about improvements in how Acts were drafted. Presenting the Bill for that Act to the House of Lords, Lord Brougham observed:

> [H]e had made frequent attempts in that House – he was going to say with more or less success, but it was hardly possible to do so with less success, unfortunately – to amend

---

1 *Acts Interpretation Act 1901* (Cth); *Interpretation Act 1987* (NSW); *Acts Interpretation Act 1954* (Qld); *Legislation Interpretation Act 2021* (SA); *Acts Interpretation Act 1931* (Tas); *Interpretation of Legislation Act 1984* (Vic); *Interpretation Act 1984* (WA); *Legislation Act 2001* (ACT); *Interpretation Act 1978* (NT).

2 For other references in this book to Interpretation Acts, see **[8.2]**, **[12.3]**, **[19.2]**, **[24]**, **[32.8]**, **[36.9]**, **[37.3]**, **[39.3]**, **[40.8]** and chapter 43.

3 *Interpretation Act 1850*, 13 & 14 Vict, c 21. For discussion of the historical background of the United Kingdom and the Commonwealth Interpretation Acts, see Nick Horn, 'Interpretation Acts: Coherent Interpretation and a Coherent Statute Book' in Jeffrey Barnes (ed), *The Coherence of Statutory Interpretation* (Federation Press 2019) 160, 160–4. For discussion of the history of particular provisions of Interpretation Acts, see Chad Jacobi, *Interpretation Acts: Origins and Meaning* (Thomson Reuters, 2019).

> the only manufacture which had received no improvement for the last 150 years – that of Acts of Parliament.[4]

Lord Brougham's Act brought about improvement in Acts by providing general statutory definitions, allowing sections of Acts to be treated as substantive enactments without any need for introductory words, simplifying how Acts may be referred to and preventing the revival of a repealed Act upon the repeal of the Act that repealed it. It only had seven sections but the elements it contained are still elements of today's Interpretation Acts.

The essential purposes of an Interpretation Act are to shorten legislation and set out in one place a number of general rules of construction applicable to legislation.[5] Examples of provisions specifically aimed at shortening legislation include those that set out definitions of terms commonly used in legislation, that provide machinery provisions to put flesh on bare-bones operative provisions (such as provisions for delegation or service of documents) and that avoid the need to set out ancillary rules such as that words in the singular include the plural and vice versa. The general rules of construction provided are many and varied, ranging from approaches to interpretation to how to calculate age, distance or time. These general rules also contribute to the shortening of legislation as, in their absence, it would be necessary to consider including specific provisions to cover the matters dealt with by them.

It is a good practice to have the relevant Interpretation Act on hand when reading legislation.

Australia's Interpretation Acts are not uniform in their scope or language. They vary in size, from more than 300 sections, in the case of the Australian Capital Territory,[6] to 60 sections in the case of South Australia.[7]

Interpretation Acts are subject to contrary intention

[25.3] The application of an Interpretation Act is subject to a contrary intention

In *Waterfront Place Pty Ltd v Minister for Planning*[8] the Victorian Court of Appeal stated that '[u]niversal application is, of course, a defining characteristic of interpretation statutes'.[9] This defining characteristic is reflected in provisions contained in each of Australia's Interpretation Acts applying their terms, unless otherwise provided, to Acts across the whole of the statute book, irrespective of when passed.[10] However, that universality is not absolute. Each Act includes

---

4 United Kingdom, *Parliamentary Debates*, House of Lords, 12 February 1850, vol 108, col 708.

5 The NSW Interpretation Act was described by the Privy Council as a 'drafting convenience' in *Blue Metal Industries Ltd v Dilley* (1969) 117 CLR 651, 658 (Lords Morris, Pearce, Wilberforce, Pearson and Diplock). For an evaluation of Interpretation Acts, see Nick Horn, 'Interpretation Acts: Coherent Interpretation and a Coherent Statute Book' in Jeffrey Barnes (ed), *The Coherence of Statutory Interpretation* (Federation Press 2019) 160; Ross Carter, 'Interpretation Acts – Are They, and (How) Do They Make for, Great Law?' [2020] (3) *The Loophole: Journal of the Commonwealth Association of Legislative Counsel* 2.

6 The *Legislation Act 2001* (ACT) covers other matters related to legislation not commonly found in Interpretation Acts such as provisions about the publication of legislation and the preparation of regulatory impact statements for delegated legislation.

7 *Legislation Interpretation Act 2021* (SA).

8 (2019) 59 VR 556.

9 Ibid 559 [6] (Maxwell ACJ, Forrest and Emerton JJA).

10 *Acts Interpretation Act 1901* (Cth) s 2(1); *Interpretation Act 1987* (NSW) s 5(1); *Acts Interpretation Act 1954* (Qld) s 2; *Legislation Interpretation Act 2021* (SA) s 3; *Acts Interpretation Act 1931* (Tas) s 4(1); *Interpretation of Legislation Act 1984* (Vic) s 4(1); *Interpretation Act 1984* (WA) s 3(1), (2); *Legislation Act 2001* (ACT) s 4; *Interpretation Act 1978* (NT) s 3(1), (4).

a general provision recognising that its provisions may be excluded or modified in their operation by any individual Act.[11]

These limiting provisions vary in their terms.

Section 2(2) of the *Acts Interpretation Act 1901* (Cth) simply provides that the application of the Act, or any of its provisions, to an Act or provision is subject to a contrary intention. The *Interpretation Act 1987* (NSW) (s 5(2)), *Legislation Interpretation Act 2021* (SA) (s 3(3)), *Interpretation of Legislation Act 1984* (Vic) (s 4(1)(a))[12] and *Interpretation Act 1978* (NT) (s 3(3)) take a similar approach. The *Acts Interpretation Act 1954* (Qld) (s 4) provides that its provisions may be displaced, wholly or partly, by a contrary intention appearing in any Act.

Section 4 of the *Acts Interpretation Act 1931* (Tas) contains a more expansive provision that focuses on textual inconsistency. It states that, except where otherwise expressly provided, the provisions of the Act apply in the interpretation and construction of every Act and regulation except in so far as

- any provision of the *Acts Interpretation Act* is inconsistent with or repugnant to the true intent and object of the particular Act or regulation, or in the case of a regulation, the enabling Act; or
- the interpretation that any provision of the *Acts Interpretation Act* would give to anything contained in the particular Act or regulation is inconsistent with its context or with a definition or interpretation contained in it, or in the case of a regulation, contained in the enabling Act.[13]

Section 3 of the *Interpretation Act 1984* (WA), similar to the Tasmanian approach, is expansive in its terms. It applies that Act to every written law unless

- express provision is made to the contrary; or
- the intent and object of the particular Act or something in the subject or context of the particular Act, or in the case of subsidiary legislation, the enabling Act, is inconsistent with that application.[14]

The *Legislation Act 2001* (ACT) classifies its provisions as either determinative or non-determinative. Under s 6 of that Act, while both kinds of provisions may be expressly displaced, in the absence of express displacement the latter simply requires a contrary intention whereas the former requires a 'more deliberate displacement' described as a 'manifest' contrary intention.[15]

---

11 *Acts Interpretation Act 1901* (Cth) s 2(2); *Interpretation Act 1987* (NSW) s 5(2); *Acts Interpretation Act 1954* (Qld) s 4; *Legislation Interpretation Act 2021* (SA) s 3(3); *Acts Interpretation Act 1931* (Tas) s 4(1); *Interpretation of Legislation Act 1984* (Vic) s 4(1)(a); *Interpretation Act 1984* (WA) s 3(1); *Legislation Act 2001* (ACT) s 6; *Interpretation Act 1978* (NT) s 3(3).

12 Some provisions of the Victorian Act are expressed as applying unless the contrary intention 'expressly' appears.

13 See *Briers v Skilled Group Ltd* (2014) 23 Tas R 305, 326 [77] (Porter J, Wood and Pearce JJ agreeing at 329 [91]–[92]).

14 See *Toolan v Metropolitan (Perth) Passenger Transport Trust* (2001) 25 WAR 1, 23 [68] (Malcolm CJ, Pidgeon, Owen and Wheeler JJ agreeing at 4 [2], 9 [20], 9 [21], 23 [72]).

15 In *O'Donnell v Environment Protection Authority* (2012) 192 LGERA 1, 31 [40] Penfold J stated that 'it is useful, in considering whether a determinative provision has been displaced by a manifest contrary intention, to ask whether the amending law "clearly contradicts" the determinative provision concerned'. Section 6(6) provides that a provision of the Act must not be taken to be displaced by a provision of an Act or statutory instrument 'so far as the provisions can operate concurrently' while s 6(7) provides that a provision of the Act must not be taken to be displaced by a provision of an Act or statutory instrument 'because the provisions deal with the same or a similar subject matter': ibid.

The onus is on a party asserting the existence of a contrary intention to show its existence.[16]

In *Blue Metal Industries Ltd v Dilley*,[17] a case involving the takeover provisions of the *Companies Act 1961* (NSW), Lord Morris, giving the judgment of the Privy Council, stated:

> [I]n considering whether a contrary intention appears there need be no confinement of attention to any one particular section of an Act. It must be appropriate to consider the section in its setting in the legislation and furthermore to consider the substance and tenor of the legislation as a whole.[18]

In *Pfeiffer v Stevens*[19] McHugh J stated that '[a]n intention contrary to the *Acts Interpretation Act* may appear not only from the express terms or necessary implication of a legislative provision but from the general character of the legislation itself'.[20]

In *Attorney-General (Qld) v Australian Industrial Relations Commission*[21] the proposition is found that there is a contrary intention when the provisions of the particular Act being considered are 'clearly inconsistent' with the *Acts Interpretation Act*.[22]

In *ADCO Constructions Pty Ltd v Goudappel*[23] Gageler J stated that the cases 'demonstrate that a contrary intention will appear with the requisite degree of certainty if it appears "clearly" or "plainly" from the text and context of the provision in question'.[24]

As in all questions of statutory interpretation, the fundamental object is to determine the legislative intention by analysing the words of the particular statute in their context and having regard to their purpose.[25]

Nick Horn, a parliamentary counsel, has made the point that legislative drafters have a high level of awareness of the operation of Interpretation Acts and, if it is intended in the drafting of a statute to depart from a default rule in such an Act, a competent modern drafter will include an express provision in the new statute to override the operation of the default rule.[26]

In *Forsyth v Deputy Commissioner of Taxation*[27] Kirby J, referring to Interpretation Acts, stated:

> If such Acts state the rules by which parliamentary counsel draft legislation, courts should generally be ready to interpret the legislation in accordance with the stated provisions.[28]

The recognition that a subsequent Act may depart from a default rule laid down by an Acts Interpretation Act is consistent with 'the basic principle that legislation enacted by one

---

16 *Graovac v Minister for Immigration and Multicultural Affairs* (1999) 56 ALD 709, 714, [11] (Madgwick J).

17 (1969) 117 CLR 651.

18 Ibid 656.

19 (2001) 209 CLR 57.

20 Ibid 73 [56].

21 (2002) 213 CLR 485.

22 Ibid 505 [52] (Gaudron, McHugh, Gummow and Hayne JJ).

23 (2014) 254 CLR 1.

24 Ibid 22 [52]. In *Dossett v TKJ Nominees Pty Ltd* (2003) 218 CLR 1 Gummow, Hayne and Heydon JJ referred to a need for a contrary intention to be 'clearly apparent': at 14 [43].

25 See **[4.2]**.

26 Nick Horn, 'Interpretation Acts: Coherent Interpretation and a Coherent Statute Book' in Jeffrey Barnes (ed), *The Coherence of Statutory Interpretation* (Federation Press, 2019) 160, 174–5.

27 (2007) 231 CLR 531.

28 Ibid 562 [95]. See also *Waterfront Place Pty Ltd v Minister for Planning* (2019) 59 VR 556, 562–6 [24]–[41] (Maxwell ACJ, Forrest and Emerton JJ).

Parliament can be repealed or modified by a subsequent Parliament'.[29] A court not readily jumping to the conclusion that there is a contrary intention is consistent with drafters being aware of the operation of Interpretation Acts and indicating an intention to override them when required.

An Interpretation Act works in tandem with other Acts. In *Attorney-General (Qld) v Australian Industrial Relations Commission*[30] Gleeson CJ stated:

> Acts of Parliament are drafted, and are intended to be read and understood, in the light of the *Acts Interpretation Act*. A particular Act, and the *Acts Interpretation Act*, do not compete for attention, or rank in any order of priority. They work together. The meaning of the particular Act is to be understood in the light of the interpretation legislation. The scheme of that legislation is to state general principles that apply unless a contrary intention is manifested in a particular Act.[31]

Acts shortening provisions

Interpretation Acts facilitate the shortening of other legislation [25.4]

The statute book of each Australian jurisdiction, large as it is, would be considerably larger if each Act had to deal with things such as definitions of terms commonly used in legislation, the service of documents under the Act and how an instrument of delegation under the Act operates.

Including in Interpretation Acts provisions that deal with these and other such matters avoids the need for particular Acts to legislate for them, resulting in a considerable shortening of the size of the statute book.

(a) Definitions of common terms

There is a large range of terms commonly used in legislation. Defining them in an Interpretation Act for the purposes of all Acts and delegated legislation in the jurisdiction saves space and ensures consistency in the meaning of these terms as used across all the jurisdiction's legislation, unless in any particular case the jurisdiction chooses to vary the meaning of the term.

Queensland and the Australian Capital Territory include extensive lists of definitions in their Interpretation Acts. The *Legislation Act 2001* (ACT) is the most comprehensive and includes in pt 1 of the dictionary to that Act definitions of terms such as 'for' (defined to include 'for the purposes of'), 'in relation to' (defined to include a range of other expressions such as 'in respect of' and 'in connection with') and 'under' (defined to include, among others, 'for or for the purposes of', 'in accordance with' and 'within the meaning of').

In Queensland and the Northern Territory 'function' is defined as including duty,[32] while in South Australia it includes 'power and duty',[33] in the Australian Capital Territory it includes 'authority, duty and power'[34] and in Western Australia it includes 'powers, duties, responsibilities,

---

29 *Re Pacific Coal; Ex parte Construction, Forestry, Mining and Energy Union* (2000) 203 CLR 346, 443–4 [284] (Kirby J). See chapter 3.

30 (2002) 213 CLR 485.

31 Ibid 492–3 [8].

32 *Acts Interpretation Act 1954* (Qld) sch 1; *Interpretation Act 1978* (NT) s 17.

33 *Legislation Interpretation Act 2021* (SA) s 4.

34 *Legislation Act 2001* (ACT) dictionary, pt 1.

authorities and jurisdictions'.[35] In Queensland legislation a reference to a state includes a territory[36] while in ACT legislation it includes the Northern Territory.[37] Queensland and the Australian Capital Territory define 'liability' as meaning 'any liability or obligation (whether liquidated or unliquidated, certain or contingent, or accrued or accruing)'.[38] A few jurisdictions even define the word 'definition' itself.[39]

The range of definitions, and the differences between jurisdictions, point to the need to refer to the relevant Interpretation Act when reading legislation of a particular jurisdiction.

In all jurisdictions, except Tasmania, there is a provision to the effect that where a term is defined as having a particular meaning, other parts of speech and grammatical forms of that term have corresponding meanings.[40]

Below is a selection of terms that commonly appear in legislation. Differences in the definitions of those terms are highlighted.

'contravene'

In all jurisdictions this is defined as including a failure to comply.[41] In Queensland and the Australian Capital Territory 'fail' is defined as including 'refuse'.[42]

'document'

The definition of this term is broadly similar across the jurisdictions and includes such things as anything on which there is writing as well as maps, plans, drawings and photographs.[43]

'land'

Most jurisdictions define 'land' in a broadly similar way as including messuages, tenements and hereditaments, corporeal and incorporeal, of any tenure or description, whatever may be the

35 *Interpretation Act 1984* (WA) s 5.

36 *Acts Interpretation Act 1954* (Qld) s 33A.

37 *Legislation Act 2001* (ACT) dictionary, pt 1.

38 *Acts Interpretation Act 1954* (Qld) sch 1; *Legislation Act 2001* (ACT) dictionary, pt 1.

39 *Interpretation Act 1987* (NSW) s 21(1); *Acts Interpretation Act 1954* (Qld) sch 1; *Interpretation Act 1984* (WA) s 5; *Legislation Act 2001* (ACT) s 130.

40 *Acts Interpretation Act 1901* (Cth) s 18A; *Interpretation Act 1987* (NSW) s 7; *Acts Interpretation Act 1954* (Qld) s 32; *Legislation Interpretation Act 2021* (SA) s 7; *Interpretation of Legislation Act 1984* (Vic) s 39; *Interpretation Act 1984* (WA) s 9; *Legislation Act 2001* (ACT) s 157; *Interpretation Act 1978* (NT) s 23.

41 *Acts Interpretation Act 1901* (Cth) s 2B; *Interpretation Act 1987* (NSW) s 21(1); *Acts Interpretation Act 1954* (Qld) sch 1; *Legislation Interpretation Act 2021* (SA) s 4; *Acts Interpretation Act 1931* (Tas) s 46 (this section also defines 'fail to comply with' as including 'contravene'); *Interpretation of Legislation Act 1984* (Vic) s 38; *Interpretation Act 1984* (WA) s 5; *Legislation Act 2001* (ACT) dictionary, pt 1; *Interpretation Act 1978* (NT) s 17.

42 *Acts Interpretation Act 1954* (Qld) sch 1; *Legislation Act 2001* (ACT) dictionary, pt 1.

43 *Acts Interpretation Act 1901* (Cth) s 2B; *Interpretation Act 1987* (NSW) s 21(1); *Acts Interpretation Act 1954* (Qld) sch 1 (does not refer to photographs as such but refers to anything from which images are capable of being produced); *Legislation Interpretation Act 2021* (SA) s 4; *Acts Interpretation Act 1931* (Tas) s 24(bb) (similar to Queensland); *Interpretation of Legislation Act 1984* (Vic) s 38 (expressly covers discs and films); *Interpretation Act 1984* (WA) s 5 (includes publications, which is defined to include things like records, films and images); *Legislation Act 2001* (ACT) dictionary, pt 1; *Interpretation Act 1978* (NT) s 17.

estate or interest in them.[44] South Australia defines 'land' as including a building or structure affixed to land, waters and airspace over land, and the bed of any body of waters and subsoil and subterranean waters.[45] Victoria and Western Australia define 'land' as including buildings and other structures, land covered with water, and any estate, interest, easement, servitude, privilege or right in or over land.[46]

'person'

In the Commonwealth,[47] New South Wales,[48] Queensland,[49] South Australia,[50] Victoria,[51] the Australian Capital Territory[52] and the Northern Territory[53] this term is defined to include a body politic or corporate as well as an individual. In Tasmania[54] and Western Australia[55] an unincorporated body of persons is included.

Some jurisdictions define the term 'entity' as including a person and an unincorporated body.[56]

References to domestic relationships

In most jurisdictions there are definitions of 'de facto partner'[57] and 'de facto relationship'.[58] In the Australian Capital Territory the defined terms are 'domestic partner' and 'domestic relationship'.[59]

---

44 *Acts Interpretation Act 1901* (Cth) s 2B; *Interpretation Act 1987* (NSW) s 21(1); *Acts Interpretation Act 1954* (Qld) sch 1; *Acts Interpretation Act 1931* (Tas) s 46 (includes houses and buildings); *Legislation Act 2001* (ACT) dictionary, pt 1; *Interpretation Act 1978* (NT) s 17.

45 *Legislation Interpretation Act 2021* (SA) s 4.

46 *Interpretation of Legislation Act 1984* (Vic) s 38 (the buildings or other structures must be permanently affixed to land); *Interpretation Act 1984* (WA) s 5.

47 *Acts Interpretation Act 1901* (Cth) s 2C.

48 *Interpretation Act 1987* (NSW) s 21(1). Also includes a corporation.

49 *Acts Interpretation Act 1954* (Qld) s 32D. Defined as including a corporation (includes a body politic or corporate) as well as an individual.

50 *Legislation Interpretation Act 2021* (SA) s 4. Defined simply as including a body corporate so does not cover bodies politic.

51 *Interpretation of Legislation Act 1984* (Vic) s 38.

52 *Legislation Act 2001* (ACT) s 160. Defined as including a corporation (includes a body politic or corporate) as well as an individual.

53 *Interpretation Act 1978* (NT) s 24AA.

54 *Acts Interpretation Act 1931* (Tas) s 41(1). Excludes the Crown from the definition.

55 *Interpretation Act 1984* (WA) s 5. Does not refer to bodies politic but includes 'public body'.

56 *Acts Interpretation Act 1954* (Qld) sch 1; *Legislation Interpretation Act 2021* (SA) s 4; *Interpretation of Legislation Act 1984* (Vic) s 38; *Legislation Act 2001* (ACT) dictionary, pt 1.

57 *Acts Interpretation Act 1901* (Cth) s 2D; *Interpretation Act 1987* (NSW) s 21C(1); *Acts Interpretation Act 1954* (Qld) s 32DA; *Interpretation Act 1984* (WA) s 13A(4), (5); *Interpretation Act 1978* (NT) s 19A(3).

58 *Acts Interpretation Act 1901* (Cth) s 2F; *Interpretation Act 1987* (NSW) s 21C(2); *Acts Interpretation Act 1954* (Qld) sch 1; *Interpretation Act 1984* (WA) s 13A; *Interpretation Act 1978* (NT) s 19A(3).

59 *Legislation Act 2001* (ACT) s 169.

References to periods of time

While not universally included, there are definitions of 'business day',[60] 'calendar month',[61] 'calendar year',[62] 'financial year',[63] 'month'[64] and 'year'[65]. South Australia defines 'day' as 'a period of 24 hours ending at the stroke of midnight'.[66]

'writing'

This term is defined in all jurisdictions as including any mode of representing or reproducing words, figures, drawings or symbols in a visible form.[67] In New South Wales and Western Australia it is defined as including printing, photography, photocopying, lithography, typewriting and any other mode of representing or reproducing words in a visible form.[68]

(b) Singular and plural

Interpretation Acts in each jurisdiction contain a provision to the effect that words in the singular include the plural and words in the plural include the singular.[69] This handy provision is subject to being displaced by a contrary intention.

In *Sherzad v Minister for Immigration and Citizenship*[70] the Full Court of the Federal Court referred to the use of the word 'words' in the Commonwealth provision.[71] The Court stated:

---

60 *Acts Interpretation Act 1901* (Cth) s 2B; *Acts Interpretation Act 1954* (Qld) sch 1; *Legislation Interpretation Act 2021* (SA) s 4; *Legislation Act 2001* (ACT) dictionary, pt 1; *Interpretation Act 1978* (NT) s 17.

61 *Acts Interpretation Act 1901* (Cth) s 2B; *Interpretation Act 1987* (NSW) s 21(1); *Acts Interpretation Act 1954* (Qld) sch 1; *Legislation Interpretation Act 2021* (SA) s 4; *Legislation Act 2001* (ACT) dictionary, pt 1; *Interpretation Act 1978* (NT) s 17.

62 *Acts Interpretation Act 1901* (Cth) s 2B; *Interpretation Act 1987* (NSW) s 21(1); *Acts Interpretation Act 1954* (Qld) sch 1; *Legislation Interpretation Act 2021* (SA) s 4; *Interpretation of Legislation Act 1984* (Vic) s 44(6); *Legislation Act 2001* (ACT) dictionary, pt 1; *Interpretation Act 1978* (NT) s 17.

63 *Acts Interpretation Act 1901* (Cth) s 2B; *Acts Interpretation Act 1954* (Qld) sch 1; *Legislation Interpretation Act 2021* (SA) s 4; *Acts Interpretation Act 1931* (Tas) s 45; *Interpretation of Legislation Act 1984* (Vic) s 44(6); *Interpretation Act 1984* (WA) s 5; *Legislation Act 2001* (ACT) dictionary, pt 1; *Interpretation Act 1978* (NT) s 17.

64 *Acts Interpretation Act 1901* (Cth) s 2B; *Interpretation Act 1987* (NSW) s 21(1); *Acts Interpretation Act 1954* (Qld) sch 1; *Legislation Interpretation Act 2021* (SA) s 4; *Acts Interpretation Act 1931* (Tas) s 46; *Interpretation of Legislation Act 1984* (Vic) s 44(6); *Interpretation Act 1984* (WA) s 5; *Legislation Act 2001* (ACT) dictionary, pt 1; *Interpretation Act 1978* (NT) s 17.

65 *Acts Interpretation Act 1954* (Qld) sch 1; *Legislation Interpretation Act 2021* (SA) s 4; *Interpretation of Legislation Act 1984* (Vic) s 44(6); *Interpretation Act 1984* (WA) s 5; *Legislation Act 2001* (ACT) dictionary, pt 1; *Interpretation Act 1978* (NT) s 17.

66 *Legislation Interpretation Act 2021* (SA) s 4.

67 *Acts Interpretation Act 1901* (Cth) s 2B; *Acts Interpretation Act 1954* (Qld) sch 1; *Legislation Interpretation Act 2021* (SA) s 4; *Acts Interpretation Act 1931* (Tas) s 24(b) (omits 'drawings'); *Interpretation of Legislation Act 1984* (Vic) s 38 (omits 'drawings'); *Legislation Act 2001* (ACT) dictionary, pt 1; *Interpretation Act 1978* (NT) s 26 (omits 'drawings' and adds 'whether or not an optical, electronic, mechanical or other means or process must be used before they can be perceived').

68 *Interpretation Act 1987* (NSW) s 21(1); *Interpretation Act 1984* (WA) s 5.

69 *Acts Interpretation Act 1901* (Cth) s 23(b); *Interpretation Act 1987* (NSW) s 8(b), (c); *Acts Interpretation Act 1954* (Qld) s 32C; *Legislation Interpretation Act 2021* (SA) s 10(1), (2); *Acts Interpretation Act 1931* (Tas) s 24(d); *Interpretation of Legislation Act 1984* (Vic) s 37(c), (d); *Interpretation Act 1984* (WA) s 10(c); *Legislation Act 2001* (ACT) s 145(b); *Interpretation Act 1978* (NT) s 24(2).

70 (2008) 170 FCR 105.

71 *Acts Interpretation Act 1901* (Cth) s 23(b).

> The word 'words' is apt to include any part of speech, including nouns, pronouns, verbs, and, of relevance in the present case, demonstrative adjectives. The word 'include' does not indicate that ... one number is necessarily to apply to the exclusion of the other. Rather, both possibilities are preserved, absent a contrary intention.[72]

In that case it was held that s 23 operated, in relation to reg 1.15(1)(c) of the *Migration Regulations 1994* (Cth), to enable the singular nouns 'relative' and 'country' to include 'relatives' and 'countries', the singular verb 'is' to include 'are', and the singular demonstrative adjective 'that' to include 'those'.[73]

In *Blue Metal Industries Ltd v Dilley*[74] the Privy Council stated in relation to a provision in the *Interpretation Act 1897* (NSW) about the singular including the plural:

> [T]he mere fact that the reading of words in a section suggests an emphasis on singularity as opposed to plurality is not enough to exclude plurality. Words in the singular will include the plural unless the contrary intention appears. But in considering whether a contrary intention appears there need be no confinement of attention to any one particular section of an Act. It must be appropriate to consider the section in its setting in the legislation and furthermore to consider the substance and tenor of the legislation as a whole.[75]

In that case the Privy Council held that there was a contrary intention in the *Companies Act 1961* (NSW) sufficient to displace the presumption. A contrary intention was also found by the Tasmanian Supreme Court in *Porter v Bryan*.[76] In that case a provision making it an offence to consort with reputed thieves was interpreted as requiring consorting with more than one reputed thief. Burbury CJ stated that 'it would be inconsistent with the true intent and object of the section to apply s 24 of the *Acts Interpretation Act* 1931' because '[c]ompanionship with one reputed thief may be equivocal as an indication of a man's character; the inference from persistent companionship with a number of reputed thieves is ordinarily inescapable'.[77]

The presumption does not need to be applied uniformly across the whole of a statute. In *No 20 Cannon St Ltd v Singer & Friedlander Ltd*[78] Megarry J held, in relation to the equivalent provision in the United Kingdom:

> I do not see why this provision should not be applied distributively. Further, to 'include' the plural does not mean that the word must discard its singularity: the Act adds to the meaning of the word, rather than changing it. It would indeed be remarkable if, for example, a statute worded in terms of 'landlord' and 'tenant' applied to every case where there was a landlord and a tenant in the singular or landlords and tenants in the plural, but not to cases where there were plural landlords and a singular tenant, or vice versa. In my judgment, subject always to the context, the Interpretation Act 1889 authorises a process of selective pluralising or, for that matter, singularising.[79]

---

72 *Sherzad v Minister for Immigration and Citizenship* (2008) 170 FCR 105 [12] (Moore, Lindgren and Buchanan JJ).

73 Ibid [13].

74 (1969) 117 CLR 651.

75 Ibid 656.

76 [1963] Tas SR 41.

77 Ibid 43.

78 [1974] 1 Ch 229.

79 Ibid 241–2.

(c) **References to gender**

Before the 1980s in Australia it was common for Interpretation Acts to contain a provision to the effect that words importing the masculine gender must be taken to include females.[80] Such provisions supported the then drafting practice of using masculine pronouns to cover individuals of any gender.

The absence of a rule that words importing the feminine gender included males occasionally caused problems. Thus, in *Ogilvie v Lowe*[81] the non-Aboriginal husband of an Aboriginal woman was convicted of an offence under the *Aborigines Regulations 1957* (Vic) of living on a reserve without a permit. The woman had a permit. While under the regulations it was provided that a permit was sufficient authority for the 'wife of the aborigine' to live with him on the reserve, that did not cover the situation at hand. Scholl J noted that s 17 of the *Acts Interpretation Act 1958* (Vic) did not provide that 'words importing the feminine gender are to be deemed and taken to include males ... Accordingly, there is no statutory warrant for reading the words "wife of the aborigine" as including the husband of the aborigine'.[82]

A Bill introduced into the Victorian Parliament in 1982, the Interpretation Bill, addressed this issue by allowing words importing either the masculine or feminine gender to include the other gender. The Bill was referred to a parliamentary committee that reported in 1983.[83] While supporting the redrafted provision, the committee recommended that legislative drafters should make every endeavour to draft in gender-neutral terms.[84] It also traced how from at least the 16th century in England grammarians had pursued a path of promoting the masculine form above the feminine form, with ultimately the *Interpretation Act 1850* (UK) adopting a provision on which s 17 of the Victorian Act was modelled.[85]

Gender-neutral drafting is now the preferred drafting approach in Australia.[86] This gives Interpretation Act provisions about gender no work to do in provisions that adopt that approach. However, for legislation not drafted gender neutrally, each jurisdiction has a provision to the effect that a reference to a gender includes every other gender.[87] Like all provisions in interpretation

80 See, eg, *Acts Interpretation Act 1958* (Vic) s 17 (repealed).

81 [1963] VR 225.

82 Ibid 227.

83 Legal and Constitutional Committee, Parliament of Victoria, *Report on Interpretation Bill 1982* (Parliamentary Report No 21/1982–83, October 1983).

84 Ibid [22.18].

85 Ibid [22.3]–[22.8].

86 See **[10.7]**.

87 *Acts Interpretation Act 1901* (Cth) s 23(a); *Interpretation Act 1987* (NSW) s 8(a); *Acts Interpretation Act 1954* (Qld) s 32B; *Legislation Interpretation Act 2021* (SA) s 9(1); *Acts Interpretation Act 1931* (Tas) s 24A; *Interpretation of Legislation Act 1984* (Vic) s 37(a); *Interpretation Act 1984* (WA) s 10(a); *Legislation Act 2001* (ACT) s 145(a); *Interpretation Act 1978* (NT) s 24(1). The Northern Territory provision arguably does not include references to the neuter gender, important when legal persons such as companies or unincorporated bodies are to be included. It provides that 'any language that indicates or could be taken to indicate a person of a particular gender or sex includes any individual, regardless of gender or sex'. Section 9(2) of the *Legislation Interpretation Act 2021* (SA) provides that every word implying a particular gender will be construed as including a body corporate as well as an individual. Section 9(3) of that Act further states that every phrase consisting of a masculine pronoun and a feminine pronoun joined by the conjunction 'or' will be construed as applicable to a body corporate as well as an individual. Section 24A(2) of the *Acts Interpretation Act 1931* (Tas) provides that a word in either the masculine or feminine gender includes a body corporate or unincorporated.

legislation, it is subject to a contrary intention.[88] The South Australian provision adds that every word implying a particular gender is also applicable to an individual who does not identify as having any particular gender.

(d) **References to 'the Minister'**

The administration of Acts in a jurisdiction is allocated by instrument among the various Ministers by their ministerial title. As the title of the Minister administering a particular Act, or a provision of an Act (and hence able to exercise powers or perform functions under it) may change from time to time, it would be inconvenient if references to the Minister by their title in the Act had to be amended each time there was a change in the title of the relevant Minister.[89] This problem is averted by the widespread practice of only referring in an Act to the relevant Minister by the expression 'the Minister'. To make this work it is necessary to have a general statutory provision that construes that expression as a reference to the Minister with responsibility for administering the provision in which it appears.

Such a general provision is to be found in an Interpretation Act in each jurisdiction.[90] These provisions (other than the South Australian, Tasmanian and Western Australian provisions) also expressly recognise that a single provision may be administered in different respects by different Ministers or (other than the South Australian, Tasmanian, Victorian and Western Australian provisions) may even be administered by two or more Ministers in the same respect.[91] Express provision is also made to ensure that acting Ministers are covered.[92]

Where the Minister administering a provision is assisted by a junior Minister, the junior Minister may exercise a power under the provision on behalf of the Minister formally responsible for its administration.[93]

(e) **References to legislation**

Legislation is a dynamic organism. It is subject to frequent change, in line with changes in underlying policy or as a response to a new or evolving state of affairs. That change may be in the

---

88 See **[25.3]**. See also *Secretary, Department of Social Security v Kozhaya Dagher* [1997] AATA 419 (Member Ettinger) (the expression 'special widow' held to only refer to a woman); *Automobile Fire and General Insurance Co of Australia Ltd v Davey* (1936) 54 CLR 534, 538 (Latham CJ) (contrary intention created by fact that words denoted a particular relationship to a person and were not just words denoting gender).

89 Of course, the title of some ministerial offices (such as Prime Minister, Premier and Treasurer) is unlikely to change so references to such Ministers by their office title can be justified.

90 *Acts Interpretation Act 1901* (Cth) s 19; *Interpretation Act 1987* (NSW) s 15; *Acts Interpretation Act 1954* (Qld) s 33; *Legislation Interpretation Act 2021* (SA) s 4 (definition of 'Minister'); *Acts Interpretation Act 1931* (Tas) s 45(1) (definition of 'the Minister'); *Interpretation of Legislation Act 1984* (Vic) s 38 (definition of 'Minister'); *Interpretation Act 1984* (WA) s 12; *Legislation Act 2001* (ACT) s 162; *Interpretation Act 1978* (NT) s 19.

91 See *Tervonen v Minister for Justice and Customs (No 2)* (2007) 98 ALD 589, 618–19, [126]–[128] (Rares J); *Mokbel v A-G (Cth)* (2007) 162 FCR 296, 298 [8]–[9] (Heerey J, North J and Jessup J agreeing at 298 [13], [14]) (*Extradition Act 1988* (Cth) administered by two Ministers).

92 *Acts Interpretation Act 1901* (Cth) s 19(4); *Interpretation Act 1987* (NSW) s 15(1)(b); *Acts Interpretation Act 1954* (Qld) s 33(1)(b); *Legislation Interpretation Act 2021* (SA) s 4 (definition of 'Minister'); *Acts Interpretation Act 1931* (Tas) s 25; *Interpretation of Legislation Act 1984* (Vic) s 38 (definition of 'Minister'); *Interpretation Act 1984* (WA) s 12(c); *Legislation Act 2001* (ACT) s 162(3); *Interpretation Act 1978* (NT) s 19(2)(b).

93 See *A-G (Cth) v Foster* (1999) 84 FCR 582, 593 [37] (von Doussa, O'Loughlin and Mansfield JJ).

form of an amendment to a provision, or a provision may be completely repealed and re-enacted (with or without modification) or a provision may simply be repealed and not re-enacted.

Cross-referencing to other legislation is a common feature in Acts and delegated legislation. The cross-reference may be to a defined term, to another provision of the same Act or instrument or to the whole or a portion of another Act or instrument. The other Act or instrument to which the cross-reference is made may be an Act or instrument of the same jurisdiction or of another Australian jurisdiction.

An Interpretation Act in each Australian jurisdiction has provisions aimed at clarifying the effect of cross-references in the various scenarios set out above. The provisions are, however, not identical across the jurisdictions. The following are types of common provisions dealing with cross-references to Acts found across Australia:

1. A reference to an Act of the same jurisdiction, which has been amended, is a reference to that Act as amended from time to time.[94]
2. A reference to an Act of another Australian jurisdiction, which has been amended, is a reference to that Act as amended from time to time.[95]
3. A reference to an Act of the same jurisdiction, which has been repealed and re-enacted, with or without modifications, is a reference to the re-enacted Act as amended from time to time.[96]
4. A reference to an Act of another Australian jurisdiction, which has been repealed and re-enacted, with or without modifications, is a reference to the re-enacted Act as amended from time to time.[97]

Sections 10(c) and 10A(c) of the *Acts Interpretation Act 1901* (Cth) construe references to a provision of a Commonwealth Act, or an Act of another Australian jurisdiction, which is repealed and re-enacted, with or without modifications, as references to the re-enacted provision.[98]

---

94 *Acts Interpretation Act 1901* (Cth) s 10(a); *Interpretation Act 1987* (NSW) s 68(1); *Acts Interpretation Act 1954* (Qld) s 14H(1)(a); *Legislation Interpretation Act 2021* (SA) s 36; *Acts Interpretation Act 1931* (Tas) s 13(5); *Interpretation of Legislation Act 1984* (Vic) s 17(1)(a); *Interpretation Act 1984* (WA) s 16(1); *Legislation Act 2001* (ACT) s 102(1)(a); *Interpretation Act 1978* (NT) s 50(1).

95 *Acts Interpretation Act 1901* (Cth) s 10A(a); *Interpretation Act 1987* (NSW) s 68(1); *Acts Interpretation Act 1954* (Qld) s 14H(1)(a); *Legislation Interpretation Act 2021* (SA) s 36; *Acts Interpretation Act 1931* (Tas) s 13(6); *Interpretation of Legislation Act 1984* (Vic) s 17(1)(a); *Interpretation Act 1984* (WA) s 16(3) (Commonwealth Acts only); *Legislation Act 2001* (ACT) s 102(1)(a).

96 *Acts Interpretation Act 1901* (Cth) s 10(b); *Interpretation Act 1987* (NSW) s 68(3)(a); *Acts Interpretation Act 1954* (Qld) s 14H(1)(b); *Legislation Interpretation Act 2021* (SA) s 36; *Acts Interpretation Act 1931* (Tas) s 13(5); *Interpretation of Legislation Act 1984* (Vic) s 17(1)(b), (c); *Legislation Act 2001* (ACT) s 102(1)(b); *Interpretation Act 1978* (NT) s 15(1). The *Interpretation of Legislation Act 1984* (Vic) s 16(1)(b) expressly provides that a subordinate instrument made under an Act, or provision of an Act, that has been repealed and re-enacted, with or without modifications, has effect as if it were made under the re-enacted Act or provision.

97 *Acts Interpretation Act 1901* (Cth) s 10A(b); *Interpretation Act 1987* (NSW) s 68(3)(a); *Acts Interpretation Act 1954* (Qld) s 14H(1)(b); *Legislation Interpretation Act 2021* (SA) s 36; *Acts Interpretation Act 1931* (Tas) s 13(6); *Interpretation of Legislation Act 1984* (Vic) s 17(1)(b), (c); *Legislation Act 2001* (ACT) s 102(1)(b); *Interpretation Act 1978* (NT) s 15(2), (3).

98 See also *Acts Interpretation Act 1931* (Tas) s 17 for references to repealed and re-enacted provisions of Tasmanian Acts.

Some jurisdictions also treat cross-references in legislation to instruments made under an Act of their jurisdiction,[99] or any other Australian jurisdiction,[100] in a similar way to how they treat references to Acts.

(f) Delegation

An important feature of legislation is the conferral on persons of functions, duties and powers of various kinds. To facilitate the performance of those functions and duties and the exercise of those powers, legislation commonly confers a power of delegation on those persons. To shorten legislation and ensure consistency in application and effect, an Interpretation Act in each jurisdiction contains detailed provisions about delegations.[101]

The following are common features of these Interpretation Acts provisions:

- A delegation may be made to a specified person or to the person holding, occupying, or performing for the time being the duties of, a specified office or position.[102]
- A delegation may be made without limitation as to how or when it may be exercised, or it may be delegated subject to compliance with specified limitations.[103]
- In relation to a provision that depends on a person's opinion, belief or state of mind about a matter when exercising a power or performing a function or duty, a delegate may act on their own opinion, belief or state of mind about the matter.[104]
- The power to delegate may not be delegated unless that is expressly provided for in the legislation conferring the power of delegation.[105]

---

99 *Acts Interpretation Act 1901* (Cth) s 10 (as applied by the *Legislation Act 2003* (Cth) s 13(1)(a)); *Interpretation Act 1987* (NSW) s 68; *Acts Interpretation Act 1954* (Qld) s 14H; *Legislation Interpretation Act 2021* (SA) s 36; *Interpretation of Legislation Act 1984* (Vic) s 17; *Interpretation Act 1984* (WA) s 16(1), (2); *Legislation Act 2001* (ACT) s 102; *Interpretation Act 1978* (NT) s 50(1).

100 *Interpretation Act 1987* (NSW) s 68; *Acts Interpretation Act 1954* (Qld) s 14H; *Legislation Interpretation Act 2021* (SA) s 36; *Interpretation of Legislation Act* 1984 (Vic) s 17; *Legislation Act 2001* (ACT) s 102.

101 *Acts Interpretation Act 1901* (Cth) ss 34AA–34A; *Interpretation Act 1987* (NSW) s 49; *Acts Interpretation Act 1954* (Qld) s 27A; *Legislation Interpretation Act 2021* (SA) s 43; *Acts Interpretation Act 1931* (Tas) ss 23AA, 23A; *Interpretation of Legislation Act 1984* (Vic) ss 42–42A; *Interpretation Act 1984* (WA) ss 58–59; *Legislation Act 2001* (ACT) pt 19.4; *Interpretation Act 1978* (NT) ss 46A, 48.

102 *Acts Interpretation Act 1901* (Cth) s 34AA; *Interpretation Act 1987* (NSW) s 49(1), (8); *Acts Interpretation Act 1954* (Qld) s 27A(1), (9); *Legislation Interpretation Act 2021* (SA) s 43(7), (8); *Acts Interpretation Act 1931* (Tas) s 23AA(1); *Interpretation of Legislation Act 1984* (Vic) s 42A(2); *Interpretation Act 1984* (WA) s 59(1)(d), (f); *Legislation Act 2001* (ACT) s 233; *Interpretation Act 1978* (NT) s 46A(1).

103 *Acts Interpretation Act 1901* (Cth) s 34AB(1)(a); *Interpretation Act 1987* (NSW) s 49(2)(a); *Acts Interpretation Act 1954* (Qld) s 27A(2)(a); *Legislation Interpretation Act 2021* (SA) s 43(2); *Acts Interpretation Act 1931* (Tas) s 23AA(2)(a); *Interpretation of Legislation Act 1984* (Vic) s 42A(1)(b); *Interpretation Act 1984* (WA) s 59(1)(b), (c); *Legislation Act 2001* (ACT) ss 234 (also expressly states that all or part of a function may be delegated), 239(1). If the power to be delegated is a single indivisible power, such as the power to determine an application, these provisions do not enable the delegation of part only of the power – for example, the power to refuse the application but not the power to approve it. See *Singh v Minister for Immigration, Local Government and Ethnic Affairs* (1989) 18 ALD 638.

104 *Acts Interpretation Act 1901* (Cth) s 34A; *Interpretation Act 1987* (NSW) s 49(7); *Acts Interpretation Act 1954* (Qld) s 27A(8); *Legislation Interpretation Act 2021* (SA) s 43(4); *Acts Interpretation Act 1931* (Tas) s 23A; *Interpretation of Legislation Act 1984* (Vic) s 42; *Interpretation Act 1984* (WA) s 58; *Legislation Act 2001* (ACT) s 239(3); *Interpretation Act 1978* (NT) s 48.

105 *Acts Interpretation Act 1901* (Cth) s 34AB(1)(b); *Interpretation Act 1987* (NSW) s 49(10); *Legislation Interpretation Act 2021* (SA) s 43(3); *Interpretation of Legislation Act 1984* (Vic) s 42AA(1)(a); *Legislation Act 2001* (ACT) ss 231(2), 236; *Interpretation Act 1978* (NT) s 46A(2). Even in the absence of such a provision, at common law a delegate of a statutory power cannot subdelegate that power unless authorised to do so by

- A function, power or duty performed or exercised by a delegate is as effective as it would have been if it had been performed or exercised by the delegator.[106]
- Delegating a function, power or duty does not prevent the delegator themselves performing or exercising that function, power or duty.[107]

Section 34AB(2) and (3) of the *Acts Interpretation Act 1901* (Cth) and s 43(9) and (10) of the *Legislation Interpretation Act 2021* (SA) cover the situation where, after a delegation is made, amending legislation confers new functions, duties or powers on the delegator or alters the functions, duties or powers of the delegator. In the former situation the additional functions, duties or powers are automatically included in the delegation if the delegation was of all of the delegator's then existing functions, duties or powers. In the latter situation the delegated functions, duties or powers are automatically altered accordingly.

Section 43(12) of the *Legislation Interpretation Act 2021* (SA) provides that the validity of a delegation 'is not affected by a grammatical error, spelling error, error of punctuation, formatting error or other minor error if the scope and meaning of the delegation is readily apparent despite the error'.

The *Legislation Act 2001* (ACT) expressly states that a function may be delegated to two or more delegates.[108] It also provides that a delegation, or anything done under a delegation, is not invalid only because of a defect or irregularity in or in relation to the delegation[109] and that anything done by a delegate is not invalid only because the delegation had been amended or revoked or the occasion for exercising it had not arisen or had ended.[110]

Some other provisions about delegation found in some Interpretation Acts are as follows:

- a delegation must be in, or be evidenced by, writing signed by or on behalf of the delegator;[111]
- a delegation may be revoked, wholly or partly, by the delegator;[112]

statute, expressly or impliedly. This principle is commonly expressed by reference to the maxim *delegatus non potest delegare*.

106 *Acts Interpretation Act 1901* (Cth) s 34AB(1)(c); *Interpretation Act 1987* (NSW) s 49(6); *Acts Interpretation Act 1954* (Qld) s 27A(3D), (7); *Legislation Interpretation Act 2021* (SA) s 43(5); *Acts Interpretation Act 1931* (Tas) s 23AA(4), (5), (8); *Interpretation of Legislation Act 1984* (Vic) s 42A(1)(c); *Interpretation Act 1984* (WA) s 59(3); *Legislation Act 2001* (ACT) s 239(2), (4); *Interpretation Act 1978* (NT) s 46A(3).

107 *Acts Interpretation Act 1901* (Cth) s 34AB(1)(d); *Interpretation Act 1987* (NSW) s 49(9); *Acts Interpretation Act 1954* (Qld) s 27A(10); *Legislation Interpretation Act 2021* (SA) s 43(6); *Acts Interpretation Act 1931* (Tas) s 23AA(6); *Interpretation of Legislation Act 1984* (Vic) s 42A(1)(a); *Interpretation Act 1984* (WA) s 59(1)(a); *Legislation Act 2001* (ACT) s 240; *Interpretation Act 1978* (NT) s 46A(4).

108 *Legislation Act 2001* (ACT) s 235.

109 Ibid s 242(1). See *Lewis v Chief Executive Department of Justice and Community Safety (ACT)* (2013) 280 FLR 118, 138–9 [111]–[113] (Refshauge ACJ); *Burridge v Chief Magistrate of the Magistrates Court (ACT) (No 2)* (2018) 338 FLR 339, 352 [78]–[79] (Elkaim, Loukas-Karlsson and Charlesworth JJ); *Sports Centres Australia Pty Ltd v Commissioner for Australian Capital Territory Revenue* (2019) 240 LGERA 311, 335–7 [121]–[127] (Crowe AJ).

110 *Legislation Act 2001* (ACT) s 242(2).

111 *Interpretation Act 1987* (NSW) s 49(2)(b); *Acts Interpretation Act 1954* (Qld) s 27A(3); *Acts Interpretation Act 1931* (Tas) s 23AA(2)(b); *Legislation Act 2001* (ACT) s 232.

112 *Interpretation Act 1987* (NSW) s 49(2)(c); *Acts Interpretation Act 1954* (Qld) s 27A(2)(c), (3A); *Legislation Interpretation Act 2021* (SA) s 43(2); *Acts Interpretation Act 1931* (Tas) s 23AA(2)(c); *Interpretation Act 1984* (WA) s 59(1)(e); *Legislation Act 2001* (ACT) s 237 (extends also to amendment).

- a delegated function may be exercised only in accordance with any conditions to which the delegation is subject;[113]
- a delegate, in the exercise of a delegated function, may exercise any incidental function;[114]
- a delegated function that purports to have been exercised by a delegate must be taken to have been duly exercised until the contrary is proved;[115]
- a change in who holds the office of a delegator, or in the membership of a delegator body, does not affect a delegation and the person for the time being occupying or acting in the office, or the body as constituted for the time being, is taken to be the delegator;[116]
- the delegation of a function or power does not relieve the delegator of the obligation to ensure that the function or power is properly performed or exercised;[117] and
- the rules that apply to a delegation apply to a subdelegation in the same way, where subdelegation is permitted.[118]

In the absence of an express power of delegation, common law principles of agency may apply. A Minister or senior public official ('the principal') may be able to authorise a person (an 'agent') to exercise or perform, on behalf of and in the name of the Minister or senior public official, a statutory power or function by relying on the *Carltona* principle.[119] Section 46 of the *Interpretation Act 1978* (NT) expressly provides for this.[120]

Section 23AAB of the *Acts Interpretation Act 1931* (Tas) conflates the concepts of delegation and authorisation by a principal. It provides that the power to delegate a function or power includes a power to authorise another person to perform the function or exercise the power on behalf of the authorising person, and it applies the provisions of that Act relating to delegation to an authorisation.

(g) **Service of documents**

Legislation frequently provides for the issue and giving of documents of various kinds. A critical feature is specifying how a document can be given to, or served on, a person. Interpretation Acts in each jurisdiction provide rules for service that apply in the absence of a contrary intention.

---

113 *Interpretation Act 1987* (NSW) s 49(3); *Acts Interpretation Act 1954* (Qld) s 27A(4); *Acts Interpretation Act 1931* (Tas) s 23AA(3).

114 *Interpretation Act 1987* (NSW) s 49(4); *Acts Interpretation Act 1954* (Qld) s 27A(5); *Interpretation Act 1984* (WA) s 59(2)(a).

115 *Interpretation Act 1987* (NSW) s 49(5); *Acts Interpretation Act 1954* (Qld) s 27A(3B), (6).

116 *Acts Interpretation Act 1954* (Qld) s 27A(8A), (8B); *Acts Interpretation Act 1931* (Tas) s 23AA(5A) (only covers change in holder of delegator office and provides that the delegation continues); *Legislation Act 2001* (ACT) s 241 (simply provides that the delegation does not end). See *Kelly v Watson* (1985) 10 FCR 305, 318–9 (Neaves J). The *Legislation Interpretation Act 2021* (SA) s 43(11) provides that a delegation made by, or to, the holder of a particular office does not cease to have effect merely because the person who held the office when the function was delegated ceases to do so.

117 *Acts Interpretation Act 1954* (Qld) s 27A(10A); *Legislation Act 2001* (ACT) s 238.

118 *Interpretation Act 1987* (NSW) s 49(10); *Acts Interpretation Act 1954* (Qld) s 27A(11), (12); *Legislation Interpretation Act 2021* (SA) s 43(9); *Acts Interpretation Act 1931* (Tas) s 23AA(7); *Legislation Act 2001* (ACT) s 231(1).

119 See *Carltona Ltd v Commissioner of Works* (1943) 2 All ER 560, 563 (Lord Greene MR). For an application of this principle, in a context where there existed a power of delegation, see *O'Reilly v State Bank of Victoria Commissioners* (1983) 153 CLR 1.

120 The *Acts Interpretation Act 1901* (Cth) s 34AAB provides for a Minister to authorise another Minister or a member of the Executive Council to act on the Minister's behalf in the performance of ministerial functions or duties or the exercise of ministerial powers.

Provisions commonly included provide for:

- personal service on a natural person;[121]
- service on a natural person by leaving the document at the person's residential or business address;[122]
- service on a natural person by post;[123]
- service on a body corporate by leaving the document at the head office, a registered office or a principal office;[124] and
- service on a body corporate by post.[125]

Section 39(1)(a)(ii) and (b) of the *Acts Interpretation Act 1954* (Qld) and ss 247(1)(c), 248(1)(c) and 250(3) and (4) of the *Legislation Act 2001* (ACT) provide for service on both natural persons and bodies corporate by fax. The latter Act also provides for such service to be effected by email.[126] The provisions of s 51(2)(c) and (3)(b) of the *Legislation Interpretation Act 2021* (SA) cover electronic service on both natural persons and bodies corporate.

The *Interpretation Act 1987* (NSW) and the *Interpretation of Legislation Act 1984* (Vic) do not provide for methods of service but do specify how service by post may be effected and when it is deemed to have been effected.[127] Section 30A of the *Acts Interpretation Act 1931* (Tas) provides for electronic service of infringement notices. Section 249 of the *Legislation Act 2001* (ACT) provides for the service of documents on agencies (administrative units, statutory office holders and other entities established for a public purpose under a law).

(h) **Appointment, suspension and removal of officers**

Legislation commonly provides for the appointment of officers of various kinds to carry out a scheme established by the legislation. Such officers include public servants, statutory office holders

---

121 *Acts Interpretation Act 1901* (Cth) s 28A(1)(a)(i); *Acts Interpretation Act 1954* (Qld) s 39(1)(a)(i); *Legislation Interpretation Act 2021* (SA) s 51(2)(a); *Acts Interpretation Act 1931* (Tas) s 29AB(1)(a)(i); *Interpretation Act 1984* (WA) s 76(a); *Legislation Act 2001* (ACT) s 247(1)(a); *Interpretation Act 1978* (NT) s 25(1)(a)(i), (iii) (includes service on a person authorised by the recipient to receive the document).

122 *Acts Interpretation Act 1954* (Qld) s 39(1)(a)(ii); *Legislation Interpretation Act 2021* (SA) s 51(2)(b) (also covers a physical address designated by the natural person for service); *Acts Interpretation Act 1931* (Tas) s 29AB(1)(a)(ii); *Interpretation Act 1984* (WA) s 76(c); *Legislation Act 2001* (ACT) ss 247(1)(e), 250(5); *Interpretation Act 1978* (NT) s 25(1)(d).

123 *Acts Interpretation Act 1901* (Cth) ss 28A(1)(a)(ii), 29; *Acts Interpretation Act 1954* (Qld) ss 39(1)(a)(ii), 39A; *Legislation Interpretation Act 2021* (SA) s 51(2); *Acts Interpretation Act 1931* (Tas) ss 29AB(1)(a)(ii), 30; *Interpretation Act 1984* (WA) ss 76(b), 75; *Legislation Act 2001* (ACT) ss 247(1)(b), 250(1); *Interpretation Act 1978* (NT) s 25(1)(b).

124 *Acts Interpretation Act 1901* (Cth) s 28A(1)(b); *Acts Interpretation Act 1954* (Qld) s 39(1)(b); *Legislation Interpretation Act 2021* (SA) s 51(3)(a) (covers registered office and another physical address designated by the body corporate for service or the last known place of business of the body corporate if another physical address is not designated); *Acts Interpretation Act 1931* (Tas) s 29AB(1)(b); *Interpretation Act 1984* (WA) s 76(d) (principal place of business or principal office in the state); *Legislation Act 2001* (ACT) ss 248(1)(e), 250(5) (registered office or other business address); *Interpretation Act 1978* (NT) s 25(1)(d), (4) (business address).

125 *Acts Interpretation Act 1901* (Cth) ss 28A(1)(b), 29; *Acts Interpretation Act 1954* (Qld) ss 39(1)(b), 39A; *Legislation Interpretation Act 2021* (SA) s 51(3)(a); *Acts Interpretation Act 1931* (Tas) ss 29AB(1)(b), 30; *Interpretation Act 1984* (WA) ss 76(b), 75; *Legislation Act 2001* (ACT) ss 248(1)(b), 250(1); *Interpretation Act 1978* (NT) s 25(1)(b), (2).

126 *Legislation Act 2001* (ACT) ss 247(1)(d), 248(1)(d), 250(3)–(4).

127 *Interpretation Act 1987* (NSW) s 76; *Interpretation of Legislation Act 1984* (Vic) s 49. Similar provision is made by the *Legislation Interpretation Act 2021* (SA) s 51(4), (5).

and employees or directors of an entity established by or under the legislation. Interpretation Acts in each jurisdiction address issues such as the procedure for appointing them and the circumstances in which they may be suspended or dismissed from office. This saves the need for express provisions in each individual item of legislation unless something different is proposed, such as limiting the circumstances in which an officer may be dismissed or suspended from office.

These are some common provisions relating to appointment etc:

- a power to appoint that includes a power to remove or suspend;[128]
- a power to appoint that includes a power to make an acting appointment to the office;[129]
- a power to appoint that includes a power to reappoint;[130] and
- protection from invalidity for things done, or purportedly done, by an appointee in a range of circumstances, including a defect or irregularity connected with the appointment.[131]

The *Acts Interpretation Act 1901* (Cth) (s 33A), *Acts Interpretation Act 1954* (Qld) (s 24B), *Interpretation of Legislation Act 1984* (Vic) (s 41AA) and *Legislation Act 2001* (ACT) (div 19.3.2) contain a range of provisions dealing with acting appointments made under a specific power contained in another Act, including (except in Victoria) a time limit of 12 months on acting in a vacant office. Under the *Interpretation Act 1987* (NSW) (s 46), *Acts Interpretation Act 1954* (Qld) (s 24A), *Legislation Interpretation Act 2021* (SA) (s 41(2)(a)), *Interpretation Act 1984* (WA) (s 53) and *Legislation Act 2001* (ACT) (s 207) an appointment may be of a person by name or of the person holding a particular office. Section 21A of the *Acts Interpretation Act 1931* (Tas) provides for eligible persons to be able to perform the duties of an office, where the office holder is unable to do so or the office is vacant, if directed to do so in writing by the appointing authority.

Section 40 of the *Interpretation Act 1978* (NT) provides that a person acting in an office (including a ministerial office) during the absence or inability of the office holder may continue to act for up to 12 months after the office holder ceases to hold office, unless the authority to act is revoked earlier.

---

128 *Acts Interpretation Act 1901* (Cth) s 33(4); *Interpretation Act 1987* (NSW) s 47(1)(b)(i), (2); *Acts Interpretation Act 1954* (Qld) s 25(1)(b), (2); *Legislation Interpretation Act 2021* (SA) s 41(2)(c); *Acts Interpretation Act 1931* (Tas) s 21(1)(a); *Interpretation of Legislation Act 1984* (Vic) s 41(1)(b)–(c), (3); *Interpretation Act 1984* (WA) s 52(1)(a); *Legislation Act 2001* (ACT) s 208; *Interpretation Act 1978* (NT) s 44. In *Director-General of Education v Suttling* (1987) 162 CLR 427 it was held by Brennan J (Mason ACJ and Deane J concurring) that the power of removal conferred by the *Interpretation Act 1987* (NSW) was general in nature and could not be exercised in derogation of rights created under the specific Act under which an officer is appointed.

129 *Acts Interpretation Act 1901* (Cth) s 33(4); *Interpretation Act 1987* (NSW) s 47(1)(b)(ii)–(iv), (3); *Acts Interpretation Act 1954* (Qld) s 25(1)(b)(ii), (iv), (v), (3), (4); *Legislation Interpretation Act 2021* (SA) s 41(2)(e), (3); *Acts Interpretation Act 1931* (Tas) s 21(1)(c)–(d), (1B); *Interpretation of Legislation Act 1984* (Vic) s 41(1)(a), (d), (2), (3); *Interpretation Act 1984* (WA) s 52(1)(b), (2); *Legislation Act 2001* (ACT) s 209, div 19.3.2; *Interpretation Act 1978* (NT) s 44A.

130 *Acts Interpretation Act 1901* (Cth) s 33AA; *Interpretation Act 1987* (NSW) s 47(1)(a) (power may be exercised from time to time); *Acts Interpretation Act 1954* (Qld) s 25(1)(c) (sch 1 defines 'appoint' as including 'reappoint'); *Legislation Interpretation Act 2021* (SA) s 41(2)(d) (power to reappoint person suspended or removed); *Acts Interpretation Act 1931* (Tas) s 21(1)(b), (3) (power to reappoint person suspended or removed or at end of fixed term); *Interpretation of Legislation Act 1984* (Vic) s 40 (power may be exercised from time to time); *Interpretation Act 1984* (WA) s 52(1)(a); *Legislation Act 2001* (ACT) s 208 (dictionary, pt 1 – defines 'appoint' as including 'reappoint'); *Interpretation Act 1978* (NT) s 41(1) (power may be exercised from time to time).

131 *Acts Interpretation Act 1901* (Cth) s 33AB; *Acts Interpretation Act 1954* (Qld) s 26 (limited to appointment defect or irregularity); *Legislation Interpretation Act 2021* (SA) s 41(8); *Interpretation Act 1984* (WA) ss 52(3) (limited to occasion for acting appointment not having arisen or having ceased) and 57(b) (limited to appointment defect); *Legislation Act 2001* (ACT) s 212 (limited to appointment defect or irregularity). See further **[37.4]**.

General interpretative rules

[25.5] **Interpretation Acts contain interpretative rules that apply generally to legislation and that are intended to help readers understand the operation of legislation**

Parliament may, as it chooses, set out interpretative rules for legislation passed by it. Other chapters have looked at such things as

- rules directed at general approaches to statutory interpretation;[132]
- the use by courts of extrinsic material in interpreting legislation;[133]
- the material that forms part of an Act;[134]
- the use of examples;[135]
- the commencement of Acts and the exercise of powers between their passing and their commencement;[136]
- the numbering and citation of Acts;[137]
- drafting styles;[138]
- the principle that a statute is always speaking;[139]
- reading and construing Acts subject to the *Constitution*;[140]
- the effect of non-compliance with statutory requirements;[141]
- the application of Acts to the Crown;[142]
- rules for construing references to places;[143] and
- delegated legislation.[144]

These rules, contained in Interpretation Acts, assist readers in understanding how Acts operate.

This chapter looks at a group of other interpretative rules commonly found in Interpretation Acts.[145]

(a) **Effect of amendment and repeal on pre-existing rights and obligations**

Chapter 39 discusses the common law presumption against the retrospective operation of legislation and the related common law rules that apply upon the repeal or amendment of an

132 See Part II, especially chapter 8.

133 See Part V.

134 See chapters 13 and 20.

135 See **[13.14]**.

136 See chapter 12.

137 See **[13.7]**, **[13.12]**, **[13.16]**.

138 See **[10.7]**, **[16]**.

139 See chapter 19 and especially chapter 24.

140 See the legislative provisions relating to severance at **[25.5](e)**. These provisions also contain the presumption about reading and construing Acts subject to the legislative power of the respective parliaments. For a broader discussion of the presumption see **[32.8]**.

141 See chapter 37.

142 See chapter 40.

143 See chapter 41.

144 See chapter 43.

145 Provisions contained in Interpretation Acts are referred to in various other chapters. See chapters 16, 19, 20, 32, 36, 37, 39, 41, 43.

Act. Informed by those rules,[146] Interpretation Acts in each jurisdiction also contain provisions expressly dealing with the effect on pre-existing rights and obligations of repealing or (except in Tasmania, Western Australia and the Northern Territory) amending[147] an Act.

While the language used in these provisions is not uniform,[148] there are several common propositions that can be extracted from them.

- The repeal of an Act that repealed another Act does not revive that other Act, unless express provision is made for revival.[149]
- The repeal or amendment of an Act does not revive anything not in force or existing at the time at which the repeal or amendment takes effect.[150]
- The repeal or amendment of an Act does not affect the previous operation of the Act, or anything duly done or suffered under it.[151]
- The repeal or amendment of an Act does not affect any right, privilege, obligation or liability acquired, accrued or incurred under it.[152]

---

146 See *Spear v Hallenstein* [2018] VSC 169, [53] (Niall JA). In *ADCO Constructions Pty Ltd v Goudappel* (2014) 254 CLR 1 it was accepted by French CJ, Crennan, Kiefel and Keane JJ that what was contained in the *Interpretation Act 1987* (NSW) s 30(1)(c) (amendment or repeal of an Act does not affect any right, privilege, obligation or liability acquired, accrued or incurred under the Act, unless the contrary intention appears) 'mirrors the common law' on the retrospective operation of statutes: at 15 [27].

147 Common law rules on retrospectivity apply, in these jurisdictions, to the amendment of an Act.

148 *Acts Interpretation Act 1901* (Cth) s 7; *Interpretation Act 1987* (NSW) ss 28, 30 (extends also to statutory rules); *Acts Interpretation Act 1954* (Qld) ss 19, 20, 20A; *Legislation Interpretation Act 2021* (SA) s 32 (extends also to legislative instruments); *Acts Interpretation Act 1931* (Tas) ss 14, 16 (extends also to regulations, rules and by-laws but applies only to repeals); *Interpretation of Legislation Act 1984* (Vic) s 14 (Acts), s 28 (subordinate instruments); *Interpretation Act 1984* (WA) ss 34, 37, 39 (extends also to subordinate legislation but applies only to repeals); *Legislation Act 2001* (ACT) ss 84, 86, 88 (extends also to statutory instruments); *Interpretation Act 1978* (NT) ss 11, 12 (applies only to repeals).

149 At common law when an Act was repealed, it was considered (except as to transactions past and closed) as if it had never existed. See *Surtees v Ellison* (1829) 9 B & C 750, 752; 109 ER 278, 279 (Lord Tenterden CJ). As to the common law rule on revival of a repealed statute on the repeal of the repealing statute, see *Tattle v Grimwood* (1826) 3 Bing 493, 496; 130 ER 603, 604–5 (Best CJ). Note that under s 109 of the *Australian Constitution*, upon the repeal of a federal Act that was inconsistent with a state Act, the state Act revives. See *Butler v A-G (Vic)* (1961) 106 CLR 268, 274 (Fullagar J), 283 (Taylor J), 286 (Menzies J and Windeyer J), 278 (Kitto J).

150 This proposition, while it overlaps with the one stated immediately before it above, is broader in scope. It has been held to prevent the revival of common law (see *Callanan v B* (2005) 1 Qd R 348, 354 [9] (McPherson JA)). At common law upon the repeal of an Act that displaced common law, the common law was revived. See *Marshall v Smith* (1907) 4 CLR 1617, 1634–5 (Barton J).

151 It was held in *Heston and Isleworth UDC v Grout* [1897] 2 Ch 306 that a notice given under a repealed Act was a thing duly done that was preserved by a provision of this kind in the *Interpretation Act 1889* (UK). See also *ISPT Nominees Pty Ltd v Chief Commissioner of State Revenue* (2003) 53 ATR 527, 570–1 [170] (Barrett J). A provision to this effect in the *Interpretation Act 1897* (NSW) s 8 was held in *Smith v Motor Discounts Ltd* (1935) 54 CLR 107 to continue the invalidation effected by a repealed Act of a personal covenant entered into by a mortgagor.

152 On the terms of the provisions, a right or privilege must have been acquired or have accrued. This may require some step to have been taken before the repeal or amendment of the relevant legislation. In *Total (Australia) Ltd v Registrar of Companies* [1969] VR 821 it was held that a company had not acquired a right to lodge a notice without a fee where it did not seek to lodge the notice until after a fee had been prescribed for a lodgement. In *Esber v Commonwealth* (1992) 174 CLR 430 the provision to this effect in the *Acts Interpretation Act 1901* (Cth) was held to protect a right to have a decision reviewed by a tribunal where a review application was made before the repeal of the provision giving that right. On the terms of the provisions also a liability must have been incurred. In *Ogden Industries Pty Ltd v Lucas* (1967) 116 CLR 537

- The repeal or amendment of an Act does not affect any penalty, forfeiture or punishment incurred in respect of any offence committed against the Act.[153]
- The repeal or amendment of an Act does not affect any investigation, legal proceeding or remedy in respect of any such right, privilege, obligation, liability, penalty, forfeiture or punishment and any such investigation, legal proceeding or remedy may be instituted, continued or enforced, and any such penalty, forfeiture or punishment may be imposed, as if the Act had not been repealed or amended.[154]

These provisions avoid the need to include specific transitional provisions to provide for the matters covered by them. Their intent is to preserve accrued rights and obligations, necessitating an indication of contrary intention in the repealing or amending Act if a different outcome is intended. The inclusion of a comprehensive set of transitional provisions in a repealing or amending Act may displace the Interpretation Act provisions from having any operative effect.[155]

On their face the Victorian provisions, ss 14 and 28 of the *Interpretation of Legislation Act 1984* (Vic), are only excluded if a contrary intention 'expressly appears'.[156] However, in *Mitchell v Latrobe Regional Hospital*[157] the Victorian Court of Appeal held that the word 'expressly' in s 14(2) is 'not be read narrowly: "expressly" means "plainly", "clearly", or "by necessary implication" and, as such, does not require a line by line reference to every part of a piece of existing legislation'.[158]

Windeyer J stated that the provision to this effect in the *Acts Interpretation Act 1901* (Cth) 'describes a liability having become complete by past events rather than a situation in which some future event must occur to make the effect of past events create a completed liability': at 584. In *Byrne v Garrisson* [1965] VR 523 (Gowans J) it was held that the word 'liability' in the relevant provision in the *Acts Interpretation Act 1958* (Vic) embraced criminal as well as civil liability: 528–9.

153 Read together with the dot points both immediately before it above and after it, this allows a prosecution to be commenced after the repeal of an enactment for an offence committed against that enactment before the repeal. See *Byrne v Garrisson* [1965] VR 523.

154 On the terms of the provisions, the investigation, legal proceeding or remedy must be in respect of a right, privilege, obligation or liability acquired, accrued or incurred, or a penalty, forfeiture or punishment incurred, before the repeal or amendment. See *Esber v Commonwealth* (1992) 174 CLR 430, 439 (Mason CJ, Deane, Toohey and Gaudron JJ). However, the procedure to be followed is not preserved. See *Yrttiaho v Public Curator of Queensland* (1971) 125 CLR 228, 244–5 (Gibbs J); *Rodway v The Queen* (1990) 169 CLR 515, 523–4 (the Court).

155 See *GF Heublein and Bro Inc v Continental Liqueurs Pty Ltd* (1962) 109 CLR 153, 161 (Dixon CJ, Taylor and Windeyer JJ). Section 37(2) of the *Interpretation Act 1984* (WA) provides that the inclusion of express saving provisions in a repealing enactment does not prejudice the operation of s 37(1) (general savings on repeals) with respect to the effect of those repeals. See *Dossett v TKJ Nominees Pty Ltd* (2003) 218 CLR 1, 13–14 [41]–[45] (Gummow, Hayne and Heydon JJ). In that case it was held that specific savings provisions in a repealing Act did not manifest an intention to oust the operation of s 37(1) of the *Interpretation Act 1984* (WA) as the phrase "unless the contrary intention appears" in s 37(1) had to be read with s 37(2) of that Act, thereby allowing s 37(1) to have any additional operation of which it was capable.

156 See also *Acts Interpretation Act 1931* (Tas) ss 14(1), 16(1), (2). The ACT provisions (*Legislation Act 2001* (ACT) ss 84, 86, 88) by s 6(2) of that Act 'may be displaced expressly or by a manifest contrary intention'. The relevant provisions in other jurisdictions may be displaced by a contrary intention simpliciter.

157 (2016) 51 VR 581, 595–6 [64] (Osborne and Beach JJA, Forrest AJA).

158 The reasons for judgment records at 593 [54] that counsel for the respondent did point out that 'other provisions in the [*Interpretation of Legislation Act*] use the expression "unless the contrary intention appears". The word "expressly", when added to that phrase, must give it a more demanding meaning'. This submission was not accepted.

(b) Statutory powers may be exercised from time to time

Section 33(1) of the *Acts Interpretation Act 1901* (Cth) provides that, subject to a contrary intention, where an Act confers a power or function or imposes a duty, then the power may be exercised, and the function or duty must be performed, from time to time as occasion requires. There are equivalent provisions in each other Australian jurisdiction.[159] The purpose of these provisions is to exclude the common law rule 'that prima facie a power is exhausted when it has been exercised'.[160]

An example of the operation of such provisions is found in *Pfeiffer v Stevens*.[161] The issue before the High Court in this case was whether a sunset period gazetted by the Minister under s 860(2) of the *Local Government Act 1993* (Qld) for the purposes of an interim local law made under s 860(1) of that Act could be extended by the Minister gazetting a further period under s 860(2). Gleeson CJ and Hayne J held that s 860(2) authorised the Minister to extend the operation of an interim local law more than once, relying on the provision in s 23(1) of the *Acts Interpretation Act 1954* (Qld). McHugh J held that the objects of the *Local Government Act 1993* (Qld) implied a power of extension but that s 23(1) 'puts the matter beyond controversy'.[162]

(c) Calculation of age, distance and time

Where legislation makes having reached a specified age a relevant criterion for something, it is necessary to have a clear rule for calculating when a person reaches that age. In all Australian jurisdictions a person attains an age expressed in years at the beginning of the anniversary of their birth – that is, at the start of their birthday.[163] Such a rule is unsurprising but at common law a different rule applied, with the age being attained at the beginning of the day immediately before their birthday.[164] Up until the commencement of the *Legislation Interpretation Act 2021* (SA) on 1 January 2022, this was the rule that applied in South Australia.[165]

The South Australian and Northern Territory provisions include a subsection directed at clarifying the rule for persons born on 29 February in a leap year. However, each provides for a different result. In South Australia the end result is that for a person born on 29 February, the anniversary of their birth in a year that is not a leap year is 1 March whereas in the Northern Territory it is

---

159 *Interpretation Act 1987* (NSW) ss 47(1)(a), 48(1); *Acts Interpretation Act 1954* (Qld) s 23(1); *Legislation Interpretation Act 2021* (SA) s 37(1) (read with the definition of 'function' in s 4); *Acts Interpretation Act 1931* (Tas) s 20(a); *Interpretation of Legislation Act 1984* (Vic) s 40(a); *Interpretation Act 1984* (WA) s 48; *Legislation Act 2001* (ACT) s 197; *Interpretation Act 1978* (NT) s 41(1).

160 *Day v Hunkin* (1938) 61 CLR 65, 73 (Latham CJ). See also *Minister for Indigenous Affairs v MJD Foundation Ltd* (2017) 250 FCR 31, 40–2 [24]–[31] (Perram J), 64–5 [140]–[142] (Mortimer J).

161 (2001) 209 CLR 57. Gleeson CJ and Hayne JJ stated that the 'purpose of such an interpretative provision is to permit economy of language': at 65.

162 Ibid 72. Gummow and Kirby JJ held that s 23(1) was excluded by a contrary intention in the *Local Government Act 1993* (Qld).

163 *Acts Interpretation Act 1901* (Cth) s 37A; *Interpretation Act 1987* (NSW) s 37; *Acts Interpretation Act 1954* (Qld) s 38A; *Legislation Interpretation Act 2021* (SA) s 49; *Age of Majority Act 1973* (Tas) s 4; *Age of Majority Act 1977* (Vic) s 2; *Age of Majority Act 1972* (WA) s 4; *Legislation Act 2001* (ACT) s 149; *Interpretation Act 1978* (NT) s 30.

164 *Prowse v McIntyre* (1961) 111 CLR 264.

165 *A-G v Smith* (1985) 39 SASR 311, 315 (King CJ), White and Millhouse JJ agreeing at 316. The statement in the second reading speech for the Legislation Interpretation Bill 2021 (SA) that the new provision 'does not change the (unstated) current position' is incorrect. See *Legislative Council Hansard*, 6 May 2021, 3369 (the Hon RI Lucas); *House of Assembly Hansard*, 26 August 2021, 6716 (the Hon VA Chapman).

28 February. The Northern Territory provision in effect is a statutory restatement of the common law rule that a person attains an age on the beginning of the day before their birthday.[166]

Despite there being no specific provision, the South Australian position applies in all Australian jurisdictions except the Northern Territory.[167]

Unless another way of measuring distance is intended for the purposes of an Act or delegated legislation,[168] the distance between two places is measured in all Australian jurisdictions in a straight line on a horizontal plane.[169]

Frequently, legislation enables or requires something to be done within a specified period. In the absence of a clear rule the calculation of that period can give rise to disputation. For example, if something could only be done within six months after a particular event, is the day of that event included or excluded or is the calculation made from the actual time at which that event occurs? After a period of conflicting outcomes in cases dealing with the calculation of time,[170] in *Lester v Garland*[171] the Court of Appeal in England held, on ordinary interpretation principles, that the day of the event was to be excluded. This avoided backdating the reckoning of the period to the beginning of the day on which the event occurred, and it was consistent with the common law approach of not taking account of fractions of a day.

The Interpretation Acts in each Australian jurisdiction contain provisions for calculating periods of time that apply in the absence of a contrary intention.

Under those Acts, where a period of time is expressed to be reckoned from a specified day,[172] that day is not included in the period.[173] With the exception of New South Wales and Tasmania, which do have an express provision in their Interpretation Act, where a period of time is expressed to end at, on or with, or to be reckoned to, a specified day, that day is included in the period.[174]

---

166 *Prowse v McIntyre* (1961) 111 CLR 264.

167 *PM v Childrens Court of the ACT* (2018) 336 FLR 379.

168 In *Re Bonner and Director-General of Health* [1983] AATA 239 determining where the nearest specialist was located was determined by reference to the shortest practical route.

169 *Acts Interpretation Act 1901* (Cth) s 35; *Interpretation Act 1987* (NSW) s 38 (for Acts passed on or after 1 September 1987); *Acts Interpretation Act 1954* (Qld) s 37; *Legislation Interpretation Act 2021* (SA) s 48; *Acts Interpretation Act 1931* (Tas) s 28; *Interpretation of Legislation Act 1984* (Vic) s 43; *Interpretation Act 1984* (WA) s 65; *Legislation Act 2001* (ACT) s 150; *Interpretation Act 1978* (NT) s 27. This mode of measurement was settled as part of English common law in *Lake v Butler* (1855) 5 El & Bl 92, 98–9; 119 ER 416, 418 (Erle J) as being more easily ascertainable than the nearest practical road, which had been the earlier rule as applied, for example, in *Wing v Earle* (1653) Cro Eliz 212, 78 ER 468. Prior to their repeal, the earlier rule had been adopted by the *Interpretation Act 1897* (NSW) s 35(1) and *Acts Interpretation Act 1954* (Qld) s 37.

170 See Chad Jacobi, *Interpretation Acts Origins and Meaning* (Thomson Reuters, 2019) 183–6. See also *Watson v Issell* (1890) 16 VLR 607, 609–10 (Higinbotham CJ).

171 (1808) 15 Ves Jun 248; 33 ER 748.

172 A day could be a given day or the day on which a given act is done or other event takes place.

173 *Acts Interpretation Act 1901* (Cth) s 36(1), table, item 5; *Interpretation Act 1987* (NSW) s 36(1); *Acts Interpretation Act 1954* (Qld) s 38(1); *Legislation Interpretation Act 2021* (SA) s 44(1), table, item 3; *Acts Interpretation Act 1931* (Tas) s 29(1); *Interpretation of Legislation Act 1984* (Vic) s 44(1); *Interpretation Act 1984* (WA) s 61(1)(b); *Legislation Act 2001* (ACT) s 151(2); *Interpretation Act 1978* (NT) s 28(1). In *Forster v Jododex Australia Pty Ltd* (1972) 127 CLR 421 the High Court held that there was a prima facie rule of construction that the term of a lease or licence, which is expressed to commence from a specified day, commences at midnight on the specified day and lasts during the whole anniversary of that day.

174 *Acts Interpretation Act 1901* (Cth) s 36(1), table, items 3, 4; *Acts Interpretation Act 1954* (Qld) s 38(1); *Legislation Interpretation Act 2021* (SA) s 44(1), table, items 4, 5; *Interpretation of Legislation Act 1984* (Vic) s 44(2); *Interpretation Act 1984* (WA) s 61(1)(d); *Legislation Act 2001* (ACT) s 151(2); *Interpretation Act 1978* (NT) s 28(1A).

However, where the period for doing a thing ends on a day that is a Saturday or Sunday or a public holiday in the place in which the thing is to be or may be done, the period extends to the next day that is not a Saturday or Sunday or a public holiday in that place.[175]

The *Acts Interpretation Act 1901* (Cth) and the *Legislation Interpretation Act 2021* (SA) each contain a table setting out rules for calculating certain other periods. A period expressed as beginning at, on or with a specified day includes that day.[176] A period expressed as beginning after a specified day does not include that day.[177] A period expressed to end before a specified day does not include that day.[178]

There are, however, some differences between the jurisdictions. In Commonwealth and South Australian legislation a period of time expressed to occur between two days includes both days whereas both those days are excluded in ACT legislation.[179] In Western Australia where there is a reference to a number of clear days, or 'at least' or 'not less than' a specified number of days, between two events, both days on which the events happen are excluded, while if not so expressed, the day of the first event is excluded and the day of the second event is included.[180] Tasmania provides that in calculating a period of time, not exceeding six days, Sundays, statutory holidays and public holidays are excluded.[181]

While these provisions for calculating periods of time apply in the absence of a contrary intention, in *Waterfront Place Pty Ltd v Minister for Planning*[182] the Victorian Court of Appeal held, in relation to the provision of the Victorian Act allowing an act to be done on the next business day where the period expires on a holiday,[183] that 'a court should be very slow to find an unstated

175 *Acts Interpretation Act 1901* (Cth) s 36(2), (3); *Interpretation Act 1987* (NSW) s 36(2); *Acts Interpretation Act 1954* (Qld) s 38(2), (3), (5); *Legislation Interpretation Act 2021* (SA) s 44(2), (2a); *Acts Interpretation Act 1931* (Tas) s 29(3); *Interpretation of Legislation Act 1984* (Vic) s 44(3), (4); *Interpretation Act 1984* (WA) s 61(1)(e), (2); *Legislation Act 2001* (ACT) s 151A; *Interpretation Act 1978* (NT) s 28(2). In *Waterfront Place Pty Ltd v Minister for Planning* (2019) 59 VR 556, 560 [12] (Maxwell ACJ, Forrest and Emerton JJ) the Victorian Court of Appeal stated that this extension rule was 'a rule of practical commonsense, reflecting the critical difference between weekdays and holidays, and is one which is relied on by those needing to comply with time limits (and their advisers)'. See *Onebev Pty Ltd v Encore Beverages Pty Ltd* (2016) 50 VR 106 as to the interpretation of *Acts Interpretation Act 1901* (Cth) s 36(3) (definition of 'holiday').

176 *Acts Interpretation Act 1901* (Cth) s 36(1), table, item 2; *Legislation Interpretation Act 2021* (SA) s 44(1), table, item 2. See also *Interpretation Act 1984* (WA) s 61(1)(a), *Legislation Act 2001* (ACT) s 151(2), table, item 1. However, *Acts Interpretation Act 1954* (Qld) s 38(1) provides that in calculating a period beginning on a specified day, that day is excluded.

177 *Acts Interpretation Act 1901* (Cth) s 36(1), table, item 6; *Legislation Interpretation Act 2021* (SA) s 44(1), table, item 6. See also *Interpretation Act 1984* (WA) s 61(1)(b), *Legislation Act 2001* (ACT) s 151(2), table, item 2 (s 151(3) provides, however, that a thing, that must or may be done within a specified period after a specified day, may be done on the specified day).

178 *Acts Interpretation Act 1901* (Cth) s 36(1), table, item 7; *Legislation Interpretation Act 2021* (SA) s 44(1), table, item 7. See also *Interpretation Act 1984* (WA) s 61(1)(c), *Legislation Act 2001* (ACT) s 151(2), table, item 4.

179 Compare the *Acts Interpretation Act 1901* (Cth) s 36(1), table, item 1 and *Legislation Interpretation Act 2021* (SA) s 44(1), table, item 1 with the *Legislation Act 2001* (ACT) s 151(2), table, item 5.

180 *Interpretation Act 1984* (WA) s 61(1)(f), (g). The *Acts Interpretation Act 1931* (Tas) s 29(2) and *Acts Interpretation Act 1954* (Qld) s 38(1)(a) have a similar rule with respect to clear days or where the term 'at least' is used in relation to the specified number of days. In *Forster v Jododex Australia Pty Ltd* (1972) 127 CLR 421 the High Court held that an instrument using the words 'at least' or 'not less than' in prescribing a period between two events should, in the absence of a contrary intention, be regarded as indicating that a clear period of time must expire between the two events.

181 *Acts Interpretation Act 1931* (Tas) s 29(6).

182 (2019) 59 VR 556.

183 *Interpretation of Legislation Act 1984* (Vic) s 44(3).

contrary intention' to such a rule of practical commonsense and that the 'threshold requirement for contrary intention . . . should be stringently applied'.[184]

Some Interpretation Acts contain other provisions. In New South Wales there is a general provision allowing a power conferred on a person or body to extend the period of time prescribed or allowed for the doing of a thing, to be exercised after the period of time has expired.[185] In Queensland, South Australia and Western Australia there is a provision stating that if no time is provided or allowed for doing a thing, the thing is to be done as soon as possible.[186]

(d) Compliance with forms

Legislation, whether primary or secondary, may prescribe a form to be used for a particular purpose.[187] This gives rise to an issue as to the effect of using a form that departs in some way from the prescribed form. While there are some differences in wording, the Interpretation Act in each jurisdiction provides that strict compliance with the prescribed form is not required and substantial compliance is sufficient.[188] Some specifically require that any deviation is not misleading.[189] Some contain additional provisions mandating compliance with a requirement for a form to be completed in a specified manner or to contain specified information.[190]

What constitutes substantial compliance depends on the circumstances. So long as no ambiguity or misunderstanding is created, it is immaterial that prescribed language is not used.[191] Specifying in a form a particular provision of an Act may, however, be necessary for

---

184 *Waterfront Place Pty Ltd v Minister for Planning* (2019) 59 VR 556, 560 [12]. The Court stated: 'Axiomatically, both the language used in statutes and their interpretation by courts should be such as will promote certainty, comprehensibility and predictability. These are foundational requirements of the rule of law. Those considerations are, we think, of particular importance in relation to provisions of this kind, which are designed to provide clarity and certainty to individuals and corporations – and public officials – engaged in a wide range of activities. A person who is aware of the extension rule, and who sees nothing in the provisions imposing the time limit to suggest that the rule does not apply, should be able to proceed on the assumption that it does': at 560 [13].

185 *Interpretation Act 1987* (NSW) s 36(3).

186 *Acts Interpretation Act 1954* (Qld) s 38(4). The *Legislation Interpretation Act 2021* (SA) s 44(3) uses the expression 'as soon as is reasonably practical' and the *Interpretation Act 1984* (WA) s 63 uses the expression 'with all convenient speed'.

187 It is now not uncommon, however, to see a provision to the effect that a form is in the 'prescribed form' if it complies with a specified number of requirements. See, eg, *Children's Services Regulations 2020* (Vic) reg 127 and *Gaming Machine Regulations 2020* (SA) sch 1.

188 *Acts Interpretation Act 1901* (Cth) s 25C; *Interpretation Act 1987* (NSW) s 80(1); *Acts Interpretation Act 1954* (Qld) s 48A(1); *Legislation Interpretation Act 2021* (SA) s 52 (forms to the same effect are sufficient provided that deviations are not calculated to mislead); *Acts Interpretation Act 1931* (Tas) s 47(2) (forms to the like effect are sufficient compliance provided that any deviation is not calculated to mislead or prejudice a person concerned); *Interpretation of Legislation Act 1984* (Vic) s 53 (forms in or to the like effect are sufficient in law); *Interpretation Act 1984* (WA) s 74 (deviations not materially affecting the substance or likely to mislead do not invalidate the form); *Legislation Act 2001* (ACT) s 255(4); *Interpretation Act 1978* (NT) s 68 (substantial compliance, or such compliance as the circumstances of a particular case allow, is sufficient).

189 *Legislation Interpretation Act 2021* (SA) s 52; *Acts Interpretation Act 1931* (Tas) s 47(2); *Interpretation Act 1984* (WA) s 74; *Legislation Act 2001* (ACT) s 255(4).

190 *Interpretation Act 1987* (NSW) s 80(2); *Acts Interpretation Act 1954* (Qld) s 48A(2); *Legislation Act 2001* (ACT) s 255(5)(c), (d).

191 *A-G (NSW) v Markisic* [2012] NSWSC 433, [92] (Schmidt J). In that case a notice to admit facts used the words 'does not admit', and not the prescribed word 'disputes', in relation to identified facts.

there to be substantial compliance.[192] The purpose for which the form is to be used may affect the degree of flexibility in language allowed.[193] A form that achieves the same practical effect as the prescribed form may be substantially compliant.[194]

These provisions are applicable even when the empowering legislation provides that the prescribed form 'must' be used.[195]

(e) **Severance**

If a provision of an Act is beyond the legislative power of the Parliament, while other provisions of the Act are within that power, there are Interpretation Acts provisions in each jurisdiction which apply. They ensure that, as far as possible, so much of the Act is preserved as is within power, while any part beyond power is to be severed.[196]

Similar provision is expressly made in each jurisdiction, other than the Australian Capital Territory and the Northern Territory, for items of delegated legislation that are beyond the legislative power of the Parliament.[197] South Australia, the Australian Capital Territory and the Northern Territory each has a provision requiring items of delegated legislation to be interpreted as operating to the full extent of, but not to exceed, the power given by the Act under which they are made. At the same time they aim to preserve so much of an instrument as is within that power.[198] This would cover a situation where a provision of delegated legislation exceeds a power purportedly given by the enabling Act, but not validly given, because for the Act to give that power would be beyond the legislative power of the Parliament.

There are also provisions in each jurisdiction, except Tasmania and Western Australia, achieving a similar outcome for items of delegated legislation any portion of which is beyond the power conferred by the enabling Act.[199]

---

192 *Adams v Lambert* (2006) 228 CLR 409, 418 [22] (Gleeson CJ, Gummow, Kirby, Hayne, Callinan, Heydon and Crennan J); *Tsolacis v McKinnon* (2012) 38 VR 260, 277–8 [65] (Cavanough J).

193 In *Klepp v Gibb* (1988) 81 ALR 383, 395 [40] it was stated by the Full Federal Court (Sweeney, Jenkinson and Neaves JJ) that a warrant to commit a person to prison, which did not appropriately adapt the prescribed form to the circumstances, was not addressed to the appropriate person in charge of the prison and did not state the designation of the person who signed the warrant lacked 'the degree of precision and clarity which should attend a warrant for the committal of a person to prison'.

194 In *Nitro Circus Touring Australia Pty Ltd v Lenzoni* [2016] NSWSC 178 Hammerschlag J stated that '[s]ubstantial compliance is a matter of degree and concerns the practical effect of what has been done, compared with the practical effect the relevant provision which has not been complied with seeks to achieve': at [30].

195 *QUYD Pty Ltd v Marvass Pty Ltd* [2009] 1 Qd R 41 [24] (Fraser JA).

196 *Acts Interpretation Act 1901* (Cth) s 15A; *Interpretation Act 1987* (NSW) s 31; *Acts Interpretation Act 1954* (Qld) s 9; *Legislation Interpretation Act 2021* (SA) s 15; *Acts Interpretation Act 1931* (Tas) s 3; *Interpretation of Legislation Act 1984* (Vic) s 6; *Interpretation Act 1984* (WA) s 7; *Legislation Act 2001* (ACT) s 120; *Interpretation Act 1978* (NT) s 59.

197 *Acts Interpretation Act 1901* (Cth) s 15A as applied by *Legislation Act 2003* (Cth) s 13(1)(a), (2); *Interpretation Act 1987* (NSW) s 31; *Acts Interpretation Act 1954* (Qld) s 9 as applied by *Statutory Instruments Act 1992* (Qld) s 14, sch 1; *Legislation Interpretation Act 2021* (SA) s 15(1); *Acts Interpretation Act 1931* (Tas) s 3 as applied by s 5(2); *Interpretation of Legislation Act 1984* (Vic) s 22; *Interpretation Act 1984* (WA) s 7.

198 *Legislation Interpretation Act 2021* (SA) s 15(2), (3); *Legislation Act 2001* (ACT) s 43; *Interpretation Act 1978* (NT) s 61.

199 *Acts Interpretation Act 1901* (Cth) s 46(2); *Interpretation Act 1987* (NSW) s 32; *Statutory Instruments Act 1992* (Qld) s 21; *Legislation Interpretation Act 2021* (SA) s 15(2), (3); *Interpretation of Legislation Act 1984* (Vic) s 22; *Legislation Act 2001* (ACT) s 43; *Interpretation Act 1978* (NT) s 61. See **[43.14]** as to the operation of the common law 'blue pencil rule' in the absence of a statutory severance provision applicable to delegated legislation.

(f) Words of permission and obligation

Each jurisdiction, other than the Northern Territory, has provisions in its Interpretation Act relating to the meaning of all or some of the words 'may', 'shall' and 'must' in legislation.[200] South Australia also construes 'may not' as being prohibitory in nature.[201] Tasmania also construes 'is to' and 'are to' and treats them as being directory in nature.[202]

The use of these words in legislation, when conferring a power, has given rise to much litigation over the years. For a discussion about their meaning see **[36.9]**.

---

200 *Acts Interpretation Act 1901* (Cth) s 33(2A) (meaning of 'may'); *Interpretation Act 1987* (NSW) s 9 (meaning of 'may' and 'shall'); *Acts Interpretation Act 1954* (Qld) s 32CA (meaning of 'may' and 'must'); *Legislation Interpretation Act 2021* (SA) s 11 (meaning of 'may', 'shall' and 'must'); *Acts Interpretation Act 1931* (Tas) s 10A (meaning of 'must' and 'may'); *Interpretation of Legislation Act 1984* (Vic) s 45 (meaning of 'may' and 'shall'); *Interpretation Act 1984* (WA) s 56 (meaning of 'may' and 'shall'); *Legislation Act 2001* (ACT) s 146 (meaning of 'may' and 'must').

201 *Legislation Interpretation Act 2021* (SA) s 11(2).

202 *Acts Interpretation Act 1931* (Tas) s 10A(1)(b).

OTHER ACTS OF GENERAL APPLICATION 26

Overview

This chapter builds on chapter 25, which examines the role played by Interpretation Acts. Unless expressly or impliedly disapplied, an Interpretation Act applies to all Acts passed by the same legislature. But an Interpretation Act is not the only Act that applies to other individual Acts. Across the statute book of a jurisdiction there is a range of Acts that support the operation of individual Acts. Some have a broad application, such as a Human Rights Act. The application of others depends on the subject matter of the individual Act. These Acts, which have an application across the statute book, are referred to in this chapter as 'Acts of General Application'. Some jurisdictions – for example, Western Australia[1] and the Commonwealth[2] – publish a list of them. [26.1]

This chapter does not purport to be an exhaustive examination of all Acts with a general application to other Acts. Its aim is to highlight and introduce the more important of them.

Human Rights Acts

In some jurisdictions Human Rights Acts impact the interpretation of legislation by requiring that legislation be interpreted compatibly with specified human rights [26.2]

In three Australian jurisdictions Human Rights Acts have been enacted that impact the interpretation of legislation, including delegated legislation. They are, in order of enactment, the *Human Rights Act 2004* (ACT), the *Charter of Human Rights and Responsibilities Act 2006* (Vic) ('the Victorian Charter') and the *Human Rights Act 2019* (Qld).[3]

---

1 See Parliamentary Counsel's Office, *How to Read Legislation: A Beginner's Guide* (Government of Western Australia, 2011). The following Acts are listed in this publication: *Criminal Investigation Act 2006* (WA); *Bail Act 1982* (WA); *Criminal Procedure Act 2004* (WA); *Criminal Code Act 1913* (WA) ss 2–5, 7, 11–17, 22–26; *Evidence Act 1906* (WA); *Sentencing Act 1995* (WA); *Fines, Penalties and Infringement Notices Enforcement Act 1994* (WA). Also included are the *Public Sector Management Act 1994* (WA) and *Financial Management Act 2006* (WA) for persons in, or dealing with, the public service. In addition, for some of the basic laws laying down how Western Australia is governed, the guide points readers to the *Australian Constitution*, *Constitution Act 1889* (WA) and *Constitution Acts Amendment Act 1899* (WA).

2 See Australian Government, *Federal Register of Legislation*, 'How to Read Legislation' (Web Page) <https://www.legislation.gov.au/content/readlegislation#general>. The following Acts are listed in this publication: *Crimes Act 1914* (Cth); *Criminal Code Act 1995* (Cth); *Freedom of Information Act 1982* (Cth); *Administrative Appeals Tribunal Act 1975* (Cth); *Administrative Decisions (Judicial Review) Act 1977* (Cth); *Judiciary Act 1903* (Cth); *Ombudsman Act 1976* (Cth); *Privacy Act 1988* (Cth); *Australian Constitution.*

3 At the Commonwealth level there is the *Human Rights (Parliamentary Scrutiny) Act 2011* (Cth). This Act establishes a Parliamentary Joint Committee on Human Rights with the function of examining Bills, legislative instruments that come before either House of the Parliament and Acts for compatibility with the rights and freedoms recognised or declared by specified international instruments. It requires Bills and

These Acts have the purpose of protecting the human rights specified in them (civil and political in each, plus economic, social and cultural in the Australian Capital Territory and Queensland).[4] The Acts recognise that human rights may be limited by legislation. However, only a limitation that is reasonable and 'can be demonstrably justified in a free and democratic society' is permitted and a list of relevant factors is specified for deciding whether a limitation is reasonable and justifiable.[5] Each of the Acts contains provisions affecting how legislation in that jurisdiction is to be interpreted compatibly with human rights.[6]

Section 30 of the *Human Rights Act 2004* (ACT) provides that, so far as it is possible to do so consistently with its purpose, a territory law must be interpreted in a way that is compatible with human rights. Section 31(1) of that Act adds: 'International law, and the judgments of foreign and international courts and tribunals, relevant to a human right may be considered in interpreting the human right.'[7]

The provisions of s 32(1) and (2) of the Victorian Charter are to the same effect as s 30 of the *Human Rights Act 2004* (ACT). But s 32(2) of the Victorian Charter also expressly includes judgments of domestic courts and tribunals in the list of relevant judgments that may be considered. Further, s 32(3) of the Victorian Charter clarifies that s 32 does not affect the validity of an Act or provision of an Act that is incompatible with a human right or the validity of a subordinate instrument or provision of a subordinate instrument that is incompatible with a human right and is empowered to be so by the Act under which it is made.[8]

Section 48 of the Queensland Act is generally to the same effect as s 32 of the Victorian Charter. But s 48(2) adds: 'If a statutory provision can not be interpreted in a way that is

---

legislative instruments to which s 42 (disallowance) of the *Legislation Act 2003* (Cth) applies to be accompanied by a statement that includes an assessment of their compatibility with those rights and freedoms. It does not, however, impact the interpretation of legislation.

4 The *Human Rights Act 2004* (ACT) sets out civil and political rights in pt 3 and economic, social and cultural rights in pt 3A. The Victorian Charter sets out civil and political rights in pt 2. The *Human Rights Act 2019* (Qld) sets out civil and political rights in div 2 of pt 2 and economic, social and cultural rights in div 3 of pt 2.

5 *Human Rights Act 2019* (Qld) s 13; Victorian Charter s 7(2); *Human Rights Act 2004* (ACT) s 28.

6 Whether the issue of reasonable and justifiable limitations is to be considered while applying these interpretative provisions (that is, applying the required interpretative approach to rights as reasonably and justifiably limited), or is only to be considered when the interpretative approach points to the statutory provision as limiting the relevant human right, is unsettled. No binding ratio on this issue is found in the decision of the High Court in *Momcilovic v The Queen* (2011) 245 CLR 1. In the decision below, *R v Momcilovic* (2010) 25 VR 436, the Victorian Court of Appeal had held that the limitation provision in s 7(2) of the Victorian Charter is to be considered only after the statutory provision in question has been interpreted in accordance with s 32(1) of that Charter as limiting a human right protected by the Charter. In *Noone v Operation Smile* (2012) 38 VR 569 Nettle JA expressed the view that it was appropriate for the Victorian Court of Appeal to adhere to the approach to this issue it had taken in *Momcilovic* until the High Court determines that approach to be incorrect: at 609 [142].

7 In *Momcilovic v The Queen* (2011) 245 CLR 1, French CJ observed: '[I]nternational and foreign domestic judgments should be consulted with discrimination and care. Such judgments are made in a variety of legal systems and constitutional settings which have to be taken into account when reading them': at 37–8 [19]. See also Gummow J at 89 [155]. See *Bare v Independent Broad-based Anti-corruption Commission* (2015) 48 VR 129, 188–9 [182]–[184] (Warren CJ).

8 In *Momcilovic v The Queen* (2011) 245 CLR 1 Crennan and Kiefel JJ held that s 32(3) of the Victorian Charter acknowledges that it may not be possible to read a provision conformably with Charter rights and, in that situation, the provision stands: at 217 [566].

compatible with human rights, the provision must, to the extent possible that is consistent with its purpose, be interpreted in a way that is most compatible with human rights.'[9]

Each of the Acts empowers the Supreme Court of its jurisdiction to declare that a statutory provision cannot be interpreted consistently with a human right and give a copy of the declaration to the Attorney-General.[10] The declaration does not affect the validity of the relevant provision or give rise to any rights or obligations.[11]

The express inclusion of a requirement in each of these Acts that statutory provisions must be *interpreted* consistently with their *purpose* has arguably helped avoid the kind of judicial legislating (albeit within limits) that has occurred in the United Kingdom under s 3(1) of the *Human Rights Act 1998* (UK). That section requires that legislation be read and given effect in a way that is compatible with rights under the *European Convention for the Protection of Human Rights and Fundamental Freedoms* so far 'as it is possible to do so' but makes no reference to statutory purpose.[12]

In *Momcilovic v The Queen*[13] Crennan and Kiefel JJ compared s 32(1) of the Victorian Charter with s 3(1) of the UK Act and stated:

> It [s 32(1)] too opens with the words 'So far as it is possible to do so' but continues 'consistently with their purpose'. The reference to statutory purpose points clearly to the task ordinarily undertaken by courts in construing legislation . . .[14]

In the same case French CJ said the following in relation to s 32(1) of the Victorian Charter:

> The subsection limits the interpretation which it directs to that which is consistent with the purpose of the statutory provision under consideration. It operates upon constructional choices which the language of the statutory provision permits. Constructional choice

---

9 Although the Victorian Charter does not contain such an express provision, it has been interpreted in the same way. Thus, in *Slaveski v Smith* (2012) 34 VR 206 the Victorian Court of Appeal (Warren CJ, Nettle and Redlich JJA) held that, under s 32(1) of the Victorian Charter, if the words of a statute were capable of more than one meaning, a court should give them whichever of those meanings best accorded with the human right in question: at 215 [24].

10 *Human Rights Act 2019* (Qld) s 53; Victorian Charter s 36; *Human Rights Act 2004* (ACT) s 32.

11 *Human Rights Act 2019* (Qld) s 54; Victorian Charter s 36(5); *Human Rights Act 2004* (ACT) s 32(3).

12 See, eg, *Ghaidan v Godin-Mendoza* [2004] 2 AC 557 where Lord Nicholls stated that s 3 of the UK Act allowed a court 'to read in words which change the meaning of the enacted legislation, so as to make it Convention-compliant' although the imported meaning 'must be compatible with the underlying thrust of the legislation being construed': at 571–2 [32]–[33]. Lord Steyn agreed at 573 [37], Lord Rodger agreed at 593 [103] and Baroness Hale agreed at 609 [145]. In *Sheldrake v DPP* [2005] 1 AC 264 (Lords Rodger and Carswell dissenting) held that, relying on s 3 of the *Human Rights Act 1998* (UK), s 11(2) of the *Terrorism Act 2000* (UK) must be read down so as to impose on the defendant an evidential burden only, even though that was not Parliament's intention when enacting the provision. In *Ahmed v HM Treasury (Justice Intervening) (Nos 1 and 2)* [2010] 2 AC 534 Lord Philips stated (at 647 [115]) that, by enacting s 3 of the 1998 Act, Parliament has been held to direct the courts to interpret legislation in a way which is compatible with Convention rights, even where such interpretation involves departing from the 'unambiguous meaning the legislation would otherwise bear', or the 'legislative intention . . . of the Parliament': see *Ghaidan v Godin-Mendoza* [2004] 2 AC 557, [30], per Lord Nicholls and *Sheldrake v Director of Public Prosecutions* [2005] 1 AC 264, [24], per Lord Bingham. Such an interpretation must, however, be one that is 'possible' having regard to the underlying thrust or intention of the legislation.

The UK Act was discussed in *Momcilovic v The Queen* (2011) 245 CLR 1, 38 [20], 48–9 [47]–[48], 50 [49] (French CJ); 180 [447], 182–3 [451]–[452] (Heydon J); 209–10 [542]–[543], 211 [546] (Crennan and Kiefel JJ).

13 (2011) 245 CLR 1.

14 Ibid 210 [544].

> subsumes the concept of ambiguity but lacks its negative connotation. It reflects the plasticity and shades of meaning and nuance that are the natural attributes of language and the legal indeterminacy that is avoided only with difficulty in statutory drafting.[15]

In *Momcilovic* Gummow J also expressed the view that the reference to 'purpose' in s 32(1) of the Victorian Charter was a limiting factor on courts as it referred 'to the legislative "intention" revealed by consideration of the subject and scope of the legislation in accordance with principles of statutory construction and interpretation'.[16] Crennan and Kiefel JJ regarded the statement in s 32(1) that all statutory provisions 'must be interpreted' in a way that is compatible with Charter rights as another limiting factor as it was

> a firm statement and one which, it may be inferred, was intended to overcome any misapprehension about the role of the courts in construing legislation. The reference to interpretation must be taken to be a reference to that process of construction as understood and ordinarily applied by courts, a process which is to be taken as accepted by the other arms of government in a system of representative democracy.[17]

The ACT courts have applied the same approach in interpreting s 30 of the *Human Rights Act 2004* (ACT). In *Andrews v Thompson*[18] the Court of Appeal observed that s 30 was 'closely equivalent' to s 32(1) of the Victorian Charter and that there was 'no basis for interpreting the two corresponding sections in any different manner'.[19]

The Queensland and Victorian Acts provide for the making by Parliament of an 'override declaration' – that is, a declaration that an Act, or provision of an Act, has effect despite being inconsistent with one or more human rights or anything else in the Act.[20] In the Queensland Act, s 48(5) expressly provides that s 48 (interpretation) 'does not apply to a statutory provision the subject of an override declaration that is in force'. The same result is achieved by s 31(6) of the Victorian Charter, which provides that if an override declaration is made in respect of a statutory provision, then to the extent of the declaration the Act has no application to that provision. This effectively excludes s 32 (interpretation).

Statutory review mechanisms

[26.3] **Administrative decisions and actions taken under an Act are subject to various kinds of investigatory mechanisms and other forms of external review provided for under other Acts**

By way of background, many Acts establish entities of various kinds to perform public functions and empower the entities to take administrative actions and make decisions of an administrative nature.

15 Ibid 50 [50]. Bell J emphasised that the task imposed by s 32(1) 'is one of interpretation and not of legislation': at 250 [684]. See also Gummow J at 92–3 [171] (Hayne J agreeing at 123 [280]). French CJ stated that s 32(1) 'applies to the interpretation of statutes in the same way as the principle of legality but with a wider field of application': at 50 [51]. See chapter 28 for the principle of legality.

16 Ibid 92 [170] (Hayne J agreeing at 123 [280]).

17 Ibid 210 [545].

18 (2018) 340 FLR 439.

19 Ibid 447 [45] (Elkaim, Loukas-Karlsson JJ, Robinson AJ).

20 See *Human Rights Act 2019* (Qld) s 43; Victorian Charter s 31.

The establishing Act does not contain the complete picture of the legal environment in which the entity will operate. Indeed, it may not even set out all its powers and functions, as one or more other Acts may confer powers, or impose functions, on the entity.[21] There is a range of other legislation that impacts on the entity by providing for its decisions to be subject to investigatory mechanisms and other forms of external review.[22]

This section looks at the external review that may be called on to examine actions taken by a public entity, including administrative decisions made by the entity.[23]

The entity may be subject to a financial or performance audit by a state-appointed Auditor-General.[24] The terms and conditions of employment of its staff may be regulated as set out in **[26.8]**. The entity may need to comply with a state-imposed financial management framework.[25]

For the review of administrative decisions, each Australian jurisdiction has by an Act ('the tribunal Act') established a general administrative appeals tribunal and vested it with jurisdiction to conduct a review, on their merits, of decisions across a range of subject areas. In doing so the tribunal reconsiders both the facts and the law and may make a fresh decision. The tribunal Act also sets out standard procedural provisions for applications to the tribunal and specifies the remedies available to the tribunal.[26] The typical nature of the legislative scheme under which such tribunals operate is that the tribunal Act provides that other Acts (enabling Acts) passed in the relevant jurisdiction may legislate for the making of applications to the tribunal for the review of decisions made by an entity under powers conferred by the enabling Act.[27]

For an application made to the tribunal as provided for by the enabling Act, the enabling Act may modify any of the standard procedural provisions contained in the tribunal Act or vary the remedial powers of the tribunal. Accordingly, to gain a proper understanding of the position with respect to administrative review by the tribunal of decisions made by an entity under an enabling Act, the enabling Act should be read together with the tribunal Act.

21 This may include an Interpretation Act. See chapter 25.

22 Judicial review of administrative decisions is also available at common law.

23 Provision may be made for an internal review of a decision to be conducted by the entity itself.

24 *Auditor-General Act 1997* (Cth); *Public Finance and Audit Act 1983* (NSW); *Auditor-General Act 2009* (Qld); *Public Finance and Audit Act 1987* (SA); *Audit Act 2008* (Tas); *Audit Act 1994* (Vic); *Auditor General Act 2006* (WA); *Auditor-General Act 1996* (ACT); *Audit Act 1995* (NT).

25 *Public Governance, Performance and Accountability Act 2013* (Cth); *Public Finance and Audit Act 1983* (NSW); *Financial Accountability Act 2009* (Qld); *Public Finance and Audit Act 1987* (SA); *Financial Management Act 2016* (Tas); *Financial Management Act 1994* (Vic); *Financial Management Act 2006* (WA); *Financial Management Act 1996* (ACT); *Financial Management Act 1995* (NT).

26 *Administrative Appeals Tribunal Act 1975* (Cth); *Civil and Administrative Tribunal Act 2013* (NSW); *Administrative Decisions Review Act 1997* (NSW); *Queensland Civil and Administrative Tribunal Act 2009* (Qld); *South Australian Civil and Administrative Tribunal Act 2013* (SA); *Tasmanian Civil and Administrative Tribunal Act 2020* (Tas); *Victorian Civil and Administrative Tribunal Act 1998* (Vic); *State Administrative Tribunal Act 2004* (WA); *ACT Civil and Administrative Tribunal Act 2008* (ACT); *Northern Territory Civil and Administrative Tribunal Act 2014* (NT).

27 *Administrative Appeals Tribunal Act 1975* (Cth) s 25; *Civil and Administrative Tribunal Act 2013* (NSW) s 30; *Administrative Decisions Review Act 1997* (NSW) s 9; *Queensland Civil and Administrative Tribunal Act 2009* (Qld) ss 6, 9; *South Australian Civil and Administrative Tribunal Act 2013* (SA) s 31; *Tasmanian Civil and Administrative Tribunal Act 2020* (Tas) s 58; *Victorian Civil and Administrative Tribunal Act 1998* (Vic) s 42; *State Administrative Tribunal Act 2004* (WA) s 13; *ACT Civil and Administrative Tribunal Act 2008* (ACT) s 9; *Northern Territory Civil and Administrative Tribunal Act 2014* (NT) ss 30, 33. See *Allan v Transurban City Link Ltd* (2001) 208 CLR 167, 172 [9] (Gleeson CJ, Gaudron, Gummow, Hayne and Callinan JJ).

Example 26.1 *Victorian Civil and Administrative Tribunal Act 1998* (Vic) and *Freedom of Information Act 1982* (Vic)

Section 40 of the *Victorian Civil and Administrative Tribunal Act 1998* (Vic) ('the VCAT Act') states that the Victorian Civil and Administrative Tribunal ('the Tribunal') established by pt 2 of the VCAT Act has two types of jurisdiction: original jurisdiction and review jurisdiction.

Section 42(1) of the VCAT Act provides that review jurisdiction is jurisdiction conferred on the Tribunal by or under an 'enabling enactment' to review a decision made by a 'decision-maker'. The term 'enabling enactment' is defined by s 3 of the VCAT Act as 'an enactment by or under which jurisdiction is conferred on the Tribunal'. Section 3 of the VCAT Act also defines 'decision-maker' as 'a person who makes, or is deemed to have made, a decision under an enabling enactment'.

Section 48(a) of the VCAT Act specifies that one of the ways in which the review jurisdiction of VCAT is invoked is by a person who is entitled to do so by or under an enabling enactment applying to VCAT for review of a decision made by an entity under that enactment (a decision-maker). Section 67 details how an application is to be made.

Section 50 of the *Freedom of Information Act 1982* (Vic) ('the FOI Act') enables applicants to apply to VCAT for review of a range of specified decisions made by a range of decision-makers. Section 52 of the FOI Act specifies the time within which an application to VCAT must be made, s 54 deals with who are parties to proceedings before VCAT and s 55 allocates the onus to establish certain matters in such proceedings. There are other provisions in the Division in which those sections are located that impact on the powers available to the Tribunal on a review.

McKechnie v Victorian Civil and Administrative Tribunal[28] involved an application under Order 56 of the *Supreme Court (General Civil Procedure) Rules 2015* (Vic) for judicial review by the Supreme Court of Victoria of a VCAT decision on requests, for access to documents, made or purportedly made by a prisoner under the FOI Act. Cavanough J, in giving judgment, stated:

> [T]he relevant 'enabling enactment' for present purposes is Part VI, Division 3 of the *FOI Act*, in that that Division provides for VCAT to have jurisdiction to review certain decisions made or deemed to have been made under the *FOI Act*. Not all decisions made or deemed to have been made under the *FOI Act* are reviewable by VCAT. The *FOI Act* is carefully drawn so as to distinguish between decisions (or deemed decisions) that are, and decisions (or deemed decisions) that are not, reviewable by VCAT. . . .
>
> Under the *VCAT Act* and the *FOI Act*, jurisdiction at VCAT in FOI matters is available only in relation to a 'decision' or deemed 'decision'. The decision or deemed decision must fall within one or other of the classes specified in s 50(1) of the *FOI Act*, as in force from time to time.[29]

Cavanough J held that, in the circumstances, there had been no reviewable decision of a kind specified in s 50(1) of the FOI Act.

The existence of such an administrative review scheme does not necessarily affect any right that a person may have at common law to seek a judicial review of a particular administrative decision in the ordinary courts.[30] On a judicial review only the legality of the decision-making

28 (2020) 62 VR 54.

29 Ibid 103–4 [121]–[122].

30 A court from which judicial review is sought may exercise a discretion to refuse to deal with the matter on the basis that an alternative remedy is available. This discretion may be expressly recognised by legislation. See, eg, *Civil and Administrative Tribunal Act 2013* (NSW) s 34.

process is considered, not its merits.[31] The right to seek judicial review for jurisdictional error is constitutionally protected.[32] This right has been traditionally enforceable through the issue of writs of various kinds (such as writs of prohibition, mandamus or certiorari).[33] Several Australian jurisdictions have also established, separate from the common law-based judicial review procedure, statutory processes for obtaining from courts an order of review in respect of certain kinds of administrative decisions.[34]

Administrative actions by public entities (not limited to decisions) may also be subject to investigation by a public official known as an Ombudsman or, in Western Australia, a Parliamentary Commissioner. Each Australian jurisdiction has established an office of Ombudsman or Parliamentary Commissioner with the function of investigating certain administrative actions of public entities, either on their own motion or in response to a complaint by a person or a referral to them by another body.[35] There is a range of other entities established by Australian jurisdictions with power to investigate administrative actions of a public entity that are alleged to involve conduct that is discriminatory in some respect[36] or to be corrupt or to otherwise constitute misconduct of some kind.[37]

---

31 See *A-G (NSW) v Quin* (1990) 170 CLR 1, 35–7 (Brennan J).

32 Section 75(v) of the *Australian Constitution* vests in the High Court original jurisdiction in any matter in which a writ of mandamus or prohibition or an injunction is sought against an officer of the Commonwealth. Section 39B(1) of the *Judiciary Act 1903* (Cth) vests similar original jurisdiction in the Federal Court. In *Plaintiff S157/2002 v Commonwealth* (2003) 211 CLR 476 the High Court held that Parliament could not oust the jurisdiction conferred by s 75(v) of the *Constitution* to review decisions involving jurisdictional error. Section 75(iii) of the *Constitution* vests in the High Court original jurisdiction in any matter in which the Commonwealth, or a person suing or being sued on behalf of the Commonwealth, is a party. Such a matter may be remitted to the Federal Court under s 44(2A) of the *Judiciary Act 1903* (Cth). In *Kirk v Industrial Court of New South Wales* (2010) 239 CLR 531 the majority in the High Court (French CJ, Gummow, Hayne, Crennan, Kiefel and Bell JJ; Heydon J agreeing at 585 [113]) held that legislation 'which would take from a State Supreme Court power to grant relief on account of jurisdictional error is beyond State legislative power': at 581 [100].

33 In certain jurisdictions, relief or remedy in judicial review proceedings is no longer granted through the issue of a writ but by way of judgment or order. See *Supreme Court Act 1970* (NSW) s 69; *Judicial Review Act 1991* (Qld) s 41; *Judicial Review Act 2000* (Tas) s 43; *Supreme Court Act 1986* (Vic) s 3(6); *Supreme Court (General Civil Procedure) Rules 2015* (Vic) r 56.01; *Court Procedures Rules 2006* (ACT) rr 3553–3554; *Supreme Court Act 1979* (NT) s 9(2)(b).

34 See *Administrative Decisions (Judicial Review) Act 1977* (Cth); *Judicial Review Act 1991* (Qld); *Judicial Review Act 2000* (Tas); *Administrative Law Act 1978* (Vic); *Administrative Decisions (Judicial Review) Act 1989* (ACT).

35 *Ombudsman Act 1976* (Cth); *Ombudsman Act 1974* (NSW); *Ombudsman Act 2001* (Qld); *Ombudsman Act 1972* (SA); *Ombudsman Act 1978* (Tas); *Ombudsman Act 1973* (Vic); *Parliamentary Commissioner Act 1971* (WA); *Ombudsman Act 1989* (ACT); *Ombudsman Act 2009* (NT).

36 For example, the Australian Human Rights Commission established under the *Australian Human Rights Commission Act 1986* (Cth); the Anti-Discrimination Board constituted under the *Anti-Discrimination Act 1977* (NSW); the Ageing and Disability Commissioner appointed under the *Ageing and Disability Commissioner Act 2019* (NSW); the Human Rights Commissioner appointed under the *Anti-Discrimination Act 1991* (Qld); the Commissioner for Equal Opportunity appointed under the *Equal Opportunity Act 1984* (SA); the Anti-Discrimination Commissioner appointed under the *Anti-Discrimination Act 1998* (Tas); the Victorian Equal Opportunity and Human Rights Commission continued in existence by the *Equal Opportunity Act 2010* (Vic) s 154; the Commissioner for Equal Opportunity appointed under the *Equal Opportunity Act 1984* (WA); the Human Rights Commission established under the *Human Rights Commission Act 2005* (ACT); the Anti-Discrimination Commissioner appointed under the *Anti-Discrimination Act 1992* (NT).

37 For example, the Integrity Commissioner appointed under the *Law Enforcement Integrity Commissioner Act 2006* (Cth); the Independent Commission Against Corruption established under the *Independent Commission Against Corruption Act 1988* (NSW); the Crime and Corruption Commission established under the *Crime and Corruption Act 2001* (Qld); the Independent Commissioner Against Corruption appointed under the *Independent Commissioner Against Corruption Act 2012* (SA); the Integrity Commission established under the *Integrity Commission Act 2009* (Tas); the Independent Broad-based Anti-corruption Commission established

Rights to obtain certain kinds of information held by public entities are also established by legislation in all Australian jurisdictions.[38] Protection for private information held by public entities, and the privacy of individuals who interact with these entities, is provided for by legislative schemes in all Australian jurisdictions[39] except South Australia[40] and Western Australia.

There are also Acts in place in all Australian jurisdictions[41] under which a royal commission or judicial inquiry may be established to examine specific actions taken by a public or private entity.[42]

Criminal and sentencing Acts

[26.4] The creation of, and punishment for, offences against individual Acts depend on the application of a range of general criminal and sentencing Acts

Acts frequently make engaging in a specified form of conduct a criminal offence and fix the punishment applicable to a person who commits such an offence. Such provisions depend for their efficacy on a suite of other legislation operating in the background dealing with the creation of, and punishment for, offences.[43]

At the Commonwealth level the Schedule to the *Criminal Code Act 1995* (Cth) contains an extensive set of provisions known as the *Criminal Code*.[44] Chapter 2 of that Code states general principles of criminal responsibility applicable to every offence created under Commonwealth legislation. It lays out what a physical or fault element of an offence may consist of and specifies default fault elements where the law creating an offence does not specify a fault element for a particular physical element. It sets out what is meant when a Commonwealth law creates an offence that is described as an offence of strict or absolute liability. It lists a range of circumstances in which a person is not criminally responsible for an offence. These various provisions

---

under the *Independent Broad-based Anti-corruption Commission Act 2011* (Vic); the Corruption and Crime Commission established under the *Corruption, Crime and Misconduct Act 2003* (WA); the ACT Integrity Commission established under the *Integrity Commission Act 2018* (ACT); the Independent Commissioner Against Corruption established under the *Independent Commissioner Against Corruption Act 2017* (NT).

38 *Freedom of Information Act 1982* (Cth); *Government Information (Public Access) Act 2009* (NSW); *Right to Information Act 2009* (Qld); *Freedom of Information Act 1991* (SA); *Right to Information Act 2009* (Tas); *Freedom of Information Act 1982* (Vic); *Freedom of Information Act 1992* (WA); *Freedom of Information Act 2016* (ACT); *Information Act 2002* (NT).

39 *Privacy Act 1988* (Cth); *Privacy and Personal Information Protection Act 1998* (NSW); *Information Privacy Act 2009* (Qld); *Personal Information Protection Act 2004* (Tas); *Privacy and Data Protection Act 2014* (Vic); *Information Privacy Act 2014* (ACT); *Information Act 2002* (NT).

40 South Australia has in place a relevant Cabinet Administrative Instruction – Information Privacy Principles ('IPPS') Instruction. See South Australian Department of Premier and Cabinet, *Information Privacy Principles (IPPS) Instruction* (South Australian Government, 2020).

41 *Royal Commissions Act 1902* (Cth); *Royal Commissions Act 1923* (NSW); *Commissions of Inquiry Act 1950* (Qld); *Royal Commissions Act 1917* (SA); *Commissions of Inquiry Act 1995* (Tas); *Inquiries Act 2014* (Vic); *Royal Commissions Act 1968* (WA); *Royal Commissions Act 1991* (ACT); *Inquiries Act 1945* (NT).

42 Recent examples include the Royal Commission into Misconduct in the Banking, Superannuation and Financial Services Industry at the Commonwealth level and in Victoria the Royal Commission into the Management of Police Informers and the COVID-19 Hotel Quarantine Inquiry.

43 See also **[41.10]** and **[42.5]**.

44 The *Criminal Code Act 1995* (Cth) sch s 1.1 provides that the only offences against Commonwealth laws are those created by, or under the authority of, the Code or another Commonwealth Act. This rules out common law offences.

operate in relation to any offence created by a Commonwealth Act. The *Criminal Code* also creates various ancillary offences (such as offences relating to attempt, incitement or conspiracy) applicable to offences created by Commonwealth Acts.

The *Criminal Code 2002* (ACT) contains similar provisions for offences created under laws of the Australian Capital Territory.[45] Schedule 1 to the *Criminal Code Act 1983* (NT) sets out the *Criminal Code of the Northern Territory of Australia*, which also contains broadly similar provisions.

There are also Criminal Codes in Queensland,[46] Tasmania[47] and Western Australia[48] that contain the more serious criminal offences in the jurisdiction and codify rules relating to criminal responsibility. In these code jurisdictions there are no common law offences,[49] but the common law power of a court to punish for contempt of court is preserved.[50]

New South Wales and Victoria each have a *Crimes Act*[51] while in South Australia there is a *Criminal Law Consolidation Act 1935* (SA). These Acts contain a broad range of criminal offences. But while they may set out provisions relevant to matters such as defences or the effect of intoxication on criminal responsibility,[52] they do not codify the law relating to the elements of offences. They may, however, create offences for conduct such as attempting or conspiring to commit, or inciting the commission of, an offence created by those Acts or by other Acts.[53] They may also provide definitions of terms used in criminal provisions across the statute book[54] and contain provisions about the necessary geographical nexus for an offence.[55]

To create consistency in sentencing across offences regarded as comparable in terms of seriousness, Victoria classifies offences by reference to the specified levels of maximum punishment attached.[56] Particular Acts may then fix the maximum period of imprisonment or maximum fine capable of being imposed for an offence created by the Act by providing that the offence attracts imprisonment, or a fine, of a specified level. South Australia has a similar scheme. There, maximum periods of imprisonment ranging from Division 1 imprisonment (15 years maximum) to Division 8 imprisonment (three months maximum), or maximum fines ranging from Division

---

45 Section 5(1), similarly to the *Criminal Code Act 1995* (Cth) sch s 1.1, provides that the only offences against ACT laws are the offences created under the Code Act or any other Act.

46 *Criminal Code Act 1899* (Qld).

47 *Criminal Code Act 1924* (Tas).

48 *Criminal Code Act Compilation Act 1913* (WA).

49 Section 4 in app B to the *Criminal Code Act Compilation Act 1913* (WA) provides that no person is liable to be tried or punished in Western Australia for an offence except under the express provisions of the *Criminal Code* or some other statute of, or that applies to, Western Australia. The *Criminal Code Act 1899* (Qld) s 5 is to the same effect. The *Criminal Code Act 1924* (Tas) s 6 abolished common law prosecutions.

50 *Criminal Code Act 1899* (Qld) s 8; *Criminal Code Act 1924* (Tas) s 10; *Criminal Code Act Compilation Act 1913* (WA) app B s 7.

51 *Crimes Act 1900* (NSW); *Crimes Act 1958* (Vic).

52 See *Crimes Act 1900* (NSW) pts 11–11A; *Criminal Law Consolidation Act 1935* (SA) pt 3 div 2, pt 8; *Crimes Act 1958* (Vic) pt IC.

53 See *Crimes Act 1900* (NSW) pts 8A, 9; *Criminal Law Consolidation Act 1935* (SA) pts 7B, 9 div 2; *Crimes Act 1958* (Vic) pt I divs 10–12.

54 For example, *Crimes Act 1900* (NSW) s 7 defines 'possession' while s 8 defines 'public place'.

55 See *Crimes Act 1900* (NSW) ss 10A–10F; *Criminal Law Consolidation Act 1935* (SA) pt 1A. See further **[41.10]**.

56 See *Sentencing Act 1991* (Vic) s 109(1)–(2). For example, s 3(1) of the *Crimes Act 1958* (Vic) provides that the punishment for murder is level 1 imprisonment (life) or imprisonment for such other term as is fixed by the court.

1 fine ($75,000 maximum) to Division 12 fine ($75 maximum), may be specified in Acts.[57] There are legislative schemes in all Australian jurisdictions, other than South Australia and Western Australia, for fixing the amount of fines by reference to units called penalty units.[58] An Act may specify an offence as meriting a fine of a specified number of penalty units that have a value set out in generally applicable legislation. This mechanism allows for the easy adjustment of the amount of fines by the simple means of adjusting the value of a penalty unit.

There are provisions that provide for bodies corporate to be subject to fines five times heavier than those applicable to natural persons convicted of the same offence.[59] There are also provisions that classify an offence as indictable or summary depending on the maximum period of imprisonment that may be imposed in respect of an offence.[60]

Evidence Acts

[26.5] **Proof of criminal or civil liability is required to be shown in accordance with rules of evidence established by Evidence Acts**

Legislation commonly provides for liability to be attached to a person engaging in specified conduct, either because of doing so with a specified state of mind (such as intentionally) or because the conduct brought about a specified circumstance or result (such as death or serious injury). The liability may be either criminal or civil. Liability is attached to the person if a court or tribunal in a proceeding finds that the person engaged in that conduct and that any other necessary requirements are satisfied.

For the conduct of such a proceeding, there needs to be rules about the standard of proof that is required and other procedural matters. These rules are supplied by Evidence Acts in each Australian jurisdiction.[61] The rules make provision about such matters as:

- who is competent to give, and who may be required to give, evidence;
- how a witness may be examined, cross-examined or re-examined;
- the kinds of evidence that are inadmissible; and
- what privileges a witness may rely on to refuse to give evidence.

Except for Queensland, South Australia and Western Australia, the Evidence Acts largely adopt common provisions and are collectively referred to as the Uniform Evidence Acts. The origin of these Acts lies in work done by the Australian Law Reform Commission in the 1980s that culminated in a final report in 1987.[62]

---

57 See *Legislation Interpretation Act 2021* (SA) s 54.

58 See *Crimes Act 1914* (Cth) s 4AA; *Crimes (Sentencing Procedure) Act 1999* (NSW) s 17; *Penalties and Sentences Act 1992* (Qld) s 5; *Penalty Units and Other Penalties Act 1987* (Tas) s 4; *Sentencing Act 1991* (Vic) s 110; *Legislation Act 2001* (ACT) s 133; *Penalty Units Act 2009* (NT) s 5.

59 See *Crimes Act 1914* (Cth) s 4B(3); *Penalties and Sentences Act 1992* (Qld) s 181B; *Sentencing Act 1991* (Vic) s 113D; *Sentencing Act 1995* (WA) ss 40(5), (5a), *Sentencing Act 1995* (NT) s 29; *Interpretation Act 1978* (NT) s 38DC.

60 See *Crimes Act 1914* (Cth) ss 4G–4H; *Criminal Procedure Act 1986* (NSW) ss 5–6; *Criminal Procedure Act 1921* (SA) s 5; *Sentencing Act 1991* (Vic) s 112; *Legislation Act 2001* (ACT) s 190; *Criminal Code Act 1983* (NT) sch 1 s 3.

61 *Evidence Act 1995* (Cth); *Evidence Act 1995* (NSW); *Evidence Act 1977* (Qld); *Evidence Act 1929* (SA); *Evidence Act 2001* (Tas); *Evidence Act 2008* (Vic); *Evidence Act 1906* (WA); *Evidence Act 2011* (ACT); *Evidence (National Uniform Legislation) Act 2011* (NT).

62 Australian Law Reform Commission, *Evidence* (Report No 83, June 1987). The NSW Law Reform Commission, *Evidence* (Report No 56, June 1988) recommended that the bulk of the ALRC's proposals be adopted in New South Wales. Following work done by the then Standing Committee of Attorneys General in consultation with

Other facilitative Acts

Electronic transactions are facilitated by legislative provisions that are common to all Australian jurisdictions [26.6]

The *Electronic Transactions Act 1999* (Cth) facilitates the use of electronic transactions in all dealings. Each state and territory has enacted legislation that substantially mirrors the Commonwealth Act.[63]

Each of those Electronic Transactions Acts (an 'ETA') provides that for the purposes of a law of the enacting jurisdiction, a transaction is not invalid only because it took place wholly or partly by means of one or more electronic communications.[64]

An Act may require a person to give information in writing,[65] provide a signature, produce a document in material form, record information in writing or retain a document in material form. Although no specific provision is made by that Act, by force of the jurisdiction's ETA, these things may be done by means of an electronic communication, subject to certain conditions.[66] These Acts also contain provisions for determining when and where an electronic communication is sent and received.[67] Such provisions are important for providing certainty as to when and where a contract formed electronically is made.

---

those jurisdictions, in 1995 the Commonwealth and New South Wales enacted uniform Evidence Acts. Subsequently Victoria, Tasmania, the Australian Capital Territory and the Northern Territory did the same.

63 *Electronic Transactions Act 2000* (NSW); *Electronic Transactions (Queensland) Act 2001* (Qld); *Electronic Transactions Act 2000* (SA); *Electronic Transactions Act 2000* (Tas); *Electronic Transactions (Victoria) Act 2000* (Vic); *Electronic Transactions Act 2011* (WA); *Electronic Transactions Act 2001* (ACT); *Electronic Transactions (Northern Territory) Act 2000* (NT).

64 See *Electronic Transactions Act 1999* (Cth) s 8; *Electronic Transactions Act 2000* (NSW) s 7; *Electronic Transactions (Queensland) Act 2001* (Qld) s 8; *Electronic Communications Act 2000* (SA) s 7; *Electronic Transactions Act 2000* (Tas) s 5; *Electronic Transactions (Victoria) Act 2000* (Vic) s 7; *Electronic Transactions Act 2011* (WA) s 8; *Electronic Transactions Act 2001* (ACT) s 7; *Electronic Transactions (Northern Territory) Act 2000* (NT) s 7. An 'electronic communication' is defined in *Electronic Transactions Act 2000* (NSW) s 5(1); *Electronic Transactions (Queensland) Act 2001* (Qld) sch 2; *Electronic Communications Act 2000* (SA) s 5(1); *Electronic Transactions Act 2000* (Tas) s 3; *Electronic Transactions (Victoria) Act 2000* (Vic) s 3(1); *Electronic Transactions Act 2011* (WA) s 5(1); *Electronic Transactions Act 2001* (ACT) dictionary; *Electronic Transactions (Northern Territory) Act 2000* (NT) s 5. In these Acts 'electronic communication' is a communication of information in the form of data, text, images or sound (where the sound is processed at its destination by an automated voice recognition system) by means of guided or unguided electromagnetic energy, or both. The *Electronic Transactions Act 1999* (Cth) s 5(1) contains a similar definition of 'electronic communication' but refers to 'speech' instead of 'sound'.

65 Examples provided by the Electronic Transactions Acts of giving information include making an application, lodging a claim, return or objection, issuing a certificate and giving a statement of reasons. The Acts also cover where a person is permitted under a law of the enacting jurisdiction to give information in writing.

66 See *Electronic Transactions Act 1999* (Cth) ss 9–12; *Electronic Transactions Act 2000* (NSW) ss 8–11; *Electronic Transactions (Queensland) Act 2001* (Qld) ch 2 pt 2; *Electronic Communications Act 2000* (SA) ss 8–11; *Electronic Transactions Act 2000* (Tas) ss 6–9; *Electronic Transactions (Victoria) Act 2000* (Vic) ss 8–11; *Electronic Transactions Act 2011* (WA) ss 9–12; *Electronic Transactions Act 2001* (ACT) ss 8–11; *Electronic Transactions (Northern Territory) Act 2000* (NT) ss 8–11.

67 See *Electronic Transactions Act 1999* (Cth) pt 2 div 3; *Electronic Transactions Act 2000* (NSW) pt 2 div 3; *Electronic Transactions (Queensland) Act 2001* (Qld) ch 2 pt 3; *Electronic Communications Act 2000* (SA) pt 2 div 3; *Electronic Transactions Act 2000* (Tas) pt 2 div 3; *Electronic Transactions (Victoria) Act 2000* (Vic) pt 2 div 3; *Electronic Transactions Act 2011* (WA) pt 2 div 3; *Electronic Transactions Act 2001* (ACT) pt 2 div 2.3; *Electronic Transactions (Northern Territory) Act 2000* (NT) pt 2 div 3.

The ETA[68] may provide for delegated legislation to make certain kinds of transactions or communications,[69] or specified laws,[70] exempt from their application.

With an ETA in place in a jurisdiction, it is unnecessary for any individual Act to provide specifically for the making under it, by electronic means, of transactions and communications unless it is intended to vary how the ETA operates or to exclude its application, wholly or partly.

[26.7] Common regulatory standards apply to the sale of goods and the carrying on of an occupation throughout Australia

The *Mutual Recognition Act 1992* (Cth) ('the MRA') provides for the recognition within each state and territory of regulatory standards adopted anywhere else in Australia regarding goods and occupations. The MRA has coverage across each jurisdiction through a mixture of state referrals of power[71] or adoption of the MRA[72] under s 52(xxxvii) of the *Australian Constitution*, and territory requests that the Commonwealth enact the MRA.[73]

The effect of the scheme is that goods that can lawfully be sold in one Australian jurisdiction can be sold in any other Australian jurisdiction[74] and persons registered in one Australian jurisdiction for an occupation are entitled to be registered in any other Australian jurisdiction (a second jurisdiction) for the equivalent occupation after notifying the local registration authority of the second jurisdiction.[75] On carrying on the occupation in the second jurisdiction, a person is required to comply with laws in force in that jurisdiction regulating the manner of carrying on the occupation in that jurisdiction.[76]

The entitlement to be registered for an occupation in a second jurisdiction is supported by s 20(1) of the MRA, which provides that the entitlement applies 'as if the law of the second State that deals with registration expressly provided that registration in the first State is a sufficient ground of entitlement to registration'.[77]

---

68 See *Electronic Transactions Act 1999* (Cth) s 7A; *Electronic Transactions Act 2000* (NSW) s 6A; *Electronic Transactions (Queensland) Act 2001* (Qld) s 7A(2); *Electronic Communications Act 2000* (SA) s 6A; *Electronic Transactions Act 2000* (Tas) s 4A; *Electronic Transactions (Victoria) Act 2000* (Vic) s 6A; *Electronic Transactions Act 2011* (WA) s 7; *Electronic Transactions Act 2001* (ACT) s 6A; *Electronic Transactions (Northern Territory) Act 2000* (NT) s 6A. Schedule 1 to the Queensland Act sets out a range of exempt transactions and communications and none are prescribed by delegated legislation.

69 Examples of exemptions at the state or territory level include requirements for a document to be served personally or to be witnessed under the signature of a person other than its author, such as the execution of a will. No exemptions are prescribed by delegated legislation for the Australian Capital Territory.

70 The *Electronic Transactions Regulations 2020* (Cth) list a range of Commonwealth laws to which specified provisions of the *Electronic Transactions Act 1999* (Cth) do not apply including the *Australian Passports Act 2005* (Cth), various provisions of the *Commonwealth Electoral Act 1918*, the *Cheques Act 1986* (Cth) and the *Corporations Act 2001* (Cth).

71 *Mutual Recognition (New South Wales) Act 1992* (NSW); *Mutual Recognition (Queensland) Act 1992* (Qld); *Mutual Recognition (Tasmania) Act 1993* (Tas) s 5 (reference of power to amend the Commonwealth Act).

72 *Mutual Recognition (South Australia) Act 1993* (SA); *Mutual Recognition (Tasmania) Act 1993* (Tas) s 4; *Mutual Recognition (Victoria) Act 1998* (Vic); *Mutual Recognition (Western Australia) Act 2020* (WA).

73 *Mutual Recognition (Australian Capital Territory) Act 1992* (ACT); *Mutual Recognition (Northern Territory) Act 1992* (NT).

74 *Mutual Recognition Act 1992* (Cth) pt 2.

75 Ibid pt 3.

76 Ibid s 17(2).

77 See *Victorian Building Authority v Andriotis* (2019) 268 CLR 168. In that case the registration authority in the second jurisdiction had purported to reject a registration application on the basis that the applicant failed to meet good character requirements in the relevant legislation of the second jurisdiction. All seven

The result is that legislation in an Australian jurisdiction (the second jurisdiction) regulating the carrying on of an occupation must be read subject to the MRA as it will allow a person registered to carry on an equivalent occupation in another jurisdiction (the first jurisdiction) to obtain registration in the second jurisdiction for that occupation as if the legislation in the second jurisdiction had expressly provided for that very circumstance.

General legislation may deal with the terms and conditions of employment, and the rights and responsibilities of employees and employers, in the public sector [26.8]

Legislation establishing a public body may provide for persons to be employed to conduct the work necessary for the functioning of the body.[78] It is unnecessary for the legislation to make any provision as to their terms and conditions of employment or their rights as employees or the rights of their employer. This is because of the existence in each Australian jurisdiction of general industrial relations legislation dealing with those matters.[79]

The regime that regulates the terms and conditions of employment of such persons, and their rights and responsibilities and those of their employers, varies from jurisdiction to jurisdiction. Public sector workers employed by the Commonwealth, the Australian Capital Territory or the Northern Territory are covered by the *Fair Work Act 2009* (Cth).[80] That Act also covers Victorian public sector workers with certain exceptions including law enforcement officers and public sector executives.[81] The employment of other state public sector workers is governed by state industrial relations legislation.[82]

References to periods of time in Acts are construed by general Acts [26.9]

Under s 8AA of the *National Measurement Act 1960* (Cth) the Chief Meteorologist must maintain Co-ordinated Universal Time ('UTC') as determined by the International Bureau of Weights and Measures. Each state and territory has legislation defining standard time in that state or territory

---

High Court judges held that registration in one jurisdiction is of itself sufficient to ground an entitlement to registration for the equivalent occupation in another jurisdiction. This ruled out any capacity for the registration authority in the second jurisdiction to consider issues of good character.

78 Public sector legislation in each jurisdiction also provides generally for the employment of public servants who can be assigned to work across the government departments and public bodies existing in that jurisdiction. See *Public Service Act 1999* (Cth); *Government Sector Employment Act 2013* (NSW); *Public Sector Act 2008* (Qld); *Public Sector Act 2009* (SA); *State Service Act 2000* (Tas); *Public Administration Act 2004* (Vic); *Public Sector Management Act 1994* (WA); *Public Sector Management Act 1994* (ACT); *Public Sector Employment and Management Act 1993* (NT). See also *Public Governance, Performance and Accountability Act 2013* (Cth); *Public Sector Ethics Act 1994* (Qld); *Public Sector (Honesty and Accountability) Act 1995* (SA).

79 Such legislation also applies to persons employed in the private sector.

80 This Act principally relies on s 51(xx) of the *Australian Constitution* (the corporations power) and on the referral of industrial relations powers to the Parliament of the Commonwealth under s 51 (xxxvii) of the *Constitution* by all states except Western Australia. See *Industrial Relations (Commonwealth Powers) Act 2009* (NSW); *Fair Work (Commonwealth Powers) and Other Provisions Act 2009* (Qld); *Fair Work (Commonwealth Powers) Act 2009* (SA); *Industrial Relations (Commonwealth Powers) Act 2009* (Tas); *Fair Work (Commonwealth Powers) Act 2009* (Vic).

81 See *Fair Work (Commonwealth Powers) Act 2009* (Vic) ss 4, 5, 5A.

82 See *Industrial Relations Act 1996* (NSW); *Industrial Relations Act 2016* (Qld); *Fair Work Act 1994* (SA); *Industrial Relations Act 1984* (Tas); *Industrial Relations Act 1979* (WA).

by reference to UTC[83] and construing references in Acts or delegated legislation to periods of time as references to standard time.[84]

Each jurisdiction (except Queensland, Western Australia and the Northern Territory) also has legislation declaring a specified part of the year as summer time (being one hour in advance of standard time)[85] and providing for references in Acts or delegated legislation to time within such a period to be construed accordingly.[86]

For Commonwealth legislation, s 37 of the *Acts Interpretation Act 1901* (Cth) provides that, unless it is otherwise specifically stated, a reference to time is deemed in each state or part of the Commonwealth to mean the legal time in that place.

[26.10] The power to make rules of court may be found in general legislation

Legislation commonly confers jurisdiction on a court to make a finding in a proceeding involving a dispute between parties. To ensure justice and fairness, the conduct of the proceeding requires rules with which parties must comply. The individual Act conferring jurisdiction on the court may be silent on this matter.

In New South Wales,[87] Victoria[88] and Western Australia[89] there is a general provision in interpretation legislation empowering the body that makes court rules in that jurisdiction to make rules, including rules with respect to costs, for the purpose of regulating the practice and procedure of a court. These rules may relate to a new jurisdiction that is conferred on a court, or an existing jurisdiction that is extended or varied, by an Act or item of delegated legislation.

In the Australian Capital Territory, s 45 of *the Legislation Act 2001* (ACT) provides that the power of an entity to make rules for a court includes power to make rules 'in relation to any matter necessary or convenient to be prescribed for carrying out or giving effect to the court's jurisdiction under any law that authorises or requires anything to be done in or in relation to the court'.

Accordingly, in those jurisdictions an Act or delegated legislation conferring jurisdiction on a court, or extending or varying a court's jurisdiction, may be silent on the need for rules. In other jurisdictions it may be necessary for provision to be made in such an Act or delegated legislation for the making of rules.

In the Commonwealth,[90] New South Wales,[91] Tasmania[92] and Western Australia[93] there is a provision in interpretation legislation to the effect that the power of the authority to make rules

83 *Standard Time Act 1987* (NSW) ss 3, 4, 5; *Standard Time Act 1894* (Qld) s 3, *Standard Time Act 2009* (SA) s 3; *Standard Time Act 1895* (Tas) s 3; *Supreme Court Act 1986* (Vic) s 43(1); *Standard Time Act 2005* (WA) s 4; *Standard Time and Summer Time Act 1972* (ACT) s 4; *Standard Time Act 2005* (NT) s 4.

84 *Standard Time Act 1987* (NSW) s 6; *Standard Time Act 1894* (Qld) s 4; *Standard Time Act 2009* (SA) s 4; *Standard Time Act 1895* (Tas) s 4; *Supreme Court Act 1986* (Vic) s 43(2); *Standard Time Act 2005* (WA) s 5; *Standard Time and Summer Time Act 1972* (ACT) s 7; *Standard Time Act 2005* (NT) s 5.

85 *Standard Time Act 1987* (NSW) ss 7, 8, 9; *Daylight Saving Act 1971* (SA) s 3; *Daylight Saving Act 2007* (Tas) s 4; *Summer Time Act 1972* (Vic) s 3; *Standard Time and Summer Time Act 1972* (ACT) s 5.

86 *Standard Time Act 1987* (NSW) s 10; *Daylight Saving Act 1971* (SA) s 4; *Daylight Saving Act 2007* (Tas) s 5; *Summer Time Act 1972* (Vic) s 4; *Standard Time and Summer Time Act 1972* (ACT) s 7.

87 *Interpretation Act 1987* (NSW) s 78(2).

88 *Interpretation of Legislation Act 1984* (Vic) s 50.

89 *Interpretation Act 1984* (WA) s 66.

90 *Acts Interpretation Act 1901* (Cth) s 2K.

91 *Interpretation Act 1987* (NSW) s 78(1).

92 *Acts Interpretation Act 1931* (Tas) s 48.

93 *Interpretation Act 1984* (WA) s 66(2).

of court includes a power to make rules for the purpose of any Act that directs or authorises anything to be done by rules of court. In the Northern Territory the general rule-making power for a court under the legislation regulating that court extends to any matter within the jurisdiction of the court, irrespective of how that jurisdiction is conferred.[94]

In each jurisdiction there exists a body of rules that regulate the general practice and procedure of courts. For civil matters in New South Wales, Queensland, South Australia and the Australian Capital Territory there is a set of uniform rules applicable to the various courts.[95] In other jurisdictions there are separate sets of rules for the various courts.[96] Indeed general rules may be separately provided for a court in the exercise of its various jurisdictions.[97] No special rules of court will be required if the conduct of the relevant proceeding is covered by such general rules.

Monitoring and investigation powers may be conferred by a general Act [26.11]

The *Regulatory Powers (Standard Provisions) Act 2014* (Cth) ('the Regulatory Powers Act') provides a databank or standard set of monitoring and investigation powers. The powers can be called up by any individual Commonwealth Act establishing a regulatory scheme to provide for the monitoring of whether provisions of that Act are being complied with or investigating suspected non-compliance with any of its provisions. The Regulatory Powers Act also provides an enforcement framework that can be called up to enforce provisions.

Importantly, the Regulatory Powers Act does not apply of its own force to any regulatory scheme. Provisions contained in that Act only apply to a scheme if triggered by a provision in the Act establishing that scheme.[98]

Part 2 of the Regulatory Powers Act creates a framework for monitoring whether the provisions of an Act have been, or are being, complied with. It includes power for authorised persons to enter premises (by consent or under a warrant), search the premises and anything on the premises and question any person on the premises.[99]

Part 3 creates a framework for gathering material that relates to contraventions of a regulatory scheme. It contains similar powers to those in pt 2 but also provides power to seize evidential material.[100]

The privileges against self-incrimination and legal professional privilege are not abrogated by pt 2 or 3.[101]

Part 4[102] creates a framework for the use of civil penalties to enforce any provision of an Act that is a 'civil penalty provision' as defined by s 79(2) of the Regulatory Powers Act. This requires

94 *Supreme Court Act 1979* (NT) s 86(3); *Local Court Act 2015* (NT) s 48(2)(a).

95 *Uniform Civil Procedure Rules 2005* (NSW); *Uniform Civil Procedure Rules 1999* (Qld); *Uniform Civil Rules 2020* (SA); *Court Procedures Rules 2006* (ACT).

96 See *High Court Rules 2004* (Cth); *Supreme Court Rules 2000* (Tas); *District Court Rules 2005* (WA); *Supreme Court Rules 1987* (NT).

97 See *Magistrates Court (Civil Division) Rules 1998* (Tas); *Magistrates' Court (Family Violence Protection) Rules 2018* (Vic); *Local Court (Adoption of Children) Rules 1994* (NT).

98 See *Regulatory Powers (Standard Provisions) Act 2014* (Cth) ss 8–10, 38, 79, 100, 111, 118.

99 Examples of the triggering of pt 2 are the *Biosecurity Act 2015* (Cth) s 481 and *Export Control Act 2020* (Cth) s 326.

100 Examples of the triggering of pt 3 are the *Biosecurity Act 2015* (Cth) s 484, *Export Control Act 2020* (Cth) s 329 and *Road Vehicle Standards Act 2018* (Cth) s 52.

101 *Regulatory Powers (Standard Provisions) Act 2014* (Cth) ss 17, 47.

102 An example of the triggering of pt 4 is the *Sport Integrity Australia Act 2020* (Cth) s 72.

that the other Act either provide that a provision is a civil penalty provision or set a penalty described as a 'civil penalty'. Part 4 allows an application to be made to a court for an order that a person pay a pecuniary penalty to the Commonwealth.[103]

Part 5 creates a framework for the use of infringement notices where an infringement officer reasonably believes a provision subject to an infringement notice has been contravened.[104] An infringement notice requires payment of the amount specified in the notice.[105] On payment being made any liability of the person for the alleged contravention is discharged.[106]

Part 6 creates a framework for accepting and enforcing undertakings relating to compliance with provisions.[107] The undertaking may be enforced by court order.[108]

Part 7 creates a framework for using injunctions to enforce provisions.[109] It provides for an authorised person to apply to a court for an injunction restraining a person from engaging in conduct, or requiring a person to do a thing, if the person has refused or failed, or is refusing or failing, or is proposing to refuse or fail, to do a thing and that refusal or failure was, is or would be a contravention of a provision.

The Regulatory Powers Act reduces the volume of individual Acts establishing regulatory schemes and ensures greater consistency in the kind of regulatory powers available across the Commonwealth statute book. However, it has a disadvantage common to all legislation that incorporates material by reference. For a reader to understand what powers are available to officials under a scheme that triggers provisions of the Regulatory Powers Act, the reader must locate the relevant provisions of the Regulatory Powers Act and read the two Acts together.

There is no equivalent of the Regulatory Powers Act at state or territory level.

---

103 *Regulatory Powers (Standard Provisions) Act 2014* (Cth) s 82.

104 An example of the triggering of pt 5 is the *Sport Integrity Australia Act 2020* (Cth) s 73B.

105 *Regulatory Powers (Standard Provisions) Act 2014* (Cth) s 104(1)(f).

106 Ibid s 107(1)(a).

107 An example of the triggering of pt 6 is the *Road Vehicle Standards Act 2018* (Cth) s 57.

108 *Regulatory Powers (Standard Provisions) Act 2014* (Cth) s 115.

109 An example of the triggering of pt 7 is the *Road Vehicle Standards Act 2018* (Cth) s 58.

PART VII

THE WIDER CONTEXT

Previous Parts have examined contextual aids beyond the Act that are supplied by the legislative history (Part V) and Interpretation Acts and other Acts of general application (Part VI). Part VII continues in the same vein and examines other interpretative criteria beyond the Act concerned.

Chapter 27 (*Consequences*) considers how a particular construction may be tested by reference to its consequences – that is, the likely operation of the statute if a particular construction were preferred. The results a court may take into account include results that are unworkable or impracticable, inconvenient, anomalous or illogical, futile or pointless, or artificial.

Chapter 28 (*The Principle of Legality*) examines a principle of the common law under which it is presumed that Parliament does not intend by legislation to abrogate or curtail fundamental common law rights or principles, or to depart to a marked degree from the general system of law.

The 'statute book' is a term commonly used to describe all Acts of Parliament in existence in a particular jurisdiction, whether or not commenced to operate. Chapter 29 (*Use of the Statute Book and Legislation of Other Jurisdictions*) examines the use of the statute book, together with legislation of other jurisdictions (interstate and international).

Chapter 30 (*Use of Precedent*) examines the use of binding and persuasive precedent in the interpretative task. Precedent here refers, broadly, to prior judicial decisions of courts on the meaning of particular legislative text.

Chapter 31 (*International Treaties and Materials*) discusses the extent to which international treaties and other international materials are aids to interpretation. It discusses the long-established common law principle that, in cases of ambiguity, a construction of a statute that is consistent with Australia's international obligations should be preferred to a construction that is not.

Chapter 32 (*Other Common Law Presumptions and Aids*) considers residual common law presumptions and aids that are potentially available. They fall into three broad categories: works of reference; surrounding law (which in this chapter takes in maxims of law, the

Australian Constitution, and the general principles governing the lawfulness of administrative action); and common sense.

Chapter 33 (*Inadmissible Considerations*) is concerned with considerations of a type that should not be taken into account in statutory interpretation. The reason why such considerations ought not be given any weight is that they do not point to the legislative intention. An example of an inadmissible consideration is a judicially constructed policy – namely, a policy of the judge's own making.

CONSEQUENCES 27

Overview

A particular construction of a statutory provision may be tested by reference to its consequences. The principle directs attention to the likely operation of a statute if that construction were preferred. In practice, cases raising the principle are more concerned with adverse consequences. [27.1]

Like other interpretative aids, the consequences of a particular construction are not determinative of themselves; they may provide (at least) reason to question whether a result was intended. In taking account of the consequences of a particular construction, what is vital is not whether a consequence is undesirable from a party's standpoint, but whether, in the court's opinion, the legislature could not have intended a statute to operate in a particular way.

There is no definitive prescription of the kinds of adverse consequences that could not have been intended, though absurd consequences are often referred to.

Defining consequences

In relation to a construction, 'consequences' refers to the likely operation of the statute if that construction were preferred [27.2]

A court will examine whether a particular construction 'may be expected to lead' to beneficial or adverse consequences.[1] Put another way, it may examine the 'evident scope' for beneficial or adverse consequences.[2] 'Consequences' here refers to the likely operation of the statute if a particular construction were preferred.[3] The court may also examine the past operation of the provision: how the provision has operated in the instant case.[4]

A synonym for the consequence of a particular construction is 'result'.[5]

---

1 *Uelese v Minister for Immigration and Border Protection* (2015) 256 CLR 203, 217 [45] (French CJ, Kiefel, Bell and Keane JJ).

2 *Shahi v Minister for Immigration and Citizenship* (2011) 246 CLR 163, 175 [31] (French CJ, Gummow, Hayne and Bell JJ).

3 *Cooper Brookes (Wollongong) Pty Ltd v Commissioner of Taxation (Cth)* (1981) 147 CLR 297, 320 (Mason and Wilson JJ); *Legal Services Board v Gillespie-Jones* (2013) 249 CLR 493, 509 [48] (French CJ, Hayne, Crennan and Kiefel JJ); *Yasmin v A-G (Cth)* (2015) 236 FCR 169, 194 [108] (the Court).

4 *Wei v Minister for Immigration and Border Protection* (2015) 257 CLR 22, 34 [31] (Gageler and Keane JJ).

5 *Shahi v Minister for Immigration and Citizenship* (2011) 246 CLR 163, 177 [38] (French CJ, Gummow, Hayne and Bell JJ); *Collector of Customs v Agfa-Gevaert Ltd* (1996) 186 CLR 389, 401 (the Court); *Minister for Immigration and Citizenship v SZJGV* (2009) 238 CLR 642, 653 [12] (French CJ and Bell J).

Taking into account consequences

[27.3] A particular construction may be tested by reference to its consequences

A court may test a particular construction 'by reference to its consequences'.[6] It is well settled that the consequences of a particular reading are relevant.[7] As Kirby J stated: 'It is both permissible, and often helpful, to look to the consequences which would flow if one construction were favoured rather than another.'[8] Statements from other members of the High Court of Australia include:

> [I]f two constructions are open, the court will obviously prefer that which will avoid what it considers to be inconvenience or injustice.[9]
>
> [T]here are cases in which inconvenience of result or improbability of result assists the court in concluding that an alternative construction which is reasonably open is to be preferred to the literal meaning because the alternative interpretation more closely conforms to the legislative intent discernible from other provisions in the statute.[10]
>
> The context of the words, the consequences of a literal or grammatical construction, the purpose of the statute or the canons of construction may require the words of a legislative provision to be read in a way that does not correspond with the literal or grammatical meaning.[11]
>
> [T]he consequences of a particular construction can be taken into account in assessing the likelihood of that construction being correct.[12]

A court takes account of consequences 'upon the hypothesis of Parliamentary rationality and good sense'.[13]

There are numerous instances of the High Court taking into account the consequences of a particular construction.[14]

---

6 *Yasmin v A-G (Cth)* (2015) 236 FCR 169, 194 [108] (the Court).

7 *Western Australia v Ward* (2002) 213 CLR 1, 354 [850] (Callinan J).

8 *Emanuele v Australian Securities Commission* (1997) 188 CLR 114, 146.

9 *Cooper Brookes (Wollongong) Pty Ltd v Commissioner of Taxation (Cth)* (1981) 147 CLR 297, 305 (Gibbs CJ).

10 Ibid 320 (Mason and Wilson JJ).

11 *Project Blue Sky Inc v Australian Broadcasting Authority* (1998) 194 CLR 355, 384 [78] (McHugh, Gummow, Kirby and Hayne JJ) (citation omitted).

12 *CTM v The Queen* (2008) 236 CLR 440, 509 [237] (Heydon J).

13 *Emanuele v Australian Securities Commission* (1997) 188 CLR 114, 147 (Kirby J).

14 See, eg, *Australian Education Union v General Manager of Fair Work Australia* (2012) 246 CLR 117, 157 [101] (Heydon J); *Independent Commission Against Corruption v Cunneen* (2015) 256 CLR 1, 27 [54] (French CJ, Hayne, Kiefel and Nettle JJ); *Legal Services Board v Gillespie-Jones* (2013) 249 CLR 493, 509 [48] (French CJ, Hayne, Crennan and Kiefel JJ); *R v Independent Broad-based Anti-corruption Commissioner* (2016) 256 CLR 459, 473–4 [49]–[52] (French CJ, Kiefel, Bell, Keane, Nettle and Gordon JJ); *North Australian Aboriginal Justice Agency Ltd v Northern Territory* (2015) 256 CLR 569, 647 [221] (Nettle and Gordon JJ); *Mansfield v The Queen* (2012) 247 CLR 86, 105 [69] (Heydon J); *Pfeiffer v Stevens* (2001) 209 CLR 57, 73 [52] (McHugh J); *Project Blue Sky Inc v Australian Broadcasting Authority* (1998) 194 CLR 355, 391–2 [96]–[98] (McHugh, Gummow, Kirby and Hayne JJ); *Shahi v Minister for Immigration and Citizenship* (2011) 246 CLR 163, 174–5 [31] (French CJ, Gummow, Hayne and Bell JJ), 180 [50] (Heydon J) (dissenting as to outcome); *Minister for Immigration and Citizenship v SZJGV* (2009) 238 CLR 642, 651 [9], 652–3 [10], 653 [12] (French CJ and Bell J); *Uelese v Minister for Immigration and Border Protection* (2015) 256 CLR 203, 217 [45], 219 [51] (French CJ, Kiefel, Bell and Keane JJ); *Wicks v State Rail Authority of New South Wales* (2010) 241 CLR 60, 77 [54] (the Court).

Cases in which a court refers to the consequences of a particular construction mainly deal with perceived adverse consequences. This may be because, inherently, adverse consequences are a sign that the construction may be amiss. Also, where the consequences are perceived to be beneficial, the presumption that remedial legislation is to be given a 'fair, large and liberal' interpretation is commonly engaged.[15]

Example 27.1 *Berenguel v Minister for Immigration and Citizenship*[16]

The plaintiff challenged, in the High Court of Australia, the refusal by a delegate of the Minister to issue him with a Skilled (Residence) (Class VB) Visa, Subclass 885 (Skilled – Independent). A criterion for the grant of the visa was that the applicant has 'vocational English': cl 885.213(a) of the *Migration Regulations 1994* (Cth).[17] That criterion appeared under a heading to a division of the Regulations that stated 'Criteria to be satisfied at time of application'. 'Vocational English' was defined in reg 1.15B. Subclause 1.15B(5) stated that 'the person has achieved, in a test conducted not more than 2 years before the day on which the application was lodged', an International English Language Testing System ('IELTS') test score of at least 5.

Pursuant to his intention to obtain the visa, the plaintiff booked an IELTS test on 26 February 2008. On 21 April 2008 he lodged his visa application and paid a prescribed fee of $2,600 to the Department of Immigration and Citizenship. The earliest date on which the English language test could be administered to him was 10 May 2008. The plaintiff sat the test on that date and secured a score of 6, which meant he satisfied the standard of vocational English. The plaintiff provided the Department with the test result on 7 June 2008. But, on 12 December 2008, a delegate refused the plaintiff's application for the reason that he had not met 'the regulatory requirement of having vocational English at [the] time of application'.[18]

The High Court considered whether it was correct to construe reg 1.15B(5) as requiring vocational English to be demonstrated at the time of application. Against this, it considered a construction of the words 'not more than 2 years before the day on which the application was lodged' as meaning 'the test was conducted no earlier than two years before the application was lodged'.[19] The Court unanimously preferred the latter alternative construction that favoured the plaintiff.[20]

In giving reasons the Court made a brief, but significant, reference to the principle that a construction may be tested by reference to its consequences. Their Honours said: 'Moreover, in this case, the construction for which the minister contends leads to such plain unfairness and absurdity that it is not to be preferred.'[21] The Court did not elaborate, presumably because the unfairness and absurdity was 'plain'. It may be inferred that unfairness existed by reason that, well before the decision was made, the plaintiff had supplied evidence of competency in the

15 See **[17.3]**.

16 (2010) 264 ALR 417.

17 Alternatively, 'competent English', but this was at a higher standard than vocational English. The delegate did not rely on this higher standard.

18 The Minister so submitted in the High Court also: *Berenguel v Minister for Immigration and Citizenship* (2010) 264 ALR 417, 422 [22] (the Court).

19 Ibid 422 [25].

20 Ibid 423 [26].

21 Ibid.

English language. Furthermore, this evidence was more recent than the evidence that would be required on the Minister's construction. And no convincing reason was advanced by counsel for the Minister to show that the Minister's construction would have fair consequences.[22]

[27.4] Like any other interpretative aid, the consequences of a particular construction are not determinative of themselves, but they may provide (at least) reason to question whether a result was intended

If a court perceives that a construction would lead to 'unattractive consequences', it may still find that, overall, the construction is the preferable one. Considering all the relevant arguments as to the meaning of the disputed provision is the tried and true judicial method for ascertaining the legislative intention.[23] As the Federal Court said of a Minister's construction that, if preferred, would bring about 'a drastic result': 'If that is, on a proper construction, what Parliament intended, then so be it.'[24] Further, a remedy for correcting any unattractive consequences lies with the Parliament. As Keane J said with respect to particular 'unattractive consequences', 'the amelioration of that state of affairs, which itself is a consequence of legislative action, is properly a matter for the legislature'.[25]

Although not determinative on its own, testing a construction by reference to its consequences can be productive. The benefits were put by the Northern Territory Supreme Court:

> [As counsel pointed out, practical] difficulties in themselves would not be sufficient reason to construe the Act in such a way as to avoid the difficulties. However, they provide some reason to question whether the legislature intended a construction which would produce such a result.[26]

If a court does not have regard to the result of a particular construction when it would be productive to do so, it may be arguable that the construction 'elevates form over substance'.[27]

---

22 In fairness, at the hearing, counsel for the Minister, Mr Lloyd, attempted to explain the purpose from the Minister's viewpoint: 'In my submission, the purpose of having it as a time of application criteria is that people do not even apply until they have passed the test. So they do not spend money and wait and spend time. If they cannot pass the test, they should not apply at all': Transcript of Proceedings, *Berenguel v Minister for Immigration and Citizenship* [2010] HCATrans 41, 7 (SB Lloyd SC). But this is not to the point when the facts show that an applicant *has passed the test* well before the decision is made.

23 See **[9.10]**.

24 *BGM16 v Minister for Immigration and Border Protection* (2017) 252 FCR 97, 110 [70] (Mortimer and Wigney JJ).

25 *King v Philcox* (2015) 255 CLR 304, 327 [43].

26 *Suich v Northern Territory* (2010) 27 NTLR 188, 193 [20] (Kelly J).

27 *Cumerlong Holdings Pty Ltd v Dalcross Properties Pty Ltd* (2010) 175 LGERA 433, 447 [79] (Handley JA) (dissenting on result).

In taking into account adverse consequences of a particular construction, what is vital is not whether a consequence is undesirable from a party's standpoint, but whether, in the court's opinion, the legislature could not have intended a statute to operate in a particular way [27.5]

(a) A court gives weight not to consequences of a construction per se, but only those consequences that in its opinion reflect Parliament's intention

Since the paramount object of statutory interpretation is to ascertain the intention of Parliament,[28] a court must be able to weigh the relative contribution of any particular aid in that regard.[29] So, a court does not give weight to consequences of a construction per se, but only those consequences that, in its opinion, reflect Parliament's intention. This is why the High Court has explained that, where allegedly adverse consequences of a particular construction are concerned, the question is whether 'the legislature could not have intended a statute to operate in a particular way'.[30] Thus, if a court refers to the operation of a statute as 'absurd', 'extraordinary', 'capricious', 'irrational' or 'obscure', a reader should infer that these are a reference to consequences that Parliament could not have intended.[31]

Hence, it is not necessarily fatal if a particular construction is likely to lead to a harsh result.[32] On the contrary, it may be that such consequences are 'reflective of a legitimate policy choice having regard to competing considerations'.[33] **Example 27.2** is illustrative.

Example 27.2 *Dietman v Brennan-Kuss*[34]

In the early 1990s the third respondent (H) lawfully caught two sharks of the species White Shark pursuant to his South Australian fishing licence. He retained their jaws and teeth. In 1998 White Shark was declared a protected species pursuant to the *Fisheries Act 1982* (SA) and, later, pursuant to a replacement legislative scheme: the *Fisheries Management (General) Regulations 2007* (SA) made under the *Fisheries Management Act 2007* (SA) ('FMA').

In 2010 H provided, to the first and second respondents, one set of the jaws and some loose teeth of a White Shark. They were on consignment to offer for sale from the first and second respondents' store in Coober Pedy (a town in South Australia). After a complaint had been laid in

28 See chapter 4.

29 See **[9.9]** for weighing of interpretative arguments.

30 *Legal Services Board v Gillespie-Jones* (2013) 249 CLR 493, 509 [48] (French CJ, Hayne, Crennan and Kiefel JJ). See also *Construction, Forestry, Mining and Energy Union v Mammoet Australia Pty Ltd* (2013) 248 CLR 619, 635 [49] (the Court); *Medical Board of Australia v Kemp* (2018) 56 VR 51, 82 [157] (Niall JA, Maxwell P agreeing at 53 [1], Tate JA agreeing at 53 [2]).

31 *Cooper Brookes (Wollongong) Pty Ltd v Commissioner of Taxation (Cth)* (1981) 147 CLR 297, 321 (Mason and Wilson JJ). This statement has subsequently been endorsed by the High Court: *Legal Services Board v Gillespie-Jones* (2013) 249 CLR 493, 509 [48] (French CJ, Hayne, Crennan and Kiefel JJ).

32 *Victims Compensation Fund Corporation v Brown* (2003) 201 ALR 260, 268 [29] (Heydon J, McHugh J agreeing at 261 [1], Gummow J agreeing at 261 [2], Kirby J agreeing at 261 [3], Hayne J agreeing at 261 [4]). See, eg, *Minister for Immigration, Citizenship, Migrant Services and Multicultural Affairs v Moorcroft* (2021) 391 ALR 270, 279 [29] (the Court).

33 See, eg, *Minister for Immigration, Citizenship, Migrant Services and Multicultural Affairs v Moorcroft* (2021) 391 ALR 270, 278 [27] (the Court).

34 (2015) 123 SASR 24.

2012 the respondents were found guilty in the Magistrates Court of having possession of, and offering for sale, an aquatic resource of a protected species, namely White Shark, in contravention of s 72(2)(b) of the FMA:

> (2) Subject to this section, if a person sells or purchases, or has possession or control of –
>
> ...
>
> (b) an aquatic resource of a protected species;
>
> ...
>
> the person is guilty of an offence.

It was common ground that H was in possession of the jaws and teeth within the meaning of s 72(2)(b).

The respondents successfully appealed to a single judge of the Supreme Court. That judge read down the scope of s 72(2)(b), 'so that it applied only to fish of a species which was protected when it was taken'.[35] On an appeal to the Full Court of the Supreme Court of South Australia by the complainant, the issue arose as to whether that construction was correct, or whether the provision 'proscribes possession of, or commercial dealing in, an aquatic resource of a species that is declared to be a protected species *at the time of the possession or other dealing*.[36]

Kourakis CJ observed that the text supported the latter, wider construction, since the text made no reference to the circumstances of the taking.[37] The consequences of the wider construction were considered by Kourakis CJ. Referring to the consequences for the fishers, he said: 'I acknowledge that it may be harsh to proscribe the marketing of fish which were lawfully taken'.[38] This was because the construction would deny such fishers the right to sell their property.[39] Yet, the Chief Justice held: 'Overall there is good reason to conclude that the plain words of s 72(2)(b) of the FMA were intended to have the meaning they bear on their face.'[40] Kourakis CJ reasoned that it was not irrational to proscribe the marketing of fish, which were lawfully taken. In this regard he referred to certain 'notorious facts' (which by definition would have been known to the legislature). They included the long coastline of South Australia that supports large and valuable fisheries; the difficulty in adequately policing the vast waters of the state; the movement of many species across long distances that cross over state and Commonwealth boundaries; and the difficulty in proving when and where fish, found exposed for sale in markets, were taken. He also noted that it is 'a globally recognised, environmental strategy to deter the taking of protected species by denying poachers a market in which to supply unlawfully taken animals'.[41]

It is apparent that the Court's evaluation of the consequences took in not only the consequences for fishers of the construction that favoured the prosecution, but also the consequences for enforcement and the wider environmental consequences of the opposing construction. Once all the consequences were taken into account the Court was persuaded that '[t]he total prohibition on the marketing of a protected species or prescribed class of fish may be both a necessary and rational measure'.[42]

35 Ibid 33–4 [31] (Kourakis CJ, Bampton J agreeing at 40 [55], Muecke DCJ agreeing at 40 [56]).

36 Ibid 26 [4] (emphasis added).

37 Ibid 33 [30].

38 Ibid.

39 Ibid.

40 Ibid 34 [32].

41 Ibid 33 [30].

42 Ibid.

(b) **In evaluating whether certain consequences of a particular construction were likely to have been intended, courts may appeal to common sense**

In a statutory interpretation case, the High Court observed: 'Appeals to common-sense ... is neither a recent nor uncommon invocation.'[43] For example, with respect to the principle that a court may take account of the consequences of a particular construction, a court may say that '[i]t cannot sensibly be the intention of the legislation that [specified consequences ensue]'.[44]

(c) **In evaluating whether the consequences of a particular construction were likely to have been intended, a court will be assisted by asking whether the consequences frustrate the legislative purpose**

Having regard to the consequences of a particular construction is closely linked to the requirement that, in interpreting a statute, a court gives weight to the construction that will advance the legislative purpose.[45] The latter is an important indicator of legislative intention. So whether the consequences of a particular construction frustrates the legislative purpose will be a key way in which to assess the construction.

Example 27.3 *Alcan (NT) Alumina Pty Ltd v Commissioner of Territory Revenue (NT)*[46]

The dispute before the High Court of Australia arose from transactions by which the appellant acquired 100 per cent of the shares in Gove Aluminium Ltd ('GAL'). The land to which GAL was entitled at the relevant date comprised leases granted under statute. All but two of the leases contained an option to renew.

Section 4(1) of the *Taxation (Administration) Act 2007* (NT) ('the Act') defined 'dutiable property' as meaning, among other things, 'land'. In turn, 'land' was defined as including 'a lease of land'. Further, 'lease' was defined as follows:

> includes a lease granted under an Act ... but does not include –
>
> ...
>
> (c) an option to renew a lease.

The respondent Commissioner determined that the options to renew a lease were within the meaning of 'land' in s 56N(2)(b) of the Act (a provision in div 8A of the Act placing a threshold for liability in the case of an acquisition of shares in a corporation). Hence, the transactions involved relevant acquisitions for the purposes of the Act. The Commissioner assessed stamp duty on the transactions in the amount of $31,050,000 and, together with a penalty of $16,467,997, the total liability of Alcan was $47,517,997.

The Court of Appeal of the Northern Territory agreed with the Commissioner's construction of 'land' in s 56N(2)(b). The Court found that the definition of lease did not apply to div 8A and to the definition of 'dutiable property', by reason of a contrary intention evinced by the context and legislative history. The essential buttress of the Court of Appeal's reasoning was an argument

43 *Collector of Customs v Agfa-Gevaert Ltd* (1996) 186 CLR 389, 400 n 43 (the Court).

44 *ZD v Secretary to the Department of Health and Human Services* [2017] VSC 806, [81] (Osborn JA).

45 See chapter 8.

46 (2009) 239 CLR 27.

based on consequences made in the light of legislative history. The Court found that since 1978 the legislature had 'consistently increased its capacity to raise revenue by closing off avoidance practices and increasing the range of transactions attracting duty'.[47] It inferred that 'it would be surprising if the legislature intended to sever from a lease something which contributed to its value on a conveyance'.[48]

The High Court unanimously allowed the appeal by Alcan. First, it noted that the Commissioner did not argue that the consequence for the revenue was an absurd result.[49] Second, it noted that the outcome had been assessed by the Court of Appeal by reference to 'the general legislative purpose of raising revenue'.[50] The High Court found that fixing upon the general legislative purpose of raising revenue was 'insufficient to support an intention to exclude a clearly expressed definition'.[51] As discussed in more detail in chapter 8, a statute is not to be construed simply on the basis of the general purpose of the statute.[52] It may be inferred that the outcome for the raising of revenue was given little weight by the High Court because it did not frustrate a specific legislative purpose of the provision concerned.

(d) When a court evaluates the consequences of a particular construction, judicial intuitions may be involved

In a case involving the *Disability Discrimination Act 1992* (Cth) that reached the High Court, the Court below (the Full Federal Court) had referred to the 'draconian consequences' of a particular construction.[53] This led McHugh and Kirby JJ to observe:

> In matters of anti-discrimination law generally, and disability law in particular, judicial intuition as to what is 'draconian' must be kept in firm check, for sometimes it will be based unconsciously on the very attitudes that the law is designed to correct and redress.[54]

But their Honours added that, '[w]here statutory provisions, or the common law, are not designed to alter common attitudes and stereotypes, intuition can sometimes afford a useful check for judicial reasoning'.[55] This indicates that intuition can be a valuable tool if used appropriately.

(e) If a party to a dispute alleges that certain consequences of a particular construction ought to be taken into account, but the consequences are particular only to that party, a court may not find the consequences of great assistance

If a party to a dispute alleges that its interests will be damaged by a particular construction being upheld, a court may not find these considerations alone to be significant. Thus, in a case involving

47 *Commissioner of Territory Revenue v Alcan (NT) Alumina Pty Ltd* (2008) 156 NTR 1, 24 [76] (Martin (BR) CJ, Angel J agreeing at 30 [104], Southwood J agreeing at 34 [121]), quoted in (2009) 239 CLR 27, 43 [36] (Hayne, Heydon, Crennan and Kiefel JJ, French CJ agreeing at 30 [1]).

48 (2009) 239 CLR 27, 48 [52] (Hayne, Heydon, Crennan and Kiefel JJ, French CJ agreeing at 30 [1]).

49 Ibid 46 [45].

50 Ibid 47 [51].

51 Ibid 48 [53].

52 See **[8.7]**.

53 *Purvis v New South Wales (Department of Education and Training)* (2002) 117 FCR 237, 247 [27] (the Court).

54 *Purvis v State of New South Wales (Department of Education and Training)* (2003) 217 CLR 92.

55 Ibid 104 [19] n 30.

s 26A of the *Fair Work (Registered Organisations) Act 2009* (Cth), in which the Australian Education Union ('AEU') was the appellant, French CJ, Crennan and Kiefel JJ said:

> In aid of its preferred construction of s 26A, the AEU pointed to the unfairness to it of the construction adopted by the Full Court. The unfairness was defined by reference to the AEU's loss of the benefit of the judgment it had secured in *Lawler* and the waste of resources expended in obtaining it. Considerations of fairness at this level of particularity are not of great assistance in the construction of a statutory rule with general application.[56]

The explanation would appear to be that a court is interested in all the relevant consequences of the operation of a provision, not a partial and potentially misleading account of the consequences on a particular party only.

(f) If a party to a dispute claims in general terms that positive or negative consequences will likely result if a particular construction is upheld, but the party does not particularise or otherwise substantiate the claim, a court will not give the claim any weight

A party to a dispute may allege in general terms that a particular construction will cause adverse consequences, such as 'unacceptable confusion'.[57] But if the allegation is not supported, such as by reference to a particular consequence, the argument will be rejected.[58] The same applies to an allegation in general terms that a favourable result will ensue if a particular construction is upheld.[59]

(g) The consequences of both constructions should be considered in an even-handed way

After evaluating the consequences of a particular construction, it is appropriate to consider any 'countervailing examples' of the consequences of taking the opposing construction.[60] If this does not happen the decision-maker may reason 'partially'.[61] This common-sense stipulation flows from the fact that each construction will likely have consequences and, if a court is able to perceive what those consequences are likely to be, it should be even-handed with both constructions under consideration.

Kinds of consequences that may be taken into account

As far as adverse consequences are concerned, there is no definitive prescription of the kinds of consequences that could not have been intended [27.6]

(a) The collective label often used to describe consequences that could not have been intended is 'absurd'

In *Collector of Customs v Agfa-Gevaert Ltd*[62] the High Court approved of the way Bennion had collectively assembled relevant adverse consequences under one head or label – 'absurdity'.[63]

56 *Australian Education Union v General Manager of Fair Work Australia* (2012) 246 CLR 117, 134 [28] (French CJ, Crennan and Kiefel JJ). See also 159 [109] (Heydon J).

57 *Registrar of Births, Deaths and Marriages (NSW) v Norrie* (2014) 250 CLR 490, 500 [41] (the Court).

58 Ibid 501 [43]–[44].

59 *Australian Education Union v Department of Education and Children's Services* (2012) 248 CLR 1, 19 [41] (Heydon J).

60 *AQO v Minister for Finance and Services* (2016) 93 NSWLR 46, 85 [169] (Basten JA, Ward JA agreeing at 87 [177]).

61 Ibid.

62 (1996) 186 CLR 389.

63 See Oliver Jones, *Bennion on Statutory Interpretation: A Code* (LexisNexis, 6th ed, 2013) Part XXI.

Bennion used the word 'absurd' (as the courts have done) in the sense of 'contrary to sense and reason'.[64] In *Collector of Customs v Agfa-Gevaert Ltd*[65] the Court spoke of 'absurd in the sense that the result may be unworkable or impracticable, inconvenient, anomalous or illogical, futile or pointless, or artificial'.[66] While helpful, the list of consequences is not complete. Other adverse or absurd consequences that have been given weight include a 'capricious' result,[67] 'discordant and inconsistent treatment',[68] 'improbability of result',[69] 'arbitrary' distinction,[70] 'contradictory' scheme,[71] 'irrational' result,[72] 'harsh and oppressive' operation,[73] 'odd result',[74] 'drastic result',[75] 'unreasonable' result,[76] 'injustice' or 'unjust' consequences,[77] 'unfairness',[78] 'draconian step',[79] 'uncertainty',[80] '[frustration of] the statutory objective',[81] 'undesirable practical consequences'[82] and 'unlikely consequence'.[83] As Mason and Wilson JJ stated in *Cooper*

64 Ibid 869.

65 (1996) 186 CLR 389.

66 Ibid 401 (the Court) (citations omitted). The footnotes supply authorities on each of those aspects.

67 *North Australian Aboriginal Justice Agency Ltd v Northern Territory* (2015) 256 CLR 569, 647 [221] (Nettle and Gordon JJ); *Tickle Industries Pty Ltd v Hann* (1974) 130 CLR 321, 331 (Barwick CJ).

68 *Footscray City College v Ruzicka* (2007) 16 VR 498, 505 [17] (Chernov JA, Warren CJ agreeing at 499 [1], Maxwell P agreeing at 499 [2]).

69 *Cooper Brookes (Wollongong) Pty Ltd v Commissioner of Taxation (Cth)* (1981) 147 CLR 297, 320 (Mason and Wilson JJ).

70 *Public Service Association v Industrial Relations Secretary* [2015] NSWCA 386, [53] (Emmett AJA, Ward JA agreeing at [19]).

71 *Probuild Constructions (Aust) Pty Ltd v Shade Systems Pty Ltd* (2018) 264 CLR 1, 32 [82] (Gageler J).

72 *Mansfield v The Queen* (2012) 247 CLR 86, 105 [68] (Heydon J); *Legal Services Board v Gillespie-Jones* (2013) 249 CLR 493, 509 [48] (French CJ, Hayne, Crennan and Kiefel JJ); *Minister for Immigration and Citizenship v SZJGV* (2009) 238 CLR 642, 652–3 [9]–[10] (French CJ and Bell J).

73 *Minister for Immigration and Multicultural and Indigenous Affairs v SZAYW* (2005) 145 FCR 523, 540 [77] (Weinberg J).

74 *R v A2* (2019) 269 CLR 507, 558 [157] (Nettle and Gordon JJ, Edelman J agreeing at 572 [193]); *Collett v Repatriation Commission* (2009) 178 FCR 39, 48 [33] (Logan J).

75 *BGM16 v Minister for Immigration and Border Protection* (2017) 252 FCR 97, 110 [70] (Mortimer and Wigney JJ).

76 *Legal Services Board v Gillespie-Jones* (2013) 249 CLR 493, 509 [48] (French CJ, Hayne, Crennan and Kiefel JJ); *R v Hannan* (2016) 259 A Crim R 558, 569 [49] (Peter Lyons J).

77 *Legal Services Board v Gillespie-Jones* (2013) 249 CLR 493, 509 [48] (French CJ, Hayne, Crennan and Kiefel JJ); *Uelese v Minister for Immigration and Border Protection* (2015) 256 CLR 203, 217 [45] (French CJ, Kiefel, Bell and Keane JJ).

78 *Berenguel v Minister for Immigration and Citizenship* (2010) 264 ALR 417, 423 [26] (the Court).

79 *Murphy v Farmer* (1988) 165 CLR 19, 28 (Deane, Dawson and Gaudron JJ).

80 *R v Independent Broad-based Anti-corruption Commissioner* (2016) (2016) 256 CLR 459, 473 [49] (French CJ, Kiefel, Bell, Keane, Nettle and Gordon JJ); *Uelese v Minister for Immigration and Border Protection* (2015) 256 CLR 203, 219 [51] (French CJ, Kiefel, Bell and Keane JJ).

81 *R v Independent Broad-based Anti-corruption Commissioner* (2016) 256 CLR 459, 474 [52] (French CJ, Kiefel, Bell, Keane, Nettle and Gordon JJ).

82 *Western Australian Planning Commission v Dungey* [2010] WASC 52, [54] (Beech J). See also *Medical Board of Australia v Kemp* (2018) 56 VR 51, 83 [167] (Niall JA, Maxwell P agreeing at 53 [1], Tate JA agreeing at 53 [2]).

83 *SAS Trustee Corporation v Miles* (2018) 265 CLR 137, 152 [27] (Kiefel CJ, Bell and Nettle JJ).

Brookes (Wollongong) Pty Ltd v Commissioner of Taxation (Cth),[84] labels such as 'absurd' are not definitive, for

> the propriety of departing from the literal interpretation is not confined to situations described by these labels. It extends to any situation in which for good reason the operation of the statute on a literal reading does not conform to the legislative intent as ascertained from the provisions of the statute, including the policy which may be discerned from those provisions.[85]

(b) **The potentially relevant consequences of a particular construction include the consequences for the enforcement of the law**

Taking into account the consequences of a particular construction includes having regard, where appropriate, to whether a construction 'would have placed a burden of proof on the prosecution which might be very difficult to discharge'.[86] If the consequence merely goes to 'greater prosecutorial convenience', this may not be compelling.[87] But if the consequences of a construction are that clear difficulties would attend the prosecution of a breach of a duty or a prohibition imposed by a provision,[88] that consequence counts against the construction.

Similarly, a court may give weight to the consequences a construction would have for the administration of the law. If one construction would lead to a complex and time-consuming evaluative assessment in a context in which fast and simple decision-making is contemplated, it is not readily to be supposed that the construction was Parliament's intention.[89]

---

84 (1981) 147 CLR 297.

85 Ibid 321.

86 *Mansfield v The Queen* (2012) 247 CLR 86, 105 [69] (Heydon J).

87 *HKSAR v Tse Man Fei* (Court of Final Appeal of the Hong Kong Special Administrative Region, FACC No 1 of 2016, 5 July 2016) [55] (Fok J, Ma CJ agreeing at [1], Ribeiro PJ agreeing at [2], Gleeson NPJ agreeing at [60]).

88 *R v A2* (2019) 269 CLR 507, 525 [48] (Kiefel CJ and Keane J, Nettle and Gordon JJ agreeing generally at 554 [148], Edelman J agreeing at 572 [193]; *DPP (Cth) v Easton* (2018) 98 NSWLR 1077, 1104 [125] (N Adams J).

89 *Minister for Immigration, Citizenship, Migrant Services and Multicultural Affairs v Moorcroft* (2021) 391 ALR 270, 276–7 [21]–[22] (the Court).

28 THE PRINCIPLE OF LEGALITY

Overview

[28.1] The principle of legality is a rule of construction under which it is presumed that Parliament does not intend by legislation to abrogate or curtail fundamental common law rights (including privileges and immunities) or principles or to depart to a marked degree from the general system of law.

The presumption at the core of the principle of legality may be rebutted by the relevant legislation, either expressly or by necessary implication.

The principle of legality operates as a restraint, not as a limitation, on Parliament's power to encroach on rights. Even when it is clear that it is an object of the legislation to encroach on a particular right, there is authority for the proposition that the principle of legality has the role of minimising the extent of that encroachment.

The strength of the presumption increases the more fundamental the court perceives the right or principle to be.

There is no catalogue of fundamental rights; nor is there a settled ongoing list of such rights. A right considered to be fundamental at one point in time may cease to be so in line with changing community values.

While accepting that Parliament can, if it wishes, abrogate or curtail fundamental common law rights or principles or markedly depart from the general system of law, courts have also signalled to Parliament that it will only be taken to intend to do so if it makes that intention unmistakably clear. They assume that this is in line with how Parliament would behave – that is, that Parliament would want to make unmistakably clear an intention to interfere with a fundamental right or principle or to depart to a marked degree from the general system of law.

Apart from the principle of legality being considered by courts to be reflective of how Parliament would behave when intending to encroach on a fundamental right or principle or depart markedly from the general system of law, courts further rationalise that the principle of legality protects such rights or principles or that system from inadvertent interference by requiring Parliament to be upfront about what it is doing and to accept the political consequences of that.

The principle of legality is not limited to primary legislation but applies also to delegated legislation. Whether it has any application to rights established by statute is not settled.

What is the principle of legality and how may it be rebutted?

The principle of legality is a common law principle that presumes that, in the absence of express words or a necessary implication, Parliament does not intend by legislation to infringe fundamental common law rights, overthrow fundamental principles or markedly depart from the general system of law [28.2]

This chapter deals with yet another presumption to which regard must be had in interpreting legislation.[1] The principal purpose of this one is to protect fundamental common law rights (including privileges and immunities) or principles, and the general system of law, from unintended interference.

Examination of the history and development of this presumption in Australia usually starts with *Potter v Minahan*.[2] In that case O'Connor J quoted with approval[3] the following passage from the then current edition of Maxwell, *The Interpretation of Statutes*:

> It is in the last degree improbable that the legislature would overthrow fundamental principles, infringe rights, or depart from the general system of law, without expressing its intention with irresistible clearness; and to give any such effect to general words, simply because they have that meaning in their widest, or usual, or natural sense, would be to give them a meaning in which they were not really used.[4]

That principle of construction, in those terms, continued to be applied over successive decades.[5] Then the principle became narrowed so that the common law rights covered by it were limited to 'fundamental' common law rights[6] and the departures from the general system of law to which it applied were limited to ones that departed from it to a marked degree.[7] This narrowing was evident in the language of the majority judgment in *Bropho v Western Australia*.[8] They described

1 In *Federal Commissioner of Taxation v Tomaras* (2018) 265 CLR 434 Edelman J stated that these presumptions arise 'because human experience has shown that Parliament has historically acted in a certain way', that they are not rules of law but standardised inferences arising from 'common probabilities of fact'. Their effect is, he stated, that a court is reluctant to give the words of a statute a meaning that 'would conflict with recognized principles that Parliament would be prima facie expected to respect': at 466 [100].

2 (1908) 7 CLR 277.

3 Ibid 304 (citations omitted).

4 J Anwyl Theobold (ed), *Maxwell on Statutes* (Sweet and Maxwell, 4th ed, 1905) 121–2. This passage of Maxwell relied on a statement of Marshall CJ in *United States v Fisher*, 6 US 358 (1805) where he stated that '[w]here rights are infringed, where fundamental principles are overthrown, where the general system of law is departed from, the legislative intention must be expressed with irresistible clearness, to induce a court of justice to suppose a design to effect such objects': at 390. See *Lee v New South Wales Crime Commission* (2013) 251 CLR 196, 307 [307] (Gageler and Keane JJ).

5 See, eg, *Sargood Brothers v Commonwealth* (1910) 11 CLR 258, 279 (O'Connor J); *Melbourne Corporation v Barry* (1922) 31 CLR 174, 206 (Higgins J); *Pyneboard Pty Ltd v Trade Practices Commission* (1983) 152 CLR 328, 341 (Mason ACJ, Wilson and Dawson JJ).

6 A use of 'important' to describe the common law rights protected by the presumption appears in the joint judgment of the majority in *Daniels Corporation International Pty Ltd v Australian Competition and Consumer Commission* (2002) 213 CLR 543, 553 [11] (Gleeson CJ, Gaudron, Gummow and Hayne JJ) and in the judgment in that case of Kirby J at 575–6 [85] –[86], 577 [90], 581 [104]–[105] and 583 [108]. See also *Lee v New South Wales Crime Commission* (2013) 251 CLR 196, 310 [313] (Gageler and Keane JJ). There would not appear to be any basis for attaching any significance to the use of the qualifier 'important' rather than 'fundamental' to describe the category of rights now protected by the presumption.

7 Fundamental principles continued to be covered by the presumption.

8 (1990) 171 CLR 1.

the presumption as 'the presumption against the modification or abolition of fundamental rights or principles'.[9]

Express articulation of the reason for this narrowing is to be found in the judgment of McHugh J in *Malika Holdings Pty Ltd v Stretton*[10] where he stated:

> [N]early every session of Parliament produces laws which infringe the existing rights of individuals. Given the frequency with which legislatures now amend or abolish rights or depart from the general system of law, it is difficult to accept that it is 'in the last degree improbable' that a legislature would intend to alter rights or depart from the general system of law unless it did so 'with irresistible clearness'.
>
> Hallowed though the rule of construction referred to in *Potter v Minahan* may be, its utility in the present age is open to doubt in respect of laws that 'infringe rights, or depart from the general system of law'. In those areas, the rule is fast becoming, if it is not already, an interpretative fiction. Such is the reach of the regulatory state that it is now difficult to assume that the legislature would not infringe rights or interfere with the general system of law.[11]

McHugh J regarded fundamental rights as the corollaries of fundamental principles (which was the term used in *Potter v Minahan*) and which were presumed to continue unless the legislative language is clear and unambiguous.[12]

The reality of McHugh J's assessment of Parliament's behaviour is borne out by a December 2015 report of the Australian Law Reform Commission.[13] That report highlighted the quite extensive encroachment of Commonwealth laws on traditional rights, freedoms and privileges recognised by the common law. It cited numerous examples of laws that encroached on rights and freedoms such as freedom of speech, freedom of religion, freedom of association and assembly, freedom of movement, property rights, the privilege against self-incrimination, legal professional privilege, access to courts and protection from retrospective laws. A review of state and territory laws is likely to show a similar pattern of behaviour.

A presumption as to behaviour only has validity so long as the pattern of behaviour continues. If experience shows that Parliament is being less respectful of certain kinds of rights and that it is no longer improbable that it would interfere with them without considering that it was necessary

---

9 Ibid 18 (Mason CJ, Deane, Dawson, Toohey, Gaudron and McHugh JJ).

10 (2001) 204 CLR 290.

11 Ibid 298–9 [28]–[29]. Kirby J agreed with McHugh J that 'contemporary applications of the principle that legislation is presumed not to erode fundamental rights unless this object is clearly expressed need to be considered in the context of the quantity and variety of legislation today': at 328 [121]. However, Kirby J observed that there was still much work for the presumption to perform as the key word in it is 'fundamental'. McHugh J returned to the theme in *Gifford v Strang Patrick Stevedoring Pty Ltd* (2003) 214 CLR 269, saying that '[given] the frequency with which legislatures now abolish or amend "ordinary" common law rights, the "presumption" of non-interference with those rights is inconsistent with modern experience and borders on fiction': at 284 [36]. See also *Electrolux Home Products Pty Ltd v Australian Workers' Union* (2004) 221 CLR 309, 328 [19] (Gleeson CJ).

12 (2001) 204 CLR 290, 298 [28]. McHugh J set out, as examples of fundamental legal principles, the principle that a civil or criminal trial is to be a fair trial, that a criminal charge is to be proved beyond reasonable doubt, that people are not to be arrested or searched arbitrarily, that laws (especially criminal laws) do not operate retrospectively and that superior courts have jurisdiction to prevent unauthorised assumptions of jurisdiction by inferior courts and tribunals.

13 Australian Law Reform Commission, *Traditional Rights and Freedoms: Encroachment by Commonwealth Laws* (Report No 129, December 2015).

to employ irresistible clearness to do so, the presumption can be expected to change to reflect that change in behaviour.

Example 28.1 is an illustration of a case in which the relevant legislation was held not to express an unmistakably clear intention to affect a fundamental common law right, the right of an owner of private residential property to exclude others from it.

Example 28.1 *Coco v The Queen*[14]

Subject to specified exceptions, s 43 of the *Invasion of Privacy Act 1971* (Qld) ('the Act') made it an offence to use a listening device to record or listen to a private conversation. There was an exception in s 43(2)(c) of the Act for a member of the police force acting in the performance of duty and authorised to use the device by a senior police officer 'under and in accordance with an approval in writing given by a judge of the Supreme Court in relation to any particular matter specified in the approval'.

Police were investigating an offence of bribing Commonwealth officers. An approval was given by a Supreme Court judge for the use of a listening device in certain premises. A condition of the approval was that any police officer engaged in the investigation of the offence was authorised to enter the premises to which the approval applied for the purpose of installing and maintaining the device.

Coco was charged with offering to bribe Commonwealth officers and at his trial recordings of conversations obtained by means of the listening device were admitted into evidence. Coco was convicted and his appeal to the Queensland Court of Appeal was dismissed. Coco applied to the High Court for special leave to appeal the conviction on various grounds including that the approval given by the judge for the use of the listening device was void as the Act did not confer authority on the judge to authorise an entry that would otherwise constitute an unlawful trespass.

The High Court granted special leave and reversed the decision of the Court of Appeal, holding that s 43 of the Act did not confer power on a judge to authorise entry onto premises where that entry would otherwise have constituted a trespass. The majority stated:

> Every unauthorized entry upon private property is a trespass, the right of a person in possession or entitled to possession of premises to exclude others from those premises being a fundamental common law right ... Statutory authority to engage in what otherwise would be tortious conduct must be clearly expressed in unmistakable and unambiguous language.[15]

In their joint judgment Deane and Dawson JJ described it as being 'settled law that a court should not impute to a legislature an intention either to abolish or to modify a fundamental common law right or privilege unless the relevant legislation makes such an intention unambiguously clear'.[16]

---

14 (1994) 179 CLR 427.

15 Ibid 435–6 (Mason CJ, Brennan, Gaudron and McHugh JJ) (citations omitted). See also *Binsaris v Northern Territory* (2020) 270 CLR 549, 561 [25] (Gageler J).

16 (1994) 179 CLR 427, 446.

Example 28.2 concerns a departure from the general system of law.

Example 28.2 *X7 v Australian Crime Commission*[17]

In this case the issue concerned the power of an examiner appointed under the *Australian Crime Commission Act 2002* (Cth) ('the Act') to coercively examine a person about offences with which he had already been charged but for which he had not yet been tried. The Act did not expressly refer to the examination of a charged person, but its terms were capable of being interpreted as extending to such an examination. Hayne and Bell JJ, in a joint judgment with which Keifel J agreed,[18] held that such a process, despite the protections built into the Act preventing the direct use of evidence obtained in an examination, would alter the accusatorial process of criminal justice to a marked degree.[19] They held that an alteration of that kind 'is not made by a statute cast in general terms' but 'must be made by express words or necessary intendment'.[20] In applying the principle of legality to the issue of statutory construction arising in that case, Hayne and Bell JJ pointed out that the rule 'is not confined to legislation which may affect rights' but was engaged in that case because of the effects which construing the Act as allowing the examination of a charged person would have on 'a defining characteristic of the criminal justice system'.[21]

[28.3] The presumption may be rebutted but doing so requires clear and unambiguous language or a necessary implication

In *Coco v The Queen*[22] the majority accepted that the presumption was rebuttable by a clear implication. They indicated, as an instance of a clear implication, where to not rebut the presumption would result in the statutory provisions becoming 'inoperative or meaningless'. They considered that general words are rarely sufficient to rebut the presumption as 'in the context in which they appear, they will often be ambiguous on the aspect of interference with fundamental rights'.[23]

In *Daniels Corporation International Pty Ltd v Australian Competition and Consumer Commission*[24] McHugh J (using language reflective of that used by the majority in *Coco*) stated:

> Courts do not construe legislation as abolishing, suspending or adversely affecting rights, freedoms and immunities that the courts have recognised as fundamental unless the legislation does so in unambiguous terms ... courts will hold that the presumption has not been overcome unless the relevant legislation expressly abolishes, suspends or adversely affects the right, freedom or immunity or does so by necessary implication. They will hold that the legislature has done so by necessary implication whenever the legislative provision would be rendered inoperative or its object largely frustrated

17 (2013) 248 CLR 92.

18 Ibid 152–3 [157].

19 Ibid 127 [70], 131 [85], 132 [87].

20 Ibid 127 [71].

21 Ibid 132 [87].

22 (1994) 179 CLR 427, 436 (Mason CJ, Brennan, Gaudron and McHugh JJ).

23 Ibid 437.

24 (2002) 213 CLR 543.

in its practical application, if the right, freedom or immunity were to prevail over the legislation.[25]

In *X7 v Australian Crime Commission*[26] Kiefel J made the point that the requirement of the principle of legality for 'irresistible clearness' was 'not a low standard', adding that it will 'usually require that it be manifest from the statute in question that the legislature has directed its attention to the question whether to so abrogate or restrict and has determined to do so'.[27]

Examples 28.3 and **28.4** are cases in which the presumption was rebutted by necessary implication. **Example 28.3** relates to the common law privilege against self-incrimination.

Example 28.3 *R v Independent Broad-based Anti-corruption Commissioner*[28]

In this case the High Court held that pt 6 of the *Independent Broad-based Anti-corruption Commission Act 2011* (Vic) ('the IBAC Act') authorised the Independent Broad-based Anti-corruption Commission ('IBAC') to compulsorily examine police officers about a matter with respect to which they had not been charged with an offence but might subsequently be and, further, that s 144 of the IBAC Act abrogated the privilege against self-incrimination in respect of persons examined by IBAC. In their High Court appeal counsel for the police officers referred to *X7 v Australian Crime Commission*[29] in which the majority of the High Court had interpreted the *Australian Crime Commission Act 2002* (Cth) ('the ACC Act') as not authorising the compulsory examination of a person charged with an offence about the circumstances of the offence while the trial for the offence was pending.[30]

The majority judgment distinguished *X7 v Australian Crime Commission* on the basis that the police officers in the present case had not been charged and to extend the common law principle that an accused person cannot be required to assist in proof of an offence charged to when a person has not been charged 'would be to fetter the pursuit and exposure of a lack of probity within the police force, which is the object of the IBAC Act'.[31]

Gageler J stated[32] that 'any common law principle or presumption of interpretation must surely have reached the limit of its operation where its application to read down legislation plain on its face would frustrate an object of that legislation[33] or render means by which the legislation sets out to achieve that object inoperative or nonsensical'[34].

---

25 Ibid 562–3 [43] (citations omitted).

26 (2013) 248 CLR 92.

27 Ibid 153 [158].

28 (2016) 256 CLR 459.

29 (2013) 248 CLR 92.

30 In *X7 v Australian Crime Commission* Hayne and Bell JJ stated that to 'hold that the general words of the relevant provision of the ACC Act authorise compulsory examination of a person charged with an indictable Commonwealth offence about the subject matter of the offence charged would thus depart in a marked degree from the 'general system of law': at 132 [87].

31 (2016) 256 CLR 459, 473 [51] (French CJ, Kiefel, Bell, Keane, Nettle and Gordon JJ).

32 Ibid 481 [77].

33 Gageler J, citing *Daniels Corporation International Pty Ltd v Australian Competition and Consumer Commission* (2002) 213 CLR 543, 563 [43].

34 Gageler J, citing *Coco v The Queen* (1994) 179 CLR 427, 438, 446.

Example 28.4 involves the common law requirement to afford natural justice to a person affected by a decision by requiring the disclosure of information relied on in making that decision.

Example 28.4 *Vella v Minister for Immigration and Border Protection*[35]

Section 503A of the *Migration Act 1958* (Cth) ('the *Migration Act*') dealt with a situation in which information might be given to a migration officer on the condition that it be treated as confidential. A migration officer to whom such information was given was prohibited by that section from communicating it to any other person, except the Minister or an authorised migration officer where the communication is relevant to the exercise of certain powers, including the power to cancel a visa and the power to revoke a decision to cancel a visa. Section 503A(2) expressly provided that if information is so communicated to the Minister, the Minister 'must not be required to divulge or communicate the information to a court, a tribunal, a parliament or parliamentary committee or any other body or person'. However, s 503A did not expressly provide that the rules of natural justice were excluded.

Mr Vella, originally from Malta, had resided in Australia for more than 40 years when he departed for a trip overseas. Despite that long period of residence, Mr Vella had not become an Australian citizen. A few days after Mr Vella's departure, the Minister decided to cancel his visa under s 501(3) of the *Migration Act* on the basis that the Minister reasonably suspected that the person did not pass the character test and the visa cancellation was in the national interest. In so deciding, the Minister relied on information protected from disclosure by s 503A ('the protected information'). Section 501(5) of the *Migration Act* provided that the rules of natural justice did not apply to visa cancellation under s 501(3).

Section 501C of the *Migration Act* set up a procedure under which a person whose visa has been cancelled is required to be given an opportunity to make representations about revoking the cancellation decision. Mr Vella was not provided with any particulars of the protected information in connection with that procedure. Mr Vella argued that it was not possible to respond in any meaningful way to the cancellation decision if, at the very least, the substance of the protected information on which the Minister had relied was not provided.

The Minister decided not to revoke the cancellation decision and, in doing so, relied on the protected information. That information was at no stage provided to Mr Vella.

Mr Vella issued a subpoena for the production of the protected information. The Minister relied on s 503A(2) in refusing to divulge or communicate that information to the Court. The Minister's refusal was upheld in an earlier proceeding. In the proceeding before the Full Federal Court, the Minister conceded that, were it not for s 503A of the *Migration Act*, natural justice would have required the disclosure of the protected information.

The Full Federal Court held unanimously that the requirements of natural justice, to the extent that they would have required Mr Vella to have been given notice of the protected information, were excluded by s 503A. It concluded that there was nothing in the text of the provision to suggest that the words 'required to' cannot extend to the requirement to afford natural justice or procedural fairness.[36] The Court stated:

35 (2015) 90 ALJR 89.

36 Ibid 77 [62].

> Whilst it may have been preferable for there to be an express reference in s 503A to the fact that the section, where applicable, may operate to exclude natural justice, nonetheless there are in s 503A 'plain words of necessary intendment'. The text is sufficiently clear to find a conclusion that the section can operate to exclude requirements to disclose which would otherwise be implied by the requirements of natural justice.[37]

Even if rebutted, the presumption may operate to limit the interference [28.4]

An issue that has arisen is whether the presumption has any work to do when it is a clear purpose of the legislation to impair a common law right.

In *Australian Securities and Investments Commission v DB Management Pty Ltd*[38] the High Court, in a unanimous judgment, upheld the validity of a modification of s 701 of the *Corporations Law* (NSW) made by the Australian Securities and Investments Commission to bring within the compulsory acquisition provisions of that section shares allotted in a company upon the exercise of options after the close of takeover offers. One of the arguments raised against its validity was a presumption that legislation is not intended to interfere with vested proprietary interests. The Court stated:

> As to the presumption that legislation is not intended to interfere with vested proprietary rights, the relevant provisions of the legislation in question have, as their primary concern, interference with vested proprietary rights. That is what compulsory acquisition is about ... It is of little assistance, in endeavouring to work out the meaning of parts of that scheme, to invoke a general presumption against the very thing which the legislation sets out to achieve.[39]

In that case the High Court considered the principle of legality as not relevant to how it interpreted the *Corporations Law* (NSW) as it was the clear purpose of the Law to interfere with vested proprietary rights.

However, in *Lee v New South Wales Crime Commission*[40] some role for the principle, albeit a limited one, was conceded by Gageler and Keane JJ:

> The principle at most can have limited application to the construction of legislation which has amongst its objects the abrogation or curtailment of the particular right, freedom or immunity in respect of which the principle is sought to be invoked.[41]

Support for the principle of legality having a role to play in minimising the impact on a fundamental right that the legislature clearly intends to encroach on may be found in several judgments of French CJ. In *Momcilovic v The Queen*[42] French CJ said that the principle of legality 'requires that statutes be construed, where constructional choices are open, to avoid or minimise

37 Ibid 81 [83] (Buchanan, Flick and Wigney JJ).

38 (2000) 199 CLR 321.

39 Ibid 340 [43] (Gleeson CJ, Gaudron, Gummow, Hayne and Callinan JJ).

40 (2013) 251 CLR 196.

41 Ibid 310–11 [314].

42 (2011) 245 CLR 1.

their encroachment upon rights and freedoms at common law'.[43] In a similar vein, in *North Australian Aboriginal Justice Agency Ltd v Northern Territory*[44] French CJ, this time together with Kiefel and Bell JJ, stated that 'the principle of legality favours a construction, if one be available, which avoids or minimises the statute's encroachment upon fundamental principles, rights and freedoms at common law'.[45] In that case those same judges made the further point that there still is a role for the principle of legality even if the purpose of the statute does involve interference with a fundamental right. They said that the principle 'is properly applied in such a case to the choice of that construction, if one be reasonably open, which involves the least interference' with that right.[46]

Fundamental rights

[28.5] **The strength of the presumption in relation to a right increases the more fundamental the right is**

The more fundamental or important the right, the greater the level of clarity that is required to abrogate or curtail it.[47] In *Federal Commissioner of Taxation v Tomaras*[48] Edelman J stated that a 'more nuanced approach than one which is all-or-nothing might calibrate the strength of the presumption to the unlikelihood of an intention to impair the particular right based on factors including the importance of the right within the legal system and the extent to which it is embedded in the fabric of the legal system within which Parliament legislates'.[49]

Example 28.5 *Probuild Constructions (Aust) Pty Ltd v Shade Systems Pty Ltd*[50]

In this case the High Court had to consider the scheme established by the *Building and Construction Industry Security of Payment Act 1999* (NSW) ('the Security of Payment Act') in relation to progress payments for construction work. Disputed claims for payment were referred to an adjudicator who could determine the amount of progress payment payable. The High Court

43 Ibid 46 [43].

44 (2015) 256 CLR 569.

45 Ibid 581 [11]. Cited in support was *Saeed v Minister for Immigration and Citizenship* (2010) 241 CLR 252, 259 [15] (French CJ, Gummow, Hayne, Crennan and Kiefel JJ); *Lacey v A-G (Qld)* (2011) 242 CLR 573, 591–2 [43] (French CJ, Gummow, Hayne, Crennan, Kiefel and Bell JJ); *Australian Crime Commission v Stoddart* (2011) 244 CLR 554, 622 [182] (Crennan, Kiefel and Bell JJ); *Australian Education Union v General Manager of Fair Work Australia* (2012) 246 CLR 117, 135 [30] (French CJ, Crennan and Kiefel JJ).

46 *North Australian Aboriginal Justice Agency Ltd v Northern Territory* (2015) 256 CLR 569, 582 [11] (French CJ, Kiefel and Bell JJ). In *DPP v Kaba* (2014) 44 VR 526 Bell J stated: 'The application of the principle of legality is essentially binary. The interpretation involving the least infringement of human rights must be preferred to any other interpretation': at 581 [194]. See also *South Australia v Totani* (2010) 242 CLR 1, 28 [31] (French CJ); *Ma v Police (SA)* (2000) 137 SASR 159, 193 [120] (Peek J).

47 *Mann v Paterson Constructions Pty Ltd* (2019) 267 CLR 560, 623 [159] (Nettle, Gordon and Edelman JJ); *Mondelez Australia Pty Ltd v Automotive, Food, Metals, Engineering, Printing and Kindred Industries Union* (2020) 94 ALJR 818, 838 [96] (Edelman J).

48 (2018) 265 CLR 434.

49 Ibid 467 [101]. In *Gifford v Strang Patrick Stevedoring Pty Ltd* (2003) 214 CLR 269 Mc Hugh J stated that the presumption 'is strong when the right is a fundamental right of our legal system; it is weak when the right is merely one to take or not take a particular course of action': at 284 [36].

50 (2018) 264 CLR 1.

held that the scheme excluded the jurisdiction of the Supreme Court, as the superior court of record in the State, to make an order in the nature of certiorari quashing an adjudicator's determination for non-jurisdictional error on the face of the record even though that was not expressly stated in the Security of Payment Act.

The majority referred to the requirement that 'an intention to alter the settled and familiar role of the superior courts must be clearly expressed'[51] but noted that the Security of Payment Act 'is not concerned with finally and conclusively determining the entitlements of parties to a construction contract'.[52] As such, they held that the question whether the Security of Payment Act 'absent an express statement but read as a whole' excluded the jurisdiction of the Supreme Court to make an order in the nature of certiorari to quash an adjudicator's determination 'depends on examination of the text, context and purpose [of the Act]'.[53]

Edelman J stated that the narrow approach to construction based on the principle of legality 'applies with very little force to legislation in the nature of the Security of Payment Act, which requires an adjudicator to determine parties' rights but, in effect, only on an interim basis.[54]

In this case the High Court interpreted the Security of Payment Act as creating an informal and speedy means for the recovery of progress payments to keep cash flowing in the construction industry but as not affecting the common law rights of the parties under the construction contract. Accordingly, it was prepared to construe that Act as excluding the jurisdiction of the Supreme Court to make an order in the nature of certiorari with respect to the determination of an adjudicator despite the absence of clear words to that effect.

The strength of the presumption in this case was effectively at the lower end of the scale as the parties' common law rights under the construction contract were not affected.[55]

The category of fundamental rights is not fixed and may vary over time [28.6]

The challenge to identifying fundamental common law rights is, as pointed out by McHugh J, that '[w]hat is fundamental in one age or place may not be regarded as fundamental in another age or place'.[56] That quotation from McHugh J continues as follows:

> When community values are undergoing radical change and few principles or rights are immune from legislative amendment or abolition, as is the case in Australia today, few principles or rights can claim to be so fundamental that it is unlikely that the legislature would want to change them.[57]

There is no complete list of principles or rights currently regarded as fundamental for the purposes of the principle of legality. Illustrations put forward on behalf of the respondent in

51 Ibid 14 [34] (Kiefel CJ, Bell, Keane, Nettle and Gordon JJ).

52 Ibid 15 [37].

53 Ibid 14 [34].

54 Ibid 35 [90].

55 See Dan Meagher, 'On the Wane? The Principle of Legality in the High Court of Australia' (2021) 32(1) *Public Law Review* 61.

56 *Malika Holdings Pty Ltd v Stretton* (2001) 204 CLR 290, 298 [28].

57 Ibid.

Momcilovic v The Queen were developed in that case by Heydon J.[58] In *Director of Public Prosecutions v Kaba*[59] Bell J doubted that a catalogue was necessary:

> It is important to know what rights and freedoms are covered by the principle of legality because this determines what legislation will be interpreted according to the protective approach that it specifies and therefore its scope as a normative rule. Up to now, the rights and freedoms covered have not been catalogued and I am not suggesting that they should be. They are generally 'informed by the history of the common law', which should continue to be so. Important guidance has been provided in scholarly writings and judgments. However, some uncertainty remains, more than is necessary or desirable, particularly as regards identifying what rights and freedoms are 'fundamental' or 'commonly accepted', how much the qualifier 'fundamental' has 'work to do' in that process and, indeed, whether it has completely outlived its usefulness.[60]

[28.7] Parliament has the power to erode fundamental common law rights should it want to do so

In *South Australia v Totani*[61] French CJ said the following in relation to the principle of legality:

> That principle, well known to the drafters of legislation, seeks to give effect to the presumed intention of the enacting Parliament not to interfere with such rights and freedoms except by clear and unequivocal language for which Parliament may be accountable to the electorate. Save to the extent that it imposes something approaching a formal requirement of clear statutory language, the principle of legality does not constrain legislative power.[62]

In *Lee v New South Wales Crime Commission*[63] Gageler and Keane JJ stated that the principle does not exist to shield important rights 'from being specifically affected in the pursuit of clearly identified legislative objects by means within the constitutional competence of the enacting legislature'.[64] Parliament can, if it wishes, affect important common law rights if it makes that intention plain.

---

58 (2011) 245 CLR 1, 177–8 [444]. The illustrations put forward were freedom from trespass by police officers on private property, procedural fairness, the conferral of jurisdiction on a court, and vested property interests. Heydon J stated that to that list might be added right of access to the courts, right to a fair trial, the writ of habeas corpus, open justice, the non-retrospectivity of statutes extending the criminal law, the non-retrospectivity of changes in rights or obligations generally, mens rea as an element of legislatively created crimes, freedom from arbitrary arrest or search, the criminal standard of proof, the liberty of the individual, the freedom of individuals to depart from and re-enter their country, the freedom of individuals to trade as they wish, the liberty of individuals to use the highways, freedom of speech, legal professional privilege, the privilege against self-incrimination, the non-existence of an appeal from an acquittal and the jurisdiction of superior courts to prevent acts by inferior courts and tribunals in excess of jurisdiction. His Honour provided citations to relevant authorities.

59 (2014) 44 VR 526.

60 Ibid 577–8 [178] (citations omitted).

61 (2010) 242 CLR 1.

62 Ibid 29 [31].

63 (2013) 251 CLR 196.

64 Ibid 310 [313].

In *Daniels Corporation International Pty Ltd v Australian Competition and Consumer Commission*[65] Kirby J referred approvingly to the following statement of Lord Hoffmann in *R v Secretary of State for the Home Department; Ex parte Simms*:

> Parliament can, if it chooses, legislate contrary to fundamental principles of human rights ... The constraints upon its exercise by Parliament are ultimately political, not legal. But the principle of legality means that Parliament must squarely confront what it is doing and accept the political cost.[66]

Kirby J has described the presumption as 'a very useful discipline for the Parliament and for those who draft legislation submitted to it for enactment'.[67] It operates as a discipline by requiring Parliament to aim for irresistible clarity in its language. Given that the presumption is 'a working hypothesis, the existence of which is known both to Parliament and the courts, upon which statutory language will be interpreted',[68] Parliament is on notice as to what it must do to exercise its undoubted power to interfere with a common law right treated by courts as fundamental. The remedy is in Parliament's own hands.

Rationale for presumption

The rationale for the presumption is that it is in line with how Parliament is presumed to wish to operate and improves the process by which it operates [28.8]

The rights that are covered by the principle of legality are rights that, in view of their importance within the system of law, are respected by courts and are assumed by courts to be respected by Parliament.[69] Respect for those rights demands that they may only be encroached on after considered deliberation.

In *Lee v New South Wales Crime Commission*[70] Gageler and Keane JJ stated that the principle of legality 'respects the distinct contemporary functions, enhances the distinct contemporary processes, and fulfils the shared contemporary expectations of the legislative and the judicial branches of government'.[71] They added:

> The principle of construction is fulfilled in accordance with its rationale where the objects or terms or context of legislation make plain that the legislature has directed its attention to the question of the abrogation or curtailment of the right, freedom or immunity in question and has made a legislative determination that the right, freedom or immunity is to be abrogated or curtailed.[72]

65 (2002) 213 CLR 543.

66 Ibid 582 [106]. The citation for this dictum of Lord Hoffmann is [2000] 2 AC 115, 131.

67 *Malika Holdings Pty Ltd v Stretton* (2001) 204 CLR 290, 328 [121].

68 *Electrolux Home Products Pty Ltd v Australian Workers' Union* (2004) 221 CLR 309, 329 [21] (Gleeson CJ). See also *North Australian Aboriginal Justice Agency Ltd v Northern Territory* (2015) 256 CLR 569, 581 [11] (French CJ, Kiefel and Bell JJ). In *A-G (SA) v Corporation of the City of Adelaide* (2013) 249 CLR 1 French CJ observed that the presumption 'can be taken to be a presumption of which those who draft legislation, regulations and by-laws are aware': at 31 [42].

69 In *Al-Kateb v Godwin* (2004) 219 CLR 562 Gleeson CJ said that the principle of legality 'governs both Parliament and the courts' and 'is an expression of a legal value, respected by the courts, and acknowledged by the courts to be respected by Parliament': at 577 [19]–[20].

70 (2013) 251 CLR 196.

71 Ibid 310 [312].

72 Ibid 310 [314].

In *Director of Public Prosecutions v Kaba*[73] Bell J stated that the 'premise of the principle of legality is that individual rights and freedoms under the common law have an anterior value which counts in, and represents the starting point of, the process of interpreting legislation impacting thereon'.[74]

The original rationale for the presumption is that it is highly improbable that Parliament would infringe fundamental rights without expressing its intention with 'irresistible clearness'.[75] In *Coco v The Queen*[76] the majority judges supplemented that rationale by pointing to a valuable by-product of the presumption and its requirement for a clear expression of an unmistakable and unambiguous intention to abrogate or curtail a fundamental freedom. They stated:

> At the same time, curial insistence on a clear expression of an unmistakable and unambiguous intention to abrogate or curtail a fundamental freedom will enhance the parliamentary process by securing a greater measure of attention to the impact of legislative proposals on fundamental rights.[77]

Being forced to be upfront with an intention to abrogate or curtail a right, freedom or immunity may be a cause of frustration in legislators. In *Yuill v Corporate Affairs Commission (NSW)*[78] Kirby P (as he then was) said, in relation to such feelings of frustration:

> [T]he delays, interruption and frustration are strictly temporary. And they have a beneficial purpose. It is to permit Parliament, which has the last say, an opportunity to clarify its purpose where the court is not satisfied that the purpose is sufficiently clear. And the opportunity is reserved to those cases where important interests are at stake, which might have been overlooked and which deserve special attention.[79]

Applicability of presumption to delegated legislation and statutory rights

[28.9] **The presumption is also applicable to delegated legislation**

Delegated legislation is made by an entity under a power delegated to it by an Act or an instrument made under an Act.[80] The principle of legality clearly applies to the empowering provision of the relevant enabling Act. But it also applies to the delegated legislation itself.[81] Thus

---

73 (2014) 44 VR 526.

74 Ibid 574 [170].

75 *Potter v Minahan* (1908) 7 CLR 277, 304 (O'Connor J); *Bropho v Western Australia* (1990) 171 CLR 1, 18 (Mason CJ, Deane, Dawson, Toohey, Gaudron and McHugh JJ); *Coco v The Queen* (1994) 179 CLR 427, 437 (Mason CJ, Brennan, Gaudron and McHugh JJ); *Electrolux Home Products Pty Ltd v Australian Workers' Union* (2004) 221 CLR 309, 329 [21] (Gleeson CJ); *North Australian Aboriginal Justice Agency Ltd v Northern Territory of Australia* (2015) 256 CLR 569, 581 [11] (French CJ, Kiefel and Bell JJ).

76 (1994) 179 CLR 427.

77 Ibid 437–8 (Mason CJ, Brennan, Gaudron and McHugh JJ).

78 (1990) 20 NSWLR 386.

79 Ibid 403. Kirby J referred to this statement in *Daniels Corporation International Pty Ltd v Australian Competition and Consumer Commission* (2002) 213 CLR 543, 581 [104] and stated: 'Viewed in this light, the courts are not usurping the democratic function of Parliament by insisting on clear provisions to abolish an important common law right' (at [105]).

80 See **[43.2]**.

81 See D Meagher and M Groves, 'The Common Law Principle of Legality and Secondary Legislation' (2016) 39 (2) *University of New South Wales Law Journal* 450.

even if the enabling Act is construed as authorising the making of delegated legislation that might abrogate or curtail fundamental common law rights or markedly depart from the general system of law, there is a necessary second step of examining whether the delegated legislation in fact exercises that power, expressly or by necessary implication.

In *Attorney-General for the State of South Australia v Corporation of the City of Adelaide*,[82] a case concerning a by-law that prohibited persons from preaching, canvassing, haranguing or distributing printed material on any road without the permission of the council, French CJ, who was part of the majority that held that the by-law was within the by-law making powers conferred by the *Local Government Act 1934* (SA), said of the principle of legality:

> It can also inform the construction of statutes generally and the construction of delegated legislation made in the purported exercise of statutory powers.[83]

The same point was made by Heydon J in his dissenting judgment. He stated:

> The principle of legality can apply both to parliamentary legislation creating a power to make delegated legislation, and to the delegated legislation itself. The consequence of applying the principle of legality to a power in parliamentary legislation to make delegated legislation will tend to be a relatively narrow construction of that power. And the consequence of applying the principle of legality to delegated legislation made under that power will tend to be a relatively narrow construction of that delegated legislation.[84]

Example 28.6 *Evans v New South Wales*[85]

This case concerned the *World Youth Day Act 2006* (NSW) ('the WYD Act') and *World Youth Day Regulation 2008* (NSW) ('the WYD Regulation'), which were enacted to put regulatory controls in place for the 2008 World Youth Day held in Sydney, an occasion when young members of the Catholic Church gather. The applicants intended to protest during the World Youth Day celebrations on various issues and submitted that the WYD Act and WYD Regulation prevented them from doing so.

Section 58 of the WYD Act gave a broad regulation-making power and specifically authorised the making of regulations for or with respect to 'regulating the use by the public of, and the conduct of the public on, World Youth Day venues and facilities'. Clause 7 of the WYD Regulation empowered the giving of a direction to a person within a World Youth Day–declared area to cease engaging in conduct that causes annoyance to participants in a World Youth Day event.

The Full Court of the Federal Court 'interpreted the WYD Act on the presumption that it was not the intention of Parliament that regulations would be made under the WYD Act preventing or interfering with the exercise of the fundamental freedom of free speech'.[86] The Court stated that

82 (2013) 249 CLR 1.

83 Ibid 32 [44]. French CJ observed that the presumption 'can be taken to be a presumption of which those who draft legislation, regulations and by-laws are aware': at 31 [42].

84 Ibid 66–7 [150].

85 (2008) 168 FCR 576.

86 Ibid 579 [7] (French, Branson and Stone JJ).

it accepted 'the general principle that a regulation should not be interpreted as conferring powers that are repugnant to fundamental rights and freedoms at common law in the absence of clear authority from Parliament'.[87]

The Court referred to the principle of legality, saying that it is 'an important principle that Acts be construed, where constructional choices are open, so as not to encroach upon common law rights and freedoms'.[88] Applying that principle, the Court read down the broad general terms of s 58 of the WYD Act, recognising that 'freedom of expression in Australia is a powerful consideration favouring restraint in the construction of broad statutory power when the terms in which that power is conferred so allow'.[89] So read down, the Court held that s 58 did not support cl 7 of the WYD Regulation, so far as it related to 'annoyance' as it extended to 'expressions of opinion which neither disrupt nor interfere with the freedom of others, nor are objectively offensive in the sense traditionally used in State criminal statutes'.[90]

[28.10] Whether the presumption applies to statutory rights is not settled

As is clear from this chapter to this point, the focus of the principle of legality has been the protection of fundamental common law principles and rights, and the general system of law, from inadvertent interference by statute. An issue that has arisen in recent years is whether the principle should be extended to offer protection to rights arising under statute.

Early support for an extension of the principle to statutory rights is to be found in obiter remarks made by Finn J in giving judgment in a case before the ACT Supreme Court, *Buck v Comcare.*[91]

In *Buck v Comcare* the Court was considering s 57(2) of the *Safety, Rehabilitation and Compensation Act 1988* (Cth). That section suspended rights to compensation, and to institute or continue any proceedings in relation to compensation, under that Act of an employee who had refused or failed, without reasonable excuse, to undergo a medical examination. The suspension continued until the examination took place. Finn J stated:

> [Section] 57(2) operates on a significant, albeit statutory, right of an employee in Mrs Buck's position. That right does not fall into the category of 'common law' rights which traditionally have been safeguarded from legislative interference etc in the absence of clear and unambiguous statutory language ... Yet it is a right of sufficient significance to the individual in my view, that, where there may be doubt as to Parliament's intention, the courts should favour an interpretation which safeguards the individual. To confine our interpretative safeguards to the protection of 'fundamental common law rights' is to ignore that we live in an age of statutes and that it is statute which, more often than not, provides the rights necessary to secure the basic amenities of life in modern society.[92]

Those remarks of Finn J were considered by the Full Federal Court in *Australian Postal Corporation v Sinnaiah.*[93] Section 37(7) of the *Safety, Rehabilitation and Compensation Act 1988*

87 Ibid 588 [48].

88 Ibid 593 [68].

89 Ibid 596 [78].

90 Ibid 597 [83].

91 (1996) 66 FCR 359.

92 Ibid 364–5.

93 (2013) 213 FCR 449 (Cowdroy, Buchanan and Katzmann JJ).

(Cth) ('the Act') suspended rights to compensation, and to institute or continue any proceedings in relation to compensation, under the Act of an employee who had refused or failed, without reasonable excuse, to undertake a rehabilitation program for an injury. The suspension continued until the employee began to undertake the program.

Ms Sinnaiah was an Australia Post employee who had suffered various injuries. Australia Post accepted liability for two of them but denied liability for others. A rehabilitation authority ordered Ms Sinnaiah to undertake a rehabilitation program for one of the injuries for which Australia Post accepted liability. She failed to undertake the program and Australia Post contended that the effect of s 37(7) was to suspend all her rights to compensation, and to institute or continue any proceedings in relation to compensation, under the Act, not just her rights with respect to the injury for which the rehabilitation program was to be undertaken. The Court stated:

> Had that been the Parliament's intention there should be no room for ambiguity; one would expect clear words, without resort to inference.[94]

The Court then referred to the remarks of Finn J in *Buck v Comcare* and stated:

> While the context in which these remarks were made was a little different, in our opinion they apply with equal force here.[95]

In *Minister for Immigration and Citizenship v Haneef*[96] the Full Federal Court, without expressly adverting to the issue covered by Finn J's remarks, proceeded to approach the interpretation of the word 'association' in s 501(6)(b) of the *Migration Act 1958* (Cth) 'in the light of the common law principles' reflected in authorities on the principle of legality such as *Coco*.[97]

Other cases show a reluctance to simply extending the principle of legality to the protection of statutory rights.

In *Brett v Director General, Department of Education*[98] the Western Australian Court of Appeal expressed the opinion that it 'is not clear that the court should apply the same approach to limitations on statutory rights as to limitations on common law rights'.[99] In any event it concluded that even if the principle of legality applied to the particular statutory right, the outcome in the case would be the same as the legislature had directly addressed the issue.[100]

In *Elliott v Minister Administering Fisheries Management Act 1994*[101] the NSW Court of Appeal held that any application of the principle of legality (referred to in that case as the 'clear statement principle')[102] to the statutory scheme for conferring rights to participate in a fishery under consideration in that case 'must be muted' so as 'to avoid imposing a constraint on legislative

94 Ibid 458 [32].

95 Ibid 458 [34]. In *DPP (WA) v GTR* [2007] WASC 318, McKechnie J referred to Finn J's remarks and stated that '[w]hile I can easily accept this statement of principle, it provides little assistance in the resolution of this case because the statute that arguably impinges on the [statutory right] has as its dominant purpose the protection of the public and so a clash with a private right is precisely what Parliament intended': at [28]–[29]. See also *Anglican Care v NSW Nurses and Midwives' Association* (2015) 231 FCR 316, 327 [59]–[60] (Bromberg and Katzmann JJ).

96 (2007) 163 FCR 414.

97 Ibid 444 [114] (Black CJ, French and Weinberg JJ).

98 [2015] WASCA 66.

99 Ibid [18] (Buss, Le Miere and Murphy JJ).

100 Ibid [20].

101 (2018) 97 NSWLR 1082.

102 See *A-G (NSW) v Melco Resorts & Entertainment Ltd* (2020) 102 NSWLR 47, 58 [45] (the Court).

power, but also because the nature of the right, being one conferred by statute, is inherently liable to alteration by statute'.[103] The Court acknowledged that 'there is no necessary constraint depriving the holder of *statutory* rights of the benefit of the principle, although it will operate differently in that context'.[104] Indeed, the Court stated that there is much to be said for, as argued by Lim,[105] applying the principle of legality to '"vulnerable rights", particularly in an environment where so many aspects of the rights and interests of individuals depend upon legislative protection'.[106]

As noted in *Elliott v Minister Administering Fisheries Management Act 1994*,[107] statutory rights are inherently liable to alteration by statute. One statute may be expressly or impliedly repealed by another, in whole or in part.[108] The impact that a statute has on existing statutory rights may be determined by construing the later statute in accordance with the ordinary principles of statutory interpretation without any need to resort to the principle of legality.[109] Interpretation Acts in each Australian jurisdiction also contain provisions that are intended to preserve accrued statutory rights and obligations from being impacted by an amending or repealing Act in the absence of an indication of a contrary intent in that Act.[110]

The enactment procedure for Acts of Parliament presents opportunity for scrutiny.[111] On top of that, the Human Rights Acts in force in Queensland, Victoria and the Australian Capital Territory protect specified human rights from unreasonable and unjustified interference by legislation.[112] The compatibility statements required to be made to Parliament under those Acts ensure scrutiny from a human rights viewpoint.[113] The end result is that, in the jurisdictions that require compatibility statements, where a relevant human right overlaps with a right or

---

103 *Elliot v Minister Administering Fisheries Management Act 1994* (2018) 97 NSWLR 1082, 1092–3 [39] (Basten JA, Beazley J agreeing at 1084 [1], Payne JA agreeing at 1105 [103]). Basten JA stated that the principle of legality 'does not override the usual exercise of statutory construction by reference to the text of the statute, its identifiable purpose and the context within which a particular provision is found': at 1093 [40].

104 Ibid 1092 [38] (Basten JA, Beazley J agreeing at 1084 [1], Payne JA agreeing at 1105 [103]) (emphasis in original).

105 See Brendan Lim, 'The Rationales for the Principle of Legality' in D Meagher and M Groves (eds), *The Principle of Legality in Australia and New Zealand* (Federation Press, 2017) 2, 9–12. Lim described vulnerable rights as 'those rights which the ordinary political process is inherently inapt to protect'. These were 'first, rights that are claimed by a politically weak minority; and secondly, rights which themselves concern the integrity of the democratic process and are therefore targets for attack from those who control the levers of power at any given time and have every incentive to entrench that control': at 10.

106 (2018) 97 NSWLR 1082, 1092 [38].

107 (2018) 97 NSWLR 1082.

108 In *Butler v A-G (Vic)* (1961) 106 CLR 268 Fullagar J stated that implied repeal – total or partial – of an earlier statute by a later statute of the same legislature 'is a comparatively rare phenomenon' and requires 'actual contrariety' to be clearly apparent: at 275. See chapter 35.

109 See also John Basten, 'The Principle of Legality – An Unhelpful Label' in D Meagher and M Groves (eds), *The Principle of Legality in Australia and New Zealand* (Federation Press, 2017) 74 where the author stated: 'When statute affects statute we are within that growing and challenging area of conflict resolution where the conflict is between laws of the same polity': at 84–5.

110 See **[25.5] (a)**.

111 See chapter 11.

112 See **[26.2]**.

113 *Human Rights Act 2019* (Qld) s 38; *Charter of Human Rights and Responsibilities Act 2006* (Vic) s 28; *Human Rights Act 2004* (ACT) s 37. The *Human Rights (Parliamentary Scrutiny) Act 2011* (Cth) requires Bills and legislative instruments to which s 42 (disallowance) of the *Legislation Act 2003* (Cth) applies to be accompanied by a statement that includes an assessment of their compatibility with rights and freedoms recognised or declared by specified international instruments.

principle protected by the principle of legality, Parliament is forced to 'squarely confront what it is doing and accept the political cost'.[114]

In the case of delegated legislation, there are provisions in New South Wales,[115] Tasmania[116] and Victoria[117] that require a parliamentary committee to scrutinise certain items of delegated legislation after their making to consider whether they unduly trespass on personal rights and liberties. At the Commonwealth level the Senate Standing Committee for the Scrutiny of Delegated Legislation scrutinises legislative instruments that are subject to disallowance, disapproval or affirmative resolution of the Senate for the same purpose.[118] This leads to a measure of accountability, albeit after the making of the delegated legislation. And, of course, the enabling Act will have gone through a scrutiny process in full public view.

---

114 See *R v Secretary of State for the Home Department; Ex parte Simms* [2000] 2 AC 115, 131 (Lord Hoffmann).

115 *Legislation Review Act 1987* (NSW) s 9(1)(b)(i).

116 *Subordinate Legislation Committee Act 1969* (Tas) s 8(1)(a)(iii).

117 *Subordinate Legislation Act 1994* (Vic) s 21(1)(f).

118 *Senate Standing Orders 2020* ord 23.

29 USE OF THE STATUTE BOOK AND LEGISLATION OF OTHER JURISDICTIONS

Overview

[29.1] 'The statute book' is a term commonly used to describe all Acts of Parliament in existence in a particular jurisdiction, whether or not commenced to operate.[1] A law on the statute book may be an aid to interpretation. The same principle applies to the use of legislation of other jurisdictions; this includes other states and territories as well as other countries. But the statute book for a jurisdiction and the legislation of other jurisdictions (the wider legislative context) are not necessarily relevant, even if the same or a similar word is used.

The situations in which the wider legislative context is of use fall into three broad categories. The first is where the two pieces of legislation are *in pari materia* (dealing with the same subject matter on the same lines). The second is where two or more statutory enactments are overlapping and form part of a single scheme. The third is where the legislation (despite contextual differences or perhaps because of them) is useful for comparative purposes.

Some uses of the statute book and other legislative context are the subject of other chapters in this work.[2]

---

1 *M v Scottish Ministers* [2012] 1 WLR 3386, 3393 [22] (the Court). For examples of Australian judicial usage consistent with this definition, see *Work Health Authority v Outback Ballooning Pty Ltd* (2019) 266 CLR 428, 467 [88] (Gageler J) ('the Commonwealth statute book'); *Communications, Electrical, Electronic, Energy, Information, Postal, Plumbing And Allied Services Union of Australia v Queensland Rail* (2015) 256 CLR 171, 185 [30] (French CJ, Hayne, Kiefel, Bell, Keane and Nettle JJ) ('the Queensland statute book'). For its use in articles by parliamentary counsel, see James Dalmau, 'Better Ways of Deciding Whether a Contested Usage is Permissible in Legislation' [2019] (1) *The Loophole: Journal of the Commonwealth Association of Legislative Counsel* 18, 20; Teri Cherkewich, 'By Sword and Shield: Legislative Counsel's Role in Advancing and Protecting Democracy One Word (and Client) at a Time' (2015) 36(3) *Statute Law Review* 253, 261–2; Sandra Markman, 'Climbing Constitution Hill – Teaching Legislative Drafting in Ireland' [2013] (3) *The Loophole: Journal of the Commonwealth Association of Legislative Counsel* 28, 31–2; Janet Erasmus, 'Keepers of the Statute Book: Lessons from the Space-Time Continuum' [2010] (1) *The Loophole: Journal of the Commonwealth Association of Legislative Counsel* 7, 7–8. The term was always a metaphor; see Sir John Baker, *An Introduction to English Legal History* (Oxford University Press, 5th ed, 2019) 217.

2 For the use of predecessor legislation, see chapter 21. For Interpretation Acts and other Acts of general application, see chapters 25 and 26 respectively. For interpretation of uniform legislation, see chapter 30. For the status of precedents on predecessor legislation, see chapter 32. For the impact of provisions of the parent statute in the interpretation of delegated legislation, see chapter 43.

Relevance of other statutes

A provision in another statute, even with similar or identical wording, is not necessarily relevant [29.2]

Because statutes must be read contextually,[3] a provision in another statute, even with similar or identical wording, is not necessarily relevant as an aid to interpretation. In other words, courts do not assume a word is used in the same way across the statute book, regardless of context. **Example 29.1**, the case of *JAD v The Queen*,[4] illustrates this proposition.

The above principle applies a fortiori (all the more) where the words on the statute book are different to the words in question. **Example 29.2**, the case of *Taylor v The Owners – Strata Plan No 11564*,[5] is illustrative.

Example 29.1 *JAD v The Queen*[6]

The appellant was charged with a sexual offence that was perpetrated on the daughter of the appellant's de facto partner. At the time the complainant was 16 years old. Section 73(1) of the *Crimes Act 1900* (NSW) provided as follows:

> (1) Any person who has sexual intercourse with another person who:
> (a) is under his or her special care, and
> (b) is of or above the age of 16 years and under the age of 17 years,
> is liable to imprisonment for 8 years.

Subsection (3) then provided a definition of 'under his or her special care':

> (3) For the purposes of this section, a person (***the victim***) is under the special care of another person (***the offender***) if, and only if:
> (a) the offender is the step-parent, guardian or foster parent of the victim,
> . . .

The defence argued that 'foster parent' in sub-s (3)(a) required an out-of-home care arrangement and did not extend 'to the situation where a couple were living in a de facto relationship together with the child of one of the people in that relationship'.[7] The minority (Whealy JA) agreed with the defence counsel submission. He held that 'the intention in the 2003 amendment was to cover situations where children were fostered out to homes at which neither of their natural parents resided'.[8] The majority of the NSW Court of Criminal Appeal took a different view. Simpson J (with whom Hoeben J agreed) held that 'the reference to "foster parent" in s 73 includes a reference to a de facto living in a familial relationship with a natural parent of a child of the ages specified in s 73'.[9]

3 *SZTAL v Minister for Immigration and Border Protection* (2017) 262 CLR 362, 368 [14] (Kiefel CJ, Nettle and Gordon JJ). See further chapter 7.

4 [2012] NSWCCA 73.

5 (2014) 253 CLR 531.

6 [2012] NSWCCA 73.

7 Ibid [7] (Whealy JA).

8 Ibid [30].

9 Ibid [160].

As mentioned in an earlier chapter,[10] a point of difference between the reasoning of the majority and the minority concerned use of the statute book and whether alternative words would have been used if Parliament had intended to include a de facto partner within the scope of 'foster parent'. The minority referred to s 19(1A) of the *Adoption of Children Act 1965* (NSW) and the *Crimes (Domestic and Personal Violence) Act 2007* (NSW) for the legislative understanding of a de facto relationship. And Whealy JA agreed[11] with the defence counsel's example of the recognition of the expression 'foster care' in the *Adoption Act 2000* (NSW) and *Children and Young Persons (Care and Protection) Act 1998* (NSW).[12]

The majority took a more orthodox view in relation to the use of the statute book. Simpson J did not find understandings of 'de facto' and 'foster parent' in these statutes helpful, reasoning that 'a word in common parlance is given a specific statutory meaning but for the limited purpose of the statute in which it is used'.[13] In other words, the different context meant the meaning of the words in question could not be applied to the present context.

Example 29.2 *Taylor v The Owners – Strata Plan 11564*[14]

This case illustrates the significance of different wording when the statute book is relied on by counsel. The interpretative issue was the meaning of s 12(2) of the *Civil Liability Act 2002* (NSW):

> (2) In the case of any such award, the court is to disregard the amount (if any) by which the claimant's gross weekly earnings would (but for the injury or death) have exceeded an amount that is 3 times the amount of average weekly earnings at the date of the award.

In an action commenced under the *Compensation to Relatives Act 1897* (NSW) ('the Relatives Act'), by the wife of a high-earning husband killed in an accident, the plaintiff argued that 'the claimant's gross weekly earnings' referred to the person claiming damages under the Relatives Act (her). The defendants contended that the phrase referred to 'the gross weekly earnings on which the claimant relies'.[15] If the latter construction were upheld, it would have applied to the earnings of the plaintiff's late husband. The cap would have been applied.

Among other things, the majority of the Court below (the NSW Court of Appeal) had taken into account the wording of three other statutory schemes that imposed a limitation on the award of damages for injury or death calculated by reference to earnings: s 9 of the *Health Care Liability Act 2001* (NSW) ('the HCL Act'); s 151I of the *Workers Compensation Act 1987* (NSW) ('the WC Act'); and s 125 of the *Motor Accidents Compensation Act 1999* (NSW) ('the MAC Act'). The WC Act referred to 'the injured or deceased worker's net weekly earnings'. The MAC Act similarly referred to 'the injured or deceased person's net weekly earnings'.[16]

10 Chapter 5 at **[5.4]**.

11 *JAD v The Queen* [2012] NSWCCA 73, [28].

12 Ibid [7].

13 Ibid [140].

14 (2014) 253 CLR 531.

15 Ibid 546 [33] (French CJ, Crennan and Bell JJ).

16 The HCL Act did not include such wording, but the majority of the New South Wales Court of Appeal was of the view that the wording in the Liability Act had been transposed, in error, from the HCL Act: see ibid 543–4 [21].

The majority of the High Court of Australia (French CJ, Crennan and Bell JJ) rejected the relevance of these schemes for two reasons. First, the subject matter of the Relatives Act was distinct: 'Relatives Act claims arising from motor accidents, by reason of their number or otherwise, may have called for a different legislative response to Relatives Act claims arising from other wrongful acts.'[17] Second, the wording was different in that the MAC Act and the WC Act, but not the Act in question, included, respectively, the words 'or deceased person's' and 'or deceased worker's'. The different wording was significant:

> [A]s Basten JA observed, the circumstance that the legislature chose to depart from the language used in s 125 of the MAC Act (and s 151I of the WC Act) does not provide a foundation for the assumption that the different words enacted in s 12 of the Liability Act (and its predecessor, s 9 of the HCL Act) are directed to the achievement of the same object.[18]

Statutes *in pari materia*

Where the Act in question is *in pari materia* with another Act (dealing with the same subject matter on the same lines) it is to be read in the same way as that other Act is understood [29.3]

In *SZTAL v Minister for Immigration and Border Protection*[19] Kiefel CJ, Nettle and Gordon JJ summarised the *in pari materia* doctrine succinctly:

> Statutes *in pari materia*, in the sense that they deal with the same subject matter along the same lines, may form part of the context for the process of construction. Acts of this kind are said to form a kind of code or scheme, which arises from the degree of similarity involved.[20] Without this feature there is no warrant to transpose the meaning of a word from one statute to another or to assume, where the same words are used in a subsequent statute, that the legislature intended to attach the same meaning to the same words. [21]

In determining whether an Act is *in pari materia* a court will take account of, among other things, the closeness of the subject matter and the expressions in question, together with any extrinsic indications that the Act was to be so regarded provided by parliamentary materials.[22]

An additional indication of whether an Act is *in pari materia* with the Act in question is the former Act's place in the statute book. If it is judged to be the central statement of law on the question this may be a powerful indication that it is to be regarded as *in pari materia* with the Act in question. In *Coverdale v West Coast Council*[23] the respondent Council challenged the refusal of the Valuer-General to value leases over parts of the seabed and waters within Macquarie Harbour

17 Ibid 550 [43].

18 Ibid (footnote omitted).

19 (2017) 262 CLR 362.

20 Oliver Jones, *Bennion on Statutory Interpretation: A Code* (LexisNexis, 6th ed, 2013) 553.

21 (2017) 262 CLR 362, 371 [24]. As the High Court noted, it drew on Bennion's account. A further footnote has been omitted.

22 *Wilson v Transport Accident Commission* (2017) 80 MVR 157, 166–7 [27] (Bell J).

23 (2016) 259 CLR 164.

on the west coast of Tasmania. The interpretative question related to s 11(1) of the *Valuation of Land Act 2001* (Tas). It provided for the valuation of 'all lands within each valuation district, including any Crown lands'. The question was whether Crown lands extended to include the sea. 'Crown lands' was not specifically defined. 'Land' was defined inclusively in s 3. That definition did not refer to the seabed and waters above it. And case law on the ordinary signification of 'land' doubted that 'land' would be understood in that sense as encompassing the seabed.[24] But in s 2 of the *Crown Lands Act 1976* (Tas) 'land' was expressly defined to include the sea. The High Court held that the *Crown Lands Act* and the *Valuation of Land Act* were *in pari materia.*[25] In reaching this conclusion the Court observed that 'the CLA is the ultimate statutory enablement of all forms of holdings of and dealings with "Crown land"'.[26]

But if two statutes use the same or very similar words in question they will not be *in pari materia* if they 'do so in different ways and for different purposes'.[27] For this reason, 'intended' and 'intentionally' in s 5(1) of the *Migration Act 1958* (Cth) were held not to be *in pari materia* with the extended definition of 'intention' in s 5.2(3) of the *Criminal Code* (Cth).[28] And 'bodily harm' in s 4(1) of the *Crimes (Victims Assistance) Act 1989* (NT) was held not to be *in pari materia* with the definition of 'bodily harm' in s 1 of the *Criminal Code* (NT)).[29]

An Act *in pari materia* can assist the interpretation of the Act in question in one of two ways. First, it may supply a legislative definition, which presumptively applies to the Act in question. For example, in *Ramaciotti v Federal Commissioner of Taxation*[30] a dispute arose about liability to income tax. Section 13 of the *Income Tax Assessment Act 1915* (Cth) provided:

> [T]his Act shall not apply to any person who is on active service during the present war with the military or naval forces of the Commonwealth ... so far as regards income derived from personal exertion and earned prior to the commencement of this Act or during the present state of war.

The *Defence Act 1903* (Cth) defined 'active service' as 'service in or with a force which is engaged in operations against the enemy and includes any naval or military service in time of war'. On the meaning of 'active service' in the *Income Tax Assessment Act*, Knox CJ held:

> The phrase is one of art in a sense; and when we find in another Act which for this purpose is *in pari materia* a definition of that phrase, I see no reason for not giving to it in the section now under consideration the same meaning as it bears in the other Act.[31]

Alternatively, as in *Wilson v Transport Accident Commission*[32] (**Example 29.3**), the Act *in pari materia* may have been the subject of judicial interpretation. In that case it is the interpretation that is presumptively transposed to the Act in question.[33]

---

24 Ibid 171 [18] (the Court), referring to *Risk v Northern Territory* (2002) 210 CLR 392, 403–4 [26].

25 Ibid 178 [43].

26 Ibid.

27 *SZTAL v Minister for Immigration and Border Protection* (2017) 262 CLR 362, 371 [25] (Kiefel CJ, Nettle and Gordon JJ).

28 Ibid. The Code is at *Criminal Code Act 1995* (Cth) sch.

29 *Alfonso v Northern Territory* (1999) 131 NTR 8, 10–11 [9]–[13] (Mildren J).

30 (1920) 29 CLR 49.

31 Ibid 53 (Knox CJ, Isaacs J agreeing at 54 and Rich J agreeing at 54).

32 (2017) 80 MVR 157.

33 Ibid 166–7 [25]–[27] (Bell J).

Example 29.3 *Wilson v Transport Accident Commission*[34]

The plaintiff and his wife lived on a farm where they were engaged in the employment of growing produce for sale to a local cooperative. On 9 July 2014, after completing some tasks associated with his farm work, he went for a bicycle ride that was purely recreational in purpose. Sadly, he collided with the rear of legally parked truck and sustained serious injuries. He had intended to work on the farm after returning from the ride.

The plaintiff applied for no-fault compensation under the *Transport Accident Act 1986* (Vic). Section 3(1A)(c) of that Act defined a 'transport accident' as including an incident 'involving a collision between a pedal cycle and a motor vehicle while the cyclist is travelling to or from his or her place of employment'. After the plaintiff's claim was rejected by the Transport Accident Commission, he appealed to the Victorian Civil and Administrative Tribunal ('the Tribunal'). It dismissed his application. An appeal on a question of law was brought to the Supreme Court of Victoria. The question was whether s 3(1A)(c) ought to be given a literal meaning, as the plaintiff contended,[35] or whether, as the Transport Accident Commission contended, it required a work connection for the travel to be regarded as being to or from the place of employment.[36]

The Court acknowledged that 'on a plain reading of those words, Mr Wilson was travelling to his place of employment when injured on the ride because he worked on the farm where he lived and that is where he was travelling'.[37]

Against this consideration, however, the Court took into account the well-established meaning of the expression 'travelling to or from his or her place of employment' and similar expressions in decisions on workers compensation legislation, such as the decision of the High Court in *Commonwealth v Wright*[38] in relation to s 9A(1) of the *Commonwealth Employees' Compensation Act 1930* (Cth). This legislation had provided that compensation was payable where personal injury by accident was caused to an employee 'while travelling to or from – (a) his employment'.[39] After a detailed review of the case law,[40] the Supreme Court found that a long-accepted meaning in these provisions of workers compensation law was in place, which is that 'a connection between the travel and employment at the place is required'.[41] The Court held that 'the provisions of the Transport Accident Act relating to compensation for cyclists involved in certain collisions with motor vehicles should be treated as being *in pari materia* with the relevant provisions of workers compensation and like legislation'.[42] The Court then summed up its reasons for so thinking:

> I have come to this conclusion because the two bodies of legislation deal with similar subject matter, the expressions requiring interpretation are identical or similar and represent compensation eligibility criteria, the expressions had been the subject of authoritative determination and had a well-accepted meaning when the Transport Accident (Amendment) Act was enacted, the extrinsic materials show that, when enacting

34 (2017) 80 MVR 157.

35 Ibid 164 [22] (Bell J).

36 Ibid 164 [23].

37 Ibid 173 [47].

38 (1956) 96 CLR 536.

39 Quoted in *Wilson v Transport Accident Commission* (2017) 80 MVR 157, 167 [30].

40 Ibid 167–73 [28]–[44].

41 Ibid 174 [51].

42 Ibid 166 [27] (italics in original).

> those amendments, Parliament was conscious of the workers compensation legislation and there is nothing to show a contrary intention. The subject matter of the two bodies of legislation is accident compensation, specifically in relation to injuries suffered by persons when travelling to or from the place of employment. The expressions in question are 'travelling to or from the place of employment' and like expressions, which form part of the eligibility criteria in the legislation concerned.[43]

The Court found the Tribunal did not err[44] in holding that *the ride itself* must be work-related.[45] Hence, the criterion was not satisfied by a rider's intention to undertake employment at the place after completing a ride that itself was not connected to that employment.[46]

Statutes forming part of a single scheme

[29.4] **Where two or more statutory enactments form part of a single scheme, the enactments should be construed together and harmoniously**

In *Commissioner of Police for New South Wales v Eaton*[47] Gageler J framed a 'principle of harmonious construction'. It has been applied beyond provisions within the one statute to the use of the wider statute book. He expressed the principle this way:

> Stated at its highest level of generality . . . statutory texts enacted by the same legislature are to be construed so far as possible to operate in harmony and not in conflict. That principle of harmonious construction applies to the construction of provisions within different statutes of the same legislature to create 'a very strong presumption that the . . . legislature did not intend to contradict itself, but intended that both . . . should operate'.[48]

The statement has been applied to the situation where two or more statutory enactments comprise an overlapping legislative scheme. After quoting the principle articulated by Gageler J, the Full Court of the Supreme Court of Western Australia held that:

> Where two or more statutory enactments comprise the overlapping legislative scheme, the enactments should be construed accordingly, and the court should endeavour to produce a rational, sensible, efficient and just operation in preference to an inefficient, conflicting or unjust operation.[49]

---

43 Ibid 166–7 [27].

44 Ibid 174 [51]

45 Cited in ibid 164 [20].

46 Ibid 174 [50]. The result in the case has been reversed by retrospective legislation. See Michael Lombard and Shyla Sivanas, 'Trust Brings Change' (2019) 93(4) *Law Institute Journal* 34, 36, citing *Treasury and Finance Legislation Amendment Act 2018* (Vic). Section 18 of that Act (inserting s 233 into the *Transport Accident Act 1986* (Vic)) backdated the amendment to 9 July 2014, the date of the accident. The amending legislation followed commentary by the Court in the case pointing out an anomaly – namely that, while drivers who run into parked cars in their motor vehicle receive transport accident compensation, riders who run into parked cars on their bicycle and suffer serious injury receive only public health and welfare benefits: at 174 [51].

47 (2013) 252 CLR 1.

48 Ibid 33 [98] (dissenting as to outcome but not on this point; footnote omitted).

49 *Mohammadi v Bethune* [2018] WASCA 98, [36] (the Court) (footnotes omitted). For support that Court cited *Trajkoski v DPP (WA)* (2010) 41 WAR 105, 116 [50]–[52] (Buss JA, Owen JA agreeing at 107 [1]). The latter

Or as put in another case, 'the Court should endeavour, so far as is possible, to secure a coherent and harmonious operation of statutes dealing with a common or overlapping subject matter'.[50]

But in order to find that two or more enactments form part of a single scheme and should be construed together, *some* connection between the two statutes such as sharing a wider common purpose is not necessarily enough.[51] *Certain Lloyd's Underwriters v Cross*[52] is a leading case in this regard. In that case Kiefel J held: 'For a scheme to be identified, it must involve two statutes … operating together. If the operation of each statute could be said to depend on the other, there would be a warrant for construing them together in this way.'[53] A court will need to examine a number of indicia, and in particular, '[i]t is necessary to consider each of the statutes and the means by which they are intended to achieve their respective objectives, in order to determine whether they form part of a single scheme'.[54] In addition to whether the Acts share a 'common purpose',[55] and are 'connected by their terms',[56] it will be relevant to consider whether the provisions in both Acts were introduced as a single package of reforms,[57] whether they regulate the same or different subject matter,[58] the extent to which the wording of the Acts correspond,[59] and the extent to which the Acts have 'co-extensive fields of operation'.[60]

Examples of overlapping schemes construed together include two Acts that were part of a suite of legislation dealing with the prevention of cruelty to animals,[61] a series of legislation relating to appeals from a final judgment of a judge of an inferior court to a Court of Appeal,[62] and four revenue Acts considered to be an integrated part of statute law.[63]

Example 29.4 *Liu v Stephen Grubits and Associates*[64]

The appellant challenged a costs order made by a judge of the Federal Circuit Court of Australia in relation to a matter arising under the *Fair Work Act 2009* (Cth). The appellant argued that the Circuit Court lacked power to make the order. The appellant laid stress on two features of the

case in turn relied on the discussion by Kirby P in *Commissioner of Stamp Duties v Permanent Trustee Co Ltd* (1987) 9 NSWLR 719, 722–4.

50 *Will v Brighton* (2020) 104 NSWLR 170, 182 [47] (Bell P, Basten JA agreeing at [109], Simpson AJA agreeing at [127]).

51 *Certain Lloyd's Underwriters v Cross* (2012) 248 CLR 378, 414 [97]–[98] (Kiefel J).

52 (2012) 248 CLR 378.

53 Ibid 414 [97].

54 Ibid 414 [98].

55 Ibid 413–4 [95]–[98].

56 Ibid 414 [96].

57 Ibid 393 [36], 394 [39] (French CJ and Hayne J).

58 Ibid 414–5 [99]–[100] (Kiefel J).

59 Ibid 393–4 [34]–[37] (French CJ and Hayne J).

60 Ibid 394 [37]–[38] (French CJ and Hayne J), 415 [101] (Kiefel J).

61 *Will v Brighton* (2020) 104 NSWLR 170, 181–2 [45]–[47], 190 [95] (Bell P, Basten JA agreeing at 192 [109], Simpson AJA agreeing at 195 [127]).

62 *Trajkoski v DPP (WA)* (2010) 41 WAR 105, 116–7 [53]–[54] (Buss JA, Owen JA agreeing at [1]).

63 *Commissioner of Stamp Duties v Permanent Trustee Co Ltd* (1987) 9 NSWLR 719, 720–4 (Kirby P).

64 (2019) 284 IR 475.

relevant Acts, the *Federal Circuit Court of Australia Act 1999* (Cth) ('the FCCA Act') and the *Fair Work Act 2009* (Cth). First, the provision in the FCCA Act dealing with the jurisdiction of the Circuit Court to award costs in proceedings before that court (s 79(1)) expressly *excluded* proceedings in relation to a matter arising under the *Fair Work Act*. Second, while the *Fair Work Act* contained a section concerning the awarding of costs in respect of proceedings 'in a court (including a court of a State or Territory)' (s 570), the section did not in terms confer *a power* to award costs. Section 570 read:

> **Costs only if proceedings instituted vexatiously etc.**
>
> (1) A party to proceedings (including an appeal) in a court (including a court of a State or Territory) in relation to a matter arising under this Act may be ordered by the court to pay costs incurred by another party to the proceedings only in accordance with subsection (2) or section 569 or 569A.
>
> Note: The Commonwealth might be ordered to pay costs under section 569. A State or Territory might be ordered to pay costs under section 569A.
>
> (2) The party may be ordered to pay the costs only if:
> (a) the court is satisfied that the party instituted the proceedings vexatiously or without reasonable cause; or
> (b) the court is satisfied that the party's unreasonable act or omission caused the other party to incur the costs; or
> (c) the court is satisfied of both of the following:
> (i) the party unreasonably refused to participate in a matter before the FWC;
> (ii) the matter arose from the same facts as the proceedings.

The appellant's construction of s 570 was that it was no more than an express limitation on the discretion to award costs if and where that power was conferred elsewhere. As s 79 of the FCCA Act did not confer such a power on the Circuit Court, it was argued that neither that Act nor the *Fair Work Act* conferred a relevant power.

In evaluating the appellant's construction and the rival construction that s 570 impliedly conferred a power on the Circuit Court to award costs in Fair Work matters the Full Federal Court paid close regard to the principle of harmonious construction articulated by Gageler J in *Commissioner of Police for New South Wales v Eaton*[65] and quoted above. The Court came to the conclusion that the wider construction s 570, which impliedly conferred on the Circuit Court the power to award costs in a Fair Work matter, gave a more harmonious operation to the two Acts and should be preferred.[66] Several reasons justified that conclusion.

First, the FCCA Act and the *Fair Work Act* overlapped in subject matter and operation. Part 4-2 of the *Fair Work Act* (in which lay s 570) dealt with the jurisdiction and powers of courts.[67] Second, read in context, the evident purpose of div 4 of pt 4-2 'was to provide a uniform set of pre-conditions which must be satisfied before any award of costs could be made [by a court]'.[68] Those conditions were so framed having regard to the fact that the *Fair Work Act* contemplated that a matter arising under that Act could be the subject of litigation in any one of a number of

65 Ibid 479 [11] (the Court).

66 Ibid.

67 Ibid.

68 Ibid 478 [10].

courts: the Federal Court, the Circuit Court or an 'eligible State or Territory court'. Each of these courts might have very different costs regimes. Third, a 'note' contained at the foot of s 79(1) of the FCCA Act expressly linked the two Acts. The note read, in part:

> See section 570 of the *Fair Work Act 2009* for proceedings in relation to matters arising under that Act.[69]

The appellant's reading could not give the note work to do, whereas the preferred construction would do so.[70] Fourth, a 'note' at the foot of s 570(1) of the *Fair Work Act*[71] indicated that s 569 was a power to award costs, and that section worked similarly to s 570.[72] Fifth, the appellant's construction would lead to 'anomalous' consequences. The result would be that costs could be awarded in Fair Work matters by the Federal Court or any eligible state or territory court, but not by the Circuit Court.[73] The Court also noted that the preferred construction was consistent with the explanatory memorandum to the Bill that led to the introduction of s 79 of the FCCA Act.[74]

Comparable statutes

Comparable statutes may be an aid to interpretation [29.5]

As seen above, the legislative context of an Act extends to Acts *in pari materia* and statutes that are part of a single scheme. It also extends to Acts of general application, such as Interpretation Acts. Other Acts – on the statute book or from another jurisdiction – may also be of assistance. An interpreter may obtain guidance (at their discretion[75]) by employing comparative analysis – that is, analysis that is employing contrast or analogy.[76] Courts are increasingly using the statute book for such wider purposes.[77] Counsel have been encouraged to assist the court where cognate statutes exist.[78] One of the reasons for the increasing use of comparative analysis is a practical one – the availability of electronic databases of legislation and of electronic search tools.

---

69 This note was part of the FCCA Act by virtue of s 13 of the *Acts Interpretation Act 1901* (Cth): ibid 479 [11]. See generally chapter 13.

70 Ibid 479 [11].

71 Notes in the *Fair Work Act* do *not* form part of the Act: s 40A of the *Fair Work Act*: ibid 479 [15]. But the Court had regard to the note under the authority of s 15AB(1)(a) of the *Acts Interpretation Act 1901* (Cth); see generally chapter 24.

72 Ibid.

73 Ibid 480 [18].

74 Ibid 479–80 [17]–[18].

75 John Bell and George Engle, *Cross: Statutory Interpretation* (Oxford University Press, 3rd ed, 2005) 151–2.

76 Ibid 151.

77 Sir Kenneth Keith, 'Sources of Law, Especially in Statutory Interpretation, with Suggestions about Distinctiveness' in John Prebble (ed), *Sir Kenneth Keith: Collected Papers* (Victoria University of Wellington Legal Research Papers, Keith Paper 26, 2018) 77, 89.

78 *New South Wales Crime Commission v Kelaita* (2008) 75 NSWLR 564, 580 [60] (Allsop P, Giles JA and Bell JA agreeing at 580). In that case Allsop P encouraged counsel whenever an issue arises in relation to the Act in question – the *Criminal Assets Recovery Act 1990* (NSW) – to assist the Court with 'understanding as to how cognate statutes in other States and the Commonwealth have dealt with the issue in question': ibid. There is no apparent reason why the observation should not apply to any problematic statute with other 'cognates'.

Two further reasons for resort to the statute book and legislation of other jurisdictions have been suggested by the New Zealand jurist Sir Kenneth Keith.[79] The first is that the statute book enables the court to be informed about 'the broader legislative practice and context'.[80] The assumption here is that 'Parliament is using principles and language in a broadly consistent way (while recognising that in this respect Parliament is not always to be seen as perfect)'.[81] Another reason is so that a court may be better informed about the policies that underpin the area. In this respect the assumption is that 'where principle and policy are relevant to judicial decision the statute book might be considered a better source than some others'.[82]

A court may find the broader legislative practice useful in a number of ways. It may find a drafting practice,[83] or a definition in an Act of another jurisdiction,[84] shows that a construction for the term in question is feasible. It may find that the absence of a defence in the offence provision in question (when defences had been provided in comparable legislation) supports a narrow reading of the provision in question.[85] Similarly, it may find that if Parliament wished to catch a broader field of conduct, it would have used additional words that are used elsewhere on the statute book.[86] And it may find that, in 'comparable statutes', Parliament has rebutted a relevant presumption using express words – fortifying the conclusion that in the provision in question (which lacked such express words) the presumption was not rebutted.[87]

A court may find the statute book to be a source of guidance about legislative policy.[88]

Relatedly, a comparison with cognate statutes in other jurisdictions may confirm to a court that it would be a step too far to accept a construction contended for. If the statute in question does not expressly support the construction, and involves a large 'reading in', while cognate

79 Sir Kenneth Keith, 'Sources of Law, Especially in Statutory Interpretation, with Suggestions about Distinctiveness' in John Prebble (ed), *Sir Kenneth Keith: Collected Papers* (Victoria University of Wellington Legal Research Papers, Keith Paper 26, 2018) 77, 89.

80 *Assistant Registrar of Companies v Moses* [2004] 3 NZLR 577, 584 (Court of Appeal) (the Court). The judgment was delivered by Sir Kenneth Keith.

81 Sir Kenneth Keith, 'Sources of Law, Especially in Statutory Interpretation, with Suggestions about Distinctiveness' in John Prebble (ed), *Sir Kenneth Keith: Collected Papers* (Victoria University of Wellington Legal Research Papers, Keith Paper 26, 2018) 77, 89. It is interesting to compare the perspective of parliamentary counsel. Several accounts by Australian and overseas parliamentary counsel broadly align: see Peter Quiggin, 'Statutory Construction: How to Construct, and Construe, a Statute' in Neil Williams (ed), *Key Issues in Judicial Review* (Federation Press, 2014) 78, 86–7; Teri Cherkewich, 'By Sword and Shield: Legislative Counsel's Role in Advancing and Protecting Democracy One Word (and Client) at a Time' (2015) 36(3) *Statute Law Review* 253, 261–2; Sandra Markman, 'Climbing Constitution Hill – Teaching Legislative Drafting in Ireland' [2013] (3) *The Loophole: Journal of the Commonwealth Association of Legislative Counsel* 28, 31–2; Janet Erasmus, 'Keepers of the Statute Book: Lessons from the Space-Time Continuum' [2010] (1) *The Loophole: Journal of the Commonwealth Association of Legislative Counsel* 7, 7–8.

82 Sir Kenneth Keith, 'Sources of Law, Especially in Statutory Interpretation, with Suggestions about Distinctiveness' in John Prebble (ed), *Sir Kenneth Keith: Collected Papers* (Victoria University of Wellington Legal Research Papers, Keith Paper 26, 2018) 77, 89.

83 *Talacko v Bennett* (2017) 260 CLR 124, 145 [66] (Kiefel CJ, Bell, Keane, Gordon and Edelman JJ). See **Example 29.5** on this case.

84 *Federal Commissioner of Taxation v Henderson* (1943) 68 CLR 29, 44 (Latham CJ, Rich J substantially agreeing at 45).

85 *Assistant Registrar of Companies v Moses* [2004] 3 NZLR 577, 583–4 [22]–[24] (Court of Appeal) (the Court).

86 *Fisher v Bell* [1961] 1 QB 394, 399 (Lord Parker CJ, Ashworth J agreeing at 401, Elwes J agreeing at 401).

87 *R (Black) v Secretary of State for Justice* [2018] AC 215, 233–4 [44]–[45] (Baroness Hale of Richmond PSC, Lord Mance, Lord Kerr of Tonaghmore, Lord Hughes and Lord Lloyd-Jones JJSC in agreement).

88 *Hughes v Janrule Pty Ltd* (2011) 177 ACTR 1, discussed in **Example 29.6**.

statutes provide a detailed section dealing with the same issue, the court may conclude that '[i]t is not a matter ... legitimately within the province of interpretation and construction of the statute'.[89]

Comparative analysis is not always fruitful. A court may find that the analysis raises more questions than it answers. For instance, the fact that different wording is provided in interstate legislation that deals with an equivalent subject matter is not itself proof of a drafting or instructing error in the Act in question. It might equally mean that the legislature's failure to include such wording was deliberate. In such a case the interstate legislation does not assist one way or the other.[90]

Two cases involving comparable statutes follow. **Example 29.5** illustrates the use of the statute book as evidence of the broader legislative practice, while **Example 29.6** illustrates the use of the statute book as a source of guidance about legislative policy.

Example 29.5 *Talacko v Bennett*[91]

The case arose after a complex family dispute over ownership of properties in Czechoslovakia that had been seized after World War II. The properties were later reinstated to one family member, Jan Emil Talacko ('Jan Emil'). After equitable suit by five other family members, the Supreme Court of Victoria in 2009 made orders for equitable compensation against Jan Emil and in favour of the plaintiffs. In 2011 Jan Emil was made bankrupt by order of the Federal Court of Australia. In 2012, on the request of the respondents (who were among the successful plaintiffs in the compensation action), the Prothonotary of the Supreme Court of Victoria issued a document entitled 'Certificate of Finality of Judgments and Orders', evidently in reliance on s 15 of the *Foreign Judgments Act 1991* (Cth). That section read:

> (1) Subject to this section, where an application is duly made by a judgment creditor who wishes to enforce in a country a judgment that has been given in an Australian court, the Registrar of the court must issue to the judgment creditor:
> (a) a certified copy of the judgment; and
> (b) a certificate with respect to the judgment containing such particulars, including:
> (i) the causes of action to which the judgment relates; and
> (ii) the rate of interest (if any) payable on any amount payable under the judgment;
>
> as are prescribed by the regulations or by Rules of Court.
>
> (2) An application may not be made until the expiration of any stay of enforcement of the judgment in question.

After the death in 2014 of Jan Emil, his widow, Judith Talacko ('Judith'), sought declarations that the Prothonotary had exceeded his authority in issuing the Certificate and a subsequent certificate.

89 *New South Wales Crime Commission v Kelaita* (2008) 75 NSWLR 564, 580 [58] (Allsop P, Giles JA agreeing at 580 and Bell JA agreeing at 580).

90 *DPP v Moreno* (2018) 57 VR 1, 25 [83] (Daly AsJ).

91 (2017) 260 CLR 124.

The proceedings brought by Judith raised the issue of the effect of s 58(3) of the *Bankruptcy Act 1966* (Cth) on the respondents' application for a certificate under s 15 of the *Foreign Judgments Act*. Section 58 relevantly stated:

> (1) Subject to this Act, where a debtor becomes a bankrupt:
> (a) the property of the bankrupt . . . vests forthwith in the Official Trustee . . .
> (3) Except as provided by this Act, after a debtor has become a bankrupt, it is not competent for a creditor:
> (a) to enforce any remedy against the person or the property of the bankrupt in respect of a provable debt; or
> (b) except with the leave of the Court and on such terms as the Court thinks fit, to commence any legal proceeding in respect of a provable debt or take any fresh step in such a proceeding.

An appeal from a decision of the Court of Appeal of Victoria to the High Court raised the question 'whether a "stay of enforcement" of a judgment within the meaning of s 15(2) of the Foreign Judgments Act is brought about by s 58(3) of the Bankruptcy Act 1966 (Cth)'.[92]

The respondents argued that 'stay of enforcement of a judgment' had a technical, legal meaning and referred to 'a stay ordered by a court that operates directly on an order or judgment and not, in contrast, on the party who might otherwise seek enforcement of that judgment'.[93] The appellant contended that 'nothing in the text of s 15(2) qualifies the words [in question] so as to limit the provision exclusively to judicially ordered stays'.[94]

The High Court agreed with the appellant's construction.[95] In holding that '[i]t is not possible to attribute to s 15(2) an intention that a foreign court should enforce a judgment by execution which would not be permitted in Australia simply because the impediment to execution is brought about by statute rather than by an order of a court',[96] the Court took account of legislative practice evident elsewhere on the Commonwealth statute book:

> In Commonwealth legislation, the use of the word 'stay' is not confined to stays imposed by courts. It appears that, in addition to s 60(2) of the *Bankruptcy Act*, as Santamaria JA noted, s 91 of the *Insurance Act 1973* (Cth), s 161 of the *Life Insurance Act 1995* (Cth), s 189AAA of the *Bankruptcy Act* itself, s 16 of the *Cross-Border Insolvency Act 2008* (Cth) and s 58DD of the *Federal Court of Australia Act 1976* (Cth) are examples of stays which operate without judicial process.[97]

92 Ibid 130 [1] (Kiefel CJ, Bell, Keane, Gordon and Edelman JJ, Gageler J agreeing at 148 [78], Nettle J agreeing at 148 [79]).

93 Ibid 143 [60].

94 Ibid 142 [57].

95 Ibid 131 [2], 146 [70].

96 Ibid 146 [70].

97 Ibid 145 [66] (footnote omitted).

Example 29.6 *Hughes v Janrule Pty Ltd*[98]

A Master of the ACT Supreme Court rejected the plaintiff's claim for damages for injury suffered as a result of a workplace accident. The plaintiff filed a notice of appeal to the Court of Appeal. The respondent to the appeal subsequently filed an application for security for costs (initially for costs of $30,000) and a stay of proceedings until that security was provided.

The application by the respondent to the appeal for security for costs was listed before the Court of Appeal constituted by a single judge. The appellant opposed any order for security for costs and argued that the power to order security for costs was not conferred on the Court of Appeal. The respondent contended that the Court of Appeal did have that jurisdiction and that it could be exercised by a single judge.

The Court found it necessary to deal with a fundamental question, being whether the Court had jurisdiction to order security for costs in a matter in the Court of Appeal. After finding that the Court of Appeal has all procedural powers necessary for it to manage appeals within its jurisdiction, the Court considered whether those procedural powers can be exercised by the Court of Appeal constituted by a single judge.

Section 37J of the *Supreme Court Act 1933* (ACT) included:

> (1) The Court of Appeal may be constituted by a single judge for hearing and deciding any of the following matters (incidental matters) in relation to an appeal:
>
> ...
>
> (k) any other question of practice and procedure in the Court of Appeal;

The interpretative issue for the Court concerned the scope of para (k). After careful analysis the Court determined that 'para 37J(1)(k) referring to questions of practice and procedure should be read as including a reference to orders for security for costs'.[99]

The Court gave three reasons for so including,[100] one of which drew on a comparative analysis of the legislative approaches taken in other Australian jurisdictions. That analysis concluded as follows:

> In summary, those jurisdictions in which it seems that security for costs may be ordered by a single judge all provide an express power to order security for costs, but adopt one of two possible approaches to conferring that power on a single judge exercising appellate jurisdiction, being:
>
> (a) a general conferral of what might loosely be called procedural or incidental powers of the Court of Appeal on a single judge (NSW and Queensland); or
>
> (b) a specific provision, either as part of, or separate from, the provision permitting security for costs orders, that permits such orders to be made in the Court of Appeal by a single judge (South Australia and Western Australia).[101]

This analysis led the Court to fortify its reasons in the following way:

> [T]he approach taken in other Australian jurisdictions except Victoria ... indicates that there is no inherent or generally-accepted policy reason why security for costs should only be ordered by a court of appeal constituted by multiple judges.[102]

98 (2011) 177 ACTR 1.

99 Ibid 12 [62] (Penfold J).

100 Ibid 12–13 [62].

101 Ibid 12 [60].

102 Ibid 13 [62].

30 USE OF PRECEDENT

Overview

[30.1] This chapter examines the use of binding and persuasive precedent in the interpretative task. Precedent here refers broadly to prior judicial decisions of courts on the meaning of particular legislative text, rather than precedent on the common law principles of statutory interpretation. The doctrine of precedent generally applies to statutory interpretation cases in the same way as it applies to common law cases. But there are some special considerations due to fundamental interpretative principles. The fundamental object of interpreting a statute is to ascertain the legislative intent. Further, the starting point for construction must always be the text of the statute. These principles affect whether a prior decision is binding, and the degree to which a non-binding decision is persuasive. Generally, a decision of a superior court in the same hierarchy will only be binding if it attributes meaning to the same text in the same statute. There is also the principle that an intermediate appellate court construing a statute that forms part of a uniform scheme or is federal legislation should follow the interpretation given by another appellate court, unless that prior decision is plainly wrong. The persuasive value of a non-binding decision on similar or identical text will depend on the logical and relevant connection that can be established between that text and the legislation being construed. This connection is established if the statutes are *in pari materia* (see **chapter 29**). A similar approach is taken to foreign judgments on foreign legislation. Finally, inversely to precedent, it has been recognised that consistent legislative development in an area can influence the development of the common law in that area.

Binding and persuasive precedent

[30.2] **The use of judicial precedent is distinct from the precedent that comprises the common law of statutory interpretation**

The use of precedent in this chapter refers to the use of judicial decisions that stand as authority for the meaning of specific legislation, whether binding or persuasive in the instant case. The precedential value of case law in this sense is distinct from the judicial decisions that comprise the law of statutory interpretation.[1]

1 See **[1.2]**.

The doctrine of precedent applies to matters of statutory interpretation, but the starting point remains the statutory text [30.3]

The doctrine of precedent has numerous layers.[2] In its 'strict sense' the doctrine requires a court to accept and apply the legal principles established by courts at a higher tier in the hierarchy in which that court exists 'whatever its own inclinations may be'.[3] In its broader sense it includes other principles and practices that facilitate the consistency and efficacy of the law. These include the principle that appellate courts follow their own decisions,[4] and the approach that departure from a long-standing authoritative decision is a relevant consideration.[5] More controversially, the High Court has stated that lower and intermediate courts must observe 'seriously considered dicta' of a majority in the High Court.[6] This broader sense is based in judicial comity – a practice of 'recognition and courtesy shown by the judiciary in one nation or state for the laws and judicial decisions of another . . . based on mutual respect rather than binding legal principles'.[7]

These precedential principles apply to statutory interpretation matters, but there are overriding 'special considerations'.[8] The judicial task in statutory construction 'differs from that in distilling the common law from past decisions'.[9] In contrast to distilling common law principles, the fundamental object of statutory interpretation is to give effect to the legislative intent of the statute.[10] The statute is not 'a stab at formulating a concept';[11] it *is* the statement of the concept. This means that, axiomatically, the starting point remains the text of the statute, not the common law.[12]

---

2 On precedent generally see Justice Michael Kirby, 'Precedent Law, Practice and Trends in Australia' (2007) 28(3) *Australian Bar Review* 243; Sir Anthony Mason, 'The Use and Abuse of Precedent' (1988) 4(2) *Australian Bar Review* 93.

3 Sir Anthony Mason, 'The Use and Abuse of Precedent' (1988) 4(2) *Australian Bar Review* 93, 95.

4 *Babaniaris v Lutony Fashions Pty Ltd* (1987) 163 CLR 1, 13–14 (Mason J); *Nguyen v Nguyen* (1990) 169 CLR 245, 268–8 (Dawson, Toohey and McHugh JJ).

5 See, eg, *Aubrey v The Queen* (2017) 260 CLR 305, 332 [55] (Bell J, dissenting though not on principle), citing *Re Bolton; Ex parte Beane* (1987) 162 CLR 514, 531 (Deane J), *Babaniaris v Lutony Fashions Pty Ltd* (1987) 163 CLR 1, 13 (Mason J), 22–3 (Wilson and Dawson JJ) and *Hanau v Ehrlich* [1912] AC 39, 41 (Earl Loreburn LC). Bell J emphasised the importance of this practice in a criminal law context. See also 338 [73].

6 *Farah Constructions Pty Ltd v Say-Dee Pty Ltd* (2007) 230 CLR 89, 151 [134] (Gleeson CJ, Gummow, Callinan, Heydon and Crennan JJ). Whether this principle moves beyond a matter of comity is unclear: *Chief Commissioner of State Revenue v Benidorm Pty Ltd* (2020) 104 NSWLR 232, 253 [103] (Leeming JA, Meagher JA agreeing at 234 [1], Payne JAA agreeing 256 [117]). See also Bernice Chen, 'Seriously Considering "Seriously Considered Dicta": Precedent after Farah Constructions' (2021) 95(3) *Australian Law Journal* 186; Matthew Harding and Ian Malkin, 'The High Court of Australia's Obiter Dicta and Decision-Making in the Lower Courts' (2012) 34(2) *Sydney Law Review* 239.

7 *Australian Law Dictionary* (online at 11 December 2021) 'judicial comity'.

8 *John v Commissioner of Taxation (Cth)* (1989) 166 CLR 417, 439 (Mason CJ, Wilson, Dawson, Toohey and Gaudron JJ).

9 *McNamara v Consumer Trader and Tenancy Tribunal* (2005) 221 CLR 646, 661 [40] (McHugh, Gummow and Heydon JJ), referring to *Ogden Industries Pty Ltd v Lucas* [1970] AC 113, 127 and *Brennan v Comcare* (1994) 50 FCR 555, 572. See also **[1.6]**.

10 See chapter 4.

11 *Brennan v Comcare* (1994) 50 FCR 555, 573 (Gummow J), citing RA Posner, *The Problems of Jurisprudence* (1990) 248.

12 *Calidad Pty Ltd v Seiko Epson Corporation* (2020) 94 ALJR 1044, 1090 [204] (Nettle, Gordon and Edelman JJ). See also 1067 [110] (Kiefel CJ, Bell and Keane JJ).

This has led the courts to caution numerous times that, just like the words in other external materials, the words of a judicial decision, or paraphrases of the statute in a judicial decision, must not be substituted for the statutory text.[13] The attribution of meaning given in a judgment, even if binding, should not be construed as if they were words in a statute. The value in the judgment lies in the explanation and reasoning provided about the meaning of the text. That should not distract from the text. So, even where there is precedent relevant to the interpretative issue, the starting point remains the statutory text. This is consistent with statutory interpretation law.[14] Accordingly, when considering a precedent

> [t]he concern is not with the ascertainment of the meaning and the application of particular words used by previous judges, so much as with gaining an understanding of the concepts to which expression was sought to be given.[15]

Example 30.1 demonstrates the importance of not substituting the words of a judgment for the statutory text.

Example 30.1 *Weiss v The Queen*[16]

The appellant was convicted of the murder of a woman. At the trial, evidence was led that sometime after the murder, the appellant had maintained a sexual relationship with a girl under 16 years of age. The appellant appealed the conviction. Section 568(1) of the *Crimes Act 1958* (Vic) provided that the Court of Appeal on any appeal against conviction shall allow the appeal in certain circumstances. But it also contained a common form proviso that

> the Court of Appeal may, notwithstanding that it is of opinion that the point raised in the appeal might be decided in favour of the appellant, dismiss the appeal if it considers that no substantial miscarriage of justice has actually occurred.

The Court of Appeal of Victoria determined that the evidence of the girl's age was irrelevant and prejudicial. It considered the proviso. Callaway JA in the Court of Appeal (Batt JA and Harper AJA agreeing) drew a distinction between a court asking whether, without the wrongly admitted evidence, the jury at the appellant's trial would inevitably have convicted him, and asking whether, without that evidence, any reasonable jury, properly instructed, would inevitably have convicted him. Callaway JA determined that the former test was the appropriate one for the proviso, and that on that test the conviction was 'inevitable' and so the proviso applied. His Honour therefore dismissed the appeal. The appellant appealed to the High Court on the ground that the proviso did not apply.

---

13 See, eg, *Military Rehabilitation and Compensation Commission v May* (2016) 257 CLR 468, 482 [52] (French CJ, Kiefel, Nettle and Gordon JJ); *Construction, Forestry, Maritime, Mining and Energy Union v Australian Building and Construction Commissioner (The Bay Street Appeal)* (2020) 282 FCR 1, 5 [4] (Allsop CJ); *Baini v The Queen* (2012) 246 CLR 469, 476 [14] (French CJ, Hayne, Crennan, Kiefel and Bell JJ). See also *Ogden Industries Pty Ltd v Lucas* [1970] AC 113, 127 (Lord Upjohn).

14 See **[6.5]**.

15 *Comcare v PVYW* (2013) 250 CLR 246, 256 [16] (French CJ, Hayne, Crennan and Kiefel JJ), citing *Brennan v Comcare* (1994) 50 FCR 555, 572 (Gummow J). See also 256 [15].

16 (2005) 224 CLR 300. There have been judicial reservations expressed about the content of the miscarriage of justice ground as determined in *Weiss*. (See, eg, *Hofer v The Queen* (2021) 95 ALJR 937, 955–64 [82]–[122] (Gageler J).) However, these reservations do not diminish the statements in *Weiss* about statutory construction.

The High Court unanimously allowed the appeal. The Court began by establishing the fundamental proposition that the 'root question' regarding the application of the proviso was 'one of statutory construction' and that it 'is the words of the statute that ultimately govern, not the many subsequent judicial expositions of that meaning which have sought to express the operation of the proviso to the common form criminal appeal provision by using other words'.[17]

The Court recognised that there were numerous cases about the meaning of the proviso. About those cases it said:

> Many statements are to be found in the decided cases that describe the task presented by the proviso ... These expressions attempt to describe the operation of the statutory language in other words. They must not be taken as substitutes for that language. They are expressions which may mask the nature of the appellate court's task in considering the application of the proviso.[18]

The Court of Appeal, the High Court said, had fallen into the error of being diverted from the question presented by the text of the proviso.[19] The Court ordered that the matter be remitted to the Court of Appeal for further consideration to apply the proviso 'by reference to language of the *Crimes Act*'.[20]

The same point was made by the High Court nearly a decade later when it considered s 276 of the *Criminal Procedure Act 2009* (Vic), which had replaced s 568(1) of the *Crimes Act 1958* (Vic) (the provision construed in *Weiss*).[21] In construing the new provision, the Court said, the task 'does *not* begin with this Court's decision in *Weiss v The Queen*'.[22]

A prior ruling on the meaning of statutory text will only be binding to the extent that it is a decision about the same text in the same textual, contextual and factual setting [30.4]

The doctrine of binding precedent means that a court must follow the decisions of courts at a higher tier in the same hierarchy. But the court is only bound to follow the ratio decidendi of that decision.[23]

In statutory interpretation cases the authority of the court's decision is 'specific to the words of the legislative text with which that authority dealt'.[24] A decision on the meaning of statutory text will only bind a subsequent court to the extent that the court is required to determine the application of the same text in the same provision in the same statute. As explained by Lord Diplock:

> The ratio decidendi of a judgment as to the meaning of particular words or combinations of words used in a particular statutory provision can have no more than a persuasive influence upon a court which is called upon to interpret the same

17 Ibid 305 [9].

18 Ibid 313 [32]–[33]. See also 312–13 [31].

19 Ibid 318 [48].

20 Ibid 321 [58].

21 *Baini v The Queen* (2012) 246 CLR 469.

22 Ibid 477 [15] (French CJ, Hayne, Crennan, Kiefel and Bell JJ) (emphasis in original).

23 See **[1.7]**.

24 Justice Michael Kirby, 'Precedent Law, Practice and Trends in Australia' (2007) 28(3) *Australian Bar Review* 243, 251.

> word or combination of words appearing in some other statutory provision. It is not determinative of the meaning of that other provision.[25]

This is a logical consequence of the nature of the interpretative task. Context and purpose both influence the preferable choice of meaning attributable to the text. Consequently, a court cannot presume that text in a different textual setting, contextual setting or historical context, or with a different object, should be given the same meaning as identical text in a different contextual or purposive setting. This is why it has been suggested that the doctrine of binding precedent only has narrow application in statutory interpretation.[26] Particular caution should be exercised with indefinite or open-textured words that rely more heavily on context for their content.[27] **Example 30.2** illustrates the importance of context.

Example 30.2 *Metricon Qld Pty Ltd v Chief Commissioner of State Revenue (No 2)*[28]

In this case the NSW Supreme Court was required to determine the meaning of the phrase 'dominant use' in relation to land in s 10AA of the *Land Tax Management Act 1956* (NSW). One of the issues raised was the meaning to be attributed to the word 'use' and whether it only referred to a physical use of the land. White J considered the High Court decision of *Minister Administering the Crown Lands Act v NSW Aboriginal Land Council*,[29] in which the High Court held that the expression 'lawfully used' in s 36(1) of the *Aboriginal Land Rights Act 1983* (NSW) referred to a physical use of land. White J identified that 'use' was a protean word and its meaning was dependent on its statutory context.[30] So, his Honour said, the High Court decision was not to be taken as holding that the only or primary meaning of the word 'use' in relation to land is the conduct of physical activities on the land.[31] White J explained:

> The High Court's decision in *Minister Administering the Crown Lands Act v NSW Aboriginal Land Council* ... is a binding precedent on the meaning of s 36(1) of the *Aboriginal Land Rights Act 1983*. It is not a binding precedent on the construction of other legislation where the word *use* or *used* is employed.[32]

On appeal, Barrett AJA (MacFarlan and Ward JJA agreeing) did not engage with the precedential value of the High Court decision to the same extent, but recognised that 'use' was a word of

25 *Carter v Bradbeer* [1975] 1 WLR 1204, 1206.

26 Ibid; Justice Michael Kirby, 'Precedent Law, Practice and Trends in Australia' (2007) 28(3) *Australian Bar Review* 243, 252. See also Lisa Burton Crawford and Dan Meagher, 'Statutory Precedents under the "Modern Approach" to Statutory Interpretation' (2020) 42(2) *Sydney Law Review* 209 who explore the idea that the modern approach to statutory interpretation allows greater scope for departure from precedent.

27 See **[16.3](d)**.

28 (2016) 102 ATR 781.

29 (2008) 237 CLR 285.

30 *Metricon Qld Pty Ltd v Chief Commissioner of State Revenue (No 2)* (2016) 102 ATR 781, 790 [40]. See also 791 [42]–[43].

31 Ibid 791 [45].

32 Ibid 792 [47].

'variable meaning and that the construction of one statutory provision concerning "use" of land may well be an unreliable guide to the correct construction of another such provision' and so 'must be treated with caution'.[33] The Court of Appeal determined that the meaning of 'use' in s 10AA differed to some extent from White J, but dismissed the appeal.[34]

The location of the text in the statute being construed is also potentially relevant. A decision on the meaning of text in one provision in an Act will not necessarily be binding on a subsequent court considering the same words in the same Act but in another provision of that Act. This was the case in *Commissioner of Taxation (Cth) v Australian Building Systems Pty Ltd (in liq)*,[35] where the High Court was required to construe the words 'which is or will become due' in s 254(1)(d) of the *Income Tax Assessment Act 1936* (Cth). The Court considered its previous decision, *Bluebottle UK Ltd v Deputy Commission of Taxation*,[36] which had construed the same words but in the context of s 255(1)(b) of the same Act. French CJ and Kiefel J observed that a previous interpretation by the Court of a particular provision 'is a powerful indicator of the correct interpretation of a provision of the same Act which serves similar purposes and uses identical or substantially similar language' but is not determinative 'if a different construction is required by the text, context and purpose of the other provision'.[37] Consequently, careful attention must be given to the ratio decidendi of the prior decision and the specific text the subject of that decision, even if the issue appears at face value to be similar.[38]

An otherwise binding precedent on statutory meaning may also be distinguishable on its facts.[39] As Justice Gageler has explained extracurially, a court is justified and obliged to attribute meaning to statutory text 'only so far as the attribution of meaning to the text is necessary to enable that court to discern the content of the law that must be applied to determine the rights of the parties who are in dispute in the individual case'.[40] When a court determines the meaning of statutory text, it only does so in the context of the specific legislation and the concrete facts before it. It does not express a meaning of the word that purports to set the parameters of the range of meaning that could arise in all possible scenarios. Where legislation has been the subject of multiple judicial decisions, the incremental attributions of meaning eventually accumulate into a body of case law about that meaning.[41]

33 *Chief Commissioner of State Revenue v Metricon Qld Pty Ltd* (2017) 105 ATR 11, 25 [45]. However, Barrett AJA noted that this does not mean that 'use' in relation to land is completely devoid of any commonly understood meaning, citing *New South Wales Aboriginal Land Council v Minister Administering the Crown Lands Act* (2016) 260 CLR 232, 256 [34] (French CJ, Kiefel, Bell and Keane JJ): at 25 [45]–[46].

34 (2017) 105 ATR 11, 34 [80].

35 (2015) 257 CLR 544.

36 (2007) 232 CLR 598.

37 Ibid 560 [27]. See also 613 [227] (Gordon J).

38 See, eg, *Cottle v Commissioner of Police (NSW)* (2020) 298 IR 202, 216–17 [58]–[59] (Bell P, Basten JA agreeing at 220 [84], Payne JA agreeing at 220 [85]), affd *NSW Commissioner of Police v Cottle* (2022) 96 ALJR 304.

39 See, eg, *Bligh Consulting Pty Ltd v Ausgrid* [2017] NSWCA 95, [123] (Sackville AJA, McColl and Basten JJA agreeing); *John v Commissioner of Taxation (Cth)* (1989) 166 CLR 417, 435 (Mason CJ, Dawson, Wilson, Toohey, Gaudron JJ); *Ogden Industries Pty Ltd v Lucas* [1970] AC 113, 127 (Lord Upjohn).

40 Justice Stephen Gageler, 'Common Law Statutes and Judicial Legislation: Statutory Interpretation as a Common Law Process' (2011) 37(2) *Monash University Law Review* 1, 3.

41 See **[1.7]**.

Decisions on uniform and federal legislation

[30.5] **A single judge or intermediate appellate court construing a statute that forms part of a national uniform scheme or that is federal legislation should follow the interpretation given to the same wording by another appellate court, unless that prior decision is plainly wrong**

If a single judge or an appellate court construes words of legislation that is part of a national uniform scheme, then that court should follow the interpretation given to those words by another appellate court construing a comparable statute that forms part of that scheme, unless that interpretation is plainly wrong. As explained by the High Court in *Australian Securities Commission v Marlborough Gold Mines Ltd* ('*Marlborough*'):[42]

> [U]niformity of decision in the interpretation of uniform national legislation such as the [Corporations] Law is a sufficiently important consideration to require that an intermediate appellate court – and all the more so a single judge – should not depart from an interpretation placed on such legislation by another Australian intermediate appellate court unless convinced that that interpretation is plainly wrong.[43]

The High Court in *Farah Constructions Pty Ltd v Say-Dee-Pty Ltd*[44] ('*Farah*') made clear that this approach to uniform legislation should also apply to Commonwealth legislation. Intermediate appellate courts and trial judges, the Court said, 'should not depart from decisions in intermediate appellate courts in another jurisdiction on the interpretation of Commonwealth legislation or uniform national legislation unless they are convinced that the interpretation is plainly wrong'.[45]

Example 30.3 *Hill v Zuda Pty Ltd*[46]

Ms Hill was the only child of her father, who died. Prior to his death the father had been in a de facto relationship with Ms Murray. Ms Hill made a claim against her father's estate. The father and Ms Murray had been the only members of a self-managed superannuation fund. In these proceedings Ms Hill contended that the trustee of the fund, Zuda Pty Ltd, of which Ms Murray was the sole director, purported to transfer the balance of the father's member account to Ms Murray. Ms Hill argued that this was not valid due to the operation of reg 6.17A of the *Superannuation Industry (Supervision) Regulations 1994* (Cth). Ms Murray and Zuda Pty Ltd argued that the regulation provisions did not apply to a self-managed superannuation fund.

The Court of Appeal of Western Australia considered a number of authorities on the federal legislation, including the Full Court of the Supreme Court of South Australia decision of *Cantor Management Services Pty Ltd v Booth* ('*Cantor*').[47] The Court in *Cantor* had determined that these

42 (1993) 177 CLR 485.

43 Ibid 492 (the Court).

44 (2007) 230 CLR 89.

45 Ibid 151–2 [135] (the Court). See also *Hili v The Queen* (2010) 242 CLR 520, 538 [57] (French CJ, Gummow, Hayne, Crennan, Kiefel and Bell JJ). Whether this is a principle of precedent or comity is not clear: Justice Mark Leeming, 'Farah and Its Progeny: Comity among Intermediate Appellate Courts' (2015) 12 *The Judicial Review* 165, 171, 185.

46 [2021] WASCA 59.

47 (2017) 106 ATR 615.

regulations did not apply to self-managed funds. The Court of Appeal of Western Australia referred to the principle in *Farah*. Although it acknowledged there was some question as to whether the observations in *Cantor* formed part of its ratio decidendi, it determined that it did.[48]

The Court rejected Ms Hill's submission that *Cantor* was 'plainly wrong' and concluded:

> [T]he principle in *Farah Constructions* applies in this case ... In our view, the decision in *Cantor Management* should be taken as settling the question of whether reg 6.17A of the SIS Regulations applies to self managed superannuation funds until such time as it is overruled by the High Court.[49]

There are difficulties with the 'plainly wrong' *Farah/Marlborough* principle as it relates to uniform legislation [30.6]

The rationale behind the *Farah/Marlborough* principle is clear. It is to support conformity between the views of different intermediate appellate courts on the meaning of federal and uniform legislation.[50] The principles of statutory interpretation law support this approach to the extent that the legislation is identical and arising from the same source. In that instance, assumptions can be made about the relevant similarity of text, subject matter, context and purpose. They can be assumed to be statutes *in pari materia* (see **[30.8]**).

But there are difficulties with the principle, especially its application to so-called uniform legislation.

First, not all 'uniform' legislation is created equal. Generally speaking, uniform law is legislation borne of a collaborative effort across jurisdictions that has a 'harmonisation purpose'.[51] This is typically done in circumstances where it is 'considered appropriate to take a nationally consistent legislative approach to an issue or matter'.[52] Uniform schemes often, though not always, emerge from the work of national bodies such as the Council of Australian Governments (now replaced by the National Federation Reform Council) or bodies consisting of Attorneys-General.[53] They are usually underpinned by an intergovernmental agreement, formal or informal.[54]

There are numerous legislative structures that can be adopted for uniform legislation.[55] Depending on the structure, not all such collaborative arrangements involve identical legislative

48 *Hill v Zuda Pty Ltd* [2021] WASCA 59, [41], noting that if it was not, it was 'seriously considered dicta to which considerable weight must be given'.

49 Ibid [49]. Special leave to appeal this decision had been granted by the High Court of Australia: [2021] HCAB 9 (12 November 2021) 32.

50 *Hill v Zuda Pty Ltd* [2021] WASCA 59, [40].

51 Legislative Council Standing Committee on Uniform Legislation and Statutes Review, Parliament of Western Australia, *Information Report: Scrutiny of Uniform Legislation* (Report No 63, June 2011) 12.

52 Ibid 4.

53 Legislative Council Standing Committee on Uniform Legislation and General Purposes, Parliament of Western Australia, *The Work of the Committee during the Second Session of the Thirty-Sixth Parliament – August 13 2002 to November 16 2004* (Report 23, November 2004) 1. See also **[11.5]**.

54 Legislative Council Standing Committee on Uniform Legislation and Statutes Review, Parliament of Western Australia, *Information Report: Scrutiny of Uniform Legislation* (Report No 63, June 2011) 9–10.

55 Ibid app 2, 41 identifies nine different structures. See also **[10.8]**.

elements.[56] Further, for numerous other reasons there may be differences between the versions of laws introduced in different jurisdictions, or that occur over time.[57] These features of the making and enactment of uniform law are a practical reality not reflected in the principle.

Next, it is unclear whether the *Farah/Marlborough* 'plainly wrong' principle applies to uniform legislation that is not 'national', in that less than all Australian jurisdictions have adopted it. An example is the uniform evidence legislation, initially enacted by the Commonwealth, and mirrored in several Australian jurisdictions but not in Queensland, South Australia and Western Australia. There seems no obvious reason of principle as to why the *Farah/Marlborough* principle should not be adopted for judicial decisions on legislation that forms part of a 'national' scheme, even if not all jurisdictions participate. For the statutes that comprise the scheme, assumptions about similarity, background and purpose are possible.[58]

Finally, it is unclear whether the principle should be applied in the instance where a court is construing legislation that is identical, or substantially similar, to legislation construed by another appellate court but the two pieces of legislation are not part of a formal, deliberative uniform scheme. This may occur, for example, when the policy and measures of legislation passed in one state are used by another state as a model for its own legislation. The legislation may be 'uniform' in the sense of being similar, but it is not uniform in the sense of being part of a deliberate and cooperative scheme that seeks a consistent legislative policy across those jurisdictions.

There appears to be some uncertainty in state authorities as to whether the *Farah/Marlborough* principle applies in this context.[59] However, there are two reasons to prefer the view that the principle does not apply here. The first is that, without the unifying and conforming structure of a national scheme, it is speculative for an interpreter to assume without appropriate analysis that the policy, intrinsic context and wider contextual background are sufficiently similar to warrant the same meaning. Second, since *Marlborough* and *Farah*, the High Court has cautioned against the unanalysed application of judicial decisions of the appellate courts of other jurisdictions in respect of similar or identical legislation, outside of the framework of a national scheme. See **[30.8]**. This would seem to reject the 'plainly wrong' approach in this context.

[30.7] The existence of a reasonably available meaning for statutory text as an alternative to the meaning given to that statutory text in a prior decision is not sufficient for that prior decision to be regarded as 'plainly wrong'

A number of precedential practices (including the *Farah/Marlborough* principle discussed in **[30.5]**) are expressed in terms of an appellate court following a prior decision unless it is persuaded that the decision is 'plainly wrong'.

56 Legislative Council Standing Committee on Uniform Legislation and Statutes Review, Parliament of Western Australia, *Information Report: Scrutiny of Uniform Legislation* (Report No 63, June 2011) 12–13.

57 Parliamentary Council's Committee, *Protocol on Drafting National Uniform Legislation* (Australasian Parliamentary Council's Committee, 2018) 19–23; Queensland Parliamentary Library, *National Scheme Legislation* (Research Brief 2011/No 27) 7.

58 There is a suggestion of a broader approach in *R v Falzon* (2018) 264 CLR 361, 380–1 [49] (the Court).

59 See, eg, *Tillman v A-G (NSW)* (2007) 70 NSWLR 448, 464–6 [106]–[110] (Giles JA and Ipp JA); cf 452 [25], 454 [46] (Mason P dissenting); *DPP v Spong* (2018) 13 ACTLR 292, 305 [79] (the Court); *AMT Planning Consultants Pty Ltd v Central Coast Council* (2018) 238 LGERA 116, 125 [31] (Basten JA); *RJE v Secretary to the Department of Justice* (2008) 21 VR 526, 541 [50]–[52] (Maxwell P and Weinberg JA); *R v XY* (2013) 84 NSWLR 363, 373 [33] (Basten JA).

In statutory interpretation the notion of what is 'plainly wrong' will be informed by the 'fundamental (and constitutional) responsibility' of the Court to attribute meaning to the statute to effect the legislative intent and 'not to allow the perpetuation of previous error in statutory construction'[60] that is inconsistent with that intent. There is considerable authority on the content of the phrase 'plainly wrong'.[61] For present purposes it is sufficient to note that the existence of a 'constructional choice' when analysing alternative statutory meanings will not be sufficient.[62] This phrase acknowledges the well-accepted notion that statutory language can be open to more than one reasonable interpretation.[63] The fact that there is an alternative construction that is reasonably open is not enough of itself to establish that a prior decision is 'plainly wrong'. In *Hill v Zuda Pty Ltd*[64] (**Example 30.3**), the Court acknowledged that the alternative construction proposed by Ms Hill was 'reasonably arguable'[65] But, the Court said:

> [T]he principle in *Farah Constructions* applies ... If this court were to adopt a contrary position merely because it prefers one of two reasonably available constructional choices, it would result in confusion for other courts.[66]

As the construction supported by *Cantor* was 'reasonably open',[67] the argument was rejected.

Determining whether a prior statutory interpretation decision is 'plainly wrong' will involve a consideration of the interpretative process engaged in by the prior court and its appropriate application of principles of statutory interpretation. An example is the decision of *Australian Investment and Development Pty Ltd v Commissioner of State Revenue*.[68] The Victorian Court of Appeal was asked to conclude that the meaning that had been attributed to the words 'greater Melbourne' in s 64 of the *Land Tax Act 2005* (Vic) in its earlier decision, *Commissioner of State Revenue v EHL Burgess Properties Pty Ltd*,[69] was wrong. The Court noted that it was a 'high barrier' to persuade it to depart from its own previous decision.[70] It concluded: '[T]he *Burgess* Court ... adopted an orthodox approach to construction based on ascertaining legislative intention from the words used in the definition, having regard to statutory context and purpose.'[71] The construction was open, and not plainly wrong.[72]

60 *McNamara v Consumer Trader and Tenancy Tribunal* (2005) 221 CLR 646, 661 [42] (McHugh, Gummow and Heydon JJ).

61 See *Minister for Immigration, Citizenship, Migrant Services and Multicultural Affairs v FAK19* [2021] FCAFC 153, [2]–[32] (Allsop CJ, Kerr and Mortimer JJ agreeing on this matter at [104]) for a review of decisions.

62 For the formulation of alternative constructions see **[9.8]**.

63 Lisa Burton Crawford and Dan Meagher, 'Statutory Precedents under the "Modern Approach" to Statutory Interpretation' (2020) 42(2) *Sydney Law Review* 209, 231.

64 [2021] WASCA 59.

65 Ibid [50].

66 Ibid [49].

67 Ibid [44].

68 [2019] VSCA 69.

69 (2015) 209 LGERA 314. The case is presented as **Example 23.1 [23.4]**.

70 [2019] VSCA 69, [59] (the Court).

71 Ibid [60] (the Court).

72 Ibid [80] (the Court).

Decisions on statutes *in pari materia*

[30.8] A prior decision, though not subject to a precedential principle, may have persuasive value if the statute being construed and the statute construed in the prior decision are statutes *in pari materia*

Even if a court is not required to follow any prior decision, the court will not arrive at a judgment 'as though the pages of the law reports were blank'.[73] Prior decisions on legislative meaning may have persuasive value. But the reasoning of a prior decision should not be regarded as being persuasive *only* because the decision attributes meaning to identical or similar text in another statute. The High Court in *Walker Corporation Pty Ltd v Sydney Harbour Foreshore Authority*[74] made this point. The Court cited comments made by McHugh J in *Marshall v Director-General, Department of Transport*,[75] in the context of his Honour considering decisions on legislation similar to the Queensland Act he was construing. McHugh J cautioned that similarity of legislation construed in a prior decision

> does not mean that the courts of Queensland, when construing the legislation of that State, should slavishly follow judicial decisions of the courts of another jurisdiction in respect of similar or even identical legislation . . . Judicial decisions on similar or identical legislation in other jurisdictions are guides to, but cannot control, the meaning of legislation in the court's jurisdiction.[76]

This caution is equally applicable to consideration of court decisions on the meaning of similar or identical text in another statute of the same jurisdiction. It also applies to decisions on legislative antecedents.[77] The persuasive value of those decisions must be determined on a case-by-case basis given 'the obligation of anyone construing legislation is that of ascertaining the meaning of the phrase in question in the context under scrutiny'.[78]

A prior decision on identical or similar text in another statute will be persuasive if a logical and relevant connection to that other statute can be established. This might be established if the statutes are *in pari materia*.[79] A 'close analysis of the critical steps in the construction of the section'[80] in the prior decision is needed.

The case of *Beadle v La Bianca*[81] is illustrative. In the Supreme Court of Western Australia Justice Pritchard was required to determine the meaning of 'place of resort' in s 119(7) of the *Liquor Control Act 1988* (WA) ('the LC Act'), which prohibited an owner of unlicensed premises from allowing those premises to be used as a 'place of resort' for the consumption of liquor. After

73 *McNamara v Consumer Trader and Tenancy Tribunal* (2005) 221 CLR 646, 661 [42] (McHugh, Gummow and Heydon JJ), citing *Queensland v Commonwealth* (1977) 139 CLR 585, 599 (Gibbs J).

74 (2008) 233 CLR 259.

75 (2001) 205 CLR 603.

76 *Walker Corporation Pty Ltd v Sydney Harbour Foreshore Authority* (2008) 233 CLR 259, 270 [31], citing *Marshall v Director-General, Department of Transport* (2001) 205 CLR 603, 632–3 [62], since cited in numerous cases.

77 *Adams v Director Fair Works Inspectorate* (2017) 258 FCR 257, 278 [55] (the Court). See chapter 21.

78 *Telstra Corporation Ltd v Australasian Performing Right Association Ltd* ('Music on hold case') (1997) 191 CLR 140, 200 (Kirby J).

79 See **[29.3]**.

80 *Commissioner of Taxation (Cth) v Australian Building Systems Pty Ltd (in liq)* (2015) 257 CLR 544, 613 [227] (Gordon J) referring to whether a decision on the construction of a phrase in one section can be applied in the construction of that phrase in another section, but the observation is equally apt for similar statutes.

81 [2012] WASC 415. More details are provided in **Example 7.2** (**[7.7]**).

analysing the intrinsic and contextual indicators of the LC Act, her Honour considered the meaning given by judicial decisions to the phrase 'place of resort' in other statutes. One was the Western Australian Supreme Court decision of *Gypsy Jokers Motorcycle Club Inc v Commissioner of Police (No 2)*,[82] which had considered the same phrase in s 72(2) of the *Corruption and Crime Commission Act 2003* (WA). Pritchard J observed that, given the different textual setting of the phrase, the decision was of 'no assistance' other than to confirm some possibilities of meaning.[83] Next, her Honour considered the Tasmanian decision of *Switzerland Insurance Australia Ltd v Mowie Fisheries Pty Ltd* [84]on the meaning of 'place of resort' in the *Marine Act 1976* (Tas). The 'very different legislative context' of that statute meant that that decision was also of no assistance.[85] Of 'more assistance' was the New Zealand decision *Police v Davis*[86] on the meaning of 'place of resort' in s 264 of the *Sale of Liquor Act 1962* (NZ).[87] While acknowledging the decision was not binding, Justice Pritchard observed:

> [T]he construction given to the words 'place of resort' in an almost identical statutory provision in the context of legislation which appears to have had a very similar legislative object to the LC Act is a useful confirmation of the construction which can similarly be discerned from the ordinary meaning of those words, and the context in which they are used, in s 119(7) of the LC Act.[88]

Commonality with the comparable statute's wider context, such as its legislative history, may also assist in drawing an analogy between the two statutes. For example, if the statute being construed has been modelled on a statute of another jurisdiction with little material change, the persuasive value of the prior judicial decision is likely to be strengthened. This was the case in *Maxcon Constructions Pty Ltd v Vadasz*,[89] where the High Court was required to construe the words 'pay when paid provisions' under s 12 of the *Building and Construction Industry Security of Payment Act 2009* (SA). The Court noted that the Act had been modelled on the *Building and Construction Industry Security of Payment Act 1999* (NSW), with no material difference between the relevant provisions of the two Acts.[90] As such, each of the judges accepted that the reasoning in their prior decision on the equivalent provision in the NSW Act was applicable for the South Australian Act.[91]

Apart from their persuasive value, prior decisions can also show the boundaries of the possibilities of meaning of the text being construed.[92] See the example of *Beadle v La Bianca* discussed above.

---

82 [2008] WASC 166.

83 [2012] WASC 415 [49].

84 (1997) 74 FCR 205.

85 [2012] WASC 415 [50].

86 [1981] 1 DCRNZ 249.

87 [2012] WASC 415 [51].

88 Ibid [52].

89 (2018) 264 CLR 46.

90 Ibid 51 [1] (Kiefel CJ, Bell, Keane, Nettle and Gordon JJ), 58–9 [34] (Gageler J), 60 [41] (Edelman J).

91 Ibid, referring to *Probuild Constructions (Aust) Pty Ltd v Shade Systems Pty Ltd* (2018) 264 CLR 1.

92 Justice Stephen Gageler, 'Common Law Statutes and Judicial Legislation: Statutory Interpretation as a Common Law Process' (2011) 37(2) *Monash University Law Review* 1, 7.

[30.9] **Foreign judicial decisions on the interpretation of legislation may have persuasive value**

Case law from non-Australian jurisdictions is not binding on Australian courts. Since 1986 this had included decisions of superior courts in the United Kingdom.[93] Foreign judgments may be useful for comparative purposes or for 'the degree of the persuasiveness of their reasoning'.[94] As French CJ has explained:

> The use of comparative materials in judicial decision-making in Australia is not novel. Courts may, without express statutory authority, refer to the judgments of international and foreign domestic courts which have logical or analogical relevance to the interpretation of a statutory provision. If such a judgment concerns a term identical to or substantially the same as that in the statutory provision being interpreted, then its potential logical or analogical relevance is apparent.[95]

Foreign decisions on similar legislation appear to be viewed similarly to Australian decisions on statutes *in pari materia*, but without the additional strengthening factor of judicial comity. Just as with decisions on domestic statutes, the persuasive value of a foreign decision may increase if the decision is on legislation that was used as a model or idea for the domestic legislation being construed.[96]

The influence of international law on Australian law, and the progressively broader and easier access to the international law itself, means that references to foreign judgments are not unusual.[97] Use of foreign judgments on similar legislation as interpretative aids is additional to references to international law as part of the wider context, and to presumptions about international law.[98]

Doctrine of analogy

[30.10] **The courts have recognised the converse of precedent: the potential for the analogical development of the common law by reference to statute**

The increasing recognition of the importance of statutes in contemporary Australian law has seen a shift in the judicial frame of reference 'from an assumption that primacy should be given to judicial statements of principle to a focus on the statutory text'.[99] This has in turn led to growing recognition of the interface between statutes and common law.

One consequence of this broader acceptance is the express recognition of what might be characterised as the converse of precedent. This is the principle that the common law may develop by analogical reference to statutes. Although a notion that has existed for some time,[100] it found express recognition in the 1999 case of *Esso Australia Resources Ltd v Federal Commissioner of*

---

93 All appeals from Australian courts to the Privy Council of the United Kingdom were finally abolished by the 1986 *Australia Acts*. See also *Bell Lawyers Pty Ltd v Pentelow* (2019) 269 CLR 333, 355 [61] (Gageler J).

94 *Perilya Broken Hill Ltd v Valuer-General* (2015) 10 ARLR 235, 248 [74] (Leeming JA), citing *Cook v Cook* (1986) 162 CLR 376, 390 (Mason, Wilson, Deane and Dawson JJ).

95 *Momcilovic v The Queen* (2011) 245 CLR 1, 36–7 [18] (citations omitted).

96 See, eg, *Vella v Commissioner of Police (NSW)* (2019) 269 CLR 219, discussed in **[21.8]**.

97 See, eg, **[26.2]** and **[31.8]** regarding international law and the Human Rights Acts.

98 See chapters 23, 31.

99 Justice John Basten, 'Statute and the Common Law' (2019) 93(12) *Australian Law Journal* 985, 985.

100 Andrew Burrows, 'The Relationship between the Common Law and Statutes in the Law of Obligations' (2012) 128 *Law Quarterly Review* 232, 250–1 refers to numerous pre-20th-century examples.

Taxation[101] where it was labelled the 'doctrine of analogy'.[102] Under this doctrine the courts may use statutes as a tool of analysis when considering the development of a common law principle.

The doctrine requires a 'consistent pattern of legislative policy' or a discernible 'steady trend in legislation' in a particular area of law to which the common law can adapt itself.[103] For example, the underlying policy of legislative developments in tort law that the Crown have responsibility for harm done by its officials, especially police officers, was regarded as 'appropriate to be factored into the contemporary expression of the common law of Australia'.[104] This doctrine appears to be well accepted[105] even if infrequently applied.

The analogical development of the common law by reference to legislation is quite different from statutory construction.[106] The operation of the doctrine gives rise to numerous questions of principle and operation and remains a 'work in progress'.[107]

---

101 (1999) 201 CLR 49.

102 Ibid 63 [28] (Gleeson CJ, Gaudron and Gummow JJ).

103 Ibid 62 [23]–[24], in part citing *Warnink v J Townend & Sons (Hull) Ltd* [1979] AC 731, 743.

104 *Binsaris v Northern Territory* (2020) 270 CLR 549, 567–8 [44] (Gageler J).

105 Ibid; *Gifford v Strang Patrick Stevedoring Pty Ltd* (2003) 214 CLR 269, 303 [94] (Hayne J); *Tame v New South Wales* (2002) 211 CLR 317, 394 [224] (Gummow and Kirby JJ). Cf *Baker v The Queen* (2012) 245 CLR 632, 667–8 [113]–[119] (Heydon J).

106 Justice Michelle Gordon, 'Analogical Reasoning by Reference to Statute: What Is the Judicial Function?' (2019) 42(1) *University of New South Wales Law Journal* 4, 8; Sir Anthony Mason, 'The Interaction of Statute Law and Common Law' (2016) 90(5) *Australian Law Journal* 324, 338.

107 Justice Michelle Gordon, 'Analogical Reasoning by Reference to Statute: What Is the Judicial Function?' (2019) 42(1) *University of New South Wales Law Journal* 4, 25.

31 INTERNATIONAL TREATIES AND MATERIALS

Overview

[31.1] Australia's international obligations are not enforceable through legal action by a person in Australia unless those obligations are incorporated into domestic legislation. If a statute does incorporate all or part of an international agreement, then, subject to a contrary intention in the statute, it is a principle of interpretation that the words in the statute are presumed to bear the same meaning as they do in the international agreement. However, even where a statute does not incorporate text from an international agreement, Australia's international obligations may still influence the interpretation of domestic legislation. A long-established common law principle provides that, in cases of ambiguity, a construction of a statute that is consistent with Australia's international obligations should be preferred to a construction that is not. This refers to Australia's obligations at the time of enactment of the domestic legislation. The principle does not operate to restrict the exercise of a provision granting discretionary power to the executive. In addition to these principles, recourse to relevant international material as an interpretative aid is permitted under the provisions of all Australian Interpretation Acts. International material may also be considered under the common law principle of context. The statutory provisions and the principle of context allow recourse to international materials beyond only international agreements. It remains unclear how the two principles of context and consistency with established international law operate together.

International obligations incorporated in domestic law

[31.2] **Australia's international obligations do not form part of Australian domestic law unless they are validly incorporated into that law**

Australian common law has adopted what is called a 'dualist' approach to the interaction between domestic legislation and international law. Dualism maintains that the sources and content of international law and domestic law differ, and so international law can never become part of the latter unless made by the legislative power of the state.[1] This has a number of consequences for legislative interpretation.

First, the legislative power of Australian parliaments, Commonwealth and state, is not constrained by Australia's obligations under international instruments.[2] Second, Australian

1 *Tajjour v New South Wales* (2014) 254 CLR 508, 554 [48] (French CJ citing numerous authorities.) See also Robert French, 'Oil and Water? International and Domestic Law in Australia' (Brennan Lecture, Bond University, 26 June 2009) 13–16.

2 *Plaintiff S195/2016 v Minister for Immigration and Border Protection* (2017) 261 CLR 622, 634 [20] (Kiefel CJ, Bell, Gageler, Keane, Nettle, Gordon and Edelman JJ); *Horta v Commonwealth* (1994) 181 CLR 183, 195 (Mason CJ, Brennan, Deane, Dawson, Toohey, Gaudron, McHugh JJ); *Polites v Commonwealth* (1945) 70 CLR 60, 69 (Latham CJ), 78 (Dixon J).

courts must apply validly enacted domestic law, even if that law is inconsistent with international law.[3] Third, executive approval of a treaty or other agreement is not sufficient to alter domestic law. Provisions of international treaties, conventions and customary international law do not form part of Australian law unless they are given the force of law by enactment of a domestic legislature.[4] An example of such an enactment is s 5(1) of the *International Tax Agreements Act 1953* (Cth), which provides:

> Subject to this Act, on and after the date of entry into force of a provision of an agreement mentioned below [which contains a table of international agreements, conventions and protocols on income taxes and fringe benefits], the provision has the force of law according to its tenor.

Where the text of an international instrument has been enacted in Australian law it is presumed that, subject to a contrary intention, the meaning of the transposed text has the same meaning as given in the international instrument [31.3]

A domestic statute may incorporate an international instrument in whole or in part or by provision or word. An example of a provision of an instrument being incorporated was provided in **[31.2]**. In all cases where the statute transposes the text of a treaty into the statute 'the prima facie legislative intention is that the transposed text should bear the same meaning in the domestic statute as it bears in the treaty'.[5]

If it is determined that the transposed text should have the same meaning as in the international instrument, then the international rules of interpretation must be used to attribute meaning to the transposed text. Generally, the principles that govern the interpretation of international agreements are found in the *Vienna Convention on the Law of Treaties* ('the *Vienna Convention*').[6] In this instance the 'rules generally applicable to the interpretation of domestic statutes give way' to the interpretative rules governing that international instrument.[7]

Example 31.1 *Comptroller-General of Customs v Pharm-A-Care Laboratories Pty Ltd*[8]

Pharm-A-Care Laboratories Pty Ltd ('Pharm-A-Care') imported vitamin preparations and garcinia (hydroxycitric acid) into Australia in the form of pastilles. The amount of customs duties to be

3 *Kartinyeri v Commonwealth* (1998) 195 CLR 337, 384 [97] (Gummow and Hayne JJ); *Koowarta v Bjelke-Petersen* (1982) 153 CLR 168, 204 (Gibbs CJ).

4 *CPCF v Minister for Immigration and Border Protection* (2015) 255 CLR 514, 644 [462] (Keane J citing numerous authorities); *Tajjour v New South Wales* (2014) 254 CLR 508, 567 [96] (Hayne J), 576 [136] (Gageler J), 606 [249] (Keane J). See also *Povey v Qantas Airways Ltd* (2005) 223 CLR 189, 199 [12] (Gleeson CJ, Gummow, Hayne and Heydon JJ), 210–11 [59] (McHugh J).

5 *Comptroller-General of Customs v Pharm-A-Care Laboratories Pty Ltd* (2020) 94 ALJR 182, 190–1 [35] (the Court), citing the principle as identified in *Applicant A v Minister for Immigration and Ethnic Affairs* (1997) 190 CLR 225, 230–1 (Brennan CJ). See also *Addy v Federal Commissioner of Taxation* (2021) 95 ALJR 911, 914 [6] (the Court), citing various further authorities.

6 Opened for signature on 23 May 1969, 1155 UNTS 331 (entered into force 27 January 1980) ('*Vienna Convention*'). See *Addy v Federal Commissioner of Taxation* (2021) 95 ALJR 911 917–8 [23] n 37 (the Court); *Povey v Qantas Airways Ltd* (2005) 223 CLR 189, 202 [24] (Gleeson CJ, Gummow, Hayne and Heydon JJ).

7 *Applicant A v Minister for Immigration and Ethnic Affairs* (1997) 190 CLR 225, 231 (Brennan CJ).

8 (2020) 94 ALJR 182.

imposed on goods imported into Australia was determined by a detailed sch 3 to the *Customs Tariff Act 1995* (Cth) ('the Tariff Act'). The Tariff Act implemented the *International Convention on the Harmonized Commodity Description and Coding System* (1983) ('the Convention'). One of the issues before the High Court was how the pastilles should be classified under sch 3.

Schedule 3 adopted the same structure and English text as the Convention, which was authenticated in both the French and English languages. In this respect the meaning of Note 1(a) to ch 30 of the schedule was a central issue. The English version stated:

> This Chapter does not cover:
>
> (a) Foods or beverages (such as dietetic, diabetic or fortified foods, food supplements, tonic beverages and mineral waters), other than . . .

The French version, in contrast, did not contain a French equivalent to the opening words 'Food or beverages (such as . . .)'. The Comptroller submitted that, among other things, both the Tribunal and then the Court of Appeal had wrongly construed the words 'such as' in the Note as referring to examples of the wider genus of 'foods or beverages'.

The High Court agreed. It stated that the '[t]ransposition of the English text' of the Convention 'into the text of Sch 3 . . . attracts the principle of statutory construction' that the legislature intended to give the same meaning to the text as should be attributed to it under the Convention.[9] This required consideration of the interpretative principles in the *Vienna Convention*. Under those principles the French text and the English text were equally authoritative, and each term is presumed to have the same meaning in each language version. On that basis the Court determined that the words 'such as' in the English version must be read as meaning 'of the following kinds' so that the Note provided that ch 30 did not cover the particular goods listed in the parentheses, rather than 'foods or beverages' generally.[10] This construction ensured that the meaning of the English text corresponded with that of the French text.[11]

If the legislature has, when implementing a convention, used exactly the same words or phrases as the convention, then it is a logical inference that the legislature 'approved' the meaning given to those words at international law. There is also a practical reason. As judicially explained:

> If the terms of an instrument enacted into Australian law were interpreted strictly in accordance with domestic principles of statutory interpretation, there would be a risk that the treaty would be interpreted differently even though other countries had adopted the same instrument.[12]

The above principle of using international rules of interpretation for transposed text extends to recourse to extraneous materials permitted by those rules. In *Comptroller-General of Customs*, for example, the Court referred to Explanatory Notes. The Court explained that, as the Explanatory Notes were prepared and approved under the *Vienna Convention* as a guide to the interpretation

9 Ibid 190–1 [35] (the Court) citing *Applicant A v Minister for Immigration and Ethnic Affairs* (1997) 190 CLR 225, 230–1 (Brennan J).

10 Ibid 191 [37].

11 Ibid.

12 *Bywater Investments Ltd v Commissioner of Taxation (Cth)* (2016) 260 CLR 169, 224–5 [148] (Gordon J), citing *Povey v Qantas Airways Ltd* (2005) 223 CLR 189, 202 [25] (Gleeson CJ, Gummow, Hayne and Crennan JJ), 230 [128] (Kirby J).

of the coding system, they were 'available to be used in the interpretation of so much of the Tariff Act as transposes the text of the ... Convention'.[13]

Similarly, where recourse to *travaux préparatoires* (the 'preparatory work of the treaty and the circumstances of its conclusion'[14]) is permitted under the *Vienna Convention* to interpret the treaty, then the domestic courts similarly have recourse.[15] Reference to customary international law as an extrinsic aid may also be permitted.[16] This might include customary international law that has developed *subsequent* to the enactment of the domestic legislation.[17] The extent to which courts may refer to other extrinsic material that comes into existence *after* the enactment of the domestic legislation, even where permitted by international law, remains open.[18]

International obligations correspond to domestic law

Where the words of an international agreement are not expressly incorporated but they correspond with the text of a statute, the circumstances surrounding the enactment of the statute may indicate a legislative intent for those words to have the same meaning as in the agreement [31.4]

A statute may not expressly refer to, or incorporate, an international agreement, but the words of the statute may correspond to the words of the agreement. In this instance, if Parliament intends to implement a treaty and the statute uses text that exists in the instrument, this may indicate that Parliament intends for those words to have the same meaning as they do in international law.[19] Textual indicia, together with contextual and purposive indicia, including the circumstances surrounding the enactment of the statute, may determine this to be Parliament's intent. For example, in *SZTAL v Minister for Immigration and Border Protection*[20] the High Court was required to determine the meaning of 'intention' in the complementary protection regime provisions of the *Migration Act 1958* (Cth), introduced by an amending Act in 2012. The new provisions referred to an international convention. The associated parliamentary materials to the Bill for that amending Act made it clear that the new provisions were intended to give effect to that convention. The majority accepted that 'where particular words are consciously imported from an international instrument into municipal law then it will generally be the case that the words in municipal law are used in the same way as an established international law meaning of those words'.[21]

---

13 *Comptroller-General of Customs v Pharm-A-Care Laboratories Pty Ltd* (2020) 94 ALJR 182, 194–5 [58].

14 *Vienna Convention* art 32.

15 See, eg, *Macoun v Commissioner of Taxation (Cth)* (2015) 257 CLR 519, 539–40 [69]–[72], 541–2 [78] (French CJ, Bell, Gageler, Nettle and Gordon JJ).

16 Customary international law comprises the international legal rules that 'have developed from the practice of states': *Encyclopaedic Australian Legal Dictionary* (online at 5 December 2021) 'customary international law'.

17 *Vienna Convention* art 31(3). See, eg, *Macoun v Commissioner of Taxation (Cth)* (2015) 257 CLR 519, 540 [71], 542–3 [80]–[82] (French CJ, Bell, Gageler, Nettle and Gordon JJ). See Patrick Wall, 'A Marked Improvement: The High Court of Australia's Approach to Treaty Interpretation in *Macoun v Commissioner of Taxation* [2015] HCA 44' (2016) 17(1) *Melbourne Journal of International Law* 170, 13–15.

18 Justin Gleeson, 'The Increasing Internationalisation of Australian Law' (2017) 28(1) *Public Law Review* 25, 30.

19 *Koowarta v Bjelke-Petersen* (1982) 153 CLR 168, 265 (Brennan J).

20 (2017) 262 CLR 362. See also **Example 7.1 [7.3]**.

21 Ibid 389 [83] (Edelman J), 369 [18] (Kiefel CJ, Nettle and Gordon JJ). Despite this acceptance, the majority concluded that there was no established international law meaning of 'intention': at 389 [84] (Edelman J), 369 [18] (Keifel CJ, Nettle and Gordon JJ).

One difficulty is drawing the line between a statute that transposes the text of an international agreement (in which case the principle in **[31.3]** applies), and a statute that purports to implement the substance of an agreement, in whole or part, and uses some of the same language.[22] In the former situation the international rules of interpretation apply to the transposed words. But in the latter the domestic rules of interpretation apply, albeit with reference to the international materials as an interpretative aid (discussed in **[31.8]**).

Primacy of the text of domestic law

[31.5] **The starting point for construction is always the text of the statute, even if the statute incorporates whole or part of an international instrument**

As seen in **[31.2]**, Australian international obligations do not form part of domestic law only because they are ratified or approved by the executive. It is for the relevant Parliament to state, by enactment, *the extent* to which those obligations are incorporated into law. Consequently, even where a domestic statute transposes the words of a treaty or convention, the proper starting point for interpretation must be the statutory text. As judicially set out:

> The *first step* is to ascertain, with precision, what the Australian law is, that is to say what and how much of an international instrument Australian law requires to be implemented, a process which will involve the ascertainment of the extent to which Australian law by constitutionally valid enactment adopts, qualifies or modifies the instrument. The *subsequent step* is the construction of so much only of the instrument, and any qualifications or modifications of it, as Australian law requires.[23]

To start with interpreting the international instrument is to invert the interpretative process.[24] This is the case whether or not the words of the instrument are expressly incorporated. **Example 31.2** illustrates this point.

Example 31.2 *FCS17 v Minister for Home Affairs*[25]

The Federal Court was required to construe s 36 of the *Migration Act 1958* (Cth). The Court noted that an earlier version of s 36 of the *Migration Act* (governing protection visas) had adopted the definition of 'refugee' from the *Convention Relating to the Status of Refugees 1951* ('the Refugee Convention'). In that case the interpretation of the definition depended on the construction that

22 See *Minister for Immigration and Multicultural and Indigenous Affairs v QAAH of 2004* (2006) 231 CLR 1, 14–15 [34] (Gummow ACJ, Callinan, Heydon and Crennan JJ); *Bywater Investments Ltd v Commissioner of Taxation (Cth)* (2016) 260 CLR 169, 224 [146] (Gordon J).

23 *NBGM v Minister for Immigration and Multicultural Affairs* (2006) 231 CLR 52, 71–2 [61] (Callinan, Heydon and Crennan J) (emphases added). See also *DQU16 v Minister for Home Affairs* (2021) 95 ALJR 352, 358–9 [19] (the Court). For a summary of the possible interactions between domestic legislation and international agreements, see *Minister for Foreign Affairs and Trade v Magno* (1992) 37 FCR 298, 303–5 (Gummow J).

24 *NBGM v Minister for Immigration and Multicultural Affairs* (2006) 231 CLR 52, 71 [61] (Callinan, Heydon and Crennan J). See also *SZTAL v Minister for Immigration and Border Protection* (2017) 262 CLR 362, 377 [44] (Gageler J, in dissent but not on principle).

25 (2020) 276 FCR 644.

the international community attributed to the word in the Refugee Convention.[26] Then the *Migration Act* was amended to incorporate a definition of 'refugee' that was no longer defined by reference to the Refugee Convention. Chief Justice Allsop noted that in either case the 'domestic Australian law upon which any ultimate question of construction depended, was the proper ultimate focus of attention' to frame the interpretative question.[27] Following the amendment, the new words demonstrated that Parliament intended to

> depart from how courts internationally . . . have . . . interpreted the reach of the words of an international convention and of Australia's obligations thereunder . . . in order to put in place a more restricted response to circumstances calling for protection [than the Refugee Convention calls for] . . . In this context, one must go to the text of the Amendment Act and the Migration Act, *against the background* of the Refugees Convention . . .[28]

Presumption of consistency

Even if legislation does not incorporate, or does not purport to implement, Australia's international obligations, those obligations may still be relevant due to the common law presumption of consistency with established international law [31.6]

Australia's international obligations have relevance to statutory interpretation even where the domestic legislation does not incorporate or purport to implement some or all of those obligations. This is because of a long-established common law presumption of interpretation dating back to the observation in the High Court decision of *Jumbunna Coal Mine NL v Victorian Coal Miners' Association*[29] in 1908 that

> every Statute is to be so interpreted and applied as far as its language admits as not to be inconsistent with . . . the established rules of international law.[30]

This canon has 'ample support' in High Court decisions.[31] The principle has been expressed narrowly by reference to consistency with Australia's treaty obligations.[32] However, there is considerable authority that extends it more generally to, as *Jumbunna* suggested, international

26 Ibid 652 [23] (White and Colvin JJ).

27 Ibid 647 [7], citing *NBGM v Minister for Immigration and Multicultural Affairs* (2006) 231 CLR 52, 58–9 [16]–[17] (Kirby J), 71–2 [61] (Callinan, Heydon and Crennan JJ).

28 Ibid 650–1 [16]–[17] (Allsop CJ) (emphasis added); see also 662 [61] 665-6 [72]–[82] (White and Colvin JJ).

29 (1908) 6 CLR 309.

30 Ibid 363 (O'Connor J). Cf *Al-Kateb v Godwin* (2004) 219 CLR 562 where McHugh J criticised the artificiality of the presumption but noted it was 'too well established to be repealed now by judicial decision': at 589–91 [63]–[65].

31 *CPCF v Minister for Immigration and Border Protection* (2015) 255 CLR 514, 526 [8] (French CJ), citing numerous authorities including *Plaintiff S157/2002 v Commonwealth* (2003) 211 CLR 476, 492 [29] (Gleeson CJ) and *Kartinyeri v Commonwealth* (1998) 195 CLR 337, 384 [97] (Gummow and Hayne JJ).

32 See, eg, *Chu Kheng Lim v Minister for Immigration, Local Government and Ethnic Affairs* (1992) 176 CLR 1, 38 (Brennan, Deane, Dawson JJ).

law and international legal obligations.[33] This includes not only treaty and convention obligations but also customary international law.[34]

Though the principle is clearly of potential relevance to Commonwealth legislation, there is authority that supports its application to state legislation.[35] This reflects the reality of contemporary global times and the influence of international law.[36] International obligations agreed by the Commonwealth executive 'bind Australia in respect to the conduct of all organs of government in Australia' including state and territory governments.[37] Consequently, international considerations are bound to influence state government policy.[38] This is evident in the area of human rights. The Human Rights Acts of Victoria, the Australian Capital Territory and Queensland require, as far as possible as is consistent with its purpose, that legislation be construed consistently with 'human rights' and contemplate reference to international law.[39]

Two conditions control the principle. First, the reference 'as far as its language admits' has been taken to mean that the legislation must be ambiguous. This was made clear in *Minister for Immigration and Ethnic Affairs v Teoh*[40] ('*Teoh*') by Mason CJ and Deane J, though they rejected 'a narrow conception of ambiguity', referring to language 'susceptible of a construction' that is in conformity with Australia's international obligations.[41] The condition has also been described as ambiguity in its 'broad sense'[42] and as language where a constructional choice is 'available' or 'open'.[43]

Given this condition, it follows that if the statutory language is clear and not open to a construction that is consistent with Australia's obligations, then there is no work for the presumption to do.[44] **Example 31.3** illustrates this limitation.

---

33 See, eg, *CPCF v Minister for Immigration and Border Protection* (2015) 255 CLR 514, 526 [8] (French CJ); *Firebird Global Master Fund II Ltd v Republic of Nauru* (2015) 258 CLR 31, 50 [44] (French CJ and Kiefel J); *Kartinyeri v Commonwealth* (1998) 195 CLR 337, 384 [97] (Gummow and Hayne JJ).

34 *Firebird Global Master Fund II Ltd v Republic of Nauru* (2015) 258 CLR 31 [134] (Gageler J); *Zhang v Zemin* (2010) 79 NSWLR 513, 535 [125] (Spigelman CJ); *Minister for Immigration and Ethnic Affairs v Teoh* (1995) 183 CLR 273, 315 (McHugh J).

35 See, eg, *Tajjour v New South Wales* (2014) 254 CLR 508, 554 [48] (French CJ); *Kartinyeri v Commonwealth* (1998) 195 CLR 337, 384 [97] (Gummow and Hayne JJ); *Yeo v A-G (Qld)* [2012] 1 Qd R 276, 298 [60]–[61] (McMurdo P, Muir and White JJA agreeing); *Royal Women's Hospital v Medical Practitioners Board of Victoria* (2006) 15 VR 22, 39 [75] (Maxwell P).

36 See, generally, Justin Gleeson, 'The Increasing Internationalisation of Australian Law' (2017) 28(1) *Public Law Review* 25.

37 Ibid 37.

38 *Yeo v A-G (Qld)* [2012] 1 Qd R 276, 298 [60] (McMurdo P, Muir and White JJA agreeing).

39 See **[26.2]**.

40 (1995) 183 CLR 273.

41 Ibid 287 (Mason CJ and Deane J).

42 *Zhang v Zemin* (2010) 79 NSWLR 513, 535 [128] (Spigelman CJ). See also *Yeo v A-G* (Qld) [2012] 1 Qd R 276 [61] (McMurdo P, Muir and White JJA agreeing).

43 *D'Arcy v Myriad Genetics Inc* (2015) 258 CLR 334, 353 [31] (French CJ, Kiefel, Bell and Keane JJ); *Minister for Immigration and Border Protection v WZAPN* (2015) 254 CLR 610, 630 [53] (French CJ, Kiefel, Bell and Keane JJ), citing *Minister for Immigration and Multicultural and Indigenous Affairs v QAAH of 2004* (2006) 231 CLR 1, 15 [34] (Gummow ACJ, Callinan, Heydon and Crennan JJ); *Macoun v Commissioner of Taxation (Cth)* (2015) 257 CLR 519, 539 [67] (French CJ, Bell, Gageler, Nettle and Gordon JJ).

44 *CPCF v Minister for Immigration and Border Protection* (2015) 255 CLR 514, 526–7 [8] (French CJ); *Re Woolley; Ex parte Applicants M276/2003* (2004) 225 CLR 1, 10 [11] (Gleeson CJ); *Minister for Immigration and Multicultural and Indigenous Affairs v B* (2004) 219 CLR 365, 422 [159] (Kirby J); *Hopkins v Minister for Immigration, Citizenship, Migrant Services and Multicultural Affairs* (2020) 275 FCR 42, 51 [32] (the Court).

Example 31.3 *Cheedy v Western Australia*[45]

The Full Court of the Federal Court considered a decision of the National Native Title Tribunal ('the Tribunal') that had determined that the State of Western Australia could grant mining leases for land in the Pilbara, Western Australia, to FMG Pilbara Pty Ltd under the *Native Title Act 1993* (Cth) ('the Act'). The appellants, the registered native title claimants of land in the Pilbara, challenged the validity of ss 38 and 39, the relevant provisions regarding the grant.

One of the appellants' arguments on appeal was that the Tribunal and primary judge had erred by not construing ss 38 and 39 of the Act consistently with the *International Covenant on Civil and Political Rights 1966* ('the ICCPR') in so far as it provides for religious freedom. The appellants argued that ss 38 and 39 prevented them from continuing their religious practices. They argued that the principle of consistency enunciated by *Teoh* was not limited to cases of ambiguity.[46] The Court rejected this argument and, following *Teoh*, stated:

> If a provision has a clear meaning then that meaning either reflects Australia's international obligations or it does not... the canon of construction only has work to do where the provision is open to more than one interpretation. ...
>
> ... there is no relevant ambiguity in ss 38 and 39 of the Act, and hence no occasion for resort to the international obligations contained in the ICCPR ...[47]

The *second* condition was also referred to in *Teoh*. It is that the principle applies

> at least in those cases in which the legislation is enacted after, or in contemplation of, entry into, or ratification of, the relevant international instrument.[48]

The rationale for this limitation is an assumption that Parliament intends to give effect to Australia's international obligations when enacting legislation.[49] For that construct to be meaningful, those obligations must exist, or be shown to be 'known' by Parliament, at the time of enactment.

An example of the impact of this temporal condition is *McGee v Gilchrist-Humphrey*.[50] The Supreme Court of South Australia was required to construe the *Royal Commissions Act 1917* (SA) ('the Act'). One of the issues was whether the relevant section of the Act abrogated the privilege against self-incrimination. The Court was referred to a provision of the *International Covenant on Civil and Political Rights* ('the ICCPR'), which provided that no one should be compelled to testify against themselves. The ICCPR was made in 1966, signed by Australia in 1972 and ratified by Australia in 1980, 'all of which events took place after the enactment of the relevant provisions of the Act'.[51] Perry J, who addressed this issue, noted that referring to the ICCPR would support the construction preferred by the Court. However,

---

45 (2011) 194 FCR 562.

46 Ibid 581–3 [98]–[101].

47 Ibid 583 [107]–[109].

48 *Minister for Immigration and Ethnic Affairs v Teoh* (1995) 183 CLR 273, 287 (Mason CJ and Deane J). See also *CPCF v Minister for Immigration and Border Protection* (2015) 255 CLR 514, 526 [8] (French CJ); *Plaintiff S157/2002 v Commonwealth* (2003) 211 CLR 476, 492 [29] (Gleeson CJ).

49 *Minister for Immigration and Ethnic Affairs v Teoh* (1995) 183 CLR 273, 287 (Mason CJ and Deane J).

50 (2005) 92 SASR 100.

51 Ibid 113 [66] (Perry J).

> [i]t must be accepted that if the underlying rationale of the principle is as was stated by Mason CJ and Deane J in *Teoh* that 'Parliament, prima facie, intends to give effect to Australia's obligations under international law', it is difficult to see how recourse to a treaty entered into after the relevant statute was passed could be justified.[52]

Consequently, his Honour concluded, it would be 'inappropriate for this Court to have regard to the terms of the ICCPR in construing the provisions of the Act'.[53]

Doubts have been expressed about this limitation. Most notably, Kirby J took a strong position in *Coleman v Power*.[54] In direct contrast to the statements of Gleeson CJ endorsing the relevance of timing,[55] Kirby J argued that statutes should be construed against a background of international law obligations that exist in a contemporary context.[56]

There is, with respect, some merit in Kirby J's position. In *Teoh* itself, Mason CJ and Deane J left open the possibility of the principle applying more broadly by using the words 'at least in those cases'.[57] Further, as discussed in chapter 19, it is well established that legislation be interpreted, as far as possible, as 'always speaking' in the present. That approach may operate so that a statutory provision is construed in the context of contemporary statutory and common law, even if that law has developed since enactment of the provision.[58] There seems to be no reason of principle why the 'always speaking' approach should not similarly permit reference to a statute's contemporary international law context. Yet the balance of authority weighs against the rejection of this temporal limitation for the presumption of consistency, rationalising that there must 'at least' be 'a basis to conclude that the law was intended to give effect to those obligations'.[59]

[31.7] The presumption of consistency with international law does not require a discretionary executive power to be exercised in conformity with international obligations, but those obligations are a permissible consideration

The particular interpretative principles that govern the interpretation of statutory powers are discussed in detail in chapter 36. The influence of Australia's international obligations deserves a brief note here. When construing the meaning of a discretionary statutory power granted to the executive, the presumption of consistency discussed in **[31.6]** directs the statute to be read, as far as the language permits, as empowering the executive officer to act in conformity with international law. But

> [t]he principle gives rise to no presumption that the statute is to be read as legislatively constraining the officer to act in conformity with international law norms as those norms might be ascertained, interpreted and then enforced by a domestic court.[60]

---

52 Ibid 115 [78].

53 Ibid 115 [79].

54 (2004) 220 CLR 1.

55 Ibid 27–8 [17]–[19].

56 Ibid 91 [240], 93–6 [243]–[249].

57 *Minister for Immigration and Ethnic Affairs v Teoh* (1995) 183 CLR 273, 287.

58 See **[19.6]**.

59 *FCS17 v Minister for Home Affairs* (2020) 276 FCR 644, 661 [59] (White and Colvin JJ).

60 *CPCF v Minister for Immigration and Border Protection* (2015) 255 CLR 514, 627 [385] (Gageler J), citing *Re Minister for Immigration and Multicultural and Indigenous Affairs; Ex parte Lam* (2003) 214 CLR 1, 33 [101] (McHugh and Gummow JJ). See also *Minister for Immigration and Border Protection v WZARH* (2015) 256 CLR 326, 335 [30] (Kiefel, Bell and Keane JJ); *Applicant S270/2019 v Minister for Immigration and Border Protection* (2020) 94 ALJR 897, 902 [33]–[35] (Nettle, Gordon and Edelman JJ). The suggestion that a discretionary

In other words, unless a statute otherwise provides, Australia's international obligations are not mandatory criteria for a decision-maker to consider when exercising a discretionary statutory power. They are only permissible considerations.

International materials as extrinsic aids

The common law and statutory law about recourse to extrinsic materials also apply to international materials [31.8]

As discussed in chapter 24, there are statutory and common law principles about recourse to parliamentary and other historical materials. That law is relevant to international materials.

By way of brief summary, the provisions of the Interpretation Acts of all Australian jurisdictions permit access to extrinsic materials if they assist in the interpretative process.[61] Some of the Acts require a certain threshold to be met before permitting recourse to the material.[62] But none of the Acts' provisions restrict the categories of material that may be considered if those thresholds are met.[63] All of the Acts concerned, except Victoria's, provide examples of extrinsic materials that include a 'treaty or other international agreement' that is 'referred to' or 'mentioned' in the Act being construed,[64] or, in the case of the Australian Capital Territory, use the broader phrase 'any relevant treaty or other international agreement to which Australia is a party'.[65] Some decisions focus on the treaty examples in the Interpretation Acts.[66] However, the statutory language of the various Acts is wide enough to encompass not only international agreements referred to in the Act being construed but also any other international agreement or material that may assist the interpretation of the relevant provision.[67] In addition, the Human Rights Acts of Queensland, Victoria and the Australian Capital Territory permit recourse to 'international law' relevant to human rights when construing statutory provisions affecting those rights.[68]

The common law permits access to extrinsic materials through the *CIC Insurance* principle of context. That principle directs the interpreter to consider the context in which the statute is enacted from the start of the interpretation task, with no requirement of ambiguity, and 'uses "context" in its widest sense'.[69] That 'widest sense' includes the historical and contextual

---

executive power be exercised in accordance with international law was made in *Minister for Immigration and Ethnic Affairs v Teoh* (1995) 183 CLR 273, 291 (Mason CJ and Deane J). *Teoh* remains good law for the presumption of consistency (**[31.6]**).

61 See **[24.2]**.

62 See **[24.7]**.

63 See **[24.5]**.

64 *Acts Interpretation Act 1901* (Cth) s 15AB(2)(d); *Interpretation Act 1987* (NSW) s 34(2)(d); *Acts Interpretation Act 1954* (Qld) s 14B(3)(d); *Legislation Interpretation Act 2021* (SA) s 16(2)(d); *Acts Interpretation Act 1931* (Tas) s 8B(3)(d); *Interpretation Act 1984* (WA) s 19(2)(d); *Interpretation Act 1978* (NT) s 62B(2)(d).

65 *Legislation Act 2001* (ACT) s 142(1) item 7.

66 See, eg, *Minister for Immigration and Multicultural and Indigenous Affairs v QAAH of 2004* (2006) 231 CLR 1, 14–15 [34] (Gummow ACJ, Callinan, Heydon and Crennan JJ).

67 See **[24.5]**.

68 *Human Rights Act 2019* (Qld) s 48(3); *Charter of Human Rights and Responsibilities Act 2006* (Vic) s 32(2); *Human Rights Act 2004* (ACT) s 31(1).

69 *CIC Insurance Ltd v Bankstown Football Club Ltd* (1997) 187 CLR 384, 408 (Brennan CJ, Dawson, Toohey and Gummow JJ). See chapter 7.

background of a statute, as well as its legislative history.[70] This principle permits consideration of 'the fabric of international law'[71] against which a statute is passed. This not only includes international agreements but also international background to the statute.[72]

The Interpretation Act provisions on extrinsic materials and the *CIC Insurance* principle of context are relatively modern.[73] The common law principles described in **[31.3]**–**[31.6]** emerged before the 'modern' approach. It is therefore unsurprising that, prior to those modern developments, those older principles were relied on as a sort of de facto authority for recourse to relevant international materials. It would have been difficult, for example, for courts to attribute a meaning consistent with Australia's international obligations if they could not consider the documents reflecting those obligations.

The now parallel existence of the older and modern authorities gives rise to a question as to how they operate together, particularly with respect to the presumption of consistency (**[31.6]**). It is difficult to identify what work the 'ambiguity' threshold in that principle has to do when considered within the framework of modern principles that require consideration of wider context, and purpose, regardless of ambiguity.[74] That state of affairs leaves the interpreter in the slightly odd position of being required to consider international materials that form part of a statute's context to inform their interpretation, but not being permitted to engage the presumption of consistency if there is no ambiguity. Reconciliation of these principles in the context of Australia's international agreements awaits clarification by the High Court.

[31.9] As with all extrinsic material, international materials must be relevant to have probative value for the interpretative task

Chapter 24 explains that there are two primary issues regarding the use of extrinsic materials. The first is to identify the legal basis authorising recourse to those materials. The second is to assess their probative value.

Like all extrinsic material, the value to be attributed to international agreements or other international material, such as international case law or committee reports, as interpretative aids will depend upon whether there is a relevant connection to the statute and the interpretative issue. When an international instrument is referred to in domestic legislation then prima facie relevance is simple to establish. Where the statute does not refer to an international instrument, relevance will need to be demonstrated from wider context. The legislative history of a statute, such as legislative antecedents, parliamentary materials and law reform reports, may be critical to establishing a relevant connection.

---

70 See Part V (chapters 21–24).

71 *Zhang v Zemin* (2010) 79 NSWLR 513, 540 [158] (Allsop P).

72 See **[23.3]**.

73 See chapter 2.

74 See Dan Meagher, 'The Common Law Presumption of Consistency with International Law: Some Observations from Australia (and Comparisons with New Zealand)' [2012] (3) *New Zealand Law Review* 465, 467–70 who notes that the ambiguity condition was abandoned in New Zealand in the 1990s.

OTHER COMMON LAW PRESUMPTIONS AND AIDS 32

Overview

The task of an interpreter is to determine the intention of Parliament 'assisted by such aids to construction as can properly be utilised'.[1] This chapter considers residual common law presumptions and aids that are potentially available. [32.1]

They fall into three broad categories: works of reference, surrounding law, and common sense. Works of reference include dictionaries, legal scholarship and literary works. Surrounding law is discussed in various chapters of this work. The present chapter principally discusses maxims of law, the *Australian Constitution* and the general principles governing the lawfulness of administrative action. Common sense includes sound knowledge of everyday matters and sound judgement.

Dictionaries and other works of reference

Citation from works of reference is permitted by the common law doctrine of judicial notice and its statutory equivalents [32.2]

Works of reference are just one of a number of interpretative aids discussed in this work that are permitted by the common law doctrine of judicial notice[2] and provisions of Evidence Acts that have codified that doctrine.[3] The significance of these laws is that they allow a court to take account of a fact in issue or relevant to the issue in a given case without the fact being proved by evidence.[4] As McHugh J has said of the common law:

> As a general rule, facts in issue or relevant to a fact in issue must be proved by admissible evidence. The doctrine of judicial notice is an exception to this rule. A court may judicially notice a fact whenever it 'is so generally known that every ordinary person may be reasonably presumed to be aware of it'. The information which the court acquires by taking judicial notice of facts is not 'evidence strictly so called'.[5]

1 *Minister for Immigration and Multicultural and Indigenous Affairs v SZAYW* (2005) 145 FCR 523, 538 [67] (Weinberg J).

2 Judicial notice is also taken of the ordinary meaning of words (**[15.9]**), of surrounding circumstances (**[23.6]**) and of knowledge of everyday matters: see **[32.2]**.

3 It has been observed that it appears there is no room for the common law doctrine of judicial notice in New South Wales, by reason of the *Evidence Act 1995* (NSW) s 144: *Gattellaro v Westpac Banking Corporation* (2004) 204 ALR 258, 262 [17] (Gleeson CJ, McHugh, Hayne and Heydon JJ). Several other Australian jurisdictions have an identical or nearly identical provision: *Evidence Act 1995* (Cth); *Evidence Act 2011* (ACT) s 144; *Evidence Act 2001* (Tas) s 144; *Evidence Act 2008* (Vic) s 144.

4 See **[23.6]**, citing JD Heydon, LexisNexis, *Cross on Evidence* (online at 29 November 2021) [3001].

5 *Woods v Multi-Sport Holdings Pty Ltd* (2002) 208 CLR 460, 478 [64] (McHugh J; dissenting as to outcome) (footnotes omitted).

The codification in the *Evidence Act 1995* (Cth) provides as follows:

> **144 Matters of common knowledge**
>
> (1) Proof is not required about knowledge that is not reasonably open to question and is:
>
> (a) common knowledge in the locality in which the proceeding is being held or generally; or
>
> (b) capable of verification by reference to a document the authority of which cannot reasonably be questioned.
>
> (2) The judge may acquire knowledge of that kind in any way the judge thinks fit.
>
> (3) The court (including, if there is a jury, the jury) is to take knowledge of that kind into account.
>
> (4) The judge is to give a party such opportunity to make submissions, and to refer to relevant information, relating to the acquiring or taking into account of knowledge of that kind as is necessary to ensure that the party is not unfairly prejudiced.

Heydon J has explained how and when works of reference are permissible aids at common law:

> [T]he general law doctrine of judicial notice is narrow. Where judicial notice is taken without inquiry, the fact noticed must be 'open and notorious'. Where judicial notice is taken after inquiry, the inquiry must be into the 'common knowledge of educated men' as revealed in 'accepted writings', 'standard works' and 'serious studies and inquiries'. The words of Dixon J just quoted were used about historical events, but they apply equally to other facts. In short, matters judicially noticed at common law must be indisputable.[6]

An English authority has summed up the sources that may be resorted to in this way: 'Judicial notice ... includes matters of a public nature such as history, social customs and public opinion which may have to be culled from works of reference.'[7]

Commonly used works of reference are dictionaries and works of legal scholarship such as treatises on statutory interpretation. Other works are also drawn upon. Each of these categories is now considered in turn.

[32.3] A dictionary may offer a reasonably authoritative source for describing the range of meanings of a word, but it is not conclusive of ordinary meaning, let alone legal meaning

(a) The use of dictionaries is well settled

While '[t]he common law has long approved of dictionary definitions to assist in statutory interpretation',[8] it is important to discern the uses for which dictionaries have been approved. 'A dictionary may offer a reasonably authoritative source for describing the range of [ordinary] meanings of a word, including obsolete meanings.'[9] A dictionary may be a useful support for what

6 *Thomas v Mowbray* (2007) 233 CLR 307, 513–4 [619]. The reference that Heydon J gave to Dixon CJ is *Australian Communist Party v Commonwealth* (1951) 83 CLR 1, 196.

7 *Stoke-on-Trent City Council v B & Q plc* [1991] Ch 48, 65 (Hoffmann J).

8 *Polo/Lauren Co LP v Ziliani Holdings Pty Ltd* (2008) 173 FCR 266, 273 [24] (the Court), approved in *Merrick Tyler Pty Ltd v Commissioner of Main Roads* [2015] WASCA 82, [40] (the Court), citing *R v Peters* (1886) 16 QBD 636, 641 (Lord Coleridge CJ).

9 *House of Peace Pty Ltd v Bankstown City Council* (2000) 48 NSWLR 498, 505 [28] (Mason P, Stein JA agreeing at 511 [56], Giles JA agreeing at 511 [57]).

(upon interpretation) a court concludes is the relevant ordinary meaning.[10] But, for the reasons given below, 'the court's task is not accomplished by surveying the range of meanings found in a dictionary and choosing that which seems most apt'.[11]

(b) A dictionary is not a conclusive source of meaning

A dictionary is not conclusive of legal meaning.[12] This is because the function of a dictionary is limited when compared with the function of a court in statutory interpretation:

> A dictionary will give a range of meanings of a word. The task of a court is to identify, from text, context and purpose, the particular meaning that a statutory provision bears. The function of a dictionary and the function performed by a court construing a statute are utterly different. It must be borne in mind that the meaning of *any* word used in a statute depends on the context and purpose of the legislation in which it appears ...[13]

In other words, 'dictionaries are no substitute for the interpretative process'.[14] Apart from supplying a range of ordinary meanings, 'consultation of a dictionary will supply no guidance to the meaning of the word or words which the legislature intended'.[15]

A judge will likely be led to error by confining themself to a dictionary and not taking account of the statutory context.[16] A famous warning, approved by the High Court of Australia on a number of occasions,[17] is by Learned Hand J:

> Of course it is true that the words used, even in their literal sense, are the primary, and ordinarily the most reliable, source of interpreting the meaning of any writing: be it a

---

10 Examples (using the AustLII database) are *Fazzolari Pty Ltd v Parramatta City Council* (2009) 237 CLR 603, 621 [49] (French CJ) ('sale'); *NT Power Generation Pty Ltd v Power and Water Authority* (2004) 219 CLR 90, 124–5 [93] ('licence') (McHugh ACJ, Gummow, Callinan and Heydon JJ); *Public Service Association and Professional Officers' Association Amalgamated (NSW) v Director of Public Employment* (2012) 250 CLR 343, 363 [39] (French CJ) ('policy'); *Fischer v Nemeske Pty Ltd* (2016) 257 CLR 615, 629 [21] (French CJ and Bell J) ('advance'); *Olin Corporation v Super Cartridge Co Pty Ltd* (1977) 180 CLR 236, 248 (Gibbs J) ('compress'); *Interlego AG v Toltoys Pty Ltd* (1974) 130 CLR 461, 467 (Stephen J) ('lateral').

11 *South Western Sydney Local Health District v Gould* (2018) 97 NSWLR 513, 531 [81] (Leeming JA, Basten JA agreeing at 516 [2], Meagher JA agreeing at 517 [8]).

12 *Polo/Lauren Co LP v Ziliani Holdings Pty Ltd* (2008) 173 FCR 266, 273 [24] (the Court), approved in *Merrick Tyler Pty Ltd v Commissioner of Main Roads* [2015] WASCA 82 [40] (the Court); *House of Peace Pty Ltd v Bankstown City Council* (2000) 48 NSWLR 498, 505 [28] (Mason P, Stein JA agreeing at 511 [56], Giles JA agreeing at 511 [57]).

13 *South Western Sydney Local Health District v Gould* (2018) 97 NSWLR 513, 530 [79] (Leeming JA, Basten JA agreeing at 516 [2], Meagher JA agreeing at 517 [8]).

14 *Tal Life Ltd v Shuetrim* (2016) 91 NSWLR 439, 458 [80] (Leeming JA, Beazley P agreeing at 443 [1], Emmett AJA agreeing at 483 [217]), quoting R McDougall, 'Construction of Contracts: the High Court's Approach' (2016) 41(2) *Australian Bar Review* 103, 115.

15 *Will v Brighton* (2020) 104 NSWLR 170, 183 [54] (Bell P, Basten JA generally agreeing at 192 [109], Simpson AJA generally agreeing at 195 [127]).

16 See, eg, *Blacktown Workers' Club Ltd v O'Shannessy* (2011) 183 LGERA 184, 194 [38] (Basten JA, Handley AJA agreeing at 198 [62], Sackville AJA agreeing at 199 [72]); *South Western Sydney Local Health District v Gould* (2018) 97 NSWLR 513, 529–30 [76]–[77] (Leeming JA, Basten JA agreeing at 516 [2], Meagher JA agreeing at 517 [8]).

17 *Kelly v The Queen* (2004) 218 CLR 216, 251 [98] (McHugh J); *Thiess v Collector of Customs* (2014) 250 CLR 664, 672 [23] (the Court); *Commissioner of Taxation (Cth) v BHP Billiton Ltd* (2011) 244 CLR 325, 340 [49] (French CJ, Heydon, Crennan and Bell JJ); *Residual Assco Group Ltd v Spalvins* (2000) 202 CLR 629, 643–4 [27] (Gleeson CJ, Gaudron, McHugh, Gummow, Hayne and Callinan JJ); *Muin v Refugee Review Tribunal* (2002) 190 ALR 601, 626 [104] (McHugh J).

> statute, a contract, or anything else. But it is one of the surest indexes of a mature and developed jurisprudence not to make a fortress out of the dictionary; but to remember that statutes always have some purpose or object to accomplish, whose sympathetic and imaginative discovery is the surest guide to their meaning.[18]

As discussed in **[15.9]** in chapter 15, dictionaries are not conclusive even of ordinary meaning. The main reason is that a judge retains the ability to determine ordinary meaning with or without resort to a dictionary.[19] At a practical level, dictionaries are not determinative because 'they do not speak with one voice'.[20] This last point is illustrated by the fact that each party may take 'refuge' in various dictionary definitions.[21] Also, it is presumed that '[s]tatutes are always speaking to the present',[22] whereas a dictionary may suffer from a time lag. And dictionaries may be found to be unpersuasive.[23] Hence, caution and good judgement are needed.[24] Among other things, an interpreter should not confine attention to a single dictionary.[25]

(c) Despite their limitations, dictionaries are frequently used

It has been judicially acknowledged that 'dictionaries are frequently used'.[26] This empirical claim is justified when resort is had to AustLII.[27] The High Court of Australia has often used dictionaries to support a finding that a word bears a particular ordinary meaning.[28]

---

18 *Cabell v Markham*, 148 F 2d 737, 739 (1945).

19 See discussion at **[15.9]**.

20 *House of Peace Pty Ltd v Bankstown City Council* (2000) 48 NSWLR 498, 505 [28] (Mason P, Stein JA agreeing at 511 [56], Giles JA agreeing at 511 [57]).

21 *Merrick Tyler Pty Ltd v Commissioner of Main Roads* [2015] WASCA 82, [40] (the Court); *Polo/Lauren Co LP v Ziliani Holdings Pty Ltd* (2008) 173 FCR 266, 273 [25] (the Court). In particular, where a party selects *part* of a dictionary definition for a submission as to ordinary usage, a court is likely to find the submission unpersuasive: see *Mansfield v The Queen* (2012) 247 CLR 86, 95 [26] n 20, 96 [30] (Hayne, Crennan, Kiefel and Bell JJ).

22 *Muin v Refugee Review Tribunal* (2002) 190 ALR 601, 626–7 [100]–[104] (McHugh J). See further chapter 19.

23 For example, in *Provincial Insurance Australia Pty Ltd v Consolidated Wood Products Pty Ltd* (1991) 25 NSWLR 541 Mahoney JA (referring to the *Shorter Oxford English Dictionary* and the *Macquarie Dictionary*) did not accept that a meaning of a 'canal' in the sense of a channel was obsolete in Australia: at 560–1. In *R v Tamawiwy (No 3)* (2015) 302 FLR 79 the Supreme Court of the Australian Capital Territory found the *Macquarie Dictionary* meaning of 'email' (the sending of messages over a computer network, especially the internet) to be 'very wide and loose': at 83 [33] (Refshauge ACJ).

24 *Polo/Lauren Co LP v Ziliani Holdings Pty Ltd* (2008) 173 FCR 266, 273 [24] (the Court), approved in *Merrick Tyler Pty Ltd v Commissioner of Main Roads* [2015] WASCA 82, [40] (the Court).

25 *Provincial Insurance Australia Pty Ltd v Consolidated Wood Products Pty Ltd* (1991) 25 NSWLR 541, 560–1 (Mahoney JA). It has been said that the *Macquarie Dictionary* is the most authoritative Australian dictionary: *House of Peace Pty Ltd v Bankstown City Council* (2000) 48 NSWLR 498, 506 [33] (Mason P, Stein JA agreeing at 511 [56], Giles JA agreeing at 511 [57]).

26 *House of Peace Pty Ltd v Bankstown City Council* (2000) 48 NSWLR 498, 504 [27] (Mason P, Stein JA agreeing at 511 [56], Giles JA agreeing at 511 [57]).

27 As mentioned in chapter 15, a search of 'dictionary' on the High Court of Australia database on AustLII alone results in 635 hits: see <http://classic.austlii.edu.au/>.

28 Examples (using the AustLII database) are *Coleman v Power* (2004) 220 CLR 1, 37 [53]–[54] (McHugh J), 71 [170] (Gummow and Hayne JJ), 86 [224] (Kirby J), 116 [307]–[308] (Heydon J) ('insult'); *Milne v The Queen* (2014) 252 CLR 149, 163 [33] (French CJ, Hayne, Bell, Gageler and Keane JJ) ('use'); *White v DPP (WA)* (2011) 243 CLR 478, 485 [10] (French CJ, Crennan and Bell JJ) ('property'); *Agius v The Queen* (2013) 248 CLR 601, 613 [42] (French CJ, Hayne, Crennan, Kiefel, Bell and Keane JJ) ('state of affairs'); *A-G (SA) v Corporation of the City of Adelaide* (2013) 249 CLR 1, 20–1 [17] ('licence'), 32–3 [45] ('preach', 'canvass',

(d) **In the near future the use of dictionaries might be supplemented, or perhaps sidelined, by the use of a 'corpus linguistics'**

A corpus linguistics is 'big data': a tool that 'measures word usage by querying databases that contain millions of naturally occurring sentences'.[29] In Australia they include the Australian Corpus of English and the Australian component of the International Corpus of English,[30] each of which contains about a million words.[31] In the United States they include the Corpus of Historical American English[32] and the Corpus of Contemporary American English.[33] The last two have been used in a small number of American cases.[34]

In statutory interpretation the advantages of a corpus linguistics are said to be that it is 'more transparent than judicial intuition and a helpful check on judges' confirmation bias';[35] it is more rigorous, as judges' sources for ordinary meanings can range beyond dictionaries and can be 'somewhat haphazard';[36] it is more wide-ranging, as a dictionary is limited to *permissible* meanings;[37] it is more up to date than a dictionary as it can 'more quickly capture changing semantic usage';[38] it can service as a cross-check in those difficult cases where 'dictionaries diverge';[39] it can search particular time periods;[40] and it can find definitively whether there is evidence of a particular usage.[41]

'harangue') (French CJ); *King v The Queen* (2012) 245 CLR 588, 605 [38] (French CJ, Crennan and Kiefel JJ) ('dangerous'); *Lithgow City Council v Jackson* (2011) 244 CLR 352, 369 [43] (French CJ, Heydon and Bell JJ) ('perceived'); *Commissioner of Taxation (Cth) v Anstis* (2010) 241 CLR 443, 455–6 [29] (French CJ, Gummow, Kiefel and Bell JJ) ('gain', 'produce'); *Wacal Developments Pty Ltd v Realty Developments Pty Ltd* (1978) 140 CLR 503, 529 (Aickin J) ('instalment'); *Pinkstone v The Queen* (2004) 219 CLR 444, 462–3 [51] (McHugh and Gummow JJ) ('send').

29 Anonymous, 'Wilson v Safelite Group Inc' (2019) 133(2) *Harvard Law Review* 691, 691.

30 Michael Haugh, 'The Australian National Corpus Initiative' (Web Page, 20 December 2013) <https://www.mq.edu.au/>.

31 This corpus is quite small by international standards. 'The British National Corpus is one hundred million words, and the Corpus of Contemporary American English is more than four hundred million words. There is now even a two billion word corpus of English held by Oxford University Press, the Oxford English Corpus': Michael Haugh, 'The Australian National Corpus Initiative', (Web Page, 20 December 2013) <https://www.mq.edu.au/>.

32 See Anonymous, 'Wilson v Safelite Group Inc' (2019) 133(2) *Harvard Law Review* 691.

33 See John D Ramer, 'Corpus Linguistics: Misfire or More Ammo for the Ordinary-Meaning Canon?' (2017) 116(2) *Michigan Law Review* 303, 306.

34 *Wilson v Safelite Group Inc*, 930 F 3d 429, 440–1 (2019) ('results in' and 'extending to'); *People v Harris*, 885 NW 2d 832 (2016) ('information'); *State of Utah v Rasabout*, 356 P 3d 1258 (2015) ('discharge').

35 Anonymous, 'Wilson v Safelite Group Inc' (2019) 133(2) *Harvard Law Review* 691, 693, citing *Wilson v Safelite Group Inc*, 930 F 3d 429, 440–1 (2019) (Thapar J). See also John D Ramer, 'Corpus Linguistics: Misfire or More Ammo for the Ordinary-Meaning Canon?' (2017) 116(2) *Michigan Law Review* 303, 308, 326.

36 John D Ramer, 'Corpus Linguistics: Misfire or More Ammo for the Ordinary-Meaning Canon?' (2017) 116(2) *Michigan Law Review* 303, 306, 323–4.

37 Ibid 307.

38 Anonymous, 'Wilson v Safelite Group Inc' (2019) 133(2) *Harvard Law Review* 691, 693, citing *Wilson v Safelite Group Inc*, 930 F 3d 429, 441 (2019) (Thapar J).

39 Ibid 693, citing *Wilson v Safelite Group Inc*, 930 F 3d 429, 440 (2019) (Thapar J).

40 Ibid 694, citing *Wilson v Safelite Group Inc*, 930 F 3d 429, 444–5 (2019) (Thapar J).

41 Ibid 694.

Arguments against its usage can be made. It is said that 'judges are ill-equipped to perform sophisticated corpus analysis'.[42] It is preferable for judges to rely on the judgement of trained experts, as expressed through dictionaries, rather than take on the role of 'armchair lexicographers'.[43] Judges can come to opposite conclusions,[44] especially if they use incorrect methods.[45] Use of a corpus also risks 'privileging the most newsworthy connotations of a term over its ordinary meaning'.[46] And the need to read through the search returns and observe how the word is used in context involves 'heavy lifting',[47] the cost of which would be borne by the parties.

It has been assumed in the American cases, where a corpus linguistic analysis was undertaken, that the material and analytical findings from analysing it are admissible. But in Australia expert evidence cannot be given as to ordinary meaning.[48] Is a corpus linguistics analysis admissible as a work of reference, in respect of which judicial notice may be taken? The answer is not clear. On the one hand, the database is likely to contain works, such as literary works, that have been admitted in the past.[49] Also, dictionaries founded on historical principles such as the *Oxford English Dictionary* (which are clearly admissible) also contain extracts of their sources (to which on occasion, references is had[50]). On the other hand, a corpus linguistics is not a reference work in the sense that it plainly sets out undisputable matters that are directly drawn upon. Rather, it is a database intended to be analysed and to be the basis for empirical judgements. Plainly, those judgements are not *in* the database but are drawn from it by a process of analysis.

[32.4] Legal scholarship is commonly cited for a variety of purposes

Legal scholarship includes treatises and scholarly journal articles. It is commonly cited in reasons for judgment for a variety of purposes.[51] Where the scholarship is thorough and thoughtful, it can be influential.[52] Journal articles can be helpful to the High Court even if the article concerns a case that is on appeal to the High Court.[53] French CJ identified the scholarship that is most directly relevant to judicial reasoning:

---

42 Ibid 694, citing *Wilson v Safelite Group Inc*, 930 F 3d 429, 445–7 (2019) (Stranch J).

43 Ibid 694, quoting *Wilson v Safelite Group Inc*, 930 F 3d 429, 447 (2019) (Stranch J).

44 John D Ramer, 'Corpus Linguistics: Misfire or More Ammo for the Ordinary-Meaning Canon?' (2017) 116(2) *Michigan Law Review* 303, 316, discussing *People v Harris*, 885 NW 2d 832 (2016) (Mich Sup Ct).

45 Ibid 321.

46 Anonymous, 'Wilson v Safelite Group Inc' (2019) 133(2) *Harvard Law Review* 691, 694, quoting *Wilson v Safelite Group Inc*, 930 F 3d 429, 445–6 (2019) (Stranch J).

47 John D Ramer, 'Corpus Linguistics: Misfire or More Ammo for the Ordinary-Meaning Canon?' (2017) 116(2) *Michigan Law Review* 303, 328.

48 See **[18.6](d)**. Cf *Wilson v Safelite Group Inc*, 930 F 3d 429, 447 (2019) (Stranch J), suggesting corpus linguistics be left for a qualified expert.

49 See **[32.5]**.

50 See *Doyle v Maypole Bakery Pty Ltd* [1981] Tas R 376 (**Example 32.1** below).

51 Chief Justice French, 'Judges and Academics: Dialogue of the Hard of Hearing' (2013) 87(2) *Australian Law Journal* 96, 101. The author postulated a variety of functions of doctrinal scholarship that the legal scholar might perform: at 103.

52 Ibid 101–2. For instance, the work of Professor William Wade, discussed below (**[32.9]**), has been influential in changing the way courts approach interpretative issues in administrative law.

53 Chief Justice French, 'Judges and Academics: Dialogue of the Hard of Hearing' (2013) 87(2) *Australian Law Journal* 96, 104. But a journal article will not be helpful 'to the extent it smacks of advocacy': at 104. For an instance of a member of the High Court drawing on academic scholarship, see *Coleman v Power* (2004) 220 CLR 1, 89 [230] n 325, 101 [264] n 378 (Kirby J). Scholarship of this nature has been influential in the United Kingdom. In *R v Bentham* [2005] 1 WLR 1057 Lord Bingham acknowledged the force of academic

> That class of scholarship which is most directly relevant to judicial reasoning is Posner's 'traditional doctrinal scholarship'. Such scholarship, not limited to treatises and restatements [sic] will offer analysis and synthesis of case law including cases turning on questions of statutory interpretation and may take a critical approach to judicial reasoning in a particular area by reference to weakness in logic, inconsistently [sic] with prior authority or unintended and undesirable results flowing from a particular case or line of cases. Such criticism may suggest ways in which an allegedly erroneous line of reasoning can be corrected.[54]

In light of the view of French CJ, a sample of the AustLII database was searched to determine the variety of purposes for which legal scholarship was used.[55] The most common use of legal scholarship was to employ it as a source supplying additional references to authority.[56] Other, more significant, uses included the following: providing historical facts that are part of the context;[57] providing a convenient source where authorities are set out;[58] explaining the law;[59] synthesising the law;[60] developing a principle that encapsulates the existing law;[61] providing critical insight;[62] and giving a source of scholarly discussion of an issue that touches, but is not directly relevant to, the case.[63]

It has been claimed that courts 'refer to and rely upon views expressed about statutory meaning by ... text writers and legal commentators'.[64] In respect of views as to what the law is, only a small number of cases in the sample cited scholarly views for this purpose.[65]

---

criticisms of the decision below: at 1061 [8] (Lord Steyn agreeing at 1062 [12], Lord Phillips agreeing at 1062 [13], Lord Carswell agreeing at 1062 [15]). The case is discussed on another basis at **Example 18.3**.

54 Chief Justice French, 'Judges and Academics: Dialogue of the Hard of Hearing' (2013) 87(2) *Australian Law Journal* 96, 101–2.

55 The AustLII database of High Court decisions was searched. The texts selected were Dennis C Pearce, *Statutory Interpretation in Australia* (1st and 2nd editions); Dennis C Pearce and Robert S Geddes, *Statutory Interpretation in Australia* (3rd–8th editions); and Francis Bennion, *Statutory Interpretation / Bennion on Statutory Interpretation* (1st–6th editions). These texts were selected on the hypothesis that they were among the most likely of scholarly works on statutory interpretation to have been cited.

56 See, eg, *Hughes v The Queen* (2017) 263 CLR 338, 409 [181] n 215 (Nettle J).

57 See, eg, *Project Blue Sky Inc v Australian Broadcasting Authority* (1998) 194 CLR 355, 391–2 [96] (McHugh, Gummow, Kirby and Hayne JJ).

58 See, eg, *Aubrey v The Queen* (2017) 260 CLR 305, 324 [35] (Kiefel CJ, Keane, Nettle and Edelman JJ).

59 See, eg, *DPP (Cth) v Keating* (2013) 248 CLR 459, 479 [48] (French CJ, Hayne, Crennan, Kiefel, Bell and Keane JJ).

60 See, eg, *Collector of Customs v Agfa-Gevaert Ltd* (1996) 186 CLR 389, 401 (Brennan CJ, Dawson, Toohey, Gaudron and McHugh JJ).

61 See, eg, *SZTAL v Minister for Immigration and Border Protection* (2017) 262 CLR 362, 371 [24] (Kiefel CJ, Nettle and Gordon JJ).

62 See, eg, *R v LK* (2010) 241 CLR 177, 219–20 [96]–[97] (Gummow, Hayne, Crennan, Kiefel and Bell JJ).

63 See, eg, *Coleman v Power* (2004) 220 CLR 1, 96 [246] n 364 (Kirby J).

64 John McMillan, 'Statutory Interpretation and Deference: An Executive Perspective' in Janina Boughey and Lisa Burton Crawford (eds), *Interpreting Executive Power* (Federation Press, 2020) 24, 33. The author does not provide any examples.

65 There were three cases: *Coleman v Power* (2004) 220 CLR 1, 95 [245] n 360 (Kirby J); *Chang v Laidley Shire Council* (2007) 234 CLR 1, 33 [113] n 102 (Hayne, Heydon and Crennan JJ); *Minister for Immigration and Border Protection v Kumar* (2017) 260 CLR 367, 396 [73] n 99 (Nettle J) (dissenting as to outcome).

[32.5] Other scholarly works are cited from diverse areas

Scholarly works have been cited from diverse areas. Historical works that have been cited include works of Australian history in a case dealing with alleged 'insulting words' to a police officer,[66] and the history of families in a case on the meaning of 'parent'.[67] Philosophical works, such as the works of Bertrand Russell, have been cited.[68] A book of political quotations has been cited.[69] More recently, scholarship on cyberbullying has been examined in detail and drawn upon.[70]

Literary works have often been cited in case law.[71] Examples in statutory interpretation cases are extracts from essays of Alexander Pope,[72] Gilbert and Sullivan's *The Pirates of Penzance*[73] and Lewis Carroll's *Through the Looking-Glass*.[74] Meehan points out that literature is used for several positive reasons, ranging from 'a repository of wisdom, an authoritative source of enduring human truths'[75] to a source of 'substantial illustrative force'.[76]

Example 32.1 *Doyle v Maypole Bakery Pty Ltd*[77]

The respondent was charged with breaching s 91(1) of the *Public Health Act 1962* (Tas) ('the Act'). The provision stated that '[n]o person shall sell an article of food . . . which is adulterated'. Section 63 of the Act further provided that an article of food is adulterated when 'it contains any substance in any quantity . . . that is foreign to the food'. The article in question was a pack of six lamingtons, wrapped in thin plastic. The offending substance was a blowfly. According to evidence from the Government Analyst, the blowfly did not penetrate the surface of the cake but was resting in an indentation in the cake. The heady question of statutory interpretation was this: did 'contains' have the narrow construction of wholly enclosed, or was it sufficient that the

66 *Coleman v Power* (2004) 220 CLR 1, 91 [239] n 338 (Kirby J), a case discussed in **Example 32.4**.

67 *H v Minister for Immigration and Citizenship* (2010) 188 FCR 393, 405 [47] (the Court).

68 *Barbosa v Di Meglio* [1999] NSWCA 307, [9] (Mason P); *Jones v Australian Competition and Consumer Commission* (2002) 76 ALD 424, 443 [112] (Weinberg J).

69 *Coleman v Power* (2004) 220 CLR 1, 46 [81] n 177 (McHugh J).

70 *Phillips v Police* (2016) 125 SASR 427, 433–5 [22]–[25] (Kourakis CJ).

71 Their use has generated a literature of their own: see Michael Meehan, 'The Good, The Bad and the Ugly: Judicial Literacy and Australian Cultural Cringe' (1990) 12(4) *Adelaide Law Review* 431; Ken Barlow, 'Alice, Humpty Dumpty and the Law' (2011) 85(6) *Australian Law Journal* 365; Steven M Oxenhandler, 'The Lady Doth Protest Too Much Methinks: The Use of Figurative Language from Shakespeare's Hamlet in American Case Law' (1999–2000) 23(2) *Hamline Law Review* 370; James L Robertson, 'Practical Benefits of Literature in Law, and Their Limits' (2016) 35(1) *Mississippi College Law Review* 266.

72 *Doyle v Maypole Bakery Pty Ltd* [1981] Tas R 376 (**Example 32.1** below).

73 *Virgin Blue Airlines Pty Ltd v Federal Commissioner of Taxation* (2010) 190 FCR 150, 164 [64] (Jessup J).

74 *Smoker v Pharmacy Restructuring Authority* (1994) 53 FCR 287, 289 (Wilcox J). For references to other Lewis Carroll works, see Ken Barlow, 'Alice, Humpty Dumpty and the Law' (2011) 85(6) *Australian Law Journal* 365.

75 Michael Meehan, 'The Good, The Bad and the Ugly: Judicial Literacy and Australian Cultural Cringe' (1990) 12 (4) *Adelaide Law Review* 431, 436. An example is the line of cases (eg, *Smoker v Pharmacy Restructuring Authority* (1994) 53 FCR 287) that use Humpty Dumpty's statement in *Through the Looking-Glass* as authority for the fact that '[p]rovided it makes its intention clear, Parliament can use any word it wishes, however much this may offend linguistic purists': at 289 (Wilcox J).

76 Michael Meehan, 'The Good, The Bad and the Ugly: Judicial Literacy and Australian Cultural Cringe' (1990) 12(4) *Adelaide Law Review* 431, 436.

77 [1981] Tas R 376.

foreign substance is attached or adheres to the article in question? The Magistrate adopted the former construction, and dismissed the charge.

On appeal the Supreme Court of Tasmania used literature to support a holding that 'it does not seem to me that the ordinary meaning of the word "contain" necessarily excludes something found on or in the surface of the cake after it is cooked'.[78] The judge cited an extract from an essay by Pope: 'So vast a throng the stage can ne'er contain.'[79] Neasey J took from this that 'a stage can be said to contain actors or people who are on its surface'. For this and other reasons his Honour preferred the wider construction and entered a conviction.[80]

Surrounding law

The surrounding law in which a statute is to operate is part of the context to be considered [32.6]

An important part of the context of a statute is the surrounding law. As Heydon J has said:

> The context [of the language the legislature has used] lies partly in the rest of the statute (which calls for interpretation of its language), partly in the pre-existing state of the law, partly in the mischief being dealt with and partly in the state of the surrounding law in which the statute is to operate.[81]

The surrounding law is all the common law and statute law that is relevant. As eloquently put by Gageler: 'The meaning of a statutory text is also informed, and reinformed, by the need for the courts to apply the text each time, not in isolation, but as part of the totality of the common law and statute law as it then exists.'[82]

Apart from the obvious fact that surrounding law is *law*, the courts need to take account of surrounding law for a fundamental reason, which is that '[c]onstruction should favour coherence in the law'.[83] It is also reasonable to impute knowledge of the relevant law to the Parliament, for 'Parliament in its wisdom in passing an Act must be taken to know the general law'.[84]

Surrounding law is a vast area. For convenience, some of the topics are dealt with separately in this work. The following topics are dealt with elsewhere:

- for legislative antecedents, see chapter 21 in Part V (*Legislative History*);
- for pre-existing common law, see chapter 22 in Part V (*Legislative History*);
- for the statute book, see chapter 29 in the current part;
- for precedent, see chapter 30 in the current part;
- for international treaties and conventions, see chapter 31 in the current part; and
- for mens rea and the *Criminal Code* provisions in the nature of mens rea, see chapter 42 in Part VIII (*Special Interpretative Issues*).

78 Ibid 378 (Neasey J).

79 Ibid. The extract was taken from the *Oxford English Dictionary*. The second edition of that dictionary (1989) states that the quotation is from Alexander Pope, *An Essay on Criticism* (1709).

80 [1981] Tas R 376, 378.

81 *Momcilovic v The Queen* (2011) 245 CLR 1, 175 [441] (Heydon J) (dissenting as to outcome).

82 Stephen Gageler, 'Common Law Statutes and Judicial Legislation: Statutory Interpretation as a Common Law Process' (2011) 37(2) *Monash University Law Review* 1, 1–2.

83 *Plaintiff S4/2014 v Minister for Immigration and Border Protection* (2014) 253 CLR 219, 236 [42] (the Court).

84 *Fisher v Bell* [1961] 1 QB 394, 399 (Lord Parker CJ, Ashworth J agreeing at 401, Elwes J agreeing at 401).

The present chapter deals with the following aspects of residual surrounding law:

- maxims of law;
- presumptions arising concerning the *Australian Constitution*;
- presumptions of administrative law; and
- other presumptions of law.

[32.7] A wide range of maxims of law are available

(a) Maxims of law are general aphorisms that are repositories of wisdom

Maxims of law,[85] mostly couched in Latin[86] (hence the term 'Latin maxims'[87]), are general aphorisms.[88] Maxims are venerated as 'repositories of that wisdom the best lawyers contribute to human welfare as they pass through life'.[89] Although expressing basic principle,[90] and often described as 'principles',[91] they are not principles in the sense that they are applied in a stand-alone fashion to the facts.[92] They are interpretative presumptions that are presumptively implied in statute law.[93] They are rebuttable.[94]

The maxims are too numerous to mention in full in this publication.[95] Maxims that are commonly encountered in statutory interpretation include *de minimis non curat lex* (the law does not concern itself with trifles);[96] *lex non cogit ad impossibilia* (the law does not compel a person to

85 The term used in *Broom's Legal Maxims* and approved in *Thompson v Groote Eylandt Mining Co Ltd* (2003) 173 FLR 72, 81 [32] (Mildren J, Martin CJ generally agreeing at 73 [1], Thomas J agreeing at 82 [39]).

86 Oliver Jones, *Bennion on Statutory Interpretation: A Code* (LexisNexis, 6th ed, 2013) 978.

87 *Chapman v Commonwealth Bank of Australia* [2012] VSCA 162, [32] (the Court); *Lockrey v Historic Houses Trust of New South Wales* (2012) 84 NSWLR 114, 131 [80] (Barrett JA, Campbell JA agreeing at 116 [1], Meagher JA agreeing at 116 [2]).

88 *Dowell Australia Ltd v Archdeacon* (1975) 132 CLR 417, 426 (McTiernan J).

89 Oliver Jones, *Bennion on Statutory Interpretation: A Code* (LexisNexis, 6th ed, 2013) 978. The author acknowledges that some judges eschew the use of Latin: at 978.

90 Ibid.

91 *Dowell Australia Ltd v Archdeacon* (1975) 132 CLR 417, 426 (McTiernan J), in relation to *lex non cogit ad impossibilia*; *Lockrey v Historic Houses Trust of New South Wales* (2012) 84 NSWLR 114, 131 [81] (Barrett JA, Campbell JA agreeing at 116 [1], Meagher JA agreeing at 116 [2]), in relation to *lex non cogit ad impossibilia*; *Van Dongen v Northern Territory* (2005) 16 NTLR 169, 177 [14] (Mildren J), in relation to *lex non cogit ad impossibilia*; *De Marco v Chief Commissioner of State Revenue* (2013) 83 NSWLR 445, 452 [33] (McColl JA) (dissenting as to outcome), in relation to *nullus commodum capere potest de injuria sua propria*.

92 See *Nicholls v Michael Wilson & Partners Ltd* (2010) 243 FLR 177, 212 [181] (Young JA), doubting that *nullus commodum capere potest de injuria sua propria* is a principle.

93 *De Marco v Chief Commissioner of State Revenue* (2013) 83 NSWLR 445, 452 [33] (McColl JA) (dissenting as to outcome), approving a statement of Bennion in *Statutory Interpretation* (LexisNexis, 5th ed, 2008) 1141 in relation to *nullus commodum capere potest de injuria sua propria*; *Pinho v Andre* (Supreme Court of Victoria, Smith J, 20 December 1994) 22, in relation to *de minimis non curat lex*, approving a statement of Bennion in *Statutory Interpretation*; *Farnell Electronic Components Pty Ltd v Collector of Customs* (1996) 72 FCR 125, 127 (Hill J), approving a statement of FAR Bennion in *Statutory Interpretation: A Code* (2nd ed, 1992) 780.

94 *Van Dongen v Northern Territory* (2005) 16 NTLR 169, 177 [14] (Mildren J), speaking of *lex non cogit ad impossibilia*. For instances of rebuttal, see *Farnell Electronic Components Pty Ltd v Collector of Customs* (1996) 72 FCR 125 (in relation to *de minimis non curat lex*); *De Marco v Chief Commissioner of State Revenue* (2013) 83 NSWLR 445 (in relation to *nullus commodum capere potest de injuria sua propria*).

95 A detailed list (with translations) appears in Lawrence G Greene (ed), *Radin Law Dictionary* (Oceana Publications, 1955) 397–408. For a discussion of several of them in the context of statutory interpretation, see Oliver Jones, *Bennion on Statutory Interpretation* (LexisNexis, 6th ed, 2013) Part XXIV.

96 See discussion below.

do that which he or she cannot possibly perform);[97] *nullus commodum capere potest de injuria sua propria* (no person can obtain an advantage by his or her own wrong);[98] and *ut res magis valeat quam pereat* ('It is better for a thing to have effect than to be made void').[99] The interaction between maxims and statute law is now illustrated.

(b) *De minimis non curat lex*: the law does not concern itself with trifles

This maxim (often shortened to '*de minimis*') means 'the law does not concern itself with trifles'.[100] It has also been translated as 'The law does not have regard to absurdly minimal matters'.[101] As indicated in this latter description, the reasons for the maxim include to discourage unnecessary litigation, to ensure time is not wasted, to keep costs down and to preserve the dignity of the law.[102]

Whether the maxim ought to be implied is a question of interpretation.[103] The presence of words in a statute such as 'exclusively', 'solely' or 'only' is not to be disregarded but is not conclusive.[104] The applicability of the maxim 'depends upon the context in which it falls to be considered'.[105] It may be found that the statute admits of no exception.[106] Even if the maxim applies, a court may find the particular non-compliance not to be of such triviality as to be ignored.[107]

The maxim 'has been applied, either expressly or by implication, in a wide variety of situations where a trivial failure to comply with a specific condition has been ignored'.[108] For instance, the maxim has been approved in relation to a 'trifling' departure from criminal procedure[109] and in relation to compliance with a regulatory offence.[110] It has been applied to a 'minor and

97 See *Van Dongen v Northern Territory* (2005) 16 NTLR 169, 177–9 [14]–[17] (Mildren J); *R v Justices of Leicestershire* (1850) 15 QB 88, 92; 117 ER 391, 392; *Lockrey v Historic Houses Trust of New South Wales* (2012) 84 NSWLR 114, 131 [80]–[83] (Barrett JA, Campbell JA agreeing at 116 [1], Meagher JA agreeing at 116 [2]).

98 See *Thompson v Groote Eylandt Mining Co Ltd* (2003) 173 FLR 72, 80–2 [31]–[35] (Mildren J, Martin CJ generally agreeing at 73 [1], Thomas J agreeing at 82 [39]); *Holden v Nuttall* [1945] VLR 171, 178 (Herring CJ); *Woodcock v South Western Electricity Board* [1975] 2 All ER 545, 548–9 (Dunn J); *De Marco v Chief Commissioner of State Revenue* (2013) 83 NSWLR 445, 452–8 [32]–[64] (McColl JA) (dissenting as to outcome), 460–1 [76] (Basten JA), 467–72 [120]–[152] (Gzell J).

99 See discussion at **[32.8](b)**.

100 *Chapman v Commonwealth Bank of Australia* [2012] VSCA 162, [32] (the Court).

101 *Dann v Gavranich* (1989) 10 MVR 148, 150 (White J, Jacobs J agreeing at 148) (dicta).

102 *Pinho v Andre* (Supreme Court of Victoria, Smith J, 20 December 1994) 22, approving a statement in Francis Bennion, *Statutory Interpretation* (edition not cited).

103 *Farnell Electronic Components Pty Ltd v Collector of Customs* (1996) 72 FCR 125, 130 (Hill J).

104 Ibid 128–9, referring to *Biga Nominees Pty Ltd v Commissioner of Taxation (Cth)* (1991) 104 FLR 74 and to *Randwick Municipal Council v Rutledge* (1959) 102 CLR 54, 94 (Windeyer J).

105 *Farnell Electronic Components Pty Ltd v Collector of Customs* (1996) 72 FCR 125, 130 (Hill J).

106 Ibid 131.

107 Ibid.

108 Ibid 128.

109 *Lloyd v Police* (2004) 89 SASR 383, 386 [2] (Doyle CJ), 394 [33] (Debelle J) (dicta).

110 *Dann v Gavranich* (1989) 10 MVR 148, 150 (White J, Jacobs J agreeing at 148) (dicta). In *Williams v The Queen* (1978) 140 CLR 591 Murphy J applied it as a basis for setting aside a criminal conviction for possessing a prohibited plant, for which imprisonment was a potential punishment: at 602. But in *Harrison v Moore* (2018) 28 Tas R 99 the Supreme Court of Tasmania, referring to *Ross on Crime*, took the view that the maxim did not apply to criminal liability as a complete defence: at 107 [33] (Brett J).

insubstantial' breach of constitutional law[111] and to determine the 'substance' of the requirements of a law governing rights of litigants in civil action.[112]

Example 32.2 *Pinho v Andre*[113]

For the purposes of purchasing a bakery business the plaintiffs and the defendants obtained a bank loan secured by two mortgages of their respective residential properties. Unfortunately, the business ran into financial difficulty and default occurred under the mortgages. The bank exercised its powers of sale and arranged auctions for the two properties. The home of the plaintiffs was sold and the bank received net proceeds of $100,861.24. At the time the debt owed under the loan was $100,868.87, resulting in a shortfall of $7.63. The home of the defendants was passed in. The defendants executed a deed under which the bank permitted them to enter into occupation of the property. The mortgage held by the bank over the property of the defendants was later transferred by it to the plaintiffs. A further transfer of the mortgage was made by the first and second plaintiff to the second plaintiff (Mrs P).

Relying on s 52(3) of the *Supreme Court Act 1986* (Vic), the plaintiffs brought an action in the Supreme Court seeking an order from the Court that the first defendant 'pay to the plaintiffs contribution . . . to the extent of one-half of the sum paid by the Plaintiffs to the Commonwealth Bank of Australia in repayment of a loan in respect of which the First Plaintiff and First Defendant were jointly liable'.[114] Section 52(3) stated as follows:

> (3) A person who pays a debt or performs a duty as referred to in subsection (1) is entitled –
>
> (a) to stand in the place of the creditor; and
>
> (b) to use all the remedies of the creditor
>
> . . .
>
> in any proceeding to obtain from the principal debtor or any co-surety, co-contractor or co-debtor (as the case requires) indemnity for the advances made and loss sustained by the person who paid the debt or performed the duty.

The phrase whose meaning was in doubt was 'pays a debt'.[115] Counsel for the second defendant argued that the provision meant paid in full, and this had not occurred.[116] The Court disagreed. One basis was that the bank had abandoned or waived its rights to total payment. That having been done, the debt had been paid.[117] In the alternative the Court held that the *de minimis* principle applied[118] and the section required that the debt be paid 'in substance'[119] or 'in a practical sense'.[120] This had occurred, the plaintiffs having paid all but $7.63 of the debt. The Court held Mrs P was entitled to an order for possession of the property the subject of the defendants' original mortgage to the bank.[121]

111 *Sharples v Arnison* (2001) 160 FLR 194, 215 [95] (Ambrose J).

112 *Pinho v Andre* (Supreme Court of Victoria, Smith J, 20 December 1994) 22. See **Example 32.2**.

113 Supreme Court of Victoria, Smith J, 20 December 1994.

114 *Pinho v Andre* (Supreme Court of Victoria, Smith J, 20 December 1994) 3.

115 Also, similarly, 'pays that debt' in s 52(1).

116 *Pinho v Andre* (Supreme Court of Victoria, Smith J, 20 December 1994) 17.

117 Ibid 22.

118 Ibid.

119 Ibid.

120 Ibid 23.

121 Ibid 30.

The *Australian Constitution* has a unique place in the interpretation of Australian legislation [32.8]

(a) In a case in which the validity of legislation is challenged, a court should ordinarily begin by construing the impugned legislation if its construction might affect the legislation's validity

Where legislation is impugned on constitutional grounds the following rule of practice is employed where possible:

> One would not ordinarily proceed to a determination of questions of constitutional validity where the case might be resolved on the basis that the impugned law, properly construed, does not have the operation and effect for which the challenger contends.[122]

The rule has been acknowledged in other cases.[123]

Example 32.3 *Zhang v Commissioner of Police*[124]

The plaintiff challenged the validity of a search warrant that identified offences against s 92.3(1) and (2) of the *Criminal Code* (Cth) (in sch to *Criminal Code Act 1995* (Cth)). As part of that challenge he argued that s 92.3(1) and (2) were invalid on the ground that the provisions impermissibly burdened the implied freedom of political communication that the High Court has recognised is a constitutional limitation on legislative power.

Put in abbreviated form, s 92.3(1) creates an offence where a person engages in certain conduct on behalf of a foreign principal, and the person is reckless as to whether the conduct will influence the political process of the Commonwealth or a state or territory. The conduct must be of a certain character, and one of the possible characters is that it is 'covert'. In the present case the warrant identified the conduct as 'covert'.

The plaintiff's case, that the implied freedom of political communication was infringed, depended on 'covert' being given a wide reading as meaning 'private' or 'not overt'.[125] The plaintiff's case failed at the outset as the Court found that the plaintiff 'did not contend that on all available constructions of the word would the permutation offend the implied freedom of political communication'.[126] Implicit in the Court's reasoning is an acknowledgement that an available construction was as put by the Attorney-General (intervening in support of the defendant): that 'covert' could be read down to mean 'involving some element of nefarious concealment or secrecy'.[127] Thus, although not required to reach a definite conclusion on the constructional issue, the Court held that '[the plaintiff's] argument that those offences do not exist can be rejected without need of determining the constitutional argument he presents'.[128]

---

122 *North Australian Aboriginal Justice Agency Ltd v Northern Territory* (2015) 256 CLR 569, 625–6 [149] (Keane J).

123 See, eg, *Coleman v Power* (2004) 220 CLR 1, 21 [3] (Gleeson CJ) (dissenting as to outcome), 68 [158] (Gummow and Hayne JJ), 84–5 [219]–[220] (Kirby J), 115 [306] (Heydon J) (dissenting as to outcome).

124 (2021) 389 ALR 363.

125 Ibid 367 [18] (the Court).

126 Ibid.

127 Ibid 367 [19].

128 Ibid 368 [20].

(b) A statute should be interpreted to avoid incompatibility with the *Australian Constitution*

A statute should be interpreted, so far as its words allow, to keep it within constitutional limits.[129] Two particular principles fit under the umbrella 'principle of constitutional conformity'.[130] According to Isaacs J, '[i]t is a received canon of judicial construction to apply in cases of this kind with more than ordinary anxiety the maxim *Ut res magis valeat quam pereat*.[131] But endeavours of this kind cannot be pushed far. The ordinary principles of statutory construction still apply.[132] A court cannot prefer 'one construction of a statutory provision over another merely to avoid constitutional doubt'.[133] Similarly, '[t]he court should not strain to give a meaning to statutes that is artificial or departs markedly from their ordinary meaning simply in order to preserve their constitutional validity'.[134]

In the same vein is s 15A of the *Acts Interpretation Act 1901* (Cth) and equivalent state and territory provisions.[135] Section 15A provides: 'Every Act shall be read and construed subject to the Constitution, and so as not to exceed the legislative power of the Commonwealth'. This section has been understood as permitting a court to save a provision from invalidity by giving it a partial operation if that had been intended. A law expressed in general terms cannot be read down if 'the law was intended to operate fully and completely according to its terms, or not at all'. But 'where a law is intended to operate in an area where Parliament's legislative power is subject to a clear limitation, it can be read as subject to that limitation'.[136]

Example 32.4 *Coleman v Power*[137]

The appellant, who loudly called a particular police officer 'a corrupt police officer' in a public place, was charged with a breach of s 7(1)(d) of the *Vagrants, Gaming and Other Offences Act 1931* (Qld). It made it an offence to use 'insulting words' in a public place. The appellant argued that he could not be convicted as the provision infringed the implied freedom of communication between people concerning political and governmental matters.

129 *K-Generation Pty Ltd v Liquor Licensing Court* (2009) 237 CLR 501, 519 [46] (French CJ). See also to similar effect *Coleman v Power* (2004) 220 CLR 1, 88 [227] (Kirby J).

130 *Coleman v Power* (2004) 220 CLR 1, 87–8 [227] (Kirby J).

131 *Federal Commissioner of Taxation v Munro* (1926) 38 CLR 153, 180 (Isaacs J). The maxim means 'It is better for a thing to have effect than to be made void': *Coleman v Power* (2004) 220 CLR 1, 88 [227] n 319 (Kirby J), quoting with approval *Jowitt's Dictionary of English Law* (2nd ed, 1977) vol 2, 1845.

132 *North Australian Aboriginal Justice Agency Ltd v Northern Territory* (2015) 256 CLR 569, 604 [76] (Gageler J) (dissenting as to outcome).

133 Ibid.

134 *International Finance Trust Co Ltd v New South Wales Crime Commission* (2009) 240 CLR 319, 349 [42] (French CJ).

135 See **[25.5](e)**.

136 *Coleman v Power* (2004) 220 CLR 1, 55 [108] (McHugh J), quoting *Victoria v Commonwealth* (1996) 187 CLR 416, 502–3. The latter case in turn had quoted *Pidoto v Victoria* (1943) 68 CLR 87, 108 (Latham CJ) for the first quotation.

137 (2004) 220 CLR 1.

The appeal was allowed, with the majority giving different reasons. One of the members of the majority, McHugh J, found that an unqualified prohibition on the use of insulting words was not compatible with the implied freedom of political communication.[138] His Honour then looked to the Queensland equivalent to s 15A of the *Acts Interpretation Act 1901* (Cth), namely s 9(1) of the *Acts Interpretation Act 1954* (Qld), which read as follows:

> (1) An Act is to be interpreted as operating –
> (a) to the full extent of, but not to exceed, Parliament's legislative power . . .

Applying this provision as read in the light of case law, McHugh J held:

> [T]he clear intention of s 9 of the Queensland *Acts Interpretation Act* is that, where possible, an invalid law should be saved to the extent that it is within the power of the Queensland legislature. In the present case, the relevant part of para (d) of s 7(1) was within the power of the Queensland legislature except to the extent that it penalised insulting words uttered in discussing or raising matters concerning politics and government in or near public places. It should be read down accordingly.[139]

(c) **If two constructions are textually available, one of which leads to constitutional invalidity while the other leads to validity, a court must opt for the construction that leads to validity**

In *Residual Assco Group Ltd v Spalvins*[140] six members of the High Court stated the following interpretative rule:

> If the choice is between reading a statutory provision in a way that will invalidate it and reading it in a way that will not, a court must always choose the latter course when it is reasonably open. Courts in a federation should approach issues of statutory construction on the basis that it is a fundamental rule of construction that the legislatures of the federation intend to enact legislation that is valid and not legislation that is invalid.[141]

In *Zhang v Commissioner of Police* (**Example 32.3**) the High Court resolved the dispute without having to apply the above rule. But the High Court indicated that the principle would have been applied had it been necessary 'to ensure validity if the wide reading for which [the appellant] contended did lead to invalidity'.[142]

---

138 Ibid 54 [105]–[106].

139 Ibid 56 [110].

140 (2000) 202 CLR 629.

141 Ibid 644 [28] (Gleeson CJ, Gaudron, McHugh, Gummow, Hayne and Callinan JJ). See also *North Australian Aboriginal Justice Agency Ltd v Northern Territory* (2015) 256 CLR 569, 605 [79] (Gageler J) (dissenting as to outcome); *Coleman v Power* (2004) 220 CLR 1, 87 [225] (Kirby J).

142 (2021) 389 ALR 363, 367 [18] (the Court).

[32.9] The general principles governing the lawfulness of administrative action surround a statutory power and are implied, unless there is a contrary legislative intention

In administrative law the usual focus is the exercise or non-exercise of a statutory power.[143] The common law and statutory principles concerning the lawfulness of administrative action are part of the surrounding law that informs the scope of the power. In Australia 'general legal principles with which administrators must comply to act lawfully ... include procedural fairness, relevant and irrelevant considerations, improper purpose, inflexible application of policy, the "rules" against delegation and dictation, error of law, jurisdictional fact, no evidence, irrationality/ illogicality in factual findings, and unreasonableness'.[144]

Traditionally, it is fair to say that these principles were generally seen as giving rise to common law duties.[145] As Bateman and McDonald put it, 'they were '"grounds of review" which exist *ex ante* a statute conferring power on an administrator'.[146] They were described as 'common law grounds of review'.[147] For instance, Mason J spoke of the 'common law doctrine of natural justice'[148] and the 'common law duty to act fairly'.[149]

An exclusive focus on the common law was reigned in. Over the course of several cases Brennan J[150] demonstrated that, if there was no contrary legislative intention, the principles were 'implied limitations on the extent or the exercise of statutory power'.[151] Thus, for instance, '[t]here is no jurisdiction to declare a purported exercise of statutory power invalid for failure to comply with procedural requirements other than those expressly or impliedly prescribed by statute'.[152] The High Court has now clearly accepted Brennan J's approach, observing that '[t]he statutory limits of the decision-making authority conferred by a statute are determined

143 See, for judicial review, *Annetts v McCann* (1990) 170 CLR 596, 604 (Brennan J), cited in Will Bateman and Leighton McDonald, 'The Normative Structure of Australian Administrative Law' (2017) 45(2) *Federal Law Review* 153, 167 n 68. The focus on statutory powers applies all the more so to merits review and ombudsman investigations.

144 Will Bateman and Leighton McDonald, 'The Normative Structure of Australian Administrative Law' (2017) 45(2) *Federal Law Review* 153, 158–9. The authors do not mention the ground of 'narrow' or 'simple' ultra vires, which is the most straightforward case of statutory interpretation. See generally Robin Creyke et al, *Control of Government Action: Text, Cases and Commentary* (LexisNexis Butterworths, 5th ed, 2019) ch 8, esp 433 [8.1.2]; Roger Douglas et al, *Douglas and Jones's Administrative Law* (Federation Press, 8th ed, 2018) ch 9; Margaret Allars, *Introduction to Australian Administrative Law* (Butterworths, 1990) 165 [5.10].

145 Cf *MZAPC v Minister for Immigration and Border Protection* (2021) 390 ALR 590, 633 [168]–[169] (Edelman J).

146 Will Bateman and Leighton McDonald, 'The Normative Structure of Australian Administrative Law' (2017) 45(2) *Federal Law Review* 153, 155.

147 *Kioa v West* (1985) 159 CLR 550, 576 (Mason J).

148 Ibid 582.

149 Ibid 584.

150 His Honour was influenced by the learned writings of Professor Sir William Wade: Stephen Gageler, 'The Underpinnings of Judicial Review of Administrative Action: Common Law or Constitution?' (2000) 28(2) *Federal Law Review* 303, 311–2. The work of Wade that Brennan J referred to was William Wade, *Administrative Law* (Clarendon Press, 6th ed, 1988). As pointed out by Gageler, Brennan J acknowledged this debt in *Walton v Gardiner* (1993) 177 CLR 378, 408.

151 *A-G (NSW) v Quin* (1990) 170 CLR 1, 36. The other seminal reasons for judgment of Brennan J are in *FAI Insurances Ltd v Winneke* (1982) 151 CLR 342 and *Kioa v West* (1985) 159 CLR 550. The development is well told in Will Bateman and Leighton McDonald, 'The Normative Structure of Australian Administrative Law' (2017) 45(2) *Federal Law Review* 153.

152 *Kioa v West* (1985) 159 CLR 550, 611 (Brennan J).

as an exercise in statutory interpretation informed by evolving common law principles of statutory interpretation'.[153] So too is the synonymous question[154] of whether an error is of such a magnitude as to amount to a 'jurisdictional error'.[155]

The idea that the general principles as to the lawfulness of administrative action are to be considered as an exercise of statutory interpretation causes some commentators to recoil.[156] But administrative law principles do not cease to exist on the 'statutory approach', as Bateman and McDonald call the dominant approach to the identification of error in decision-making.[157] On the contrary, the principles are part of the surrounding law that a court is to take into account. In the words of Edelman J:

> That exercise of construction is not dependent solely on the literal text. Rather, the statute is construed in light of the background principles and history of judicial review, as well as common law principles, including the principle that the consequences of an error that a legislature will be taken to intend will usually depend on the gravity of the error.[158]

Therefore, it is too crude to say that the common law grounds of review have been replaced by legislative intention.[159] As the High Court recognised with natural justice, to see the choice of the source of duty in terms of extremes – a bare common law duty, or a bare implication from statute uninformed by the common law presumptions and principles – is to proceed upon a false

153 *MZAPC v Minister for Immigration and Border Protection* (2021) 390 ALR 590, 597 [30] (Kiefel CJ, Gageler, Keane and Gleeson JJ). See to same effect *Hossain v Minister for Immigration and Border Protection* (2018) 264 CLR 123, 133–4 [27]–[28] (Kiefel CJ, Gageler and Keane JJ). The principles have been explicitly recognised as 'presumptions of law'. For natural justice, see *Plaintiff S10/2011 v Minister for Immigration and Citizenship* (2012) 246 CLR 636, 658 [66] (Gummow, Hayne, Crennan and Bell JJ), quoting with approval *Kioa v West* (1985) 159 CLR 550, 619 (Brennan J). For reasonableness, see *Minister for Immigration and Citizenship v Li* (2013) 249 CLR 332, 362 [63], 369 [86] (Hayne, Kiefel and Bell JJ), 371 [92] (Gageler J). For other principles, see 'the general and deeply rooted common law principle of construction that such decision-making authority as is conferred by statute must be exercised according to law and to *reason* within limits set by the subject matter, scope and purposes of the statute': *Minister for Immigration and Citizenship v Li* (2013) 249 CLR 332, 370–1 [90] (Gageler J) (emphasis in original).

154 *MZAPC v Minister for Immigration and Border Protection* (2021) 390 ALR 590, 597 [29] (Kiefel CJ, Gageler, Keane and Gleeson JJ).

155 *Hossain v Minister for Immigration and Border Protection* (2018) 264 CLR 123, 133–4 [27] (Kiefel CJ, Gageler and Keane JJ). The significance of an error being regarded as a jurisdictional error is that a privative clause cannot prevent the decision being challenged by judicial review: see *Plaintiff S157/2002 v Commonwealth* (2003) 211 CLR 476. It also usually results in the challenged decision being invalid ab initio; cf *Project Blue Sky Inc v Australian Broadcasting Authority* (1998) 194 CLR 355 (example of non-jurisdictional error).

156 Justice MJ Beazley, 'Administrative Law and Statutory Interpretation: Room for the Rule of Law?' (2018) 93 *AIAL Forum* 1, 7; cf Will Bateman and Leighton McDonald, 'The Normative Structure of Australian Administrative Law' (2017) 45(2) *Federal Law Review* 153, 179, who tend to lament the rise of the statutory approach. Given that common law principles condition statutory powers presumptively, their criticism seems misplaced or overstated.

157 The authors recognise that the High Court continues to refer to the principles: Will Bateman and Leighton McDonald, 'The Normative Structure of Australian Administrative Law' (2017) 45(2) *Federal Law Review* 153, 156.

158 *Hossain v Minister for Immigration and Border Protection* (2018) 264 CLR 123, 144 [64] (footnotes omitted).

159 Cf Will Bateman and Leighton McDonald, 'The Normative Structure of Australian Administrative Law' (2017) 45(2) *Federal Law Review* 153, 167.

dichotomy.[160] Seeing each principle as a presumption or as a 'default position'[161] explains one part of the implication process. The other part is the examination for any contrary legislative intention. Of course, in some cases the statute may establish a different or more particular condition and in exceptional cases the statute may expressly or impliedly oust the principle altogether.[162]

[32.10] **Other presumptions of law exist in a number of areas**

In addition to presumptions of law dealt with elsewhere in this work,[163] a number of areas of law contain substantive presumptions that, if there is no contrary legislative intention, are impliedly imported into a statutory provision where relevant. They include the 'presumption of law that every person is of sound mind'[164] and the presumption as to when a missing person should be found to be dead.[165]

Common sense

[32.11] **Common sense is a commonplace factor in statutory interpretation, though not always identified as such**

An English judge has said (with deliberate understatement) that 'it is not necessary, in construing a statutory expression, to take leave of one's common sense'.[166] In *Collector of Customs v Agfa-Gevaert Ltd*[167] the High Court unanimously agreed with that observation. It noted that there was nothing new in it, saying, '[a]ppeals to "common-sense" in matters of statutory construction is neither a recent nor uncommon invocation'.[168] Other phrases that are similar to common sense

160 *Plaintiff S10/2011 v Minister for Immigration and Citizenship* (2012) 246 CLR 636, 666 [97] (Gummow, Hayne, Crennan and Bell JJ). For the resolution, see *Minister for Immigration and Border Protection v SZSSJ* (2016) 259 CLR 180, 205 [75] (the Court) (demonstrating that if procedural fairness is implied, this occurs through the application of a 'common law principle of statutory interpretation'). This accommodation of statutory power and common law principle through a statutory interpretation framework was correctly anticipated in Stephen Gageler, 'The Underpinnings of Judicial Review of Administrative Action: Common Law or Constitution?' (2000) 28(2) *Federal Law Review* 303, 312–3.

161 *Minister for Immigration and Citizenship v Li* (2013) 249 CLR 332, 371 [92] (Gageler J), discussing the common law principle of reasonableness.

162 Ibid. For an example of implied exclusion of natural justice, see *Plaintiff S10/2011 v Minister for Immigration and Citizenship* (2012) 246 CLR 636. For discussion of this issue, see Jeffrey Barnes, 'How Statutory Interpretation Sustains Administrative Law' (2015) 22(3) *Australian Journal of Administrative Law* 163, 167–9; Matthew Groves, 'Exclusion of the Rules of Natural Justice' (2013) 39(2) *Monash University Law Review* 285.

163 For the presumption against retrospective operation of legislation, see chapter 39. For the 'presumption of law that mens rea is required before a person can be held guilty of a criminal offence' (*He Kaw Teh v The Queen* (1985) 157 CLR 523, 566–7 (Brennan J, quoting with approval *Gammon Ltd v A-G of Hong Kong* [1985] 1 AC 1, 14 (Lord Scarman)), see chapter 42.

164 *R v Falconer* (1990) 171 CLR 30, 61 (Deane and Dawson JJ).

165 *Axon v Axon* (1937) 59 CLR 395, 405 (Dixon J), 414 (Evatt J).

166 *Exxon Corporation v Exxon Insurance Ltd* [1982] Ch 119, 144 (Oliver LJ), quoted with approval in *Collector of Customs v Agfa-Gevaert Ltd* (1996) 186 CLR 389, 400 (the Court).

167 (1996) 186 CLR 389.

168 Ibid 400 n 43. For other High Court applications of or references to common sense in statutory interpretation, see *Kirk v Industrial Court of New South Wales* (2010) 239 CLR 531, 555 [18] (French CJ, Gummow, Hayne, Crennan, Kiefel and Bell JJ); *Sheahan v Carrier Air Conditioning Pty Ltd* (1997) 189 CLR 407, 441 (Kirby J) (dissenting as to outcome); *Saraswati v The Queen* (1991) 172 CLR 1, 5 (Deane J) (dissenting

include 'common knowledge',[169] 'common experience'[170] and references to good sense.[171] 'Common sense' is presently discussed as a specific interpretative criterion.[172]

Inherently, 'common sense' has, or is assumed to have, an obviously true quality about it.[173] But its deployment in statutory interpretation has possible downsides.[174] Sometimes the concept is simply cited in a conclusory way. What is obvious to the judge is not always obvious to the reader. As the High Court opined in *Wallace v Kam*:[175] 'Resort to "common sense" will ordinarily be of limited utility unless the perceptions or experience informing the sense that is common can be unpacked and explained.'[176]

Because of (as shall be demonstrated) the everyday subject matter with which it deals and the simple, logical reasoning it captures, '[i]t is difficult to overstate the role of common sense in statutory interpretation'.[177] At the same time, because it is often not explicitly referred to in judgments, its use may not be immediately obvious.

Dictionary definitions of common sense are a useful starting point.[178] Cogent appeals to common sense in statutory interpretation can be divided into two broad categories. As a noun, it is an appeal based on knowledge of everyday matters. The *Australian Oxford Dictionary* gives this definition: 'sound practical sense, especially in everyday matters'.[179] In a second adjectival sense it

---

as to outcome). For its use in relation to administrative law principles, see *CRI026 v Republic of Nauru* (2018) 355 ALR 216, 230 [49] (the Court); *Minister for Immigration and Citizenship v Li* (2013) 249 CLR 332, 351 [28] (French CJ). For its deployment in interpreting the *Australian Constitution*, see *Love v Commonwealth* (2020) 270 CLR 152, 287 [392] (Edelman J); *Wong v Commonwealth* (2009) 236 CLR 573, 609 [110] (Kirby J). For English authorities, see *R v Secretary of State for the Home Department; Ex parte Naughton* [1997] 1 WLR 118, 130 (Popplewell J), citing with approval *Barnes v Jarvis* [1953] 1 WLR 649, 652 (Lord Goddard CJ) and David Lowe and Charlie Potter, *Understanding Legislation: A Practical Guide to Statutory Interpretation* (Hart, 2018) 59 [4.2].

169 *Milanes v Minister for Immigration and Border Protection* (2015) 234 FCR 508, 528–9 [122] (Katzmann J).

170 *Pinkstone v The Queen* (2004) 219 CLR 444, 463 [52] (McHugh and Gummow JJ).

171 *ZD v Secretary to the Department of Health and Human Services* [2017] VSC 806, [81] (Osborn JA).

172 This present section is not discussing the issue of whether, or to what extent, *the interpretative criteria of the law of interpretation as a whole* are based on 'common sense'. On this, some commentators are sceptical: see John Basten, 'Construing Statutes Conferring Powers – A Process of Implication or Applying Values?' in Janina Boughey and Lisa Burton Crawford (eds), *Interpreting Executive Power* (Federation Press, 2020) 54, 56; John Basten, 'Legislative Intention' (2019) 93(5) *Australian Law Journal* 367, 367; Neil Duxbury, *Elements of Legislation* (Cambridge University Press, 2013) 139. Cf Justice John Middleton, 'Statutory Interpretation: Mostly Common Sense?' (2016) 40(2) *Melbourne University Law Review* 626: 'In the main [the rules of construction] are based upon common sense, and our constitutional values (which will have varied over time)' (at 637).

173 Ruth Sullivan, *Statutory Interpretation* (Irwin Law, 3rd ed, 2016) 36.

174 See further ibid 37.

175 (2013) 250 CLR 375.

176 Ibid 385 [23] (the Court). Their Honours were discussing the use of 'common sense' in a particular statutory context.

177 Ruth Sullivan, *Statutory Interpretation* (Irwin Law, 3rd ed, 2016) 36.

178 It is a misunderstanding that common sense refers to universally held or inherently held knowledge or reasoning. The *Oxford English Dictionary* (3rd ed, 2016, online at 8 May 2022) states that the 'meanings' of '[n]atural intelligence possessed by a typical person; innate understanding' and '[a] generally held belief or opinion' are all obsolete.

179 The *Australian Oxford Dictionary* (Oxford University Press, 2nd ed, 2004). The *Oxford English Dictionary* (3rd ed, 2016, online) gives a similar meaning: 'Intelligence or sagacity in relation to practical matters arising in everyday life.'

describes a particular way of thinking: 'reasonable, sensible; appealing to or in accordance with instinctive understanding or sound judgement'.[180]

Knowledge of everyday matters that have figured in statutory interpretation cases cover a multitude of matters.[181] They include that a depression in the ground may contain water,[182] the existence of severe chronic illnesses in the community,[183] the use of the internet for forming relationships,[184] the increase of 'domestic partnerships' (de facto relationships) in modern life,[185] how identity cards are used,[186] what is involved in sending a parcel through the post,[187] the properties of some imitation or replica firearms[188] and whether certain countries are English-speaking.[189]

Exercising reasoning powers on a reasonable, sensible basis is often self-evident when courts take account of the likely consequences of a particular construction.[190] Instinctive understanding is evident when the court places itself in the shoes of the audience addressed by the law in question and asks what the audience would take from that law.[191]

Two cases concerning common sense follow. **Example 32.5** illustrates the use of knowledge of everyday matters, while **Example 32.6** illustrates the use of sound judgement.

Example 32.5 *Minister for Immigration and Citizenship v Yucesan*[192]

In this case the question was whether a man who lived in and was a citizen of Turkey was eligible for a Prospective Marriage (Temporary) visa when he had never met in person his fiancee, a Sydney woman (the first respondent). The *Migration Regulations 1994* (Cth) determined eligibility by requiring that the parties to the proposed marriage must 'have met and be known to each other personally'.[193] Counsel for the first respondent argued that it was sufficient that the parties were known to each other personally. The Court agreed that the word 'met' was ambiguous. On the one hand, it might have the meaning of having been in each other's physical presence. In another sense, the Court conceded, 'met' might not require the parties to have been in each other's physical presence. In this regard the Court acknowledged that the internet facilitated people 'meeting' for the first time:

180 *Oxford English Dictionary* (3rd ed, 2016, online at 8 May 2022).

181 For English illustrations, see Oliver Jones, *Bennion on Statutory Interpretation: A Code* (LexisNexis, 6th ed, 2013) 105–7.

182 *Doyle v Maypole Bakery Pty Ltd* [1981] Tas R 376, 378 (**Example 32.1** above).

183 *ZD v Secretary to the Department of Health and Human Services* [2017] VSC 806, [81] (Osborn JA) ('sensibly').

184 *Minister for Immigration and Citizenship v Yucesan* (2008) 169 FCR 202, 207 [17] (the Court).

185 *Scott-Mackenzie v Bail* (2017) 16 ASTLR 449, 461 [47] (the Court).

186 *ABC Developmental Learning Centres Pty Ltd v Secretary, Department of Human Services* (2007) 15 VR 489, 494 [30] (Hollingworth J).

187 *Pinkstone v The Queen* (2004) 219 CLR 444, 463 [52] (McHugh and Gummow JJ) ('common experience').

188 *DPP v Scheele* (2016) 12 ACTLR 1, 10 [43] (the Court).

189 *Milanes v Minister for Immigration and Border Protection* (2015) 234 FCR 508, 528–9 [122] (Katzmann J) ('common knowledge').

190 See **[27.5]**.

191 See *Collector of Customs v Agfa-Gevaert Ltd* (1996) 186 CLR 389, 398–402 (the Court).

192 (2008) 169 FCR 202. See chapters 1, 5.

193 *Migration Regulations 1994* (Cth) cl 300.214.

> [I]t is true that the meaning of words evolves with time and also with technological progress. With the growth of the internet, the comment, 'We met over the internet' would not surprise.[194]

But, for various reasons, the Court preferred the construction that 'met' meant having been in each other's presence.[195]

Example 32.6 *ABC Developmental Learning Centres Pty Ltd v Secretary, Department of Human Services*[196]

In response to certain alleged incidents at two of the plaintiff's child care centres, an authorised officer of the respondent Department requested the head office of the plaintiff company in Brisbane to answer certain questions and provide information. Section 36(1)(f) of the *Children's Services Act 1996* (Vic) ('the Act') stated that an authorised person may require a 'person' to answer a question and provide information for the purpose of ascertaining whether the Act was being complied with.

In the Supreme Court the interpretative question was whether an exercise of the power in s 36(1)(f) could apply to *any* person, as the Department contended, or only a person at the licensed premises at the time of the request, as the company contended.[197] The Court preferred the construction of the company and declared the requests to be invalid.[198]

The commonsensical aspect of the Court's reasoning concerned s 41 of the Act. Under that provision the power in question (s 36(1)(f)) could not be exercised if the authorised officer failed to produce, on request, their identity card 'for the inspection by the occupier of the premises'. The Court reflected: 'One might ask rhetorically: how could s 41 be complied with, if an authorised officer could ask a question by mail, email or over the telephone?'[199] In short, using simple logic that illustrated sound judgement, the Court demonstrated how the presence of s 41 pointed towards the narrow construction put by the company.

194 (2008) 169 FCR 202, 207 [17].
195 Ibid 209 [28].
196 (2007) 15 VR 489.
197 Ibid 493 [18] (Hollingworth J).
198 Ibid 495 [32].
199 Ibid 494 [30].

33 INADMISSIBLE CONSIDERATIONS

Overview

[33.1] Put simply, inadmissible considerations are considerations of a type that ought not be taken into account in statutory interpretation. The reason why such considerations ought not be given any weight is that they do not point to the legislative intention.

This chapter is concerned with considerations that have been found to be inadmissible (other than those dealt with in earlier chapters[1]). A judicial policy, such as a policy of the judge's own making, is not admissible. Additionally, the following executive government sources are not admissible:

- a post-enactment statement by a member of the executive (even if uttered in Parliament) purporting to set out the effect of a law (its meaning);
- delegated legislation, in relation to the interpretation of the Act that authorised it (subject to very limited exceptions); and
- administrative (governmental) processes created after the Act in question was passed.

Finally, a court is not permitted to take into account a matter of speculation.

What makes a consideration inadmissible

[33.2] **Inadmissible considerations are considerations of a type that ought not be taken into account**

Put simply, the law of interpretation consists of the principles that may be taken into account, and the methods by which an interpretation is reached, in arriving at the intention of Parliament or the legal meaning of statutory provisions in question. The principles have been more accurately described as 'the interpretative criteria',[2] and more loosely as so-called rules of interpretation. Indications of meaning in a particular statutory and factual context that are derived from such criteria, or are applications of them, are called 'interpretative factors'. By contrast, inadmissible considerations are purportedly lawful considerations, not supported by or derived from the interpretative criteria of the law. At a general level, inadmissible considerations are of a type that ought not be taken into account. On the face of it, such considerations are endless, since they are

1 Inadmissible considerations discussed elsewhere in this work are the following: statements of meaning in Hansard, and in other parliamentary materials accompanying or associated with the Bill that became the Act in question (chapter 24); international agreements entered into after the Act in question has been passed (chapter 31). Inadmissible evidence in relation to a word used in a statute in accordance with its ordinary English meaning is discussed in **[18.6](d)**.

2 At **[1.2]**, **[9.6]**.

in theory all the possible considerations beyond the interpretative criteria. For convenience this chapter is concerned with considerations that from time to time are wrongly assumed to be relevant.

The reason why certain considerations are inadmissible is that they do not point to the legislative intention [33.3]

To be admitted as an interpretative criterion of the law, a criterion must have the potential to point to the legislative intention in an objective way. This is because ascertaining the legislative intention is 'the duty of a court'[3] and '[t]he fundamental object of statutory construction'.[4] On a number of occasions courts have rejected arguments about the meaning of legislative provisions for the reason that they were based on considerations of a type that could not be reasonably attributed to the legislature.

In *Harrison v Melhem*[5] the Court of Appeal of the NSW Supreme Court rejected the relevance, under both the common law and the *Interpretation Act 1987* (NSW),[6] of a statement of meaning made by a Minister in the course of a second reading speech.[7] It did so because the subjective intention of Ministers or parliamentarians is not relevant to the task of ascertaining the objective intention of Parliament.[8]

Another illustration relates to international treaties and conventions.[9] Kiefel J (as her Honour then was) has held that 'a statute is to be interpreted and applied, so far as its language permits, so that it is in conformity, and not in conflict, with *established* rules of international law'.[10] Earlier, in *Coleman v Power*,[11] Gleeson CJ considered the proposition that an international treaty to which Australia is a party is a relevant consideration when the treaty was entered into *after* the relevant Act was passed. The Chief Justice used the concept of legislative intention to critique the proposition. He found it difficult to reconcile the proposition with the duty to give effect to the legislative intention.[12]

3 *Project Blue Sky Inc v Australian Broadcasting Authority* (1998) 194 CLR 355, 384 [78] (McHugh, Gummow, Kirby and Hayne JJ).

4 *Cooper Brookes (Wollongong) Pty Ltd v Commissioner of Taxation (Cth)* (1981) 147 CLR 297, 320 (Mason and Wilson JJ); *Certain Lloyd's Underwriters v Cross* (2012) 248 CLR 378, 411 [88] (Kiefel J). See further chapter 4.

5 (2008) 72 NSWLR 380.

6 Ibid 401 [172] (Mason P, Spigelman CJ agreeing at 382 [1], Beazley JA generally agreeing at 403 [191], Giles JA agreeing at 403 [192]). For other authorities see chapter 24.

7 Ibid 399 [162], 401 [172] (Mason P, Spigelman CJ agreeing at 382 [1], Beazley JA generally agreeing at 403 [191], Giles JA agreeing at 403 [192]). Mason P's views were dicta: at 398 [157] (viii). Accepting the views in *Harrison*, a statement of meaning is not necessarily irrelevant. It can still be used for the purpose of inferring the mischief or the purpose, as the High Court did in *Berenguel v Minister for Immigration and Citizenship* (2010) 264 ALR 417, 422 [21] (the Court); see further chapter 24 and the discussion of that case in Jeffrey Barnes, 'Contextualism: The "Modern Approach to Statutory Interpretation"' (2018) 41(4) *University of New South Wales Law Journal* 1083, 1097-9.

8 (2008) 72 NSWLR 380, 384 [14] (Spigelman CJ), citing *Eastman v The Queen* (2000) 203 CLR 1, 46 [146]–[147] (McHugh J). See also Mason P at 398–9 [159]–[160] (Spigelman CJ agreeing at 382 [1], Beazley JA generally agreeing at 403 [191], Giles JA agreeing at 403 [192]).

9 See chapter 31.

10 *Plaintiff M70/2011 v Minister for Immigration and Citizenship* (2011) 244 CLR 144, 234 [247] (emphasis added).

11 (2004) 220 CLR 1.

12 Ibid 28 [19]. See chapter 31 for other authorities on the circumstances when international agreements are admissible.

Judicial policy

[33.4] A judicially constructed policy is not admissible

In developing and maintaining the law of interpretation the courts are obliged to respect underlying constitutional principles.[13] If a court had a freewheeling power to consider policy considerations in interpreting legislation, such as policy of its own making, '[t]he reciprocal functions of legislation by Parliament and interpretation by the courts could hardly be separated'.[14]

Also, to accord with the rule of law, a court needs to apply statutory and common law principles of interpretation in interpreting the law, by reason that the principles of interpretation are part of the law of the land.[15] As courts are allowed to base their decisions on law only, policies and preferences that are not recognised in law are not admissible.

As a consequence, 'in the interpretation of statutes, judicial policy is alien to the task of exegesis'.[16] A judicial policy (contrasted with a legislative policy[17]) is one that is 'judicially constructed':

> This approach, with respect, emphasised a judicially constructed policy at the expense of the requisite consideration of the statutory text and its relatively clear purpose. In construing a statute it is not for a court to construct its own idea of a desirable policy, impute it to the legislature, and then characterise it as a statutory purpose.[18]

A judicially constructed policy is not admissible either as evidence of a statutory purpose[19] or to support a finding as to legislative intention.[20] It is not sufficient for a court purportedly to impute the policy to Parliament – that is, for it to *say* the 'purpose' is a legislative purpose.[21]

The High Court has similarly warned about making 'a priori'[22] assumptions about purpose:

> A second and not unrelated danger that must be avoided in identifying a statute's purpose is the making of some *a priori* assumption about its purpose. The purpose of legislation

13 See generally chapter 3.

14 *Barker v Campbell* (1983) 153 CLR 52, 104 (Brennan J), approved in *Australian Education Union v Department of Education and Children's Services* (2012) 248 CLR 1, 14 [28] (French CJ, Hayne, Kiefel and Bell JJ).

15 *Electrolux Home Products Pty Ltd v Australian Workers' Union* (2004) 221 CLR 309, 329 [21] (Gleeson CJ), approved in *Saeed v Minister for Immigration and Citizenship* (2010) 241 CLR 252, 259 [15] (French CJ, Gummow, Hayne, Crennan and Kiefel JJ); *Building Construction Employees v Minister for Industrial Relations* (1986) 7 NSWLR 372, 405–6 (Kirby P). See further **[1.2]**.

16 *Theophanous v Herald & Weekly Times Ltd* (1994) 182 CLR 104, 143 (Brennan J). His Honour acknowledged that in the development of the common law judicial policy had a limited role: ibid.

17 Ibid.

18 *Australian Education Union v Department of Education and Children's Services* (2012) 248 CLR 1, 14 [28] (French CJ, Hayne, Kiefel and Bell JJ). This holding was applied in *Williams v Wreck Bay Aboriginal Community Council* (2019) 266 CLR 499, 527 [79] (Kiefel CJ, Keane, Nettle and Gordon JJ).

19 *Australian Education Union v Department of Education and Children's Services* (2012) 248 CLR 1, 14 [28] (French CJ, Hayne, Kiefel and Bell JJ).

20 *Sovar v Henry Lane Pty Ltd* (1967) 116 CLR 397, 405 (Kitto J, Owen J agreeing at 417), approved in *Australian Education Union v Department of Education and Children's Services* (2012) 248 CLR 1, 14 [28] (French CJ, Hayne, Kiefel and Bell JJ).

21 *Australian Education Union v Department of Education and Children's Services* (2012) 248 CLR 1, 14 [28] (French CJ, Hayne, Kiefel and Bell JJ).

22 'A priori' relevantly means 'reasoning or arguing . . . from propositions or assumed axioms (and not from experience)' (*Oxford English Dictionary* [2021, online]); 'claiming to report matters of fact but actually not supported by factual study' (*Macquarie Dictionary* [online]).

> must be derived from what the legislation says, and not from any assumption about the desired or desirable reach or operation of the relevant provisions.[23]

The above restrictions make plain that the taking into account of 'public policy' in statutory interpretation is much more limited than it is in the development of the common law.[24] As noted by Derrington J, '[t]he primary "policy" to be adopted in the interpretation of legislation is that emerging (expressly or impliedly) from the enactment itself'.[25]

In this regard the High Court and other appellate courts have criticised lower courts in a number of areas. In anti-discrimination law a court cannot apply policy, which may have been considered prior to the enactment of the Act in question, where that policy is not reflected in the Act.[26] And in the migration arena a court cannot allow its view of what are appropriate requirements for a visa to influence the result, at the expense of the stated requirements, properly interpreted.[27]

The same kind of restrictions apply to counsel in the making of submissions on how a particular Act ought to be interpreted. Counsel cannot, under the guise of interpretation, effectively ask the court to construct its own policy. For instance, when there is no evidence that the Act in question was based on any particular overseas legislative model, an argument by counsel that its construction is supported by international regulatory practice in overseas jurisdictions is not relevant. It is not a question of how much weight the material should be accorded. The material simply 'does not assist'[28] and relying on it is an 'invalid approach'.[29]

Example 33.1 *Australian Education Union v Department of Education and Children's Services*[30]

For many years the Minister of Education of South Australia appointed persons as temporary 'contract teachers' purportedly under a general power to appoint 'officers and employees' conferred by s 9(4) of the *Education Act 1972* (SA) ('the Act'):

> The Minister may appoint such officers and employees (in addition to the employees and officers of the Department and the teaching service) as he considers necessary for the proper administration of this Act or for the welfare of the students of any school.

The Australian Education Union contended that the only mechanism that the Act provided for the appointment of teachers was the one found in s 15 of the Act, which at the relevant time stated:

> (1) Subject to this Act, the Minister may appoint such teachers to be officers of the teaching service as he thinks fit.
> (2) An officer may be so appointed on a permanent or temporary basis.

---

23 *Certain Lloyd's Underwriters v Cross* (2012) 248 CLR 378, 390 [26] (French CJ and Hayne J) (emphasis added). See further chapter 8, esp **[8.5]**. For a case on an a priori assumption about meaning see *Perera-Cathcart v The Queen* (2017) 260 CLR 595, 613–4 [40] (Kiefel, Bell and Keane JJ).

24 *HZCP v Minister for Immigration and Border Protection* (2019) 273 FCR 121, 156 [144] (Derrington J) (dissenting as to outcome).

25 Ibid. As an example, his Honour cited s 15AA of the *Acts Interpretation Act 1901* (Cth).

26 *AB v Western Australia* (2011) 244 CLR 390, 406 [38] (the Court).

27 *Minister for Immigration and Citizenship v Yucesan* (2008) 169 FCR 202, 205 [7], 209 [28] (the Court).

28 *Mansfield v The Queen* (2012) 247 CLR 86, 100 [50] (Hayne, Crennan, Kiefel and Bell JJ).

29 Ibid 106 [75] (Heydon J).

30 (2012) 248 CLR 1.

...

(5) No officer appointed on a permanent basis (other than an officer appointed on probation) shall be dismissed or retired from the teaching service except in accordance with the provisions of this Act.

(6) An officer appointed on a temporary basis or appointed on probation shall hold office at the pleasure of the Minister.

The significance of the dispute over the relevant power was that the long service leave entitlements of officers and employees appointed under s 9(4) were less favourable than the entitlements enjoyed by officers of the teaching service appointed under s 15.

The dispute was referred by the Industrial Relations Commission of South Australia to the Industrial Relations Court of South Australia ('the IRC'). Two judges held that s 15 did not necessarily give the Minister all of the flexibility necessary to fulfil the Minister's obligations under the Act, and pt III of the Act (which contained s 15) conferred detailed rights on members of the teaching service that might be thought unnecessarily prescriptive in respect of the ad hoc appointment of relief teachers in diverse circumstances. On appeal to the Supreme Court of South Australia, as found by the High Court, the Supreme Court justices

> emphasised what their Honours considered to be the benefits flowing from the Minister's construction of s 9(4). Those benefits, expressed in terms of flexibility, were elevated to a statutory purpose.

The High Court did not find the above reasoning of the IRC and the Supreme Court relevant. As to the IRC's reasoning the High Court described it as emphasising a 'judicially constructed policy'.[31] Similarly, it found that the argument of the Supreme Court was not correct. The High Court held that the 'purpose' referred to 'lacked a foundation in the text of the Act'.[32] Upholding the Union's contention, the High Court held that '[t]he textual and contextual indicators and the purpose of the statutory scheme lead to the conclusion that the authority of the Minister to appoint teachers under the Act was at all times to be found in s 15 and that s 9(4) did not authorise such appointments'.[33]

Certain executive government sources

[33.5] **Post-enactment statements by members of the executive about the effect of a law (even if uttered by Ministers in Parliament) are not of themselves of assistance to a court or tribunal**

(a) Ministerial statements in Parliament

Unless Parliament otherwise provides,[34] post-enactment statements by a member of the executive government about the effect of a law, even if uttered by Ministers during the course of parliamentary proceedings in Parliament, are not an admissible aid in court or tribunal

31 Ibid 14 [28] (French CJ, Hayne, Kiefel and Bell JJ).

32 Ibid 14 [29].

33 Ibid 15 [31].

34 Exceptionally, Parliament may give a statement of ministerial or governmental 'policy' legal force. Examples are *Tasmanian Development Act 1983* (Tas) s 11(1); *Transport Integration Act 2010* (Vic) ss 22, 23(d); *Victorian Civil and Administrative Tribunal Act 1998* (Vic) s 57; and the (now repealed) *Broadcasting Services Act 1992* (Cth) s 160(b) that was considered in *Project Blue Sky Inc v Australian Broadcasting Authority* (1998)

proceedings.[35] The High Court has not followed the *Chevron* doctrine in the United States of America in according weight, let alone deference, to executive government opinions as to the meaning of statutory provisions.[36]

A leading case in which the matter was squarely raised is *Australian Education Union v Department of Education and Children's Services* (**Example 33.1** above). That case, it will be recalled, concerned the interpretation of ss 9(4) and 15 of the *Education Act 1972* (SA). In this case the Solicitor-General for South Australia submitted that the Court should have regard to a statement made by the Minister in the second reading speech for the Bill, which upon enactment became the *Education (Part-time Remuneration) Amendment Act 1991* (SA). In the course of his speech the Minister referred to 'casual teachers who, unlike the permanent teachers appointed under section 15 of the Education Act ("officers of the teaching service"), are engaged under contracts of service pursuant to section 9(4) of the Act'. The Court refused to consider the material, stating: 'There is no basis at common law or otherwise for resorting to a ministerial statement, about the effect of a law in force at the time of the statement, as an aid to the interpretation of that law.'[37]

Two points may be made about the High Court's statement. First, the Court's prohibition extended to a statement as to the *effect* of a law. Here the Court is referring to the legal effect of a law, or in short, its legal meaning. The Court is not, of course, ruling on *arguments* by the executive government as to the meaning of a law. The Court's ruling is restricted to the admissibility of a bare statement of the meaning or effect of the law in question. Second, the words 'or otherwise' suggest the Court was holding that the same result would occur if legislation governing extrinsic materials (rather than the common law) was purportedly relied on.

Other High Court cases support and explain the law behind the ruling in *Australian Education Union*.[38] In *Dossett v TKJ Nominees Pty Ltd*[39] a party tendered an extract from a speech to the Legislative Assembly of Western Australia. The speech had been made 16 days after the relevant law had been enacted. The Minister made the statement, she so thought, to clarify the law. The reasons for judgment of McHugh J are notable for the explanation of why such speeches are not admissible:

> There is no requirement in the law of Western Australia that a court should give any special weight to a Minister's opinion concerning the meaning of legislation that has been enacted by the Legislature. And it would be contrary to the rule of law, the supremacy of Parliament and the doctrine of the separation of powers to give any special weight to a Minister's opinion as to what an enacted law meant.[40]

---

194 CLR 355, 384 [79], 385 [81] (McHugh, Gummow, Kirby and Hayne JJ). Unpublished government policies also may be given legal force in certain circumstances: see, eg, *Freedom of Information Act 1982* (Cth) s 10.

35 The treatment of statements of meaning made in the course of parliamentary debates or in documents accompanying or associated with a Bill is the subject of chapter 24.

36 See discussion of *Chevron USA Inc v Natural Resources Defense Council Inc*, 467 US 837 (1984) in **[5.2]**. The discussion of that case in *Corporation of the City of Enfield v Development Assessment Commission* (2000) 199 CLR 135 was dicta.

37 (2012) 248 CLR 1, 16 [33].

38 See also *Hunter Resources Ltd v Melville* (1988) 164 CLR 234, 241 (Mason CJ and Gaudron J), 245 (Wilson J). Wilson J dissented as to the outcome.

39 (2003) 218 CLR 1. The speech is extracted at 20 [67]–[68] (Kirby J).

40 Ibid 6 [10]. The use of the word 'special' is unfortunate. It is most unlikely that his Honour intended to give the statement *any* weight. This would be consistent with his emphatic reference to constitutional principles, and in the light of other High Court authorities that are clearly against giving weight to post-enactment statements of meaning.

(b) **Opinions by other members of the executive government**

Opinions as to the effect of a law, uttered by other members of the executive government, are also of no weight as far as a court is concerned. For instance, a legal opinion of a statutory agency or of a Crown Solicitor receives no weight.[41] Similarly, unless an Act indicates otherwise, a departmental policy that interprets the law carries no weight. As the Full Federal Court said in a case involving Child Support Agency guidelines:

> The primary judge was correct to say that the CSA ['Child Support Agency'] guidelines are not a permissible aid to the construction of the CSA Act ['the *Child Support (Assessment) Act 1989* (Cth)'].[42]

The impact of these authorities has been felt in the work of the Administrative Appeals Tribunal. Early in its history, in the well-known case of *Re Drake and Minister for Immigration and Ethnic Affairs (No 2)*,[43] the President of the Tribunal, Brennan J, propounded a 'general practice' of ordinarily applying a ministerial policy guiding the exercise of a discretionary power.[44] But the Tribunal has subsequently pointed out that a 'policy' document may set out an interpretation of the law.[45] In this light the Federal Court has redrawn the *Drake* doctrine. It has stated that the *Drake case* 'does not suggest ... that guidelines or policy documents which express a view about the scope or meaning of legislation provide a tool or aid in construing the legislation'.[46] In the words of the Tribunal the general practices propounded in *Drake* 'do *not* apply to the interpretation of the enactment conferring the discretionary power'.[47]

---

41 *South Australia v Lampard-Trevorrow* (2010) 106 SASR 331, 377 [217] (the Court).

42 *P v Child Support Registrar* (2014) 225 FCR 378, 391 [49] (the Court). See also *Port of Brisbane Corporation v Commissioner of Taxation* (2004) 140 FCR 375, 386 [26] (Moore J).

43 (1979) 2 ALD 634.

44 Ibid 645. An exception was if 'the policy was unlawful or ... its application tends to produce an unjust decision in the circumstances of the particular case': at 645. The *Drake* case was subsequently applied to departmental policy.

45 *Re Sapronov and Minister for Immigration and Citizenship* (2011) 120 ALD 362, 376 [61] (Fice SM). This case concerned the Australian Citizenship Instructions, which purport to 'provide guidance on policy in relation to the interpretation of, and the exercise of powers under, the Act and the Regulations': at 376 [61]. See also *P v Child Support Registrar* (2014) 225 FCR 378, which concerned the Child Support Guide. The Guide purports to contain 'some hints on how to interpret difficult clauses and commonly used expressions': <https://guides.dss.gov.au/child-support-guide>.

46 *Port of Brisbane Corporation v Commissioner of Taxation* (2004) 140 FCR 375, 386 [26] (Moore J).

47 *Barrie and Minister for Immigration, Citizenship, Migrant Services and Multicultural Affairs (Citizenship)* [2020] AATA 287, [36] (Forgie DP) (emphasis in original). For other applications of the *Port of Brisbane* principle in the Tribunal, see *Burchell and National Disability Insurance Agency* [2019] AATA 1256, [50] (Rayment DP); *Fei and Minister for Immigration and Border Protection (Citizenship)* [2016] AATA 624, [42] (Webb M); *Re Sapronov and Minister for Immigration and Citizenship* (2011) 120 ALD 362, 376 [61] (Fice SM); *Re Petroulias and Commissioner of Taxation* (2010) 122 ALD 153, 161 [35] (Britton SM); *Re Rebmik Contractors Pty Ltd and Commissioner of Taxation* (2008) 101 ALD 445, 448 [15] (Fice M); *Kay and Child Support Registrar* [2015] AATA 429, [33] (Forgie DP and Cremean SM); *Re Kumar and Minister for Immigration and Citizenship* (2009) 107 ALD 178, 200–1 [79] (Forgie DP). The Tribunal has noted that departmental officers are free to develop an interpretation *for themselves*: *Re Sapronov and Minister for Immigration and Citizenship* (2011) 120 ALD 362, 376 [61] (Fice SM).

The above principles apply to published policy,[48] such as an Excise Bulletin published by the Australian Taxation Office,[49] Diesel Fuel Rebate Scheme Eligibility Guidelines published by the Commissioner of Taxation[50] and the Child Support Guide published by the Child Support Agency.[51] In other words, the fact that an executive government interpretation of legislation is officially published does not give it legal status for the purpose of interpreting the law on which the government seeks to advise.

Except in limited circumstances, delegated legislation cannot be used to construe a statute [33.6]

(a) As a general rule, delegated legislation cannot be used to construe a statute

Subject to limited exceptions discussed below, delegated legislation made under an Act is not admissible to construe the Act. This general principle is long-standing[52] and has been confirmed by the High Court:

> The regulations ... cannot be used to construe, and thereby to alter, provisions of the Act which created them.[53]

A rationale for the principle is hinted at in the above statement – since delegated legislation is the product of a statute, it is not suitable material with which to construe the statute. Another reason for the principle is to respect the separation of powers. Speaking of regulations, the Full Court of the Supreme Court of South Australia has observed that 'regulations are made by the Executive Government based on *its* determination of the scope of the statute and the regulation-making power'.[54]

It has been held that it is also impermissible to read down a provision of an Act 'to avoid what [the judge] thought were the incongruous or irrational consequences of [the provision of the Act] on the Regulations made by the government'.[55]

---

48 For critical commentaries see Janina Boughey, 'The Case for "Deference" to (Some) Executive Interpretations of Law' in Janina Boughey and Lisa Burton Crawford (eds), *Interpreting Executive Power* (Federation Press, 2020) 34; John McMillan, 'Statutory Interpretation and Deference: An Executive Perspective' in Janina Boughey and Lisa Burton Crawford (eds), *Interpreting Executive Power* (Federation Press, 2020) 24. The latter argues for less aversion to the views expressed by a domestic executive agency, partly on the ground that '[i]t is commonplace that courts refer to and rely upon views expressed about statutory meaning by foreign courts, international bodies, text writers and legal commentators': at 33. The writer does not cite any authorities and, in its reference to text writers and legal commentators, the argument is not persuasive. Text writers and legal commentators enjoy no status as authorities on the meaning of statutory expressions – see the research at **[32.4]**. It is true that the opinions of foreign courts and international bodies may receive weight if the text they interpret is relevant and comparable, but such bodies are interpreting other texts and their interpretations are not potentially self-serving as are executive interpretations. See also **[33.7]** and **Example 33.4**.

49 *Port of Brisbane Corporation v Commissioner of Taxation* (2004) 140 FCR 375.

50 *Re Rebmik Contractors Pty Ltd and Commissioner of Taxation* (2008) 101 ALD 445.

51 *P v Child Support Registrar* (2014) 225 FCR 378.

52 *The Great Fingall Consolidated Ltd v Sheehan* (1905) 3 CLR 176, 184 (Griffith CJ, Barton J agreeing at 190, O'Connor J agreeing at 190).

53 *Wallaby Grip Ltd v QBE Insurance (Australia) Ltd* (2010) 240 CLR 444 [21] (the Court). See also *Master Education Services Pty Ltd v Ketchell* (2008) 236 CLR 101, 110 [19] (the Court).

54 *Dietman v Brennan-Kuss* (2015) 123 SASR 24, 38 [45] (Kourakis CJ, Bampton J agreeing at 40 [55], Muecke DCJ agreeing at 40 [56]) (emphasis added).

55 Ibid 38 [47].

Example 33.2 *Tom and Bill Waterhouse Pty Ltd v Racing New South Wales*[56]

The plaintiff, a bookmaker licensed by Racing NSW to operate in respect of races conducted in New South Wales, sought a declaration from the NSW Supreme Court that the way it conducted its business did not require it to apply to Racing NSW for an approval under an amendment to the *Racing Administration Act 1998* (NSW) ('the Act'). Racing NSW contended to the contrary. As amended, s 33 of the Act provided:

> **33 Publication of NSW race fields restricted**
>
> A person must not, whether in New South Wales or elsewhere, publish a NSW race field unless the person:
>
> (a) is authorised to do so by a race field publication approval and complies with the conditions (if any) to which the approval is subject, or
> (b) is authorised to do so by or under the regulations.

Breach of the provision was punishable by a fine or imprisonment: s 33. A fee may be payable as a condition of a grant of approval: s 33A.

One of the issues in the case concerned the meaning of 'publish'. The issue arose because the defendant contended that it meant communicate to *any* person, whether inside or outside the plaintiff company. Hence, on that construction, communication of information relating to a race field among directors and staff of the plaintiff constituted a publication, and a fee was payable if approval was to be granted. The plaintiff contended that 'publish' meant communicate to the world at large, or at least to a person outside the plaintiff company.

In the course of submissions the defendant contended that support for its construction of 'publish' was to be found in exemptions provided for by reg 15(1)(b) of the *Racing Administration Regulation 2005* (NSW) ('the Regulation'), as authorised by s 33(b) of the Act (emphasis added):

> **15 Authorisations to publish NSW race fields: s 33(b)**
>
> (1) The following publications of NSW race fields, whether in New South Wales or elsewhere, are authorised:
>
> ...
>
> (b) a publication by any of the following bodies for its internal administrative or regulatory purposes:
> (i) a relevant racing control body,
> (ii) a body that corresponds to a relevant racing control body under the legislation of another State or Territory,
> (iii) the Australian Racing Board,
> (iv) Harness Racing Australia Inc.,
> (v) Greyhounds Australasia Limited,
>
> ...

The defendant submitted that, by its reference to 'internal administrative or regulatory purposes', the Regulation indicated that, but for such exemption, such internal uses would be publications within the meaning of s 33.

56 (2008) 72 NSWLR 577.

In interpreting that section of the Act, the Court gave no weight to the Regulation.[57] Among its reasons was that delegated legislation was not usually to be invoked to construe words used in the principal legislation (the Act), unless the Act and regulations together formed a cohesive, unified scheme. This was not such a case.[58]

(b) An exception to the general rule against the admissibility of delegated legislation in construing an Act arises in respect of identifying the nature of a legislative scheme

Mason J (as he then was) observed that '[o]ne looks at regulations, not to construe an overall scheme or to throw light on ambiguity in a statutory provision, but to ascertain what the scheme is'.[59] This pithy observation was approved of by the High Court in *Master Education Services Pty Ltd v Ketchell*,[60] where the Court stated that '[i]t may be useful to read together regulations and the Act with which they were made, in order to identify the nature of a legislative scheme which they comprise'.[61]

Examples of the exception were given by Kourakis CJ in *Dietman v Brennan-Kuss*.[62] He mentioned how '[a] consideration of both the Act and the regulations made thereunder may be necessary properly to understand the scope and elements of an offence which is created by the joint operation of a statutory provision and regulations'.[63]

In addition, on 'very rare occasions'[64] it might not be possible to understand the policy underlying an entire Act without identifying and taking account of the scheme created by the joint operation of the Act and delegated legislation. In such a case, as noted in the *Dietman* case, the delegated legislation necessarily assists in the interpretative process: '[T]he legislative policy so elucidated might then aid in the construction of the statute.'[65] An example is *Deputy Federal Commissioner of Taxation (SA) v Ellis & Clark Ltd*.[66] In that case Dixon J (Rich J agreeing) found it necessary to use the regulations to understand the legislative policy behind the scheme created jointly by the Sales Tax Assessment Acts and the regulations made thereunder. He found as follows:

> [T]he legislation depends in a remarkable degree upon the regulations made under the power which it confers on the Executive. Without the regulations, not only is it unworkable, but the expression of legislative policy is so inadequate as almost to be unintelligible.[67]

---

57 Ibid 590 [41] (Palmer J).

58 Ibid 590–1 [41]–[44].

59 *Brayson Motors Pty Ltd (in liq) v Commissioner of Taxation (Cth)* (1985) 156 CLR 651, 652.

60 (2008) 236 CLR 101.

61 Ibid 110 [19] (the Court).

62 (2015) 123 SASR 24, 37–8 [42]–[44] (Bampton J agreeing at 40 [55], Muecke DCJ agreeing at 40 [56]).

63 Ibid 37 [42]. See **Example 33.3**.

64 Ibid 37 [43].

65 Ibid.

66 (1934) 52 CLR 85.

67 Ibid 89 (Rich J agreeing at 87).

Example 33.3 *Turner v Keegan*[68]

The respondent was charged with failing to keep four rounds of ammunition secured separately from a firearm, contrary to the provisions of s 23(9)(d)(ii) of the *Firearms Act 1973* (WA) ('the Act'). Section 23(9) read as follows (emphasis added):

> (9) A person who, –
>
> . . .
>
> (d) being responsible for the storage of any firearm or ammunition, fails –
>
> . . .
>
> (ii) where prescribed requirements as to security are specified in relation to a firearm or ammunition *of a prescribed kind*, to ensure that those requirements are observed;
>
> . . . commits an offence.

The reference to 'prescribed kind' was taken up in the *Firearms Regulations 1974* (WA) ('the Regulations'). Regulation 11A provided (emphasis added):

> **11A** (1) A person entitled to possess *firearms or ammunition of any kind* is to ensure that the firearms or ammunition are stored in accordance with this regulation.
>
> . . .
>
> (8) Ammunition is not to be stored in a cabinet or container in which a firearm is stored unless the ammunition is in another locked metal container in which no firearm is stored and which is securely affixed so as to prevent its removal from the cabinet or container.

The issue was the scope of s 23(9)(d)(ii): did 'prescribed kind' mean *something less* than all firearms or ammunition (the respondent/defendant's construction) or did it allow prescription of *all* kinds of firearms and ammunition (as had purportedly occurred under reg 11A(1)) (the appellant's construction)? The respondent argued (as the Magistrate had held) that no offence could be committed if no lawful prescription under s 23(9)(d)(ii) had occurred.

The Supreme Court observed that the offence was created by the joint operation of the Act and the Regulations:

> it being at all material times understood that the offence alleged was created by the provisions of s 23(9)(d)(ii) of the Act when read in conjunction with the provisions of reg 11A(8) of the Regulations.[69]

The Court agreed with the appellant's submission that it was open to the legislature to prescribe by reg 11A(1) all firearms and/or ammunition within the meaning of s 23(9)(d)(ii) of the Act.[70] The Court directed a verdict of conviction be entered.[71]

(c) A further exception arises in relation to 'Henry VIII' clauses: statutory provisions that authorise the making of delegated legislation that amends the empowering Act

A peculiar type of joint operation of an Act and delegated legislation is facilitated by a statutory provision, pejoratively called a 'Henry VIII' clause. This is a clause in an Act 'authorising delegated

68 [2001] WASCA 9.

69 Ibid [1] (Miller J).

70 Ibid [17].

71 Ibid [18].

legislation which may be inconsistent with, or amend, the empowering statute'.[72] The High Court has observed that although 'frequently criticised for good reason', they have been upheld in a number of cases.[73] These provisions are considered further in this work in chapter 43 **[43.9]**.

Where a government agency, based on its own interpretation of an Act that it administers, creates administrative processes to administer the Act, the agency cannot then point to those administrative processes as support for its interpretation [33.7]

A government agency may, based on its own interpretation of an Act that it administers, set up administrative processes for dealing with the operation of a provision of the Act. As mentioned above, the government's post-enactment interpretation of the Act is accorded no weight in the courts.[74] It follows, as **Example 33.4** illustrates, that, on the assumption that Parliament did not legislate in the knowledge of such administrative processes, the processes themselves are not admissible in the interpretation of the provision concerned.

Example 33.4 *Barnes v Victoria*[75]

In this case the Court of Appeal of the Supreme Court of Victoria was asked to determine the meaning of 'agree to the request' in s 49(2)(a) of the *Disability Act 2006* (Vic), set out below:

> **49 Request for disability services**
>
> (1) A person with a disability or a person on behalf of a person with a disability may request disability services from a disability service provider.
>
> (2) If a disability service provider receives a request under subsection (1), the disability service provider may –
>
> (a) agree to the request; or
>
> (b) refuse the request.

The applicant, who had been diagnosed with primary progressive multiple sclerosis, made a request for disability services. The Secretary to the Department of Health and Human Services (Victoria) eventually wrote to the applicant, stating:

> I can confirm that DHS Disability Services agrees to the request ... in accordance with section 49(2) of the Disability Act 2006, and have placed the need for the additional individual support package on the Disability Support Register (DSR). As you are aware, registration on the DSR does not result in the automatic allocation of a resource, however you will be considered along with others who have a registered need for this support.

The Court summed up the rival contentions as to meaning. The applicant contended that

> when a disability service provider 'agrees' to a request to provide disability services, it takes a step for which the Act specifically provides, and the statutory agreement is binding in nature. The disability service provider falls under a duty to comply with the request as agreed.

72 *ADCO Constructions Pty Ltd v Goudappel* (2014) 254 CLR 1, 6 [2] n 1 (French CJ, Crennan, Kiefel and Keane JJ).

73 Ibid 16 [31].

74 See **[33.5]**.

75 [2015] VSCA 343.

In opposing that contention, the Secretary effectively contended that 'agreeing to a request creates no statutory duty but only indicates assent to a proposal, in effect indicating the disability service provider's preparedness to provide the services requested, but no more'.[76]

The Court preferred the Secretary's construction.[77] But the Court did not agree with all of the Secretary's arguments. The Secretary had drawn the Court's attention to documents setting out policies and procedures by which the Department handles requests for disability services. The nature of the documents was outlined as follows:

> Consistently with s 8(2)(d), these documents are directed to determining priority of access to disability services. The documents describe the operation of the 'Disability Services Register'. This register is an administrative tool, not provided for under the Act, by which the Secretary records those requests for disability services to which she has agreed under s 49(2)(a). As the correspondence with the applicant indicated, the recording of a request on the register is not treated as entitling the person in question to receive the relevant services.

The Secretary submitted that these arrangements, and the processes for which these documents provide, reflect the fact that the demand for disability services exceeds available funding and that the executive government must determine how the funding should be allocated. Section 9 of the Act confirms this as the role of the Secretary.

The Court assessed the argument based on the department's administrative arrangements against the paramount duty of a court to give effect to the intention of Parliament. The Court found that acceding to the argument would not assist in identifying that intention:

> [T]he administrative processes are founded upon the Department's interpretation of s 49. There is no suggestion that Parliament legislated in the knowledge of such processes or in the expectation that they would be applied. As such, the evidence as to how the Department applies s 49 falls well short of identifying 'the intention manifested by the legislation', and is ultimately self-serving.[78]

Speculative matters

[33.8] Matters of speculation are not admissible

In determining whether there is present in a statutory context an interpretative factor that points to one of the competing constructions, a judge examines whether there is material or evidence to support the drawing of the appropriate inference.[79] According to Dixon CJ, an inference is 'a deduction which may reasonably be drawn from [the established facts]'. If 'the state of facts inferred leaves room for conflicting conjectures or hypotheses', it will not be appropriate for a court to draw an inference.[80]

---

76 Ibid [53] (the Court).

77 Ibid [54].

78 Ibid [46]. The Court quoted *Saeed v Minister for Immigration and Citizenship* (2010) 241 CLR 252, 264 [31] (French CJ, Gummow, Hayne, Crennan and Kiefel JJ), who in turn cited *Wik Peoples v Queensland* (1996) 187 CLR 1, 168–9 (Gummow J).

79 See, eg, *R v A2* (2019) 269 CLR 507, 549 [134] (Bell and Gageler JJ) (dissenting) (mischief); *Berenguel v Minister for Immigration and Citizenship* (2010) 264 ALR 417, 422 [21] (the Court) (legislative purpose).

80 *Holloway v McFeeters* (1956) 94 CLR 470, 476–7 (Dixon CJ, dissenting as to outcome).

For example, let us assume that the meaning of a provision of Act A (the unit of inquiry) is in issue. The question is whether a decision made under the unit of inquiry is subject to the provisions of Act B. Now Act B has a provision for the making of regulations that could, if exercised, exclude a decision under the unit of inquiry from the operation of Act B. (Such an exclusion has not taken place.) Further, Act B has been subjected on several occasions to amendments touching upon Act A without excluding the operation of the unit of inquiry from Act B. In this context, can a court draw an inference from such established facts that Parliament intended an exercise of power under the unit of inquiry to be subject to the provisions of Act B? In *Commissioner of Police for New South Wales v Eaton*,[81] such a question arose. The High Court answered in the negative, holding:

> These are matters of speculation. No proper inferences helpful to the process of construction are available.[82]

81 (2013) 252 CLR 1.

82 Ibid 28 [79] (Crennan, Kiefel and Bell JJ).

PART VIII

SPECIAL INTERPRETATIVE ISSUES

Previous Parts have dealt with general principles of statutory interpretation. These principles potentially apply to all problems that may be solved by interpretation. Part VIII deals with special interpretative issues. These are issues arising in the case of particular interpretative problems.

Chapter 34 (*Remedial Constructions for Drafting Errors*) examines the extent to which the courts are prepared to read legislation as if the statutory text were modified, in order to address an apparent drafting error.

Chapter 35 (*Provisions in Apparent Conflict*) deals with the resolution of statutory provisions in apparent conflict – whether provisions of the one statute or of different statutes. In resolving apparent conflict courts draw on a range of interpretative techniques in addition to ordinary principles of interpretation.

Chapter 36 (*Statutory Powers and Their Characterisation: Discretion or Duty?*) considers the meanings of 'may', 'shall' and 'must'. It focuses on the question of characterisation that often arises in relation to 'may' and 'shall': namely, should the words be characterised as conferring a discretion or as imposing a duty, at least in certain circumstances?

Chapter 37 (*The Effect of Non-compliance with a Statutory Requirement*) deals with the situation when Parliament has not unambiguously stated whether or not a breach of a statutory requirement invalidates a related act. In such a case whether Parliament intended invalidity may arise as a question of interpretation.

Chapter 38 (*Statutory Reasonableness*) is a case study of the interpretation of a broad term: the reasonableness standard in legislation. As with other broad terms, it may not be possible to define it exhaustively, but its scope may be confined by interpretation.

Statute law is considered to be 'retrospective' if it has one of two general operations: it is retroactive, or it impairs an existing right or obligation. Most disputes deal with the second operation, and chapter 39 (*Presumption Against Retrospective Operation*) discusses the statutory and common law presumptions that are called into play.

Chapter 40 (*Presumption Against Application to Government and Other Crown Entities*) considers the application of legislation to the Crown. At common law there is a presumption that general words in a statute do not apply to the Crown in any capacity. The term 'the

Crown' has a broad meaning for this purpose. The presumption covers executive governments, government agencies and staff, as well as the Sovereign and her direct representatives in Australia.

Chapter 41 (*Presumption Against Extraterritorial Operation*) deals with the question of whether Parliament intended that a statute or certain of its provisions should have an operation wholly outside the territory of the enacting legislature (whether state, territory or Commonwealth), or partly within and partly outside the territory. At common law there is a presumption against extraterritorial operation. In respect of offences, however, statutes of general operation in most Australian jurisdictions have defined the territorial nexus in a way that allows some extraterritorial operation.

Chapter 42 (*Mental Ingredient of Statutory Offences*) discusses how surrounding law (principles of criminal responsibility) when read with a statutory offence determines whether or not the offence contains a mental ingredient or a ground of exculpation for honest and reasonable mistake of fact (mens rea). The chapter also outlines the comparable law in jurisdictions in which the common law of mens rea has been supplanted by criminal codes.

Chapter 43 (*Delegated Legislation*) considers the interpretation of instruments of a legislative character that are made under an Act. Generally, the ordinary principles of statutory interpretation, both statutory and common law, apply to delegated legislation. However, courts may take into consideration some different contextual factors, and some distinct interpretation legislation provisions are applicable to delegated legislation.

REMEDIAL CONSTRUCTIONS FOR DRAFTING ERRORS

34

Overview

This chapter addresses the extent to which the courts are prepared to read legislation as if the statutory text is modified in order to address an apparent drafting error. This is known as 'remedial construction'. The doctrine of the separation of powers and the notion of legislative intent are central to remedial constructions. Drafting deficiencies can be viewed on a spectrum. At one end of the spectrum are obvious and simple printing or grammatical errors, which courts will readily read as corrected. Further along the spectrum are less straightforward instances of drafting errors where determining the line between interpretation and legislation may involve the application of particular guiding factors. In these instances courts may be willing to read legislation as if it contained additional words, substituted words or omitted words. Permissible remedial constructions are still characterised as constructions of the text enacted by Parliament. At the other end of the spectrum are drafting inadvertences that have led to a 'gap' in the legislation. Courts will not adopt a remedial construction for these oversights as they require conjecture about how Parliament might have addressed the gap – a legislative, not a judicial, function. Remedial constructions are sometimes referred to as 'strained' constructions, but this label is ambiguous. [34.1]

Concepts central to remedial construction

The doctrine of the separation of powers and the concept of legislative intent are central to the issue of whether a court will read a statutory provision as if a drafting error is corrected [34.2]

In certain circumstances courts are willing to construe legislation as if a drafting defect is corrected. The High Court has called a construction that corrects a drafting deficiency a 'remedial construction'.[1]

There are two fundamental concepts that influence the law on remedial constructions. The first is the doctrine of the separation of powers. Briefly, this doctrine states that the legislature has the function of making or amending legislation, and the courts' function is to determine the legal meaning of that legislation.[2] Accordingly, courts must be mindful that a remedial construction is not 'de facto' legislating, or 'judicial legislation'.[3]

1 *Taylor v The Owners – Strata Plan No 11564* (2014) 253 CLR 531, 549 [39] (French CJ, Crennan and Bell JJ).

2 See **[3.3]**.

3 *Inco Europe Ltd v First Choice Distribution (A Firm)* [2000] 1 WLR 586, 592 (Lord Nicholls). See also **[6.10]**.

The second concept is legislative intent. The fundamental object of statutory interpretation is to discern Parliament's 'intent'.[4] To adopt a remedial construction a court must be convinced that is it necessary to achieve a clear legislative intent.

The notion of a 'drafting error' can encompass a spectrum of legislative inadvertence. Not all these errors are open to a remedial construction. The point at which a remedial construction becomes impermissible is a matter of identifying when the line between interpretation and 'judicial legislation' is crossed. This explains why the notion of remedial construction is an issue of 'longstanding controversy'.[5] Determining when a remedial construction is within the boundaries of interpretation necessarily 'involves a judgment of matters of degree'.[6] The High Court has identified two ends of a spectrum of legislative inadvertence for making that judgement. It is

> readily answered in favour of addition or omission in the case of simple, grammatical, drafting errors which if uncorrected would defeat the object of the provision. It is answered against a construction that fills 'gaps disclosed in legislation' ...[7]

Sections **[34.4]**–**[34.8]** discuss different points on this spectrum.

[34.3] **Identifying a drafting deficiency is a matter of statutory interpretation, not factual empirical evidence**

It is not necessary for there to be factual empirical evidence of a drafting error or inadvertence in order to have a remedial construction, except to the extent that such 'evidence' is identified from the process of interpretation. That is, the inadvertence must be detectable as a result of considering the statutory text in its context and having regard to its purpose. As explained by the Court of Appeal of Western Australia:

> Identification of purpose and drafting errors is ... a matter of statutory construction, giving effect to the whole of the statutory text in its context. Where there is an obvious drafting error, the true meaning of the language is apparent from the statutory text understood as a whole in its relevant context, even though that meaning is not literal or grammatical.[8]

Simple and obvious drafting errors

[34.4] **It is well established that where there is an obvious and simple drafting error, the courts will generally read the legislation as if the error is corrected**

As noted in the High Court quote in **[34.2]**, the courts will 'readily' read legislation as if it is corrected in the case of simple and obvious drafting errors. Whether an error is simple and obvious is largely a matter of impression that arises from the interpretative exercise. It may be obvious because the grammatical meaning of the uncorrected text would, for example, defeat the purpose of the legislation,[9] leave a provision as having no work to do,[10] lead to an absurd or

4 See chapter 4.

5 *Lawson v Western Australia [No 3]* [2018] WASCA 129, [75] (the Court).

6 *Taylor v The Owners – Strata Plan No 11564* (2014) 253 CLR 531, 548 [38] (French CJ, Crennan and Bell JJ).

7 Ibid (citations omitted).

8 *Australian Unity Property Ltd v City of Busselton* (2018) 237 LGERA 333, 355 [90].

9 *New South Wales Crime Commission v Kelly* (2003) 58 NSWLR 71, 76 [24] (Sheller JA, Santow JA agreeing at 77 [72], Tobias JA agreeing at 77 [73]).

10 *Day v Harness Racing New South Wales* (2014) 88 NSWLR 594, 610 [77]–[78] (Leeming JA, McColl JA agreeing at 597 [1], Macfarlan JA agreeing at 597 [2]).

irrational operation[11] or be repugnant to the rest of the statute.[12] The obviousness of the error alleviates separation of powers concerns. In reading the legislation as corrected, the court is giving a construction that is 'indubitably' intended by Parliament.[13]

For example, in *Day v Harness Racing New South Wales*[14] delegated legislation contained a rule about prohibited substances for racing horses. The rule created a prohibition of a certain level of concentration of 'cobalt chloride' in horse urine. The Court found that there was a clear and simple drafting error in that the rule should have referred to 'cobalt' only. This was because it was 'meaningless to speak of, and impossible to measure, a concentration of dissolved "cobalt chloride"'.[15] A literal construction would leave the rule as having no work to do,[16] and clearly defeat the 'manifest intention' of the rule.[17] Other examples of simple and obvious errors in legislation that have been read as corrected include the incorrect placement of a word,[18] an incorrect word,[19] a superfluous word[20] and an erroneous cross reference.[21] It is not unusual in these instances for there to be scant or limited analysis supporting the remedial reading, due to the blatant obviousness and uncomplicated nature of the error.

The courts may more readily acknowledge the existence of a simple and obvious drafting error when the instrument being construed is delegated legislation that has been drafted by persons other than parliamentary counsel. This is regarded as a relevant contextual factor.[22] It may indicate that the instrument has not been as carefully and precisely drafted as it would otherwise be. For example, in *Day v Harness Racing New South Wales* (discussed above) the Court noted that, in identifying an error, it was legitimate to have regard to the fact that the rules had been drafted by members of the body corporate 'Harness Racing New South Wales', not parliamentary counsel.[23]

In addition to the judicial practice of correcting simple errors, there is legislation in some states and territories that grants limited powers to authorised officers, usually parliamentary

---

11 *F, BV v Magistrates Court of South Australia* (2013) 115 SASR 232, 241 [13] (Kourakis CJ); *Cooper Brookes (Wollongong) Pty Ltd v Commissioner of Taxation (Cth)* (1981) 147 CLR 297, 320 (Mason and Wilson JJ).

12 *New South Wales Crime Commission v Kelly* (2003) 58 NSWLR 71, 76 [23] (Sheller JA, Santow JA agreeing at 77 [72], Tobias JA agreeing at 77 [73]).

13 *Day v Harness Racing New South Wales* (2014) 88 NSWLR 594, 611 [84] (Leeming JA, McColl JA agreeing at 597 [1], Macfarlan JA agreeing at 597 [2]).

14 Ibid.

15 Ibid 601 [22].

16 Ibid 610 [77].

17 Ibid 607 [55], citing *H Jones and Co Pty Ltd v Warden, Councillors and Electors of the Municipality of Kingborough* (1950) 82 CLR 282, 318 (Dixon J).

18 *DPP (Nauru) v Fowler* (1984) 154 CLR 627, 630 (Gibbs CJ, Murphy, Wilson, Deane and Dawson JJ).

19 *New South Wales Crime Commission v Kelly* (2003) 58 NSWLR 71, 76 [20]–[23] (Sheller JA, Santow JA agreeing at 77 [72], Tobias JA agreeing at 77 [73]); *Minister for Immigration and Citizenship v SZJGV* (2009) 238 CLR 642, 651–3 [9]–[12] (French CJ and Bell J).

20 *CGX20 v Minister for Immigration, Citizenship, Migrant Services and Multicultural Affairs* (2021) 284 FCR 416, 422 [23] (the Court).

21 *Dome Resources NL v Silver* (2008) 72 NSWLR 693, 703 [32] (Basten and Bell JJA), citing *Lindner v Wright* (1976) 14 ALR 105, 109 (Muirhead J).

22 *City of Swan v West Australian Shalom Group Inc* [2017] WASC 217, [37] (Banks-Smith J). See **[43.3]** for contextual factors particular to delegated legislation.

23 *Day v Harness Racing New South Wales* (2014) 88 NSWLR 594, 610 [79] (Leeming JA, McColl JA agreeing at 597 [1], McFarlan JA agreeing at 597 [2]).

counsel, to make stylistic changes or to correct simple errors (such as grammar and punctuation) in reprints or compilations of legislation.[24]

Guidance for remedial construction beyond simple errors

[34.5] **Where the drafting error is not simple and obvious, the common law has developed guidelines for assisting the evaluation of whether a remedial construction is permissible**

Where the drafting error is not immediately obvious and simple, determining whether a remedial construction is permissible involves more extended analysis. The analysis must identify textual, contextual, purposive and other interpretative indicia that anchors the conclusion that there is a drafting inadvertence, and that it is clear what Parliament wished to achieve but did not do so due to that inadvertence. Given that the result of the analysis is to read the text in a modified form (beyond the correction of a simple and obvious grammatical error), a strong and clear argument supported by interpretative criteria must be made to convince the court of the legitimacy of a remedial construction. To this end the common law has developed guidance, in the form of three so-called conditions. These conditions assist the interpreter to determine whether there is a legislative error that can be legitimately corrected as a matter of construction, or whether it is one beyond the judicial function.[25] The three 'conditions' were initially formulated by Lord Diplock in the 1980 House of Lords decision *Wentworth Securities Ltd v Jones*.[26] The third condition was subsequently modified by Lord Nicholls in the 2000 House of Lords decision *Inco Europe Ltd v First Choice Distribution (A Firm)*.[27] As modified, this approach states that the court must be 'abundantly sure'[28] that

1. it is possible to determine from a consideration of the provisions of the Act read as a whole precisely what the intended purpose of the provision or Act is;
2. it is apparent from that consideration that the drafter and Parliament had by inadvertence overlooked an eventuality that must be dealt with if the purpose of the provision or statute is to be achieved; and
3. it is possible to state the substance of the provision that Parliament would have made, though not necessarily the precise words, if the attention of Parliament had been drawn to the error prior to enactment.

24 See, eg, *Legislation Act 2003* (Cth) div 3; *Interpretation Act 1987* (NSW) s 45E; *Reprints Act 1992* (Qld) pt 4; *Legislation Revision and Publication Act 2002* (SA) ss 4–7; *Interpretation of Legislation Act 1984* (Vic) s 54A sch 1; *Reprints Act 1984* (WA) ss 7, 7A (to be replaced by the *Legislation Act 2021* (WA) (pts 2–5 not commenced at time of writing); *Legislation Act 2001* (ACT) ss 114–118. The correction of simple and obvious errors in these contexts is sometimes referred to as the 'slip' rule: Explanatory Memorandum, Statute Law Revision (Spring 2016) Bill 2016, 4.

25 These conditions can also be used for the simple and obvious errors discussed in **[34.4]**. But the obviousness of those errors and the clarity of the legislative intent allows the court to adopt the pragmatic approach of correcting the error without more.

26 [1980] AC 74, 105 (Lord Diplock).

27 [2000] 1 WLR 586, 592 (Lord Nicholls). Lord Diplock in *Wentworth* stated that it must be possible to state 'with certainty' what additional words Parliament would have used. In *Inco Europe* Lord Nicholls softened this by referring to the 'substance' of the words Parliament would have used.

28 Ibid.

From conditions one and two, it is clear that unambiguous identification of the purpose of the relevant provision or statute is central.[29] It is highly relevant to determining whether there has been an error that can be rectified. It must be 'abundantly plain'[30] what the provision is seeking to achieve, but is unable to achieve, due to a drafting inadvertence.

That importance is demonstrated in the relatively uncommon instances where the courts have adopted a remedial construction. For example, in *Lowe v The Queen*[31] Warren CJ determined that a word could be read into s 25 of the *Jury Directions Act 2013* (Vic), which concerned directions by a trial judge to the jury.[32] One basis of Her Honour's reasoning was that the ordinary meaning of the provision, without a remedial construction, would undermine the purposes of the Act (which included to simplify and clarify the duties of the trial judge) and the purpose of the provision (to enhance the certainty of the cases that require a mandatory direction) and would result in a reversion to the previous common law position, even though other provisions indicated Parliament's intent to abolish it.[33] Another example is *Coleman v Caesarstone Australia Pty Ltd*[34] where Bowskill J was required to construe the definition of 'personal injury' in the *Personal Injuries Proceedings Act 2002* (Qld). Bowskill J determined that the definition should be read as if it contained additional words. The main reason was that a remedial construction gave full effect to the clear purpose of s 6(3)(b) and the intention of Parliament.[35] To read otherwise would be 'illogical, unreasonable and inconsistent'.[36]

The third condition is significant as indicia of whether the court is transcending its judicial function.[37] There must be a 'high degree of exactitude' about the words the court determines must be implied or modified.[38] For example, in *Lowe* and *Coleman* Warren CJ and Bowskill J, respectively, were able to identify without difficulty the words to be read into the relevant sections.[39] This indicia is relevant because if the court cannot be certain about the substance of the language of the corrective reading, then it enters the realm of conjecture. Conjecture necessitates a choice of language, which is a legislative not a judicial function.

The guidance provided by the Diplock Conditions has been clarified by the High Court in at least three ways [34.6]

Following their formulation, the three 'conditions' ('Diplock Conditions') were adopted as an approach in Australia to remedial constructions.[40] Prior to 2014 there was some uncertainty

---

29 *Mills v Meeking* (1990) 169 CLR 214, 235 (Dawson J). The development of the 'Diplock Conditions' has been linked to the ascendency of the requirement to have regard to the purpose of the statute: Benedict Coxon, 'Open to Interpretation: The Implication of Words into Statutes' (2009) 30(1) *Statute Law Review* 1, 4, 11.

30 *Inco Europe Ltd v First Choice Distribution (A Firm)* [2000] 1 WLR 586, 589 (Lord Nicholls).

31 (2015) 48 VR 351.

32 Redlick JA and Robson AJA determined the appeal on an alternative ground, but stated that if they were incorrect, they agreed with Warren CJ that the remedial construction should be adopted to give effect to the 'unmistakable legislative intent': Ibid 391 [146].

33 Ibid 371–2 [61]–[64].

34 [2021] QSC 125.

35 Ibid [29]–[31].

36 Ibid [29].

37 *Inco Europe Ltd v First Choice Distribution (A Firm)* [2000] 1 WLR 586, 592 (Lord Nicholls).

38 *DPP v Leys* (2012) 44 VR 1, 25 [73] (the Court).

39 (2015) 48 VR 351, 371–2 [59] [67] and [2021] QSC 125 [38].

40 See, eg, *Momcilovic v The Queen* (2011) 245 CLR 1, 221 [580] (Crennan and Kiefel JJ), citing *Newcastle City Council v GIO General Ltd* (1997) 191 CLR 85, 113 (McHugh J); *Minister for Immigration and Citizenship v*

about their application. In 2014 the High Court of Australia had the opportunity to consider them in *Taylor v The Owners – Strata Plan No 11564* ('*Taylor*').[41]

Taylor was an appeal from the NSW Court of Appeal. The facts of *Taylor* are detailed elsewhere in this book.[42] The interpretative issue was the meaning of words in s 12(2) of the *Civil Liability Act 2002* (NSW), which, in relation to an award of damages, required the court to disregard the amount by which the 'claimant's gross weekly earnings' would exceed a certain amount. The plaintiff argued that 'the claimant's gross weekly earnings' be given their ordinary meaning and as such referred to the earnings of the person claiming damages (the plaintiff). The defendants contended that the words should be read as referring to the gross weekly earnings on which the claimant relies (being the plaintiff's deceased high-earning husband).

In the Court of Appeal, McColl JA (with whom Hoeben JA agreed) had determined that there was a plain drafting mistake in s 12(2) and, using the Diplock Conditions, construed s 12(2) as if it contained additional words to read 'the claimant's *or deceased person's* gross weekly earnings'.[43] The plaintiff appealed.

The majority decision of French CJ, Crennan and Bell JJ (the '*Taylor* majority') rejected the defendants' argument. In the course of doing so, they addressed the Diplock Conditions and clarified them in the following ways.

(a) Satisfaction of the three conditions is not necessarily required nor sufficient to adopt a remedial construction

The *Taylor* majority acknowledged that the Diplock Conditions accorded with principles previously enunciated by the High Court on drafting errors.[44] They also stated that McColl JA had been 'right to consider that satisfaction of each [of the three conditions as reformulated in *Inco Europe*] could be treated as a prerequisite' for a remedial construction.[45] But they made two qualifying points.

First, they said, it was 'unnecessary to decide whether Lord Diplock's three conditions are always, or even usually, necessary and sufficient'.[46] In other words, satisfaction of the conditions is not mandatory for adopting a remedial construction. This is because the central concern is whether the remedial construction could be characterised as one 'consistent with the language in fact used by the legislature'.[47] This proposition is discussed further in **[34.7]**.

Second, they noted that even if the Diplock Conditions were satisfied, the court may still be 'inhibited from interpreting a provision in accordance with what it is satisfied was the underlying

SZJGV (2009) 238 CLR 642, 651–2 [9] (French CJ and Bell J); *Carr v Western Australia* (2007) 232 CLR 138, 147 [17] (Gleeson CJ); *Mills v Meeking* (1990) 169 CLR 214, 243 (McHugh J); *F, BV v Magistrates Court of South Australia* (2013) 115 SASR 232, 242 [17] (Kourakis CJ); *DPP v Leys* (2012) 44 VR 1, 38 [109] (the Court); *Kingston v Keprose Pty Ltd* (1987) 11 NSWLR 404, 422–3 (McHugh JA).

41 (2014) 253 CLR 531.

42 See **Example 29.2** in chapter 29.

43 *Taylor v The Owners – Strata Plan No 11564* (2013) 83 NSWLR 1, 11 [43].

44 (2014) 253 CLR 531, 548–9 [39], referring to *Cooper Brookes (Wollongong) Pty Ltd v Commissioner of Taxation (Cth)* (1981) 147 CLR 297.

45 *Taylor v The Owners – Strata Plan No 11564* (2014) 253 CLR 531, 549 [39].

46 Ibid 549 [39].

47 Ibid.

intention of Parliament' if the alteration to the statutory language is 'too far reaching'.[48] This means that the extent to which the language must be read in a modified manner is relevant to the court's assessment of whether it would transcend its judicial function. The more substantial or extensive the words to be read in 'the more difficult it will be to reach the conclusion that the words used by Parliament manifest an intention to include the words omitted'.[49]

These qualifications indicate that, despite the label of 'condition', the Diplock Conditions are not rules, but are best viewed as 'in the nature of guidelines'.[50] The 'guidelines' continue to be referred to by Australian courts when addressing instances of apparent drafting error.[51] This is likely because they are useful indicia of the high threshold needed to justify a remedial construction when it involves more than an obvious textual error.

(b) There may be a fourth 'condition', but, like the Diplock Conditions, this is neither a prerequisite nor determinative

In addition to the Diplock Conditions, a possible fourth condition was addressed by the *Taylor* majority.[52] The Court of Appeal had referred to an additional requirement to the Diplock Conditions that the *modified* construction must be consistent with the words of the statutory scheme.[53] The *Taylor* majority did not reject its relevance, but noted that, even against a background of satisfaction of the Diplock Conditions, it would not necessarily be sufficient.[54]

This so-called fourth condition is sometimes referred to by intermediate courts.[55] However, similar to the Diplock Conditions, it is neither determinative nor necessary.[56] The fourth condition is best viewed as another potentially relevant factor in determining whether a remedial construction is available.

---

48 Ibid 549 [40], citing in part *Inco Europe Ltd v First Choice Distribution (A Firm)* [2000] 1 WLR 586, 592 (Lord Nicholls). See also the *Taylor* majority's reference to an alteration that is 'too big, or too much at variance with the language in fact used by the legislature', citing *Western Bank Ltd v Schindler* [1977] Ch 1, 18 (Scarman LJ): at 548 [38].

49 *Pilbara Infrastructure Pty Ltd v Brockman Iron Pty Ltd (No 2)* [2014] WASC 345, [143] (Edelman J), affd *Pilbara Infrastructure Pty Ltd v Brockman Iron Pty Ltd* [2016] WASCA 36. See, eg, *Australian Unity Property Ltd v City of Busselton* (2018) 237 LGERA 333, 360 [107] (the Court).

50 *Commissioner for Corrective Services (WA) v Raj* (2014) 244 A Crim R 558, 566 [45] (Beech J).

51 See, eg, *Taylor v A-G (Cth)* (2019) 268 CLR 224, 275 [143] (Edelman J); *Tohi v Minister for Immigration, Citizenship, Migrant Services and Multicultural Affairs* (2021) 285 FCR 187, 236–7, [164] (O'Bryan J, Katzmann J agreeing at 191 [1]); *Redman v Return to Work Corp (SA)* (2021) 305 IR 326, 331–6 [11]–[24] (Kourakis CJ), 359–61 [124]–[127] (Livesey JA, Bleby JA agreeing at 365 [149]; *Hall v The Queen* (2020) 136 SASR 535, 542–4 [26]–[30] (the Court); *Hart v Commissioner of Taxation* (2019) 272 FCR 612, 637 [116]–[117] (the Court); *Kiriwina Investment Co Pty Ltd v Green Lees Developments Pty Ltd* [2018] NSWCA 210, [48] (White JA, Gleeson JA agreeing at [1]); *Lawson v Western Australia [No 3]* [2018] WASCA 129, [76–80] (the Court); *Department for Health and Ageing v Li* (2018) 130 SASR 578, 599–602 [94]–[98] (Stanley J, Bampton J agreeing at 603 [107]).

52 *Taylor v The Owners – Strata Plan No 11564* (2014) 253 CLR 531, 544–5 [25].

53 *Taylor v The Owners – Strata Plan No 11564* (2013) 83 NSWLR 1, 10 [40] (McColl JA, Hoeben JA agreeing at 22 [98]), drawing on statements in *DPP v Leys* (2012) 44 VR 1 and *Mills v Meeking* (1990) 169 CLR 214.

54 *Taylor v The Owners – Strata Plan No 11564* (2014) 253 CLR 531, 549 [39].

55 See, eg, *Merck Sharp & Dohme Corporation v Sandoz Pty Ltd* [2021] FCA 947, [70]–[76] (Jagot J); *Re Joybay Pty Ltd* [2019] VSC 620, [57] (Daly AsJ); *DPP v Moreno* (2018) 57 VR 1, 23 [71]–[72] (Daly AsJ); *DPP v Scheele* (2016) 12 ACTLR 1, 9 [33] (the Court).

56 *Lowe v The Queen* (2015) 48 VR 351, 363, [29] (Warren CJ).

(c) Remedial constructions can be adopted to expand or narrow the operation of a provision

Prior to *Taylor* there was divergence in intermediate appellate court authorities as to whether it was permissible for a remedial construction to expand the scope of operation of a provision.[57] This issue primarily arose from statements made by Chief Justice Spigelman in the NSW Court of Criminal Appeal.[58] His Honour contended that a provision could only be read as if it contained additional words or omitted words if the effect was to 'read down' (or narrow) the scope of the provision (or to give it an ambulatory construction). The Court in *Director of Public Prosecution v Leys*[59] had rejected this limitation.[60] The *Taylor* majority preferred the broader approach of *Leys* and said:

> Consistently with this Court's rejection of the adoption of rigid rules in statutory construction, it should not be accepted that purposive construction may never allow of reading a provision as if it contained additional words (or omitted words) with the effect of expanding its field of operation. As the review of the authorities in *Leys* demonstrates, it is possible to point to decisions in which courts have adopted a purposive construction having that effect.[61]

Although dissenting as to outcome, Gageler and Keane JJ made similar statements.[62] These statements by the Court effectively reject the limitation endorsed by Chief Justice Spigelman.[63]

[34.7] The courts characterise a permissible remedial construction as a construction of the language in fact used by the legislature; this statement seems contradictory, but can be explained

The High Court is clear that a remedial construction must be '[a] construction of the words the legislature has enacted'.[64] If the statutory text is intractable and is not capable of a construction that accords with the apparent legislative intent, then the ordinary or grammatical meaning must prevail.

On its face this qualification appears inconsistent with the nature of a remedial construction, which involves reading statutory language as if it is modified. One way to reconcile remedial constructions with this qualification is to view the former as 'explaining' or 'expounding' the meaning of the statutory text.[65] To put it another way, the application of ordinary principles of

---

57 For a discussion of this divergence, see Benedict Coxon, 'Open to Interpretation: The Implication of Words into Statutes' (2009) 30(1) *Statute Law Review* 1.

58 *R v Young* (1999) 46 NSWLR 681, 686–90 [8]–[32]; *R v PLV* (2001) 51 NSWLR 736, 742–4 [80]–[89] (Simpson J agreeing at 745 [98]).

59 (2012) 44 VR 1.

60 Ibid 34–5 [98].

61 *Taylor v The Owners – Strata Plan No 11564* (2014) 253 CLR 531, 548 [37] (citations omitted).

62 Ibid 556–7 [65].

63 *Redman v Return to Work Corp (SA)* (2021) 305 IR 326, 361 [127] (Livesey JA, Bleby JA agreeing at 365 [149]).

64 *Taylor v The Owners – Strata Plan No 11564* (2014) 253 CLR 531, 549 [39] (French CJ, Crennan and Bell JJ), 556–7 [65] (Gageler and Keane JJ). See also *HFM043 v Republic of Nauru* (2018) 92 ALJR 817, 820 [24] (the Court).

65 *HFM043 v Republic of Nauru* (2018) 92 ALJR 817, 820 [24] (the Court). See also *Taylor v The Owners – Strata Plan No 11564* (2014) 253 CLR 531, 556–7 [65] (Gageler and Keane JJ), citing *Cooper Brookes (Wollongong) Pty Ltd v Commissioner of Taxation (Cth)* (1981) 147 CLR 297, 310–11, 319–21 and *MacAlister v The Queen* (1990) 169 CLR 324, 330.

construction, together with the guidance of the Diplock Conditions, allows the court to come to a view about meaning that is manifestly consistent with legislative intent, but not immediately apparent from the actual statutory text due to drafting inadvertence.[66] The interpretative process provides the abundantly clear basis for the judicial exegesis of the remedial construction. That said, it may be plainer for the courts to acknowledge that permissible remedial constructions are a form of rectification and, while a construct, in effect there is modification of statutory language to achieve the legislative intent.

Gaps in legislation distinguished

The courts will not adopt a remedial construction for a drafting inadvertence that has left a 'gap' or omission in the legislation; this is clearly inconsistent with the judicial function [34.8]

Section **[34.4]** addresses one end of the spectrum, being simple and obvious drafting errors. Further along the spectrum, the purported errors become less straightforward and require more developed analysis (**[34.5]**–**[34.6]**). These types of inadvertences may be open to remedial constructions because they consist 'not in a failure to address the problem and determine what should be done, but in the failure to provide in the instrument express words appropriate to give effect to it'.[67] To put it another way, there has been an error in the statutory text to reflect an otherwise clear legislative intent on a particular matter.

At some point along the spectrum, the inadvertence moves into a sphere that the courts are not prepared to enter. This type of drafting inadvertence, as indicated in the quotation from *Taylor* (**[34.2]**), is often referred to as a 'gap' in the legislation. The older concept of a *casus omissus* ('omitted case') is similar.[68] A 'gap' in this instance describes an inadvertence with respect to a particular matter, or class of things, or state of affairs that the reader would expect to be addressed in the legislation, but has not been due to legislative inadvertence or inattention.[69] That is, it can be inferred that Parliament had not turned its attention to that particular matter, thing or state. It is not the court's role to remedy a provision by reference to what Parliament might have done if it had considered the class of matter before the Court.[70] To read the statute as if that gap was filled (ie the matter addressed) may further, or be consistent with, the purpose of the statute. But as the gap is not addressed it is not possible to state with certainty how and to what extent Parliament would have addressed it. Filling the gap therefore requires the court to 'divine *unexpressed* legislative intention'.[71] This involves judicial speculation or a judicial choice about what the legislature might have done about the matter or state of affairs overlooked: an exercise that is a legislative, not judicial, function.[72] **Example 34.1** is an illustration of such a gap.

66 *Country Carbon Pty Ltd v Clean Energy Regulator* (2018) 267 FCR 126, 156 [126] (Mortimer J).

67 *Taylor v Centennial Newstan Pty Ltd* (2009) 76 NSWLR 379, 395 [61] (Beazley JA), citing *Tokyo Mart Pty Ltd v Campbell* (1988) 15 NSWLR 275, 283 (Mahoney JA).

68 *Kurnell Passenger & Transport Service Pty Ltd v Randwick City Council* (2009) 230 FLR 336, 350 [57] (McColl JA).

69 *Taylor v Centennial Newstan Pty Ltd* (2009) 76 NSWLR 379, 395 [61] (Beazley JA), citing *Tokyo Mart Pty Ltd v Campbell* (1988) 15 NSWLR 275, 283 (Mahoney JA).

70 *Esso Australia Pty Ltd v Australian Workers' Union* (2017) 263 CLR 551, 582 [52] (Kiefel CJ, Keane, Nettle and Edelman JJ).

71 *Taylor v The Owners – Strata Plan No 11564* (2014) 253 CLR 531, 556–7 [65] (Gageler and Keane JJ) (emphasis added).

72 *HFM043 v Republic of Nauru* (2018) 92 ALJR 817, 820–1 [24] (the Court).

Example 34.1 *Commissioner for Corrective Services (WA) v Raj*[73]

In April 2013 the defendant, then under 18 years old, was sentenced to a term of detention in a youth detention centre under the *Young Offenders Act 1994* (WA). In April 2014, after he had turned 18 years old, he was convicted of assaulting a youth custodial officer and sentenced to imprisonment for one month. The magistrate ordered that the one-month imprisonment be cumulative (rather than be served concurrently) upon the detention. The Commissioner for Corrective Services sought a declaration from the Supreme Court as to whether the magistrate had the power to make such an order.

Section 88(3) of the *Sentencing Act 1995* (WA) ('the *Sentencing Act*') provided the power for a magistrate to make orders that one 'fixed term' could be served cumulatively with another. Section 85 defined 'term' as 'a term of imprisonment imposed on an offender by a court as a sentence'.

The interpretative issue was whether 'fixed term' included a detention order for the purposes of s 88(3). If this 'wide' construction was appropriate, then the magistrate had the power to order that the imprisonment and detention be served cumulatively. If it was not, then the magistrate's power under the section was confined to orders about terms of 'imprisonment' under the *Sentencing Act*.

The Court was required to consider the *Sentencing Act* as part of a complementary scheme that included the *Sentence Administration Act 2003* (WA) (the '*SAA*') and *Young Offenders Act 1994* (WA).[74] So, as well as considering the *Sentencing Act*, Beech J was required to consider the effect of a wide construction on s 7 of the *SAA*, which governed the order of service of two fixed terms. Beech J identified 'significant difficulties' for s 7 of the *SAA*.[75] In particular, his Honour considered the use in s 7 of the terms '*parole term*' and '*non-parole period*', which were defined as follows:

> ***non-parole period***, in relation to a parole term, means the period that under section 93(1) of the *Sentencing Act 1995* the prisoner has to serve before he or she is eligible to be released on parole.
>
> ***parole term*** means a term to which a parole eligibility order applies.

The defined terms did not on their face accommodate a sentence of detention. This led to difficulties with the operation of s 7 and other provisions of the *SAA*. The Commissioner argued that the difficulties could be addressed by construing s 7 as if it contained additional words, to include detention. The Commissioner proposed that the definition of 'non-parole period' could be amended by adding 'or, in the case of a term of detention under the Young Offenders Act, the period that the prisoner has to serve before he or she can be released under a supervised release order' while the definition of 'parole term' could be changed by adding 'or a sentence of detention'.[76]

73 (2014) 244 A Crim R 558.

74 For legislative schemes see **[29.4]**.

75 (2014) 244 A Crim R 558, 572 [93].

76 Ibid 572 [96].

His Honour stated that the construction proposed by the Commissioner for s 7 required an 'unacceptably radical recasting of the text'.[77] Further, to adopt that construction was to fill a 'gap' that was, he said, beyond the judicial function to fill:

> The language of s 7 . . . 'covers only one state of affairs' and it would not be legitimate to construe the words in 'a tortured and unrealistic manner to cover another set of circumstances'. In my view, to adopt the wider construction of s 88(3) of the *Sentencing Act*, and the proposed construction of s 7 of the *Sentence Administration Act* would be for the court to intrude into the legislative function. The legislative scheme has what, I am satisfied, is an unintended gap.[78]

In this instance the proposal to remedy the 'gap' was not an exercise that involved adopting a construction consistent with what Parliament had clearly intended. Parliament had failed to address a particular 'state of affairs' – a policy gap. While the gap could be identified, the Court could only speculate about how Parliament intended to address the gap. Whether and in what circumstances a sentence of detention could be aggregated was a 'matter in respect of which there are policy choices to be made'.[79] Such choices 'are matters for Parliament'.[80] Accordingly, the Court determined that s 88(3) did not encompass sentences of detention.

Strained construction

Sometimes the label of 'strained' construction is used in the context of remedial construction; it is unclear whether this is a distinct device but the issue may be of little practical consequence [34.9]

The label of 'straining' the meaning of statutory text generally refers to giving that text an unusual or ungrammatical meaning.[81] It is well accepted that a 'strained' or ungrammatical meaning may be the outcome of ordinary processes of statutory interpretation.[82] For example, 'reading down' a word so that it is attributed an unusual, narrow meaning, and therefore a more confined scope than its ordinary meaning, may be characterised as 'strained'.

The description of a 'strained' meaning is sometimes used to describe a remedial construction.[83] Other commentary suggests the label is inappropriate.[84] The terminology of 'straining' for a remedial construction is problematic. Straining meaning implies attributing a meaning to the text that is ungrammatical or unnatural but nevertheless is a meaning attributable to the text in

77 Ibid 573 [98]. See also 573–4 [101].

78 Ibid 573–4 [101]–[102] (citations omitted).

79 Ibid 574 [106].

80 Ibid.

81 See **[6.9]**. For an interesting perspective on what it means for meaning to be 'strained' see Adam Perry, 'Strained Interpretations' (2019) 39(2) *Oxford Journal of Legal Studies* 316.

82 *Project Blue Sky Inc v Australian Broadcasting Authority* (1998) 194 CLR 355, 384 [78] (McHugh, Gummow, Kirby and Hayne JJ).

83 See, eg, *Department for Health and Ageing v Li* (2018) 130 SASR 578, 587 [40] (Kourakis CJ); *DPP v Scheele* (2016) 12 ACTLR 1, 8 [32] (the Court); *Newcastle City Council v GIO General Ltd* (1997) 191 CLR 85, 113 (McHugh J).

84 *DPP v Leys* (2012) 44 VR 1, 39 [111] (the Court).

its unmodified form. Remedial constructions attribute meaning to text as if the language was rearranged or modified. That modification produces the 'ungrammatical' meaning.

In the end the distinction, if any, between characterisations is 'a fine one'[85] and may have little practical import. For example, in *Taylor* the majority determined that a remedial construction was not available. In contrast, Gageler and Keane JJ determined that an ungrammatical meaning was permissible, but characterised it as 'straining' the meaning of the text.[86]

85 Stephen Lumb and Sharon Christensen, 'Reading Words into Statutes: When Homer Nods' (2014) 88(9) *Australian Law Journal* 661, 664.

86 *Taylor v The Owners – Strata Plan No 11564* (2014) 253 CLR 531, 557 [68].

PROVISIONS IN APPARENT CONFLICT 35

Overview

In a society in which it is often said that the quantity, variety and sources of law made by or under the authority of parliaments is expanding at a significant rate, resolving apparent conflict is a staple activity of the courts. Interpretative resources are drawn on to resolve such conflict. [35.1]

Courts work from the presumption that the provisions of one statute, or of two statutes made by the one Parliament, are intended to work together. This leads to the main principle in the resolution of apparent conflict between statutory provisions: that statutory texts enacted by the same Parliament (whether provisions of the one statute or of different statutes) are to be construed so far as possible to operate in harmony and not in conflict. This principle is known as the principle of harmonious construction or the principle of consistency. The basis of the principle is the need to maintain coherence in the law.

In resolving apparent conflict – that is, achieving the most harmonious construction overall – courts draw on a range of interpretative techniques. Some techniques apply both to a conflict between multiple provisions of the one statute and to a conflict between different statutes. Other techniques apply only to one of these conflicts. One technique is the linguistic canon *generalia specialibus non derogant* – that if there is an apparent conflict between a general law and special law, the presumption is that the special law prevails and the general law is cut back accordingly. Ordinary principles of statutory interpretation may also be brought into play. An interpretative technique applicable to conflicts between multiple provisions of the one statute is to determine which is the leading provision and which is the subordinate provision that must give way. And, where the conflict between statutes is found to be irreconcilable, then, as a last resort, a court may conclude that the later law has impliedly repealed the earlier law.

Apparent conflict is an interpretative problem

Where apparent conflict between statutory provisions is perceived, courts draw on interpretative resources to resolve the conflict [35.2]

Resolving apparent or actual conflict between legislation is 'a staple activity of Australian courts'.[1] Kirby J has suggested why this is the case: 'In a society in which the quantity, variety and sources

1 *Ferdinands v Commissioner for Public Employment* (2006) 225 CLR 130, 149 [59] (Kirby J) (dissenting as to outcome). Many other commentators have analysed what Justice McHugh has called the 'almost exponential' growth in Australian legislation: Justice MH McHugh, 'The Growth of Legislation and Litigation' (1995) 69(1) *Australian Law Journal* 37, 37. Justice McHugh points out that 'the increase has not been so much in the *number* of Acts passed as in the *length* of legislation passed': (at 38, emphases in original). His data on Commonwealth and a selection of state Acts (at 38) are consistent with other findings: see, eg, Senate Standing Committee on Legal and Constitutional Affairs, *The Cost of Justice: Second Report: Checks and*

of law made by or under parliaments (already great) expands at a significant rate, it is unsurprising that suggested incompatibilities frequently need to be resolved.'[2]

In dealing with apparent conflict, courts call on interpretative resources.[3] Whether a conflict is between multiple provisions of the one statute or between two statutes, a court seeks to determine the interrelationship of the provisions or the statutes through the test of legislative intention. In *Commissioner of Police for New South Wales v Eaton*[4] (a case of two statutes), Crennan, Kiefel and Bell JJ pointed out that '[t]he question of the relationship between the two statutes [in apparent conflict] is one of legislative intention'.[5] So too did the High Court in the earlier *Project Blue Sky* case (a case of multiple provisions of the one statute). There the plurality stated that 'the duty of a court is to give the words of a statutory provision the meaning that the legislature is taken to have intended them to have'.[6]

The approach an interpreter may make to deal with apparent conflict may be affected by the kind of conflict. Two broad types may be identified. First, there may be apparent conflict between statutory provisions in the one statute.[7] Second, there may be apparent conflict between provisions of different statutes of the one Parliament.[8] Care needs to be taken in applying the principles of this chapter. While most of the principles apply to both situations, some principles apply only to one, while other principles apply only to the other.

'Apparent' conflict may also be compared with 'actual' conflict. In the first instance, when conflict between legislative provisions is *alleged*, it is appropriate to refer to such conflict being apparent rather than actual. This is because, as was noted in a case dealing with different statutes

---

Imbalances: The Role of Parliament and the Executive (Parliament of the Commonwealth of Australia, 1993) 18–19 [2.11]–[2.13], 28–9 [2.36]); Catriona Cook et al, *Laying Down the Law* (LexisNexis, 8th ed, 2012) 233; Office of Parliamentary Counsel, *Reducing Complexity in Legislation* (Australian Government, Document Release 2.1, 2016) [12], Attachment A. Cf Prue Vines and M Scott Donald, 'Introduction: Is Statutory Interpretation in Private Law Distinctive?' in Prue Vines and M Scott Donald (eds), *Statutory Interpretation in Private Law* (Federation Press, 2019) 2, 3.

2 *Ferdinands v Commissioner for Public Employment* (2006) 225 CLR 130, 149 [59] (Kirby J) (dissenting as to outcome) (footnote omitted).

3 Sometimes, state parliaments have attempted to avoid interpretative processes being brought into play to resolve a potential conflict between statutes. The parliaments have laid down either a 'magic formula' by which amendments to a particular Act are to be taken to have occurred (*South-Eastern Drainage Board (South Australia) v Savings Bank of South Australia* (1939) 62 CLR 603, 634 (Evatt J)), or have required an Act to be amended 'expressly' for the Act to be taken to be amended (see *Rose v Hvric* (1963) 108 CLR 353). These attempts have not succeeded in avoiding an interpretative solution. The question of apparent conflict is determined not simply by whether the Parliament has satisfied the formula or by an express requirement that the Parliament had purported to lay down, but by the 'true construction' of the provisions concerned, taking into account all available indications: *Rose v Hvric* (1963) 108 CLR 353, 357 (the Court).

4 (2013) 252 CLR 1.

5 Ibid 18 [45] (Crennan, Kiefel and Bell JJ).

6 *Project Blue Sky Inc v Australian Broadcasting Authority* (1998) 194 CLR 355, 384 [78] (McHugh, Gummow, Kirby and Hayne JJ). In this chapter 'plurality' is understood to refer to the leading reasons for judgment among the reasons for judgment of those members of a court who agree with the proposed orders of the court.

7 An example discussed below (**Example 35.1**) is *Project Blue Sky Inc v Australian Broadcasting Authority* (1998) 194 CLR 355.

8 Examples discussed below are *Commissioner of Police for New South Wales v Eaton* (2013) 252 CLR 1 (**Example 35.2**, **[35.8]**) and *Saliba v Aziz* (2013) 281 FLR 278 (**Example 35.3**).

in apparent conflict, 'every attempt should be made to reconcile competing statutes'.[9] In the case of provisions of the one statute in apparent conflict, a similar duty arises. Here the duty is 'to construe the relevant provision so that it is consistent with the language and purpose of all the provisions of the statute'.[10] But if conflict between provisions of different statutes is found to be irreconcilable, the provisions should be held to be in conflict.[11] The later Act will take preference.[12] Similarly, in the case of apparent conflict between provisions of the one statute, it may not be possible to completely reconcile the provisions. For instance, a provision of the Act may be left with little or no work to do.[13]

The language in this area varies according to whether the later or earlier Act takes priority. Where a later Act takes preference over an earlier Act, it will be appropriate to describe the effect as 'implied repeal'.[14] But where an *earlier* Act causes an implication to be made in a later Act, cutting back the operation the later Act would otherwise have had, a court may describe the result as the 'non-application' of the later Act to matters the subject of the earlier Act.[15]

Basic presumptions applied in resolving apparent conflict

It is presumed that provisions of one statute, or of two statutes made by the one Parliament, are intended to work together [35.3]

The most basic presumption in this area was articulated by Gummow and Hayne JJ in *Ferdinands v Commissioner for Public Employment*.[16] Here they pointed out how apparent conflict between statutory provisions is to be approached:

> The question in the present case is not whether one law enacted by one legislature prevails over a law enacted by another legislature; it is whether the presumption that two laws made by the one legislature are intended to work together is displaced.[17]

That case concerned two statutes in apparent conflict. The presumption that laws are intended to work together applies equally to the construction of multiple provisions within a single

---

9 *North Australian Aboriginal Justice Agency Ltd v Northern Territory* (2015) 256 CLR 569, 649 [227] (Nettle and Gordon JJ), referring to *Butler v A-G (Vic)* (1961) 106 CLR 268, 276 (Fullagar J).

10 *Project Blue Sky Inc v Australian Broadcasting Authority* (1998) 194 CLR 355, 381 [69] (McHugh, Gummow, Kirby and Hayne JJ).

11 *North Australian Aboriginal Justice Agency Ltd v Northern Territory* (2015) 256 CLR 569, 649 [227] (Nettle and Gordon JJ).

12 See **[35.10]**.

13 As occurred in *DPP v Scheele* (2016) 12 ACTLR 1 (CA), where the preferred construction of provisions of the *Firearms Act 1996* (ACT) left an item in sch 1 to that Act with 'little or no work to do': 13 [58].

14 See, eg, *Butler v A-G (Vic)* (1961) 106 CLR 268, 280 (Kitto J, Menzies J agreeing at 286); *Ferdinands v Commissioner for Public Employment* (2006) 225 CLR 130, 139 [20] (Gummow and Hayne JJ); *McNeill v The Queen* (2008) 168 FCR 198, 212 [76] (the Court); *Saliba v Aziz* (2013) 281 FLR 278, 284 [22]–[23], 288 [47] (the Court). In *John Beever (Aust) Pty Ltd v Paper Australia Pty Ltd (No 2)* [2019] VSC 575, [10] the Court used a different form of expression, namely that 'the later and more specific Act displaces or supersedes the earlier'.

15 *Commissioner of Police for New South Wales v Eaton* (2013) 252 CLR 1, 32 [92] (Crennan, Kiefel and Bell JJ). This case is discussed below: **Example 35.2**.

16 (2006) 225 CLR 130.

17 Ibid 146 [49], approved in *Commissioner of Police for New South Wales v Eaton* (2013) 252 CLR 1, 19 [48] (Crennan, Kiefel and Bell JJ).

statute.[18] As Gaudron J said in a case dealing with apparent conflict in the one statute, 'there is a general presumption that the legislature intended that both provisions should operate'.[19] Nevertheless, the reality is that apparent, and in some cases actual, conflict occurs. In such cases additional principles are brought into play.

[35.4] **Statutory texts enacted by the same Parliament (whether provisions of the one statute or of different statutes) are to be construed so far as possible to operate in harmony and not in conflict (the principle of harmonious construction or the principle of consistency)**

The principle of harmonious construction,[20] also known as the principle of consistency,[21] applies to the construction of different statutes in apparent conflict as well as the construction of multiple provisions within the one statute. In *Project Blue Sky Inc v Australian Broadcasting Authority*[22] (a case of the latter), McHugh, Gummow, Kirby and Hayne JJ (the plurality) held:

> The primary object of statutory construction is to construe the relevant provision so that it is consistent with the language and purpose of all the provisions of the statute. The meaning of the provision must be determined 'by reference to the language of the instrument viewed as a whole' ... A legislative instrument must be construed on the prima facie basis that its provisions are intended to give effect to harmonious goals.[23]

This principle was extended to the construction of different statutes in apparent conflict in *Commissioner of Police for New South Wales v Eaton*:[24]

> In accordance with ordinary rules of construction concerning the internal operation of a statute, the *Police Act* should be construed in a way which best achieves a harmonious result. The same principle of consistency informs the construction of two statutes which may share a field of operation.[25]

The principle of harmonious construction is a high priority of courts. It has been called the 'primary object of statutory construction'.[26] Thus, if a court can read provisions consistently it should do so. In other words, if one construction favours consistency and the other does not, the principle favours the former construction.

---

18 *Commissioner of Police for New South Wales v Eaton* (2013) 252 CLR 1, 33 [98] (Gageler J) (dissenting as to outcome).

19 *Saraswati v The Queen* (1991) 172 CLR 1, 17 (Gaudron J), approved in *Ferdinands v Commissioner for Public Employment* (2006) 225 CLR 130, 138 [18] (Gummow and Hayne JJ), 163 [109] (Kirby J) (dissenting as to outcome).

20 *Commissioner of Police for New South Wales v Eaton* (2013) 252 CLR 1, 33 [98] (Gageler J) (dissenting as to outcome).

21 Ibid 28 [78] (Crennan, Kiefel and Bell JJ).

22 (1998) 194 CLR 355.

23 Ibid 381 [69], 381–2 [70] (McHugh, Gummow, Kirby and Hayne JJ) (footnotes omitted).

24 (2013) 252 CLR 1.

25 Ibid 28 [78] (Crennan, Kiefel and Bell JJ) (footnote omitted).

26 *Project Blue Sky Inc v Australian Broadcasting Authority* (1998) 194 CLR 355, 381 [69] (McHugh, Gummow, Kirby and Hayne JJ); *Western Australian Planning Commission v Southregal Pty Ltd* (2017) 259 CLR 106, 121 [52] (Kiefel and Bell JJ).

The achievability of the *Project Blue Sky* doctrine – of a court striving to give effect to 'harmonious goals' – has been colourfully described as a 'vision splendid'.[27] Since that commentary, however, the High Court has restated the principle of harmonious construction. It has said that a court is not aiming to achieve 'absolute validity'.[28] A court may have to be satisfied with 'relative consistency'.[29] In other words, a court is seeking no more than 'to determine which of the two competing constructions ... is more harmonious overall'.[30] It follows from this restatement of the principle of harmonious construction that, inevitably, there will be cases when no available construction is without difficulty.[31]

In achieving the most harmonious construction, courts draw on a range of techniques. These techniques are elaborated on and illustrated at **[35.6]–[35.10]**.

The principle of harmonious construction is illustrated with the leading case, the subject of **Example 35.1**.

Example 35.1 *Project Blue Sky Inc v Australian Broadcasting Authority*[32]

Section 158 of the *Broadcasting Services Act 1992* (Cth) ('the Act') set out the primary functions of the Australian Broadcasting Authority ('ABA'). They included:

(j) to develop program standards relating to broadcasting in Australia; and
(k) to monitor compliance with those standards.

The Authority made a program standard under s 122 of the Act. That section stated:

(1) The ABA must, by notice in writing:
  (a) determine standards that are to be observed by commercial television broadcasting licensees ...
  ...
...
(4) Standards must not be inconsistent with this Act or the regulations.

The standard required Australian programs to comprise a certain percentage of all programming broadcast. The validity of the standard was challenged by companies involved in the New Zealand film industry. The companies relied on s 160(d) of the Act and an international

27 Justice Nye Perram, 'The Perils of Complexity: Why More Law is Bad Law' (2010) 39(4) *Australian Tax Review* 179, 184. This is a reference to part of a line from AB (Banjo) Paterson's famous poem, first published in 1889, 'Clancy of the Overflow': 'And he sees the vision splendid of the sunlit plains extended': William H Wilde, Joy Hooton and Barry Andrews (eds), *The Oxford Companion to Australian Literature* (Oxford University Press, 2nd ed, 2005).

28 *Independent Commission Against Corruption v Cunneen* (2015) 256 CLR 1, 22 [35] (French CJ, Hayne, Kiefel and Nettle JJ).

29 Ibid.

30 Ibid.

31 In *Bull v The Queen* (2000) 201 CLR 443 three constructions were considered by the plurality and none were entirely satisfactory: at 468 [85] (McHugh, Gummow and Hayne JJ). See also *DPP v Scheele* (2016) 12 ACTLR 1 (CA), where the preferred construction left an item in sch 1 to the *Firearms Act 1996* (ACT) with little or no work to do: at 13 [58]. In that latter case the legislature subsequently responded by extensively amending the Act: see *Crimes (Serious and Organised Crime) Legislation Amendment Act 2016* (ACT); Supplementary Explanatory Statement, Crimes (Serious and Organised Crime) Legislation Amendment Bill 2016 (ACT) 2, 3.

32 (1998) 194 CLR 355.

agreement between Australia and New Zealand given force under that provision. Section 160(d) provided as follows:

> The ABA is to perform its functions in a manner consistent with:
>
> ...
>
> (d) Australia's obligations under any convention to which Australia is a party or any agreement between Australia and a foreign country.

An international agreement, the *Australia–New Zealand Closer Economic Relations Trade Agreement*, had come into force in 1983 and the Protocol on Trade in Services to the Australia–New Zealand Closer Economic Relations Trade Agreement had come into effect in 1989. It was common ground between the parties that the provisions of cl 9 of the Australian Content Standard were in conflict with the provisions of arts 4 and 5 of the Protocol.

According to the plurality of the High Court, the first question in the case[33] was 'is cl 9 of the Australian Content Standard in breach of s 160(d) of the Act?'[34] In the court below, a majority of the Federal Court had held 'that there was "an irreconcilable conflict between the special provision constituted by s 122(2)(b) of the Act and the general provision of s 160(d), as applied to the [Trade Agreement]" and that s 122(2)(b) must prevail'.[35] The plurality disagreed.[36] They held that that s 122 was impliedly cut back by s 160:

> When s 122 is read with s 160, the legal meaning of s 122 is that the ABA must determine standards relating to the Australian content of programs but only to the extent that those standards are consistent with the directions in s 160.[37]

In reasoning to this conclusion, their Honours began by seeing if one of the provisions was the 'leading provision'.[38] The leading provision is the dominant provision, to which the other provision is subordinate. Their Honours determined it was s 160:

> [Section] 160 and s 122 ... They are interlocking provisions, with s 160 – the dominant provision – directing how the function conferred by s 122 is to be carried out.[39]

Section 160 was the dominant provision because Parliament had indicated such a hierarchy through the terms of ss 122 and 160. As for s 160:

> The express words of s 160 require the ABA to carry out its functions in accordance with the directions given by that section. Section 160 therefore provides the conceptual framework in which the functions conferred by s 158 are to be carried out.[40]

---

33 The case raised a second question: if the standard is in breach of s 160(d) of the Act, is the standard invalid? That second question is the subject of chapter 37.

34 (1998) 194 CLR 355, 380 [66] (McHugh, Gummow, Kirby and Hayne JJ).

35 Ibid 381 [68].

36 Brennan CJ also allowed the appeal, but for different reasons.

37 (1998) 194 CLR 355, 385 [80] (McHugh, Gummow, Kirby and Hayne JJ).

38 Ibid 382 [70], quoting *Institute of Patent Agents v Lockwood* [1894] AC 347, 360 (Lord Herschell LC).

39 Ibid 385 [81] (McHugh, Gummow, Kirby and Hayne JJ).

40 Ibid 384 [79].

Section 122 confirmed this hierarchy,[41] for sub-s (4) required that '[s]tandards must not be inconsistent with this Act or the regulations'.

The next step they took was to seek a construction of the provisions that would give both provisions an operation in the sense that neither was redundant, and that was also consistent with the objects of the Act. The plurality did not read s 122, as the Full Federal Court had done, as providing for preferential treatment of Australian programs. By a close attention to the words of s 122 and having regard to case law on the meaning of 'relate to', the plurality read 'relate to' as requiring the 'existence of a connection or association between the content of the Standard and the Australian content of programs'.[42] It followed that '[a] standard can relate to the Australian content of programs although it also regulates other matters'.[43] Further, a standard did not have to give preference to be one that 'related to' the Australian content of programs. Thus, a standard could be made that was consistent with s 122 (must relate to Australian content of programs) *and* s 160(d) (must not discriminate against persons of New Zealand nationality or another nationality protected by agreements similar to those contained in the Protocol).[44] For instance, the ABA could determine a standard that required that 'Australian and New Zealand programs should each be given a fixed percentage of viewing time'.[45]

Finally, the plurality had regard to the objects provision in the Act, which included 'to promote the role of broadcasting services in developing and reflecting a sense of Australian identity, character and cultural diversity': s 3(e). The plurality noted that the construction it favoured was consistent with that object.[46]

The basis of the principle of harmonious construction (principle of consistency) is the need to maintain coherence in the law [35.5]

For obvious reasons courts must avoid interpreting provisions in a way that would perpetuate conflict, whether it is between multiple provisions in the one statute or between different statutes. As regards the former, Dixon J has opined:

> [W]hen two apparently inconsistent provisions occur in one Act of Parliament, to reconcile them by interpretation is the only course open. They cannot both receive their full meaning as it is expressed.[47]

In the case of conflict between different statutes, a court asks whether the provisions can 'stand together'.[48] If they cannot, the earlier one falls.[49]

The underlying basis for this stance appears to be that '[c]onstruction should favour coherence in the law'.[50]

---

41 Ibid 385 [80].

42 Ibid 387 [87] (footnote omitted).

43 Ibid.

44 Ibid 388 [89].

45 Ibid 388 [90].

46 Ibid.

47 *South-Eastern Drainage Board (South Australia) v Savings Bank of South Australia* (1939) 62 CLR 603, 626.

48 *Ferdinands v Commissioner for Public Employment* (2006) 225 CLR 130, 138 [18] (Gummow and Hayne JJ); *Butler v A-G (Vic)* (1961) 106 CLR 268, 280 (Kitto J, Menzies J agreeing at 286).

49 See **[35.10]**.

50 *Plaintiff S4/2014 v Minister for Immigration and Border Protection* (2014) 253 CLR 219, 236 [42] (the Court).

Techniques for resolving apparent conflict

[35.6] **In resolving apparent or actual conflict – achieving the most harmonious construction overall – courts draw on a range of interpretative techniques**

The overarching technique of preferring a construction that operates consistently (the principle of harmonious construction) has been cited and illustrated above.[51] In addition, a court has available to it a number of particular tools to resolve apparent conflict. These are now briefly outlined.

In the case of conflict between multiple provisions of the one statute or of conflict between different statutes, a court can

- work out which is the general law and which is the special law, and prefer the special law to the extent necessary; and
- use 'ordinary'[52] principles of statutory interpretation to find the most harmonious construction.

Additionally,

- in the case of conflict between multiple provisions of the one statute, a court can work out which is intended to be the leading provision and which is intended to be the subordinate provision, and prefer the leading provision to the extent necessary; and
- in the case of irreconcilable conflict between an earlier Act and a later Act, a court will, as a last resort, prefer the later Act and hold that that Act impliedly repeals the earlier Act.

Each of these techniques is now elaborated on.

[35.7] **If there is apparent conflict between a general law and a special law, the presumption is that the special law prevails and the general law is cut back accordingly: *generalia specialibus non derogant***

The *generalia specialibus non derogant* canon has been described in an earlier chapter.[53] As **Example 35.2** shows, the *generalia specialibus* canon also assists in resolving apparent conflict between provisions of different statutes.[54]

Example 35.2 *Commissioner of Police for New South Wales v Eaton*[55]

A probationary constable was dismissed by the Commissioner of Police for New South Wales. The constable attempted to challenge his dismissal by applying to the Industrial Relations Commission. Section 81(4) of the *Industrial Relations Act 1996* (NSW) ('the IR Act') provided: 'If an employer dismisses an employee and the employee claims that the dismissal is harsh, unreasonable or unjust, the employee may apply to the Commission for the claim to be dealt with under this Part [ie, ch 2 pt 6].' At the same time, s 80(3) of the *Police Act 1990* (NSW) provided:

51 At **[35.4]** and **Example 35.1**.

52 Here 'ordinary' signifies principles not specifically designed to resolve conflict.

53 At **[18.14]**.

54 See *Commissioner of Police for New South Wales v Eaton* (2013) 252 CLR 1 (**Example 35.2**); *DPP v Gibson* (2012) 61 MVR 261.

55 (2013) 252 CLR 1.

'The Commissioner [of Police] may dismiss any such probationary police officer from the NSW Police Force at any time and without giving any reason.'

The question was whether s 80(3) of the *Police Act* impliedly excluded the review under ch 2 pt 6 of the IR Act by the Commission of a decision to dismiss a probationary police officer. By majority the High Court held that the necessary implication of reading the two Acts together was that the *Police Act* had that effect.[56] Among the reasons they gave was the indication provided by the *generalia specialibus* canon. Heydon J held that s 80(3) 'deals with the specific and relatively narrow subject of dismissing probationary constables', while '[s]ection 84(1) of the IR Act deals with the general subject of the remedies open to a broad range of employees dismissed harshly, unreasonably or unjustly'.[57] He held that this indicated that 'the general provision must give way to the particular provision'.[58] Crennan, Kiefel and Bell JJ similarly held that 'the general provisions of the IR Act do not apply in the face of the special, and inconsistent, terms of s 80(3) of the *Police Act*'.[59]

Ordinary principles of statutory interpretation are brought into play in order to find the most harmonious construction overall [35.8]

A court resolves apparent conflict between statutory provisions by ascertaining the presumed legislative intention: this was discussed at **[35.2]**. Accordingly, in order for that intention to be found, 'all available indications' are brought into play.[60] This includes factors derived by applying ordinary principles of interpretation.

The case of *Commissioner of Police for New South Wales v Eaton* (introduced above at **Example 35.2**) illustrates the deployment of ordinary principles of statutory interpretation in the search for the most harmonious resolution of an apparent conflict between provisions of two Acts.[61] It will be recalled that the case concerned the interaction between s 80(3) of the *Police Act 1990* (NSW) and ch 2 pt 6 of the *Industrial Relations Act 1996* (NSW) ('the IR Act'). The question was whether the provisions of the IR Act did not apply by reason of inconsistency with s 80(3) of the *Police Act*. In the reasoning of the majority of the Court, several interpretative factors derived from ordinary principles of interpretation were relied on in order to produce the most harmonious result: that ch 2 pt 6 of the IR Act did not apply to a decision made under s 80(3) of the *Police Act*[62] or, put another way, s 80(3) impliedly excluded review under ch 2 pt 6 of the IR Act.[63]

---

56 Ibid 7 [10], 14 [31] (Heydon J), 32 [92] (Crennan, Kiefel and Bell JJ). Gageler J at 37 [106] dissented.

57 Ibid 10–11 [21].

58 Ibid 11 [21].

59 Ibid 32 [92] (Crennan, Kiefel and Bell JJ).

60 *Commissioner of Police for New South Wales v Eaton* (2013) 252 CLR 1, 19 [46] (Crennan, Kiefel and Bell JJ), quoting *Associated Minerals Consolidated Ltd v Wyong Shire Council* [1975] AC 538, 553–4 (Lord Wilberforce).

61 For an illustration of the application of ordinary principles of interpretation to the resolution of apparent conflict between provisions of the same Act, see *Dolheguy v Becker* (2009) 52 MVR 462.

62 (2013) 252 CLR 1, 32 [92] (Crennan, Kiefel and Bell JJ).

63 Ibid 14 [31] (Heydon J).

Upon an examination of s 80(3), its language pointed to 'an unfettered power to dismiss'.[64] Their Honours highlighted the words 'at any time'[65] and 'without giving any reason'.[66] The subject matter – 'the probationary status of probationary constables'[67] – was another factor pointing to the conclusion that the provisions of the IR Act did not apply to probationary constables.[68] Other provisions in the *Police Act* were relied on. The regime that provided for the claims of confirmed police officers also maintained a focus on the decision of the Commissioner of Police.[69] Beyond the Acts concerned, a High Court case on comparable legislation had also found there was an 'unfettered power to dismiss' a probationary constable.[70] Finally, adverse consequences of reading the power to dismiss as subject to the IR Act were outlined. They included the difficulty of the NSW Industrial Relations Commission carrying out its task when no reason was given,[71] and the anomalous consequence that a probationary constable would enjoy a right of review superior to that of a confirmed constable.[72]

[35.9] **In the case of apparent conflict between provisions of the one statute, a court may employ the technique of determining which is the leading provision and which is the subordinate provision that must give way**

One technique to deal with apparent conflict between legislative provisions was expounded in *Institute of Patent Agents v Lockwood*:[73]

> [T]here is a conflict sometimes between two sections to be found in the same Act. You have to try and reconcile them as best you may. If you cannot, you have to determine which is the leading provision and which the subordinate provision, and which must give way to the other.[74]

As noted, it is a technique to deal with conflict between provisions of the one statute. In the *Project Blue Sky* case the plurality quoted with approval this statement of Lord Herschell.[75] Their Honours then opined: 'Only by determining the hierarchy of the provisions will it be possible in many cases to give each provision the meaning which best gives effect to its purpose and language while maintaining the unity of the statutory scheme.'[76]

This method is itself interpretative. That is to say, a court determines the hierarchy of provisions by determining which provision Parliament can be taken to have intended to be the leading provision, and which provision Parliament can be taken to have intended to be the subordinate provision.

---

64 Ibid 27 [74] (Crennan, Kiefel and Bell JJ).

65 Ibid 7–8 [12] (Heydon J).

66 Ibid 8 [13] (Heydon J), 27 [74] (Crennan, Kiefel and Bell JJ).

67 Ibid 9 [16] (Heydon J).

68 Ibid 9–10 [15]–[16].

69 Ibid 27 [76] (Crennan, Kiefel and Bell JJ).

70 Ibid 7–8 [12] (Heydon J).

71 Ibid 8 [14].

72 Ibid 11–14 [22]–[30] (Heydon J), 27–8 [76]–[77] (Crennan, Kiefel and Bell JJ).

73 [1894] AC 347.

74 Ibid 360 (Lord Herschell LC).

75 *Project Blue Sky Inc v Australian Broadcasting Authority* (1998) 194 CLR 355, 382 [70].

76 Ibid. See also *Western Australian Planning Commission v Southregal Pty Ltd* (2017) 259 CLR 106, 152 [137] (Keane J) (dissenting as to outcome).

It is not always necessary to use this technique when attempting to find the most harmonious construction.[77] But as the *Project Blue Sky* case (**Example 35.1**) and others[78] have showed, it can be a useful technique.

Where the conflict between different statutes is found to be 'irreconcilable', then, as a last resort, a court may conclude that the earlier law has been impliedly repealed by the later law [35.10]

Express repeal is not the only method by which an Act may be repealed. For a long time it has been recognised that an Act may be held by a court to have been impliedly repealed.[79] Implied repeal is a determination reached by a court that an earlier Act is to 'be taken to be repealed by implication',[80] or, as the Latin maxim puts it, *leges posteriores priores contrarias abrogant*.[81] The root explanation is inconsistency.[82]

The consequence of implied repeal is supported by basic constitutional principle: the supremacy of Parliament. Under the doctrine, '[i]t is recognized as a general principle of English constitutional law that one parliament cannot bind its successors'.[83] The doctrine applies to parliaments within a federation, within their own sphere.[84]

A finding of implied repeal is a comparatively rare event in the courts. In the 1961 case of *Butler v Attorney-General (Vic)*,[85] Fullagar J stated that it was a 'comparatively rare phenomenon'.[86] In the 2003 case of *Dossett v TKJ Nominees Pty Ltd*[87] McHugh J stated that it was 'a rare and unlikely event'.[88] Still, as these statements imply, in small number of cases a court has found it has occurred.[89]

---

77 *Western Australian Planning Commission v Southregal Pty Ltd* (2017) 259 CLR 106, 122 [54] (Kiefel and Bell JJ).

78 *Plaintiff S297/2013 v Minister for Immigration and Border Protection* (2014) 255 CLR 179, 196 [64] (Crennan, Bell, Gageler and Keane JJ); *Financial Services Council Ltd v Industry Super Australia* (2014) 222 FCR 455, 460 [23] (the Court).

79 *Ferdinands v Commissioner for Public Employment* (2006) 225 CLR 130, 137–8 [18] (Gummow and Hayne JJ), citing *Foster's Case* (1614) 11 Co Rep 56 b [77 ER 1222]; *Garnett v Bradley* (1877–78) LR 3 App Cas 944, 965–6.

80 *Goodwin v Phillips* (1908) 7 CLR 1, 7 (Griffith CJ).

81 'Later laws abrogate prior contrary laws': *Ferdinands v Commissioner for Public Employment* (2006) 225 CLR 130, 161 [105] n 97 (Kirby J) (dissenting as to outcome).

82 Ibid 137–8 [18] (Gummow and Hayne JJ).

83 *South-Eastern Drainage Board (South Australia) v Savings Bank of South Australia* (1939) 62 CLR 603, 617 (Latham CJ).

84 *Butler v A-G (Vic)* (1961) 106 CLR 268, 276 (Fullagar J) (dissenting as to outcome).

85 (1961) 106 CLR 268.

86 Ibid 275.

87 (2003) 218 CLR 1.

88 Ibid 7 [14].

89 See, eg, *Butler v A-G (Vic)* (1961) 106 CLR 268, 280 (Kitto J, Menzies J agreeing at 286); *Ferdinands v Commissioner for Public Employment* (2006) 225 CLR 130, 139 [20] (Gummow and Hayne JJ); *McNeill v The Queen* (2008) 168 FCR 198, 212 [79], 213 [81] (the Court); *Saliba v Aziz* (2013) 281 FLR 278, 282–3 [12]–[13], 288 [47] (the Court).

The test for determining whether implied repeal has occurred has been variously expressed.[90] In *Butler v Attorney-General (Vic)*[91] Fullagar J (dissenting as to outcome) stated that '[implied] repeal will not be held to have been effected unless actual contrariety is clearly apparent'.[92] This language was approved of and applied by four members of the High Court in *Dossett v TKJ Nominees Pty Ltd*.[93] Other similar tests are used. Some were referred to with approval in *Ferdinands v Commissioner for Public Employment*.[94] They are 'repugnancy' and 'the two cannot stand or live together (or cannot be "reconciled")'.[95] Other tests include 'wholly inconsistent',[96] 'really contradictory enactments'[97] and 'not possible to comply with both Acts simultaneously'.[98]

As a finding of implied repeal is a drastic step for a court to take, a court strives to avoid having to make such a finding. Accordingly, there must be 'very strong grounds to support that implication'.[99] In *Ferdinands v Commissioner for Public Employment*[100] Gummow and Hayne JJ held that '[n]o conclusion can be reached about whether a later statutory provision contradicts an earlier without first construing both provisions'.[101] A court will not hold an implied repeal to have occurred if constructions of the provisions are available that avoid taking that step. Thus, '[i]f . . . there is fairly open on the words of the later Act, a construction by adopting which the earlier Act may be saved from repeal, that construction is to be adopted'.[102]

Example 35.3 ***Saliba v Aziz***[103]

On 24 February 2011 the respondent, who was the holder of an ACT driver licence, was issued with a notice immediately suspending his driver licence. Later, on 18 May 2011, the respondent was seen by police to be driving a vehicle. He was arrested and charged under s 32(2)(a) of the *Road Transport (Driver Licensing) Act 1999* (ACT) ('the *Driver Licensing Act*'). Section 32 included the following provisions:

90 A 'covering the field' test, used in applying s 109 of the *Commonwealth Constitution*, has not been applied: *Ferdinands v Commissioner for Public Employment* (2006) 225 CLR 130, 146 [49] (Gummow and Hayne JJ).

91 (1961) 106 CLR 268.

92 Ibid 275.

93 (2003) 218 CLR 1, 7 [14] (McHugh J), 14 [43]–[44] (Gummow, Hayne and Heydon JJ).

94 (2006) 225 CLR 130.

95 Ibid 138 [18] (Gummow and Hayne JJ).

96 *Goodwin v Phillips* (1908) 7 CLR 1, 7 (Griffith CJ).

97 *Butler v A-G (Vic)* (1961) 106 CLR 268, 290 (Windeyer J) (dissenting as to outcome), quoting *Maxwell on the Interpretation of Statutes* (8th ed, 1937) 147.

98 *Ferdinands v Commissioner for Public Employment* (2006) 225 CLR 130, 146 [47] (Gummow and Hayne JJ).

99 *Saraswati v The Queen* (1991) 172 CLR 1, 17 (Gaudron J), approved in *Ferdinands v Commissioner for Public Employment* (2006) 225 CLR 130, 134 [4] (Gleeson CJ), 138 [18] (Gummow and Hayne JJ), 163 [109] (Kirby J) (dissenting as to outcome).

100 (2006) 225 CLR 130.

101 Ibid 145 [47].

102 *Goodwin v Phillips* (1908) 7 CLR 1, 10 (Barton J). See, to the same effect, *Saraswati v The Queen* (1991) 172 CLR 1, 17–18 (Gaudron J), quoting *Seward v The 'Vera Cruz'* (1884) 10 App Cas 59, 68 (Lord Selbourne).

103 (2013) 281 FLR 278.

> **32 Offences committed by disqualified drivers etc**
>
> . . .
>
> (2) A person whose Australian driver licence is suspended by a court in Australia or under the law of any jurisdiction must not –
>
> (a) drive a motor vehicle on a road or road related area during the period of suspension except in accordance with a restricted licence issued to the person;
>
> . . .
>
> . . .
>
> (5) If a court convicts a person of an offence against subsection (1) or (3), the person is automatically disqualified from holding or obtaining a driver licence –
>
> (a) for a first offender – for 12 months or, if the court orders a longer period, the longer period . . .

Also on the statute book at the time of the offence were ss 61B(4)(d) and 61C of the *Road Transport (General) Act 1999* (ACT) ('the *General Act*'). These provisions had been inserted in 2010. Section 61B(4)(d) imposed a duty on a person, who had been issued with an immediate suspension notice, not to drive a vehicle. Section 61C created an offence of breaching that duty. It provided:

> **61C Drive while suspension notice in effect**
>
> (1) A person commits an offence if –
>
> (a) the person has been served with an immediate suspension notice; and
>
> (b) the notice has not ceased to have effect; and
>
> (c) the person contravenes section 61B (4) (d) . . .
>
> Maximum penalty: 20 penalty units.

Section 64 provided for additional punishment:

> **64 Court may order disqualification for other offences**
>
> (1) A court that convicts a person, or finds a person guilty, of an offence against the road transport legislation may disqualify the person from holding or obtaining a driver licence for the period the court considers appropriate.

While the *Driver Licensing Act* and the *General Act* both concerned driving a vehicle while a driver licence was suspended, the Acts' operations differed. A conviction for an offence under s 61C of the *General Act* might result in no disqualification at all, unless the Court imposed one under s 64 of that Act. Under the earlier Act with which the respondent was charged, the *Driver Licensing Act*, conviction was accompanied by an automatic disqualification from holding or obtaining a licence for at least 12 months. In addition, that Act imposed a heavier fine.

The primary judge set aside the conviction and sentence imposed on the respondent, for the reason that s 32(2) of the *Driver Licensing Act* had been impliedly repealed by s 61C of the *General Act*. Upon a further appeal to the ACT Court of Appeal, the issue was whether the primary judge had been correct in so holding.

The Court observed that the respective provisions – s 32(2) of the *Driver Licensing Act* and s 61C of the *General Act* – dealt with the same conduct – that is, driving while an ACT driver licence was suspended.[104] The Court agreed[105] with the reasoning in a Federal Court case that dealt with a similar issue.[106] That case had dealt with a charge under a provision of the *Defence Force Discipline Act 1982* (Cth) where the elements of the charged offence were identical to another offence in the same Act in respect of which the maximum penalty was lower. Employing consequential reasoning,[107] the Federal Court had stated:

> It is hardly likely that the legislature intended to allow the same conduct to be treated differently, where there is no relevant aggravating or distinguishing circumstance, dependent upon the whim of the prosecuting authority. Such a result would be capricious and arbitrary.[108]

The Federal Court distinguished the case from the 'commonplace' situation where

> the one act or course of conduct might lead to a variety of offences created by the same statute. However, those offences would all be different in character, one from the other, usually with an ascending order of gravity.[109]

In the present case, the finding of implied repeal was upheld and the appeal against the decision of the primary judge was accordingly dismissed.[110]

104 Ibid 286 [33].

105 Ibid.

106 *Hoffmann v Chief of Army* (2004) 137 FCR 520.

107 See chapter 27.

108 (2013) 281 FLR 278, 286 [32] (the Court), quoting *Hoffmann v Chief of Army* (2004) 137 FCR 520, 528 [11].

109 Ibid, quoting *Hoffmann v Chief of Army* (2004) 137 FCR 520, 528 [11].

110 Ibid 288 [47]–[48].

STATUTORY POWERS AND THEIR CHARACTERISATION: DISCRETION OR DUTY?

36

Overview

Statutory powers confer authority that enables a person or body to do what would otherwise be illegal or ineffective. They do so in two broad ways: by conferring discretions and imposing duties. This chapter focuses on the meanings of 'may', 'shall' and 'must' and on a question of characterisation that often arises in relation to them: namely, should the words be characterised as conferring a discretion or as imposing a duty, at least in certain circumstances?[1] [36.1]

Developments in legislative drafting, a result of the plain language movement, have tended to reduce interpretative disputes in relation to the characterisation of statutory powers. But they have not eliminated the need for interpreting them in all situations.

Although a statutory power is often expressed in a word in common use, whether it is characterised as a discretion or a duty is a matter of interpretation, to be determined according to the intention of the legislature. At common law the prima facie meaning of 'may' is that it is permissive – an authority to do something that otherwise a person or authority could not lawfully do. But where a power, expressed by 'may', is conditioned upon the existence of an event or upon the formation of a particular opinion by the repository of the power, the condition may sometimes be taken to specify the circumstances in which the power must be exercised. In other words, even though the word 'may' is used in the power, the context may indicate that the power must be exercised once the condition is met. With the word 'shall', its prima facie meaning is that it is used in a mandatory sense. Similarly, the prima facie meaning of 'must' imports an imperative.

Most Interpretation Acts in Australia make provision for determining the meaning of 'may', 'shall' and 'must'. Although their terms differ somewhat, in substance they reflect the common law.

Functions of statutory powers

Statutory powers fulfil two broad functions: conferring discretions and imposing duties [36.2]

Statutory powers are ubiquitous in statute law. They may be conferred on whomever Parliament sees fit.[2] Commonly, they include public officials or bodies,[3] bodies corporate[4] and natural persons in their private capacity.[5]

1 For an elaboration of this issue in relation to the making of delegated legislation, see **[43.15]**.

2 The possibility of conferring power on an algorithmic system is discussed in Will Bateman, 'Algorithmic Decision-Making and Legality: Public Law Dimensions' (2020) 94(7) *Australian Law Journal* 520, 529–30.

3 See, eg, Commissioner of Taxation (*Income Tax Assessment Act 1997* (Cth)) and Secretary of the Department of Social Services (*Social Security Act 1991* (Cth)).

4 See, eg, *Fundraising Act 1998* (Vic) s 18 (body corporate may apply for registration as a fundraiser).

5 See, eg, *Administration and Probate Act 1958* (Vic) s 90A(1) (eligible person may apply to the Supreme Court for a family provision order).

A statutory power 'enables an authority to do what would otherwise be illegal or ineffective'.[6] A power '[makes] legal and possible [that] which there would otherwise be no right or authority to do'.[7]

Powers may be conferred expressly or impliedly. Commonly, powers are expressly conferred by 'may', 'shall', 'must' and similar terms. Powers, including incidental powers,[8] may be implied.[9] An example of an implied power is taken from *Pfeiffer v Stevens*,[10] where s 860(2) of the *Local Government Act 1993* (Qld) was at issue:

> (2) The proposed local law must include a sunset provision stating the law will expire –
> (a) 6 months after its commencement; or
> (b) at the end of a longer period gazetted by the Minister.

In this case McHugh J (semble, Gleeson CJ and Hayne J[11]) held that the Minister was impliedly empowered to extend the period of the proposed local law *a second time*.[12]

Powers may be broken down, broadly speaking, into two categories: discretions and duties. In this area a discretion is defined as 'a capacity to choose between alternative courses of action'.[13] Thus, if a person has a discretion, the power may be exercised or not. The following is an example of a discretion:

> The Director-General may suspend or cancel a licence or authority . . .[14]

Conceptually, duties are a special type of power. The imposition of a duty on a person or body impliedly enables the duty-holder to carry out the act that constitutes the performance of the

6 *Yarmirr v Australian Telecommunications Corporation* (1990) 96 ALR 739, 749 (Burchett J, quoting with approval *Wade on Administrative Law* (6th ed, 1988) 614). See similar definition in *Finance Facilities Pty Ltd v Commissioner of Taxation (Cth)* (1971) 127 CLR 106, 134 (Windeyer J, Barwick CJ agreeing at 128).

7 *Julius v Lord Bishop of Oxford* (1880) 5 App Cas 214, 222 (Earl Cairns LC).

8 *Johns v Australian Securities Commission* (1993) 178 CLR 408, 428–9 (Brennan J, Dawson J agreeing generally at 435, Gaudron J agreeing generally at 458). Statutes often codify this principle: see, eg, *Australian Crime Commission Act 2002* (Cth) s 19.

9 See, eg, *Federal Commissioner of Taxation v Multiflex Pty Ltd* (2011) 197 FCR 580, 592–3 [40] (the Court).

10 (2001) 209 CLR 57.

11 Ibid 63 [17] (Gleeson CJ and Hayne J).

12 Ibid 68 [40] (McHugh J). The presumption in the *Acts Interpretation Act 1954* (Qld) s 23(1) (a power may be exercised as occasion requires) was applied in the absence of a contrary intention: at 63–5 [19]–[26] (Gleeson CJ and Hayne J), 65–6 [28]–[29], 72 [51] (McHugh J). The role of Interpretation Acts in extending statutory powers is discussed in chapter 25.

13 *Samad v District Court of New South Wales* (2002) 209 CLR 140, 152 [31] (Gleeson CJ and McHugh J). The High Court has recognised that 'discretion' has a number of senses in law: *Baiada Poultry Pty Ltd v The Queen* (2012) 246 CLR 92, 103–4 [26] (French CJ, Gummow, Hayne and Crennan JJ). One usage has been criticised. The Court has deprecated the use of the word 'discretionary' to describe a 'judgment' as to whether a proviso such as 'substantial miscarriage of justice' is satisfied, where the satisfaction of the proviso could enliven a duty to act. Their Honours said that '[i]t is distracting because the description requires consideration of which of the several different ways in which the concept of "discretion" can be used is intended'. And, they added, '[i]t invites error if it suggests that the proviso need not be applied even if no substantial miscarriage of justice has actually occurred': *Baiada Poultry Pty Ltd v The Queen* (2012) 246 CLR 92, 103–4 [26] (French CJ, Gummow, Hayne and Crennan JJ).

14 *Poisons and Therapeutic Goods Regulation 1994* (NSW) cl 149, discussed in *Samad v District Court of New South Wales* (2002) 209 CLR 140.

duty.[15] Of course, a statutory duty to do an act requires a person to perform the act when the circumstances call for it.[16] The following is an example of such a duty:

> **Notice of hearing of application**
> As soon as practicable after the application is filed, a registrar must give written notice to the person whose protection is sought and defendant of the time and place for the hearing of the application.[17]

In practice, powers are not necessarily entirely a discretion or a duty; often a power will contain a mixture of the two capacities.[18] Even where a power is apparently discretionary, implied limits always exist and consequential duties to observe those limits will arise. Put another way, a discretion that is unfettered on its face is never at large;[19] it is not unlimited.[20] A court might be presented with a question as to whether there is an implied duty to *consider* exercising the power.[21] It might be a question of whether the conferral of a power is coupled with a duty not to exercise it more than once or again.[22] Or it might be a question as to whether the repository of the power is impliedly bound to take into account a particular consideration in the exercise of the discretion conferred, or is duty-bound not to take into account a particular consideration.[23] Ascertaining implied considerations to be taken into account, or not to be taken into account, by public bodies is 'determined by construction of the statute conferring the discretion'.[24]

Statutory discretions and statutory duties are also subject to various limits determined by interpretation. Many of these questions are part of the day-to-day operation of administrative law. It has been said that 'statutory construction is the key to most administrative law'.[25] The present chapter focuses on the meaning of 'may', 'shall' and 'must' respectively and whether a statutory power

15 *Re Davis* (1947) 75 CLR 409, 418 (Starke J) ('shall').

16 Exceptionally, a statutory provision using imperative language is not legally enforceable. See **[37.4]**. And the enforcement of a breach of duty by a public official or body is subject in any case to remedial law, and remedies are often discretionary.

17 *Personal Violence Restraining Orders Act 2016* (NT) s 13, briefly discussed in *Atkinson v Bardon* (2018) 41 NTLR 35, 48–9 [40] (Mildren AJ).

18 Christopher Enright, *Federal Administrative Law* (Federation Press, 2001) 80 [7.7].

19 *Re Settree Estates* (2018) 98 NSWLR 910, 936 [113] (Lindsay J).

20 *Ballantyne v Workcover Authority of New South Wales* [2007] NSWCA 239, [90]. See generally *Padfield v Minister for Agriculture, Fisheries and Food* [1968] AC 997, 1029–30 (Lord Reid), 1060 (Lord Upjohn); *North Australian Aboriginal Justice Agency Ltd v Northern Territory* (2015) 256 CLR 569, 591 [34] (French CJ, Keifel and Bell JJ), quoting with approval *Gerlach v Clifton Bricks Pty Ltd* (2002) 209 CLR 478, 504 [70] (Kirby and Callinan JJ).

21 Cases that have discussed this question include the following: *Minister for Immigration and Citizenship v SZGUR* (2011) 241 CLR 594; *Carter v Minister for Aboriginal Affairs* (2005) 143 FCR 383; *West Australian Field and Game Association Inc v Pearce* (1992) 8 WAR 64; *Re Kierath, Minister for Heritage; Ex parte City of Fremantle* (2000) 22 WAR 342.

22 *Minister for Immigration and Multicultural Affairs v Bhardwaj* (2002) 209 CLR 597; *Kabourakis v Medical Practitioners Board of Victoria* [2006] VSCA 301; Stephen J Moloney, 'Finality of Administrative Decisions and Decisions of the Statutory Tribunal' (2010) 61 *AIAL Forum* 35. See also chapter 25.

23 *Samad v District Court of New South Wales* (2002) 209 CLR 140, 152 [32] (Gleeson CJ and McHugh J). In public law these considerations are respectively called 'relevant' and 'irrelevant' considerations.

24 *Minister for Aboriginal Affairs v Peko-Wallsend Ltd* (1986) 162 CLR 24, 39 (Mason J, Gibbs CJ generally agreeing at 30, Dawson J agreeing at 71).

25 Kristen Walker, 'Jurisdictional Error Since Craig' (2016) *AIAL Forum* 35, 39. For other illustrative analyses see Justice John Basten, 'Modern Judicial Review – An Overview' (Speech, Western Australian Bar Association CPD Conference, 4 November 2015); Jeffrey Barnes, 'How Statutory Interpretation Sustains Administrative Law' (2015) 22(3) *Australian Journal of Administrative Law* 163; Jeffrey Barnes, 'Statutory Interpretation

should be characterised as a discretion or a duty. For other limits on statutory powers (especially discretions) determined by interpretation, administrative law treatises may be examined.[26]

Example 36.1 ***North Australian Aboriginal Justice Agency Ltd v Northern Territory***[27]

Section 133AB of the *Police Administration Act 1978* (NT) provided a regime for holding a person in custody for a period of up to four hours (or, in the case of intoxication, 'for a period longer than 4 hours until the member believes on reasonable grounds that the person is no longer intoxicated'). The section applied if the person was arrested without a warrant and 'the person was arrested because the member [of the Police Force] believed on reasonable grounds that the person had committed, was committing or was about to commit, an offence that is an infringement notice offence'. On the expiry of the four-hour period or the longer period, a power in sub-s (3) was enlivened:

> (3) The member, or any other member, on the expiry of the period mentioned in subsection (2), may:
> (a) release the person unconditionally; or
> (b) release the person and issue the person with an infringement notice in relation to the infringement notice offence; or
> (c) release the person on bail; or
> (d) under section 137, bring the person before a justice or court for the infringement notice offence or another offence allegedly committed by the person.

The subsection was examined by the High Court. Nettle and Gordon JJ recognised the dual role played by the statutory power in sub-s (3). They held that, while the provision conferred a discretion to choose among a set of options, it also, impliedly, imposed an obligation:

> [The word] *may* in s 133AB(3) has the purpose of imposing an obligation on police officers to adopt one of the four options identified in s 133AB(3)(a)–(d) and so should be read as *must*.[28]

Developments in drafting of statutory powers

[36.3] **Developments in legislative drafting have reduced, but not eliminated, interpretative disputes in relation to the characterisation of statutory powers and in relation to 'may' and 'shall' in particular**

Interpretative difficulties have often arisen with the use of both 'shall' and 'may'. 'Shall' in particular became one of the foci of the plain language movement's challenge to traditional

and Administrative Law' in Matthew Groves (ed), *Modern Administrative Law in Australia: Concepts and Context* (Cambridge University Press, 2014) 119.

26 See, eg, Mark Aronson, Matthew Groves and Greg Weeks, *Judicial Review of Administrative Action and Government Liability* (Thomson Reuters, 6th ed, 2017); Robin Creyke et al, *Control of Government Action: Text, Cases and Commentary* (LexisNexis Butterworths, 5th ed, 2019).

27 (2015) 256 CLR 569.

28 Ibid 645 [209] (emphases in original; footnote omitted).

legislative drafting. A leading critic of traditional drafting called 'shall' the 'most misused word in the legal vocabulary'.[29] The Full Family Court noted that the problems with the use of 'shall' in legislation were 'notorious'.[30] The avoidance of 'shall' is a feature of many plain language legislative drafting manuals.[31]

One of the causes of difficulty with 'shall' is its lexical or semantic ambiguity: does it express an imperative, or does it express futurity?[32] To make matters more complicated, 'shall' has been evidently used in legislation in several senses.[33] An example is given by Barnes.[34] He looked at the use of 'shall' in the *Magistrates Act 1983* (SA) in the light of amendments by the *Magistrates (Miscellaneous) Amendment Act 2013* (SA). The amendments were designed to clarify the meaning of 'shall' in line with current (plain language) drafting style.[35] As expected, some amendments replaced 'shall' with 'must'. But other amendments pointed to a number of different senses in which 'shall' had been apparently deployed, for it was variously replaced with a present tense verb, with the future tense 'will' and with the discretionary 'may'. Cases in which 'shall' was found to confer a discretion[36] exemplified the problem with 'shall'.

To minimise problems with 'shall' recurring, parliamentary counsel in Australia and New Zealand now use 'must' and other terms instead of 'shall' to impose a duty. 'Shall' has virtually been abandoned altogether. The changed practice is evident in a survey of Australian, New

29 Michele M Asprey, *Plain Language for Lawyers* (Federation Press, 4th ed, 2010) 213, quoting Professor Joseph Kimble.

30 *In the Marriage of Harris* (1987) 11 Fam LR 629, 635 (the Court).

31 Jeffrey Barnes, 'Duties and Discretions: How Have "Plain English" Legislative Drafting Techniques Fared in Administrative Law?' (2016) 83 *AIAL Forum* 36, 42. The author cites manuals from Australia, Canada, Hong Kong, New Zealand, South Africa, the United Kingdom and the United States. For Australia see Office of Parliamentary Counsel, *Plain English Manual* (Australian Government, 2016) 20–1 [83]–[84].

32 *Varverakis v Police* (2003) 38 MVR 247, 251 [15] (Gray J), quoting *International Union v Massey-Ferguson Industries Ltd* (1979) 94 DLR (3d) 743, 745–6 (Reid J); Office of Parliamentary Counsel, *Plain English Manual* (Australian Government, 2016) [83]. And see the example of the amendments to the *Magistrates Act 1983* (SA), discussed above. See further Jeffrey Barnes, 'Duties and Discretions: How Have "Plain English" Legislative Drafting Techniques Fared in Administrative Law?' (2016) 83 *AIAL Forum* 36, 38–9.

33 Jeffrey Barnes, 'Duties and Discretions: How Have "Plain English" Legislative Drafting Techniques Fared in Administrative Law?' (2016) 83 *AIAL Forum* 36, 39, citing Elmer A Driedger, *The Composition of Legislation: Legislative Forms and Precedents* (Department of Justice (Canada), 2nd ed, 1976) 12–15. See also Nick Horn, 'And Yet More on the Thorny Business of Auxiliary Verbs . . .' (2002) 48 *Clarity* 35, 35.

34 Jeffrey Barnes, 'Duties and Discretions: How Have "Plain English" Legislative Drafting Techniques Fared in Administrative Law?' (2016) 83 *AIAL Forum* 36, 44–5.

35 The Minister described the purpose of the amendments as 'to convert various outdated references and to make other technical changes to accommodate current drafting practices': South Australia, *Parliamentary Debates*, House of Assembly, Magistrates (Miscellaneous) Amendment Bill 2013, 2 May 2013 (JR Rau). The South Australian Office of Parliamentary Counsel drafts in a plain English style: Nick Horn, 'Legislative Drafting in Australia, New Zealand and Ontario: Notes on an Informal Survey' [2005] (1) *The Loophole: Journal of the Commonwealth Association of Legislative Counsel* 55, 85.

36 See, eg, *Re Davis* (1947) 75 CLR 409; *Re Griffiths* [1991] 2 Qd R 29, 37 (Byrne J) (discussed below); *Newcastle City Council v A-G (NSW)* (1983) 52 LGRA 75, 78 (Kearney J); *R v Moylan; Ex parte Jenkins* [1974] WAR 176, 178–9 (Jackson CJ, Wickham J and Wallace J agreeing at 179); *Wallersteiner v Moir* [1974] 1 WLR 991, 1030 (Scarman LJ); *Re Lord Thurlow; Ex parte Official Receiver* [1895] 1 QB 724, 729–31 (Lord Esher MR).

Zealand and Ontario parliamentary counsel,[37] in drafting manuals[38] and in surveys of the statute book.[39]

As the South Australian example above illustrates, it is important to emphasise that parliamentary counsel have not simply replaced 'shall' with 'must'. To do this would have only created further problems. To impose a duty they use a word ('must') not prone to the semantic ambiguity that potentially arose with 'shall'. But, in addition, they have been 'much more careful and precise with modal auxiliaries'.[40]

The use of 'must' and 'must not' has been widely welcomed.[41] Members of the High Court have observed that the use of 'must' avoided 'constructional difficulty' associated with 'may'.[42] A judge of the Supreme Court of the Northern Territory has noted the care that parliamentary counsel take with 'must',[43] an observation that was not made by judges with respect to 'shall'. Few cases raise the issue of whether 'must' imposes a duty or confers a discretion,[44] and cases where 'must' conferred a discretion have been rare.[45] As regards 'must not', a search of the AustLII database did not reveal a case where that phrase was interpreted as anything other than a prohibition.

As this chapter demonstrates, 'may' can be ambiguous too. It can enable the doing of the thing authorised at discretion. Or it can be a 'simple empowering word'.[46] In the latter case 'the effect

---

37 Jeffrey Barnes, 'Duties and Discretions: How Have "Plain English" Legislative Drafting Techniques Fared in Administrative Law?' (2016) 83 *AIAL Forum* 36, 42, citing Nick Horn, 'Legislative Drafting in Australia, New Zealand and Ontario: Notes on an Informal Survey' [2005] (1) *The Loophole: Journal of the Commonwealth Association of Legislative Counsel* 55, 92.

38 Jeffrey Barnes, 'Duties and Discretions: How Have "Plain English" Legislative Drafting Techniques Fared in Administrative Law?' (2016) 83 *AIAL Forum* 36, 42.

39 See survey reported in Jeffrey Barnes, 'Duties and Discretions: How Have "Plain English" Legislative Drafting Techniques Fared in Administrative Law?' (2016) 83 *AIAL Forum* 36. The only state using 'shall' in 2013 (in a very limited degree) was Victoria. A subsequent survey for this chapter by Barnes, of 2019 Acts of the Victorian Parliament, found only two Acts used the word.

40 Ibid 48. See also this article at 44, citing Michele M Asprey, *Plain Language for Lawyers* (Federation Press, 4th ed, 2010) 207.

41 A few judges have expressed reservations about the use of 'must' and 'must not' in legislation. In *Halwood Corporation Ltd v Roads Corporation* [1998] 2 VR 439 Tadgell JA argued that while '"must" as a modal auxiliary may often appropriately express an obligation . . . the mere addition of "not" may fail as an apt expression of a prohibition': at 445–6 (Brooking JA agreeing at 440). Dowsett J thought it inappropriate that mandatory language be directed to the courts rather than prescribing that in certain circumstances a party has a particular right or obligation: Justice JA Dowsett, 'Lawyers and Legislation' (Speech, Bar Practice Course, Banco Court, Brisbane, 19 July 2013) 25–6.

42 *International Finance Trust Co Ltd v New South Wales Crime Commission* (2009) 240 CLR 319, 373 [121] (Hayne, Crennan and Kiefel JJ) (dissenting as to outcome).

43 *Atkinson v Bardon* (2018) 41 NTLR 35 [40] (Mildren AJ). See also *DPP v Dickfoss* (2011) 249 FLR 374, 396 [90] (Mildren J).

44 See *DPP v George* (2008) 102 SASR 246; *DPP v Dickfoss* (2011) 249 FLR 374, 395 [87] (Mildren J); *Radojevic v JDA Design Group Pty Ltd (No 2)* [2017] VSC 796, [60] (Ginnane J); *Coffs Harbour and District Local Aboriginal Land Council v Lynwood* [2017] NSWCA 317, [31] (Meagher JA, Simpson JA agreeing at [43]).

45 One case (arguably dicta) is *DPP v George* (2008) 102 SASR 246. The case is discussed in Jeffrey Barnes, 'Duties and Discretions: How Have "Plain English" Legislative Drafting Techniques Fared in Administrative Law?' (2016) 83 *AIAL Forum* 36, 43. In *D v Chief Executive Officer, Department for Child Protection and Family Support* [2016] WASC 289 'must' in *Children and Community Services Act 2004* (WA) ss 36(2) and 38(2), (4) was held to be intended to be 'exhortatory and not mandatory': at [82] (Corboy J).

46 *Victorian Building Authority v Andriotis* (2019) 268 CLR 168, 182 [43] (Kiefel CJ, Bell and Keane JJ).

[of the provision as a whole read in context is] to impose an obligation, or, at least, an obligation that must be performed in certain circumstances'.[47]

As mentioned above, parliamentary counsel in Australia and New Zealand now eschew 'shall' when their intention is to confer a discretion. Another drafting suggestion from a leading plain language proponent is to add a specific reference to a 'discretion' when 'may' is used.[48] Commonwealth legislation contains many examples of this drafting practice. For instance,

> 'The Inspector-General may, in his or her discretion'[49]
>
> 'The Authority may, at the discretion of the Authority,'[50]
>
> 'The Minister may, in his or her absolute discretion,'.[51]

Alternatively, a drafter may separately provide, in the subsection following a conferral of a power, a reference to 'In exercising its discretion under subsection (1)'.[52]

A broader response is to provide a general interpretative rule for the Act, such as the following:

> **Exercise of powers in Minister's discretion**
> Where a provision of this Act provides that the Minister may do a particular act or thing, and the word ***may*** is used, the act or thing may be done at the Minister's discretion.[53]

It is true that these drafting techniques are not without some effect. They are a more forceful indication of meaning than the prima facie meaning that arises from the use of the word 'may' alone in a provision. Their inclusion may assist a judge in reaching a view as to whether a power confers a discretion.[54] But there is no evidence that these drafting devices eliminate the issue of determining whether the power must be performed in certain circumstances. The references to 'in his or her discretion' and the like are themselves subject to interpretation. If there is no apparent justification for a discretion in the circumstances – that is, if the discretion has, as the High Court has said, 'effectively run out'[55] – a court would not allow form to triumph over substance. The explicit reference to 'in his or her discretion' would be read as a *general* conferral of discretion.[56] As regards the interpretative rule about the meaning of 'may' in a particular Act, this rule would be read in the manner of a definition – as subject to a contrary intention.[57]

---

47 *Samad v District Court of New South Wales* (2002) 209 CLR 140, 152 [32] (Gleeson CJ and McHugh J).

48 Jeffrey Barnes, 'Duties and Discretions: How Have "Plain English" Legislative Drafting Techniques Fared in Administrative Law?' (2016) 83 *AIAL Forum* 36, 46, drawing on Peter Butt, 'Recent Decisions' (2002) 48 *Clarity* 34, 35.

49 *Inspector-General of Taxation Act 2003* (Cth) s 9.

50 *Food Standards Australia New Zealand Act 1991* (Cth) s 111(1).

51 *National Radioactive Waste Management Act 2012* (Cth) s 17.

52 *National Consumer Credit Protection Act 2009* (Cth) s 278(2).

53 *Child Care Act 1972* (Cth) s 22A.

54 *Minister for Immigration and Multicultural Affairs v Bhardwaj* (2002) 209 CLR 597, 640 [130] (Kirby J) (dissenting as to outcome).

55 *Samad v District Court of New South Wales* (2002) 209 CLR 140, 164 [77] (Gaudron, Gummow and Callinan JJ), quoting Mark Aronson and Bruce Dyer, *Judicial Review of Administrative Action* (LBC Information Services, 2nd ed, 2000) 588.

56 Cf *WABZ v Minister for Immigration and Multicultural and Indigenous Affairs* (2004) 134 FCR 271, 294 [67] (French and Lee JJ).

57 See chapter 13.

Interpreting statutory powers – discretion or duty?

[36.4] Although a statutory power is often expressed by a word in common use, whether it is characterised as a discretion or a duty is a matter of interpretation, to be determined according to the intention of the legislature

Words commonly employed to confer a statutory discretion and impose a statutory duty are respectively 'may' and 'must'. In older statutes, 'shall' is commonly employed in a number of senses. Words in law, including words that are in common use, take their legal meanings. These are often, but not always, their popular or grammatical meanings.[58] The intention of Parliament, which takes in all relevant legal considerations, is brought to bear.[59] As Brennan J said in relation to statutory powers: 'The question whether the repository of a discretionary power is under a duty to exercise the power depends on the intention of the legislature as revealed in the language of the statute.'[60]

It follows that if there is to be departure from the prima facie meaning of a word expressing a statutory power, indications must be found in the 'statutory context in which the power is created'.[61] Some of these indications were referred to in the leading case of *Julius v Lord Bishop of Oxford*[62] (in which the words 'it shall be lawful' were at issue):

> [T]here may be something in the nature of the thing empowered to be done, something in the object for which it is to be done, something in the conditions under which it is to be done, something in the title of the person or persons for whose benefit the power is to be exercised, which may couple the power with a duty, and make it the duty of the person in whom the power is reposed, to exercise that power when called upon to do so.[63]

Prior law may also be of assistance. If an amending Act replaces 'shall' with 'may', that is an indication that a discretion was intended.[64]

[36.5] The meaning of 'may' depends on its context

(a) The prima facie meaning of 'may' is that it is permissive, entailing an authority to do something that otherwise a person or authority could not lawfully do

The starting point in statutory interpretation is the text in question (**[6.5]**) – that is, the ordinary and grammatical meaning or the natural and ordinary meaning of the words in question

58 *Project Blue Sky Inc v Australian Broadcasting Authority* (1998) 194 CLR 355, 384 [78] (McHugh, Gummow, Kirby and Hayne JJ). Cf Colin Howard, 'The Language of the Law' (1993) 86 *Victorian Bar News* 21, arguing for the 'superficially close connection' legal language has with the ordinary language of everyday.

59 This concept is multifaceted. See chapter 4 of this work.

60 *Commissioner of State Revenue (Vic) v Royal Insurance Australia Ltd* (1994) 182 CLR 51, 84 (Brennan J, Toohey J agreeing at 103, McHugh J agreeing at 103). See also *Ward v Williams* (1955) 92 CLR 496, 505, quoted at **[36.5](a)** below.

61 *Commissioner of State Revenue (Vic) v Royal Insurance Australia Ltd* (1994) 182 CLR 51, 85 (Brennan J, Toohey J agreeing at 103, McHugh J agreeing at 103).

62 (1880) 5 App Cas 214.

63 Ibid 222–3 (Earl Cairns LC). This statement has often been approved by members of the High Court – see, eg, *Commissioner of State Revenue (Vic) v Royal Insurance Australia Ltd* (1994) 182 CLR 51, 88 (Brennan J, Toohey J agreeing at 103, McHugh J agreeing at 103); *O'Donoghue v Ireland* (2008) 234 CLR 599, 642–3 [129] (Kirby J; dissenting as to outcome); *Graham Barclay Oysters Pty Ltd v Ryan* (2002) 211 CLR 540, 658 [310] (Callinan J).

64 *Commissioner of State Revenue (Vic) v Royal Insurance Australia Ltd* (1994) 182 CLR 51, 64 (Mason CJ), 85 (Brennan J, Toohey J agreeing at 103, McHugh J agreeing at 103).

(**[15.2]**). Where 'may' is concerned there is clear High Court authority on the ordinary meaning that is the starting point:

> In considering the correctness of this interpretation it is necessary to bear steadily in mind that it is the real intention of the legislature that must be ascertained and that in ascertaining it you begin with the prima facie presumption that permissive or facultative expressions operate according to their ordinary natural meaning. 'The authorities clearly indicate that it lies on those who assert that the word "may" has a compulsory meaning to show, as a matter of construction of the Act, taken as a whole, that the word was intended to have such a meaning' – per *Cussen* J: *Re Gleeson*.[65]

(b) If a power, conferred by 'may', is conditioned upon the existence of an event or upon the formation of a particular opinion by the repository of the power, it is an interpretative question as to whether the condition specifies the circumstances in which the power must be exercised

A power that is conferred in permissive terms ('may') may be expressly or impliedly 'conditioned upon the existence of an event or upon the formation of a particular opinion by the repository of the power'.[66]

Although the fact that the event specified has occurred, or the opinion has been formed, does not necessarily generate a duty to exercise the power,[67] such conditions have potential significance for the characterisation of statutory powers. The condition may sometimes be taken to specify the circumstances in which the power must be exercised.[68] In other words, the provision *may* be read as 'conferr[ing] a power coupled with an implied duty to exercise the power, once properly engaged'.[69] Thus, the condition may specify the circumstances in which the duty will arise, or when 'an obligation is engaged by law'.[70]

Whether the condition, if satisfied, does generate a duty depends on whether 'such an intention [arises] by reference to the context in which the word [may] is used'.[71]

In cases where a court has found that an implied duty arises, the following considerations have been influential in reaching that conclusion:

---

65 *Ward v Williams* (1955) 92 CLR 496, 505 (the Court); footnote omitted. This statement has been approved of in subsequent High Court cases: *Samad v District Court of New South Wales* (2002) 209 CLR 140, 160–1 [66] (Gaudron, Gummow and Callinan JJ); *Commissioner of State Revenue (Vic) v Royal Insurance Australia Ltd* (1994) 182 CLR 51, 84–5 (Brennan J, Toohey J agreeing at 103, McHugh J agreeing at 103).

66 *Commissioner of State Revenue (Vic) v Royal Insurance Australia Ltd* (1994) 182 CLR 51, 85 (Brennan J, Toohey J agreeing at 103, McHugh J agreeing at 103).

67 *Samad v District Court of New South Wales* (2002) 209 CLR 140, 161 [69] (Gaudron, Gummow and Callinan JJ).

68 *Commissioner of State Revenue (Vic) v Royal Insurance Australia Ltd* (1994) 182 CLR 51, 85 (Brennan J, Toohey J agreeing at 103, McHugh J agreeing at 103).

69 *Trinh v The Queen* [2016] NSWCCA 110, [12] (Basten JA).

70 *Ballantyne v Workcover Authority of New South Wales* [2007] NSWCA 239, [90] (Basten JA; dissenting as to outcome).

71 *Victorian Building Authority v Andriotis* (2019) 268 CLR 168, 182 [43] (Kiefel CJ, Bell and Keane JJ). See to similar effect *Commissioner of State Revenue (Vic) v Royal Insurance Australia Ltd* (1994) 182 CLR 51, 85 (Brennan J, Toohey J agreeing at 103, McHugh J agreeing at 103).

- the apparent stringency of the criteria;[72]
- the fact that the condition is expressed in terms of a general entitlement;[73]
- consistency with a ground in the immediate context;[74]
- comparable provisions in the Act;[75]
- the scheme of the Act;[76] and
- an assessment by the court that no satisfactory criterion or criteria could be devised that would guide the exercise of the supposed discretion.[77]

The lack of cogency of a particular justification advanced by the party contending for a discretion can confirm the court's conclusion in this regard.[78]

Where a court has dismissed the case for a duty, the perception that, if the power were read as giving rise to a duty, odd consequences would ensue, has been influential.[79]

If satisfaction of the condition is found to generate an implied duty, it may be expressed in the same provision as the power.[80] But not necessarily. It may be

- implied in the same provision by means of a common law presumption;[81] or
- expressed in another subsection of the same section,[82] in another provision of the Act concerned[83] or even in another Act that is to be read with the Act in question.[84]

---

72 *Commissioner of Australian Federal Police v Hart* (2018) 262 CLR 76, 109 [104] (Gordon J, Kiefel CJ, Bell, Gageler and Edelman JJ agreeing at 82 [2]).

73 *John Fairfax Publications Pty Ltd v Gacic* (2007) 230 CLR 291, 302 [28] (Gummow and Hayne JJ, Kirby J agreeing at 329 [128]); *Victorian Building Authority v Andriotis* (2019) 268 CLR 168, 181 [39] (Kiefel CJ, Bell and Keane JJ).

74 *Finance Facilities Pty Ltd v Commissioner of Taxation (Cth)* (1971) 127 CLR 106, 138 (Owen J).

75 Ibid 134 (Windeyer J, Barwick CJ agreeing at 128).

76 *Victorian Building Authority v Andriotis* (2019) 268 CLR 168, 181–2 [37]–[44] (Kiefel CJ, Bell and Keane JJ), 207 [132] (Nettle and Gordon JJ).

77 *Pilbara Infrastructure Pty Ltd v Australian Competition Tribunal* (2012) 246 CLR 379, 423–4 [116] (French CJ, Gummow, Hayne, Crennan, Kiefel and Bell JJ).

78 *Finance Facilities Pty Ltd v Commissioner of Taxation (Cth)* (1971) 127 CLR 106, 136 (Windeyer J, Barwick CJ agreeing at 128).

79 *Samad v District Court of New South Wales* (2002) 209 CLR 140, 162 [72] (Gaudron, Gummow and Callinan JJ).

80 *Finance Facilities Pty Ltd v Commissioner of Taxation (Cth)* (1971) 127 CLR 106, 135, 136 (Windeyer J, Barwick CJ agreeing at 128), 139 (Owen J); *Leach v The Queen* (2007) 230 CLR 1, 17–18 [36]–[38] (Gummow, Hayne, Heydon and Crennan JJ) (discussed in **Example 36.2**); *Commissioner of Australian Federal Police v Hart* (2018) 262 CLR 76, 109 [104] (Gordon J, Kiefel CJ, Bell, Gageler and Edelman JJ agreeing 82 [2]); *Baiada Poultry Pty Ltd v The Queen* (2012) 246 CLR 92, 103 [25] (French CJ, Gummow, Hayne and Crennan JJ); *John Fairfax Publications Pty Ltd v Gacic* (2007) 230 CLR 291, 302 [28], 303 [30] (Gummow and Hayne JJ, Kirby J agreeing at 329 [128]); *R v Skinner* (2016) 126 SASR 120, 136 [82] (Doyle J, Kelly J agreeing at 122 [1]); *DPP (WA) v Williams* (2007) 35 WAR 297, 314 [68], 315 [72] (Wheeler JA, Le Miere AJA agreeing at 319 [89]).

81 *Saeed v Minister for Immigration and Citizenship* (2010) 241 CLR 252, 262 [23], 269 [50] (French CJ, Gummow, Hayne, Crennan and Kiefel JJ) (dicta).

82 *Pilbara Infrastructure Pty Ltd v Australian Competition Tribunal* (2012) 246 CLR 379, 423–4 [116], 424 [119] (French CJ, Gummow, Hayne, Crennan, Kiefel and Bell JJ);

83 *Commissioner of State Revenue (Vic) v Royal Insurance Australia Ltd* (1994) 182 CLR 51, 87–8 (Brennan J, Toohey J agreeing at 103, McHugh J agreeing at 103); *Victorian Building Authority v Andriotis* (2019) 268 CLR 168, 182 [43] (Kiefel CJ, Bell and Keane JJ).

84 *Jordan v Criminal Injuries Compensation Commissioner Neasey* [2018] TASFC 10, [9]–[11] (The Court); *Culve Engineering Pty Ltd v Apollo General Engineering (Aust) Pty Ltd (in liq)* (2017) 53 VR 219, 232 [59], [62] (the Court).

Example 36.2 *Leach v The Queen*[85]

The appellant was found guilty of committing two murders. At the time of the appellant's offending in 1983, s 5 of the *Criminal Law Consolidation Act 1978* (NT) provided that the mandatory sentence for murder was life imprisonment. In 2003 the *Sentencing (Crime of Murder) and Parole Reform Act 2003* (NT) was passed. It provided in s 18 that the sentence of a prisoner, who at the commencement of the 2003 Act was serving a sentence of life imprisonment for two or more convictions for murder, 'is taken to include a non-parole period of 25 years'. Section 19 permitted the Director of Public Prosecutions to apply to the Supreme Court of the Northern Territory to revoke the non-parole period set by s 18, and to fix a non-parole period longer than 25 years or to refuse to fix any non-parole period.

An issue raised in this case concerned the meaning of 'may' in s 19(5), which read (emphasis added):

> The Supreme Court *may* refuse to fix a non-parole period if satisfied the level of culpability in the commission of the offence is so extreme the community interest in retribution, punishment, protection and deterrence can only be met if the offender is imprisoned for the term of his or her natural life without the possibility of release on parole.

It was argued by the appellant that, through the word 'may', the subsection conferred a discretion on the Supreme Court to consider what were described as 'ordinary sentencing considerations'. The High Court disagreed. The plurality held:

> [Section] 19(5) is a provision of the kind considered in *Finance Facilities Pty Ltd v Federal Commissioner of Taxation* and *Mitchell v The Queen*. The word 'may' is used, not to give a discretion, but to confer a power which is to be exercised upon the Court being satisfied of the matters described in the provision.[86]

The reasons of the plurality focused on the text of the provision, the nature of the condition, and the adverse consequences that would result if a separate discretion were held to exist:

> [T]he appellant's submission would require reading s 19(5) as presenting a conundrum for the Court considering an application under s 19. Central to the appellant's contention was the proposition that the Court may be satisfied that 'the community interest in retribution, punishment, protection and deterrence can *only* be met if the offender is imprisoned for the term of his or her natural life without the possibility of release on parole', yet conclude that a non-parole period should be fixed. That proposition should be rejected. Section 19(5) is not to be read as requiring the Court to consider the exercise of some separate or additional discretion after, or despite, its having reached the conclusion that the level of the prisoner's culpability was as described in the provisions: 'so extreme' that the community interest in the specified considerations could 'only be met' by imprisonment for life.[87]

85 (2007) 230 CLR 1.

86 Ibid 17 [38] (Gummow, Hayne, Heydon and Crennan JJ) (footnotes omitted). Gleeson CJ similarly held at 9 [13] and 12 [19]. 'Plurality' is here understood to refer to the leading reasons for judgment among the reasons for judgment of those members of a court who agree with the proposed orders of the court.

87 Ibid 17 [37] (Gummow, Hayne, Heydon and Crennan JJ) (emphasis in original).

(c) Even if a power to do an act is generally discretionary, in the proper exercise of a discretion in a particular case there may be only one possible outcome; in this situation a court will be obliged to command that outcome

The High Court has approved the proposition that in particular circumstances a 'discretion [can] effectively run out'.[88] In the same case Gleeson CJ and McHugh J used equivalent language. They referred to the situation where 'in the proper exercise of a discretion, there [is] only one possible outcome'.[89]

Example 36.3 *Hall v Sheiban Pty Ltd*[90]

The applicants, all receptionists in the second respondent's (S's) general medical practice, complained to the Human Rights and Equal Opportunity Commission that the second respondent had sexually harassed them before and during their employment. The Commission made a declaration that during their employments each of them was sexually harassed by the respondents. But the Commission made a further declaration that 'it is inappropriate to take any further action in those matters, including that damages by way of compensation be payable by the respondent(s) to any of the complainants'.

The Commission declined to make an order for damages, purportedly under s 81(1) of the *Sex Discrimination Act 1984* (Cth). That subsection read in part as follows:

> (1) After holding an inquiry, the Commission may –
> (a) dismiss the complaint the subject of the inquiry; or
> (b) find the complaint substantiated and make a determination, which may include any one or more of the following:
> ...
> (iv) except where the complaint was dealt with as a representative complaint – a declaration that the respondent should pay to the complainant damages by way of compensation for any loss or damage suffered by reason of the conduct of the respondent;
> ...
> (vii) a declaration that it would be inappropriate for any further action to be taken in the matter.

The Commission determined that, on the facts, the behaviour of S complained of by the applicants was insignificant, sporadic and trivial. On the law, the Commission reasoned to the effect that no reasonable woman could in the light of that conduct assert that she had suffered loss or damage in consequence of it.

On judicial review the Full Federal Court disagreed. On the facts found by the President, the Full Court found that there was evidence of significant loss and damage.[91] As regards the law, the Court found that the Commission's approach to the awarding of damages was untenable and

88 *Samad v District Court of New South Wales* (2002) 209 CLR 140, 164 [77] (Gaudron, Gummow and Callinan JJ).

89 Ibid 156 [46].

90 (1989) 20 FCR 217.

91 Ibid 242, 244 (Lockhart J), 284 (French J).

demonstrated an error of law.[92] The measure of the compensation was to be found in the words of the statute, and not by reference to a supposed principle of the reasonableness of the victim's response to the conduct in question. The statute required 'no more to attract the exercise of the Commission's discretion than that the loss or damage be "by reason of" the conduct complained of'.[93] The fact that the powers of the Commission were introduced by the word 'may' did not preclude a finding that a duty to award damages arose in the circumstances of the case.[94] The purpose of the legislation was to establish a 'statutory tort'[95] and it was the purpose of the legislation that 'where a complaint is substantiated and loss or damage is suffered some form of redress is contemplated in the ordinary course'.[96] Hence, the exercise of the discretion on the question of compensation miscarried.[97] In this case there was only one possible outcome: 'It is plain in this case . . . that the only appropriate form of redress for such loss or damage as has been suffered by the applicants, is compensation by way of damages.'[98] The Court accordingly directed the Commission to declare that the first and second respondents should pay to each of the applicants damages by way of compensation for any loss or damage suffered by her by reason of the conduct rendered unlawful by s 28 of the *Sex Discrimination Act 1984* (Cth).[99]

(d) 'May' may have a distributive operation in a particular section or subsection

Powers may be expressed in various ways. One way is by commencing with a chapeau[100] that contains 'may', and then providing detail on the power with a number of indented paragraphs, each of which has an independent operation. For example, in *Samad v District Court of New South Wales*[101] cl 149 of the *Poisons and Therapeutic Goods Regulation 1994* (NSW) provided (emphasis added):

> The Director-General *may* suspend or cancel a licence or authority on any one or more of the following grounds:
>
> . . .
>
> (e) the annual fee for the licence is not duly paid,
>
> (f) in the case of a licence or authority to supply methadone, the supply of methadone is causing disruption to the amenity of the area in which the premises from which it is being supplied are situated.

A question can arise as to whether 'may' in a chapeau has the same meaning in its application to all the paragraphs, or whether it has a 'distributive operation'[102] – that is, a meaning that can vary depending on which paragraph applies. In *Samad* the plurality held (without formally

92 Ibid 239, 242 (Lockhart J), 281 (French J).

93 Ibid 281 (French J).

94 Ibid 261 (Wilcox J).

95 Ibid.

96 Ibid 282 (French J).

97 Ibid 284.

98 Ibid 283. See also 261 (Wilcox J).

99 Ibid 287.

100 A chapeau is the opening words at the top of a section or subsection conferring a power, the words being common to all operations of the indented paragraphs which follow immediately afterwards.

101 (2002) 209 CLR 140.

102 *Samad v District Court of New South Wales* (2002) 209 CLR 140, 162 [71] (Gaudron, Gummow and Callinan JJ).

deciding) that 'may' in cl 149 of the *Poisons and Therapeutic Goods Regulation 1994* (NSW) had a distributive operation.[103]

[36.6] **The prima facie meaning of 'shall' is that it is used in a mandatory sense**

The prima facie meaning of 'shall' is that it 'is used in an Act in a mandatory sense'.[104] Like the word 'may', '[t]he word "shall" cannot be construed without reference to its context'.[105] The context includes 'the subject matter, [and] the purpose and effect of the section in which it appears'.[106]

As noted above (**[36.3]**), 'shall' is now seldom used in contemporary Australian and New Zealand legislation, but its popularity in older legislation means that interpreters need to be able to interpret it where required.

Example 36.4 *Re Griffiths*[107]

Section 52A(1) of the *Builders' Registration and Home-owners' Protection Act 1979* (Qld) ('the Act') provided for the Registrar of the Builders' Registration Board of Queensland to take enforcement action where a person had commenced building construction in contravention of the Act. The application was to be made to a judge of the Supreme Court of Queensland in chambers for an order that the person concerned cease building construction. Subsection (2) stated (emphasis added):

> (2) An application referred to in subsection (1) shall be made and in the first instance *shall* be dealt with ex parte.
>
> If it is made to appear to the Judge in Chambers that the building construction in question has been commenced or is being performed in contravention of any of the provisions of this Act he *shall* –
>
> (a) make an interim order of the description sought by the applicant;
> (b) adjourn the matter of the application for a period of seven days or as near as practicable thereto; and
> (c) make an order directed to the person who has commenced or is performing that building construction to show cause why the interim order should not be made absolute.

The Registrar made an application to a judge in chambers under s 52A(1). The evidence adduced in support of the application revealed a prima facie case that a man (CS) was building a house in contravention of the Act. CS had not been informed, however, of an intention to seek an order against him. The issues in the case were, first, whether the application must be dealt with ex parte; and second, where a relevant contravention was established, whether the Court was obliged to make an interim order. Both issues raised the meaning of 'shall' in sub-s (2) (as indicated above). The applicant laid emphasis on the word 'shall' in sub-s (2) and on the use of 'may' in sub-s (1).

103 Ibid 162 [71].

104 *Re Davis* (1947) 75 CLR 409, 428 (Williams J); *Grunwick Processing Laboratories Ltd v Advisory, Conciliation and Arbitration Service* [1978] AC 655, 690 (Lord Diplock), 698 (Lord Salmon).

105 *Re Davis* (1947) 75 CLR 409, 419 (Starke J). See also *Grunwick Processing Laboratories Ltd v Advisory, Conciliation and Arbitration Service* [1978] AC 655, 698 (Lord Salmon).

106 *Grunwick Processing Laboratories Ltd v Advisory, Conciliation and Arbitration Service* [1978] AC 655, 698 (Lord Salmon).

107 [1991] 2 Qd R 29.

The Court acknowledged that '[i]n legislation, "shall" ordinarily signifies must'.[108] But the Court was not persuaded by the applicant's arguments, holding that Parliament did not intend to compel ex parte applications in every case (as distinct from permitting them in necessitous cases),[109] and there was a discretion to withhold making an interim order.[110] The Court referred to the presumption against imputing to the legislature an intention to deny elementary natural justice, and to the potential for undesirable consequences for the builder and the homeowner, and for inconvenience to the applicant, if all applications had to be made and heard ex parte. Similarly, if there were no discretion to refuse an interim order, curious consequences might arise for the homeowner and third parties such as subcontractors. Having found a discretion to refuse the order, the Court proceeded to exercise it against the applicant on the grounds that the applicant declined to offer an undertaking as to damages, and the case was not so urgent as to deny some notice of the hearing to the person against whom the proposed order was directed.

The prima facie meaning of 'must' and like words imports an imperative [36.7]

Like the word 'shall', '[p]rima facie, the word "must" does not confer a discretion on the Court but is used to indicate an imperative; a command, obligation, duty, necessity or inevitability'.[111]

And like other words conferring a power, 'whether or not it is used in [its prima facie] sense depends upon the context'.[112] The context includes the consistency of use of the words 'may' and 'must' across the Act as a whole.[113] But, as noted above (**[36.3]**), cases raising the question of whether 'must' is imperative or discretionary have been rare, and cases holding that it is not an enforceable command have been extremely rare.

The words 'is to' are, in addition to 'must', a further plain language alternative to 'shall' when a duty is sought to be imposed.[114] The words are described as 'a gentler form' than 'must'.[115] An example of its use is the former s 160 of the *Broadcasting Services Act 1992* (Cth), the subject of the well-known *Project Blue Sky* case (emphasis added):

> The ABA *is to* perform its functions in a manner consistent with:
>
> ...
>
> (d) Australia's obligations under any convention to which Australia is a party or any agreement between Australia and a foreign country.

A number of courts have held that the words 'is to' are equivalent to 'must'.[116]

108 Ibid 33 (Byrne J).

109 Ibid 35.

110 Ibid 32.

111 *DPP v Dickfoss* (2011) 249 FLR 374, 395 [87] (Mildren J). See also *Atkinson v Bardon* (2018) 41 NTLR 35, 48–9 [40] (Mildren AJ).

112 *DPP v Dickfoss* (2011) 249 FLR 374, 395 [87] (Mildren J).

113 Ibid 396 [90].

114 Office of Parliamentary Counsel, *Plain English Manual* (Australian Government, 2016) [83].

115 Ibid.

116 *Cleary v Australian Co-operative Foods (No 2)* (1999) 32 ACSR 701, 709 [18] (Austin J); *Tasmanian Heritage Council v Cita Property Group Pty Ltd* (2010) 181 LGERA 429, 435 [24] (Wood J). See also *Commissioner of Police v Reid* (2000) 9 Tas R 418, 432 [17] (Cox CJ) ('courts tend to treat as mandatory').

The words 'may not' are sometimes used in legislation, such as the following:

> The Minister *may not* publish a notification under subsection (1) unless at least 14 days have elapsed after notice of intention to publish the notification has been published in a newspaper circulating in the locality in which the land is situated or in a newspaper circulating generally in the State.[117]

It has been held that, prima facie, 'may not' carries the same meaning as 'cannot', 'shall not' and 'must not'.[118]

[36.8] 'Should' is an ambiguous word

The word 'should' in legislation has proved troublesome. There is no uniform approach to its prima facie meaning. The Full Court of the South Australian Supreme Court has held that, prima facie, the word 'should' is not mandatory.[119] Somewhat differently, the Court of Appeal of the NSW Supreme Court has started with the assumption that 'should' is ambiguous:

> [T]he expression 'should consider' ... could mean shall or must consider, indicating obligation, or could, in a weaker form, indicate advisability or likelihood of an outcome.[120]

In that case the Court was considering s 10 of the *Judicial Officers Act 1986* (NSW) and the powers of the Judicial Commission (emphasis added):

> **10 Guidelines**
>
> (1) In addition to its functions under Part 6 in relation to complaints –
>
> (a) the Commission may formulate guidelines to assist both it and the Conduct Division in the exercise of their functions ...
>
> ...
>
> (2) The guidelines for the Conduct Division may include provisions with respect to any one or more of the following matters –
>
> ...
>
> (c) the criteria that the Conduct Division *should consider* when determining whether a hearing should be held in public or in private ...

The difficulty with 'should consider' in s 10(2)(c) was solved by reading the words in question in context. The Court reasoned that, having regard to the term 'guidelines', to their purpose ('assist': s 10(1)(a)) and to the word 'should' itself, the words 'should consider' did not create mandatory considerations.[121]

---

117 *Crown Lands Act 1989* (NSW) s 90(2) (emphasis added), discussed in *New South Wales Aboriginal Land Council v Minister Administering the Crown Lands Act* [2016] NSWLEC 157.

118 *New South Wales Aboriginal Land Council v Minister Administering the Crown Lands Act* [2016] NSWLEC 157, [63] (Pepper J). In South Australia the words have been given a presumptive legislative meaning. The *Legislation Interpretation Act 2021* (SA) s 11(2) states that 'if an Act or a legislative instrument specifies that an entity "may not" perform a function, the entity is prohibited from performing it'.

119 *South Australia Housing Trust v Development Assessment Commission* (1994) 63 SASR 35, 38 (King CJ, Perry J agreeing at 41).

120 *AB v Conduct Division of the Judicial Commission* (NSW) (2018) 365 ALR 163, 174 [48] (the Court). The Court came to the conclusion that read in context it did not express mandatory considerations: at 175 [49].

121 Ibid 175 [49].

The terms of Australian Interpretation Acts' provisions on the meaning of 'may', 'shall' and 'must' differ somewhat, but in substance they reflect the common law [36.9]

All Australian jurisdictions other than the Northern Territory state interpretative rules in their Interpretation Act regarding the meaning of expressions conferring powers.[122]

All of the jurisdictions concerned state rules regarding the interpretation of 'may'.[123] Putting aside the added layer afforded by the rules in Queensland and Victoria (discussed below), the rules are generally similar.[124] The Commonwealth's rule is typical:

> Where an Act assented to after the commencement of this subsection provides that a person, court or body may do a particular act or thing, and the word ***may*** is used, the act or thing may be done at the discretion of the person, court or body.

Four jurisdictions provide rules regarding the meaning of 'shall'.[125] Putting aside again the added layer afforded by the rule in Victoria, the rules for three of the jurisdictions (South Australia, Victoria and Western Australia) are similar. For instance, South Australia's states:

> If, in an Act or a legislative instrument, the word ... 'shall' ... is used in conferring a function, the entity on which the function is conferred is required to perform it.[126]

The NSW version – which defines 'shall', 'if used to impose a duty' – does not have the same (or any) effect as it is circular.[127]

Putting aside the added layer provided by the Queensland version, four of the jurisdictions provide for the meaning of 'must' in a generally similar way.[128] The ACT provision (in s 146(2) of the *Legislation Act 2001* (ACT)) is typical:

> (2) In an Act or statutory instrument, the word must, or a similar term, used in relation to a function indicates that the function is required to be exercised.

The reference in the ACT provision to 'or a similar term' has been held to extend to 'shall'.[129] The Tasmanian version makes separate provision for the meaning of the comparable

---

122 *Acts Interpretation Act 1901* (Cth) s 33(2A); *Interpretation Act 1987* (NSW) s 9; *Acts Interpretation Act 1954* (Qld) s 32CA; *Legislation Interpretation Act 2021* (SA) s 11; *Acts Interpretation Act 1931* (Tas) s 10A; *Interpretation of Legislation Act 1984* (Vic) s 45; *Interpretation Act 1984* (WA) s 56; *Legislation Act 2001* (ACT) s 146.

123 *Acts Interpretation Act 1901* (Cth) s 33(2A); *Interpretation Act 1987* (NSW) s 9(1); *Acts Interpretation Act 1954* (Qld) s 32CA(1); *Legislation Interpretation Act 2021* (SA) s 11(1); *Acts Interpretation Act 1931* (Tas) s 10A(1)(c); *Interpretation of Legislation Act 1984* (Vic) s 45(1); *Interpretation Act 1984* (WA) s 56(1); *Legislation Act 2001* (ACT) s 146(1).

124 The Tasmanian provision (*Acts Interpretation Act 1931* (Tas) s 10A(1)(c)) is different. It does not presume a discretion is conferred.

125 *Interpretation Act 1987* (NSW) s 9(2); *Legislation Interpretation Act 2021* (SA) s 11(3); *Interpretation of Legislation Act 1984* (Vic) s 45(2); *Interpretation Act 1984* (WA) s 56(2).

126 *Legislation Interpretation Act 2021* (SA) s 11(3).

127 *Coffs Harbour and District Local Aboriginal Land Council v Lynwood* [2017] NSWCA 317, [8] (Basten JA), speaking of *Interpretation Act 1987* (NSW) s 9(2).

128 *Legislation Act 2001* (ACT) s 146(2); *Acts Interpretation Act 1954* (Qld) s 32CA(2); *Legislation Interpretation Act 2021* (SA) s 11(3); *Acts Interpretation Act 1931* (Tas) s 10A(1)(a).

129 *R v Thompson (No 3)* [2017] ACTSC 53, [44] (Refshauge J).

expressions 'is to' and 'are to'.[130] The Tasmanian provision has been held to extend to 'must not'.[131]

The Interpretation Acts provide that their provisions are subject to a contrary intention in the substantive Act in question.[132] In other words, the relevant provisions of the Interpretation Acts are presumptive, not conclusive of legal meaning.[133] They do not provide an 'absolute rule of construction'.[134]

The assistance that the rules provide has been doubted. One court stated that the rules were 'a restatement of the common law and are no assistance in discerning the intention and object of the relevant statute'.[135] More recently, courts are discovering some efficacy in the statutory rules. The rule regarding 'may' is said to be 'a legal principle, which must be applied unless a contrary intention appears from the Act in which the word is found';[136] the rules are 'a powerful starting point to consideration';[137] and the rules 'reinforc[e] the prima facie presumption'.[138]

Finally, the Queensland and Victorian Interpretation Acts contain unusual provisions regarding the interpretation of statutory powers. The *Acts Interpretation Act 1954* (Qld) states:

> **32CA Meaning of *may* and *must* etc.**
>
> (1) In an Act, the word ***may***, or a similar word or expression, used in relation to a power indicates that the power may be exercised or not exercised, at discretion.
>
> (2) In an Act, the word ***must***, or a similar word or expression, used in relation to a power indicates that the power is required to be exercised.
>
> (3) To remove any doubt, it is declared that this section applies to an Act passed after 1 January 1992 despite any presumption or rule of interpretation.

130 *Acts Interpretation Act 1931* (Tas) s 10A(1)(b). This states the provision is presumptively to be 'directory'. This has been held to mean not discretionary: *Mulholland v Tasmania* (2017) 25 Tas R 313, 323 [24] (Pearce J, Tennent J agreeing at 315 [1]; Brett J agreeing at 326 [34]).

131 *Tasmania v Joseph* (2017) 25 Tas R 327, 337 [27] (Brett J); *Mitchell v Marshall* (2014) 27 Tas R 1, 11 [36] (Blow CJ).

132 *Acts Interpretation Act 1901* (Cth) s 2(2); *Interpretation Act 1987* (NSW) s 5(2), *Acts Interpretation Act 1954* (Qld) s 4; *Legislation Interpretation Act 2021* (SA) s 3(3); *Acts Interpretation Act 1931* (Tas) s 4(1); *Interpretation of Legislation Act 1984* (Vic) s 4; *Interpretation Act 1984* (WA) s 3(1); *Legislation Act 2001* (ACT) s 6(2).

133 *Kim v Minister for Immigration and Multicultural and Indigenous Affairs* (2004) 38 AAR 304, 308 [9] (Kiefel J) (speaking of *Acts Interpretation Act 1901* (Cth) s 33(2A)).

134 *Victorian Building Authority v Andriotis* (2019) 268 CLR 168, 182 [43] (Kiefel CJ, Bell and Keane JJ) (speaking of *Acts Interpretation Act 1901* (Cth) s 33(2A)).

135 *Re Dunsborough Districts Country Club Inc* [1982] WAR 321, 329 (Olney J) (speaking of *Interpretation Act 1981* (WA) s 32).

136 *Mack Fleet Pty Ltd v Transport for NSW* (2020) 93 MVR 242, 247 [6] (Basten JA, Ward JA agreeing at 255 [50], Leeming JA agreeing at 255 [51]).

137 *ICI Australia Operations Pty Ltd v Workcover Authority of New South Wales* (2004) 60 NSWLR 18, 77 [314] (McColl JA, Mason P agreeing at 22 [1], Meagher JA agreeing generally at 22 [3] (speaking of *Interpretation Act 1987* (NSW) s 9); see also *Question of Law Reserved (No 1 of 2018)* [2018] SASCFC 128, [115] (Hinton J, Lovell J agreeing at [46]) (speaking of the *Acts Interpretation Act 1915* (SA) s 34, the predecessor to *Legislation Interpretation Act 1915* (SA) s 11(1), (3)).

138 *Shiel v Secretary, Department of Social Security* (1999) 56 ALD 465, 473 [42] (Katz J) (speaking of *Acts Interpretation Act 1901* (Cth) s 33(2A)).

The *Interpretation of Legislation Act 1984* (Vic) states:

45 Construction of 'may' and 'shall'

(1) Where in this Act or any Act passed or subordinate instrument made on or after the commencement of this Act the word 'may' is used in conferring a power, that word shall be construed as meaning that the power so conferred may be exercised, or not, at discretion.

(2) Where in this Act or any Act passed or subordinate instrument made on or after the commencement of this Act the word 'shall' is used in conferring a power, that word shall be construed as meaning that the power so conferred must be exercised.

(3) The provisions of this section shall have effect notwithstanding any rule of construction to the contrary and any such rule is hereby abrogated with respect to this Act and any Act passed or subordinate instrument made on or after the commencement of this Act.

In both jurisdictions extrinsic material indicates that the intention of the proponents was to lay down an absolute rule of construction in relation to 'may' and 'must' in Queensland and 'may' and 'shall' in Victoria.[139]

The better view is that these intentions have not been achieved.[140] First, the preponderance of Full Court authority regarding the Victorian provision favours the view that a later Parliament may express a contrary intention to the Interpretation Act provision.[141] Second, High Court dicta indicates that if a provision is laid down in 'mandatory terms' in an Interpretation Act, it

> would necessarily give way to the provisions of a subsequent enactment which, notwithstanding the earlier provision, disclosed a contrary legislative intent since the subsequent enactment would represent a pro tanto repeal or amendment of the earlier provision.[142]

---

139 For the Victorian provision see Victoria, *Parliamentary Debates*, Legislative Assembly, 7 March 1984, 3051, 3056 (Mr Cain). For the Queensland provision see *Statute Law (Miscellaneous Provisions) Act 1991* (Qld) s 34 (explanatory note to proposed s 32CA(1), (2)).

140 For a broader discussion see Jeffrey Barnes, 'Duties and Discretions: How Have "Plain English" Legislative Drafting Techniques Fared in Administrative Law?' (2016) 83 *AIAL Forum* 36, 45–6. For a trenchant criticism of the Victorian rule, see *Encyclopaedia Britannica (Australia) Inc v Director of Consumer Affairs* [1988] VR 904, 912–3 (Fullagar J, Murray J agreeing at 905), approved in *Telstra Corporation Ltd v Hurstville City Council* (2002) 118 FCR 198, 233 [78] (the Court).

141 *Telstra Corporation Ltd v Hurstville City Council* (2002) 118 FCR 198, 232–3 [78] (the Court) (speaking of s 45(3) of the *Interpretation of Legislation Act 1984* (Vic)). Consistent with this decision is *Culve Engineering Pty Ltd v Apollo General Engineering (Aust) Pty Ltd (in liq)* (2017) 53 VR 219, 232 [59]–[62] (the Court). A legislative provision expressed in the form of 'may' (legislation A) is to be read in context including other legislation (legislation B). Giving effect to legislation B meant that legislation A gave rise to a prima facie entitlement. Absent 'disentitling circumstances', legislation A was not discretionary. Cf *Accident Compensation Commission v Murphy* [1988] VR 444, 447 (the Court) (dicta). The Queensland provision has been held to reinforce the common law and not lay down an absolute rule: *R v Holley; Ex parte Attorney-General* [1997] 2 Qd R 407, 433 (Fryberg J) (dicta); *Leahy v Barnes* [2013] QSC 226, [31] (Henry J).

142 *Bropho v Western Australia* (1990) 171 CLR 1, 22 (the Court). Although this dicta was made in the context of rules in Interpretation Acts regarding statutes binding the Crown (*Acts Interpretation Act 1931* (Tas) s 6(6) and *Acts Interpretation Act 1954* (Qld) s 13), the Court's reference to rules laid down in 'mandatory terms' is apposite to the Queensland and Victorian provisions.

37 THE EFFECT OF NON-COMPLIANCE WITH A STATUTORY REQUIREMENT

Overview

[37.1] The effect of non-compliance with a statutory requirement is an issue that arises in a variety of ways.

Most commonly, it is an issue as to whether Parliament intended that the breach of a requirement would invalidate a public or private act to which it is related. Relevant public acts include delegated legislation, an administrative decision and the holding of a criminal trial. A private act includes a contract. The question as to whether it was intended that the breach has this effect (the interpretative question) is distinct from the prior question of whether the requirement has been breached. The interpretative question does not necessarily arise. Parliament may unambiguously state whether or not a breach of a statutory requirement invalidates a related act. In such a case, by definition, the interpretative question does not arise. But if Parliament does not expressly state whether or not a breach of a statutory requirement invalidates a related act, then whether Parliament intended invalidity may arise as a question of interpretation. This question is commonly known as 'the *Project Blue Sky* inquiry', after the leading case of that name. This inquiry has a wide application in the law. It includes determining whether a breach of a statutory requirement invalidates an administrative decision and whether a breach of criminal procedure invalidates a trial. But the inquiry has little, if any, application to breaches of civil procedure. Where the inquiry is applicable, a number of interpretative factors are commonly employed. Some Interpretation Acts and other Acts attempt to provide for the effect of a 'defect or irregularity'. But these provisions, if relevant at all to the *Project Blue Sky* inquiry, are not determinative.

In an exceptional way non-compliance with a statutory 'requirement' may also raise an issue as to whether it was intended that the requirement be legally enforceable. Put another way, a question may be raised as to whether the due operation of the provision has been left to political, rather than judicial, oversight.

How the issue of the effect of non-compliance may arise

[37.2] **The effect of non-compliance with a statutory requirement is an issue that arises in a variety of ways**

If there is non-compliance with a statutory requirement, this may raise the issue of whether the non-compliance invalidates a related public or private act. Relevant public acts include delegated legislation, an administrative decision and the holding of a criminal trial. A private act includes a contract. As stated above, this issue is commonly referred to as the *Project Blue Sky* inquiry.

Exceptionally, non-compliance with a statutory requirement may raise the issue as to whether it was intended that the requirement be legally enforceable *at all*. Specifically, is the 'requirement' enforceable by proceedings in a court, or has the due operation of the provision been left entirely to political oversight?

Non-compliance with a statutory requirement may also affect duties in tort law.[1] For instance, it may raise the defence of illegality at common law[2] and it may raise the tort of breach of statutory duty.[3]

Is the requirement an essential condition?

Whether non-compliance with a statutory requirement invalidates a related act may be an interpretative question [37.3]

(a) Whether non-compliance with a statutory requirement invalidates a related act is distinct from the threshold question of whether non-compliance has occurred

It is a commonplace that the validity of some public or private act that impinges on a person's rights or obligations is impugned in legal proceedings. The relevant act is '"the act" upon which [the applicant] fixes for relief'.[4] The 'act' could be an administrative decision, delegated legislation, the holding of a criminal trial, or a private agreement. In the present context, if the act is invalid it is void ab initio (from its inception).[5] It is not enforceable.

One way by which an aggrieved person might seek to impugn the validity of the act in question is to point to a breach of a related statutory requirement and to argue that the breach has the effect of invalidating the impugned act. Examples of a requirement the breach of which has led to a related act being invalidated include a requirement to consult a certain organisation before making a decision,[6] a time limit for making an application to a tribunal,[7] and the requirement to make available a copy of a search warrant to the occupier of the relevant premises at the commencement of the execution of the warrant.[8]

It is important to emphasise that the question of whether a statutory requirement has been breached[9] is distinct from the present question of the *effect* of the breach – that is, whether the breach of a statutory requirement invalidates a related act.[10] As Spigelman CJ has observed:

> Parliament always intends that its procedural stipulations will be complied with. That does not mean that it intends that every failure to comply with such a stipulation has the

1 Specialist works on tort law should be consulted. See, eg, Martin Davies and Ian Malkin, *Torts* (LexisNexis Butterworths, 8th ed, 2018).

2 See *Miller v Miller* (2011) 242 CLR 446. Legislation that deals with the effect of illegality on the recovery of damages for personal injury is the *Civil Liability Act 2002* (NSW) s 54; *Civil Liability Act 2003* (Qld) s 45; *Civil Liability Act 1936* (SA) s 43; *Civil Liability Act 2002* (Tas) s 6; *Wrongs Act 1958* (Vic) s 14G; *Personal Injuries (Liabilities and Damages) Act 2003* (NT) s 10.

3 For a recent illustration and a review of authorities see *Srikantha v Commonwealth (No 2)* (2020) 299 IR 302.

4 *Re Minister for Immigration and Multicultural and Indigenous Affairs; Ex parte Palme* (2003) 216 CLR 212, 225 [45] (Gleeson CJ, Gummow and Heydon JJ).

5 But a decision found to be void is not legally non-existent for all purposes. Unless and until duly challenged the decision is valid and operative. See discussion of case law in *Minister for Immigration and Multicultural Affairs v Bhardwaj* (2002) 209 CLR 597, 631–2 [102]–[103] (Kirby J) (dissenting as to outcome).

6 *Kutlu v Director of Professional Services Review* (2011) 197 FCR 177.

7 *Fernando v Minister for Immigration and Multicultural Affairs* (2000) 97 FCR 407.

8 *Commissioner, Australian Federal Police v Oke* (2007) 159 FCR 441.

9 Chapter 36 examined the question of whether a provision imposes a duty or confers a discretion.

10 *Gnych v Polish Club Ltd* (2015) 255 CLR 414, 431 [63] (Gageler J).

> consequence that events subsequent to the failure are invalid. It is necessary to identify a legislative intent or purpose that that be so.[11]

The question of whether non-compliance with a statutory requirement invalidates a related act assumes one has found non-compliance. In other words, whether there has been non-compliance is a prior determination.[12]

The following are two examples of cases where the distinction has arisen:

- Whether the Australian Broadcasting Authority has fulfilled its duty, under s 160(d) of the *Broadcasting Services Act 1992* (Cth), of performing its functions consistent with Australia's obligations under an agreement between Australia and a foreign country, is distinct from the question of whether the (assumed) non-compliance with s 160(d) invalidates a provision of a standard purportedly determined by it under s 122 of that Act.[13]
- Whether the Minister has fulfilled their duty to consult the Australian Medical Association about a proposed appointment of a medical practitioner to the Professional Services Review Panel under s 84(3) of the *Health Insurance Act 1973* (Cth) is distinct from the question of whether the (assumed) non-compliance with s 84(3) invalidates appointments to the Panel.[14]

(b) **Parliament may unambiguously state whether or not a breach of a statutory requirement invalidates a related act, in which case an interpretative issue as to what is the effect of the breach does not arise**

Three broad types of case for this scenario may be identified.

Parliament may link the performance of the statutory requirement with the validity or enforceability of the related act. For instance, Parliament may require a rule-maker to lodge a legislative instrument for registration, and separately state that, if a legislative instrument is not registered, the instrument is not enforceable.[15]

At the other end of the spectrum, Parliament may state that there is no link between performance of a statutory requirement and the validity of a related act. For instance, Parliament may require a rule-maker to be satisfied that certain consultation has occurred before making a legislative instrument, and separately state that the fact that consultation does not occur does not affect the validity or enforceability of the instrument.[16]

Or Parliament can adopt a halfway-house position. For instance, it may require a legislative instrument to be laid before each house of Parliament within a certain number of sitting days of that house after the registration of the instrument, and separately state that '[i]f a copy of the legislative instrument is not so laid the instrument ceases to have effect immediately after the last day for it to be so laid'.[17]

---

11 *R v Janceski* (2005) 64 NSWLR 10, 21 [44].

12 *Lloyd v Police* (2004) 89 SASR 383, 402 [70] (White J) (dissenting as to outcome).

13 *Project Blue Sky Inc v Australian Broadcasting Authority* (1998) 194 CLR 355.

14 *Kutlu v Director of Professional Services Review* (2011) 197 FCR 177.

15 *Legislation Act 2003* (Cth) ss 15G, 15K. See also *Petroleum Act 1984* (Cth) s 57D; *Native Title Act 1993* (Cth) s 28; *Life Insurance Act 1995* (Cth) s 165A; *Lands Acquisition Act 1978* (NT).

16 *Legislation Act 2003* (Cth) ss 17, 19.

17 Ibid s 38.

(c) If Parliament does not unambiguously state whether or not non-compliance with a statutory requirement invalidates a related act, then whether the non-compliance has that effect may arise as a question of interpretation[18]

'The statutory limits of the decision-making authority conferred by a statute are determined as an exercise in statutory interpretation.'[19] The same applies to the question of whether non-compliance with a statutory requirement leads to invalidity:

> Whether, and if so in what circumstances, non-compliance results in a decision that exceeds the limits of the decision-making authority conferred by the statute is itself a question of statutory interpretation.[20]

The leading case is *Project Blue Sky Inc v Australian Broadcasting Authority*.[21] In that case McHugh, Gummow, Kirby and Hayne JJ articulated the problem and the test as follows:

> An act done in breach of a condition regulating the exercise of a statutory power is not necessarily invalid and of no effect. Whether it is depends upon whether there can be discerned a legislative purpose to invalidate any act that fails to comply with the condition. The existence of the purpose is ascertained by reference to the language of the statute, its subject matter and objects, and the consequences for the parties of holding void every act done in breach of the condition.[22]

The question as to whether non-compliance with a statutory requirement invalidates a related act is often called the '*Project Blue Sky* inquiry'[23] or the '*Project Blue Sky* question'.[24]

Several features of the test propounded by McHugh, Gummow, Kirby and Hayne JJ may be noted.[25] First, when assessing whether non-compliance with a statutory requirement invalidates

18 As observed in *Kutlu v Director of Professional Services Review* (2011) 197 FCR 177, in this area Parliament has not given thought to the question at issue: at 187 [25] (Rares and Katzmann JJ). This indicates that 'legislative intention' is something that is attributed to Parliament based on objective 'indications' rather than something 'found' like an object. See chapter 4.

19 *MZAPC v Minister for Immigration and Border Protection* (2021) 390 ALR 590, 597 [30] (Kiefel CJ, Gageler, Keane and Gleeson JJ). See further **[32.9]**.

20 Ibid.

21 (1998) 194 CLR 355.

22 Ibid 388–9 [91] (McHugh, Gummow, Kirby and Hayne JJ). Brennan CJ, while agreeing that the appeal ought to be allowed, dissented on the consequences of the effect of the breach.

23 See, eg, Justice Nye Perram, 'Project Blue Sky: Invalidity and the Evolution of Consequences for Unlawful Administrative Action' [2012] *Federal Judicial Scholarship* 35; *Minister for Immigration and Citizenship v SZIZO* [2009] HCATrans 71 (BW Walker SC).

24 See, eg, *New South Wales v Corbett* [2007] HCATrans 119 (Gummow J); *Ko v Hall* [2020] VSCA 224, [38] (Maxwell P and Beach JA); *Randren House Pty Ltd v Water Administration Ministerial Corporation* [2020] NSWCA 14, [140] (Leeming JA); *Buzzacott v Minister for Sustainability, Environment, Water, Population and Communities* (2013) 215 FCR 301, 324 [119] (the Court).

25 The *Project Blue Sky* inquiry (or its earlier incarnation) has occasionally been criticised by judges. See *Hatton v Beaumont* [1977] 2 NSWLR 211, 225 (Mahoney JA); *Ian Street Developer Pty Ltd v Arrow International Pty Ltd* [2018] VSCA 294 [43]–[65] (Maxwell P). Cf the attempt to show the rigour of the inquiry in Graeme Hill, 'Applying Project Blue Sky – When Does Breach of a Statutory Requirement Affect the Validity of an Administrative Decision?' (2015) 80 *AIAL Forum* 54.

a related act, the unit of inquiry (the provision whose meaning is in question) is the statutory requirement that has been breached.[26]

Second, the test applies in respect of a 'condition regulating the exercise of a statutory power'. Their Honours did not restrict it to a discrete act or event and nor did Brennan CJ.[27]

Third, the test is not restricted to assessing the validity of public law 'acts' such as the exercise of statutory powers. The *Project Blue Sky* inquiry may arise in private law. It has been applied to determine whether a breach of a statutory requirement invalidated tenancy agreements[28] and a franchise agreement.[29]

Fourth, their Honours opted to frame the inquiry at this point as a question of 'whether there can be discerned a legislative *purpose* to invalidate any act' (emphasis added). Though not referring in terms to legislative intent at this point, later cases have confirmed that the 'purpose' was used in that sense.[30] In *Forrest & Forrest Pty Ltd v Wilson*[31] the High Court expressed the *Project Blue Sky* test in terms of whether 'a statutory requirement . . . was *intended* to invalidate an act done in breach of the requirement'.[32]

Fifth, ascertaining whether Parliament intended that a breach of a statutory requirement should invalidate a related act is a matter of implication.[33]

Finally, their Honours disapproved of the labels 'mandatory' and 'directory' to classify provisions the breach of which leads respectively to invalidity or not to invalidity.[34] Despite this move the High Court has subsequently begun reusing the 'mandatory' label.[35]

(d) The *Project Blue Sky* inquiry applies to breaches of criminal procedure, but it has little, if any, application to breaches of civil procedure

It has been observed that 'the *Project Blue Sky* approach is relevant not only with respect to administrative decision-makers (such as in *Project Blue Sky* itself) but also with respect to statutory requirements relating to the jurisdiction or powers of the courts'.[36] But that observation was made in a case involving an alleged breach of criminal procedure. The *Project Blue Sky* inquiry has little, if any, application in relation to breaches of civil procedure. In *Berowa Holdings*

26 See *Project Blue Sky Inc v Australian Broadcasting Authority* (1998) 194 CLR 355, 392–3 [99]. See also *Forrest & Forrest Pty Ltd v Wilson* (2017) 262 CLR 510, 528 [62] (Kiefel CJ, Bell, Gageler and Keane JJ).

27 Brennan CJ made a distinction between, on the one hand, 'a provision which prescribes an act or the occurrence of an event as a condition on the power' and, on the other hand, '[a] provision which directs the manner of the exercise of a power': *Project Blue Sky Inc v Australian Broadcasting Authority* (1998) 194 CLR 355, 373 [37]. In his view the former, but not the latter, lent itself to analysis of the consequences. In the case of the latter there was only one result: 'A purported exercise of a power in breach of the provision which governs the manner of its exercise is invalid': at 373 [34].

28 *Australian Broadcasting Corporation v Redmore Pty Ltd* (1989) 166 CLR 454 (agreement not invalid); *Gnych v Polish Club Ltd* (2015) 255 CLR 414 (agreement not invalid).

29 *Master Education Services Pty Ltd v Ketchell* (2008) 236 CLR 101 (agreement not invalid).

30 On the centrality of legislative intent, see chapter 4.

31 (2017) 262 CLR 510.

32 Ibid 528 [62] (Kiefel CJ, Bell, Gageler and Keane JJ) (emphasis added). See also *MZAPC v Minister for Immigration and Border Protection* (2021) 390 ALR 590, referring to the leading judgment in the *Project Blue Sky case* as reiterating a 'focus upon legislative intention': at 634 [173] (Edelman J).

33 *Gnych v Polish Club Ltd* (2015) 255 CLR 414, 431 [63] (Gageler J).

34 (1998) 194 CLR 355, 390–1 [93] (McHugh, Gummow, Kirby and Hayne JJ).

35 *PM v The Queen* (2007) 232 CLR 370, 381 [31] (Gleeson CJ, Hayne, Heydon and Crennan JJ); *Wei v Minister for Immigration and Border Protection* (2015) 257 CLR 22, 33 [25] (Gageler and Keane JJ).

36 *Davis (A Pseudonym) v The Queen* (2016) 55 VR 1, 22 [87] (the Court).

Pty Ltd v Gordon[37] the plurality of the High Court explained why '[t]here ... is a very real difficulty in characterising [civil] proceedings as "invalid"'.[38] It pointed out that the institution of an action or other proceeding 'engages the procedural law appurtenant to the relevant court, which in modern times is found primarily in the Rules'. Under that law, if a procedural rule expressed in mandatory form is breached, 'the normal outcome is that a choice accrues to the other party either to do nothing or to seek an appropriate order from the court'.[39] Their Honours acknowledged 'the possibility of a defendant denying the plaintiff's right to invoke the jurisdiction of the court, for example where the plaintiff's right is conditional upon there being an action cognisable within that jurisdiction'. But any such denial 'must be made within the structure of the relevantly engaged procedural law, and not outside it'.[40]

A breach of criminal procedure is treated differently. The *Project Blue Sky* inquiry readily applies.[41] Kirby P (as he then was) explained the general approach:

> Criminal procedure in our tradition is generally strict. The peril of liberty and the risk to reputation have imposed on criminal trials over the centuries a rigorous discipline so that procedural requirements are strictly complied with in the defence of the regularity of criminal process and the acceptability of its outcome. Rules of practical commonsense and flexibility, which have become increasingly acceptable in civil trials, must be viewed with reservation and care in the context of criminal trials. The fact that a point may be 'technical' is irrelevant. The strict application of the rule of law in criminal proceedings is the essence of the way in which, in our legal system, courts have defended due process. ... The procedural error or omission may, in some cases, be so significant that it strikes at the heart of the jurisdiction of the court ...[42]

In *R v Janceski*[43] it was said that 'there is still a rigorous approach taken by this and other courts to the fundamental requirements of a criminal trial regardless of the consequences'.[44] Nevertheless, not all breaches of criminal procedure will undermine the validity of a trial:

> Technicalities are not enforced for their own sake. They have a purpose; if they do not, they should go. Accordingly, one is in my opinion entitled to look to the function which an instant technicality is said to serve. If insistence upon the technicality in the instant case will not serve that purpose, it should not be used to defeat a trial.[45]

Examples of breaches of criminal procedure that were held to invalidate the trial include the failure of a trial judge adequately to instruct the jury in compliance with s 21AW(2) of the *Evidence Act 1977* (Qld) (relating to the manner of giving of evidence by a child complainant),[46]

37 (2006) 225 CLR 364.

38 Ibid 370 [13] (Gleeson CJ, Gummow, Hayne, Heydon and Crennan JJ).

39 Ibid 371 [14].

40 Ibid 371 [16].

41 *PM v The Queen* (2007) 232 CLR 370, 381 [31] (Gleeson CJ, Hayne, Heydon and Crennan JJ).

42 *R v Birlut* (1995) 39 NSWLR 1, 5, approved in *R v Deng* (1996) 91 A Crim R 80, 85 (Mahoney P).

43 (2005) 64 NSWLR 10.

44 Ibid 43 [224] (Howie J, Hunt AJA agreeing at [212], Johnson J agreeing at [287]).

45 *R v Deng* (1996) 91 A Crim R 80, 86, approved in *R v Janceski* (2005) 64 NSWLR 10, 54 [272] (Howie J, Hunt AJA agreeing at [212], Johnson J agreeing at [287]).

46 *R v Hellwig* [2007] 1 Qd R 17.

and where an indictment was not signed by a person authorised to do so, contrary to s 126 of the *Criminal Procedure Act 1986* (NSW).[47]

(e) A number of interpretative criteria are commonly employed in this area

Two preliminary points may be noted about the determination of the *Project Blue Sky* inquiry. First, it is not compelling that 'must' is used in the statutory requirement.[48] Breach of such a requirement may not lead to invalidity.[49] The same applies to other imperative language: 'shall'[50] and 'is to'.[51] Similarly, it is not conclusive that the requirement is stated in the form of a prohibition such as 'may not'[52] or 'must not'.[53] Second, it is also not conclusive that the legislation provides expressly for certain consequences of the breach of the statutory requirement in question (such as making the breach a criminal offence). If some consequences are provided for, the provision may or may not be exhaustive in this regard.[54]

Drawing on published research,[55] courts have recognised a number of interpretative criteria that are commonly employed in this area.[56] As each statute throws up different factors,[57] there is not one set of factors that are applicable in every case. A list of interpretative criteria that have been employed is provided below.[58]

---

47 *R v Janceski* (2005) 64 NSWLR 10.

48 *Commissioner, Australian Federal Police v Oke* (2007) 159 FCR 441, 447 [32] (Branson and Lindgren JJ, Besanko J agreeing generally at 450 [47]); *Ian Street Developer Pty Ltd v Arrow International Pty Ltd* [2018] VSCA 294, [66] (Maxwell P, McLeish JA agreeing at [88], Niall JA agreeing at [91]).

49 *Re Minister for Immigration and Multicultural and Indigenous Affairs; Ex parte Palme* (2003) 216 CLR 212; *Registrar of Motor Vehicles v Vu* (2013) 115 SASR 385; *Ko v Hall* [2020] VSCA 224, [37] (dicta); *Davis (A Pseudonym) v The Queen* (2016) 55 VR 1, [56] (the Court) (dicta).

50 *Tasker v Fullwood* [1978] 1 NSWLR 20.

51 *Project Blue Sky Inc v Australian Broadcasting Authority* (1998) 194 CLR 355; *Ian Street Developer Pty Ltd v Arrow International Pty Ltd* [2018] VSCA 294.

52 *Kirkham v Industrial Relations Commission* (2015) 121 SASR 471, 482–3 [36] (Kourakis CJ, Bampton J agreeing at 484 [48]) (dicta).

53 *Master Education Services Pty Ltd v Ketchell* (2008) 236 CLR 101. See also *Project Blue Sky Inc v Australian Broadcasting Authority* (1998) 194 CLR 355. In that case s 122(4) of the *Broadcasting Services Act 1992* (Cth) provided that 'Standards must not be inconsistent with this Act . . .'. The statutory requirement that had been breached was laid down by the Act concerned.

54 *Gnych v Polish Club Ltd* (2015) 255 CLR 414, 431 [63] (Gageler J).

55 Graeme Hill, 'Applying Project Blue Sky – When Does Breach of a Statutory Requirement Affect the Validity of an Administrative Decision?' (2015) 80 *AIAL Forum* 54.

56 *Davis (A Pseudonym) v The Queen* (2016) 55 VR 1, 23 [88] (the Court); *Keenan v The Queen* [2020] VSCA 105, [64] (the Court). The identified factors were also applied in *Ko v Hall* [2020] VSCA 224, [64] (Maxwell P and Beach JA).

57 *Project Blue Sky Inc v Australian Broadcasting Authority* (1998) 194 CLR 355, 389 [91] (McHugh, Gummow, Kirby and Hayne JJ).

58 The research by Hill (Graeme Hill, 'Applying Project Blue Sky – When Does Breach of a Statutory Requirement Affect the Validity of an Administrative Decision?' (2015) 80 *AIAL Forum* 54) has been helpful in the preparation of this chapter.

Whether the statutory requirement in question has a 'rule-like quality which can be easily identified and applied'.[59] If so, this points towards invalidity.[60] If not, it points away from invalidity.[61]

Whether the language of the requirement 'speak[s] of the exercise . . ., rather than the existence, of power'.[62] The latter is evidenced by 'shall not be empowered to enter into any agreement'[63] and 'may not terminate . . . unless'.[64] If the former, this points away from invalidity.[65] If the latter, this points towards invalidity.[66]

Whether the statutory purpose of the requirement would be advanced by holding the impugned act invalid. Although this was referred to by the High Court in *Wei*,[67] the factor is not discriminating since it has been pointed out that, in every case, attaching the consequence of invalidity would better serve the purpose of the requirement.[68]

Whether the requirement was stated in an Interpretation Act or other Act of general application, rather than in the Act under which the impugned act was made. If the former, this points away from invalidity.[69]

Whether compliance with the statutory requirement is within the control of the party who is aggrieved by the decision, or *whether the control is 'internal to government'.*[70] If the former, this

---

59 *Project Blue Sky Inc v Australian Broadcasting Authority* (1998) 194 CLR 355, 391 [95] (McHugh, Gummow, Kirby and Hayne JJ).

60 *Kutlu v Director of Professional Services Review* (2011) 197 FCR 177, 188–9 [27]–[28] (Rares and Katzmann JJ); *Commissioner, Australian Federal Police v Oke* (2007) 159 FCR 441, 447 [34] (Branson and Lindgren JJ, Besanko J agreeing generally at 450 [47]).

61 *Project Blue Sky Inc v Australian Broadcasting Authority* (1998) 194 CLR 355, 391–2 [95]–[96] (McHugh, Gummow, Kirby and Hayne JJ); *Kirkham v Industrial Relations Commission* (2015) 121 SASR 471, 482 [31] (Kourakis CJ, Bampton J agreeing at 484 [48]); *Ko v Hall* [2020] VSCA 224, [66] (Maxwell P and Beach JA); *Registrar of Motor Vehicles v Vu* (2013) 115 SASR 385, 395–6 [27], 396–7 [32]–[33], 397 [37] (Kourakis CJ, Anderson J agreeing generally at 398 [40]).

62 *Australian Broadcasting Corporation v Redmore Pty Ltd* (1989) 166 CLR 454, 457 (Mason CJ, Deane and Gaudron JJ).

63 Ibid 459.

64 *Kirkham v Industrial Relations Commission* (2015) 121 SASR 471, 480 [24]–[25] (Kourakis CJ, Bampton J agreeing at 484 [48]).

65 *Australian Broadcasting Corporation v Redmore Pty Ltd* (1989) 166 CLR 454, 457 (Mason CJ, Deane and Gaudron JJ).

66 *Kirkham v Industrial Relations Commission* (2015) 121 SASR 471, 480 [24]–[25] (Kourakis CJ, Bampton J agreeing at 484 [48]).

67 *Wei v Minister for Immigration and Border Protection* (2015) 257 CLR 22, 33 [26], 34 [29]–[30] (Gageler and Keane JJ).

68 *Kirkham v Industrial Relations Commission* (2015) 121 SASR 471, 482 [34] (Kourakis CJ, Bampton J agreeing at 484 [48]). This also illustrates the fallacy of reasoning by reference solely to legislative purpose or by reference to a simplistic view of the Interpretation Act provision regarding legislative purpose.

69 *Registrar of Motor Vehicles v Vu* (2013) 115 SASR 385, 395 [26] (Kourakis CJ, Anderson J agreeing generally at 398 [40]).

70 *Kirkham v Industrial Relations Commission* (2015) 121 SASR 471, 481 [29] (Kourakis CJ, Bampton J agreeing at 484 [48]).

points towards invalidity.[71] If the latter, then, when breached, it points away from invalidating dealings with innocent outsiders and affected parties.[72]

Whether '[the provision that has been breached] has useful purposes to serve even if non-compliance does not result in invalidity'.[73] If so, this points away from invalidity.[74] If not, this points towards invalidity.[75]

Whether the condition is a preliminary requirement in that it 'logically and temporally' precedes the impugned act, or does the condition succeed the impugned act?[76] If the former, this points towards invalidity.[77] If the latter, it points away from invalidity.[78]

Whether the requirement is 'pivotal to the operation' of the statute,[79] *whether non-compliance would 'frustrate the legislative purpose of the scheme',*[80] *or whether fulfilment of the requirement is 'so cardinal to the object of the statute as to disclose an intention that its complete non-observance should invalidate [the related act]'.*[81] If it is pivotal in this sense, its breach points towards invalidity.

Whether the requirement is part of a statutory regime that, due to its special nature, is ordinarily read as essential to the making of the impugned act.[82]

Whether there are 'other sections of the . . . Act which provide expressly that a failure to comply with the section does not affect the validity of what is done under the section'.[83] If so, this is indicative of an intention that the breach of the requirement in question invalidates the related act.[84]

---

71 *Fernando v Minister for Immigration and Multicultural Affairs* (2000) 97 FCR 407, 413–4 [28] (Heerey J, Dowsett J agreeing generally at 420 [55]).

72 *Kirkham v Industrial Relations Commission* (2015) 121 SASR 471, 481 [29] (Kourakis CJ, Bampton J agreeing at 484 [48]); *Australian Broadcasting Corporation v Redmore Pty Ltd* (1989) 166 CLR 454, 457 (Mason CJ, Deane and Gaudron JJ); *Ko v Hall* [2020] VSCA 224, [70] (Maxwell P and Beach JA).

73 *Kirkham v Industrial Relations Commission* (2015) 121 SASR 471, 482 [32] (Kourakis CJ, Bampton J agreeing at 484 [48]). This is an application of the presumption against surplusage. See **[18.3]**.

74 In *Ko v Hall* [2020] VSCA 224, it was suggested that the time limit would be exhortatory: [59]–[60] (Maxwell P and Beach JA).

75 *Kutlu v Director of Professional Services Review* (2011) 197 FCR 177, 190 [32] (Rares and Katzmann JJ).

76 *Re Minister for Immigration and Multicultural and Indigenous Affairs; Ex parte Palme* (2003) 216 CLR 212, 225 [44] (Gleeson CJ, Gummow and Heydon JJ).

77 *Kutlu v Director of Professional Services Review* (2011) 197 FCR 177, 188 [27] (Rares and Katzmann JJ); *Fernando v Minister for Immigration and Multicultural Affairs* (2000) 97 FCR 407, 410 [11], 415 [31] (Heerey J, Dowsett J agreeing generally at 420 [55]); *Kirkham v Industrial Relations Commission* (2015) 121 SASR 471, 480 [24]–[25] (Kourakis CJ, Bampton J agreeing at 484 [48]).

78 *Re Minister for Immigration and Multicultural and Indigenous Affairs; Ex parte Palme* (2003) 216 CLR 212, 224–5 [42], 225 [44] (Gleeson CJ, Gummow and Heydon JJ).

79 *Kutlu v Director of Professional Services Review* (2011) 197 FCR 177, 201 [81] (Rares and Katzmann JJ).

80 *Registrar of Motor Vehicles v Vu* (2013) 115 SASR 385, 397 [36] (Kourakis CJ, Anderson J agreeing generally at 398 [40]).

81 *Tasker v Fullwood* [1978] 1 NSWLR 20, 24 (the Court).

82 *Forrest & Forrest Pty Ltd v Wilson* (2017) 262 CLR 510, 529 [64], 534 [81] (Kiefel CJ, Bell, Gageler and Keane JJ). The regime of a special nature in that case (the *Mining Act 1978* (WA)) was 'a statutory regime [that] confers power on the executive government of a State to grant exclusive rights to exploit the resources of the State': at 529 [64].

83 *Commissioner, Australian Federal Police v Oke* (2007) 159 FCR 441, 447 [33] (Branson and Lindgren JJ, Besanko J agreeing generally at 450 [47]). This is an application of the *expressio unius est exclusio alterius* canon. See **[18.10]**.

84 *Forrest & Forrest Pty Ltd v Wilson* (2017) 262 CLR 510, 532 [74] (Kiefel CJ, Bell, Gageler and Keane JJ); *Kutlu v Director of Professional Services Review* (2011) 197 FCR 177, 190–1 [37] (Rares and Katzmann JJ).

Whether invalidity would be consistent with the broad statutory goals. If so, this points towards invalidity.[85]

Whether 'public inconvenience would be a result of the invalidity of the act'.[86] If so, this points away from invalidity.[87]

Whether injustice would be a consequence if the impugned act was not found to be invalid. If so, this points towards invalidity.[88]

Whether the breach can be directly remedied by other legal or administrative action. If so, this points away from invalidity.[89]

It is probable that the criteria can be ranked. While in *Project Blue Sky* the plurality observed that the courts had not ranked the criteria in the abstract,[90] a researcher (Hill) has since found that in practice the case law contains a hierarchy. According to Hill,[91]

> [t]he most important factor is the court's assessment of the significance of the statutory requirement. Non-compliance is likely to impinge on the effectiveness of a decision if:
>
> - a requirement is an essential element of a statutory scheme; or
> - the requirement contains a procedural safeguard for persons affected by the statutory scheme (such as a provision that gives effect to the requirements of procedural fairness), or affects private property rights.[92]

85 *Fernando v Minister for Immigration and Multicultural Affairs* (2000) 97 FCR 407, 412 [22] (Heerey J, Dowsett J agreeing generally at 420 [55]); *Kutlu v Director of Professional Services Review* (2011) 197 FCR 177, 186 [20] (Rares and Katzmann JJ), 203 [84] (Flick J) (legislative history); *Commissioner, Australian Federal Police v Oke* (2007) 159 FCR 441, 447–8 [34] (Branson and Lindgren JJ, Besanko J agreeing generally at 450 [47]).

86 *Project Blue Sky Inc v Australian Broadcasting Authority* (1998) 194 CLR 355, 392 [97] (McHugh, Gummow, Kirby and Hayne JJ). But if the inconvenience 'would enure only to those with some responsibility for the non-observance', the factor has little or no weight: *Forrest & Forrest Pty Ltd v Wilson* (2017) 262 CLR 510, 528–9 [63], 532–3 [77] (Kiefel CJ, Bell, Gageler and Keane JJ). See also *Kutlu v Director of Professional Services Review* (2011) 197 FCR 177, 187 [25] (Rares and Katzmann JJ).

87 *Project Blue Sky Inc v Australian Broadcasting Authority* (1998) 194 CLR 355, 391–2 [96]–[98] (McHugh, Gummow, Kirby and Hayne JJ); *Ko v Hall* [2020] VSCA 224, [42], [67] (Maxwell P and Beach JA).

88 *Wei v Minister for Immigration and Border Protection* (2015) 257 CLR 22, 34 [28], [31]) (Gageler and Keane JJ).

89 *Ko v Hall* [2020] VSCA 224, [62], [68] (Maxwell P and Beach JA); *Re Minister for Immigration and Multicultural and Indigenous Affairs; Ex parte Palme* (2003) 216 CLR 212, 224 [41], 226 [48] (Gleeson CJ, Gummow and Heydon JJ); *Australian Broadcasting Corporation v Redmore Pty Ltd* (1989) 166 CLR 454, 459–60 (Mason CJ, Deane and Gaudron JJ).

90 (1998) 194 CLR 355, 389 [91] (McHugh, Gummow, Kirby and Hayne JJ).

91 Graeme Hill, 'Applying Project Blue Sky – When Does Breach of a Statutory Requirement Affect the Validity of an Administrative Decision?' (2015) 80 *AIAL Forum* 54, 70–1. Hill's thesis is supported in Paul Daly, 'A Typology of Materiality' (2019) 26(3) *Australian Journal of Administrative Law* 134, 136. While Hill's article presents important and valuable research, the article does not disclose what method of selection was made for the case law. See further the discussion of doctrinal legal research that makes empirical claims in Theunis Roux, 'Judging the Quality of Legal Research: A Qualified Response to the Demand for Greater Methodological Rigour' (2014) 24(1) *Legal Education Review* 177.

92 Graeme Hill, 'Applying Project Blue Sky – When Does Breach of a Statutory Requirement Affect the Validity of an Administrative Decision?' (2015) 80 *AIAL Forum* 54, 70.

To resolve competing indications, as in other areas of statutory interpretation (**[9.10]**), a court makes a 'judgment'[93] by ascertaining 'where the balance lies'.[94]

(f) In considering whether the breach of a statutory requirement invalidates an impugned decision, a court will also consider the extent and consequences of the departure on the facts of the case, and the decision will not ordinarily be invalid if complying with the requirement could have made no difference to the decision

In *Minister for Immigration and Citizenship v SZIZO*[95] the High Court had regard to 'the extent and consequences of the departure' from a statutory requirement.[96] Thus, if the extent of the non-compliance is 'by no means egregious',[97] this points away from invalidity.[98]

Relatedly, in later cases the High Court has developed a requirement of materiality that a plaintiff must normally discharge in challenging judicial and administrative acts.[99] In a statute 'there will . . . be a usual implication that an act is not invalid if the non-compliance is immaterial'.[100] Put in a positive way, a statute is 'ordinarily to be interpreted as incorporating a threshold of materiality in the event of non-compliance'.[101] What the threshold standard is can depend on the statute.[102] Ordinarily, however, a decision will not be invalid 'if complying with the condition could have made no difference to the decision that was made in the circumstances in which that decision was made'.[103]

(g) Some Interpretation Act provisions and some individual Acts provide for the effect of a defect or irregularity, but these provisions, if relevant at all, are not determinative of the *Project Blue Sky* inquiry

Some Interpretation Acts provide, in a limited way, for the effect of a defect or irregularity in relation to an appointment.[104] For instance, s 33AB of the *Acts Interpretation Act 1901* (Cth) provides:

> Anything done by or in relation to a person purporting to act under an appointment (including an acting appointment) under an Act is not invalid merely because:

93 *Project Blue Sky Inc v Australian Broadcasting Authority* (1998) 194 CLR 355, 389 [91] (McHugh, Gummow, Kirby and Hayne JJ).

94 *R v Janceski* (2005) 64 NSWLR 10, 23 [57] (Spigelman CJ). See also *Kirkham v Industrial Relations Commission* (2015) 121 SASR 471, 482 [35] (Kourakis CJ, Bampton J agreeing at 484 [48]).

95 (2009) 238 CLR 627.

96 Ibid 640 [35] (the Court).

97 *Davis (A Pseudonym) v The Queen* (2016) 55 VR 1, 25 [97] (the Court).

98 *Ko v Hall* [2020] VSCA 224, [41], [69] (Maxwell P and Beach JA).

99 *MZAPC v Minister for Immigration and Border Protection* (2021) 390 ALR 590, 592 [1]–[3] (Kiefel CJ, Gageler, Keane and Gleeson JJ), referring to *Hossain v Minister for Immigration and Border Protection* (2018) 264 CLR 123 and *Minister for Immigration and Border Protection v SZMTA* (2019) 264 CLR 421.

100 *MZAPC v Minister for Immigration and Border Protection* (2021) 390 ALR 590, 635 [174] (Edelman J).

101 Ibid 597 [31] (Kiefel CJ, Gageler, Keane and Gleeson JJ), quoting *Hossain v Minister for Immigration and Border Protection* (2018) 264 CLR 123, 134–5 [29]–[30].

102 *Hossain v Minister for Immigration and Border Protection* (2018) 264 CLR 123, 134 [30] (Kiefel CJ, Gageler and Keane JJ).

103 Ibid 134–5 [30], followed in *MZAPC v Minister for Immigration and Border Protection* (2021) 390 ALR 590, 598 [34] (Kiefel CJ, Gageler, Keane and Gleeson JJ).

104 Cf an individual Act (not an Interpretation Act) that may provide binding rules in this area: eg, *Local Government (Whittlesea City Council) Act 2020* (Vic) s 7(d).

(a) for any appointment – the occasion for the appointment had not arisen; or
(b) for any appointment – there was a defect or irregularity in connection with the appointment; or
(c) for any appointment – the appointment had ceased to have effect; or
(d) for an acting appointment – the occasion to act had not arisen or had ceased.[105]

Some other jurisdictions, including the Australian Capital Territory, have comparable provisions.[106]

Some other Acts make similar provision. For instance, s 116(2) of the *Mining Act 1978* (WA) provides:

> Except in the case of fraud, a mining tenement granted or renewed under this Act shall not be impeached or defeasible by reason or on account of *any informality or irregularity* in the application . . .

The High Court has held that 'informality' and 'irregularity' in the above provision described minor defects that did not remove the need for a *Project Blue Sky* inquiry where it was apt:

> 'Informality' means a want of legal form as distinct from a want of legal substance. The term 'irregularity' refers to a lack of regularity in the method or manner in which a power is exercised: it is a term used in deliberate contrast to an act beyond power.[107]

In respect of the Interpretation Act provisions, which are wider in their scope (though related only to anything done by a person purporting to act under an appointment), the ACT Supreme Court has held that 'the terms of [the relevant Interpretation Act provision] may be added to the material cited by the plurality [in the *Project Blue Sky* case] as relevant to determining the legislative intention'.[108]

Example 37.1 *Ian Street Developer Pty Ltd v Arrow International Pty Ltd*[109]

The *Building and Construction Industry Security of Payment Act 2002* (Vic) ('the Act') regulates payments in the building and construction industry. Section 3 states that the object of the Act is

> to ensure that any person who undertakes to carry out construction work or who undertakes to supply related goods and services under a construction contract is entitled to receive, and is able to recover, progress payments in relation to the carrying out of that work and the supplying of those goods and services.

The Act establishes a procedure for claiming the progress payment. In the case of a dispute, the Act provides for an application for adjudication of a payment claim (s 18). In s 22(4) the Act specifies a time limit within which an adjudication must be completed:

105 The amendment that inserted s 33AB is discussed in Anna Lehane and Robert Orr, 'Amendments to the Commonwealth Acts Interpretation Act' (2013) 73 *AIAL Forum* 40, 47–8.

106 *Interpretation Act 1987* (NSW) s 52; *Acts Interpretation Act 1954* (Qld) s 26; *Interpretation Act 1984* (WA) s 57; *Legislation Act 2001* (ACT) s 212.

107 *Forrest & Forrest Pty Ltd v Wilson* (2017) 262 CLR 510, 532 [76] (Kiefel CJ, Bell, Gageler and Keane JJ).

108 *Hill v Council of Law Society of ACT* [2019] ACTSC 79, [29] (Burns J). The primary judge's decision was affirmed on appeal for different reasons: (2020) 15 ACTLR 1. Section 212 was not referred to.

109 [2018] VSCA 294.

[A]n adjudicator is to determine an adjudication application as expeditiously as possible and, in any case –

(a) within 10 business days after the date on which the acceptance by the adjudicator of the application takes effect in accordance with section 20(2); or
(b) within any further time, not exceeding 15 business days after that date, to which the claimant agrees.

The adjudicator accepted the application on 30 June 2017. On 7 July the claimant agreed to extend, to 31 July 2017, the time for the adjudicator to determine the adjudication application. The proprietor and the builder were informed on 28 July 2017 that the adjudicator had made the determination. The adjudicator determined that the proprietor was liable to pay the builder $381.446.78 (excluding GST, interest and 50 per cent of the adjudicator's fee).

The first question was whether there had been a breach of s 22(4). The builder submitted there had not been a breach. It was argued that s 22(4)(b) allows up to 25 days after the acceptance date, by reason that the words 'that date' in that provision referred to the date commencing at the expiry of the 10 days referred to in para (a). The Court disagreed. It was held, by the primary judge and on appeal, that the words 'that date' in para (a) referred to 'the date on which the acceptance by the adjudicator of the application takes effect in accordance with section 20(2)'.[110] This gave a total of just 15 days from the acceptance date for the making of the determination. It was common ground that on this construction there had been a breach of s 22(4).

The next question was the *Project Blue Sky* inquiry: whether the breach of s 22(4) invalidated the adjudication. On the one hand, the imperative language of the provision ('is to'), while not determinative, pointed to invalidity.

On the other hand, several factors pointed away from invalidity. First, in a number of provisions of the Act Parliament had dealt specifically with the circumstances in which an adjudicator's determination would be void.[111] Second, s 28(2) of the Act permitted the claimant to withdraw the application if the adjudicator failed to determine the application within the time allowed. Third, to hold that the expiry of the time limit terminated the adjudicator's jurisdiction would frustrate the specified legislative purpose of 'ensuring' a person entitled to a progress payment was able to recover it. Fourth, invalidity would bring unjust consequences as the adjudicator's conduct was wholly beyond the control of the claimant. Finally, the Court was not persuaded by the applicant's argument that invalidity was conducive to certainty for all concerned. More weighty were the adverse consequences for the effectiveness of the scheme and the maintenance of confidence of participants in the building industry if an adjudicator's delay operated to nullify the process of adjudication. The Court held that the breach of s 22(4) did not invalidate the adjudication.[112]

110 Ibid [85] (Maxwell P, McLeish JA agreeing at [88] and Niall JA agreeing at [91].)

111 This is effectively an application of the *expressio unius est exclusio alterius* canon: see **[18.10]**.

112 [2018] VSCA 294, [67] (Maxwell P, McLeish JA agreeing at [88], Niall JA agreeing at [91].)

Is breach of the requirement legally enforceable?

Exceptionally, with some statutory requirements, non-compliance is not enforceable by proceedings in a court; rather, the due operation of the provision is left to political oversight [37.4]

Exceptionally, non-compliance with a statutory 'requirement' may raise an issue as to whether it was intended that the requirement should be legally enforceable. Put another way, a question may be raised as to whether the due operation of the provision has been left to political, rather than judicial, oversight.

A statutory requirement may not be legally enforceable as a result of an unambiguous statement to that effect by Parliament. Alternatively, a requirement may not be enforceable by reason that Parliament is to be taken to have intended that the requirement is not enforceable by proceedings in a court, at least in the circumstances of the case.

Provisions setting out requirements that are not enforceable in a court have been called 'political duties',[113] 'general exhortatory provisions',[114] provisions that are 'aspirational and incapable of enforcement'[115] and, somewhat misleadingly, a 'duty ... of imperfect obligation'.[116]

Exhortatory provisions raise a number of issues.[117] For instance, it might be asked why the statute book should contain such provisions. If Acts are archetypal sources of law, says Feldman, the phenomenon seems counterintuitive.[118] In a fine-grained analysis of 'legislation which bears no law', Feldman points out that

> the doctrine of parliamentary sovereignty merely asserts that law carried by an Act of Parliament is the highest form of law ... in the United Kingdom. It does not assert that every provision in an Act of Parliament bears law.[119]

Through United Kingdom examples, he argues that non-law-bearing legislation

> can generate effects in the real world by psychological means. To legislate is to assert a special type of impersonal and institutional authority, tapping into a reservoir of respect for the legitimacy of the state and its institutions.[120]

---

113 *Yarmirr v Australian Telecommunications Corporation* (1990) 96 ALR 739, 749 (Burchett J), quoting with approval *Wade on Administrative Law* (6th ed, 1988) 614.

114 *Minister for Immigration and Multicultural Affairs v Eshetu* (1999) 197 CLR 611, 642 [108] (Gummow J), quoting with approval *Sun Zhan Qui v Minister for Immigration and Ethnic Affairs* [1997] FCA 324 (Lindgren J).

115 *Environment East Gippsland Inc v VicForests* (2010) 30 VR 1, 69 [312] (Osborn J).

116 *Re Minister for Immigration and Multicultural and Indigenous Affairs; Ex parte Palme* (2003) 216 CLR 212, 224 [41] (Gleeson CJ, Gummow and Heydon JJ); *Environment East Gippsland Inc v VicForests* (2010) 30 VR 1, 68 [305], 69 [311] (Osborn J). But, confusingly, the High Court has also used this term to describe an *enforceable* duty, the breach of which does not invalidate a related, impugned act: *Glennan v Commissioner of Taxation* (2003) 198 ALR 250, 253 [13] (the Court).

117 See David Feldman, 'Legislation Which Bears No Law' (2016) 37(3) *Statute Law Review* 212.

118 Ibid 223.

119 Ibid. The freedom of the UK Parliament may not be shared to that degree by the Commonwealth Parliament. The High Court of Australia has questioned whether an entire Commonwealth Act containing non-binding guidelines would be valid by reason that the Act would lack a connection with a head of legislative power: *Plaintiff S157/2002 v Commonwealth* (2003) 211 CLR 476, 512–3 [101]–[102] (Gaudron, McHugh, Gummow, Kirby and Hayne JJ).

120 David Feldman, 'Legislation Which Bears No Law' (2016) 37(3) *Statute Law Review* 212, 223. The idea of a 'reservoir of respect' for ordinary (enforceable) law is well supported in the literature: see David Miers and Alan C Page, *Legislation* (Sweet & Maxwell, 2nd ed, 1990) 232; Ross Cranston, *Law, Government and Public*

Accordingly, a question may arise for interpreters: is the performance of a duty intended to be justiciable? Although the phenomenon of non-law-bearing legislation is exceptional in the broad scheme of things, it is sufficiently common to warrant some research and analysis.

(a) Parliament may declare a statutory 'requirement' to be unenforceable in the courts

In *Minister for Immigration and Multicultural Affairs v Bhardwaj*[121] Gaudron and Gummow JJ held that '[s]ubject to the Constitution ... the Parliament may give an administrative decision whatever force it wishes'.[122] The same principle applies to any other statutory provision. In some statutes[123] Parliament has declared that a specified provision does not impose a duty that is enforceable by proceedings in a court. For example, s 8 of the *Australian Broadcasting Corporation Act 1983* (Cth) states, in relation to the Australian Broadcasting Corporation Board:

> **Duties of the Board**
>
> (1) It is the duty of the Board:
>
> (a) to ensure that the functions of the Corporation are performed efficiently and with the maximum benefit to the people of Australia;
>
> (b) to maintain the independence and integrity of the Corporation;
>
> (c) to ensure that the gathering and presentation by the Corporation of news and information is accurate and impartial according to the recognized standards of objective journalism; ...
>
> ...
>
> ...
>
> (3) Nothing in subsection (1) or (2) is to be taken to impose on the Board a duty that is enforceable by proceedings in a court.

It is true that, in some statutes, a statement that specified provisions do not create duties that are legally enforceable in judicial proceedings is made with respect to provisions having such language as 'Parliament expects' or 'should'.[124] Weaker still are provisions expressing Parliament's 'support' for particular measures.[125] These provisions do not in terms lay down a legal duty. But

Policy (OUP, 1987) 34–5; Jeffrey Barnes, 'The Role of Legislation in the Advancement of Community Education: Pt 2: Is Exhortation the Key?' (1999) 14(2) *Australian Journal of Emergency Management* 56; Patrick Parkinson, *Tradition and Change in Australian Law* (LBC Information Services, 2nd ed, 2001) 24–5. Parkinson points out that 'the law commands a high level of respect in western societies which is independent of popular acceptance either of the merits of particular laws or of the level of respect shown to the law makers': at 24.

121 (2002) 209 CLR 597.

122 Ibid 613 [47].

123 For reasons of space the examples below are from research of the statute books of the Commonwealth and the State of Victoria using AustLII databases.

124 *Enhancing Online Safety for Children Act 2015* (Cth) s 22.

125 *Gambling Measures Act 2012* (Cth) ss 19(2), 198.

in many other instances Parliament has used imperative language such as 'duty',[126] 'shall',[127] 'must'[128] and 'is to',[129] and still provided that the provision does not impose a duty that is legally enforceable.[130]

Though not directly legally enforceable, many 'exhortatory provisions' may inform the interpretation of the Act to which they relate.[131] They may do so by setting down 'guiding principles' or other general 'principles'.[132] Or they may provide a statement of values,[133] a 'vision statement',[134] 'objectives'[135] or a 'flow chart'.[136]

But some Acts go further and deliberately state that the provisions do not affect even the interpretation of any Act or law.[137] Sometimes, the Parliament will indicate the purpose of such non-legally enforceable, non-interpretative principles. With respect to certain 'principles for the wellbeing of children', s 4(1) of the *Child Wellbeing and Safety Act 2005* (Vic) states:

> It is the intention of Parliament that the principles set out in this Part should be used for guidance in the development and provision of Government, Government-funded and community services for children and their families.

(b) **Through interpretation, a court may find that Parliament did not intend that a provision in the form of a duty should be capable of legal enforcement**

Even if an Act does not on its face state that a provision, which is in the form of a duty, does not impose a duty that is enforceable by proceedings in a court, exceptionally a question may arise as to whether Parliament intended that the performance of the duty, or the manner of its performance, is subject to the supervision of the courts.

---

126 *Australian Broadcasting Corporation Act 1983* (Cth) s 8(1), (3); *Special Broadcasting Service Act 1991* (Cth) s 10(1), (2).

127 *Australian Broadcasting Corporation Act 1983* (Cth) ss 6(2), (4), 8(2), (3).

128 *Parliamentary Service Act 1999* (Cth) ss 64KA(3), (6), 64MB(4), (9); *Special Broadcasting Service Act 1991* (Cth) s 6(2), (4); *Trans-Tasman Mutual Recognition Act 1997* (Cth) s 39(4), (5); *Members of Parliament (Standards) Act 1978* (Vic) ss 5(1), 5A(a); *Serious Offenders Act 2018* (Vic) pt 21 s 339.

129 *Charter of Budget Honesty Act 1998* (Cth) s 3(2), sch 1.

130 *Defence Housing Australia Act 1987* (Cth) s 62.

131 *Minister for Immigration and Multicultural Affairs v Eshetu* (1999) 197 CLR 611, 635 [76] (Gaudron and Kirby JJ).

132 Examples of Victorian statutory provisions are *Family Violence Protection Act 2008* (Vic) s 144J(2), (3), (4)(a); *Prevention of Family Violence Act 2018* (Vic) s 4; *Commercial Passenger Vehicle Industry Act 2017* (Vic) pt 2 div 1 s 21; *Creative Victoria Act 2017* (Vic) ss 4, 5; *Victorian Fisheries Authority Act 2016* (Vic) s 5, pt 2 divs 2–3; *Education and Training Reform Act 2006* (Vic) ss 1.2.1–1.2.3; *Filming Approval Act 2014* (Vic) ss 5, 8; *Marine Safety Act 2010* (Vic) pt 1.4 s 22; *Multicultural Victoria Act 2011* (Vic) ss 4, 5.

133 Victorian examples are *Parliamentary Administration Act 2005* (Vic) s 5(1), (3); *Public Administration Act 2004* (Vic) s 7(1), (4).

134 *Transport Integration Act 2010* (Vic) ss 6, 28.

135 Ibid ss 7–13, 28.

136 *Workplace Injury Rehabilitation and Compensation Act 2013* (Vic) ss 13, 14.

137 Examples of Victorian statutory provisions are *Child Wellbeing and Safety Act 2005* (Vic) pt 2, ss 4(2)(b), 41U(2), (3)(b); *Constitution Act 1975* (Vic) s 1A(3)(b); *Family Violence Protection Act 2008* (Vic) s 144J(2), (3), (4)(b); *Members of Parliament (Standards) Act 1978 (Vic)* pt 3 s 5A(b); *Serious Offenders Act 2018* (Vic) pt 21 s 339(b); *Victims' Charter Act 2006* (Vic) s 22(1)(b). Some of these provisions have exceptions: eg, *Victims' Charter Act 2006* (Vic) s 22(2); *Members of Parliament (Standards) Act 1978* (Vic) s 5A(b).

In determining whether such a provision imposes a duty that is enforceable by proceedings in a court, the court may have regard to a number of considerations. First, the form and character of the duty. If it involves an extremely broad judgement, that points against judicial supervision,[138] as does a duty having a 'general and indefinite character'.[139] If the provision contains objectives that may be inconsistent as between themselves and require adjustment, that also points away from direct enforcement.[140] And if the duty is expressed as an ideal that cannot be achieved absolutely, this indicates against judicial supervision.[141] So too does a duty for which it is difficult, perhaps impossible, to prove a failure of performance.[142]

Second, the statutory context. If a supervisory role is committed to an executive body, that points against detailed supervision by the courts.[143]

Third, the consequences for the achievement of the statutory goals if a private right such as that which the applicants claim were recognised. If recognising a private right could only obstruct the goals, this points away from such recognition.[144]

Fourth, the separation of powers is a general consideration, as it is necessary to consider 'the rules of law which courts are capable and fitted to enforce'.[145] There may be no practicable alternative but to leave the administration of the provision to the executive,[146] subject to political supervision.[147]

If a court encounters some of these factors, the stance it takes depends on the circumstances. Sometimes a court may regard a duty as inherently not suitable for direct enforcement.[148] At other times a court may recoil from ruling out that possibility in all circumstances. It may hold that no breach has been made out in the circumstances, while indicating that, except in the case of total default, 'detailed supervision by the courts of the manner of performance of the duty is not likely to have been intended'.[149]

---

138 *Yarmirr v Australian Telecommunications Corporation* (1990) 96 ALR 739, 747 (Burchett J).

139 Ibid 749, quoting with approval *Wade on Administrative Law* (6th ed, 1988) 614.

140 *Minister for Immigration and Multicultural Affairs v Eshetu* (1999) 197 CLR 611, 643 [109] (Gummow J), 665 [176] (Callinan J), quoting with approval *Sun Zhan Qui v Minister for Immigration and Ethnic Affairs* [1997] FCA 324 (Lindgren J).

141 *Yarmirr v Australian Telecommunications Corporation* (1990) 96 ALR 739, 749 (Burchett J).

142 *Minister for Immigration and Multicultural Affairs v Eshetu* (1999) 197 CLR 611, 643 [109] (Gummow J), 665 [176] (Callinan J), quoting with approval *Sun Zhan Qui v Minister for Immigration and Ethnic Affairs* [1997] FCA 324 (Lindgren J).

143 *Yarmirr v Australian Telecommunications Corporation* (1990) 96 ALR 739, 750 (Burchett J). See also *Shiel v Secretary, Department of Social Security* (1999) 56 ALD 465, 472 [36] (Katz J).

144 *Yarmirr v Australian Telecommunications Corporation* (1990) 96 ALR 739, 748 (Burchett J).

145 Ibid 749, quoting with approval *Re Citizen Limbo* (1989) 92 ALR 81, 82 (Brennan J).

146 Ibid 748.

147 Ibid 749.

148 *Shiel v Secretary, Department of Social Security* (1999) 56 ALD 465, 471 [32] (Katz J); *Minister for Immigration and Multicultural Affairs v Eshetu* (1999) 197 CLR 611, 635 [76] (Gaudron and Kirby JJ), 642–4 [106]–[109] (Gummow J), 664–8 [176]–[179] (Callinan J).

149 *Yarmirr v Australian Telecommunications Corporation* (1990) 96 ALR 739, 749 (Burchett J).

Example 37.2 *Yarmirr v Australian Telecommunications Corporation*[150]

The applicants, who were, or represented, Aboriginal communities in remote areas of the Northern Territory, contended that s 27 of the *Australian Telecommunications Corporation Act 1989* (Cth) had been breached. The provision stated:

Community service obligations

27. (1) Telecom shall supply a standard telephone service between places within Australia.

(2) The public switched telephone service shall be the standard telephone service.

(3) Telecom shall supply the standard telephone service as efficiently and economically as practicable.

(4) Telecom shall ensure:

(a) that, in view of the social importance of the standard telephone service, the service is reasonably accessible to all people in Australia on an equitable basis, wherever they reside or carry on business; and

(b) that the performance standards for the standard telephone service reasonably meet the social, industrial and commercial needs of the Australian community.

The Federal Court held that it was likely that the duty was not enforceable.[151] The following sums up the Court's reasons:

> When parliament imposes on a functionary a broad duty involving the development and application of policy, to be performed nationally, the fulfilment of which must be subject to many constraints and may be achieved in many different ways, according to the measure allowed to those constraints, but cannot be achieved absolutely, if only because it involves an ideal, detailed supervision by the courts of the manner of performance of the duty is not likely to have been intended.[152]

The Court further held that, in any case, there was no evidence the duty had been breached.[153]

150 Ibid.

151 Ibid 749.

152 Ibid.

153 Ibid 750.

38 STATUTORY REASONABLENESS

Overview

[38.1] Statutory reasonableness refers to the use in legislation of the 'reasonableness' standard in its various forms. The concept of statutory reasonableness may be profitably examined, taking in its general characteristics and its special interpretative aspects. The importance of examining it is underlined by the fact that, for a number of compelling reasons, it is widely used in statute law.

Courts discourage a particular form of statutory reasonableness being defined. Rather, in applying the standard it is preferable to ask the statutory question in terms of the language itself rather than a paraphrase of it. The general characteristics of statutory reasonableness are principally three: it is a legal standard, it has an objective component and it is flexible.

Although disputes with respect to statutory reasonableness occur most often with its application to the facts, it is not free of interpretation. Statutory reasonableness is interpreted in the same broad way as other statutory terms, but the interpreter is more reliant on the context and the legislative purpose in particular.

Concept

[38.2] **Statutory reasonableness refers to the use, in legislation, of the 'reasonableness' standard in its various forms**

'Statutory reasonableness' refers to use of a reasonableness standard in legislation. Legislation may require something be 'reasonable' or 'unreasonable'. Similarly, it may use the adverbs 'reasonably' and 'unreasonably'. For example, the *Social Security Act 1991* (Cth) provides for, among others, 'reasonable costs of living', 'reasonable distance' (s 543A(2A)(f)), 'reasonable excuse' (s 500J) and 'unreasonable for the person to make the journey' (s 1061ZAAK(5)(a)).

[38.3] **The concept of statutory reasonableness may be profitably examined**

Statutory reasonableness is expressed in a variety of forms in an enormous number of contexts. Some have been mentioned already. It is not practicable to examine each and every form and use.[1] Instead, the focus here is on the concept: the general characteristics of statutory reasonableness and its special interpretative aspects.

1 Many particular uses are the subject of works covering the area concerned. An example is s 15(2) of the *Freedom of Information Act 1982* (Cth). It states that '[t]he request must . . . provide such information concerning the document as is *reasonably* necessary to enable a responsible officer of the agency, or the Minister, to identify it' (emphasis added). Texts on freedom of information elaborate the law and practice on this requirement: see, eg, Moira Paterson, *Freedom of Information and Privacy in Australia: Information Access 2.0* (LexisNexis Butterworths, 2nd ed, 2015) [3.24].

Statutory reasonableness presents a case study of the interpretation of general principles drafting.[2] The special interpretative issue it illustrates is how the law approaches the interpretation of terms that, when read in isolation, are vague and indeterminate.

Apart from its interpretative aspects, statutory reasonableness, like other legal standards,[3] also raises significant issues concerning the application of a standard to the facts.[4] With a legal standard '[t]he solution often emerges from a careful description of the facts'.[5] Unravelling and identifying the salient facts are 'all-important'.[6] But in difficult cases 'where the relevant facts afford argument both ways', their resolution requires a 'value judgment'.[7] These matters, which are beyond the scope of this chapter, are discussed elsewhere.[8]

Importance in statute law

Statutory reasonableness is a widely used measure in statute law [38.4]

Reasonableness provides a test that is 'well-known in both criminal and civil law'.[9] It has been described as the 'great workhorse of the common law'.[10] Commentators suggest that it is often used in statute law.[11]

To measure its usage in the Commonwealth statute book, an Act that is commonly used, the *Social Security Act 1991* (Cth), was chosen as a sample. References to 'reasonable', 'unreasonable',

2 See chapters 10 (**[10.7]**), 14 (**[14.7]**) and 16. For recognition that statutory reasonableness is an instance of general principles drafting or some synonym, see **[38.4]**. Nevertheless, statutory reasonableness is not typical general principles drafting. Unless defined to an extent, it lies towards the broader end of the spectrum of general principles drafting: Oliver Jones, *Bennion on Statutory Interpretation* (LexisNexis Butterworths, 6th ed, 2013) 1042.

3 For a definition of a legal standard see **[38.7]**.

4 For the general distinction between interpretation and application to the facts, see **[1.4]**.

5 Justice John Fogarty, 'Giving Effect to Values Used in Statutes' in Jeremy Finn and Stephen Todd (eds), *Law, Liberty, Legislation: Essays in Honour of John Burrows QC* (LexisNexis NZ Ltd, 2008) 1, 10.

6 Ibid 7, quoting with approval *Gillies v Keogh* [1989] 2 NZLR 327, 330 (Cooke P).

7 Ibid 7.

8 Ibid 1; Joachim Dietrich, 'Statutory Interpretation and Private Law Obligations' in Prue Vines and M Scott Donald (eds), *Statutory Interpretation in Private Law* (Federation Press, 2019) 58; Justice Timothy Ginnane, 'Indefinite Terms and Broad Discretions: Statutory Interpretation Against an "Infinite Variety of Facts"' in Jeffrey Barnes (ed), *The Coherence of Statutory Interpretation* (Federation Press, 2019) 95; Julius Stone, *Legal System and Lawyers' Reasonings* (Maitland Publications, 1968) 263–4. Each of these writers gives different emphases to application as opposed to interpretation of legal standards.

9 *Taikato v The Queen* (1996) 186 CLR 454, 470 (Dawson J) (dissenting as to outcome). See also *Canadian Foundation for Children, Youth and the Law v A-G (Canada)* [2004] 1 SCR 76, 99–100 [27] (McLachlin CJ, Gonthier, Iacobucci, Major, Bastarache and LeBel JJ).

10 *Thomas v Mowbray* (2007) 233 CLR 307, 352 [100] (Gummow and Crennan JJ).

11 Commentators point to the popularity of general principles drafting and instance reasonableness. See, eg, Dennis Murphy, 'Plain English in Drafting Legislation and Regulations' (Speech, Plain Legal Language for Public Sector Administrators', Parliament House, Sydney, 29 July 1992) 10; Joachim Dietrich, 'Statutory Interpretation and Private Law Obligations' in Prue Vines and M Scott Donald (eds), *Statutory Interpretation in Private Law* (Federation Press, 2019) 48, 62 n 23; Joachim Dietrich, 'Giving Content to General Concepts' (2005) 29 *Melbourne University Law Review* 218, 218; Justice Timothy Ginnane, 'Indefinite Terms and Broad Discretions: Statutory Interpretation Against an "Infinite Variety of Facts"' in Jeffrey Barnes (ed), *The Coherence of Statutory Interpretation* (Federation Press, 2019) 95, 97. The Canadian Supreme Court opined that 'the [Canadian] criminal law is thick with the notion of "reasonableness"' in *Canadian Foundation for Children, Youth and the Law v A-G (Canada)* [2004] 1 SCR 76, 100 [27] (McLachlin CJ, Gonthier, Iacobucci, Major, Bastarache and LeBel JJ).

'reasonably' and 'unreasonably' were checked.[12] It was found that the Act contains 253 individual references.[13] Another finding is the wide variety of terms with which 'reasonable' or a variation is partnered. For instance, there are 32 different terms with which 'reasonable' is partnered. The most popular use of 'reasonable' is in the term 'reasonable excuse'.

[38.5] **Statutory reasonableness is used in statute law for a number of compelling reasons**

On occasion, judges express a little frustration with reasonableness standards that are open-ended.[14] Yet they are commonly used in legal systems,[15] and there are compelling reasons why this is so. From a drafting point of view the use of reasonableness is a product of the drafter's constant search for the level of generality that is appropriate to the subject matter and consistent with the instructions.[16] As with other instances of general principles drafting, statutory reasonableness is used by the drafter when they need to express the statute at a high or relatively high level of generality. The drafter will have such a need when the circumstances that the Parliament wishes to regulate are so complex or unpredictable that a precise rule cannot be sensibly formulated or agreed upon.[17] Statutory reasonableness fills this need because it is capable of 'ready application in widely differing circumstances'.[18]

Definition and general characteristics

[38.6] **Courts discourage statutory reasonableness being defined; it is preferable, in applying statutory reasonableness, to ask the question in terms of the language itself rather than a paraphrase of it**

Statutory reasonableness has occasionally been essayed by judges. For instance, Windeyer J said:[19]

> [T]he idea of reasonableness seems to be here amorphous. It is, of course, true that, as a measure in fact of time, space, quantity and conduct, reasonableness is a concept deeply rooted in the common law: and so, in such cases, is the power of a court to say whether a particular decision of that fact is or is not within the bounds of reason.[20]

---

12 Research carried out by, and data drawn on held on file by, the author primarily responsible for this chapter. Based on the *Social Security Act 1991* (Cth) version registered 26 October 2020.

13 Excluded from the count were use in headings and cross-references.

14 See, eg, *Taikato v The Queen* (1996) 186 CLR 454, 466 (Brennan CJ, Toohey, McHugh and Gummow JJ).

15 *Bropho v Human Rights and Equal Opportunity Commission* (2004) 135 FCR 105, 127–8 [76] (French J), quoting with approval Julius Stone, *Legal System and Lawyers' Reasonings* (Maitland Publications, 1968) 21–2.

16 Stephen Laws, 'Drawing the Line' in Constantin Stefanou and Helen Xanthaki (eds), *Drafting Legislation: A Modern Approach* (Ashgate, 2008) 19, 30–2; Jack Stark, 'The Proper Level of Generality for Statutes' (2004) 25(1) *Statute Law Review* 77; Paul Yowell, 'Legislation, Common Law and the Virtue of Clarity' in Richard Ekins (ed), *Modern Challenges to the Rule of Law* (LexisNexis NZ Ltd, 2011) 101. This is also why statutory reasonableness may be structured (by specific criteria) to reduce the level of its generality.

17 Justice John Fogarty, 'Giving Effect to Values Used in Statutes' in Jeremy Finn and Stephen Todd (eds), *Law, Liberty, Legislation: Essays in Honour of John Burrows QC* (LexisNexis NZ Ltd, 2008) 1, 5; Justice Timothy Ginnane, 'Indefinite Terms and Broad Discretions: Statutory Interpretation Against an "Infinite Variety of Facts"' in Jeffrey Barnes (ed), *The Coherence of Statutory Interpretation* (Federation Press, 2019) 95, 97–8; Paul Yowell, 'Legislation, Common Law and the Virtue of Clarity' in Richard Ekins (ed), *Modern Challenges to the Rule of Law* (LexisNexis NZ Ltd, 2011) 101, 120.

18 *Taikato v The Queen* (1996) 186 CLR 454, 470 (Dawson J) (dissenting as to outcome).

19 In relation to the *Income Tax Assessment Act 1936* (Cth) s 99A.

20 *Giris Pty Ltd v Commissioner of Taxation (Cth)* (1969) 119 CLR 365, 383–4.

And French J (as he then was), after analysing definitions of 'reasonable' in the *Shorter Oxford English Dictionary*, observed that '[t]here are elements of rationality and proportionality in the relevant definitions of reasonably'.[21]

More recently, however, in *McKinnon v Secretary, Department of Treasury*[22] the High Court expressed a preference for applying the language rather than a paraphrase. Hayne J said:

> The statutory words are to be given their ordinary meaning. It will seldom be helpful, and it will often be misleading, to adopt some paraphrase of them.[23]

Callinan and Heydon JJ specifically addressed the reference, by the Federal Court at first instance, to 'the mind of a person guided by reason'.[24] Their Honours said that '[w]e would prefer to ask the question in terms of the language of the legislation itself, rather than any adaptation of it'.[25]

But there is nothing wrong with saying what reasonableness is *not*. Absurd, irrational or ridiculous grounds are not reasonable grounds.[26] Stating that reasonableness is distinct from such grounds is acceptable.[27]

Statutory reasonableness is a legal standard [38.7]

Statutory reasonableness is a legal standard.[28] A standard imposes a 'requirement that the courts shall evaluate the concrete situation rather than apply a formula mechanically'.[29] Other standards include indecency, obscenity and dangerousness.[30] A standard involves the making of a 'value judgment':

> Where, as here, a statutory provision requires that some act or thing be reasonable, without specifying the criteria to be applied, that issue is determined by the making of a value judgment in the light of all the circumstances save those which, by reason of the subject-matter concerned, are wholly extraneous.[31]

---

21 *Bropho v Human Rights and Equal Opportunity Commission* (2004) 135 FCR 105, 128 [79] (speaking of 'anything said or done reasonably' in s 18D of the *Racial Discrimination Act 1975* (Cth)).

22 (2006) 228 CLR 423.

23 Ibid 445 [60].

24 As quoted by Hayne J at Ibid 447 [68].

25 Ibid 468 [131].

26 Ibid 445 [60] (Hayne J).

27 Ibid 445–6 [61].

28 *Prior v Mole* (2017) 261 CLR 265, 304 [128] (Gordon J); *Bropho v Human Rights and Equal Opportunity Commission* (2004) 135 FCR 105, 127 [76] (French J).

29 Julius Stone, *Legal System and Lawyers' Reasonings* (Maitland Publications, 1968) 263. By 'mechanically', Stone means 'logical formulations and deductions': at 263–4.

30 *Alqudsi v The Queen* (2016) 258 CLR 203, 210–11 [10] (French CJ), citing the *Criminal Procedure Act 1986* (NSW) s 132(5). For other standards see Julius Stone, *Legal System and Lawyers' Reasonings* (Maitland Publications, 1968) 263.

31 *Chakravarti v Advertiser Newspapers Ltd* (1998) 193 CLR 519, 555 [86] (Gaudron and Gummow JJ) (speaking of 'reasonable letter or statement'). See also *Taiapa v The Queen* (2009) 240 CLR 95, 106 [30] (the Court), quoting Professor Glanville Williams, *Textbook of Criminal Law* (Stevens and Sons, 2nd ed, 1983) 49; *Solomons v District Court (NSW)* (2002) 211 CLR 119, 143 [50] (McHugh J).

[38.8] A reasonableness standard has an objective component

By reason of the ordinary meaning of 'reasonable',[32] statutory reasonableness ordinarily imports an objective standard.[33] This means 'a judgment independent of that which the [statutory] actor thinks is reasonable'.[34] Or, as Gleeson CJ and Kirby J said of a 'reasonable grounds' test in s 58(5) of the *Freedom of Information Act 1982* (Cth):

> The point of the objectivity of such a test, when it is necessary to consider whether a primary decision-maker had reasonable grounds for a given state of mind, is that the question is not whether the primary decision-maker thinks he or she has reasonable grounds.[35]

Although judges often refer to reasonableness as an objective standard, test or judgment,[36] this is shorthand. More precisely, statutory reasonableness has an objective *component*: the 'objective circumstances' necessary to found reasonableness.[37]

[38.9] Statutory reasonableness is a flexible concept

Statutory reasonableness is a flexible concept in several respects.[38] First, statutory reasonableness will vary according to whichever thing reasonableness is partnered with. So, for instance, a statute may refer to 'reasonable grounds for suspecting' and 'reasonable grounds for believing'.

---

32 *Liversidge v Anderson* [1942] AC 206, 228, 231, 244 (Lord Atkin) ('If the Secretary of State has reasonable cause to believe'). Though dissenting as to the interpretation, his reasons for judgment are now regarded as 'orthodox' when a statute prescribes that there must be 'reasonable grounds' for a state of mind: *George v Rockett* (1990) 170 CLR 104, 112 (the Court).

33 See *Prior v Mole* (2017) 261 CLR 265, 278 [27] (Gageler J) ('reasonable grounds for believing'); *McKinnon v Secretary, Department of Treasury* (2006) 228 CLR 423, 429 [10], 430 [12] (Gleeson CJ and Kirby J) ('reasonable grounds for the claim'); *Shapowloff v Dunn* (1981) 148 CLR 72, 85 (Wilson J, Gibbs CJ agreeing at 75, Stephen J agreeing at 79, Murphy J agreeing at 79) ('no reasonable or probable ground of expectation'); *Greiner v Independent Commission Against Corruption* (1992) 28 NSWLR 125, 145 (Gleeson CJ), 171–2 (Mahoney JA), 193 (Priestley JA) ('reasonable grounds for dismissing . . . a public official'). Only in an unusually drawn statute would reasonableness effectively allow a subjective judgment – that is, allow the decision-maker to determine for themself whether the reasonableness test is satisfied. In *Liversidge v Anderson* [1942] AC 206 Lord Atkin conceded that reg 42C(1) of the *Defence (General) Regulations 1939* (UK) was 'subjective': at 235. It read: '[A chief officer of police if authorized by the Secretary of State] may, if he is satisfied in the case of any premises in his district that there is reasonable cause to believe that [premises are unlawfully used may close them]'. And in *Greiner v Independent Commission Against Corruption* (1992) 28 NSWLR 125 Mahoney JA intimated that, if the Act in question (*Independent Commission Against Corruption Act 1988* (NSW)) had provided that the conduct in question was 'to be judged according to what "in the opinion of the Commission" could constitute reasonable', the test would not be objective: at 171–2.

34 *Bropho v Human Rights and Equal Opportunity Commission* (2004) 135 FCR 105, 128 [79] (French J) ('anything said or done reasonably').

35 *McKinnon v Secretary, Department of Treasury* (2006) 228 CLR 423, 429 [10].

36 *Ainsworth v Albrecht* (2016) 261 CLR 167, 198 [101] (Nettle J); *Solomons v District Court of New South Wales* (2002) 211 CLR 119, 143 [50] (McHugh J); *Bropho v Human Rights and Equal Opportunity Commission* (2004) 135 FCR 105, 128 [79] (French J).

37 *Prior v Mole* (2017) 261 CLR 265, 292 [73] (Nettle J), referring to *George v Rockett* (1990) 170 CLR 104, 116 (the Court).

38 *Taikato v The Queen* (1996) 186 CLR 454, 491 (Kirby J) (dissenting as to outcome) (speaking of 'reasonable excuse'); *Minister for Immigration and Multicultural and Indigenous Affairs v Al Masri* (2003) 126 FCR 54, 86 [129] (the Court) (speaking of 'reasonably practicable').

The High Court has held that '[t]he facts which can reasonably ground a suspicion may be quite insufficient reasonably to ground a belief'.[39]

Second, in general, the standard for the one term will depend on the facts rather than some preordained line. So it is said to be a 'fact dependent'[40] or 'fact-intensive exercise'.[41] For example, let us assume that there is a defence of 'reasonable excuse' for being in possession of an explosive fuse or detonator, or of a small cannister capable of emitting an irritant liquid. A more substantial excuse would be needed for the former than for the latter.[42]

Third, statutory reasonableness may vary in its application over time, for it permits contemporary values and contemporary circumstances to be taken into account.[43]

Fourth, statutory reasonableness may, or may not, involve a decision-maker striking a balance between competing positions. As Gleeson CJ and Kirby J pointed out in *McKinnon* v *Secretary, Department of the Treasury*,[44] the image of the scales of justice is pervasive in legal thinking, but 'balancing' is not always an apt description of what statutory reasonableness is about.[45] In other words, it is a misconception to assume that every deployment by a drafter of statutory reasonableness will involve a decision-maker striking a balance between competing positions. Courts recognise that the drafter has the ability to widen or narrow the reasonableness issue. Two contrasting cases illustrate the drafter's different uses of statutory reasonableness in this regard.

Waters v Public Transport Corporation[46] illustrates the drafter employing the 'striking a balance' approach. Section 17(5) of the *Equal Opportunity Act 1984* (Vic) provided as follows:

> (5) For the purposes of sub-section (1) a person discriminates against another person on the ground of the status or by reason of the private life of the other person if –
>
> ...
>
> (c) the requirement or condition is not reasonable.

The majority held that 'reasonable' meant reasonable in all the circumstances of the case. This was described as striking a balance between the putative discriminator's legal freedom and the interests of persons in a protected category,[47] and as involving 'weighing all the relevant factors'.[48]

The ruling in the *Waters case* was distinguished in *Ainsworth v Albrecht*.[49] This case concerned interpretation of the *Body Corporate and Community Management Act 1997* (Qld). A dispute arose

---

39 *George v Rockett* (1990) 170 CLR 104, 115 (the Court).

40 *National Disability Insurance Agency v McGarrigle* (2017) 157 ALD 458, 459 [4] (the Court) ('reasonable and necessary supports').

41 *National Disability Insurance Agency v WRMF* (2020) 276 FCR 415, 449 [152] (the Court) ('reasonable and necessary supports').

42 *Taikato v The Queen* (1996) 186 CLR 454, 491 (Kirby J) (dissenting as to outcome).

43 *Bropho v Human Rights and Equal Opportunity Commission* (2004) 135 FCR 105, 127–8 [76] (French J), quoting Julius Stone, *Legal System and Lawyers' Reasonings* (Maitland Publications, 1968) 21–2; *Canadian Foundation for Children, Youth and the Law v A-G (Canada)* [2004] 1 SCR 76, 103 [36], 104 [39] (McLachlin CJ, Gonthier, Iacobucci, Major, Bastarache and LeBel JJ). An example is given in *Taikato v The Queen* (1996) 186 CLR 454, 492 (Kirby J) (dissenting as to outcome) ('reasonable excuse'). See further chapter 19.

44 (2006) 228 CLR 423.

45 Ibid 433 [19].

46 (1991) 173 CLR 349.

47 Ibid 379 (Brennan J).

48 Ibid 395 (Dawson and Toohey JJ, Deane J agreeing at 383–4).

49 (2016) 261 CLR 167. For another case involving legislation that required a different and narrower approach, see *A-G v Fardon* [2019] 2 Qd R 487, 499–500 [47]–[48] (the Court).

between owners of lots in a community titles scheme. Section 276 of that Act stated that an adjudicator may make an order mentioned in sch 5. Item 10 of that schedule described the order as follows:

> If satisfied a motion ... considered by a general meeting of the body corporate and requiring a resolution without dissent was not passed because of opposition that in the circumstances is unreasonable – an order giving effect to the motion as proposed, or a variation of the motion as proposed.

The adjudicator described the issue that she was required to address as being 'whether the opposition to [the] motion was unreasonable in the circumstances and whether the Body Corporate acted reasonably in refusing to give approval'. In the High Court the first respondent (whose proposal led to the dispute) invited the Court to adopt the same approach as in *Waters*: to strike a balance between competing positions and 'weigh all the relevant factors'. The Court refused to do so. The plurality (French CJ, Bell, Keane and Gordon JJ) held that reliance upon the reasons for judgment in *Waters* was misplaced. They said that *Waters* was a case 'concerned with the duty of a decision-making body to reach a reasonable decision taking into account competing considerations'.[50] They pointed out that, under item 10, '[a] lot owner voting his or her opposition to a motion is not a decision-maker of this kind'. They held that the adjudicator had addressed the wrong question. In the present case the statute was narrowly drawn:

> The adjudicator's task under Item 10 of Sched 5 is not to determine whether the outcome of the vote of the general meeting of the Body Corporate was a reasonable balancing of competing considerations, but whether the opposition of lot owners to the proposal was unreasonable.[51]

Interpretation

[38.10] **Although disputes with respect to statutory reasonableness occur most often with its application to the facts, it is not free of interpretation**

A commentator has asked – in respect of general concepts operating through statute – 'how do the courts give effect to those broad concepts?'[52] Put simply they give effect to broad concepts largely through application to the facts ('a value judgment'[53]) with interpretation playing a lesser role.[54] But general principles drafting is still subject to interpretation[55] and statutory

50 *Ainsworth v Albrecht* (2016) 261 CLR 167, 184 [51].

51 Ibid.

52 Joachim Dietrich, 'Giving Content to General Concepts' (2005) 29(1) *Melbourne University Law Review* 218, 233.

53 Justice John Fogarty, 'Giving Effect to Values Used in Statutes' in Jeremy Finn and Stephen Todd (eds), *Law, Liberty, Legislation: Essays in Honour of John Burrows QC* (LexisNexis NZ Ltd, 2008) 1, 7.

54 See the brief discussion on application of legal standards to the facts at **[38.3]**. For different views as to the relative importance of interpretation in regard to legal standards, see Justice John Fogarty, 'Giving Effect to Values Used in Statutes' in Jeremy Finn and Stephen Todd (eds), *Law, Liberty, Legislation: Essays in Honour of John Burrows QC* (LexisNexis NZ Ltd, 2008) 1, 7; Joachim Dietrich, 'Statutory Interpretation and Private Law Obligations' in Prue Vines and M Scott Donald (eds), *Statutory Interpretation in Private Law* (Federation Press, 2019) 58. Dietrich demonstrates that it is difficult to generalise and the role of interpretation is context-dependent.

55 See chapter 16.

reasonableness is no exception. As Gordon J has stated: 'The legal standard of reasonableness is the standard indicated by the proper construction of the statute in issue.'[56]

Of note at the outset is that it is most unlikely that statutory reasonableness in a particular context can be defined in an exhaustive sense. This is because of its vagueness and potential breadth. As the High Court said of the indefinite term 'just and equitable' in the *Family Law Act 1975* (Cth): 'It is not possible to chart its metes and bounds.'[57] This statement does not, however, mean that broad terms such as 'just and equitable' and statutory reasonableness cannot by a process of interpretation be 'confined'.[58] The reference to 'confined' suggests that standards may be given an interpretation that *partially* defines them, such as something a particular form of statutory reasonableness does generally include or something the term does not generally include.

An example of a case determining what reasonableness positively includes[59] is *Taikato v The Queen*[60] (**Example 38.1** below). An example of a case determining what reasonableness does *not* include is *Australian Securities and Investments Commission v Albarran*.[61] In the latter case the Federal Court interpreted 'reasonable excuse' in s 219(2A) of the *Australian Securities and Investments Commission Act 2001* (Cth). This was a defence to a charge of an individual refusing or failing to answer a question that he or she is required to answer by the chairperson at a hearing of the Companies Auditors and Liquidators Disciplinary Board. One alleged reasonable excuse pertained to reliance on legal advice. The Court did not agree. It held that 'reliance on legal advice cannot amount to "reasonable excuse"'.[62]

Statutory reasonableness is interpreted in the same broad way as other statutory terms, but the interpreter is more reliant on the context and legislative purpose in particular [38.11]

As this chapter is dealing with a concept that is used in widely different contexts, it is difficult to generalise about its interpretation. So much depends on the particular statutory context.[63] Nevertheless, a few general points may be made, with the proviso that, strictly speaking, the authorities generally relate to particular terms and particular contexts.

Like other terms in legislation, statutory reasonableness cannot be defined solely using the dictionary. As L Hand J famously said, one cannot 'make a fortress out of the dictionary'.[64] In

56 *Prior v Mole* (2017) 261 CLR 265, 304 [128] (Gordon J). But in statutes that have codified the calculus of negligence, such as the *Civil Liability Act 2002* (NSW), 'little has changed in the courts' approaches to determining reasonableness': Joachim Dietrich, 'Statutory Interpretation and Private Law Obligations' in Prue Vines and M Scott Donald (eds), *Statutory Interpretation in Private Law* (Federation Press, 2019) 58, 70.

57 *Stanford v Stanford* (2012) 247 CLR 108, 120 [36] (French CJ, Hayne, Kiefel and Bell JJ).

58 *Taikato v The Queen* (1996) 186 CLR 454, 470 (Dawson J) (dissenting as to outcome). Cf Joachim Dietrich, 'Statutory Interpretation and Private Law Obligations' in Prue Vines and M Scott Donald (eds), *Statutory Interpretation in Private Law* (Federation Press, 2019) 58, who states that 'many, or perhaps most, general concepts cannot be *defined*' (emphasis in original): at 62.

59 See also *Prior v Mole* (2017) 261 CLR 265, 275 [18] (Kiefel and Bell JJ), 290 [69], 290–1 [71] (Nettle J), 300 [108], 301 [113] (Gordon J).

60 (1996) 186 CLR 454. Another example is *Canadian Foundation for Children, Youth and the Law v A-G (Canada)* [2004] 1 SCR 76 ('reasonable force' in the *Criminal Code*, RSC 1985 (Canada), c C-46, s 43).

61 (2008) 169 FCR 448.

62 Ibid 463 [84], 464 [98] (Jacobson J).

63 *Taikato v The Queen* (1996) 186 CLR 454, 479 (Kirby J) (dissenting as to outcome); *Comcare v Martinez (No 2)* (2013) 212 FCR 272, 290 [68] (Robertson J).

64 *Cabell v Markham* (1945) 148 F 2d 737, 739. For discussion of this observation see **[32.3](b)**.

Comcare v Martinez (No 2)[65] the meaning of 'administrative action taken in a reasonable manner in respect of the employee's employment' was at issue.[66] The Federal Court found that the Administrative Appeals Tribunal had taken the legal meaning of 'reasonable' from the dictionary rather than having considered the particular statutory context.[67]

Given the difficulty (if not impossibility) of defining a particular statutory reasonableness requirement exhaustively, a decision-maker is also prone to err if they purport to define it exhaustively. In *He v Minister for Immigration and Citizenship*[68] reg 1.15(1)(c)(ii) of the *Migration Regulations 1994* (Cth) specified, as one of the criteria for eligibility for a certain visa, non-contact with an overseas near relative within 'a reasonable period before making the application'. The Migration Review Tribunal applied a Departmental 'policy', which stated that a 'reasonable period' is taken to be three years. The Federal Magistrates Court found that the Tribunal erred. The policy was legally irrelevant to the determination,[69] as (it seems) the policy fixed an arbitrary line instead of directing decision-makers to consider the circumstances of the case.[70]

While the text (the words in question) remains the starting point with statutory reasonableness, the words themselves are less important indications of meaning.[71] Decisions on the same words in other statutes are of even less assistance.[72]

An important factor is the legislative purpose. Justice Ginnane suggested this extracurially in his study of indefinite terms.[73] His thesis is supported by judicial use in relation to 'reasonable excuse'. In *Taikato v The Queen* the majority said: '[W]hat is a reasonable excuse depends not only on the circumstances of the individual case but also on the purpose of the provision to which the defence of "reasonable excuse" is an exception.'[74] *Taikato* involved interpretation of criminal law. In *Dordevic v Moore*[75] the ACT Supreme Court applied this approach to 'reasonable excuse' in civil law (claims for personal injury).[76]

---

65 (2013) 212 FCR 272.

66 The relevant provision was the *Safety, Rehabilitation and Compensation Act 1988* (Cth) s 5A(1).

67 (2013) 212 FCR 272, 289–90 [66]–[69] (Robertson J). The Tribunal took the meaning from an earlier Tribunal case which had relied on the dictionary.

68 (2009) 112 ALD 635.

69 Ibid 655 [154] (Nicholls FM).

70 Ibid 654 [146].

71 Justice Timothy Ginnane, 'Indefinite Terms and Broad Discretions: Statutory Interpretation Against an "Infinite Variety of Facts"' in Jeffrey Barnes (ed), *The Coherence of Statutory Interpretation* (Federation Press, 2019) 95, 97, 110 (speaking of indefinite terms). See further chapter 22. Cf Joachim Dietrich, 'Giving Content to General Concepts' (2005) 29(1) *Melbourne University Law Review* 218, 234.

72 *Taikato v The Queen* (1996) 186 CLR 454, 464 (Brennan CJ, Toohey, McHugh and Gummow JJ) ('no guidance') ('reasonable excuse').

73 Justice Timothy Ginnane, 'Indefinite Terms and Broad Discretions: Statutory Interpretation Against an "Infinite Variety of Facts"' in Jeffrey Barnes (ed), *The Coherence of Statutory Interpretation* (Federation Press, 2019) 95, 95, 102, 110.

74 (1996) 186 CLR 454, 464 (Brennan CJ, Toohey, McHugh and Gummow JJ).

75 (2017) 12 ACTLR 282.

76 Ibid 296 [44] (Burns J).

If a particular statutory reasonableness requirement has a common law background, the common law will also be of assistance,[77] whether the legislation reinforces the common law[78] or cuts across it.[79]

Example 38.1 *Taikato v The Queen*[80]

The appellant was found by police officers, at midday on a public street, to be carrying a pressurised canister of formaldehyde to defend herself if she happened to be attacked. She had carried the canister for a few years but had not used it. At the time she was found to be in possession, there was no perceived or immediate threat to her. Some years before the day in question, the appellant had been the subject of an attempted attack on her at her home. The appellant was charged with an offence under s 545E of the *Crimes Act 1900* (NSW). Subsection (1) made it an offence for a person to possess in a public place a thing 'capable of discharging ... irritant matter in liquid, powder, gas or chemical form'. Relevantly, sub-s (2) provided a defence of 'reasonable excuse' for possessing the thing. The appellant was convicted by a magistrate. An appeal to the District Court, and a case stated for the Court of Criminal Appeal, raised, among other things, the issue of the defence of 'reasonable excuse'. At both of those levels it was held that the defence was not established.

An issue for the High Court was whether the appellant had a reasonable excuse for possessing the canister at the time. The majority (Brennan CJ, Toohey, McHugh and Gummow JJ) construed 'reasonable excuse'.[81] For starters the purpose of the section as a whole was inferred:

> One purpose of s 545E is to protect the public from the use of certain dangerous weapons which are analogous to, but not as dangerous as, guns. It strikes at the person who goes into a public place armed with such a weapon.[82]

In addition, though, the defence of 'reasonable excuse' entailed its own purpose: to ensure that the reach of the section is not 'intolerable in a free society'.[83] Common sense suggested some clear and easy cases that fell within the defence,[84] and the purpose indicated cases clearly falling

77 Justice Timothy Ginnane, 'Indefinite Terms and Broad Discretions: Statutory Interpretation Against an "Infinite Variety of Facts"' in Jeffrey Barnes (ed), *The Coherence of Statutory Interpretation* (Federation Press, 2019) 95, 102 (speaking of indefinite terms).

78 *Australian Securities Commission v Gallagher* (1993) 11 WAR 105, 114–6 (Pidgeon J, Franklyn J agreeing at 123 and Walsh J agreeing at 123) ('reasonable degree of care and diligence' by a non-executive director of a company).

79 *George v Rockett* (1990) 170 CLR 104, 110–1 (the Court) ('reasonable grounds' for the issue of a search warrant).

80 (1996) 186 CLR 454.

81 As they held the view that counsel for the appellant had not relied on the 'reasonable excuse' limb (at 464), their holding appears to be obiter dicta. A view contrary to the majority on this score was expressed by Dawson J (at 469) and Kirby J (at 490). See generally **[1.6]** for a discussion of formulating the rule of a case.

82 (1996) 186 CLR 454, 464.

83 See chapter 28 for a discussion of the principle of legality, which has been described as, in part, 'a common sense guide to what a Parliament in a liberal democracy is likely to have intended': *Electrolux Home Products Pty Ltd v Australian Workers' Union* (2004) 221 CLR 309, 329 [21] (Gleeson CJ).

84 (1996) 186 CLR 454, 464–5. See also 491 (Kirby J) (dissenting as to outcome).

outside it.[85] But their Honours were of the view that it would be wrong for a person's guilt to depend on a value judgment by a court.[86] The rule of law, and the principle that '[t]he operation of the criminal law should be as certain as possible',[87] indicated that, in the light of the facts, the section needed confining in a principled way. They held that 'a well-founded fear of attack in the public place in question would have to be a minimum requirement'.[88] For that requirement the majority drew strength from the legislative purpose, observing that if the defence was not so confined 'the purpose of the section would be too easily defeated'.[89] By majority the appeal was dismissed.

85 Ibid 465.

86 Ibid.

87 See **[17.4](g)**.

88 (1996) 186 CLR 454, 466.

89 Ibid.

PRESUMPTION AGAINST RETROSPECTIVE OPERATION

39

Overview

Statute law is considered to be 'retrospective' if it has one of two general operations: it is retroactive, *or* it impairs an existing right or obligation. [39.1]

The concept of retrospectivity is reflected in the interpretative presumption that a statute ought not be given a retrospective operation. The presumption exists at common law and in Interpretation Acts.

The presumption is derived from certain values, which pull in different directions to a certain extent.

To fall within the presumption a right must have vested, and an obligation must have been incurred, immediately before the old law was repealed or amended. A vested right (a 'right acquired') and an incurred obligation for the purposes of the presumption have special meanings. In particular, the presumption is inapplicable to statutes that affect mere matters of procedure.

Finally, if the presumption is attracted, it is subject to any contrary intention in the new law.

Concept of retrospectivity

Statute law is 'retrospective' if it has one of two general operations [39.2]

The common law provides for a 'rule ... that a statute ought not be given a retrospective operation where to do so would affect an existing right or obligation unless the language of the statute expressly or by necessary implication requires such construction'.[1] The Interpretation Acts provide similarly. Before setting out the details of the presumption, it is convenient to describe, in general, what the concept of retrospectivity entails in the law of interpretation. The concept recognises two operations of statute law as retrospective:[2] one narrow, and the other 'extended'.[3]

As regards the narrow operation, Gageler J has helpfully stated that 'a provision [of legislation] might be said to have retrospective operation if, and to the extent that, the provision is taken to have had legal operation at or from a past date'.[4] This equates with what commentators

1 *Rodway v The Queen* (1990) 169 CLR 515, 518 (the Court).

2 *ADCO Constructions Pty Ltd v Goudappel* (2014) 254 CLR 1, 20–1 [44]–[48] (Gageler J). See also Lord Alan Rodger, 'A Time for Everything Under the Law: Some Reflections on Retrospectivity' (2005) 121 *Law Quarterly Review* 57, 64.

3 *ADCO Constructions Pty Ltd v Goudappel* (2014) 254 CLR 1, 15 [26] (French CJ, Crennan, Kiefel and Keane JJ).

4 Ibid 20 [45].

refer to as a 'retroactive law'.[5] A retroactive law may have a backdated commencement date (a date prior to the date of assent).[6] Or it may validate certain 'past acts' that occurred before that date and that may have been invalid. For example, it may say that the past act is 'valid, and is taken always to have been valid'.[7]

A retrospective law in an extended sense is not deemed to take effect from a prior date. In other words, it is prospective in operation.[8] But it is considered retrospective because of its impact on 'vested' rights and liabilities from the date of commencement of the new law. To quote Gageler J again: '[A] provision of [legislation] might be said to have retrospective operation if, and to the extent that, the [provision] operates to alter rights or liabilities which have already come into existence by operation of prior law on past events.'[9] For example, a law (the new law) is retrospective if, after a person is injured and is conditionally entitled to recover damages under the then existing (prior) law upon proof of liability and quantum, the new law removes that entitlement.[10] The extended sense is referred to as 'divesting vested rights'[11] or 'impair[ing] an existing right or obligation'.[12] The meaning of what is a vested right (also called a 'right acquired' and sometimes an 'accrued right'[13]) is elaborated on below (**[39.5]**). The term is technical and is not equivalent to *any* legal right.[14]

---

5 Lord Alan Rodger, 'A Time for Everything Under the Law: Some Reflections on Retrospectivity' (2005) 121 *Law Quarterly Review* 57, 64; Australian Law Reform Commission, *Traditional Rights and Freedoms – Encroachments by Commonwealth Laws* (Report 129, December 2015) 364–5 [13.29]–[13.31], drawing on Elmer Driedger, 'Statutes: Retroactive Retrospective Reflections' (1978) 56(1) *Canadian Bar Review* 264; Lon L Fuller, *The Morality of Law* (Yale University Press, rev ed, 1969) 53, 59.

6 See, eg, *Criminal Code Amendment (Offences Against Australians) Act 2002* (Cth), discussed in Australian Law Reform Commission, *Traditional Rights and Freedoms – Encroachments by Commonwealth Laws* (Report 129, December 2015) 365 [13.30].

7 *Native Title Act 1993* (Cth) s 14, quoted in Australian Law Reform Commission, *Traditional Rights and Freedoms – Encroachments by Commonwealth Laws* (Report 129, December 2015) 365 [13.31].

8 *Gustavson Drilling (1964) Ltd v Minister of National Revenue* [1977] 1 SCR 271, 282 (Martland, Judson and Dickson JJ); Australian Law Reform Commission, *Traditional Rights and Freedoms – Encroachments by Commonwealth Laws* (Report 129, December 2015) 364–5 [13.29], quoting with approval Elmer Driedger, 'Statutes: Retroactive Retrospective Reflections' (1978) 56(1) *Canadian Bar Review* 264, 268–9.

9 *ADCO Constructions Pty Ltd v Goudappel* (2014) 254 CLR 1, 21 [48]. See also to similar effect *Coleman v Shell Co of Australia* (1943) 45 SR (NSW) 27, 31 (Jordan CJ, Davidson and Halse Rogers JJ agreeing at 35).

10 *Free Lanka Insurance Co Ltd v Ranasinghe* [1964] AC 541 (PC), approved in *Esber v Commonwealth* (1992) 174 CLR 430, 440 (Mason CJ, Deane, Toohey and Gaudron JJ). See also *Resort Management Services Ltd v Noosa Shire Council* [1997] 2 Qd R 291, 298 (McPherson JA).

11 *Maxwell v Murphy* (1957) 96 CLR 261, 270 (Dixon CJ), quoting *Dixie v Royal Columbian Hospital* (1941) 2 DLR 138, 139–40 (Sloane JA). See also *South Australia v Collings* (1996) 65 SASR 432, 435 (Doyle CJ, Millhouse J agreeing at 438 and Williams J agreeing at 438).

12 *Mathieson v Burton* (1971) 124 CLR 1, 22 (Gibbs J), quoting with approval *Re Athlumney; Ex parte Wilson* [1898] 2 QB 547, 551–2 (Wright J).

13 *Chang v Laidley Shire Council* (2007) 234 CLR 1, 6 [5] (Kirby J), quoting *A-G (Qld) v Australian Industrial Relations Commission* (2002) 213 CLR 485, 522 [108]. Some decisions have made a conceptual distinction between, on the one hand, a vested right or right acquired, and, on the other hand, an accrued right. The former includes a conditional right within the protection of the presumption. The latter is a 'fully enforceable' right, all conditions for enforcement having been fulfilled: *Hamilton Gell v White* [1922] 2 KB 422, 431 (Atkin LJ); *Chief Adjudication Officer v Maguire* [1999] 1 WLR 1778, 1788–9 (Waller LJ), 1790–1 (Clarke LJ).

14 *ADCO Constructions Pty Ltd v Goudappel* (2014) 254 CLR 1, 15 [26] (French CJ, Crennan, Kiefel and Keane JJ), quoting with approval *Australian Education Union v General Manager of Fair Work Australia* (2012) 246 CLR 117, 133 [26] (French CJ, Crennan and Kiefel JJ).

Sources of the presumption

A presumption against retrospective operation exists at common law and in Interpretation Acts [39.3]

(a) Subject to an exception for matters of mere procedure, at common law a presumption against retrospective operation arises if, under the old law, that law had defined rights or liabilities by reference to past events

As judicially observed,[15] the classic statement of the general principle at common law is by Dixon CJ in *Maxwell v Murphy*:[16]

> The general rule of the common law is that a statute changing the law ought not, unless the intention appears with reasonable certainty, to be understood as applying to facts or events that have already occurred, in such a way as to confer or impose or otherwise affect rights or liabilities which the law had defined by reference to the past events. But, given rights and liabilities fixed by reference to past facts, matters or events, the law appointing or regulating the manner in which they are to be enforced or their enjoyment is to be secured by judicial remedy is not within the application of such a presumption.[17]

It can be seen that the presumption is composed of two main principles. First, generally speaking, it applies to legislation that affects 'rights or liabilities which the law had defined by reference to the past events'. The second main principle is the exception. Dixon CJ described a law to which the presumption is inapplicable as a 'law appointing or regulating the manner in which [rights or liabilities] are to be enforced or their enjoyment is to be secured by judicial remedy'. In *Rodway v The Queen*[18] the exception was pithily expressed this way: '[T]here is no presumption against retrospectivity in the case of statutes which affect mere matters of procedure.'[19] The rights with which the presumption is concerned are hence 'rights of a substantive kind'.[20]

(b) Interpretation Acts lay down a statutory presumption in the case of repeals, and in some cases for amendments

The Interpretation Acts lay down a similar presumption against retrospective operation.[21] An extract of the Commonwealth provision in the *Acts Interpretation Act 1901* (Cth) follows:

> **7 Effect of repeal or amendment of Act**
>
> ...
>
> *No effect on previous operation of Act or part*

---

15 *Jurd v Public Trustee* [2001] NSWSC 632, [10] (MacReady M).

16 (1957) 96 CLR 261.

17 Ibid 267. This statement was approved in *Rodway v The Queen* (1990) 169 CLR 515, 519–20 (the Court).

18 (1990) 169 CLR 515.

19 Ibid 518 (the Court).

20 *Yrttiaho v Public Curator of Queensland* (1971) 125 CLR 228, 244–5 (Gibbs J, Menzies J agreeing at 236, Windeyer J agreeing at 236, Walsh J agreeing at 436) (speaking of the *Acts Interpretation Act 1954* (Qld) but also holding at 245–6 that the statute did not reverse the established rule of the common law); *Torrac Nominees Pty Ltd v Karabay* (2007) 69 NSWLR 669, 675 [43] (Young CJ in Eq, Ipp JA agreeing at 671, Handley AJA agreeing at 679) (speaking of the *Interpretation Act 1987* (NSW)).

21 *Legislation Act 2001* (ACT) s 84; *Interpretation Act 1987* (NSW) s 30; *Acts Interpretation Act 1954* (Qld) s 20; *Legislation Interpretation Act 2021* (SA) s 32; *Acts Interpretation Act 1931* (Tas) s 16; *Interpretation of Legislation Act 1984* (Vic) s 14; *Interpretation Act 1984* (WA) s 37; *Interpretation Act 1978* (NT) s 12.

(2) If an Act, or an instrument under an Act, repeals or amends an Act (the ***affected Act***) or a part of an Act, then the repeal or amendment does not:

...

(c) affect any right, privilege, obligation or liability acquired, accrued or incurred under the affected Act or part ...

Some differences between the various provisions exist. While most jurisdictions apply to both repeals and amendments, the Tasmanian, Western Australian and the Northern Territory Interpretation Acts provide only for the effect of a repeal.[22] Most jurisdictions make provision simply for the statutory presumption to be rebutted by a contrary intention. In this regard two jurisdictions are different in form. The Tasmanian provision requires a contrary intention to be 'expressly provided'.[23] The Victorian provision requires that a contrary intention 'expressly appears'.[24] The Victorian Court of Appeal, however, has interpreted this requirement broadly, as follows:

> In our view, the authorities stretching over many decades and the application of common sense support the interpretation of the word 'expressly' which requires that s 14(2) not be read narrowly: 'expressly' means 'plainly', 'clearly', or 'by necessary implication' and, as such, does not require a line by line reference to every part of a piece of existing legislation.[25]

Some matters that are covered by the common law presumption are the subject of particular statutory provision. All jurisdictions provide that an increase in a penalty since an offence was committed does not apply to the offence.[26] Some jurisdictions provide that, if a law makes an act or omission an offence, the act or omission is only an offence if done or not done after the law commences.[27] And the Victorian and ACT Interpretation Acts state that they apply to a repeal or amendment that affects an immunity.[28]

In addition, most Interpretation Acts have provisions that *overcome* the presumption in the case of a law that *reduces* the maximum penalty or the penalty for an offence.[29] As a result, the reduction applies to an offence committed before the law commences (but the new rule does not affect any penalty imposed before the law commences).

---

22 This limitation only has significance where the common law presumption does not apply. See discussion of differences below. The High Court of Australia has held that, in the case of the Western Australian *Interpretation Act*, the substitution of a provision by another provision is not an amendment; it is a repeal: *Dossett v TKJ Nominees Pty Ltd* (2003) 218 CLR 1, 5–6 [8]–[9] (McHugh J), 12–13 [36]–[39] (Gummow, Hayne and Heydon JJ), 25 [83] (Kirby J). The question of '[w]hether an Act has been repealed or amended is a matter of substance and not one of form only': *Mathieson v Burton* (1971) 124 CLR 1, 20 (Gibbs J), quoting with approval *Beaumont v Yeomans* (1934) 34 SR (NSW) 562, 569 (Jordan CJ, Stephen J agreeing at 570, Maxwell J agreeing at 570).

23 *Acts Interpretation Act 1931* (Tas) s 16(1).

24 *Interpretation of Legislation Act 1984* (Vic) s 14(2).

25 *Mitchell v Latrobe Regional Hospital* (2016) 51 VR 581, 596 [64] (the Court).

26 *Crimes Act 1914* (Cth) s 4F(1); *Crimes (Sentencing Procedure) Act 1999* (NSW) s 19(1); *Acts Interpretation Act 1954* (Qld) s 20C(3); *Legislation Interpretation Act 2021* (SA) s 53(2)(a); *Sentencing Act 1997* (Tas) s 99(1); *Sentencing Act 1991* (Vic) s 114(1); *Sentencing Act 1995* (WA) s 10; *Legislation Act 2001* (ACT) s 84A(2); *Sentencing Act 1995* (NT) s 121(1).

27 *Acts Interpretation Act 1954* (Qld) s 20C(2); *Legislation Act 2001* (ACT) s 84A(1).

28 *Interpretation of Legislation Act 1984* (Vic) s 14(2)(ea); *Legislation Act 2001* (ACT) s 84(6).

29 *Crimes Act 1914* (Cth) s 4F(2); *Crimes (Sentencing Procedure) Act 1999* (NSW) s 19(2); *Legislation Interpretation Act 2021* (SA) s 53(2)(b); *Sentencing Act 1997* (Tas) s 99(2); *Sentencing Act 1991* (Vic) s 114(2); *Legislation Act 2001* (ACT) s 84A(3); *Sentencing Act 1995* (NT) s 121(2). For common law see **[39.6]**.

(c) The contents of the common law and statutory presumptions overlap with each other

In respect of the NSW *Interpretation Act* the High Court has said that 'the protection of accrued rights provided by s 30(1)(c) of the *Interpretation Act* (read with s 5(2) of that Act) mirrors the common law as enunciated by Dixon CJ in both *Maxwell v Murphy* and *Chang Jeeng v Nuffield (Australia) Pty Ltd*'.[30] As an example, the Queensland Interpretation Act does not reveal an intention to reverse the exclusion at common law, whereby a merely procedural statute does not fall within the presumption.[31]

There are some differences between the common law and statutory presumptions. In one respect the statutory presumption is wider; in another respect that mantle is taken by the common law.

At common law 'a liability to punishment for contravention of a penal statute did not continue after the repeal of the enactment which imposed it'.[32] The Interpretation Acts changed this.[33] Thus, Dixon J observed that, before the *Acts Interpretation Act 1901* (Cth), 'a liability to punishment for contravention of a penal statute did not continue after the repeal of the enactment which imposed it unless expressly saved by the repealing statute'.[34]

The statutory presumption does not apply to a statute that 'imposes an entirely new obligation'.[35] Put another way, if the repeal is of a common law principle, it is the common law presumption that is relevant.[36]

Justification for the presumption

The presumption against retrospective operation is derived from certain values, which pull in different directions to a certain extent [39.4]

In a wide-ranging address, Allsop CJ pointed out that '[l]aw, at its very foundation, is conceived and derived from values'.[37] Underlying the presumption against retrospective operation are values that have influenced the shape of the doctrine.

---

30 *ADCO Constructions Pty Ltd v Goudappel* (2014) 254 CLR 1, 15 [27] (French CJ, Crennan, Kiefel and Keane JJ) (footnotes omitted). See also to similar effect *Ogden Industries Pty Ltd v Lucas* (1967) 116 CLR 537, 582 (Windeyer J).

31 *Yrttiaho v Public Curator of Queensland* (1971) 125 CLR 228, 245–6 (Gibbs J, Menzies J agreeing at 235, Windeyer J agreeing at 236, Walsh J agreeing at 236).

32 *Byrne v Garrisson* [1965] VR 523, 525 (Gowans J). See also to similar effect *R v Scarlett; Ex parte McMillan* (1972) 20 FLR 349, 352 (Fox J); *Terasof Pty Ltd v Roads Corporation* [2011] VSC 199, [48] (Robson J). But a conviction by a court does not lapse with the revocation of the law under which it arose because 'its operation does not depend upon the law creating the offence, but upon the authority belonging to a judgment or sentence of a competent Court': *Victorian Stevedoring and General Contracting Co Pty Ltd v Dignan* (1931) 46 CLR 73, 106 (Dixon J).

33 For the United Kingdom, see *R v Scarlett; Ex parte McMillan* (1972) 20 FLR 349, 352 (Fox J). For the Commonwealth of Australia, see *Victorian Stevedoring and General Contracting Co Pty Ltd v Dignan* (1931) 46 CLR 73, 105 (Dixon J). For Victoria, see *Byrne v Garrisson* [1965] VR 523, 525 (Gowans J).

34 *Victorian Stevedoring and General Contracting Co Pty Ltd v Dignan* (1931) 46 CLR 73, 105.

35 *Robertson v City of Nunawading* [1973] VR 819, 827 (the Court).

36 *Western Australia v Richards* (2008) 37 WAR 229, 238 [34] (Steytler P, Martin CJ agreeing at 231–2 [1], McClure JA agreeing at 243 [54], Buss JA agreeing at 243 [55]).

37 Chief Justice James Allsop, 'Values in Law: How They Influence and Shape Rules and the Application of Law' (Centre for Comparative and Public Law, Faculty of Law, University of Hong Kong Hochelaga Lecture Series 2016) 1.

At a simple level it is often stated that the reason for the presumption is that 'in a well ordered and civilised society the legislature would not intend what is unjust'.[38]

It is convenient to consider retroactive laws (see **[39.2]**) first. A retroactive law (unless it is remedial) is clearly unjust as it 'falsifies ... existing legal rules upon which people have ordered their affairs, exercised their rights and incurred liabilities and obligations'.[39] This is particularly the case with a retroactive criminal statute. As Fuller says, commanding a person today to do something yesterday is a 'brutal absurdity'.[40]

An opposition to retrospectivity in the sense of retroactivity is also supported by rule of law considerations. The first principle in Raz's elaboration of the rule of law is as follows:

> *All laws should be prospective, open and clear*. One cannot be guided by a retroactive law. It does not exist at the time of action.[41]

A law that is retrospective in the extended sense (**[39.2]**) may also be considered unjust by the ordinary citizen on the basis that affected persons have arranged their affairs in reliance on the existing law.[42]

These values need to be balanced against other public values that pull in the opposite direction to a certain extent. One affects the content of the presumption, the other its rebuttal. The scope of the presumption – how far the presumption is to extend – is affected by the need to ensure the whole body of law is not ossified forever under the guise of concerns about 'retrospectivity'.[43] If there were a vested right to continuance of the law as it stood in the past, this would be at odds with the policy that 'legislation conform to changing social needs and governmental policy'.[44] In keeping with such considerations, the presumption should not be 'far-reaching'.[45] Thus, if the presumption accorded recognition to a person who resorted to an enactment by the making of an application under it, for the expectancy of a benefit from the application but without some right otherwise existing, it is feared that 'there could be no effective repeal or amendment of any such enactment'.[46]

---

38 *Doro v Victorian Railways Commissioners* [1960] VR 84, 86 (Adam J), approved in *R v Boland* [1974] VR 849, 859 (the Court). See also to similar effect *Dossett v TKJ Nominees Pty Ltd* (2003) 218 CLR 1, 17 [55] (Kirby J).

39 *Australian Education Union v General Manager of Fair Work Australia* (2012) 246 CLR 117, 134–5 [30] (French CJ, Crennan and Kiefel JJ).

40 Lon L Fuller, *The Morality of Law* (Yale University Press, rev ed, 1969) 59.

41 Joseph Raz, 'The Rule of Law and its Virtue' (1977) 93 *Law Quarterly Review* 195, 198 (emphasis in original). The High Court has also noted that a retroactive law is not consistent with the rule of law: *Australian Education Union v General Manager of Fair Work Australia* (2012) 246 CLR 117, 134–5 [30] (French CJ, Crennan and Kiefel JJ).

42 *EWP Ltd v Moore* [1992] 1 QB 460, 474 (Staughton LJ, Bingham LJ agreeing at 475); Lon L Fuller, *The Morality of Law* (Yale University Press, rev ed, 1969) 59, 60.

43 Lon L Fuller, *The Morality of Law* (Yale University Press, rev ed, 1969) 60.

44 *Gustavson Drilling (1964) Ltd v Minister of National Revenue* [1977] 1 SCR 271, 282–3 (Martland, Judson and Dickson JJ). The comment was made in relation to tax law, but the comment has a wider applicability.

45 *Abbott v Minister for Lands* [1895] AC 425, 431 (PC).

46 *Robertson v City of Nunawading* [1973] VR 819, 825 (the Court).

Another consideration, which may weigh against the presumption, arises if a retrospective law is 'curative'.[47] In such a case 'justice may lay [sic] almost wholly upon the side of giving remedial legislation a retrospective operation where that is possible'.[48]

When will the presumption be attracted?

A vested right and an incurred obligation for the purposes of the presumption have special meanings [39.5]

As a result of balancing the underlying values, parliaments and the courts have arrived at a particular understanding of the nature of the 'existing right or obligation' that is sufficient for the statutory and common law presumption to be attracted.

(a) In ascertaining whether a right or obligation was acquired or was incurred under the old law, it is helpful to start with ordinary principles of interpretation

At this point the analysis is of the right or obligation possessed under the old (repealed) law.[49] Courts have pointed out that it is helpful, as a starting point, to consider, under ordinary principles of interpretation, the nature of the right or obligation:

> In his clear and helpful argument Mr Neil, for the claimant, submitted that the Court should approach the case in three steps. It should first determine the nature of the right possessed by a potential applicant for relief under s 106 ..., then whether such an applicant has an accrued or acquired right within s 30(1)(c) [of the *Interpretation Act 1987* (NSW)], and then whether s 30 has been excluded by a contrary intention ... (*Interpretation Act* s 5(2)).[50]

For example, if under the old law an official is conferred an 'absolute discretion' in a matter, such that, on an informed reading, no right at all, not even a conditional right, was conferred on the plaintiff, that person cannot lay claim to a vested right.[51]

(b) The relevant point in time to evaluate the right or obligation under the old law is immediately before its repeal

In order to consider whether a right or obligation falls within the presumption, the relevant date is immediately before the law was repealed.[52] Thus, if a party had a right to take action within a specified period under the old law but, immediately before its repeal, had lost that right by reason

47 Lon L Fuller, *The Morality of Law* (Yale University Press, rev ed, 1969) 53–4.

48 *Polyukhovich v Commonwealth of Australia* (1991) 172 CLR 501, 642–3 (Dawson J). See also Lon L Fuller, *The Morality of Law* (Yale University Press, rev ed, 1969) 53–4.

49 *Esber v Commonwealth* (1992) 174 CLR 430, 439 (Mason CJ, Deane, Toohey and Gaudron JJ); *Spear v Hallenstein* [2018] VSC 169, [46] (Niall JA).

50 *Colley v Futurebrand FHA Pty Ltd* (2005) 63 NSWLR 291, 295 [12] (Handley JA, Giles JA agreeing at 299 [36]). See to similar effect *Telford v Severin* (2007) 98 SASR 70, 75 [21] (Duggan J, White J agreeing at 78 [39], Kelly J agreeing at 78 [40]; *Barminco Investments Pty Ltd v O'Brien* [2006] WASCA 88, [19] (Steytler P, McLure JA agreeing at [41]).

51 *Telford v Severin* (2007) 98 SASR 70, 76 [23], 77 [30] (Duggan J, White J agreeing at [39], Kelly J agreeing at [40]).

52 *Dossett v TKJ Nominees Pty Ltd* (2003) 218 CLR 1, 12 [35] (Gummow, Hayne and Heydon JJ); *Esber v Commonwealth* (1992) 174 CLR 430, 440 (Mason CJ, Deane, Toohey and Gaudron JJ); *Maxwell v Murphy* (1957) 96 CLR 261, 268 (Dixon CJ); *Director of Public Works v Ho Po Sang* [1961] AC 901, 925 (PC).

that the time period had expired without the right being availed of, the presumption is not attracted as there is no 'existing right or obligation' immediately before the repeal.[53]

(c) **A right is understood broadly in certain respects**

At common law a 'right' is read in a general way[54] – that is, not according to the dictates of analytical jurisprudence.[55] It includes an immunity or exemption from legal consequences.[56]

And a right may be 'of a qualified, limited and transitory nature'.[57] For example, it may be 'personal and temporary', such as a right of the child of a lessee of prescribed premises to continue in possession of the premises after the death of the lessee, until probate or letters of administration of the estate of the deceased lessee are granted.[58]

(d) **By definition, a person cannot be said to have acquired a right to a particular thing if the acquisition of that right depended on a favourable exercise of a discretion, and immediately before the repeal of the old law the discretion had not been exercised**

For the purposes of the presumption, the distinction between discretionary and non-discretionary decisions that are outstanding at the date of repeal is crucial.[59] The distinction is 'between what can be called an accrued right and what is no more than the hope of obtaining some discretionary remedy'.[60] Thus, if the remedy is discretionary then (by definition) a right to the remedy cannot accrue while the power remains unexercised.

When a remedy is discretionary a party will properly concede that no right to the remedy arises. Among instances of this is *Minogue v Victoria*.[61] A prisoner applied for parole. At the time of the application the prisoner was eligible for parole but the grant of parole was discretionary. After he made his application, the conditions for obtaining parole were changed and (on the face of them) the prisoner could no longer obtain parole. The High Court noted that the plaintiff accepted that parole was 'in the grant of the Executive' (discretionary) and there was no right to parole.[62] The leading judgment added that eligibility for parole merely 'constituted a factum by reference to which a statutory parole system operates'.[63]

---

53 *Maxwell v Murphy* (1957) 96 CLR 261, 268 (Dixon CJ).

54 *Boyce v Hughes* (1970) 72 SR (NSW) 54, 57 (Sugerman P, Holmes JA agreeing at 59–60).

55 *Mathieson v Burton* (1971) 124 CLR 1, 12 (Windeyer J); *Wellington Diocesan Board of Trustees v Wairarapa Market Buildings Ltd* [1974] 2 NZLR 562, 571 (Cooke J).

56 *Mathieson v Burton* (1971) 124 CLR 1, 12–13 (Windeyer J); *Boyce v Hughes* (1970) 72 SR (NSW) 54, 57 (Sugerman P, Holmes JA agreeing at 59–60).

57 *Boyce v Hughes* (1970) 91 WN (NSW) 171, 173 (Sugerman P), approved in *Mathieson v Burton* (1971) 124 CLR 1, 23 (Gibbs J).

58 *Mathieson v Burton* (1971) 124 CLR 1, 23 (Gibbs J).

59 *Durham Holdings Pty Ltd v New South Wales* (1999) 47 NSWLR 340, 351 [28] (Spigelman CJ, Handley JA agreeing at 365 [109], Giles JA agreeing at 365 [110]). In this area the conferral of 'discretion' is not to be equated with a question that is difficult to resolve or a requirement to exercise judgment: *New South Wales Aboriginal Land Council v Minister Administering the Crown Lands (Consolidation) Act and the Western Lands Act* (1988) 14 NSWLR 685, 691–2 (Hope JA, Samuels JA agreeing at 697, Clarke JA agreeing at 697). Here discretion is understood as 'a capacity to choose between alternative courses of action': see **[36.2]**.

60 *Convex Ltd's Patent* [1980] RPC 423, 437 (Buckley LJ, Ackner LJ agreeing at 438, Oliver LJ agreeing at 438).

61 (2018) 264 CLR 252. Another example is *Re Rocha Pty Ltd (No 2)* (2016) 312 FLR 309, 311–2 [4]–[5], 317 [26] (Brereton J).

62 (2018) 264 CLR 252, 263 [17]–[18] (Keifel CJ, Bell, Keane, Nettle and Edelman JJ), 284 [104] (Gordon J)).

63 Ibid 263 [17] (Keifel CJ, Bell, Keane, Nettle and Edelman JJ).

(e) To be a vested right the right must be 'specific', not abstract or general

Just because a person has a freedom to do a particular act does not mean that that freedom will fall within and be protected by the presumption. *Starey v Graham*[64] is a foundational case.[65] The new law required a person describing themself as a patent agent to pay a fee. The appellant, who had been describing himself as a patent agent before and after the new law had commenced, had not paid the fee. The new law preserved a 'right acquired'. The issue was whether the 'patent agent' had a right acquired immediately before the new law commenced. It was held that

> 'right acquired' means some specific right which in one way or another has been acquired by an individual, and which some persons have got and others have not got. It does not mean 'right' in the sense in which it is often popularly used.[66]

It was held that the 'right' to something that arose merely because the law had not forbidden it (such as wearing spectacles or in this case calling oneself a patent agent) did not qualify as a 'right acquired'.[67] A specific right is one conferred by law. It does not arise from 'a mere gap in the field covered by the legislation which left the person concerned free of statutory control in that area'.[68]

Specific rights include 'specific rights given to an individual upon the happening of one or other of the events specified in the statute'.[69] Examples that fall within this category are a notice to quit served on a tenant by their landlord[70] and the death of a lessee of prescribed premises.[71] The taking of 'appropriate steps' has also been mentioned as triggering a specific right.[72] However (as discussed in (g) below), 'even if a person has taken steps to put statutory machinery in motion, 'the statutory proceedings may only at the date of repeal have reached the stage when he has a hope or expectation or acquiring a right'.[73]

A person does not have a specific right if it is 'abstract' in the sense of notional. For instance, the fact that a statute is passed to protect a class or group (such as tenants generally) does not itself confer on each member of the group anything more than 'abstract rights'.[74]

---

64 [1899] 1 QB 406.

65 The reasoning in this case was approved in *Resort Management Services Ltd v Noosa Shire Council* [1997] 2 Qd R 291, 304 (Fryberg J, McPherson JA agreeing at 295, Moynihan J agreeing at 299) and in *Barminco Investments Pty Ltd v O'Brien* [2006] WASCA 88, [20] (Steytler P, McLure JA agreeing at [41]).

66 [1899] 1 QB 406, 411 (Channell J). See also to similar effect *Hamilton Gell v White* [1922] 2 KB 422, 431 (Atkin LJ).

67 [1899] 1 QB 406, 411 (Channell J).

68 *Robertson v City of Nunawading* [1973] VR 819, 825 (the Court).

69 *Hamilton Gell v White* [1922] 2 KB 422, 431 (Atkin LJ).

70 *Hamilton Gell v White* [1922] 2 KB 422.

71 *Mathieson v Burton* (1971) 124 CLR 1, 24 (Gibbs J).

72 *Resort Management Services Ltd v Noosa Shire Council* [1997] 2 Qd R 291, 303 (Fryberg J, McPherson JA agreeing at 295, Moynihan J agreeing at 299); *Abbott v Minister for Lands* [1895] AC 425, 431. The taking of an appropriate step (making a claim for claimable Crown lands) secured a conditional right in *New South Wales Aboriginal Land Council v Minister Administering the Crown Lands (Consolidation) Act and the Western Lands Act* (1988) 14 NSWLR 685, 691–3 (Hope JA, Samuels JA agreeing at 697, Clarke JA agreeing at 697). Cf *Abbott v Minister for Lands* [1895] AC 425 where the appellant failed to take an appropriate step under the old law (tender for conditional purchase of Crown lands). To same effect is *Chang v Laidley Shire Council* (2007) 234 CLR 1. The appellant failed to take an appropriate step under the old law (make a development application that if not granted gave rise to a right of compensation).

73 *County Council of the County of Moray v Maclean* [1962] SC 601, 606 (Lord Hunter).

74 *Hamilton Gell v White* [1922] 2 KB 422, 431 (Atkin LJ).

Similarly, a person does not have a specific right if their right is merely 'general',[75] such as a 'right' available to 'the public in general'.[76] In *Abbott v Minister for Lands*[77] legislation provided that 'any person' might tender for a conditional purchase of unsold lands.[78] The plaintiff tendered after one of the statutory conditions was altered. He asserted that he had a 'right accrued' on the basis of the now-repealed law. It was held that

> the mere right (assuming it to be properly so called) existing in the members of the community or any class of them to take advantage of an enactment, without any act done by an individual towards availing himself of that right, cannot properly be deemed a 'right accrued' within the meaning of the enactment.[79]

Abbott was applied in *Spear v Hallenstein*.[80] Under the old law, s 59 of the *Coroners Act 1985* (Vic), 'any person' could apply to the Supreme Court of Victoria for an order that some or all of the findings of a coronial inquest are void. No application having been made by the plaintiff under that law prior to its repeal, it was held that the plaintiff did not have a right protected by s 14 of the *Interpretation of Legislation Act 1984* or the common law.[81] One of the reasons for so holding was that 'the putative right to bring an application under s 59 was shared by the world at large'.[82]

(f) Merely because conduct is lawful at the time that it is engaged in does not give rise to a specific immunity from future liability with respect to that conduct

A similar result occurs where the new law imposes a liability on a person who under the old law was not liable. More specifically, merely because conduct is lawful at the time it is engaged in (under the old law) does not mean that that conduct is immune from future liability under a new law. The leading case is *Re A Solicitor's Clerk*.[83] A solicitor's clerk was convicted of larceny. At the time of the offence, disciplinary action could be taken *only* for larceny of the property of the clerk's employer or employer's clients. The clerk did not fall within this provision. The new law provided that the Law Society may apply for an order disciplining a clerk for an offence of larceny, whether of the employer or anyone else. The issue was whether the clerk could be disciplined for past misbehaviour or whether they were protected by the presumption against retrospective operation. It was held that the clerk could be disciplined:

> [T]his Act is not in truth retrospective. It enables an order to be made disqualifying a person from acting as a solicitor's clerk in the future and what happened in the past is the cause or reason for the making of the order, but the order has no retrospective effect.[84]

---

75 *Resort Management Services Ltd v Noosa Shire Council* [1997] 2 Qd R 291, 303–4 (Fryberg J, McPherson JA agreeing at 295, Moynihan J agreeing at 299).

76 Ibid 303. This proposition was expressly based on *Abbott v Minister for Lands* [1895] AC 425. See also, to same effect, *Barminco Investments Pty Ltd v O'Brien* [2006] WASCA 88: '[A] statutory right available to the public at large is unlikely to be regarded as an accrued right': at [20] (Steytler P, McLure JA agreeing at [41]).

77 [1895] AC 425.

78 *Crown Lands Alienation Act 1861* (NSW) s 13.

79 [1895] AC 425, 431 (PC).

80 [2018] VSC 169.

81 Ibid [8] (Niall JA).

82 Ibid [58].

83 [1957] 1 WLR 1219.

84 Ibid 1222 (Lord Goddard CJ, Barry J agreeing at 1223, Havers J agreeing at 1223).

The case has been applied a number of times in Australian courts.[85] In one of these cases, *Geschke v Del-Monte Home Furnishers Pty Ltd*,[86] the Court explained its decision in terms of the absence of a relevant right. The new law, the *Market Court Act 1978* (Vic) stated:

> Where the Court is satisfied that a trader has repeatedly engaged in unfair conduct within the meaning of section 15 it may make an order prohibiting the trader from engaging in such conduct.

The issue was whether unfair conduct of a trader occurring before the commencement of the Act could be looked at in an application to prohibit unfair conduct in the future. The Court conceded that '[i]n one sense such legislation may appear to attach new consequences to past acts'.[87] Nevertheless, the legislation did not impair an existing right or obligation because '[i]n no meaningful sense was the trader here the holder of an accrued right to trade without risk of future restraint based on past conduct'.[88]

The Victorian Court of Appeal took a similar approach to *Geschke* in *Yarra City Council v Metropolitan Fire and Emergency Services Board*.[89] Section 62A(2) of the *Environment Protection Act 1970* (Vic) provides that a court may order a person who has caused or permitted pollution to occur at premises to compensate the occupier who has been served with a clean-up notice. The issue was whether the Act applied to pollution-causing conduct that occurred prior to the commencement of the section. The Court held:

> While liability did not attach to the pollution-creating conduct at the time it was engaged in, and the conduct was therefore lawful, there was no relevant 'right' to engage in that conduct in the sense of an exemption or immunity from future liability under statute in respect of the pollution.[90]

(g) A person does not have a 'right acquired' if, in the absence of some pre-existing substantive right, the person merely sets in train a statutory procedure investigating whether some right should or should not be given

The Interpretation Acts make it clear that the act of beginning a proceeding in a court, tribunal or other statutory body does not *itself* generate a vested right to have that proceeding determined on the basis of the law in force at the time the application was made. The Commonwealth Act is typical. Section 7(2) provides (emphasis added) that the repeal or amendment does not

> (c) affect any right, privilege, obligation or liability acquired, accrued or incurred under the affected Act …
>
> …

85 *La Macchia v Minister for Primary Industry* (1986) 72 ALR 23, 26–7 (Toohey J, Bowen CJ agreeing at 24); *Geschke v Del-Monte Home Furnishers Pty Ltd* [1981] VR 856, 860 (Gobbo J); *Re McInnes* (2014) 241 IR 158, 162–3 [15] (the Full Bench); *Yarra City Council v Metropolitan Fire and Emergency Services Board* (2017) 223 LGERA 135.

86 [1981] VR 856.

87 Ibid 860 (Gobbo J).

88 Ibid.

89 (2017) 223 LGERA 135.

90 Ibid 183 [218] (the Court).

(e) affect any investigation, legal proceeding or remedy *in respect of any such* right, privilege, obligation, liability . . .[91]

It can be seen that the legal proceeding referred to in para (e) is only 'in respect of any such right' – that is, as has been held, 'in respect of an accrued right'.[92] In other words, para (e) only operates in relation to proceedings 'initiated after the amendment in respect of substantive rights acquired before the amendment took effect'.[93]

Since the Interpretation Acts mirror the common law in respect of vested rights (see **[39.3](c)**), there is no reason to doubt that the common law position is the same. Case law confirms this. The taking of a step to have a matter put before an administrative body did not itself generate a right in *Director of Public Works v Ho Po Sang*.[94] This ruling was followed by the Full Court of the Supreme Court of Victoria in *Robertson v City of Nunawading*,[95] which held:

> Resort to the enactment by the making of an application under it which looks to an expectancy of benefit from the application . . . sets in train a procedure, but in the absence of some right otherwise existing, there is no right to have the procedure continued in the face of the repeal of the enactment under which it was instituted.[96]

But, purportedly on the basis of a later High Court of Australia authority, some courts have thought that a vested right to have a procedure continued on the basis of the law in force at the time of making an application to a statutory body arises merely upon the making of an application to such a body (without there needing to be a pre-existing right or liability).[97] In this regard, dicta by the majority in *Esber v Commonwealth*[98] has been purportedly relied on. But (putting aside the fact that the relevant statements in *Esber* were dicta), *Esber* did not stand for, or no longer stands for, such a proposition.

In *Esber* the appellant had applied under the *Compensation (Commonwealth Government Employees) Act 1971* (Cth) to redeem weekly payments of compensation so that he might receive in lieu a lump sum. The application was refused. The appellant applied to the Administrative Appeals Tribunal for review of the decision. After his application to the Tribunal, the 1971 Act was repealed and replaced by the *Commonwealth Employees' Rehabilitation and Compensation Act 1988* (Cth), under which the applicant did not qualify for a redemption. The question was whether, in the Tribunal, the appellant could continue to rely on the 1971 Act.

Some statements in the reasons for judgment of the majority of the High Court (read in isolation) appear to rest the right to redemption solely on the application to the Tribunal having

---

91 *Acts Interpretation Act 1901* (Cth) s 7(2).

92 *Yrttiaho v Public Curator of Queensland* (1971) 125 CLR 228, 244 (Gibbs J, Menzies J agreeing at 236, Windeyer J agreeing at 236, Walsh J agreeing at 436).

93 Ibid 245. See also, to similar effect, *Director of Public Works v Ho Po Sang* [1961] AC 901, 922 (PC).

94 [1961] AC 901.

95 [1973] VR 819.

96 Ibid 825 (the Court).

97 *Gerrard v Mayne Nickless Ltd* (1996) 135 ALR 494, 512–3 (the Court); *Felman v Law Institute of Victoria* [1998] 4 VR 324, 333, 335 (Kenny JA, Winneke P agreeing at 326, Brooking JA agreeing at 326); *Colley v Futurebrand FHA Pty Ltd* (2005) 63 NSWLR 291, 296 [18], 298 [31] (Handley JA, Giles JA agreeing at 299 [36]); *Combined Gunggandji People v Queensland* (2009) 179 FCR 187, 207 [73]; *Re Rocha Pty Ltd (No 2)* (2016) 312 FLR 309, 316 [23], 318 [29] (Brereton J); *Spear v Hallenstein* [2018] VSC 169, [8], [70], [73], [76], [80], [84] (Niall JA). See also *Re McIntyre v Transport Workers' Union of Australia; Ex parte A-G (Qld)* (2000) 105 FCR 584, 590–601 (the Court) (reversed by *A-G (Qld) v Australian Industrial Relations Commission* (2002) 213 CLR 485).

98 (1992) 174 CLR 430.

been made.[99] There are three reasons why the High Court should not be taken to have so held. First, if so, it would be contrary to interpretations of the Interpretation Acts in *Yrttiaho* and *Director of Public Works* cases referred to above, yet there was no statement to that effect in *Esber*.

Second, in *Esber* the majority had earlier held that '[the appellant] had a right to have his claim to redemption determined in his favour if the delegate had wrongly refused his claim'.[100] This holding was followed by its approval of a statement that a right for the purposes of the *Acts Interpretation Act* may be conditional if it is 'conditional upon the relevant facts being established'.[101] This strongly suggests that the majority was not purporting to break new ground, but was following the *Free Lanka Insurance Co* line of cases. These authorities hold that, if at the date of repeal all that remains is '[t]he proof of matters of fact on which a right and its extent depends',[102] a conditional right is in existence at that date.

Third, in 2002, in *Attorney-General (Qld) v Australian Industrial Relations Commission*,[103] the High Court revisited *Esber* and clarified the effect of that case. The 2002 case involved an application to an arbitral body, the Australian Industrial Relations Commission, for the making of an award, the law having changed after the making of the application. The issue was whether the relevant law was the law at the time the application was made, or the law at the time the matter was dealt with by the Commission. The Court distinguished *Esber* by saying that the present case did not involve a determination of existing rights and liabilities, but of conditions to prevail in the future.[104] In contrast, it observed, *Esber* concerned 'Mr Esber's entitlement to redeem his rights to further payments of compensation under the earlier legislation'.[105] The Court went on to explain that the right in the present case was merely 'a public law right to require the Commission to observe its duty to comply with the law *as it exists from time to time*'.[106] In other words, interpolating from that case, the making of an application to a statutory body could not, in the absence of a pre-existing right at stake, give rise to a vested right to a determination based on the old law immediately before its repeal, and *Esber* cannot stand for the proposition for which a number of cases have so held or assumed. The High Court has repeated its analysis of the effect of an application to a statutory body in *Minogue v Victoria*,[107] and it must be taken now to be settled law.

---

99 'Once the appellant lodged an application to the Tribunal to review the delegate's decision, he had a right to have the decision of the delegate reconsidered and determined by the Tribunal ... it was a substantive right': ibid 440 (Mason CJ, Deane, Toohey and Gaudron JJ).

100 Ibid.

101 Ibid, approving *New South Wales Aboriginal Land Council v Minister Administering the Crown Lands (Consolidation) Act and the Western Lands Act* (1988) 14 NSWLR 685, 694.

102 *Australand Corporation (Qld) Pty Ltd v Johnson* [2008] 1 Qd R 203, 251 [133] (Keane JA).

103 (2002) 213 CLR 485.

104 Ibid 503 [45] (Gaudron, McHugh, Gummow and Hayne JJ).

105 Ibid 505 [50]. For judicial analysis of *Esber* that supports the present analysis, see *Jagroop v Minister for Immigration and Border Protection* (2016) 241 FCR 461, 475–6 [70]–[72] (Kenny and Mortimer JJ, Dowsett J agreeing at 463 [1]). For commentary that is supportive, see JS Douglas, 'Accrued Rights and Statutory Interpretation: The Chicken-Catcher's Case' [2003] *Queensland Judicial Scholarship* 51, 10.

106 (2002) 213 CLR 485, 502 [40] (Gaudron, McHugh, Gummow and Hayne JJ) (emphasis added).

107 (2018) 264 CLR 252, 264 [19] (Kiefel CJ, Bell, Keane, Nettle and Edelman JJ).

(h) **A vested right does not need to be an immediately enforceable legal right at the date of the repeal of the old law; it is sufficient if the right is contingent or inchoate**

A vested right 'may fall short of an immediately enforceable legal right in the strict sense'.[108] An important early case was *Hamilton Gell v White*.[109] In this case Scrutton LJ distinguished between 'the acquisition of the right' and 'its enforcement'.[110] In other words, a right could be acquired notwithstanding steps to its enforcement might not have been taken prior to the repeal of the old law.

The notions of what constitutes the 'acquisition' of the right and what constitutes its 'enforcement' were elaborated on in later cases. In *Free Lanka Insurance Co Ltd v Ranasinghe*[111] the Privy Council held that a right may satisfy the relevant Interpretation Act 'although that right might fairly be called inchoate or contingent'.[112] This statement was approved, for the *Acts Interpretation Act 1901* (Cth), by the High Court of Australia in *Esber v Commonwealth*.[113] The same principle applies to an obligation or liability.[114]

It is now well accepted that a right may be regarded as inchoate or contingent when all that is left is '[t]he proof of matters of fact on which a right and its extent depends'.[115] Put another way, 'a right has accrued when all that is left for it to be given effect is the operation of procedural machinery for its enforcement'.[116] Here 'enforcement' has the meaning of an investigation in respect of an *existing* right. In *Director of Public Works v Ho Po Sang*[117] it was observed that 'there is a manifest distinction between an investigation in respect of a right and an investigation which is to decide whether some right should or should not be given'.[118] It follows that a right may be acquired notwithstanding it is contingent on a 'non-discretionary decision of an official or a court'.[119] A non-discretionary decision includes the exercise of judgement even though different persons may arrive at different conclusions.[120]

---

108 *Chang v Laidley Shire Council* (2007) 234 CLR 1, 15 [40] (Kirby J).

109 [1922] 2 KB 422.

110 Ibid 430.

111 [1964] AC 541.

112 Ibid 552.

113 (1992) 174 CLR 430, 440 (Mason CJ, Deane, Toohey and Gaudron JJ).

114 *Chang v Laidley Shire Council* (2007) 234 CLR 1, 15–16 [40] (Kirby J, citing *Plewa v Chief Adjudication Officer* [1995] 1 AC 249, 259 (Lord Woolf)).

115 *Australand Corporation (Qld) Pty Ltd v Johnson* [2008] 1 Qd R 203, 251 [133] (Keane JA).

116 Ibid.

117 [1961] AC 901.

118 Ibid 922.

119 *New South Wales Aboriginal Land Council v Minister Administering the Crown Lands (Consolidation) Act and the Western Lands Act* (1988) 14 NSWLR 685, 696 (Hope JA, Samuels JA agreeing at 697, Clarke JA agreeing at 697). The meaning of discretion is discussed above at **[39.5](d)**. In the *New South Wales Aboriginal Land Council* case the Court added a proviso that the statutory machinery for obtaining that decision has been set in train before the repeal or amendment. But it will not be necessary to set in train statutory machinery if an individual substantive right is in existence at the date of repeal: *Torrac Nominees Pty Ltd v Karabay* (2007) 69 NSWLR 669, 675 [43] (Young CJ in Eq, Ipp JA agreeing at 671, Handley AJA agreeing at 679); *Combined Gunggandji People v Queensland* (2009) 179 FCR 187, 208 [78] (Dowsett J).

120 *New South Wales Aboriginal Land Council v Minister Administering the Crown Lands (Consolidation) Act and the Western Lands Act* (1988) 14 NSWLR 685, 691–2 (Hope JA, Samuels JA agreeing at 697, Clarke JA agreeing at 697).

In the cases there are a number of examples where what remained at the date of repeal was proof of matters of fact or the operation of procedural machinery for the enforcement of a right.[121]

The distinctions in the case law – between acquisition of the right and its enforcement – are determined by interpretation.[122] More straightforward are cases where the legislation specifically states that an entitlement arises, and the statement is separate from provision for the taking of procedural steps that are necessary for the right to fully accrue. *Hamilton Gell v White*[123] concerned s 11 of the *Agricultural Holdings Act 1908* (UK), which stated that on a certain event 'the tenant . . . shall . . . be entitled to compensation'. In a proviso the section provided that 'no compensation shall be payable' unless certain procedural steps were taken, not all of which had been taken at the date of repeal. Similarly, *Chief Adjudication Officer v Maguire*[124] concerned s 60 of the *Social Security Act 1975* (UK), which provided that 'the weekly rate of a disability pension shall . . . be increased' if the result of a disability was as specified. Section 165A of the Act provided that 'no person shall be entitled to any benefit unless . . . he makes a claim for it'. In both of these cases it was recognised that a conditional right had arisen notwithstanding procedural steps had not been taken at the date of repeal.

More difficult are cases where the substantive criteria and the procedural steps are expressed together. In *Resort Management Services Ltd v Noosa Shire Council*[125] the Queensland Court of Appeal considered s 33(10)(a) of the *Local Government Act 1936* (Qld), which stated that a person, whose estate or interest in land was injuriously affected by a change in a planning scheme 'shall, if he makes a claim therefor within the time prescribed, be entitled to obtain from the Local Authority compensation in respect of such injurious affection'. It was observed that '[t]he question is whether making a claim is itself a part of the definition of the right you have or whether it's merely a procedure that applies to enable your right to be vindicated'.[126] The Court held a conditional right arose in this case because

> [m]aking a timely claim is not one of the elements defining the right but is merely a condition of its exercise. The function of the condition is not to limit the class of people

121 See, eg, *Dossett v TKJ Nominees Pty Ltd* (2003) 218 CLR 1, discussed in **Example 39.1**. For other examples, see *Free Lanka Insurance Co Ltd v Ranasinghe* [1964] AC 541 (PC) (proof of negligence); *Chief Adjudication Officer v Maguire* [1999] 1 WLR 1778 (CA) (submission of claim to social security benefit); *Resort Management Services Ltd v Noosa Shire Council* [1997] 2 Qd R 291 (lodging of claim for compensation); *County Council of the County of Moray v Maclean* [1962] SC 601 (making of demand for repayment); *Combined Gunggandji People v Queensland* (2009) 179 FCR 187 (right to a lease subject to certain authorities being satisfied to such); *Esber v Commonwealth* (1992) 174 CLR 430 (proof of right to redemption); *Convex Ltd's Patent* [1980] RPC 423 (proof of entitlement to have patent restored); *New South Wales Aboriginal Land Council v Minister Administering the Crown Lands (Consolidation) Act and the Western Lands Act* (1988) 14 NSWLR 685 (proof of entitlement to claimable Crown Lands). A party has not acquired a conditional right if, immediately before the repeal of the old law that the party seeks to rely on, the party 'maintained a choice to hold and enjoy a diametrically opposed right': *Australand Corporation (Qld) Pty Ltd v Johnson* [2008] 1 Qd R 203, 251 [133] (Keane JA) (option to avoid a contract and return to pre-contractual position); see also at 245 [122] (Keane JA).

122 *Chief Adjudication Officer v Maguire* [1999] 1 WLR 1778, 1789–90 (Clarke LJ); *Resort Management Services Ltd v Noosa Shire Council* [1997] 2 Qd R 291, 301 (Fryberg J, McPherson JA agreeing at 295, Moynihan J agreeing at 299).

123 [1922] 2 KB 422.

124 [1999] 1 WLR 1778.

125 [1997] 2 Qd R 291.

126 *Resort Management Services Ltd v Noosa Shire Council* [1997] 2 Qd R 291, 301 (Fryberg J, McPherson JA agreeing at 295, Moynihan J agreeing at 299), quoting McPherson JA during the argument.

> who would otherwise acquire the right – that was achieved by the other elements of s 33(10)(a). It is to provide a cross-reference to the procedure prescribed for the exercise of the right.[127]

But in *Chang v Laidley Shire Council*[128] the High Court unanimously dismissed the appeal by a landowner adversely affected by a change in a planning scheme. The appellant had not made a development application under the old law. That law (s 5.4.2 of the *Integrated Planning Act 1997* (Qld)) stated:

> An owner of an interest in land is entitled to be paid reasonable compensation by a local government if –
>
> (a) a change reduces the value of the interest; and
> (b) a development application (superseded planning scheme) for a development permit relating to the land has been made; and
> (c) the application is assessed having regard to the planning scheme and planning scheme policies in effect when the application was made; and
> (d) the assessment manager, or, on appeal, the court –
> (i) refuses the application; or
> (ii) approves the application in part or subject to conditions or both in part and subject to conditions.

Hayne, Heydon and Crennan JJ were adamant that the legislation did not recognise any right, conditional or fully accrued, until the development application had been made. They held: 'The statutory right to compensation for which that section provided depended on a particular form of development application having been made and its having been dealt with in a particular way.'[129] It was not up to the Court to work out on its own a fair result. Rather, a right for the purpose of the statutory presumption was 'to be understood by reference to the statute that has been amended or repealed'.[130] So, as Kirby J acknowledged, if '[a] procedural step [was] designated by Parliament as essential to an entitlement' a court should not undermine 'the apparent statutory objectives'.[131]

[39.6] The presumption against retrospective operation is inapplicable to statutes that affect mere matters of procedure

The presumption against retrospectivity does not apply to statutes that affect mere matters of procedure. Courts have sometimes had difficulty in applying this exception.[132] Its rationale is not entirely clear. But it may be related to when the right is acquired, for '[a] right to a particular procedure is acquired only when the occasion for the application of that procedure arises'.[133]

Characterising a change as merely procedural is more clearly indicated if the substantive right that is regulated by the procedure is identified. For example, in *Yrttiaho v Public Curator of Queensland*[134] an amending rule to the Rules of the Supreme Court reduced from six years to

127 Ibid 308 (Fryberg J, McPherson JA agreeing at 295, Moynihan J agreeing at 299).

128 (2007) 234 CLR 1.

129 Ibid 34 [117].

130 Ibid.

131 Ibid 23 [68], 24 [75].

132 *Maxwell v Murphy* (1957) 96 CLR 261, 267 (Dixon CJ); *Rodway v The Queen* (1990) 169 CLR 515, 518 (the Court).

133 *Rodway v The Queen* (1990) 169 CLR 515, 523 (the Court).

134 (1971) 125 CLR 228.

three years the period after which leave to take a fresh step in an action was required. On the instant facts, on the commencement of the new law the reduction still left the appellant (the plaintiff in the action) with time to take a fresh step in the action without leave. Gibbs J pointed out that the cause of action was not barred. His substantive right remained enforceable. The change merely altered the manner in which the action had to be conducted.[135]

It has been observed that '[m]atters described as of "practice and procedure" are not necessarily of insignificant consequence for the person affected'.[136] Nevertheless, the fact that a procedure provides fundamental protection against wrongful conviction ordinarily provides no reason to alter the classification as merely procedural.[137]

Cases dealing with the same or similar subject matter may be persuasive precedents.[138]

It may not be enough simply to characterise the amending law as either procedural or substantive. A provision's operation is *merely* procedural only if 'it would not, if given unconfined operation, affect pre-existing substantive rights or liabilities'.[139] Hence, a court looks also at the operation of the amendment on the instant facts to see if (despite its prima facie characterisation as procedural) the repealing law impairs any existing right or liability. For example, it is convenient to consider an amendment to a statute of limitations. It is ordinarily procedural.[140] But if the amendment, at the time it commences, revives a cause of action that had previously become barred, or deprives a person of the opportunity of instituting an action that is otherwise within time, it impairs existing substantive rights and is not merely procedural.[141]

The following are examples of laws impairing an existing *substantive* right: a section abolishing a common law rule that ordinarily resulted in a court imposing a lesser sentence on a state government appeal than in its opinion should have been imposed at first instance;[142] an amendment to a Compensation Act that took away a right to redeem weekly payments of compensation for a lump sum;[143] an amendment to an Aboriginal Land Rights Act that changed a transfer of lands from one effected by the granting of an estate in fee simple into one effected by the granting of a lease in perpetuity;[144] a law depriving a person of an immunity to legal action;[145] an increase in penalties for a statutory offence;[146] a more restrictive legislative regime applying to the recovery

---

135 Ibid 241.

136 *Jagroop v Minister for Immigration and Border Protection* (2016) 241 FCR 461, 475 [66] (Kenny and Mortimer JJ, Dowsett J agreeing at 463 [1]).

137 *Rodway v The Queen* (1990) 169 CLR 515, 522 (the Court).

138 The example of costs orders is illustrative: see *Hancock v Edgell Birdseye (Ulverstone) Division of Petersville Industries Ltd* [1998] TASSC 10.

139 *Victrawl Pty Ltd v Telstra Corporation Ltd* (1995) 183 CLR 595, 615 (Deane, Dawson, Toohey and Gaudron JJ).

140 *Re Athlumney; Ex parte Wilson* [1898] 2 QB 547, 553 (Wright J), quoted with approval in *Yrttiaho v Public Curator of Queensland* (1971) 125 CLR 228, 246 (Gibbs J, Menzies J agreeing at 236, Windeyer J agreeing at 236, Walsh J agreeing at 436).

141 *Rodway v The Queen* (1990) 169 CLR 515, 519 (the Court). An example of the latter is *McCarthy v Tasmania* [1998] TASSC 124.

142 *Western Australia v Richards* (2008) 37 WAR 229, 239 [36], 240 [41] (Steytler P, Martin CJ agreeing at 231–2 [1], McLure JA agreeing at 243 [54], Buss JA agreeing at 243 [55]).

143 *Esber v Commonwealth* (1992) 174 CLR 430, 440 (Mason CJ, Deane, Toohey and Gaudron JJ).

144 *New South Wales Aboriginal Land Council v Minister Administering the Crown Lands (Consolidation) Act and the Western Lands Act* (1988) 14 NSWLR 685, 697 (Hope JA, Samuels JA agreeing at 697, Clarke JA agreeing at 697).

145 *Maxwell v Murphy* (1957) 96 CLR 261, 283 (Williams J).

146 *Samuels v Songaila* (1977) 16 SASR 397, 400 (Bray CJ).

of damages for personal injury;[147] and a change in a Statement of Principles that, though evidentiary in subject matter, operated as a bar or threshold test on the right to a pension.[148]

Examples of merely *procedural* laws include: 'an amendment to the practice and procedure of a court, including the admissibility of evidence and the effect to be given to evidence';[149] a law conferring a power to award costs against any party where previously there was none;[150] a change in the way a court decision was made as to whether to activate a suspended sentence of imprisonment;[151] and a change in a Ministerial Direction in migration law that, though prescriptive and directed to the content of a discretion, did not result in the loss of any right.[152]

Ousting the presumption

[39.7] **If the presumption against retrospective operation is attracted, it is subject to any contrary intention in the new law**

If the presumption against retrospective operation is attracted, this establishes the 'prima facie position' of the law to which the affected person is subject.[153] But if satisfied, the presumption is subject to any contrary intention in the new law. A contrary intention might exist in the amending law's savings and transitional provisions, or in other substantive terms of the new law.[154]

Where a savings or transitional provision is said to be the source of a contrary intention, this will be the case if the provision is read as exhaustive. Referring to the Commonwealth Act, the High Court gave this brief reason: 'An exhaustive express transitional provision of this nature leaves no room for s 8 of the Interpretation Act to operate.'[155]

Where the repealing law is otherwise said to evidence a contrary intention, the test is inconsistency: '[W]here the provisions of a repealing statute are clearly inconsistent with the survival of accrued rights, those provisions are controlling, and any presumption erected by s 8 is displaced.'[156]

In either case, whether a contrary intention exists depends on ordinary principles of interpretation:

> [A] contrary intention will appear with the requisite degree of certainty if it appears 'clearly' or 'plainly' from the text and context of the provision in question that the provision is designed to operate in a manner which is inconsistent with the maintenance of an existing right or liability.[157]

147 *Dossett v TKJ Nominees Pty Ltd* (2003) 218 CLR 1, 24 [80] (Kirby J).

148 *Repatriation Commission v Keeley* (2000) 98 FCR 108, 122–3 [42] (Lee and Cooper JJ), 130 [72], 130–1 [76]–[78] (Kiefel J).

149 *Rodway v The Queen* (1990) 169 CLR 515, 521 (the Court). This case dealt with alterations to the law formerly requiring certain evidence to be corroborated.

150 *Hancock v Edgell Birdseye (Ulverstone) Division of Petersville Industries Ltd* [1998] TASSC 10.

151 *Tasmania v Thorpe* [2011] TASSC 18.

152 *Jagroop v Minister for Immigration and Border Protection* (2016) 241 FCR 461, 477–8 [78]–[80] (Kenny and Mortimer JJ, Dowsett J agreeing at 463 [1]).

153 *Spear v Hallenstein* [2018] VSC 169, [85] (Niall JA).

154 See, eg, *A-G (Qld) v Australian Industrial Relations Commission* (2002) 213 CLR 485.

155 Ibid 510 [65] (Gaudron, McHugh, Gummow and Hayne JJ). The then s 8 of the *Acts Interpretation Act 1901* (Cth) is now s 7 of that Act.

156 Ibid 505 [52].

157 *ADCO Constructions Pty Ltd v Goudappel* (2014) 254 CLR 1, 22 [52] (Gageler J).

The presumption is harder to rebut where the repealing law purports to affect individual rights and privileges.[158] But if it is conferring a benefit it may be easier to find a contrary intention.[159]

Difficulties have arisen with a provision that identifies particular savings but does not state expressly that it is exhaustive.[160] It is a question of interpretation whether it is to be read as exhaustive.[161] It is open for a court to construe such a provision as merely identifying categories for which *express* savings are enacted.[162] Judges may point out that alternative words could have been used if it were Parliament's intention to make the savings exhaustive.[163] On the other hand, a particularised savings provision may be interpreted as impliedly exhaustive.[164] To reach such a conclusion more is required than particular savings. The Court needs to find that the context supports such an effect.[165]

Western Australia's *Interpretation Act 1984* has a unique Interpretation Act provision dealing with the effect of legislative change.[166] After setting out a general savings provision (s 37(1)), sub-s (2) provides:

> The inclusion in the repealing provisions of an enactment of any express saving with respect to the repeals effected thereby shall not be taken to prejudice the operation of this section with respect to the effect of those repeals.

Because of that provision, it is harder to find a contrary intention from the inclusion in the new law of particular savings. This is because the Interpretation Act provision neutralises the argument that might otherwise be made that the particularity of savings provisions should be read as impliedly exhaustive. The effect of s 37(2) can only be overcome by the new law being held to impliedly repeal s 37(2) itself.[167]

---

158 *Dossett v TKJ Nominees Pty Ltd* (2003) 218 CLR 1, 24 [80] (Kirby J).

159 *R v Morton* [1986] VR 863, 867 (the Court). See also dicta relating to reduced penalties in *Samuels v Songaila* (1977) 16 SASR 397, 404 (Bray CJ), 420–1 (King J). But liberalising civil law for plaintiffs at the same time as relieving defendants of an immunity does not demonstrate a retrospective operation was intended: see *Maxwell v Murphy* (1957) 96 CLR 261.

160 See, eg, *Dossett v TKJ Nominees Pty Ltd* (2003) 218 CLR 1; *A-G (Qld) v Australian Industrial Relations Commission* (2002) 213 CLR 485.

161 *IOOF Holdings Ltd v Federal Commissioner of Taxation* (2014) 224 FCR 535, 559 [96] (Robertson J, Davies J agreeing in principle at 566 [130]).

162 As McHugh J and Kirby J respectively so held in *Dossett v TKJ Nominees Pty Ltd* (2003) 218 CLR 1, 6–7 [11], 23 [77].

163 See ibid 7 [15] (McHugh J), 23 [77], 24–5 [81] (Kirby J). On the 'alternative words could have been used' approach, see **[18.4]**.

164 See, eg, *A-G (Qld) v Australian Industrial Relations Commission* (2002) 213 CLR 485, 510 [65] (Gaudron, McHugh, Gummow and Hayne JJ); *GF Heublein and Bro Inc v Continental Liqueurs Pty Ltd* (1962) 109 CLR 153, 161–2 (the Court).

165 As the High Court found in *A-G (Qld) v Australian Industrial Relations Commission* (2002) 213 CLR 485, 509–11 [65]–[69] (Gaudron, McHugh, Gummow and Hayne JJ).

166 To similar effect, some other jurisdictions have included in particular repealing or amending Acts a statement that the general savings provisions in the relevant interpretation Act are not affected. An example is the *Local Government Act 2020* (Vic) s 328(5).

167 *Dossett v TKJ Nominees Pty Ltd* (2003) 218 CLR 1, 7 [14] (McHugh J), 13–14 [43]–[44] (Gummow, Hayne and Heydon JJ). On implied repeal see **[35.10]**.

Example 39.1 *Dossett v TKJ Nominees Pty Ltd*[168]

The appellant was injured at work. At the time of the injury, pursuant to the *Workers' Compensation and Rehabilitation Act 1981* (WA) ('the 1981 Act'), leave of the District Court of Western Australia was required for the commencement by the appellant of proceedings at common law to recover damages for personal injury. The appellant sought leave on 1 July 1998. On 5 October 1999 his application for leave had not been determined. On that day the *Workers' Compensation and Rehabilitation Amendment Act 1999* (WA) ('the 1999 Act') commenced. This Act amended the 1981 Act and enacted a more restrictive legislative regime applying to the appellant's common law rights. After the commencement of the 1999 Act the District Court held that the amended provision applied to the appellant's application and the Court had no power to give him leave to commence proceedings under the law in force immediately before the commencement of the 1999 Act.

The respondent (defendant) conceded that, immediately before the 1999 Act commenced, the appellant had a vested right to obtain damages.[169] In other words, it conceded the presumption against retrospective operation was attracted and, prima facie, the old law continued to apply to the appellant.

The case in the High Court of Australia turned on whether an intention contrary to the presumption ('a contrary intention') was expressed in the transitional provisions in the 1999 Act. Section 32(7) of that Act ('the transitional provision') stated as follows:

> (7) The amended provisions do not affect the awarding of damages in proceedings –
> (a) commenced before the assent day; or
> (b) for the commencement of which the District Court gave leave under the former provisions before the assent day,
>
> and the former provisions continue to apply in relation to those proceedings.

Three members of the Court decided the case on the basis of s 37(2) of the *Interpretation Act 1984* (WA).[170] As discussed above, this provision has no counterpart in other Australian jurisdictions. But two other members of the Court (McHugh and Kirby JJ) considered whether the transitional provision expressed a contrary intention to the general savings provision in s 37(1) of the *Interpretation Act*, a provision that has counterparts in other Australian jurisdictions and many other common law countries. McHugh J held that the transitional provision did not express a contrary intention to s 37(1)[171] and Kirby J was also so inclined.

McHugh J considered the argument that the transitional provision had identified with particularity the claims for damages that may proceed under the earlier regime and that an 'irresistible inference' was that the claims so identified were the only claims of this nature that can proceed. In response, he pointed out that the transitional provision said nothing about pending *applications* for leave to commence proceedings for damages. Further, it did not contain a statement that the two classes of proceedings were the *only* proceedings to which the former provisions continue to apply. And it did not address s 37(1), such as by stating that the

168 (2003) 218 CLR 1.

169 Ibid 12 [35], where Gummow, Hayne and Heydon JJ observed that the concession was properly made. Note that it was a contingent right to damages: contingent on the non-discretionary decision of the District Court granting leave and the proof of matters of fact on which the right depended. See **[39.5](h)**.

170 Ibid 13–14 [41]–[45] (Gummow, Hayne and Heydon JJ).

171 Ibid 6 [11].

transitional provision applied 'despite anything in any other statute'.[172] He concluded this discussion of general principles by saying that 's 32 contains no foundation for the inference of contrary intention upon which [the respondent] relies'.[173]

Kirby J considered s 37(2) of the *Interpretation Act* alongside s 37(1) of the same Act. But it is a fair reading of Kirby J's reasons to say that he would have came to the same conclusion without considering s 37(2). He made similar textual arguments as made by McHugh J[174] and referred to the importance of the principle of legality when it applies to individual rights and privileges.[175]

172 Ibid 6–7 [11], 7 [15].

173 Ibid 6 [11].

174 Ibid 23 [77], 24–5 [81].

175 Ibid 24 [80], 25–6 [85]–[86].

40 PRESUMPTION AGAINST APPLICATION TO GOVERNMENT AND OTHER CROWN ENTITIES

Overview

[40.1] There is a common law presumption that general words in a statute do not apply to the Crown in any capacity. The term 'the Crown' has a broad meaning for this purpose. It covers executive governments, government agencies and staff as well as the Sovereign and the Sovereign's direct representatives in Australia.

The presumption is displaced if a legislative intent to bind the Crown is found in the statute, irrespective of when it was passed. Such intent may be limited to part of the statute or to the Crown in certain respects only.

The common law presumption has been reversed by statute in two jurisdictions and an earlier form of the presumption is encapsulated in legislation in two others. Such statutory provisions are subject to being modified or displaced by subsequent enactments.

An immunity that the Crown has from legislation relating to a matter does not extend to a party dealing with the Crown on that matter.

The presumption and its displacement

[40.2] General words in a statute are presumed not to apply to the Crown

Many Acts contain a statement along the lines of 'This Act binds the Crown in each of its capacities'[1] or 'This Acts binds the Crown in right of [the enacting jurisdiction] and, so far as the legislative power of Parliament permits, the Crown in all its other capacities'.[2] The full scope of such statements is not immediately apparent.[3]

These statements are included to rebut a presumption that general words in a statute (such as a provision imposing an obligation on a 'person', 'an employer', a 'landlord', a 'factory owner' or a 'manufacturer of goods' to do or refrain from doing something) do not bind the Crown in any capacity. This long-standing presumption has its roots in the common law.[4] It has been described as 'a sacred maxim'.[5]

---

1 See, eg, *National Sports Tribunal Act 2019* (Cth) s 7(1).

2 See, eg, *Melbourne Strategic Assessment (Environment Mitigation Levy) Act 2020* (Vic) s 9; *Local Government Act 2019* (NT) s 3.

3 See **[40.6]** as to the lack of clarity of the term 'the Crown'.

4 See **[40.8]** for statutory modifications and reversals.

5 *Moore v Smith* (1859) 5 Jur NS 892; 120 ER 1034, 1035 (Lord Campbell CJ).

In *Federal Commissioner of Taxation v Tomaras*[6] Gageler J stated that '[u]nderlying the presumption is the understanding that a statute applicable to a citizen has the potential to operate with different force and with different consequences if applied to a government'.[7]

An evolving issue over the years has been how the presumption may be displaced. The modern rule as to displacement was arrived at by the High Court in *Bropho v Western Australia*.[8] In that case it was held by the majority that the presumption is displaced if a legislative intent to bind the Crown is found 'in the provisions of the statute – including its subject matter and disclosed purpose and policy – when construed in a context that includes permissible extrinsic aids'.[9] An express provision one way or the other simplifies the search for legislative intent.[10]

In *Bropho* the High Court was construing s 17 of the *Aboriginal Heritage Act 1972* (WA) ('the AHA'). That section made it an offence for a person to do certain things to an Aboriginal site (including destroying or damaging any object on or under it) without authorisation by trustees or ministerial consent. A government agency had commenced tunnelling and excavation works on an Aboriginal site without authorisation or consent.

Mr Bropho, a person of Aboriginal descent, instituted proceedings against the agency and the State of Western Australia under the AHA. By virtue of s 6 the AHA applied to 'all objects . . . irrespective of where found or situated in the State' of sacred, ritual or ceremonial significance to persons of Aboriginal descent. Section 10 required the Minister to ensure that 'all places in Western Australia' that were of significance to persons of Aboriginal descent were recorded and their relative importance evaluated. Section 18(1) defined 'the owner of any land' to include a lessee from the Crown. The issue before the High Court was whether the general reference to 'a person' in s 17 included government employees acting in the course of their duties.

The High Court held that it did. The majority stated that there was 'no difficulty in discerning in the provisions of the Act a legislative intent that those provisions apply generally to Crown land and to objects on such land'[11] and, given that, 'the conclusion that it was the legislative intent that the general words of s 17 should apply indifferently to natural persons in Western Australia, including government employees, is all but inevitable'.[12] *Bropho* remains good law to this day.[13]

---

6 (2018) 265 CLR 434.

7 Ibid 443–4. See also *Roberts v Ahern* (1904) 1 CLR 406, 418 (the High Court); *Bradken Consolidated Ltd v Broken Hill Pty Co Ltd* (1979) 145 CLR 107, 122 (Gibbs ACJ).

8 (1990) 171 CLR 1. Before *Bropho* the general rule of construction was that the Crown was not bound by a statute unless it was expressly so provided, or it appeared by necessary implication that the statute was intended to bind the Crown. To constitute a necessary implication, the intention to bind the Crown must be manifest from the terms of the statute or its purpose must be wholly frustrated if the Crown were not bound. See *Brisbane City Council v Group Projects Pty Ltd* (1979) 145 CLR 143, 167 (Wilson J); *Bradken Consolidated Ltd v Broken Hill Pty Co Ltd* (1979) 145 CLR 107, 116 (Gibbs ACJ), 127 (Stephen J), 135 (Mason and Jacobs JJ); *China Ocean Shipping Co v South Australia* (1979) 145 CLR 172, 187 (Barwick CJ), 199–200 (Gibbs J), 221–2 (Stephen J), 240 (Aickin J). In these cases the courts applied a narrow concept of 'necessary implication' as set out by the Privy Council in *Province of Bombay v Municipal Corporation of Bombay* [1947] AC 58.

9 (1990) 171 CLR 1, 22 (Mason CJ, Deane, Dawson, Toohey, Gaudron and McHugh JJ).

10 Office of Parliamentary Counsel, *Drafting Direction No 3.10 – Legislation that Refers to or Affects Australian Governments or Jurisdictions* (Australian Government, 2018) states that 'all Bills in which the Crown is to be bound should clearly state this intention, and should specify the extent to which the Crown is to be bound': at para 3.

11 (1990) 171 CLR 1, 24.

12 Ibid 25.

13 See *Federal Commissioner of Taxation v Tomaras* (2018) 265 CLR 434, 439–40 (Kiefel CJ and Keane J), 443–4 (Gageler J), 451–2 (Gordon J).

In *Bropho* the majority took the view that the strength of the presumption against a legislative intent to bind the Crown depends 'upon the circumstances, including the content and purpose of the particular provision and the identity of the entity in respect of which the question of the applicability of the provision arises'.[14] In that case they took cognisance of the fact that 93 per cent of land in Western Australia was Crown land and that, if the AHA only applied to land that was not Crown land, 'the Act would be extraordinarily ineffective to achieve its stated purpose of preserving Western Australia's Aboriginal sites and objects'.[15] They also recognised the increased scope of Crown activities.[16]

They contrasted a question of whether the Sovereign themself is subject to a provision imposing criminal liability with a question of the kind arising in that case (whether employees of a governmental corporation engaged in commercial and developmental activities are bound by general provisions safeguarding places or objects significant to a particular community group). In the former case the presumption is 'extraordinarily strong', whereas in the latter case the presumption 'will represent little more than the starting point of the ascertainment of the relevant legislative intent'.[17]

In *Commonwealth v Anti-Discrimination Tribunal (Tas)*[18] Weinberg J stated that, even if the Crown is not 'bound' by an Act, it 'might, however, unless the contrary intention appeared, take advantage of an Act if it chose to do so'.[19] However, in *Federal Commissioner of Taxation v Tomaras*[20] Edelman J treated the issue of benefit as being just another aspect of the basic presumption but with the force of the presumption being weakened in those circumstances.[21]

[40.3] The rule in *Bropho* applies to legislation whenever passed

The majority in *Bropho* stated that earlier judicial pronouncements based on the view of the law as expounded in *Province of Bombay v Municipal Corporation of Bombay*[22] 'should be read as applying to the context of the particular statutory provisions involved in the cases in which they

---

14 (1990) 171 CLR 1, 23 (Mason CJ and Deane, Dawson, Toohey, Gaudron and McHugh JJ).

15 Ibid 24.

16 The majority noted that the operations of the Crown have moved from encompassing 'little more than the Sovereign, his or her direct representatives and the basic organs of government' to a position 'where the activities of the executive government reach into almost all aspects of commercial, industrial and developmental endeavour' and 'where it is commonplace for governmental commercial, industrial and developmental instrumentalities and their servants and agents . . . to compete and have commercial dealings on the same basis as private enterprise': at 18–19. See also *Downs v Williams* (1971) 126 CLR 61, 71 (Windeyer J).

17 Ibid 23. In *Registrar of the Accident Compensation Tribunal v Commissioner of Taxation (Cth)* (1993) 178 CLR 145 Mason CJ, Deane, Toohey and Gaudron JJ stated that it was clear from *Bropho* that the presumption must yield to the circumstances involved, including the content and purpose of the provision, the way the provision would operate and whether the provision would bind servants or agents of the government in relation to acts they do or property which they own or occupy in that capacity: at 171–2. In *Federal Commissioner of Taxation v Tomaras* (2018) 265 CLR 434 Edelman J stated that 'if the presumption applies, the circumstances will also dictate its strength': at 470 [107].

18 (2008) 169 FCR 85.

19 Ibid 110 [120].

20 (2018) 265 CLR 434.

21 He stated that '[t]he force of the presumption will also be much weaker if the statute operates to the benefit of the Crown or, to a lesser degree, if it does not necessarily operate to the detriment of the Crown': ibid 470 [109]. He further stated: '[It] is also possible that the general presumption might apply even if the relevant provision does not necessarily operate to the detriment of the Crown.' (at 473 [118]).

22 [1947] AC 58. See n 8 above.

were made'.[23] While expressing that it was not intended 'to overturn the settled construction of particular existing legislation',[24] the majority further stated:

> [I]t must be acknowledged that, in the period since the *Province of Bombay Case*, the tests of 'manifest from the very terms of the statute' and 'purposes of the statute being otherwise wholly frustrated' came to be established as decisive of the question whether, in the absence of express reference, the general words in a statute bind the Crown. That being so, it may be necessary, in construing a legislative provision enacted before the publication of the decision in the present case, to take account of the fact that those tests were seen as of general application at the time when the particular provision was enacted. If, however, a legislative intent that the Crown should be bound is apparent notwithstanding that those tests are not satisfied, the legislative intent must prevail.[25]

Accordingly, the rule in *Bropho* applies to the construction of legislation, whether enacted before or after the decision in that case.[26] The question in all cases is whether there is a legislative intent to bind the Crown.

The presumption applies to the Crown in all its capacities and not just that of the enacting jurisdiction [40.4]

A State may be bound by a valid Commonwealth law[27] and may in turn bind the Commonwealth by a valid State law.[28] An ACT or Northern Territory Act may bind the Crown in right of the Commonwealth[29] or in right of a state or of the other territory. Unless otherwise specifically provided, a Commonwealth Act that binds the Crown in right of each state, binds the Crown in right of the Australian Capital Territory[30] and the Northern Territory.[31]

The presumption about general words in an Act not applying to the Crown applies to the Crown in every capacity and not just in the capacity of the Crown in right of the enacting jurisdiction.[32] In *Commonwealth v Western Australia (Mining Act Case)*[33] the presumption was expressed as 'a presumption that a statute which regulates the conduct or rights of individuals does not apply to members of the executive government of any of the polities in the federation, government instrumentalities and authorities intended to have the same legal status as the executive government, their servants or agents'.[34]

---

23 (1990) 171 CLR 1, 22.

24 Ibid 22.

25 Ibid 23.

26 See *Federal Commissioner of Taxation v Tomaras* (2018) 265 CLR 434, 469 [105] (Edelman J).

27 *Amalgamated Society of Engineers v Adelaide Steamship Co Ltd* (1920) 28 CLR 129.

28 *Pirrie v McFarlane* (1925) 36 CLR 170. See also *Commonwealth v Western Australia (Mining Act Case)* (1999) 196 CLR 392, 472 (Hayne J).

29 For the Australian Capital Territory this can only be done to the extent provided by regulations made under the *Australian Capital Territory (Self-Government) Act 1988* (Cth). See s 69A(1) of that Act.

30 *Australian Capital Territory (Self-Government) Act 1988* (Cth) s 27.

31 *Northern Territory (Self-Government) Act 1978* (Cth) s 51(1).

32 *Bradken Consolidated Ltd v Broken Hill Pty Co Ltd* (1979) 145 CLR 107, 122–3 (Gibbs ACJ), 129 (Stephen J), 136 (Mason and Jacobs JJ).

33 (1999) 196 CLR 392.

34 Ibid 410 (Gleeson CJ and Gaudron J).

In that case it was held that the *Mining Act 1978* (WA), despite applying expressly to 'Crown land', did not apply to land held by the Commonwealth. Hayne J, with whom McHugh and Callinan JJ agreed,[35] read the definition of 'Crown land' as referring only to land held by the state and opined that it 'is only if the definition of Crown land is read in that way that effect is given to the presumption that the legislature of one polity does not intend to bind the other polities in the federation'.[36]

In *Federal Commissioner of Taxation v Tomaras*[37] Gageler J expressed:

> Stated sufficiently for present purposes, the presumption of the common law of Australia that a statute does not 'bind the Crown' is a presumption that a statute enacted by an Australian legislature does not operate to impair the legal position of the body politic or executive government of the Commonwealth, a State or a self-governing Territory . . . the presumption is displaced simply where an affirmative intention to alter the legal position of the Commonwealth, State or self-governing Territory appears from the text, structure, subject matter or context of the statute.[38]

While all polities in the federation are covered by the presumption, separate consideration must be given to the Crown in right of the enacting jurisdiction and the Crown in right of any other polity. The fact that an Act is expressed as not binding on the Crown in right of the enacting jurisdiction, and is silent as to the position in relation to other polities, does not mean that the Act binds the Crown in right of any of the other polities in the federation.[39]

In *AGU v Commonwealth (No 2)*[40] the NSW Court of Appeal held that a provision stating that a statute binds the Crown 'while effective to rebut the general presumption that a statute does not bind the government which passed it, will be a factor, not necessarily determinative, in determining whether specific provisions apply in relation to other bodies politic'.[41]

A reference to 'the Crown' in NSW legislation is a reference to the Crown in right of New South Wales.[42] Similarly, a reference to the Crown in Victorian legislation is a reference to the Crown in right of Victoria[43] and a reference to the Crown in South Australian legislation is a reference to the Crown in right of South Australia.[44] This reflects the common law position.[45] If it is intended to refer to the Crown in another capacity, that intent must be expressed clearly so as to create a contrary intention.

35 Ibid 421 (McHugh J), 479 (Callinan J).

36 (1999) 196 CLR 392, 475.

37 (2018) 265 CLR 434.

38 Ibid 443–4 [18].

39 *Commonwealth v Western Australia (Mining Act Case)* (1999) 196 CLR 392, [39]–[40] (Gleeson CJ and Gaudron J).

40 (2013) 86 NSWLR 348.

41 Ibid 356 [29] (Basten JA). Leeming JA and Sackville AJA agreed at 359 [44]–[45].

42 *Interpretation Act 1987* (NSW) s 13(b).

43 *Interpretation of Legislation Act 1984* (Vic) s 38.

44 *Legislation Interpretation Act 2021* (SA) s 4.

45 *Superannuation Fund Investment Trust v Commissioner of Stamps (SA)* (1979) 145 CLR 330, 355 (Mason J), 357 (Murphy J).

What is meant by the term 'the Crown' in this context?

The Crown includes the executive branch of government and government bodies together with their employees and agents [40.5]

While the presumption applies to statutes that impact the Sovereign[46] or the Sovereign's direct representatives in Australia[47] or a prerogative right or privilege of the Crown,[48] its coverage is much greater than that. It applies to the executive branch of government[49] and any other body satisfying the tests for being regarded as part of the Crown for this purpose together with their employees and agents. With the growth in government activities, this is a large group.[50]

Entities that are part of the Crown are sometimes described as being within 'the shield of the Crown' or as 'representing the Crown'. Various tests are applied by courts to determine whether an entity is part of the Crown for the purposes of the presumption.

In *Australian Competition and Consumer Commission v Australian Egg Corporation Ltd*[51] the Federal Court stated:

> The determination of whether an entity is part of the Crown as executive is made by reference to the legislation by which the body is established or governed and, in particular, the legislative intention, the activities which it undertakes and the nature and extent of the governmental or ministerial control over the body.[52]

The nature and degree of control of the entity by the government is an important element to be considered in determining whether it is part of the Crown.[53] In the *Australian Egg Corporation* case the Australian Egg Corporation was held not to be an agency of the Crown because of the level of its independence from the government. It was incorporated under the *Corporations Act 2001* (Cth) and so not a statutory corporation, the ability of government to exercise direct control over its activities was limited, none of its directors were appointed by government and government had no control over the appointment of its directors. These factors outweighed the fact that under statutory funding agreements between the corporation and the government there was provision for monitoring and review by the government of its activities to ensure accountability of government funds that it received.

---

46 See, eg, *Succession to the Crown Act 2015* (Cth).

47 See, eg, *Constitution Act 1975* (Vic) pt 1.

48 See, eg, *Copyright Act 1968* (Cth) ss 8A, 182A.

49 In *Roberts v Ahern* (1904) 1 CLR 406 the High Court held that '[t]he modern sense of the rule, at any rate, is that the Executive Government of the State is not bound by Statute unless that intention is apparent': at 418.

50 See n 16 above.

51 (2016) 337 ALR 573.

52 Ibid 593 [97] (White J). An appeal against the decision of White J was dismissed by the Full Court of the Federal Court in *Australian Competition and Consumer Commission v Australian Egg Corporation Ltd* (2017) 254 FCR 311 but the issue of whether the Australian Egg Corporation Ltd was part of the Crown was not a subject of that appeal.

53 In *NT Power Generation Pty Ltd v Power & Water Authority* (2002) 122 FCR 399 Finkelstein J stated: 'If the Crown is able to control the activities of the corporation (whether directly, by instruction or direction, or indirectly, pursuant to a power to remove those in control of its operation otherwise than for misconduct or incapacity) the corporation will usually be the alter ego of the Crown' (at 431 [126]).

Courts do not readily conclude that an entity is part of the Crown. In *Townsville Hospitals Board v Townsville City Council* [54] Gibbs CJ stated:

> All persons should prima facie be regarded as equal before the law, and no statutory body should be accorded special privileges and immunities unless it clearly appears that it was the intention of the legislature to confer them. It is not difficult for the legislature to provide in express terms that a corporation shall have the privileges and immunities of the Crown, and where it does not do so it should not readily be concluded that it had that intention.[55]

Legislation occasionally provides that a specified body does, or does not, represent the Crown.[56] It had been assumed that such a provision confers on the body the status, immunities and privileges of the Crown.[57] The decision of the High Court in *McNamara v Consumer Trader and Tenancy Tribunal*[58] undermined that assumption.

In *McNamara* the High Court had to consider whether the *Landlord and Tenant (Amendment) Act 1948* (NSW) ('the LTA Act') applied to the Roads and Traffic Authority of New South Wales ('the RTA'). Section 5(a) of the LTA Act provided that the Act did not bind the Crown in right of the State. Section 46(2)(b) of the *Transport Administration Act 1988* (NSW) provided that the RTA 'is, for the purposes of any Act, a statutory body representing the Crown'.

McHugh, Gummow and Heydon JJ, in their joint judgment,[59] said there was no automatic congruence between the phrase 'representing the Crown' and an entitlement to the privileges and immunities of the Crown. That phrase simply had the effect that it brought a body to which it applied within the scope of any statutory provision dealing with bodies so described. In their opinion the RTA could only rely on the Crown's immunity under the LTA if the application of that Act to the RTA would impair the State's legal situation. As no impairment would result to the Crown in right of the State, the RTA was bound by the LTA.

Within less than a year after judgment in that case, both New South Wales and Victoria passed legislation to effectively overturn it by providing that a statement in an Act that an entity represents the Crown means that the entity has the status, privileges and immunities of the Crown.[60]

---

54 (1982) 149 CLR 282.

55 Ibid 291. Murphy, Wilson and Brennan JJ agreeing, 292.

56 See, eg, *Building and Construction Industry Training Fund and Levy Collection Act 1990* (WA) s 6(3); *Darwin Waterfront Corporation Act 2006* (NT) s 7. The latter Act also stated that the relevant body does not enjoy any privileges, rights or immunities of the Crown and is not within the shield of the Crown.

57 See Explanatory Note to the Interpretation Amendment Bill 2006 (NSW). In *Wynyard Investments Pty Ltd v Commissioner for Railways (NSW)* (1955) 93 CLR 376 the High Court, by majority (Williams, Webb and Taylor JJ), held that the Commissioner for Railways was the Crown in right of the State of New South Wales. The majority based this conclusion on s 4(2) of the *Transport (Division of Functions) Act 1932* (NSW), which provided that 'for the purposes of any Act' the Commissioner 'shall be deemed to be a statutory body representing the Crown'. The majority interpreted the word 'represent' as meaning that the Commissioner must act as the agent or servant of the Crown.

58 (2005) 221 CLR 646.

59 Ibid 662 (Gleeson CJ agreeing at 650 [1], Hayne J agreeing at 668 [61]).

60 See now *Interpretation Amendment Act 2006* (NSW) s 13A; *Interpretation of Legislation Act 1984* (Vic) s 46A.

The term 'the Crown' in the presumption lacks clarity [40.6]

Given the scope of the presumption, it is legitimate to ask whether a more directly informative term than 'the Crown', such as 'government', might be used in its formulation. The majority did just that in *Bass v Permanent Trustee Co Ltd*[61] where they stated:

> Where the legislative provisions in question are concerned with the regulation of the conduct of persons or individuals, it will often be more appropriate to ask whether it was intended that they should regulate the conduct of the members, servants and agents of the executive government of the polity concerned, rather than whether they bind the Crown in one or other of its capacities. In other legislative contexts, slightly different questions may emerge. Thus, for example, where legislation regulates the use of land or other property, it will usually be more pertinent to ask whether the legislation was intended to apply to land or property owned by or on behalf of the polity in question.[62]

In referencing the Crown, the presumption is referencing a concept rooted in constitutional theory derived from the United Kingdom. In the joint judgment of Gleeson CJ, Gummow and Hayne JJ in *Sue v Hill*[63] five senses in which the expression 'the Crown' is used are identified including the Sovereign, the body politic and the executive branch of government.[64] In relation to the usage of the term 'the Crown' to refer to the body politic, the joint judgment notes:[65] 'Writing in 1903, Professor Pitt Cobbett[66] identified this [usage] as involving a "defective conception" which was "the outcome of an attempt on the part of English law to dispense with the recognition of the State as a juristic person, and to make the Crown do service in its stead".' The joint judgment[67] also references Harrison Moore's statement in 1904[68] that it was likely that Australian drafters would avoid using the term 'Crown' and use 'Commonwealth' and 'State' instead but added that this optimism has proved misplaced.

It would have made perfect sense for Australian drafters to have chosen that course, and for Australian courts to have reformulated the presumption in terms more revealing of its meaning, given Australia's status as a federation and how the polities constituting the federation are recognised in the *Constitution*.[69]

---

61 (1999) 198 CLR 334.

62 Ibid 346 [18] (Gleeson CJ, Gaudron, McHugh, Gummow, Hayne and Callinan JJ). Gleeson CJ and Gaudron J had adopted the same approach a few months earlier in *Commonwealth v Western Australia (Mining Act Case)* (1999) 196 CLR 392, in stating: 'It would be preferable, in our view, and more consonant with our constitutional arrangements, if the presumption that a statute "does not bind the Crown" were expressed as a presumption that a statute which regulates the conduct or rights of individuals does not apply to members of the executive government of any of the polities in the federation, government instrumentalities and authorities intended to have the same legal status as the executive government, their servants or agents': at 410.

63 (1999) 199 CLR 462.

64 Ibid 497–503 [83]–[94].

65 Ibid 498–9 [84].

66 P Cobbett, '"The Crown" as Representing "the State"' (1903) 1(1) *Commonwealth Law Review* 23, 30.

67 *Sue v Hill* (1999) 199 CLR 462, 502 [92].

68 Harrison Moore, 'The Crown as Corporation' (1904) 20(4) *Law Quarterly Review* 351, 362.

69 In *Bank of New South Wales v Commonwealth* (1948) 76 CLR 1 Dixon J noted that while the Commonwealth and the States may not formally be juristic persons, the Constitution treats them 'as organizations or institutions of government possessing distinct individualities': at 363.

In *Australian Competition and Consumer Commission v Baxter Healthcare Pty Ltd*[70] Kirby J argued that to treat the Commonwealth, states and territories as manifestations of the Crown was incompatible with the text, structure and character of the Constitution. These were new constitutional entities constituting a new nation and deriving their existence from the Constitution.

The majority in *Bass v Permanent Trustee Co Ltd*[71] observed that 'the nature of our federal structure [makes] expressions such as "shield of the Crown", "binding the Crown" and, more particularly, "binding the Crown in right of the Commonwealth" and "binding the Crown in right of the States" inappropriate and potentially misleading when the issue is whether the legislation of one polity in the federation applies to another'.

Act may be binding on the Crown only partially or only in certain respects

[40.7] **The application of an Act to the Crown need not be uniform throughout the Act**

Even in the face of an express statement in an Act that it binds the Crown, it is still necessary to consider whether, on examining the Act as a whole, the Crown is subject to all obligations to which the Act gives rise.[72] The Crown may be bound by some provisions but not others[73] or a provision may bind the Crown only in certain respects such as not in relation to the Sovereign themself or not in relation to employees of a governmental agency as distinct from the agency itself[74] or not in relation to any criminal liability.[75]

In *Victorian Railway Commissioners v Herbert*[76] the Full Court of the Victorian Supreme Court stated:

> The fact is, we think, that where statutory bodies are set up to conduct Governmental undertakings, it may be that they should be treated as representing the Crown or as agents of the Crown for one purpose and not for another. Such a body may be held liable in tort and denied the Crown's immunity in this respect, but may on the other hand be allowed to claim the Crown's priority for debts owing to it.[77]

70 (2007) 232 CLR 1, 45–55.

71 (1999) 198 CLR 334, 347 (Gleeson CJ, Gaudron, McHugh, Gummow, Hayne and Callinan JJ).

72 *Telstra Corporation Ltd v Worthing* (1999) 197 CLR 61.

73 In *Federal Commissioner of Taxation v Tomaras* (2018) 265 CLR 434 Edelman J stated: 'It is also possible for the general presumption to apply so that part of a statute binds the Crown while another part does not' (at 473 [118]).

74 *Bropho v Western Australia* (1990) 171 CLR 1, 23–4 (Mason CJ, Deane, Dawson, Toohey, Gaudron and McHugh JJ).

75 *State Authorities Superannuation Board v Commissioner of State Taxation (WA)* (1996) 189 CLR 253, 269–70 (Brennan CJ, Dawson, Toohey and Gaudron JJ). In concluding that the *Stamp Act 1921* (WA) bound the Crown except to the extent that it created a criminal offence, the Court held that this differential application was brought about not by the *Bropho* presumption but by 'a different presumption based upon the inherent unlikelihood that the legislature should seek to render the Crown liable to a criminal penalty': at 270. See *Cain v Doyle* (1946) 72 CLR 409 where Dixon J stated that there was 'the strongest presumption against attaching to a statutory provision a meaning which would amount to an attempt to impose upon the Crown a liability of a criminal nature': at 424.

76 [1949] VLR 211.

77 Ibid 213.

Example 40.1 *Commonwealth v Anti-Discrimination Tribunal (Tas)*[78]

Mr Nichols complained to the Tasmanian Anti-Discrimination Commissioner that Centrelink had discriminated against him on the grounds of his disability in providing 'facilities, goods and services'. There was a long queue in the Centrelink office. His request to be allowed to wait without standing in line, as he was in constant pain due to prostate cancer, was denied. His complaint was referred to the Anti-Discrimination Tribunal under the *Anti-Discrimination Act 1998* (Tas) ('the *Anti-Discrimination Act*'). Section 16 of the *Anti-Discrimination Act* provides that a person must not discriminate against another person on certain specified grounds including disability.

Section 4 of the *Anti-Discrimination Act* provided that the Act 'binds the Crown in the right of Tasmania and, so far as the legislative power of Parliament permits, in all its other capacities'. The Commonwealth sought a declaration that neither it nor Centrelink was a 'person' to whom the Act applied. The Federal Court made the declaration sought by the Commonwealth.[79]

Section 3 of the *Anti-Discrimination Act* defined 'person' as including 'an organisation'. The latter term was in turn defined as including 'a council', 'a Government Department' and 'a State authority'. Section 41(1) of the *Acts Interpretation Act 1931* (Tas) provided that in an Act the expression 'person' includes a body of persons (corporate or unincorporated) other than the Crown.

The Commonwealth had argued that s 4 of the *Anti-Discrimination Act* was intended to do no more than override the presumption in favour of Crown immunity that had been given statutory force in Tasmania by s 6(6) of the *Acts Interpretation Act 1931* (Tas). It did not establish as a matter of construction that the *Anti-Discrimination Act* was intended to bind the Commonwealth. The Act had to be read as a whole and interpreted in accordance with ordinary principles of construction.

Kenny J pointed out that the judgment of the majority in *Bropho*[80] 'demonstrates that, in determining whether or not the Tasmanian Parliament intended that the obligation to which s 16 gives rise applies to the Crown in right of the Commonwealth, it is necessary to consider the *Anti-Discrimination Act* in its entirety, including its subject matter and purpose'.[81] Upon doing so, Kenny J concluded that the word 'person' in s 16 did not embrace the Commonwealth. The considerations that led her to that conclusion included:[82]

- the absence of any reference to Commonwealth departments or authorities in the definition of 'organisation';
- the fact that there were references in that definition to state authorities and state departments – this indicated that Parliament was not relying on s 4 to extend the meaning of 'person' to the Crown in any capacity;
- the fact that s 16 only prohibited discrimination in activities connected with specified matters. One such matter was discrimination in administering state laws and programs on certain specified grounds not including disability. This indicated 'that, in the field of governmental administration of laws and programs, the Tasmanian Parliament was

78 (2008) 169 FCR 85.

79 Ibid 117–19 [151]–[160] (Weinberg J), 150 [263] (Kenny J), 98 [49] (Goldberg J dissenting).

80 (1990) 171 CLR 1, 21–2.

81 *Commonwealth v Anti-Discrimination Tribunal (Tas)* (2008) 169 FCR 85, 124 [178].

82 Ibid 117–19 [151]–[160]. Weinberg J also held that the *Anti-Discrimination Act* did not, on its proper construction, bind the Crown in right of the Commonwealth largely for the same reasons: at 113–18 [145]–[156].

concerned only with discrimination on the part of Tasmania and, even here, only with respect to a small subset of the grounds for which s 16 provides'.[83] This showed that '[t]he Tasmanian Parliament recognised that the administration of State laws and programs should not be subject to the same regime as applied to other regulated activities. Since it said nothing of other bodies politic, such as the Commonwealth, it can be inferred that it did not intend them to be "persons" for the purposes of s 16 of the *Anti-Discrimination Act* and related provisions';[84] and

- the fact that s 3 defined 'services' to include services provided by a state authority or a council but did not include any reference to a Commonwealth authority; and
- the fact that the orders that the Tribunal could make on finding a complaint substantiated included imposing a penalty provision and ordering re-employment.

Presumption may be modified or reversed by legislation

[40.8] **The presumption is a common law 'rule' of statutory construction and as such may be modified or reversed by legislation**

In *Bropho* the majority rejected the view that the presumption reflects a prerogative power of the Crown to override words in a statute capable of applying to it.[85] They stated that this view 'certainly has no place in the law of this country where it has been consistently accepted that the rule that legislative provisions worded in general terms are prima facie inapplicable to the Crown is a rule of statutory construction which identifies a presumption to be applied in ascertaining the relevant legislative intent'.[86]

As a mere common law 'rule' of statutory construction, the presumption may be 'supplemented, modified or reversed by legislative provision'.[87] Supplementation[88] or modification has happened in Queensland and South Australia while reversal has happened in Tasmania and the Australian Capital Territory.

Section 13 of the *Acts Interpretation Act 1954* (Qld) provides: 'No Act passed after the commencement of this Act shall be binding on the Crown or derogate from any prerogative right of the Crown unless express words are included in the Act for that purpose.' Section 6(6) of the *Acts Interpretation Act 1931* (Tas) is to the same effect.

The Queensland and Tasmanian provisions were enacted before *Bropho*. The general rule of construction at the time of their enactment was that the Crown was not bound by a statute

83 Ibid 126 [184].

84 Ibid 127 [186].

85 *Bropho v Western Australia* (1990) 171 CLR 1, 15–16 (Mason CJ, Deane, Dawson, Toohey, Gaudron and McHugh JJ). This view had been put forward by Lord Keith in *Madras Electric Supply Corporation Ltd v Boarland* [1955] AC 667, 694.

86 *Bropho v Western Australia* (1990) 171 CLR 1, 15. *R v Sutton* (1908) 5 CLR 789, 795 (Griffth CJ), 800 (Barton J), 805–6 (O'Connor J) and *Minister for Works (WA) v Gulson* (1944) 69 CLR 338, 347 (Latham CJ), 359 (McTiernan J) are cited in support of that proposition. See also *Federal Commissioner of Taxation v Tomaras* (2018) 265 CLR 434, 451–2 [52] (Gordon J).

87 *Bropho v Western Australia* (1990) 171 CLR 1, 15 (Mason CJ, Deane, Dawson, Toohey, Gaudron and McHugh JJ).

88 In *Commonwealth v Anti-Discrimination Tribunal (Tasmania)* (2008) 169 FCR 85 Kenny J referred to s 6(6) of the *Acts Interpretation Act 1931* (Tas) as supplementing the pre-*Bropho* understanding of the general law: at 123 [177].

unless it was expressly so provided or it appeared by necessary implication that the statute was intended to bind the Crown.[89] In referring to the necessity for express words, it seems likely that the intention was to exclude 'necessary implication' as a basis for displacing the presumption against the Crown being bound.[90] Indeed, in *Bradken Consolidated Ltd v Broken Hill Pty Co Ltd*[91] Stephen J described the Queensland provision as an instance of a version of the common law that was 'even more favourable to the Crown than the rule itself'.[92]

However, in *Kaye v Attorney-General (Tas)*[93] Williams J, referring to the Tasmanian provision, observed that the 'words of an Act could, no doubt, be sufficiently express to derogate from such a right although they did not in terms refer to the prerogative if their operation necessarily or naturally had that effect'.[94] He further stated that the legal significance of the general principle applicable at the time and the Tasmanian provision 'would not appear to differ'.[95]

The effect of these provisions, as they have generally been interpreted by the courts, is to freeze the pre-*Bropho* common law statement of the presumption.[96]

In South Australia s 22 of the *Legislation Interpretation Act 2021* (SA) reverses the presumption with respect to Acts passed after 20 June 1990,[97] not only in relation to the Crown in right of South Australia but also 'so far as the legislative power of the State permits' the Crown in any other capacity. It provides that Acts passed after that date 'will, unless the contrary intention appears (either expressly or by implication), be taken to bind the Crown, but not so as to impose any criminal liability on the Crown'. Any immunity that the Crown has extends 'to an agent of the

89 See n 8.

90 In *Re Commissioner of Water Resources and Leighton Contractors Pty Ltd* [1991] 1 Qd R 549 the Queensland Supreme Court (Byrne J) recognised that the choice of language in the Queensland provision 'may perhaps have been endeavouring to exclude the doctrine that the Crown could be bound by statute if it so appeared by necessary implication': at 551.

91 (1979) 145 CLR 107.

92 Ibid 127. In *Northbuild Construction Pty Ltd v Lockton* [2000] 2 Qd R 600 Thomas JA referred to Stephen J's observation and treated the Queensland provision as requiring express words for the Crown to be bound: at [9]–[10], [28]. In *Commonwealth v Anti-Discrimination Tribunal (Tasmania)* (2008) 169 FCR 85 Goldberg J seemed to accept that express words were required for the purposes of the Tasmanian provision: at 94 [23].

93 (1956) 94 CLR 193.

94 Ibid 204. In *Brisbane City Council v Group Projects Pty Ltd* (1979) 145 CLR 143 Wilson J referred to that observation of Williams J in *Kaye* and expressed the view that the identical Queensland provision restated the then common law that a statute does not bind the Crown unless an intention that the Crown be bound appears either expressly or by necessary implication from the words of the statute: at 167, Gibbs J agreeing at 152 and Mason J agreeing at 164. See also *BMG Resources Ltd v Municipality of Beaconsfield* [1988] Tas R 142, where Green CJ treated the Tasmanian provision as having the effect that a provision restricting the development of land by a person did not apply to Crown land as an intention to bind the Crown 'does not appear either expressly or by necessary implication from the words of the statute' (at 145) and *Re Commissioner of Water Resources and Leighton Contractors Pty Ltd* [1991] 1 Qd R 549 where the Queensland Supreme Court (Byrne J) held that the Queensland provision 'does not mean that the Crown cannot be bound where it appears to be a necessary implication that the Crown is to be bound': at 551.

95 *Kaye v A-G (Tas)* (1956) 94 CLR 193, 205.

96 In *Commonwealth v Anti-Discrimination Tribunal (Tasmania)* (2008) 169 FCR 85, Weinberg J referred to the conclusion in DC Pearce and RS Geddes, *Statutory Interpretation in Australia* (6th ed, 2006), that the Tasmanian provision is 'on the same footing as the common law presumption as originally formulated before its displacement in *Bropho*': at 112–3 [139].

97 This was the judgment date in *Bropho*.

Crown[98] in respect of an act within the scope of the agent's obligations', unless the contrary intention is expressed.[99]

In the Australian Capital Territory s 121(1) of the *Legislation Act 2001* (ACT) provides that an Act 'binds everyone, including people who are not Australian citizens and all governments'.[100] Section 121(4) of that Act provides that to 'the extent that an Act does not bind a government, the same degree of immunity extends to a government entity in relation to an authorised act or omission of the entity'.

The enactment of statutory provisions covering the subject matter of the presumption (whether affirming a version of it or reversing it) does not obviate the need for statutory construction of a later Act to determine the application of that Act to the Crown. In *Bropho* the majority stated:

> [E]ven if such a rule of statutory construction had been laid down in completely unqualified and mandatory terms by legislative provision, it would necessarily give way to the provisions of a subsequent enactment which, notwithstanding the earlier provision, disclosed a contrary legislative intent since the subsequent enactment would represent a pro tanto repeal or amendment of the earlier provision.[101]

Immunity does not extend to a party dealing with the Crown

[40.9] **A person contracting with an exempt Crown entity does not enjoy any derivative Crown immunity**

The issue has arisen under the *Trade Practices Act 1974* (Cth) ('the TPA') as to whether, if a government is not bound by a provision of an Act relating to a matter, that immunity extends to a party dealing with that government in relation to that matter. Section 46 of the TPA dealt with misuse of market power and s 47 provided that a corporation must not, in trade or commerce, engage in the practice of exclusive dealing.

In *Bradken Consolidated Ltd v Broken Hill Pty Co Ltd*,[102] decided before *Bropho*, the High Court held that the whole of the TPA did not bind the Crown in right of a state as an intention to do so did not appear by express words or necessary implication.[103] The majority judges went further by recognising a form of derivative immunity in parties contracting with the Crown in right of a state so as not to prejudicially affect the Crown by the invalidation of those contracts even though the TPA applied to those parties.[104] This was regarded as a corollary of the principle about Crown immunity.

98 This term is defined as extending to 'an instrumentality, officer or employee of the Crown or a contractor or other person who carries out functions on behalf of the Crown'.

99 The pre-*Bropho* general rule of construction is preserved by s 22(3) of the *Legislation Interpretation Act 2021* (SA) for Acts passed on or before 20 June 1990. It provides that such an Act will only be taken to bind the Crown if it 'expressly, or by necessary implication, binds the Crown'.

100 The section makes an exception for certain money provisions and provisions imposing criminal liability. Also, under the *Australian Capital Territory (Self-Government) Act 1988* (Cth) s 27 an ACT enactment does not bind the Crown in right of the Commonwealth except as provided by regulations made under that Act.

101 *Bropho v Western Australia* (1990) 171 CLR 1, 22.

102 (1979) 145 CLR 107.

103 At the time of *Bradken*, the TPA contained s 2A, which stated that the Act bound the Crown in right of the Commonwealth in so far as it was carrying on a business. No express reference was made to the Crown in right of a state or territory.

104 (1979) 145 CLR 107, 123 (Gibbs ACJ), 129 (Stephen J), 138 (Mason and Jacobs JJ)

After *Bradken* a new s 2B was added to the TPA that provided that certain provisions of the Act (including ss 46 and 47) bound the Crown in right of a state or territory when carrying on a business. The soundness of the corollary proposition came before the High Court in *Australian Competition and Consumer Commission v Baxter Healthcare Pty Ltd* (**Example 40.2**) where six of the seven judges rejected it and, in so doing, disapproved of *Bradken.*

It is now clearly established that a person dealing with the Crown, or a Crown instrumentality or agent, is not relieved from complying with a statutory provision that relates to the dealing just because the Crown, or Crown instrumentality or agent, is not bound by that provision with respect to that dealing.

Example 40.2 *Australian Competition and Consumer Commission v Baxter Healthcare Pty Ltd*[105]

This case concerned dealings that a manufacturer and wholesaler of medical fluids and equipment, Baxter, had with various state and territory governments. South Australia wished to be supplied with only certain sterile fluids and sought a volume discount on those fluids. Baxter offered to provide that discount if South Australia entered into a further exclusive arrangement for the supply of other fluids and equipment. South Australia rejected that offer. Meanwhile, Baxter negotiated contracts with certain other states and the Australian Capital Territory for the supply of medical fluids and equipment on a sole and exclusive, or near exclusive, basis. The Australian Competition and Consumer Commission brought proceedings against Baxter in the Federal Court alleging a contravention of ss 46 and 47 of the *Trade Practices Act 1974* (Cth) ('the TPA').

In the Federal Court reliance was placed upon the *Bradken* doctrine of 'derived immunity' to hold that ss 46 and 47 did not apply to Baxter's conduct as that conduct related to dealings with state and territory governments who, in those dealings, were not carrying on a business and, accordingly, were not bound by those sections. On appeal to the High Court, the majority rejected the 'derived immunity' argument and held that Baxter, in its dealings with those governments, was bound by ss 46 and 47 of the TPA. They expressed the view that the proposition that the TPA did not bind governments 'does not require, as a corollary, that it does not bind corporations dealing with [governments]'.[106]

In their joint judgment Gleeson CJ and Gummow, Hayne and Crennan JJ stated:

> The first respondent was a trading corporation. A conclusion that, in carrying on dealings with a government in the course of its own business, it enjoyed a general immunity not available to the government when the government was carrying on business itself would be remarkable ...
>
> It is one thing to read the Act so as not to divest the Crown of legal right. It is another thing altogether to read the Act as giving an executive government ... including all its servants and agents, a freedom not enjoyed when the government itself is carrying on business, from any impact of laws enacted for the promotion of competition and fair trading in the public interest. And it is even more unlikely that that freedom extends to all persons dealing with that executive government.[107]

105 (2007) 232 CLR 1.

106 Ibid 40 [76].

107 Ibid 36–7 [64]–[68].

41 PRESUMPTION AGAINST EXTRATERRITORIAL OPERATION

Overview

[41.1] A statute has extraterritorial operation if it operates on, or purports to regulate, occurrences or conduct that occur either wholly outside the territory of the enacting legislature (whether federal or state), or partly within and partly outside the territory.

Parliament may make unambiguously clear that a statute or certain of its provisions is to have an extraterritorial operation. But if Parliament does not specify the territorial reach of a particular statute, a presumption against extraterritorial operation arises at common law. Most Interpretation Acts contain a provision to similar effect.

The presumption deals with the problem that statutory language, on its face, applies to the whole world. The rationale for the presumption depends on whether the relevant law is federal or state. The social context of the presumption and attitudes towards it have changed, however, and as a result the presumption is now more readily rebutted.

In applying the presumption it is erroneous to conflate, on the one hand, the legislative *capacity* of a Parliament to make a law with, on the other hand, ascertaining whether Parliament *intended* the law in question to be subject to a territorial limitation as to its application. At common law the presumption has greater weight in respect of offences, but statutes of general operation in most Australian jurisdictions define the territorial nexus in a way that allows some extraterritorial operation.

If the presumption is raised it may be rebutted by sufficient evidence of a contrary legislative intention.

What is extraterritorial operation?

[41.2] **Extraterritorial operation refers to the operation of a statute outside the territory of the enacting legislature**

A statute has extraterritorial operation if it operates on, or purports to regulate, occurrences or conduct that occur either wholly outside the territory of the enacting legislature (whether federal or state), or partly within and partly outside the territory.[1]

An example of a statute regulating conduct that may occur wholly outside the territory of the enacting legislature was the subject of *XYZ v Commonwealth*.[2] Section 50BA(1) of the *Crimes Act 1914* (Cth) stated:

1 *DRJ v Commissioner of Victims Rights (No 2)* (2020) 103 NSWLR 692, 701 [23], [25] (Bell P).

2 (2006) 227 CLR 532.

> A person must not, while outside Australia, engage in sexual intercourse with a person who is under 16.
> Penalty: Imprisonment for 17 years.

In the case the plaintiff, an Australian citizen, had been committed for trial in Victoria for an offence against this law. The offence was said to have occurred in Thailand. The alleged victim was neither a citizen or a resident of Australia. Gleeson CJ observed that the legislation clearly had, or purported to have, extraterritorial effect.[3]

A statute that operated partly within and partly outside the territory of the enacting legislature was the subject of *Director of Public Prosecutions v Sutcliffe*.[4] The respondent had been charged with stalking a person, contrary to s 21A of the *Crimes Act 1958* (Vic) ('the Act'):

> **Stalking**.
>
> (1) A person must not stalk another person.
> Penalty: Level 5 imprisonment (10 years maximum).

The alleged actions of the respondent (a resident of Victoria) all took place in the State of Victoria. The effect of the stalking was allegedly experienced outside the territory (in Canada) via various means including email. The Court held that the legislature intended the Act to have extraterritorial operation where all the elements of the offence except proof of the harmful effect occurred within the territory of the enacting legislature.[5]

The reverse operation occurred in *Brownlie v State Pollution Control Commission*.[6] Section 16 of the *Clean Waters Act 1970* (NSW) prohibited pollution of 'any waters'. The charge related to pollution of the Barwon River on the NSW side of the river, the boundary between New South Wales and Queensland lying in the middle of the river. The conduct alleged to have caused the pollution occurred extraterritorially in Queensland. The Court held that the NSW Act applied to the conduct.[7]

A statute does not have extraterritorial operation merely because, within the territory of the enacting legislature, it may catch a person who is a resident of another state.[8]

To determine whether a statute has an extraterritorial operation it is sometimes necessary to know precisely where the boundary lies between the territories concerned.[9] Some cases have established some of the boundary lines.[10]

As indicated above, in a federation such as Australia, for a statute's operation to be 'extraterritorial' it need not occur outside the Commonwealth of Australia. In the case of state or territory

---

3 Ibid 535–6 [4]. By majority the legislation was also held to be constitutionally valid.

4 [2001] VSC 43.

5 Ibid [102]–[103] (Gillard J).

6 (1992) 27 NSWLR 78.

7 Ibid 87–8 (Gleeson CJ, Carruthers J agreeing at 90, Lee AJ agreeing at 90).

8 *Chubb Insurance Co of Australia Ltd v Moore* (2013) 302 ALR 101, 132 [146] (Emmett JA and Ball J, Bathurst CJ agreeing at 103 [1], Beazley P agreeing at 104 [2], Macfarlan JA agreeing at 104 [3]).

9 Mark Moshinsky, 'State Extraterritorial Legislation and the Australia Acts 1986' (1987) 61(12) *Australian Law Journal* 779, 780.

10 See, eg, *Ward v The Queen* (1980) 142 CLR 308 (boundary between New South Wales and Victoria); *New South Wales v Commonwealth (Seas and Submerged Land Act Case)* (1975) 135 CLR 337 (boundary between Australian states and the Commonwealth).

legislation, extraterritorial operation may occur in another state or territory[11] or in the federal sphere.[12]

A law may have an extraterritorial operation in respect of a tangible or intangible thing. An example of a tangible thing is a place of abode.[13] Examples of an intangible property or thing, which lacks any natural geographical sense, are an obligation to pay interest and a contract for the supply of recreational services.[14]

The presumption and when, how and why it arises

[41.3] Parliament may make unambiguously clear that a statute or certain of its provisions may have an extraterritorial operation

In a number of instances Parliament has indicated, in an unambiguous fashion, that the Act may have extraterritorial operation.[15] For example, s 5(1) of the *Competition and Consumer Act 2010* (Cth) provides:

> **5 Extended application of this Act to conduct outside Australia**
>
> (1) Each of the following provisions ... extends to the engaging in conduct outside Australia by:
>
> ...
>
> (g) bodies corporate incorporated or carrying on business within Australia; or
>
> (h) Australian citizens; or
>
> (i) persons ordinarily resident in Australia ...

In such a case, by definition no interpretative issue arises as to whether extraterritorial operation was intended.

On a broader scale, parliaments in most Australian jurisdictions have passed general laws that effectively give statutory offences an extraterritorial operation unless a contrary intention is indicated.[16]

---

11 See, eg, *Brownlie v State Pollution Control Commission* (1992) 27 NSWLR 78; *Vickers v Queensland Building and Construction Commission* [2019] QCA 66; *Law Society of New South Wales v Glenorcy Pty Ltd* (2006) 67 NSWLR 169; *O'Connor v Healey* (1967) 69 SR (NSW) 111.

12 *D151 v New South Wales Crime Commission* (2017) 94 NSWLR 738. The case dealt with the meaning of 'offence' in s 35A of the *Crime Commission Act 2012* (NSW). The provision placed restrictions on the New South Wales Crime Commission taking evidence from a person the subject of a current charge for an offence. The question was whether the word in question extended to an offence under federal law.

13 *O'Connor v Healey* (1967) 69 SR (NSW) 111.

14 *DRJ v Commissioner of Victims Rights (No 2)* (2020) 103 NSWLR 692, 718 [100], 719 [104] (Leeming JA, Bell P agreeing at 695 [1], Meagher JA agreeing at 706 [42]). The reference to obligation to pay interest is a reference to *Wanganui-Rangitikei Electric Power Board* (1934) 50 CLR 581. The reference to contract is a reference to *Insight Vacations Pty Ltd v Young* (2011) 243 CLR 149.

15 For further examples, see *DRJ v Commissioner of Victims Rights (No 2)* (2020) 103 NSWLR 692, 702–4 [29]–[31] (Bell P); *XYZ v Commonwealth* (2006) 227 CLR 532, 535 [2], [4] (Gleeson CJ); *DPP (WA) v Hafner* (2004) 28 WAR 486, 493 [43] (Pullin J); *Lipohar v The Queen* (1999) 200 CLR 485, 523 [96] (Gaudron, Gummow and Hayne JJ).

16 See **[41.10]**.

If Parliament does not specify the territorial reach of a particular statute, a presumption against extraterritorial operation arises at common law [41.4]

Longstanding common law authority is *Jumbunna Coal Mine NL v Victorian Coal Miners' Association*,[17] where O'Connor J stated:

> In the interpretation of general words in a statute there is always a presumption that the legislature does not intend to exceed its jurisdiction. Most statutes, if their general words were taken literally in their widest sense, would apply to the whole world, but they are always read as being prima facie restricted in their operation within territorial limits.[18]

In *Meyer Heine Pty Ltd v China Navigation Co Ltd*[19] several members of the High Court propounded a similar proposition.[20] One of its members, Taylor J, said:

> The words of the section are general but, prima facie, 'the persons, property, and events in respect of which Parliament has legislated are presumed to be limited to those in the territory over which it has jurisdiction'.[21]

More recently, Gleeson CJ has stated:

> Legislation, including criminal legislation, is commonly expressed without territorial reference, and is construed and applied on the understanding 'that the legislature of a country is not intending to deal with persons or matters over which, according to the comity of nations, the jurisdiction properly belongs to some other sovereign or State'.[22]

And in *Insight Vacations Pty Ltd v Young*[23] the High Court pointed out that, independently of any comparable Interpretation Act provision that applies (see **[41.5]**), the common law presumption against extraterritorial operation can arise.[24] Other appellate court authorities can also be found in support of the common law presumption.[25]

17 (1908) 6 CLR 309.

18 Ibid 363.

19 (1966) 115 CLR 10.

20 Ibid 23 (Kitto J), 30–1 (Taylor J), 38 (Menzies J) (referring to penal laws), 43 (Windeyer J).

21 Ibid 30–1, quoting *Morgan v White* (1912) 15 CLR 1, 13 (Isaacs J).

22 *XYZ v Commonwealth* (2006) 227 CLR 532, 537–8 [7], quoting *Niboyet v Niboyet* (1878) 4 PD 1, 7 and citing Dixon J in *Barcelo v Electrolytic Zinc Co of Australasia Ltd* (1932) 48 CLR 391, 424.

23 (2011) 243 CLR 149.

24 Ibid 159 [28] (the Court).

25 *Melville v Chief Executive Officer, Department of Health and Families* (2011) 30 NTLR 98, 108 [37] (the Court); *Bray v F Hoffman-La Roche Ltd* (2003) 130 FCR 317, 352 [162] (Branson J, Carr J agreeing at 328 [29]); *Chubb Insurance Co of Australia Ltd v Moore* (2013) 302 ALR 101, 132 [145] (Emmett JA and Ball J, Bathurst CJ agreeing at 103 [1], Beazley P agreeing at 104 [2], Macfarlan JA agreeing at 104 [3]); *Waller v Freehills* (2009) 177 FCR 507, 519–20 [50] (the Court).

Example 41.1 *R v Nationwide News Pty Ltd*[26]

In the course of a committal hearing, the Magistrates' Court of Victoria prohibited publication of the true identity of a witness and publication of any information that could reveal that identity. The order was made pursuant to s 126(2) of the *Magistrates' Court Act 1989* (Vic):

> (2) The Court may in the circumstances mentioned in subsection (1) –
>
> ...
>
> (c) make an order prohibiting the publication of a report of the whole or any part of a proceeding or of any information derived from a proceeding; ...

Subsection (4) made contravention of the order an offence:

> (4) A person must not contravene an order made and posted under this section.

The defendants published newspapers. The Director of Public Prosecutions sought orders for contempt of court against the defendants on the basis of certain articles published by the defendants in New South Wales and Queensland. It was alleged that the articles contained information that was, to the defendants' knowledge, the subject of a non-publication order by the Magistrates' Court. Applying the common law presumption against extraterritorial operation, the Court held that the power under s 126(2) proscribed conduct occurring in Victoria,[27] and the Director had accordingly failed to establish a breach of the orders.[28]

[41.5] Most Interpretation Acts contain a provision to similar effect as the common law presumption

Except in South Australia and Western Australia, Australian Interpretation Acts contain a presumption similar in effect to that applying under the common law.[29] For example, the *Acts Interpretation Act 1901* (Cth) provides:

> **21 Office etc. means office etc. of the Commonwealth**
>
> (1) In any Act:
>
> (a) references to any officer or office shall be construed as references to such officer or office in and for the Commonwealth; and
>
> (b) references to localities jurisdictions and other matters and things shall be construed as references to such localities jurisdictions and other matters and things in and of the Commonwealth.

---

26 (2008) 22 VR 116.

27 Ibid 132 [71] (Mandie J).

28 Ibid 132 [75].

29 *Acts Interpretation Act 1901* (Cth) s 21; *Interpretation Act 1987* (NSW) s 12; *Acts Interpretation Act 1954* (Qld) s 35; *Acts Interpretation Act 1931* (Tas) s 27; *Interpretation of Legislation Act 1984* (Vic) s 48; *Legislation Act 2001* (ACT) s 122; *Interpretation Act 1978* (NT) s 38(1).

The Interpretation Act provisions reinforce, but do not supersede, the common law.[30] It has been observed that the absence of a statutory presumption in South Australia 'probably does not alter the way in which South Australian legislation is construed'.[31]

The statutory presumption provides a starting point for the inquiry[32] or prima facie position.[33] This means that, like other provisions of Interpretation Acts,[34] the presumption does not alone dictate the answer.[35]

The statutory presumption was applied in *Mercorella v Secretary to the Department of Justice*.[36] Section 77(6A) of the *Corrections Act 1986* (Vic) stated:

> If a prisoner is sentenced to another prison sentence while on parole, the prisoner's parole is taken to have been cancelled on the sentence being imposed.

The question was whether the words 'another prison sentence' extended to a prison sentence imposed by a court outside Victoria (on the facts, South Australia). Applying the presumption[37] and other factors, it was held that it did not.[38]

The presumption against extraterritorial operation deals with the problem that statutory language, on its face, applies to the whole world [41.6]

Legislative drafters frequently employ 'general or apparently universal language'.[39] At the same time, 'the subject matter which the statute addresses may occur or exist outside as well as within the territory in which the relevant legislature is located'.[40] If the general words were taken literally in their widest sense, the provisions 'would apply to the whole world'.[41] Therefore, a question may arise as to the extent to which the statute is intended to apply 'to property which may be situated, or conduct which occurs, either outside the territory of the enacting legislature or partly outside that territory'.[42]

30 *Brownlie v State Pollution Control Commission* (1992) 27 NSWLR 78, 83 (Gleeson CJ, Carruthers J agreeing at 90, Lee AJ agreeing at 90), speaking of the NSW provision. See also to same effect *R v Nationwide News Pty Ltd* (2008) 22 VR 116, 132 [71] (Mandie J).

31 *DRJ v Commissioner of Victims Rights (No 2)* (2020) 103 NSWLR 692, 721 [118] (Leeming JA, Bell P agreeing at 695 [1], Meagher JA agreeing at 706 [42]).

32 *D151 v New South Wales Crime Commission* (2017) 94 NSWLR 738, 744 [18] (Basten JA, Beazley ACJ agreeing at 740 [1]); *DRJ v Commissioner of Victims Rights (No 2)* (2020) 103 NSWLR 692, 698 [11] (Bell P) (speaking of the NSW provision).

33 *DRJ v Commissioner of Victims Rights (No 2)* (2020) 103 NSWLR 692, 719 [108] (Leeming JA, Bell P agreeing at 695 [1], Meagher JA agreeing at 706 [42]).

34 See **[25.3]**.

35 *D151 v New South Wales Crime Commission* (2017) 94 NSWLR 738, 744 [18] (Basten JA, Beazley ACJ agreeing at 740 [1]) (speaking of the NSW provision). Whether legislative drafters ought to do more than rely on the statutory presumption was discussed in *DRJ v Commissioner of Victims Rights (No 2)* (2020) 103 NSWLR 692, 701–6 [23]–[41] (Bell P).

36 (2015) 46 VR 646.

37 Ibid 653 [37] (Weinberg JA).

38 Ibid 655 [46].

39 *DRJ v Commissioner of Victims Rights (No 2)* (2020) 103 NSWLR 692, 696 [4] (Bell P).

40 Ibid.

41 *Jumbunna Coal Mine NL v Victorian Coal Miners' Association* (1908) 6 CLR 309, 363 (O'Connor J).

42 *DRJ v Commissioner of Victims Rights (No 2)* (2020) 103 NSWLR 692, 696 [4] (Bell P).

[41.7] The rationale for the presumption differs according to whether the relevant law is federal or state

The presumption in the common law of Australia is derived from English law. English courts (which at the time did not have to concern themselves with devolution) had expressed the rationale in terms of 'the comity of nations'. For example, in *Barcelo v Electrolytic Zinc Co of Australasia Ltd*[43] Dixon J quoted with approval the following statement of James LJ in *Niboyet v Niboyet*:

> It is always to be understood and implied that the legislature of a country is not intending to deal with persons or matters over which, according to the comity of nations, the jurisdiction properly belongs to some other sovereign or State.[44]

As implied in this statement, the comity of nations is threatened by the assertion of jurisdiction by a court of one nation over the residents of another nation, since that assertion 'invades the sovereignty of the latter nation'.[45]

Despite the above justification, the presumption also applies to legislatures whose legislative competence is limited territorially.[46] Put another way, the presumption applies to a state or territory legislature in relation to the operation of its legislation in another state or territory. Concerns based on the comity of nations do not apply here.[47] In this case the rationale for the presumption is found elsewhere – in 'the Constitution, its text and structure'.[48] This basis has been explained as recognising 'the territorial divisions of the Commonwealth and the limited law-making responsibilities established for each "law area"'.[49]

[41.8] The social context of the presumption and attitudes towards it have changed, and as a result the presumption is more readily rebutted

Globalisation has been described as the 'phenomenon of our times'.[50] Globalising factors, such as international trade and travel, foreign investment and modern communications technologies, are internationalising institutions, finance and, inevitably, criminal activity. Nation states are increasingly asserting extraterritorial jurisdiction.[51] These social and political changes have led to legislation that has eroded the presumption in respect of statutory offences in most Australian jurisdictions.[52]

At an interpretative level, Bell P has observed that the 'value and utility [of the presumption] has ... diminished, both with the times and with changing attitudes to the extraterritorial

43 (1932) 48 CLR 391.

44 Ibid 424 (Dixon J), quoting *Niboyet v Niboyet* (1878) 4 PD 1, 7 (James LJ). For more recent statements and approval see *Lipohar v The Queen* (1999) 200 CLR 485, 497 [15] (Gleeson CJ), 522–3 [95] (Gaudron, Gummow and Hayne JJ).

45 *Waller v Freehills* (2009) 177 FCR 507, 517 [44] (the Court).

46 *Lipohar v The Queen* (1999) 200 CLR 485, 497 [15] (Gleeson CJ).

47 Ibid 525 [99], 525–6 [101], 526 [102] (Gaudron, Gummow and Hayne JJ), 551 [165] (Kirby J) (dissenting as to outcome).

48 Ibid 525 [99] (Gaudron, Gummow and Hayne JJ); see also Kirby J at 551 [165] (dissenting as to outcome).

49 Ibid 553 [170] (Kirby J) (dissenting as to outcome).

50 Danielle Ireland-Piper, 'Extraterritorial Criminal Jurisdiction: Does the Long Arm of the Law Undermine the Rule of Law?' (2012) 13 *Melbourne Journal of International Law* 1, 6 quoting Spencer Zifcak, *Globalisation and the Rule of Law* (Routledge Press, 2005) 1.

51 Ibid 3, 8–9.

52 See **[41.10]**.

operation of laws'.[53] In the 19th century Lord Halsbury once propounded that '[a]ll crime is local'.[54] But as has been judicially observed, we live in a 'shrinking world'.[55] Since the 19th century, immense developments in transport and technology have meant that vastly more commercial activity traverses territorial borders and boundaries than when the statutory and common law presumptions were laid down.[56] These influences have also affected transborder crime.[57] It has been observed that '[c]rime is now established on an international scale'.[58] As a result, the courts are more ready to apply the law 'in a manner which accommodates the [new] reality, especially in relation to transactions occurring within the Federation'.[59] The changing attitude to extraterritorial operation of laws is denoted by the reasonable regularity with which Parliament specifies that a law may have an extraterritorial operation.[60] As a result of these changes, it has been said that the presumption 'may be readily rebutted'.[61]

It is erroneous to conflate, on the one hand, the legislative *capacity* of a Parliament to make a law with, on the other hand, ascertaining whether Parliament *intended* the law in question to be subject to a territorial limitation as to its application [41.9]

The presumption against extraterritorial operation is a presumption used to work out what ambit was *intended* by the Parliament. This interpretative question may be contrasted with a constitutional question as to the limits of legislative power. While the Commonwealth Parliament is not restricted territorially,[62] state and territory parliaments continue to be so. In other words, while

53 *DRJ v Commissioner of Victims Rights (No 2)* (2020) 103 NSWLR 692, 702 [27].

54 *Macleod v A-G (NSW)* [1891] AC 455, 458, quoted in *Lipohar v The Queen* (1999) 200 CLR 485, 497 [15] (Gleeson CJ).

55 *Lipohar v The Queen* (1999) 200 CLR 485, 559 [184] (Kirby J), quoting *Libman v The Queen* [1985] 2 SCR 178, 213–4 (La Forest J).

56 *DRJ v Commissioner of Victims Rights (No 2)* (2020) 103 NSWLR 692, 701–2 [26] (Bell P).

57 *Lipohar v The Queen* (1999) 200 CLR 485, 502 [34], 503 [37] (Gleeson CJ), 548–50 [160]–[162] (Kirby J) (dissenting as to outcome); *DPP v Sutcliffe* [2001] VSC 43, [60]–[66] (Gillard J).

58 *Lipohar v The Queen* (1999) 200 CLR 485, 503 [37] (Gleeson CJ), quoting with approval *Liangsiriprasert v United States* [1991] 1 AC 225, 251 (Lord Griffiths, speaking for the Privy Council).

59 Ibid 503 [37].

60 For examples of legislation in the Commonwealth sphere see *DRJ v Commissioner of Victims Rights (No 2)* (2020) 103 NSWLR 692, 702–3 [30] (Bell P). For examples of legislation at the State level see *DRJ v Commissioner of Victims Rights (No 2)* (2020) 103 NSWLR 692, 703–4 [31] (Bell P) and *DPP v Sutcliffe* [2001] VSC 43, [98] (Gillard J). See also *Waller v Freehills* (2009) 177 FCR 507, 518 [45] (the Court), referring to laws of the United States of America.

61 *DRJ v Commissioner of Victims Rights (No 2)* (2020) 103 NSWLR 692, 704 [33] (Bell P). This remark was made in the context of the relevant statutory presumption, but there is no reason why it ought not apply equally to the common law presumption. It was also stated in a case dealing with civil law. Cf authority that holds that at common law the presumption is stronger in relation to offences: see **[41.10]**.

62 *Polyukhovich v Commonwealth of Australia* (1991) 172 CLR 501 determined that the words 'for the peace, order, and good government of the Commonwealth' in s 51 of the *Australian Constitution* imposed no territorial limitation: at 529 (Mason CJ), 550 (Brennan J), 605–6 (Deane J), 635–6 (Dawson J), 695 (Gaudron J), 713–4 (McHugh J). Hence, 'once a subject matter is found to be within the terms of s 51, the Commonwealth has, and always has had, power to give extraterritorial operation to a law on that subject matter': at 713 (McHugh J). See also *Bray v F Hoffman-La Roche Ltd* (2003) 130 FCR 317, 352 [162] (Branson J, Carr J agreeing at 328 [29]).

state[63] and territory[64] parliaments may legislate extraterritorially there are limits in doing so and as a result some forms of extraterritorial legislation are beyond their power to enact. For state legislatures, the source of the limitation is the grant of power to the legislatures in their respective constitutions.[65] The leading judicial statement is by Gibbs J in *Pearce v Florenca*,[66] holding that a state has extraterritorial legislative competence if 'there is any real connection – even a remote or general connection – between the subject matter of the legislation and the State'.[67]

What Parliament intended as to their territorial reach is *not* answered by asking whether a Parliament has the 'legislative capacity'[68] or 'constitutional power'[69] to make the law in question.[70] In other words,

> it would be erroneous to conflate constitutional power with statutory interpretation. The ambit of particular legislation is not a question of constitutional power but one of statutory interpretation. The question is not what the Parliament of New South Wales could have done but what, as a matter of construction, it has done, in enacting the relevant legislation.[71]

Similarly, the question of interpretation – the ambit which was intended – is not answered by asking whether a court would have jurisdiction, for '[t]he jurisdiction of a court to hear and determine a charge of a criminal offence and the territorial ambit of a law which creates or defines the offence charged are two distinct questions'.[72]

Thus, a court may observe that the legislature would have had extraterritorial legislative competence or power to make a law of the character in question, while determining that the legislature did not intend the law in question to have an extraterritorial ambit.[73]

---

63 *Australia Act 1986* (Cth) s 2(1); *Union Steamship Co of Australia Pty Ltd v King* (1988) 166 CLR 1, 14 (the Court).

64 *Lucas-Smith v Coroners' Court* (ACT) (2009) 166 ACTR 42, 47 [32] (Higgins CJ).

65 *Union Steamship Co of Australia Pty Ltd v King* (1988) 166 CLR 1, 13–14 (the Court), referring to the words 'peace, order and good government'; *Lipohar v The Queen* (1999) 200 CLR 485, 524 [97] (Gaudron, Gummow and Hayne JJ). For the territory legislatures, the limitation is found in grants of power in respective self-government Acts passed by the Commonwealth Parliament.

66 (1976) 135 CLR 507.

67 Ibid 518. This statement was approved in *Union Steamship Co of Australia Pty Ltd v King* (1988) 166 CLR 1, 14 (the Court). The law on this topic is summarised in *DRJ v Commissioner of Victims Rights (No 2)* (2020) 103 NSWLR 692, 723–4 [128]–[129] (Leeming JA, Bell P agreeing at 695 [1], Meagher JA agreeing at 706 [42]).

68 *DRJ v Commissioner of Victims Rights (No 2)* (2020) 103 NSWLR 692, 726 [137] (Leeming JA, Bell P agreeing at 695 [1], Meagher JA agreeing at 706 [42]).

69 *Chubb Insurance Co of Australia Ltd v Moore* (2013) 302 ALR 101, 133 [147] (Emmett JA and Ball J, Bathurst CJ agreeing at 103 [1], Beazley P agreeing at 104 [2], Macfarlan JA agreeing at 104 [3]).

70 *DRJ v Commissioner of Victims Rights (No 2)* (2020) 103 NSWLR 692, 726 [137] (Leeming JA, Bell P agreeing at 695 [1], Meagher JA agreeing at 706 [42]).

71 *Chubb Insurance Co of Australia Ltd v Moore* (2013) 302 ALR 101, 133 [147] (Emmett JA and Ball J, Bathurst CJ agreeing at 103 [1], Beazley P agreeing at 104 [2], Macfarlan JA agreeing at 104 [3]).

72 *Thompson v The Queen* (1989) 169 CLR 1, 19, 23 (Brennan J). The extract at 19 was quoted with approval in *Lipohar v The Queen* (1999) 200 CLR 485, 520 [87] (Gaudron, Gummow and Hayne JJ).

73 *DRJ v Commissioner of Victims Rights (No 2)* (2020) 103 NSWLR 692, 725 [135] (Leeming JA, Bell P agreeing at 695 [1], Meagher JA agreeing at 706 [42]).

But constitutional limits do raise questions of territorial restrictions if no connection with the state or territory is apparent. As stated above, without *some* territorial connection a state or territory law is invalid. But constitutional law does not indicate *which* of several elements of the law in question is to be territorially restricted.[74] The constitutional need for some territorial connection does not translate to every element. Nor is such a result required by the presumption against extraterritorial operation. It is a 'fallacy' that the statutory presumption '[requires] each and every word of a statute to have the territorial connection'.[75] Therefore, if no connection with the state is apparent, an issue that may arise is *which* element of the relevant law is to have a 'geographical limitation to which the legislative power of a State Parliament is subject'.[76]

Statutes of general operation in most Australian jurisdictions define the territorial nexus for offences in a way that allows some extraterritorial operation [41.10]

It has been held that the 'general presumption at common law is that crime is local'.[77] Where Parliament creates an offence, and Parliament does not make clear whether the offence has an extraterritorial operation, some judicial statements describe the presumption as 'strong'.[78] The presumption has been said to be 'even stronger' against a parliamentary intention to make acts *done by foreigners abroad* triable in a domestic court.[79]

But, for crimes, the presumption at common law has been eroded by statutory developments in most Australian jurisdictions. In all jurisdictions other than Victoria,[80] statutes of general operation define what is variously referred to as 'geographical jurisdiction', 'geographical nexus', 'territorial nexus' or 'territorial application'. The regimes in Queensland, Tasmania and Western Australia are similar. They define the nexus as existing between the state concerned and at least one element of the crime[81] or at least one of the acts or omissions that make up the elements.[82] Other jurisdictions have similar provisions.[83]

74 *Barcelo v Electrolytic Zinc Co of Australasia Ltd* (1932) 48 CLR 391, 428 (Dixon J).

75 *DRJ v Commissioner of Victims Rights (No 2)* (2020) 103 NSWLR 692, 713 [75] (Leeming JA, Bell P agreeing at 695 [1], Meagher JA agreeing at 706 [42]), citing *O'Connor v Healey* (1967) 69 SR (NSW) 111, 114 (Jacobs JA, Wallace P agreeing at 115, Holmes JA agreeing at 115), and *Law Society of New South Wales v Glenorcy Pty Ltd* (2006) 67 NSWLR 169, 177 [37] (Mason P, McColl JA agreeing at 186 [85], Basten JA agreeing at 186 [86]).

76 *Insight Vacations Pty Ltd v Young* (2011) 243 CLR 149, 159–60 [29] (the Court). See also *DRJ v Commissioner of Victims Rights (No 2)* (2020) 103 NSWLR 692, 721 [116] (Leeming JA, Bell P agreeing at 695 [1], Meagher JA agreeing at 706 [42]). *DRJ v Commissioner of Victims Rights (No 2)* (2020) 103 NSWLR 692 is a particularly good example and contains an insightful discussion by Leeming JA at 729–35 [148]–[176]. Among the cases his Honour discusses in this regard, apart from *Insight Vacations*, are *O'Connor v Healey* (1967) 69 SR (NSW) 111 and *Old UGC Inc v Industrial Relations Commission (NSW)* (2006) 225 CLR 274.

77 *Lipohar v The Queen* (1999) 200 CLR 485, 527 [106] (Gaudron, Gummow and Hayne JJ), quoting *Brownlie v State Pollution Control Commission* (1992) 27 NSWLR 78, 83. See also *Thompson v The Queen* (1989) 169 CLR 1, 23–4 (Brennan J); *Grannall v C George Kellaway and Sons Pty Ltd* (1955) 93 CLR 36, 52 (the Court).

78 *Treacy v DPP* [1971] AC 537, 551 (Lord Reid), approved in *Thompson v The Queen* (1989) 169 CLR 1, 24 (Brennan J), 33 (Deane J) and in *Lipohar v The Queen* (1999) 200 CLR 485, 497 [16] (Gleeson CJ).

79 *Air-India v Wiggins* [1980] 1 WLR 815, 819 (Lord Diplock), approved in *Thompson v The Queen* (1989) 169 CLR 1, 24 (Brennan J).

80 *R v Nationwide News Pty Ltd* (2008) 22 VR 116, 131 [67] (Mandie J).

81 *Criminal Law (Territorial Application) Act 1995* (Tas) s 4.

82 *Criminal Code Act 1899* (Qld) sch 1 s 12; *Criminal Code Act Compilation Act 1913* (WA) app B sch s 12.

83 *Criminal Code Act 1995* (Cth) sch s 14.1(2)(a) (restricted to certain offences); *Crimes Act 1900* (NSW) s 10C(2)(a); *Criminal Law Consolidation Act 1935* (SA) s 5G(2)(a); *Criminal Code 2002* (ACT) s 64(2)(a); *Criminal Code Act 1983* (NT) sch 1 s 43CA(2)(a).

The Australian Capital Territory, New South Wales and Northern Territory go further.[84] They additionally provide, in the words of the NSW provision, that the geographical nexus is satisfied 'if the offence is committed wholly outside the State, but the offence has an effect in the State'.[85] South Australia makes similar provision.[86]

For offences against a law of the Commonwealth, the *Criminal Code* defines a 'standard geographical jurisdiction'.[87] It applies to certain offences.[88] The Code separately defines various geographical jurisdictions for which a law of the Commonwealth may provide that the particular jurisdiction applies.[89]

Rebutting the presumption

[41.11] **If the presumption is raised, it may be rebutted by sufficient evidence of a contrary legislative intention**

Like other presumptions, the presumption may be rebutted expressly or impliedly.[90] In a simple case, plain words rebut the presumption.[91]

A contrary intention may be found by implication in the context and subject matter.[92] The fact that there is a comparable law in the extraterritorial jurisdiction is relevant but not determinative.[93] The legislative purpose can be an important factor,[94] among others.[95]

---

84 The Commonwealth also makes further provision in the *Criminal Code Act 1995* (Cth) sch pt 2.7.

85 *Crimes Act 1900* (NSW) s 10C(2)(b). Equivalent provisions are the *Criminal Code 2002* (ACT) s 64(2)(b); *Criminal Code Act 1983* (NT) sch 1 s 43CA(2)(b). The place in which an offence has an effect is defined: *Crimes Act 1900* (NSW) s 10B(3); *Criminal Code 2002* (ACT) s 63(3); *Criminal Code Act 1983* (NT) sch 1 s 43BZ(3). See also qualifications in the *Criminal Code 2002* (ACT) s 65(2); *Crimes Act 1900* (NSW) s 10D(2); *Criminal Code Act 1983* (NT) sch 1 s 43CB(2).

86 *Criminal Law Consolidation Act 1935* (SA) s 5G(2)(b), (c). The legislation was found to be within the constitutional limits of the State of South Australia in *Thai v DPP (No 2)* (2009) 229 FLR 294, 313 [71] (Gray J).

87 *Criminal Code Act 1995* (Cth) sch s 14.1.

88 Offences created by provisions commencing at or after the commencement of the relevant section (24 May 2001).

89 *Criminal Code Act 1995* (Cth) pt 2.7.

90 *R v Franke* [1929] VLR 285, 288 (the Court), quoting with approval John W Salmond, 'The Limitations of Colonial Legislative Power' (1917) 33(2) *Law Quarterly Review* 117, 119; *Australian Securities Commission v Bank Leumi Le-Israel* (1995) 134 ALR 101, 123–4 (Sackville J), affirmed on appeal: (1996) 139 ALR 527, 546 (Lehane J, Lockhart J agreeing at 529, Foster J agreeing at 529).

91 *Vickers v Queensland Building and Construction Commission* [2019] QCA 66, [80] (Morrison JA, Holmes CJ agreeing at [1], Gotterson JA agreeing at [2]).

92 *Wanganui-Rangitikei Electric Power Board* (1934) 50 CLR 581, 601 (Dixon J); *Melville v Chief Executive Officer, Department of Health and Families* (2011) 30 NTLR 98, 108–9 [37] (the Court).

93 *Brownlie v State Pollution Control Commission* (1992) 27 NSWLR 78, 85 (Gleeson CJ, Carruthers J agreeing at 90, Lee AJ agreeing at 90). More broadly, the federal structure does not inhibit the extraterritorial operation of state or territory legislation in another state or territory: *Mobil Oil Australia Pty Ltd v Victoria* (2002) 211 CLR 1, 26 [16] (Gleeson CJ).

94 *Brownlie v State Pollution Control Commission* (1992) 27 NSWLR 78, 87–8 (Gleeson CJ, Carruthers J agreeing at 90, Lee AJ agreeing at 90); *Vickers v Queensland Building and Construction Commission* [2019] QCA 66, [80] (Morrison JA, Holmes CJ agreeing at [1], Gotterson JA agreeing at [2]); *D151 v New South Wales Crime Commission* (2017) 94 NSWLR 738, 746 [26] (Basten JA), 759 [91]–[92] (Simpson JA), Beazley ACJ agreeing with Basten JA and Simpson JA at 740 [1].

95 See analysis of case law in *DRJ v Commissioner of Victims Rights (No 2)* (2020) 103 NSWLR 692, 698 [10] (Bell P).

Example 41.2 *DPP v Sutcliffe*[96]

As mentioned above (**[41.2]**), the respondent had been charged with stalking a person, in breach of s 21A of the *Crimes Act 1958* (Vic) ('the Act'). The alleged actions of the respondent (a resident of Victoria) all took place in the State of Victoria. The effect of the stalking was allegedly experienced outside the territory (in Canada) via various means including email. The question of construction was whether s 21A extended to conduct where an essential ingredient of the offence of stalking a person – proof of the harmful effect – occurred outside the State.

The Court held that, by necessary implication, the Parliament intended s 21A to have an extraterritorial operation where all ingredients except the harmful effect were alleged to have occurred within the territory.[97] Drawing from the provision, the Court referred to how the definition of stalking in s 21A(2) was non-exclusive. It also pointed to specific parts of that definition that provided for communications where the victim and the offender could be separated by a large distance. The communications included 'telephoning and sending electronic messages'. The Court also pointed to the proscribed conduct being 'a course of conduct', as 'the conduct could take place in a variety of ways, through a variety of means, and over a long period of time'.[98] After considering other provisions of the Act, the Court held that, contrary to the submissions of the respondent, the provisions 'do not establish a legislative pattern leading to the conclusion that, unless the Victorian Parliament expressly enacts that a statutory provision creating an offence may have an extraterritorial operation, it does not do so'.[99] This was because the other provisions of the Act referred to by the respondent were concerned with *conduct* occurring outside the state and not with the *effect* of the conduct. After examining the legislative history, namely the parliamentary debates concerning the Bill that became the Act in question, the Court discerned that Parliament was aware that the mischief could occur in a diversity of situations where people had been stalked. And after reflecting on the wider context, the Court considered that the respondent's construction could have absurd consequences and rob the provision of much of its effect.

96 [2001] VSC 43.

97 Ibid [102]–[103] (Gillard J).

98 Ibid [87].

99 Ibid [102].

42 MENTAL INGREDIENT OF STATUTORY OFFENCES

Overview

[42.1] A statutory offence may contain, expressly or by implication, a proposition as to a state of mind. At common law the state of mind that an offence contains is known as 'mens rea'.

The common law provides two presumptions as to mens rea. First, there is a presumption that mens rea is an essential ingredient in every offence. If it is not an essential ingredient, a further presumption arises: an honest and reasonable belief in a state of facts that, if they existed, would make the defendant's act innocent, is to be treated as a ground of exculpation. The rationale for the presumptions as to mens rea is to avoid a primitive response of punishing a person for engaging in prohibited conduct when, due to lack of knowledge or intent, the person is morally innocent.

Disputes as to mens rea generally involve one or both of two main issues: applicability (whether mens rea is part of the offence in some way) and content (if mens rea is applicable, the specific state of mind). Both issues are approached as a matter of statutory interpretation. The applicability of mens rea turns on a number of factors and takes account of the entire statutory context. The determination of the content is regulated by prima facie requirements.

The common law doctrine of mens rea applies in the 'common law jurisdictions' of Australia, which for this purpose comprise New South Wales, South Australia and Victoria. The common law has been supplanted by exclusive criminal Codes in the 'code jurisdictions': the Commonwealth, Queensland, Tasmania,[1] Western Australia, the Australian Capital Territory and the Northern Territory. In these jurisdictions offences may have mental elements in the nature of mens rea.

How state of mind for an offence is addressed in criminal law

[42.2] **A statutory offence may contain, expressly or by implication, a proposition as to a state of mind**

Australian authorities recognise that a statutory offence may contain 'expressly or by implication a proposition as to a state of mind'.[2] At common law the state of mind that an offence may

1 Tasmania is a hybrid common law/code jurisdiction.

2 *R v Tolson* (1889) 23 QBD 168, 187 (Stephen J), approved in *He Kaw Teh v The Queen* (1985) 157 CLR 523, 565 (Brennan J) and in *CTM v The Queen* (2008) 236 CLR 440, 486 [159] (Hayne J), 462 [61] (Kirby J) (dissenting as to outcome).

contain is referred to as 'mens rea'.[3] Mens rea is also referred to as the 'appropriate fault element'.[4]

Legislation may mark an offence with one or more of a variety of mental states, such as 'maliciously', 'fraudulently', 'negligently' and 'knowingly'.[5]

Where a positive state of mind is implied, knowledge is most often required.[6] The presumptive knowledge requirement was authoritatively stated by Jordan CJ:

> [I]t is also necessary at common law for the prosecution to prove that he knew that he was doing the criminal act which is charged against him, that is, that he *knew that all the facts constituting the ingredients necessary to make the act criminal were involved in what he was doing.*[7]

An older, influential authority defined mens rea in terms of 'knowledge of the wrongfulness of the act'.[8] But unless Parliament otherwise requires, mens rea does *not* require knowledge of the illegality of the act or that what the accused is doing is wrong.[9] At common law, ignorance of the law is no excuse.[10]

Determining whether a state of mind is part of an offence (and if so what it is) is approached differently across Australian jurisdictions [42.3]

For the purposes of determining whether a state of mind is part of an offence and if so, what it is, Australia divides into 'common law jurisdictions' and 'code jurisdictions'.

Common law jurisdictions are jurisdictions in which the common law doctrine of mens rea has not been supplanted by criminal codes.[11] In Australia, the common law jurisdictions are New South Wales, South Australia and Victoria. In these jurisdictions, where Parliament has not unambiguously made it clear whether an offence contains a mental ingredient, the courts are empowered, through statutory interpretation, to determine whether the offence contains such an ingredient and, if so, what it is.

---

3 *He Kaw Teh v The Queen* (1985) 157 CLR 523, 529, 531 (Gibbs CJ, Mason J agreeing at 546), 565 (Brennan J), 590–1 (Dawson J). But mens rea is beset with problems of definition: *He Kaw Teh v The Queen* (1985) 157 CLR 523, 568 (Brennan J). Brennan J there included voluntariness within its ambit: at 568–70. See also other mental states referred to in *CTM v The Queen* (2008) 236 CLR 440, 486 [159] (Hayne J).

4 *R v Bo (No 3)* [2016] ACTSC 175, [34] (Refshauge J).

5 *CTM v The Queen* (2008) 236 CLR 440, 486 (Hayne J).

6 *Question of Law Reserved (No 2 of 1998)* (1998) 70 SASR 502, 513 (Duggan J).

7 *R v Turnbull* (1943) 44 SR (NSW) 108, 109 (Jordan CJ) (emphasis added), quoted with approval in *He Kaw Teh v The Queen* (1985) 157 CLR 523, 531 (Gibbs CJ, Mason J agreeing at 546), 572 (Brennan J).

8 *Sherras v De Rutzen* [1895] 1 QB 918, 921 (Wright J). Cf Day J at 920: an 'intention to do a wrongful act'.

9 *He Kaw Teh v The Queen* (1985) 157 CLR 523, 588 (Brennan J); *Leask v Commonwealth* (1996) 187 CLR 579, 598 (Dawson J); *DPP (Cth) Reference No 1 of 2008* (2008) 21 VR 111, 115 [21] (the Court); *Question of Law Reserved (No 2 of 1998)* (1998) 70 SASR 502, 511 (Doyle CJ, Cox J agreeing at 512, Duggan J generally agreeing at 512). Although the High Court approved *Sherras v De Rutzen* in *He Kaw Teh v The Queen* (1985) 157 CLR 523, 528 (Gibbs CJ, Mason J agreeing at 546), 566 (Brennan J). Dawson J noted in *Leask v Commonwealth* (1996) 187 CLR 579 that the reference to 'wrongfulness' in *Sherras v De Rutzen* must now be read in the light of the modern statement that knowledge pertains to 'knowledge of the circumstances which give the act its character when an act is voluntarily done', quoting *He Kaw Teh v The Queen* (1985) 157 CLR 523, 570 (Brennan J): at 598.

10 *Ostrowski v Palmer* (2004) 218 CLR 493, 500–1 [1]–[2] (Gleeson CJ and Kirby J). The position under the Criminal Codes is the same: see below **[42.7]**.

11 A statutory 'code' is a statute that replaces the previous law on a subject and purports to be a comprehensive statement of the law on that subject: see **[22.4]**.

In the code jurisdictions (the Commonwealth, Queensland, Tasmania, Western Australia, the Australian Capital Territory and the Northern Territory), the common law doctrine of mens rea has been supplanted by codes (with a partial exception in the case of Tasmania). In these jurisdictions a mental ingredient in the nature of mens rea may apply to a statutory offence.[12] In the Commonwealth *Criminal Code* they are known as 'fault elements'.[13] The codes are outlined below (**[42.7]**).

The common law principle of mens rea

[42.4] Mens rea expresses, at common law, the state of mind that an offence contains

(a) The principle of mens rea breaks down into twin presumptions

The common law provides two presumptions as to mens rea. In the first place, there is a presumption that mens rea is an essential ingredient in every offence. Wright J in *Sherras v De Rutzen*[14] propounded:

> There is a presumption that mens rea ... is an essential ingredient in every offence; but that presumption is liable to be displaced either by the words of the statute creating the offence or by the subject-matter with which it deals, and both must be considered.[15]

Sherras v De Rutzen was approved in the leading Australian case of *He Kaw Teh v The Queen.*[16] Brennan J similarly held in his own words:

> It is now firmly established that mens rea is an essential element in every statutory offence unless, having regard to the language of the statute and to its subject-matter, it is excluded expressly or by necessary implication ...[17]

The *Sherras v De Rutzen* presumption states an 'original obligation on the prosecution to prove mens rea'.[18] In *He Kaw Teh v the Queen*[19] Gibbs CJ described this sense of mens rea as 'full mens rea', or 'mens rea, in the sense of guilty intention or guilty knowledge'.[20]

If mens rea is not an essential ingredient in a statutory offence, a further presumption arises.[21] The relevant principle is known as the '*Proudman v Dayman* defence',[22] after the leading case of that name. In that case Dixon J observed:

12 *R v Martin* [1963] Tas SR 103, 114 (Burbury CJ) (speaking of the Tasmanian *Criminal Code*).

13 *Criminal Code Act 1995* (Cth) sch ch 2.

14 [1895] 1 QB 918.

15 Ibid 921.

16 (1985) 157 CLR 523, 528 (Gibbs CJ, Mason J agreeing at 546), 566 (Brennan J). Dawson J was more equivocal: at 594.

17 Ibid 566. In *CTM v The Queen* (2008) 236 CLR 440 Hayne J approved of this statement of Brennan J: at 484 [148]. Kirby J similarly so held: at 462 [61].

18 *R v Wampfler* (1987) 11 NSWLR 541, 546 (Street CJ, Hunt J agreeing at 550, McInerney J agreeing at 550).

19 (1985) 157 CLR 523.

20 Ibid 535. Gibbs CJ was following the approach of Lord Reid in *Sweet v Parsley* [1970] AC 132, 150.

21 *He Kaw Teh v The Queen* (1985) 157 CLR 523, 533 (Gibbs CJ, Mason J agreeing at 546), 582 (Brennan J), 590 (Dawson J).

22 *CTM v The Queen* (2008) 236 CLR 440, 446 [6] (Gleeson CJ, Gummow, Crennan and Kiefel JJ).

> As a general rule an honest and reasonable belief in a state of facts which, if they existed, would make the defendant's act innocent affords an excuse for doing what would otherwise be an offence.[23]

The *Proudman v Dayman* principle has been affirmed by the High Court of Australia.[24] In *He Kaw Teh* Dawson J said: 'In this country it is well established by authority that . . . there does exist a presumption that honest and reasonable mistake is to be treated as a ground of exculpation.'[25]

The *Proudman v Dayman* principle recognises a 'middle course',[26] 'middle position'[27] or 'half-way house'[28] between full mens rea and absolute liability.[29]

The *Proudman v Dayman* principle does not operate, in the way the *Sherras v De Rutzen* proposition does, as a presumptive 'element' or 'essential ingredient' of a statutory offence. This is because, with the former, 'the evidentiary onus of raising the ground of exculpation is on the accused'.[30] Importantly though, if the evidential burden is satisfied, 'the onus of proving the absence of [an honest and reasonable] belief lies on the prosecution'.[31] But if the evidential burden is not satisfied, that is the end of the matter.[32] The evidential onus on the accused explains why the principle is often referred to, in a loose sense,[33] as a 'defence'.

Although mens rea can be regarded as comprising twin propositions – the presumption in the *Sherras v De Rutzen* sense and the presumption comprising the '*Proudman v Dayman* defence' – only one will apply to any particular external or physical element. Of the two, the presumption as to full mens rea is the 'prima facie' requirement.[34] It is more likely if an offence is one of a serious kind.[35]

23 *Proudman v Dayman* (1941) 67 CLR 536, 540. The details of the principle – the scope of its particular elements — are beyond the scope of this chapter. See further Simon Bronitt and Bernadette McSherry, *Principles of Criminal Law* (Lawbook Co, 4th ed, 2017) ch 3; Penny Crofts, *Criminal Law Elements* (LexisNexis Butterworths, 6th ed, 2017) 24–5 [2.46]–[2.48]; *Bell v Tasmania* (2021) 395 ALR 589.

24 *He Kaw Teh v The Queen* (1985) 157 CLR 523, 532, 533 (Gibbs CJ, Mason J agreeing at 546), 582 (Brennan J), 591 (Dawson J); *CTM v The Queen* (2008) 236 CLR 440, 446 [5], 456 [35] (Gleeson CJ, Gummow, Crennan and Kiefel JJ), 463–4 [66] (Kirby J) (dissenting as to outcome), 483 [146] (Hayne J).

25 *He Kaw Teh v The Queen* (1985) 157 CLR 523, 591.

26 Ibid 533 (Gibbs CJ, Mason J agreeing at 546).

27 Ibid.

28 Ibid 591 (Dawson J).

29 In *He Kaw Teh v The Queen* (1985) 157 CLR 523 the High Court did not formally decide whether, semantically, the *Proudman v Dayman* principle was to be seen as an aspect of 'mens rea'. Brennan J and Dawson J included it ('the wide view'): at 573 and 590 respectively. Wilson J (dissenting as to outcome) appeared not to: at 551. Gibbs CJ (with Mason J agreeing at 546) did not decide the point: at 534. But Gibbs CJ seemingly approved a statement of the Supreme Court of Canada endorsing the wide view in *R v Corporation of City of Ste Marie* [1978] 2 SCR 1299, 1325–6 (the Court): at 533–4.

30 *CTM v The Queen* (2008) 236 CLR 440, 447 [8] (Gleeson CJ, Gummow, Crennan and Kiefel JJ). See also *He Kaw Teh v The Queen* (1985) 157 CLR 523, 534, 535 (Gibbs CJ, Mason J agreeing at 546), 592–3 (Dawson J). In *He Kaw Teh* Dawson J pointed out that the onus on the prosecution might arise as a result of evidence elicited by way of cross-examination during the case for the prosecution: at 592.

31 *He Kaw Teh v The Queen* (1985) 157 CLR 523, 534. See to same effect Brennan J at 574 and Dawson J at 593. The statement of Gibbs CJ was followed in *CTM v The Queen* (2008) 236 CLR 440, 447 (Gleeson CJ, Gummow, Crennan and Kiefel JJ).

32 *CTM v The Queen* (2008) 236 CLR 440, 456 [36] (Gleeson CJ, Gummow, Crennan and Kiefel JJ), 480 [136] (Hayne J).

33 Ibid 446 [6] (Gleeson CJ, Gummow, Crennan and Kiefel JJ).

34 *He Kaw Teh v The Queen* (1985) 157 CLR 523, 575, 578, 582 (Brennan J).

35 Ibid 535 (Gibbs CJ, Mason J agreeing at 546).

Both presumptions are regarded as basic legal principles. In *CTM v the Queen*[36] the High Court emphasised that the *Proudman v Dayman* middle course was a 'basic legal principle of criminal responsibility'[37] and 'reflects fundamental values as to criminal responsibility'.[38] It might be asked how two presumptions that share a similar field (the state of mind that an offence in one way or another prescribes) can both be basic. Part of the answer lies in the fact that the presumptions cannot be availed of in relation to the one set of facts. As Brennan J said, 'knowledge and mistaken belief cannot co-exist in relation to the same fact'.[39]

(b) **The rationale for the presumptions as to mens rea is to avoid a primitive approach to criminal punishment**

Punishment for the actus reus alone (the acts or omissions constituting a crime) is seen as primitive.[40] The purpose for implying mens rea is to provide 'a humane protection for persons who unwittingly engage in prohibited conduct'.[41] The courts wish to avoid 'the public scandal of convicting on a serious charge persons who are in no way blameworthy'.[42] A person is not blameworthy if the person is 'morally innocent'.[43]

The rationale applies equally to the *Proudman v Dayman* ground of exculpation for an honest and reasonable mistake of fact.[44]

When absolute liability is contemplated – that is, the statute does not require any mental state to accompany the prohibited act and the 'defence' of honest and reasonable mistake of fact is not available – the rationale for omitting mens rea lies in aiding the achievement of the purpose of the statute. But absolute liability is not appropriate if the persons concerned cannot 'govern their behaviour accordingly'.[45] In other words, 'there must be something he can do, directly or indirectly ... which will promote the observance of [the law]'.[46]

(c) **Disputes as to mens rea generally involve one or both of two main issues: its applicability and its content**

A threshold issue with respect to mens rea is whether it is applicable. Put another way, it is 'whether the Parliament intended that the forbidden conduct should be punishable even in

36 (2008) 236 CLR 440.

37 Ibid 446 [5] (Gleeson CJ, Gummow, Crennan and Kiefel JJ).

38 Ibid 456 [35]. It would be a mistake to see the highlighting of the *Proudman v Dayman* principle in *CTM* as transforming or overhauling the principles laid down in *He Kaw Teh*. There is no suggestion in *CTM* that the propositions about full mens rea in *He Kaw Teh* are to be doubted. In *CTM* counsel for the accused disclaimed reliance on full mens rea (at 480 [140]), so there was no call for its judicial consideration.

39 *He Kaw Teh v The Queen* (1985) 157 CLR 523, 575.

40 *Leary v The Queen* (1977) 74 DLR (3d) 103, 122 (Dickson J), quoted with approval in *R v O'Connor* (1980) 146 CLR 64, 96 (Stephen J) and in *He Kaw Teh v The Queen* (1985) 157 CLR 523, 565 (Brennan J).

41 *He Kaw Teh v The Queen* (1985) 157 CLR 523, 568 (Brennan J).

42 *Sweet v Parsley* [1970] AC 132, 150 (Lord Reid), quoted with approval in *He Kaw Teh v The Queen* (1985) 157 CLR 523, 565 (Brennan J).

43 Ibid 157 (Lord Pearce). See similar remarks by Lord Reid at 149.

44 *Thomas v The King* (1937) 59 CLR 279, 309 (Dixon J), approved in *CTM v The Queen* (2008) 236 CLR 440, 481 [142] (Hayne J).

45 *He Kaw Teh v The Queen* (1985) 157 CLR 523, 595 (Dawson J).

46 *Lim Chin Aik v The Queen* [1963] AC 160, 174, approved in *He Kaw Teh v The Queen* (1985) 157 CLR 523, 530 (Gibbs CJ, Mason J agreeing at 546), 568 (Brennan J).

the absence of some blameworthy state of mind'.[47] The relevant factors are considered below (**[42.5]**).

If mens rea is applicable, its content will need to be determined. If content is an issue a court will be faced with 'deciding exactly what mental state is imported'.[48] As Brennan J suggested, the second stage should not be underestimated for '[i]t is the "beginning of wisdom", as Lord Hailsham of St Marylebone said in *Reg v Morgan*, to see "that 'mens rea' means a number of quite different things in relation to different crimes"'.[49] The determination of content is considered below (**[42.6]**).

(d) Issues as to mens rea are approached as a matter of statutory interpretation

The applicability of mens rea can be raised as part of the determination of the scope of express words of the statute. The question here is whether 'the words describing the offence ... themselves necessarily import a mental element'.[50] Examples of words raising such an issue are 'wilfully demands',[51] 'possession',[52] 'intention'[53] 'threat'[54] and 'is concerned in the management of premises used for the purpose of smoking cannabis'.[55] If the language is found to import mens rea it is not necessary to rely on the common law presumption to found an implication in the offence as a whole.[56]

If the mental element is not stated directly or through language that necessarily imports it, the applicability of mens rea may still be raised. Here the interpretative issue is whether mens rea is to be implied in the offence as a whole.[57] Fundamentally, this question arises because a statute is to be read in the light of surrounding law.[58] Mens rea is a common law doctrine, forming part of the 'general principles of the common law which govern criminal responsibility'.[59] As we have seen, the common law supplies a presumption as to mens rea. Whether the presumption is displaced is 'a question of the interpretation of the statute creating the offence'.[60] Of course the language of the statute is controlling.[61]

---

47 *He Kaw Teh v The Queen* (1985) 157 CLR 523, 529 (Gibbs CJ, Mason J agreeing at 546).

48 Ibid.

49 Ibid 568 (Brennan J).

50 Ibid 539 (Gibbs CJ, Mason J agreeing at 546).

51 *Iannella v French* (1968) 119 CLR 84.

52 *He Kaw Teh v The Queen* (1985) 157 CLR 523, 537–9 (Gibbs CJ, Mason J agreeing at 546), referring to the *Customs Act 1901* (Cth) s 233B(1)(c).

53 *Will v Brighton* (2020) 104 NSWLR 170, 184–6 [59]–[74] (Bell P, Basten JA generally agreeing at 192 [109]).

54 *DPP v Acme Storage Pty Ltd* (2017) 264 IR 215, 224–6 [34]–[41] (the Court).

55 *Sweet v Parsley* [1970] AC 132, 156 (Lord Morris), 159 (Lord Pearce), 161 (Lord Wilberforce), 165 (Lord Diplock).

56 *He Kaw Teh v The Queen* (1985) 157 CLR 523, 539 (Gibbs CJ, Mason J agreeing at 546).

57 *Proudman v Dayman* (1941) 67 CLR 536, 540–1 (Dixon J); *He Kaw Teh v The Queen* (1985) 157 CLR 523, 565, 582 (Brennan J).

58 See chapter 32 at **[32.6]**.

59 *He Kaw Teh v The Queen* (1985) 157 CLR 523, 528 (Gibbs CJ, Mason J agreeing at 546). See also to similar effect Dawson J at 590.

60 Ibid 590 (Dawson J). See to similar effect Brennan J at 567. See also *CTM v The Queen* (2008) 236 CLR 440, 446 [5] (Gleeson CJ, Gummow, Crennan and Kiefel JJ).

61 *CTM v The Queen* (2008) 236 CLR 440, 446 [5] (Gleeson CJ, Gummow, Crennan and Kiefel JJ). See generally chapter 6.

The same general process applies to the determination of its content. Here the question is what is the legislative intention as to the mental state to be implied.[62]

(e) If mens rea applies, it applies to a particular external element of a statutorily defined offence

In *Vallance v The Queen*[63] Dixon CJ explained 'the external elements necessary to form the crime' as the elements of an offence other than any mental ingredient – that is, conduct, circumstances and results. Brennan J amplified this analysis in *He Kaw Teh*, saying that a statute ordinarily creates and defines an offence only by reference to 'the prohibited act or omission (conduct), the circumstances in which the act is done or the omission is made and, in some instances, the results of the act or omission'.[64]

If mens rea applies, it applies to a particular external element. It follows that 'it may connote different states of mind in respect of the several external elements of the same crime'.[65]

Applicability of the common law principle

[42.5] **The applicability of mens rea turns on a number of factors**[66]

(a) Courts have regard to a tripartite classification of offences

In *He Kaw Teh v The Queen*[67] the High Court 'recognised a tripartite categorisation of statutory offences, based upon the mental ingredient necessary'.[68] The categories of offences are as follows:

- 'Offences in which mens rea, consisting of some positive state of mind such as intent, knowledge, or recklessness, must be proved by the prosecution'.[69] In these offences mens rea has been referred to as 'full mens rea'.[70]
- Offences 'which, whilst not requiring the prosecution to prove mens rea in order to make out a case, [allow] the accused to raise honest and reasonable mistake [of fact] by way of exculpation'.[71] These are commonly known as 'strict liability' offences.[72] They involve the *Proudman v Dayman* 'middle position'.[73]

---

62 *He Kaw Teh v The Queen* (1985) 157 CLR 523, 576 (Brennan J).

63 (1961) 108 CLR 56, 59.

64 *He Kaw Teh v The Queen* (1985) 157 CLR 523, 565.

65 Ibid 568 (Brennan J).

66 The common law process of determining legislative intention in this area has been criticised as 'tortuous': *Hawthorne (Department of Health) v Morcam Pty Ltd* (1992) 29 NSWLR 120, 131 (Hunt CJ at CL, Sully J generally agreeing at 133). An academic criticism (the criteria are imprecise and defy consistent application) is Brent Fisse, *Howard's Criminal Law* (Law Book Co, 5th ed, 1990) 524, 532–3.

67 See (1985) 157 CLR 523, 533–4 (Gibbs CJ, Mason J agreeing at 546), 590 (Dawson J).

68 *Selectrix Pty Ltd v Humphrys* (2001) 159 FLR 348, 350 [5] (Hedigan J). To similar effect is *R v Wampfler* (1987) 11 NSWLR 541, 546 (Street CJ, Hunt J agreeing at 550, McInerney J agreeing at 550). For *He Kaw Teh v The Queen*, see (1985) 157 CLR 523, 533 (Gibbs CJ, Mason J agreeing at 546), 590 (Dawson J).

69 *R v Corporation of City of Ste Marie* [1978] 2 SCR 1299, 1325 (the Court), referred to with approval in *He Kaw Teh v The Queen* (1985) 157 CLR 523, 533 (Gibbs CJ, Mason J agreeing at 546).

70 *He Kaw Teh v The Queen* (1985) 157 CLR 523, 533, 535 (Gibbs CJ, Mason J agreeing at 546).

71 Ibid 590 (Dawson J). See to similar effect Gibbs CJ at 533 (Mason J agreeing at 546).

72 Ibid 590 (Dawson J). See also Gibbs CJ at 534 (Mason J agreeing at 546).

73 Ibid.

- Offences where 'the offence is . . . complete once the prohibited act . . . is proved'[74] *and* where the statute does not expressly or impliedly contain a 'full mens rea' element nor does it permit the defendant to raise the honest and reasonable mistake of fact as a ground of exculpation.[75]

(b) **Courts take account of the entire statutory context**

In general the same general interpretative criteria apply, whether it is the presumption as to full mens rea or the *Proudman v Dayman* principle whose displacement is at issue.[76] So, a court may treat the two presumptions in a similar manner. For example, if serious penal consequences would occur if no mens rea is involved this is an indication that Parliament did not intend to displace the presumption of full mens rea[77] and the *Proudman v Dayman* ground of exculpation.[78]

In answering the question whether the presumption as to mens rea is displaced[79] or mens rea is excluded[80] courts have 'regard to the whole of the statutory context'.[81] There is no fixed set of factors across all contexts.[82] Legislative history may be relevant in one case but not in another.[83] A term in the offence may be defined in one statute but not in another.[84] And so on. With these riders, criteria that have been mentioned in leading High Court cases[85] are set out below. The case examples that follow instance particulars as well as further criteria.

Words of the offence. In *He Kaw Teh*, Gibbs CJ stated that 'one must have regard to the words of the statute creating the offence'.[86] For example, a word may necessarily import a mental element.[87]

Mischief and purpose. If the section is enacted to deal with a grave social mischief, this suggests an absolute liability.[88] If the offence is 'for the purpose of regulating social or industrial conditions or to protect the revenue . . . [the provision] may also more easily be regarded as imposing absolute liability'.[89] A court will ask whether absolute liability would give added efficacy to the provision – in other words, whether 'the purpose of the statute is not merely to deter a person from engaging in prohibited conduct but to compel him to take preventive measures to

74 Ibid 590 (Dawson J). See to similar effect Wilson J at 556 (dissenting as to outcome).

75 Ibid 590 (Dawson J). See to similar effect Gibbs CJ at 534 (Mason J agreeing at 546), Wilson J at 556 (dissenting as to outcome).

76 Ibid 576 (Brennan J); *Tsolacis v McKinnon* (2012) 38 VR 260, 286 [97] (Cavanough J); David Lanham et al, *Criminal Laws in Australia* (Federation Press, 2006) 385.

77 *He Kaw Teh v The Queen* (1985) 157 CLR 523, 530, 535 (Gibbs CJ, Mason J agreeing at 546), 583 (Brennan J).

78 *CTM v The Queen* (2008) 236 CLR 440, 447 [7] (Gleeson CJ, Gummow, Crennan and Kiefel JJ).

79 *Sherras v De Rutzen* [1895] 1 QB 918, 921 (Wright J), approved in *He Kaw Teh v The Queen* (1985) 157 CLR 523, 528 (Gibbs CJ, Mason J agreeing at 546).

80 *He Kaw Teh v The Queen* (1985) 157 CLR 523, 566, 567 (Brennan J).

81 Ibid.

82 Judges sometimes take the factors mentioned by Gibbs CJ in *He Kaw Teh v the Queen* (1985) 157 CLR 523 as the relevant factors for the instant case, but the factors identified in another context can only at best be a general guide.

83 Respectively, *CTM v The Queen* (2008) 236 CLR 440 and *He Kaw Teh v The Queen* (1985) 157 CLR 523.

84 Respectively, *DPP v Hazelwood Pacific Pty Ltd (Ruling 2)* [2019] VSC 871 and *He Kaw Teh v the Queen* (1985) 157 CLR 523.

85 *He Kaw Teh v the Queen* (1985) 157 CLR 523; *CTM v The Queen* (2008) 236 CLR 440.

86 (1985) 157 CLR 523, 529 (Gibbs CJ, Mason J agreeing at 546).

87 Ibid 539 (Gibbs CJ, Mason J agreeing at 546).

88 Ibid 529 (Gibbs CJ, Mason J agreeing at 546), 595 (Dawson J).

89 Ibid 595 (Dawson J).

avoid the possibility that, without deliberate conduct on his part, the external elements of the offence might occur'.[90]

Surrounding statutory provisions.[91] The penalty for the offence is important. A 'severe'[92] or 'serious'[93] penalty tends to suggest that the presumption is not displaced.[94] An offence with a penalty that is monetary and not more than moderately sized is more easily regarded as imposing absolute liability.[95] A court may also have regard to the terms of a related offence in the same Act.[96]

Social consequences falling on the accused. If 'a convicted offender is exposed to obloquy and disgrace' this points away from the presumption being displaced.[97]

Consequences for enforcement. A court may have regard to whether a particular mental state 'would represent a real impediment to the successful prosecution of offenders'.[98] But mere difficulties are not enough; the court will examine the degree of difficulty involved and give weight accordingly.[99]

The case law contains many examples of the application of these and other relevant criteria. In some cases courts have found that the presumption as to full or original mens rea has not been rebutted.[100] In others, courts have found that the middle course *Proudman v Dayman* principle has not been ousted.[101] And in others still, the offence has been found to be of absolute liability.[102]

---

90 Ibid 567 (Brennan J). See to similar effect Gibbs CJ at 535–6 (Mason J agreeing at 546), Dawson J at 595 citing *Lim Chin Aik v The Queen* [1963] AC 160.

91 Ibid 576 (Brennan J).

92 Ibid 583 (Brennan J).

93 *CTM v The Queen* (2008) 236 CLR 440, 447 [7] (Gleeson CJ, Gummow, Crennan and Kiefel JJ), 462 [61] (Kirby J) (dissenting as to outcome).

94 See to similar effect *He Kaw Teh v The Queen* (1985) 157 CLR 523, 530, 535 ('gravity of the offence') (Gibbs CJ, Mason J agreeing at 546).

95 Ibid 595 (Dawson J).

96 See, eg, *R v Lagan* (2001) 127 A Crim R 262.

97 *He Kaw Teh v The Queen* (1985) 157 CLR 523, 530 (Gibbs CJ, Mason J agreeing at 546). See to similar effect Brennan J at 583.

98 Ibid 595 (Dawson J).

99 Ibid 536–7 (Gibbs CJ, Mason J agreeing at 546), 597 (Dawson J). Cf Brennan J at 580–1.

100 Ibid 537 (Gibbs CJ, Mason J agreeing at 546), 583–4 (Brennan J), 597 (Dawson J) (importation of narcotic goods); *Petch v The Queen* (2020) 103 NSWLR 1, 18 [47] (Hamill J, Hoeben CJ agreeing at 3 [1]) (blackmail); *R v Lagan* (2001) 127 A Crim R 262, 270–1 [78], 272 [88] (administering an injurious substance likely to endanger human life); *Question of Law Reserved (No 2 of 1998)* (1998) 70 SASR 502 (transfer of currency).

101 *CTM v The Queen* (2008) 236 CLR 440, 456 [35] (Gleeson CJ, Gummow, Crennan and Kiefel JJ), 462–3 [61] (Kirby J), 489 [168], 490 [172] (Hayne J) (sexual intercourse with a person who is above 14 years and under 16 years of age); *Proudman v Dayman* (1941) 67 CLR 536, 541 (Dixon J) (permitting an unlicensed person to drive a motor vehicle); *Hawthorne (Department of Health) v Morcam Pty Ltd* (1992) 29 NSWLR 120, 129 (Mahoney JA), 133 (Hunt CJ at CL, Sully J generally agreeing at 133) (selling any food that does not comply with a prescribed standard); *DPP v Bone* (2005) 64 NSWLR 735, 749 [35]–[37] (Adams J) (driving a motor vehicle while there is present in driver's blood the middle range prescribed concentration of alcohol); *Giachin v Sandon* (2013) 233 A Crim R 490, 508 [79] (Penfold J) (prescribed blood alcohol concentration exceeded); *DPP v Hazelwood Pacific Pty Ltd (Ruling 2)* [2019] VSC 871, [55] (pollution of atmosphere); *Strathfield Municipal Council v Elvy* (1992) 25 NSWLR 745, 750 (Gleeson CJ, Clarke JA agreeing at 752, Lee AJ agreeing at 752) (failure by member of a council to disclose to a council meeting pecuniary interest in a matter with which the council is concerned). See other examples cited in *DPP v Bone* (2005) 64 NSWLR 735, 746 [26] (Adams J).

102 *Stanojlovic v DPP* (2018) 273 A Crim R 215, 224 [45] (the Court) (probationary driver not displaying an appropriate P plate); *Tsolacis v McKinnon* (2012) 38 VR 260, 262 [9] (Cavanough J) (dicta) (driving an unregistered motor vehicle on a highway); *Kearon v Grant* [1991] 1 VR 321, 323 (Brooking J, Kaye J agreeing at 324, Murphy J agreeing at 324) (exceeding a speed limit); *Ambrose v Edmonds-Wilson* (1998) 48 SASR 514,

Three case examples, one for each of these categories, follow.

Example 42.1 *R v Lagan*[103] (full mens rea)

The accused, who was an experienced heroin user, was found by the ACT Supreme Court to have injected a neighbour, Ms E, with heroin. As a result Ms E suffered a potentially fatal overdose. The accused was charged with breaching s 27(3)(b) of the *Crimes Act 1900* (ACT), which read as follows:

> (3) A person who intentionally and unlawfully –
>
> . . .
>
> (b) administers to, or causes to be taken by, another person any stupefying or overpowering drug or poison or any other injurious substance likely to endanger human life or cause a person grievous bodily harm . . .
>
> . . .
>
> is guilty of an offence punishable, on conviction, by imprisonment for 10 years.

There was no issue concerning the intentional and unlawful administering of a drug. The question was whether it was to be implied in the offence that at the time of the alleged offence the accused knew that the administration of the drug was likely to endanger the person's life.

The prosecution argued that it was not necessary that the accused was aware of the danger in administering the drug. It was enough that the substance, objectively, was likely to endanger human life or cause a person grievous bodily harm.

The Court disagreed with this submission.[104] After extracting at length passages from the reasons for judgment of Brennan J in *He Kaw Teh*, the Court pointed to s 28(2)(a) in the same Act for guidance. It read as follows (emphasis added):

> (2) A person who intentionally and unlawfully –
>
> (a) administers to, or causes to be taken by, another person any poison or other injurious substance *with intent to injure or cause pain or discomfort to that person . . .*
>
> is guilty of an offence punishable, on conviction, by imprisonment for 5 years.

The Court reasoned that 'it is not credible that it was intended that the higher penalty should apply [to a charge under s 27(3)(b)] if there is not present, at least, the intent referred to in the s 28 offence'.[105] In summary, the Court used the surrounding statutory provisions (the penalty and a provision in the same Act: s 28(2)(a)) to guide it in answering the question of whether the presumption as to mens rea had been displaced.

---

519 (Bollen J) (failure to furnish a tax return); *Wilson v Gahan* [1999] VSC 72, [39] (Warren J) (agricultural spraying which damages plants or stock outside the target area); *R v Clarke* (2008) 100 SASR 363, 377 [59] (Doyle CJ, David J agreeing at 387 [106]), 386 [105] (Bleby J) (production of child pornography and inciting a child to commit an indecent act).

103 (2001) 127 A Crim R 262.

104 Ibid 271 [79], 272 [88] (Higgins J).

105 Ibid 271 [79].

On the facts the court found the implied mental ingredient was not made out:

> [T]he intent shown by the evidence, was not to injure or to cause any pain or annoyance to Ms E. In fact, the only conclusion that can sensibly be drawn from the evidence was that the administration of the heroin was intended to relieve Ms E's feelings of depression, to dull her awareness of emotional pain. That is, to 'help' not harm her.

Example 42.2 *DPP v Hazelwood Pacific Pty Ltd (Ruling No 2)*[106] (middle position)

A fire or fires ignited in Hazelwood mine on 9 February 2014. The fire was not declared 'safe' until 25 March 2014. In the meantime, it was alleged, the fire polluted the atmosphere over, and nearby, the township of Morwell in Victoria.

The accused were each registered proprietors of the land on which the Hazelwood mine is situated. Each faced charges that they had offended against s 41(1)(a), (b) and (e) of the *Environment Protection Act 1970* (Vic) ('the Act'), which read as follows:

> **Pollution of atmosphere**
>
> (1) A person shall not pollute the atmosphere so that the condition of the atmosphere is so changed as to make or be reasonably expected to make the atmosphere –
>   (a) noxious or poisonous or offensive to the senses of human beings;
>   (b) harmful or potentially harmful to the health, welfare, safety or property of human beings;
>   . . .; or
>   (e) detrimental to any beneficial use made of the atmosphere.

An issue for preliminary determination by the Supreme Court of Victoria was whether s 41 created an offence of strict liability *or* an offence of absolute liability.

The Court held that the offence was one of strict liability.[107] In other words, honest and reasonable mistake of fact was a basis of exculpation.

The Court gave several reasons supporting its holding in this regard. It had regard to the words of the offence. It held that the words 'shall not pollute' did not in themselves strongly indicate an intention that liability is absolute rather than strict. Indeed, the definition of 'pollute' included 'causing or permitting pollution' and the Court regarded exculpation by reason of honest and reasonable mistake as supported by the definition.[108]

Read in context, the statutory purpose was not consistent with absolute liability. The Court had regard to an amending Act, which changed the offence from summary to indictable and increased the penalty,[109] and to the Minister's second reading speech to the amending Bill. The Minister had seen the purpose as providing 'adequate deterrents to potential environmental offenders' and 'effective enforcement of environmental laws'. The Court took note of what would occur if the offence was one of absolute liability. If a business attempted to do the right thing but was operating

106 [2019] VSC 871.

107 Ibid [55] (Keogh J).

108 Ibid [42].

109 *Environment Protection (Enforcement and Penalties) Act 2000* (Vic).

under an honest and reasonable mistake of fact, it would be subject to criminal penalty.[110] A section of the Act providing a 'principle of enforcement'[111] was to like effect. It stated that enforcement of environmental requirements should be undertaken for the purpose of 'influencing the attitude and behaviour of persons whose actions may have adverse environmental impacts'.

Certain surrounding statutory provisions did not provide the support the prosecution had claimed. Section 62C provided an occupier of a commercial undertaking with a defence if the discharge from its premises was unrelated to the undertaking. The prosecution argued that the narrowness of that defence counted against a broader 'defence' of honest and reasonable mistake of fact. The Court disagreed, saying that s 62C was not a defence to s 41 and applied to a restricted class of alleged polluters. The prosecution also claimed that the Act set up a hierarchy of offences, with s 59E requiring proof of intention, recklessness or negligence and providing for far harsher penalties. The Court disagreed with the inference, pointing out that prescribing a specific mental element was unsurprising given the maximum penalty of up to seven years' gaol.

A previous authority on a comparable provision in the Act in question[112] ought not be followed.[113] The prosecution had argued that, as that authority had found that the relevant offence was one of absolute liability, and as amendments to s 41 had subsequently occurred without expressly making the offence one of strict liability, Parliament had not intended to change the nature of the offence. The Court disagreed for several reasons, including that the words of the comparable provision at the time of the earlier authority were not re-enacted or repeated in the amending legislation.[114]

Authorities on the interpretation of a comparable statute of New South Wales (*Clean Waters Act 1970*) had held for strict liability.

Lastly, in a point that anticipates the next case example, the Court contrasted the circumstances the subject of the present offence with circumstances that are typically subject to absolute liability:

> As the present case demonstrates, pollution events will often result from a complex set of circumstances playing out over a period of time. Consideration of what acts will cause or prevent pollution may be equally complex. By contrast, absolute liability offences usually involve circumstances in which the acts necessary to ensure compliance with the provision in order to avoid conviction are more obvious and straightforward.[115]

Example 42.3 *Stanojlovic v DPP*[116] (absolute liability)

The applicant (defendant), who was employed as a tow-truck driver, arrived at the scene of a multiple vehicle collision. At the time he held a probationary driver's licence. At the time of his

110 [2019] VSC 871, [45] (Keogh J).

111 Section 1K. This appears to be a general principle intended to aid interpretation.

112 *Allen v United Carpet Mills Pty Ltd* [1989] VR 323 considered s 39(1) of the *Environment Protection Act 1970* (Vic).

113 [2019] VSC 871, [55] (Keogh J).

114 Ibid [48]. For discussion of the re-enactment presumption see **[21.8]**.

115 Ibid [49].

116 (2018) 273 A Crim R 215.

arrival, his tow truck did not have a P plate displayed facing out from the front of the vehicle. He was issued with an infringement notice for breaching reg 55(1) of the *Road Safety (Drivers) Regulations 2009* (Vic):

> **Probationary driver must display P plates**
>
> (1) A person who holds a probationary driver licence … must not drive a motor vehicle … on a highway unless
>
> …
>
> (b) … an appropriate P plate is displayed facing out from the front of the vehicle …
>
> Penalty: 3 penalty units.

The applicant contested the infringement notice in the Magistrates' Court but was convicted. The applicant appealed to the County Court. The Court accepted that the offence created by reg 55(1) did not exclude the '*Proudman v Dayman* defence'. Further, the Court found that the applicant had an honestly and reasonably held belief that a P plate was affixed to the front of his vehicle. The Court allowed the appeal and ordered the charge be dismissed.

The Director of Public Prosecutions sought judicial review of the County Court's order. A judge of the Trial Division of the Supreme Court held that absolute liability applied to the element of the offence that involved not displaying a P plate facing out from the front or rear of the vehicle.

On appeal to the Court of Appeal, that Court agreed with the decision and reasons of the judge of the Trial Division. Several indications from the offence and its statutory context pointed to absolute liability. The words of the offence were drawn upon. '[T]he mandatory language of the regulation'[117] was a factor, there being no particular words that incorporated a mental element such as 'intentionally', 'knowingly' or 'without reasonable excuse'.[118]

The subject matter of the offence was drawn upon. In this case it was found that the character of the offence was more regulatory than criminal.[119] In support it observed that 'the potential penalties for the offence were low (with no risk of imprisonment) and no significant moral stigma attached to the offence'.[120]

Absolute liability would give added efficacy to the statutory purpose. In this regime, it found that 'the important public safety purpose of the regulation … is directed to risky driving behaviour by young and/or inexperienced drivers by providing police and other road users with a means of easily identifying probationary drivers'.[121] Imposition of absolute liability would aid compliance because 'compliance … is likely to be more effective if a charge for failure to display the applicable P plate brooks no argument about the honesty and reasonableness of the belief of the driver'.[122]

The surrounding legislative provisions were called in aid. Reading the *Road Safety Act 1986* (Vic) and the Regulations as a whole it held that 'the interests of the individual need to be subjugated to the welfare of the public as a whole if the graduated licensing scheme is to operate effectively'.[123]

117 Ibid 224 [46].

118 Ibid 221 [28].

119 Ibid 224 [46]

120 Ibid 222 [32].

121 Ibid 224 [46].

122 Ibid 225 [49].

123 Ibid 222 [31], 224 [46].

Finally, the consequences upon potential accused (drivers) were taken into account. Agreeing with the Court below, the Court of Appeal found that imposition of absolute liability would not be 'overly onerous in circumstances where the commission of the offence is "largely avoidable by a conscientious probationary driver"'.[124]

Content of the common law principle

The content of 'full mens rea' is regulated by prima facie requirements [42.6]

If an offence is found by implication to consist of some positive state of mind, the state of mind may be ascertained to be that '[the accused] knew that all the facts constituting the ingredients necessary to make the act criminal were involved in what he was doing'.[125]

In *He Kaw Teh* Brennan J essayed a detailed statement of the 'prima facie' requirements,[126] making a distinction between an act, the circumstances in which a relevant act is done or omission is made, and results:

> [V]oluntariness and intent are the mental states ordinarily applicable to *an act* involved in an offence, [while] knowledge or the absence of an honest and reasonable but mistaken belief is the mental state ordinarily applicable to *the circumstances* in which a relevant act is done or omission is made and, where a mental state is applicable to *results*, it may be either foresight of the possibility of their occurrence (if recklessness is an element) or knowledge of the probability (or likelihood) of their occurrence or an intention to cause them (if a specific intent is an element).[127]

These are subject to actual expressions of legislative intention.[128]

The case of *He Kaw Teh* affords a simple illustration of ascertaining the content of mens rea. The offence in question was s 233B(1)(b) of the *Customs Act 1901* (Cth), which read as follows:

> (1) Any person who –
>
> ...
>
> (b) imports, or attempts to import, into Australia any prohibited imports to which this section applies or exports, or attempts to export, from Australia any prohibited exports to which this section applies;

The maximum penalty for the offence was life imprisonment. Brennan J noted that it was appropriate first to 'identify the acts respectively involved in the offences defined in paras (b) and (c) and to ascertain the form of mens rea applicable to them and to the accompanying circumstances (if any) which are prescribed by those paragraphs'.[129] He proceeded to reason as follows:

> Importing simpliciter is not an act nor is it defined to be a prohibited act in para (b). Importing narcotic goods is an act; it is the act referred to in para (b). The character of the act involved in the offence depends on the nature of the object imported. The paragraph

124 Ibid 222 [31]. See also 224 [46].

125 *He Kaw Teh v The Queen* (1985) 157 CLR 523, 531 (Gibbs CJ, Mason J agreeing at 546), 572 (Brennan J), quoting with approval *R v Turnbull* (1943) 44 SR (NSW) 108, 109 (Jordan CJ).

126 Ibid 572, 575, 578.

127 Ibid 568 (Brennan J) (emphases added).

128 Ibid 594 (Dawson J).

129 Ibid 584.

> thus impliedly requires an intent to do the prohibited act – importing narcotic goods – and thus requires knowledge of the nature of the object imported.

Dawson J similarly reasoned from the 'forbidden act', holding:

> [T]he prosecution is required to prove that the accused intended to do the forbidden act which, in the case of s 233B(1)(b), is importing narcotic goods into Australia. Thus the intent must go not only to the act of importation but also to the nature and quality of the goods imported.[130]

Gibbs CJ also agreed on the specific state of mind, holding that 'the prosecution on a charge under [para (b)] bears the onus of proving that the accused knew that he was importing a narcotic substance'.[131]

Another illustration is *R v Lagan,* the facts and legislation for which were set out above (**Example 42.1**). In that case the Court suggested that 'the essence of the offence is the administration of a substance *known by the offender to be likely to endanger life or, at least, to cause grievous bodily harm*'.[132] It may be observed that this holding applies the prima facie principle set out in *He Kaw Teh* pertaining to circumstances in which a relevant act is done – namely, that, in relation to an ingredient necessary to make an act criminal, there be knowledge of the facts constituting the ingredient. The required intent not being present, the Court upheld the submission that the Crown had failed to make out a prima facie case and it directed an acquittal on the charge under s 27(3)(b) of the *Crimes Act 1900* (ACT).

Position under the Criminal Codes

[42.7] **The Criminal Codes exclude the common law doctrine of mens rea but comparable general provisions in the nature of mens rea do not entirely remove the need for statutory interpretation**[133]

The code jurisdictions of Australia in respect of criminal law are the Commonwealth,[134] Queensland,[135] Tasmania,[136] Western Australia,[137] the Australian Capital Territory[138] and the Northern Territory.[139]

Speaking of the Tasmanian Code, Windeyer J said that it 'supplants' the common law doctrine of mens rea.[140] In other words, the Code is exhaustive in terms of mental elements in the nature

130 Ibid 596.

131 Ibid 537.

132 (2001) 127 A Crim R 262, 271 [84] (Higgins J), quoting from an earlier decision of the Court: *R v Hughes* [2000] ACTSC 112, [7] (emphasis added).

133 For background to the Codes and a general evaluation of them, see Simon Bronitt and Bernadette McSherry, *Principles of Criminal Law* (Lawbook Co, 4th ed, 2017) ch 2.

134 *Criminal Code Act 1995* (Cth).

135 *Criminal Code Act 1899* (Qld).

136 *Criminal Code Act 1924* (Tas). But the Tasmanian 'Code' can be seen as a hybrid code/common law jurisdiction, for it expressly saves common law justifications, excuses and defences: *Criminal Code Act 1924* (Tas) s 8.

137 *Criminal Code Act Compilation Act 1913* (WA).

138 *Criminal Code 2002* (ACT).

139 *Criminal Code Act 1983* (NT).

140 *Vallance v The Queen* (1961) 108 CLR 56, 78 (Windeyer J) (speaking of the *Criminal Code* established by the *Criminal Code Act 1924* (Tas)).

of mens rea.[141] This means that '[a]ny mental element as a positive ingredient of a crime must be found within the *Code* itself'.[142] Similar rulings as to mental elements in code provisions have been made about the codes of the Commonwealth,[143] Queensland,[144] Western Australia[145] and the Northern Territory.[146]

But the comprehensive content of the mental ingredients is not supplied in every case by the Code expressly stating mental ingredients in each of the offences themselves (though this is done for some offences). It is supplied by general rules set out separately in the Code. These rules are 'intended to have general application and to state fundamental principles of criminal responsibility'.[147] Thus, the terms of particular offences have to be read with the separate rules of general application. Therefore, the Codes too rely on statutory interpretation to some extent.

The exclusive coverage of the rules of general application varies. The Commonwealth[148] and Western Australian[149] Codes are comprehensive. The ACT Code is planned to be comprehensive.[150] The Queensland Code applies to indictable offences.[151] The Tasmanian Code does not apply to summary offences.[152] The Northern Territory Code applies only to certain offences.[153]

The Codes generally declare that they are exclusive to all or certain classes of offence.[154]

The content of the rules of general application varies from Code to Code. They include a positive requirement of intention,[155] an exclusion for unintended consequences,[156] and various rules allowing a reasonable mistake of fact as a ground of exculpation.[157]

---

141 *R v Martin* [1963] Tas SR 103, 114 (Burbury CJ) (speaking of the Tasmanian *Criminal Code).*

142 Ibid.

143 *DPP (Cth) Reference No 1 of 2008* (2008) 21 VR 111, 115 [21] (the Court); *Mei Ying Su v Australian Fisheries Management Authority (No 2)* (2008) 251 ALR 135, 141 [17] (Reeves J) (affirmed by *Australian Fisheries Management Authority v Su* (2009) 176 FCR 95).

144 *Widgee Shire Council v Bonney* (1907) 4 CLR 977, 981 (Griffith CJ); *R v Barlow* (1997) 188 CLR 1, 18 (McHugh J).

145 *Brennan v The King* (1936) 55 CLR 253, 263 (Dixon and Evatt JJ); *Binetti v Feasey* (2015) 249 A Crim R 305, 316 [48] (Corboy J).

146 *Pregelj v Manison* (1987) 31 A Crim R 383, 393 (Nader J, Kearney J agreeing generally at 399).

147 *Vallance v The Queen* (1961) 108 CLR 56, 78 (Windeyer J) (speaking of the Tasmanian Code).

148 *Criminal Code Act 1995* (Cth) sch s 2.2.

149 *Criminal Code Act Compilation Act 1913* (WA) app B s 4.

150 *Criminal Code 2002* (ACT) s 7 (but delayed application: s 8).

151 *Criminal Code Act 1899* (Qld) sch 1 s 5; *R v Scarth* [1945] St R Qd 38, 48 (Philp J).

152 *Criminal Code Act 1924* (Tas) s 4(3).

153 *Criminal Code Act 1983* (NT) sch 1 s 43AA.

154 *Criminal Code Act 1995* (Cth), sch ss 1.1, 2.1; *Criminal Code 2002* (ACT) s 6 (but application is at the time of writing delayed and is subject to a declaration by the Minister: ss 8, 10(1); *Criminal Code Act 1899* (Qld) sch 1 s 5; *Criminal Code Act 1924* (Tas) s 4(1) (prosecutions on indictment or information); *Criminal Code Act Compilation Act 1913* (WA) app B s 4. Cf the Northern Territory Act, which simply establishes a 'Code': *Criminal Code Act 1983* (NT) s 5.

155 *Criminal Code Act 1995* (Cth) sch s 5.6 (default fault element); *Criminal Code Act 1924* (Tas) sch 1 s 13(1); *Criminal Code 2002* (ACT) s 22; *Criminal Code Act 1983* (NT) sch 1 s 43AM.

156 *Criminal Code Act 1899* (Qld) sch 1 s 23(1)(b)(i).

157 *Criminal Code Act 1995* (Cth) sch ss 6.1, 9.2; *Criminal Code Act 1899* (Qld) sch 1 s 24; *Criminal Code Act 1924* (Tas) sch 1 s 14; *Criminal Code Act Compilation Act 1913* (WA) app B sch s 24; *Criminal Code 2002* (ACT) ss 23, 36; *Criminal Code Act 1983* (NT) sch 1 ss 43AN, 43AX. Although Dixon J in *Thomas v The King* (1937) 59 CLR 279 was of the opinion that the Tasmanian, Queensland and Western Australian provisions were in the same

The way in which the rules of general application apply to a particular offence varies in the extent to which statutory interpretation is required to determine if the general rule applies. The Codes of the Commonwealth, the Australian Capital Territory and the Northern Territory rely least on statutory interpretation in this regard. The Commonwealth,[158] ACT[159] and Northern Territory[160] Codes provide definitions of an 'offence of strict liability' and 'an offence of absolute liability'. (These definitions are consonant with the common law.) If a law creating a particular offence expressly provides that the offence is an offence of strict liability or an offence of absolute liability, the relevant definition is automatically attracted. If no such provision is made, the default general rule as to the 'fault element' (state of mind) applies.[161] Therefore, under these Codes the determination of whether an offence has a fault element, a defence of reasonable mistake of fact, or is an offence is one of absolute liability is a matter of simply applying the general rules in the Codes rather than employing the common law technique of applying a presumption and looking for any contrary intention from the provision and its context.[162]

In contrast, the Queensland, Western Australian and Tasmanian Codes rely on statutory interpretation to determine if the statutory equivalent of the *Proudman v Dayman* 'defence' is available. The Queensland[163] and Western Australian[164] Codes include a general rule providing for the prima facie availability of mistake of fact as a ground of exculpation. But that prima facie availability is subject to interpretation, for the Codes state that '[t]he operation of this [prima facie] rule may be excluded by the express or implied provisions of the law relating to the subject'.[165] The Tasmanian Code is even more reliant on statutory interpretation. It does not impose a prima facie rule in this regard; rather, it provides that whether criminal responsibility is entailed by an act or omission done or made under a mistake of fact is 'a question of law, to be determined on the construction of the statute constituting the offence'.[166]

terms and restated the common law 'with complete accuracy' (at 305–6), Kiefel CJ and Keane JJ disagreed in *Bell v Tasmania* (2021) 395 ALR 589, 594–6 [16]–[23]. They pointed out, first, that the terms of the Tasmanian provision were different to the Queensland provision and, second, that Queensland courts had (rightly) consistently held that the Queensland provision had a different operation: at 595 [20]. What their Honours had to say about the Queensland provision would apply to the Western Australian provision as it is in the same terms.

158 *Criminal Code Act 1995* (Cth) sch s 6.1 (strict liability), s 6.2 (absolute liability).

159 *Criminal Code 2002* (ACT) s 23 (strict liability), s 24 (absolute liability).

160 *Criminal Code Act 1983* (NT) sch 1 s 43AN (strict liability), s 43AO (absolute liability).

161 *Criminal Code Act 1995* (Cth) sch s 5.6; *Criminal Code 2002* (ACT) s 22; *Criminal Code Act 1983* (NT) sch 1 s 43AM. In these Codes the default rule varies according to whether an element of an offence consists of, on the one hand, 'conduct' or, on the other hand, 'a circumstance or a result'. For conduct, the fault (mental) element is intention; for a circumstance or a result, the element is recklessness. Each of these mental elements is defined in turn in the Codes. Interpretation may be necessary to ascertain what is an element for this purpose and whether the element consists of conduct, circumstance or a result. See, eg, *PJ v The Queen* (2012) 36 VR 402.

162 *Mei Ying Su v Australian Fisheries Management Authority (No 2)* (2008) 251 ALR 135, 141 [17] (Reeves J) (affirmed by *Australian Fisheries Management Authority v Su* (2009) 176 FCR 95).

163 *Criminal Code Act 1899* (Qld) sch 1 s 24.

164 *Criminal Code Act Compilation Act 1913* (WA) app B sch s 24.

165 *Criminal Code Act 1899* (Qld) sch 1 s 24(2); *Criminal Code Act Compilation Act 1913* (WA) app B sch s 24.

166 *Criminal Code Act 1924* (Tas) sch 1 s 14. See also *Criminal Code Act 1924* (Tas) s 8 (saving of common law justifications).

Even with the apparently more restricted Commonwealth Code and its equivalents in the territories, interpretative disputes can arise in the application of the default rule.[167] Such disputes are resolved not by reading an element of the offence in isolation but 'in the context of the provision, and the Act, as a whole'.[168]

Finally, most of the code jurisdictions restate the common law rule that ignorance of the law is no excuse.[169]

167 See, eg, *PJ v The Queen* (2012) 36 VR 402.

168 Ibid 412 [36] (the Court). In this regard the Court quoted the leading authority on the ordinary principles of statutory interpretation, *Project Blue Sky Inc v Australian Broadcasting Authority* (1998) 194 CLR 355, 381 [69].

169 *Criminal Code Act 1995* (Cth) sch ss 9.3, 9.4; *Criminal Code Act 1899* (Qld) sch 1 s 22; *Criminal Code Act 1924* (Tas) sch 1 s 12; *Criminal Code Act Compilation Act 1913* (WA) app B sch s 22; *Criminal Code Act 1983* (NT) sch 1 s 43AY.

43 DELEGATED LEGISLATION

Overview

[43.1] Most Acts include a section empowering the making of other instruments under the Act. Such instruments, when of a legislative character, are known as delegated legislation. A wide variety of terms is used across Australian jurisdictions to describe delegated legislation.

Generally, the ordinary principles of statutory interpretation, both statutory and common law, apply to delegated legislation. However, courts may take into consideration some different contextual factors, and there are some distinct Interpretation Act provisions applicable to delegated legislation. Terms used in delegated legislation have the same meaning as in the enabling Act. Delegated legislation may be given a retrospective operation through a backdated commencement or by altering accrued rights or liabilities. However, there is a common law presumption against retrospective operation and statutory provisions exist to limit retrospective operation.

There are several grounds on which delegated legislation may, in full or in part, be held to be invalid. The process followed by courts in considering a validity issue involves determining the meaning of the enabling Act, then that of the delegated legislation and finally considering whether, so construed, the delegated legislation is empowered by the enabling Act, as so construed. An invalid portion may be severed by relying upon, in some jurisdictions, statutory severance provisions and, in others, common law.

The legal effect of not making delegated legislation as contemplated by the enabling Act depends on the nature, purpose and language of the authorising provision and on the context.

What is delegated legislation?

[43.2] **Delegated legislation covers a broad spectrum of instruments**

The term 'delegated legislation' is used in this chapter to refer to any instrument of a legislative character made by an entity under a power delegated to the entity by an Act or an instrument made under an Act.[1] Such instruments differ from instruments of an administrative character made in the execution of legislation. In *Commonwealth v Grunseit*[2] Latham CJ stated:

1 Delegated legislation is sometimes referred to as subordinate legislation or subsidiary legislation. For a discussion of the reasons why Parliament makes use of delegated legislation, see Dennis Pearce and Stephen Argument, *Delegated Legislation in Australia* (LexisNexis Butterworths, 5th ed, 2017) [1.9].

2 (1943) 67 CLR 58.

> The general distinction between legislation and the execution of legislation is that legislation determines the content of a law as a rule of conduct or a declaration as to power, right or duty, whereas executive authority applies the law in particular cases.[3]

Delegated legislation has a wide variety of names across Australia. Names commonly found are regulation, order, rule, by-law, local law, scheme, code and notice.

The Commonwealth has adopted the term 'legislative instrument' as its key descriptor for Commonwealth delegated legislation.[4] However, the Commonwealth includes as 'legislative instruments' instruments that are not of a legislative character.[5] The Commonwealth maintains a Federal Register of Legislation, including legislative instruments.[6] A legislative instrument is not enforceable by or against any person (including the Commonwealth) unless the instrument is registered as a legislative instrument.[7] Legislative instruments must be tabled in Parliament and, with some limited exceptions,[8] may be disallowed by Parliament.[9] They are also automatically repealed after a fixed period of time, generally 10 years.[10]

Other Australian jurisdictions continue to use traditional names for delegated legislation such as regulation, rule and by-law. New South Wales, Queensland and Victoria group together the more important items of delegated legislation (including any made, or required to be approved, by the Governor) into a class of instrument referred to as statutory rules.[11] They must be published on an official website or in a government gazette[12] and laid (or notice of them laid) before Parliament.[13] Statutory rules may be disallowed by Parliament[14] and expire after a specified period.[15]

3 Ibid 82. Latham CJ's classification has been described as the 'hallmark of the exercise of legislative power': see *Plaintiff S157/2002 v Commonwealth* (2003) 211 CLR 476, 512–3 [102] (Gaudron, McHugh, Gummow, Kirby & Hayne JJ); *Plaintiff M79/2012 v Minister for Immigration and Citizenship* (2013) 252 CLR 336, 367 [88] (Hayne J).

4 There are also 'notifiable instruments', which include commencement instruments. These are not subject to parliamentary scrutiny: see *Legislation Act 2003* (Cth) pt 2.

5 Ibid s 9.

6 Ibid ch 2 pt 1.

7 Ibid s 15K(1).

8 Ibid s 44.

9 Ibid ch 3 pt 2.

10 Ibid s 50.

11 *Interpretation Act 1987* (NSW) s 21(1); *Statutory Instruments Act 1992* (Qld) s 8; *Subordinate Legislation Act 1994* (Vic) s 3(1).

12 *Interpretation Act 1987* (NSW) s 39; *Statutory Instruments Act 1992* (Qld) s 47; *Subordinate Legislation Act 1994* (Vic) s 17.

13 *Interpretation Act 1987* (NSW) s 40; *Statutory Instruments Act 1992* (Qld) s 49; *Subordinate Legislation Act 1994* (Vic) s 15.

14 *Interpretation Act 1987* (NSW) s 41; *Statutory Instruments Act 1992* (Qld) s 50; *Subordinate Legislation Act 1994* (Vic) s 23.

15 *Subordinate Legislation Act 1989* (NSW) s 10; *Statutory Instruments Act 1992* (Qld) s 54; *Subordinate Legislation Act 1994* (Vic) s 5.

Tasmania[16] applies a similar regime to regulations, rules and by-laws. Western Australia[17] does too with respect to regulations, rules, local laws and by-laws.[18]

South Australia recently adopted a new standardised terminology of 'legislative instrument'. That term is defined by the *Legislation Interpretation Act 2021* (SA) s 4 broadly to include regulations, rules, by-laws, proclamations, other instruments of a legislative character and other instruments of a kind prescribed by regulation.[19]

The Australian Capital Territory, like the Commonwealth, maintains a register of Acts, statutory instruments and other instruments.[20] Statutory instruments include regulations, rules and commencement notices.[21] They must be presented to the Legislative Assembly and may be disallowed or amended by the Assembly.[22]

In the Northern Territory the term 'subordinate legislation' is used to cover regulations, rules, by-laws and other instruments to which s 63 or 63A of the *Interpretation Act 1978* (NT) applies. Under those sections, subordinate legislation must be published (on the legislation website in the case of regulations), notified in the Gazette and tabled in the Legislative Assembly. The Legislative Assembly may disallow the whole, or specified portions, of the subordinate legislation.[23]

Ordinary interpretation principles generally apply

[43.3] **The ordinary principles of statutory interpretation generally apply to delegated legislation but there are some different contextual factors, and some specific statutory provisions, to consider**

The same general common law principles applicable to the interpretation of Acts apply to the interpretation of delegated legislation.[24] In *ADCO Constructions Pty Ltd v Goudappel*[25] French CJ, Crennan, Kiefel and Keane JJ stated:

> The appropriate inquiry in the construction of delegated legislation is directed to the text, context and purpose of the regulation, the discernment of relevant constructional

16 The *Subordinate Legislation Act 1992* (Tas) covers regulations, rules and by-laws made, or required to be approved, affirmed or consented to, by the Governor and other instruments of a legislative character to which the Act is applied by notice of the Treasurer. The requirement to lay regulations, rules and by-laws before Parliament is contained in the *Acts Interpretation Act 1931* (Tas) s 47.

17 *Interpretation Act 1984* (WA) pt VI. See also Department of Treasury, *Better Regulation Program: Information Paper for Agencies* (Western Australian Government, 2020).

18 In Western Australia the term 'subsidiary legislation' is defined by the *Interpretation Act 1984* (WA) s 5 to cover all instruments made under a written law that have legislative effect. However, only regulations, rules, local laws and by-laws are required to be tabled in Parliament and subject to disallowance. See *Interpretation Act 1984* (WA) s 42.

19 *Legislative Instruments Act 1978* (SA). See also South Australian Department of the Premier and Cabinet and Department of Treasury and Finance, *Better Regulation Handbook: How to Design and Review Regulation, and Prepare a Regulatory Impact Statement* (Government of South Australia, 2011).

20 *Legislation Act 2001* (ACT) s 18.

21 Ibid s 13.

22 See, eg, ibid ch 7.

23 *Interpretation Act 1978* (NT) s 63C.

24 *Collector of Customs v Agfa-Gevaert Ltd* (1996) 186 CLR 389, 398 (the Court); *Pilbara Infrastructure Pty Ltd v Brockman Iron Pty Ltd* [2016] WASCA 36, [131] (Buss JA); *City of Swan v West Australian Shalom Group Inc* [2017] WASC 217, [36] (Banks-Smith J).

25 (2014) 254 CLR 1.

> choices, if they exist, and the determination of the construction that, according to established rules of interpretation, best serves the statutory purpose.[26]

Similarly, the same statutory principles applicable to the interpretation of Acts generally apply also to the interpretation of delegated legislation.[27] Queensland,[28] Victoria[29] and the Australian Capital Territory[30] have also each enacted a provision requiring that delegated legislation, just like Acts, is to be interpreted in a way that is compatible with the human rights recognised in their human rights legislation.[31]

In *Master Education Services Pty Ltd v Ketchell*[32] the High Court stated that regulations must be placed in their statutory context, which 'includes the legislation under which they are enacted and with which they are required to be consistent'.[33] This is in contradistinction to the position applicable to the construction of Acts where generally delegated legislation made under an Act is not admissible to construe the Act.[34]

Other contextual aspects relevant to the construction of delegated legislation relate to its drafting and the nature of the audience to which it is directed.

Much delegated legislation is drafted by persons unskilled in drafting but knowledgeable in the field to which the legislation relates. Cognisance is taken of the fact that as a result the quality of drafting tends to be lower, meriting a more relaxed approach to construction.[35] As stated by Leeming JA in *4Nature Inc v Centennial Springvale Pty Ltd*:[36] 'It is a general proposition that if legal language has been used less than carefully, it may be appropriate to give rather less weight to precise textual considerations.'[37]

---

26 Ibid 14–15.

27 *Legislation Act 2003* (Cth) s 13(1)(a); *Interpretation Act 1987* (NSW) s 5; *Statutory Instruments Act 1992* (Qld) pt 4 div 1 (provisions of *Acts Interpretation Act 1954* (Qld) that apply to statutory instruments); *Statutory Instruments Act 1992* (Qld) pt 4 div 2 (provisions of *Acts Interpretation Act 1954* (Qld) that do not apply to statutory instruments); *Legislation Interpretation Act 2021* (SA) s 3; *Acts Interpretation Act 1931* (Tas) s 4; *Interpretation of Legislation Act 1984* (Vic) s 4; *Interpretation Act 1984* (WA) s 3; *Legislation Act 2001* (ACT) s 4; *Interpretation Act 1978* (NT) s 4. See *Comcare v Lilley* (2013) 216 FCR 214, 230 [66] (the Court). See also chapter 25 of this work.

28 *Human Rights Act 2019* (Qld) s 48.

29 *Charter of Human Rights and Responsibilities Act 2006* (Vic) s 32.

30 *Human Rights Act 2004* (ACT) s 30.

31 See **[26.2]**.

32 (2008) 236 CLR 101.

33 Ibid 109–10 [19]. See also *One.Tel Ltd v Australian Communications Authority* (2001) 110 FCR 125, 141 [64] (Hill J).

34 *Hunter Resources Ltd v Melville* (1988) 164 CLR 234, 244 (Mason CJ and Gaudron J), cited by French CJ in *Plaintiff M47/2012 v Director-General of Security* (2012) 251 CLR 1, 42 [56]. See also **[33.6]** of this work.

35 *Tovir Investments Pty Ltd v Waverley Council* [2014] NSWCA 379, [54]–[55] (Leeming JA); *Echunga Football Club Inc v Hills Football League Inc* (2014) 121 SASR 449, 454–5 [18] (Stanley J); *Day v Harness Racing New South Wales* (2014) 88 NSWLR 594, 610–11 [79]–[84] (Leeming JA with whom McColl agreed at [1] and MacFarlan JJA agreed at [2]); *Channel Seven Brisbane Pty Ltd v Australian Communications and Media Authority* (2014) 227 FCR 162 [53] (Mortimer J); *City of Swan v West Australian Shalom Group Inc* [2017] WASC 217, [37] (Banks-Smith J).

36 (2017) 95 NSWLR 361.

37 Ibid 387 [107]. However, in that case, as the language in the instrument required to be interpreted was based directly on language used in the enabling Act, it could not be said to be drafted less carefully than primary legislation: at 372–3 [45] (Basten JA, Beazley P agreeing at 363 [1], Leeming JA agreeing at 387 [108]).

The nature of the likely audience can influence a court to allow delegated legislation to 'be read with a little latitude'[38] having regard to 'the need to keep in mind that regulations are often addressed to practical people skilled in a particular trade and hence often exhibit minor inconsistencies which ought to lead to their interpretation in light of practical considerations'.[39] This leads to courts taking a practical approach to the construction of delegated legislation.[40]

Terms have same meaning as in enabling Act

[43.4] Terms used have the same meaning as in the enabling Act

At the Commonwealth level[41] and in Queensland,[42] South Australia,[43] Victoria[44] and the Australian Capital Territory,[45] terms used in delegated legislation have the same meaning as in the enabling Act *as in force from time to time*. Thus, if the meaning in the enabling Act changes after the delegated legislation is made, the changed meaning flows through to the delegated legislation. This is in line with the position arrived at unanimously by the High Court in *Birch v Allen*.[46] Getting to this outcome in New South Wales,[47] Tasmania,[48] Western Australia[49] and the Northern Territory[50] depends on reading references to 'the Act' in the relevant provision as referring to the Act as in force from time to time.[51]

---

38 *Minister for Immigration and Citizenship v Anochie* (2012) 209 FCR 497, 505 [26] (Perram J). In that case, Perram J held that reading 'with a little latitude' was inapplicable to a direction given by the Minister under the *Migration Act 1958* (Cth) on the basis that the intended readership of the direction were ministerial delegates making complex administrative decisions as well as tribunals and courts reviewing such decisions.

39 Ibid 504 [25].

40 See *Langton v Independent Commission Against Corruption* (2000) 49 NSWLR 164, 167 [12] (Stein and Giles JJA); *Australian Tea Tree Oil Research Institute v Industry Research and Development Board* (2002) 124 FCR 316, 328–9 [37]–[38] (Stone J); *Marina Bay Developments Pty Ltd v Pittwater Council* [2007] NSWLEC 41, [19]–[20] (Lloyd J); *Telstra Corporation Ltd v Australian Competition and Consumer Commission* (2008) 176 FCR 153, 194 [164] (Rares J); *Comcare v Lilley* (2013) 216 FCR 214, 230 [67] (the Court).

41 *Legislation Act 2003* (Cth) s 13(1)(b).

42 *Statutory Instruments Act 1992* (Qld) s 37.

43 *Legislation Interpretation Act 2021* (SA) s 12.

44 *Interpretation of Legislation Act 1984* (Vic) s 23.

45 *Legislation Act 2001* (ACT) s 148.

46 (1942) 65 CLR 621. At the time of this decision the *Acts Interpretation Act 1901* (Cth) s 46 provided that expressions in regulations have the same meaning as in the enabling Act but did not contain the words 'as in force from time to time'. In *Kostrzewa v Southern Electric Authority of Queensland* (1969) 120 CLR 653, without referring to *Birch v Allen*, Barwick CJ at 656 and Windeyer J at 658 expressed the view that it was the definition of a term in the parent Act as at the time a regulation was made that applied, not that definition as subsequently amended.

47 *Interpretation Act 1987* (NSW) s 11.

48 *Acts Interpretation Act 1931* (Tas) s 19.

49 *Interpretation Act 1984* (WA) s 44(1).

50 *Interpretation Act 1978* (NT) s 20(1). Section 23A of that Act allows the spelling in an item of delegated legislation of a word defined in the enabling Act to be updated to current practice without affecting its meaning.

51 *Interpretation Act 1987* (NSW) s 68(1) provides that in any Act a reference to some other Act extends to the other Act as in force for the time being. The *Acts Interpretation Act 1931* (Tas) s 13(5) provides that a reference in an Act to an Act includes a reference to all subsequent enactments that amend, or are passed in substitution for, the Act referred to. The *Interpretation Act 1984* (WA) s 16(1) provides that a reference in a written law (which includes Acts) to a written law is a reference to that written law as amended. The

These useful provisions avoid the need to include definitions in delegated legislation of terms defined in the enabling Act. However, all these various provisions are displaced if a contrary intention appears.[52]

Retrospective operation

Whether delegated legislation can have a retrospective operation depends on what is provided by the enabling Act, but it is presumed not to have such an operation [43.5]

The common law presumption against the retrospective operation of legislation is dealt with in chapter 39. This presumption also applies to delegated legislation.[53] It is displaced if the intention to do so sufficiently appears in the enabling Act.[54]

The capacity to provide for retrospective operation by altering accrued rights or liabilities is also affected by Interpretation Act provisions in each jurisdiction.[55] Like all provisions in such Acts, they are subject to exclusion or modification by individual Acts.[56]

An enabling Act may delegate power to an entity to make legislation that regulates matters retrospectively.[57] The validity of such delegated legislation depends on the meaning of the enabling Act – whether properly construed that Act empowers giving delegated legislation made under it a retrospective operation.[58]

There are two ways in which delegated legislation may have retrospective operation.[59] One is through backdating the commencement of its legal operation so that it is taken to have had legal

---

Interpretation Act 1978 (NT) s 50(1) provides that a reference in an Act to other legislation is a reference to the other legislation as amended from time to time.

52 *Interpretation Act 1987* (NSW) s 5(2); *Statutory Instruments Act 1992* (Qld) s 4; *Acts Interpretation Act 1931* (Tas) s 4; *Interpretation of Legislation Act 1984* (Vic) s 23; *Interpretation Act 1984* (WA) s 3(1); *Legislation Act 2001* (ACT) s 6(3), (6); *Interpretation Act 1978* (NT) s 3(3). In those provisions it is expressly made clear that the contrary intention may appear in the delegated legislation. While the *Legislation Act 2003* (Cth) s 13(1) states 'unless the contrary intention appears' without stating where that contrary intention may be found, nothing in that section excludes a contrary intention being found in the delegated legislation. The same situation applies under the *Legislation Interpretation Act 2021* (SA) s 12. That section, like all provisions of that Act, is 'subject to a contrary intention'. See s 3(3) of that Act.

A similar approach was taken at common law. In *Blashill v Chambers* (1884) 14 QBD 479 Grove J stated: 'I do not say that there may not be words in by-laws which are so obviously used in a different sense to the same words in the Act that the Court may properly, reading them with the context, put a different construction upon them; but prima facie I should say that the proper mode of construction is to apply the same interpretation to terms used in a by-law which is applied to the same terms in the Act under the powers of which the by-law is framed' (at 485–6). For all these provisions, a contrary intention may, of course, also appear in the enabling Act.

53 *ADCO Constructions Pty Ltd v Goudappel* (2014) 254 CLR 1, 21 [51] (Gageler J).

54 Ibid 22 [52] (Gageler J). In that case the accrued right of a worker to lump sum compensation was held to be extinguished by a regulation.

55 *Acts Interpretation Act 1901* (Cth) s 7; *Legislation Act 2003* (Cth) s 13(1)(a); *Interpretation Act 1987* (NSW) s 30; *Acts Interpretation Act 1954* (Qld) s 20; *Statutory Instruments Act 1992* (Qld) s 14(1), sch 1; *Legislation Interpretation Act 2021* (SA) s 32; *Acts Interpretation Act 1931* (Tas) s 16; *Interpretation of Legislation Act 1984* (Vic) s 28(2); *Interpretation Act 1984* (WA) s 37; *Legislation Act 2001* (ACT) s 84; *Interpretation Act 1978* (NT) s 12.

56 See **[25.3]**.

57 *Broadcasting Co of Australia Pty Ltd v Commonwealth* (1935) 52 CLR 52, 67 (Starke J).

58 Ibid 60 (Gavan Duffy CJ, Evatt and McTiernan JJ).

59 See *ADCO Constructions Pty Ltd v Goudappel* (2014) 254 CLR 1, 20 (Gageler J).

operation at or from a date before it is made, registered or published. The second way is by altering rights or liabilities that existed immediately before that date without backdating the commencement of the legislation.

There are statutory provisions in New South Wales, Victoria and the Northern Territory that expressly prevent the commencement of delegated legislation being backdated without specific authorisation in the enabling Act.[60] South Australia expressly recognises that backdating may happen in the case of legislative instruments other than regulations if authorised by the enabling Act.[61] The Commonwealth[62] and Tasmania[63] allow backdating (provided existing rights or privileges of a non-government person are not prejudiced or liabilities or obligations are not imposed on such a person in respect of things already done or omitted to be done) unless the enabling Act provides otherwise. Queensland[64] and the Australian Capital Territory[65] provide for prospective commencement but allow the retrospective commencement of a provision of delegated legislation that does not adversely affect the rights of, or impose liabilities on, a non-government person. Western Australia[66] simply provides that delegated legislation commences on publication, or another day specified or provided for in the instrument. This could, therefore, be a day earlier than the day of publication.

A distinction needs to be drawn between an instrument affecting existing rights or imposing liabilities defined by reference to past events, such as one removing a right of appeal,[67] and an instrument changing practice and procedure, such as one altering the standard of proof required in a disciplinary proceeding.[68] The former kind of instrument is subject to a presumption against it having retrospective effect whereas the latter kind of instrument is unaffected by such a presumption.[69]

Grounds for invalidity

[43.6] A three-step process is applied in determining whether delegated legislation is invalid

It has been said that authorities are of little use in determining the validity of delegated legislation.[70] The outcome in any particular case depends on the meaning of the terms used in the enabling Act to empower the making of the delegated legislation.

Determining that meaning is the first step in a three-step process when the validity of delegated legislation is in issue. The second step is to determine the meaning of the delegated legislation and the final step is to consider whether the delegated legislation, so construed, is within the power given by the enabling provision.[71]

60 *Interpretation Act 1987* (NSW) s 39(1); *Subordinate Legislation Act 1994* (Vic) s 16(1); *Interpretation Act 1978* (NT) s 63B(3), (4).

61 *Legislative Instruments Act 1978* (SA) s 16D.

62 *Legislation Act 2003* (Cth) s 12(1A), (2), (4).

63 *Acts Interpretation Act 1931* (Tas) s 47(3).

64 *Statutory Instruments Act 1992* (Qld) ss 32, 34.

65 *Legislation Act 2001* (ACT) ss 75B, 76.

66 *Interpretation Act 1984* (WA) s 41(1).

67 See, eg, *Australian Coal & Shale Employees Federation v Aberfield Coal Mining Co Ltd* (1942) 66 CLR 161.

68 See, eg, *O'Connell v Palmer* (1994) 53 FCR 429.

69 *Rodway v The Queen* (1990) 169 CLR 515, 518–9 (the Court).

70 *Footscray Corporation v Maize Products Pty Ltd* (1943) 67 CLR 301, 308 (Rich J).

71 *South Australia v Tanner* (1989) 166 CLR 161, 173 [3] (Brennan J). See also *Evans v New South Wales* (2008) 168 FCR 576, 591 [60]; *Enernoc Australia Pty Ltd v Minister for Energy (WA) (No 2)* [2017] WASC 113, [17].

The next few sections look at the grounds on which, following those steps, delegated legislation may be held to be invalid.

Delegated legislation is invalid to the extent that it deals with a matter outside the scope of the enabling Act [43.7]

To be valid delegated legislation must be 'within the scope of what the Parliament intended when enacting the statute which empowers the subordinate authority to make certain laws'.[72] Scope defines the boundaries of the subject areas beyond which the delegated legislation must not stray. The legal and practical effect of the delegated legislation is relevant to determining whether it is within the scope of the empowering provision.[73] Invalidity results from dealing with a subject that is outside that scope.[74]

The terms in which authority is given to make delegated legislation, whether specific or general, are of crucial importance in determining scope. There are certain commonly used empowering provisions.

One commonly used expression is empowering the making of delegated legislation to prescribe such matters as are 'required or permitted' to be prescribed. This can only be relied on to make delegated legislation about a matter where there is a provision in the enabling Act providing for, or expressly permitting, that matter to be prescribed.[75] Delegated legislation made under such a power has 'to fall within a proper construction of the breadth allowed by the permission (or requirement) granted'.[76]

Another commonly used expression is empowering the making of delegated legislation that is 'necessary or convenient to be prescribed for giving effect to' the enabling Act. In *Morton v Union Steamship Co of New Zealand Ltd*[77] the High Court said the following of such a power:

> A power expressed in such terms to make regulations enables the Governor-General in Council to make regulations incidental to the administration of the Act. Regulations may be adopted for the more effective administration of the provisions actually contained in the Act, but not regulations which vary or depart from the positive provisions made by the Act or regulations which go outside the field of operation which the Act marks out for itself.[78]

In *Carbines v Powell*[79] the relevant head of power was to prescribe matters 'necessary or convenient to be prescribed for carrying out or giving effect to' the Act. Isaacs J stated:

> To 'carry out' the Act means to enforce its provisions. To 'give effect' to an Act is to enable its provisions to be effectively administered. There is little, if any, difference between the two expressions. They both connote that the Governor-General's regulations are to be

72 *Minister of Resources v Dover Fisheries Pty Ltd* (1993) 43 FCR 565, 577 [46] (Gummow J).

73 *Williams v Melbourne Corporation* (1933) 49 CLR 142, 155–6 (Dixon J); *A-G (SA) v Corporation of the City of Adelaide* (2013) 249 CLR 1, 57 (Hayne J).

74 *Young v Toacassie* (1905) 2 CLR 470, 477 (Griffith CJ for the Court); *Minister of Resources v Dover Fisheries Pty Ltd* (1993) 43 FCR 565, 577 [46] (Gummow J).

75 *Morton v Union Steamship Co of New Zealand Ltd* (1951) 83 CLR 402, 410 (Dixon, McTiernan, Williams, Webb, Fullagar and Kitto JJ).

76 *R v Goreng-Goreng* (2008) 220 FLR 21, 254 [77] (Refshauge J).

77 (1951) 83 CLR 402.

78 Ibid 410.

79 (1925) 36 CLR 88.

> confined to the same field of operations as that marked out by the Act itself. It cannot be supposed that Parliament gave permission to the Executive to enlarge legislatively that field at discretion.[80]

Later in that same passage, Isaacs J quoted what he had said in an earlier case,[81] that 'in the absence of express statement to the contrary, you may complement, but you may not supplement, a granted power'.

In *Shanahan v Scott*[82] the relevant head of power was 'providing for all or any purposes ... necessary or expedient for the administration of this Act or for carrying out the objects of this Act'. The majority stated that such a power authorises what is strictly ancillary and does not 'support attempts to widen the purposes of the Act, to add new and different means of carrying them out or to depart from or vary the plan which the legislature has adopted to attain its ends'.[83]

The more detail the enabling Act itself contains on a matter, the less scope there is for delegated legislation to be made about that matter relying on a necessary or convenient (or expedient) head of power.[84]

The test of what is 'required or permitted' or 'necessary or convenient' to be prescribed is an objective test.[85] In *Re Sonnadere*[86] the Western Australian Supreme Court held invalid a regulation made under a 'necessary' power that purported to exclude persons of a particular race from registering under an Act on the basis that the exclusion 'was not in any way necessary in order to carry out the objects of the Act'.[87]

[43.8] Delegated legislation is invalid if repugnant to the enabling Act

Unless authorised by the enabling Act,[88] delegated legislation is invalid if it is repugnant to that Act. Examples of repugnancy at common law[89] include making unlawful something that the Act

80 Ibid 91–2. Rich J noted that there was 'no doubt, a considerable deal of elasticity in the words "necessary or convenient" on account of the discretion always given to the Executive. But that discretion is limited to carrying out and giving effect to "this Act". [It] does not give carte blanche to enact independent legislation. Independent legislation is a matter for Parliament itself': at 96.

81 *Australian Boot Trade Employees' Federation v Whybrow & Co* (1910) 11 CLR 311, 338.

82 (1957) 96 CLR 245.

83 Ibid 250 (Dixon CJ, Williams, Webb and Fullagar JJ). In *Binsaris v Northern Territory* (2020) 270 CLR 549 Gordon and Edelman JJ stated that the 'phrase "necessary or convenient" indicates an ancillary power to carry into effect what is enacted in the statute': at 583 [100].

84 *Morton v Union Steamship Co of New Zealand Ltd* (1951) 83 CLR 402, 410 (the Court).

85 In *Commonwealth v Progress Advertising and Press Agency Co Pty Ltd* (1910) 10 CLR 457 Higgins J stated in relation to a 'necessary' regulation-making power that 'the word "necessary" may be construed liberally, not as meaning absolutely or essentially necessary, but as meaning appropriate, plainly adapted to the needs of the Department – to "the carrying out" of the Act ... But the power does not extend to everything which the Governor-General in Council *considers* to be necessary. The regulation must *be* necessary, in the sense which I have stated': at 469. See also *Esmonds Motors Pty Ltd v Commonwealth* (1970) 120 CLR 463 where Barwick CJ stated that regulations made under such a power must be 'such as may reasonably be thought to be necessary or convenient for carrying out or giving effect to the Ordinance': at 467.

86 (1903) 5 WALR 11.

87 Ibid 13.

88 See **[43.9]**.

89 The *Interpretation Act 1984* (WA) s 43(1) expressly provides that subsidiary legislation must not be inconsistent with the enabling Act and is void to the extent that it is.

says is lawful and adding something that is inconsistent with the Act.[90] There is no difference between repugnancy and inconsistency.[91] Inconsistency arises when the delegated legislation 'varies or departs from (in other words alters, impairs or detracts from) the provisions of the Act'.[92]

Example 43.1 *Plaintiff M47/2012 v Director-General of Security*[93]

Section 36 of the *Migration Act 1958* (Cth) ('the *Migration Act*') provided for the issue of protection visas to non-citizens in respect of whom the Minister was satisfied that Australia had protection obligations under the *Convention Relating to the Status of Refugees* ('the Refugee Convention'). Section 501 gave the Minister power to refuse to grant a visa to an applicant who did not pass a test known as the 'character test'. One of the circumstances in which a person might not pass the character test was on national security grounds recognised by the Refugee Convention. Such a refusal was, however, subject to a merits review in the Administrative Appeals Tribunal unless the Minister had personally made the decision and declared the refugee to be an excluded person.

Section 504 authorised the Governor-General to make regulations 'not inconsistent with this Act, prescribing all matters which by this Act are required or permitted to be prescribed or which are necessary or convenient to be prescribed for carrying out or giving effect to this Act'. Section 31(3) set out one of the matters permitted to be prescribed, namely, criteria for specified classes of visa.

Clause 866.225 of the *Migration Regulations 1994* ('the Regulations') prescribed public interest criterion 4002 as a criterion for the grant of a protection visa. That criterion required that an applicant not be assessed by the Australian Security Intelligence Organisation ('ASIO') as a direct or indirect risk to security. Under the Regulations such an assessment required the Minister to refuse to grant a protection visa. The merits of the ASIO assessment could not be challenged.

M47, a Sri Lankan national, applied for a protection visa but was refused even though he had been granted refugee status under the Refugee Convention. The basis of the refusal was that he did not satisfy public interest criterion 4002. M47 argued that the criterion was invalid. The High Court, in a 4:3 majority decision,[94] held that cl 866.225 was invalid to the extent that it prescribed public interest criterion 4002, because the criterion was inconsistent with the *Migration Act*.

The inconsistency arose because the criterion subsumed the national security criteria that were an element of the character test, thus allowing the *Migration Act* to be administered in a way that avoided the making by the Minister of a decision under the character test to refuse an application based on national security grounds. Effectively, decision-making on national security grounds was shifted from the Minister to ASIO, as an ASIO assessment for public interest criterion 4002 left the Minister no choice but to refuse the application. Further, inconsistently with the scheme for merits review provided by the *Migration Act* of refusals based on failing the character test, no

90 *Clyde Engineering Co Ltd v Cowburn* (1926) 37 CLR 466, 511 (Higgins J), referring to *Gentel v Rapps* [1902] 1 KB 160, 166.

91 *Plaintiff M47/2012 v Director-General of Security* (2012) 251 CLR 1, 41 [54] (French CJ).

92 Ibid 77 [174] (Hayne J).

93 (2012) 251 CLR 1.

94 Ibid 48 (French CJ), 91 (Hayne J), 155 (Crennan J) and 170 (Kiefel J) (Gummow J at 69, Heydon at 128 and Bell J at 180 dissenting).

merits review was available in respect of the ASIO assessment. Public interest criterion 4002 therefore negated important elements of the statutory scheme and was inconsistent with that scheme.

[43.9] An Act may empower the making of delegated legislation inconsistent with, or that directly amends, the enabling Act

An Act may authorise delegated legislation that qualifies or provides exceptions to, or otherwise is inconsistent with, provisions of that Act.[95] It may even permit a direct amendment of the Act.[96] A provision authorising a direct amendment is known as a 'Henry VIII' clause.[97]

Capacity to qualify a provision in an Act may arise where the Act states that the provision is 'subject to the regulations'. *O'Connell v Nixon*[98] provides an example of this. Section 8AA(1) of the *Police Regulation Act 1958* (Vic) ('the Act') enabled a member of the police force who considered that they had a better claim to a promotion or transfer than the member selected for promotion or transfer, to appeal to the Police Appeals Board, '[s]ubject to the regulations'. A regulation was made to the effect that a member was not entitled to appeal if they had not applied for the promotion or transfer. The Victorian Court of Appeal unanimously upheld the validity of the regulation on the basis that the Act and the regulations together constituted the statutory scheme governing rights of appeal and, accordingly, the regulations might limit or restrict the right of appeal provided by the Act.[99]

ADCO Constructions Pty Ltd v Goudappel[100] is an example of how an accrued right to lump sum compensation for a work injury arising by force of savings and transitional provisions inserted in an Act by an amending Act was extinguished by a regulation. The amending Act provided for savings or transitional provisions to be made by regulation that were inconsistent with those in the principal Act or that deemed the principal Act to be amended with effect from a date earlier than the date of assent to the amending Act.[101]

The extent to which delegated legislation may amend the enabling statute 'is confined by the subject matter, scope and purpose of the statute'.[102] It has been held that any ambiguity in the

95 *Oates v A-G (Cth)* (2003) 214 CLR 496, 508–9 [31] (Gleeson CJ, McHugh, Gummow, Kirby, Hayne and Heydon JJ).

96 *ADCO Constructions Pty Ltd v Goudappel* (2014) 254 CLR 1, 16 (French CJ, Crennan, Kiefel and Keane JJ), 19–20 (Gageler J), all referring to *Victorian Stevedoring and General Contracting Co Pty Ltd v Dignan* (1931) 46 CLR 73 and *Public Service Association and Professional Officers' Association Amalgamated (NSW) v Director of Public Employment* (2012) 250 CLR 343, 355 [18] (French CJ) in support of this proposition.

97 These clauses are so named because of their use by Henry VIII of England during his reign (1509–1547). In *ADCO Constructions Pty Ltd v Goudappel* (2014) 254 CLR 1 Gageler J defended the use of a clause allowing a regulation to amend an Act as 'striking a legislated balance between flexibility and accountability in the working out of the detail of replacing one modern complex statutory scheme with another' given the scope for both parliamentary scrutiny of the regulation and judicial review of the exercise of the regulation-making power: at 25.

98 (2007) 16 VR 440.

99 Ibid 441 [1] (Chernov JA), 444 [19], 446 [26], 447 [28], 448 [32] (Nettle JA), 453 [49] (Redlich JA).

100 (2014) 254 CLR 1.

101 *Workers Compensation Legislation Amendment Act 2012* (NSW) sch 12[1], inserting cl 5 of a new pt 19H in the *Workers Compensation Act 1987* (NSW).

102 *North Australian Aboriginal Justice Agency Ltd v Northern Territory* (2015) 256 CLR 569, 591 [34] (French CJ, Kiefel and Bell JJ).

provision authorising an amendment should be resolved in favour of the narrower interpretation as 'Parliament does not lightly delegate to the executive the power to amend primary legislation'.[103]

Delegated legislation is invalid if made for an unauthorised purpose [43.10]

A statutory power may only be exercised for the purposes for which it is conferred, and an exercise of that power for a different purpose results in invalidity.[104] This applies irrespective of who makes the delegated legislation, including a representative of the Crown.

> **Example 43.2 *R v Toohey; Ex parte Northern Land Council*[105]**
>
> The Northern Land Council had made a traditional land claim under the *Aboriginal Land Rights (Northern Territory) Act 1976* (Cth) to a substantial area of land in the Cox Peninsula in the Northern Territory. Under that Act a claim could not be made in respect of land in a town, defined as having the same meaning as in the planning law of the Northern Territory. After the claim was made a regulation was made under the *Planning Act 1979* (NT) specifying areas of land that were to be treated as towns, including most of the land in the Cox Peninsula. The majority in the High Court held that the powers conferred by the *Planning Act* could only be exercised for planning purposes.[106] An exercise of that power for the purpose of defeating a traditional land claim would be invalid. Courts can inquire into the purpose for which a power is exercised, even if that power is exercised by a representative of the Crown such as the Administrator of the Northern Territory.

Delegated legislation is invalid if it adopts a means not reasonably proportionate to the end to be achieved or if it satisfies a high threshold test for unreasonableness [43.11]

Section **[43.10]** sets out how delegated legislation is invalid if made for a purpose other than one for which it is authorised to be made. Delegated legislation is also invalid if made for an authorised purpose but the means adopted by it for achieving that purpose are not reasonably proportionate.[107] Colloquially this situation has been described as 'using a sledgehammer to crack a nut'.[108] The test of reasonable proportionality is directed to the particular purpose for which it

103 *R v Secretary of State for the Environment, Transport and the Regions; Ex parte Spath Holme Ltd* [2001] 2 AC 349, 382 (Lord Bingham).

104 *Arthur Yates & Co Pty Ltd v Vegetable Seeds Committee* (1945) 72 CLR 37.

105 (1981) 151 CLR 170.

106 Ibid 186 (Gibbs CJ), 215 (Stephen J), 217 (Mason J), 183–4 (Wilson J).

107 Recent cases often trace this back to Dixon J in *Williams v Melbourne Corporation* (1933) 49 CLR 142 where he expressed the view that 'it is not always enough to ascertain the subject matter of the power and consider whether the by-law appears on its face to relate to that subject' but that it 'must often be necessary to examine the operation of the by-law in the local circumstances to which it is intended to apply' and, upon doing that, its true character 'may then appear to be such that it could not reasonably have been adopted as a means of attaining the ends of the power': at 155.

108 *Vanstone v Clark* (2005) 147 FCR 299, 346 [172] (Weinberg J).

is intended that the power to make the delegated legislation may be exercised.[109] That purpose may be expressly stated in the enabling Act or may need to be implied from the scope of that Act. An express statement of purpose makes it easier to run an argument based on reasonable proportionality.[110]

Aside from invalidity arising from a lack of reasonable proportionality, delegated legislation may be held to be invalid on the ground of unreasonableness. A 'high threshold test' is set for unreasonableness in this context.[111] This helps prevent courts from becoming engaged in 'merits review under the guise of judicial review'.[112]

The test for unreasonableness in the case of delegated legislation has been described in *Brunswick Corporation v Stewart*[113] as 'so oppressive and capricious that no reasonable mind can justify it'[114] and as involving 'such oppressive or gratuitous interference with the rights of those who are subject to it as could find no justification in the minds of reasonable men'.[115] In *Re Minister of Primary Industries and Energy v Austral Fisheries Pty Ltd*[116] Lockhart J stated that delegated legislation 'may be declared to be invalid on the grounds of unreasonableness if it leads to manifest arbitrariness, injustice or partiality'.[117]

Because of the high threshold an argument that delegated legislation is invalid for unreasonableness is rarely successful.

Neither test provides a separate and distinct ground of invalidity.[118] Invalidity arises because the enabling Act does not empower the adoption of means of achieving the purpose of the legislation that are not reasonably proportionate[119] or the making of legislation that meets a 'high threshold test' for unreasonableness.[120]

---

109 In *Vanstone v Clark* (2005) 147 FCR 299 Weinberg J held an item of delegated legislation invalid on a proportionality test. Under the *Aboriginal and Torres Strait Islander Commission Act 1989* (Cth) the Minister was empowered to specify conduct as constituting 'misbehaviour'. An office holder under that Act could be suspended from office for 'misbehaviour'. The Minister made a determination that defined 'misbehaviour' by reference to a conviction for an offence for which there is a penalty of imprisonment. This brought in such a broad range of offences that it lacked reasonable proportionality.

110 Ibid 332 [110]–[112].

111 *A-G (SA) v Corporation of the City of Adelaide* (2013) 249 CLR 1, 34 (French CJ).

112 *Vanstone v Clark* (2005) 147 FCR 299, 346 [172] (Weinberg J). See also *A-G (SA) v Corporation of the City of Adelaide* (2013) 249 CLR 1, 34 [48] (French CJ).

113 (1941) 65 CLR 88.

114 Ibid 97 (Starke J).

115 Ibid 99 (Williams J), stating that such an interference 'would be an abuse of power and therefore not within it'.

116 (1993) 40 FCR 381.

117 Ibid 384. In this case the Federal Court held that a mistake in a formula in a management plan led to unreasonableness on the application of the plan.

118 As to unreasonableness see *Williams v Melbourne Corporation* (1933) 49 CLR 142, 149–50 (Starke J), 154–5 (Dixon J), 158 (Evatt J), 159 (McTiernan J).

119 In *South Australia v Tanner* (1989) 166 CLR 161 Wilson, Dawson, Toohey and Gaudron JJ noted that 'the parties accepted the reasonable proportionality test of validity . . . namely, whether the regulation is capable of being considered to be reasonably proportionate to the pursuit of the enabling purpose' (at 165) and stated that the regulation 'must be so lacking in reasonable proportionality as not to be a real exercise of the power': at 168. See also *Williams v Melbourne Corporation* (1933) 49 CLR 142, 155 (Dixon J).

120 In *Vanstone v Clark* (2005) 147 FCR 299 Weinberg J stated that delegated legislation 'may be invalid because its effect is so unreasonable that it cannot be regarded as falling within the contemplation of the legislature in enacting the empowering Act': at 332 [105]. In *Re Minister of Primary Industries and Energy v Austral Fisheries Pty Ltd* (1993) 40 FCR 381 Lockhart J gave as 'the underlying rationale' for the invalidity on the ground

Delegated legislation is invalid if it subdelegates a legislative power without authorisation [43.12]

The maxim *delegatus non potest delegare* (an entity to whom a power is delegated is not authorised to delegate that power to another entity) applies to the power to make delegated legislation. However, in *Dainford Ltd v Smith*[121] Gibbs CJ stated:

> I am not convinced that recourse to the maxim delegatus non potest delegare is of much assistance in deciding upon the validity of an exercise of statutory powers. It is simpler to ask directly whether the power has been exercised by the person upon whom it has been conferred and whether it has been exercised in the manner and within the limits laid down by the statute conferring the power.[122]

The issue arises where, for example, an Act empowers the Governor-General to determine a matter by regulation and the Governor-General makes a regulation that leaves the determination of that matter to someone else. It is necessary to examine the enabling Act to decide whether it permits subdelegation of the legislative power. If it does not, the regulation is invalid.[123] It is also relevant to consider whether what has purportedly been subdelegated is in fact an administrative power and not a legislative power. Leaving an administrative decision to be made by another entity within prescribed limits does not give rise to an issue of subdelegation of a legislative power.[124]

A related issue concerns the capacity for delegated legislation to provide for a matter, wholly or partly, by incorporating by reference material contained in another document without setting out that material within the body of the instrument. That material could be a national standard, an industry code of practice, a building specification or material of any other kind. The material may have been published by a public body or by a private body. It may be widely available or be difficult to find.

Against a background of conflicting common law decisions on the validity of this approach,[125] except for Tasmania and Western Australia all Australian jurisdictions have legislated to provide clarity.

It is generally the case in the Commonwealth, New South Wales, South Australia and the Australian Capital Territory that material in Acts and certain kinds of delegated legislation can be incorporated as in force at a particular time or as in force from time to time. But material in other documents can only be incorporated as in force at the time the delegated legislation takes effect

---

of unreasonableness that 'legislation of this offending kind cannot be within the scope of what Parliament intended when authorizing the subordinate legislative authority to enact laws': at 384.

121 (1985) 155 CLR 342.

122 Ibid 349.

123 *Turner v Owen* (1990) 26 FCR 366, 372–4 (Pinctus J), 388–90 (French J); *Stuart v O'Connor* [2016] NSWSC 1179, [118]–[119].

124 *Welsbach Light Co of Australasia Ltd v Commonwealth* (1916) 22 CLR 268, 281 (Isaacs J), 283–4 (Higgins J); *R v McLennan; Ex parte Carr* (1952) 86 CLR 46, 59 (Dixon CJ, Williams, Fullagar and Kitto JJ); *Dainford Ltd v Smith* (1985) 155 CLR 342, 357 (Wilson J).

125 Cf *Wright v TIL Services Pty Ltd* (1956) 56 SR (NSW) 413, 421–2 (Walsh J) and *Dainford Ltd v Smith* (1985) 155 CLR 342, 348 (Gibbs CJ) with *McDevitt v McArthur* (1919) 15 Tas LR 6, *McIvor v Allen* (1943) 43 SR (NSW) 266 and *Arnold v Hunt* (1943) 67 CLR 429.

or an earlier time but not as in force from time to time unless such incorporation is specifically authorised.[126]

Queensland allows material in any document to be incorporated as in force at a particular time or from time to time.[127] Victoria requires specific authorisation to incorporate material from non-legislative material and attaches tabling requirements to that material and provisions requiring that it be kept available for inspection.[128] The Northern Territory, while allowing the provisions of any Northern Territory or Commonwealth Act, or statutory instrument under such an Act, to be incorporated as in force at a particular time or from time to time, allows material in any other document to only be incorporated as in force when the incorporating instrument takes effect.[129]

All these provisions may, of course, be displaced by a contrary intention in the enabling Act.[130]

[43.13] Delegated legislation is not invalid for uncertainty as to its meaning but is invalid if, once interpreted, its operation is uncertain

An item of delegated legislation may provide difficult interpretative challenges to be resolved by the application of the ordinary principles of statutory interpretation.[131] These challenges do not lead to invalidity. What may lead to invalidity is a provision that, even when interpreted by applying those principles, results in an uncertain outcome. In this situation the invalidity results from the fact that the instrument has not effectively exercised the power to fix an outcome in the particular circumstances. The text, context and purpose of the enabling Act determines what operation the delegated legislation made under it is intended to have. To the extent that the delegated legislation fails to deliver in its operation the certainty of outcome contemplated by the enabling Act, the delegated legislation is invalid.[132]

Example 43.3 *King Gee Clothing Co Pty Ltd v Commonwealth*[133]

Regulation 23 of the *National Security (Prices) Regulations* (Cth) gave the Prices Commissioner power, by order, to fix the maximum price at which certain goods may be sold. An order was made

126 *Legislation Act 2003* (Cth) s 14; *Interpretation Act 1987* (NSW) ss 42, 69; *Legislative Instruments Act 1978* (SA) s 16E(3); *Legislation Act 2001* (ACT) s 47.

127 *Statutory Instruments Act 1992* (Qld) s 23.

128 *Interpretation of Legislation Act 1984* (Vic) s 32.

129 *Interpretation Act 1978* (NT) s 66.

130 See **[25.3]**.

131 See **[43.3]**.

132 See the discussion about uncertainty in *Comcare v Lilley* (2013) 216 FCR 214, 234–5 [84]–[89] (the Court).

133 (1945) 71 CLR 184. See also *Cann's Pty Ltd v Commonwealth* (1946) 71 CLR 210. In *Richard G Bejah Insurance & Financial Services Pty Ltd v Maning* [2002] TASSC 36 Crawford J referred to *King Gee* and *Cann's* in holding ultra vires for uncertainty so much of a State Coastal Policy as depended on the meaning of the expression 'coastal zone'. Because it was not possible to determine which land formed part of the 'coastal zone', the operation of the legislation was uncertain: at [24]. In *Sunland Group Ltd v Gold Coast City Council* (2021) 95 ALJR 922 Gordon J stated that '[t]he fact that there is no void-for-vagueness doctrine in Australia is not inconsistent with the proposition that there may be a failure to exercise power pursuant to a statutory provision if, properly construed, the statutory provision requires that the exercise of the power possess certainty in some respect in order for there to be a valid exercise of power': at 926–7 [19].

that, by paras 6, 7 and 11, fixed the prices at which certain items of clothing might be sold. Under provisos to those paragraphs, the calculation involved estimating certain matters relying on judgement and experience. The provisos were declared void as not being a proper exercise of the power conferred by reg 23.

Dixon J distinguished the resolution by construction and interpretation of ambiguities and uncertainties in an instrument from the situation where 'the basis of the price, however clearly described, involves . . . a matter of estimate, assessment, discretionary allocation, or apportionment, resulting in the attribution of an amount or figure as a matter of judgment'. The former situation does not go to power but in the latter situation 'the power has not been pursued and is not well exercised'.[134] Rich J stated that the provisos did not contain 'any adequate statement of the integers from which a calculation of the controlling price can be made'.[135] Starke J said that 'the subject cannot certainly ascertain the price that is fixed'.[136]

Severance of invalid portion

An invalid portion of delegated legislation may be severed [43.14]

Each jurisdiction, other than Tasmania and Western Australia, has enacted a provision to the effect that delegated legislation is to be construed as operating to the full extent of, but so as not to exceed, the power conferred by the Act under which it is made, and if an instrument would otherwise be construed as being in excess of that power, it is to be taken to be a valid instrument to the extent to which it is not in excess of that power.[137]

The effect of these provisions is to reverse the common law presumption that the instrument is to operate as a whole.[138] Any part of the instrument that is beyond power is severed unless doing so would have the result that the remaining provisions 'would operate differently upon the persons, matters or things falling under it or in some other way would produce a different result'.[139] In that situation the whole instrument is invalid.

The position was described as follows by the Victorian Full Court in *Olsen v City of Camberwell*:[140]

> If the enactment, with the invalid portion omitted, is so radically or substantially different a law as to the subject-matter dealt with by what remains from what it would be with the omitted portions forming part of it as to warrant a belief that the legislative body intended it as a whole only, or, in other words, to warrant a belief that if all could not be carried into effect the legislative body would not have enacted the remainder independently, then the whole must fail.[141]

---

134 *King Gee Clothing Co Pty Ltd v Commonwealth* (1945) 71 CLR 184, 197. Williams J referred approvingly to Dixon J's analysis: at 207.

135 Ibid 190.

136 Ibid 192.

137 *Legislation Act 2003* (Cth) s 13; *Interpretation Act 1987* (NSW) s 32; *Statutory Instruments Act 1992* (Qld) s 21; *Legislation Interpretation Act 2021* (SA) s 15(2), (3); *Interpretation of Legislation Act 1984* (Vic) s 22; *Legislation Act 2001* (ACT) s 43; *Interpretation Act 1978* (NT) s 61.

138 *Bank of New South Wales v Commonwealth* (1948) 76 CLR 1, 369–70 (Dixon J).

139 Ibid 371 (Dixon J).

140 [1926] VLR 58.

141 Ibid 68.

In Tasmania and Western Australia, where there is not a statutory severance provision, the common law makes a 'blue pencil rule' applicable. This was described in *Harrington v Lowe*[142] as follows:

> As to the common law in Australia, the position ... appears to be that a valid operation for the sub-rules might be preserved after textual surgery by operation of the 'blue pencil' rule so that the valid portion could operate independently of the invalid portion, or failing that, by treating the text as modified so as to achieve severance. But this latter step may be taken only where in so doing there is effected no change to the substantial purpose and effect of the impugned provision, and, in particular, there is not left substantially a different law as to the subject-matter dealt with from what it would otherwise be.[143]

Effect of not making delegated legislation contemplated by the enabling Act

[43.15] **The legal effect of not making delegated legislation as contemplated by the enabling Act depends on the nature, purpose and language of the authorising provision and on the context**

Generally speaking, an Act conferring power on an entity to make delegated legislation does so by using the expression 'may make' and then proceeding to list particular matters for which the delegated legislation 'may' provide.[144] The use of the word 'may' indicates that the power may be exercised, or not exercised, at the discretion of the entity vested with the power.[145]

Occasionally, an issue arises as to the legal effect of a failure to make an item of delegated legislation that the enabling Act contemplated being made.

In *Commonwealth v Huon Transport Pty Ltd*[146] the High Court had to consider the effect of a failure to make regulations under the *Defence Act 1903* (Cth) authorising a person to requisition a vessel required for naval or military purposes and fixing how the owner was to be compensated. The majority held that the failure did not render unlawful a requisitioning of vessels under the provision around the time of the outbreak of the Second World War.[147] Despite the lack of regulations, the owner had a right to be compensated with the amount of that compensation being worked out on general legal principles.[148]

---

142 (1996) 190 CLR 311.

143 Ibid 328 (Brennan CJ, Dawson, Toohey, Gaudron, McHugh and Gummow JJ). This statement was taken to represent the common law in *Messages On Hold Australia Pty Ltd v City of Perth* [2007] WASC 226, [96] (Beech J). This was also the position taken by the Victorian Court of Appeal in *R v Ng* (2002) 5 VR 257, 287 [58] (Winneke P, Batt and Eames JJA).

144 See, eg, the *COVID-19 Emergency Response Act 2020* (SA) s 19.

145 See chapter 36 of this work, esp **[36.5]** and **[36.9]**. See also *Commissioner of Police v Thayli Pty Ltd* [2020] WASC 43, [64]–[65] (Smith J).

146 (1945) 70 CLR 293.

147 Ibid Rich J (305–6), Dixon J (316). Starke J (at 312) and Williams J (at 330) limited their consideration to the compensation issue as the lawfulness of the requisition had not been challenged by any of the parties. Dissenting, Latham CJ (at 297) and McTiernan J (at 327) held that the operation of the provision depended on regulations giving authority to an officer to do the requisitioning.

148 Ibid 306 (Rich J), 312 (Starke J), 316 (Dixon J), 331 (Williams J). Latham CJ (at 297) and McTiernan J (at 327) proceeded on the basis that the vessels had been taken, not under the statutory power, but based on an implied promise to pay a fair hire for them.

Dixon J stated:

> The provision is expressed in a form which might perhaps be thought to suggest that regulations authorizing officers to act under it and prescribing the manner of recompense to the owners are indispensable to its operation. But the nature and purpose of the power conferred by the section furnish strong reasons against so interpreting it . . . clear words alone should lead us to regard such a power as in abeyance until there had been time for the production from the *officina ordinatorum*[149] of a suitable regulation.[150]

The lack of prescription of a method of inspecting a council's books under s 215 of the *Local Government Act 1919* (NSW) did not prevent the right to inspect arising under that section as 'nothing but the clearest language could justify the conclusion that Parliament intended that the Executive not only might decide whether and how the right of inspection should be regulated but might, by preferring silence, deny to the section all operation'.[151] Similarly, in *Insurance Commissioner of the State Motor Car Insurance Office v Denning*[152] the failure to prescribe the form of a contract of insurance was held not to prevent a policy coming into existence.[153]

In *GBT v Western Australia*[154] the Court of Appeal in Western Australia reviewed the above cases and stated that those cases

> indicate that the legal effect of a failure to make a prescription contemplated by an enabling Act will very much depend on the context in which the question is asked. In some cases, even where the more natural literal meaning of the provision suggests it may not operate in the absence of a regulation, the subject matter, purpose or context of the legislation may lead the court to a different view. The answer to the question will turn on the application of the rules of statutory construction to the particular statute in question.[155]

It has been held in a series of cases in the United Kingdom that, in circumstances where the failure to make regulations prevents a person effectively exercising a right conferred by an Act,

---

149 Roughly translated, this means the place where those who make rules work.

150 *Commonwealth v Huon Transport Pty Ltd* (1945) 70 CLR 293, 316. Rich J stated: 'I am unable to think that the legislature intended to suspend the operation of so important a power until regulations laying down procedure and scales of compensation were forthcoming' (at 305–6).

151 *Downey v Pryor* (1960) 103 CLR 353, 363 (Kitto J). Windeyer J expressed the view that the words 'as prescribed' do not make s 215 'depend for its effectual operation on something being prescribed' and that this was not a case 'where a prescription of something pursuant to a statute is necessary to complete a statutory right': at 364. Dissenting, McTiernan J stated the view that 'no complete right of inspection arises' in the absence of a prescribed method: at 359.

152 (1970) 120 CLR 437. Kitto J stated that to interpret the Act otherwise would result in it being left to the Executive to determine whether the owner had a right to effect an insurance in the way set out in the Act and 'no machinery would have been provided for constraining [it] to perform this delegated function': at 451–3.

153 In *Lynch v Rainbird* [1968] Tas SR 30 a failure to prescribe a method of breath analysis for a breathalyser did not prevent a charge of drink driving being made out. Burbury CJ stated that to hold that until regulations are made the legislative scheme cannot be effectively implemented would be to frustrate the clear purpose of the legislature when it enacted the legislation: at 36.

154 [2019] WASCA 40. In this case a failure to prescribe qualifications or accreditations needed to be a 'qualified psychologist' resulted in a person not being a 'qualified psychologist', and therefore not a 'qualified expert', for the purpose of a proceeding under the *Dangerous Sexual Offenders Act 2006* (WA). The Court concluded that this construction did not 'produce an unreasonable or unusual outcome' as the Act could still operate by two psychiatrists being appointed as qualified experts: at [71].

155 Ibid [62].

the person empowered to make regulations has a duty to do so. The Australian courts, in the cases referred to above, did not consider whether there was a duty to make the delegated legislation. They opted for a different solution.

In *Singh v Secretary of State for the Home Department*[156] the House of Lords held that the Secretary of State had a duty to make regulations under s 18(1) of the *Immigration Act 1971* (UK) as, in the absence of regulations, a person against whom a deportation order had been made could not effectively exercise the power to appeal against the decision to make the order. This was because the regulations were intended to provide for the giving of a conclusive statement of reasons and of a statement giving particulars of the rights of appeal available and how they may be exercised.

In *M v Scottish Ministers*[157] the Supreme Court held that the Ministers were under an obligation to make regulations by the date on which certain provisions of the *Mental Health (Care and Treatment) (Scotland) Act 2003* (Scotland) came into force as, without the regulations, rights created by those provisions for patients to appeal against the conditions of their detention in hospital could not be effectively exercised.

156 [1992] 1 WLR 1052.

157 [20212] 1 WLR 3386.

GLOSSARY

absolute liability offence: A statutory offence where the statute does not require any mental state to accompany the prohibited act, nor does it encompass strict liability. The offence is complete once the prohibited act is proved (source: *He Kaw Teh v The Queen* at **[42.4](b)**). See also MENS REA. Cf STRICT LIABILITY OFFENCE.

absolute rule of construction: A statutory rule that purports to set out conclusively the meaning of a word or phrase in another statute (source: **[36.9]**).

absurdity: The consequences of a particular CONSTRUCTION where the result is contrary to sense and reason, such as where it would be unworkable or impracticable, inconvenient, anomalous or illogical, futile or pointless, or artificial (sources: *Bennion on Statutory Interpretation* and *Collector of Customs v Agfa Gevaert Ltd* at **[27.6]**). See CONSEQUENCES.

Act of general application: An Act, such as an INTERPRETATION ACT, that applies to other individual Acts and supports their operation (source: **[261]**).

alternative words: An interpretative technique by which a court may show that if Parliament had intended an alternative meaning, it could have used particular (alternative) words that would have made such an intention clear (source: **[18.4]**). See generally LINGUISTIC CANONS.

always speaking: An interpretative principle propounding that, where possible, a court should approach the INTERPRETATION of TEXT as if it is speaking continuously in the present. The principle may enable the text to apply to a state of affairs that did not exist at the time of enactment (source: **[19.2]**). See also AMBULATORY. Cf *CONTEMPORANEA EXPOSITIO EST OPTIMA ET FORTISSIMO IN LEGE*.

ambulatory: A description of the nature and character of the language of a TEXT that is ALWAYS SPEAKING (source: **[19.2]**).

amending Act: An Act that amends, or repeals, one or more provisions in an existing Act or Acts (source: **[11.6]**). Cf PRINCIPAL ACT.

application: The process of matching the facts in the instant case to the relevant legislation to determine whether the facts fall within or outside the legislation (source: **[1.4]**). Cf INTERPRETATION.

assent: The consent of the Queen (which in practical terms in Australia occurs through her representative), allowing the conversion of a Bill into an Act (source: *R v The Commissioner for Transport; Ex parte Cobb & Co Ltd* at **[11.2]**). See STATUTE BOOK. Cf COMMENCEMENT DATE.

automatic commencement: The provision for commencement of an Act, or of a provision of an Act, after a specified period that is provided for by INTERPRETATION ACTS in Australian jurisdictions where an earlier commencement date is not otherwise fixed for the Act or provision (source: **[12.5]**). Cf COMMENCEMENT NOTICE and PROCLAMATION.

***Carltona* principle:** A principle whereby a Minister or senior public official ('the principal') may be able to authorise a person (an 'agent') to exercise or perform, on behalf of and in the name of the Minister or senior public official, a statutory power or function (source: *Carltona Ltd v Commissioner of Works* at **[25.4](f)**).

cascading definitions: A form of LEGISLATIVE CHAIN comprising a series of definition provisions operating at successive levels. For instance, a term is defined ('first-level definition'), following which, separately, an element of that definition is itself defined ('second-level definition'), and then, further still, an element of that second definition is itself defined ('third-level definition') (source: *Gibbs v Mercantile Mutual Insurance (Australia) Ltd* at **[9.5](e)**).

cassus omissus: See GAP.

chapeau: The opening words at the top of a section or subsection immediately preceding indented paragraphs, those words applying to each of the indented paragraphs (sources: **[13.8]**, **[36.5](d)**). See also DISTRIBUTIVE OPERATION.

clauses: The fundamental way in which a Bill is divided. Clauses are proposed sections, and deal with a single theme or topic (source: **[13.8]**).

clear drafting: Drafting of a Bill that does not have the effect of requiring the reader to resolve an ambiguity or uncertainty through the application of canons of interpretation or presumptions of LEGISLATIVE INTENT (sources: generally **[10.10]** and *Smith v Watson* at **[10.10]**). Cf PLAIN LANGUAGE STYLE.

code: A statute that replaces the previous law on a subject and purports to be a comprehensive statement of the law on that subject (source: **[22.4]**). See also CODE JURISDICTIONS and CODIFYING ACT.

code jurisdictions: The Australian jurisdictions that have stated the mental element of a statutory offence exhaustively in CODES (source: **[42.3]**). Cf COMMON LAW JURISDICTIONS.

codifying Act: An Act that consolidates an area of law into an exhaustive CODE. Codifying Acts usually include a statutory restatement of the common law (source: **[11.6]**). See also CODE JURISDICTIONS. Cf CONSOLIDATION.

commencement date: The date an Act, or a provision of an Act, comes into force (source: **[12.2]**). Cf PASSING DATE.

commencement notice: An instrument, made under authority of an Act, that provides for the date of commencement of the Act or a provision of the Act. It may also fix the time on a day for the commencement (sources: **[12.3]** generally and *McKenzie v Huybers* at **[12.3]**). See PROCLAMATION.

common law jurisdictions: In relation to the mental ingredient of statutory offences, the Australian jurisdictions that do not have criminal codes that state the mental element exhaustively or exclusively (source: **[42.3]**). Cf CODE JURISDICTIONS.

common sense: **1.** Noun. An appeal based on knowledge of everyday matters. **2.** Adjective. Describes a particular way of thinking that is reasonable, sensible, or appealing to or in accordance with instinctive understanding or sound judgement (sources: *Australian Oxford Dictionary* and *Oxford English Dictionary* at **[32.11]**).

composite expression: A compound expression or composite phrase, created out of at least two elements or integers, that is different from each of them (source: *Victims Compensation Fund Corporation v Brown* at **[18.5]**). See generally LINGUISTIC CANONS.

connotation: The essential meaning or essential attributes of a word or phrase (source: *Chubb Insurance Company of Australia Ltd v Moore* at **[19.4]**). Cf DENOTATION.

consequences: In relation to a particular CONSTRUCTION of a statutory provision, the likely effect or operation of the provision if that construction were preferred (source: **[27.2]**). See ABSURDITY. Cf PURPOSE.

consistency, principle of: See HARMONIOUS CONSTRUCTION.

consolidation: **1.** In a formal sense, an Act that gathers together, in one place, other Acts and provisions scattered across a number of other Acts to consolidate the law in an area into a single Act. It does not have the purpose of changing the law (sources: **[11.6]**, **[21.4]**). Cf CODIFYING ACT. **2.** An online version of an Act that incorporates all amendments and repeals currently in force, so that, for the convenience of the user, the Act is a complete and current version (source: **[21.4]**).

construction: **1.** Generally, a synonym for INTERPRETATION (source: **[1.4]**). See also **[9.8](a)**. **2.** A contention as to the meaning of the words in question (source: *Inland Revenue Commissioners v Hinchy* at **[9.8](a)**). **3.** The specific, final interpretation reached by a court or interpreter (source: **[9.8](a)**).

constructional choice: **1.** The alternative CONSTRUCTIONS that the TEXT, read in CONTEXT, yields (sources: *Coverdale v West Coast Council* and *Berenguel v Minister for Immigration and Citizenship* at **[9.8]**). **2.** The task of choosing between the rival contentions as to meaning (source: *Coverdale v West Coast Council* at **[9.8]**).

construe: Synonym for interpret (source: **[1.4]**). See CONSTRUCTION and INTERPRETATION.

contemporanea expositio est optima et fortissimo in lege: A maxim that in effect propounds that the original intent of the words in question should be sought. If the maxim still has relevance, it is now confined to very old statutes (source: **[19.3]**). Cf ALWAYS SPEAKING.

context: Those matters of relevance to be considered together with the TEXT; notionally separate from (that is, outside) the text (source: *SAS Trustee Corporation v Miles* at **[7.2]**). See also **[7.3]**. See further INTRINSIC CONTEXT and EXTRINSIC CONTEXT. See generally chapter 7.

contrary intention: In relation to an INTERPRETATION ACT, an intention in an Act that excludes or modifies the operation of provisions of the interpretation Act. A contrary intention may appear not only from the express terms or NECESSARY IMPLICATION of a legislative provision but from the general character of the legislation itself (sources: **[25.3]** generally and *Pfeiffer v Stevens* at **[25.3]**).

corpus linguistics: A tool that measures word usage by querying databases that contain a tremendous number of naturally occurring sentences (source: *Harvard Law Review* at **[32.3](d)**).

critical thinking: The process by which a court evaluates the relevance and WEIGHT of an interpretative argument (source: **[9.9]**).

Crown: For the purposes of the presumption that general words in a statute do not apply to the crown in any capacity, the term refers to executive governments, government agencies and staff as well as the Sovereign and the Sovereign's direct representatives in Australia (sources: **[40.1]**, **[40.5]**). See also **[40.6]** and SHIELD OF THE CROWN.

***de minimis non curat lex*:** A MAXIM OF LAW or a LATIN MAXIM, propounding that the law does not concern itself with trifles (source: *Chapman v Commonwealth Bank of Australia* at **[32.7]**).

declaratory Act: An Act that merely declares what the law is (source: **[11.6]**).

delegated legislation: Instruments of a legislative character that are made under the authority of an Act. Examples include regulations, orders, rules, by-laws, local laws, schemes, statutory rules, codes and notices (source: chapter 43). See also **[3.2]**. Also known as SUBORDINATE LEGISLATION.

denotation: In reference to a word or phrase, the class of things that, from time to time, may be seen to possess the essential attributes (CONNOTATION) of a word or phrase sufficiently to justify the application of the word or phrase to them (source: *Chubb Insurance Company of Australia Ltd v Moore* at **[19.4]**). Cf CONNOTATION.

directory provision: A legislative provision imposing a duty, the breach of which does not lead to invalidity of a related public or private act (source: **[37.3](c)**). Cf MANDATORY PROVISION.

discretion: A capacity, conferred by legislation, to choose between alternative courses of action (source: *Samad v District Court of New South Wales* at **[36.2]**). See also STATUTORY POWER. Cf STATUTORY DUTY.

distributive operation: An operation of a provision where a word or phrase appears in the CHAPEAU to the provision, following which are indented paragraphs, each having an independent operation. The meaning of the word or phrase can vary according to which paragraph applies in the circumstances (source: **[36.5](d)**).

drafting style: The way in which legislation is written by PARLIAMENTARY COUNSEL (sources: **[10.7]**, **[16.2]**). See also **[14.7]**. See further GENERAL PRINCIPLES STYLE, PLAIN LANGUAGE STYLE and TRADITIONAL STYLE.

dualist (n dualism): In relation to international law and domestic law, an approach to law that assumes the sources and content of each differ. Accordingly, international law can never become part of domestic law unless enacted as an exercise of the legislative power of the state (source: *Tajjour v New South Wales* at **[31.2]**).

***ejusdem generis*:** A LINGUISTIC CANON specifying that, where there are general words following two or more specifics, the general words should be confined to things of the same kind or genus as those specified (sources: *Cody v JH Nelson Pty Ltd* and *Director of Public Prosecutions v Williams* at **[18.8]**). See also *NOSCITUR A SOCIIS*.

enabling Act: An Act that confers jurisdiction or a power to do a specified thing (source: **[26.3]**). Where the thing is the making of DELEGATED LEGISLATION, see generally chapter 43.

enacting words: See WORDS OF ENACTMENT.

exhortatory provision: A provision containing a requirement that is not enforceable by proceedings in a court. Also called a 'political duty' or a provision that is 'aspirational and incapable of enforcement' (source: **[37.4]**).

expectation of clarity in penal provisions: An idea, fundamental to criminal responsibility, that the criminal law should be certain and its reach ascertainable by those who are subject to it (sources: *Director of Public Prosecutions (Cth) v Keating* and *Brown v Tasmania* at **[17.4](g)**). See PENAL PROVISION.

***expressio unius est exclusio alterius*:** A LINGUISTIC CANON that treats the express mention of one thing as indicating the exclusion of another (source: *Spence v Queensland* at **[18.10]**).

***expressum facit cessare tacitum*:** A LINGUISTIC CANON that provides that, where there is specific statutory provision on a topic, there is no room for implication of any further matter on that same topic (source: *John v Commissioner of Taxation of Commonwealth of Australia* at **[18.11]**).

extraterritorial operation: The operation of a statute where it operates on, or purports to regulate, occurrences or conduct that occur either wholly outside the territory of the enacting legislature, or partly within and partly outside that territory (source: *DRJ v Commissioner of Victims Rights (No 2)* at **[41.2]**).

extrinsic context: The CONTEXT of the words in question beyond the Act concerned (sources: **[7.3]** and see Parts V–VII generally). Cf INTRINSIC CONTEXT.

extrinsic material: Material that is extraneous to, or not forming part of, the Act in question (sources: **[24.5]**, **[24.11]**). Cf **[24.2]**.

factor: See INTERPRETATIVE FACTOR.

first reading: The stage at which a Bill is formally introduced into a House of Parliament. No debate on the contents of the Bill occurs at this stage (source: **[11.4]**). See also READING STAGES, SECOND READING and THIRD READING.

gap: A drafting inadvertence with respect to a particular matter, class of things or state of affairs that the reader would expect to be addressed in the legislation but, due to legislative inadvertence or inattention, was not so addressed (source: *Taylor v Centennial Newstan* at **[34.8]**). The older term of *cassus omissus* (omitted case) is similar.

general principles style: A DRAFTING STYLE where the law is drafted deliberately in general or broad terms. In drafting in this style the drafter contemplates that detailed elaboration will be addressed elsewhere (source: **[16.2]**). See also **[10.7]**, **[14.7]**. Cf TRADITIONAL STYLE and PLAIN LANGUAGE STYLE.

***generalia specialibus non derogant*:** A LINGUISTIC CANON that provides that a general statutory provision will not normally be taken to override a special statutory provision that governs the circumstances with greater particularity. If the canon applies, the special provision is read as a proviso to the general provision (sources: *Ferdinands v Commissioner for Public Employment* and *Goodwin v Phillips* at **[18.14]**).

golden rule: A so-called interpretative rule that emerged in the 19th century. It provided that the GRAMMATICAL MEANING be adopted, unless it led to some ABSURDITY, or some repugnance or inconsistency with the rest of the instrument (source: *Grey v Pearson* at **[2.3]**). The rule has since been superseded.

grammatical meaning: The meaning of a provision derived from reading the provision as a piece of English prose, and with an emphasis on the rules and usages of grammar (sources: *Bennion on Statutory Interpretation* and *Project Blue Sky Inc v Australian Broadcasting Authority* at **[15.3]**). Cf LITERAL MEANING, NATURAL MEANING and ORDINARY MEANING.

harmonious construction: An INTERPRETATION of an Act that involves a preference for the CONSTRUCTION that is more harmonious overall, and that best achieves a harmonious result (sources: *Independent Commission Against Corruption v Cunneen* and *Commissioner of Police for New South Wales v Eaton* at **[35.4]**).

Henry VIII clause: A provision in an Act authorising DELEGATED LEGISLATION that qualifies or provides exceptions to, or otherwise is inconsistent with, provisions of that Act (sources: *ADCO Constructions Pty Ltd v Goudappel* at **[33.6](c)** and **[43.9]**).

Human Rights Act: An Act that has the purpose of protecting the human rights specified in it and that contains provisions affecting how legislation is to be interpreted compatibly with human rights (source: **[26.2]**).

implied repeal: The effective repeal of an Act, not by Parliament, but following upon a determination by a court that the Act is in a state of actual contrarity with a later Act (source: *Goodwin v Phillips* at **[35.10]**). See *LEGES POSTERIORES PRIORES CONTRARIAS ABROGANT*.

***in pari materia*:** Describes a situation where an Act deals with the same subject matter on the same lines as another Act (sources: *SZTAL v Minister for Immigration and Border Protection* and *Bennion on Statutory Interpretation* at **[29.3]**).

inadmissible consideration: A consideration of a type that ought not be taken into account in STATUTORY INTERPRETATION (source: **[33.2]**).

inference: In law generally, a deduction that may reasonably be drawn from the established facts (source: *Holloway v McFeeters* at **[33.8]**). In STATUTORY INTERPRETATION it includes a conclusion that there is evidence of a relevant INTERPRETATIVE FACTOR (source: **[33.8]**).

intention of Parliament: See LEGISLATIVE INTENT.

interpretation: The process by which a court or other interpreter determines the meaning of legislation for the purpose of applying it to the facts of the instant case (source: **[1.4]**). See CONSTRUCTION. Cf APPLICATION.

Interpretation Act: An Act of a particular jurisdiction, dealing with the INTERPRETATION of Acts of that jurisdiction. The main purposes of such an Act are, first, to shorten other legislation, by enacting provisions that apply across the STATUTE BOOK without any need for them to be specifically set out, and, second, to put in place general interpretative principles applicable to legislation (source: **[25.1]**). See also ACT OF GENERAL APPLICATION.

interpretative criteria: The general guides to LEGISLATIVE INTENT established by common law and statute law (source: *Bennion on Statutory Interpretation* at **[7.3]**, **[9.6]**). Cf INTERPRETATIVE FACTOR.

interpretative factor: An indication of the meaning of words in question that is derived from (that is, an application of) an INTERPRETATIVE CRITERION and that is relevant to a dispute over meaning. To be relevant the factor must be manifested in the statutory context read in the light of the circumstances of the case (source: *Bennion on Statutory Interpretation* at **[9.6]**).

intractable (opp tractable): Used to refer to TEXT that, after being read in CONTEXT, is not capable of bearing a CONSTRUCTION contended for. Other similar phrases are not 'open on the language', cannot be 'reconciled with the language' and not 'compatible with the language' (source: **[6.10]**).

intrinsic context: In relation to the words in question, the CONTEXT provided by the Act concerned (source: **[7.3]**. See also **[7.7]**). Cf EXTRINSIC CONTEXT.

irresistible clearness: With respect to the PRINCIPLE OF LEGALITY, the standard to be met if that principle is to be overthrown or departed from (sources: **[28.3]** generally; *X7 v Australian Crime Commission*; *R v Independent Broad-based Anti-corruption Commissioner*; and *Vella v Minister for Immigration and Border Protection* at **[28.3]**).

judicial notice, doctrine of: 1. At common law, a doctrine that permits a court to judicially notice, without being proved by evidence, a fact that is open and notorious, together with matters of a public nature set out in works of reference (sources: *Cross on Evidence* at **[23.6]**, and *Thomas v Mowbray* and *Stoke-on-Trent City Council v B & Q plc* at **[32.2]**). **2.** As codified under Evidence Acts in most Australian jurisdictions, a doctrine that allows a court to judicially notice (without being proved by evidence) knowledge that is not reasonably open to question, and is (a) common knowledge in the locality in which the proceeding is being held or generally, or (b) capable of verification by reference to a document the authority of which cannot reasonably be questioned (source: **[32.2]**).

Latin maxim: A general aphorism relating to law (source: *Dowell Australia Ltd v Archdeacon* at **[32.7]**). See also MAXIM OF LAW.

leading provision: In a case of apparent conflict between provisions of the same statute, the provision that is intended to be hierarchically superior (source: **[35.9]**). Cf SUBORDINATE PROVISION.

legal meaning: The meaning of words that the court takes Parliament to have intended (source: *Project Blue Sky Inc v Australian Broadcasting Authority* at **[1.4]**). See also **[4.7]**. See also LEGISLATIVE INTENT.

legal term: A term of art in the law that attracts the presumption with respect to words or phrases of TECHNICAL MEANING (source: **[18.6]**). See generally LINGUISTIC CANONS.

***leges posteriores priores contrarias abrogant*:** Later laws abrogate prior contrary laws (source: *Ferdinands v Commissioner for Public Employment* at **[35.10]**). See also IMPLIED REPEAL.

legislation by reference: See REFERENTIAL AMENDMENT.

legislative antecedents: The enactments that constitute the historical legislative development of the statute or statutory provision being interpreted (source: **[21.3]**).

legislative chain: A series of legislative provisions that are linked, such as by CASCADING DEFINITIONS, or where a rule is subject to exceptions, and the exceptions are themselves subject to exceptions (source: *AQO v Minister for Finance and Services* at **[9.5](e)**).

legislative drafting: The preparation of a Bill, usually by PARLIAMENTARY COUNSEL on the instructions of the government (source: **[10.2]**).

legislative evolution: See LEGISLATIVE ANTECEDENTS.

legislative history: The historical background to a statute, including LEGISLATIVE ANTECEDENTS, pre-parliamentary materials, parliamentary materials, the surrounding circumstances relating to the Bill that became the Act in question, and the pre-existing common law (source: Part V Introduction).

legislative intent: Also known as the intention of Parliament. **1.** The fundamental object of STATUTORY INTERPRETATION (source: *Certain Lloyd's Underwriters v Cross* at **[4.2]**). Also referred to as the central question in statutory interpretation (source: *Momcilovic v The Queen* at **[4.2]**). **2.** The final conclusion about the meaning of words in question, attributable to the legislature, that is reached after applying the principles of statutory interpretation (sources: **[4.5]**, **[4.7]**, **[8.3]**). An objective construct, it refers to the presumed or imputed intent of Parliament. It does not refer to the subjective thought-processes of the individuals involved in making legislation, nor to the aggregation of their collective individual mental states (source: *Lacey* v *Attorney-General of Queensland* at **[4.4]**). Equivalent in this sense to LEGAL MEANING. Cf PURPOSE and STATEMENT OF LEGISLATIVE INTENT.

legislative purpose: See PURPOSE.

***lex non cogit ad impossibilia*:** A LATIN MAXIM or a MAXIM OF LAW that means the law does not compel a person to do that which they cannot possibly perform (source: *Van Dongen v Northern Territory of Australia* at **[32.7]**).

linguistic canons: General language conventions that are recognised and put into effect as presumptions in STATUTORY INTERPRETATION. See chapters 15, 18.

literal meaning: The meaning of words in question readily ascertained from the language used (source: *Plaintiff S157/2002 v Commonwealth* at **[15.3]**). Cf GRAMMATICAL MEANING, NATURAL MEANING and ORDINARY MEANING.

literal rule: An interpretative 'rule', which came to prominence in the 19th century, stating that, if the words of the statute are in themselves precise and unambiguous, then no more can be necessary than to expound those words in their natural and ordinary sense (source: *Sussex Peerage Case* at **[2.3]**). The 'rule' has since been superseded. See further NATURAL MEANING and ORDINARY MEANING.

long title: A title to a Bill, placed at the start of the Bill, that describes the Bill's general objects. During the passage of the Bill through the Parliament, each CLAUSE of a Bill must come within the scope of the Bill as defined by the long title (source: **[13.4]**). Cf SHORT TITLE.

mandatory provision: A legislative provision imposing a duty, the breach of which leads to the invalidity of a related public or private act (source: **[37.3]**). Cf DIRECTORY PROVISION.

manner and form requirements: Special requirements that are provided in a Constitution Act for a Bill to be passed by Parliament, and that are over and above that of a vote by simple majority. The stipulations may include, but are not limited to, a requirement for a Bill to be passed only by an absolute majority vote or approval at a referendum (sources: **[11.7]** generally and *South-Eastern Drainage Board (South Australia) v Savings Bank of South Australia* at **[11.7]**).

marginal notes: Notes found in the margins of the printed page of an Act and briefly indicating the contents of the section opposite the note (sources: **[13.11]** generally and *Chandler v Director of Public Prosecutions* at **[13.11]**). Also known as SIDE NOTES.

maxim of law: A general aphorism relating to law and expressed in Latin (source: *Dowell Australia Ltd v Archdeacon* at **[32.7]**). Also known as a LATIN MAXIM.

means (n): The provisions that the law lays down for achieving the legislative PURPOSE (source: **[8.3]**).

mens rea: At common law, the state of mind that a statutory offence contains (source: **[42.2]**). In some usage it includes the *PROUDMAN V DAYMAN* PRINCIPLE or STRICT LIABILITY (source: *He Kaw Teh v The Queen* at **[42.4]**).

mischief: A defect or gap in the existing law that needs to be addressed (source: *R v A2* at **[8.3]**). See also MISCHIEF RULE.

mischief rule: An interpretative 'rule' established in the 16th century. It provided that where the language of a statute is ambiguous on its face, the courts are to be guided by the MISCHIEF that the common law did not provide for and by the remedy that Parliament had resolved by statute to 'cure' that mischief (source: *Heydon's Case* at **[2.3](c)**). The rule has since been superseded.

mutual recognition Act: An Act that provides for the recognition within each state and territory of regulatory standards adopted anywhere else in Australia regarding goods and occupations (source: **[26.7]**).

national uniform legislation: Legislation on a particular subject matter that operates uniformly across Australia. Such legislation can be achieved either by one jurisdiction enacting legislation and the remaining jurisdictions applying it as a law of their jurisdiction, or by all or multiple jurisdictions enacting the same legislation that has been drafted as model legislation (source: **[10.8]**).

natural meaning: The meaning of words in question arrived at after the provision in question is simply read through as a whole (source: *Canadian Pacific Air Lines Ltd v Canadian Air Line Pilots Association* at **[15.3]**). Cf GRAMMATICAL MEANING, LITERAL MEANING and ORDINARY MEANING.

necessary implication: With respect to the PRINCIPLE OF LEGALITY, the intention that must be found for that principle to be rebutted in the absence of clear and unambiguous language (sources: chapter 28 generally and *Daniels Corporation International Pty Ltd v Australian Competition and Consumer Commission* at **[28.3]**).

***noscitur a sociis*:** A LINGUISTIC CANON pointing to the immediate context of the words in question as an indication of meaning (source: *Pac-Rim Printing Pty Ltd v Australian Postal Corporation* at **[18.7]**).

***nullus commodum capere potest de injuria sua propria*:** A LATIN MAXIM or MAXIM OF LAW that means no person can obtain an advantage by their own wrong (source: *Thompson v Groote Eylandt Mining Co Ltd* at **[32.7]**).

objects clause: A section of an Act that expressly states the PURPOSES for which the Act is enacted or the object or objects it seeks to achieve, and that is treated as relevant to the CONSTRUCTION of the Act (sources: **[8.5](a)**, **[20.7]** generally and *Tickner v Bropho* at **[20.7]**). Also known as a PURPOSE PROVISION.

ordinary meaning: In relation to words in question, the meaning the words ordinarily convey in society (source: *Wicks v State Rail Authority of New South Wales* at **[15.4]**). Cf GRAMMATICAL MEANING, LITERAL MEANING and NATURAL MEANING.

override declaration: A declaration in an Act that the Act, or provision of the Act, has effect despite being inconsistent with one or more human rights or anything else in a HUMAN RIGHTS ACT (source: **[26.2]**).

parliamentary counsel: Specialist government lawyers who are charged with the task of LEGISLATIVE DRAFTING, usually on the instructions of government (sources: **[10.4]**, **[10.5]**). In jurisdictions with a legislature that is not a Parliament, the term 'legislative counsel' is applicable.

passing date: The date on which the final stage of the passage of a Bill through parliament is completed (source: **[12.2]**). Cf COMMENCEMENT DATE.

penal presumption rule: A SECOND-ORDER PRINCIPLE that ambiguity in the meaning of a PENAL PROVISION is to be resolved in favour of the CONSTRUCTION favouring the subject (source: *Aubrey v The Queen* at **[17.4](c)**).

penal provision: A provision creating a criminal offence, or a provision providing for a civil penalty (source: **[17.4](e)**).

plain language style: A DRAFTING STYLE where the drafter focuses on drafting in language that is clear and effective for its intended audience (source: Butt at **[16.2]**). See also **[10.7]**, **[14.7]**. Cf TRADITIONAL STYLE, GENERAL PRINCIPLES STYLE and CLEAR DRAFTING.

plain meaning: The meaning of a provision when, after regard to the CONTEXT, it is concluded that the relevant words are not open to more than one INTERPRETATION (source: *Cheedy v Western Australia* at **[15.11]**).

preamble: Words inserted in a Bill before the WORDS OF ENACTMENT that explain the background to the Bill and the reason why the legislation is desirable (source: **[13.6]**).

precedent: 1. A judicial decision that stands as authority for the meaning of specific legislation (whether binding or persuasive in the instant case). **2.** Judicial decisions that comprise the common law principles of the law of STATUTORY INTERPRETATION (sources: **[30.1]**, **[30.2]**).

principal Act: An Act comprised completely of new substantive provisions: a new Act. It may also contain provisions that make amendments to other Acts consequential on the new substantive provisions (source: **[11.6]**). Cf AMENDING ACT.

principle of legality: A common law principle that presumes that, in the absence of express words or a NECESSARY IMPLICATION, Parliament does not intend by legislation to abrogate or curtail fundamental common law rights or principles, or to depart to a marked degree from the general system of law (source: *Potter v Minahan* at **[28.2]**).

private Bill: A Bill introduced into Parliament for the benefit of particular individuals or organisations. Private Bills are peculiar to New South Wales and Victoria (source: **[11.5]**). Cf PUBLIC BILL.

proclamation: An instrument, made under authority of an Act, that provides for the date of commencement of the Act or a provision of the Act. It may also provide for the time of the commencement (sources: **[12.3]** generally and *McKenzie v Huybers* at **[12.3]**). See also COMMENCEMENT NOTICE.

***Project Blue Sky* question:** If there is non-compliance with a statutory requirement, the question of whether the non-compliance invalidates a related public or private act (named after the leading case *Project Blue Sky Inc v Australian Broadcasting Authority*) (source: **[37.3]**).

***Proudman v Dayman* principle:** The general rule of criminal law propounding that an honest and reasonable belief in a state of facts that, if they existed, would make the defendant's act innocent, affords an excuse for doing what would otherwise be an offence (source: *Proudman v Dayman* at **[42.4](a)**). See also STRICT LIABILITY OFFENCE.

public Bill: A Bill that applies to the general community (source: **[11.5]**). Cf PRIVATE BILL.

purpose: In relation to a law, the goal that the law is designed to achieve (source: *Richardson v Forestry Commission* at **[8.3]**). Cf CONSEQUENCES, MEANS and MISCHIEF.

purpose provision: See OBJECTS CLAUSE.

read down: An INTERPRETATION of a provision that narrows the scope that the provision might otherwise have been accorded (source: **[34.6]**).

reading stages: The three stages relating to the passage of a Bill through each House of Parliament. Those stages are a FIRST READING, a SECOND READING and a THIRD READING (source: **[11.4]**).

***reddendo singula singulis*:** A LINGUISTIC CANON providing that distinct matters with particular objects should be assigned distributively (source: *Schenker & Co (Aust) Pty Ltd v Maplas Equipment and Services Pty Ltd* at **[18.9]**).

re-enactment presumption: The presumption that, where Parliament re-enacts a provision containing words that have been given a meaning by a court, Parliament can be taken to have intended the meaning given by the court (source: **[21.8]**).

referential amendment: A drafting technique employed where a statute modifies the operation of an existing provision, but where the amendments do not in a textual way become part of the statute it amends (source: Renton Committee at **[16.6]**). Also known as LEGISLATION BY REFERENCE. Cf TEXTUAL AMENDMENT.

remedial construction: An INTERPRETATION of legislation that corrects a drafting deficiency (source: *Taylor v The Owners – Strata Plan No 1564* at **[34.2]**).

remedial legislation: Legislation providing benefits and remedies (source: *IW v City of Perth* at **[17.3](a)**).

retrospective legislation: 1. Legislation that is taken to have had legal operation at or from a past date (retroactive legislation). **2.** Legislation that alters rights or liabilities that had already come into existence by operation of prior law on past events (extended sense) (source: *ADCO Constructions Pty Ltd v Goudappel* at **[39.2]**). See also VESTED RIGHT.

revenue Act: Taxation legislation or legislation imposing a duty (source: *Brunton v Commissioner of Stamp Duties* at **[17.5](a)**).

schedule: The part of an Act appended to the body of legislation. It may set out ancillary or technical matters or matters of detail. It may also contain provisions that repeal or amend other legislation or provisions of a savings or transitional nature (source: **[13.9]**).

scheme: 1. A high-level overview of the structure or framework of an Act that is deduced from looking at the overall arrangement of its components and their general content (source: **[20.2]**). **2.** Two or more statutes that depend on each other and operate together (source: *Certain Lloyd's Underwriters v Cross* at **[29.4]**).

second-order principle: An interpretative principle to be applied as a last resort when the normal principles of interpretation have 'run out' and failed to resolve the issue (source: *Brown v Tasmania* at **[17.4](c)** and **(g)**). See also PENAL PRESUMPTION RULE.

second reading: The stage of the passage of a Bill through Parliament during which the broad principles of a Bill are debated (source: **[11.4]**). See also READING STAGES, FIRST READING and THIRD READING.

shield of the Crown: Entities that are part of the CROWN. Also known as entities 'representing the crown' (source: **[40.5]**).

short title: The name of an Act. Except in Victoria, it appears in a separate section of the Act concerned (source: **[13.7]**). Cf LONG TITLE.

side notes: See MARGINAL NOTES.

source of doubt: A root cause of interpretative doubt; a socio-legal phenomenon (source: **[14.2]**).

statement of legislative intent: A statement in legislation about how that legislation is intended to operate (source: **[4.8]**). It is an intrinsic aid to INTERPRETATION. Cf LEGISLATIVE INTENT.

statute book: The entire body of all the Acts of Parliament in existence in a particular jurisdiction, whether or not they have commenced to operate (source: *M v Scottish Ministers* at **[29.1]**). See further COMMENCEMENT DATE.

statute law revision Act: An Act that formally repeals spent Acts, or corrects minor errors, or otherwise tidies up the STATUTE BOOK without effecting any substantive changes (source: **[11.6]**). See generally AMENDING ACT.

statutory duty: A requirement, imposed by statute, to perform an act when the circumstances call for it (source: **[36.2]**). See generally STATUTORY POWER. Cf DISCRETION.

statutory interpretation: The process that determines the meaning of legislation (source: **[1.4]**). See LEGAL MEANING.

statutory power: An authority, conferred by statute, to do what would otherwise be illegal or ineffective (sources: *Wade on Administrative Law* and *Yarmirr v Australian Telecommunications Corporation* at **[36.2]**). See also DISCRETION and STATUTORY DUTY.

statutory reasonableness: A term in legislation that uses a 'reasonableness' standard in one of a number of forms (source: **[38.2]**).

strained construction: An unusual or non-grammatical CONSTRUCTION (sources: **[6.9]**, **[34.9]**). See also **[15.3]** and GRAMMATICAL MEANING.

strict liability: See STRICT LIABILITY OFFENCE.

strict liability offence: A statutory offence that, while not requiring the prosecution in every case to prove a specific state of mind (MENS REA), allows the accused to raise honest and reasonable mistake of fact as a ground of exculpation (source: *He Kaw Teh v The Queen* at **[42.5]**). See also *PROUDMAN V DAYMAN* PRINCIPLE. Cf ABSOLUTE LIABILITY OFFENCE.

subdelegation: In relation to legislative power, the conferral of that power by an Act (an ENABLING ACT) (source: **[43.12]**).

subordinate legislation: An alternative name for DELEGATED LEGISLATION (source: **[43.2]**).

subordinate provision: In a case of apparent conflict between two or more provisions of the same statute, the provision that a court determines Parliament intended to be the one that is subject to the other (leading) provision (source: *Institute of Patent Agents v Lockwood* at **[35.9]**). Cf LEADING PROVISION.

surplusage, presumption against: The presumption (LINGUISTIC CANON) that a court should endeavour to avoid words chosen by the legislature being rendered redundant (sources: *Project Blue Sky Inc v Australian Broadcasting Authority* and *R v Berchet* at **[18.3]**).

surrounding law: Common law and statute law, lying outside the statute in question, that are relevant to resolving an interpretative dispute (source: **[32.6]**).

technical meaning: In relation to a word or phrase whose meaning is in question, the meaning it has previously acquired in relation to a particular expertise. It is the presumed LEGAL MEANING (source: *Clegg v Western Australia (No 2)* at **[18.6]**). See generally LINGUISTIC CANONS. See also LEGAL TERM.

text: The words of legislation whose meaning is in question (source: *R v A2* at **[6.3]**). The term UNIT OF INQUIRY is synonymous.

text-based: An interpretative process in which the TEXT of legislation is central to, and a constraint on, INTERPRETATION (source: **[6.2]**). See further chapter 6.

textual amendment: A drafting technique for amending legislation that involves identifying particular text in the existing legislation, and one of the following: inserting or adding other text; omitting the existing text; or omitting that text and substituting other text for it (source: Office of Parliamentary Counsel (Commonwealth) at **[16.6]**). Cf REFERENTIAL AMENDMENT.

third reading: The stage of the passage of a Bill through Parliament at which a vote is taken to accept or reject the Bill in its final form (source: **[11.4]**). See also READING STAGES, FIRST READING and SECOND READING.

traditional style: A DRAFTING STYLE where the drafter focuses on preparing a Bill or delegated legislation in a way that is precisely expressed, detailed, and certain in its effect (source: **[16.2]**). See also **[10.7]**, **[14.7]**). Cf PLAIN LANGUAGE STYLE and GENERAL PRINCIPLES STYLE.

uncommenced Act: An Act that has not yet come into force. An uncommenced Act can have legal relevance for particular purposes (source: *Queensland v Central Queensland Land Council Aboriginal Corporation* at **[12.9]**). See also UNPROCLAIMED AMENDMENT.

unit of inquiry: A term synonymous with TEXT (source: *Bennion on Statutory Interpretation* at **[6.3]**). See also **[9.5](a)**.

unproclaimed amendment: An amendment to an Act that is yet to come into force. Unproclaimed amendments can contribute, though in a limited way, to the interpretative process (sources: **[12.9]** generally, *Wilson v Dagnall; R v Walsall Justices, Ex parte W* and *Hersfield Developments Corporation Pty Ltd v Melbourne and Metropolitan Board of Works* at **[12.9]**). See also UNCOMMENCED ACT.

vested right: A right that is covered by the presumption against retrospective operation. Also called a 'right acquired' (source: **[39.2]**). See also extended sense of RETROSPECTIVE LEGISLATION.

weight: **1.** The level of support an INTERPRETATIVE FACTOR can give to a CONSTRUCTION to which the factor points, after it has been evaluated using CRITICAL THINKING (source: **[9.9]**). **2.** The overall support that a particular construction receives from interpretative factors (source: **[9.10]**).

will of Parliament: See LEGISLATIVE INTENT.

words of enactment: Words that appear at the start of a Bill for the purpose of evidencing, when the Bill is passed, that Parliament has approved the Bill, and that any other consent necessary for the making of a valid Act has been obtained (source: **[13.5]**). Also referred to as ENACTING WORDS.

BIBLIOGRAPHY

These are the works referred to in various chapters

ACT Parliamentary Counsel's Office, *Developing Legislation and Working with PCO* (ACT Government, 2020)

ACT Parliamentary Counsel's Office, *Words and Phrases Guide: A Guide to Plain Legal Language* (ACT Government, 2016)

Adler, Mark and Daphne Perry, *Clarity for Lawyers: Effective Legal Language* (The Law Society, 3rd ed, 2017)

Administrative Review Council, *Report to the Attorney-General: Rule Making by Commonwealth Agencies* (Report No 35, Australian Government Publishing Service, 1992)

Alexander, Larry, 'Goldsworthy on Interpretation of Statutes and Constitutions: Public Meaning, Intended Meaning and the Bogey of Aggregation' in Lisa Burton Crawford, Patrick Emerton and Dale Smith (eds), *Law Under a Democratic Constitution: Essays in Honour of Jeffrey Goldsworthy* (Hart Publishing, 2019) 5

Allars, Margaret, *Introduction to Australian Administrative Law* (Butterworths, 1990)

Allen, Carlton, *Law in Making* (Oxford University Press, 7th ed, 1964)

Allsop, Chief Justice James, 'Values in Law: How They Influence and Shape Rules and the Application of Law' (Centre for Comparative and Public Law, Faculty of Law, University of Hong Kong Hochelaga Lecture Series 2016)

Allsop, Justice James, 'Statutes: Context, Meaning and Pre-enactment History' [2005] (Winter) *Bar News* 19

Anonymous, 'Statutory Guidelines for Interpreting Commonwealth Statutes (Current Topics)' (1981) 55 *Australian Law Journal* 711

Anonymous, 'Wilson v Safelite Group Inc' (2019) 133(2) *Harvard Law Review* 691

Appleby, Gabrielle and Joanna Howe, 'Scrutinising Parliament's Scrutiny of Delegated Legislative Power' (2015) 15(1) *Oxford University Commonwealth Law Journal* 3

Aronson, Mark, Matthew Groves and Greg Weeks, *Judicial Review of Administrative Action and Government Liability* (Thomson Reuters, 6th ed, 2017)

Asimakis, John-Patrick, '"Always Speaking" Statutes' (2021) 95(11) *Australian Law Journal* 869

Asprey, Michele M, *Plain Language for Lawyers* (Federation Press, 4th ed, 2010)

Attorney-General (Cth), *New Guidelines for the Interpretation of Commonwealth Laws* (Press Release 35/81, 27 May 1981)

Attorney-General's Department, *Another Look at Statutory Interpretation* (Australian Government Publishing Service, 1982)

Attorney-General's Department, *Statutory Interpretation: Extrinsic Aids* (Policy Discussion Paper No 285/1982, Attorney-General's Department, October 1982)

Attorney-General's Department, *Symposium on Statutory Interpretation* (Australian Government Publishing Service, 1983)

Attorney-General's Department and Office of Parliamentary Counsel, *Review of the Commonwealth Acts Interpretation Act 1901* (Commonwealth of Australia, 1998)

Australian Capital Territory, *Parliamentary Debates*, Legislative Assembly, 13 March 2003, 999 (Mr Stanhope)

Australian Government, *How to Read Legislation* <https://www.legislation.gov.au/content/readlegislation#general>

Australian Law Reform Commission, *Evidence* (Report No 83, June 1987)

Australian Law Reform Commission, *Traditional Rights and Freedoms: Encroachments by Commonwealth Laws* (Report No 129, December 2015)

Australian Law Dictionary (Oxford University Press, online)

Australian Oxford Dictionary (Oxford University Press, 2nd ed, 2004)

Bailey, Diggory, 'Bridging the Gap: Legislative Drafting Practice and Statutory Interpretation' [2020] (April) *Public Law* 220

Bailey, Diggory, 'Interpreting Parliamentary Inaction' (2020) 79(2) *Cambridge Law Journal* 245

Bailey, Diggory and Luke Norbury, *Bennion on Statutory Interpretation* (LexisNexis, 7th ed, 2017)

Baker, JH, *An Introduction to English Legal History* (Oxford University Press, 4th ed, 2002)

Baker, Sir John, *An Introduction to English Legal History* (Oxford University Press, 5th ed, 2019)

Balkin, JM, 'Interdisciplinarity as Colonization' (1996) 53(3) *Washington and Lee Law Review* 949

Barak, Aharon, *Purposive Interpretation in Law* (Trans Sari Bashi, Princeton University Press, 2005)

Barlow, Ken, 'Alice, Humpty Dumpty and the Law' (2011) 85(6) *Australian Law Journal* 365

Barnes, Jeffrey, 'Contextualism: "The Modern Approach to Statutory Interpretation"' (2018) 41(4) *University of New South Wales Law Journal* 1083

Barnes, Jeffrey, 'Crimes Act 1914 (Cth) – Part VIIC – Division 3: Sections 85ZV, 85ZW and Associated Definitions: Potential Interpretative Issues and Their Impact' DOI 10.5281/zenodo.3271515

Barnes, Jeffrey, 'Duties and Discretions: How Have "Plain English" Legislative Drafting Techniques Fared in Administrative Law?' (2016) 83 *AIAL Forum* 36

Barnes, Jeffrey, 'How Statutory Interpretation Sustains Administrative Law' (2015) 22 *Australian Journal of Administrative Law* 163

Barnes, Jeffrey, 'Is There an Overall Method to Interpreting Legislation?' in Jeffrey Barnes (ed), *The Coherence of Statutory Interpretation* (Federation Press, 2019) 78

Barnes, Jeffrey, 'Sources of Doubt and the Quest for Legal Certainty' (2008) 2(2) *Legisprudence: International Journal for the Study of Legislation* 119

Barnes, Jeffrey, 'Statements of Meaning in Parliamentary Debates: Revisiting *Harrison v Melhem*' [2018] 5 *University of New South Wales Law Journal Forum* 1

Barnes, Jeffrey, 'Statutory Interpretation' in Ian Freckelton and Hugh Selby (eds), *Appealing to the Future: Michael Kirby and his Legacy* (Lawbook Co, 2009) 721

Barnes, Jeffrey, 'Statutory Interpretation and Administrative Law' in Matthew Groves (ed), *Modern Administrative Law in Australia: Concepts and Context* (Cambridge University Press, 2014) 119

Barnes, Jeffrey, 'Statutory Interpretation, Law Reform and Sampford's Theory of the Disorder of Law – Part One' (1994) 22(1) *Federal Law Review* 116

Barnes, Jeffrey, 'Statutory Objects Provisions: How Cogent is the Research and Commentary?' (2013) 34(1) *Statute Law Review* 12

Barnes, Jeffrey, 'The Continuing Debate about "Plain Language" Legislation: A Law Reform Conundrum' (2006) 27(2) *Statute Law Review* 83

Barnes, Jeffrey, 'The Plain Language Movement and Legislation: Does Plain Language Work?' (PhD Thesis, La Trobe University, 2013)

Barnes, Jeffrey, 'The Role of Legislation in the Advancement of Community Education: Pt 2: Is Exhortation the Key?' (1999) 14(2) *Australian Journal of Emergency Management* 56

Barnes, Jeffrey, 'When "Plain Language" Legislation is Ambiguous – Sources of Doubt and Lessons for the Plain Language Movement' (2010) 34(3) *Melbourne University Law Review* 671

Barnes, Jeffrey et al, *Council of Australian Law Deans Good Practice Guide to Teaching Statutory Interpretation* (Council of Australian Law Deans, 2015)

Barwick, Sir Garfield, 'Foreword to the First Edition' in DC Pearce and RS Geddes, *Statutory Interpretation in Australia* (Butterworths, 3rd ed, 1988) vii

Basten, John, 'Constitutional Dimensions of Statutory Interpretation' (Speech, Centre for Comparative Constitutional Studies, Melbourne Law School, 24 July 2015)

Basten, John, 'Construing Statutes Conferring Powers – A Process of Implication or Applying Values?' in Janina Boughey and Lisa Burton Crawford (eds), *Interpreting Executive Power* (Federation Press, 2020) 54

Basten, John, 'Legislative Intention' (2019) 93 *Australian Law Journal* 367

Basten, John, 'Separation of Powers – Dialogue and Deference' (2018) 25 *Australian Journal of Administrative Law* 91

Basten, John, 'The Principle of Legality – An Unhelpful Label' in Dan Meagher and Matthew Groves (eds), *The Principle of Legality in Australia and New Zealand* (Federation Press, 2017) 74

Basten, Justice John, 'Constitutional Dimensions of Statutory Interpretation' (Speech, Constitutional Law Conference, Centre for Comparative Constitutional Studies, Melbourne Law School, 24 July 2015)

Basten, Justice John, 'Modern Judicial Review – An Overview' (Western Australian Bar Association CPD Conference, 4 November 2015)

Basten, Justice John, 'Statute and the Common Law' (2019) 93 *Australian Law Journal* 985

Basten, Justice John, 'Statutory Interpretation: Choosing Principles of Interpretation' (2017) 91 *Australian Law Journal* 881

Bateman, Will, 'Algorithmic Decision-Making and Legality: Public Law Dimensions' (2020) 94 *Australian Law Journal* 520

Bateman, Will and Leighton McDonald, 'The Normative Structure of Australian Administrative Law' (2017) 45 *Federal Law Review* 153

Bayne, Peter, 'Fuzzy Drafting and the Interpretation of Statutes in the Administrative State' (1992) 66 *Australian Law Journal* 523

Beazley, Justice MJ, 'Administrative Law and Statutory Interpretation: Room for the Rule of Law?' (2018) 93 *AIAL Forum* 1

Bell, John and George Engle, *Cross: Statutory Interpretation* (Oxford University Press, 3rd ed, 2005)

Bennion, FAR, *Bennion on Statute Law* (Longman, 3rd ed, 1990)

Bennion, FAR, *Bennion on Statutory Interpretation: A Code* (LexisNexis, 5th ed, 2008)

Bennion, FAR, *Understanding Common Law Legislation: Drafting and Interpretation* (Oxford University Press, 2009)

Benson, Robert W, *The Interpretation Game: How Judges and Lawyers Make the Law* (Carolina Academic Press, 2008)

Berry, Duncan, 'A Comparative Study of Legal Jargon in Australian Statutes' [2014] (3) *The Loophole: Journal of the Commonwealth Association of Legislative Counsel* 3

Bertlin, Alison, 'What Works Best for the Reader? A Study on Drafting and Presenting Legislation' [2014] (2) *The Loophole: Journal of the Commonwealth Association of Legislative Counsel* 25

Bingham, Tom, *The Rule of Law* (Penguin Books, 2010)

Black, Ashley, 'Development of Principles of Statutory Interpretation' (Speech, Francis Forbes Society for Australian Legal History, 1 October 2013)

Blaker, Jamie, 'Is Intentionalist Theory Indispensable to Statutory Interpretation?' (2017) 43 *Monash University Law Review* 238

Bott, Bruce and Ruth Talbot-Stokes, *Nemes and Coss' Effective Legal Research* (LexisNexis Butterworths, 6th ed, 2015)

Bottomley, Stephen and Simon Bronitt, *Law in Context* (Federation Press, 4th ed, 2012)

Boud, David, Ruth Cohen and David Walker, 'Introduction: Understanding Learning from Experience' in David Boud, Ruth Cohen and David Walker (eds), *Using Experience for Learning* (Society for Research into Higher Education & Open University Press, 1993) 1

Boughey, Janina, 'The Case for "Deference" to (Some) Executive Interpretations of Law' in Janina Boughey and Lisa Burton Crawford (eds), *Interpreting Executive Power* (Federation Press, 2020) 34

Bowman, Geoffrey, 'The Art of Legislative Drafting' (2005) 7(1–2) *European Journal of Law Reform* 3

Bradley, Timothy J, 'Getting into Mischief: Reflections on Statutory Interpretation and the Mischief Rule' (2021) 109 *Georgetown Law Journal Online* 199

Braithwaite, John, 'Rules and Principles: A Theory of Legal Certainty' (2002) 27 *Australian Journal of Legal Philosophy* 47

Bray, Samuel L, 'The Mischief Rule' (2021) 109 *Georgetown Law Journal* 967

Brazil, P, 'Legislative History and the Sure and True Interpretation of Statutes in General and the Constitution in Particular' (1961) 4 *University of Queensland Law Journal* 1

Brazil, P, 'Opening of Seminar' in Attorney-General's Department, *Another Look at Statutory Interpretation: A Symposium* (Australian Government Publishing Service, 1982) 1

Brazil, P, 'Purposive Versus Literal Approach' in Attorney-General's Department, *Another Look at Statutory Interpretation: A Symposium* (Australian Government Publishing Service, 1982) 18

Brett, Peter, 'The Theory of Interpreting Statutes' (1953) 2(2) *University of Queensland Law Journal* 99

Bronitt, Simon and Bernadette McSherry, *Principles of Criminal Law* (Lawbook Co, 4th ed, 2017)

Brown, Catherine, Judith McNamara and Cheryl Treloar, *Good Practice Guide (Bachelor of Laws): Statutory Interpretation* (Australian Learning and Teaching Council, 2011)

Bryson, Justice John, 'Statutory Interpretation: An Australian Judicial Perspective' (1992) 13 (3) *Statute Law Review* 187

Burridge, Kate and Alexander Bergs, *Understanding Language Change* (Routledge, 2016)

Burrows, Andrew, *Thinking About Statutes: Interpretation, Interaction, Improvement* (Cambridge University Press, 2018)

Burrows, Andrew, 'The Relationship between the Common Law and Statutes in the Law of Obligations" (2012) 128 *Law Quarterly Review* 232

Butt, Peter, *Modern Legal Drafting: A Guide to Using Clearer Language* (Cambridge University Press, 3rd ed, 2013)

Callaway, Justice Frank, 'Judges and Statutes' [2005] (Winter) *Bar News* 25

Campbell, Joseph and Richard Campbell, 'Why Statutory Interpretation Is Done as It Is Done' (2014) 39 *Australian Bar Review* 1

Campbell, Lisbeth, 'Legal Drafting Styles: Fuzzy or Fussy?' (1996) 3(2) *Murdoch University Electronic Journal of Law* 17

Carroll, Lewis, *Through the Looking-Glass and What Alice Found There?* (Macmillan, 1872)

Carston, Robyn, 'Legal Texts and Canons of Construction: A View from Current Pragmatic Theory' in Michael Freeman and Fiona Smith (eds), *Law and Language: Current Legal Issues* (Oxford University Press, 2013) vol 15, 8

Carter, RI, *Burrows and Carter: Statute Law in New Zealand* (LexisNexis NZ Ltd, 5th ed, 2015)

Carter, Ross, 'Interpretation Acts – Are They, and (How) Do They Make for, Great Law?' [2020] (3) *The Loophole: Journal of the Commonwealth Association of Legislative Counsel* 2

Chen, Bernice, 'Seriously Considering "Seriously Considered Dicta": Precedent after Farah Constructions' (2021) 95 *Australian Law Journal* 186

Chen, Bruce, 'The Principle of Legality: Protecting Statutory Rights from Statutory Infringement?' (2019) 41 *Sydney Law Review* 73

Cherkewich, Teri, 'By Sword and Shield: Legislative Counsel's Role in Advancing and Protecting Democracy One Word (and Client) at a Time' (2015) 36(3) *Statute Law Review* 253

Chernov, Alex, 'The Lawyer and Morality' (1991) 18(1) *Brief* 6

Cobbett, P, '"The Crown" as Representing "the State"' (1903) 1 *Commonwealth Law Review* 23

Cogan, Robert, 'Preface' in Robert Cogan, *Critical Thinking: Step by Step* (University Press of America, 1998)

Committee Appointed by the Lord President of the Council, *Committee on The Preparation of Legislation* (Cmnd 6053, May 1975)

Commonwealth, *Gazette: Special*, No S 85, 2 March 1986

Commonwealth, *Parliamentary Debates*, House of Representatives, 6 June 1901, 789 (Attorney-General Deakin)

Commonwealth, *Parliamentary Debates*, House of Representatives, 24 October 1963, 2263 (Sir Garfield Barwick)

Commonwealth, *Parliamentary Debates*, Senate, 27 May 1981, 2166–7 (Attorney-General Durack)

Commonwealth, *Parliamentary Debates*, Senate, 28 May 1981, 2166 (Attorney-General Durack)

Commonwealth, *Parliamentary Debates*, Senate, 28 May 1981, 2312 (Senator Evans)

Commonwealth, *Parliamentary Debates*, Senate, 8 March 1984, 582 (Attorney-General Evans)

Commonwealth, House of Representatives, *Votes and Proceedings No 2* (10 May 1901)

Connors, Robert J, 'The Differences Between Speech and Writing: Ethos, Pathos, and Logos' (1979) 30(3) *College Composition and Communication* 285

Coode, George, *On Legislative Expression: Or, The Language of the Written Law* (William Benning and Co, 1845)

Cook, Catriona et al, *Laying Down the Law* (LexisNexis, 8th ed, 2012)

Corbett-Jarvis, Nichola and Brendan Grigg, *Effective Legal Writing: A Practical Guide* (LexisNexis Butterworths, 2nd ed, 2017)

Cormacain, Ronan, 'Legislation, Legislative Drafting and the Rule of Law' (2017) 5(2) *The Theory and Practice of Legislation* 115

Cotterrell, Roger, 'Why Must Legal Ideas Be Interpreted Sociologically?' (1998) 25(2) *Journal of Law and Society* 171

Coxon, Benedict, 'Open to Interpretation: The Implication of Words into Statutes' (2009) 30(1) *Statute Law Review* 1

Cranston, Ross, *Law, Government and Public Policy* (Oxford University Press, 1987)

Crawford, Lisa Burton, *The Rule of Law and the Australian Constitution* (Federation Press, 2017)

Crawford, Lisa Burton and Dan Meagher, 'Statutory Precedents Under the "Modern Approach" to Statutory Interpretation' (2020) 42 *Sydney Law Review* 209

Crennan, Justice Susan, 'Blackstone's "Signs" and Statutory Interpretation' (CLE Lecture, Victorian Bar, Melbourne, 28 November 2007)

Creyke, Robin et al, *Control of Government Action: Text, Cases and Commentary* (LexisNexis Butterworths, 5th ed, 2019)

Creyke, Robin et al, *Laying Down the Law* (LexisNexis Butterworths, 10th ed, 2018)

Crofts, Penny, *Criminal Law Elements* (LexisNexis Butterworths, 6th ed, 2017)

Cross, R and JW Harris, *Precedent in English Law* (Clarendon Press, 4th ed, 1991)

Crowe, Jonathan, 'Not-So-Easy Cases' (2019) 40(1) *Statute Law Review* 75

Cutts, Martin, *Oxford Guide to Plain English* (Oxford University Press, 4th ed, 2013)

Dalmau, James, 'Better Ways of Deciding Whether a Contested Usage is Permissible in Legislation' [2019] (1) *The Loophole: Journal of the Commonwealth Association of Legislative Counsel* 18

Daly, Paul, 'A Typology of Materiality' (2019) 26 *Australian Journal of Administrative Law* 134

Davies, Margaret, 'Authority, Meaning, Legitimacy' in Jeffrey Goldsworthy and Tom Campbell (eds), *Legal Interpretation in Democratic States* (Ashgate, 2002) 115

Davies, Martin and Ian Malkin, *Torts* (LexisNexis Butterworths, 8th ed, 2018)

Department of Premier and Cabinet, *The Legislation Handbook* (Queensland Government, 2019)

Department of Prime Minister and Cabinet, *Legislation Handbook* (Australian Government, 2017)

Department of Prime Minister and Cabinet, *Report on Unproclaimed Legislation* (Australian Government, August 2019)

Department of Treasury, *Better Regulation Program: Information Paper for Agencies* (Western Australian Government, 2020)

Dharmananda, Jacinta, 'Drafting Statutes and Statutory Interpretation: Express or Assumed Rules?' (2019) 45(2) *Monash University Law Review* 401

Dharmananda, Jacinta, 'Outside the Text: Inside the Use of Extrinsic Materials in Statutory Interpretation' (2014) 32 *Federal Law Review* 333

Dharmananda, Jacinta, 'The "Always Speaking" Principle: Not Always Needed?' (2017) 28 *Public Law Review* 199

Dharmananda, Jacinta, 'The Commonwealth Strikes Back: Clarifying Amendments to the *Acts Interpretation Act 1901* (Cth)' (2011) 35 *Australian Bar Review* 116

Dharmananda, Jacinta, 'Using Parliamentary Materials in Interpretation: Insights from Parliamentary Process' (2018) 41 *University of New South Wales Law Journal* 4

Dharmananda, Jacinta and Patricia Lane, 'Teaching Statutory Interpretation in Australia: What's Next?' (2018) 39(1) *Statute Law Review* 27

Dicey, AV, *Introduction to the Study of the Law of the Constitution* (Macmillan & Co, 1885)

Dicey, AV, *Introduction to the Study of the Law of the Constitution* (Macmillan & Co, 8th ed, 1915)

Dick, Robert C, *Legal Drafting in Plain Language* (Carswell, 3rd ed, 1995)

Dickerson, Reed, 'Statutory Interpretation: The Uses and Anatomy of Context' (1972) 23 *Case Western Reserve Law Review* 353

Dickerson, Reed, *The Interpretation and Application of Statutes* (Little, Brown, & Co, 1975)

Dietrich, Joachim, 'Giving Content to General Concepts' (2005) 29 *Melbourne University Law Review* 218

Dietrich, Joachim, 'Statutory Interpretation and Private Law Obligations' in Prue Vines and M Scott Donald (eds), *Statutory Interpretation in Private Law* (Federation Press, 2019) 48

Diplock, Sir Kenneth, 'The Courts as Legislators' in Brian W Harvey (ed), *The Lawyer and Justice* (Sweet & Maxwell, 1978) 263

Dirkis, Michael and Brett Bondfield, 'At the Extremes of a Good Tax Policy Process: A Case Study Contrasting the Role Accorded to Consultation in Tax Policy Development in Australia and New Zealand' (2005) 11(2) *New Zealand Journal of Taxation Law and Policy* 250

Douglas, JS, 'Accrued Rights and Statutory Interpretation: The Chicken-Catcher's Case' [2003] *Queensland Judicial Scholarship* 51

Douglas, Roger et al, *Douglas and Jones's Administrative Law* (Federation Press, 8th ed, 2018)

Dowsett, Justice JA, 'Lawyers and Legislation' (Bar Practice Course, Banco Court, Brisbane, 19 July 2013)

Driedger, EA, 'Statutes: The Mischievous Literal Golden Rule' (1981) 59(4) *Canadian Bar Review* 780

Driedger, Elmer, 'Statutes: Retroactive Retrospective Reflections' (1978) 56 *Canadian Bar Review* 264

Driedger, Elmer A, *The Composition of Legislation: Legislative Forms and Precedents* (Department of Justice (Canada), 2nd ed, 1976)

Duxbury, Neil, *Elements of Legislation* (Cambridge University Press, 2013)

Dworkin, Ronald, *Law's Empire* (Hart, 1998)

Dworsky, Alan L, *The Little Book on Legal Writing* (FB Rothman, 2nd ed, 1992)

Dyson, Sir John, 'The Shifting Sands of Statutory Interpretation' (Conference Paper, Legislation and the Supreme Court, 9 October 2010)

Eagleson, Robert, 'Drafting Matters – Letters of Advice' (2007) 58 *Clarity* 23

Eagleson, Robert D, 'Efficiency in Legal Drafting' in David St L Kelly (ed), *Essays on Legislative Drafting* (Adelaide Law Review Association, 1988) 13

Edelman, Justice James, '2018 Winterton Lecture Constitutional Interpretation' (2019) 45(1) *University of Western Australia Law Review* 1

Edelman, Justice James, 'Uncommon Statutory Interpretation' (2012) 11(1) *The Judicial Review* 71

Ekins, Richard, 'Case Comment – Updating the Meaning of Violence' (2013) 129 (January) *Law Quarterly Review* 17

Ekins, Richard, 'Intentions and Reflections: The Nature of Legislative Intent Revisited' (2019) 64(1) *The American Journal of Jurisprudence* 139

Ekins, Richard, 'Statutes, Intentions and the Legislature: A Reply to Justice Hayne' (2014) 14(1) *Oxford University Commonwealth Law Journal* 3

Ekins, Richard, *The Nature of Legislative Intent* (Oxford University Press, 2012)

Ekins, Richard and Jeffrey Goldsworthy, 'The Reality and Indispensability of Legislative Intentions' (2014) 36(1) *Sydney Law Review* 39

Elder, David, (ed), *House of Representatives Practice* (Department of the House of Representatives Canberra, 7th ed, 2018)

Ellis, Elizabeth, *Principles and Practice of Australian Law* (Thomson Reuters, 3rd ed, 2013)

Emerton, Patrick and Lisa Burton Crawford, 'Statutory Meaning without Parliamentary Intention: Defending the High Court's "Alternative Approach" to Statutory Interpretation' in Lisa Burton Crawford, Patrick Emerton and Dale Smith (eds), *Law Under a Democratic Constitution* (Hart Publishing, 2019) 39

Emig, Janet, 'Writing as a Mode of Learning' (1977) 28 *College Composition and Communication* 124

Emmett, JS, 'Early Statutes Shaping the Common Law' in JT Gleeson, JA Watson and RCA Higgins (eds), *Historical Foundations of Australian Law – Volume 1 Institutions, Concepts and Personalities* (Federation Press, 2013) 115

Encyclopaedic Australian Legal Dictionary (LexisNexis, online)

Ennis, Robert H, 'A Taxonomy of Critical Thinking Dispositions and Abilities' in Joan Boykoff Baron and Robert J Sternberg (eds), *Teaching Thinking Skills: Theory and Practice* (W H Freeman & Co, 1987) 9

Ennis, Robert H, 'The Degree to Which Critical Thinking is Subject Specific: Clarification and Needed Research' in Stephen P Norris (ed), *The Generalizability of Critical Thinking: Multiple Perspectives on an Educational Ideal* (Teachers College Press, 1992) 21

Enright, Christopher, *Federal Administrative Law* (Federation Press, 2001)

Enright, Christopher, *Legal Technique* (Federation Press, 2002)

Erasmus, Janet, 'Keepers of the Statute Book: Lessons from the Space-Time Continuum' [2010] (1) *The Loophole: Journal of the Commonwealth Association of Legislative Counsel* 7

Facione, Peter A, *Critical Thinking: A Statement of Expert Consensus for Purposes of Educational Assessment and Instruction: Executive Summary: The Delphi Report* (California Academic Press, 1990)

Fallon Jr, Richard H, '"The Rule of Law" as a Concept in Constitutional Discourse' (1997) 97 *Columbia Law Review* 1

Feldman, David, 'Beginning at the Beginning: The Relationships between Politics and Law' in David Feldman (ed), *Law in Politics, Politics in Law* (Hart Publishing, 2015) xxvii

Feldman, David, 'Legislation Which Bears No Law' (2016) 37(3) *Statute Law Review* 212

Finkelstein, Ray and David Hamer (eds), *LexisNexis Concise Australian Legal Dictionary* (LexisNexis Butterworths, 5th ed, 2015)

Fish, Stanley, *Doing What Comes Naturally: Change, Rhetoric, and the Practice of Theory in Literary and Legal Studies* (Clarendon Press, 1989)

Fish, Stanley, 'Intention Is All There Is: A Critical Analysis of Aharon Barak's Purposive Interpretation in Law' (2008) 29(3) *Cardozo Law Review* 1109

Fisse, Brent, *Howard's Criminal Law* (Law Book Co, 5th ed, 1990)

Fogarty, Justice John, 'Giving Effect to Values Used in Statutes' in Jeremy Finn and Stephen Todd (eds), *Law, Liberty, Legislation: Essays in Honour of John Burrows QC* (LexisNexis NZ Ltd, 2008) 1

Frankfurter, Felix, 'Some Reflections on the Reading of Statutes' (1947) 47 *Columbia Law Review* 527

French, Chief Justice Robert, 'Judges and Academics: Dialogue of the Hard of Hearing' (2013) 87 *Australian Law Journal* 96

French, Chief Justice Robert, 'The Courts and the Parliament' (Speech, Queensland Supreme Court Seminar, Brisbane, 4 August 2012)

French, Chief Justice Robert, 'The Courts and the Parliament' (2013) 87(12) *Australian Law Journal* 820

French, Chief Justice Robert, 'The Judicial Function in an Age of Statutes' (2011 Goldring Memorial Lecture, Wollongong, 18 November 2011)

French, Chief Justice RS, 'Oil and Water? International and Domestic Law in Australia' (Brennan Lecture, Bond University, 26 June 2009)

French, Robert, 'Rights and Freedoms and the Rule of Law' (2017) 28(2) *Public Law Review* 109

French, Robert, 'The Principle of Legality and Legislative Intention' (2019) 40 *Statute Law Review* 40

Fried, Charles, 'Sonnet LXV and the "Black Ink" of the Framers' Intention' (1987) 100 *Harvard Law Review* 751

Fuller, Lon L, 'Positivism and Fidelity to Law – A Reply to Professor Hart' (1957) 71(4) *Harvard Law Review* 630

Fuller, Lon L, *The Morality of Law* (Yale University Press, rev ed, 1969)

Gageler, Justice Stephen, 'Deference' (2015) 22 *Australian Journal of Administrative Law* 151

Gageler, Justice Stephen, 'Legislative Intention' (2015) 41(1) *Monash University Law Review* 1

Gageler, Stephen, 'Common Law Statutes and Judicial Legislation: Statutory Interpretation as a Common Law Process' (2011) 37 *Monash University Law Review* 1

Gageler, Stephen, 'The Underpinnings of Judicial Review of Administrative Action: Common Law or Constitution?' (2000) 28 *Federal Law Review* 303

Geddes, RS, 'Purpose and Context in Statutory Interpretation' (2005) 2(1) *University of New England Law Journal* 5

General Counsel for the New South Wales Department of Premier and Cabinet, *Ministerial Handbook* (New South Wales Department of Premier and Cabinet, 2011)

Gensler, Howard, 'Law School Examinations and Factual Analysis' (1997) 31(2) *The Law Teacher* 198

Gerangelos, Peter A et al, *Winterton's Australian Federal Constitutional Law: Commentary and Materials* (Thomson Reuters, 4th ed, 2017)

Ginnane, Justice Timothy, 'Indefinite Terms and Broad Discretions: Statutory Interpretation Against an "Infinite Variety of Facts"' in Jeffrey Barnes (ed), *The Coherence of Statutory Interpretation* (Federation Press, 2019) 95

Glazebrook, Justice Susan, 'Filling the Gaps' in Rick Bigwood (ed), *The Statute: Making and Meaning* (LexisNexis, 2004) 153

Gleeson, Justin, 'The Increasing Internationalisation of Australian Law' (2017) 28 *Public Law Review* 25

Gleeson, Murray, 'Statutory Interpretation' (Speech, Justice Hill Memorial Lecture, Taxation Institute of Australia, 24th National Convention, 11 March 2009)

Gleeson, Murray, 'The Meaning of Legislation: Context, Purpose, and Respect for Fundamental Rights' (2009) 20 *Public Law Review* 26

Gleeson, Murray, *The Rule of Law and the Constitution: Boyer Lectures 2000* (ABC Books, 2000)

Godwin, Andrew, Vivienne Brand and Rosemary Teele Lanford, 'Legislative Design – Clarifying the Legislative Porridge' (2021) 38 *Company and Securities Law Journal* 280

Goldfarb, Neal, '"Always Speaking"?' Interpreting the Present Tense in Statutes' (2013) 58(1) *Canadian Journal of Linguistics* 63

Goldsworthy, Jeffrey, 'Is Legislative Supremacy Under Threat? Statutory Interpretation, Legislative Intention and Common-Law Principles' (2016) 60(11) *Quadrant* 56

Goldsworthy, Jeffrey, 'Lord Burrows on Legislative Intention, Statutory Purpose, and the "Always Speaking" Principle' [2020] *Statute Law Review* doi:10.1093/slr/hmaa019

Goldsworthy, Jeffrey, 'Parliamentary Sovereignty and Statutory Interpretation' in Rick Bigwood (ed), *The Statute: Making and Meaning* (LexisNexis, 2004) 187

Goldsworthy, Jeffrey, *Parliamentary Sovereignty: Contemporary Debates* (Cambridge University Press, 2010)

Goldsworthy, Jeffrey, 'Response to Contributors' in Lisa Burton Crawford, Patrick Emerton and Dale Smith (eds), *Law Under a Democratic Constitution: Essays in Honour of Jeffrey Goldsworthy* (Hart Publishing, 2019) 269

Gordon, Justice Michelle, 'Analogical Reasoning by Reference to Statute: What Is the Judicial Function?' (2019) 42 *University of New South Wales Law Journal* 4

Greenawalt, Kent, *Statutory and Common Law Interpretation* (Oxford University Press, 2013)

Greene, Lawrence G, (ed), *Radin Law Dictionary* (Oceana Publications, 1955)

Groves, Matthew, 'Exclusion of the Rules of Natural Justice' (2013) 39 *Monash University Law Review* 285

Hackett-Jones, Geoffrey, 'The Scar of Odysseus and the Role of Parliamentary Counsel in the Legislative Process' in David St L Kelly (ed), *Essays on Legislative Drafting in Honour of J Q Ewens* (1988) 43

Handford, Peter and Brenda McGivern, 'Two Problems of Occupiers' Liability: Part One – The Occupiers' Liability Acts and the Common Law' (2015) 39(2) *Melbourne University Law Review* 128

Harding, Matthew and Ian Malkin, 'The High Court of Australia's Obiter Dicta and Decision-Making in the Lower Courts' (2012) 34 *Sydney Law Review* 239

Haugh, Michael, 'The Australian National Corpus Initiative' <https://www.mq.edu.au/> (accessed 21 February 2020)

Hayne, Justice Kenneth, 'Statutes, Intentions and the Courts: What Place Does the Notion of Intention (Legislative or Parliamentary) Have in Statutory Construction?' (2013) 13 *Oxford University Commonwealth Law Journal* 271

Heydon, JD, *Cross on Evidence* (LexisNexis, online)

Hill, Graeme, 'Applying Project Blue Sky – When Does Breach of a Statutory Requirement Affect the Validity of an Administrative Decision?' (2015) 80 *AIAL Forum* 54

Hiltunen, Risto, 'The Grammar and Structure of Legal Texts' in Peter M Tiersma and Lawrence M Solan (eds), *The Oxford Handbook of Language and Law* (Oxford University Press, 2012) 39

Hoffmann, Leonard, 'Language and Lawyers' (2018) 134 (October) *Law Quarterly Review* 553

Horn, Nick, 'And Yet More on the Thorny Business of Auxiliary Verbs . . .' (2002) 48 *Clarity* 35

Horn, Nick, 'Interpretation Acts: Coherent Interpretation and a Coherent Statute Book' in Jeffrey Barnes (ed), *The Coherence of Statutory Interpretation* (Federation Press, 2019) 160

Horn, Nick, 'Legislative Drafting in Australia, New Zealand and Ontario: Notes on an Informal Survey' [2005] (1) *The Loophole: Journal of the Commonwealth Association of Legislative Counsel* 55

House of Representatives Standing Committee on Legal and Constitutional Affairs, Parliament of Australia, *Clearer Commonwealth Law: Report of the Inquiry into Legislative Drafting by the Commonwealth* (Final Report, September 1993)

Howard, Colin, 'The Language of the Law' (1993) 86 *Victorian Bar News* 21

Hurst, James Willard, *Dealing with Statutes* (Columbia University Press, 1982)

Inns of Court School of Law, *Case Preparation* (Blackstone Press, 1996)

Inns of Court School of Law, *Opinion Writing* (Blackstone Press, 1996)

Ireland-Piper, Danielle, 'Extraterritorial Criminal Jurisdiction: Does the Long Arm of the Law Undermine the Rule of Law?' (2012) 13 *Melbourne Journal of International Law* 1

Jackson, Bernard S, *Making Sense in Law: Linguistic, Psychological and Semiotic Perspectives* (Deborah Charles Publications, 1995)

Jackson, Sir Gilbert HB, *Maxwell on the Interpretation of Statutes* (Sweet and Maxwell, 8th ed, 1937)

Jacobi, Chad, *Interpretation Acts: Origins and Meaning* (Thomson Reuters, 2019)

Jenkins, Christopher, 'The Language of Legislation' [1997] (December) *The Loophole: Journal of the Commonwealth Association of Legislative Counsel* 9

Jones, Oliver, *Bennion on Statutory Interpretation: A Code* (LexisNexis, 6th ed, 2013)

Jones, Oliver, 'Statutory Interpretation: The Case for a Core Subject' (2007) 5(2) *Journal of Commonwealth Law and Legal Education* 85

Kenneth, Keith, 'Sources of Law, Especially in Statutory Interpretation, with Suggestions about Distinctiveness' in John Prebble (ed), *Sir Kenneth Keith: Collected Papers* (Keith Paper 26, Victoria University of Wellington) 77

Kenny, Justice Susan, 'Constitutional Role of the Judge: Statutory Interpretation' (2014) 1 *Judicial College of Victoria Online Journal* 4

Kenny, Justice Susan, 'Current Issues in the Interpretation of Federal Legislation' (Seminar Paper, National Commercial Law Seminar Series, The Victorian Bar, 3 September 2013)

Kidd, CJF, 'The Construction of Consolidating Statutes and the *Barras* Principle: The Significance of *Farrell v Alexander*' (1977) 51 *Australian Law Journal* 256

Kirby, Justice Michael, 'Precedent Law, Practice and Trends in Australia' (2007) 28(3) *Australian Bar Review* 243

Kirby, Michael, 'The Never-Ending Challenges of Drafting and Interpreting Statutes – A Meditation on the Career of John Finemore QC' (2012) 36(1) *Melbourne University Law Review* 140

Laing, Rosemary (ed), *Odgers' Australian Senate Practice* (Department of the Senate Canberra, 14th ed, 2016)

Lane, Patricia, 'Colloquium on Teaching Legal Interpretation: A Report' (2013) 87 *Australian Law Journal* 575

Langacker, Ronald W, 'Possession and Possessive Constructions' in John R Taylor and Robert E MacLaury (eds), *Language and the Cognitive Construal of the World* (Mouton de Gruyter, 1995) 51

Lanham, DJ, *Criminal Laws in Australia* (Federation Press, 2006)

Law Commission and the Scottish Law Commission, *The Interpretation of Statutes* (Report, Law Com No 21, Scot Law Com No 11, 9 June 1969)

Law Drafting Division, *Drafting Legislation in Hong Kong: A Guide to Styles and Practices* (Hong Kong Department of Justice, 2012)

Law Reform Commission of Victoria, *Access to the Law: The Structure and Format of Legislation* (Report No 33, Law Reform Commission of Victoria, May 1990)

Law Reform Commission of Victoria, *Legislation, Legal Rights and Plain English* (Discussion Paper No 1, Law Reform Commission of Victoria, August 1986)

Law Reform Commission of Victoria, *Plain English and the Law* (Report No 9, Law Reform Commission of Victoria, 1987)

Law Reform Commission of Victoria, *Plain Language and the Law: The 1987 Report Republished* (Report, Law Reform Commission of Victoria, 2017)

Law Reform Committee of South Australia, *Law Relating to Construction of Statutes* (Ninth Report, 1970)

Laws, Stephen, 'Drawing the Line' in Constantin Stefanou and Helen Xanthaki (eds), *Drafting Legislation: A Modern Approach* (Ashgate, 2008) 19

Leeming, Justice Mark, 'Equity: Ageless in the "Age of Statutes"' (2015) 9(2) *Journal of Equity* 108

Leeming, Justice Mark, 'Farah and its Progeny: Comity Among Intermediate Appellate Courts' (2015) 12 *The Judicial Review* 165

Leeming, Mark, *Resolving Conflicts of Laws* (Federation Press, 2011)

Legal & Constitutional Committee, Parliament of Victoria, *Report on Interpretation Bill 1982* (Report No 21/1982–83, October 1983)

Legislative Council Standing Committee on Uniform Legislation and General Purposes, Parliament of Western Australia, *The Work of the Committee During the Second Session of the Thirty-Sixth Parliament – August 13 2002 to November 16 2004* (Report 23, November 2004)

Legislative Council Standing Committee on Uniform Legislation and Statutes Review, Parliament of Western Australia, *Information Report: Scrutiny of Uniform Legislation* (Report No 63, June 2011)

Lehane, Anna and Robert Orr, 'Amendments to the Commonwealth Acts Interpretation Act' (2013) 73 *AIAL Forum* 40

Lim, Brendan, 'The Rationales for the Principle of Legality' in Dan Meagher and Matthew Groves (eds), *The Principle of Legality in Australia and New Zealand* (Federation Press, 2017) 2

Lindell, Geoffrey, 'Assent or Refusal to Assent to Legislation – On Whose Advice? (2009) 11(3) *Constitutional Law and Policy Review* 126

List, Christian, 'Collective Wisdom: Lessons From the Theory of Judgment Aggregation' in Hélène Landemore and Jon Elster (eds), *Collective Wisdom: Principles and Mechanisms* (Cambridge University Press, 2012) 203

List, Christian and Philip Pettit, *Group Agency: The Possibility, Design and Status of Corporate Agents* (Oxford University Press, 2011)

Logan, Justice John, 'Statutory Construction – Panel Discussion Presentation' [2016] *Federal Judicial Scholarship* 6

Lombard, Michael and Shyla Sivanas, 'Trust Brings Change' (2019) 93(4) *Law Institute Journal* 34

Lovric, Daniel, 'Legislative Counsel and the Judiciary: Divergences in Statutory Interpretation?' [2015] (2) *The Loophole: Journal of the Commonwealth Association of Legislative Counsel* 42

Lovric, Daniel, 'Principles-Based Drafting: Experiences from Tax Drafting' [2010] (3) *The Loophole: Journal of the Commonwealth Association of Legislative Counsel* 16

Lowe, David and Charlie Potter, *Understanding Legislation: A Practical Guide to Statutory Interpretation* (Hart, 2018)

Lucke, Horst, 'Statutes and the Intention of the Lawmaker as the Ultimate Guide to Their Applicability: History and Prospects' (2010) 45 *Supreme Court History Program Yearbook* 1

Lumb, Stephen and Sharon Christensen, 'Reading Words into Statutes: When Homer Nods' (2014) 88(9) *Australian Law Journal* 661

MacCallum Jr, Gerald C, 'Legislative Intent' (1966) 75 *Yale Law Journal* 754

MacCormick, Neil, *Legal Reasoning and Legal Theory* (Oxford University Press, 1994)

MacCormick, Neil D and Robert S Summers, 'Interpretation and Justification' in Neil D MacCormick and Robert S Summers (eds), *Interpreting Statutes: A Comparative Study* (Dartmouth, 1991) 511

MacCormick, Neil D and Robert S Summers (eds), *Interpreting Statutes: A Comparative Study* (Dartmouth, 1991)

MacKenzie, Madeleine and David Purdie (eds), *Thring's Practical Legislation: The Composition and Language of Acts of Parliament and Business Documents* (Luath Press Limited, 3rd ed, 2015)

MacLeod, Thomas, *The High Court on the Interpretation of Statutes* (Law Book Co, 1924)

Macquarie Concise Dictionary (7th ed, 2017)

Macquarie Dictionary (5th ed, 2009)

Macquarie Dictionary (online)

Magyar, John J, 'Debunking *Millar v Taylor*: The History of the Prohibition of Legislative History' (2020) 41 *Statute Law Review* 32

Mann, Trischa, (ed), *Australian Law Dictionary* (Oxford University Press, 3rd ed, 2017)

Manning, John F, 'What Divides Textualists from Purposivists' (2006) 106(1) *Columbia Law Review* 70

Manning, John F, 'Without the Pretense of Legislative Intent' (2017) 130 *Harvard Law Review* 2397

Mantel, Hilary, *Bring Up the Bodies* (Fourth Estate, 2012)

Markman, Sandra, 'Climbing Constitution Hill – Teaching Legislative Drafting in Ireland' [2013] (3) *The Loophole: Journal of the Commonwealth Association of Legislative Counsel* 28

Markman, Sandra C, 'Legislative Drafting: Art, Science or Discipline?' [2011] (4) *The Loophole: Journal of the Commonwealth Association of Legislative Counsel* 5

Mason, Justice Keith, 'The Intent of Legislators' in Tom Gotsis (ed), *Statutory Interpretation: Principles and Pragmatism for a New Age*, Education Monograph 4 (Judicial Commission of NSW, 2007) 33

Mason, Justice Keith, 'The Intent of Legislators: How Judges Discern it and What They Do if They Find it' (2006) 27 *Australian Bar Review* 253

Mason, Mark, 'Critical Thinking and Learning' (2007) 39(4) *Educational Philosophy and Theory* 339

Mason, Sir Anthony, 'Changing the Law in a Changing Society' (1993) 67(8) *Australian Law Journal* 568

Mason, Sir Anthony, 'Rights, Values and Legal Institutions: Reshaping Australian Institutions' in Geoffrey Lindell (ed), *The Mason Papers: Selected Articles and Speeches by Sir Anthony Mason AC, KBE* (Federation Press, 2007) 80

Mason, Sir Anthony, 'The Interaction of Statute Law and Common Law' (2016) 90 *Australian Law Journal* 324

Mason, Sir Anthony, 'The Use and Abuse of Precedent' (1988) 4(2) *Australian Bar Review* 93

Mayo, Herbert, 'The Interpretation of Statutes' (1955) 29(4) *Australian Law Journal* 204

McDonald, Barbara, 'Legislative Intervention in the Law of Negligence: The Common Law, Statutory Interpretation and Tort Reform in Australia' (2005) 27(3) *Sydney Law Review* 443

McHugh, Justice MH, 'The Growth of Legislation and Litigation' (1995) 69 *Australian Law Journal* 37

McMillan, John, 'Statutory Interpretation and Deference: An Executive Perspective' in Janina Boughey and Lisa Burton Crawford (eds), *Interpreting Executive Power* (Federation Press, 2020) 24

Meagher, Dan, 'On the Wane? The Principle of Legality in the High Court of Australia' (2021) 32 *Public Law Review* 61

Meagher, Dan, 'The "Always Speaking" Approach to Statutes (and the Significance of Its Misapplication in *Aubrey v The Queen*)' (2020) 43(1) *University of New South Wales Law Journal* 191

Meagher, Dan, 'The Common Law Presumption of Consistency with International Law: Some Observations from Australia (and Comparisons with New Zealand)' [2012] (3) *New Zealand Law Review* 465

Meagher, Dan, 'The "Modern Approach" to Statutory Interpretation and the Principle of Legality: An Issue of Coherence?' (2018) 46(3) *Federal Law Review* 397

Meagher, Dan and Matthew Groves, 'The Common Law Principle of Legality and Secondary Legislation' (2016) 39(2) *University of New South Wales Law Journal* 450

Meehan, Michael, 'The Good, The Bad and the Ugly: Judicial Literacy and Australian Cultural Cringe' (1990) 12 *Adelaide Law Review* 431

Meehan, Michael and Graham Tulloch, *Grammar for Lawyers* (LexisNexis Butterworths, 3rd ed, 2013)

Meiklejohn, Carmel, *Fitting the Bill: A History of Commonwealth Parliamentary Drafting* (Office of Parliamentary Counsel, 2012)

Meyerson, Denise, 'Rethinking the Constitutionality of Delegated Legislation' (2003) 11 *Australian Journal of Administrative Law* 45

Middleton, Justice John, 'Statutory Interpretation: Mostly Common Sense?' (2016) 40 *Melbourne University Law Review* 626

Miers, David and Alan C Page, *Legislation* (Sweet & Maxwell, 2nd ed, 1990)

Moloney, Stephen J, 'Finality of Administrative Decisions and Decisions of the Statutory Tribunal' (2010) 61 *AIAL Forum* 35

Moore, Harrison, 'The Crown as Corporation' (1904) 20 *Law Quarterly Review* 351

Moran, Eamonn, 'The Coherence of Statutory Interpretation: Drafting Perspectives' in Jeffrey Barnes (ed), *The Coherence of Statutory Interpretation* (Federation Press, 2019) 50

Moshinsky, Mark, 'State Extraterritorial Legislation and the Australia Acts 1986' (1987) 61 *Australian Law Journal* 779

Murphy, Dennis, 'Plain English in Drafting Legislation and Regulations' (Speech, Plain Legal Language for Public Sector Administrators', Parliament House, Sydney, 29 July 1992)

New South Wales, *Parliamentary Debates*, Legislative Council, 16 November 1995, 3322 (Jeff Shaw)

Northern Territory Law Reform Commission, *Report on Statutory Interpretation* (Report No 12, December 1987)

Nourse, Victoria, 'Elementary Statutory Interpretation: Rethinking Legislative Intent and History' (2014) 55 *Boston College Law Review* 1613

Nourse, Victoria F, 'A Decision Theory of Statutory Interpretation: Legislative History by the Rules' (2012) 122 *Yale Law Journal* 70

NSW Law Reform Commission, *Evidence* (Report No 56, June 1988)

NSW Parliamentary Counsel's Office, *DP1: Using PCO Drafting Practice Documents* (NSW Government, 2017)

NSW Parliamentary Counsel's Office, *DP2: PCO Plain Language Policy* (NSW Parliamentary Counsel's Office, 2017)

NSW Parliamentary Counsel's Office, *DP3: PCO Gender Neutral Language Policy* (NSW Parliamentary Counsel's Office, 2017)

O'Brien, Paul, 'Legislative Titles – What's in A Name?' [2012] (3) *The Loophole: Journal of the Commonwealth Association of Legislative Counsel* 17

Office of Parliamentary Counsel, *Amending Forms Manual* (Australian Government, 15th ed, 2019)

Office of Parliamentary Counsel, *Drafting Direction No 1.3* (Australian Government, 2017)

Office of Parliamentary Counsel, *Drafting Direction No 1.3A: Simplified Outlines* (Commonwealth of Australia, November 2016)

Office of Parliamentary Counsel, *Drafting Direction No 2.1: English Usage, Gender-Specific and Gender-Neutral Language, Grammar, Punctuation and Spelling* (Australian Government, 2016)

Office of Parliamentary Counsel, *Drafting Direction No 3.10: Legislation that Refers to or Affects Australian Governments or Jurisdictions* (Australian Government, 2018)

Office of Parliamentary Counsel, *Manual for the Preparation of Bills* (Tasmanian Government, 2011)

Office of Parliamentary Counsel, *OPC Drafting Manual* (Australian Government, 2019)

Office of Parliamentary Counsel, *OPC's Drafting Services: A Guide for Clients* (Australian Government, 2016)

Office of Parliamentary Counsel, *Plain English Manual* (Australian Government, 2016)

Office of Parliamentary Counsel, *Reducing Complexity in Legislation* (Australian Government, 2016)

Office of Shadow Attorney-General, *Interpreting Tax Laws* (Press Release, 28 May 1981)

Office of the Chief Parliamentary Counsel of Victoria, *Notes for Guidance on the Preparation of Statutory Rules* (Victorian Government, 2017)

Office of the Chief Parliamentary Counsel of Victoria, *The Legislative Process* (Victorian Government, June 2020)

Office of the Parliamentary Counsel of the United Kingdom, *Drafting Guidance* (The National Archives, 2020)

Oliver, Lord of Aylmerton, 'A Judicial View of Modern Legislation' (1993) 14(1) *Statute Law Review* 1

Oxenhandler, Steven M, 'The Lady Doth Protest Too Much Methinks: The Use of Figurative Language from Shakespeare's Hamlet in American Case Law' (1999-2000) 23 *Hamline Law Review* 370

Oxford English Dictionary (3rd ed, 2009, online)

Oxford English Dictionary (3rd ed, 2011, online)

Oxford English Dictionary (3rd ed, 2016, online)

Parkinson, Patrick, *Tradition and Change in Australian Law* (LBC Information Services, 2nd ed, 2001)

Parliamentary Counsel's Committee, *Protocol on Drafting National Uniform Legislation* (Australasian Parliamentary Counsel's Committee, 2018)

Parliamentary Counsel's Office of Western Australia, *How to Read Legislation: A Beginner's Guide* (Western Australian Government, 2011)

Paterson, Moira, *Freedom of Information and Privacy in Australia: Information Access 2.0* (LexisNexis Butterworths, 2nd ed, 2015)

Paul, Richard, *Critical Thinking: What Every Person Needs to Survive in a Rapidly Changing World* (Center for Critical Thinking and Moral Critique, Sonoma State University, 1990)

Pearce, DC, *Statutory Interpretation in Australia* (Butterworths, 1st ed, 1974)

Pearce, DC, *Statutory Interpretation in Australia* (Butterworths, 2nd ed, 1981)

Pearce, DC, *Statutory Interpretation in Australia* (LexisNexis Butterworths, 9th ed, 2019)

Pearce, DC and RS Geddes, *Statutory Interpretation in Australia* (Butterworths, 3rd ed, 1988)

Pearce, DC and RS Geddes, *Statutory Interpretation in Australia* (Butterworths, 4th ed, 1996)

Pearce, DC and RS Geddes, *Statutory Interpretation in Australia* (Butterworths, 5th ed, 2001)

Pearce, DC and RS Geddes, *Statutory Interpretation in Australia* (LexisNexis Butterworths, 6th ed, 2006)

Pearce, DC and RS Geddes, *Statutory Interpretation in Australia* (LexisNexis Butterworths, 7th ed, 2011)

Pearce, DC and RS Geddes, *Statutory Interpretation in Australia* (LexisNexis Butterworths, 8th ed, 2014)

Pearce, Dennis, *Interpretation Acts in Australia* (LexisNexis Butterworths, 2018)
Pearce, Dennis and Stephen Argument, *Delegated Legislation in Australia* (LexisNexis Butterworths, 5th ed, 2017)
Penfold, Hilary, 'Legislation in the Courts' [2019] (1) *The Loophole: Journal of the Commonwealth Association of Legislative Counsel* 2
Penfold, Hilary, 'Legislative Drafting and Statutory Interpretation' (2006) 7 *The Judicial Review* 471
Pengilley, Warren, *Credit Act 1984* (Longman Professional, 1984)
Perram, Justice Nye, 'Project Blue Sky: Invalidity and the Evolution of Consequences for Unlawful Administrative Action' [2012] *Federal Judicial Scholarship* 35
Perram, Justice Nye, 'The Perils of Complexity: Why More Law is Bad Law' (2010) 39 *Australian Tax Review* 179
Perry, Adam, 'Strained Interpretations' (2019) 39(2) *Oxford Journal of Legal Studies* 316
Pinder, Greg, 'The Coherent Principles Approach to Tax Law Design' [2005] *Treasury Economic Roundup* (Autumn) 75
Pinker, Steven, *The Sense of Style: The Thinking Person's Guide to Writing in the 21st Century* (Penguin Books, 2014)
Plucknett, Theodore FT, *Concise History of the Common Law* (Little, Brown, & Co, 1956)
Plucknett, Theodore FT, *Statutes and Their Interpretation in the First Half of the Fourteenth Century* (Cambridge University Press, 1922)
Popkin, William, *Statutes in Court: The History and Theory of Statutory Interpretation* (Duke University Press, 1999)
Prebble, John, (ed), *Sir Kenneth Keith: Collected Papers* (Victoria University of Wellington Legal Research Papers, Keith Paper 26, 2018)
Queensland, *Parliamentary Debates*, Legislative Assembly, 21 May 1991
Queensland Department of the Premier and Cabinet, *The Queensland Legislation Handbook* (Queensland Government, 6th ed, 2019)
Queensland Parliamentary Library, *National Scheme Legislation* (Research Brief 2011/No 27)
Quiggin, Peter, 'A Survey of User Attitudes to the Use of Aids to Understanding in Legislation' [2011] (1) *The Loophole: Journal of the Commonwealth Association of Legislative Counsel* 96
Quiggin, Peter, 'Statutory Construction: How to Construct, and Construe, a Statute' in Neil Williams (ed), *Key Issues in Judicial Review* (Federation Press, 2014) 78
Radin, Max, 'Statutory Interpretation' (1930) 43 *Harvard Law Review* 863
Ramer, John D, 'Corpus Linguistics: Misfire or More Ammo for the Ordinary-Meaning Canon?' (2017) 116(2) *Michigan Law Review* 303
Rares, Justice Steven, 'Legality, Rights and Statutory Interpretation' (Conference Paper, 2013 AGS Administrative Law Conference, Canberra, 20–21 June 2013)
Raz, Joseph, *Between Authority and Interpretation: On the Theory of Law and Practical Reason* (Oxford University Press, 2009)
Raz, Joseph, 'The Rule of Law and Its Virtue' (1977) 93 *Law Quarterly Review* 195
Renton Committee, *The Preparation of Legislation* (Cmd 6053, 1975)
Robertson, David, *Judicial Discretion in the House of Lords* (Clarendon Press, 1998)
Robertson, James L, 'Practical Benefits of Literature in Law, and Their Limits' (2016) 35(1) *Mississippi College Law Review* 266
Rodger, Lord Alan, 'A Time for Everything Under the Law: Some Reflections on Retrospectivity' (2005) 121 *Law Quarterly Review* 57
Roux, Theunis, 'Judging the Quality of Legal Research: A Qualified Response to the Demand for Greater Methodological Rigour' (2014) 24(1) *Legal Education Review* 177

Sales, Lord Justice Philip, 'In Defence of Legislative Intention' (2019) 48(1) *Australian Bar Review* 6

Sales, Lord Justice Philip, 'Legislative Intention, Interpretation, and the Principle of Legality' (2019) 40(1) *Statute Law Review* 53

Sales, Lord Justice Philip, 'Modern Statutory Interpretation' (2017) 38(2) *Statute Law Review* 125

Salmond, John W, 'The Limitations of Colonial Legislative Power' (1917) 33 *Law Quarterly Review* 117

Samek, RA, 'A Case for Social Law Reform' (1977) 55(3) *Canadian Bar Review* 409

Sanson, Michelle, *Statutory Interpretation* (Oxford University Press, 2nd ed, 2016)

Saunders, Cheryl, 'Constitutional Dimensions of Statutory Interpretation' in Anthony J Connolly and Daniel Stewart (eds), *Public Law in the Age of Statutes: Essays in Honour of Dennis Pearce* (Federation Press, 2015) 27

Saunders, Cheryl, *The Constitution of Australia: A Contextual Analysis* (Hart Publishing, 2011)

Schane, Sanford A, *Language and the Law* (Continuum, 2006)

Scutt, Jocelynne A, 'Statutory Interpretation and Recourse to Extrinsic Aids' (1984) 58 *Australian Law Journal* 483

Scrutiny of Acts and Regulations Committee, Parliament of Victoria, *Practice Note* (26 May 2014)

Scrutiny of Acts and Regulations Committee, Parliament of Victoria, *Report on Commencement by Proclamation* (Report No 37, April 1993)

Senate Standing Committee on Legal and Constitutional Affairs, *The Cost of Justice: Second Report: Checks and Imbalances: The Role of Parliament and the Executive* (Parliament of the Commonwealth of Australia, 1993)

Shepsle, Kenneth A, 'Congress Is a "They," Not an "It": Legislative Intent as Oxymoron' (1992) 12(2) *International Review of Law and Economics* 239

Slocum, Brian G, 'Ordinary Meaning and Empiricism' (2019) 40(1) *Statute Law Review* 13

Smith, Dale, 'What is Statutory Purpose?' in Lisa Burton Crawford, Patrick Emerton, and Dale Smith (eds), *Law Under a Democratic Constitution: Essays in Honour of Jeffrey Goldsworthy* (Hart Publishing, 2019) 13

Smith, Emma, *This is Shakespeare* (Pelican Books, 2019)

Solomon, David, 'The Legislative Record of the Australian Parliament' in JR Nethercote (ed), *Parliament and Bureaucracy: Parliamentary Scrutiny of Administration: Prospects and Problems in the 1980s* (Hale & Iremonger, 1982) 135

Sourdin, Tania, 'Judge v Robot? Artificial Intelligence and Judicial Decision-Making' (2018) 41 *University of New South Wales Law Journal* 1114

South, Jim, 'Are Legislative Intentions Real?' (2014) 40(3) *Monash University Law Review* 853

South Australia, *Parliamentary Debates*, House of Assembly, Magistrates (Miscellaneous) Amendment Bill 2013, 2 May 2013 (JR Rau)

South Australia, *Parliamentary Debates*, Legislative Council, Explanation of Clauses, 6 May 2021, 3367 (RI Lucas, Treasurer)

South Australian Department of the Premier and Cabinet and the Department of Treasury and Finance, *Better Regulation Handbook: How to Design and Review Regulation, and Prepare a Regulatory Impact Statement* (Government of South Australia, 2011)

Spigelman, Chief Justice JJ, 'Principle of Legality and the Clear Statement Principle' (2005) 79 *Australian Law Journal* 769

Spigelman, Chief Justice JJ, 'The Intolerable Wrestle: Developments in Statutory Interpretation' (2010) 84 *Australian Law Journal* 822

Standing Committee on Administration and Procedure, Parliament of the Australian Capital Territory, *Omnibus Bills* (Report 2, May 2017)

Stark, Jack, 'The Proper Level of Generality for Statutes' (2004) 25(1) *Statute Law Review* 77

Steele, James, 'Statutory Forebears: Legislative Evolution as a Means of Statutory Interpretation' (2018) 39(3) *Statute Law Review* 303

Stellios, James, *Zines's the High Court and the Constitution* (Federation Press, 6th ed, 2015)

Steyn, Lord Johan, 'Interpretation: Legal Texts and Their Landscape' in BS Markesinis (ed), *The Clifford Chance Millennium Lectures: The Coming Together of the Common Law and the Civil Law* (Hart Publishing, 2000) 79

Steyn, Lord Johan, 'The Intractable Problem of the Interpretation of Legal Texts' (2003) 25(1) *Sydney Law Review* 5

Stone, Julius, *Legal System and Lawyers' Reasonings* (Maitland Publications, 1968)

Stone, Julius, *Precedent and Law* (Butterworths, 1985)

Strong, SI, *How to Write Law Essays and Exams* (Oxford University Press, 3rd ed, 2010)

Stubbs, Matthew T, 'From Foreign Circumstances to First Instance Considerations: Extrinsic Material and the Law of Statutory Interpretation' (2006) 34 *Federal Law Review* 103

Sullivan, Ruth, 'Foreword to the Fourth Edition' in Ruth Sullivan, *Sullivan on the Construction of Statutes* (LexisNexis, 5th ed, 2008) ix

Sullivan, Ruth, *Statutory Interpretation* (Irwin Law, 3rd ed, 2016)

Sullivan, Ruth, 'Statutory Interpretation in a New Nutshell' (2003) 82 *Canadian Bar Review* 51

Sullivan, Ruth, 'Statutory Interpretation in Canada' in Tom Gotsis (ed), *Statutory Interpretation: Principles and Pragmatism for a New Age* (Education Monograph 4) (Judicial Commission of New South Wales, 2007) 105

Sullivan, Ruth, *Sullivan on the Construction of Statutes* (LexisNexis Canada, 5th ed, 2008)

Sullivan, Ruth, *Sullivan on the Construction of Statutes* (LexisNexis Canada, 6th ed, 2014)

Theobold, J Anwyl, *Maxwell on Statutes* (Sweet and Maxwell, 4th ed, 1905)

Thorne, Samuel E, *A Discourse upon the Exposicion & Understandinge of Statutes, with Sir Thomas Egerton's Additions* (Huntington Library, 1942)

Thorne, SE, 'Equity of a Statute and Heydon's Case' (1936) 31 *Illinois Law Review* 202

Thring, Henry, *Practical Legislation: The Composition and Language of Acts of Parliament and Business Documents* (John Murray, 1902)

Tiersma, Peter M, *Legal Language* (University of Chicago Press, 1999)

Turnbull, I, 'Legislative Drafting in Plain Language and Statements of General Principle' (1997) 18(1) *Statute Law Review* 21

Turnbull, Ian, 'Plain Language and Drafting in General Principles' [1995] *The Loophole: Journal of the Commonwealth Association of Legislative Counsel* 25

Turnbull, IML, 'Clear Legislative Drafting: New Approaches in Australia' (1990) 11(3) *Statute Law Review* 161

Twining, William and David Miers, *How to Do Things with Rules: A Primer of Interpretation* (Cambridge University Press, 5th ed, 2010)

Twomey, Anne, 'The Refusal or Deferral of Royal Assent' [2006] *Public Law* 580

United Kingdom, *Parliamentary Debates*, House of Lords, 12 February 1850, vol 108

Victoria, *Gazette*, No 63, 28 July 1986

Victoria, *Parliamentary Debates*, Legislative Assembly, 7 March 1984, 3051, 3056 (Mr Cain)

Victoria, *Parliamentary Debates*, Legislative Council, 28 February 1984, 1602 (Attorney-General Kennan)

Victoria, *Parliamentary Debates*, Legislative Council, 7 May 1985, 432–7 (JH Kennan, Attorney General)

Vienna Convention of the Law of Treaties, opened for signature on 23 May 1969, 1155 UNTS 331 (entered into force 27 January 1980)

Vines, Prue and M Scott Donald, 'Introduction: Is Statutory Interpretation in Private Law Distinctive?' in Prue Vines and M Scott Donald (eds), *Statutory Interpretation in Private Law* (Federation Press, 2019) 2

Voermans, Wim, 'Styles of Legislation and Their Effects' (2011) 32(1) *Statute Law Review* 38

Wade, William, *Administrative Law* (Clarendon Press, 6th ed, 1988)

Walker, Kristen, 'Jurisdictional Error Since Craig' (2016) 86 *AIAL Forum* 35

Wall, Patrick, 'A Marked Improvement: The High Court of Australia's Approach to Treaty Interpretation in *Macoun v Commissioner of Taxation* [2015] HCA 44' (2016) 17(1) *Melbourne Journal of International Law* 1

Webb, Thomas E and Robert Greyer, 'The Drafters' Dance: The Complexity of Drafting Legislation and the Limitations of "Plain Language" and "Good Law" Initiatives' (2020) 41(2) *Statute Law Review* 129

Weinberg, Justice Mark, 'Of Mozart, Modern Drafting and the Criminal Lawyers' Lament' (Speech, Victoria Law Foundation Oration, Supreme Court of Victoria, Melbourne, 21 July 2016)

White, James Boyd, *Justice as Translation: An Essay in Cultural and Legal Criticism* (University of Chicago Press, 1990)

Wilberforce, Lord, 'A Judicial Viewpoint' in Attorney-General's Department, *Symposium on Statutory Interpretation* (Australian Government Publishing Service, 1983) 5

Wilde, William H, Joy Hooton and Barry Andrews (eds), *The Oxford Companion to Australian Literature* (Oxford University Press, 2nd ed, 2005)

Williams, George, Sean Brennan and Andrew Lynch, *Blackshield and Williams: Australian Constitutional Law and Theory: Commentary and Materials* (Federation Press, 7th ed, 2018)

Williams, Glanville, *Textbook of Criminal Law* (Stevens and Sons, 2nd ed, 1983)

Wilson, Roy and Brian Galpin, *Maxwell on the Interpretation of Statutes* (Sweet & Maxwell, 11th ed, 1962)

Winckel, Anne, 'The Contextual Role of a Preamble in Statutory Interpretation' (1999) 23(1) *Melbourne University Law Review* 184

Wittgenstein, Ludwig, *Philosophical Investigations*, tr GEM Anscombe (Basil Blackwell, 1953)

Xanthaki, Helen, *Drafting Legislation: Art and Technology of Rules for Regulation* (Hart Publishing, 2014)

Yowell, Paul, 'Legislation, Common Law and the Virtue of Clarity' in Richard Ekins (ed), *Modern Challenges to the Rule of Law* (LexisNexis NZ Ltd, 2011) 101

Zander, Michael, *The Law-Making Process* (Hart Publishing, 7th ed, 2015)

INDEX

A

abstract rights, 609
Act analysis
  close attention to text, 126
  determine object of interpretation, 123–6
  elemental analysis, 127
  grammatical analysis, 127–8
  tracing in complex legislation, 129–30
Acts
  access to, 178–80
  background facts and circumstances. *See* background facts and circumstances
  classification of, 174–5
  common law as part of history of. *See* pre-existing common law
  components of. *See* components of an Act
  consolidation Acts. *See* consolidation Acts
  Crown copyright in, 178–9
  future Acts, 177
  historical legislative development of, 316–17
  Human Rights Acts, 177
  legislative evolution of, 317
  making of. *See* making of an Act
  preamble, 296–7
  principal and amending Acts, 175
  public general Act, 175
  revenue Acts. *See* revenue Acts
  status of pre-commencement, 190–3
  structure of. *See* structure of an Act
  subsequent amending Acts, 315, 327–9
  wider context of, 85, 88–9
Acts of general application
  criminal and sentencing Acts, 410–12
  electronic transactions Acts, 413–14
  employment Acts, 415
  evidence Acts, 412
  goods and occupations Acts, 414–15
  Human Rights Acts, 403–6
  monitoring and investigative powers, 417–18
  other facilitative Acts, 413–18
  power to make rules of court, 416–17
  references to periods of time construed by general Acts, 415–16
  statutory review mechanisms, 406–10
Acts shortening provisions, 381
  appointment, suspension and removal of officers, 392–3
  definitions of common terms, 381–4
  delegation, 389–91
  references to gender, 386–7
  references to legislation, 387–9
  references to 'the Minister', 387
  service of documents, 391–2
  singular or plural, 384–5
administrative decisions and actions
  constitutional lawfulness of, 504–6
  investigative mechanisms and other forms of external review, 406–10
alternative constructions
  as form of legal drafting, 139–40
  as rival contentions to meaning of the words, 135–6
  centrality to practice of interpretation, 136–7
  form of, 140
  formulated to resolve a dispute, 137–8
  interpreter always employs words not in text, 138
  methods to formulate, 138–9
  not applications, 137
  related to text, 139
'always speaking' approach
  ambulatory, description, 285
  circumstances unknown at enactment and, 283–5
  contemporanea expositio est optima et fortissimo in lege and, 285–6
  distinguishing connotation from denotation, 286–9
  generality of text and, 288–9
  international law context, 486
  limitations of, 292–4
  not licence to 'update' meaning of text, 292–4
  overview, 283
  penal nature of provision and, 294
  provision construed in context of contemporary law, 289–92

B

background facts and circumstances
  as part of wider context, 340–1
  commercial context, 343–4
  constitutional context, 344–5
  international context, 344
  overview, 340
  politicial context, 343
  range of matters, 342–5
  rationality and parliamentary awareness, 345–8
  social context, 343
  specialist field context, 342
  'surrounding circumstances', 23–4, 342
  use of judicial notice, 348–9
Bills
  agreed to in same terms by each House of Parliament, 166–8
  approval for introduction of, 152
  assent, 206
  classification of, 172–4
  consent, New South Wales, 166
  consent, Victoria, 167
  'disputed', Victoria, 167
  divided components have headings, 201–3
  drafts of, 151
  introduction of, 152
  legislative drafting and, 149–50
  must be divided into clauses, 199–200
  must have long title, 196–8
  non-government, Crown copyright in, 179
  passage through Commowealth Parliament, 169–72
  passage through House of Representatives, 169–71
  passage through Senate, 171–2
  preamble, 198–9
  private Bills, 172–4
  public Bills, 173
  read three times in each House of Parliament, 168
  referral to Federation Chamber, 170–1
  structural rules dictate form of, 195–6
  structure of in drafting, 155

C

Carltona principle, 391
Chevron doctrine, 63–4, 515
codes
  interpretation of, 333–5
cogency, 141
commencement
  Act may be amended before it commences, 191
  day(s) fixed by or under Act or by interpretation legislation, 182–5
  difference to enactment, 181
  Executive's power to delay may be limited, 186–9
  internal references to commencment construed differently across Australia, 189–90
  limited powers may be exercised between passing and commencement, 190–1
  overview, 181
  provision operative even if not expressly commenced, 185–6
  uncommenced legislation and courts, 191–3
common sense
  statutory interpretation and, 506–9
Commonwealth Office of Parliamentary Counsel
  Plain English Manual, 158, 160, 195, 233, 236
components of an Act, 295
  chapters, parts, divisions and subdivisions, 201
  date of passing, 206
  definitions, 203–4, 302–4
  examples, notes and reader's aids, 204–5, 305–7
  interpretative value of individual components, 296–308
  long title, 296
  number when passed, 206
  numbering of, 203
  objects clause, 299
  part, division and subdivision headings, 300–2
  preamble, 296–7
  provision location's impact on interpretation, 308–11
  punctuation, 205, 307–8
  schedules, 200–1, 310–11
  short title, 199, 298
  simplified outlines, 305
  statement of fact in preamble, 297
composite expressions, 265–7
conflict, provisions in apparent. *See* provisions in apparent conflict
consequences
  'absurd', 429–31
  appeal to common sense, 427
  consequences for the enforcement of the law, 431
  considered in an even-handed way, 429
  construction tested by reference to, 422–4
  definition, 421
  frustration of legislative purpose, 427–8
  judicial intuitions, 428
  may provide reason to question whether result intended, 424
  not of great assistance, where, 428–9
  positive or negative claims not substantiated, 429
  reflect Paliament's intention, 425–6
consolidation Acts, 175, 318–19
  re-enacted words and, 327

Constitution
  constitutional validity interpretation rule, 503
  context, as part of, 344–5
  framework, relevance to statutory interpretation, 37–8
  lawfulness of administrative action, 504–6
  legislation impugned on constitutional grounds, 501
  statute interpretation to avoid incompatability with, 502–3
  unique place of in interpretation of Australian legislation, 501–3
  construction. *See* alternative constructions
contemporanea expositio maxim, 285–6
context
  as integral step in interpretative process, 32
  consequences of contextualism, 90–3
  consideration of, 88
  contextual disputes, 96–7
  duty to have regard to, 86–90
  fixing meaning and, 93–5
  indications of meaning and, 88–90, 95–6
  meaning and, 87–8
  meaning of, 84–6
  merging of 'context' and 'text', 84
  notion of, 32
  overview, 32
  presumptive rules and, 95–6
  relevance and, 84–6
  surrounding provisions and, 308–10
  utility of regard to, 93–7
contextual principle, 106
copyright
  Crown copyright in non-government Bills, 179
  in legislation, 178–9
courts
  applicability of mens rea, 444–9
  ascertaining sources of doubt and, 211–15
  consequences and. *See* consequences
  determination of remedial legislation, 315–16
  extrinsic materials and fundamental rights, 370–1
  implied repeal of legislation and, 550
  independence in reaching a decision, 64–6
  interpretative techniques for resolution of conflict, 546
  law-making ability of, 14–15
  legislative antecedents and, 315–16
  non-compliance with a statutory requirement and, 582, 587–9
  sole authoritative arbiters of legislative meaning, 62–4
  special categories of legislation and, 246
  subordinate provisions that must give way, 548–9
  uncommenced legislation and, 191–3
critical thinking, 141–2

D

de minimis non curat lex, 499–500
definitions of common terms
  'contravene', 382
  'document', 382
  'land', 382–3
  'person', 383
  references to domestic relationships, 383
  references to periods of time, 384
delegated legislation, 666–8
  Act may make inconsistent with enabling Act, 676–7
  cannot be used to construe a statute, 517–19
  contextual factors and specific provisions, 668–70
  drafting of, 669
  effect of failure to make delegated legislation, 682–4
  exception to general rule against admissibility of, 519–20
  'Henry VIII' clauses exception, 520–1, 676
  invalid portion may be severed, 681–2
  invalidity
    high threshold test for unreasonableness, 678
    matter outside scope of enabling Act, 673–4
    means not reasonably proportionate to end to be achieved, 677–8
    repugnant to enabling Act, 674–6
    subdelegation of legislative power without authorisation, 679–80
    unauthorised purpose, 677
  invalidity, process to determine, 672–3
  nature of likely audience and, 670
  overview, 666
  parliamentary counsel and, 152
  principle of legality and, 444–6
  retrospective operation, 671–2
  separation of powers and, 41–2
  terms used have same meaning as in enabling Act, 670–1
  uncertain outcome, 680–1
delegatus non potest delegare, 679
dictionaries
  determining presumptive meaning and, 227
  frequent use of, 492
  not conclusive source of meaning, 491–2
  ordinary meaning and, 24
  use of a 'corpus linguistics' and, 493–4
  use of well settled, 490–1
Diplock Conditions, 530–4
  clarification of by High Court, 531–2
  remedial construction. *See* remedial construction
  satisfaction of not necessarily required to adopt a remedial construction, 532–3
doctrine of analogy, 476–7
doctrine of judicial notice, 348–9

works of reference and, 489
doctrine of legislative supremacy, 37, 45, 330, 332
See also parliamentary supremacy
doctrine of parliamentary privilege, 178, 351–2
drafting errors, 40
remedial constructions for. *See* remedial construction
drafting styles
amending Acts, 244
contemporary legislative drafting, 237
conventions of Australian Parliamentary Counsel, 243–4
gender neutral drafting, 386
general principles-based drafting, 235–6
influence on interpretation. *See* influence of drafting styles on interpretation
main drafting styles, 231
overview, 231
plain language drafting, 233–5
re-enacted words and, 326–7
traditional style, 232–3

E

ejusdem generis, 271–3
enactment procedure, 163
exclusionary rule, 24
expert evidence on technical meaning admissible, 268–70
explanatory memorandum, 33, 58, 74, 131
passage of Bill and, 169
proclamation policy and, 187
supplementary or revised, 354
expressio unius est exclusio alterius, 274–5
expressum facit cessare tacitum, 275–7
extraneous materials, 19, 24, 29, 32, 366, 480
extrinsic materials
can support a non-ordinary or strained meaning of text, 369–70
cannot displace clear meaning of text, 367–8
desirability of persons relying on ordinary meaning, 363
determining probative value, 360–2
enactment of Interpretation Acts and, 28–30
identification of purpose and, 109–10
international materials, 487–8
legislative intent and, 58–61
ordinary meaning and, 43
pre-parliamentary and parliamentary materials. *See* pre-parliamentary and parliamentary materials
resilience of common law and, 31
statements about meaning or effect of legislation already enacted, 362

F

Farah/Marlborough 'plainly wrong' principle, 471–2
uniform legislation and, 471–2
Federal Register of Legislation, 179, 667
focus on the word in question
'alternative words could have been used', 264–5
composite expressions, 265–7
expert evidence on technical meaning admissable, 268–70
linguistic canons that focus on the word in question, 262–70
presumption against surplusage, 262–3
technical meanings presumption applies to legal terms, 268
words used in a technical sense, 267–8
foreign judicial decisions
persuasive value of, 476

G

general rights, 610
generalia specialibus non derogant, 279–80, 546–7
golden rule, 22–3, 31, 33, 92
grammatical analysis, 127–8
grammatical meaning, 222, 224

H

Hansard, 29, 92, 325
Henry VIII clauses, 520–1, 676
High Court of Australia, 37
1970s literalist approach, 26
attribution of meaning to statutory text and, 38
clarification of Diplock Conditions by, 531–2
legislative intent and, 53
relevance of constitutional framework to statutory interpretation and, 37
text-based principle and, 74
history of key concepts of statutory interpretation
1900s to 1970s approach, 17–25
1980s Interpretation Acts amendments, 25–30
1990s 'modern' approach, 31–3
2000s changes to some Interpretation Acts, 33–5
basis in English law, 18
common law developments, 31–3
focus on text within intrinsic context, 20–3
importance of understanding of, 18
inconsistencies with respect to extrinsic context, 23–4
legislative intent, 19–20
limited regard to mischief or purpose, 23

history of key concepts of statutory interpretation (cont.)
  literal, mischief and golden rules superceded, 33
  overview, 17
  whole instrument approach, 20–1
House of Representatives
  passage of a Bill through, 169–71
human rights
  rule of law and protection of, 43
Human Rights Acts, 177, 403–6

I

implied repeal of legislation, 4, 541, 549
  courts and, 550
  test for, 550
inadmissible considerations, 510–11
  certain executive government sources, 514–22
  delegated legislation and, 517–19
  exceptions to general rule, 519–20
  government agency administrative processes, 521–2
  'Henry VIII' clauses exception, 520–1
  international treaties, 511
  judicially constructed policy, 512–14
  legislative intention and, 511
  ministerial statements in Parliament, 514–15
  opinions by other members of the executive government, 516–17
  overview, 510
  speculative matters, 522–3
influence of drafting styles on interpretation, 237, 243
  detailed and precise drafting, 237–8
  general principles drafting, 240–2
  plain language drafting, 239–40
international law
  'always speaking' approach and, 486
  state to comply with, 43
international treaties and materials
  customary international law, 481
  domestic law and international obligations, 478–82
  inadmissable considerations and, 511
  international materials as extrinsic aids, 487–8
  overview, 478
  presumption of consistency, 483–7
  primacy of domestic law text, 482–3
  travaux préparatoires, 481
Interpretation Acts, 37
  Acts shortening provisions. *See* Acts shortening provisions
  calculation of age, distance and time, 397–400
  Commonwealth developments, 25–9
  compliance with forms, 400–1
  early, 24–5
  effect of amendment and repeal on pre-existing rights and obligations, 394–6
  enactment in other jurisdictions, 27–30
  general interpretative rules, 394–402
  non-compliance with a statutory requirement and, 582–4
  overview, 377
  presumption against extraterritorial operation and, 640–1
  provisions on 'may', 'shall' and 'must', 569–71
  purpose of, 377–8
  relationship with common law, 37
  rules for understanding operation of legislation, 394
  separation of powers and, 38
  severance, 401
  statutory powers may be exercised from time to time, 397
  subject to contrary intention, 378–81
  words of permission and obligation, 402
interpreting statutory powers, 560–71
  ambiguity of 'should', 568
  characterisation as discretion or duty a matter of interpretation, 560
  distributive operation of 'may', 565–6
  Interpretation Acts provisions on 'may', 'shall' and 'must', 569–71
  power conferred by 'may', 561–3
  prima facie meaning of 'may', 560–1
  prima facie meaning of 'must', 567–8
  prima facie meaning of 'shall', 566–7
  proper exercise of discretion, 564–5
interpretative factors
  distinction between interpretative criteria, 131
  identification of, 130–2
  methods to assist identification of, 132–5

J

judicial duty of independence
  independent reasoning, 66–7
  individual judgements and, 67–71
  overview, 62
judicial notice. *See* doctrine of judicial notice

L

language of the provision
  determining the presumptive meaning, 226–9
  literal, grammatical, natural and ordinary meaning read in isolation, 223–5
  ordinary meanings, 225–6
  overcoming the presumptive meaning, 229
  overview, 221

presumptive meaning, 222–3
when text has 'plain meaning', 229–30
last resort principle, 253
legal research, 121–3
legal scholarship, citation of, 494–5
leges posteriores priores contrarias abrogant, 549
legislative antecedents
as part of wider context, 330–2
common strands about use, 319–21
considered with other legislative history, 321–3
consolidation Acts, 318–19
courts and, 315–16
ordinary meaning and, 320–1
overview, 315
pre-enactment history of Act or provision, 316–18
presumptions about re-enacted words, 323–7
purpose and, 319–20
subsequent amending Acts, 315, 327–9
use as interpretative aids, 319–23
legislative drafting
alternative constructions as form of, 139–40
Bills, 149–50
drafting styles. *See* drafting styles
evolution of styles over time, 156–8
overview, 149
publishing practices and techniques, 160–1
relationship between drafting and interpretation, 161–2
role of parliamentary counsel, 153–6
sources of doubt and, 215–18
variance of practices and techniques across jurisdictions, 158–60
legislative drafting process
as function of executive government, 149–52
as integral part of law-making process, 152–3
legislative history
purpose and, 109–10
legislative instruments, 667
legislative intent
as fundamental object of statutory interpretation, 49–50
constitutional significance of, 50
distinct from purpose, 56–7
extrinsic materials and, 58–61
historical approach to, 19–20
objective concept of, 50–2
objective inference of, 52–4
overview, 49
remedial construction and, 528
statements of, 57–8
text-based principle and, 77–8
usefulness of, 55–6
legislative proposals
drafting instructions, 150
sources of, 150
legislative supremacy. *See* doctrine of legislative supremacy
linguistic canons, 260
Act to be read as a whole and consideration given to all relevant provisions, 280–2
canons that focus on the word in question, 262–70
definition, 261
espressio unius est exclusio alterius, 274–5
expressum facit cessare tacitum, 275–7
general words at end of specific items list, 271–3
generalia specialibus non derogant, 279–80
immediate context indication of meaning, 270–1
legislature intends different words to have different meanings, 279
nature of, 261–2
presumption that same word used with same meaning in a statute, 278–9
reddendo singula singulis, 273
literal meaning, 223
literal rule, 20, 33, 91–2
reduced to literal reading, 91
long title, 21, 23, 105, 107, 296
Bills must have, 196–8

M

making of an Act
access to Acts, 178–80
Acts made by constitutionally vested bodies with legislative power, 163–6
classification of Bills and Acts, 172–5
consent of Crown, 164–5
date of assent, 206
passage of Bill through Commonwealth Parliament, 166–72
powers and privileges of Parliament, 175–8
maxims of law
as part of surrounding law, 498–9
mens rea, 648–9
application and external elements, 654
disputes involve applicability and content, 652–4
full mens rea, 650–1, 654–5, 661–2
position under the criminal codes, 662–5
primitive approach to criminal punishment, avoidance of, 652
Proudman v Dayman principle, 650–2, 655
Sherras v De Rutzen presumption, 650–1
statutory context, 655–61
tripartite classification of offences, 654–5
twin presumptions of principle, 650–2

mental ingredient of statutory offences
common law principle of mens rea. *See* mens rea
overview, 648
state of mind offence determined differently across Australian jurisdictions, 649–50
statutory offence may contain proposition as to state of mind, 648–9
mischief
concept of, 101
mischief rule, 23–4, 26–7, 33

N

natural meaning, 224
non-compliance with a statutory requirement
court may find Parliament did not intend legal enforcement, 587–9
courts and, 582
generally not enforceable by court proceedings, 585–6
Interpretation Act provisions and, 582–4
interpretative criteria employed, 578–82
issues, 572–3
overview, 572
Parliament may declare 'requirement' unenforceable in the courts, 586–7
Parliament may state whether related act invalidated, 574
Project Blue Sky inquiry and. *See Project Blue Sky* inquiry
where Parliament does not unambiguously state whether related act invalidated, 574–6
whether non-compliance has occurred, 573–4
noscitur a sociis, 270–1

O

objects clause of an Act, 299
ordinary meaning, 11, 20, 33, 42, 221–2, 225–6, 241, 321
desirability of persons relying on, 363
dictionaries and, 24
extrinsic materials and, 43
legislative antecedents and, 320–1
may change over time, 228
plain language drafting and, 239–40
text-based principle and, 74–5

P

Parliament
'awareness' of, 347–8
ministerial statements in, 514–15
non-compliance with a statutory requirement and, 574–6
power to erode fundamental common law rights, 442–3
powers and privileges of, 175–8
presumption against extraterritorial operation and, 638–40, 643–5
'real' intent of, 54
parliamentary counsel
art and science of legislative drafting and, 154–6
Bill structure and, 155
delegated legislation and, 152
drafting conventions of, 243–4
drafting instructions and, 150
drafting manuals of, 160–1, 243–4
limitations on literary choices of, 155–6
non-political role of, 153
outsourcing of drafting to consultants by, 152
plain language policies, 158
policy analysis by, 151
provision of legal advice by, 153–4
parliamentary privilege. *See* doctrine of parliamentary privilege
Parliamentary Counsel's Committee
Protocol on Drafting, 159–60
parliamentary debates, 25, 178, 354, 362
parliamentary statements
admissibility of, 364–6
parliamentary supremacy
implied repeal of legislation and, 549
statutory interpretation and, 43–5
penal provisions, 245
construction of an offence provision, 253
construed by reference to ordinary 'rules' of construction, 250–1
construed in favour of the subject as last resort, 251–3
penal consequences part of legislation context, 254
reading of, 254–6
scope of last resort principle and, 253
plain English
drafting style, 157
presenting a legal opinion or reasons for judgment, 144–6
plain meaning, 221, 229–30
practical techniques of statutory interpretation
analysing the Act, 123–4
determining the preferable construction, 143–4
evaluating alternative arguments, 140–3
formulating alternative constructions, 135–40
identifying interpretative factors, 130–5
legal research, 121–3
models of interpretative skills, 117–18
overall method, 118–21
overview, 117
presenting a legal opinion or reasons for judgment, 144–6

preamble of an Act, 296–7
statement of fact in, 297
precedent
binding and persuasive precedent, 464–9
decisions on statutes *in pari materia*, 474–6
decisions on uniform and federal legislation, 470–3
doctrine of analogy, 476–7
Farah/Marlborough 'plainly wrong' principle, 470–2
judicial precedent distinct from law of statutory interpretation, 464
overview, 464
persuasive value of foreign judicial decisions, 476
'plainly wrong' interpretations, 472–3
prior ruling on statutory text and, 467–9
single judge or immediate appellate court, 470–1
statutory text as starting point, 465–7
pre-existing common law
as part of wider context, 330–3
common law that triggers legislative enactment, 338–9
impact of statute on, 335–8
interpretation of codes, 333–5
ordinary proccess of statutory interpretation and, 332–3
overview, 330
where statute abolishes common law, 335–6
where statute incorporates common law, 336–7
where statute modifies or supplements common law, 337–8
pre-parliamentary and parliamentary materials
admissability of parliamentary statements, 364–6
authorities for recourse to extrinsic materials, 352
common law authority, 351
common law principle of 'wider' context, 353
common law requirements, 358–9
inference from parliamentary inaction, 371–3
interpretation starts and end with the text, 366–7
judicial observations about, 361
overview, 350
parliamentary awareness of materials, 359–60
parliamentary debates, 26, 178, 354, 362
parliamentary privilege and, 351–2
'post-enactment' materials, 372–3
probative value, guidance on, 360–6
purpose and, 362
range of materials, 353–5
second reading speech, 58, 353–4
statutory authority, 351, 352–3
statutory requirements, 355–8
text still paramount, 366–71
use of, 362
presumption against application to government and other Crown entities
application need not be uniform throughout Act, 630–2
applies to Crown in all its capacities, 625–6
definition of the Crown, 627–30
derivative immunity, 645–6
general words in a statute, 622–4
may be modified by legislation, 632–4
overview, 622
rule in *Bropho*, 624–5
presumption against extraterritorial operation
ambit intended by Parliament and, 643–5
changing social context and attitude to, 642–3
common law and, 639–40
extraterritorial operation, 638, 658–60
Interpretation Acts and, 640–1
overview, 636
rationale, 642
rebutting the presumption, 646–7
statutes of general operation, 645–6
statutory language and, 641
presumption against retrospective operation
acquisition of a right, 608
common law and statutory presumptions overlap, 605
common law presumption, 603
concept of retrospectivity, 601–2
enforceability of vested right at repeal of old law, 614–16
inapplicable to statutes affecting mere matters of procedure, 616–18
Interpretation Acts, 603–4
justification for, 605–7
ousting the presumption, 618–21
relevant point in time, 607–8
'right acquired', 611–13
right must be 'specific' to be vested, 609–10
right understood broadly in certain respects, 608
sources of, 603–5
specific immunity from future liability, 610–11
vested rights and incurred obligations, 607
when presumption attracted, 607–18
whether right or obligation acquired or incurred under old law, 607
presumption against surplusage, 262–3
presumption of consistency (international materials), 483–7
presumption of consistency (language), 278–9
presumptive meaning, 222–3
dictionaries and other scholarly works and, 227
intuitive element of, 226–7
judge's capacity to determine meaning, 228–9
ordinary meaning of words may change over time, 228
overcoming the presumptive meaning, 229

presumptive meaning (cont.)
  primary ordinary meaning or usage of word, 227–8
  professional training and, 226–7
  text as piece of English, 222–3
principle of harmonious construction, 542–5
  coherence in the law and, 545
principle of legality, 43, 96
  delegated legislation and statutory rights, 444–9
  fundamental rights and, 440–3
  history and development of in Australia, 433–6
  limiting interference, 439–40
  overview, 432
  Parliament and common law rights, 442–3
  presumption in relation to a right, 440–1
  rationale for presumption, 443–4
  rebuttal of presumption, 436–9
  variation of fundamental rights over time, 441–2
Project Blue Sky inquiry, 572, 575–7, 582–4
  determination of, 578
  features of, 575–6
provisions in apparent conflict
  basic presumptions applied in resolution of, 541–5
  compared with 'actual' conflict, 540–1
  conflict between a general law and a special law, 546–7
  interpretative problem, 539–41
  'irreconcilable' conflict, 549–52
  ordinary principles of statutory interpretation and, 547–8
  overview, 539
  principle of harmonious construction, 542–5
  resolution techniques, 546
  statutes made by one Parliament are intended to work together, 541–2
  subordinate provisions, 548–9
purpose
  1970s approach to, 25–6
  assistance given by, 102–4
  balance with text, 115–16
  common law requirement of consideration of, 100
  convergence with context, 32
  difference in statutory provisions, 99–100
  distinct from legislative intent, 56–7
  early Australian approach to, 19
  elusive or unhelpful, 115
  finding the purpose, 104–10
  language of purpose provision, 99–100
  legislative antecedents and, 319–20
  legislative history and, 109–10
  limitations of assistance given by, 110–15
  meaning of, 101–2
  multiple or competing purposes, 111–12
  notion of mischief and, 33
  obligation to consider at common law, 31
  overview, 98
  pre-parliamentary and parliamentary materials, 362
  purpose provision, 105–9
  reference to extrinsic materials to identify, 109–10
  s 15AA and, 26–7
  separation of powers and, 40, 103
  specificity of, 112–15
  states and territories, 27–8, 30, 33–4
  statutory and common law requirement, 98–100
  statutory requirement in each jurisdiction, 98–9
purpose provision, 105–9

R

reddendo singula singulis, 56–7
re-enacted words
  change in drafting style and, 326–7
  consolidation Acts and, 327
  presumption Parliament intended to incorporate same concept, 323
  re-enactment presumption, 324–5
re-enactment presumption, 92, 315, 324–6, 347
remedial construction
  common law guidelines, 530–1
  concepts central to, 527–8
  Diplock Conditions, 531–3, 535
  'drafting error' and, 528
  fourth 'condition', 533
  gaps in legislation distinguished, 535–7
  guidance for, 530–5
  legislative intent and, 528
  overview, 527
  permissible remedial construction, 534–5
  scope of operation of a provision and, 534
  separation of powers and, 527
  simple and obvious drafting errors, 528–30
  strained construction, 537–8
remedial legislation, 245
  court determination of, 247
  exceptions in, 250
  expansive construction and, 250
  liberally construed, 247–9
  presumption limited by text and purpose of Act, 249
  widespread coverage of, 246–7
Renton Committee, 156–7
Renton Report, 25–6, 156
retroactive laws, 601–2, 606
retrospective laws, 602, 606
  'curative', 607
revenue Acts, 245

special rules formerly applied to, 256–7
special rules not applied in contemporary law, 257–8
taxation context, 258–9
rule of law
statutory interpretation and, 42–3

S

scholarly works
cited from diverse areas, 496–7
second reading speech, 58, 354
Senate
passage of a Bill through, 171–2
separation of powers, 37–8
as rationale for some statutory interpretation principles, 38–40
doctrine of, 38
Interpretation Acts and, 38
interpretation of delegated legislation and, 41–2
purpose and, 40, 103
relevance of to states and territories, 40–1
remedial construction and, 527
text-based principle and, 73
short title, 84
ease of reference and, 199
interpretative value of, 298
sources of doubt
ascertaining
appropriate drafting style and, 216–18
court's understanding of interpretative problem and, 211–15
locating responsibility for errors in legislation and, 215–16
presumptions used to justify legal meaning and, 210–11
differing origins of, 208–10
nature of, 207–8
overview, 207
specific rights, 609–10
Standing Comittee for the Scrutiny of Bills, 170
statute book
comparable statutes, 459–63
definition, 450
overview, 450
relevance of similarly worded provision in another statute, 451–3
statutes forming part of a single scheme, 456–9
statutes *in pari materia*, 453–6
wider legislative context of use, 450
statutes *in pari materia*, 24, 323, 471, 476
precedent and, 474–6
statute book and, 453–6
statutory interpretation
Act definitions, 302–4
'always speaking' approach. *See* 'always speaking' approach
as process involving skill set, 5–6
as substantive body of law, 3–4
background circumstances and, 345
basic composition, 3–6
checklists, 134
common sense and, 506–9
comparisons, 6–13
constitutional framework of legislation and, 36
contribution to law making, 14–16
dissimilar from formulating the rule of a case, 12–13
distinct from application of the law, 6–9
examples, notes and reader's aids, 305–7
extrinsic materials. *See* extrinsic materials
functions of, 14–16
history of key concepts of. *See* history of key concepts of statutory interpretation
impact of provision location on, 308–11
importance of Act's schedule, 310–11
inferences from subsections, 310
influence of drafting styles on. *See* influence of drafting styles on interpretation
international materials as extrinsic aids, 487–8
interpretation of ordinary speech and, 9–12
language of the provision. *See* language of the provision
legislative intent as fundamental object of, 49–50
overview, 3
parliamentary supremacy and, 45
part, division and subdivision headings, 300–2
practical techniques. *See* practical techniques of statutory interpretation
precedent and, 14
pre-existing common law and, 332–3
punctuation of an Act and, 307–8
relationship between interpretation and legislative drafting, 161–2
rule of law and, 42–3
separation of powers and. *See* separation of powers
simplified outlines of an Act, 305
sources of law and, 36–7
'spiral' approach, 133–4
text-based principle. *See* text-based principle
'text, context and purpose' approach, 134
'wider context' principle, 317, 353, 358
statutory powers
developments in drafting of, 556–9
functions of, 553–6
interpreting statutory powers. *See* interpreting statutory powers
overview, 553

statutory reasonableness
  definition, 592–3
  importance in statute law, 591–2
  interpretation, 596–7
  interpreter reliant on context and legislative purpose, 597–600
  is a flexible concept, 594–6
  is a legal standard, 593
  may be profitably examined, 590–1
  overview, 590
  standard has objective component, 594
  use of 'reasonableness' standard, 590
  used for compelling reasons, 592
  widely used measure in statute law, 591–2
statutory rights
  principle of legality and, 446–9
strained meaning, 224
structure of an Act
  provisions organised in a logical way, 194–5
  structural rules dictate form of a Bill, 195–6
subsequent amending Acts, 315, 327–9
surrounding law
  as part of context to be considered, 497–8
  de minimis non curat lex, 499–500
  maxims of law, 498–9

T

technical meaning
  applies to legal terms, 268
  expert evidence admissable, 268–70
  presumption that legislature used technical sense of word, 267–8
  words may be used in technical sense, 402
text-based principle
  consequences of transgressing the text, 79–82
  consideration of text and, 72
  constitutional principles, 73–4
  intention of Parliament paramount object, 77–9
  legislative intent and, 77–8
  meaning of 'text', 73
  ordinary or grammatical meaning and, 74–5
  overview, 72
  presumptive and weighty meaning of text, 75
  separation of powers and, 73
  text as starting point of interpretation, 74
  text where meaning resides, 75–7

U

uniform legislation
  Farah/Marlborough 'plainly wrong' principle and, 470–2

V

validity, 141
vested rights, 607
  enforceability of, 614–16
  must be specific, 609–10

W

works of reference
  citation from, 489–90

For EU product safety concerns, contact us at Calle de José Abascal, 56–1°,
28003 Madrid, Spain or eugpsr@cambridge.org.

www.ingramcontent.com/pod-product-compliance
Lightning Source LLC
LaVergne TN
LVHW081959200926
848481LV00010B/2770
* 9 7 8 1 1 0 8 8 1 6 0 2 1 *